STRONG ON MUSIC

Repercussions

GTS, October 1863

STRONG ON MUSIC

The New York Music Scene in the Days of
George Templeton Strong

~~~~~~~~~~

VOLUME III

REPERCUSSIONS
1857–1862

Vera Brodsky Lawrence

THE UNIVERSITY OF CHICAGO PRESS
Chicago and London

STRONG ON MUSIC
The New York Music Scene
in the Days of George Templeton Strong

VOLUME I: RESONANCES, 1836–1849

VOLUME II: REVERBERATIONS, 1850–1856

VOLUME III: REPERCUSSIONS, 1857–1862

The University of Chicago Press, Chicago 60637
The University of Chicago Press, Ltd., London
© 1999 by the Estate of Vera Brodsky Lawrence
All rights reserved. Published 1999
Printed in the United States of America

08 07 06 05 04 03 02 01 00 99   1 2 3 4 5

ISBN (cloth): 0-226-47015-6
ISBN (paper): 0-226-47016-4

This publication has been supported by grants from the National Endowment
for the Humanities, an independent federal agency, and from the Billy Rose
Foundation.

Library of Congress Cataloging-in-Publication Data

Lawrence, Vera Brodsky.
    Repercussions, 1857–1862 / Vera Brodsky Lawrence.
        p.   cm.—(Strong on music ; v. 3)
    Includes index.
    ISBN 0-226-47015-6. — ISBN 0-226-47016-4 (pbk.)
    1. Music—New York (N.Y.)—19th century—History and criticism.
    2. Strong, George Templeton, 1820–1875—Diaries.   3. Musicians—New
York (N.Y.)—Diaries.   4. New York (N.Y.)—Intellectual life.
    I. Strong, George Templeton, 1820–1875.   II. Title.   III. Series:
Lawrence, Vera Brodsky.   Strong on music ; v. 2.
    ML200.8.N5L4   1995 vol. 2
    780'.9747'109034—dc20   91-14828
                                                        CIP
                                                        MN

To
Dorothy Arnof
and
Brooks McNamara

Music is essentially a language which has its patois *and its purity, and those who are acquainted with, and readily understand, the one cannot always understand the other.*

Wilkes' Spirit of the Times
May 26, 1860

Altogether, with the congregation of fashion and folly, trade and commerce, flâneurs *and Bohemians, artists and loungers, saints and sinners, we may expect to see a lively time during the gay season in this city, which is the concentrating point of everything interesting in this country, and the leading watering place as well as the commercial emporium of the Union.*

New York Herald
September 1, 1858

CONTENTS

5

6

ILLUSTRATIONS

ACKNOWLEDGMENTS

MANY OF THE individuals and institutions that Vera Brodsky Lawrence would have thanked, if she had lived to write these acknowledgments, are known; but inevitably there are some that will be overlooked. Those of us who have helped see this volume through the press hope that any such omissions will be pardoned.

Thanks go, first of all, to the National Endowment for the Humanities—for its faithful support of this project in the form of four grants beginning in 1978—and to Elizabeth Arndt, the NEH program officer whom Lawrence praised in Volume 2 for "her unfailing kindness, helpfulness, solicitude, and her valued friendship." Next, profound thanks must be given to the Billy Rose Foundation for a generous subvention that made the publication of this third volume possible. And, finally, Lawrence would wish mention to be made of the John Simon Guggenheim Memorial Foundation for the Fellowship that enabled her to start work on this project in 1976 and for a publication subvention (for illustrations and index) that she managed to budget so wisely that it has been of assistance for all three volumes.

The institutions that played the greatest roles in the research for this volume—as for the previous volumes—are the New-York Historical Society, the Music Division of the New York Public Library, and the Archives of the New York Philharmonic. Until Lawrence was no longer able to make the journey across town to the New-York Historical Society, she was a regular (often daily) reader there; since she possessed a photocopy of Strong's diary (the original of which is housed in the Society's library), what she mainly consulted on these visits were newspapers and illustrations. She would wish to thank Jean Ashton, former librarian of the Society, Margaret Heilbrun, its present librarian, Wendy Shadwell, curator of prints, and all the other "gallant staff members" (to use her words from Volume 2) for their "cooperation and splendid assistance, through thick and thin." Jean Bowen, formerly chief of the Music Division of the New York Public Library, and the staff of that Division also deserve appreciative thanks. And Barbara Haws, archivist of the New York Philharmonic, should receive a special tribute for her unfailing interest, cooperation, and friendship; among the signs of her loyal respect for Lawrence were her Lincoln Center exhibition that called attention to Lawrence's work and, after Lawrence's death, the program she arranged at the New-York Historical Society in celebration of Lawrence's accomplishments.

For permission to reproduce illustrative material from their collections, acknowledgment is made to the New-York Historical Society, the New York Public Library, the Dartmouth College Library, and Girvice Archer, Jr. Jennifer Nelson, Storage Library Supervisor of Dartmouth College Library, deserves special thanks for her cordial cooperation. And Dr. Archer, who had generously contributed to Volume 2 by supplying items from his remarkable collection of pictures, has taken a lively and sympathetic interest in Volume 3, helping to select appropriate illustrations and making nearly three dozen of them available. Heartfelt gratitude is extended to him.

Among the persons to whom thanks are owed for advice and information on specific points are John G. Doyle and S. Frederick Starr (authorities on Gottschalk), D. W. Fostle (authority on the Steinway family), Thomas G. Kaufman (expert on Italian operas and opera singers, who contributed some two dozen notes, printed as an appendix), Mark Piel (librarian of the New York Society Library), Gary Schmidgall (authority on Walt Whitman and opera), Larry Sullivan (formerly chief of the Rare Book and Special Collections Division of the Library of Congress), and Robert Tuggle (director of the Metropolitan Opera Archives). The knowledgeable and conscientious readers secured by the University of Chicago Press—Dena J. Epstein and Wayne Shirley—also provided invaluable and greatly appreciated help, as did Marilyn Bliss (superb indexer), Pauline Fox (expert copy-editor and proofreader), and Kathleen Hansell (concerned and understanding editor). Lawrence's circle of friends who contributed what (in Volume 2) she called "moral support" include James R. Cherry, Richard Glavin, Nancy Groce, Robin Hicks, Martin Pearl, and Barbara Schneider. Their assistance took many forms, such as trips to a library or a grocery store; all in all, their many attentions greatly eased her life in a difficult time.

I have held until last the names of two other members of that circle because they are the ones to whom Lawrence wished this volume to be dedicated: Dorothy Arnof and Brooks McNamara. Professor McNamara, the distinguished historian of the American theater, was an esteemed adviser and friend to Lawrence, who enjoyed his company and valued his scholarly suggestions. During her final illness, he was a frequent visitor to her bedside and encouraged her with discussion of their proposed joint projects. Dorothy Shapiro Arnof was Lawrence's closest friend, in touch with her every day in her last years. Their acquaintance went back to childhood, when they were first-grade classmates in Norfolk, Virginia; then they lost track of each other for over six decades, and it was not until the 1982 Joplin concert at the New York Public Library at Lincoln Center (celebrating the expanded version of Lawrence's Joplin edition) that they met again and learned they were living one block apart in the East Fifties. Mrs. Arnof is herself a prominent editor, having had a forty-five-year career in publishing, first at Harper and then at Macmillan; and she was the obvious person, both professionally and personally, to handle the details of shepherding into print the manuscript of this third volume of *Strong on Music*. She has worked tirelessly on selecting the illustrations, tying up loose ends in the text, and proofreading; but she has always been respectful of her friend's marvelous prose and did not change a word or a mark of punctuation except when they were unquestionably erroneous. Vera Brodsky Lawrence would not only approve of what Mrs. Arnof has done; she would also be moved by the devotion it represents.

G.T.T.

NOTE

Throughout this book, small superscript musical notes are used to indicate that more information on the subject so tagged can be found in previous volumes of *Strong on Music:* one eighth note refers to the first volume, two beamed eighth notes to the second. The asterisks attached to the names of some operas and opera singers indicate that further information can be found in the appendix, supplied by Thomas G. Kaufman.

Vera Brodsky Lawrence

INTRODUCTION

Vera Brodsky Lawrence, 1909–1996

VERA BRODSKY LAWRENCE died on September 18, 1996, leaving six unpublished chapters of her George Templeton Strong chronicle, enough to form this third volume of *Strong on Music*. Her death brought to an end a remarkable career, for she achieved distinction both as a performer and as a music historian. For over three decades she was an admired concert pianist; then, in a radical change of direction, she turned to scholarship, and for another three decades she was a pioneering historian of American music. At the time of her death, she was best known for her scholarly achievements, such as *The Piano Works of Louis Moreau Gottschalk* (in five volumes, 1969), apparently the first collected edition of an American composer, and *The Collected Works of Scott Joplin* (in two volumes, 1971), which precipitated the worldwide revival of Joplin's music and his recognition as a great American composer.

Her renown as a scholar, however, will ultimately rest—as she wished it to—on her final work, *Strong on Music*. She lived long enough to observe the enthusiastic reception accorded its first two volumes, and she took great delight in knowing that her landmark contribution was beginning to make its way. Its method was to use the entries on music in George Templeton Strong's voluminous diary (1835–75) as a springboard for a detailed account of the New York musical scene in the mid-nineteenth century; in the process she not only took a major step in dealing with a neglected field but also showed how an overlooked source, the vast body of music criticism in the newspapers, could profitably be used. The depth of her knowledge, as revealed here, came as no surprise to a network of scholars who repeatedly consulted her, for they had discovered that the contents of her mind and her files constituted one of the major reference sources for the study of music in America.

Vera R. Brodsky was born in Norfolk, Virginia, on July 1, 1909, the only child of Simon and Rosa Brodsky, second cousins who had been born in Russia. Her mother had emigrated first, and her father—so the family story goes—saw a picture of Rosa and decided to move to America and marry her. Rosa Brodsky determined early that her daughter was to be a concert pianist, and the daughter later described her mother as "extremely ambitious" for her. Simon Brodsky was, at various times, a grocer, a dealer in store fixtures, and a jobber of dry goods; as a lover of music himself, he also encouraged his daughter's musical talent (shown by her ability to play without instruction) and started her on piano lessons at a young age. Although her general education began in public school, the bulk of it was by private tutoring to allow her to concentrate on music study. By the time she was eleven, her father's jobbing business had become so successful that he moved it and the family to New York, largely in order to give her access to outstanding music teachers.

Her first piano instructor there was Alexander Lambert, with whom she studied for five years (1921–26). Under his direction she made her first public appearance at the age of fifteen, in a December 1924 recital of his students. But her official debut came two months later, again under Lambert's supervision, when she and Hanna Lefkowitz played a concert at Aeolian Hall on February 6, 1925; the *New York Times* the next day reported the occasion under the heading "Two Girl Pianists in Debuts," noting that these "young Russian-American girls" presented "an unusual piano program." "Miss Brodsky," the reviewer said, "showed fluency and forceful musicianship" in her renditions of Debussy and Liszt. After Lambert, she worked with Josef and Rosina Lhévinne, first as a private student (1926–28) and then as a fellowship student at the Juilliard School (1928–30), where she also studied chamber music with Felix Salmond and harmony and theory with Rubin Goldmark and Bernard Wagenaar.

She embarked on a professional concert career immediately; and, when her father died six years later (on May 18, 1936, at the age of fifty-two, after a long illness), she had already received considerable attention. The *Musical Courier,* reporting his death, said that her success was "the great joy" of his life. She actively pursued her career as a pianist for thirty-four years (1930–64), performing to acclaim as a soloist with symphony orchestras and chamber music groups in the United States and Europe. When, for example, she presented Mozart's first piano quartet with the Roth Quartet at Barbizon-Plaza Hall on January 12, 1932, the *New York Times* reported that she "played with verve and understanding" and "distinctly won her audience through her delicate feeling and skill."

On a tour abroad in the summer of 1932 (following a schedule that included playing for the former crown prince of Germany at Mondsee and appearing with the Roth Quartet in Paris), she met Harold Triggs, another former Lhévinne student, at the Salzburg festival, and they decided to form a piano duo. It achieved rapid success: according to the *New York Times,* the two were already well known by February 14, 1933, when they played the premiere of Nicolai Berezowsky's *Fantasie* with the National Orchestral Association (organized to encourage young performers and composers), conducted by Leo Barzin at Carnegie Hall. Their first concert without an orchestra came on February 22, 1935, at Town Hall, with a program that included a number of transcriptions for two pianos, four of the pieces being played for the first time. One of them, added at the last minute, was Leopold Godowsky's just-completed duet transcription of his "Alt Wien"; Godowsky dedicated the piece to the two pianists and was in the audience to hear the performance. During their four years together (1932–36), Brodsky and Triggs appeared on numerous radio programs (including repeated visits to Fred Waring's show), and among their concert performances were a two-week engagement at the Radio City Music Hall and a 1936 nationwide tour.

The publicity they received came not only from their performances but also from their assumed role as champions of younger American composers. On November 14, 1933, the *New York World-Telegram* reported that the pair had been "making quiet but effective assaults upon the high-brow attitude of the self-styled high priests of music," and the accompanying picture of them carried the caption "At Bat for Younger Composers." By that time they had introduced the work of at least ten composers under the age of 35. Brodsky was quoted as explaining their mission in this way: "We feel it is the duty of young musicians to study and perform the works of the younger writers. The older musicians won't do it. We must." And she added, "We are not forsaking the classics, by any means. We just felt there was newer music which should be given its chance, too, if music is to be sustained and extended." She noted that they also liked historical "discoveries" and were planning to play an unperformed concerto of Ferdinand Bach (son of the great composer), using photocopies of the manuscript in the New York Public Library. These two concerns—publicizing the work of contemporary composers and resurrecting neglected works of the past—remained with her all her life: they were the motivating force behind the editions she produced nearly four decades later.

At the time of the New York World's Fair (1939–40), her interest in the new was displayed by her membership in Ferde Grofé's New World Ensemble, which played nightly in the Garden Court of the Ford Exposition (on the balcony of which she once held a large party that was attended by a number of New York musical celebrities). For the next six years (1939–45) she served on the Columbia Broadcasting System music staff as a performer on the CBS radio network (and an occasional performer on television). As staff pianist, one of her responsibilities was to be prepared to play as needed between radio programs, and she was on the air extensively and reached a huge audience. But her playing was by no means limited to such filling in; she was also a featured soloist, and on one occasion CBS held up its schedule by fifteen minutes to allow her to play the complete Brahms F-minor sonata. By January 1942 she was being called "the popular radio pianist" in *The Etude* magazine, and during the war years she had her own half-hour program on Sunday mornings at 11:00. Alfred Lindsay Morgan, writing on radio music for *The Etude,* ended his February 1945 comments on the fourth season of her show by saying, "Devotees of piano music as well as students of that instrument have acclaimed Miss Brodsky's playing and her interesting and able program making."

Through her numerous radio and concert appearances, she displayed an enormous repertoire, and her performance credits included many premieres. The most famous occurred on her radio broadcast of Wednesday, September 29, 1943, at 11:30 P.M., when she played Shostakovich's second piano sonata—a world premiere, according to the *New York Times,* which had reported the previous Sunday that the score "has just arrived from Russia by airplane." A few weeks later, on October 24, she played it for the first time in an American concert hall, on the occasion of an evening of Soviet instrumental and vocal works at Carnegie Hall, sponsored by the American-Russian Institute and attended by Ambassador Andrei Gromyko. The next day's *New York Times* reported that the Shostakovich piece was "splendidly played by Vera Brodsky." Many of her performances were recorded for the CBS archives, but some commercial recordings emerged as well. For instance, the broadcast on July 5, 1942, of Johnny Green's *Music for Elizabeth: Fantasia for Piano and Orchestra* (in which she played with the CBS Symphony Orchestra, conducted by the composer) was brought out in two long-playing records under the Rockhill Radio label; another performance of this piece, with her and Walter Gross forming a piano duo, was released by Victor.

While she was employed by CBS, she met Theodore Lawrence, son of Mr. and

Mrs. William T. Lawrence of New York and chief of the engineering department of the British Broadcasting Corporation in the United States; on February 22, 1944, they were married in Newark. Her husband, two years older than she, became—over the next two decades—successively an independent consultant to applicants for television licenses from the Federal Communications Commission (FCC), a technical director with Metro-Goldwyn-Mayer International, a technical director on lighting for CBS television, and a lighting expert with Kliegel Brothers Universal Electric Stage Lighting Company (Long Island City). She continued to make concert appearances after her marriage (though less frequently), but she soon gave up her CBS job. Among her musical activities in these years was participation in the National Association of American Composers and Conductors, which presented free concerts of American music at Town Hall; the program on January 13, 1952, for example, included her performance of a sonata by her former partner, Harold Triggs. Three months later (on April 20) she was one of the performers who presented a concert of contemporary Dutch chamber music at the Public Library in honor of Queen Juliana's visit to New York.

For a short time in the late 1940s, during her husband's FCC consultancy, the couple lived in the Washington suburb of Bethesda, Maryland. After that, they moved to a house on Quaker Road in the Rockland County village of Pomona, thirty miles from Manhattan, and in later life she spoke of her enjoyment of country living, particularly of her gardening and of the dog that accompanied them on cross-country automobile trips. All this came abruptly to an end on January 11, 1964, when her husband died in St. Clare's Hospital from injuries suffered in an automobile accident on 52nd Street near Eighth Avenue. The report of his death, with which she was suddenly confronted, haunted her the rest of her life, and she never after that played the piano. "Somehow I didn't want to do this any more. I changed just about everything in my life," she told Lindsy Van Gelder in an interview for the *New York Post* (November 6, 1975). Even piano playing at home was ruled out: a few months earlier (June 8, 1975), she had commented to a *New York Sunday News* interviewer, Robert Jones, "It's no pleasure being a weekend pianist when you've been a perfectionist." From that time forward, her earlier life was a topic she generally insisted on avoiding: "I hate talking about the past," she said in the same interview; "I've thrown away all my scrapbooks." She came to regard the twenty years of her marriage as an idyllic interlude between two careers.

She moved back into Manhattan and immersed herself in activity, immediately taking a job for the rest of 1964 as a lecturer on music history in the New York University School of Continuing Education. (She had in fact taught twice before for institutions, in addition to offering occasional private instruction: in 1936–37 she taught two-piano performance at the Curtis Institute of Music, and in 1948–50 she was a piano instructor at the Juilliard School.) In 1965 she began a five-year period of employment as an editor for music publishers, first (1965–67) with the Galaxy Music Publishing Corporation and then (1967–70) with the Contemporary Music Project (CMP), chaired by Norman Dello Joio and sponsored from its inception in 1958 by the Ford Foundation and the Music Educators National Conference. The quality of her work for Galaxy is suggested by Robert Ward's acknowledgment in *Sacred Songs for Pantheists* (1966): "I wish to acknowledge my debt to Vera Brodsky, who so devotedly revised and edited my reduction of the orchestral score for the piano." As administrator of

publications for the CMP and editor of the CMP Library, she devised and saw through
the press the three-volume *CMP Library Catalog* (1968; 2nd ed., 1969), describing
some five hundred works by most of the seventy-three composers who served in the
pathbreaking Composers in Public Schools Project. For this large and complex undertaking, which also involved editing the music itself and making it available in photocopy form, she supervised a staff of six editors working at picnic tables in her apartment. Her enthusiasm for the project is conveyed by her account of it in the March
1970 number of the Music Library Association's *Notes,* where she spoke of "the widely
diversified ripples it set into motion." Not the least of her accomplishments was her
recognition of the need for "a new kind of music-publishing technology which could
accommodate the unusual demands presented here" and her identification of University Microfilms of Ann Arbor as the firm that could provide the solution through its
experience in microfilming and xerography.

　　While finishing her work with CMP, she also brought to completion two independent projects, both published under the Arno Press/New York Times imprint:
in 1969, the Gottschalk edition mentioned earlier, which printed in facsimile 112
of Gottschalk's then out-of-print piano works; and in 1970, *The Wa-Wan Press,* a five-
volume facsimile reprinting of Arthur Farwell's historic series (1901–11) that published
compositions by thirty-six of his American contemporaries. (The first carried a biographical essay by Robert Offergeld, the second an introduction by Gilbert Chase; for
both, Richard Jackson was the editorial adviser.) Both editions were enthusiastically
received: H. Wiley Hitchcock (in *Notes* for March 1971) called the Gottschalk "exemplary" and said, "Bouquets should go to its editor"; and Edward N. Waters declared
that the Wa-Wan Press volumes "should be in every reference library in the land"
(*Notes,* June 1971). The idea for these editions had occurred to her when she visited
University Microfilms in connection with the CMP project and observed the firm's
system of making out-of-print books available in photographic reproductions; this
style of facsimile reprinting has since been widely adopted by music publishers, and her
editions have had a profound effect as a stimulus in the movement to recover neglected
American musical figures.

　　These two important publications were the first fruits of her determination to be
an independent scholar of American music history, and from then on she was able to
support herself primarily with a series of grants and fellowships and thus to pursue her
scholarly projects full-time. Her first two grants were from the Rockefeller Foundation, in 1970 and 1971. Under the first of them, she conducted an ingenious, determined, and wide-ranging search for all of Scott Joplin's music, and the result was her
Joplin edition, published in 1971 by the New York Public Library (with Richard Jackson as editorial consultant and with an introduction by Rudi Blesh and a preface to
the second volume by Carman Moore). A paperback entitled *Collected Piano Works* followed in 1972, along with a separate edition of Joplin's opera *Treemonisha* (edited with
William Bolcom, the composer and pianist who had introduced her to Joplin, for the
Dramatic Publishing Company); and in 1975 she brought out a "Vocal Selection" from
Treemonisha under her Fanfare Press imprint through the Chappell Music Company.
Gilbert Chase, reviewing the Joplin edition in *Notes* (December 1972), said that Law-
rence's "editorial vision, skill, and dedication are unsurpassed in the field of musical
Americana reprints."

Renewed interest in Joplin had been stirrng since the 1950s, but it took on particular force in the early 1970s, with performances by Joshua Rifkin, William Bolcom, and Dan Paget and recordings from Nonesuch Records. Her publication of the original sheet music in corrected facsimile was an esssential element in accelerating the revival, which has resulted in numerous performances throughout the world during the past quarter-century—beginning with what she called "the untrammeled emotional spree that was the Joplin mania of the '70s". As Joplin's fame spread, so did hers, and she was soon being called "the queen of ragtime," a title she always complained about. One of the journalists who interviewed her, Robert Jones, entitled a *Sunday News* column "Ragtime's Reluctant Queen" (June 8, 1975) and wrote, "Ms. Lawrence is the one who dug Scott Joplin out of the dust of libraries, took him away from the specialists and set him loose on the world. Without her, *The Sting* would have had music by somebody else and there wouldn't be sixteen listings of ragtime music under Joplin's name in the classical section of Schwann's catalogue. So—whether she likes it or not—Ms. Lawrence is the queen of ragtime."

Desirable, even inevitable, as the publication of Joplin seems to us now, it did not seem so in 1971, and her proposal was turned down by twenty-four commercial publishers before being accepted by the Public Library. She recounted, in concise form, the story of her "whole improbable Joplin adventure" for the printed program accompanying a Joplin concert at the New York Public Library on April 15, 1982, performed by the New England Ragtime Ensemble under Gunther Schuller's direction. The occasion for the concert was the 1981 republication of her Joplin edition with the word "Complete" replacing "Collected" in the title, for she had finally been able to include the three rags ("Fig Leaf Rag," "Rose Leaf Rag," and "Searchlight Rag") that she was forced to leave out of the original publication through the refusal of Jerry Vogel, their copyright owner, to cooperate.

Among her other activities on behalf of Joplin's reputation was her uncompromising insistence on a proper production of *Treemonisha,* after a January 1972 Atlanta premiere (produced by the music department of Morehouse College, with the Atlanta Symphony conducted by Robert Shaw) that she considered "one-dimensional." As artistic adviser to the Joplin estate, she steadfastly refused all performance requests (many of them from advertising agencies wishing to use the music in television commercials) until she could put together an appropriate team—which eventually included Gunther Schuller as orchestrator and conductor, Frank Corsaro as director, Franco Colavecchia as designer, and Louis Johnson as choreographer. The Houston Grand Opera mounted this production in May 1975 at the large outdoor Miller Theater, where the last of its seven performances drew 25,000 people. This success was repeated in Washington and New York later in the year, and in 1976 the Deutsche Grammophon cast recording, for which Lawrence was the artistic consultant, was the best-selling opera record of the year.

Her second Rockefeller Foundation grant (for 1971–72) allowed her to undertake research for a book on American patriotic and political songs from 1776 to 1876. Originally intended as a volume of campaign music to appear during the 1972 campaign, it grew into a much more ambitious historical work; when Macmillan finally brought it out in early November 1975 (just when *Treemonisha* was opening in New York), it bore the title *Music for Patriots, Politicians, and Presidents: Harmonies and Discords of the*

First Hundred Years. In it she showed how popular songs have always reflected the issues of the day, and her deft explanation of the background of each of the selected songs amounts to "a step-by-step narrative of American history" (as she said in the preface). Her text was accompanied by more than five hundred illustrations, some in color. Indeed, the proportion of illustrations to text and the large page size make this handsome volume appear a "coffee-table book"; but anyone who reads the text and understands the original research it embodies will know that the book is a serious work of scholarship. Although her previous publications had given her considerable experience in research, this was the first time that she revealed her skill in constructing detailed historical narratives from diverse sources, writing them up in a lively style that reflected a wry intelligence (she always maintained that scholarship and readability were not incompatible), and supplementing them with a generous selection of illustrations that clearly resulted from painstaking and imaginative searching in many libraries and collections.

Advance attention had been drawn to the book by Macmillan's February 1975 announcement of a new performing-arts division, the first endeavor of which was to be a musical based on her book and written by Edward Albee (a project that never materialized). Then, four months later, she arranged a program of twenty political songs to be performed by the John Motley Singers at the Diamond Jubilee Banquet of the American Booksellers Association convention (held in the New York Hilton on May 28); the printed program for the occasion, which used the same cover design as the jacket for her book, contained her comments on each song and listed her as a guest of honor. The great enthusiasm with which these songs were greeted, coming just after the success of *Treemonisha* in Houston, made the early summer of 1975 one of the most satisfying moments of her life, for she took these events as evidence that her campaign to rescue the American musical past for a wide audience was gaining momentum. She gave numerous radio and newspaper interviews about the book, which was actively promoted by Macmillan as a contribution to the Bicentennial and was widely and favorably reviewed in newspapers and magazines. The impact of the new book was further increased through its choice as an offering of the History Book Club and its winning the 1976 Deems Taylor Award of the American Society of Composers, Authors, and Publishers, as well as through Lawrence's preparation of an accompanying songbook, *Themes and Variations for Patriots, Politicians, and Presidents,* published by Fanfare Press and Macmillan and distributed by Schirmer in 1976. It was at this time that the New England Conservatory of Music recognized the whole body of her work by conferring on her an honorary Doctor of Music degree.

By 1976 she had behind her an extraordinary series of publications of increasing complexity, and she was ready to tackle a still more ambitious project. She applied to the John Simon Guggenheim Memorial Foundation with a proposal for the initial work on *Strong on Music* and received a Guggenheim Fellowship for 1976–77. Once begun, this work became her consuming passion, and she pursued it indefatigably for the remaining two decades of her life, supported generously and attentively by the National Endowment for the Humanities (four grants, 1978–80, 1980–82, 1989–93, and 1993–94). Her initial idea had been to bring together the largely unpublished entries on music from the famous diary of George Templeton Strong, weave them into a narrative, and annotate them to supplement the details provided by Strong. But in preparing herself for this task she discovered (as she put it in the preface to the first volume) "a fascinating, unfamiliar area of American sociocultural history—far beyond Strong's personal experience—that demanded to be chronicled."

Thus she conceived what she called a "binary form," in which each year would be covered by two essays: the first, labeled "GTS," would discuss the performances that Strong attended (and include the full texts of his comments), and the second, entitled "Obbligato," would cover (to quote from the preface to the second volume) "the thousand-and-one concurrent music happenings outside (often beneath) Strong's notice." Given the previous neglect of nineteenth-century American music history, about which she eloquently and repeatedly complained, she had to assemble this information from the rich array of contemporary sources, such as newspapers (her favorite and most used source), printed concert programs, city directories, records of music societies, music publishers' catalogues, letters and memoirs, and so on. Her immersion in the material was such that she could identify the authors of many of the anonymous newspapers reviews, and she felt strongly about the value of this largely overlooked mass of music criticism, which is "crucial to the understanding of our musical foundations" (as she said in her second-volume prefatory plea for more work on these critics).

Such research is time-consuming, and it was not until early 1988, when she was 78 (and thirteen years after the project was conceived), that the first volume was published by Oxford University Press. The title given to the series was *Strong on Music: The New York Music Scene in the Days of George Templeton Strong,* and each volume was to have its own title. The first volume, covering 1836–49 in 600 pages, was entitled *Resonances;* the longer (750-page) second volume, published by the University of Chicago Press in 1995 (along with paperbacks of both volumes), covered 1850–56 as *Reverberations;* and a third volume, now published posthumously with her designated title *Repercussions,* covers 1857–62 and contains all the material she completed before her death.

Accounting for this magnificent three-volume work in this way does not do justice to its distinctive strengths—its inclusiveness (taking in the music of beer gardens, parades, circuses, and the like as well as of concert halls); its firm sense of how all these "diverse musics" (as she called them) play their part in cultural history; and its controlling style, the articulate and witty voice of an intelligent, sophisticated, knowledgeable, even-handed, shrewd, impassioned, clear-headed, unsentimental, generous observer. Her command of style and her balance are suggested by her assessment of Strong in the preface to the first volume: "I have not allowed my admiration for Strong's dazzling journal to deafen me to the dissonant ostinato of social snobbery, intellectual intolerance, and religious and ethnic bigotry with which his otherwise witty and graceful pages are tainted." The work is music history in depth, but it is more than music history; it is cultural history laced with a wealth of beguiling anecdotes and personalities that should be contemplated by anyone who wishes to understand nineteenth-century America. As its author said in introducing the second volume, Strong's journal serves as "a passport to a bygone world." Harold C. Schonberg, reviewing the first volume in the *New York Times Book Review* (March 13, 1988), spoke for many others when he called the work "marvelous" and concluded, "There is nothing like it in the literature of American music."

This record of the highlights of Vera Brodsky Lawrence's life omits many details that would round out the picture—such as, to name a few, her liberal political activism, her piano playing for political rallies, her adaptation of fifteen neglected Offenbach pieces to produce the score for the musical *Bon Voyage* (with lyrics by Edward Mabley, it was performed by the York Players Company at the Church of the Heavenly Rest, New York, in November and December 1977), her record liner and program notes, her service (1977–80) on the Policy and Planning Panel of the National Endowment for the Arts, her membership on the Board of Advisors of the Publishing Center for Cultural Resources, her delight in the theater. And there are many other examples of her untiring efforts to revive America's musical heritage—such as her numerous articles in magazines, encyclopedias, and scholarly journals and her preparation of the program and program notes for several concerts by the Paul Hill Chorale, under the general title "Prelude to the Bicentennial." The first of them, "The Music Has Always Been There," presented at the Kennedy Center on May 23, 1972, attracted national attention (causing *Time* to review it on June 5 and to refer to her "mania for musical Americana"); its success vindicated her belief "that if people only have a chance to hear it, they'll love this music out of our past."

She had a circle of loyal friends, though they often felt sorely tried by her stubbornness, her hypercritical attitudes, and her unyielding frankness; these traits, however, were combined with feelings of great warmth and devotion toward those who had gained her respect. Her scholarly relationships had a similar edge: knowing that her time was limited, she nevertheless agreed to read manuscripts, in which she generally found much to criticize and correct; but her severe judgments were the products of great generosity, because she freely gave her precious time to upholding standards in her field and enhancing the reputations of her correspondents. In the same spirit, she gladly took the trouble to extract large quantities of information from her files upon request. She was aware that her tenacious pursuit of excellence (which had been as characteristic of her concert career as of her scholarly one) tested the patience of those she dealt with. "I can be a stubborn, persistent, demanding woman," she said to Halsey Melone in an interview for the *Washington Post* (August 6, 1972). "But," she added, "I'm not a bit harder on anyone else than I am on myself." Another interviewer, Ellen Pfeifer, concisely depicted her as "small, elegantly spoken, and lady-like, but with a discernible steely perfectionism" (*Boston Sunday Herald Advertiser,* November 2, 1975). One of her friends recently pointed out that her motto could appropriately have been "Don't fake," the instruction sometimes issued to performers by ragtime composers; she was constitutionally incapable of fakery in any form and became incensed when she detected it in the work of others. Her perfectionism and perseverance, it should be added, were always matched by enthusiasm for her work and a firm conviction of its importance.

Many of these points were heard in conversation among the friends and colleagues who gathered for a memorial program to celebrate her achievements, held on January 28, 1997, at the New-York Historical Society, where the Strong diary is housed and where much of her research was carried out. (Some of her own papers and files are now located there, and others are in the Archives of the New York Philharmonic and the Music Division of the New York Public Library.) The evening, arranged by Barbara Haws (archivist of the Philharmonic), consisted of reminiscences by her and by Frank Corsaro (who also read from *Strong on Music*), along with three musical performances: selections from Gottschalk's piano music, played by Robert DeGaetano; "The Sacred Tree" from *Treemonisha,* sung by Geraldine McMillian, accompanied by Wayne Sanders; and, as the finale, the recording of Lawrence's 1943 premiere performance of Shostakovich's *Piano Sonata No. 2.* Most of the audience had never before heard her play.

Vera Brodsky Lawrence lived to see that her scholarly labors were appreciated, and she was always gratified by such tangible signs of recognition as an Honorary Membership in the Sonneck Society (1986) and an award for *Strong on Music* from the Victorian Society in New York (1996). During the last decade of her life she suffered from increasingly severe pains, the cause of which was never discovered. But she continued to work on *Strong on Music;* indeed, writing and polishing it were what kept her going for a long time, and the last date on her computer files for Volume 3 was December 20, 1995. In the remaining nine months she was unable to work, but she had completed enough material for a third volume. At the beginning of the first one she had said that the project was taking her on a journey from which she might never return; she did not, in fact, reach her destination—the ending year of Strong's diary—but she had covered more than a quarter of the nineteenth century in unprecedented depth. Witnessing the publication of the third volume would have given her immense pleasure, as would the thought (to use her words from the previous volume) that it might inspire others "to carry forward what has been begun here." Certainly the presence of the three volumes will be an enduring source of astonished satisfaction to future scholars.

G. THOMAS TANSELLE

Repercussions

I

GTS: 1857

More marching and countermarching of the Operatic hosts! Sudden invasions, doubtful conflicts, brilliant victories leading to no results, unexpected retreats—such has been the recent course of Operatic history in New York.

Raimond
The Albion
May 16, 1857

A s 1857 UNFOLDED, the escalating sectional discord and economic disaster besetting all aspects of life in America commensurately afflicted the world of music. Concert-giving in New York—except for the periodic incursions of Sigismund Thalberg,♪ later with Henri Vieuxtemps♪—was severely curtailed. Opera, lacking the domination of Max Maretzek♪♪ for the first time in nearly a decade, stumbled along an even more precarious path than usual, at first with a succession of fleeting "seasons" under a motley assortment of presenters, then monopolized, or rather swamped—despite the hard times—by a spasmodic deluge of operas and opera-cum-concert extravaganzas unleashed by Bernard Ullman,♪♪ at last in possession of the entrepreneurial supremacy he had so long coveted.[1]

This musical instability scarcely affected George Templeton Strong, who continued unperturbedly to listen to the music he preferred—at public rehearsals and concerts of the Philharmonic Society at the Academy of Music (conducted this year by Theodore Eisfeld);♪♪[2] at Eisfeld's chamber music *soirées,* now in their seventh season;[3] at an occasional choral concert; now and then at a recherché private musicale at someone's residence; and once in a great while at the opera, usually for social, rather than musical, reasons.

[1] Achieved with funds gained from his tremendously successful management of Thalberg's American tour, with the further aid of Thalberg's ready financial backing for Ullman's various other managerial schemes, and with the timely interventions of the perennial opera angel, William H. Paine,♪ and apparently, too, of Ullman's longtime confrere John C. Jacobson (the erstwhile Jacobsohn).♪

[2] The Philharmonic seasons were now alternately conducted by Eisfeld and Carl Bergmann.♪♪

[3] Eisfeld's quartet consisted, as before, of Joseph Noll and Charles Reyer (violins), Eisfeld (viola), and Frederick Bergner (cello), all Philharmonic musicians. Their *soirées* were given at Dodworth's Rooms.

3

January 11, 1857. . . . Heard Mozart's lovely ["Jupiter"] Symphony at the Philharmonic rehearsal yesterday morning and did not go to the evening concert [the second of the Society's fifteenth season]—too great a crowd anticipated and nothing I
cared to hear but the symphony.

⁓

Particularly, Strong did not care to hear the star soloist of the evening, Louis Moreau Gottschalk,♪⁴ whom he categorically detested. Nor was he attracted by the prospect of hearing the first New York performance of Richard Wagner's *Faust* Overture
(1839–40, revised 1855):⁵ Strong was by no means a lover of contemporary music.

Nor, apparently, were the majority of the local music critics. Reviewing the concert on January 12, Charles Bailey Seymour,♪ the longtime critic of the *New-York
Times,* wrote: "After the symphony we had an overture labeled 'Faust' and written by
Mr. R. Wagner—a gentleman who supplies nightmares to the present generation—
and what he facetiously calls 'music for the future.'" Worthy of its source, added Seymour, the overture was "an effort of laborious dullness. It contains a vast amount of
sound and displays excellent mechanical skill in the precise use of instruments," keeping the musicians "at it, in factory style, until they come out at the other end of the
score." This might have been tolerable had there been "something tangible to work
upon, but in the absence of the solitary grain of wheat, this pitiless elaboration of the
chaff is somewhat hideous." The critic could find no justification for calling the work
a "Faust" Overture; it might as appropriately have been called an overture to "Pongo,
or the Intelligent Ape."⁶ The other novelty on the program—the Overture to Karl
Gutzkow's play *Uriel Acosta* (1846), by the minor German composer Louis Schindel-
meisser (1811–1864)—was, according to Seymour, "a respectable, *Lager-Bier-Garden*
sort of work."

Gottschalk played the first movement of Adolf Henselt's Piano Concerto in F minor, op. 16, a work rarely heard because of its reputedly insurmountable difficulties.
Performed by so superb a virtuoso as Gottschalk, wrote Seymour, it revealed the delightful freshness, grace, and melodious clearness that characterized its composer,
whom he held—in contrast to Wagner—to be a genius. Additionally, with Sigismund
Thalberg's pupil Emile Guyon♪ at the second piano, Gottschalk repeated the razzle-
dazzle Fantasy on themes from *Il trovatore* that he had composed for his recent "farewell" appearance with Thalberg, at Niblo's Saloon on December 26, 1856.♪⁷

True to form, Theodore Hagen,♪ Seymour's staunchly Germanic opposite num-

⁴Although Gottschalk had been elected an honorary member of the Philharmonic Society in
1855—and although he had been frequently invited—this was his first (and only) appearance with
the Society.

⁵Also appearing was Madame Bertha Sheerer-Johannsen,♪ *prima donna* of the unsuccessful German Opera Company♪ now in its expiring throes at the Broadway Theatre. She sang arias from Giovanni Pacini's *Niobe*♪ and from Mozart's *La clemenza di Tito,*♪ with clarinet *obbligato* played by Xavier
Kiefer.♪ Madame Johannsen received a generally commendatory press.

⁶The title of a currently favorite pantomime performed by the "Wonderful Ravels" at Niblo's
Garden.

⁷Gottschalk was twitted in the press for his endlessly repetitive *concerts d'adieux.* Like Paul Julien,♪ wrote Dwight's New York correspondent, *Trovator,* he seemed "determined *never* to leave the
country" (*Dwight's,* January 17, 1857, p. 127). Before his eventual departure for Cuba on February

Girvice Archer, Jr.

*Louis Moreau Gottschalk, as composer
and pianist, earned both praise and
scorn for his performances.*

ber on the *New-York Musical Review and Gazette,* gave an opposing assessment of the program (January 24, 1857, pp. 18–19). Mozart's Symphony, he wrote (echoing current avant-garde gospel), was an archaic work so simple and naive as to make its designation of "Jupiter" seem "almost comical." Yet, the symphony had caused a great deal of confusion to its earlier hearers—just as the works of Berlioz, Schumann, and Wagner were now causing a consternation that would be laughed at fifty years hence.

14 he would make yet more "farewell" appearances: on January 13 at Dodworth's for the benefit of his agent D. S. Bookstaver,♪ assisted by Clara Brinkerhoff, by fourteen-year-old Adelina Patti,♪ his future touring colleague, and by Guyon, with whom he repeated his *Trovatore* Fantasy; on January 16 with little Patti and Guyon at the Brooklyn Athenaeum; and on January 17—along with two debutant singers, Henrietta Simon, a young soprano from Cincinnati, and Mr. Rivarde, a baritone—as assisting artist at Guyon's concert at Niblo's Saloon. Illness prevented Gottschalk from appearing on January 24 at Eisfeld's *soirée,* for which he had been announced (see below).

And just as Beethoven had dispensed with "all unnecessary phrases in his music," so did Wagner: "Every trait in [the *Faust* Overture] is to the point; every *motivo*, every run and figure serves only to add to the characteristics of the whole." To Hagen, Goethe's words were implicit in every phrase. "The immense amount of melody scattered all over the work is a noble specimen of Wagner's happiest inspirations," he wrote. Hagen proudly quoted John Sullivan Dwight,♪♫ who—overwhelmed upon hearing the *Faust* Overture in Boston a few days before its New York premiere[8]—had found it to possess traits akin to Beethoven's Fifth and Ninth Symphonies, and the Overture to *Coriolanus*. To Dwight, Wagner's overture represented "something of the same sublime struggle of the soul with destiny" (*Dwight's Journal of Music,* January 10, 1857, p. 115).

Gottschalk, whom Hagen despised as cordially as did George Templeton Strong, "*attempted* to play the first part of Henselt's Concerto. We say 'attempted,'" stressed Hagen, "not because [Gottschalk] substituted for the difficult runs in the middle part his usual easy ones, nor because he dropped a great many notes, but because, in spite of all these abbreviations and simplifications, the remaining difficulties of the piece seemed to be so immense to him that he could not afford to show the least expression, nor anything of an artist-like conception and treatment." Although Henselt's concerto was concededly difficult, wrote Hagen, it had nonetheless been mastered by several first-rate pianists in Europe, none of whom had stooped to such shameless evasions as had Gottschalk—insulting to public and composer alike. And if Gottschalk had supposed that nobody among the New York critics would know the difference, well, he was not quite correct. Henry C. Watson,♪♫ in *Leslie's Illustrated Newspaper,* had also detected Gottschalk's shameful misrepresentations, exulted Hagen.[9] As for the duo on *Il trovatore,* it was, in Hagen's opinion, not only grossly inappropriate at a Philharmonic concert, but "it was the thinnest music for *two* pianos we were ever obliged to listen to."[10]

Watson, in fact, had characterized Wagner's music as "the music of indigestion, a scientific nightmare in which melody is so inhumanly treated that, torn limb from limb, we stumble occasionally upon a broken member here and there; but so disfigured by unnatural treatment, impaled now by one harmony, then crowded down and almost obliterated by some excruciating dissonance, that it is no longer to be recognized as a thing of form and meaning." Watson wondered who might be able to "bring Wagner's chaotic material into form and order, should Wagner, while groping in the dark, occasionally turn up diamonds from out of his heap of rubbish" (*Leslie's,* January 24, 1857, p. 123).

In the *Daily Tribune* (January 12, 1857), William Henry Fry♪♫—despite his well-publicized championship of American music a passionate disciple of contemporary

[8] Performed on January 3, 1857, by the Boston Philharmonic, conducted by Carl Zerrahn.

[9] Not exactly. Watson, most ardent of Gottschalkians, had in truth complained, not of a lapse in his hero's virtuosity, but of the textual embroideries that he had allowed himself "under the mistaken notion of increasing the effect. In any case," Watson had written, "the taste [was] very questionable" (*Leslie's,* January 24, 1857, p. 123).

[10] With this, at least, Watson agreed: "How it came upon a Philharmonic programme we are at a loss to conceive (*ibid.*)."

Italian opera—expressed unaccustomed, albeit chilly, tolerance of Mozart's "Jupiter" Symphony. Although he habitually damned Mozart as a primitive old fogy lacking the ability adequately to orchestrate an opera, in this instance Fry granted Mozart some "dominant good sense and good taste" in the use of melody—a capability Mozart had acquired in his youth from "setting music to Italian meters." As for "pooh-poohing down the claims, the aspirations, or even the shortcomings of such men as Wagner, Berlioz, and the others, it [was] simply ridiculous. They are divers and delvers for pearls beneath the surface, and good comes of such daring." But, qualified Fry, they were on the wrong track in neglecting "the spontaneity of melody." The sharp contrast between Mozart's melodiousness and Wagner's dissonance clearly indicated that "the new school must connect more of the beautiful with its emotional aspirations if it wishes to become popular. . . . In speaking thus," hedged Fry, temporarily attempting to be all things to all men, "we do not wish to be understood as warring against the new school or considering the old [to be] inimitably fine. But," he added with atypical sweet reasonableness, "if musical composition take any direction in this country, it should steer clear of fanaticism for either. At present," he concluded, "there is no danger of any polemical war on the subject such as has raged in Germany, for we will do our public the justice to say that they are absolutely indifferent to all artistic discussion of the kind."

Fry, no lover of concertos, minced no words in calling Henselt's concerto, "like other concertos accompanied by the orchestra . . . , a bore. The piano in the Academy was a farce, and its incapacity to fill such a large building was heightened by being overlaid by an orchestra. The composition of Henselt has some beautiful melodic bits, but is patchy in its piano and orchestra sequences. It was exquisitely difficult, and was well played, of course," by Gottschalk. Fry did not stay to hear the two-piano offering.

To the *Evening Post* critic[11] the *Trovatore* Fantasy, despite the rapturous encore it received, sounded like nothing but "two grand pianos with two skillful pianists gymnasticizing vigorously at the opposite ends." Venturing to censure the contemporary *idée fixe* in solo instrumental music—the fantasy on themes from the operas—he wrote: "We hate to quarrel with our dear public, but *fiat justitia ruat coelum:*[12] Verdi's airs require for good effect the apparatus of the opera—scenery, costume, gaslight, and warbling prima donnas; it is cruel to drag them forth in shivering nakedness [the airs, presumably], to be tortured on the six-and-fifty teeth of Chickering's mahogany monsters before the ruthless audience of the Academy. What the public really admires, or ought to in this performance, is not the dying wail of the tormented arias, but only the surpassing skill of Mr. Gottschalk as chief executioner" (*Evening Post,* January 12, 1857).

Pronouncing Wagner's *Faust* Overture to be "deficient in definiteness and clear intention," the *Post* critic closed his review with the fervent hope that the Philharmonic doorkeepers would "contrive some less objectionable way of taking tickets in

---

[11] It might have been Nathaniel Parker Willis,♪♫ who, according to his brother Richard Storrs Willis,♫ wrote an occasional music review for the *Post* (see *New-York Musical World,* March 14, 1857, p. 162).

[12] "Let justice be done though the heavens should fall."

THE NEW THEATRE.

Constance (reads Advertisement to Alice)—" ' The orchestra stalls will be exceedingly commodious. Each person will have a separate arm-chair, or occupying a space of two feet in breadth.' H'm—I don't see that that's so exceedingly commodious—eh, dear ?"—Punch.

Even ladies in crinolines worried about the size of seats in the theatre.

the first rush[13] at the entrance than by lifting the ladies and gentlemen—great coats, hoops, and all—through eighteen inches of doorway. Ladies' dresses [the crinoline was then in full, space-consuming fling], after going through the process, look anything but new."[14]

And *Raimond,* the monumentally chatty, manifestly Gallic, critic of the *Albion,* although he was reluctant to pass judgment on Wagner's overture after only a single hearing, admitted to having been more "stunned" than "seduced" by it: "It left us positively *beshrieked* with strident instrumentation," he wrote. But more strident still was the deafening "*chuchotement* of multitudinous little treble voices" belonging to the hordes of irrepressibly loquacious young ladies who had made the Philharmonic rehearsals and concerts their official meeting place for the exchange of gossip and flirtation with their male opposite numbers; they had managed to drown out Wagner even at his most vociferous. *Raimond* appealed to the Philharmonic elders to do something

[13] "We understand that there is no telling [in this year of the Philharmonic's inordinate popularity] at what hour the Philharmonic audiences begin to assemble," complained Watson (*Leslie's,* January 24, 1857, p. 123). "Much as we love these concerts, we do not enjoy them. . . . For who could enjoy classical or any other kind of music while employed in balancing oneself first on one foot and then on the other. . . . A full half hour did we arrive before the time of commencement, but we found every seat occupied."

[14] For a satirical survey of the current crinoline madness, see the delectable cartoons appearing in *Harper's Weekly* throughout 1857.

to curb this adolescent menace to the essential, serious purpose of the Society. The police! Anything! (*Albion,* January 17, 1857, p. 52).

January 22. . . . Tuesday night [January 20] Eisfeld's third [chamber music] concert [of his seventh series]: Quartet in F—Beethoven's op. 19[15]—not intelligible to me, but admirable in the well-informed judgment of others (e.g., J. J. Post,♪ who had heard it before)—[Carl] Eckert's Trio [*concertante,* op. 58], [Richard] Hoffman♪♫ at the piano, extemporized substitute for the [still present] great Gottschalk, who was ill.[16] Clear, fluent, and pretty, particularly the Scherzo, manifestly the germ of the old "Gaily the Troubadour" melody;[17] Haydn's Quartet in G, no. 63 [*sic*], very familiar and genial.[18]

January 24. . . . At Philharmonic rehearsal at 3:30 P.M. Met Ellie there. Schumann's [Second] Symphony [op. 61; first performed by the Philharmonic in 1854].♪ Cleared out after an Allegro and Scherzo "most tolerable and not to be endured,"[19] proving that Herr Schumann had worked very hard to produce something great and genial and had panted and sweated in hope of doing what Beethoven did easily, and had not done it, and had produced something troublesome to play and dismal to hear.

No human creature should do pictures or poetry or music if he can *help* it. If the inspiration is on him and the gift is in him and the power is with him he *can't* help it, and he will produce something worth producing. Otherwise he won't, and had better expend his energies on the production of potatoes, or the promotion of a railroad or canal, by the use of pickaxe and spade and flexor extensor muscles [rather] than on the desecration and degradation of Art by second-rate song or symphony or picture.

⌁

As might be expected, Strong did not attend the concert proper, given at the Academy of Music on March 7. To *Raimond,* who did attend, the Schumann Symphony, with its "learned combinations and gyratory harmonies," was alone to blame for a less than delightful evening. Not that the symphony was deficient in "evidences

---

[15] It was in fact Beethoven's "Razoumovsky" Quartet in F, op. 59, no. 1 (1806), a misidentification in the program, perpetuated by Watson in *Leslie's* (January 31, 1857, p. 131) as op. 19. Despite being announced as a first New York performance, the work had been played in 1855 at the second Mason/Bergmann matinée.♪

[16] Replacing Gottschalk at the last minute, Hoffman gave a remarkable exhibition of his extraordinary gifts as a sight-reader, wrote Watson. It was a "masterly" performance despite Hoffman's lack of rehearsal with the string players.

[17] Hoffman played the work admirably, wrote Hagen (*Review and Gazette,* January 24, 1857, p. 19), but "as to the musical merit of the trio, we feel confident that Mr. Hoffman would not have chosen of his own accord to play such a trashy composition between pieces of Beethoven, Gluck, and Haydn." (A not too thinly veiled thrust at Gottschalk's musical taste.)

[18] Additionally, Clara Brinkerhoff sang a recitative and aria from Gluck's *Iphigenia in Aulis* (in French) and one of Beethoven's *Egmont* songs♪ (in German). "Mrs. Brinkerhoff is a good singer," wrote *Raimond,* "but the quality of her voice is too strident and sharp, and her style is too abrupt, and (if we may borrow an expression from a sister art) her treatment of light and shade is too *stippled* for the performance of music so warmly-coloured and so vigorously fluent as Gluck's" (*Albion,* January 24, 1857, p. 44). The *Times* (January 21, 1857), on the contrary, found Mrs. Brinkerhoff's Gluck aria to have been given with "feeling and a strict regard for the sentiment."

[19] Strong's perennial put-down for music that he disapproved was borrowed from Dogberry in *Much Ado About Nothing,* act 3, scene 3, line 36.

of profound musical knowledge, nor even unilluminated by rays of musical genius, or unquickened by an air of inspiration," he elaborately explained (*Albion,* March 14, 1857, pp. 127–28). But it dispensed, particularly in its Larghetto, "enough tediousness and bewilderment to annihilate one's powers for the space of a whole evening. . . . What it signified, or whereof it affirmed, we neither know, nor ever expect to know. The *Schumannic* dislike of melody (let us call it rather contempt) amounts to an antipathetic and constitutional difficulty," wrote *Raimond,* who would even rather have listened to the "incoherencies and clangours of Wagner [than to Schumann's] incomprehensibilities and deliberate mystifications."

But Hagen, fiery defender of the German muse, gloried in the grandeur of Schumann's concept: "Every part, every sentence, every phrase, is laid out on the grandest scale," he wrote, although (a surprising admission) "what the author intended to illustrate, we do not know." But it was easy to conjecture from its "fanfares" and the martial character of some of its *motivos* that the symphony aspired to be "a sort of second *Eroica*." Not that it could compete with that sublime masterpiece in terms of what Hagen designated as "so-called melody." Yet, as an example of polyphonic perfection it stood supreme. Hagen urged all young students of music earnestly to study it and follow its example (*Review and Gazette,* March 21, 1857, pp. 82–83).

The program also included the Concert Overture, op. 7, by the contemporary German composer Julius Rietz,♩ according to Hagen an intelligent but commonplace work; two inconsequential violin solos played by Edward Mollenhauer,♩ "of which one would have been more than sufficient"; and two arias, sung by Marie de Roode, a recent arrival from Holland—"On Mighty Pens" from Haydn's *The Creation* and "Ocean, Thou Mighty Monster" from Weber's *Oberon,* "both of which perhaps were too much." Although she evinced a certain amount of intelligence, Miss de Roode (who received a mixed press) would have made a more favorable impression, wrote Hagen, had she not lacked "the first requisite of a singer—a voice" (*Review and Gazette,* January 24, 1857, pp. 18–19). The concert concluded, after a five-minute intermission to accommodate early departures, with Beethoven's Overture to *Egmont.*

By now, opera, restored to the Academy of Music after only a brief hiatus, was completing a short and characteristically hazardous season.

February 14. . . . Last night Walter Cutting[20] dined here and went with us to the Opera. *Trovatore.* I think there is some gleam of melodic feeling in a small way discernible toward its finale. So far, it's an improvement on Verdi's characteristic style of work, but after all—whether musically or dramatically considered—what monstrous and wonderful imbecility it is for the reigning fashionable amusement of a "cultivated" society! Plot below the standard of a minor shilling theatre, text that would be repudiated by the "Poet's Corner" of the New-York *Sun,* and music below everything. I was going to say below Nigger-Minstrelsy, but the latter implies great injustice to the latter form of Art. These are thy gods, O Fifth Avenue!

Verdi has one or two tricks that a respectable composer might introduce into an Opera once or twice with effect, but he constructs the whole Opera with them.

---

[20] An old friend and associate from the early days in Strong's paternal law office.'

In December 1856, upon Max Maretzek's sensational final break with the directors of the Academy of Music, followed by his precipitate departure with his opera company to Havana,♪ the resourceful pianist/impresario Maurice Strakosch♪ (Maretzek's cousin) had lost no time in securing the Academy for "twelve nights of Italian opera,"[21] to begin under his direction[22] on January 19. Possessing the nucleus of an able opera company in the members of his highly successful "Grand Concert Company"♪—the celebrated soprano Teresa Parodi,[23]★ the tenor Mario Tiberini,♪★ the mezzo-soprano Amalia Patti-Strakosch♪ (Strakosch's wife), and the baritone Oswald Bernardi♪—Strakosch easily assembled a supporting cast from the populous local colony of idled Italian opera singers: the contralto Giuseppina Martini d'Ormy,♪ the baritone Vincenzo Morino,♪ and one of the Barili brothers,♪★ most likely Nicolò, a bass (Amalia Strakosch's half brother). They were joined by the baritone Filippo Morelli♪★ upon completion of his tour of New England with Sigismund Thalberg.[24] Additionally, and of particular interest, Strakosch announced among his attractions the first appearance in opera of the favored young New York soprano Cora de Wilhorst,♪ briefly a member of Thalberg's touring company.

Strakosch's engagement of de Wilhorst indicates that by now he had joined forces with his longtime adversary, the redoubtable Bernard Ullman, Wilhorst's manager (and, of course, Thalberg's). Indeed, Strakosch's two opera seasons at the Academy most probably served as a kind of trial-balloon-*cum*-holding-action, with Strakosch acting as front man in a three-cornered partnership with Ullman and Thalberg, who—in any case—were soon to be announced as joint lessees of the Academy of Music, effective September 1.[25]

In the meantime, the *Herald* proclaimed Strakosch's reinstatement of opera at the Academy in a burst of vintage *Heraldese* (January 6, 1857): "The announcement has created a cheerful sensation in the world of fashion and trade. The dealers in opera cloaks, gloves, lorgnettes, *bijouterie, etc., etc.,* skip like young lambs, and all the musical ladies in the Fifth Avenue sing out of tune for joy."

Adopting an ostensibly protective attitude toward Strakosch after long years of hostility, the *Herald* plied him with advice on how to profit from the mistakes and ex-

---

[21] To be given on the customary opera nights: Mondays, Wednesdays, and Fridays. Admission prices were $1 for seats in the parquet, dress circle, and first tier, 50 cents extra for reserved seats; 50 cents for tickets in the family circle (second tier); 25 cents for the amphitheatre, as the uppermost tier was euphemistically called; and $5–$20 for private boxes.

[22] An act of audacity. Strakosch, although a good keyboard accompanist, had little experience as a conductor.

[23] Not locally heard in opera since 1851, when she had been introduced by Maretzek as a rival to Jenny Lind.♪

[24] A star of Maretzek's opera company, Morelli had not accompanied Maretzek's group to Havana, choosing instead to continue touring with Thalberg.

[25] "On the twenty-fourth day of February," writes Max Maretzek (*Sharps and Flats,* p. 37): "Mr. Bernard Ullman and Sigismund Thalberg became the lesees of the Academy, but before the expiration of one week Mr. Thalberg, for the sum of $1 paid in hand, 'did sell, assign and transfer all his rights, titles, etc.' of said lease to Mr. Ullman." In Thalberg's place, continues Maretzek, "Mr. Maurice Strakosch, till then a confirmed enemy of Ullman, stepped in and formed a partnership with the very man he had for years abused publicly and privately." (Thalberg's abdication was apparently not made known in the press.)

travagances of his predecessors (meaning Maretzek), "all of whom ran against some snag or other and were more or less shipwrecked"; Strakosch was solicitously instructed in how to avoid such errors and conduct "a strictly legitimate, and we trust, a perfectly successful operatic campaign."

The *Herald*'s overblown solicitude, more moderately echoed in the *Times* and the *Tribune,* by no means signified selfless journalistic concern for the future of opera in New York. Strakosch had decided, for reasons of economy, to limit his advertising to the above three principal morning papers—thus earning him the furious enmity of the spurned lesser dailies and weeklies. "Left-handed puffs," the *Herald* blithely dubbed their spiteful attacks, and taunted them with more and greater eulogies of Strakosch for his wisdom in "declining to advertise in newspapers of little or no circulation."[26] The press controversy raged unabated throughout Strakosch's tenure of the Academy, with the three chosen papers defending him against the vicious assaults of the others.

But not as allies: "We have already commented on the disposition of the *Herald* to avail itself of the incident for the purpose of waging a crusade against the City press and have spoken of it as exceedingly selfish, unjust, and illiberal," declared the *Times* on February 11. Yet, "the manner in which the affair has been treated by a portion of the journals concerned is still more obnoxious to censure. They have devoted their utmost energies to abuse of Mr. Strakosch, denunciation of the Opera, sweeping condemnation of the performances, and the most unscrupulous statements concerning the size and character of the audiences; and this openly and avowedly because he does not advertise in their columns."[27]

Nonetheless, despite strife, hazards, and tribulations, Strakosch's shoestring operation, with a repertory of tried-and-true operatic chestnuts, was claimed—at least by his partisans—to have succeeded surprisingly well. Opening with *Lucrezia Borgia,*[28] on January 21 (postponed from January 19 because of a severe snowstorm),[29] in the course of his short season Strakosch presented *Il trovatore, La favorita, Norma,* and *Ernani,* all

[26] "Their views upon art," wrote the *Herald* (March 24, 1857), "are dictated by the soul-inspiring motives of five dollars for an advertisement, or twenty-five cents per line for editorial notices" (puffs).

[27] "Now please *do,* dear, good, clever, darling, handsome, and amiable friend Strakosch, *do* send us your advertisement, if only for a dollar a week," gibed Charles Burkhardt (*New York Dispatch,* January 28, 1857). "If your Scotch master [James Gordon Bennett, the editor/publisher of the *Herald*] grants you permission, we will lend you the dollar to pay for it 'in advance,' whenever you may be short, or become so under the brilliant patronage you now enjoy."

[28] With Parodi (Lucrezia), Martini d'Ormy (Maffio Orsini), Tiberini (Gennaro), and Morino (Duke Alfonso). Reviewing the opening, Hagen, who predicted dire disaster for the season, found Parodi's "execution" to be "heavy and clumsy." He advised her—as long as her "executive powers" remained so defective—to "abstain from singing on the stage." To Hagen, the "greatest feature" of the *Lucrezia* performance was the sight of a benighted couple in the audience actually following the entire opera with a copy of the score. A score to listen to Donizetti! How bizarre! (*Review and Gazette,* January 24, 1857, p. 19.)

[29] A fairly well-attended opening, despite the seductive "tinkle-tinkle-tinkle of sleigh bells" that echoed throughout the freshly snow-covered city, wrote the *Times* (January 22, 1857): "It is agreeable enough to see Lucrezia Borgia gliding upon the stage in a gondola; but it is nothing to the splendid pageant to be seen in Broadway, where sleigh-loads of beautiful women are flying past to the merry music of silver bells." The *Times* feared that "the fine sleighing, the soft weather, and mulled wine [would] prove stronger attractions for our nocturnal pleasure-seekers than the syrens of the Academy of Music."

Teresa Parodi, a celebrated soprano honored by a Mazurka named after her and by her picture on the sheet music.

featuring Parodi and Tiberini,[30] and on January 28, for Cora de Wilhorst's purportedly sold-out debut, *Lucia di Lammermoor,* the surprise triumph of the season.

As Seymour later recapitulated the season (*Times,* February 17, 1857): "In spite of bad weather, unfavorable season, old operas, hostile papers, etc., M. Strakosch has made a pecuniary success. His experimental campaign of twelve nights has resulted in five moderately bad houses and seven large and remunerative ones. . . . Thanks to the economy of his arrangements, M. Strakosch has made both ends meet in a very satisfactory manner."[31] As if to bear this out, Strakosch, promptly upon the close of his first season, announced a second, again of twelve performances, to open on February 23 with Cora de Wilhorst in *Lucia di Lammermoor,* "by demand."[32]

Indeed, with her opera debut, the fledgling American *prima donna,* until only recently a diva of the drawing rooms, had instantly become all the rage. Disinherited by her intransigent, upper-caste father upon her marriage to an impecunious German nobleman, the pretty, twenty-four-year-old de Wilhorst had captured the public's sympathy with her gallant (and expertly publicized) efforts to support herself, her husband, and their baby by becoming a professional singer.

The public was by no means permitted to become unmindful of these irresistible facts. In a nicely timed letter to the editor, appearing in the *Herald* the day before her debut, Wilhorst confided her piteous plight to the world, in meek, even self-abasing, terms, more evocative of the guileful impresario than the timorous debutante. She begged the public's indulgence toward her unworthy efforts, beseeched them to bear in mind the harsh need that compelled them, and humbly confessed her musical faults and shortcomings and her blasted hopes of correcting them through music study in Italy; she told (disingenuously) of her astonishment and fright, undeserving as she was, on receiving Mr. Strakosch's offer of $1000 a month to appear in opera; of her fear of public ridicule; and of her rash agreement, in a moment of weakness, to undertake the arduous role of *Lucia* at only ten days notice—a feat, she less modestly added, unequaled in the past or future annals of opera. In closing, Wilhorst humbly begged Mr. Bennett and the press in general "to regard my advent at the Academy of Music . . . in the light of an amateur—not commanding public favor but struggling to earn an

---

[30] Parodi's Leonora (in *Il trovatore*) surpassed any he had ever heard, wrote Seymour (*Times,* January 24, 1857). With the "fresh and delicious quality of her voice, the admirable roundness of her phrasing, and the perfectly pure Italian style of her vocalization, she was the very best Leonora ever heard in New York." And Tiberini, wrote Watson: "took everyone by surprise. . . . On his former appearance [the year before] the opinion of the public and the press was decidedly lukewarm" because Tiberini was not endowed with "monster bellows-lungs." In Watson's opinion Tiberini was not inferior to Lorenzo Salvi♪ or even Mario:♪ "His entire performance was a triumph of genius over prejudice and party spirit" (*Leslie's,* January 31, 1857, p. 131).

[31] By "packing" his house with "dead-heads," claimed Hagen. Except for the two de Wilhorst performances, he asserted, Strakosch's actual receipts had not exceeded $700 a night, not enough to cover expenses (*Review and Gazette,* February 21, 1857, p. 51). According to *Trovator,* "Parodi and Tiberini and Morelli [had] been singing away to swarms of dead-heads at every evening's performance, entailing a considerable pecuniary loss upon the unlucky manager. Strakosch has made a great mistake in refusing to advertise in other than the three prominent morning dailies" (*Dwight's,* February 14, p. 156, partly quoted in the *Courier and Enquirer,* February 19, 1857).

[32] With Tiberini (Edgar), Morelli (Ashton), Attilio Arnoldi♪♪ (Arthur), and Barili (Raymond).

honest maintenance—and to spare me, therefore, the cruel effects of just, though crushing, criticism."[33] The letter evidently produced the desired effect; as Seymour wrote in the *Times* on January 31, the day after her second triumphant performance of *Lucia:* "Mme. de Wilhorst is the especial pet of the moment. She has drifted from the drawing room to the stage, and people are as glad to meet her there as though she had escaped some dire shipwreck on a dismal shore." Seymour hoped, however, that she would not be misled by "the kindly feeling" that prompted this warm public response. No longer "the accomplished *belle*" of the "privileged circles," he wrote, she must now face the judgment of the "great, clamorous, and uncompromising public."

Yet, continued Seymour, the petite and pretty Wilhorst, with her "fresh, elastic quality of voice," undeniably possessed "the pure art-instinct."[34] And if at times one might have wished for a better-trained singer, or for the absence of her occasional (slight) tremolo, her "tact and musical instinct" always came to the rescue. Indeed, in the scant two days between her first and second appearances as Lucia she had shown a noticeable improvement. "If Mme. Wilhorst is not beguiled from the hard work and intense application of an artist's career by the injudicious rapture of her friends," lectured Seymour, "she will in a very short time become a worthy exponent of the art she has adopted."[35] And even now she was, "with one or two illustrious exceptions," the best Lucia seen in New York in some years.

Even Hagen, reviewing Wilhorst's debut, went so far as to grant her the possession of "a great amount of execution . . . such as would entitle her already to compare most favorably with most of the Italian singers who are forced upon us as stars" (a palpable stab at Parodi). Of course, Cora de Wilhorst had made frequent blunders, but that was attributable to first-night nerves. Her woeful lack of acting ability, however, was not so easily condoned: "She lacks inspiration and that warmth of feeling which are the germs of great dramatic display," wrote Hagen. The great emotional roles, the Lucias, Lindas, and Lucrezias, were not for her, nor would they ever be (*Review and Gazette,* February 7, 1857, p. 35).

Whatever her limitations, there was no denying that Madame de Wilhorst had been the hit of Strakosch's season; indeed it was due to her extraordinary box-office

[33] Burkhardt, a fiery supporter of Madame de Wilhorst, scathingly referred to the "contemptible, sneaking letter addressed to the Ishmaelite of the press, begging his (disreputable) countenance and protection" as one that "no New York—no American—woman ever wrote . . . of her own volition. It was the dictation either of one of the Ghoul's own satellites, or of the person who—a stranger among us—does not know better and expects to 'make money in the provinces' out of the *Herald's* endorsement" (evidently meaning the fortune-hunting Count de Wilhorst) (*Dispatch,* February 1, 1857). *Porter's Spirit of the Times* (January 31, 1857, p. 360), too, disapprovingly referred to Madame Wilhorst's "long, [self-] deprecatory letter."

[34] Maretzek refers to her as "a charming little American society lady, with a charming little voice and a charming little temper" (*Sharps and Flats,* pp. 37–38). Watson unequivocally proclaimed her a "genius, a decided genius" (*Leslie's,* February 7, 1857, p. 147).

[35] Burkhardt, too, after exhausting his vocabulary of praise, cautioned Madame de Wilhorst against succumbing to the intoxication of the moment. "Let her turn a deaf ear to flattery, leave off letter writing to newspapers, especially to disreputable ones, keep the one great goal ever before her eyes, and study, study, study" (*Dispatch,* February 1, 1857).

Girvice Archer, Jr.

Cora de Wilhorst, a prima donna
with box-office appeal.

appeal that the venture was extended. Opening on February 23[36] to another large and
enthusiastic house with *Lucia* (evidently the only opera at the newly minted diva's
command), on February 27 she bravely ventured into the unknown, appearing as
Amina in *La sonnambula,*[37] a role in which she elicited increasingly ambivalent, if still
mostly lenient, reviews. An obviously unwilling Seymour, for example, almost apologetically admitted that Wilhorst had not added to her stature with her Amina: "In the
first place she seemed to be imperfectly acquainted with the music, her memory failing

[36] The opening was preceded on February 19 by a fund-raising ball at the Academy, magnificently transformed by the great Italian set designer Joseph Allegri to include a belvedere, an architectural scene, a night scene, a fountain, and a "parterre of choice flowers from the Conservatory of
Mr. Buchanan." Tickets, at $2, were on sale at all the music shops. The imposing list of elite patrons
included—among the managers of the event—the name of Mrs. George Templeton Strong, who
may or may not have been present; her husband's private journal makes no mention of the occasion.
[37] With Patti-Strakosch as Teresa, Tiberini as Elvino, and Morelli as the Count.

her at moments where it was most needed. In the second place her manner of delivering the text and her intonation were by no means so perfect as in *Lucia,*" and her tremolo, which was unpleasantly prevalent throughout the opera, had become "harder and more unmanageable." Yet, "the fresh quality of her voice and the natural grace and ease with which she uses it, combined with much exquisitely coquettish acting,[38] reconciled the audience to any little deficiencies, and kept them in mind of the fact that Mme. de Wilhorst is, after all, only a *debutante*. It is perhaps her misfortune that she already sings so well that she must be judged by a high standard" (*Times*, February 28, 1857).

The other reviewers similarly mixed the bitter with the sweet—disapproving, making allowances, then retreating behind great outpourings of well-meant, fatherly advice. Watson, for example, still maintaining that Wilhorst possessed genius, "unhesitatingly" stated that although her Amina was immature and lacked intensity and verisimilitude, it was, "all circumstances considered, a decided success." All she needed was a few years of study in Italy to make America proud of "its child of the soil" (*Leslie's*, March 14, 1857, p. 222).

Burkhardt, Wilhorst's most determined advocate, was forced, however, to admit that "her Amina was by no means equal to her performance of Lucia." Although she had sung her arias in "nice and correct style . . . it was the style of the drawing-room, or amateur concert singing, not that of the grand lyric stage" (*Dispatch*, March 1, 1857).

After a second performance of *La sonnambula*, Wilhorst, apparently a woman of boundless daring, appeared on March 9—to a further assortment of self-contradictory critiques—as Marie in *La figlia del reggimento*[39] (a role she was supposed to have learned in two weeks). Both the character of the *vivandière* and the music were unsuited to her "voice, style, or *physique*," wrote the *Evening Post* (March 10); yet she acquitted herself "in a manner which did credit to her industry." Although "her performance could hardly be called a success," it was nonetheless a "very commendable effort"; and while dramatically it was an improvement over her former performances, she rendered the music less effectively, doubtless due to hasty and insufficient preparation.[40]

Nothing daunted, brave little Madame Wilhorst repeated *La figlia* to an "overflowing" and enthusiastic audience at her benefit, on March 11,[41] and again on March 13, with, as an added attraction incongruously inserted between the first and second

[38] "There was a great deal of acting on the part of the debutante," wrote Hagen (*Review and Gazette*, March 7, 1857, p. 67), "but very little to the point. . . . She was altogether too fidgety in the first act, but doubtless she will improve by time and study, although we do not think she will ever become a great actress."

[39] With Tiberini as Tonio and Morelli as Sulpizio.

[40] "The opera," wrote Watson, "was, as a whole, very badly given, a necessary consequence of inadequate rehearsal. But Cora de Wilhorst made a decided hit, sustaining herself admirably to the end" (*Leslie's*, March 28, 1857, p. 254). Burkhardt, on the other hand, reported that with her "petite, graceful figure, her handsome face, coquettish but never broad style, her fresh, pure, and sympathetic voice," she was "the most naive, saucy, piquant, and clever" Marie ever seen (*Dispatch*, March 15, 1857).

[41] Reported by Watson to have netted more than $3000 at the box office (*Leslie's*, March 28, 1857, p. 254).

acts, a Grand Scena and Duetto from *Norma,* sung by Parodi, Patti-Strakosch, Tiberini, and Morelli.[42]

The subscription season closed on March 20 with *Don Giovanni,* by now the traditional closing work for opera seasons. Unmistakably confirming Ullman's impresarial presence, the advertising for this unexceptional opera production promised a gala offering, boasting "three prima donnas" in Parodi (Donna Anna), Patti-Strakosch (Donna Elvira), and Wilhorst (Zerlina);[43] an all-star cast of Tiberini (Ottavio), Morelli (Don Giovanni), the stage-manager/singer Amati Dubreuil♪ (Leporello), Morino (Masetto), and Barili (the Commendatore); and—the ultimate attraction—the first appearance at the Academy of Sigismund Thalberg,[44] who would play one of his exquisite compositions "between the acts."

This ambitious production was eclipsed the very next evening, when, with Ullman very obviously in command, Thalberg again appeared, this time with not three, but five, *prime donne*—Parodi, Patti-Strakosch, Wilhorst, Elena d'Angri, and Bertha Johannsen—and with two opera companies, Strakosch's aggregation and the all-but-defunct German opera company.[45] The monster program offered, in the following order, the first act of *Norma,* with Parodi and the Strakosch company; a "Grand Concert" of piano solos by Thalberg and opera arias by Elena d'Angri; the second act of *Don Giovanni,* with the previous night's cast, the first (or second) act of *Fidelio,* with Johannsen, Beutler, Weinlich, and Oehrlein of the German company; and finally, the last act of *Il trovatore,* with again the Strakosch cast. Strakosch would conduct for his own company, Signor Pedro de Abella for Thalberg and D'Angri, and Carl Bergmann for the German singers.

At least, that is how it was advertised in the newspapers. According to ——t——, however, the event demonstrated the depths to which Thalberg had sunk in his subservience to the American god Humbug (under the guidance of its high priest Ullman). On Monday, March 16, Thalberg had appeared in a so-called "Grand Combination Festival, *nominally* for the benefit of the German Society." Ostensibly for the same cause, a repeat concert, with a few program changes chiefly having to do with whether the first or second acts—or the entirety—of *Fidelio,* had been promised for Saturday,

---

[42] Reciprocally, on March 16, Wilhorst performed the Mad Scene from *Lucia di Lammermoor* between the third and fourth acts of *Il trovatore,* with Parodi, Patti-Strakosch (a highly praised Azucena), Tiberini, Morelli, and Barili. All told, Wilhorst appropriated the lion's share of featured appearances during Strakosch's second season, being starred in at least seven out of the twelve presentations.

[43] Who, much to Burkhardt's horror, added fancy *fioriture* to her already transposed *Batti, batti.* Perhaps the spirit of the immortal Mozart would forgive the sacrilege, but Burkhardt could not (*Dispatch,* March 22, 1857).

[44] But by far not his first appearance of the season, nor even his first collaborative appearance with the opera company.

[45] Inactive since their unsuccessful engagement at the Broadway Theatre, where during the month of January they had appeared on alternate nights with the actor Edwin Forrest. In addition to their *Fidelio♪* (December 29, 1856) and *Der Freischütz♪* (December 31), they had presented productions in German of Auber's *The Mason and the Locksmith (Le Maçon),* Lortzing's *The Czar and the Carpenter (Zar und Zimmermann),* and Donizetti's *The Daughter of the Regiment (Regimentstochter).* Too, at the Broadway, they gave "sacred" Sunday evening concerts on January 11 and 18, with the *Arion* Society assisting and Carl Bergmann conducting, and again on March 1, with Julius Unger♪ conducting. Now apparently absorbed by Ullman, they were soon to give seasons of German opera in Philadelphia and Boston (see *Dwight's,* April 4, 1857, pp. 5–7).

Playbill for Thalberg Testimonial.

Sigismund Thalberg, called by many critics the greatest living pianist.

Both: Girvice Archer, Jr.

March 21, again at Niblo's. "But when Saturday came," reported ——t——, "behold the following change: The concert was transferred to the Academy, and the aid of the functionaries of that institution [rather than of the German Society] announced 'Mr. Thalberg—prime donne—German and Italian Opera, etc. etc.'. . . On account of the length of the programme, the performances would begin at 7:30 P.M.; when they were to end, no one could know. . . . In the end, *Fidelio* was left out" (*Dwight's*, April 4, 1857, p. 32; also see below).

Following this stupendous event, Wilhorst, after two successful fund-raising concerts. departed for Europe to pursue her studies; Strakosch went on the road to book Thalberg's coming Western tour;[46] Ullman went to Europe to engage fresh talent for his approaching fall and winter campaign at the Academy of Music, and (for a brief period) the sound of opera was stilled in New York.

Among the many conflicting postmortems on Strakosch's problematic venture into opera, Watson stated that although the undertaking had been fraught with every possible disadvantage,[47] no financial loss had been reported, and thus none should be assumed.[48] With rare objectivity he continued: "That the performances, in an art-view, have not been what we have a right to expect is certain, but we have been lenient to the shortcomings of a management which had to use the resources immediately at hand, and with but little time to make the necessary preparations. . . . The capacity of [Strakosch's] company was measured in advance, and if in one instance [Parodi?] the expectation was not realized, in all other members of the company it was exceeded. The engagement of Cora de Wilhorst was undoubtedly the salvation of the undertaking. Her unexpected success, and the sympathy for her position, which extended into every representation, created an excitement favorable to the interests of the Opera. . . . Mr. Strakosch's want of experience in the department he assumed was no doubt a serious drawback to the efficiency of the representations," admitted Watson.[49] "Yet, under the circumstances, he did better than might have been expected." According to Watson, Strakosch had tried to engage a famous European conductor,

[46] A tremendously lucrative undertaking: in ten weeks they covered some "six or seven thousand miles, and gave fifty-nine concerts." Mesdames Parodi and Strakosch completed the touring company, and impresario Strakosch occasionally pitched in at a second piano in performances of Thalberg's two-piano fantasies.

[47] "Snow-storms, wind-storms, rain-storms, and oceans of mud have interposed insurmountable obstructions to amusement-seekers," wrote Watson (*Leslie's*, March 21, 1857, p. 238). "If omnibus routes passed the Academy of Music, bad weather would not prove so eminently injurious to its interests, but the one or two blocks of mud and slush that must be walked or swam [*sic*], unless we use our private conveyance, is as fatal as though a mile intervened."

[48] "Mr. Strakosch attempted to save money by niggardly management," conversely wrote Richard Grant White, "and the performances of his company were miserable indeed, as all persons competent to express an opinion acknowledged. Consequently, he was obliged to fill his houses with audiences which, as admitted in the *Tribune* and other journals, were not 'genuine'; and those who have the interests of the Academy at heart are obliged to give two eleemosynary balls in its aid" (*Courier and Enquirer*, April 11, 1857). The *Herald*, however, reported a clear profit on the undertaking of about $2000.

[49] And not only his conducting. If Strakosch "would provide the money and secure the services of a competent business man, a good stage manager, and a capable music director," asserted Richard Grant White, "we do not doubt that he would make a passable *impresario*" (*Courier and Enquirer*, February 19, 1857).

but finding him unavailable, had himself undertaken the conductorship. "We admire him for his courage," wrote Watson, "even while we cannot applaud the results."

Strong seems to have ignored Strakosch's second season, even the closing *Don Giovanni*. Nor, surprisingly, did he attend any of the numberless concerts with which Thalberg flooded the city upon his return from his New England tour in mid-February. For some time before his reappearance a "Card of the Management" (a "Manifesto," as Dwight's New York correspondent caustically termed it) repetitively announced Thalberg's impending Farewell Concerts in New York, Philadelphia, Boston, Baltimore, and Washington, to be followed by a farewell tour of the West before his return to Europe in May.

Thalberg's "farewell" campaign completely monopolized the New York music scene: "How many [concerts] this artist has given during the last fortnight," wrote Hagen in the *Review and Gazette* on March 7 (p. 67), "here, in Brooklyn, Williamsburg, at Niblo's, at Dodworth's, in the morning, in the afternoon, and in the evening, to children, to grown-up people—sometimes for nothing, but generally, *very* generally, for much money—it is difficult to say."[50] According to the *Herald* (February 21, 1857), since his arrival in November 1856 the phenomenally durable Thalberg, in just three months, had given eighteen concerts in New York, with three additional free concerts for school children; fifteen in Philadelphia and three for the schools; seven in Baltimore and one for the schools; four in Washington; six in Boston, with additionally three matinées and three for the schools; he had also played in Albany, Troy, New Haven, Providence, Salem, Wilmington, New Bedford, Harrisburg, Lancaster, Worcester, Hartford, Springfield, and Newark.[51] "The management, like the busy bee, improves each shining hour," added the *Herald,* "and is preparing to astonish the public with further novelties."[52]

Among the novelties were "new" additions to Thalberg's repertory for his forthcoming concerts at Niblo's Saloon—four opera fantasies, six *morceaux de salon,* two duets, as well as established classics by Beethoven, Mendelssohn, Bach,[53] Chopin, and Hummel. Of Ullman's more audience-catching innovations—although it meant the selfless sacrifice of a hundred seats—was the relocation of the stage to the center of

---

[50] Burkhardt was equally bemused: "At Niblo's Saloon, at Niblo's theatre, at New Haven, at Boston, now in an afternoon at Dodworth's rooms, at night in Brooklyn, anon in Philadelphia, and presto at Hartford again—here, there, and everywhere—now in a fashionable *matinée* by himself alone, again at a grand evening concert with all the best artists assisting him, and next day delighting thousands of little schoolchildren, we confess it goes beyond our powers to . . . give to our readers a due record of Mr. Thalberg's movements and triumphs. He seems ubiquitous, and wherever he appears, his rooms are always overflowing with auditors" (*Dispatch,* February 22, 1957).

[51] It should be remembered that Thalberg, always surrounded by a corps of assisting artists, played an average of only three pieces (and, of course, some encores) at each concert.

[52] Recovering from his ancient enmity toward Ullman, Burkhardt paid tribute to the genius with which he conducted Thalberg's American tour: "It were folly to deny that the management of [Thalberg's] business affairs, the arrangements of his concerts and matinées, the quickness of his movements, the combinations of attractions, the selection of hours and places for performance, the economy of time, are all more perfect, more closely calculated, and more energetically carried out than was ever any similar in this or any other country" (*Dispatch,* March 1, 1857).

[53] Bach was listed, but, to my knowledge, not played.

the hall. At either end of the platform was placed an Érard grand, upon which Thalberg would alternately perform, thus allowing all parts of the audience a closer-than-usual view of his miracle-working hands.[54]

To a blaze of introductory super-superlatives in the press, Thalberg commenced his "farewell series" on February 16 with an assisting cast that featured Madame d'Angri in opera arias, Madame Johannsen in German *Lieder,* Joseph Burke in violin solos, and the tragedienne Mrs. E. L. Davenport in declamations of elevated poems by celebrated authors (as customary at the most recherché Parisian salons).[55]

Ullman outdid even himself in the aesthetical/philosophical verbiage with which he adorned his announcement of a subscription series of three super-recherché matinées to be given by Thalberg at Dodworth's Hall on February 20, 24,and 27, concurrently with his evening concerts.[56] The subscribership would be limited to 400 carefully screened auditors and would cost five dollars each.

Always mindful of snob appeal, Ullman rather overdid things with his "Important Notice" issued on February 17 (a tactic that was adamantly rejected in Boston and Philadelphia as "impudent, offensive, foreign snobbery"): "Nearly nine-tenths of the tickets have been subscribed for by ladies belonging to the first families in the City. In view of the responsibility this devolves upon the Management, a correct [home] address will be required from every subscriber—a determination which will insure the utmost respectability of the audience and will be appreciated by no one more than the subscribers themselves." At the same time Ullman advertised that the remaining eighty subscriptions would be sold to the first bidders, so hurry, hurry, hurry!

At each matinée Thalberg, appearing without assisting artists, would perform seven gems of the piano literature, mostly consisting, as it turned out, of his too-familiar compositions and transcriptions, his oft-repeated smatterings of Beethoven (again the "Moonlight" Sonata) and Chopin (the Funeral March and a mazurka or two); three movements of a Beethoven trio in B-flat major (probably the "Archduke") with Joseph Burke and Carl Bergmann, and three (insufficiently rehearsed) movements of the Hummel Septet, op. 74, with members of the Philharmonic; he also played his fantasies on "sacred" music from Verdi and Donizetti operas on the Alexandre Organ♪ (purportedly capable of mimicking the violin, flute, oboe, clarinet, horn, bassoon, and the human voice); with William Mason, he played his *Norma* Fantasy for two pianos.

Not the least titillating of Ullman's promotional contrivances for this matinée series was his announcement that, under the impeccable supervision of Sexton Isaac

---

[54] And of his face: "It was marvelous to notice how, during the most difficult passages, he would calmly raise his eyes and pass them over the audience, as if he were but twirling his thumbs, instead of . . . 'playing a different variation with each of his fingers,'" wrote ——t—— (*Dwight's,* February 21, 1857, p. 164).

[55] "Mrs. Davenport ranted, and gasped, and whispered, and mouthed out Longfellow's 'Skeleton in Armor.' . . . I do not think our public would be much offended if this part of the performance were omitted," cruelly wrote ——t—— (*Dwight's,* February 21, 1857, p. 164).

[56] On the evening of February 20, Thalberg additionally gave a "*soirée* musicale," exactly like his matinées, with the same number of piano pieces, except that Madame d'Angri assisted. It was a short program because he appeared at Niblo's on the same evening for the benefit of the St. George's Society, as did Strakosch's singers: Parodi, Patti-Strakosch, Tiberini, and Morelli, conducted by Strakosch; and also Paul Julien and William Mason,♪ the Harmonic Society, conducted by George Frederick Bristow,♪♪ and Dodworth's Band,♪♪ presumably conducted by Harvey Dodworth.

Brown, the all-powerful arbiter of social ceremonial to the Upper Ten, "lunch" would be served during the intermission. As Edward G. P. Wilkins (*Herald,* February 21, 1857) memorably recalls the scene: "The hall was filled with the most fashionable ladies of the city . . . there were not over forty gentlemen in the audience. Brown, the expansive sexton of Grace Church, distinguished as a general manager for christenings, weddings, parties, balls, funerals, and similar gay and festive arrangements, conducted the fair auditors to their places with that Grandisonian *empressement*[57] for which he is so eminently noted. His coat could not have been glossier, or his manner more dignified, if he had been managing the funeral of a millionaire. Brown made a speech to the ladies—told them that Mr. Thalberg was happy to meet them, and if they desired a piece not on the programme, he would be happy to oblige them by playing it.[58] The ladies laughed irreverently at Brown, whose oratory is not felicitous. Brown subsided."

The concert, needless to say, was in every way "delicious." Just after Thalberg's performance of one of his opera fantasies on the Alexandre Organ "there was lunch served to the audience by Ethiopian servants dressed in black, with knee breeches, white gloves, and [white] stockings. Some of the Ethiopians . . . [were] down at the heel, and this made matter of sport for the younger ladies. So they laughed, chatted, sipped their coffee, nibbled at their lunch,[59] voted Thalberg 'such a dear,' and altogether had a happy time of it . . . [chattering] away like spring robins. These *matinées* will be very popular as reunions for the ladies who are bored to death by having nothing to do for a couple of hours in the middle of the day," commented Wilkins. "They generally go to pay calls, shop, and lunch after, but at the *matinée* they can lunch, meet all their friends, and hear Thalberg as well. It is a great institution, the Thalberg *matinée-musicale,* and so popular has it already become that a new series is already announced."

Not only a new series (two matinées, February 26 and March 3) and an "extra and single" matinée (on March 4), but a third series (March 2 and March 5) to follow. On the evening of March 5, Thalberg, with the assistance of Strakosch's opera company, appeared at a Grand Miscellaneous Concert at Niblo's Theatre; then, after a concert in Newark on March 6 (and who knows how many others!), he appeared again at Niblo's Theatre on March 10 and 12 (again his "last concert"), this time with not only the opera company but also the New York Harmonic Society, in a program consisting of a sadly underrehearsed "Lenten performance" of Rossini's *Stabat*

[57] A reference to the stalwart hero of *The History of Sir Charles Grandison* (1753–54) a popular novel by the English author Samuel Richardson (1689–1761).

[58] "Prattle and Tattle," as a gossipy/satirical column of sociomusical criticism in *Harper's Weekly* was titled, reported (March 14, 1857, p. 164) that Thalberg had charmingly obliged his fair listeners with his *Tarantella,* after a rather confused contest among them in choosing an encore most pleasing to the majority. "'Shall I play the *Tarantella,?*' asks Thalberg, with his most beaming smile. 'Yes, yes!' And then the *Tarantella* he plays." Ecstasy!

[59] Consisting, according to "Prattle and Tattle," of "fairy cups of chocolate" and "dice-sized" bits of pound cake, dispensed from a noisy pantry across the hall from the auditorium, and handed around by the three reluctant Negro servitors in questionable stockings and knee-breeches, "urged on from the rear by the pompous Brown." Only those sitting conveniently near the aisles were fortunate enough to be served, while the others looked hungrily on. But after all, among his many miracles, no one expected "dear Mr. Thalberg" to accomplish that of the loaves and fishes, did one? (*Harper's Weekly,* March 14, 1857, p. 164).

Mater,♪♫[60] conducted by George Frederick Bristow, and a conventional miscellaneous program, conducted by Abella and Strakosch.[61]

On the evening of March 16, after another "last matinée but one," Thalberg appeared (with D'Angri) at Niblo's Theatre at the gala concert, mentioned above, purportedly given for the German Society. Although sponsored by a committee of forty-three prominent members of the German community, "it was so well understood that *only half the profits* were to be applied to this object, while the other half were to fill certain private pockets," wrote ——t—— (*Dwight's,* April 4, 1857, p. 3) "that many persons would not countenance the proceeding at all, who would otherwise have contributed largely." Nonetheless, a great crowd had attended and heard "a miscellaneous concert by the orchestra, Thalberg, D'Angri, and various German singing societies (the best of which, however, had withdrawn their services in view of the above mentioned condition), and the first act of *Fidelio.*[62] At the foot of the programme it was announced that on Saturday the concert would be repeated, with various alterations, and the second act of *Fidelio.*" As we know, the concert was shifted to the Academy of Music, where no part of *Fidelio* was heard.

Although it had been announced that after his Western tour Thalberg would pay a flying trip to Europe for a few weeks and return for the opening of the Academy of Music's fall season, he was reported in July to be busily giving concerts with D'Angri at Cape May, Saratoga Springs, Newport, Nahant, Rockaway, Sharon Springs, Niagara Falls, and other select watering places.

And although *Harper's Monthly* (May 1857, pp. 849–50) enjoyed poking irreverent fun at Thalberg for the more shoddy exploits to which he cheerfully lent himself— and although *Harper's* chided him for his limited and persistently repetitive repertory— yet the writer conceded that with his glorious artistry Thalberg, after all, wove a profound magical spell, making one wonder whether he had not "touched the utmost possibility of the piano, and ask whether, when he is gone, we have not seen and lost the most perfect pianist that ever was, or ever can be."

Attempting to evoke for his readers the quality of Thalberg's magic, the critic for the *Evening Post,* in his review of an earlier Thalberg concert (the sixteenth) on February 18, could remember "nothing in the way of piano forte playing so touching and expressive" as his arrangement of "Home, Sweet Home," gloriously played as an en-

---

[60] An unruly, indeed, a "disgraceful" performance, during which the opera singers reportedly chatted merrily whenever they were not required to sing (*Dwight's,* March 21, 1857, p. 196).

[61] In an angry letter to the *Evening Post* (March 11, 1857) an offended listener protested the insult to artists and audience alike of following the noble *Stabat Mater* with such claptrap as "Yankee Doodle with variations," sung by D'Angri, and "encored in the midst of . . . shouts and catcalls which transported one . . . to the classic purlieus of the Bowery." The writer imagined that Thalberg, who with his exquisite Fantasy on *Lucrezia Borgia* had followed a duet by Patti-Strakosch and Parodi of another vulgar tune, "The Star-Spangled Banner," looked unhappy. This seems hardly commensurate with Thalberg's enthusiastic cooperation with any scheme that Ullman devised, however musically degrading. The program was repeated at the Brooklyn Athenaeum on March 19.

[62] Members of the eleven local German singing societies currently comprising the *Sängerbund* were announced to sing choral works by Mozart *(The Magic Flute)* and Rossini *(William Tell),* members of the German opera company to present the first act of *Fidelio,* and Carl Bergmann to conduct the Andante of Beethoven's Fourth Symphony and the *Tannhäuser* Overture.

core to his "subtle and refined" rendering of his *Masaniello* Fantasy. "It was the triumph of Thalberg's genius . . . as simply and tenderly played as we can imagine it to have been. The air was tolled out . . . full and clear, as if on evening bells, unencumbered by any superfluous notes, while far below, faint and dreamy, these came harmonious, multitudinous, and incessant, like the songs of a thousand birds, and as sweet, till the whole instrument seemed tremulous with sad and tender musical memories. People near us became fixed in their places, as if by a charm—not a muscle moving until the lips began to quiver, and the breast heave with stifled sobbing, and the tears stole in their eyes. . . . Ah! Sigismund Thalberg! Your skill and power never gave you a triumph equal to that which your imagination and poetic feeling gave you last night, in that, to us, most fortunate encore" (*Evening Post,* February 19, 1857).

Strong, with his well-known disdain for virtuosos, seems to have remained untouched by the all-pervading Thalberg madness.

March 8. . . . Quite a respectable little musical party here a week or ten days ago. Miss de Roode, a late importation from Holland, sang [from] *Der Freischütz* and very brilliantly (heard her also at Eisfeld's last). [Robert] Goldbeck♪ [the recently emigrated young German composer/pianist] played, and the evening was said to be very pleasant.[63]

March 23. . . . Heard the "Eroica" Saturday afternoon with Ellie—Philharmonic rehearsal.

April 25. . . . At Philharmonic rehearsal with Ellie an hour and a half this morning—long enough to hear the "Eroica" and most of the lovely *Midsummer Night's Dream* music—the finest thing, *me judice,* Mendelssohn ever produced—far outweighing legions of *St. Pauls* and *Elijahs* and tons of his symphonies. As to the "Eroica," human speech can't adequately characterize it. What a pity that opportunities of hearing such works are so rare. This must be heard a dozen times to be in any degree appreciated.[64] Only within the last five years have I acquired any real *knowledge* of the significance of that great and beautiful creation. Every year of life spent without that knowledge is appreciably less worth living, for it is a substantial addition to one's means of happiness to carry with him—as his own—the memory and perception of so glorious a work. Came from the rehearsal absolutely tingling with enjoyment.

---

[63] Marie de Roode and Goldbeck had evidently been engaged to supply the music at the Strongs' musicale. Prior to her Philharmonic appearance (in March) Miss de Roode had been heard at Eisfeld's soirée (the fourth of the series) at Dodworth's on February 24. According to *Trovator* (*Dwight's,* February 28, 1857, p. 174), she was currently supporting herself as a governess with "an uptown family." Reviewing this appearance, Hagen approved of her "full, round, rich soprano voice of much power" and her use of it in performances of Haydn's "With Verdure Clad" and Schubert's *Ave Maria* (*Review and Gazette,* March 7, 1857, p. 68). The program had included, besides, Beethoven's String Quartet in C minor, op.18, no. 4; Anton Rubinstein's String Quartet in G major, op. 17, no. 1, and Schumann's Piano Quintet, op. 44 (a work "utterly bewildering" to *Raimond*), with Henry C. Timm♪♪ at the piano.

[64] Since the Philharmonic's founding in 1842 this was their seventh performance of the "Eroica" Symphony.

Strong was wise to forgo the repetition of that bliss, for at the concert that evening every corridor of the Academy of Music was so crowded with the "striped legs of Young New York *male* . . . continually oscillating back and forth" and every box so crammed with the "Spring hats of Young New York *female,* quivering like flowers with bees in their cups," that, as Watson reported (*Leslie's,* May 9, 1857, p. 351), hundreds of extra chairs had to be supplied, besides the "hosts of the visitors [who] brought their own chairs, or camp stools; but still the supply fell short of the demand, and very many had to stand the whole evening." The resultant babel of flirtatious chatter was so thunderous that Hagen was unable to hear the performances—not that, in his opinion, they were worth listening to (*Review and Gazette,* May 2, 1857, p. 131). And *Raimond's* musical consciousness—just as he was beginning to submerge himself in the opening glories of the "Eroica"—was rudely invaded by the following conversation: "'Oh! how are you, you naughty fellow? Why didn't you come to see us?' Followed by idiotic simperings offered in explanation of such inexcusable neglect!" (*Albion,* May 2, 1857, p. 211.) And on and on throughout the concert.[65]

The Philharmonic government was universally censured for its ineffectual handling of this unfortunate phenomenon, contrary as it was to the basic mission of the Society. Arguing for a more restrictive subscribership, Watson wrote: "To insure a large dividend should not be the one great aim of the Philharmonic Society. It should have a higher mission—a more ennobling purpose; but it goes the same way as many admirable enterprises which, commenced for the encouragement of art, have degenerated into mere money speculations." While it was, of course, desirable that everyone be justly paid for his labor, what about a little "voluntary sacrifice for the glory of art"?

May 5. . . . Eisfeld's last [chamber music] concert [sixth of the seventh series] tonight[66] with Ellie. . . . Very satisfactory. Mozart's Quartet, no. 4 [probably no. 3], in E-flat, among his finest. Andante—very rich, grandiose, grave, and earnest—in strong contrast with the third movement, which is like the Scherzo of the "Pastorale" Symphony in sentiment, but furious in its jollity—Pastoral festivities in a pothouse—Shepherds on a spree. Beethoven's Trio, op. 70 [no. 1], D major, [for piano, violin, and cello] disappointed me a little.[67] His Septuor (four movements only of the seven) made

[65] Besides the "Eroica" Symphony and the *Midsummer Night's Dream* music, the program that evening included the first American performance of Henry Litolff's Overture, *Chant des Belges* (op. 101), a work that to Hagen imitated the *Tannhäuser* Overture but lacked its content; to Watson, however, it was "the sheerest nonsense." Amid the buzz of conversation, too, the young American soprano Maria Brainerd inaudibly sang "Hear ye, Israel," from Mendelssohn's *Elijah* and an aria from *Roberto il diavolo,* and Henry Timm inaudibly played the solo part in the first American performance of Schumann's Introduction and Allegro Appassionato *(Concertstück)* for Piano and Orchestra, op. 92 (1849).

[66] Strong seems to have missed Eisfeld's fifth concert, at Dodworth's on March 24, at which had been heard the promising young soprano from Cincinnati, Henrietta Simon, in an aria from *Robert le diable* and Cherubini's *Ave Maria;* the members of the quartet in Mozart's Quartet in G major (K. 387) and, by "very particular request," Beethoven's Quintet for Strings in C, op. 29, with Joseph Burke splendidly playing the first violin. Additionally, William Mason joined Noll and Bergner in a fine performance of Rubinstein's *Trio concertante* in G minor, a work he had introduced at a Mason/Bergmann matinée the year before.

[67] To Hagen the trio was the high point of the program; its Largo might have been the work of some composer of the Schumann school, he wrote. Jan Pychowski, who splendidly played the piano part, deserved credit for having chosen to play it (*Review and Gazette,* May 16, 1857, p. 147).

ample amends.[68] Hardly any composition is so crowded with beauty—so elaborate and so fresh and genial at the same time. It's like the most gorgeous of tropical forests. Arranged with Eisfeld to do it again, *here,* next week.

~~~

By this time Maretzek, who had returned to the United States in mid-February after a purportedly successful engagement in Havana,[69] was nearing the end of the opera season he had been conducting at Niblo's Theatre since April 13. Having returned without his longtime *prima donna,* Anna de LaGrange,♪[70] Maretzek and his company,[71] after a few performances in Charleston, had gone directly to Philadelphia. There, on February 25, with a new *prima donna,* Marietta Gazzaniga (1824–1884), hastily imported from Europe upon LaGrange's departure, they triumphantly opened at the beautiful new Philadelphia Academy of Music,[72] under the joint auspices of the incurable opera patron William H. Paine, Maretzek's former backer, and the New York theatre manager E. A. Marshall,♪ lessee of the new Academy. Representatives of the New York press sent to cover the opening *(Il trovatore)* grudgingly admitted that the Philadelphia Academy, with its splendid sight lines and fine acoustics, its walls and seats handsomely upholstered in a vibrant red, was perhaps the most magnificent opera house on the continent, with perhaps no superior in the world.[73]

Maretzek and his company,[74] particularly Gazzaniga, were a tremendous hit in Philadelphia. Indeed, so unwilling were the euphoric Philadelphians to let them go that their season was repeatedly renewed, and thus it was not until mid-April that— still under Paine's management—they at last made their appearance at Niblo's Theatre (Maretzek being *persona non grata* at the Academy), and then for only fifteen performances before returning to Philadelphia for yet another successful engagement before going on to Boston.[75]

---

[68] The performers of the septet were not named. The vocal soloist of the evening was a greatly improved Henrietta Behrend,♪ who sang an aria from Rossini's *William Tell* and an unidentified song by Eisfeld. Hagen concluded his review of the concert with a tribute to Eisfeld, without whose efforts "New York would be actually without any public performance of classical chamber music."

[69] Maretzek's detractors gossiped, however, that his singers had been deserting him because he had been unable to pay their salaries (*Dwight's,* February 7, 1857, p. 151).

[70] Maretzek gives no clue to the cause or circumstances of the break, nor have I seen it discussed in the press.

[71] Now consisting of Adelaide Phillips♪ and Zoë Aldini,♪ contraltos; Pasquale Brignoli,♪ tenor, Alessandro Amodio,♪ baritone, and Domenico Coletti,♪ bass/baritone.

[72] Designed by the Philadelphia architects Napoleon E. Lebrun (1821–1900) and Gustav Runge (1822–1900).

[73] This unwilling admission was offset by supercilious comments on the maladroit manners practiced in "that interior Iowa," as Wilkins arrogantly chose to refer to the City of Brotherly Love. "They applauded in the wrong places, made loud noise in the lobbies, and otherwise displayed a provincial lack of [opera-house] cultivation," derided the critic (*Herald,* February 26, 1857). This, of course, was jingoistic misrepresentation: Philadelphia (and Boston) had enjoyed seasons of opera, albeit usually imported from New York, since the lyric drama's earliest days in the United States.♪

[74] His Philadelphia cast included as *seconda donna* Caroline Richings,♪ adoptive daughter of the veteran actor/singer Peter Richings♪ and a source of pride to her townspeople.

[75] An underhanded proceeding that required meticulous timing, as Maretzek, no trifling adversary, shamelessly explains in *Sharps and Flats* (p. 41). To prevent the Ullman/Strakosch opera company from appearing in Philadelphia or Boston, Maretzek saw to it that they remained "hemmed in and bottled up in New York" [by means of] "a special arrangement with Mr. E. A. Marshall, lessee

Leslie's, Dartmouth College Library

Marietta Gazzaniga, prima donna,
favorite of the press and the public.

Maretzek's New York opening on April 13, an "aggressively rainy" Easter Monday, was not auspicious,[76] particularly not for the eagerly awaited new *prima donna,*
who was suffering from a vocally debilitating cold. Yet, despite her obvious physical
handicap, it was the critical consensus that Marietta Gazzaniga was an extraordinary
apparition on the opera scene. First appearing as Violetta in *La traviata*[77] (regarded by
some local critics as "Verdi's weakest work"), Gazzaniga's style was found to be a radical departure from the accepted *opera seria* norm, as represented by the *Puritani*s, *Nor-*

---

of the new Philadelphia Academy of Music, to produce my Havana Opera Companies exclusively
at that house; and [I] usually stole a march on the New York managers by getting before the end of
their New York season to Boston and to take off the cream of the Boston patronage." Bringing his
company into New York was less simple.

    [76] Among the hardy souls who braved the weather to hear the new *prima donna* was Maurice
Strakosch, who, as *Raimond* ornately reported, "gazed down with a sympathizing and friendly countenance from his aerial perch in the stage-box upon the new aspirant for public favor" (*Albion,* April
18, 1857, p. 187).

    [77] With Susan Pyne, a temporary addition to the company (looking more like Queen Victoria
than ever), as Flora, Brignoli (Alfredo), Amodio (Germont), both noticeably improved since their
Cuban adventure, and Coletti (Baron Douphol).

mas, and *Favorita*s in which Grisi,♪ Steffanone,♪ and Parodi had excelled. "Gazzaniga stands alone," proclaimed Wilkins (*Herald,* April 15, 1857). "We have never had anything like her. . . . The new school of operas, which, like the new school of plays, is serio-comic, requires a new school of artists—singers who are capable of the most sudden transitions from joy to grief, from a drinking song to a prayer." Gazzaniga was such an artist, and while, technically speaking, many young ladies in boarding schools could sing scale passages and arpeggios better than Gazzaniga, but few *prima donna*s could approach her in true dramatic expression of the composer's ideas.

If Madame Gazzaniga was deficient in the vocal acrobatics indigenous to contemporary *prima donna*s, she nonetheless possessed, in the opinions of most of the critics, a beautiful voice.[78] "To be so poor a vocalist," wrote Richard Grant White with his customary perversity, "Madame Gazzaniga is one of the most remarkable artists we have had upon our lyric stage . . . she possesses that rarity in music, a truly sympathetic soprano voice. . . . She has a great range, quite two octaves and a half . . . and more power than any soprano we have heard, except Jenny Lind. Her volume of voice, too, seems to be all music; very little of it runs to waste in mere noise."[79]

"Madame Gazzaniga's style is the purely declamatory dramatic style which has been brought into vogue by the latest compositions of Donizetti and by those with which Verdi alternately delights and offends us," continued White. And although she vocalized "very badly," and although her intonation was "not reliable," and although her scales and arpeggios could be exceeded by any schoolgirl, and although her "alternations of despair and exultation in the last act [were] somewhat extravagant,"[80] there was, throughout her performance, "the charm of a voice of rare quality, of a fine, free declamation, of great tenderness of vocal expression, and a remarkable sweetness of manner. As an actress she has much merit, and her person—she is blonde and has a very pretty figure[81]—wins her favor before she sings." Gazzaniga's style was "somewhat new," and would take some getting used to (*Courier and Enquirer,* April 14, 1857).

---

[78] "Her voice is an absolute soprano—rich, full, loud, portant, true, steady, tearful, passionate, heroic," wrote Fry from Philadelphia, "and although deficient in some respects, she [was] in others the greatest singer that has ever been in America" (quoted in the *Courier and Enquirer,* April 11, 1857).

[79] "Her voice is the most womanly and sympathetic we remember to have heard on the Italian stage," wrote Fry, "but cannot be classed under the head of brilliant organs" (*Tribune,* April 21, 1857). Apparently, "brilliance" was synonymous with the agile delivery of *fioriture.*

[80] In a footnote to *Raimond*'s review of *La traviata* on April 18 (pp. 187–88), John R. Young, editor of the *Albion,* intruded to inquire whether Gazzaniga did not spoil her vocalization in the third act by "over-doing the hospital business." But in Maretzek's opinion, Gazzaniga "surpassed any other Violetta on the stage, especially in the last act" (*Sharps and Flats,* p. 32).

[81] The *Herald* found her face "unexpressive and not at all handsome"; the *Evening Post* referred to her "pleasing and expressive face"; the *Albion* credited her with "a style of beauty which is rather more effective upon the stage than the beauty of blondes usually is"; the *Times* found her personal appearance to be "at times . . . positively beautiful, radiant with intelligence and sentiment, at others . . . unimpressive and commonplace." Burkhardt thought her, although "not especially beautiful," appealing because of the naturalness of her acting; Watson saw in her face "the mirror of every emotion of her heart and mind . . . if it is not beauty, [it] is certainly the sublimed essence to the beautiful" (*Herald,* April 15; *Evening Post,* April 14; *Albion,* April 18; *Times,* April 21; *Dispatch,* April 19; *Leslie's,* May 2, 1857, p. 335).

The *Evening Post* critic (April 14, 1857), on the contrary, described Gazzaniga's voice as a mezzo-soprano of "no extraordinary range," and her style "a sort of artless simplicity with a self-complacency and assurance which must have been derived from her late successes." Although she possessed "the true dramatic fire, and "walked the stage with a freedom and swing which [contrasted] singularly with the ladylike airs and stiffness of LaGrange in the same character," she did not "justify the encomiums of the Philadelphians," whose admiration, the writer spitefully added, must have been conditioned by the sparseness of their previous "operatic enjoyment." And although Gazzaniga might become a leading favorite, she would never take the place of LaGrange.

Because of Gazzaniga's persistent illness, and having no alternate soprano, Maretzek was obliged to suspend performances until April 20, again a day of torrential rain, when *La traviata* was repeated. This time, according to the *Times* (April 21, 1857), a recovered Gazzaniga "exceeded in a remarkable degree her feeble efforts" of the week before. "This lady has had much to contend against: in Philadelphia, the Philadelphians; in New-York, the weather—both, we imagine, calculated to spoil the artist. The former raised her much above the standard of her merits, the latter dragged her much beneath it." But, promised Seymour, in New York she would not be "deprived of what is her due." Thus, he wrote, although she could not control her voice, could not vocalize, and moved slowly in the "production and delivery of her best notes," her voice was "naturally grand, and . . . capable of giving infinite pleasure. Her declamation . . . in the highest degree noble." Only when brilliance was required was there something to regret. It was then that we mourned the lost LaGrange. As an actress, however, Madame Gazzaniga had no equal on the Italian stage in America.

Watson unconditionally hailed her as "the greatest dramatic vocalist that has visited America since the days of the youthful Malibran," whom, by-the-by, she equals, nay, perhaps surpasses, in intense force of passionate declamation. . . . She may not be able to sing scales, diatonic or chromatic, with the fluent frivolity of some boarding-school misses," he pointedly added, "but in all that constitutes a singer—intensity, earnestness, strong individuality, enthusiastic *abandon* to the situation, and lightning flashes of impetuous genius, she stands without a rival" (*Leslie's*, May 2, 1857, p. 335).[82]

But to Hagen her singing was worse than any of the Italian or other singers in this country, and as for her acting, "we could not discover any trait which showed more spirit and more intelligence than is generally shown by all our *prime donne*" (*Review and Gazette*, April 18, 1857, p. 115). Now, upon Gazzaniga's reappearance as Violetta and her following performance of Leonora in *Il trovatore*,[83] Hagen was driven to lay bare his suffering soul. "Our readers are aware," he wrote, "that we do not admire the modern Italian opera school. Therefore, our task of witnessing performances of

---

[82] "Madame Gazzaniga is a dramatic vocalist of the modern Italian School, in which the *trillos, roulades, cadenzas,* and *fioriture* passages of Rossini and of the French school have been sacrificed to Verdi and dramatic declamation," wrote Burkhardt. "She is not a LaGrange nor a Sontag, yet with abundant dramatic genius she excels them in vocal means. She exhibits a declamatory style and action in which each word and gesture is given with a distinctness and propriety that has fairly taken the public by storm, and made her, without puff or humbug, the favorite of the city" (*Dispatch*, May 3, 1857).

[83] With Adelaide Phillips (Azucena), Brignoli (Manrico), Morelli (replacing an ailing Amodio) as the Count de Luna, and Coletti (Ferrando).

Verdi and other operas of the same school for the purpose of criticizing them is not a very pleasant one. It is for this reason that we look upon the necessity of listening to operas like *La traviata* and singers like Madame Gazzaniga with perfect dread, which can not even be softened down with the announcement of a short season." Imagine, then, Hagen's surprise and delight when he was denied entrance to Niblo's Theatre by a man he took to be the manager.[84] "Alas! that man little thought what a perfect boon of happiness he bestowed upon us that night."

After this cozy warm-up, Hagen got down to cases. After hearing Gazzaniga in *Il trovatore* (April 24), it was more than ever obvious that she was totally incompetent: she did not sing the role of Leonora, "but howled, screamed, and *sobbed* it." Her performance of *Lucrezia Borgia* (April 27)[85] only confirmed this opinion. Yet, to do her justice, her voice was good enough to inspire regret that she did not know what to do with it. She also possessed "that outburst of passionate feeling which is one of the first requisites in Verdi's operas. . . . Voice and individuality are the elements of the modern school of operatic singing in Italy. This [was] in perfect accordance with the exhibition of physical strength and individuality in the modern dramatic compositions of that country. Strange," mused Hagen, "that the land which, only a hundred years ago, saw the greatest accomplishment in musical art, should have gone down so far as to be actually satisfied with its elements" (*Review and Gazette,* May 3, 1857, pp. 130–31).

Inspiring a broad assortment of further critical cavils, Gazzaniga appeared as Norma on April 29, with Caroline Richings as Adalgisa,[86] and on May 1 triumphantly as Linda di Chamounix,[87] with Adelaide Phillips as Pierotto, Brignoli as Carlo, Amodio as Antonio, a debutant Mauro Assoni (according to Seymour a "buffo with more humor and less buffoonery than most buffos") as the Marquis, and Attilio Arnoldi as the Prefect. On May 4, *Il trovatore* was repeated, and on May 6, *La traviata,* the latter with the incongruous interpolation, between the second and third acts, of the madhouse scene from *Il ritorno di Columella* (1837, revised 1842), a "comic" opera by Vincenzo Fioravanti (1799–1877), performed by Signor Assoni and the chorus.

On May 8, George Templeton Strong attended the closing performance of the season, for once, not *Don Giovanni.*

May 10. . . . Friday night at the Opera with Murray Hoffman and Ellie, of course. *Lucrezia Borgia,* well sung. Perhaps from association always pleasant to hear. A scene from *Columella* by Fioravanti, of whom I know nothing, but whom I suppose to be pretty profoundly debased, morally and artistically. This was a grotesque scene *in*

---

[84] Was Maretzek (or Paine) employing Ullman's habitual tactic of barring entrance to hostile critics?

[85] With Adelaide Phillipps (Maffio Orsini), Brignoli (Gennaro), and a barely recovered Amodio (Duke Alfonso).

[86] Probably a token appearance to keep in the good graces of Maretzek's Philadelphia constituents. In the thankless role of Adalgisa, Richings sang with "more accuracy than verve," wrote *Raimond,* but she appeared to have "both voice and culture enough to fill a respectable position on the Stage" (*Albion,* May 2, 1857, p. 211).

[87] To *Raimond* the memorable event of the entire season; in this role Gazzaniga magically redeemed herself (*Albion,* May 9, 1857, p. 223).

a madhouse—dance and chorus of lunatics.[88] Music of an order more suitable had it been an asylum for idiots. Also an act of *Masaniello,* which was refreshing.

—～—

As Maretzek's season approached its end, the schizoid gentlemen of the New York press began to bemoan his departure. "Why should the opera be closed?" lamented *Raimond.* "The house has been nightly filled, and with increasing crowds. The audiences have begun to assume the genuine 'Opera' air, and everything prognosticates a continued and brilliant success for the management. By all means let us have more opera" (*Albion,* May 9, 1857, p. 223).

Watson, who regarded Gazzaniga as nothing less than divine, was utterly disconsolate at the thought of losing her; his only solace was his "belief that we shall hear Gazzaniga in New York before she returns to Europe; we should indeed be grieved to think that we had heard the last of her" (*Leslie's,* May 16, p. 367; May 23, 1857, p. 383).[89]

No sooner had the Maretzek company departed than the baritone Filippo Morelli, "with a bravery that astonished the initiated," announced a "season" of three nights of opera—May 18, 20, and 22—under his own management at the Academy of Music.[90] The dual purpose of the enterprise was to bid farewell to Cora de Wilhorst, who was sailing for Europe on May 30, and to introduce an American tenor calling himself Carlo Jacopi. Purportedly a great success in Europe, where he had been studying and performing at the "theatres of Florence, Naples, and London," a fair amount of rumor had preceded Jacopi's return: that he would appear together with Wilhorst in a summer season of English opera at Wallack's Theatre, that he would head a season of German opera, and—no mere rumor—that his name was not Carlo Jacopi but Charles Jacobs, and that he was the son (or brother) of a Broadway jeweler locally advertised as the "Original Jacobs." The members of the supporting cast were Zoë Aldini,[91] the veteran comprimaria Angiolina Morra,♪♫ and the baritones Gasparoni♫ and Morelli; the conductor was Signor G. Nicolao,♫ announced as a newcomer to New York although he had appeared locally as long ago as 1852. The announced operas

---

[88] According to the *Musical World* (May 9, 1857, p. 290): "Signor [Assoni] appears as a madman, solus, sings an aria in which the gibbering, the crying, and the insane laughter of a madman are introduced, and then is attacked by a crazed and mocking crowd of people, who issue from the cells around him. They make sport of him, they beat him, they compel him to dance with them, and finally rush back to their cells, from which they bring various orchestral instruments, he leading them, while they perform one of Rossini's compositions. They afterward seize him and carry him triumphantly off the stage." One of the male inmates, wearing a nightgown over a hoop, caused "considerable merriment among the lady auditors," observed the reviewer. "A revolting picture of a mad-house," wrote Seymour (*Times,* May 9, 1857).

[89] Watson might have spared himself the anguish: Gazzaniga's career in America would continue over the following two decades.

[90] A three-night season was a wise plan, wrote Burkhardt, because the first night and the "positively last two nights" had always been the most remunerative and successful performances at the Academy (*Dispatch,* May 17, 1857).

[91] An in-and-out member of Maretzek's company, Aldini was supposed to have been dropped after her rumored disappearance (or attempted disappearance) in a fit of stage fright on the Philadelphia Academy's opening night, when she had been scheduled to appear as Azucena.

were the indispensable *Il trovatore,* and (apparently to accommodate Wilhorst's repertory) *Lucia di Lammermoor* and *La figlia del reggimento.*

Attracting an "over-full house" curious to hear the new tenor (including Brignoli
and Amodio, who had come all the way from Philadelphia), Jacopi's debut was a disaster before he ever set foot on the stage.[92] "Scarcely had the *debutant* sung the first bar"
of Manrico's offstage opening serenade, *Deserto sulla terra,* "before there was a general
laugh throughout the house at the extreme deficiency of voice and musical education.
[And] throughout the entire evening his most vigorous efforts only met with the ironi-
cal *bravi* of ridicule" (*Home Journal,* May 30, 1857).

Only Watson maintained that the reaction had been unfair. Although Jacopi/Ja-
cobs, with a small voice, had fatally erred in appearing in a house "so vastly dispropor-
tioned to his vocal powers . . . in many subdued passages, where his natural force alone
was used, he sang both smoothly and tastefully." Moreover: "The buzz of disappointment that filled the house after his first effort was disheartening enough to paralyze the
powers of a much older and more experienced singer. For the first time within our
memory the public of New York offered no encouragement to a young debutant. The
first four bars of his serenade sealed his fate; and not the shadow of encouragement
attended his subsequent efforts, some of which were certainly worthy of recognition"
(*Leslie's,* June 3, 1857, p. 410).

Wilhorst, the Leonora, was generally criticized for attempting a role for which she
was totally unfitted.[93] Hagen seized the occasion to assert that Verdi's music was at any
rate best suited to singers who had no claim to being artists—Gazzaniga, for instance.
"We hope for Madame de Wilhorst that her ambition does not urge her in this direction," he wrote. "Verdi's music ought to be a sealed book for her, at least for the present." After studying in Paris and gaining a firm and artistic basis, "she may sing Verdi
as if she was obliged to perform an unpleasant task, [but] would do it decently, at least"
(*Review and Gazette,* May 30, 1857, p. 163).

So crushing was Jacopi's failure that he immediately withdrew (or was withdrawn)
from the cast, and it was rumored that Morelli frantically sped to Philadelphia to obtain
Maretzek's permission for Brignoli to assume the leading tenor roles for the remaining
two operas. It was probably granted, for on May 20 Morelli advertised in the morning
papers that Brignoli would appear as Edgardo in that evening's performance of *Lucia.*
Prematurely, as it turned out, for the evening papers carried Brignoli's disclaimer, to
the effect that he had made no such arrangement with Morelli, and that besides, his
health made it "totally impossible" for him to sing that evening. Thus, there was no
performance at the Academy that evening.

But Morelli was not a man to accept defeat. As the *Times* announced on May 22:
"Mr. Morelli is on his legs again and bravely snaps his fingers at the inflexible Brignoli,
and brings forth a new tenor tonight in the person of Mlle. Aldini." And indeed, for
the final performance of that calamitous season, Aldini, against her better judgment,

---

[92] "The most melancholy failure ever witnessed here or elsewhere," Burkhardt called it (*Dispatch,*
May 24, 1857).

[93] Criticized by all except Watson, in whose estimation she had sung and acted the difficult role
far beyond reasonable expectations. All she needed, insisted Watson, was a year or two of study in
Europe to "place her in a position far in advance of any than has yet been attained by any American
vocalist" (*Leslie's,* June 3, 1857, p. 410).

ingloriously took on the tenor role of Tonio in *La figlia del reggimento*. As an added attraction, during an intermission Morelli and Gasparoni performed the famed "Liberty Duet"♪ from *I puritani,* presumably complete with flag-waving. Hagen angrily labeled the whole comedy of errors "an outrage upon common sense and decency"; he wished "that our public would learn better how to requite the insults which managers are apt to inflict upon it" (*Review and Gazette,* May 30, 1857, p. 163).

The Academy would not remain silent for long. By some arcane manipulation, it was opened on June 3 and 5 for two improbable benefits to two unlikely beneficiaries—the principals of the fiercely competitive Philadelphia Academy of Music—E. A. Marshall and, of all people, Max Maretzek. For Marshall's evening (June 3) the gargantuan program consisted of John Poole's classic comedy *Simpson and Co.* (London 1823), played by a cast of topnotch actors associated with Marshal during his managership of the Broadway Theatre; then *Il trovatore* under Maretzek's direction, with Gazzaniga, Adelaide Phillipps, Brignoli, and Amodio; and in conclusion a French vaudeville *Edgard et sa bonne,* played by a cast of French actors from New Orleans. At Maretzek's benefit, *Simpson and Co.* was repeated; then *La traviata,* then another French vaudeville, *La Corde sensible.*[94]

Announced as his farewell to New York—after a further short season of nine performances in Boston he would be going to Cuba, perhaps not to return for some years, if ever—Maretzek's benefit, in fact, called out great numbers of his friends and well-wishers. "We are sincerely sorry to lose Maretzek," wrote Watson, "for he has been a faithful and enterprising public servant, and to all who knew him a courteous gentleman and a good friend."[95] But in Cuba, where Maretzek's merits were perhaps better appreciated, he would doubtless gain the fortune that had eluded him during his many years of service in New York (*Leslie's,* June 13, 1857, p. 19).

In fact, even before his Boston engagement was completed, Maretzek had departed—not for Cuba but for Europe, to engage important singers for forthcoming big seasons in Philadelphia, Boston, and Havana. Before leaving, he had reportedly signed contracts with Gazzaniga, Brignoli, and Amodio for a period of nine months, to begin in September;[96] he had also formed a tripartite partnership with E. A. Marshall and Thomas Barry, manager of the Boston Theatre (at some unstated time Paine had bowed out), and it was to be all-out warfare against Ullman and Strakosch.

Scarcely had Maretzek departed when Anna de LaGrange★ rematerialized. Since her return from Havana, Madame LaGrange had been touring the United States—giv-

---

[94] Reporting a disappointing attendance at both these benefits, Burkhardt blamed the overlong, overdiverse programs: "There was too much for the price [$1 for the parquet and 50 cents for the amphitheatre] and too much variety of opposite character for any price," he wrote. People wanting to hear opera were unlikely to be interested in English farce or French vaudeville, and vice versa. "When the public goes cat-fishing, they don't want to catch trout" (*Dispatch,* June 7, 1857).

[95] The *Times* referred to Maretzek as "a conductor, a manager, an author, a composer, a disputant, a farmer, and a patriot." Burkhardt depicted him as the great unrequited martyr/ savior of opera in New York (*Times,* June 4; *Dispatch,* May 31, 1857).

[96] It was rumored that he made overtures as well to LaGrange to rejoin his company for this period (*Dwight's,* June 27, 1857, p. 102).

Girvice Archer, Jr.

Anna de LaGrange, a soprano with an
"infallible voice" said to span three octaves.

ing concerts in New Orleans, St. Louis, Cincinnati, and Chicago—and now she was back to gratify her faithful New York admirers with a few farewell concerts before sailing for Europe. After only two appearances (at Niblo's Saloon, June 11 and 22), however, she announced that she would put off her departure in order to give a season of seven operas at the Academy of Music under her own management,[97] with a company consisting of her old colleagues Brignoli, Amodio, and Coletti, the German soprano Elise Siedenburg,♪ Adelaide Phillips, and, to conduct, Maretzek's former chorusmaster Angelo Torriani.♪ No opera would be repeated during the engagement, she vainly promised.

LaGrange's announcement had taken people by surprise,[98] wrote Wilkins in the *Herald* on June 30; the "farewell concerts," he explained, had been intended to make

[97] And, according to Hagen, with the invaluable help of her agent Jacob Gosche,♪ Ullman's colleague and erstwhile co-editor of the short-lived theatrical newspaper *L'Entr'acte*♪ (*Review and Gazette,* July 25, 1857, p. 225).

[98] But not *Dwight's* New York correspondent, *Trovator.* To ensnare audiences, he wrote, LaGrange had resorted to the "usual silly humbug of giving 'farewell concerts' previous to her departure for Europe. It was even stated that she had engaged passage in the steamer of the 24th of June," her "last" concert being announced for June 22 (*Dwight's,* July 11, 1857, p. 117).

people believe that only this brief opportunity remained to enjoy this exquisite artist. It was now two years since LaGrange had first appeared at Niblo's and asserted her superiority over any other singer on this continent (Grisi, of course, excepted). "In the natural course of operatic things we must doubtless lose her presence at the Irving Place," philosophized Wilkins. "This one more opportunity should therefore be regarded with due value, especially," he sardonically added, "by those who have not fully posted themselves for a particularly useful conversational and society requisite—the exact points upon which comparison will be made of her powers with the new arrivals—with [whom] Ullman (now abroad) and Thalberg intend to open the next season of opera at the Academy."[99]

On June 29, LaGrange opened her opera season with *I puritani,* to an "astonishingly good house," worth "upwards of $1500" at the box office, continued Wilkins. She was in her "accustomed infallible voice [and] elicited the old enthusiasm," being required repeatedly to give encores and receiving showers of bouquets. Indeed, the enthusiasm she evoked signified that her tour of the provinces had exerted a "material influence on the culture of her auditors" (probably meaning that her opera audience consisted mainly of summer visitors to the city).

In rapid succession LaGrange performed a formidable, if familiar, repertory: *Norma* (July 1) with Elise Siedenburg as Adalgisa; *Lucia di Lammermoor* (July 6); *La sonnambula* (July 8); *Il trovatore* (July 10), with Adelaide Phillips as Azucena; *Lucrezia Borgia* (July 12); "by request"; again *I puritani* (July 14); "by general desire" *Il trovatore* (July 17); and, for LaGrange's farewell benefit, *Norma* (July 20).

Her season was a phenomenal success. Testifying to the perversity of audiences who ignored the opera during the more conventional and comfortable months, the Academy was jammed with happy perspiring multitudes during this unusually hot month of July. "One of the most remarkable houses we have ever seen at the Academy of Music assembled last night to witness the performance of the terribly popular opera, the 'Trovatore,'" wrote Seymour in the *Times* on July 11. "Long before the hour of commencement, every desirable seat in the building was filled, and impatient agitation for the conductor manifested itself. The curtain rose on a perfectly dense mass of human beings, all eager for the opera and determined to enjoy it at any hazard. Such a spectacle in the dog days we have never experienced, and even in the wildest times of the regular season it has not been exceeded. It was found necessary to suspend the sale of tickets, and it is said that five or six hundred people were turned from the doors! This in July!"

"Capricious . . . is the public in operatic matters," wrote a baffled Fry after this same performance (*Tribune,* July 11, 1857). "The very harvest of the Italian Opera is at this heated, blazing season of July. When probabilities induce the supposition that emptiness and desolation should preside over the Academy of Music, come the thick, sweltering, smoking crowds. They overshadow the broad pit, they perch in the loftier boxes, they roost in the cerulean cockloft of the muses. What though the thermometer rise with each tier, and on high represents the animal economy of a roasting ox, there

---

[99] Concurrent with LaGrange's reappearance in opera came Ullman's first announcements from abroad of his having engaged Erminia Frezzolini (1818–1884), the famed *prima donna assoluta* of the Italian Opera in Paris, for a four-month American tour, to begin in September.

stick the summer-flies of the Opera, through four mortal acts of the coincidentally hot *Il trovatore,* with its seething vagabonds of gipsies, boiling furies of knights, red-hot anvils, and lurid cauldron, wherein one brother immolates another. A fuller house was probably never seen at the Academy. . . . Under present auspices the Opera Troupe will do well to sing and perspire for some time to come."

Seymour took "particular pleasure in mentioning these events. Madame La-Grange, whose enterprise is thus crowned with success," he wrote, "deserves all that the intelligence and liberality of the public can shower upon her. She has worked val-iantly for the position she enjoys, and it is but right that she should gather in the fruits. . . . The company under her control is excellent, the artists tried and reliable, the conductor modest and efficient, the chorus powerful, and the performances smooth and satisfactory. With the single exception of Madame Sontag's Castle Garden campaign♪ [in 1853], we have never had a better summer company. The thousands [of summer visitors] who fill our hotels seem to be aware of this fact."[100]

In the July 11 issue of *Harper's Weekly* (p. 435) "Prattle and Tattle" proffered something new in music criticism.[101] A keen satire on local opera-giving, its faults and foibles, slyly masquerading behind the facade of a petulant young lady of fashion, the article mocked the current operatic proceedings at the Academy: Why did they have to chose such unsuitable months for their seasons? How could they hope to succeed in an opera house where there was no place to sit, for it was surely the most uncom-fortable theatre ever built, with about half its seats "being out of view of the stage," and all of them cramped, unreachable without disturbing all one's neighbors, and once reached, so disastrous to one's crinolines! Too, the writer was "tired of *prima donna*s who were neither young or handsome—either too fat or too thin—and without voices"; "she" was tired of "long, thin throats that merely [threw] off sky-rockets" but lacked sweetness upon descending from the altitudes (meaning LaGrange); tired of their turned-up eyes directed to the "press-gang in the pit," that is, "the critics in the parquette"; tired of loud tenors with snub noses and feet planted far apart to assert their manliness (meaning Brignoli); tired of over-fat bassos (meaning Amodio). In sum: the critic demanded a different and more handsome soprano with some flesh on her bones; a tenor who would control his legs and not go black in the face showing off his dramatic prowess; a basso of reasonably moderate dimensions, wearing draperies ample enough to cover the more conspicuous and rotund parts of his body; and seats ample enough to receive the most delectable, outsize, sartorial confections. Perhaps it would be helpful if the size of the seats were gauged by the extra-ample measurements of Amodio: "I doubt if he could be better employed . . . and we should all feel the benefit."

At Madame de LaGrange's closing performance, between acts one and two of *Norma,* she was crowned with a gold chaplet, or, as its presenter Colonel Hiram Fuller

---

[100] Watson reported that during LaGrange's current tenure the Academy's receipts had averaged between two and three thousand dollars a night (*Leslie's,* July 18, 1857, p. 102).

[101] The column might have been written by George William Curtis, a music critic from way back, an adept social satirist, and now a member of the *Harper's* editorial staff.

called it, a "lyric crown."[102] Fuller, the editor/publisher of the New-York *Evening Mirror,* accompanied the coronation ceremony with a "neat speech, well-deserved praise to Madame LaGrange, both of which," reported the *Times* (July 21, 1857) she accepted with "becoming modesty," while "the house was almost rent with plaudits. Madame LaGrange leaves us for another hemisphere, and takes with her the warm regards of the many thousands whom she has enchanted by her genius." Once again, the affecting leavetaking turned out to be premature. By far!

Throughout the foregoing period, with the Philharmonic and Eisfeld's chamber-music seasons in summer recess, George Templeton Strong's music listening was confined to ceremonial and social functions, the latter often taking the form of amateur musicales at his upper-caste friends' houses.

May 12. Attended the "inauguration" of the new Columbia College[103] this morning. Six or eight of the Trustees present. Prayer by our chaplain [Cornelius Roosevelt] Duffie, and "Old Hundred" sung by the boys with much energy. Introduction of the little organ[104] and of singing seems likely to work well. . . .

Big reception tonight at the Robert L. Cuttings, Fifth Avenue. I went with Ellie and Mrs. Ruggles. Very crowded. Very musical—too much music, in fact, and out of place. Mrs. Mary Wright's exquisitely delicate voice is outraged and profaned when it has to force its way through clatter and clack.[105] There is a something about that lady's singing—I don't know what—of modesty and tenderness and refinement—an absence of bravura style—that is very precious and should not be thrown away on a mere garrulous mob. It's like a bouquet of violets in a ballroom.

May 26. . . . Tonight with Ellie and Miss Rosalie [Ruggles, Ellen's cousin] to an aesthetic and musical tea at [Régis de] Trobriand's.♪ Much singing; mostly pretty bad; wails and cries of pain; mournful minor ululations (which amateurs are often perverse enough to select as appropriate to social meetings), suggesting "the wolf's long howl from Oonalaska's shore"; dreary tours de force; idiotic gibberings. Burke gave us something (from Schubert, I believe), on his violin. Had a pleasant evening.

July 5. . . . Walked downtown this morning, stopping at three Papistical churches on my way (St. Patrick's, Canal Street, and Barclay Street) in hope of hearing some good music. Disappointed. Best thing I heard was the Canal Street *Gloria,* which may have been one of Cherubini's.

July 7. . . . Yesterday morning I was a spectator of a strange, weird, painful scene [at a construction site at 20th Street and Fourth Avenue]. The earth had caved in a few minutes before and crushed the breath out of a pair of ill-starred Celtic laborers. They had just been dragged, or dug out and lay white and stark on the ground where they

---

[102] Purchased at Tiffany's for $500, an amount representing one-dollar subscriptions contributed by five hundred of Madame Lagrange's devoted admirers (*Dispatch,* July 19, 1857).

[103] The occasion was the relocation of Columbia College from Park Place, where it had stood since 1760, to the refurbished quarters of the old Deaf and Dumb Asylum, far uptown at Madison Avenue and 49th Street.

[104] And of a new organist, William H. Walter, the organist of Trinity Chapel.

[105] Mrs. Wright had been a special star of the "Mass-meetings" at Strong's home on Gramercy Park in 1855.♪

had been working, ten or twelve feet below the level of the street. Around them were a few men who had got them out, I suppose, and fifteen or twenty Irishwomen—wives, kinfolk, or friends, who had got down there in some inexplicable way. The men were listless and inert enough, but not the women. I suppose they were *"keening."* All together were raising a wild, unearthly cry—half shriek and half song—wailing as a score of daylight banshees—clapping their hands and gesticulating passionately. Now and then one of them would throw herself down on one of the corpses or wipe some trace of defilement from the dead face with her apron, slowly and carefully, and then resume her lament. It was an uncanny sound to hear, quite new to me. Beethoven would have interpreted it into music worse than the Allegretto of the Seventh Symphony.[106] Our Celtic fellow citizens are almost as remote from us in temperament and constitution as the Chinese.

August 17. [en route to Brattleboro for a summer holiday] I fled the City by Hartford boat Friday afternoon, and the sensation of leaving it . . . the delight of going swiftly *away* over sunny water and beside bright wholesome shores, made me perform an inward *Te Deum* and *Sinfonia Pastorale* together, all the way up the Sound.

Strong had reason to be grateful for this momentary respite from Wall Street, where financial calamity had struck within the past week and now threatened to engulf the entire nation. With the collapse on August 11 of the Ohio Life Insurance & Trust Company, a reputable bank with a branch in New York, the country was fast descending into a chaos of bank failures, business failures, personal bankruptcies, unemployment, and general economic pandemonium. Scarcely a propitious moment for the launching of new opera ventures, one might suppose;[107] yet, on August 12 the *Tribune* announced that William Burton's handsome new playhouse, the former Metropolitan Theatre, more recently Laura Keene's Varieties, had been leased to Maretzek and his Philadelphia and Boston partners, E. A. Marshall and Thomas Barry, for a two-month season of Italian opera, to begin in October, in opposition to Ullman's forthcoming season at the Academy of Music.[108] Maretzek's prospective cast would feature—besides Madame Gazzaniga, Brignoli, Amodio, and Coletti—such European stars as the legendary baritone Giorgio Ronconi (1810–1890), the tenor Enrico Tamberlik (1820–1889), and the basso Joseph Tagliafico (1821–1900).

Burton's was taken over instead for a shorter season of opera by a less stratospheric company headed by the spectacular Polish contralto and *impresaria* Felicita Vestvali,♪ now the star and manager of the Mexico City opera. Her supporting cast included the soprano Luigia Caranti (locally heard in '47 and '49 as Luigia Caranti di Vita),♪ a new tenor, one Alessandro Maccaferri, Maretzek's singers Amodio and Coletti, and later the *buffo* Mauro Assoni. As it turned out, not Maccaferri but Brignoli sang the leading

[106] A work that Strong persistently regarded with a certain amount of superstitious dread.
[107] But, wishfully reported ——t—— in *Dwight's* (October 24, 1857, p. 239): "The 'hard times' seem to have less effect upon public amusements than on anything else in this city. A week or two ago it was estimated that an average of $10,000 was nightly taken at the different theatres, concerts, and other exhibitions open to the public."
[108] The announcement might have been a deliberate red herring to diminish Ullman, Maretzek's abiding enemy.

Both: Girvice Archer, Jr.

Felicita Vestvali, a handsome woman who liked to play such male roles as this Maffio Orsini.

tenor roles,[109] implying a sub-rosa connection between Vestvali and Maretzek, as did the conductorship of Angelo Torriani.

Vestvali's season followed a disastrous week of would-be Jullien-like promenade concerts♩ at Burton's, "Monster Musical Festivals and Fêtes de Promenade," as Burton elegantly advertised them, "so popular during the summer season in London and Paris" (and at only twenty-five cents admission). At great cost, he had transformed the parquet of his theatre into a promenade, installed a fountain that perpetually played upon "a glacier of real ice," and engaged the singers Henrietta Behrend and Carlo Jacopi (the latter gamely, but vainly, trying again), the Brothers Mollenhauer, various instrumental virtuosos from the Philharmonic, and the currently idled chorus and orchestra of the Academy of Music, all under the musical direction of Joseph Noll. Burton's losses on his week of promenades reportedly amounted to an astronomical $1200 (*Review and Gazette,* August 8, 1857, p. 241).

Vestvali, however, attracted large audiences to Burton's. Although somewhat debatably billed as "the Queen of the Lyric Stage," with only one exception—Azucena in *Il trovatore* (August 19)—Vestvali gratified her predilection for dashing transvestite roles: Maffio Orsini in *Lucrezia Borgia* (August 17), Romeo in Bellini's *I Capuleti ed i*

---

[109] In the first of which (Gennaro in *Lucrezia Borgia*) he interpolated a *romanza* from Arditi's "American" opera *La spia.*♩

Montecchi (August 21), Pierotto in *Linda di Chamounix* (August 24); and even the baritone role of Don Carlos in *Ernani* (August 28 and 29).

In this masculine role Vestvali encompassed "all the martial character that inches and bearing can impart," wrote Seymour (*Times,* August 29, 1857). "She is magnificent in her appearance and fills the eye splendidly. Those who would see a superb woman to advantage cannot have a better opportunity." But, despite Vestvali's very noticeable vocal improvement: "In a musical point of view, the performance was not remarkable for completeness, evidently lacking additional rehearsals." John Darcie,♪ in *Porter's Spirit of the Times* (September 5, 1957, p. 15) agreed—as did everyone—that Vestvali was visually breathtaking in the role, but nonetheless found the substitution of the contralto for the baritone voice to be unsatisfying, especially in the vocal ensembles. Moreover, in order to pad out the too-slender role of Don Carlos, Vestvali had appropriated "one or two [of Ernani's] tenor arias," which she reportedly delivered with "considerable effect."

"The opera of "'Romeo e Giulietta'" [*sic*]," disapprovingly wrote Seymour (*Times,* August 22, 1857), "is one that seems to possess unusual attractions for *contralti,* all of whom insist on its production, as though the public really cared to see it, which we fancy is not strictly the case. There are several reasons why American and English audiences cannot warm to this opera, foremost among which is a lingering veneration for the name of Shakespeare and a wholesome horror of operatic versions of his works. . . . Still, 'Romeo' offers a fine opportunity for the display of a dashing contralto like Vestvali, and the large and fashionable attendance of last night was owing, we believe, as much to the fact of her presence in the cast as to the performance of the opera itself, which under any circumstances is a dull affair."[110] Vestvali, in addition to possessing the vocal requirements of the role, was to an unusual degree a "gallant impersonator of the hero," wrote Seymour, but try as he would, he could not place her Romeo on a level with her Orsini or her Azucena.

Caranti, the Juliet, did her best (not good enough), and a Signor Giannoni, a tenor until now heard only in concerts with Ole Bull,♪♪ was a sympathetic Tybalt, although he sang distressingly out of tune (perhaps debutant nerves).[111] Both Brignoli and Amodio were praised, as usual, for their "improvement," apparently a self-perpetuating condition since their return from Havana.

Despite the spectacular failure of Burton's promenade experiment, local theatre managers seemed to have been hopelessly seized with the compulsion to offer low-priced musical entertainment to ambulatory masses amid Jullienesque dream-world surroundings of make-believe splendor. An unoriginal breed, the *Home Journal* tagged

---

[110] But an irascible Fry pronounced it "a depraved taste which dresses a fine woman in men's clothes, and makes her sing throughout a whole piece in accents which are supposed to be manly love, but have the same resemblance to nature that Juliet would have if done by a bearded man with a deep bass voice." Vestvali's Pierotto was more acceptable to Fry since it at least portrayed merely a boy, not a full-fledged man (*Tribune,* August 25, 1857).

[111] In June, Giannoni had been dropped from Maretzek's company after a single disastrous appearance at the Philadelphia Academy of Music (*Dwight's,* June 13, 1857, p. 87).

them (August 1, 1857): "As soon as one of them gets hold of a new idea in amusement, the rest adopt it *instanter*—especially when it promises to pay."[112]

Thus it was that a superspectacular new series of promenades, provocatively (if inappropriately) named "Choral Opera," made a heavily ballyhooed appearance at the New York Academy of Music on August 5. A tardy appearance, for the very opening had to be delayed two days beyond the originally announced date in order to iron out certain financial difficulties with the orchestra, grown wary, reported the *Times* (August 3, 1857), since being "deprived of their recompense for services rendered during [Burton's] recent series of Promenade Concerts."

The guiding spirits of the new venture—William Stuart, manager of Wallack's Theatre, and Dion Boucicault (1820?–1890), the brilliant Irish actor and playwright—in their efforts to outdo the comparatively primitive promenade concerts at the Philadelphia Academy of Music and the Boston Music Hall advertised attractions that transcended mere fountains and flowers and gauzy draperies. Magnificently redecorated in scarlet and gold, the New York Academy of Music offered such enticements as "Ice Cream Saloons" administered by Mr. Wagner's Broadway confectionery establishment; wines and beverages dispensed by Mr. Dunn, recently of Delmonico's; and an up-to-the-minute "Telegraphic Bulletin" to disseminate the latest news from all over the United States.[113] Too, "entirely new acoustic features" designed by Boucicault would be displayed for inspection by architects and the general public.

The entertainers at the Choral Operas were recruited from various branches of the music and theatre worlds: the popular singing actresses Miss Agnes Robertson (Mrs. Boucicault) and Mrs. John Wood for ballads and ethnic dialect songs, a German male quartet from the *Sängerbund* for German specialties, and a mixed quartet of singers of moderate repute—Henrietta Simon, Agnes Spinola, Attilio Arnoldi, and Charles Guilmette♪—for loftier operatic and sacred fare. A chorus and orchestra of 120 persons was conducted by Robert Stoepel,♪ and a just-completed, great cathedral organ built by Henry Erben♪ for the Chicago Universalist Church was generously lent by that community for the duration of the Choral Opera season.

The program, a vast hodgepodge, was changed from day to day. On August 16, a Sunday, an afternoon session featured Elder Hyde, a former dignitary of the Mormon Church, who discoursed on "The Prophet Brigham Young and the Mormons in Utah." At the Grand Sacred Concert that evening Rossini's complete *Stabat Mater* was performed by the third-string *prima donna*s Madame Chome,♪ and Madame Hyatt (the former Miss Emmeline De Luce♪♪), with Messrs. Arnoldi and Guilmette, a chorus of 150, and the veteran organist William A. King,♪♪ who presided at Erben's great organ. Imminent performances of *The Creation* and *Messiah* were promised.

But little time remained for such brave intentions. As William Henry Fry informed his readers on August 18, the Choral Opera's days were numbered. Just when the orchestra had finally achieved "unanimity of expression, these concerts [were] to be stopped suddenly and prematurely on account of the want of public patronage. The

---

[112] At least Niblo had reportedly succeeded with his own version of promenade entertainment, given in his "illuminated garden of beautiful trees, with ballet and comic pantomimes" performed by the unceasingly Wonderful Ravels.

[113] A precursor of the television set in the twentieth-century bar.

splendid Academy is splendidly decorated for the purpose," wrote Fry, "a crowded orchestra is engaged—an immense chorus—and now some of the very newest stars from
Europe, and the admission price next to nothing [twenty-five cents]—and yet, with
all this, the concerts are to be stopped."

Fresh by the last steamer from Europe the "very newest stars" were presented on
August 17: the admirable English violinist Henry C. Cooper, former concertmaster of
the London Philharmonic and a member of the eminent Beethoven Quartet Society
of London, and his young wife, the mezzo-soprano Annie Milner. Fry described her
as looking about nineteen years old, "blooming as an English rose, with intensely English light hair, fair complexion, and general style." A pupil of Mrs. Joseph Wood,⌐
Milner—like Mrs. Wood—possessed a voice of "rare beauty—Anglican beauty—
without a ragged, jagged note . . . the style not exactly heroic or ecstatic, but liberal
and elegant." Cooper was a musician of high excellence, whose gift for playing a simple melody "with passionate humanity, [made] the violin resemble an inspired being—
a linguist without words" (Tribune, August 18, 1857).

But the promenades were doomed. "Evidently," as Hagen observed, "promenade
concerts will not do for the New-Yorkers, even if they are called 'Choral Operas'"
(Review and Gazette, August 22, 1857, p. 259).

Beginning in July with the first announcements from Europe of Erminia Frezzolini's engagement for the coming opera season at the Academy, Ullman issued a continuous stream of communiqués from Europe naming other world-famous concert and
opera artists he had signed, or would sign, for the approaching season. Now, upon his
return at the beginning of August, despite the bleak economic outlook, Ullman intensified his campaign, ceaselessly impressing upon the public consciousness—in newspaper puffs, on ubiquitous placards and posters, and in the display windows of photogra-
phers, picture galleries, and music stores—the names and likenesses of his superlative
coming artists: Frezzolini, prima donna assoluta of the Théâtre des Italiens in Paris; Gustave Roger (1815–1879), the world-famed tenor of the Paris Opéra; Louis Gassier★
(1820–1872), first baritone of the Italian Opera, London; Domenico Labocetta,★ primo
tenore di grazia at La Scala, Milan; Carl Formes (1815–1889), the renowned basso of
Covent Garden and the major European opera houses; the soprano Juliana May, a
young native of Washington, D.C., who had been studying music abroad; Carl Anschütz (1815–1870), conductor of Italian, German, and English Opera at the Drury
Lane Theatre in London; the cellist Feri Kletzer, of the Beethoven Rooms, London;
and, above all, the supreme violinist Henri Vieuxtemps,⌐ not heard in the United
States since 1844.

Not to be outdone, the opposing Maretzek/Marshall group allowed scarcely a day
to pass without publicizing their own imposing roster of new artists—the magnificent
Ronzani Ballet of Turin, engaged in Europe by Maretzek on behalf of E. A. Marshall,
besides Ronconi, Tamberlik,[114] and Tagliafico.

With so lavish an embarrassment of riches, wrote Wilkins (Herald, August 8,
1857), "we could have a combination that would set the Fifth Avenue wild with de-

---

[114] The two famous tenors, Roger, claimed by Ullman, and Tamberlik, by Maretzek, although
reported to have signed iron-bound contracts, did not arrive.

light." And, he added, with tongue in cheek: "We presume that there will be no un-friendly opposition between the two operatic chiefs, but that a treaty of amity will be arranged."

Apprehensions of conflict were, however, expressed on all sides. "As the opening of the fall season approaches, we hear more and more rumours of a new operatic war," wrote *Raimond* (*Albion*, August 21, 1857, p. 415), "and although the combined capital, good sense, and musical experience of Messrs. Thalberg and Ullman have been brought to bear upon the management of the coming opera,[115] it appears that we are not yet to be delivered from the 'curse of a granted prayer.'"

The granted prayer (for new singers) had unfortunately brought with it "the hos-tility of ex-managers and of our former singers, and already our placid friends of the *City of Brotherly Love* are rejoicing over the possibility that the Broadway [Theatre, managed by Marshall, controlling also the theatres of Boston and Philadelphia] may bring Mr. Ullman's enterprise at the Academy to a disastrous termination."

Exasperated, the *Times* (September 2, 1857) exploded: "It is in the highest degree trying and unaccountable that, with two operatic managers who abhor each other most cordially and who desire nothing better in this world than to see each other's ruin, we are yet in a state of gloomy uncertainty as to that bone of contention, the Opera, which the public cunningly contrives to snatch up whilst its managers are fighting about it." Ullman and Maretzek held the cards, and could, at will, "play a profitable game at the expense of the dear public, but they [quarrel] like brigands. . . . It was bad enough when we had one manager, but now that we have two it becomes depressing and irrational.[116]

"Operatic matters were never in a worse position . . . in spite, too, of an amount of diplomacy which would drive Machiavelli to despair if he were now in the flesh and in the opera business." As Seymour saw it, the problem lay in the absence of good will: Ullman, possessing the lease of the Academy (doubtless to Maretzek's great cha-grin), had imported a great *prima donna* (Frezzolini) and engaged several European sup-porting artists, none of whom had yet arrived.[117] "For the present, therefore, he has only Signorina Frezzolini on whom he can rely for a grand musical convulsion."

Purportedly, on endeavoring to engage a temporary supporting cast from the en-emy ranks, Ullman had soon discovered that Marshall, acting for the imminently re-turning Maretzek, had no inclination to oblige him (Ullman)—at least, not "without an equivalent, or something more." As matters stood, Ullman needed some of Maret-zek's singers to begin his season; Maretzek needed Ullman's Academy of Music for his New York performances.

---

[115] Although Thalberg was nominally (and doubtless financially) a partner in the enterprise, it is unlikely that he engaged in its actual administration. Strakosch apparently worked in the background, while Ullman noticeably occupied the spotlight.

[116] "We do devoutly hope," earlier wrote *Raimond,* "that if we are to have two Italian Companies singing at one and the same time in New York, they will, at least, have the grace to fight each other behind the scenes, and not drive the public to take sides with the one or the other by running a senseless 'opposition' against each other and placarding the same Opera on the same nights" (*Albion,* March 7, 1857, p. 116).

[117] Frezzolini had in fact arrived on August 22 and the following evening had been serenaded at her hotel, the Union Place, on Union Square.

"Both parties being fully aware of this state of things," it had been suggested that the two companies unite, alternately to occupy each other's opera houses for a month and to share each other's stars.[118] To what extent this plan was actually attempted at the time remains considerably shrouded in confusion and obscurity. As *Dwight's* wisely observed: ". . . our experience as collector of musical news has not increased our confidence in the thousand and one newspaper reports circulated by operatic managers and agents. They love to excite and mystify the public" (September 5, 1857, p. 181).

Might it, then, have been Maretzekian strategy to spread in advance the rumor that the thirty-nine-year-old Frezzolini had long since passed her vocal prime?—"that we are to have the same disappointment with her as with Grisi, Sontag, and others, who have come to us with voices more than mellow, even far gone in their 'sere and yellow' autumn?" ungallantly speculated the *Evening Post* (September 5, 1857).[119]

Therefore, when—thanks to the providential last-minute arrivals of Labocetta, Gassier, and Anschütz—the Academy opened with *La sonnambula* on September 7 (only a week late) the critics were "pleasantly disappointed" by the new *prima donna:* "There has been so much said about the failure of Madame Frezzolini's powers that we were prepared to hear nothing but a wreck of a voice," wrote Fry (*Tribune,* September 8; *Dwight's,* September 12, 1857, p. 187). Not that it was by any means a fresh voice: it had been injured, wrote Fry, by the "ultra-declamatory school which has grown up within the last few years" (meaning Verdi's). Yet enough of her voice had remained to establish her as a "great artist." And although Madame Frezzolini had failed to produce "one full, voluminous, luscious note, surcharged with lyrical passion, frenzied with beauty, [she nonetheless possessed] great delicacy, refined intensity, and pathos within a quiet sphere." It was, however, Fry's opinion that Frezzolini had come "a few years too late to this country to do herself full justice." Unlike Europe, the United States, being a young country, demanded "fresh voices as the symbol of youth and love." In appearance, at least, Frezzolini was still attractive, having "a fine Roman face, a well-delineated figure, good carriage, and a *distingué* style."

The new tenor, Domenico Labocetta, confirmed his La Scala billing as *tenore di grazia,* a graceful—as opposed to robust—tenor; he possessed a voice of great sweetness, obscured—unfortunately for his debut—by hoarseness due to a bad cold, as a published note from Dr. Mott testified. But it was the baritone, Louis Gassier, who was the great hit of the evening, with his "good, round, sympathetic, manly voice. . . . He sings very well, too," wrote Fry, drawing a favorite fine distinction. Last, and far from least, the conductor Carl Anschütz instantly established himself as a "master of

[118] "Mr. Ullman, among his other gifts of 'management,' has that of knowing when his head is off, of seeing when the enemy are too strong for him," declared *Dwight's* (September 5, 1857, p. 181). "Finding himself limited to the New York Academy, with the other strongholds occupied against him, he has well nigh come to terms, happy to share the advantages possessed by Messrs. Barry and Marshall. Should this happy union come about, even if no more of the promised stars arrive, our three cities will enjoy in turn by far the finest operatic company ever yet heard in America."

[119] The *Herald* (September 8, 1857), however, attributed the large attendance at the Academy opening to the "warmth with which the merits of Madame Frezzolini . . . had been discussed previous to her arrival in this country." The *Albion* (September 12, 1857, p. 440) remarked that the house had been "considerably 'packed,'" although it conceded that the "paying audience" was comparatively large, being mostly visitors to the city.

his profession . . . quick, firm, mercurial, precise, and all alive. His readings were frequently remarkable."[120] The opera, it seems, had after all opened "brilliantly."

The critics generally agreed on the merits of everyone in the company but Frezzolini: they made allowances for Labocetta's hoarseness, declared Gassier the best baritone to have been heard in New York since Cesare Badiali,♪ and highly praised Anschütz's superb and sensitive musicianship. Writing about Frezzolini, Richard Grant White, that master of ambiguity, surpassed himself: "She appeared before an audience not only willing but anxious to be pleased, and under these circumstances she pleased them. We cannot say that she did much more. Her voice is still so good that we can see how good it must have been, though it could never have been of the very first class." Then the inevitable comparisons: "The imperial quality of Jenny Lind's voice . . . the luscious richness of Alboni's, the exquisite sweetness and flexibility of Sontag's, the dramatic utterance of Grisi—these Madame Frezzolini has not, nor were they ever hers." What she did have was a fine, true soprano voice, an unexceptionable method, acting ability, an attractive appearance, and, most particularly, a fascinating quality of vocal elegance impossible to describe. Her very fine acting and singing would have been better still, had her voice been equal to it; all the same, she was by far "the greatest prima donna, save one, yet heard in the Academy of Music" (*Courier and Enquirer,* September 8; reprinted in *Dwight's,* September 12, 1857, p. 187).

Seymour, after commenting on her "Oriental" features, her "pale and thoughtful complexion," and her figure "sufficiently decided for the milliners," declared that Frezzolini "sang sweetly, pleasantly, and artistically, but without displaying any of the power either as an actress or a singer which the audience expected." Yet, in the same breath Seymour credited Frezzolini with a delicacy and elegance not heard since Sontag.[121] "Of late, we have been somewhat coarsely addicted to screaming. . . . There is not the faintest approach to a scream or a bawl in Madame Frezzolini's method. She sings truly; with sentiment, with passion, with intelligence." Perhaps it was only nervousness that had rendered her voice so feeble at her debut (*Times,* September 8; reprinted in *Dwight's,* September 12, 1857, p. 187).

Frezzolini was less reservedly praised by Watson (in *Leslie's*), Darcie (in *Porter's Spirit*), Burkhardt (in the *Dispatch*), the anonymous critic of the *Evening Post,* and particularly by Hagen, who, although he remarked that she had lost brilliance in the past ten years, nonetheless reveled in the purity of her style, both vocal and histrionic; she sang in the true, noble style of the old Italian school, "with a preservation of melodiousness for each tone [rather than] dashing runs which would have produced only a smile upon the face of a master of the old Italian method of singing"[122] (*Review and Gazette,* September 19, 1857, p. 291). Yet, others blamed her for attempting to seduce her audiences with injudicious interpolations of showy *fioriture* where it did not belong.

La sonnambula was repeated on September 9; on September 11, in a house so

---

[120] Anschütz was "lovable" for two reasons, wrote Seymour: "He can produce a perfect *pianissimo* and he does not allow his fiddlers to scrape" (*Times,* September 8, 1857).

[121] Deified since her death in 1854, Sontag had been harshly judged by the critics when she appeared in New York in 1852–53.♪

[122] Frezzolini had studied with the younger Manuel Garcia.♪♪

Girvice Archer, Jr.

*Louis Gassier, a splendid baritone, was
compared to Bodiali—who, though Italian,
had played Macbeth in 1850.*

jammed that many had to stand,[123] Frezzolini appeared as a ladylike Lucrezia Borgia with Vestvali, who had been added to Ullman's company, as a sensational Maffio Orsini. Carlo Scola,★ a member of the Lima opera company (and the second husband of Clotilda Barili♪) was a sorry replacement for Labocetta as Gennaro,[124] Gassier was splendid as the Duke, and Frezzolini was again admired for her indescribable vocal elegance and delicacy. But even her faithful adherent in the *Evening Post* (September 12, 1857) sadly missed "the power, the devilish energy, and withering fire of the haughty and desperate Borgia."[125]

[123]Ullman, it was universally recognized, had elevated the skillful distribution of free tickets to a fine art.

[124]"It was very kind of Signor Scola to throw himself in the breach in this desperate way," unkindly wrote the *Evening Post* (September 12, 1857), but "we can only pray, devoutly, that no circumstances may ever induce him to do it again."

[125]Despite Frezzolini's vocal superiority, *Raimond* longed for Gazzaniga's overwhelming passion as Lucrezia, a quality Frezzolini did not begin to possess (*Albion*, September 19, 1857, p. 451).

Vestvali was a "superb" Orsini, although she rather overdid the "unaccustomed freedom of doublet and hose." She sang her drinking song with "a fire and abandon such as we have never heard given to it before, but a little closer adherence to the score would have done no harm." And although she was encored in her interpolated cavatina from *Maria de Rohan,* the *Post* critic wondered if it had really been necessary to "make the part worth Miss Vestvali's taking by introducing [the cavatina] into an opera that already ran until eleven o'clock."[126]

On September 14, *Il trovatore* was given with Frezzolini as a surprisingly spirited Leonora, Vestvali as Azucena (overacting the role and the audience loving it), the questionable new tenor Maccaferri replacing the still ailing Labocetta as Manrico, and Oswald Bernardi, a quick replacement for one Egisio Vieri, as the Count di Luna.[127]

Making a virtue of necessity, after a repetition of *Il trovatore* on September 16, Ullman announced—with full fanfare—that he had engaged Madame LaGrange (still present) for his opera company;[128] she would make her first appearance with them in *Norma* on September 18:[129] "The Directors [Ullman and Strakosch] trust," he trumpeted, "that their efforts to present to their patrons such an unprecedented combination of the highest celebrities in the musical world will be duly appreciated. Those who are familiar with operatic matters will readily acknowledge that no Opera House in Europe possesses two prima donnas of such rank and reputation as Mlle. Frezzolini and Mme. de LaGrange, and it has been reserved for the New-York Academy of Music to inscribe on its banner such famous names." Now it would be possible to present new operas as well as the great masterpieces of Mozart, Meyerbeer, and Rossini—that is, as soon as Messrs. Roger and Formes arrived. Indeed, the Academy would then possess "an array of vocal strength such as has never appeared, or is ever likely to appear at any Opera-House during a single season."

But for the present, the Directors would confidently continue to rely on "the liberality of their patrons, of which, until now," they claimed, "they have received ample proof, the season, thus far—thanks to the sensation produced by Mlle. Frezzolini—

[126] And was it necessary—a cause of general complaint—to prolong the intermissions to fifteen, and even twenty, minutes, causing the performances often to run past midnight?

[127] Vieri had a two-month contract as first baritone at the Academy of Music for a fee of $250 a month. At the first rehearsal of *Il trovatore* he had sung so excruciatingly out of tune that "the other performers laughed at him, and the rehearsal broke up in confusion." He was dismissed, upon which he brought suit in the Marine Court for breach of contract but lost on the basis of having misrepresented himself as a good singer (*Evening Post,* October 21, 1857).

[128] A move obviously intended both to fill his grievous lack of a strong *prima donna* and to snatch LaGrange from Maretzek's clutches, to say nothing of stimulating his own sagging box office.

[129] "After the pretty and artistic, but emasculated, renditions of Madame Frezzolini," wrote Darcie, a LaGrange devotee, "the fine, vigorous, and impressive style of LaGrange was more acceptable than ever—the notes fell refreshingly on the ear—the fire and brilliance of the cantatrice found a sympathetic chord in the hearts of all present." LaGrange was second only to Grisi in the role, he wrote, and in some of the vocal effects her superior. Amalia Patti-Strakosch, the Adalgisa, was highly praised, as was Gassier as Oroveso, but Scola, the Pollione, broke down in his first cavatina and fled from the stage, leaving Anschütz to cope with the disaster as best he could. Fortunately Maccaferri was in the audience and, quickly exchanging clothes with Scola, he completed the opera "in his most robust style" (*Porter's Spirit,* September 26, 1857, p. 64).

having exceeded in brilliancy and attendance any other since the Academy of Music has been opened."[130]

It was announced that henceforth the two *prime donne* would be heard on alternate opera nights. Thus, on September 21, Frezzolini appeared as a charming and genteel Adina in Donizetti's seldom heard *L'elisir d'amore*,[131] with a recovered Labocetta as Nemorino, Gassier as Belcore and the long absent, extrovert *basso buffo* Luigi Rocco♩ (just back from Europe) as Dr. Dulcamara. On September 23, LaGrange created a furor with her brilliant performance of Rosina in *Il barbiere di Siviglia*,[132] with Labocetta, hailed as an ideal Almaviva; Gassier a superb Figaro; and Rocco an overacted Bartolo. In sum, the best opera performance heard in years.

By September 22 the Academy directors officially announced their "amicable" arrangement with the directors of the Philadelphia Academy of Music, wherein a mutual exchange of some of their artists had been agreed upon. For starters, Brignoli (manna to the tenor-starved Ullman) and Amodio would appear with Frezzolini and Vestvali on September 25 in a performance of the overworked *Trovatore* (*positively* its last of the season). Because Maccaferri was indisposed, the scheduled performance of *Ernani,* on September 26, was replaced by the *Barber of Seville;* on September 28, a Saturday,[133] the "positively last night" of *Lucrezia Borgia* was given, with Frezzolini as Lucrezia and Brignoli as Gennaro; and on September 30, the delayed performance of *Ernani,* with LaGrange as Elvira, a recovered Maccaferri as Ernani, Gassier as Silva, and Vestvali again as Don Carlos in what Burkhardt disgustedly called "a hermaphroditical version" of *Ernani.*[134]

It was, however, not solely the re-entry upon the New York opera stage of LaGrange, Brignoli, and Amodio that bolstered the faltering Academy. It was, rather, one of Ullman's more superb inspirations that injected a new excitement into the wilting music scene—the pairing together as a concert team of two of the world's greatest virtuosos, Sigismund Thalberg and Henri Vieuxtemps.[135]

In early September, upon the synchronous arrival from Europe of Vieuxtemps and the return from the West of his "twin brother in art" Thalberg, the two musical

[130] But the press was not fooled: "The inability of Madame Frezzolini to sustain, with satisfaction to the public, the heroines of grand or tragic operas has induced the management to enter into arrangements with Madame LaGrange," wrote Darcie (*ibid.*). Besides, he spitefully added—by now well launched on his systematic persecution of Ullman—it was well known that the huge audiences at the Academy had consisted mostly of "dead heads."

[131] To Darcie it was "the same pretty, namby-pamby, lady-like assumption, as far as the acting went, as Frezzolini's preceding parts." And although her performance of Adina was as "charming as a singing lesson," she disappointed him by not reminding him in the least of Fanny Persiani (1812–1867), as he had hoped she would (*ibid.*).

[132] Pulling out all the stops, in the Lesson Scene Madame LaGrange sang her famed "Hungarian Variations" and at the end of the opera "The LaGrange Polka."

[133] The opera nights were now Mondays, Wednesdays, Fridays, and Saturdays.

[134] So repelled was Burkhardt that he could not bring himself to attend the performance (*Dispatch,* October 4, 1857).

[135] In fact a replay of Ullman's brilliant exploit in 1847 of pairing Henri Herz and Camillo Sivori as a joint concert attraction.♪

Henri Vieuxtemps, a violinist so great "he had nothing more to achieve—a master."

Girvice Archer, Jr.

giants, according to Ullman's mellifluous promotional prose, had "effected a union," and on September 15, an opera off night, they sensationally appeared at Niblo's Saloon for the first time, "on one and the same evening." They were "supported (it is almost shameful to use the word)," apologized the *Times* (September 14), by artists from the Academy of Music: Gassier, Rocco, and Anschütz (all making their local concert debuts),[136] and the Academy orchestra of forty men. Also appearing, but without prior announcement or billing, was a young debutante, Claudina Cairoli, later briefly to join Ullman's opera company.

A masterstroke on Ullman's part! The electrifying combination of Thalberg and Vieuxtemps all but deprived the critics of their superlatives. Vieuxtemps, being the greater novelty, received the greater attention. After all, as the somewhat jaded critic for the *Evening Post* (September 16, 1857) commented: Thalberg "played precisely the

[136] Great publicity value seems to have been attached to first and last appearances in various categories, to say nothing of "last appearances but one" (or two).

same pieces in precisely the same way as last season;[137] for particulars," he added, "see the columns of any musical paper for last winter."[138]

But Vieuxtemps! With the "steady, clear, and searching quality of his bowing," wrote the *Post* reviewer, he created "a certain fine resonance by which the violin in his hands [was] no longer a mere fiddle, but almost [ceased] to be an instrument at all." Accompanied by the orchestra,[139] Vieuxtemps played the first movement of his Concerto in A major, op. 25 (1844), and with Madame Vieuxtemps at the piano, his Fantasy on *I Lombardi,* Paganini's *Le streghe,* and, for an encore—a reminiscence of his earlier visit—"The Carnival of Venice."♪

Vieuxtemps was described in the *Musical World,* (September 19, 1857, p. 604), probably by its current co-editor, the Trinity Church organist, Edward Hodges,♪ as "a quiet-looking gentleman, close-shorn, neat, grave, and of entirely unassuming and modest manner. . . . He has that intense concentration in his art when he plays, which seems never to turn the eye outward to an admiring public, or to be conscious of aught but the music which absorbs him. He has no clap-trap, no attitudinizing, no pantomime or harlequinizing, no listening to 'the soul of his mother imprisoned in his violin' [a thrust at Ole Bull]. . . . He plays straightforward, with the most immaculate musical tone, with the most unerring precision, and with that intense depth of feeling and musical significance peculiar to no other man that we know of, except Vieuxtemps. He is, in a word, a master."

In the *Tribune* (September 17, 1857), Fry wrote: "He does not scratch, or play out of tune, like some others of reputation. His style is pure, large, and grand. He does not miss a note. In the region of pure healthiness he has had no equal here as a player." Vieuxtemps's technical equipment was phenomenal: "In all the machinery of violin-playing invented by Paganini—rolling up distant octaves in juxtaposition—playing without the bow, as well as [playing] the devil generally in 'The Witches' Dance' (the 'Streghe'), Vieuxtemps is at home. His octaves, too, are marvelous. In his arpeggios, rapid iterations, pinkings, and all the nomenclature of the violin pushed to its utmost limits, Mr. Vieuxtemps is a great artist."

And Richard Grant White: "He will cut out eight square-edged notes in a second with the point of an up-bow, and not move his wrist half a finger's breadth. Thus it is

---

[137] But Wilkins asserted that "any instrumental performer who can secure for two seasons [as had Thalberg] our mercurial, fitful public must be more than good—he must be great. Mr. Thalberg is now so far familiar to all of us that criticism upon his performance is unnecessary." And, the ultimate, all-inclusive tribute: "M. Vieuxtemps is to the violin what Thalberg is to the piano" (*Herald,* September 16, 1857).

[138] "Mr. Thalberg played his old pieces, which we really think ought to be laid aside for awhile," wrote Hagen (*Review and Gazette,* September 19, 1857, pp. 291–92). "The piano-forte literature is too rich to justify a constant repetition of the same compositions." But, of course, Thalberg had played magnificently, especially his Fantasia on *L'elisir d'amore,* and also his fantasies on *Moses* and *Masaniello.*

[139] But not well: in two identical passages, reported the *Musical World* (September 19, 1857, p. 604), the woodwinds had made the same wrong entrance, creating a "direful chaos of the harmony. Vieuxtemps turned around to the orchestra in astonishment, and Mr. Anschütz must have been deeply mortified at the disgrace of such a thing. . . ." Henceforth Vieuxtemps preferred to play works with piano accompaniment splendidly rendered by his attractive wife.

Ginnie Archer, Jr.

*Erminia Frezzolini, a ladylike Lucretia
Borgia—with vocal elegance and
purity of style, the critics said.*

ever with a great master; he is as unimpeachable in detail as he is admirable in design, always illustrating the axiom that the greater includes the less." And more significantly: "His style may be justly called classic—a term much abused in art and constantly used merely as a synonym for 'good.' Symmetry, grace, a serene expression of power, singleness of purpose, a sparing use of ornament, and the highest finish even of the minutest detail—these are the characteristic traits of Mr. Vieuxtemps's style, both as a composer and a performer" (*Courier and Enquirer,* September 17, 1857).

Any attempt to enumerate the thousand and one felicities of Vieuxtemps's technical mastery, wrote Watson (*Leslie's,* September 19, 1857, p. 247) could best be summed up in a single sentence: "His mechanism is perfect—he has nothing to achieve . . . and in soul and sentiment and passion[140] he reaches the sublime in expression. We confess to an ecstacy of emotion, which, as we looked from face to face, we found was shared. Murmurs of irrepressible delight burst forth during his performance, and at the close every hand and every voice was raised to do him honor."

Watson had lauds, as well, for Thalberg: As always, "immaculate and unapproachable in his art, [he] seemed inspired by the presence of a talent as grand as his own, and played as we have never heard him play in this country. . . . Thalberg is more popular than ever; the public never tire of hearing him, and the artists crowd his concerts, for he is a prophet in his art."

[140] Qualities in which he had immeasurably gained since his earlier visit, observed Watson.

Splendid, too, were the assisting artists: Gassier, though Gallic, rendered his aria from *Il barbiere* in the crisp accents of the true Italian; and Rocco, accompanying himself at the piano, uninhibitedly displayed his "buffo-tricks and grimaces" in a comic aria *Il ballo di famiglia* by Vincenzo Gabussi (1800–1846). But it was the young soprano Claudina Cairoli, a native of Milan, who especially captivated the critics. Everyone agreed that, with a limited, but sweet, voice, she was an enchanting singer.[141] Wilkins was especially charmed: "first, by a modest attitude; secondly, by a vocal organ which was as pure as her appearance; thirdly, by an entire absence of crinoline" (*Herald,* September 16, 1857).

On September 17, Thalberg and Vieuxtemps again mesmerized an audience at Niblo's Saloon, so numerous that the outside corridors and even the stairs were crowded. This time Vieuxtemps played his Adagio, his Tarantella, and, to close the program, his Fantasy on *Lucia di Lammermoor;* Thalberg played his Barcarole and his Fantasies on *Don Pasquale* and *Lucrezia Borgia;* and, with the addition of Labocetta, the same cast sang an assortment of arias, duets, and trios from the most popular operas.

The third concert, scheduled for September 19, was canceled because of a severe rainstorm, frustrating a number of disgruntled enthusiasts who had braved the weather in vain. But a consolatory "Grand Combination Concert," featuring "an unprecedented combination of artists," was announced for September 24, Vieuxtemps and Thalberg's last joint appearance before going on a lightning-swift sweep of Philadelphia, Baltimore, and Washington. On this occasion they were assisted by Madame LaGrange, and again by Gassier and Rocco.[142]

On September 26, Ullman hinted that Frezzolini (less than a sensation in opera) would soon appear in the Concert Room for the first time in America. "The high celebrity of Mlle. Frezzolini as the leading star of the *soirées* given by the Emperor of the French, [and] of the far-famed Concerts of the *Conservatoire* in Paris," he proclaimed, "justifies the Directors in believing that this announcement will meet with approbation."

Frezzolini made her local concert debut on October 2 at a Grand Combination Concert with Vieuxtemps and Thalberg, Amalia Patti-Strakosch (henceforth known as Madame Strakosch), Gassier, and Rocco.[143] And as a come-on: "In order to give the audience every possible comfort, six rows of chairs, amounting to over 200 seats, will be struck off the [Seating] Diagram.[144] The utmost care will be taken not to have the Saloon crowded. For this reason [the directors] announce to cut off the free list, with the exception of the press."

---

[141] Cairoli sang an aria from *L'elisir d'amore* and, with Rocco, a duet from the same opera.

[142] LaGrange was announced to sing the *Grâce* from *Robert le diable* and the Rode Variations; Thalberg to play his Fantasies on *La sonnambula* and *Norma,* his Tarantelle, op. 65, and his enormously popular arrangement of "Home, Sweet Home"; Vieuxtemps to play his *Fantaisie caprice,* his Fantasy on *I Lombardi,* and his composition *Les Arpèges;* and Rocco would repeat his *buffo* hit.

[143] Frezzolini was announced to sing a *romanza* from Verdi's *Giovanna d'Arco,* an aria from *I Lombardi,* with Madame Strakosch a duet from Donizetti's *Maria Padilla,* and with Rocco one from *L'elisir d'amore;* Thalberg would play his Fantasies on *Semiramide, Les Huguenots,* and *Lucrezia Borgia;* and Vieuxtemps his Fantasy on *Lucia di Lammermoor* and Paganini's "Witches' Dance."

[144] This might have been an artful Ullmanesque dodge to conceal a less than capacity audience, for the hard times were beginning to make themselves felt, even at the Thalberg/Vieuxtemps level.

Frezzolini in fact pleased the critics more as a concert singer than she had done in opera. In her encore—the finale to *La sonnambula*—she was no less great than Henriette Sontag, wrote her ardent supporter, presumably Wilkins, in the *Herald* (October 3, 1857). Her manner, too, was "more like that of a lady entertaining a party of friends than an artist singing to the public, and her *toilette* was sufficiently exquisite to excite even the admiration of her own sex." It was, of course, superfluous to mention the greatness of Thalberg and Vieuxtemps.

The *Times* (October 3, 1857) wondered how these "extraordinary, monster affairs," for which Ullman had already become famous, could possibly pay, especially in these hard times, with so many artists participating in each.[145] It was a source of wonderment, too, that the audiences were so insatiable for music: "If there are a dozen pieces, they want twenty-four, and if there are twenty-four, they want forty-eight." At only one dollar a ticket, with no extra charge for reserved seats, these concerts were "the cheapest and best in America," and the *Times* hoped to see them fully patronized.

Cheaper yet was the Grand Oratorio that followed at the Academy of Music on Sunday evening, October 4. "No one will say that listening to an oratorio provokes unholy thought of the world and its vanities," defensively wrote the *Times* (October 3, 1857), to forestall inevitable religious objections to being entertained on the Sabbath. "The managers of the Academy of Music have determined (from the highest motives, of course) on making the experiment of cheap Sunday concerts" with the very best in programing and choice of artists. With an orchestra of "sixty professors" and a chorus of fifty singers conducted by Anschütz, the program consisted of Beethoven's "Pastoral" Symphony; Rossini's *Stabat Mater* sung by LaGrange, Vestvali, Mme. Strakosch, Labocetta, Gassier, Scola, Rocco, and an unidentified Barili;★ and, to close, the March from Meyerbeer's *Le Prophète*. All for fifty cents—a concession to current economic conditions.[146]

This "dangerous experiment," as the *Times* playfully called it (October 5, 1857), turned out to be a "success which promises perpetuity." The program had indeed offered nothing unsuitable for Sabbath consumption; Anschütz and his sixty professors had given an excellent performance of the Beethoven symphony; and with the exception of a too-loud accompaniment, the performance of the *Stabat Mater*—both by the singers and the orchestra—was the best ever heard in New York.[147] The house had been "completely filled."

---

[145] Probably because Ullman was exacting maximum service from all of his artists. On that same evening (October 2) LaGrange appeared at the Academy in *I puritani;* on the following evening Frezzolini was heard in *Lucia di Lammermoor,* while Thalberg/Vieuxtemps/LaGrange, together with Rocco, were giving a Grand Combination Concert at the Brooklyn Athenaeum.

[146] At Niblo's Theatre, for the same reason, tickets for the upper tier had been reduced to 25 cents.

[147] Following Beethoven's "idyl," as Hagen referred to the "Pastoral" Symphony, the March from *The Prophet* reminded him of the fireworks that usually ended popular out-of-doors entertainments: "It seemed to be an indication that the whole affair was intended to end in smoke, which considering the present state of matters at the Academy, was after all, quite *àpropos*" (*Review and Gazette,* October 17, 1857, pp. 322–23).

Ullman needed all the well-attended performances he could muster, for, despite his elaborate efforts to present to the world the semblance of a booming opera season, symptoms of the growing economic depression had become frighteningly visible at the Academy and even at the Thalberg/Vieuxtemps concerts. Thus, after Frezzolini repeated her greatest success, *L'elisir d'amore,* on October 5, the opera management abruptly announced that the following performance—*Don Giovanni* on October 7— would be "last night but two" of the present opera season.

"The spasmodic production of Mozart's *Don Giovanni* is the sure sign of a waning management," commented an increasingly hostile Darcie[148] (*Porter's Spirit,* October 17, 1857, p. 112), and this was conspicuously true of the present effort. "Scared by a succession of bad houses, the Academic 'powers that be' bethought themselves of the immortal *Don,* and up he went, with a flourish of trumpets and display of posters that was something astounding."

The result was a large and, for once, a paying house: "People who had not been to the opera before, this season, went on this occasion; others who had not often been absent were there as usual; some of the customary dead-heads, even, unable to obtain the usual freedom of *entrée,* were shamed into paying; whilst not a few attended for the express purpose of witnessing a lyric set-to between LaGrange and Frezzolini, in which public opinion was all in favor of the former." Besides, claimed Darcie, it was the fashion to go once in a season to hear *Don Giovanni.*

October 8. . . . Yesterday Miss Leavenworth and Murray Hoffman dined here and [we] went to *Don Giovanni.* Satisfactory evening. Leporello [Rocco] and the Don [Gassier] severally respectable—*decent,* at least. LaGrange executed Donna Anna's music honestly. Elvira [Mme. Strakosch] and the tenor [Labocetta] did their work fairly. I think I've never heard the opera performed with fewer flagrancies of defect—or more tamely. But that glorious music can stand feeble rendering.[149]

⚫

To attract an audience to the second *Don Giovanni* performance (October 9), Vieuxtemps and Thalberg appeared "between the acts," Vieuxtemps playing a movement of one of his concertos "in his happiest and most admirable vein," and as an encore "a quaint version of the Irish melody 'The Prince's Day'—an eccentricity peculiarly Paganinish and very amusing." After Vieuxtemps, the greatest violinist, came Mr. Thalberg, the greatest pianist, who played his Fantasy on *Lucrezia* and as an encore his arrangement of "The Last Rose of Summer" (*Times,* October 10, 1857).

The following evening they appeared again (to a slim attendance) at the closing Grand Combination Opera Gala, wherein the entire company appeared in single acts

---

[148] As former partners in the publication of opera librettos and the short-lived theatrical sheet *L'Entr'acte,* Ullman and Darcie had apparently parted on less than amicable terms. A vengeful Darcie—playing upon Ullman's inability to accept adverse criticism—now made every attempt as a newspaper critic to undermine Ullman's efforts in all he attempted.

[149] Especially feeble, according to the critics, was Frezzolini's Zerlina, overdressed in satin and gold. Notably, in this performance Labocetta, in addition to *Il mio tesoro,* splendidly sang the aria *Dalla sua pace,* composed by Mozart for Don Ottavio but rarely sung (*Dispatch,* October 11, 1857).

of *Norma, La sonnambula, Il barbiere di Siviglia,* and *L'elisir d'amore.* In the interval, between *La sonnambula* and *Il barbiere,* Thalberg and Vieuxtemps appeared and as usual brought down the house.

On Sunday, October 11, the Academy presented a final Oratorio, this time including both Frezzolini and LaGrange, supported by "all the great artists of the Academy," its chorus, and its orchestra, again splendidly conducted by Anschütz. The program opened with Mozart's "Jupiter" Symphony, then the Prayer from *Mosè* sung by Frezzolini, with Labocetta, Gassier, Barili, and the chorus and orchestra of 100; then Schubert's *Ave Maria* sung by Amalia Strakosch; the *Miserere* from *Il trovatore* by Frezzolini and Labocetta with the chorus; then again Rossini's *Stabat Mater* sung by LaGrange, Strakosch, Labocetta, Gassier, Scola, Rocco, Barili, *et al.,* and to close, the March from Mendelssohn's *Athalie.*♪♫

After a projected tour of Philadelphia, Boston, and Baltimore, promised Ullman, the company would return to the Academy (on an unspecified date), when no effort would be spared to give the most brilliant performances possible with the "unparalleled resources of this great establishment." But Darcie (*Porter's Spirit,* October 10, p. 96), proceeded ruthlessly to puncture the Ullmanian bubble: "Notwithstanding the 'crowded and brilliant audiences,' concerning which so much has been said and written, the season has not proved a sufficiently paying one to warrant its continuance. The financial pressure in commercial circles has materially affected the receipts at the opera house; and although, numerically, the attendances have shown, on the regular nights, but little falling off, there has been a sad deterioration in the cash balance in the treasurer's hands. We believe the management has proposed to reduce salaries all round. . . . This does not accord with the triumphant paeans of the directors at the commencement of the season; nor are the operatic artists—always exigent in their demands . . . very likely to consent to the breaking of a bargain made in good faith."

The directors had made their initial mistake in relying on Madame Frezzolini to carry the weight of the opera season, continued Darcie, gathering momentum, "and ere the third night came, they found out what anybody conversant with European operatic affairs could have told them beforehand, that this artiste, however acceptable in light operas and as a concert singer, was physically and artistically incapable of carrying on her fair shoulders the weight of a lyric campaign." Thus, the management had been compelled to double their "expense of prima donnas" by engaging LaGrange, without gaining any corresponding benefit, since LaGrange sang only the operas that Frezzolini was unable to deal with. But in whatever she sang, LaGrange had "killed Frezzolini."

The directors had shown the same poor judgment in choosing their tenors, continued Darcie. Labocetta, short and stout, with merely a "pretty," drawing-room sort of voice, was physically unfitted for grand opera, and the others, Maccaferri and Scola, were dismal failures and could only be regarded as fourth-raters. Only Gassier, among the new singers, could be considered a truly first-class artist.

Watson, on the other hand, defended the opera management. The unprecedented pressures of the money market that had affected all aspects of the entertainment scene, he wrote, had affected opera more seriously than any other form of amusement, because, with the enormous sums needed to run an opera establishment, "a scarcity of money is more immediately felt than in the houses of cheaper amusement." While a night's expenses at a theatre, including one good artist—"a star, of course"—would not exceed one hundred and fifty dollars, "the Italian opera cannot be opened under a nightly cost of from eleven [hundred] to thirteen hundred dollars." And managers could scarcely economize on singers for a public that had "thought Grisi terribly *passé,* tolerated Bosio,♪ and endured Steffanone." The Academy had to attempt to satisfy, too, "the cynical and painfully cultivated taste of our musical critics, most of whom judge singers as they would horses, by their pedigree—who, having no standard of judgment but what pleases them . . . prefer to sneer and grumble. . . . Perfection is demanded by these gentlemen, but perfection is a dear article; and then, with a consistency quite compatible with their general conduct, they berate and blackguard the managers for charging a price by which alone their outlay and expenses can be covered. The Management of the Italian opera is not an enviable position. . . . We can only wonder at and admire the man who from choice undertakes to manage the New York Opera House. He must be in love with martyrdom and greedy for trouble" (*Leslie's,* October 17, 1857, p. 311).

After an ensuing period laden with rumors, editorials, surmises, and hidden negotiations—and after a concert (announced as the "last concert but one") by Thalberg and Vieuxtemps at Niblo's on October 23,[150] at which appeared also Madame Frezzolini (making her "positively last appearance in the Concert Room"), Labocetta, Gassier, Rocco, and the new cellist Feri Kletzer[151]—it was at last announced that the Academy would reopen on October 28 for a "Winter Opera Season." (Ullman had apparently landed a new backer.)

The Academy did not in fact reopen until November 2. By then, as Darcie reported (*Spirit,* October 31, 1857, p. 144), an intramural upheaval had taken place: "Maurice Strakosch, heartily sick of managing an opera troupe, resigns his chair at the director's table[152] in favor of Mr. W. H. Paine (who has returned from Europe with an artist or two). . . . Madame Frezzolini secedes with Strakosch and accompanies him on a concert tour through the South and West,[153] Madame de LaGrange remaining as *prima donna assoluta.* Madame D'Angri, who has not yet been heard on the lyric stage in America, has been engaged as contralto, in lieu of Vestvali,[154] and will make her debut as Arsace in the *Semiramide* of Rossini. . . . *Rigoletto, Mosè in Egitto, Otello,* and other operas differing from the customary *répertoire* are spoken of as likely to be produced during the coming season." About the previously promised combined effort with Maretzek and his company, an eloquent silence.

Perhaps it was this development at the Academy, added to the dismal state of the economy, that had convinced Maretzek, whose short and apparently unprofitable sea-

---

[150] At which they performed for the first time their newly composed violin and piano duet on themes from *Les Huguenots.*

[151] Kletzer played his Fantasia on Styrian Airs, a piece Hagen characterized as "trash," accompanied at the piano by Anschütz, who so unmercifully pounded the instrument that, reported Watson, the soloist was drowned (*Review and Gazette,* October 31, p. 338; *Leslie's,* October 31, 1857, p. 343).

[152] But evidently retaining his partnership with Ullman.

[153] Madame Frezzolini's destination was in fact Havana, where she became a major diva in Maretzek's opera company.

[154] Who had recently departed for Matanzas, Cuba, with her new opera company, among them the failed tenor Scola, the baritone Bernardi, and Weinlich,♪ the bass of last year's ill-fated German opera company (*Musical World,* November 21, 1857, p. 721).

son in Philadelphia had closed on October 2, to abandon his plan of bringing his company to New York for a season at the Broadway Theatre. Instead, on November 2 they embarked for Havana, where they proceeded to give a reportedly successful three-month season at the Tacón Theatre.[155]

Thus uncontested, and heralded by flights of Ullman's most untrammeled prose, the Academy launched its winter season on November 2 with Rossini's *Semiramide*. Featuring LaGrange in the title role, the occasion included both the opera debut of Elena d'Angri as Arsace and the first appearance in America of Fortini, reputed to be "*primo basso* of Covent Garden," evidently one of Paine's new singers, as Oroe. Although the papers had wishfully noted a slight improvement in theatre attendance during the previous week, it was observed that the opening-night attendance at the Academy, while adequate, "considering the Wall-street thermometer"—and comparatively free of deadheads—hardly matched the voluminous forces assembled on the stage: the chorus, the supernumeraries, and the instrumental band.

D'Angri was, of course, the focus of critical interest. With her powerful, rich contralto voice, second only to Alboni's, and with her superb musicality, she was unanimously hailed as a magnificent singer of opera, although there were differences of opinion about her acting. And even if she made a less handsome young man than did Vestvali in the role of Arsace, she was immeasurably a better singer.

LaGrange, however, for the first time since her return to New York, was criticized for her growingly noticeable tremolo—albeit "kindly and forgivingly" by the critic for the *Musical World* (November 21, 1857, p. 721), who pardoned her "tremulousness and unsteadiness of tone in consideration of that marvelous Art, of which she is mistress." But Watson (*Leslie's,* November 7, 1857, p. 359) harshly accused her—although she sang the music with her accustomed brilliance—of not having indulged her hearers with "one pure, steady, unbrokenly sustained note. She trembled on the minims, and she trembled on the demi-semiquavers; in fact, no note was so short but Madame LaGrange managed to tremble upon it." This was nothing but self-indulgence, claimed Watson. and he demanded that she immediately discard this "disagreeable eccentricity and come back again to the style of excellence which won her the high reputation she enjoys."[156]

Like his colleagues, Watson proclaimed D'Angri a great artist; he praised Gassier's Assur and Labocetta's Idreno, but Fortini, the Oroe, "did not shine to advantage—indeed, he did not shine at all."[157] Besides, the choice of *Semiramide* as an opening attraction for the new opera season was perhaps not quite appropriate. It was late in the

---

[155] Maretzek's company now included a new soprano Signora Ramos (apparently a failure), the preeminent basso Giorgio Ronconi (who for some reason had not appeared during the Philadelphia season); Stecchi-Bottardi, a tenor (good enough to rival Brignoli, it was said, but by far no Tamberlik); Tagliafico, baritone; and, of course, Gazzaniga, Brignoli, Amodio, and Coletti.

[156] "It is my misfortune to dislike the *tremolo* style of LaGrange so much that, while everybody else was in ecstacies, I sat upon thorns and fervently wished never to hear her open her lips again," wrote Dwight's Diarist, Alexander Wheelock Thayer,♪ after a performance of *Lucrezia Borgia* (*Dwight's,* December 5, 1857, p. 283). But Burkhardt steadfastly denied the existence of Madame La-Grange's notorious tremolo.

[157] With his virtually inaudible voice, Fortini should have been named "Signor *Piano*-Fortini," quipped the sharp-tongued critic for the *Spirit of the Times*.

day to criticize Rossini's music, wrote Watson, "still, we cannot but remark that with all its beauties, the more we hear it, the more soulless it appears to us. Passages, passages, nothing but passages, outside glitter and no real depth."

The critic for the *Evening Post* (November 3, 1857) agreed: with all its pomp, luxury, and barbaric splendor, the total effect of *Semiramide* was "heavy." Of course, the opera was splendid, "but the audience never fail to experience a feeling of relief when the . . . curtain falls upon the last act of the obscure tragedy."[158]

It was a relief, too, after the trying sublimities of *Semiramide,* wrote *Raimond,* to enjoy the complete and refreshing contrast when *Rigoletto* was presented on November 4 (*Albion,* November 7, 1857, p. 536). Not heard since its unsuccessful first performances at the Academy during the momentary regime of Ole Bull in 1855,♪[159] it was in a very real sense now being heard for the first time, this being its first performance with Verdi's own instrumentation.[160] The cast included Madame Frezzolini as Gilda, for the "first time in America"; Pietro Bignardi, a new tenor from "the great Opera in Florence" (another of Paine's singers?) as the Duke of Mantua; and Francesco Taffanelli,♪ a longtime minor member of the local Italian opera community, as Rigoletto. Frezzolini was, for once, unanimously praised, even by her most enthusiastic detractors—even by Hagen—who found her a "very acceptable Gilda"[161] (*Review and Gazette,* November 14, 1857, p. 355).

But Hagen denied that *Rigoletto* was music: "Can an attempt to characterize, to dramatize the most horrid scenes of social life by means of sounds leave any impression which may approach to what we are accustomed to derive from music?" he thundered (*Review and Gazette,* November 14, 1957, p. 355). Burkhardt could tolerate *Rigoletto,* but barely: "If we must have our regular dose of [Verdi]," he wrote, "we prefer him in *Rigoletto,* not that we love him more, but that we hate him less in this, than in most of his other popular works. . . . *Rigoletto* is certainly no masterpiece, as it is full of plagiarisms and faults, and yet abounds with fascinating trifles. Verdi," commented Burkhardt, "is merely a successful writer of melodramatic music, of fanciful nightmare compositions" (*Dispatch,* November 8, 1857).

Seymour playfully hailed the handsome new tenor, Bignardi: There are "some phenomena connected with this gentleman," he stated. "In the first place, he has got a voice; in the second, he does not appear to be afflicted with a chronic cold; in the

[158] A yawning audience was an axiomatic component of a *Semiramide* performance, wrote Burkhardt, who regarded the work, despite its intermittent lovely melodies, as "uninteresting and wearisome" (*Dispatch,* November 8, 1857).

[159] "It was not a success then," wrote Watson, "and, we believe . . . that it will never be a favorite with a New York audience. The music in the first three acts is irredeemably dull—one or two effective pieces being only observable during a dreary waste of over two hours." Only the Quartet in the last act, with its "exquisite and passionate melody," was truly first rate (*Leslie's,* November 14, 1857, p. 375).

[160] For its 1855 production, under Maretzek, it will be remembered, an orchestration had been locally concocted from the piano score by Julius Unger.♪

[161] This was her swan song at the Academy: after a final concert with Thalberg and Vieuxtemps at Niblo's on November 5, Madame Frezzolini departed with Strakosch and Madame Strakosch, not, as announced, on a concert tour of the South and West, but to Havana to join Maretzek's opera company. (For the ensuing Gazzaniga/Frezzolini rivalry at the Tacón Theatre, see *Sharps and Flats,* pp. 32–36).

third, he sings like a man and not like a whining monk. Such an unusual combination of attributes excited an audience not over-used to their influence, and Signor Bignardi obtained a well merited success. His voice is of the *robusto* kind, but with a more delicate vein of sentiment in it than we have had in his predecessors. . . . We look on Signor Bignardi as one of the most desirable members of the company"[162] (*Times*, November 5, 1857). Taffanelli, too, was more tolerable than in the past,[163] and Anschütz was universally lauded. It seemed that a legitimate opera season was at last under way. Because of Frezzolini's indisposition, *Semiramide*, not *Rigoletto*, was repeated.

With the resumption of opera, Ullman announced the resumption of his Sunday concerts in characteristic style: "The great success of the Sunday performances given last month, which have been attended by the élite of the City, including the most prominent stockholders," he significantly added, "has induced the Directors to give a Grand Sacred and Oratorio Concert on Sunday, November 8, on which will be presented a programme on a scale of unequaled splendor and magnificence." The performers were LaGrange, D'Angri, Labocetta, and Gassier, the oratorio singers Annie Milner and the newly arrived English tenor Ernest Perring; also Henri Vieuxtemps, who outdid himself in his performance of his *Fantaisie caprice,* and Anschütz, who splendidly conducted Beethoven's Fifth Symphony. Tickets for this event were fifty cents for the parquette and boxes, and twenty-five cents for the amphitheatre.

The opera bill for the following week was a representative bit of Ullmanesque flimflam: three "Star Performaces" of *Il trovatore,* on November 9, 11, and 13, featuring for the first time LaGrange as Leonora, D'Angri as Azucena, Bignardi as Manrico, a new baritone, Achille Ardavani, as the Count di Luna, and, to preserve the truly All-Star quality of the occasion, Gassier had consented to sing the lesser role of Ferrando.

Despite this luminous array of stars, wrote Hagen, Verdi's music left him in the dark. Surprisingly, he had words of praise for the cast, particularly for D'Angri and Bignardi, both of whom sang with passion and feeling. About Ardavani, the company's latest acquisition, Hagen chose to be enigmatic: he, "of course, did not please that part of the public which, at our Academy, arrogates to itself the role of the umpire in such matters." But although Ardavani had a "sweet, good voice" and knew how to use it "pretty well," he could not approach Amodio, neither in voice nor in girth (*Review and Gazette,* November 14, 1857, p. 355).

On November 13, Ullman (desperately fighting a deteriorating financial situation) informed the public of "a plan which has been suggested to [the Directors] in consequence of the furor created last season by Mr. Thalberg's Matinées and the well established success of the public rehearsals of the Philharmonic Society."[164] Ullman proposed to present a monster monthly Saturday matinée comprising two or more single acts of operas, with a between-the-acts concert featuring his concert and opera artists. The fifty-cent admission would be good for seats in all parts of the house, except the

[162] Hagen, too, credited Bignardi with a "fine voice, elegance and finish, and spirit and intelligence, qualities in which most of our tenors at the Academy have been wanting" (*Review and Gazette,* November 14, 1857, p. 355).

[163] Except to Watson. to whom Taffanelli seemed a "sorry jester. He would hardly have passed for a humorous undertaker" (*Leslie's,* November 14, 1857, p. 375).

[164] An organization that Ullman evidently regarded as a rival; he refused to allow either Thalberg or Vieuxtemps to appear with the Society.

amphitheatre, which on these occasions would be closed off, as would the barroom. To accomplish this extraordinary undertaking, wrote Ullman, the artists, "desirous of assisting . . . in elevating the standard of music, [had] most liberally consented to volunteer their valuable services." The first of these magnificent entertainments, to be presented the following day, November 14, consisted of single acts from *Lucia di Lammermoor,* with LaGrange as Lucia,[165] and *The Barber of Seville,* with D'Angri as Rosina; the male roles in both operas to be filled by Labocetta, Gassier, Fortini, and (for the *Barber*) Rocco. The concert part of the program would be performed by Annie Milner, Claudine Cairoli, Ernest Perring, and by Henri Vieuxtemps, no less, who would open proceedings with his *Fantaisie caprice* and close them with Paganini's "Witches' Dance."

The experiment was a resounding success. The house was crowded, reported the *Times* (November 15, 1857), with "at least fourteen hundred ladies" present. This statistic had evidently been issued from Ullman's information manufactury, for Watson, too, reported it, further identifying the fourteen hundred ladies as musically disadvantaged suburbanites, starved for culture because the local railroads shut down at eight P.M., making it impossible for them to attend the regularly scheduled opera. "These morning operas, commencing at two P.M., will enable them to reach the city, hear all the musical novelties, and return by the five o'clock trains," wrote Watson. He urged Ullman to publicize the matinées far and wide as a boon to culture-starved, out-of-town ladies.

On Sunday evening, November 15, Vieuxtemps—together with his concert companions of the day before, and with the addition of Madame D'Angri—appeared at the second Grand Classical and Sacred Performance at the Academy. In addition to Vieuxtemps's *Fantaisie caprice,* the program included opera and oratorio arias by Beethoven, Handel, and Meyerbeer; with Anschütz conducting his "orchestra of fifty," Beethoven's Overture to *Fidelio,* Mendelssohn's *Meerestille und glückliche Fahrt,* and, to close the program, Beethoven's Seventh Symphony.[166] A potent object lesson to the Philharmonic, preached Hagen: all these riches for only fifty cents, while a dollar at the Philharmonic bought only "an old symphony by Spohr and Mr. Mollenhauer" (*Review and Gazette,* November 28, 1857, p. 371).

Aside from its narrow programing practices, the Philharmonic, like everyone else, was affected by the deplorable state of the economy: "All occasion for the fear expressed in the late report of the Philharmonic Society of the 'perils of success,' seems likely to be removed," spitefully commented Hagen (*Review and Gazette,* October 31, 1857, p. 337). "The directors will no longer have to complain of the crowds of 'youth and vivacity,' or of the 'exciting attrition of so many elements of beauty and attractiveness,'[167] for their subscribers are leaving in mass. The returning of tickets by former subscribers who do not wish to renew seems to have become a perfect epidemic." Ac-

---

[165] As it turned out, Cairoli replaced LaGrange, who suffered an unprecedented last-minute indisposition.

[166] About one-quarter of the audience left before the symphony, wrote *Dwight's* newly acquired New York—or rather, Brooklyn—correspondent *Bellini;* one quarter more after the second movement, and the last movement was played to "an extremely small, though select, audience" (*Dwight's,* November 21, 1857, p. 269).

[167] A reference to the Philharmonic's recently published, overly euphoric, Annual Report.

cording to Hagen's distorted report, nearly two-thirds of the Philharmonic subscribership, including all those living in Brooklyn, had canceled.[168] Although the money pressure was largely to blame, the Philharmonic itself was to a great extent responsible, wrote Hagen. It had failed in its stated mission as an "educating institution," particularly with its frequent repetitions of such creaky old chestnuts as Spohr's *Die Weihe der Töne* "mixed with Verdi arias and garden overtures." Strong did not share Hagen's contempt for Spohr's hackneyed symphony.

October 26. . . . Saturday afternoon I went through soaking rain to the Philharmonic rehearsal at the Academy of Music[169] to hear Spohr's *Weihe der Töne* symphony. It is melodic and genial, and stands high among second-rate works. But compositions that require explanatory notes are essentially wrong.[170] The necessity of labeled memoranda shows that the composer has attempted something outside the sphere of his Art, or else that he has done his work ill, like a painter whose landscape is made intelligible only by inscriptions that *this* is a tree and this is a house. Nobody wants a printed commentary on the C-minor, the "Eroica," or the Overture to *Der Freischütz.* Each speaks for itself most eloquently. The printed explanations prefixed to the movements of the "Pastorale" are generally felt to be an offense, for each movement tells the story indicated by its heading, and a great deal more. The "Scene beside a Brook" and the "Joyous Assembling of the Country People" merely limit and restrict Beethoven's music to one form of "Pastoral," or rural, expression out of many.

November 21. . . . Went with Ellie to the Philharmonic concert. Crowd. Clack.[171] At last an excited individual—Teutonic—rose up in the midst of a dreary *Adagio*[172] on the violoncello by one of those inevitable Mollenhauers and exclaimed, with much emphasis —as if in continuation of some fruitless private remonstrance— "Well, I can talk, too. So the every *bodies* can hear *me!* Is it not possible for us to have some place where we can *hear* [the music]?" And then subsided with like abruptness. People were still as mice in that neighborhood for some time. This self-sacrificing champion of silence should receive some testimonial.[173] At these concerts, especially,

---

[168] Not uninfluenced by the advent of the Brooklyn Philharmonic Society, recruited predominantly from New York Philharmonic musicians and conducted by Eisfeld.

[169] Despite their thorny relationship with Ullman, the Philharmonic—in the absence of another suitable auditorium—had renewed their sublease for another season's use of the Academy for both rehearsals and concerts. With their original offer of $2000 apparently having been refused, they resolved, at their board of directors' meeting on August 25, to pay no more than $2500 for the 1858 season, presumably the sum finally agreed upon (Philharmonic Archives).

[170] More than explanatory notes, the composer demanded that the poem by Carl Pfeiffer, upon which this composition was based, be read to the audience before the work was performed—in this instance in an English translation.

[171] A smaller crowd than usual, reported the *Musical World* (November 28, 1857), but evidently of undiminished loquacity.

[172] A movement of a concerto by the German cellist/composer Georg Goltermann (1824–1898), played by Henry Mollenhauer, who in addition played a Grand Fantasia for cello by François Servais (1807–1866).

[173] The incident was reported both in *Dwight's* (November 28, 1857, p. 277) and the *Musical Times* (November 28, 1857, p. 736).

the music is drowned—or at least one's capacity for enjoying it is paralyzed with vexation by excessive, ill-bred, obstreperous gabblings.[174] Spohr's *Weihe der Töne* is a very pretty symphony. The Prayer and Allegro from *Der Freischütz* [were] very feebly rendered by one Miss Annie Milner; *Qui la voce* (from *Puritani*) rather better done. A second-rate singer finds *fioriture* and vocalization easier than real music. Schumann's Overture to *Manfred* heavy and dead—mere diligent dullness. Beethoven's Overture to *Leonora* (no. 2, in C) was the finale. It's long and elaborate—seems not among the *Hirnbesitzer's* most genial works—evidently needs to be heard more than once—but is full of life and strength. It abounds in those magical little single phrases, made up of two or three notes, that can hardly be called melody, but seem something higher and more intense.

•••

At the Academy, *Lucrezia Borgia* was given on November 16, with LaGrange, D'Angri, and Bignardi (a sensational Gennaro); on November 18 the despised *Rigoletto* was repeated, with LaGrange for the first time as Gilda, and D'Angri, who had "kindly consented" to take the minor role of Magdalena; also Bignardi, Taffanelli, Rocco, and Amati Dubreuil. For the comparatively unballyhooed "Extra" matinée[175] the following day, the "star performance" of *Il trovatore* was exhumed. Then, once again, amid all this seemingly fruitful activity came the shocking announcement that the November 20 performance of *La sonnambula* (with LaGrange, Labocetta, and Gassier) would terminate the season.[176]

As the *Herald* (November 19, 1857) explained this latest fiasco: "Recently, only a few of the performances have paid expenses, and on several there has been a dead loss of five or six hundred dollars per night. *Rigoletto* was admirably done, at an expense of twelve hundred dollars, to an audience which only paid six hundred."

Following the example of the other stricken New York theatres, "a proposition was made [by Ullman] to the artists having the larger salaries to submit to a reduction of one third of their pay; to those having small salaries, with the chorus and orchestra, a reduction of one fourth was proposed. The alternative of a refusal of these propositions was the closing of the house, to take place this week."

General dismay! "The 'gentlemen of the chorus' refused outright. . . . The orchestra at first refused, but finally concluded to think about it until today. The managers offered, in case they agreed to a reduction, to give extra performances enough to make up nearly the amount of their regular salaries.

"The artists have not yet been heard from, with the exception of Madame La-Grange, who, like a sensible person, saw the state of things and offered a reduction

---

[174] It was a pity, observed ——t——, that the lost part of the subscribership had not included these remorseless conversationalists (*Dwight's,* November 28, 1857, p. 277).

[175] "Extra," it was explained, to accommodate those who had missed the first matinée because of the short advance notice it had received.

[176] "The last night of the present season gave us the 'Sonnambula,'" disgustedly wrote the *Times* (November 21, 1857), "thus terminating a brief and disastrous campaign with the opera that inaugurated it." The only cast change—the replacement of Frezzolini by LaGrange—was, however, "by no means to be regretted."

without being asked.[177] Madame D'Angri likewise evinced the same spirit." The proposed reduction would save about $4000 a month, and, if accepted, the management gave its pledge to go on paying as promptly as it had done in the past.

The threat to close the Academy might have been a stratagem on Ullman's part to coerce, or frighten, his cast into accepting his offer. Or it might truly have been a last-ditch stand. On November 23, Ullman continued his one-sided colloquy with the public: "The public are respectfully informed that although not all the artists have accepted the proposition made to them for a reduction of salaries in conformity with the commercial stringency, yet a temporary arrangement has been concluded by which the director believes to be enabled [with what behind-the-scenes manipulations?] to give the opera a further trial of two weeks longer, which, if successful may induce a continuance of the season." The chorus, orchestra, and the minor employees of the Academy, he tactfully asserted, had shown "great readiness in making a proportionate reduction on their respective salaries." Several of the artists, too, had "voluntarily come forward to prevent the sudden close of the season, while one or two of them [refused] to sing unless paid in advance and in full."

Although he had determined not to open the house unless the artists unanimously agreed to accept the reduction in pay, yet, magnanimously wishing to "prevent a catastrophe by which some hundred and fifty people with families should be suddenly thrown out of employment, and from a legitimate desire to afford the American public the opportunity of hearing for at least a few nights one of the world's greatest artists in a celebrated work, which has been for nearly two months in active preparation," Ullman changed his mind. He was therefore announcing the American debut on November 30 of the peerless German basso Carl Formes[178] in his world-renowned role of Bertram in Meyerbeer's *Robert le diable* (in Italian), with two further performances on December 2 and 4. Appearing with Formes would be LaGrange as Alice, Claudina Cairoli as Isabelle, Bignardi as Robert, Labocetta as Raimbaut, with Teresa Rolla, the popular *danseuse* from Niblo's, as the ghostly abbess, who, with a *corps de ballet,* would perform a *divertissement* especially choreographed by Paul Brillant.

Despite his protestations of dire financial peril, Ullman announced a superspectacular production for *Robert,* with hundreds of gorgeous new costumes, new properties, new machinery, and new scenery painted by Hannibal W. Calyo, the American star pupil of the great Joseph Allegri.[179] Should the production succeed, Ullman promised a long list of unhackneyed operas to follow. "Should he, however, be disappointed in his expectations, the season will close after seven nights more, which, with

---

[177] LaGrange's generous willingness to relinquish one-fifth of her salary still left her with "a cozy $2000 a month," observed R. Storrs Willis; it was hardly commensurate with a proportionate reduction of a chorus singer's or orchestra musician's salary, which averaged, at most, only about fifteen dollars a week (*Musical World,* November 28, 1857, p. 733).

[178] Since his duly serenaded arrival from Europe on November 5, Formes had been nursing a severe cold, or "catarrhical fever," that had prevented him from making his debut at the Academy until now—a great sorrow to Ullman, especially in the present circumstances.

[179] In May, Allegri returned to Europe "after a lengthened residence in this city, where he [had] painted a great deal of fine scenery and made a great deal of money and a great many friends" (*Herald,* May 25, 1857).

Carl Formes, peerless German basso, admired by Strong.

SIGNORINA TERESA ROLLA, PREMIERE DANSEUSE. PHOTOGRAPHED BY FREDRICKS. SEE PAGE 211.

Signorina Teresa Rolla, popular dancer who appeared with Formes.

the thirty-three already given will complete the number of forty, to which he is bound by his lease."

As Darcie venomously reported the ensuing phenomenon (*Porter's Spirit,* December 19, 1857, p. 256): "The little individual of Teutonic extraction, whose name occupies a conspicuous place on the posters and is continually paraded in cards and advertisements as the present lessee and manager of the Academy of Music, was beginning, for the second time in two or three months, to learn that the couch managerial is no bed of roses, and that the direction of grand opera performances is a very different thing to the management of a concert troupe." With the protracted indisposition of Formes throwing his plans into confusion, and with the earlier failure of Frezzolini, the mediocrity of Labocetta, and the inescapable inroads made by the financial "revulsion," Ullman had been forced to seek extraordinary ways and means of saving the Academy—both for himself "and his friend [William H. Paine] 'the man with the monish,'[180] who, although he has vowed time and again never to have anything more to do with opera, cannot refrain from dabbling in it—all, of course, for the love of art, and with the sole desire of assisting to establish Italian opera on 'a firm and permanent basis.'" Thus, sneered Darcie, the production of *Robert le diable* had been a desperate last stand, a "sink or swim business." Owing entirely to Formes, it had turned out to be an unprecedented triumph.

"Even in the 'golden prime' of Grisi and Mario, we do not recollect having seen audiences so vast[181] as those of Monday and last evening," reported the *Evening Post* (December 3, 1857), after the second performance of *Robert le diable.*[182] "A few more such houses will atone for weeks of empty benches."

Although Formes had not yet completely recovered, it was obvious that he possessed a more magnificent bass voice than had ever been heard in America (at least a bigger one, wrote Willis),[183] an almost miraculous ability to use it (according to Willis he lacked "style and school" and seemed to be "deficient in ear" as well), and he was a consummate actor.

Except for Willis's carping comments, Formes was unanimously acclaimed the greatest of great artists, both vocally and histrionically: "His voice is plenteous in quantity, beautiful in quality . . . and as an actor he has had no equal among the operatic artists who have preceded him," wrote Richard Grant White (*Courier and Enquirer,* De-

---

[180] Contemporary slang for *money,* in mockery of a Jewish accent.

[181] Seymour reported a first-night ticket sale of $4000, "the largest amount, we believe, ever taken at a single operatic performance here or elsewhere. A few such gatherings will bring happiness to the heart of Mr. Ullman" (*Times,* December 1, 1857).

[182] Yielding to public demand, following the "positively last" (third) performance of *Robert le diable,* two more were given, on December 7 and 9. (In all, it was performed seven times.) For the December 9 performance, it was planned to run special excursion trains to transport opera-goers from Philadelphia, Albany, Troy, New Haven, Hartford, and intermediate places—or at least so Ullman promised. On clouds of lyrical prose, as a concession to the hard times he also introduced a new pricing policy for the remainder of the season, setting aside 400 reserved seats at $1, to be sold on the day of performance.

[183] Willis, who reveled in showing off his familiarity with Germany and things German, informed his readers that Formes had studied in Cologne with the formerly famous basso Oehrlein, the same Oehrlein who for some years past was a member of New York's German singing community (*Musical World,* December 5; *Dwight's,* December 12, 1957, pp. 291–92).

cember 2, 1857). "Formes is a genius. . . . Seldom has nature given to one man so much as to this singer," wrote Hagen (*Review and Gazette,* December 12, p. 388). "After Marini♪ there was but one man who could remove the impression his magnificent organ created—and that one is Herr Formes," wrote Seymour (*Times,* December 1). "He is not only a consummate musical artist, with the voice of the true *basso profundo,* of great compass, full, rich, and mellow, but he is most decidedly a man of commanding presence and looks the soldier and the hero, not one of your lady-killers, but a man of mark, who, if he could not sing a note, would, as an actor alone, become a feature in any dramatic performance," wrote Darcie (*Porter's Spirit,* December 5, 1857).

Of Formes's supporting cast, LaGrange as Alice was again both lauded for her mastery of everything she attempted and censured for her increasingly unmanageable wobble; Cairoli as Isabelle was generally treated as an unmemorable novice whose voice possessed only about three legitimate notes; Bignardi did not shine as Robert, nor did Labocetta excel as Raimbaut; Anschütz turned in an admirable job; and the production was pronounced to be magnificent. That is, except for its "curtailment and disarrangement"—the displacement of its second act into its fourth, and the division of the third act into "two separate acts, and shortened at that" (*Musical World,* December 5, 1857, pp. 757–58).[184]

Apparently unaware of these disfigurements was George Templeton Strong.

November 30. . . . Dined with us Miss Josephine Strong and Murray Hoffman, and went to the Academy of Music. Season opening with *Robert le diable* and Formes making his debut here as Bertram. There was the biggest operatic crowd ever got together in New York. No standing place was unoccupied. *Deutschland* thronged the galleries and endorsed Herr Formes with vociferous bellowings. The opera was well done. LaGrange admirable in the part of Alice, as she is in every role. Only Isabella's music was imperfectly rendered, by one Cairoli, a debutante. . . . Formes is evidently very strong, though Bertram's work is rather musical declamation (and faces)[185] than music. I'd like to hear him in the *Freischutz.* How he'd sing *Hier im ird'schen Jammerthal!* But *Robert* doesn't attract me much. The Music is like Robert Browning's poetry, ungenial and ungrateful, without fluency or *song.* It suggests tedious, toilsome effort to create—weary vigils in hope of inspiration. You feel that Meyerbeer worked long and faithfully, and was heartily glad when the drudgery of composition was over. As to the Ballet, words can't express the idiocy of an age that tolerates so preposterous an exhibition.

But all Opera, with or without ballet, is in truth a mere childish phantasmagoria, embellished by music, good or bad. *Don Giovanni* itself is not an exception. Its music

---

[184] Despite the production's pretensions of grandeur, the celebrated graveyard scene "lacked graves and tombstones," complained Willis. "The ghosts, therefore, were denied the privilege of rising out of them, and had to walk out from behind the scenes. The change of ghosts into nymphs, which abroad is usually accomplished by machinery—the ghostly dress being whisked off like a flash of lightning—had here to be accomplished by the poor ghosts themselves—with their own hands. The times are hard, however," quipped Willis, "and it is not strange that even the ghosts have to undress themselves" (*Musical World,* December 5, p. 745, quoted in *Dwight's,* December 12, 1857, pp. 291–92).

[185] Formes's makeup as the fiendish Bertram was reportedly fearful to behold.

is celestial, but considered as a whole—plot, text, and acting—it is beneath contempt, fit for an audience of South Sea Islanders or Esquimaux.

December 8. . . . Saturday at Philharmonic rehearsal Beethoven's brilliant and beautiful Eighth Symphony (in F), including the gem of an Allegretto that Jullien's orchestra used to play so effectively♪ and Mendelssohn's "Caves of Staffa" ["Fingal's Cave"] Overture.

Following the initial five performances of *Robert le diable, La traviata* was revived on December 11, with LaGrange single-handedly redeeming haphazard performances by Bignardi, Ardavani, Rocco, and even Anschütz. For the present, however, German opera in German chiefly possessed the Academy. Flotow's *Martha*♪ was presented on December 12, with the incredibly versatile and indefatigable LaGrange as Martha,♪ and Formes, for whom the role had been composed, as Plunkett; they were supported by Minna von Berkel♪ (Nancy) and Hugo Pickaneser♪ (Lionel), both from Ullman's peripheral German opera company. As a piquant added enticement, *Martha* was performed from the composer's own score, as revised by him for an imminent Paris production.[186]

As Plunkett, Formes's personification of the quintessential rural Englishman was uncanny. "His apotheose of the English porter [beer], responded to by the chorus with a tremendous cheer for Lager, electrified the audience," wrote Hagen. "The trill he had to sing was good; however," Hagen compulsively added: "we have heard it done better" (*Review and Gazette,* December 26, 1857, p. 403).

December 12. . . . With Ellie tonight, and Murray Hoffman (who dined here) to the Academy of Music to hear *Martha* (Flotow). Full house and most enthusiastic. Music very pleasant to hear—very fresh, brilliant, melodic, and lively, and pretty uniformly good throughout. Flotow is very copious in phrases of melody, generally above commonplace, and sometimes decidedly original and vigorous. His style, I think, is eclectic. The Teutonic element predominates, but his way of working up a melody with orchestral effects of light and shadow suggested reminiscences of that lovely *Giuramento,*♪ and he introduces vocal unisons occasionally that were like Verdi. On the whole, I've seldom been more pleased with an Opera heard for the first time.

Because of Formes's lingering illness, on December 14 *Lucrezia Borgia* was substituted for *Martha;* for the same reason, on December 15 *Il trovatore* replaced *I puritani* at the benefit of the Hebrew Benevolent Society; on December 18 *Norma* was given as another fifty-cent "Ladies' Matinée." On December 19, in collaboration with the New York Harmonic Society,♪ a super-elaborate performance of Haydn's *The Creation* was sponsored by thirty-three members of the New York and Brooklyn clergy[187] and attended by some 4000 people. Perched upon a giant platform elevated to a height of

---

[186] It was announced that no other German opera would be presented during Formes's stay.

[187] Recalling a tactic employed by Ullman in his management of Henriette Sontag in 1852,♪ hardly necessary as an endorsement for *The Creation,* commented ——t—— (*Dwight's,* December 19, 1857, p. 303).

twelve feet (in purported imitation of Exeter Hall in London) were the soloists: La-Grange, who sang Eve;[188] Annie Milner (Gabriel); Ernest Perring (Uriel); Formes (noted as an oratorio singer), "looking like several pulpits," as Raphael and Adam;[189] the 350 members of the Harmonic Society,[190] conducted by George Frederick Bristow; the Academy orchestra, conducted by Anschütz; and a large organ, built by Richard M. Ferris and Company.

December 24. . . . Heard *The Creation* Saturday night with Ellie . . . very satisfying performance. Choruses superb, orchestra ditto. Solo parts all decently respectable. Not even Formes was entitled to much higher praise, and the still, small voice of the tenor [Ernest Perring] hardly deserved even that. Philharmonic rehearsal same afternoon. [Beethoven's] Eighth Symphony and Mendelssohn's ("Fingal's Cave") Overture.

Now that Ullman had hit his stride, his productions more and more thickly crowded the remaining days and nights of the holiday season. On December 23 he presented the seventh performance of *Robert le diable,* a benefit for LaGrange, with the beneficiary singing the roles of both Alice and Isabelle; on December 24 another triumphant *Martha;* on Christmas Day another fifty-cent "Ladies' Matinée" of *Norma;* on Christmas Night a greatly magnified production of the Harmonic Society's annual *Messiah,* featuring Ullman's newest *prima donna* Anetta Caradori (1823–?),[191] Elena d'Angri, Annie Kemp,♪ Ernest Perring, and Carl Formes; on December 26 again *Martha;* on December 28, *I puritani,* with Formes as an unprecedentedly magnificent Sir

---

[188] Her first essay of oratorio sung in English. "Madame LaGrange [showed] more signs of decay in this kind of music than in any other," wrote *Bellini.* "The pulsation in the voice, when the tone is to be sustained, is painful" (*Dwight's,* January 2, 1858, p. 316).

[189] Fry, who regarded contemporary oratorio as an obsolete relic of the "dead and departed . . . middle ages," protested against the incongruity of "the Prophets and Apostles [being represented by] gentlemen in citizens' dresses, with music-books in their hands; Angels and Prophetesses . . . by young ladies in white crinolines [with] blue sashes, likewise with music-books. Adam, even . . . in a black coat and trousers and white cravat; and Eve in russet silks. Adam, with a music-book in his hand, sings his love to Eve, with a music-book in her hand; and the grand passion under such circumstances reminds us of two owls in an ivy bush" (*Tribune,* December 21, 1857). Hagen objected to the graduated volume of gaslight during the "Let there be Light" section of the work; if "any such miserable Punch and Judy trick should ever again be attempted," he hoped at least that the "public would not again applaud it" (*Review and Gazette,* December 26, 1857, p. 404).

[190] "Numbers are very valuable in grand choruses *provided they sing,*" wrote Burkhardt, "but where is the use of three hundred upturned faces and open mouths when only 20 or 30 of the three hundred actually sing or can be heard? A smaller number of choristers *with* voices and with sufficient cleverness to sing together might greatly improve the New York Harmonic Society" (*Dispatch,* December 27, 1857).

[191] Not to be confused with the Maria Rosalba Caradori Allan who captivated New York audiences in 1839.♪ The current Caradori, born in Pest of Italian parents, had been a longtime colleague of Formes at Drury Lane (*Dwight's,* January 30, 1858, p. 347–49). She was the possessor, according to Seymour (*Times,* December 26, 1857) of a "strong mezzo-soprano voice of a somewhat hard quality." To Hagen, despite her strong voice, she sang "indifferently, and gave every moment the impression that she would rather have sung something else" (*Review and Gazette,* January 9, 1858, p. 2).

George Walton,[192] and, between the acts, Thalberg and Vieuxtemps, in the first of another heavily ballyhooed series of Thalberg's farewell appearances.[193]

As his crowning achievement, on December 30 "the little autocrat of Fourteenth Street" presented Beethoven's *Fidelio,* with Formes in the role of Rocco, Anetta Caradori as Leonora, and members of the German opera company—Minna von Berkel as Marcellina, Pickaneser as Florestan, Beutler as Jacquino, and one Behringer (said to be a member of the chorus) as Pizarro. As an added attraction, the orchestra played all three *Leonore* overtures. A difficult opera such as *Fidelio,* requiring intelligent and accomplished actor/singers able to cope with its uncompromising musical and dramatic demands,[194] wrote Hagen (*Review and Gazette,* January 9, 1858), was unlikely to be well received because the Academy lacked the requisite high caliber not only of singers and actors, but of audiences. "Every attempt at German opera in this country has to be a failure," he asserted, "not only for the insufficiency of the singers, but especially for the incompleteness of the entire troupe." Perpetually lacking a baritone, on this occasion they had taken a man from the chorus to sing—what? the difficult part of the Governor: "The result was frightful; not only for the poor victim but for those who had to sing with him, and consequently for the success of the whole opera."[195]

It had been especially unfair to Madame Caradori, who, just as she was about to declare herself the wife of the prisoner, found her efforts drowning in torrents of explosive laughter, a circumstance unlikely to lend verisimilitude to a moment of high drama. Hagen doubted, however, that Caradori would have been more convincing, even with more able colleagues. None of this referred, of course, to Formes, whose Rocco was an ideal model of all that was good, true, and beautiful.

December 30. . . . Tonight with Ellie, Miss Anne Leavenworth, and George Anthon to hear *Fidelio,* my first introduction to that work. House scantily filled and not at all interested. All the parts badly filled but Rocco, in which Formes was very strong indeed. Leonora was lubberly and sang false; the other woman and Florestan hardly respectable; Jacquino faint and feeble; Pizarro absurd. One of his ambitious failures was greeted with a loud, derisive giggle by the whole house, and caused mortal agony and shame, doubtless, to the unhappy wretch.

We can scarcely recognize the inhumanity of the crowded spectators at an old Roman Amphitheatre, turning down their thumbs and condemning to death the de-

---

[192] "Such a Sir George has never been seen and heard here," wrote Hagen, "and we doubt if any Italian singer will ever represent this character as Mr. Formes does" (*Review and Gazette,* January 9, 1858).

[193] During the month of December, Thalberg had been announced to give two matinées and two soirées, advertised as his final appearances before departing for Europe in early January.

[194] "The work is almost devoid of ornamentation, and is therefore seemingly ungracious to the singers," wrote the *Evening Post* critic (December 31, 1857). "There is neither climax nor a cadence, a very high note or a very low note, nor a single vocal trick, from first to last, of which they can take advantage to win favor from the house. Whatever applause is gained must be won by straightforward, truthful, good singing."

[195] "The quite important and difficult character of Pizarro was entrusted to a mere chorus singer, who, as soon as he began to sing, was hooted and hissed, and hardly allowed to proceed," reported ——t—— (*Dwight's,* January 9, 1858, p. 324).

feated gladiator whose exertions had not been sufficiently entertaining. But our audiences inflict, in mere thoughtlessness, pangs almost as bitter as death.

. . . *Fidelio* heard for the first time under the disadvantages of so feeble a performance is not very impressive. I render quite a tribute to Beethoven when I record my wish to hear it again—my vague perception of strength and beauty beneath its surface. Tonight I felt only portions of Formes's role—a trio (Leonora, Florestan, Rocco), and the choral effects that precede the finale. These last are very powerful and beautiful.

. . . It's not strange *Fidelio* should have disappointed me, for whenever I hear a "new" work of Beethoven's I am unreasonable enough to expect something of the same order with his greatest symphonies. I caught myself tonight more than once harboring a dreadful doubt whether it were not in fact *Heavy* music!!! "From all false doctrine, heresy and schism . . ."

OBBLIGATO: 1857

We do not yet expect "American Music" to rival the productions of the great masters of Europe. Every school must have a beginning . . . the American school of composition has taken a vast stride forward since the days when Billings *was looked upon as the grand musical authority of New England.*

New York Musical World
January 10, 1857

FACED WITH THE Thalberg/Ullman juggernaut and the deepening economic crisis, concert-giving by local musicians suffered a sharp decline in 1857.[1] Only the established performing organizations—the Philharmonic, the Mendelssohn Union,♪ the Harmonic Society, and Eisfeld's chamber-music concerts—despite depleted subscriberships—attempted to maintain their accustomed schedules. The fledgling New-York American-Music Association,♪ too, continued with undiminished fervor to pursue their stated purpose—to provide music by native or naturalized American composers with a chance to be heard.

The first concert of their second season, at Dodworth's Hall on December 30, 1856, had been a "creditable affair, all things considered," wrote the critic of the *Musical World* (January 10, 1857, p. 10), presumably R. Storrs Willis (himself a member of the organization); at least it indicated an encouraging advance in American composition since the days of the New England singing schools. Among the performers on this occasion were the American soprano Mrs. Jameson;♪ the recently imported Scottish bass/baritone of the Pyne/Harrison English Opera Company, Charles Guilmette; the highly regarded pianist Candido Berti;♪ and the Association's chorus of thirty-five singers. Among the compositions heard were an anthem by William H. Walter, organist of Trinity Chapel and Columbia College,[2] a song by G. F. Bristow, and "A Death

---

[1] "That the present 'financial crisis' should greatly injure the interests of musicians and the musical trade is a matter of course," wrote Hagen. "At a time when 'to economize' seems to be almost a national feeling, music, whether as a public amusement or as a means of education, will be most likely the first to suffer from it" (*Review and Gazette,* October 31, 1857, p. 337).

[2] And a native New Yorker. Announcing Walter's appointment as organist at Columbia College, the *Musical World* (June 6, 1857, p. 355) hoped that "we shall some day have the gratification of announcing a musical professorship at Columbia College, at present a *desideratum* in that venerable and flourishing institution."

Bed Rhapsody," a curiously named work whose rationale eluded the reviewer, by the irrepressible president of the Association, Charles Jerome Hopkins.♪[3] Also performed was a Christmas carol attributed to one "Jr.," in fact Hopkins's older brother "Deacon" John Henry Hopkins, Jr. (1820–1891), the formidable editor of the *Church Journal*.[4]

Appearing at the Association's following concert, at Dodworth's Hall on February 27, were the singers Mrs. Emma Bostwick,♪ Misses Caroline M. Shepard and Ada Robjohn, Messrs. Guilmette, Loomis, Tucker, and James A. Johnson;♪ the pianists Henry C. Timm, William Mason, and Candido Berti;♪ and the Philharmonic clarinetist Xavier Kiefer. A "Consecration Anthem" by Edward Hodges was highly praised; the other works performed (not specified by title) were composed by C. J. Hopkins, G. F. Bristow, J. N. Pychowski, T. J. Cook, and the Baltimore composer James Monroe Deems (1818–1901); W. H. Fry was represented by an excerpt from his *Stabat Mater*♪ sung by Guilmette and chorus, and, of all composers—although "he had never visited this country"—Franz Liszt, whose two-piano transcription of his orchestral tone poem *Les Préludes* (1854), played by Mason and Berti, was pronounced the hit of the evening (*Times*, March 2, 1857).[5]

Despite its specifically American orientation, the infant Association received support and encouragement from most of the critics, albeit diluted with inevitable quibbles. Even if their present efforts were "feeble," wrote *Trovator*, it was hoped that the up-and-coming organization—with the right effort—might eventually form the nucleus of an American Conservatory of Music and be an honor to the country (*Dwight's*, March 21, 1857, p. 196).

On April 17, at the Association's third Grand Concert, again at Dodworth's, Candido Berti played an *Allegro de concert* by the naturalized American, Pychowski, "with fine effect"; Richard Hoffman♪♪ played his own *Fantaisie* for piano; W. H. Walter's Anthem was well sung by the chorus; and Miss Shepard nobly replaced Mrs. Georgiana Stuart Leach,♪ who, like Mrs. Jameson, was too ill to sing. At least, so reported the *Musical World* (April 25, 1857, p. 259), but the *Review and Gazette* (May 2, 1857, p. 132) confusedly (and confusingly) reported instead a performance of the String Quartet in D minor by Charles Hommann (misidentified as "Hoffman") performed by Anthony A. Reiff, Jr.,♪ and associates. An unidentified song was given by the allegedly absent Mrs. Leach; an unnamed vocal quartet by William Mason was rendered "with spirit and power" by Misses Thomas and Robjohn with Messrs. Loomis and Tucker; and Gottschalk's *Valse di bravura* and *Sérenade* were splendidly played (by Richard Hoffman? Candido Berti?).

At the fourth and final concert of their second season, at Dodworth's on May 29, the New-York American-Music Association presented a lengthy program of native works, consisting—as listed in the *Musical World* (June 6, 1857, p. 354) and *Dwight's* (June 13, 1857, p. 84)—of the *Kyrie Eleison* from a Mass in D, composed by a Dr.

---

[3] C. Jerome Hopkins was characterized as that rarety of rareties, a real American-born musician.

[4] This might have been the first public hearing of his classic Christmas carol "Three Kings of Orient."

[5] According to Hagen, eight of the eleven works performed were by native-born Americans, two by naturalized citizens, and one by the outlander Liszt (*Review and Gazette*, March 7, 1857, p. 68).

R. F. Halsted[6] and performed by the oratorio singers Mrs. Crump and James A. Johnson, with chorus; Gottschalk's *Souvenirs d'Andalousie* was played by Berti;[7] an *Ave Maria*
by W. A. King,♪♫ sung by Henrietta Simon; a *Grand scena ed aria* by Anthony A. Reiff,
Jr., sung by Guilmette; a song "Come, love with me" composed and sung by J. A.
Johnson; a setting of a Hymn (no. 156 in the Book of Common Prayer) by "Jerome,"
sung by Henrietta Simon and chorus; a "Hymn to the Virgin" by J. M. Deems, sung
by Mrs. Crump, J. A. Johnson, and the chorus; a flute Fantasie on *Lucrezia* and *Lucia*
composed by Felice Eben,♪♫ played by him on the Boehm flute; a Song by W. H. Walter, sung by J. A. Johnson; and a Duet from Deems's opera *Esther,* sung by Henrietta
Simon and Charles Guilmette. W. A. King was "Conductor at the Piano," and Guilmette, now appointed the Association's conductor, led the chorus.

"The American-Music Association seems to be in a flourishing condition, judging
by the funds and the manuscript music which are sent to us for transfer to the proper
officers,"[8] wrote R. Storrs Willis in the *Musical World* (June 6, 1857), by way of summing up their second season. But although he praised the "indefatigable efforts" of Mr.
Hopkins, who seemed to be "the soul of the institution,"[9] Willis disapproved the Association's method of raising funds by imposing a five-dollar fee upon each composer for
each manuscript submitted. "A musical association should make its appeal [for] subscription to those who are able to pay, and not by exactions upon composers, who are
not, ordinarily, blessed with an abundance of this world's goods," wrote Willis. Moreover: "A composition that is fit to be performed ought not to be subjected to the
ordeal of being pitted against its decided inferior simply because the latter has been
whistled in to the tune of $5."

Henry C. Watson, who throughout their second season had ignored the Association's efforts, at last delivered himself of an ill-tempered summation (in *Leslie's,* June 13,
1857, p. 19)—not of their performances but of their method of choosing the works to
be performed and of the committee they had elected to implement it: "We were not
much impressed by the selection made for this responsible office last year," wrote Watson, who apparently had not been invited to serve on the committee. He had been

---

[6] A versatile New York physician who served as organist at the Church of the Holy Apostles
(Ninth Avenue at 28th Street), Dr. Halsted was proudly described as a "Native-American" who had
never been abroad. His *Kyrie* revealed "fine musical feeling and a refined and cultivated taste," wrote
the *Musical World,* but it was "somewhat overspiced with dissonances . . . the flat-sixth, particularly,
in its various harmonic combinations being over-used and over-prominent." The reviewer trusted
that Dr. Halsted would soon "fall into a more diatonic style of writing."

[7] From a note appearing with the *Musical World*'s June 6 review, we learn that Gottschalk's faithful disciple Berti was currently going to law school and supporting himself by giving piano lessons.

[8] Together with the mandatory five-dollar membership fee, manuscripts were submitted at the
offices of the *Musical World.*

[9] "'Jerome' is the President of the Society; or rather," continued Willis, "he is the Vice-President, Financier, all the Directors, Agent, and almost Door-keeper and Type-setter of the programmes—in short, he is the Society itself. He started it, keeps it in a state of active vitality, lives in
it and for it; in a very close sense he is engaged to it, and one of these days, for aught we see to
prevent, will marry it." Hopkins had "always been contending two antagonistic biases—Chemistry
and Music." Willis had "advised him, some time since, to strike the flag of his inclinations to chemistry, but he would not heed us."

"much amused," after their first concert, he wrote, to see "a criticism in a musical paper, signed with the initials of one of the committee" disparaging one of the very
pieces they had selected, and "virtually acknowledging that these selected works were
unfit to place before the public."

Not that Watson disapproved the Association's long-term objective—to encourage and disseminate American music (Watson was himself both a composer and a naturalized American). He recognized the difficulties of their quest—the hostilities to be
endured, the hazards and the pitfalls—but, he believed, after a few years the effort
would surely be carried along by its own momentum. (It wasn't.) In the meantime,
the Association's constitution would need to be revised and vigilance exerted to keep
the friends they had already made and to increase their number.

Hagen, inevitably missing the point in his own summing-up of the Association's
second season—although he conceded that they had made progress since their founding—objected to the "too strict observance" of their rule to present compositions exclusively by native-born, or naturalized, American composers: "We should rather
think," he rationalized, that "it would be much better to choose only such compositions for public performance as are really good; and if these can be had only in small
numbers for each concert, to make the rest of the programme up by pieces of the real
masters of the art." What good, he asked, were eight American compositions, of which
only two or three showed real talent? It would be better to play only those three, and
fill the remainder of the program with "the best of old and modern masters," performed by able foreigners, if need be (*Review and Gazette,* June 13, 1857, p. 178).

At the Association's annual election, on October 22, they again chose Hopkins as
president, elected Candido Berti vice-president, W. H. Walter secretary, and reelected
one J. Allen Stewart treasurer. On November 12, at Dodworth's, they presented the
first concert of their third season. Among the performers were the Misses Madeline
and Mary Gellie and Mary Gibson, and Messrs. J. N. Pychowski, William A. King,
Theodore Thomas,♪ David Griswold,♪♪ and Charles Guilmette and chorus. Tickets, as
before, were fifty cents.

Since their founding in late 1856, according to the *Musical World* (October 24,
1857, p. 673), the New-York American-Music Association had performed fifty-seven
manuscript works by American composers: two sonatas for violin and piano, one string
quintet, one string quartet, one fugue for piano, three vocal fugues and "several works
in the strict style," various solos for cornet, flute, piano, violin, clarinet, and works
for voice.

The critics looked upon these efforts for American music with a kind of amused
tolerance (or less amused intolerance), but the performance on December 23 of
George Frederick Root's *The Flower Queen, or Coronation of the Rose,*♪ by the black
congregation of the Shiloh Presbyterian Church, under the direction of a Mr. E. Di-
nas, was treated as a hilarious curiosity (*Review and Gazette,* December 25, 1857,
p. 402).

Apart from the above cooperative efforts, and with Gottschalk having departed
for the Caribbean, few other American artists ventured to announce concerts during

that problematical year. In April there was a slight flurry when Harry Sanderson (1837?–1871), a sometime pupil of Gottschalk who had assisted at two of his concerts in 1856, made what might be called an official debut at Niblo's Saloon on April 21. Sanderson was an uncommonly gifted young man, indeed something of a genius, wrote Watson (*Leslie's,* May 9, 1857, p. 351), but he had been thoroughly spoiled by the adulation heaped upon him because of the "schottisches, quicksteps, and operatic arrangements" that had spontaneously poured from his fingers since childhood, even before he knew his notes. Possessing this "fatal facility," he had "closed his heart against study, and he went on acquiring new powers in his fingers, but leaving his mind, musically, almost a blank." Within the past two years he had studied a little (first with Carl Wels,♪♫ then with Gottschalk), but not enough to make up for his musical deficiencies. "He has a most dexterous finger," wrote Watson, "indulges in wild difficulties, and flings out octave passages with the speed of an express train;[10] he has great power and dashes through everything with infinite spirit," arousing his hearers to a near frenzy. "There is yet time for Mr. Sanderson to become a brilliant pianist and an accomplished musician," wrote Watson, if the young man would show "sufficient earnestness of character to make the trial."[11]

Sanderson's assisting artists were Cora de Wilhorst, whose voice, wrote Watson, "rang through the hall with the clearness of a trumpet"; also the tenor Giannoni, the baritone Morelli, and the harpist Aptommas.♪ The accompanist, Mariano Manzocchi♪ (variously phoneticized in the advertisements as "Manzocki" and "Manzouki"), was, in Watson's opinion, "very intolerable. . . . We are compelled to say that he does not play well enough to accompany, and should advise him to leave that business to more competent hands."

Also in April—on the 16th—Maria Brainerd appeared at Niblo's Saloon in a run-of-the-mill concert, singing arias by Verdi and Meyerbeer, the "Jerusalem" from Mendelssohn's *St. Paul,* a Scottish folk song, and, with Filippo Morelli, a duet from *Il trovatore;* she was assisted as well by Robert Goldbeck, who played his Fantasia on *Le Prophète* and two of his études. Edward Mollenhauer, who was scheduled to appear, defaulted, and thus his announced performance with Miss Brainerd's indispensable mentor and alter ego Clare W. Beames♪ and the Philharmonic cellist Frederick Bergner♪ of Gounod's *Méditation* on Bach's C-major Prelude from the *Well-Tempered Clavier* (still a curiosity), arranged this time for piano, Alexandre Organ, and cello, was not heard.

On April 29, Mrs. Jameson, "at the request of many friends," uneventfully ap-

---

[10] Sanderson's specialty, noted the *Tribune* (April 21, 1857), was "the performance of octaves with each hand, a grand *tour de force* in which he is almost, if not quite, unrivaled. He is an American by birth," added the writer (doubtless Fry), "and other things equal, that should give him the preference in his own country."

[11] Hagen was less tolerant. Sanderson, although talented, was by far not ready to appear in public, he wrote. "He has neither style, finish, elegance, individuality, nor any of those higher requirements for a pianist in our days." Why had he chosen to play such chestnuts as a "potpourri from *Il trovatore,* the familiar March from the *Prophète,* and two easier pieces of Gottschalk and Mason? There are hundreds of amateurs who can play the same compositions at least as well as Mr. Sanderson does. We repeat, wherefore this concert?" In Hagen's opinion, it had been given at least five years too soon (*Review and Gazette,* May 2, 1857, p. 132).

Girvice Archer, Jr.

Filippo Morelli, who sang
a duet with Brainerd.

peared at Dodworth's Hall, with the assistance of Charles Guilmette, the violinist Henry Appy,♪ the hornist Henry Schmitz♪♫, and with G. Washbourn Morgan and W. T. Walter as accompanists.

More notable were Cora de Wilhorst's two valedictory concerts[12] at Niblo's Saloon on May 16 and 21 (wedged between her disastrous appearances at the Morelli/ Jacopi fiasco), before her departure for Europe on May 30. A "moderately large and perfectly contented audience" were charmed by her renderings of "thoroughly familiar pieces from popular operas," reported the *Times* (May 22, 1857), and by songs by Émile Millet,♪♫ Wilhorst's proud teacher, performed by two of her talented classmates: Mr. Rivarde, and one of the Misses Gellie, a contralto.[13]

Later in the year, on September 22, Juliana May, another native, and a would-be

[12] Sponsored by a socially elite committee who put the sales of subscriptions to Wilhorst's concerts in the able hands of the ubiquitous Sexton Isaac Brown of Grace Church.

[13] They had been heard at Millet's recent concert of his own compositions, given at Dodworth's on April 28.

prima donna, outrageously puffed as a socially elevated Washingtonian, made her anti-climactic debut at Niblo's Saloon. Like all Americans returning from vocal study abroad, she had purportedly reaped epoch-making triumphs in the great European opera houses. Also—with Ullman ostensibly in charge—her advance publicity leaned heavily upon her elite origins: "The more special attraction which she will bring for our American public," ghostwrote Ullman (or was it Nathaniel P. Willis?) in the convoluted jargon of the *Home Journal* (August 22, 1857), "is the elevation that will be given to the sentiment and expression of her music by the charms of refinement and education. A daughter of one of the best educated and most intellectually high-toned families in our country, she has all that can infuse soul and meaning into else more animal or mechanical music, and this, we venture to say, will be as great a difference as is made by the same elements in manner and character."[14]

Miss May's overinflated social credentials did not, however, bring her the approval of the critics. On the contrary, as Watson wrote: "No amount of money expended in Italy or elsewhere can supply natural deficiencies. The social position of Miss May has, we think, been a serious drawback to her hopes of a professional career. To grasp at a position in art, much has to be endured, much to be abandoned, and much to be sacrificed, which a lady of refined instincts and one used from childhood to the beautiful amenities of the elegant home-circle, would find hard, if not impossible, to endure, abandon, or sacrifice." More to the point, Miss May's studies in Europe had taught her little of proper tone production, style, taste, phrasing, emphasis—and yes—of "the general refinement which springs from intellectual culture."

Even her more indulgent critics agreed that Juliana May was by far no ripe artist.

Undeterred, Miss May's manager immediately announced a second concert at Niblo's Saloon ("previous to her departure"), because, unrealistically went the promotional prose: "The success achieved by this young American artist on her first appearance, has gone so far to remove received opinions that none but foreign Talent will be appreciated by our concert and opera-visiting public." This second event was postponed from September 29 to October 6 in deference to the Horticultural Society's prior claim to the hall. Again Miss May sang opera arias—from *Lucia, Linda di Chamounix,* and *Les Vêpres siciliennes;* flamboyant Harry Sanderson, who assisted, played the March from *Le Prophète* and a hot-off-the-griddle "Juliana Polka" of his own invention; Taffanelli (with a big voice) and Alaimo (with a small one) sang arias by Verdi, Donizetti, and Mercadante—Taffanelli all but vocally annihilating a piteously cowering Alaimo in a duet from Donizetti's *Belisario* (*Musical World,* October 17, 1857, p. 667); Henry C. Timm accompanied.

The American singers who participated in the American-Music Association's events were interchangeably heard at the concerts of the city's two principal choral societies, the Harmonic Society and the Mendelssohn Union. As we know, in 1857 the Harmonic Society had been preempted by Ullman—early in the year with perfor-

---

[14] At her first concert Juliana May sang opera arias by Rossini, Verdi, and Meyerbeer; her assisting artists were Brignoli (replacing an apparently indisposed Antonio Alaimo♪); the leather-lunged baritone Francesco Taffanelli; and John A. Kyle,♪♩ temporarily emerging from his retirement job at the Customs House to reaffirm his mastery of the flute.

mances of Rossini's *Stabat Mater* and in December with *The Creation* and *Messiah*. These collaborations represented only a part of Ullman's scheme, announced in September, of presenting some eight grand oratorios[15] or other large-scale choral works, featuring his opera stars supported by the Harmonic Society and the Academy Orchestra conducted by Anschütz (or Berlioz, who was rumored to have been engaged, or was on the verge of being engaged, by Ullman).

At the Harmonic Society's single independent concert of the season they presented *The Seven Sleepers* by Carl Loewe,♪ and a *Te Deum* and *Jubilate* by Bristow, for soprano, vocal quartet, and chorus; also the "Jerusalem" from Mendelssohn's *St. Paul*, sung by Maria Brainerd. This program, mired in a confusion of announcements and postponements, was at last given twice—at Dodworth's on April 13, accompanied at the piano by Anthony Reiff, Jr., and at the City Assembly Rooms on May 15, accompanied by an orchestra of Philharmonic musicians conducted by Bristow.

The Seven Sleepers (first heard in New York in 1846) was excellently performed, presumably on both occasions, by Mrs. Crump, the Misses Brainerd, Andem, and Robjohn, and the Messrs. Gardner, Hassel, F. H. Nash,♪♪ Holloway, Wooster, H. Tucker, and the chorus. Bristow's *Te Deum and Jubilate* was found to be a "very pleasing and well-harmonized work." and Miss Andem, who at the first concert splendidly replaced the ailing Boston singer Anna Stone Eliot as solo soprano, was singled out for special praise (*Dwight's,* June 6, 1857, p. 77).

On September 7 the now incorporated Harmonic Society held their annual directors' meeting and issued their annual report, showing the Society to be "flourishing." Bristow was reappointed conductor, and promptly began rehearsals for coming performances of *The Creation* and *Messiah*.

American music was occasionally performed by the Harmonic Society's most important rival, the splendid Mendelssohn Union, now grown to "about 75 to 100 voices." At the second concert of their third season,[16] at the City Assembly Rooms on February 21, they gave Rossini's *Stabat Mater,* a repeat performance of Mendelssohn's incidental music to Racine's *Athalie,*♪ and William Mason's serenade "Slumber Sweetly," composed for vocal quartet but performed by the entire chorus. The cast included Mesdames Brinkerhoff, Crump, and Shepard, the Misses Andem, Shepard and Leach, and Messrs. Guidi,♪ Kemp, Wernecke, and Smith; G. Washbourn Morgan conducted and William Berge,♪ the organist of the Church of St. Francis Xavier, accompanied at the piano—the hall still lacking an organ, a fact deplored by the *Musical World* (February 28, 1857, pp. 183–84).

In a heavy-handed review (probably by Hodges) Mason's serenade was described as "fluent and pleasing, giving one the idea, however, rather of a vocal study in semitones than an out-gushing of the heart in serenade." A gallant serenader would surely be less likely to express his emotions in half tones than in "hearty *whole* tones," claimed the critic.

He also characterized Mendelssohn's *Athalie,* having heard only the instrumental

---

[15] A means of utilizing his cast on Sundays, otherwise a loss, by providing pious entertainment acceptable to those whose religious scruples forbade the contaminating influences of opera.

[16] They had venturesomely inaugurated their third season with a performance of Costa's *Eli*♪ on December 13, 1856.

introduction (due to the excessive length of the program), as a work "pompous and grandiose . . . King Harmony reigning supreme, and the Angel of Melody rendering small service." But then: "Mendelssohn, after all, had not saliently the gift of melody" (*Musical World,* February 28, 1857, p. 183–84).

Seymour, however, could find no fault with the concert except that was "too much of a good thing," exhausting both the performers and an over-polite audience who seemed not only determined to see it through to the bitter end but were "afflicted with a mania for encores." The Mendelssohn Union nonetheless deserved applause: "Their music, particularly in its choral effects, is remarkably good," wrote Seymour (*Times,* February 23, 1857), it showed "careful cultivation and a share of individual, personal musical talent much greater than is generally vouchsafed to the constitution of our native Musical Societies."

At their third concert, on May 7, again at the City Assembly Rooms, the Mendelssohn Union presented Mozart's *Requiem* and the first performance of a *Magnificat* composed especially for the occasion by William Berge and accompanied by an orchestra conducted by Morgan, with Berge at the piano; the solos were sung by the Misses Tingle, Dingley, and Hawley and the Messrs. Simpson and Wernecke.

To the *Musical World* it seemed that the *Requiem* was "more strictly *executed* than performed—the lack of adequate rehearsal, particularly of the voices with the instruments *ensemble* being such as hardly to justify a public performance." It was hoped that they would eventually be capable of a performance of Mozart's *Requiem* "which will not make the immortal Maestro turn (so to speak) in his coffin."

These harsh words were the merest warm-up for the critic's denunciation of Berge's *Magnificat,* a work magnificent only as a musical joke—that is, if the composer had been capable of humor. More like a "jolly little operetta," it was composed of "reminiscences from most of the modern stage pieces." Berge, clumsily punned the critic, "to an exhilarating degree" had utilized the technique of "imitation," more properly reserved in music for counterpoint.

At the fourth and last concert of their third season, on June 25, again at the City Assembly Rooms and again with orchestra, the Mendelssohn Union presented Haydn's *The Creation,* with Misses Tingle, Dingley, and Maria Leach, and Messrs. Marcus Colburn,♪♫ Stephen W. Leach,♪♫ and Charles Wernecke. As before, Morgan conducted and Berge accompanied at the piano.

The Mendelssohn Union additionally appeared at the Annual Exhibition and Festival of the New-York Horticultural Society at Niblo's Saloon on October 1, and on December 28 at the "new-old" Mozart Hall (at 663 Broadway),[17] where, as the first concert of their fourth season, the Union presented Rossini's opera *Moses in Egypt* as an oratorio. Of the soloists, the tenor Mr. William Henry Cooke and the basso Charles Wernecke were good and Miss Dingley, Mrs. Crump, and Mr. McConkey merely fair. While it was commendable to have produced the work entire, wrote the *Times* (December 29, 1857), the performance was afflicted with faults, chief among them a reduced chorus to accommodate the limited dimensions of the injudiciously chosen

---

[17] Recently opened, Mozart Hall, with a capacity of about 1200, occupied the former premises of the National Academy of Design (*Times,* November 11, 1857).

hall.[18] The Union was advised to return to their roomier former locale despite its lack of an organ.

Not ballyhooed as an American composition, Carl Wels's new Christmas Mass was given for the first time on Christmas Day at an overflowing St. Stephen's Church, where Wels, a naturalized American citizen, served as organist. Nearly all the musicians in the city attended, reported the *Herald* (December 30, 1857). Dedicated to Dr. Cumming, the music-loving pastor of the church, the Mass, in five parts, was performed by the St. Stephen's principal singers: Madame Victor Chome, soprano; Mr. Dubos, tenor; Philip Mayer,♪♫ bass, and the choir. Wels displayed his splendid keyboard virtuosity in a score that was "much more delicate, agile, and graceful than organ music generally," wrote the *Herald*.

In 1857, resident musicians of all origins, probably prompted by the example of Gottschalk (if not of Thalberg), tended more and more to give their concerts in series rather than singly. On January 6 the harp virtuoso Aptommas♪ played the second of a monthly series of harp *soirées* he had inaugurated on December 2, 1856, at Dodworth's Hall, when he was assisted by the gifted Hungarian pianist Madame Florentine Spaczek♪ (as she was currently spelled), two of the Mollenhauers, and the German singer Otto Feder♪ (replacing an indisposed Madame von Berkel). It was, however, very much Aptommas's evening: with Madame Spaczek he played the "celebrated duet" for harp and piano by Carl Czerny and Elias Parish-Alvars on themes from *Linda di Chamounix;* with the Mollenhauers the Trio in C by George Onslow, originally composed for piano, violin, and cello; and several solos—*La mandolina* and the spectacular Fantasia on *Lucrezia Borgia* by Parish-Alvars, and transcriptions of piano music, Jacob Blumenthal's *La Source* and Gottschalk's *Marche de nuit*.

To a degree, wrote *Raimond*, Aptommas had achieved for the harp what Thalberg had achieved for the piano: "He has enlarged our faith in its capacity. His delicacy of touch is as remarkable as his grasp and control" (*Albion*, January 10, 1857, p. 20). Seymour agreed: "Mr. Aptommas is one of the greatest of living players, and it is a luxury of an unusual kind to listen to his masterly performance on the harp" (*Times*, January 9, 1857).

On February 8, again at Dodworth's Hall, Aptommas gave the third (and last) *soirée* of his series, assisted by Madame von Berkel, Henry C. Timm, and the youthful composer/pianist Robert Goldbeck. Aptommas, obviously a scholarly and inventive musician, had other interesting projects up his sleeve. On May 13 he presented a "Harp Lecture" at the Spingler Institute (7 Union Square), wherein he outlined the history of the harp from the earliest times, "its relation to the social and political development of mankind, [and] the influence it exercised upon even art and literature" (*Review and Gazette*, May 16, 1857, p. 146). Musical illustrations were supplied by Aptommas, Charles Guilmette, and an unidentified lady. A splendid occasion.

On tour during the summer, Aptommas gave concert/lectures on the music of

---

[18]Mozart Hall needed "only to be as broad as it is long, and to be furnished with seats instead of fence-rails, to be a really excellent saloon," sardonically wrote *Raimond,* who had come away from there with "a pair of excruciated legs" (*Albion,* November 21, 1957, p. 560).

Strong on Music: Repercussions

his native Wales. Then, falling in with another current trend—that of giving public performances in private surroundings—on November 19 he returned to his original historical subject matter and delivered concert/lectures in the more intimate environment of his recently established "*conservatoire de la harpe*" (his home), at 48 West 24th Street. Aptommas's first lecture was attended by a "large representation of fair listeners from Madame Chegary's School [as well as] many of the unfair, sterner sex." The *Musical World* (November 28, 1857, p. 733) advised "those who would pass a pleasant evening and find themselves in attractive company" to attend Aptommas's series. Tickets at fifty cents were available at his *conservatoire*.

Following this trend, three matinées were announced by Robert Goldbeck, to take place on January 17, February 7, and February 21 at the residence of a friend[19] (at 43 East 23rd Street). Tickets, at $2 for the series or $1 for a single event, were on sale at all the usual music stores. At Goldbeck's first matinée a small but select audience[20] assembled in "small, but tastefully arranged, rooms,[21] filled with Art-reminiscences of every kind, [which] shed a very home-like atmosphere over the whole affair,[22] which was also most satisfactory in a musical point of view," wrote ——t——, obviously a wholehearted supporter of young Goldbeck. Not only was Goldbeck a remarkable pianist for his tender years, but a composer of genius. His lovely little "Aquarelles," of which he played two, and also a few of his other compositions, were most refreshing "after some very modern piano compositions which are often inflicted upon us nowadays, and which I fear are destined to be still more 'the rage'" (*Dwight's*, January 24, 1857, pp. 131–32).

Goldbeck was also an exemplary performer of the classics: one would not want to hear the Adagio of Beethoven's Sonata in D minor, op. 31, no. 2 (1802), better played, wrote ——t——.[23] The young pianist shone, too—as his partner William Doehler did not—in Mendelssohn's Violin and Piano Sonata in F minor, op. 4 (1825). Also appearing on the program was Madame Johannsen, who was rather too loud in *Una voce poco fa*, but redeemed herself with her admirable rendering of Schubert's *Aufenthalt* (*Schwanengesang*, no. 5) (1828) and *Barcarolle* (perhaps *Auf dem Wasser zu singen*, op. 72) (1823).

Following Goldbeck's second matinée, assisted by Maria Brainerd (accompanied as always by Dr. Clare W. Beames), Aptommas, and Doehler,[24] the *Evening Post* critic

---

[19] According to the *Musical World*, a Mr. Neill; according to the *Post*, a Mr. Charles Brace.

[20] Present were "some of our very best lady amateur pianists," formidable judges of piano playing, and celebrities, reported the *Musical World* (January 10, 1857, p. 50); among them Ole Bull and the American historian and music-lover George Bancroft [1800–1891].

[21] "We have seen small concert rooms," wrote Hagen, "but these in which Mr. Goldbeck receives his friends and admirers are decidedly the smallest we have ever attempted to enter. . . . These were, of course, crowded, and as far as hoops, crinolines, bonnets, and shawls allowed us to see, by ladies alone." Hagen complained, too, of "one of the most rattling pianos which ever went under the name of *grands*" (*Review and Gazette*, February 7, 1857, p. 35).

[22] As did the gaslight that softly lit the curtained room.

[23] Not according to Hagen, who deplored Goldbeck's indifference to the contrasts of light and shade and of fast and slow (*Review and Gazette*, February 7, 1957, p. 35).

[24] Besides two more of his *Aquarelles*, Goldbeck, a prolific composer, played his *La Complainte* and *Valse Interrompe;* also two Chopin pieces, the Prelude in D-flat (the "Raindrop"), op. 28, and the Étude in sixths, op. 25, no. 8; and Beethoven's "Pastorale" Sonata, op. 28 (1801). Aptommas played

(February 3, 1857), commenting on Goldbeck's compositional affinity with such advanced composers as Schumann, Chopin, and Mendelssohn, delivered himself of a blast against the dominating musical idols of the day (meaning Thalberg and Gottschalk): "As the early Christians were driven to assemble at night in obscure haunts of the city, or in dens and caves of the wilderness, to worship in spirit or in truth," he ranted, "so is it at present with piano-forte music, when those who love the works of those great *tone prophets,* Mendelssohn, Chopin, and Beethoven, are generally obliged to assemble in obscure nooks and corners, leaving the open concert hall to the undisturbed sway of those worse-than-heathen deities' potpourris and fantasias. Why will not piano-forte players learn that skill is not inspiration, and that one may be a faithful acolyte and sincere worshiper without possessing the slightest qualifications for the office of high priest. This, for the whole tribe of fantasia-makers at large!"

On February 26 (instead of February 21, as previously announced) the final matinée of Goldbeck's series was shifted "for personal reasons" to a new locale, the Spingler Institute. With Marie de Roode, Otto Feder, and once again with William Doehler assisting, the precocious Goldbeck again played Beethoven—the Piano Sonata in A-flat, op. 26, and (with Doehler) the Violin and Piano Sonata in F, op. 24; he also gave a group of Mendelssohn's Songs Without Words and a group of his own *Aquarelles;* Feder sang three new songs by Goldbeck, which would have fared better had Feder omitted "his usual very unpleasant grimaces and gestures," wrote ——t—— (*Dwight's,* March 7, 1857, p. 179); and Miss de Roode, accompanied by her younger sister Eugénie, a gifted pianist, satisfactorily performed music by Haydn, Weber, and Mendelssohn.

Although Goldbeck's matinées did not earn him a vast sum, ——t—— commented, they succeeded in making him known to the public and being accepted by "influential society. He is already a great favorite of the ladies, and has quite a number of pupils." As his subsequent career shows, Goldbeck perfectly exemplifies that special breed of mid-nineteenth-century musical emigrant destined to occupy a special place in a young country thirsting for European polish.

In June, independent of the American-Music Association, the Reverend Charles Jerome Hopkins, as he was listed in the City Directory, held a private *soirée* at his residence (995 Broadway), at which several of his compositions were performed—by himself, Mesdames Brinkerhoff and Crump, Miss Kemp, Charles Guilmette, and the Philharmonic cellist Frederick Bergner.

And in October the basso Stephen Leach♪♫ announced a series of Musical Evenings,[25] to be given on Tuesdays and Fridays at his "Home Concert Room," at 29 East 29th Street. The performers were Leach, his wife Georgiana Stuart Leach,♫ his sister Maria Leach,♪♫ the up-and-coming tenor and future clergyman William Henry Cooke, and George Frederick Bristow. Tickets, presumably available at the Home Concert Room, were fifty cents.

Parish-Alvars's *Lucrezia* Fantasy and Blumenthal's *La Source;* Miss Brainerd sang Cherubini's *Ave Maria* and some German *Lieder,* and Doehler played a Nocturne by Spohr.

[25] Presumably a continuation of the series of "Madrigal Union" concerts in which the Leaches had engaged, with John Frazer and G. Washbourn Morgan, at the Hope Chapel in 1856.♫

Charity concerts, too, were known on special occasions to invade the privacy of the home. The most grandiose of these events took place on January 22 at the Fifth Avenue palace of a Mr. S. P. Townsend, a tycoon who, according to *Trovator*, had "soared aloft to fame and wealth on the wings of a Sarsaparilla bottle." To assure the uncompromisingly *recherché* tone of the occasion (although technically a "public event," inasmuch as tickets were sold at an astronomical $2), no advance word of it had been allowed to escape into the newspapers,[26] for, as *Trovator* satirically put it: "the *élite* and the *bon ton, et cetera*, were particularly desirous that the *soirée* should be exceedingly *recherché* and *comme il faut, et cetera*, and that the *verve* and *empressement, et cetera*, which the [mostly amateur] performers were expected to throw into their *arias* and *cavatinas* and *romanzas, et cetera*, should be by no means diminished by the fears of the *critiques* and *résumés, et cetera*, of the daily papers."

Trovator named a long list of amateur performers, vocal and pianistic *demoiselles* of the *beau monde* who had enjoyed the advantages of study with the most expensive European *maîtres*. The three token professional performers who kept things musically afloat were Aptommas the harpist, Guidi the tenor, and Kyle the flutist. "The program was long," wrote *Trovator*, "and many of the audience dropped away before it was finished, the last piece being listened to with a sense of relief."

But while the *élite* basked in the radiance of sweet charity within the walls of the well-heated and brilliantly lit mansion, outside, "with the mercury an incredible distance below zero, a biting wind blowing, and snow lying on the ground . . . were over two hundred coachmen, shivering and freezing . . . awaiting the departure of their masters and mistresses."

What price charity, mused *Trovator* as he went out into the "dark, gloomy night and saw these men waiting and paralyzed with cold." It seemed to him that the "fashionable music floating from the other end of the noble hall sounded very much like a sounding brass, or a tinkling cymbal" (*Dwight's*, January 31, 1857, pp. 140–41).[27]

More modestly, concerts were given for a diversity of complimentary and charitable causes: on March 20, for the organ fund of the South Dutch Church in Fifth Avenue by the Misses Marie de Roode and Olivia Sconcia, Charles Guilmette, Richard

---

[26] George Templeton Strong would attempt to echo this reticence in the '70s with the super-recherché musicales of his Church Music Association, given at first at his home and later as "private" concerts at Steinway Hall.

[27] Happily at a more benign temperature, in early March an army of coachmen paralyzed the traffic at Fifth Avenue and 34th Street as they awaited the departures of "nearly two thousand" guests of these same Townsends at a gargantuan ball that was the talk of New York. With the connivance and assistance of the formidable Sexton Brown, their entire house had been thrown open for the awesome occasion: the first floor was devoted to dancing (with the band playing out in an adjoining hall); in the picture gallery a moving panorama of the Hudson was kept in constant motion throughout the evening; the upper floors "were arranged for conversation, whist, etc. The basement was appropriated to refreshments, billiards, bowling, etc. The large number of carriages which thronged Fifth Avenue and Thirty-fourth Street rendered access to the house tedious and difficult. The whistle of the outside guard, as usual, announced arrivals, which caused the doors to open as the visitors approached. Mr. Brown, surrounded by policemen, stood near the entrance, to protect, direct, and suggest—indeed, he seems to have become a necessity at fashionable entertainments," observed the *Home Journal* (March 7, 1857).

Hoffman, and members of the Mendelssohn Union, under the direction of G. Washbourn Morgan. On April 24 at Academy Hall (663 Broadway) a group called the "Spiritualists of New York" appeared in compliment to the English actress Emma Hardinge, "Directress of the Music at Dodworth's Hall." The program featured *The Song of the Stars,*" described as a "Spiritual Apologue" because its words and music, scored for fifty voices and piano, were said to have been composed by Miss Hardinge while in a trance. On April 28, for the benefit of the Ladies' Society for the Relief of Widows and Orphans, Robert Goldbeck appeared at the City Assembly Rooms, together with the tenor J. B. Beutler, the baritone Leopold von Gilsa, the German *Liederkranz* under Agricol Paur,♪ and an orchestra conducted by Joseph Noll.

On May 1 the Pyne/Harrison English Opera Company,♪ at Burton's Theatre, assisted by Stephen Leach, Edward Mollenhauer, Aptommas, James G. Maeder,♪♪ and Dodworth's Band,♪♪ appeared "for the last time in America," for the benefit of the Widows and Orphans Fund of the New York Fire Department. On May 3, at Niblo's Saloon, Cora de Wilhorst, Giannoni, Morelli, Doehler, the duo-pianistic brothers L. and V. Dachauer-Gaspard,♪ with an apparently additional Mr. Gaspard who played the Alexandre Organ, and Manzocchi, appeared for the benefit of the Ladies Benevolent Society of St. Vincent de Paul. On May 7, Susan Pyne received, or rather gave, her "first and farewell" benefit concert at Niblo's Saloon before returning to England with—again "positively for the last time in New York"—the assistance of Louisa Pyne and William Harrison,♪ also Stephen Leach, Alfred Sedgwick,♪ and George F. Bristow. On May 19, at Niblo's Saloon, a complimentary concert was tendered by the members of her church to a Miss Ada Robinson, another candidate for vocal study abroad; assisting were Filippo Morelli, William Mason, F. N. Crouch,♪ Frederick Mollenhauer, and Felice Eben; and on June 30 a trio of American singers consisting of Stephen and Georgiana Leach and Mrs. Leach's sister Anna Griswold, with G. Washbourn Morgan and William Berge as accompanists, appeared at the New Home Chapel (50th Street near Madison Avenue) in aid of the Home for the Friendless. (As a special attraction, the painting "The Court of Death," by the venerable Rembrandt Peale (1778–1860), was exhibited at this event.) On July 2 at Dodworth's Hall, Madame Chome, First Soprano at the Church of St. Francis Xavier, was honored by her colleagues with a complimentary concert.

More spectacularly, on November 10 Madame de LaGrange opened Mozart Hall[28] with a benefit for Henrietta Simon, who was about to make the requisite pilgrimage to Europe to complete her musical education; the assisting artists were Rocco, Labocetta, Gassier, and Fortini, the pianist Emile Guyon, the newly emigrated composer/violinist Julius Eichberg (1824–1893), and the beneficiary herself. Again at Mozart Hall, a second Grand Concert was given on November 24 for the benefit of the Woman's Hospital. The cast included Maria Brainerd, Maria Hadley, and the Messrs. Clementi, Donnizetti (*sic*), Morino, Sedgwick, Sedgwick's talented little concertina-playing son Charles, Anthony Reiff, Jr., and C. W. Beames.

---

[28] Despite its faults, it was advertised as a "Magnificent *Salle de Concert* with a seating capacity of two thousand, large, elegantly furnished parlors and dressing rooms . . . a fine and well ventilated supper room capable of seating five hundred persons," and a ballroom, "the largest in the city and lighted by five magnificent chandeliers."

Louisa (right) and Susan Pyne,
sisters who (with William Harrison)
initiated a new era of English opera.

Both: Girvice, Archer, Jr.

Also in November an impromptu private concert took place at the residence of a Mrs. Baldwin, in 25th Street. Given as a kind of farewell to Mrs. Bostwick, who was moving from Brooklyn to Chicago (as it turned out, only temporarily), the performers, besides Mrs. Bostwick, were Madame Spaczek and the promising young tenor George Simpson (barely out of his teens). As a farewell gift, Mrs. Bostwick's friends presented her with "a purse of about one hundred and fifty dollars, a much larger sum," tellingly commented the *Musical World* (November 28, 1857, p. 733), "than is often realized from concerts on the largest scale in New York."

Signifying the hard times,[29] an ultra-fashionable concert for the relief of "the poor in the northwestern section of the city" was given on December 1 at the Baptist Church at Fifth Avenue and 35th Street, generously lent by its pastor to the Committee of Ladies of the Church of the Holy Innocents (West 37th Street, near Broadway), who organized the event. The performers were Theodore Eisfeld and his quartet party, the singers Hattie Andem, Maria Brainerd (a last-minute replacement for an ailing Anna J. Warren), Guilmette, and George Simpson, the pianist Richard Hoffman, the violinist Joseph Burke, the harpist Aptommas, the Sedgwicks—father and son—and the accompanists Henry C. Timm and C. W. Beames.

As we know, on December 15 at the Academy of Music, due to Formes's stubborn illness, *Il trovatore* replaced *I puritani* for the Hebrew Benevolent Society's benefit. And on November 28, to assist the New York Fire Department Fund, a combination opera and concert extravaganza took place at the Academy, consisting of acts of *Il trovatore, Lucia di Lammermoor,* and *La sonnambula,* sung by LaGrange, D'Angri, Bignardi, Ardavani, Gassier, and Labocetta; songs by Annie Milner and Ernest Perring; and miraculous piano and violin performances by Thalberg and Vieuxtemps.

Individual concerts by resident musicians were few and far between. In February an unpublicized *soirée* was given at the Stuyvesant Institute by Charles Guilmette, a man of infinite capacities. Briefly a member of the Pyne/Harrison English opera company, prior to that, the purported "*Basso Assoluto* to his Excellency Dom Pedro II of Brazil," now budding conductor of the New-York American-Music Association chorus, Guilmette further revealed that he held a medical degree and intended, "as soon as a sufficient list of subscribers should be obtained," to deliver a course of lectures on his specialty "the physical education of the voice." This, wrote the *Musical World* (February 21, 1857, p. 116), would be of inestimable value to persons dependent on their voices— clergymen, singers, and public speakers. "The medical and surgical education of Dr. Guilmette and his own experience as a vocalist qualify him in an eminent degree to render such lectures a public boon."

Thus, in addition to his frequent concert appearances, on March 23, the versatile Dr. Guilmette delivered his first lecture at the University Medical College (Fourteenth

---

[29] "The 'hard times' have served to develop the kindness and generosity of the musical profession to a degree which no other cause could have done," wrote Hagen (*Review and Gazette,* December 26, 1857, p. 402). In these arduous days when everyone was striving to "take care of himself," the musicians were always ready to announce a benefit concert; indeed they were often the only ones willing to help the poor and suffering. As the depression deepened, reported Hagen, benefit concerts were being given throughout the nation, from Maine to California.

Street, next door to the Academy of Music).[30] By October he had established a thriving practice, operating a weekly "vocal clinique," free to the public, for speakers and singers at his institute, no. 6 Union Square. In addition he was available for lectures and instruction given in public or private institutions to classes not exceeding fifty students, at $10 an hour. Private lessons to single students were $5 an hour; daily medical consultations, held from eight to eleven A.M. and from five to seven P.M., were $5 for the first consultation with treatment, and $1 for "subsequent advice."

Four exceptionally gifted women ventured to display their pianistic prowess in this Thalberg year, three of them newcomers and one an infrequently heard resident. On March 24, Eugénie de Roode, a prize-winner at the Paris *Conservatoire,* although described as little more than a child, made her debut at Niblo's Saloon, playing a movement of Chopin's E-minor Concerto,♪ op. 11 (1830), accompanied by a string quintet composed of the three Mollenhauers and Messrs. Herzog and Besig of the Philharmonic; with Edward Mollenhauer, Miss de Roode played a piano and violin duo by Osborne and de Bériot; and alone a concert étude by Alexandre Goria and Thalberg's Fantasia on *The Huguenots,* op. 20. She was assisted by her sister Marie, who sang arias by Proch and Meyerbeer.

On May 14, Madame Florentine Spaczek, a resident since 1851 (when she had arrived as a member of Kossuth's entourage♪), gave a concert at Niblo's saloon, assisted by Emma Gillingham Bostwick, Aptommas, Edward Mollenhauer, and Timm, who "conducted at the piano." With Aptommas, Spaczek performed Parish-Alvars's Grand Duo on *Anna Bolena* and *La sonnambula;* alone she played a set of *Variations brillants* on *I puritani* by Joseph Christoph Kessler (1800–1872) and "The Banjo" by Louis Moreau Gottschalk; Mrs. Bostwick sang an aria from *Il trovatore* and songs by Eckert and Luigi Venzano; Mollenhauer played one of his endless supply of violin fantasies, and Aptommas performed an Andantino by Parish-Alvars and his own arrangement of "Home, Sweet Home."

In October a Madame de Bienville, despite her name, a native of Portland, Maine,[31] arrived from Europe and announced a concert at Dodworth's for October 27, apparently postponed to December 3, when she gave an ambitious and unconventional program. Accompanied by "artists of the Academy" (a double quartet of string players from the Academy orchestra), she played not only a movement of Hummel's Piano Concerto in A minor, op. 85, but also a movement of Mendelssohn's Concerto in G minor, op. 25, and with the gentlemen from the Academy and Ranieri Villanova♪ at the Alexandre Organ (called the "orgue-melodium"), she performed a "curious arrangement" by Gounod of Schubert's song "The Young Nun" (*Die junge Nonne,* op. 43 [1825]) and a "trashy one" of the *Miserere* from *Il trovatore* contrived by the contemporary French composer Jules Cohen (1835–1901). Madame de Bienville's unhackneyed solos were a Chaconne by Handel, *Le Tambourin* (programed as an "aria of the

<hr/>

[30] At his second lecture, on March 31, Guilmette disclosed his "discoveries on the formation and health of the voice, with ocular and auricular demonstrations." Tickets, at 25 cents, could be obtained from the janitor of the Medical College.

[31] Bereft of her American mother and French father at the age of four, Madame de Bienville, *née* Nourtie de Bock, had grown up in France, where she received her musical education at the *conservatoires* of Marseilles and Paris; she had recently returned to reside in her native land.

village") by Jean Philippe Rameau (1683–1764),[32] and a composition of her own, aptly named "Return to America." Rivarde and Alaimo assisted, singing, respectively, arias by Mercadante and Verdi; William Dressler (now organist of the Fourth Avenue Presbyterian Church) presided at the piano.

Hagen, who expressed surprise that a French lady showed so great a leaning toward "classical music," nonetheless found Madame de Bienville—although she possessed a "good deal of execution"—to be "deficient in taste, conception, expression, and in the somewhat necessary art of keeping time." Having been privileged to hear such legendary keyboard artistes as Wilhelmine Clauss (1834–1907), Arabella Goddard (1836–1922), Marie Pleyel (1811–1875), and—above all—Clara Schumann (1819–1896), he could not regard Madame Bienville as anything more than a very good amateur. He gave her high marks, however, for her good "instrumental taste" and her courage in submitting it to a modern audience (*Review and Gazette,* December 12, 1857, p. 388).

The remaining member of this pianistic foursome, despite her sex, was received virtually without reservations. Amsterdam-born Madeleine Graever-Johnson (1830–?), a pupil of Henry Litolff, turned out—to the great surprise of the local cognoscenti—to be the best "lady pianiste we have yet had in this country. We call it a surprise, it was truly such," wrote the *Musical World* (December 19, 1857, p. 770) following her debut at Niblo's Saloon on December 8.[33] "The quality of this lady's playing was altogether unexpected.

"By her uncommon executive ability"—particularly in her performance (with an orchestra conducted by Eisfeld) of Litolff's Third Piano Concerto[34]—Madame Graever-Johnson, "by her taste, elegance, and finish, [and] her perfect mastership of the instrument in a piece of most disheartening difficulty, made converts of a very fastidious and critical audience."

Appearing as she did in the thick of Thalbergian supersaturation,[35] "it was indeed a great satisfaction to hear a new player play something *new*," pointedly commented the *Musical World.* Particularly interesting was the Litolff concerto, wherein "the piano seemed not oversubordinated by the orchestra, and yet the orchestra was treated independently and as a musical power in itself."

Hagen, too, saluted Madame Graever as a "true artist." She played her long and difficult part in the arresting Litolff work finely, displaying "a nice touch, a fine *piano,*

[32] The first American performance of Rameau encountered in my research.

[33] At her debut Madame Graever-Johnson was assisted by Ullman's opera singers: Claudina Cairoli, Luigi Rocco, and Louis Gassier, who sang arias by Donizetti, Meyerbeer, Mercadante, and Verdi; Eisfeld conducted performances of Weber's *Jubel* Overture, Meyerbeer's Overture to *Les Huguenots,* and Eisfeld's own *Concerto polonaise.*

[34] Litolff's *Concerto symphonique,* or "Concerto Symphony," no. 3, op. 45, on Dutch national airs, was composed in Holland, where the composer had fled upon his escape from debtor's prison in England in 1846.

[35] All signs point to Ullman as Madame Graever-Johnson's manager, particularly the elaborate wording of her first advertisement: "Flattered by the complete success she achieved at her concerts in Paris and London, and being desirous to add to her European reputation, also the fame of having been appreciated by an American public, so distinguished for their highly cultivated musical tastes and accomplishments, [Madame Graever-Johnson] begs to announce that she will give a grand concert," etc.

and great execution." The same qualities were evident in her performance of the last movement of the Mendelssohn Concerto in G minor. But Hagen was less pleased with her rendition of Liszt's Fantasie on *Les Patineurs* from *Le Prophète* (Searle 414) (1849); it betrayed her feminine lack of physical strength. She played it more *"en miniature"*; indeed, in Hagen's opinion, only one woman had ever been able to meet its physical demands—Madame Pleyel. Madame Graever was, nonetheless, a "very valuable addition to our number of first-rate pianists; if we are not mistaken, the best lady pianist who ever came to this country" (*Review and Gazette,* December 12, 1857, p. 387).

Contrary to Hagen, ——t—— asserted that Madame Graever possessed unusual strength "for a woman," but also "great delicacy and fluency of execution." If she lacked "clearness," it was probably caused by "the nervousness almost inevitable in a lady's first appearance before a public new to her." But she played with tremendous expression and, what is more, displayed great taste in choosing at least two of her pieces for their musical worth, and not merely for showing off her mechanical powers. (A new era of pianism was dawning.) Those who had heard her would be happy to learn that Madame Graever was to appear at the delayed first *soirée* of Eisfeld's eighth season, at last set for December 29 (*Dwight's,* December 26, 1857, p. 306).

On that occasion (apparently not attended by Strong), Madame Graever again participated in a work by Litolff, his Trio in D minor, op. 47, a choice mystifying to ——t——, who found Litolff's compositions "often rather far-fetched than original, with more phrases than melodies, and though very difficult, rarely very 'grateful,' as the Germans say." Madame Graever nonetheless triumphed even more greatly than at her debut. "The degree of force which she possesses is really remarkable," ——t—— wrote. "It surpassed even the strength of many male pianists, and she played with an *élan* and spirit that quite carried one away"; her performance of the Scherzo of the Litolff trio, described by ——t—— as "a bold, dashing, reckless piece in broken triplets, and requiring force and yet lightness and untiring skill, was magnificent. . . . She is, so to speak, the *only* female pianist we have ever heard, for all who have visited us before dwindle into nothing before her" (*Dwight's,* January 9, 1858, p. 324).[36]

Only rarely during this year did the Italian opera singers give concerts, and then usually to bid farewell. Thus, on April 8 Tiberini appeared at Niblo's Saloon, assisted by de Wilhorst, Morelli, and others, before leaving to fill an engagement in New Orleans. On April 28, Madame Patania,♪ long since divorced from the Academy of Music, sang her swan song before returning to Europe. Appearing with her at Niblo's Saloon were Marietta Gazzaniga and Pasquale Brignoli (both by special permission of Mr. Paine), Ranieri Villanova with the Alexandre Harmonium, and Luciano Albites, who accompanied. On June 9, as we know, Madame de LaGrange commenced her series of "farewell" concerts before becoming opera impresaria. And on June 27, just before LaGrange's accession to the Academy, Gazzaniga made her sensational concert debut at Dodworth's, with the assistance of Brignoli, Amodio, Guyon, Villanova, and

---

[36] Also appearing at Eisfeld's *soirée, Dwight's* further noted, was Henriette Behrend, "said, by the way, to be *Madame* Somebody now, at best a mediocre singer, [who performed] a lively, dashing number from Rossini's *Soirées musicales*" and an inferior song by Eisfeld; the quartets were Mozart's no. 8 in F (K. 590), and one of Beethoven's op. 18 series, no. 2 in G.

Albites. Gazzaniga sang only twice that evening—with Brignoli in a duet from *Linda di Chamounix* and alone in a "dramatic romance" called "Mother and Child." "In the first she was excellent, in the second immense," wrote Seymour (*Times,* June 29, 1857).

Just as the year 1843 had coincidentally brought the two historic giants of the violin—Henri Vieuxtemps and Ole Bornemann Bull♪♫—to the United States for the first time, so did both reappear in 1857, but with a great difference. In 1843 the electrifying Bull had swept American audiences off their feet, while the more reserved Vieuxtemps (Bull's junior by ten years) had received a more restricted reception. After their respective tours, both had returned to Europe—Vieuxtemps in 1844, Bull in 1845.

Bull had returned to the United States in 1852♫ for the double purpose of establishing his Norwegian colony in Pennsylvania and tapping the limitless American concert bonanza to finance the project. As matters turned out, without clear title to the vast lands Bull thought he had purchased, he spent the following five years trying to disentangle himself financially and legally from the morass into which he had thoughtlessly plunged.

Now, in March 1857, six months before Vieuxtemps's triumphant reappearance, a financially defeated and physically depleted Bull returned to New York after a long absence, and, in a desperate final attempt to mend his fractured fortunes, announced a series of three farewell concerts before going back to Norway. Although ravaged by illness (said to be Chagres fever), Bull had lost none of his flamboyant performing virtuosity, if his sympathizers among the New York critics are to believed. Nor had he lost his wild impetuosity, considering that he undertook to compete with the Thalbergian steamroller then at its most formidable.

At Bull's first concert, at Dodworth's Hall on March 6: "There was, we are happy to say, a large attendance," reported a sympathetic Seymour (*Times,* March 7, 1857). "With the best of intentions toward the world, he has been sadly buffeted by it. As a violinist he stands almost alone—the representative of the ultra romantic or supernatural school, which everyone imitates but few can master. His playing last night was unequal but at times superb—and always sufficiently good and peculiar [distinctive] to merit the wonder and admiration of the audience."

"Bull drew the same magic and magnetic bow,[37] only, if possible, intensified by suffering to a still more tearful pathos," wrote Richard Storrs Willis in the *Musical World* (March 14, 1857, p. 162), and noncommittally added: "Without scrutinizing the *why* of his effects, they are certainly *effects,* and of irresistible power. Bull believes in himself and therefore people believe in him."

In his persona, wrote Watson (*Leslie's,* March 31, 1857, p. 238), Bull was still the "same strange, excitable being" who first trod the boards of the Park Theatre in 1843. Although his appearance revealed the passage of time[38] and betrayed his illness, "the

---

[37] And fabulously costly: in its tip was set a "dazzling diamond," which flashed "upon the eyes of his audience with every movement of the bow across the strings." It had been a gift from the Duke of Devonshire, reported *Trovator,* who judged the aggregate worth of Bull's three favorite violins to be at least $3000 (*Dwight's,* April 11, 1857, p. 12).

[38] Bull was now forty-seven years old.

Ole Bull, Norwegian violinist, who ranked with Vieuxtemps as a talented performer and who attempted to establish a Norwegian colony in Pennsylvania.

fire in his eyes still [spoke] of an enthusiasm as burning and unquenchable as ever." And as for his performance, Watson had rarely heard him play better.

Watson gives a compelling description of Bull's playing at this difficult time: "His intonation was perfect and his execution brilliant, clear, and full of vigor. His school, though not classic, is highly attractive and interesting, and the difficulties that he accomplishes with such easy freedom are only to be achieved by a master hand. In his slow movements he has great breadth and grandeur of style, and profound sentiment and passion. In the wonderful soliloquies which are peculiar to his school . . . he has no superior, and perhaps, save [Heinrich] Ernst, no equal; the tones vibrate with passion; they become eloquent of sorrow and sing a sad, sweet cadence, which lingers upon the memory long after the sounds have died away. It is this earnest expression of sentiment that charms his hearers like a spell of enchantment, and in this earnestness lies the secret of his success."

Hagen, true to form, while granting that Bull's playing was unchanged, pointed out that it had not improved either, because, he claimed, Bull's peculiar kind of art permitted of no improvement: "The Swedish [*sic*] performer moves continually on that delicate line which separates the sublime and fantastic world from the most ridiculous and absurd efforts, so that a step further would bring upon him a heap of ridicule and laughter." Bull, in Hagen's view, was the last representative of what he called the "polichinelle school of violin playing," now that Camillo Sivori² had given it up (*Review and Gazette,* March 21, 1857, p. 83).

Bull's repertory, if anything, was even more limited than Thalberg's; indeed it had apparently remained stationary since his first appearances in 1843. At his March 6 concert, accompanied by George Washbourn Morgan at the organ and one Franz Roth (reported to be a merciless "keyboard-thumper") at the piano, he played—as of old—his Concerto in A, Paganini's Introduction and Variations on "Hope told a Flattering Tale" *(Nel cor più non mi sento),* from Paisiello's opera *La molinara,* and Bull's apparently inexhaustible compositions "The Mother's Prayer" and the *Polacca guerriera.* His assisting artists, who sang Verdi/Bellini/Donizetti/Rossini opera arias and simple ballads (such as "Home, Sweet Home") were a young and prepossessing New York soprano Miss Victoria (or Victorine) Giller and two "second-rate" opera singers—the basso Gasparoni and the tenor Giannoni.

Bull's second concert had to be postponed to March 31 from March 20, when he suffered a severe physical relapse. With the same cast, except for Roth, who was replaced by Henry C. Timm, he again appeared to a sold-out house, wearing "all the appearance of extreme disability," as Watson noted (*Leslie's,* April 11, 1857, p. 286). His first long concerto (presumably again the Concerto in A) seemed to overtax his strength, yet he played the adagio movement "magnificently"; Watson doubted if that movement "could be more intelligently and truthfully rendered by any living artist. . . . A new enthusiasm for an old favorite has sprung up," asserted Watson, "and if his health permits, we have no doubt that Ole Bull will make a new fortune, which we hope he will have the good sense to retain." That is, if he would "discard all worthless Italian hangers-on and religiously eschew the cormorant lawyers."

Bull gave his third concert at Dodworth's Hall on April 3, as announced; he then appeared at the Brooklyn Athenaeum on April 4; and on April 11 at Niblo's Saloon he bade farewell to New York at a Grand Concert for the benefit of the Masonic Board of Relief.³⁹ Appearing with Bull on the heterogeneous program, besides his concert troupe, were the Mendelssohn Union and a "grand orchestra" composed of Philharmonic musicians conducted by G. W. Morgan. Shamelessly, Bull yet again played his Concerto in A, Paganini's Introduction and Variations on "Hope told a Flattering Tale," and the *Polacca guerriera;* his company sang the customary Italian arias; Morgan conducted the orchestra in the overtures to Weber's *Oberon* and Mozart's *Die Zauberflöte* and, with the Mendelssohn Union, two Mendelssohn works: the first act finale of his unfinished opera *Loreley,* op. 98 (1847), and excerpts from his incidental music to Racine's play *Athalie.*♪ The solos were sung by the Mendelssohn Union stars, Mrs. Clara Brinkerhoff and the Misses Mary Hawley, Hattie Andem, Caroline Dingley, and Maria Leach. On July 29, following a final tour of New England and Canada, Bull sailed for Norway, not to return to the United States until 1867.

Also returning home after a brilliantly successful sojourn of more than two years in the United States were the stars of the Pyne/Harrison English Opera Company. Ap-

---

³⁹ Reaffirming Bull's longtime affiliation with the Masons, who might, in all probability, have assisted him in this, his time of adversity.

pearing nightly (except Sundays) at Niblo's through January (1857), toward the end of the month their performances surprisingly came to be so disappointingly attended that—much to the regret of the critics—their engagement was not renewed.[40] During this final season at Niblo's they presented their past hits—*Cinderella, Daughter of the Regiment, Maritana,* and *Fra diavolo*—and new productions in English of *Lucy of Lammermoor* and *Don Pasquale,* concluding on January 27 with a gala testimonial performance, tendered by Niblo, of John Barnett's fairy opera *The Mountain Sylph.*

In strong terms, *Porter's Spirit* (January 31, 1857, p. 360) condemned their "lack of patronage by the public of New York, on whose appreciation we cannot but consider such a charge both a stigma and a disgrace. Let us not talk again of our musical taste or the establishment of English Opera in our midst . . . whilst such an artiste as Louisa Pyne, who has no superior (if even an equal) in either the old or new world—is compelled to discontinue her performances simply because the receipts of the house, night after night, are not sufficient in amount to cover the expenses."[41]

In April, after some two months in enforced limbo, doubtless attributable to their sudden break with Dr. Guilmette,[42] the Pyne/Harrison company, with Stephen Leach replacing Guilmette and with Edward Mollenhauer conducting, reappeared for six farewell nights of English opera at Burton's Theatre before finally returning to England. They performed their greatest American successes: *The Crown Diamonds, The Bohemian Girl, The Daughter of the Regiment, La sonnambula, Fra diavolo,* followed by *Midas,*[43] and, notably, William Vincent Wallace's *Maritana,* conducted by the composer.[44] Then, after their two benefit concerts, as we know—on May 1 for the New

[40] The lack of attendance was justified, wrote *Trovator,* by the deteriorated quality—apart from Louisa Pyne's always superlative artistry—of the productions: "The orchestra is wretched, the chorus microscopic, the opera hackneyed [*sic*], and it is to be wondered that they should draw as good business as they have" (*Dwight's,* January 24, 1857, p. 133).

[41] In contrast to the majority of self-indulgent Italian opera singers, wrote Burkhardt (*Dispatch,* January 18, 1857): "The [English] *prima donna* doesn't insist on postponing performances in consequence of a sore finger, which is supposed to affect her voice, nor do tight boots interfere with the vocal attempts of the tenor. Six operas a week and no disappointment to the public is the rule of the Pyne and Harrison troupe."

[42] According to a story appearing in the Boston *Bee,* reprinted in the *Times* on May 25, Guilmette, referred to as "a singer of bass notes," had refused after having fulfilled four months of his six-month contract with the company to continue unless he were paid double the sum agreed upon. This was refused and Guilmette was dropped. But before Louisa Pyne left the United States, he purportedly "trusteed [attached] $418 of her money, which had been deposited in one of the banks, resting his claim upon a charge of $225 for *medical services*." This sum would have sufficed to cover Guilmette's original claim, but in the meantime he had sued Miss Pyne for an additional $500 in damages and Harrison for $600. "All for *medical* services, no doubt," sneered the *Bee.*

[43] Announced as a "first and only" performance, *Midas* (Dublin 1762) by Kane O'Hara (1714?–1782) had been performed in New York at the John Street Theatre back in 1773.

[44] Wallace, too, planned soon to depart for England, to promote the square piano, which, in the course of his current sojourn in the United States, he had undertaken to manufacture. On July 9, 1857, at the warerooms of the Wallace Piano Forte Company, at 467 Broome Street, Wallace held a memorable unveiling of his product, designed by Spencer Driggs (the fertile inventor in 1855 of the "Linguine"), for a group of musical and theatrical luminaries that included Maurice Strakosch, Harry Sanderson, W. H. Fry, Robert Stoepel, the venerable Denis-Germain Étienne, an unspecified Mollenhauer, James Gaspard Maeder, Henry C. Watson, John Brougham, Dion Boucicault, and, acting as principal examiner, Sigismund Thalberg. "At the hands of Mr. Thalberg the Pianos underwent the

York Fire Department's Widow's and Orphan's Fund and on May 7 for Susan Pyne—Louisa Pyne and William Harrison went on to future triumphs in England.

With the Pyne/Harrison company's departure went the best of local music theatre. And although well-known musicians presided over the various theatre orchestras—Signor La Manna♪♫ and Robert Stoepel♫[45] at Wallack's, Anthony Reiff, Jr., at the New Olympic, and Thomas Baker♫ at Laura Keene's New Theatre—few musical productions of any significance seem to have taken place.[46] Except for the minstrel shows.

Nothing could rival the popularity of the minstrel shows. Through thick and thin they continued to dominate the entertainment scene over the course of this difficult year. Again the principal troupes were Buckley's Serenaders, White's Serenaders, George Christy and Henry Wood's Minstrels, Bryant's Minstrels, to a lesser degree Prendergast's Minstrels, and, briefly, at the beginning of the year, the "Original Christy's Minstrels."

From January through June, and again for five nights in August (after which they went on an extended tour), Buckley's Serenaders were in residence at their "beautiful temple of minstrelsy" at 585 Broadway.♫ Their programs consisted of indispensable minstrel-show fare—songs, dances, jokes, banjo solos, bones solos, parodies, and whatnot—followed (with Caroline Hiffert♫ as *prima-donna*-in-blackface) by one of their famous opera burlesques: *Cinderella; La sonnambula; Maritana; Don(e) Juan, or, A Ghost on a High Horse (Don Giovanni); Il trovatore; Lucrezia Borgia* (sharing a split bill with *The Essence of Old Virginny*)—or by a burlesque of an Old Folks♫ concert, or of the Hutchinson Family♪♫—or a skit, often a takeoff on current events. Among their most successful newer productions in 1857 were *Aladdin, or, The Wonderful Lamp,*[47] and, idiosyncratically, *Honor to Dr. Kane,* advertised as an "Allegorical, Operatic, Patriotic, and Melo-dramatic" tribute to the recently deceased Arctic explorer Dr. Elisha Kent Kane (1820–1857).[48] On Sunday evenings, without benefit of burnt cork, the

---

most severe tests in every way," wrote Burkhardt, who was privileged to attend. "The great pianist tried them as to volume of tone, delicacy, softness, etc., and played many *fortissimo* passages with even greater power and force than he would perhaps choose to apply to his own Érards" (*Dispatch,* July 12, 1857). A detailed description of the construction of the Wallace piano by Watson appeared in *Leslie's* (August 1, 1857, p. 135).

[45] At Wallack's, Stoepel composed—and La Manna conducted—incidental glees, choruses, and marches to a spectacular production of the play *Rienzi* (London 1828), by Mary Russell Mitford (1787–1855).

[46] Histrionically, however, despite the hard times it was a banner year, with a parade of such historically acclaimed thespians as Charlotte Cushman, Edwin Booth, Joseph Jefferson, Charles J. Mathews, John Brougham, William Burton, and, among many others, Frances Anne Kemble (described by Strong as a "truculent Amazon"), who gave her Shakespearian readings in the lecture room of University Medical College (on 14th Street, next door to the Academy of Music).

[47] Advertised as a "Glorious Chinese Feast," costing "upwards of Seven Thousand Dollars" to produce. In order to safeguard the authenticity of this superextravaganza, the public was informed that "the company will color [their faces] a la Chinese" (*Dispatch,* May 24, 1857).

[48] "A queer title for an Ethiopian peculiarity," observed Burkhardt, but he found the skit—despite "the idea of so grave a subject being turned into a burlesque—a marvel and a gem of humor." It was shocking only in the light of "so earnest a theme being handled by caricaturists" (*Dispatch,*

Buckley's gave "sacred" concerts (of popular secular music), assisted by Dodworth's Band or by Joseph Noll and his orchestra.

Upon the Buckleys' departure in June, their theatre was taken over for the summer by a group of whiteface thespians headed by Thaddeus W. Meighan and Francis S. Chanfrau,♪ who renamed it the New Olympic and, with an orchestra conducted by Anthony Reiff, Jr., attempted to resurrect some of the fondly remembered miniature comedic and musical gems produced at the original Olympic Theatre in the 1840s and earlier 1850s by the legendary William Mitchell:♪♫ among them *The Pet of the Petticoats, Amilie, The Swiss Cottage, Buy It Dear, 'tis Made of Cashmere,* and *The King of Coney Island;* also a reminiscent, new "local extravaganza" *Olympiana, or, A Night with Mitchell.*

Fading out of the picture by the beginning of August, this company was replaced on August 24—following a Buckley's five-night intermezzo—by a group managed by the actor/manager T. B. Johnston, who somehow managed to survive until early October with a repertory of light operettas: *The Swiss Cottage, Kate Kearney,* and the farces *Jenny Lind* and *King Lager, or, The Sons of Malt.* Then, on October 19, the New Olympic was taken over by Prendergast's Minstrels, a company that included such distinguished alumni of the best minstrel troupes as T. B. Prendergast, J. H. Budworth, Charlie White,♪♫ John Mulligan, and Franz Stoepel.♪♫ As always, the turnover within the minstrel community was immense.

On December 21, Buckley's Serenaders returned from their tour, heralded by flamboyant advertisements couched in jolly minstrelese:

> Although we look ragged and black are our faces.
> As free and as fair as the best we are found;
> And our hearts are as white as those in fine places,
> Although we're poor niggers dat trabel around.[49]

The Buckleys' most important competitors, the Christy and Wood Minstrels, began the year at their theatre at 444 Broadway♫ with a smash hit, appropriately titled *New Year's Calls,* wherein George Christy played a "fast 'Young New York boy'" to perfection. On the fourth week of its run they added a burlesque "Concert *à la* Maretzek," featuring songs, dances, and solos on different instruments.[50] Among Christy and Wood's numberless hits that season were hilarious burlesques of Jullien and Hutchinson Family concerts.

In mid-August, Christy and Wood's company departed for a short season in Phila-

---

February 8, February 15, 1857). The "principal scenes" of Dr. Kane's widely celebrated "philanthropic" Arctic adventure (a second vain search for the lost explorer Sir John Franklin) also supplied the subject of an elaborate panorama exhibited to the public at Empire Hall (*ibid.,* November 8, 1857).

[49] "Real niggers," is the way Burkhardt referred to seven black "Minstrel Slaves from Alabama," who—ballyhooed as a "Philanthropic Novelty"—appeared in a program of songs at the Broadway Tabernacle on April 30 (*Dispatch,* April 26, 1857). According to Odell (VI, 598), they were "singing to buy their freedom."

[50] In June the Maretzek burlesque was evidently brought up to date to include irresistibly comic George Christy as Max, beating his time "to a dot," and gifted Master Eugene doing a "most artistic" takeoff of Madame Gazzaniga singing the *Brindisi* from *Lucrezia Borgia* (*Dispatch,* June 14, 1857).

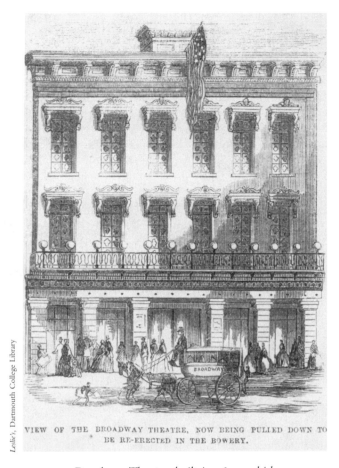

VIEW OF THE BROADWAY THEATRE, NOW BEING PULLED DOWN TO BE RE-ERECTED IN THE BOWERY.

Broadway Theatre, built in 1857, which became a fashionable place where many minstrels, as well as actors, appeared.

delphia. Temporarily returning to 444 Broadway at the beginning of September, on October 15 they then moved into their handsome new theatre at 561–63 Broadway, near Prince Street. Designed by the preeminent American theatre architect John M. Trimble,♩ the new house surprised the *Evening Post* reporter with the "completeness, beauty, and elegance of all its arrangements. The theatre will hold over two thousand persons seated on velvet cushions and is ornamented with a profusion of cupids and gilded carvings," he wrote. "The stage . . . has all the appurtenances of a first-class theatre.[51] There is a richly carpeted drawing room for ladies, with large mirrors, lounges, and marble-topped tables; and pianos are to be placed in it when the walls are thor-

---

[51] "The auditorium consists of a roomy parquette and two tiers of boxes," described Burkhardt (*Dispatch,* November 15, 1857), who marveled that "a full view of the stage may be had, or the slightest whisper heard, from any point" in the house.

oughly dry." And all this elegance and luxury could be had for only twenty-five cents—to all parts of the house (*Evening Post,* October 15, 1857).

Among the features of the Christy/Wood opening program[52] was a "Concert *à la* Jullien," concocted by their longtime violinist Leopold Meyer.♪ Its characters included "Madame Fretsoleani," played by Master Eugene, "Signor Bottleseeni, contrabass," played by G. W. H. Griffin, and "Conductor Anshoot," played by the ineffably comic George Christy. For the remainder of the year and into the next, the troupe attracted large audiences to Wood's Buildings, as their new home was grandly named.

Charlie White was, alas, less fortunate. In January his "opera house" (at 49 Bowery) burned down, and he was obliged to rely on his many well-wishers for help in raising funds to rebuild it. To this end a great benefit was held on January 30 at the Broadway Tabernacle; and for the following month, until his theatre was rebuilt, White and his Serenaders appeared at various small halls in Manhattan and Brooklyn. On February 28 he reopened his opera house, where one of his hits was *The Black Camille, or, The Fate of a Washer-woman,*[53] with John Mulligan hilarious as "Cammy." Later departing from the classic minstrel format, White presented more varied entertainment, with performances by a Signor Rockey, who played a flute solo while balancing himself fifteen feet above the stage on a pyramid of glass decanters; and a versatile Signor Martinetti, billed as the "Modern William Tell," who was not only a thespian but a phenomenal knife thrower and performer "on the rings." In July, White's Serenaders appeared at Barnum's "Lecture Room,"♪♪ and in November they announced an impending tour "through the States."

Most consistently present throughout 1857 were the Bryant Minstrels, headed by the gifted brothers Jerry, Neil, and Dan Bryant. In February they settled into E. P. Christy's old stronghold, Mechanics' Hall (472 Broadway), upon the departure, after a month's engagement, of the remnant company of "Christy's Original Minstrels," headed by J. W. Raynor and E. H. Pierce. Remaining through the end of the year and beyond, the Bryants brought out an immense repertory, much of it original, and much that was promptly appropriated by their burnt-cork brethren. Among their hundred-and-one musical concoctions they "warbled" a burlesque of the Tyrolian Rainer Family♪ and presented a travesty on a Mullenhauer (*sic*) Brothers Violin Duet fiddled by their Messrs. Isaacs and "Sivori."

Although the low-priced minstrel shows managed to survive, despite the hard times, the legitimate theatre suffered acutely. In December, drastically testifying to the gravity of the situation, the veteran English comedian George Holland, beloved of New York theatre-goers for the past three decades,[54] applied burnt cork and—astoundingly—went to work for Christy and Wood. "George Holland, late of Wallack's Theatre," stated a card in the various newspapers on December 18, "respectfully informs his friends and the public, that in consequence of the unfortunate state of the times—which has prevented the managers of what are termed the legitimate theatres

---

[52] Consisting of musical and choreographic solos and ensembles and a new farce *Married and Buried*.

[53] Dramatized versions of *Camille* were played at a number of legitimate theatres during the course of the season.

[54] Holland had made his debut at the Bowery Theatre on September 12, 1827.

from fulfilling their contracts, and thus caused him to be unable to provide those com-
forts for his family as heretofore—he has made an engagement with Wood and Christy's Minstrels. . . . He . . . begs to assure his friends and the public that he will appear
before them in the same public capacity—in the same or similar pieces in the line of
low comedy—the only difference will be that instead of coloring his face with red
paint, it will appear black; which, when washed off, he hopes they will perceive the
same honest countenance he has hitherto maintained." On December 21, Holland appeared as Black George, in *My Friend Black George from White Plains;* he was later seen
in *The Rogueries of Thomas,* a blackface version of his great former hit *The Secret.* "Only
think of it," exulted the Christy and Wood's advertisements. "Holland has taken Africa.
Cork Up. Legitimate Drama stand back. The veritable George Holland, late of Wallack's Theatre, has joined the Minstrels at Wood's Buildings. . . . Only think of it!
Only think of it! Only think of it. . . ."

Genuinely ethnic entertainment, usually plentiful, was sharply reduced in 1857.
In April the eternal Scottish troubadour William Dempster♪ returned from another of
his countless trips abroad and appeared at the expiring Broadway Tabernacle for the
last times on April 13 and 15, and again on April 20, in the lachrymose ballads for
which he was noted—"The May Queen," "The Mother's First Grief," "The Lament
of the Irish Immigrant," "The Blind Boy," "The Dying Child." Tickets for these tear-
jerking attractions were fifty cents.

On May 6 a Mr. Crawford, with William A. King at the piano, gave a first
"Grand Night of Scottish Song" at Dodworth's and, by request, a second on May 22
at the City Assembly Rooms. Attired in "full Highland costume" and accompanied at
the piano by Anthony Reiff, Jr., he stirringly sang "Draw the Sword, Scotland." Tickets for his first concert were fifty cents; for the second they were cut to twenty-five
cents.

Even more pronouncedly chauvinistic was the "Scottish Nightingale," Miss Agnes
Sutherland, who appeared at Dodworth's on September 24 in a program ballyhooed
as being "of probably more National interest than any of the kind ever before attempted in this country." Also in September—in the lecture room at Barnum's American Museum—appeared, "at great expense," a Miss E. L. Williams, billed as "the
Welsh Nightingale" in an entertainment especially written for her by the eminent Irish
song writer and *diseur* Samuel Lover.♪ In this vehicle Miss Williams portrayed twelve
different characters and sang seventeen different songs, all by Lover.

Proliferating at a speed too dizzying to record, and outstripping the minstrel
shows in popularity, were the drinking establishments♪ that offered so-called "Free
Concerts" to a thirsty, lower-caste clientele. The aggressively genteel advertisements
for these "free-and-easies," or "concert saloons," crowded the newspapers' amusement
columns as tightly as their disreputable premises crowded the Bowery and adjacent
streets.[55]

"Free concerts are to be found in great and constantly increasing numbers in the
lower part of this city," wrote a "Mr. Podhammer," who investigated the phenomenon

---

[55] For a list (or partial list) of these establishments, see Odell, VI, 501, 189–92; VII, 92–93.

for the *Home Journal*[56] (May 16, 1857): "While their proprietors generously offer the poorer classes musical entertainments *gratis,* they further their pecuniary interest by thus augmenting the sale of their *Lager-Bier,* rum, and bad cigars."

Inviting us to their tour of these shoddy establishments, Podhammer and his friend Smith, after having partaken of the massive Teutonic jollity dispensed at the *Deutscher Volksgarten* (45 Bowery), next visited a "low, dirty basement in the Bowery," where "two sooty imps vigorously [operated] on banjo and bones, to the intense delight of a diabolical-looking crowd of all shades of color, though the varieties of complexion were rendered scarcely distinguishable by a uniform coating of dirt—that leveler of distinctions." They seemed "doubly demoniac" as seen through a "dense crowd of tobacco smoke," so suffocating and nauseating as to drive the overfastidious Podhammer and Smith to the street "in search of fresh air."

"A little farther up the Bowery," continues Podhammer, "we were attracted by a tremendous transparency, which read: 'Musical Hall—Free Concert Every Evening—Sacred Music on Sunday Evening.' We hopefully ascended to a spacious apartment on the third story, furnished with long rows of tables and chairs, a bar at one end, and a stage at the other, at which a melancholy pianist and a grim fiddler were hard at work. The audience consisted of about two hundred Teutons, luxuriating, as usual, in music and lager. They were being waited on by a number of pug-nosed, red-faced damsels, whose style of dress may be described . . . as *décolleté.* Placards were conspicuously posted up about the room to this effect: 'Notice—Gentlemen are requested not to applaud on Sunday Evening.'

"Presently the star of the evening, 'Signorina Johnson,' made her appearance on the stage and the melancholy pianist (no Thalberg) struck up an accompaniment. Signorina Johnson was remarkable for the generous abundance of red paint on her cheeks, the unpainted red on her nose, and for her Herculean breadth and development of chest." Not unlike certain more fashionable artists whom Podhammer had heard, the Signorina expended from her prodigious chest a prodigious amount of breath on every vowel, as, for instance, in the first stanza of "The Old Arm-Chair":

> Hi lo-hove it, hi lo-hove it,
>   And who-oo sha—hall da-hare
> To-hoo chi-hi-hide me for lo-hoving
>   That o-ho-hold a-harm Cha-hair.

"She was succeeded by a starved-looking male musician in gray coat, striped pantaloons, and cotton neckerchief, during whose performance" Podhammer and Smith made their exit.

Crossing over to Broadway, via Grand Street, our guides visited a bar whose entertainment consisted of Comic Songs delivered by a Hideous Hibernian; they then proceeded to a more ambitious establishment occupying a Broadway basement, where a scene from an English Opera was being performed amid a confusion of unsteady scenery by a *prima donna,* obviously *passée* but with her gaunt cheek-bones "bravely be-

---

[56]Another version of this article, credited to "Mr. 'Paul Potter,' the witty and delightful correspondent of the [Boston] *Courier,*" was reprinted from that paper in *Dwight's* on May 2, 1857 (p. 36).

smeared with red paint . . . robed in a juvenile short dress of dirty lace, bordered with dirty tinsel, displaying formidable ankles enshrined in dirty hose." After receiving her due applause, which she shared with a gentleman vocalist, both soloists made themselves useful by carrying lager to the customers, while the melancholy pianist and grim violinist who had accompanied them received their bounty of lager; and a bevy of "ballet-girls" (doubtless "in *decolleté*") solicited contributions from the impecunious customers "for the encouragement of art."

Cheap summer entertainment of all ethnicities flourished at increasing numbers of summer gardens, as some of the free-and-easies were seasonally classified, as, for example, "Hitchcock's Summer Garden," at 172 Canal Street, in winter the locale of his Fountain Cafe. Prominent among the multitudinous German resorts, Bellevue Gardens♩ in Yorkville was reopened in May, with concerts, as before, by Shelton's Band.♩

Dodworth's Band transferred their summer concerts to the Metropolitan Garden, a new establishment on Second Avenue between 30th and 31st Streets, where—as earlier at the Atlantic Garden—in order to attract a "more select audience," an admission price of twelve cents was charged, for which "refreshments" were provided. For the duration of the 29th Annual Great Fair of the American Institute, for which the problematical Crystal Palace was again reopened, concerts by Dodworth's Cornet Band were featured as an Extra Attraction.[57]

On February 5, 1857, the *Times* announced that—"much to the public grief"— the now comparatively disused Broadway Tabernacle, succumbing to the inexorable fate of aging New York landmarks, had been sold and would be "rebuilt for stores." On that very evening (February 5) the Hutchinson Family—Judson, John, and Asa, en route to Philadelphia—appeared at the Tabernacle; then returned on February 17, and on March 7, when, "for 'Auld Lang Syne'" (at twenty-five and fifty cents a head) they bade their sentimental farewell to the historic old hall.

It was explained in the *Home Journal* (March 7, 1857) that the Tabernacle (at 340 Broadway, between Leonard and Worth Streets) had been purchased in a private transaction by one John J. Phelps for $125,000, together with accompanying property consisting of five lots, two included in the price and three on a 21-year lease at a ground rent of $500 a year each. Additionally, the adjoining lot at 342 Broadway had been sold, presumably to the same purchaser, for $70,000. "Several splendid stores" were planned to replace the shabby old Tabernacle, a unique combination of Congregational Church and non-sectarian, non-racially-restricted, public auditorium, that for two decades had so nobly served—as Philip Hone memorably remarked in 1841—as "the *omnium gatherum* and holdall of the city."[58]

The Tabernacle's final musical attractions were a singing group—on March 5 and

---

[57] An improved version of the steam calliope, introduced in 1856,♩ was a widely discussed item among the Fair's musical attractions.

[58] A New Broadway Tabernacle was planned at a more up-to-date location—the intersection of Broadway and Sixth Avenue, at 34th Street. Until it was completed, services would be held, according to the *Times* (December 5, 1857) at the lecture hall of the Home for the Friendless, in 29th Street.

6—calling themselves the "Old Folks,"[59] and, as we know, William Dempster, who appeared there for the last time on April 20.

On April 26 more than four thousand New Yorkers reportedly crowded into the Tabernacle for a final leavetaking. Many who, through the years, had sung in its successive choirs had been invited to assist at this, its swan song; thus a fine choir of some two hundred, accompanied at the organ by John W. Crane,[60] splendidly sang a new anthem composed for the occasion and conducted by William Bradbury,♪♫ longtime music director of the Tabernacle. A second anthem "Old Denmark," composed by a Dr. Madden, was conducted by George Andrews, another former director of the Tabernacle choir, and, after an affecting valedictory sermon by the Tabernacle's pastor, Dr. J. P. Thompson, a third anthem "The Voice of Angels" was sung by Marcus Colburn and the choir, with the present music director Francis H. Nash conducting (*Tribune*, April 27, 1857).[61] After a final prayer the entire congregation rose and sang the 117th Psalm to the tune of "Old Hundred" with "overwhelming" effect.

Thus passed the Broadway Tabernacle, with its matchless memories, into history.[62] For New York it marked the end of an era.

[59] They may or may not have been the same Old Folks who had been heard in 1856: they identified themselves—under the heading "Old Folks, Old Times, and Old Hundred!"—as the "'Reading Opera Chorus Class,' the Original Old Folks Concert Troupe . . . who first gave a series of crowded Concerts last Winter at the Tremont Temple" in Boston. Claiming to recreate eighteenth-century New England performance practice as handed down by their forefathers, their advertising tactics evoked the minstrel show rather than the old singing school, at least in Hagen's disgusted opinion (see *Review and Gazette,* August 8, 1857, p. 243).

[60] Crane was the last in an illustrious line of organists that included Samuel Priestly Taylor,♪ William A. Alpers,♪ James J. Ensign,♪♫ George F. Bristow, E. J. Connolly, and Charles Crozat Converse (1832–1918). The *Review and Gazette* (May 2, 1857, p. 133) also recalled that Thomas Hastings♪ had in the past directed the music at the Tabernacle, as had a Mr. Seely, now of Bristol, Connecticut.

[61] It should be noted that the *Review and Gazette*'s account of the event differs in several details from the reports in the *Tribune* (April 27, 1857) and later in the *Times* (December 5, 1857).

[62] The Tabernacle organ, reported the *Review and Gazette* (May 2, 1857, pp. 132–33), had been sold to the Second Reformed Church in Po'keepsie (*sic*) at less than half its original cost, and it was hoped "that the singers in Po'keepsie [would] prize it very highly on account of its associations."

2

GTS: 1858

. . . the opera is a luxury that shivers in a current of disapprobation, and threatens to fall. It must be corseted and propped up by extraordinary means, and even then its performance is precarious, and its profit— except to a very few and rarely—is not at all extraordinary.

Harper's Weekly
December 4, 1858

The attempt to prove the Italian opera an institution that fosters a pure taste for music is simply absurd, Nine-tenths of the habitués of the opera go because it is the fashion, or to show their dresses, or to flirt, or to kill time, and a large proportion of these hardly know the difference between the baritone and the soprano.

Henry C. Watson
Frank Leslie's Illustrated Newspaper
November 27, 1858

January 3, 1858. Last night with Ellie, Mrs. ["Georgey"] Peters,[1] and [Murray] Hoffman to the Academy of Music. [Beethoven's] C-minor Symphony (never felt it more), some miscellaneous matters by Formes, Thalberg and Vieuxtemps, and Mozart's Mass of *Requiem,* tolerably well done. Formes did the *Tuba mirum* simply and grandly; orchestra and chorus were very effective. Still, I can't recognize this as quite up to the Twelfth Mass.[2] It's far more elaborate, cost twice the labor, but seems less genial and fresh. No doubt I'm quite wrong. . . .

Forgot to mention an Overture of Beethoven's which I never heard of till it was played Saturday night—*Die Weihe des Hauses*—["Consecration of the House," op. 124 (Vienna 1822)], seemingly a very strong and beautiful composition.[3]

[1] Mrs. Peters, the former Georgiana Snelling, was the wife of Dr. John Charles Peters, the Strongs' family physician.

[2] Strong's allegiance to the counterfeit "Twelfth Mass"♪♫ continued unshakable throughout his life.

[3] Apparently its first performance in the United States, the overture was acclaimed "one of the most powerfully brilliant compositions [that Beethoven] has left to the world" (*Times,* January 4, 1858).

~~~

Strong failed to mention, too, that the occasion of these splendid performances had been Ullman's heavily ballyhooed, superspectacular "Grand Farewell Testimonial" to Sigismund Thalberg,[4] who was supposedly about to depart on yet another farewell tour before yet another alleged final departure to Europe. The Testimonial, a multifaceted event employing the full range of Ullman's resources, began at one P.M. with a matinée performance of *Lucia di Lammermoor* (LaGrange/Labocetta/Gassier); it resumed in the evening at seven-thirty with a huge, three-pronged concert,[5] consisting first of a misleadingly designated "philharmonic concert," performed not by the New York Philharmonic Society[6] but by Anschütz and the opera orchestra; then a "Miscellaneous Concert" (Thalberg/Vieuxtemps/Formes/Caradori); and finally a "Sacred Concert" consisting of Mozart's *Requiem* (Caradori/d'Angri/Milner/Formes/Perring/Labocetta/Bignardi/Simpson and "the full force of the *Liederkranz*").[7]

The honors of the evening unquestionably belonged to Formes, who, with Thalberg accompanying at the piano, "sang, interpreted, declaimed, acted, or recited (whichever you please, for it was all these)" Schubert's song *The Wanderer* in a manner magnificent beyond Burkhardt's powers of description (*Dispatch*, January 10, 1858). The honoree, on the other hand, made less than his usual brilliant showing with "a couple of solos," one of which—his fantasia on the popular tune "Lilly Dale," composed by one H. S. Thompson (1852),[8] purportedly whipped up especially for the occasion—was universally judged to be "entirely unworthy of him" (*Times*, January 4, 1858).

The Testimonial was so heavily attended that a repeat Testimonial was needed to accommodate the overflow.[9] To this happy necessity Ullman "vivaciously responded" on January 4 with a somewhat altered bill: the matinée opera was changed to *La traviata* (LaGrange/Bignardi/Ardavani/Rocco) and minor substitutions were effected in the miscellaneous program. Beethoven's Fifth, Mozart's *Requiem,* and Schubert's *The Wanderer,* however, were repeated.

Following this colossal dual event Thalberg departed and the Academy resumed its nightly opera schedule[10] with a performance on January 6 of *Il barbiere di Siviglia*

[4]Darcie ridiculed Ullman's "egotistically outrageous, fulsome nonsense" in promoting Thalberg's farewell celebration as something that should preserved among the "modern 'Curiosities of Literature'" (*Porter's Spirit*, December 19, 1857).

[5]Those hardy souls attempting to brave the entire event were provided with separate, transferrable tickets for the afternoon and evening performances.

[6]A mighty friction was brewing between Ullman and his subtenants, the New York Philharmonic Society, whom he evidently wished to engulf, as he had already engulfed the Harmonic Society, the *Liederkranz,* and just about everything else within hearing range in New York.

[7]Again perched atop the twelve-foot-high platform reminiscent of Exeter Hall, and again accompanied by R. M. Ferris's organ.

[8]"Lilly Dale," Thalberg's op. 74, was one of the three "American" transcriptions he concocted during his sojourn in the United States; the others were "Home, Sweet Home" (op. 72) and "The Last Rose of Summer" (op. 73).

[9]The box-office receipts for the first Thalberg Testimonial reportedly amounted to some $4000 (*Dwight's*, January 9, 1858, p. 324); the repeat netted considerably less.

[10]The 1858 winter opera season had begun on January 1 with one of Ullman's popular "cheap nights": *Lucrezia Borgia,* with Anetta Caradori, D'Angri, Bignardi, and Gassier.

with Formes as a memorable Don Basilio; on January 7 (at cheap prices) *Martha,* again with Formes; and on January 8 (full prices) Rossini's *L'Italiana in Algeri* (Venice 1813), the last erroneously heralded in heartfelt Ullmanese as its first performance in New York since the legendary Garcia company had introduced it at the Park Theatre in 1826. Ullman might have confused it with Rossini's *Il Turco in Italia* (Milan 1814), performed by the Garcias at the Park Theatre on March 14, 1826. *L'Italiana* had in fact not been heard in America until 1832, when it was given at the Richmond Hill Theatre by a later and lesser opera company, imported at the instigation of Lorenzo da Ponte.[11]

The critics welcomed Ullman's departures from the usual, repetitious opera repertory: "After the large surfeit of Verdi's nightmare lobster salad," rejoiced Burkhardt in the *Dispatch* (January 10, 1959), "the manager, during the past week, has treated his patrons to the delightful *méringues* of Rossini, the tasty *créme* of Flotow, and a slight dash of ever glorious Mozart" (the *Requiem?*). But the *Evening Post* critic (January 9, 1858), deplored the poor public response to these delectable confections: "It is somewhat singular," he wrote, "that the Americans, for the most part a mirth-loving race—fond of looking at the humorous side of everything—should slight the comic opera. They will fill the Academy, at Verdi's call, to witness the most aggravated scenes of fratricide, patricide, or suicide, and come away with a splendid relish of the evening's entertainment, but let Rossini write ever so gaily, so drolly, or so charmingly . . . and the good people of New York stay sedulously away."

On the present occasion, following the overture (admirably conducted by Signor Abella), Amati Dubreuil, Ullman's stage manager/comprimario, appeared onstage and, speaking for his chief, announced that several male members of the chorus had at the last moment refused to sing unless they received extra pay.[12] Inasmuch as this was hardly an appropriate time for such negotiations, it was decided to give the opera with a "reduced" chorus;[13] in any case, it would not greatly alter the total effect.[14] Ullman trusted that the public would approve his determination "not to submit to any extortion brought forward only a few minutes before the raising of the curtain." The audience responded with deafening applause (*Herald,* January 9, 1858).[15]

Except for *Porter's Spirit of the Times,* the press sided with Ullman, who now

[11] On that distant evening Philip Hone, a recent (and unwilling) convert to Italian opera, had come home from its first performance "ashamed of having passed an evening so unprofitably. The story is contemptible, beneath criticism," he wrote in his diary, "and the music, albeit composed by the great 'Maestro,' appeared to me dull and uninteresting, without a redeeming passage; but this may have been the fault of the performers, who, with the exception of [Luciano] Fornasari the tenor, and [Ernesto] Orlandi the buffo, were 'pretty middling bad, I tell you'" (Hone, MS diary, November 5, 1832). *L'Italiana* was subsequently given in 1844 by Laure Cinti-Damoreau, three times at Palmo's Opera House, and again at the end of the historic American tour she shared with the violinist Joseph Artôt.

[12] Owed, according to the *Times* (January 11, 1858), for the repeat performance of Mozart's *Requiem* on January 4.

[13] Reduced indeed! Only three male chorus singers remained for the performance, reported the *Tribune* (January 11, 1858).

[14] Despite this untoward circumstance, the "spirited and enjoyable" performances of Madame D'Angri (who as a special attraction ended the opera with the Rondo from *Cenerentola*), and of Labocetta, Rocco, and Gassier, were enthusiastically approved by the audience and praised by the critics.

[15] Strong, who was present, makes no mention of the incident, noting only that *L'Italiana* was a "very pretty, graceful, buffo opera" (Private Journal, January 8, 1858).

flooded the papers with self-justifications and bitter indictments of the "few unscrupulous individuals" whose "sordid and villainous" demands[16] were now depriving some three hundred persons of their livelihoods. At great personal sacrifice, claimed Ullman, he had sustained these ingrates through the worst of the recent economic "revulsion" (despite their callous refusal to accept a crucially needed reduction in pay), but now he gave his solemn pledge not to yield "one iota" to their outrageous demands.

"Considering how execrably bad [the opera] chorus has been on all important occasions," commented the *Times* (January 11, 1858), "the public may at least be grateful that it has disbanded." But why didn't Ullman revert to the provisions of the Academy's charter and create a true "Academy of Music" that would educate its own chorus singers and orchestra musicians? In March, Ullman in fact announced a free singing school to be inaugurated at the Academy after the close of the spring opera season.[17]

Although Ullman had begun negotiations with Agricol Paur to form a new men's chorus from the *Liederkranz,* he decided to suspend further opera performances at the Academy for the time being; *Don Giovanni* was accordingly announced for January 15.

Even for the Upper Ten, opera-going had its trying moments.

January 15. . . . Just from *Don Giovanni* . . . Immensely crowded house[18] and endless detention waiting for carriage. The din and confusion of conflicting coaches, infuriated drivers, and desperate patrons of the opera rushing recklessly about in white gloves and patent leathers, vainly seeking their respective charioteers and vainly adjuring them to drive up, would have given Haydn new ideas for his "Chaos" Overture in the *Creation.* The opera [was] better performed than it has been in my time and in this city. Every part respectable and some attempt to make parts of it effective by display on the stage—especially the finale of the first act and the third.[19] Formes is a capital Leporello—neither he nor the Don [Gassier] more indecent than imperatively necessary. LaGrange admirable, of course, as Donna Anna, and D'Angri as Zerlina (bating ugliness and obesity). Elvira [Caradori], Masetto [Rocco], and the Commendatore [Ardavani] were quite as good as one ought to expect, and Ottavio (Labocetta), though without force enough for the part, did his exquisite music very creditably.[20]

~~~

[16] Not only the chorus, but also the orchestra, according to the *Times* (January 11, 1858), harbored the same grievances and made the same demands.

[17] On March 3, Strong noted in his private journal that his brother-in-law Jem Ruggles "was drafting a petition to the Legislature to exempt the Academy of Music from taxation, as an institution expressly designed to educate and elevate the people by them in the noblest of the liberal arts and sciences."

[18] Prompting Ullman to advertise the following day that no extra chairs or stools would be permitted in the aisles at the Academy at the repeat farewell performance of *Don Giovanni* on January 18. Gentlemen intending to bring ladies were cautioned to secure their seats in advance.

[19] New dresses! New Props! 20 candelabra! 300 lights! Chorus of 150 (the *Liederkranz*)! Two extra orchestras numbering 100 musicians in all on the stage! 250 performers! A *corps de ballet!* One of the most brilliant productions ever mounted in the U.S. (*Evening Post.* January 16, 1858). Without specifying his objections, the *Post* critic took exception, however, to the "representation of Hell"; he strongly urged that it be omitted in future performances. Hagen agreed (*Review and Gazette,* January 23, 1858, p. 20).

[20] To Burkhardt, "take it for all in all, the performance was the best ever witnessed on this side of the Atlantic, and in many respects the best ever witnessed anywhere" (*Dispatch,* January 17, 1858).

On January 19, Strong attended the penultimate offering of the curtailed opera season, a "cheap" performance of *The Barber of Seville;* it was "refreshingly sung," he wrote, with Formes "superb as Don Basilio." The following night the company bade their final farewell with another *Don Giovanni,* then headed for Philadelphia, where Ullman's extraordinary promotional tactics were later merrily lampooned by a local journalist: "Mr. Ullman adopts all sorts of attitudes towards the public. He prostrates himself before them. Tears are in his eyes, his lip quivers, and his whole frame is convulsed with sobs as he refers to the pure and splendid character he has sustained in past time and asks to be informed whether there is anything he has done not to deserve their endorsement of his *William Tell* on this occasion. He woos most tenderly. He represents himself to be devoured by respect and love for this discriminating public and seductively presses his claims to a place in its affections. . . . He paints, in sparkling and gorgeous hues, the music and action and the apparel of the stage. . . . He hints at the slovenliness and disrespect with which any other manager but Ullman would have produced Rossini's masterpiece. . . . He makes his *William Tell* a matter of conscience and duty with the community. With a sublime burst of eloquence he closes his appeal, not before he has depicted, in graphic and agitating terms, the perils of not procuring seats early, and laid down a strict code of laws for cabmen, policemen, and the city authorities generally" (quoted in *Dwight's,* May 1, 1858, p. 39).

All the same, the termination of their New York season elicited a rarely unified crop of commendatory summings-up from the critics. Despite its many spasmodic halts and recommencements, wrote the *Times* (January 21, 1858), Ullman's overall effort deserved "commemoration," if only for the sixty-four more-or-less consecutive performances he had mounted at the Academy of Music since September:[21] fifty Italian operas; four German operas, six oratorios, and four events of miscellaneous character, such as the Thalberg Testimonials and the benefits for the Fire Department. The operas performed had been Bellini's *La sonnambula, Norma,* and *I puritani;* Verdi's *Il trovatore, Rigoletto, La traviata,* and *Ernani;* Rossini's *Barber of Seville* and *L'Italiana in Algeri;* Donizetti's *Lucia di Lammermoor, Lucrezia Borgia,* and *L'elisir d'amore;* Flotow's *Martha;* Beethoven's *Fidelio;* Meyerbeer's *Robert le diable;* and Mozart's *Don Giovanni.* A formidable showing.

"If Mr. Ullman has not made money, at least he has paid his way and obtained a valuable and admirable theatrical wardrobe," continued the *Times.* Ullman was justified in seeking an extended lease of the Academy for five years; in the writer's opinion he deserved the esteem of the public and of the Academy stockholders, whose property he had "greatly enhanced in value. For instance, last night, seats were sold at four and five dollars premium."[22]

But *Porter's Spirit of the Times*—since George Wilkes's accession as editor, a bastion of ethnic bias—now openly declared war[23] on "the little wandering musical Jew," Ullman. On January 16 (*Porter's Spirit,* p. 313), in a blistering editorial, Wilkes furiously

---

[21] A feat lightsomely equated by *Harper's Weekly* with the victory of our glorious forefathers at Bunker Hill (January 23, 1858, p. 51).

[22] Watson reported box-office receipts of "nearly sixteen thousand dollars" for the three or four closing nights of the season (*Leslie's,* January 30, 1858, p. 139).

[23] In harmonious concord with his music and drama critic John Darcie.

attacked the impudent "little creature"[24] for attempting to mold the New York press to his will by barring from the Academy of Music any critic who dared to write opera reviews "contrary to his liking."[25] This prohibition applied not only to journalists on the free list, but to those who, like Wilkes's "gentlemanly and unexceptionable" drama and music critic Darcie, had on three occasions been turned away by the doorkeeper upon presenting his (purchased) tickets. Other editors might be willing to tolerate this insult to the journalistic establishment but not Wilkes, who gave fair warning that he intended to "contest and to ascertain, by course of law, whether the Press is to be treated in this way by any foreign musical adventurer who may have the luck to get possession of a playhouse and a license."

Darcie, on his part in the double-pronged attack, branded the Philadelphia opera season nothing more than a nefarious scheme concocted by "the little Hebrew Ullman" and his Semitic friend Jacobsohn ("the man mit de monish")[26] to defraud the naive Philadelphians of their "loose change." Furthermore, wrote Darcie, Ullman's objective, in "playing for a long lease" of the New York Academy, was to defile that temple of art by the introduction into its hallowed precincts of lewd and licentious masked balls.[27] "Heaven help the stockholders and preserve the Academy if it is turned over to the tender mercies of the Israelites for a series of years," raged Darcie. "The class of people that would assemble, and the scenes of riot which would take place, if masquerades were permitted, can be readily imagined" (*Porter's Spirit,* January 29, 1858, p. 352).

Notwithstanding this pernicious propaganda, Ullman's demonstrated ability to survive in the face of all hazards won him the Academy stockholders' approval, and by late February, when he returned from his well-publicized successes in Philadelphia and Baltimore,[28] he was in sole possession of a lease for the Academy of Music[29] extending

----

[24] According to Wilkes, Ullman was "but little over four feet high." He was later described as measuring "five feet nothing" and weighing scarcely more than seventy or eighty pounds, "snuff box and eye glass included" (*Dispatch,* October 8, 1859).

[25] True, in 1847, Ullman had barred an abusive Richard Grant White from Camillo Sivori's concerts, and similarly in 1853, Charles Burkhardt was not admitted to Henriette Sontag's concert and opera performances.

[26] Allegedly derived from his profitable secondhand clothing business in Chatham Street, New York's "Old Clo'" center.

[27] Ullman had announced that, beginning in April, his next great attraction, Musard, the famed Parisian dance conductor and director of the fabled masked balls at the Paris Opéra, would—in addition to a series of concerts—superintend the giving of a few fashionable masquerades at the Academy.

[28] But not Boston. Only Formes and the oratorio contingent (Caradori/Milner/Hawley/Perring) had been briefly dispatched there for two ecstatically received performances of Mendelssohn's *Elijah* with the Handel and Haydn Society, conducted by Carl Zerrahn (see *Dwight's,* January 30, 1858, p. 349); they then joined their colleagues in Philadelphia.

[29] Evidently a furious behind-the-scenes battle for possession of the Academy lease had concurrently been raging between Ullman and the rival Maretzek/Marshall partnership. Indeed, it had been a foregone conclusion that "Max the Magnificent" would take over the Academy upon his return from Havana, where he had reportedly been reaping a golden harvest. Perhaps so, wrote Watson, "but as operatic managers break contracts with as much facility as an old toper breaks a pipe stem, the chances are that the whole matter is off, and has been off and on a dozen times since the first rumor" (*Leslie's,* February 20, 1858, p. 187).

to September 1861, with the option to renew for a further two years (*Herald*, February 22, 1858).[30]

To Strong, who continued imperturbably to follow his own musical path, it was a matter of utter indifference whether the opera stayed or went.

January 25. . . . Ellie spent the evening at the Reverend Anthon's—went after her and found the athletic Madame Graever- Johnson pounding *Moïse* out of the tortured, reluctant piano with ten pile-driver power. She followed it up with one of Mendelssohn's *Lieder [ohne Wörte],* exquisitely played.

〰

Strong had evidently not stayed to hear Madame Graever-Johnson when, on January 9, he had "looked in awhile at the crowded Philharmonic concert" at the Academy of Music and heard Beethoven's Eighth Symphony and Mendelssohn's "Staffa" ("Fingal's Cave") Overture. "The last two movements of the former are a little shallow, considering it's Beethoven," he had written in his journal (January 11, 1858), "but the first is most glowing and magnificent, and the second—the memorable little Allegretto—an absolute gem without a flaw." On that occasion Madame Graever had once again performed Litolff's Concerto Symphony on Dutch Themes, a repetition irksome to Hagen (see *Review and Gazette,* January 23, 1858, p. 19). Also appearing at the concert were Ullman's singers—Labocetta and Gassier who, respectively, had sung arias from *The Magic Flute,* and Mercadante's *Il bravo* (Milan 1839), the latter accompanied at the piano by Signor Abella.

February 5. . . . At Mozart Hall last night was a scanty audience,[31] but rather larger than I expected. Its name is rather suggestive of *Lagerbier* saloons and *Lustgartens,* but it is a respectable room for concerts and meetings.

February 23. . . . At Eisfeld's [third chamber-music] concert with Ellie tonight.[32] [George] Onslow Quartette, op. 4, no 1, was pleasant and clear; Mendelssohn's Andante and Rondo, op. 43 (with Richard Hoffman at the piano) very nice; Beethoven's Quartette, op. 18, no. 5, in A, bored me, though I believe one's duty is to admire it, and I did my best. One Mrs. Anna Warren entertained the audience with a series of

---

[30] "Many have been called to the management of the Opera," philosophized the *Herald* (February 23, 1858), "but none but he have [*sic*] been chosen."

[31] Assembled not to listen to music, but to witness the installation of new faculty members at Columbia College. At least, wrote Strong of the dismal showing, "the students were present in force and acted as claquers."

[32] Strong had evidently missed Eisfeld's second *soirée,* at Dodworth's Rooms on February 2, when the program had included Haydn's universally beloved String Quartet, op. 76, no. 3; repeat performances of Rubinstein's Quartet, op. 17; and Goldbeck's Grand Trio, op. 39. Clara Brinkerhoff "pleasantly varied, by her singing [of songs by Brahms, Eisfeld, William Vincent Wallace, and one Zeller (or Zeiller)], what would otherwise have been monotonously instrumental," wrote the *Evening Post* (February 3, 1858). To *Raimond,* it was a "positive relief to turn from the realistic mannerisms and sentimental technicalities of the Schumanns and the would-be Mendelssohns to a composer so fresh and vigorous [as Rubinstein], who evidently draws from a deep well and not from a broken cistern" (*Albion,* February 6, 1858, p. 67).

wild and distressing outcries suggestive of the sharpest bodily anguish—the wail of the Banshee, or a dog shut on its tail.[33]

Question: Is there anything in the notion that Musical Language differs from articulate speech as that differs from the Language of Mathematics? That *precision* diminishes as the power of expressing sentiment increases? Grand opening for a page of fog.

~~~

Strong seems not to have attended the remaining three *soirées* of Eisfeld's season: on March 23 consisting of Schumann's String Quartet in A minor, op. 41, no. 1 (1842); Mozart's String Quartet, designated as No. 1; an aria from *Robert le diable* and Robert Franz's *Ave Maria* sung by Maria Brainerd; and Schubert's Trio in E-flat for piano, violin, and cello, op. 100 (1827), played by the recently recurred Gustav Satter,♪ with Noll and Bergner. On April 13 they gave Schubert's String Quartet in D minor ("Death and the Maiden"); Beethoven's String Quartet, op. 18, no. 6; a trio for piano and strings on Byron's *Sardanapalus,* composed by Satter and played by him with Noll and Bergner; and *Dove sono* from *The Marriage of Figaro* and Kücken's ballad "The Jewish Maiden," sung by Hattie Andem. On May 11 the program consisted of Haydn's String Quartet in B-flat, no. 78; Beethoven's String Quintet in C, op. 29 (1801), with Joseph Burke playing first violin; an air from *Elijah* and a *romanza* from *Anna Bolena,* sung by Annie Kemp; and Schumann's Quartet in E-flat for piano and strings, op. 47 (1842).

On February 22, when a triumphant Ullman brought his opera company back to the Academy of Music, creating, as Burkhardt commented (*Dispatch,* February 28, 1858), a sudden demand for "opera cloaks and light kid gloves although it was Lent," he opened with a tightly packed week of operas. Beginning with *I puritani,*[34] featuring Formes, who was now entering his "farewell season" at the Academy, performances followed—variously at cheap and full prices—of *L'Italiana in Algeri, Don Giovanni, Robert le diable, Ernani,*[35] and Rossini's infrequently heard *Otello.*[36] Subscriptions for these six operas, at eight dollars, additionally included a coupon for a reserved seat and complimentary tickets to two extra matinée performances.[37]

The *Otello* was not well given, reported the *Times* (March 2, 1858). Despite the excellent cast (LaGrange/Tiberini/Labocetta/Gassier/Formes), "the chorus was bad and the orchestra by no means what we have a right to expect from Mr. Anschütz."

[33] More charitably, Hagen reported that Mrs. Warren, who sang a *canzonetta* by Donizetti and a ballad by the minor German composer Friedrich Truhn (1811–1886), showed "some good training but little beauty of voice" (*Review and Gazette,* March 6, 1858, p. 67).

[34] The cast included LaGrange, Gassier, and—added to the company while on tour—Tiberini.

[35] With D'Angri courageously, if ill-advisedly, emulating the more shapely Vestvali in the role of Carlo V.

[36] Ullman seems to have been studying Garcia's 1825–26 repertory: on February 7, 1826, Rossini's *Otello* (Naples 1816) had been presented at the Park Theatre, with Manuel Garcia as Otello and his fabled daughter Maria Felicitá (the future Malibran) as Desdemona. Since then, *Otello* had been successfully produced in 1849 by Max Maretzek at the Astor Place Opera House,♪ with a harp-playing Bertucca as Desdemona, Giuseppe Guidi as Otello, and the rambunctious Benevantano as Iago.

[37] In effect bringing the price of a reserved seat down to only $1 for each opera. "This is the true secret of management," approved Henry C. Watson (*Leslie's,* February 27, 1858, p. 203).

Besides, continued Seymour: "It is a fact that operas bearing Shakespearean titles do not succeed with Anglo-Saxon audiences."[38] *Otello* was not repeated.

After a further cheap performance of *L'Italiana in Algeri* on March 2 and a full-priced *Robert le diable* on March 3, a recess was called to allow the Academy forces to devote full attention to final preparations for the great event of the season—a mammoth production of Meyerbeer's *Les Huguenots,*♪♪[39] promising to eclipse in splendor anything that had ever been seen on the opera stage in the United States, or anywhere else.

To induce the desired degree of public receptivity, Ullman's advertisements for this event outdid his previous efforts in both intensity of pathos and trusting confidences.[40] Through the worst of the financial revulsion, he poignantly reminded his readers—in the face of the greatest obstacles ever to beset an impresario, and at an astronomical monthly outlay of $25,000—he had bravely sustained "the longest and most brilliant season of grand Opera" ever to have taken place in America. The present magnificent production of *The Huguenots* had imposed an even more crushing burden upon his resources: "the new scenery and dresses alone cost over $6000 . . . the extra chorus, extra orchestra, and extra rehearsals . . . $10,000."

In a supplementary "Synopsis of the *mise en scene*" Ullman elaborated: a force of 200 persons had been working on *The Huguenots* for the past three months; five new sets—mostly copies of the original Paris designs, had been painted by the master scenic artists Allegri, Calyo, and Heister—and some 300 new costumes had been ordered, some from Paris, and all authentic.[41] The chorus had been increased from thirty-five to seventy singers (later claimed to be 100), and in "the Conjuration Scene" to 200—the largest chorus ever to appear in an opera anywhere. The orchestra had been enlarged from thirty to forty players, and the enormous cast included LaGrange (Valentine), D'Angri (Urbain), Siedenburg (Marguerite de Valois), Tiberini (Raoul), Gassier (Count de St. Bris), Taffanelli (Count de Nevers), Rocco (Merú), Pickaneser (Cossé), Beutler (Tavannes), Oehrlein (de Retz), Barattini (Thoré), and, above all, Formes (Marcel). Angiolina Morra and Amati Dubreuil played minor roles.[42]

---

[38] Darcie labeled Rossini's once popular *Otello* a "dead letter in the operatic repertoire" (*Porter's Spirit,* March 6, 1858, p. 16).

[39] It was not the work's first performance in New York: in 1845 *Les Huguenots* had been produced in French at the Park Theatre by a splendid visiting opera company from New Orleans;♪ and in 1850, as *Gli Ugonotti,* it was successfully given in Italian at the Astor Place Opera House by Don Francisco Martí's magnificent Havana opera company: Bosio, Steffanone, Vietti, Salvi, and Marini.♪

[40] "When an operatic manager or an impresario of any kind becomes impressively confidential—detailing and explaining his plans and prospects—rest assured he is trying to humbug you and gives this fake information for a special purpose," cynically commented Watson (*Leslie's,* February 20, 1858, p. 187).

[41] In addition to the customary libretto, giving the text and musical illustrations, a "Scenic Synopsis" was sold at the Academy, offering a "thorough and clear explanation of every scene."

[42] On a more exalted plane, Ullman, in a later advertisement, sought to entice a more erudite clientele by assigning to Meyerbeer and *The Huguenots* their proper places in the hierarchy of High Art: "Meyerbeer, like Mozart and Beethoven," he wrote, "endeavored to portray in each of his compositions one of those grand ideas which at different epochs had agitated mankind." This was illustrated by Meyerbeer's contrasting treatments of "Luther's Choral": austere when sung by the Protestants, recklessly merry when sung by the Catholics—thus creating in music "a *chiaroscuro* which has its only parallel in the pictures of a Raphael or a Correggio."

The total outlay represented the greatest sum ever expended on an opera production in this country, and although Ullman expected an "immense" attendance, he could at best never hope to recover his investment. A sorry recompense for his Herculean efforts to provide New York with opera productions equal to the best in Europe. Surely the generous and compassionate New York public would never exact so great a sacrifice.

Besides, Ullman pointed out (wiping away a tear), he had never claimed one of the personally lucrative benefits customarily assigned to themselves by fellow-impresarios (meaning Maretzek). The only reward Ullman now sought was the insignificant surcharge of fifty cents on the $1 admissions to *The Huguenots*,[43] a sum so minuscule as to be scarcely perceptible to the individual ticket purchaser, but representing to the manager a hypothetical extra $5000 toward offsetting his extraordinary expenses.

"Do you think I have some claim on you?" he disingenuously asked his public. "Will you pay the price? And will you pay it cheerfully? You have done so for Sontag, Alboni, Mario and Grisi, and the old and worn-out operas they have appeared in."[44] In Paris, he pointed out, $3 was cheerfully paid, and in London $5, to witness inferior opera productions. And if, after the first performance of *The Huguenots,* there should be dissatisfaction with the new admission price, he would promptly reduce it back to $1.

A "grand *coup de théâtre*," applauded the *Herald* (March 1, 1858), now, for arcane reasons of its own, Ullman's warmest supporter.[45] In a long and flattering editorial, that volatile journal painted the coming opera season in the rosiest of rosy hues—social, economic, and musical. The other papers, too, mostly sided with the "little Napoleon," as Ullman was popularly nicknamed, but to Wilkes the surcharge provided fresh ammunition for his relentless attacks on "the little musical Hebrew." Ullman's plot to add an extra charge to his already exorbitant price of $1 for opera tickets was an outrage, fumed Wilkes, when the normal maximum admission to "all other public entertainments given in this country by the most intellectual, worthy, and talented philosophers, lecturers, actors, and actresses" was only fifty cents. It was all the fault of the inordinate fees paid foreign opera singers.[46] Wilkes saw "no reason why a greasy, foreign bohemian,[47] who is only capable, between overfeeding and wine-bibbing, of roll-

---

[43] Reserved seats still cost an additional fifty cents.

[44] Here Ullman went too far, exploded Wilkes. How dared this little Hebrew upstart compare himself to such divinities as Sontag, Mario, and Grisi! And what an affront to "the People!" Ullman's cool demand for an extra half-dollar was an insult, equally to those to whom the sum represented a day's pay as to the select few who "could not be tempted into the [Academy] even in the name of charity." Wilkes furthermore cautioned the "foolish of the latter class not to be misled into the notion that the extra 'half-dollar' will make the Opera more fashionable and exclusive" (*Porter's Spirit,* March 6, 1858, p. 9).

[45] Burkhardt sarcastically referred to the *Herald* as "the official organ of the Ullman opera administration."

[46] Although a few major theatrical stars received as much as $250 a week, actors' weekly salaries normally ran from fifteen to fifty dollars, usually "nearer to the smaller than to the larger amount," reported the *Herald* (March 29, 1858). "At the Opera," on the other hand, "the principal singers [received] six hundred, five hundred, and four hundred dollars per week, while the smallest pipe of them all [did] not deign to emit its harmony under two hundred dollars per month."

[47] The term *bohemian* to describe such aberrant types as writers, artists, and musicians, had now reached the United States.

ing sound through his fat throat three nights a week, [should be] paid at a rate that would be a recompense for the President of the United States, or a Foreign Minister, at least." Rather than "fattening the frangipanni [sic] of the opera with . . . additional half-dollars," stormed Wilkes, "better let the gipsies" return to their native "tambou-rines, triangles, and hand organs" (*Porter's Spirit,* March 6, 1858, p. 9).

Nonetheless, on March 8 a large audience braved "a violent snowstorm, which very much interfered with locomotion on foot or on wheels,"[48] to attend the opening of *The Huguenots*. What they witnessed, according to the *Evening Post* (March 9, 1858), was "an epoch in our musical history," not only because it was more perfectly pre-sented than any preceding opera production at the Academy, but because it brilliantly displayed "the abundance of resources at the command of the director, and his skill and liberality in applying them." And, the writer continued, lapsing into the cultural defensiveness indigenous to nineteenth-century America, the production demon-strated the "high degree of musical culture which our people have attained, when it is found necessary to minister to their tastes with a splendor and completeness rarely witnessed in European capitals."[49]

The critics vied with each other, not only in their praises of the spectacular pro-duction but in their windy, "learned" lauds of Meyerbeer. According to some he was the supreme creator of music drama of all time, although a venturesome few dared irreverently to suggest that perhaps, after all, his operas were "rather dull than de-lightful."[50] The cast (with a few exceptions) was pronounced unsurpassable: LaGrange was vocally and dramatically magnificent in her portrayal of Valentine,[51] D'Angri was perfection itself as the page Urbain, and Formes, the Marcel, as always, was beyond perfection.[52] Anschütz's conducting of the augmented orchestra dramatically demon-strated how a proper orchestra should sound in an opera house, and Hannibal Calyo's sets—particularly his renderings of the Castle of Chenonceaux and the facade of the Cathedral of Notre Dame—were superb.[53] The production, drastically shortened but still too long, was infallibly compared—both favorably and unfavorably—with the

---

[48] Had it not snowed, ruefully confided Ullman in his advertisement for the second performance of *The Huguenots* (given on March 10), the first-night receipts would have amounted to "over $5000." But even so, despite the weather, the ticket sales had reached $2500.

[49] "It is very droll," keenly commented the "Lounger" in *Harper's Weekly* (March 20, 1858, p. 178), "to observe what particular attention is called to the fact—what half skeptical, half despairing, appeals are made to the public to come forward and show—that New York has as much taste, and sentiment, and musical appreciation as Paris, or St. Petersburg, or Madrid."

[50] Meyerbeer's music was essentially Teutonic, wrote the Francophile Darcie, and, like German philosophy, it contained much that was heavy and incomprehensible, "causing vulgar, uneducated people to yawn, whilst a few *savants* listen with wrapt [sic] attention" (*Porter's Spirit,* March 13, 1858, p. 32).

[51] Only Darcie complained that Valentine's music—transposed up to suit her voice—did not suit LaGrange, nor did she, with her florid, French style of vocalization, suit the music; she was no match for Grisi in the role (*ibid.*).

[52] But Tiberini, it was generally thought, was not up to the demands of his role—nor did his persistent influenza improve his unfortunate performance of it as the run went on.

[53] Only Burkhardt, who had been prevented by illness from hearing *The Huguenots* until nearly the end of its run, found fault with the production. Despite his rapturous advance buildup, he now found the sets, costumes, general staging, and dramatic direction to be woefully vulgar (*Dispatch,* March 28, 1959).

Paris production, with whose most minute details all the critics seemed somehow to be personally familiar.

The *Huguenots* was performed three times weekly for a grand total of nine consecutive performances,[54] a killing schedule for all concerned,[55] except, apparently, the opera-going public, who, with each performance, willingly enriched Ullmans's coffers by a purported $3000.[56]

Immediately after *The Huguenots* opened, Ullman (for once dispensing with his usual fanfare) quietly rescinded his surcharge,[57] a double triumph for Wilkes, who exulted in "the Failure of the Old Clo' Principle": "Little Ullman," he sneered, had missed in his attempt to play upon the folly of "the flies who flutter in the amber of the Academy dress circle" (*Porter's Spirit,* March 13, 1858, p. 25).

The "most positively final" performance of *The Huguenots* was announced for March 26 as the first part of an elaborate farewell benefit for Formes, purportedly about to return to Europe.[58] Those purchasing $1 seats for this gala event would receive a free ticket for the following day's matinée performance of *Martha,*[59] featuring Formes and—replacing the also imminently departing LaGrange—Madame Bertha Johannsen, just returned from a grand tour of the South with Thalberg—yes, Thalberg.

That *The Huguenots,* as an essentially French work by a German composer, should be performed in Italian was standard opera procedure; but that William Henry Fry's embattled opera *Leonora,*♪♫ Ullman's closing offering of the season,[60] should—after its long exclusion from the New York stage[61]—at last materialize in an Italian translation seems nothing less than a supreme irony. Unperformed since 1845, when it was first given in his native Philadelphia, *Leonora* was claimed by Fry, a fanatical crusader for opera in English, to be a cultural landmark or icon—not only as the "first American grand opera" ("grand" because every word of it was sung) but because it was, he

<hr/>

[54] The inexorable progression of *The Huguenots* was momentarily interrupted on March 13 by a cheap performance of *Semiramide,* and on March 20 by *Lucrezia Borgia,* the last cheap matinée of the season.

[55] On March 19 the indestructible LaGrange briefly succumbed to influenza and had to be replaced for that one performance by Anetta Caradori, unfortunately also ailing. Caradori's occasional attacks of hoarseness "excited the wrath of the audience," wrote Seymour, who gallantly observed that "a little more consideration might have been shown for a lady who was palpably indisposed" (*Times,* March 20, 1858).

[56] "Twenty or thirty thousand persons have witnessed the performance of [*The Huguenots*]," wrote Watson, "and the receipts must have been very large, for [with the exception of the critics] the 'free ticket system' has been almost entirely suspended," a development eliciting considerable pro-and-con discussion in the press (*Leslie's,* March 27, 1858, p. 267).

[57] Watson, among others, maintained that a continuation of the surcharge would have been well justified by the magnificence of the production (*Leslie's,* March 20, 1858, p. 254).

[58] Closely following upon the return to Europe of the highly regarded tenor Pietro Bignardi, Formes's rumored departure foretold the ultimate dissolution of Ullman's opera company, wrote Darcie in his role of public Iago (*Porter's Spirit,* March 20, 1858, p. 48).

[59] For those not attending *The Huguenots,* the admission to *Martha,* a cheap matinée, was fifty cents, with no reserved seats.

[60] Darcie quoted a colleague's quip that "Fry's opera would close any season" (*Porter's Spirit,* March 20, 1858, p. 48).

[61] Attributed to the evil machinations of James Gordon Bennett, implacable enemy of all members of the Fry family.

shamelessly maintained, the first "authentic grand opera" ever to have been composed in English.[62] It was only through opera in English, Fry had vehemently preached through the years, that America would at last establish her musical identity. Thus to repudiate his dearest obsession and permit *Leonora* to be performed in Italian signifies the extent of Fry's hunger to see his work produced, at any sacrifice.

But it was perhaps not so wrenching a sacrifice, after all. A New York correspondent of *Dwight's*[63] disclosed (April 3, 1858, p. 7) that the Italian libretto used in this production had been obligingly supplied by Fry himself—that it was the same libretto that he had vainly offered to the director of the Paris Opéra more than a decade earlier,♪ the same that he had provided for the thwarted production of *Leonora* at the Astor Place Opera House in 1848,[64] and doubtless the same that he had again unsuccessfully offered to the Academy of Music in 1855.♪ What behind-the-scenes maneuverings lay behind this current production were not revealed,[65] nor is it known how they ever managed to elude the hostile scrutiny of James Gordon Bennett.

Triumphantly announcing the close of the "longest and most prosperous season ever given at the Academy of Music," Ullman, a virtuoso paradoxist, thus ushered in Holy Week (the year's most unproductive week at the box office) with "a tribute to American achievement in Lyrical Art: the production for the first time in the Italian language [on March 29 and 31] of *Leonora,* Fry's grand opera in four acts,"[66] touted as the first technically grand opera of the modern school.

"Originally adapted to English words, with a view of proving the noble qualities of that language and its capability to answer all the requirements of the lyrical drama," it was "especially gratifying," declared Ullman, to be "the first to present in the New York Academy of Music, the work of an American composer [albeit in Italian] and thus in a measure to fulfill the pleasing duty imposed on him by the charter of the Institution,♪ a duty heretofore neglected by his predecessors."

This salute to American art, hastily put together amid the rigors of the ongoing

[62] The libretto of *Leonora* was adapted by Fry's brother, Joseph Reese Fry, from Edward Bulwer-Lytton's play *The Lady of Lyons.* W. H. Fry's prefatory remarks to the original vocal score, published in Philadelphia (1846) by E. Ferrett and Co, are cited in William Treat Upton's *Fry* (pp. 327–31).

[63] Newly acquired by the Boston firm of Oliver Ditson and Company, its publisher for the following twenty years.

[64] A fiasco directly attributed by Fry to James Gordon Bennett's evil connivance.

[65] Darcie wondered who had "smoothed away the difficulties—what friendly hand poured oil, what Machiavellian diplomacy been exerted—to enable Piccolo Ullman even to announce this work as his closing subject" (*Porter's Spirit,* March 20, 1858, p. 48).

[66] Originally in three acts. There is disagreement about the extent of Fry's revisions for this performance. His contemporaries consistently reported only a new aria for D'Angri and a few inconsequential odds and ends. Burkhardt, in the *Dispatch* (April 4, 1858), claimed, however, that Fry refused to change his original score, "preferring to stand by its merits or imperfections as they first appeared." And Seymour (*Times,* March 30, 1858): "Not a note in the score has been changed since the time when it was first played in Philadelphia." But William Treat Upton, nearly a century later, claimed extensive alterations: "It must have given Fry great satisfaction to hear his opera revised to fit his present taste," wrote Upton in his enthusiastic biography of Fry (p. 158), adding, after an examination of the score: "It is quite apparent that the original full score and original orchestra parts were used in [the Academy] performance, with the necessary changes cued in and new material interleaved in both score and parts," creating an arduous task for Anschütz and the orchestra musicians. Upton does not reckon with the many changes reportedly made immediately after the first performance in 1845.♪

Huguenots, was performed by LaGrange (Leonora), D'Angri (Mariana), Signora Morra (Martina), Tiberini (Julio) Gassier (Montalvo), Rocco (Valdor), and Barattini (Alferez).

The critics generally responded to both the work and the production with unaccustomed moderation. The *Evening Post* (March 31, 1858) congratulated Fry on being the first American composer to be honored by having his opera performed in Italian, a departure that indicated the coming of age of American opera. It was "no longer a thing so vague and unsubstantial that the present generation [could] scarcely hope to see it realized," noted the *Post.* And even if Fry composed nothing more, the performance of *Leonora* in Italian entitled him to be known as "the Father and Founder of [American] national opera."

Although more lenient toward Fry than on the occasion of *Leonora*'s Philadelphia production, most of the critics—now Fry's colleagues—nonetheless maintained, as before, that the fluent and pleasing melodies in which the work abounded[67] (although perhaps too persistently in the major mode) were unmistakably derived from Bellini and Donizetti—not out-and-out plagiarisms, but familiar enough to be readily recognized.[68] And why not? wrote Richard Grant White. Although composed by an American, *Leonora* was "as much an Italian opera as *La sonnambula* or *Lucia* are Italian operas, or *Fidelio* or *Oberon* are German operas—the latter, by the way," White pointedly remarked, "having been written to English words."[69] If, during the interim, Fry had composed two or three additional operas containing nothing more original than the most important scenes of *Leonora,* "we should say that he was not an inspired composer." But as matters stood, continued White (himself no mean paradoxist), this judgment did not apply: *Leonora* remained a first effort superior to anything by Nicolai or any other modern writer of his rank. Of course, it was not equal to *Lucia* or *Lucrezia*— or even *Parisina,*♪ but it stacked up pretty well against "the least known half of Donizetti's operas" (*Courier and Enquirer,* March 31, 1858).

Most of the critics tolerantly pointed out that Fry's opera, although not devoid of talent, was obviously the work of a young and inexperienced hand and lacked the skill that would surely have marked a more mature effort,[70] as Fry's recent orchestra works attested. Some complained of his excessive use of brass in the orchestra (and as Seymour slyly observed, elsewhere as well) that in noisiness rivaled Verdi at his most deafening.

Unexpectedly, Darcie (probably because of the friendship both he and Fry bore for Jullien) had unstinting words of praise for *Leonora* and its composer. Hagen, however, delivered himself of a diatribe, uttering, in the harshest of Hagenisms, sentiments that the other critics had more gently clothed in clouds of euphemism. Much as Hagen admired Fry as an *homme de lettres,* he could find no parallel to the quality of his literary

---

[67] "Melodic" rather than "melodious," wrote *Harper's Weekly* (April 10, 1858, p. 227), delicately splitting hairs. Fry's airs had the "movement and construction of melodies," but were not catchy tunes. People would not be heard whistling them, or hand-organs grinding them, or "young Misses banging them upon pianos."

[68] Considering Fry's youth when he composed *Leonora,* such leanings on the most popular composers of the day were only to be expected and condoned, magnanimously agreed most of the critics.

[69] The libretto to Weber's *Oberon,* composed and first performed in England in 1826, had been written in English by the English playwright James Robinson Planché (1796–1880).

[70] A supposition that Fry hotly rejected.

achievements in this immature self-indulgence that he elected to call an opera. And despite his excellent command of the written and spoken language, Fry obviously had no inkling of "the technical requisites for writing an opera," else he would never have tolerated a work as poor as *Leonora;* indeed it was mystifying to Hagen that Fry did not recognize it as "one of the weaknesses of his youth, and think it best to put it in oblivion forever."[71] Whether or not Fry possessed the true vocation for composing a valid opera could only be determined by his composing one; the example of *Leonora* made Hagen fear that he did not possess the faculty (*Review and Gazette,* April 3, 1859, pp. 98–99).

Hagen reported a thin house, betokening "on the part of the public an unjust neglect with regard to American art and its patronage," as did James Gordon Bennett's *Herald,* which beforehand had noticeably all but ignored the production of Fry's opera.[72] But to Fry the production of his opera at the Academy of Music, despite any misgivings he might have felt, doubtless represented a moment of high fulfillment. At the first performance he was called out after each of its four acts; at the second performance, after three curtain calls, at the public's insistence he made his inevitable speech.

"Ladies and gentlemen," Fry began archly: "What is the matter? I hope I have not done anything wrong. (Cheers.)" Then, lapsing into his old refrain: "In regard to your judgment upon my music, it becomes me to say nothing—for art asks no favors. (Great cheering). . . . An American in my own country, I may be permitted to say that if we are to become a great nation it will not be from the number of things we import from Europe, but from the number of things we produce ourselves. (Applause.)"

Although there existed a ready—indeed eager—market for American literature and art, claimed Fry, "our dramatic music may lie dead. In my own case, in this instance, it has lain by for twenty-five years[73] because I could not get anybody to take hold of it. What I can do now, I could do when I was seventeen years of age. In this instance the manager of this house has thrown aside the conventional rules, and to him you are indebted for this American opera." Fry thanked the foreigners who had participated in this tribute to American art, despite the crushing demands—morning, noon, and night—of their *Martha*s, their *Messiah*s and *Trovatore*s (*Tribune,* April 1, 1858).

On March 30, between the two *Leonora* performances, the solemn Lenten season was observed at the Academy with an eventful rendition (presumably in English) of Handel's *Messiah,* by Caradori, D'Angri, George Simpson, Formes (still present), and the Harmonic Society. As the performance neared its conclusion, the occasion degenerated into a riotous clash of wills between the audience, who demanded an encore (taboo at oratorio performances) of Formes's "trumpet aria," and Anschütz, who refused to repeat it. As the *Evening Post* tells it (March 31, 1858), upon the encore being

[71] *Raimond* agreed: "*Leonora* should be now a reminiscence for its author as well as for ourselves" (*Albion,* April 3, 1858, pp. 163–64).

[72] Reporting a considerable loss at the box office, on April 2, after the second performance, the *Herald,* with forked tongue, summarized the critical consensus: *Leonora* was "a very fair first attempt, but . . . made up of reminiscences from other composers—Bellini, Donizetti, and Rossini." And because people preferred to take their Bellini, Donizetti, and Rossini unadulterated, the opera had been a failure thirteen years ago, as it was again now.

[73] More accurately, thirteen years.

refused, "the audience stormed. Mr. Anschütz furiously flourished his baton and insisted that the music should go on. For three or four minutes the Academy was filled with a horrible din of violent instrumentation, frenzied vocalization, shouts, stamping, catcalls, brass trumpets, and German gutterals. Mr. Anschütz's temper was up. So was that of the audience." Anschütz, "shattered by passion," at this point addressed the audience: "Zhentlemen and ladeez, it is *nevair* customary to repeat ze sacred music," and forthwith attempted to proceed with the performance. "The first note was a signal for the renewal of the uproar, which was now aided by some obstreperous youths upon the stage." In disgust, Anschütz threw down his baton and stormed off. After a brief pause for backstage consultation, an unidentified gentleman appeared and informed the audience that the trumpet accompaniment was too difficult to repeat. Whereupon an "injured and irate Anschütz returned to the scene of his former triumphs, the audience behaved itself, and the performance proceeded successfully to its close."

On April 1, Ullman at last closed his spectacularly successful opera season with a reprise of the "positively last performance" of *The Huguenots.* The occasion marked LaGrange's farewell to the Academy, an event that went curiously unobserved by Ullman.[74] Thus, despite her triumphant years within its walls, her announced swan song at the Academy went all but unnoticed in the press.

Recapitulating Ullman's spring opera season, the *Herald* (April 2, 1858) reported unheard-of box-office receipts of some $30,000 for *The Huguenots* alone. Despite a very considerable increase in expenses, the proceeds at the Academy had commensurately grown, chiefly because of *The Huguenots, Robert le diable,* and *Don Giovanni,* the three productions that, according to the *Herald,* had "saved the season." Ullman, with his opulent offerings and his splendid artists, had sustained a "very long" opera season,[75] giving more than satisfaction to everyone concerned. And with the likelihood of longer and more secure engagements, famous European opera singers would be more willing to accept lower fees. The *Herald* envisaged an operatic paradise-to-come, entirely brought about by Ullman's splendid management.

As a fitting coda to these triumphs, Ullman, who could not bear to see the Academy—or an artist under his management—idle for a single day, unabashedly ignored his recent rites of farewell to Thalberg and, hailing the great pianist's return from his vastly lucrative tour of the South, announced Thalberg's first popular-priced matinée at the Academy, on April 3 (tickets at fifty cents to all parts of the house). The assisting artists were Annie Milner, Henry C. Cooper, and the opera orchestra conducted by Anschütz.

Following this concert, sparsely noticed by the jaded critics, the Academy was closed for renovations preparatory to the loudly heralded visit of "the great Musard," a subject of widespread advance (and subsequent) controversy, chiefly engineered by the malevolent George Wilkes.

Strong, in the meantime, had continued to maintain the serenity of his musical pace.

---

[74] Suggesting that they were already engaged in the dispute that ended in litigation in Paris the following summer, from which Ullman emerged victorious.

[75] "Success unprecedented has attended the efforts of Mr. Ullman," wrote Fry, for the time being Ullman's friend and ally. "He has had but few slim or simply fair houses; one cause of which is the excellence of the entertainments he has offered, and another is the splendid weather with the absence of rain, by which ladies could walk to the Academy" (*Tribune,* April 2, 1858).

March 7. . . . Spent half an hour last night at the Philharmonic concert—[at the Academy of Music] crowded and garrulous—like a square mile of tropical forest with its floods of squalling paroquets and troops of chattering monkeys. Young America loves the Philharmonic. Acres of pretty little half-fledged girls frequent these solemnities for the sake of Mr. Timm or Mr. Eisfeld, who's teaching them music, and they are followed by cohorts of ill-bred, juvenile males, whose gabble drowns the music. I heard part of a pretty symphony by [Ferdinand] Hiller [1811–1885];[76] *Voi che sapete* [sung by Madame D'Angri, by permission of Ullman] and *Vedrai carino* (substituted when the former was encored); a dismal clarinet and orchestra concerto [composed by Eisfeld and played by Xavier Kiefer]; and Beethoven's Overture to *Coriolanus* (which I could not comprehend).[77]

March 14. . . . [returning from a spiritualistic séance, currently all the rage][78] "Spiritual Music" is said to be no uncommon manifestation. It seems to occur more frequently than any other first-class prodigy. Its name is very suggestive and full of promise—reminds one of Prospero's Island "full of noises"—of "Come unto these yellow sands"[79] and of the

> Sound of a hidden brook
> In the leafy month of June[80]

that floated around Coleridge's "Mariner" in his loneliness, and of the tune played to the Witch of Fife and her company, that

> rang so sweit through the grein Lommond
>   that the nycht-winde lowner blew,
> and it soupit along the Loch Leven
>   and walkinit the white sea mew.
> It rang so sweit through the grein Lommond,
>   So sweitly butt and so shrill
> That the weazilis laup out of their mouldy holis
>   And dancit on the mydnycht hill.[81]

A solo or a symphony from the World of Spirits would be something unearthly and of keen and searching beauty, one would think. Tieck's Explorer into the *Mundus*

---

[76] According to Seymour (*Times*, March 6, 1858): "a composer who enjoys an ample fortune, a remarkable amount of scientific attainment, and a limited number of ideas." Performed from a manuscript graciously sent from Germany by the composer, the symphony "fell dead upon the audience," reported ——t—— in *Dwight's* (March 13, 1858, p. 397).

[77] Its first performance by the Philharmonic, the *Coriolanus* Overture was "played magnificently and was the special luxury of the programme," wrote Seymour (*Times,* March 6, 1858). For the rest, Madame D'Angri sang the *Ah, mon fils!* from *Le Prophète,* repeating it as an encore; William Mason played the Larghetto and Presto movements of Adolf Henselt's "difficult" Piano Concerto in F minor, op. 16 (its first movement had been played by Gottschalk in 1857); and Eisfeld conducted the *Faust* Overture, op. 80, by Lindpaintner.

[78] Not only spiritualism but a great wave of religious revivalism had currently seized the populace.

[79] Shakespeare: *The Tempest,* act 1, scene 2, line 375.

[80] More properly, "A noise like of a hidden brook / In the leafy month of June"; Samuel Taylor Coleridge: "The Rime of the Ancient Mariner" (1798), part 5, lines 369–70.

[81] Lines from "The Witch of Fife," sung by the Eighth Bard in *The Queen's Wake* (1813), an epic poem celebrating Mary Queen of Scots, by the Scottish poet James Hogg (1770–1835), known as "the Ettrick Shepherd."

subterraneus heard it, and speaks of "*die tiefen Klänge und Tönen, hier einzeln und verborgen, aus denen die irdische Musik entsteht*"[82]—the reality, that is, which Beethoven and Mozart have obscurely paraphrased into earthly music hampered and embarrassed not only by the dimness of their own mortal perception—the feebleness of their own faculty of expression —but by the awkward material tools for which they wrote. It must be most like the weird music of an Aeolian harp, but infinitely higher and more varied. Whoso has but once heard it can take no pleasure thereafter in earthly orchestras. The C-minor Symphony rendered at the *Conservatoire* itself will be to him mere *dudelei* [tootling]—an array of hurdy-gurdies grinding out *Trovatore*. What do these fortunate people who have heard the melodies and harmonies wherein Spirits delight tell us about them? Generally something like this: "The Banjo or Accordion," as the case may be, "circulated around the room far over our heads and then fell on the table, where nobody could have touched it, and played 'Hail Columbia,' 'Old Virginny,' and 'Jordan is a hard road to travel' almost as well as a musician could have done!!!" Amen. Spiritualism is an unquestionable marvel.

~~~

No less a marvel was Ullman's sensational buildup for his following attraction at the Academy of Music. Heralded as the "Most Colossal and Artistic Entertainment ever introduced in America," a month of Monster Concerts and Balls was announced to begin in early or mid-April under the inspired direction of "Musard, *Le Roi du Quadrille*." The (not unintentional) omission of Musard's given name led many to believe that it was the legendary Philippe Musard (1793–1859)♪♫—the true Quadrille King in bygone days—who was meant, not his less illustrious son Alfred (1828–1881).[83] Consequently, the newspapers were bombarded with letters to the editor from those who knew better, not a few of whom accused Ullman of deliberate deception for his own selfish gains (grist to the Wilkes/Darcie mill). Ullman, in an answering deluge of defensive prose reinforced by mountains of corroborative documentation, claimed that Alfred Musard, a hero in fun-loving Paris[84]—with his celebrated promenade concerts at the Hôtel d'Osmond and his longtime directorship of the madcap Paris Opéra Balls—was currently as much "the true Musard" as his father had ever been in his day.[85]

To evoke the "true Musard" sound, a "monster orchestra" of 120 players (the minimum purportedly required for Musard's "monster quadrilles") was engaged,[86] to

[82] "The deep sounds and tones, here individual and secret, out of which earthly music arises."

[83] Among the misled was Burkhardt, who misinformed his readers that this present Musard had introduced to London and Paris "those monster concerts . . . of which Jullien has thus far been [the] only imitator" (*Dispatch,* February 7, 1858).

[84] Musard was "the delight of Parisian grisettes and those ladies who quaff champagne, smoke cigarettes, [and] are not particular in their small-talk," sneered Darcie (*Porter's Spirit,* April 17, 1858, p. 112).

[85] Although this Musard was conclusively proved to be the son rather than the father, some critics credited him with "admirable abilities and powers" of his own: "Alfred Musard, *the* Musard of today," saluted Watson, "we give you welcome and snub your stupid, poke-nose detractors" (*Leslie's,* April 18, p. 331).

[86] Ullman's "*monstre orchestre,*" disparaged Darcie, was "a *monstre* collection of the *debris* of the different New York bands, backed up by a few musicians of real talent," doubtless including some members of the Philharmonic (*Porter's Spirit,* April 17, 1858, p. 112).

consist of "sixty first-rate violins, thirty contrabasses and cellos, nine trombones and twenty drums, exclusive of the usual number of wind and brass instruments,"[87] and of Musard's virtuoso solo players brought from Paris, à la Jullien (or so Ullman hoped).

The descriptive noises demanded by Musard's programmatic war-horses were supplied by a variety of musical and extra-musical devices: in "The Grand Battle Quadrille," for example, the bombing in the recent Crimean War of the impregnable Malakoff Fortress by French Zouaves[88] was simulated by a mighty artillery of percussion; in "The Cattle Show Quadrille" *(Quadrille des Boeufs et Moutons),* the cackles and brays of the barnyard menagerie were realistically reproduced with various whistles and rattles; and the "Express Galop" (later called the "Express Train Galop") employed "extensive and new machinery" imported from Paris to evoke the sounds of a choochoo train and the general noisy bustle endemic to that up-to-date mode of travel.[89]

To accommodate these vast forces, the Academy stage was transformed by the noted stage designer Giuseppe Guidicini into a huge octagonal "Concert-Room," with "plenty of gas lights" and a closed ceiling to act as a "sounding board." The general illumination was enhanced, too, by twenty-five new and splendid "monster candelabras" and chandeliers (specially manufactured by a Mr. Cornelius of Philadelphia),[90] in whose radiance the more news-conscious concert-goers might read the evening papers, purchased (at regular prices) from one of twenty uniformed young gentlemen. For those disposed to "lounge," a hundred luxurious sofas and divans were strewn throughout the lushly carpeted corridors; for those seized in mid-performance with a desire for refreshments, twenty liveried black waiters were stationed at various points in the parquet and balconies, waiting to be dispatched for "ice creams" and other delicacies; for those wishing (nonalcoholic) stimulants, twenty young ladies "of prepossessing appearance," dispensed them in a tastefully decorated Tea and Coffee Room on the first tier.[91]

Among Ullman's further allurements was "a new contrivance," consisting of large transparent placards, by which the evening's program was announced from the stage;

[87] Careless arithmetic, clumsily joshed Burkhardt (*Dispatch,* April 11, 1858): with the already specified instrumentation adding up to 119 players, how could one remaining musician "do the duty of cornets, horns, bassoons, trumpet, bugle, etc.?"

[88] The original Zouaves, in 1848, were native Algerian soldiers recruited by the French from the Kabyle tribe of Zouaoua. The name and exotic oriental uniform (gaiters, baggy red trousers, short open-fronted jacket, and a tasseled cap or turban) were subsequently given to the elite French fighters who so spectacularly served in the Crimean War. And still later to American forces in the Civil War.

[89] To maintain local verisimilitude, the foreign sound effects were soon replaced by devices of American manufacture, evoking more familiar railroad noises.

[90] An echo of Ullman's "thousand-candles" exploit, devised for Henri Herz's concerts in the 1840s.

[91] Not all of these refinements were products of Ullman's fertile imagination. Adam Carse cites a traveler's description in the London *Musical World* of a Philippe Musard promenade concert in 1837 at the *Salle Valentino* in Paris: "For one franc [one] was admitted to . . . a musical paradise, a spacious hall furnished with mirrors, couches, ottomans, statues, fountains, and floral decoration, and at one end a *café* attended by a troupe of 'perfumed waiters.'" An orchestra of eighty players was seated on a platform in the center of the hall, around which "strolled promenaders of all nations, and in the recesses they formed themselves into groups, chatting, eating, drinking, reading, and sleeping" (Carse, *Life of Jullien,* p. 6).

Leslie's, Dartmouth College Library

ALFRED MUSARD, CONDUCTOR OF THE CELEBRATED MUSARD CONCERTS.

Alfred Musard, Le Roi du Quadrille, *imperturbable
leader of dance music and "monster quadrilles."*

1000 fans were distributed gratis to ladies at each performance by the liveried waiters; and twenty-minute promenades were held (along the carpeted corridors) during inter-missions, from which the promenaders were innovatively summoned back to their seats by the "sounding of a gong." Souvenir booklets containing the various quadrille scenarios, the words of the vocal works performed, and simple piano arrangements of the "Zouaves'" and the "Cattle Show" quadrilles, were sold for twenty-five cents. At the opening concert, on April 12, a biography of Musard was found on every seat, together with a description of the first projected "Opera Ball,"[92] announced for April 29 despite Wilkes's violent threats and imprecations.[93]

[92] For some weeks past, model masks and costumes had been exhibited at the Academy and other places, reported the *Herald* (March 24, 1858).

[93] Wilkes had resuscitated and belabored an all-but-forgotten (and long unobserved) statute passed in 1829—a year when a fad for licentious masked balls had threatened to compromise the city's morality—forbidding masquerading of any kind in New York at the penalty of $1000 fine. At Wilkes's instigation, Police Justice James H. Welsh wrote a dire open letter to Ullman warning him against breaking this law. Wilkes went so far as to claim that this momentous threat to decency had sent the State Legislature in Albany scurrying into extraordinary session, unanimously to pass a bill making the giving of a masked ball a penitentiary offense (*Porter's Spirit,* April 17, 1858, p. 105). (What with one thing and another, no fancy dress ball, with or without masks, was given.)

To satisfy those of elevated musical tastes, at each of the first ten concerts the prevailing *gaieté Parisienne* would be "relieved"—as the advertisements felicitously put it—by a solo from Thalberg[94] and two from D'Angri. Additional solos for flute, piccolo, *cornet à pistons,* oboe, bassoon, and ophicleide would be performed from time to time by Musard's virtuosos.[95]

Accordingly, at Musard's opening concert on April 12, incongruously wedged among the overtures to *William Tell* and *Fra diavolo,* Musard *père*'s quadrille *Le centième Suisse,* the "Express Train Galop," "Célestine," a polka-rondo for cornet, and "*Les Zouaves,* or The Malakoff,*" D'Angri sang the Page's aria from *The Huguenots.* And, after the prescribed promenade and sounding of the gong—between a set of variations for the ophicleide and Musard's "Military Polka"—Thalberg exquisitely played his Fantasia on *L'elisir d'amore.*

Despite all the novelty, the attractiveness of the setting, the famous soloists, and Ullman's promotional persuasiveness, the Musard concerts—instead of becoming the expected "rage"—were disappointingly received. Their poor attendance was generally attributed to the persistent cold and rain that, according to Watson, "kept the ladies indoors and the Academy of Music consequently thinly attended" (*Leslie's,* May 1, 1858, p. 347). And although the critics commented most favorably on the personable Musard's graceful and elegantly detached conducting style, his refreshing avoidance of conductorial shenanigans, his imperturbable control of his splendid orchestra,[96] and his entrancing repertory of quadrilles, polkas, waltzes and galops, it was generally hoped that—following Jullien's example—he would soon mingle his lilting dance tunes with the more meaningful music that New York audiences purportedly preferred.[97] But Musard—strictly a leader of dance music—was clearly no Jullien. And besides, as *Raimond* astutely pointed out (*Albion,* April 17, 1858, pp. 187–88), it required a great deal of adapting on both Musard's and New York's parts to reconcile their intrinsic cultural differences.[98] Thus, almost before Musard had given his first graceful downbeat, Ullman, having recognized the handwriting on the wall, lost no time in donning his mantle of kindly musical mentor to the masses, and, explaining in one of his advertisements that—now that he had successfully established Musard's supremacy as the world's greatest interpreter of music "appealing principally to the ear"—he (Ullman) would

[94] It had been a particularly formidable coup, boasted Ullman, to have captured Thalberg, who "had to be largely indemnified, as he had to give up his concert tour, which, since his arrival in this country, has netted him an average profit of $10,000 per month." Thalberg's incongruous participation in these concerts, oddly enough, raised no critical eyebrows.

[95] Consisting of Legendre (cornet), Moreau (ophicleide), Demersmann (flute), Hubens (oboe), and Artus (bassoon).

[96] At last permitting Burkhardt blissfully to imbibe that *pianissimo* for which he had endlessly thirsted, a *pianissimo* that, although produced by a great number of strings, caressed the ear "like the breath of zephyr through a leafy forest" (*Dispatch,* April 18, 1858).

[97] "His quadrilles are capital and take well with the people and are played better than any quadrille music that we ever heard," wrote Watson (*Leslie's,* April 24, 1858, p. 331), but he hoped that "evenings of classical music [would] be embraced in the month's programme of Mr. Musard's concerts. They will pay well, for the majority of our concert visitors really like the higher class of music."

[98] For all of Musard's admirable qualities, no critic was willing to accept his deafening monster quadrilles as music.

focus his attention, regardless of expense, upon the sort of "cheap and first-class permanent entertainment which ultimately must greatly contribute towards the full development of [the public's] musical taste, which, in an incredibly short time, has made such rapid progress." It had been to this admirable end, he claimed, that he had in the first place engaged Thalberg and D'Angri for the Musard concerts, and to this end, he announced, Carl Anschütz would henceforth "divide the conductorship with Mr. Musard."[99]

Whereupon, on April 15 Anschütz conducted token performances of the Overture to *Oberon* and the American premiere of a *Fackeltanz* ("Torch Dance") by Meyerbeer[100] in a program of Musard's quadrilles, otherwise "relieved" by Thalberg's *Masaniello* Fantasy and D'Angri's arias from *La cenerentola* and *Lucrezia Borgia.*

On April 19, Anschütz initiated a series of "Grand Classical Nights" with a "Berlioz Night,"[101] not only presenting four works by that problematical and seldom-heard composer but featuring—in addition to Thalberg and D'Angri—the return of Vieuxtemps, "the monarch of the violin," who had now completed his American tour and was planning an early return to Europe.[102]

Taking over the first two parts of the three-part program, Anschütz, with a "slightly reduced" orchestra,[103] conducted four works by Berlioz,[104] his Overture to *Les Francs-Juges,* the *Carnaval romain* Overture, and his orchestrations of Weber's "Invitation to the Dance" and the less familiar "Rákóczy March," listed in the papers as "Faust and Rakotzy [sic] March";[105] D'Angri sang an aria from Rossini's *Tancredi;* Thalberg played his Fantasy on *Lucrezia Borgia;* and Vieuxtemps played de Bériot's *Le Tremolo*—so magnificently, according to the *Times* (April 21, 1858), that the stalwart few who had braved that evening's violent rainstorm were "sent quite frantic."[106] The program's third part—encompassing the "dance department," as the *Times* called it—"under the graceful *batôn* of Musard, went off like a bottle of champagne."

---

[99] "Mr. Napoleon Ullman certainly understands his business," commented *Harper's Weekly* (May 1, 1858, p. 275). "Quite undismayed by the [merely] moderate success of the pure Musard music, he has not betaken himself to denouncing the public taste, but has somewhat changed his programme." This might have been a superficial reading of the situation: Ullman might indeed have been trying to establish character in the face of the mounting controversy over his projected masked balls.

[100] Which of Meyerbeer's three *Fackeltänze*—composed respectively in 1846, 1850, and 1853—was not specified.

[101] The unusual choice of the controversial composer was attributed to Ullman's projected importation of Berlioz to the United States, never, alas, realized.

[102] Reminiscent of Herz and Sivori in 1847, wherever their tours had intersected, Thalberg and Vieuxtemps had appeared together, invariably creating great sensations.

[103] "A number of superfluous drums and trombones have been dismissed and their places filled with stringed instrument performers," explained Seymour (*Times,* April 19, 1858).

[104] A program scheme disapproved by Seymour: "It is not good for the classical, nor is it beneficial to the popular portion of the programme, to have each section distinct and, as it were, warring with the other. It would be better to permit them to mingle like good friends, first an intellectual classical work, then a sparkling dance piece" (*Times,* April 26, 1858).

[105] Composed during a visit to Austro-Hungary in 1846, the "Rákóczy March" was soon incorporated by Berlioz into his "Dramatic Legend," *The Damnation of Faust* (Paris 1846).

[106] And consequently demanding "The Carnival of Venice" as an encore, to which Vieuxtemps "good-naturedly" yielded.

The Berlioz Night was repeated on April 21 and 23, and, after a rapid sequence of tempestuous events, it was followed on April 27 by an even more memorable "Beethoven Night."

But first: on April 22, immediately after the second Berlioz Night, Ullman introduced a series of Musard matinées. Considered in Paris a time of day unsuitable for this kind of musical entertainment, wrote *Raimond* (*Albion*, April 24, 1858, p. 199), here it was regarded not only as a boon to ladies but an emancipation to their spouses "from the fatal necessity of doing escort duty after dinner and sitting in a state of somnolence, like so many connubial Arguses." Too, the matinées enabled "all manner of unyoked maidens to spend their mornings [afternoons] in something more satisfactory and useful than social forays upon the characters of their friends and neighbors, or aimless 'shopping,' up and down Broadway."[107]

The program of Musard's first matinée differed little from his nightly concerts:[108] the soloists were Thalberg (*Masaniello* Fantasy), Vieuxtemps (Carnival of Venice), and D'Angri (an unidentified opera aria); Musard conducted the *William Tell* Overture and his "Zouaves," "Cattle Show," and "Express Train" quadrilles.

The second matinée precipitated a scandalous attack upon the Philharmonic Society by Ullman, their landlord at the Academy of Music, with whom relations—never harmonious—had steadily been deteriorating. At a Philharmonic Board of Directors' meeting on April 20 it had been decided to refuse Ullman's request to use the Academy for Musard's second matinée, on the afternoon of Saturday, April 24—the date of the Philharmonic's final concert of their 1857–58 season.[109] In refusing, the Society were legally within their rights: their lease with Ullman/Thalberg/Strakosch granted them the uninterrupted use of the Academy for the full day of a Philharmonic concert,[110] at the exorbitant rental of $625, customarily turned over to Ullman during the intermission of the given concert.

Although the matinée apparently did take place,[111] a vengeful Ullman—giving no advance warning—ordered the doors of the Academy, customarily opened at 7 P.M. on Philharmonic nights, to be kept locked until the rent was paid, in advance and in cash. Standing in the crowd of disgruntled and frustrated ticketholders "shivering" outside the locked Academy doors was Daniel Walker, the Philharmonic treasurer, who had brought the money for the usual payment but was unable to gain entrance to the

[107] The *Times* agreed: "No better provision can be made for these bright spring mornings than these entertainments, at which you may talk about the fashions without being frowned at by a surly amateur, or scowled at by an irate professor, as at the serious Philharmonic" (April 23, 1858).

[108] It was announced that no evening performance would be given on matinée days.

[109] The minutes of the same meeting disclose, as well, that the Philharmonic officers rejected Ullman's request to borrow some musical scores from the Society (Philharmonic Archives).

[110] Beginning with their public rehearsal in the morning and ending with the evening concert. Since the Musard orchestra employed several members of the Philharmonic, an added afternoon appearance would put a great strain upon those players and seriously compromise the quality of the Philharmonic's performance.

[111] "The poor fiddlers had a hard time of it," wrote the *Times* (April 26, 1858), "almost twelve hours of sawing. At 10 o'clock in the morning the final [public] rehearsal of the Philharmonic Society; at 3 o'clock the Musard Matinée; at 8 the concert of the Philharmonic Society."

building to satisfy Ullman's outrageous demand. Exactly how the impasse was eventually resolved is not clearly explained in the newspaper reports of the incident.

Responding to the Society's self-absolving explanation of the unfortunate affair, later issued to their subscribership and the press, Watson wrote: "This statement entirely exonerates the Philharmonic Society from all blame and throws the explanation upon Mr. Ullman. It is very evident to all that Mr. Ullman is desirous to kill off all musical entertainments but those emanating from his bureau of management. Whatever success he may have with smaller affairs, the Philharmonic Society is altogether too strong for him. Its existence is based upon the high character it has maintained through many years; it has the sympathy of the public, and it is as much an institution of New York as the Astor Place Library" (*Leslie's,* May 15, 1858, p. 379).

Strong, who, with Ellen, attended the concert, for some reason makes no mention in his journal of the contretemps.[112] His short entry for April 24 merely lists the evening's program: Mendelssohn's A-minor Symphony [no 3, op. 56]; the Overture, Scherzo, and Finale, op. 52 by Schumann (1840); and Wagner's *Tannhäuser* Overture; and adds: "This last gains on better acquaintance."[113]

The very next evening Ullman dispensed soothing unction at the scene of last night's hostilities with an Oratorio Night, Anschütz conducting, wherein sacred arias by Handel and Haydn, and—with the assistance of the *Liederkranz*—Mozart's *Requiem* were performed by D'Angri, Caradori, Tiberini, and Formes (just returned to New York, not from Europe but from a profitable tour of Boston and New England); Thalberg contributed magnificently with his *Mosè Fantasy,* as did Vieuxtemps with an unspecified "difficult fantasia." The event "only needed the 'dim, religious light' and the surroundings of a cathedral service, to make the *Requiem* the great feature of the present month's music," wrote the impressionable *Evening Post* critic (April 26, 1868). Mendelssohn's *Elijah,* announced to be in "active rehearsal," was scheduled to follow in a few days.

But on the following evening, April 26, hostilities—this time evoking physical violence—erupted in the lobby of the Academy of Music when the debarred critic John Darcie, accompanied by George Wilkes, attempted, in militant assertion of their civil rights, to present their purchased tickets to the doorkeeper. Their visit was by no means unexpected: Wilkes, who for months had been viciously pounding away at Ullman, had coolly advised him in a stiffly correct open letter, dated April 23, that on April 26 he meant to pay this unwelcome visit to the Academy together with his employee Darcie, to ascertain that Darcie was permitted the unhindered exercise of his

---

[112] Strong had recently been paying less than his usual attention to musical matters, mentioning only, on April 17, that he had "stopped at Erben's factory to hear a first-class organ just completed and destined for some Presbyterian conventicle at San Francisco."

[113] Not in Willis's opinion. Although a work of great genius, the *Tannhäuser* Overture had been overplayed, he wrote, and "After repeated hearing, the appoggiatural climax of the orchestra, ascending as it does, augmenting as it does in force, piling the musical Ossa-upon-Pelion as it continues to do, lets slip, at last, the imagination. You begin to grow weary of it, and think that it *might* have been less demonstrative; that a little less of that sort of thing would have been better" (*Musical World,* May 1, 1858, p. 277). The remainder of the program consisted of Spohr's Violin Concerto *In modo di scena cantante (Gesangsscene),* op. 47, superbly played by Henry Cooper; an English song to substitute for the *Non mi dir,* from *Don Giovanni,* sung by his vocally indisposed wife Annie Milner; and Giovanni Pacini's Duet for voice and violin, in which they collaborated. The Coopers were managed by Ullman.

honorable profession: to write his opinion of the performance for publication in Wilkes's paper.

Ullman, forewarned, prepared for their visit with a warrant for Darcie's arrest[114] and a supplementary squad of police to enforce it. Nor did Wilkes come unprepared, judging by the fortuitous presence of some of his heftier prize-fighting friends, among them the champions Johnny Lyng and Billy Mulligan, presumably no habitués of the Academy of Music.[115]

As the *Tribune* (April 27, 1858) reported the incident: Darcie, upon presenting his ticket, was roughly seized by two deputy sheriffs, and in his struggle to free himself Wilkes went to his assistance. By the time Wilkes was quelled and Darcie forcibly removed from the Academy, the melee had spread to include some of the onlookers— both casual and interested—and spilled out to the street. Among those witnessing the disturbance was Judge Russell himself, who, according to the *Herald,* happened by co- incidence to be in the Academy audience with his family that evening, but who, ac- cording to the Wilkes faction, had played a sinister part in the unsavory plot against Wilkes and Darcie.[116]

Darcie, followed by an infuriated Wilkes and his companions, was taken to a nearby station house and put in jail, but was soon released on $500 bail. Wilkes and his crew, quickly disentangling themselves from the threatening clutches of the law, defiantly returned to the Academy, where without further interference, they witnessed the remainder of the program.[117]

Although more trouble had been predicted for the following evening, the Bee- thoven Night, it went off on schedule and serenely, and Darcie was there to review it. Following the Beethoven part of the program, reported the *Evening Post* (April 28, 1858), the doorkeeper of the Academy (it was in fact Ullman's lawyer) appeared on- stage and, speaking for the Director, apologetically explained that "the difficulty which occurred last night between the Management and the Editor of *Porter's Spirit of the Times* was entirely unpremeditated and was not intended as any mark of disrespect to that gentleman, or to the honorable profession to which he belongs."[118]

Coyly referring to the recent contentiousness, Darcie wrote: "We had intended to pay a visit to this house on the Monday evening of last week, but the fates were

[114] Issued to Ullman by his alleged friend, City Judge Abraham D. Russell, on the grounds that Darcie had been "annoying [Ullman] within his place of business, and that he [Darcie] [threatened] to do so again on the evening of the 26th of April, and [that Ullman had] reasonable grounds to apprehend disturbance, difficulty, and riot, so as to interrupt his business" (*Evening Post,* July 7, 1858).

[115] In the spate of exaggerated reports that followed, the pro-Ullman *Herald* multiplied Wilkes's henchmen to a "mob of twenty-five armed rowdies."

[116] In the endless aftermath of the affair, Russell was indicted on charges trumped up by Wilkes and Darcie; the indictment was eventually quashed.

[117] The incident spawned an endless trail of legal proceedings, and—needless to say—of abusive editorials and defamatory music reviews in *Porter's Spirit of the Times.*

[118] Wilkes's account of the event claimed that Ullman had made an apology to him in person and offered to provide him and Darcie with free tickets in the future. "This we declined," declared punctilious Wilkes, "preferring to adhere to our role of entering like the rest of the general public, by paying our way." It was then that Ullman, entirely of his own volition, caused his apology to be read to the audience, asserted Wilkes, but the general wisdom had it that he had demanded Ullman's apology, or else!

adverse to our intentions, and we were compelled to postpone our visit to the following evening, when the first part of the program was devoted to that leviathan of the
old-school composers, Beethoven."

The twin glories of the evening, of course, had been the performances by Thalberg of the first movement of Beethoven's Piano Concerto in C minor and by Vieuxtemps of the first movement of the Violin Concerto, each playing his own cadenza.
Anschütz's readings of two minor Beethoven works—the overtures to Kotzebue's play
King Stephen, op. 117 (1811), and to *Die Namensfeier,* op. 115 (1814), both being heard
for the first time in the United States—were judged to be "fair" but elicited little enthusiasm. The "Pastoral" Symphony was better received because it was more familiar,
but it was just too long to sit through all four movements, especially by an audience
that would have preferred "a sprightly polka or a waltz."

In an unwontedly reflective vein (perhaps his jail experience had exerted a temporary sobering influence), Darcie maintained that serious music-listening was not yet to
be found in New York, except for the "large infusion of the German element among
us . . . [who] as scholarly musicians . . . are far ahead of all other nations in the knowledge of music, although they indulge in philosophical vagaries which are occasionally
incomprehensible to the rest of the world." The German influence, combined with
that of "melodious Italy," wrote Darcie, brought "every prospect that in another quarter of a century America will be more musically enlightened than France or England
. . . but the time has not yet come, and it is folly for us to profess a taste and discrimination in musical matters." To be absolutely honest, it had to be admitted that we
in America preferred a good tune—the *Puritani* "Liberty Duet," the *Trovatore* "Anvil
Chorus," even a good Negro melody—to the most sublime symphony ever composed.
"Every boy whistles them, but how many men who run the risk of damaging their
'Alexanders'[119] by a profuse display of applause can hum eight bars of Berlioz or Beethoven?"

Not that Darcie found fault with the introduction of serious music into a popular
program, but in doing so Ullman was merely making another clumsy attempt to imitate Jullien. And Jullien had wisely dispensed his "classic doses on homeopathic principals," choosing such works as would catch the popular fancy, and even then never performing more than a single movement at a time (*Porter's Spirit,* May 8, 1858, p. 160).

A group of Musard's fizzy dance tunes, concluding with what an irate listener
called the "Grand Slambang Galop," topped off Beethoven, and among their gaudy
cadences was interpolated an aria from Verdi's *Ernani* sung by the soprano Juliana May.
Of her performance, wrote Darcie, "the less said, the better." The other critics con-
curred.

Considering the shocking upheaval of the night before, it was surprising that Ellen Strong had gone "with Miss Leavenworth and George Anthon . . . to *Musard's* tonight," wrote her husband in his journal on April 27. "Her report is not favorable,"
he added.[120]

---

[119]*Alexandres* were a fashionable brand of French gloves, evidently preferred by opera-going
members of the Upper Ten.
[120]On April 30, Strong again chose not to accompany his wife, this time to a musical party, because "I couldn't persuade myself to . . . undergo Verdi."

The "Beethoven Night" was repeated on April 28, and on the following evening Mendelssohn's *Elijah* was presented with Formes and D'Angri, Caradori, Andem, Milner, Perring, Simpson, and the Harmonic Society. Bristow, who conducted, was evidently more amenable to encores than Anschütz; indeed so unbounded was his compliance that the concert had to be terminated before the oratorio was completed (*Evening Post,* April 30, 1858).[121]

On May 1, Thalberg and Vieuxtemps played their duo on *La sonnambula* at Musard's concert, and the next night made their "most positively last appearance in New York for the present" before departing on a joint tour of the Midwest. On this valedictory occasion—being a Sunday it was solemnly classified a "Sacred and Classical Concert"—they performed their duo on *The Huguenots* and Vieuxtemps played a properly pious solo; D'Angri and Formes sang serious arias by Haydn, Mozart, and Meyerbeer; and Anschütz repeated Beethoven's "Pastoral" Symphony, the *King Stephen* Overture, Berlioz's *Francs-Juges* Overture, and a March by Mendelssohn. Doubtless owing to the solemnity of the occasion, Musard and his quadrilles, for once, were absent.

The following Thalberg/Vieuxtemps tour, successively assisted by Juliana May, Anetta Caradori, and particularly by Elena D'Angri, came to an abrupt halt in mid-June when Madame Thalberg unexpectedly materialized from Europe and—reportedly after a chase—once and for all spirited the frolicsome Titan of the Keyboard off to the safe seclusion of the Italian vineyards she had inherited from her father, the supreme opera basso Luigi Lablache. "Private family circumstances," it was explained in the papers, had compelled Thalberg's sudden departure.[122] Vieuxtemps returned to Europe in July 1858—apparently voluntarily.

Succeeding Thalberg as the star of what remained of Musard's problematical engagement in New York, Carl Formes made his "debut as a concert singer" the following evening, May 3. He reportedly captivated Musard's audience with his great performance of Sarastro's aria from *The Magic Flute, In diesen heil'gen Hallen* (borrowed from last night's sacred concert), Schubert's "The Wanderer," and—despite his funny German accent—an exciting (according to Darcie, highly ludicrous) rendition of the elder Charles Dibdin's nautical song, "The Bay of Biscay, O."[123] In the two latter pieces Formes was excellently accompanied at the piano by his versatile colleague, the fine oratorio tenor Ernest Perring; the other soloists were Madame D'Angri and Henry Cooper, a splendid violinist, but by no means another Vieuxtemps.

On May 3, too, Musard unveiled "The Gotham Quadrille, and the Telegraph

[121] The sprightly *Post* critic found encores to be absurd in general but especially so in works of dramatic content, as in *Elijah* after he "has sung 'It is enough,' and hoped to die, going over the song and contradicting his first assertion and getting more than enough." Or *The Huguenots,* when Marcel "redouble[s] the slaughters of the final scene and the agonies of dissolution; or [when] some accommodating Richard III [has] two nightmares, instead of the one put down in acting editions of that much mutilated play."

[122] Twenty years later, as Maretzek slyly relates in *Sharps and Flats* (pp. 42–43), Madame D'Angri's granddaughter, a Mlle. Thalberg, made her debut in London as Zerlina in—most appropriately—*Don Giovanni.*

[123] Despite his limitless admiration of Formes, Burkhardt begged him not to go on giving the "Bay of Biscay, Oh-ho-ho"—wonderful as it was—as an encore to Mozart's *Heil'gen Hallen* (*Dispatch,* May 9, 1858).

Potpourri," his great American composition (obviously intended to parallel, if not surpass, Jullien's phenomenally successful "American Quadrille").♩ Beginning with "The
Star-Spangled Banner" and closing with "Yankee Doodle," the complete work comprised a few bars each of some thirty-six loosely strung together tunes. The knack of
successfully combining so many tunes, wrote Burkhardt, consisted mainly in knowing
when to stop, evidently a knack Musard did not possess.

Although his "Gotham Quadrille" was dismissed by the critics as "a musical
chaos," it was nonetheless repeated at all of Musard's remaining concerts in New York.
And, as an extra inducement, at his "Presentation Matinée" on May 8, every lady in
the audience received a gift copy of the "Express Train Galop," arranged for piano.[124]

During the concluding week of Musard's season, coinciding with Anniversary
Week,[125] two oratorios were appropriately given, *Messiah* on May 11 and—after an
intervening "Mendelssohn Night" and another all-Musard concert—*Elijah* repeated
on May 14, with the assistance of the Harmonic Society and the "patronage" of intim-
idating numbers of clergymen of New York and Brooklyn, listed in massive columns
in Ullman's newspaper advertisements.

May 11. . . . With Ellie tonight at Academy of Music. Heard the *Messiah* excellently well rendered. Formes and D'Angri and a very respectable tenor (Perring) and
soprano (Miss Milner) doing solos. It's an immense work—the *Divina commedia* of music, surviving all contemporary production.

May 12. . . . About a dozen people here tonight . . . to meet Timm, Scharfenberg, and Hoffman. . . . They gave us some vigorous four-handed music: Mozart's B-
flat [G-minor] Symphony, Mendelssohn's *Midsummer Night* music, from the Overture
to the *Hochzeits-Marsch,* and some things by Schubert. That ineffable trio of the Mozart
symphony came out as clearly on Ellie's Érard as when rendered by the Philharmonic.

Musard took his leave of New York with a matinée on May 15;[126] then, fortified
by Formes, his graceful baton, and his two remaining Parisian virtuosos, he headed for
Philadelphia, where his orchestra consisted of local musicians, and the haberdashers'
windows were bursting with "Musard caps."[127]

"The Musard concerts have been a very bad failure," on which Ullman lost his
shirt, summarized Dwight's caustic correspondent *Bellini.* The New York audiences
had been small and their enthusiasm only lukewarm when it was not absolutely zero.

[124] *"What* an inducement!" sneered ——t——. "Surely, 'Humbug is great, and Ullman is its
prophet!'" (*Dwight's,* May 8, 1858, p. 45).

[125] A giant annual celebration of Holy Week, marked by a convocation of religious and benevolent societies active throughout the Union and beyond. Thousands of delegates—predominantly
members of the clergy—not only participated in a massive schedule of meetings, conferences, delib-
erations, and lectures held in the various churches and auditoriums, but enjoyed the city's culturally
edifying activities and the hospitality officially proffered by city dignitaries and by prominent clergymen and representatives of the local philanthropic societies.

[126] At which incongruously appeared Madame Graever-Johnson.

[127] A promotional item allegedly peddled to the mens' hat trade personally by Ullman. *Dwight's*
(May 29, 1858, p. 71) described them as "frightful slouches . . . offered to snobs for 37½ cents."

But "Mons. Musard is always intensely graceful, never in earnest, for fear it might be vulgar. The ladies think him 'such a love of a man,' and *Mons.* thinks the 'American poobleek don't know good mooseek'" (*Dwight's,* May 15, 1858, pp. 52–53).

Yet, Seymour, deploring New York's backwardness in the appreciation of instrumental music, credited the Musard concerts with making a greater contribution to the cause of good music in a single week than had the Philharmonic been able to accomplish in more than half the span of their existence with their "miserable routine of four concerts a year." Burkhardt angrily disagreed (*Times,* April 19; *Dispatch,* April 25, 1858).

Nor—as Darcie had so truly observed—was the "couch managerial" an ideal bed of roses. In February, Ullman—in one of those provocative little personal asides with which he liked to pepper the amusement columns—prematurely confided to the public that his negotiations with the fabled, but still unheard, opera baritone Giorgio Ronconi had so far progressed that he might with confidence announce four opera appearances by Ronconi at the New York Academy of Music. But Ronconi unaccountably chose to remain with the Maretzek/Marshall forces, currently in the toils of a seriously disheveled season at the Philadelphia Academy of Music.[128]

When Ronconi at last appeared, he electrified Philadelphia audiences with his breathtaking portrayals of Chevreuse in *Maria de Rohan* (a role composed for him by Donizetti in 1843), William Tell in Rossini's opera, Dr. Dulcamara in *L'elisir d'amore,* Sir George Walton in *I puritani,* and Antonio in *Linda di Chamounix.* Described as unprepossessing in appearance, small in stature, neither handsome nor graceful, with a harsh, far from powerful, and not too skillfully handled, voice, and tending to sing flat, Ronconi was nonetheless hailed, after appearing as Chevreuse, as "the most extraordinary and impressive performer that . . . ever appeared on the American lyric stage. [His] every nerve seemed to thrill with intense vitality, every motion and every look was a study. No one thought of Ronconi, his figure or his voice, but became absorbed in the passion of Chevreuse" (*Philadelphia Bulletin,* cited in *Dwight's,* April 17, 1858, p. 22).

In early May, upon the stormy breakup of the Philadelphia spring opera season,[129] Ronconi, unwilling to leave the United States without having appeared in New York,[130] together with Madame de LaGrange[131]—who at last seemed truly ready to depart—bypassed Ullman and, without undue fanfare, jointly announced three autonomous opera performances at Burton's Theatre. Concurrent with Musard's farewell week at the Academy they presented, on May 10, *L'elisir d'amore;* on May 12, *Il barbiere*

---

[128] A season fraught with internecine hostilities, scandalous accusations, litigations, and finally the resignation of E. A. Marshall as business manager and backer of the Maretzek company.

[129] "The Opera season . . . came to a most unpleasant conclusion," reported *Dwight's* Philadelphia correspondent (May 15, 1858, p. 53). "Pecuniary difficulties, intrigues, plots and counterplots, quarrels, and many other concomitant features . . . hurried it to a finale somewhat premature."

[130] It would have been unthinkable, wrote Burkhardt: like visiting Rome without seeing the Pope, or being in France without going to Paris (*Dispatch,* May 9, 1858).

[131] Upon the close of Ullman's opera season, Madame de LaGrange had joined Maretzek's embattled company in Philadelphia.

di Siviglia; and on May 14, *Linda di Chamounix;* then, yielding to the public's anguished plea for at least one more performance, they repeated *L'elisir d'amore* on the afternoon of May 15, and on May 19 sailed from Boston on the *Europa,* promptly on schedule.[132]

It was, of course, Ronconi's show. No artist of his quality had ever before been seen in America (nor apparently anywhere), and the critics, breathless with wonder, vainly sought words to express their wonderment, for Ronconi functioned on a plane beyond the local critical experience. The very soul of comedy, Ronconi's personification of the quack Dr. Dulcamara, in *The Elixir of Love,* was so exquisitely conceived, wrote the critic for the *Evening Post* (May 11, 1858), that "it bordered on the painful."

To Seymour, Ronconi's voluntary "flexibility of facial muscle . . . and the remarkable facility with which he can cause a series of the most maddening wrinkles to gravitate to any given point of his face—to say nothing of a prodigious wink which he delivers with the certainty of an artillery man"—elicited such "manifestations of hearty delight" as to defy description (*Times,* May 11, 13, 1858).

Ronconi's Figaro in the *Barber of Seville*—in contrast to the popular concept of the character as "a buffoon of vehement vitality, with unequaled power of lungs and limbs"—was "altogether more finished and exact and at the same time infinitely more humorous, without being in the slightest degree boisterous," continued Seymour. "An inexhaustible fund of by-play supplies this gentleman with an absolute command of 'situations'; he makes them as he goes along, and with so little effort that it is difficult to believe they are not specified in the text. His Figaro is much more a gentleman than his Dulcamara, but as an impersonation it is equally funny. The house was kept in a constant roar. . . . There was no single drawback to a very magnificent performance."

"As a comedian, Burton could well afford to take lessons from him," wrote Darcie.[133] "He possesses a greater amount of facial flexibility and genuine humor than any other actor that we remember in modern times." And as a tragedian, "his terrible earnestness and impulsive vigour lend epic truthfulness to his portrayals, which has rarely been equaled, never excelled" (*Porter's Spirit,* May 15, 1858, p. 172).[134]

And Fry: "Great as are his powers, [Ronconi] leaves the impression of much greater things unexpressed. His force is genius and not talent—it is a spring and not a reservoir" (*Tribune,* May 11, 1858).

With the sole exception of Hagen, the critics were all happily surprised to find Ronconi's much maligned voice to be capable beyond their fondest expectations. And, with the exception of Signor Nicolao,[135] who noisily conducted a poor pickup orchestra and chorus, their cast—consisting of Claudina Cairoli, the ever-utilitarian Ma-

---

[132] Madame de LaGrange was headed, after France, for Brazil, where she reportedly received a colossal $120,000 for a two-year engagement at the Rio de Janeiro opera. She would not return to the United States until the mid-1860s, nor would Ronconi.

[133] A suggestion tantamount in the twentieth century to giving comedy lessons to Charlie Chaplin.

[134] "Who could imagine," wrote Darcie, "that the magniloquent *Dulcamara* or the gay and dashing *Figaro* was before them in the person of the heart-stricken, woebegone old man [Antonio, in *Linda di Chamounix*], whose sorrows caused the eyes to glisten, and whose intensity of emotion compelled the sympathy of all present. . . . A finer piece of acting was never witnessed" (*Porter's Spirit,* May 22, 1858, p. 192). Ronconi was indeed, as Darcie said, the Edmund Kean of the opera stage.

[135] "The conductor [was] a most excited gentleman, who treated his desk in the most violent manner," wrote Hagen (*Review and Gazette,* May 15, 1858).

dame Avogadro, Tiberini (who, too, was returning to Europe), Coletti, and an unspecified Barili—were tolerantly received.

Madame de LaGrange, who, to all intents and purposes, was departing forever, was treated with great deference (never a mention of her tremolo) and with due recognition of her extraordinary career in the United States, her goodly deeds, and her indestructible ladylikeness.[136] There was widespread condemnation, however, of her substitution of a vulgar vocal polka (presumably the "LaGrange Polka") for Donizetti's finale in *L'elisir d'amore* and, as a conclusion to *Il barbiere,* another of her razzle-dazzle display pieces.

But Ronconi! "We heard him but four times in New York," lamented Watson, "and this brief visit taught us how great a loss we were about to sustain.[137] His proper place was New York during his stay in America . . . his greatness has been wasted in the provinces" (*Leslie's,* May 20, 1858, p. 411). Watson did not mention that in New York—without benefit of managerial apparatus—Ronconi wrought his miracles before rows of empty seats.

Early in April, Ullman—albeit smarting from Ronconi's cruel defection—published joyful news in another of his little private/public confidences: he had received word from the legendary English opera impresario Benjamin Lumley (1811–1875), confirming Lumley's long-contemplated visit to the United States in September with the "entire and immense" personnel[138] of Her Majesty's Theatre, the world-famed opera house that he managed in London. The consummation of this colossal project was a great personal satisfaction, crowed Ullman, implying his active involvement in the project; it had, he claimed, been the principal purpose of his most recent visit to England.

But Ullman's euphoria turned to chagrin when Phineas T. Barnum[139] promptly stepped forward and with huge Barnumesque fanfare advertised—in a flood of pamphlets and newspaper advertisements—that at the unimaginable expenditure of some $300,000 he, Barnum, was importing Lumley and his opera and ballet forces, amounting to 148 people. Scheduled to arrive in September, informed Barnum, the company would appear in New York, Philadelphia, and Boston. The project was not a new one, he claimed: it had been the subject of long and frequent consultations with Lumley in London.[140]

---

[136] For a bittersweet account of LaGrange's tearful departure from New York, see the *Review and Gazette,* "A Scene in Broadway" (May 29, 1858, p. 163).

[137] "Somebody ought to serve an injunction on the Cunard [Steamship] Company to restrain them from taking away Ronconi," wrote the *Times* (May 17, 1858).

[138] Lumley planned to bring everyone, from his great singers and ineffable ballerinas to his scene painters, dressers, librarians; in short, the complete complex population of a major opera establishment.

[139] Barnum, who was just emerging from a sequence of financial disasters—the collapse of the Jerome Clock Company in 1856 and the subsequent destruction by fire of his palatial Connecticut estate, Iranistan—was desperately in need of a spectacular new project.

[140] As early as the year before it had been rumored that Lumley intended to bring his company to the United States (*Home Journal,* July 4, 1857), but at that time no reference was made to a collaboration with either Barnum or Ullman. It is far from unlikely, however, that then and/or later the canny Lumley had encouragingly, if not downright misleadingly, explored the comparative advantages offered by each of the competing impresarios.

Leslie's, Dartmouth College Library

At Barnum's Museum there were startling mechanical effects and splendor of mise en scène
showing the resources of his opera and ballet enterprises.

The feasibility of Barnum's scheme depended entirely upon the immediate sale, in each of the three cities—before June 10, in fact—of 800 subscriptions, each to consist of twenty tickets, one to each of twenty Lumley productions, at an outrageous five dollars apiece.[141] For local performances, continued Barnum's announcement, arrangements had been "conditionally made with Mr. Ullman, the Lessee of the Academy of Music in New York, for the use of that edifice, in which event he [would] contribute his talent and personal exertions toward carrying out this great enterprise to a successful issue."

As might be expected, Ullman did not passively accept Barnum's attempted takeover of the Lumley project. Nor did the press: "If the manager [Barnum] hopes to get five dollars admission, he is grievously mistaken," fumed the *Times* (May 17, 1858). "For an entertainment which is largely patronized by the masses, it is altogether a preposterous demand. . . . To ask five dollars where the highest price heretofore has been but two is ridiculous." Besides, we could raise a better opera company ourselves for less. And, "by the way," needled the *Times,* "it is a little curious that we do not hear Mr. Ullman's name mentioned in connection with this undertaking. He was the first to propose the scheme."

---

[141] Or, as the interesting, frustratingly unidentified new *Albion* critic (*Raimond's* unidentified successor) succinctly put it: "It seems that everything . . . will go merry as a marriage-bell if eight hundred goodly citizens and burgesses will step forward boldly and guarantee to pay one hundred dollars a piece for a season of twenty nights" (*Albion,* May 29, 1858, p. 260).

FRANK LESLIE'S ILLUSTRATED NEWSPAPER.

BARNUM'S AMERICAN MUSEUM.—
         WYMAN, THE WONDERFUL,
in his entirely new series of
                    MIRACLES,
in the way of Fascination, Divination, Demonology, Witchcraft, Spirit Rapping,
Enchantment, Ventriloquism, Magic, &c.
     Every Afternoon and Evening at 3 and at 7¾ o'clock during the week.
     Also, the GRAND AQUARIA, or Ocean and River Gardens; Living Serpents,
Happy Family, &c. &c.
          Admittance. 25 cents; Children under ten, 13 cents.

Newspaper advertisement showing the variety of entertainments Barnum offered.

Whoever might had originated the scheme soon became beside the point in the ensuing argument. Each of the men, finding himself in a tight financial squeeze and facing serious professional embarrassment, was playing a hazardous game to save his entrepreneurial skin. In the *Review and Gazette* of June 12 (p. 179), Hagen observed: 'We are afraid the $80,000 subscription required by Mr. Barnum will not be forthcoming; something," he added, wickedly twisting his double-edged knife, "which Mr. Ullman might have anticipated, as he figures in this scheme only as the lessee of the house."

In any case, Ullman's imperiled reign as supreme opera dictator depended on the defeat of Barnum's "Mammoth Opera Scheme." It is therefore not unlikely that the ensuing barrage of fault-finding newspaper editorials might have been instigated—or at least insinuated—from behind the scenes by Ullman; no less the avalanche of letters-to-the-editor, attacking the question from every conceivable point of view. Barnum, the great hero/villain of the age, was not only vilified and ridiculed, but also bombarded with friendly advice. Opera as an entity was praised, maligned, glorified. Even Luigi Arditi,♪♫ now conducting at Lumley's far-off opera house, was unkindly designated by *An Opera-Goer* as "the worst conductor in London," far inferior to Maretzek or Anschütz, and certainly the last thing we needed over here.[142]

Then, at the peak of the hullabaloo, a startling announcement in the *Times* (June 7): "Mr. Ullman left suddenly for Europe at a moment's notice, in an overcrowded steamer, and in circumstances which indicate some extraordinary inducements. It is hinted that he is to proceed posthaste to London to effect a speedy engagement with certain stars.[143] Mr. Barnum is also to leave for Europe in a day or two, probably to

[142] As, wrote the *Opera-goer,* was the opera ballet: "that pet attraction of an aristocracy past the middle age, but yet vicious. Hitherto we [Americans] have denied the soft impeachment of twinkling legs and have failed to appreciate that stimulating 'poetry in motion' which bald-headed peers discover through the powerful glasses of their lorgnettes." But never fear. "If Mr. Lumley supplies the same conveniences for going behind the scenes at the Academy that he does at his London establishment, we may pick up something of a special knowledge" (*Times,* June 2, 1858).

[143] Particularly Lumley's most celebrated *prima donna,* Marietta Piccolomini (1834–1899), who would make her debut at the Academy of Music on October 20, 1858.

give attention to his enterprise.[144] In the meantime," slyly added the *Times,* "the opera at the Academy gets on famously, without a manager."

Notwithstanding the tensions attendant on his sudden departure, Ullman had found a suitable, if surprising, tenant to occupy the Academy while he was away. As it expediently came about, his mortal enemy Max Maretzek, with a dispossessed opera troupe on his hands, was in as great need of a performance place as Ullman was in need of a subtenant. At last the partners Ullman and Maurice Strakosch, as Maretzek relates in *Sharps and Flats* (p. 44), "had come to the conclusion to arrange a *modus vivendi* between ourselves."

"How Maretzek and Ullman could so far forget their time-honoured feuds as to permit an arrangement of this description," reproached an aggrieved Darcie, "is a mystery only known to opera *impresarios* who declare war to the knife upon each other one day, and kiss and make up the next" (*Porter's Spirit,* May 15, 1858, p. 172). Thus it transpired, despite all previous hostilities, that Maretzek and the key members of his opera troupe—Gazzaniga, Brignoli, Gassier, and Amodio—once again moved into the Academy of Music. Now presumably without a backer, for the remaining month of their contract with Maretzek the singers had organized as a "Commonwealth," or co-operative,[145] with a paternal William H. Paine to look after their business affairs. On May 31 they opened with a fine performance of *La favorita,* "certainly among Donizetti's best, poor and thin as it is," patronizingly wrote George Templeton Strong, who was present.

Unlike Strong, to the true opera aficionado it was like old times—so comforting to have Max, resplendent in white neckcloth and all, again in the conductor's chair where he belonged—and such balm to the soul to hear again the Verdi and Donizetti standbys so beautifully performed by one's old favorites. As soon as they reappeared at the Academy, wrote the *Albion* (June 5, 1858, pp. 271–72), the Barnum/Lumley chimera faded—suddenly it ceased to evoke even a "bubble of excitement." Perhaps if it had been possible to withhold all opera from New York until September, the infamous five-dollar tickets might have "gone off as rapidly as cheap soup-tickets in a hard winter." But now we had been saved. There were lessons to be learned: by Ullman, to produce palatable operas that people wanted to hear instead of ersatz, "strong infu-

---

[144] There never was an enterprise as far as Lumley was concerned, later contended the *Herald* (August 31, 1858). An unrelenting foe of Barnum's, the *Herald* alleged that on the flimsy basis of a single, casual conversation with Lumley, Barnum had issued his famous prospectus, with its infamous subscription scheme. In fact, Lumley had been mostly silent on the entire matter: "He simply allowed Barnum to try the temper of the American people and pave the way for the joint enterprise of Lumley and Ullman," wrote the *Herald.* Barnum had been "out-generaled and completely knocked off his feet by this English manager."

[145] The very opera artists who in past times of need had disdained a reduction of salary, wrote Darcie, now agreed to "do a little of the speculative on their own accounts, singing for the nightly receipts, after payment of current and necessary expenses of rent, gas, printing, and payment of necessary subordinates," a likely supply of whom were always available in New York (*Porter's Spirit,* May 29, 1858, p. 208). With crowds of visitors pouring into New York at this season, the Commonwealth's financial success was assured, he wrote: going to the Italian opera was a prerequisite of the out-of-town visitor's sightseeing agenda.

sions" by Meyerbeer; by Barnum, that "the soul of Speculation is Monopoly" (something he should have known).

For a short spell the "Commonwealth," or "Associated Artists," as they variably called themselves, performed the good old chestnuts in a radiant atmosphere of peace and amity. Gazzaniga (recently widowed while in Havana) enjoyed the ideal privilege of being the only *prima donna* in town:[146] Adelaide Phillips beautifully performed the big contralto roles—the Azucenas and the Maffio Orsinis; wooden Brignoli and fat Amodio were sounding gloriously these days; Gassier was a perpetual delight; and Max was reported, between operas, to be happily cultivating his farm on Staten Island.[147]

On June 21—after performances of *La favorita, La traviata, Linda di Chamounix, Lucrezia Borgia,* two acts of *Masaniello* (with an unlikely Amodio dancing an obese tarantella) paired with the last act of *La favorita* at a fifty-cent matinée, and, of course, *Il trovatore*—the Commonwealth came forth with a new opera, *Saffo* (Naples 1840),♪ by the contemporary Italian composer Giovanni Pacini. At least, it was advertised as a new opera, but some still remembered its inauspicious local premiere in 1847 by the great visiting Havana Opera Company, when the title role had been sung by Fortunata Tedesco.♪♫

This time receiving a more favorable press, the work reportedly allowed Gazzaniga great dramatic scope. She was supported by Adelaide Phillips (receiving ever more laudatory reviews), Brignoli, Gassier, and, from the local opera storehouse, the tenor Timoleone Barattini and the baritone William Müller. *Saffo* received three performances, the second of which was unhappily attended by George Templeton Strong.

June 24. . . . Went with Ellie, Miss Josephine Strong, and George Anthon to hear the driveling opera of *Saffo* by Pacini. Such absolutely *galling* commonplace is fortunately uncommon. The Gazzaniga, who is very pleasant to hear and see, did her best to redeem it, but the performance was dreary and afflictive.

On June 26, the Associated Artists closed their season with a performance of *La traviata,* given as a matinée at the request of a group of out-of-town visitors. Then followed the benefits, now more needful than ever, it was explained, for, despite the surface euphoria, the seventeen opera performances of the past month had brought in

---

[146] A position she had not enjoyed in Havana, where her rivalry with Frezzolini had bordered on violence. But in New York she created a "furore" all her own, defined in the *Albion* as a "state of being called out after every act and subjected to a vast amount of noise, punctuated with bouquets. On Wednesday night [after her performance of *Lucrezia Borgia*], the members of the orchestra and chorus became enthusiastic. . . . They prepared an ambuscade for Madame Gazzaniga, and when that lady left the Academy, she was instantly seized, placed in a carriage, surrounded by blazing torches, headed by a brass band, and thus carried in triumph to her residence at the Everett House, where, under the flimsy pretext of a serenade, the enthusiasts presented the lady with big drums and trumpets" (*Albion,* June 12, 1858, p. 283).

[147] "All our opera managers are in Europe, with the solitary exception of Mr. Maretzek, who, secure of his Cuba, reposes like a voluptuary in the fragrant groves of Staten Island, and takes the world at his ease. Mr. Ullman, Mr. Barnum, and Mr. Strakosch are essaying all sorts of pretty coquetries with Mr. Lumley, who appears to be the despot of the European operatic world" (*Albion,* July 10, 1858, pp. 331–32).

barely enough to pay the "working expenses of the house," and left nothing for the artists,[148] splendid though they had been (*Herald,* June 30, 1858).

The *Herald* sought excuses for this failure: the expected droves of out-of-town visitors had been fewer and more frugal than expected; the rains had discouraged attendance, as had the scalding temperatures—95 degrees and higher. Too, the *Herald* regarded the parsimonious reduction of the orchestra and chorus as a severe audience deterrent: a dollar saved by this means effectively kept another ten dollars out of the box office. But the most important obstacle to the season's financial success had been not the lack of a manager, but "too many managers." No self-managed cooperative theatrical company had ever succeeded, wrote the *Herald,* citing the failure of the splendid Artists' Union Italian Opera Company in 1852.♪

Yet, managers had their place in the world: "Artists want an energetic manager to rule over them, and the public must be stirred up by the manager before they will go. The success of the Opera lies just as much with the manager as with anything else. Ronconi failed to attract, simply because he was not well managed."

Unhappily, this truism did not apply to Musard, who, despite a surfeit of management,[149] attracted fewer and lesser audiences in Philadelphia than in New York, and after returning to New York, still fewer and lesser than in Philadelphia. Left in the care of Ullman's friend and assistant Jacob Gosche, Musard "the imperturbable," and his incongruous musical mate Anschütz, after their disastrous "tour," launched a short-lived season of promenade concerts[150] at a newly resplendent New York Academy of Music on July 12. During the two weeks' interval since the close of the Commonwealth opera season,[151] the Academy had undergone another of its transformations, appearing now as a brightly colored *jardin d'été,* a Promenade Fairyland, fragrant with flowers, trees, exotic plants, and shrubbery.[152] "The entire parquette had been floored over level with the footlights," reported the *Musical World* (July 24, 1858, p. 466), "thus offering to the audience a magnificent promenade round the orchestra . . . but nothing could induce them to avail themselves of the opportunity thus afforded; a few solitary individuals did occasionally make an attempt to cross the platform, but, finding themselves objects of attraction . . . they speedily made inglorious retreat to the back of the lobbies." (Americans were evidently as temperamentally unfitted for promenade concerts as was George Templeton Strong for Italian opera.) Thus, despite the magnificent

[148] Worse, the artists had reportedly sustained actual losses: Gazzaniga, $68; Brignoli, $31; Gassier, $25; and Amodio, $15.68 (*Herald,* July 7, 1858). Maretzek had unwittingly donated his services for the season, and it may be that he and his former company, which now disbanded, parted on less than amicable terms.

[149] "Musard perished (popularly) of aggravated puffing," wrote *Dwight's* gossip columnist (September 6, 1858, p. 163).

[150] In ill-considered competition with the nightly promenade concerts conducted by Thomas Baker at the Palace Garden (or Gardens), a popular new open-air establishment at Sixth Avenue and Fourteenth Street.

[151] Giving way to the great German Festival Concert given at the Academy of Music on June 27, with its attendant "pic-nic" the following day at Jones's Wood, and subsequent German festivities held there involving Anschütz and Maretzek; see following OBBLIGATO.

[152] Contributing further to the delightful atmosphere at the Academy, it was noted that "the rustling of the ladies dresses [kept] up a novel and pleasing system [or illusion] of ventilation" (*Times,* July 12, 1858).

ambience, the fine orchestra of sixty of the city's best musicians, and the excellent soloists—Madame Zimmermann (Madame Anschütz), Messrs. Perring, Weinlich, Sedgwick, and little Master Sedgwick—and despite the solicitous puffing of the *New-York
Times,* the promenade concerts struggled on for a scant week, then ceased to be.

Their demise occurred at a most unfortunate moment (at least, from a managerial
point of view), leaving the Academy empty at a time when the city was bursting with
visitors in carnival spirits, deliriously celebrating the joining, in mid-Atlantic on August 5, 1858, of the American and British ends of the transatlantic cable. The achievement, crowning four years of trial and error, was largely credited to the inextinguishable courage and determination of the visionary American financier, Cyrus W. Field
(1819–1892); it was therefore regarded (on this side of the cable, at least) as an American national achievement. It was hoped (alas, prematurely) that the two continents
were now indissolubly joined in eternal communication,[153] but after the exchange of
a few congratulatory greetings between Queen Victoria and President Buchanan, the
cable came apart and the dialogue was interrupted, not to be durably resumed until
1866.

For now, however, the nation was ablaze with celebratory fervor. In New York,
on August 17, great masses of people assembled to witness the spectacular fireworks:
"showers of rockets, which attained an incredible altitude" set off—of all places—
from the roof of City Hall, which "like the transformation of a fairy castle, became a
palace of light. All the windows were simultaneously illuminated, and, with the aid of
three thousand, seven hundred, candles, the Hall of the City Fathers shone resplendent
in the surrounding gloom. A shout of admiration followed, and cheers for the cable
succeeded.

"Dodworth's Band, which were stationed on a commodious stand near the East
Gate, then struck up 'Hail Columbia,' which was followed by 'God Save the Queen,'
and they continued during the night to play popular and enlivening airs. At each gate,
crimson, green, and other [colored] fires were ignited, and until the close of the evening, continued to burn brilliantly. Rockets, shells, balloons of candles, shells with colored stars, colored bengaloos [*sic*], and flights were then fired from the roof of the Hall
until it presented the appearance of a roaring crater . . . of a smoking Vesuvius" (*Herald,* quoted in *Harper's Weekly,* August 28, 1858, p. 550).

It was not long before this thrilling illusion became unfortunate fact. At a replay
of the event a week later, as we learn from an acerbic Strong, the "triumphant pyrotechnics with which our city fathers celebrated this final and complete subjugation by
man of all the powers of nature—space and time included," precipitated the incinera-
tion of the cupola and half the roof of New York's City Hall, which consequently pre-

---

[153] The news from two continents now,
Is sent through the depths of the sea,
While the fishes, all wagging their tails,
Cry, Gracious, how Wise we shall be.
Times, August 7, 1858

Pulling Atlantic Cable ashore in small rowboats.

Salute of rowboat men to Captain who hauled it ashore.

Telegraphic messages of the Queen and the President.

sented "a most draggled and crestfallen appearance, all singed and reeky and shorn of its headpiece" (Private Journal, August 24, 1858; *Diary,* II, 410).[154]

On August 30, at the peak of the cable excitement, Max Maretzek, with an unaccustomed minimum of fanfare, reopened the Academy of Music for a "short season"

[154] At Trinity Church, where a more restrained commemoration was held on September 1, Strong admired the magnificent floral decorations but did not attend the ceremonies, wherein the city dignitaries—not only of New York, but of Brooklyn, Jersey City, and Hoboken—joined in stately procession with an assemblage of clergymen in white surplices. With Hodges at the organ, a choir of twenty-eight singers and soloists supplied the music, which consisted—besides the requisite "Hail Columbia" and "God Save the Queen"—mostly of Hodges's sacred compositions (*Musical World,* September 11, 1858, p. 578; Messiter, pp. 66–67). For the great official celebratory concert by the Harmonic Society on September 1, see the following OBBLIGATO.

Celebration of Atlantic Cable in Trinity Church.

SEPT. 18. 1858.]

MISCELLANEOUS.

TIFFANY & CO.,

No 550 BROADWAY, NEW YORK,
announce that they have secured the entire balance
of the
ATLANTIC TELEGRAPH SUBMARINE CABLE,
Now on board the
U S STEAM FRIGATE NIAGARA.

In order to place it within the reach of all classes, and
that every family in the United States may possess a specimen of this wonderful mechanical curiosity, they propose
to cut the Cable into pieces of four inches in length, and
mount them neatly with brass ferules.
Each piece will be accompanied with a copyrighted facsimile certificate of
CYRUS W. FIELD, ESQ.,
that it is cut from the genuine Cable. Twenty miles of it
have been actually submerged and taken up from the
bottom of the Ocean. This will be first sold in precisely
the condition in which the great Cable now lies in the bed
of the Atlantic.
Orders will be received from dealers and others for not
less than 100 pieces at a time, at $25 per hundred. Retail
price, 50 cents each.
Each order must be accompanied by the money, in funds
current in New York, as it will not be possible to open accounts. A register will be kept of the orders as they are
received, which will be filled in turn without favor or par-
tiality.
A large portion of the specimens will be ready, it is expected, for delivery within a week.
NEW YORK, August 21st, 1858.   144-146

Tiffany advertisement on
the celebration day.

Celebration in the street.

of opera, not, as one might expect, with his longtime stars Gazzaniga, Brignoli, and Amodio, but with two newcomers: a Spanish *prima donna* Pepita (*née* Josefa) Gassier★ (1821–1866), popular in London,[155] and a tenor Luigi Stefani★ (or Steffani) from the San Carlo and La Scala opera houses. Both, announced Maretzek, were engaged for his coming winter season in Havana, for which the present engagement would serve as a kind of dress rehearsal/preview.

According to Maretzek (*Sharps and Flats,* p. 44), his truce with Ullman and Strakosch provided, in exchange for relinquishing his spring and summer seasons in Philadelphia and Boston, and "for a small sum of money . . . that I might have a preliminary fall season [at the Academy] to rehearse and prepare my company for Havana, and that sometimes we should exchange artists. This agreement" he adds, "was kept on both sides for more than a year."

"The impresarii of the Italian opera have harmonized, for once," corroborated the *Herald* (September 1, 1858), and explained that their agreement had been based on a non-invasive division of territory: Maretzek to possess Havana; Strakosch the "rising cities of the West," and Ullman the Academy of Music, with such superstars as Piccolomini and Formes (see *Sharps and Flats,* p. 44).

The agreement did not, however, prevent the mounting of an immediate, concurrent, and highly competitive opera season by one of the co-signatories. On the heels of Maretzek's opening at the Academy, his kinsman, former protégé, sometime partner, and present rival, Maurice Strakosch, brought his touring opera company[156] into Burton's Theatre for a "short season." Strakosch, too, was introducing two new artists: a vivacious "French" (Belgian) *prima donna,* Pauline Colson (1833–?), whom he puffed as the possessor not only of a glorious voice, but of "youth, beauty, and genius" (a rubric that for some reason aroused the collective outrage of the critical/journalistic fraternity),[157] and, less controversially, Marcel Junca, a massive French *basso profundo.* Both were popular favorites in New Orleans, where for the past three years they had been appearing at the Théâtre d'Orleans.[158] Strakosch had also acquired Maretzek's former stars Brignoli and Amodio, and would soon acquire Gazzaniga as well, thus—in despite of Maretzek and Ullman—gaining a monopoly of the opera field with a company unrivaled in the United States.

To create the illusory appearance of fraternal goodwill, Strakosch scheduled his performances at Burton's on the "off nights" at the Academy, allowing opera-loving New Yorkers to hear as many as six different operas in a given week without prejudice to either company. "There is such a wonderful amount of amiability in the selection of the opera nights at [Burton's]—Tuesday, Thursday, and Saturday"—babbled the New-York *Times* (September 15, 1858), "that we are justified in believing it is more

---

[155] Madame Gassier, the wife of the baritone Louis Gassier, had enjoyed operatic triumphs at Drury Lane in 1855; she later appeared as the vocal soloist at Jullien's Covent Garden concerts.

[156] An offshoot of his successful concert company.

[157] This three-word "preparatory announcement," as Watson called it, had "given great offense to some of the writers of the press." What humbug! he indignantly wrote. The critics notoriously depended upon the managers for information upon which to base their critical judgments, and now this! (*Leslie's,* September 25, 1858, p. 265).

[158] Upon being engaged by Strakosch, Madame Colson reportedly hastened from New Orleans to Paris to study her opera roles in Italian, a language she did not until then command.

MAX MARETZEK, THE GREAT AMERICAN IMPRESARIO.
FROM AN AMBROTYPE BY BRADY.

Leslie's, Dartmouth College Library

Max Maretzek.

in a spirit of good fellowship than of opposition that Mr. Strakosch has inaugurated his 'season'." Not so, as soon became all too evident.

Maretzek, in the meantime, scheduled to open on August 30 with *La sonnam-bula,*[159] was faced with a desperate problem. Due to the unfortunately delayed arrival of his *primo tenore,* and with no likely alternate available, he had no choice but to cast Ernest Perring as Elvino, opposite the Madame Gassier's debut as Amina. An improb-able substitute:[160] worthy oratorio singer though he was, Perring had never before trodden the operatic boards, nor, purportedly, had he—until three days prior to the

[159] *La sonnambula* had been scheduled to be repeated on September 1, but was shifted to August 31 to avoid conflict with the great Atlantic cable celebration.

[160] Maretzek's advertisements artfully treated his unlikely choice of Perring as a response to "the demands of many professional persons and intelligent connoisseurs who appreciate the young and rising young *tenore,* Mr. Perring" (currently the solo tenor in the Calvary Church Choir). It offered Perring "a fair chance in Opera" before the arrival of Signor Stefani.

performance—ever been faced with the role of Elvino. A terrifying ordeal for Perring, it could hardly have been less frightening for Madame Gassier, but she bore it admirably and was more than favorably compared with Madame de LaGrange.[161]

Although it was known that she was the wife of Louis Gassier, who had made a lightning trip to England to fetch her, and although she was said to enjoy an enviable reputation in the opera houses of London and the Continent, Madame Gassier was not known here; the tenor Stefani even less so; and still less the other new members of the cast, Giovanni Garibaldi, a splendid young baritone, and one Pierini, a dubious *basso buffo*.[162] Yet, Maretzek did not supply the extravagant introductory ballyhoo to which the public had become conditioned.

On the day of his opening, ostensibly to justify his reticence but actually to disparage his adversary's advertising tactics, Maretzek—a subtle Machiavelli—explained in a card that he had wished to avoid being accused of "preliminary puff and notice, from a conviction that of late years it has been so excessively and commonly employed for every class of artist [that] it had become rather injurious than otherwise. . . . Many recent failures had convinced him that no degree of written reputation may insure a success."[163] It was, he implied, actually a service to his singers not to have praised them in advance.[164]

Both Madame Gassier and Stefani, once safely arrived, were glowingly received by the critics. Not only was Madame Gassier said to equal—even surpass—LaGrange in vocal pyrotechnics, but to possess the best voice locally heard in many a year. Hers was the most successful debut within the *Times*'s (apparently restricted) memory (August 31, 1858).

Although not handsome, Madame Gassier possessed "excellent points. . . . Her raven hair and dark eyes, full of enthusiasm and passion, [betokened] her Spanish nativity," wrote the *Post* (August 31, 1858). Darcie, however, described her as "the plumpest little rice-bird in the world, with the throat of a nightingale" and a face of "that type of Spanish beauty and figure [possessing] that charming *embonpoint*, which would," he leered, "win a hermit from his cell, or a monk from his cloister" (*Porter's Spirit*, September 4, 1858, p. 16). And vocally she was as exact and certain as was Madame de LaGrange (whose style she recalled), but "without being nearly so worn" (*Albion*, September 4, 1858, pp. 427–28).

On September 3, Luigi Stefani created a furor as the Duke of Mantua in *Rigoletto*. Combining a fine stage presence and great ease of manner with a perfectly magnificent voice (he was said to have mastered the secret of singing without getting red in the

[161] Except by Watson, who found her execution, although reasonably "rapid and brilliant," to be less perfect than those of LaGrange, Laborde, or Sontag (*Leslie's*, September 11, 1858, p. 233).

[162] For the rest, the company included, of course, Louis Gassier and Adelaide Phillips, also Alessandro Gasparoni, Mauro Assoni, and sundry utility singers drawn from the local opera bank, as the occasion demanded. Maretzek's co-conductor was again Angelo Torriani, a casualty of the recent Philadelphia opera fiasco; his stage manager was Amati Dubreuil.

[163] The failure of Musard being a case in point.

[164] "It is something in [Madame Gassier's] favor," wrote the suggestible *Times* (August 30, 1858), "that Mr. Maretzek has not thought it necessary to resort to the low circus-trick of publishing her 'points' [in posters] on every dead wall in the city," as, presumably, Madame Colson's points had been exhibited.

face), he offered yet another best debut ever witnessed by the *Times* (September 4, 1858). And again: "We have had no such singer of late years." So great was the furor over Stefani, wrote the *Times,* that Madame Gassier, the excellent Gilda, was nearly overlooked.

But not by Darcie, who found her to be a divine Gilda; he particularly admired her womanly modesty in shunning the usual male attire in the last act, and instead wrapping herself in a mantle, in which she could perfectly well pass for a man without resorting to all that indecent exposure (*Porter's Spirit,* September 11, 1858, p. 32).

Darcie was enchanted, too, as were his colleagues, with the *Barber of Seville,* which followed on September 6. Such a Rosina as Madame Gassier's, he wrote, had not been seen since the days of Malibran and Sontag. In the lesson scene she breathtakingly sang the "Carnival of Venice," vocalizing to perfection Vieuxtemps's diabolically difficult violin variations, and as a finale she sensationally negotiated the acrobatics of the spectacular waltz composed for her by Luigi Venzano.[165] Gothamites, wrote Darcie, should swear out a collective warrant prohibiting Madame Gassier from ever going to Cuba.

Louis Gassier, superb as Figaro (as in every role he sang) surpassed himself in this performance; Pierini, a tall, thin, comic/lugubrious-looking fellow, made a wonderfully eccentric Don Basilio; Gasparoni was an indifferent Dr. Bartolo; and Domenico Labocetta—"courteously" loaned for the occasion (according to the terms of the agreement) by his manager Maurice Strakosch—was, as always, an ideal Almaviva.

On September 10, Maretzek added to his repertory the operatic hit of hits, *Il trovatore,*[166] with Stefani creating "a second furore" as Manrico; on September 11 *The Barber of Seville* was repeated as a fifty-cent matinée; and on September 13, on the eve of Strakosch's opening, *Lucia di Lammermoor* was presented with Madame Gassier as a brilliant Lucia and Stefani a sensational Edgardo.[167]

The following evening Pauline Colson made her bow at Burton's in *La figlia del reggimento.* Carefully scrutinized for her three highly mooted attributes,[168] she was judged indeed to possess youth and beauty and perhaps a tiny, future germ of the third attribute. For the present, she had a fresh soprano voice,[169] knew how to use it, was a splendid actress, was vividly—perhaps too vividly—"Frenchy" in vocal delivery and persona (a characteristic that would take some getting used to), dressed tastefully, and carried herself with great self assurance; she radiated "an immense amount of dash."

[165] Patania, with Gottschalk at the piano, had lamely attempted it in 1856, remembered Darcie.

[166] "That everlasting and horrible *Trovatore,* with which every manager and every street organ-grinder has nauseated the city," raged Burkhardt. "Let them do the sledge hammer chorus at free concerts, in bar-rooms, or at the Ethiopian performances—let them do *Trovatore* in English at minor theatres, or in French, or in German, or in Greek—we have done writing about it" (*Dispatch,* September 18, 1858).

[167] Indeed, almost too sensational: "He acts with such fervor, and is so easily stimulated by applause, that he is very apt to go a step beyond the boundaries of true art," and of his voice. But Stefani had "the finest tenor voice ever heard in New York," and in the "tearful finale" of *Lucia,* although a bit vigorous for a death scene, he had been excelled only by Salvi and Mario (*Times,* September 18, 1858).

[168] By now, "youth-beauty-genius" had become a catch phrase on the lips of all New York.

[169] Despite, according to some critics, a wobble, indulgently referred to, in her case, as a typically Gallic vocal trait.

*Pauline Colson in two different
costumes for her performances.
Having made her first appearance
on stage at 13 during a youth
of poverty, she had grown into
an indomitable presence.*

With a cast that included Labocetta as Tonio (mediocre), Ettore Barili as Sergeant Sulpizio (bad, bad) and a chorus and orchestra miserably conducted by an unspecified Mollenhauer (probably Edward),[170] Strakosch's opera season got off to a middling start. On September 18, however, after a repeat performance of *La figlia* (September 16), Colson appeared as Violetta in *La traviata* and suddenly—startlingly—she manifested her full possession of the third attribute.[171]

Why had she not made her debut in this role? demanded the stunned critics, most of whom found her Violetta of a magnificence to excel even Gazzaniga's. Although Colson still retained some of her essential "Frenchiness" in the role, the *Times* (September 20, 1858) doubted "if the music [had] ever been more accurately sung, or the play more truly acted, as a whole." Undeniably, "there were *scenas* which could not, of course, be compared with Mme. Gazzaniga's, but while we missed the superb Italian genius of that lady, we were spared many of the inaccuracies which always marred her efforts in brilliant vocalization."

To the less susceptible *Albion* critic, however, it was unthinkable that Colson should be permitted to appear as Violetta "when the company boasts of Madame Gazzaniga, who is unquestionably the finest impersonation of that character we have ever had in this city." There was no comparison, he wrote, between Gazzaniga's towering tragic genius and the obvious tricks of a "second class French actress, playing constantly to the audience . . . and generally overdoing things in a piquant way. . . . In many points of pure art, however," abruptly about-faced the critic, "Madame Colson is decidedly the best Violetta we have yet heard" (*Albion*, September 25, 1858, p. 464).

Gazzaniga, purportedly about to return to Europe, appeared with the Strakosch company on September 21 as Leonora in *Il trovatore,* repeating the role on September 24 and 27, with Amalia Strakosch as Azucena, and Brignoli and Amodio, as of old, in the roles of Manrico and the Count di Luna. On September 28, Gazzaniga appeared as Lucrezia Borgia at the mangled opera debut of the new basso Marcel Junca,[172] and on September 30, at her benefit, she took her leave of the company with again the first two acts of *Lucrezia Borgia* followed this time by the last act of *La favorita,* movingly performed with Brignoli.

Ignoring Strakosch's performance schedule, Maretzek, on September 18, a Saturday, diminished the attendance at Colson's debut in *La traviata* that evening by giving a fifty-cent matinée of *Lucrezia Borgia* at the Academy.[173] Suddenly, all pretence of an amicable professional relationship between the two men was abandoned.

[170] "We have seldom listened to a performance more wretchedly dissonant," complained the *Albion* (September 25, 1858, p. 464). "Why does not Mr. Strakosch conduct? Compared with Mr. Mollenhauer he is a perfect [Michael] Costa."

[171] Appearing with Colson were Brignoli, a good Alfredo, and Amodio, a superb Germont.

[172] "After the second act the stage manager, Mr. Moore, announced that in consequence of unavoidable consequences the last act of 'Lucrezia' would be omitted and the fourth act of the 'Trovatore' substituted for it. It was said that the orchestra parts of the last act of 'Lucrezia' were missing and that Mr. Strakosch's illness . . . prevented the rectifying of the error of some of his subordinates. At any rate, there was no more 'Lucrezia'" (*Herald,* September 29, 1858).

[173] Featuring Anetta Caradori, who, according to Burkhardt (*Dispatch,* September 25, 1858), was a great artist. Unfairly treated by Ullman and correspondingly overlooked by the journalists, he wrote, she had been recognized for her true worth by Maretzek, who had secured her for Havana. Maretzek's old tenor, Giuseppe Guidi, also engaged for Havana, was the Gennaro, Adelaide Phillips the excellent Orsini, and Giovanni Garibaldi the Duke Alfonso.

A musical tug of war had been inevitable from the start, wrote the *Times* (September 21, 1858), adding, with tongue in cheek: "The first tug, we feel bound to confess, came from Mr. Strakosch. It was a sinful thing in that gentleman to announce that he possessed the only artist who combined youth and beauty with genius. No responsible manager could be expected to thus having his nose tweaked without dreaming of revenge." Although on the surface Maretzek's reaction had been a model of gentle forbearance combined with "a fine manly sorrow and lamentation anent the arts of the deceiver . . . everyone knew that it was nothing more than the graceful curling of the smoke from a lighted fusee, and that presently there would be an explosion."

The *Times* listed the troops marshalled beneath the opposing operatic banners,[174] referring to the Ullman and Maretzek forces as a united army, suggesting that a radical—indeed inconceivable—shift in managerial alliances had come about[175] with the emergence of Strakosch as a serious common threat. Compromise had evidently not been possible: "Mr. Strakosch is determined to go on, and Messrs. Maretzek and Ullman are determined to give him a lesson. The slightest provocation," wrote the *Times,* "will lead to operatic performances six times a week at Burton's and at the Academy. A hasty word will certainly provoke a like number of matinées, whilst a trifling act of indiscretion will bring down the prices to fifty cents."[176]

And that is just how the ugly situation evolved: "Strakosch one evening reduced his prices to fifty cents, and Maretzek immediately followed his example. Thereupon did Strakosch resume his old prices and insert in his advertisements [for his closing performance] a cutting remark about the success of the opera at a theatre [Burton's] where people *could see and hear*—a bit of irony that is calculated to make the monstrous human shaped caryatides♩ of the Academy of Music hang down their heads and blush for very shame" (*Dwight's,* October 2, 1858, p. 221).

These tit-for-tat tactics became further aggravated when Maretzek on September 24 (at full prices) produced his major effort of the season, an ambitious revival of Rossini's *William Tell,* a work he had introduced with great success in 1855.♩ In addition to a huge cast headed by Gassier as a splendid Tell and Stefani as a fine, although vocally ailing,[177] Arnoldo, Bertucca Maretzek as Matilda and Elise Siedenburg as Jemmy,

---

[174] The Strakosch corps consisted of Mesdames Colson, Gazzaniga, Parodi, de Wilhorst, and Messrs. Brignoli, Amodio, Junca, and Labocetta; the Maretzek/Ullman forces, counting the newly engaged artists yet to appear, comprised Piccolomini, Laborde, Euphrosine Poinsot, Johanna Wagner (a no-show), the Gassiers, Stefani, Formes, Adelaide Phillips, and "a park of smaller guns, to say nothing of four redoubtable conductors: Messrs. Maretzek, Torriani, Anschütz, and [Emanuele] Muzio" (1825–1890)—the last a friend, pupil, and worshipful disciple of Verdi.

[175] Ullman, after a productive four-month stay in Europe, had returned—full of schemes—in mid-September. The Ullman/Maretzek rapprochement was confirmed in the *Musical World* (November 6, 1858, p. 707).

[176] In an editorial headed "The Fight for the Operatic Championship," George Wilkes, in *Porter's Spirit of the Times,* reported the operatic duel in boxing-ring lingo: "Maretzek first made a movement with his powerful Gassiers, then feinted with Perring, following up this stratagem with a good hit with his Stefani. Strakosch stopped him cleverly with Colson, and then countered heavily, right and left, with Amodio and Brignoli, at the same time bringing his Gazzaniga into play with good effect. The consequences of these rapid exchanges were plainly visible; and both combatants retired to their respective corners, slightly puffing—in the newspapers" (September 25, 1858, p. 57).

[177] Attributed by some to a cold, by others to Stefani's unfortunate compulsion to strain his voice beyond its already large capabilities. Due to his indisposition on this occasion, the better part of the last act had to be curtailed.

the production offered the superlative Ronzani Ballet, featuring their *prima ballerina* Mlle. Louise Lamoureaux,[178] an augmented chorus of "upwards of fifty voices," an orchestra of forty-five musicians,[179] and, as a special feature, some of Joseph Allegri's beautiful sets remaining from the former production. To compete with the gala opening of *William Tell,* Strakosch on the same night scheduled a fifty-cent performance of *La Figlia del Reggimento,* whereupon an enraged Maretzek announced that cheap prices would prevail at the Academy for the remainder of Strakosch's season, now in its final week.

Into this short remaining period Strakosch crowded cheap afternoon and evening performances of operas; a fifty-cent sacred concert on Sunday, September 26, the inappropriate occasion of his new basso Marcel Junca's debut in Rossini's *Stabat Mater* (preceding Junca's abridged opera debut);[180] a concert at the Brooklyn Athenaeum on October 1;[181] and finally on October 2 the tauntingly advertised, full-priced performance of *La traviata* for Colson's benefit (referred to above). Following the last act, as an extra treat, the stirring "Liberty Duet" *(Suoni la tromba)* from *I puritani* was performed by Junca and Amodio.[182] Strakosch then departed with his company for a short season in opera-starved Boston.[183]

The *Albion* (October 2, 1868, p. 375) deplored the unseemly conflict: "An absurd pugnacity has provoked a state of hostility between the two opera managements of the city, and we have had cheap opera *ad nauseam.* . . . It is pretty well known that although Mr. Strakosch retires from the contest for a time, he will return speedily, and the foolish fight will be resumed."[184]

But by mid-October, when Strakosch and his troupe reappeared at Burton's for a four-performance stopover[185] between Boston and Baltimore, Maretzek had completed his season and was out of reach, and Ullman was again in command of the Academy and in full blast over the approaching debut of his new star, Marietta Piccolomini.

[178] "A good ballet is a most pleasant episode, and tends to lighten up the tedium which is inevitable in the old style of grand opera," observed Watson (*Leslie's,* October 2, 1858, p. 281). Darcie praised the "glorious ballet" in the first act, a *pas de deux* performed by Mlle. Lamoureux and the American dancer George Washington Smith, the like of which he had never seen "in the palmiest days of the Ronzani troupe" (*Porter's Spirit,* October 2, 1858, p. 80).

[179] The *Albion* (October 2, 1858, p. 475) angrily compared this sophisticated production with the primitive opposition at Burton's, where a skimpy orchestra of twenty-eight performers under a conductor who knew nothing of his business, scraped its way "through all sorts of noisy dissonances"; where a chorus of twenty singers "complacently [added] their mite to the confusion"; and where, "without any reason being assigned, the last act of the Opera is omitted! . . . Clearly, if the public can be induced to patronize such discreditable exhibitions, there is no future for Art in this city."

[180] Junca, thus unceremoniously squeezed into the end of the season, was judged to be more a *basso cantante* than a *basso profundo,* as announced; he was a fine artist and a splendid actor, but decidedly French.

[181] Where no facilities for giving opera yet existed.

[182] It was not to Junca's advantage, it was noted, to be paired with Amodio, whose tremendous voice all but drowned him out, powerful though he was.

[183] Where Teresa Parodi, recently returned from a concert tour of the West Indies, replaced Gazzaniga, who did not, however, return to Europe.

[184] "These skirmishing seasons are injurious to art, and scarcely merit the support of the public," wrote the disgusted *Albion* critic (October 16, 1858, p. 500).

[185] A season, in the opinion of the *Musical World* (October 23, 1858, p. 675), "briefer than a Scotchman's unmentionables."

Strakosch opened on October 16 and closed on the 21st[186] with Colson in *La traviata;* on October 18 and 19 he presented Cora de Wilhorst, just returned from Europe, as Elvira in *I puritani.* Heralding her appearance as the triumphant homecoming of the only American *prima donna* to have successfully appeared at the Théâtre des Italiens in Paris, he assured the public that she was much improved in voice and method through study with the best teachers in Europe. She was now one of the very best singers of the day, either in Europe or America, and thus entitled, as a native New Yorker, to "the first claim of the audience."

In the same advertisement, Strakosch—Ullman-like—aired some of his resentments, asserting, apparently in answer to the *Albion*'s cavil over the meagerness of his chorus, that, while it was not as numerous as the one "at some other establishments," it nonetheless consisted of the best musicians in the city, was suited to the size of Burton's Theatre, and consequently "strong enough for those who prefer music to noise."

And in answer to "recent publications in which his late [New York] opera season [had] been referred to as a species of senseless opposition," it had not been his intention, he wrote, to oppose anyone, but merely "to compete. . . . Certainly the divine right to perform Italian opera does not rest in the hands of any single person or persons," he wrote. "Mr. Strakosch claims simply that he has a right to give the Opera, and the public has an equal right to come or stay away."

Although good audiences were reported at Strakosch's performances, de Wilhorst's return was perfunctorily treated by the critics, focused as they now were upon the advent of Piccolomini.[187]

Maretzek, free at last of Strakosch during his final week at the Academy, had presented, at full prices, the first of two "new" operas: *La traviata* on October 4 and 6 with Pepita Gassier appearing for the first time as Violetta, and Giovanni Sbriglia★ (1832–1916), a handsome new tenor,[188] making his American debut as Alfredo. Madame Gassier, who had sung the role in Europe, was judged a better Violetta than expected, but certainly no match for Colson or Gazzaniga; Sbriglia was a graceful and elegant tenor, but too lightweight in concept for Alfredo, and in volume for the vast reaches of the Academy. In *Linda di Chamounix,* which followed on October 8, Madame Gassier was a surpassingly enchanting Linda; Sbriglia an inadequate Carlo.

Linda was repeated on October 11,[189] as the matinée segment of a monster two-opera Farewell Testimonial Benefit for Maretzek, a festival toward which both Stra-

---

[186] Ill-advisedly colliding with the first performances of Piccolomini in the same role on October 20 and 22.

[187] "Very favorably received [de Wilhorst] was, but it can not be expected that she should cause more than a day's talk in the presence of the pet of London and the niece of a cardinal," a reference to Piccolomini's much-disputed familial relationship to the current Cardinal Piccolomini (*Review and Gazette,* October 30, 1858, p. 337).

[188] With Ullman temporarily usurping Stefani, Sbriglia and the resurrected Maccaferri were engaged as the tenors for Maretzek's Havana company. A Signorina Caroline Alaimo, too, would join the company in Havana, to assume the more dramatic soprano roles for which Madame Gassier was not especially fitted.

[189] A rather stormy performance: when Sbriglia "came before the curtain to appropriate a share of the applause, which the prima donna [Madame Gassier] thought was all her own, indicating to him rather plainly to retire, whereupon Sbriglia got angry, refused to sing any more, and the tenor music for the rest of the opera was omitted" (*Evening Post,* October 12, 1858).

kosch and Ullman evinced brotherly solicitude by publicly offering their assistance and their devoted sentiments.[190] In the evening opera, *Ernani,* the second of Maretzek's new artists, Cesare Nanni (or Nani),★ a *basso profundo,* made a promising first appearance as Silva. During the several intermissions a diversity of terpsichorean entertainments was offered by the Ronzani Ballet, a "Bohemian Polka" by Louise Lamoureux and G. W. Smith, and vivacious Spanish songs by Pepita and Louis Gassier, among them a duet, *La jota de los torreros,* that so "tickled the audience" that a "triple encore" was demanded (*Times,* October 12, 1858). At about midnight, following the performance of *Ernani,* the exhausting program incongruously concluded with "The Death of Ugolino," a tragic pantomime composed by Signor Ronzani, and finally the "Liberty Duet" from *I puritani,* with Gassier and Nanni waving the flags.

Maretzek's hard-won euphoria was of short duration. Planning immediately to depart with his company for Havana,[191] at the last minute he received a message from the Cuban Governor General peremptorily canceling the Havana opera season: the Tacón Theatre had been severely damaged by the explosion of a nearby powder magazine and was unfit for use.

Finding himself with a large, suddenly unemployed and homeless opera company on his hands, Maretzek—heroically rising to the occasion—sped to Havana on the first available steamer. Once there, after three hours of impassioned persuasion he emerged not only in possession of a lease for the city's second-best theatre, the Villa nueva, but with official permission—in compensation for its lesser seating capacity—to double his usual prices of admission.[192] By November 12, after only a month's hiatus, Maretzek and his company were on their way south.

In mid-October, scarcely a week after Maretzek vacated the Academy, it was grandly reopened by Ullman, who with Ullmanesque flourishes galore, presented the legendary Marietta Piccolomini in her breathlessly awaited bow to the American public as Violetta in *La traviata,* the role that had brought her universal fame.

Thanks to Ullman's advance indoctrination, New Yorkers were by now well grounded in Piccolomini lore: they knew that she was of noble Italian ancestry;[193] that she had been born in Siena in 1834; that as a child she had evinced so great a passion for singing and acting that, despite her elevated station, she was permitted to study for

---

[190] "Only a week ago, our operatic managers were trying to cut each other's throats in the most vigorous, entertaining, and determined manner," wrote the *Albion* (October 9, 1959, p. 487). "The possibility of a reconciliation seemed entirely out of the question. Today it is announced that Mr. Maretzek will take a Farewell benefit . . . and lo and behold! the opposition places itself upon the stool of repentance and indites an affectionate epistle full of the softest hopes and breathing the loveliest good will. This lying down of the Lion with the Lamb would be very charming if it were only sincere."

[191] With stopover performances booked for Baltimore, Washington, Charleston, and other intermediate places.

[192] "It is thought, by persons whose profession it is to interpret the sentiments of others," quipped the *Musical World* (November 6, 1858, p. 707), "that Mr. Maretzek would not object to have a magazine explode every year."

[193] Since the twelfth century the Piccolomini dynasty had produced numberless heroes, two popes, and currently a cardinal. Prince Ottavio Piccolomini (1599–1656) had been immortalized by Schiller in his plays *The Piccolomini* and *The Death of Wallenstein.* In New York, Marietta Piccolomini's title of "princess" (a title she did not use) was discredited by Ullman's detractors, among them George Wilkes.

the stage;[194] that at the tender age of seventeen she had made her successful debut in Florence as a precocious Lucrezia Borgia; that in 1855 her even more precocious Violetta in *La traviata* had attracted the attention of Benjamin Lumley, who engaged her for Her Majesty's Theatre in London; that there, in 1856, she had created an unprecedented sensation in that naughty opera, becoming—with her appealingly tiny physique, her irresistible magnetism, and her spellbinding acting—the pet and idol of the English public.[195]

Opera-going New Yorkers had awaited her arrival in breathless suspense: "There can be no doubt that a prodigious excitement already stirs the roseate depths of Upper Tendom," tartly commented the *Times* (October 13, 1858). "The Piccolomini fever has set in, and it will rage in the best blood in the land until relief has been obtained by the old fashioned method of depletion [bloodletting]. Mr. Ullman stands ready with lancet and basin, and his fee, we are informed, will be but two dollars" (the new price for reserved seats).[196]

In advertising his season, to open on October 20, Ullman justified his increased price on the basis of the "most lavish expense . . . incurred to make the debut of Mlle. Piccolomini and the opening of the winter season one of extraordinary interest." Perhaps heeding Strakosch's snide reference to the Academy's faulty sight lines, Ullman initiated expensive improvements in at least a part of the seating arrangements—the all-important part henceforth to be reserved for the stockholders (our first "diamond horseshoe"). Clearing the first circle in the parquet (albeit regretfully at the sacrifice of "several hundreds of good seats"), the entire area was converted into two rows of "neat private boxes," thirty-five in the front row, and forty-five in the back; each box to seat four persons, and each seat (allegedly) to command an unobstructed view of the stage.[197] A spacious passageway between the rows permitted easy access to all parts of the circle, allowing the wearers of even the most capacious crinolines to exchange the elegant little amenities that so delightfully betokened visits to the recherché opera houses of Italy and France.

Recalling the preparations for Musard, the Academy corridors were "handsomely

[194] This was Ullman's version; according to other sources, she studied for the stage in defiance of her family's objections.

[195] But Wilkes (or Darcie), now in full cry after Ullman, maintained that Piccolomini was "neither a princess nor a Piccolomini; that she was not allowed to perform in the critical towns of Italy; that in Paris they wouldn't have her at any price; and that she can only act about three operas respectably, whilst her singing alone would not procure her a prominent position, not even in the chorus" (*Porter's Spirit*, October 23, 1858, p. 121).

[196] Admission remained at $1, tickets in the family circle 50 cents, and in the amphitheatre 25 cents; the free list was "rigidly suspended." From the outset, the Piccolomini season was plagued by ticket speculators, who—often by subterfuge—bought up blocks of tickets and, at outrageous prices, brazenly hawked them at the very doors of the Academy. Ullman, who was accused by his enemies of complicity with the speculators, fought a ceaseless battle, authorizing twenty ticket offices in the city and even enlisting the help of the police to eliminate the nuisance, as injurious to himself as to the public.

[197] On opening night: "The new boxes in the first tier absolutely blazed with beauty," reported the *Herald* (October 21, 1858), "and we doubt if any theatre in the world ever presented such an array of pretty women. Almost everyone was in full dress, and the effect was worth going miles to see." The *Times*, however, voiced "an artistic objection . . . to the yellow lining of the proscenium boxes. Its direct effect is to turn the complexion of the fair occupants to a dingy green" (October 21, 1858).

This program announces that Piccolomini is scheduled for appearance in two other operas at the Academy of Music.

Marietta Piccolomini, a legendary figure, appearing here as Paulina in Poliuto.

ACADEMY of MUSIC

LESSEE AND DIRECTOR.................................B. ULLMAN

FRIDAY EVENING, FEB. 11, 1859

AT 8 O'CLOCK,
Donizetti's Sparkling Opera,

DON PASQUALE

Norina.........................Mlle. Piccolomini
Ernest...............................Sig. Lorini
Doctor Malatesta....................Sig. Florenza
Don Pasquale.....................Sig. Maggiorotti
Charles................................

THE SCENE IS LAID IN ROME.

ON SATURDAY, FEBRUARY 12th
AT ONE O'CLOCK

GRAND MATINEE

When the Opera of

DON PASQUALE

Will be repeated.

The price of admission for the

MATINEE

ONE DOLLAR TO ALL PARTS OF THE HOUSE.
(NO RESERVED SEATS.)

The sale of tickets for the Matinee commences this morning, at the regular ticket offices. Tickets for the Matinee may also be obtained at the principal hotels and music stores.

Mlle. PICCOLOMINI

Leaves for Albany immediately after the Matinee.

Ticket Offices for the sale of Matinee Tickets:

HOTELS.	NEW YORK MUSIC AND BOOK STORES.
Clarendon,	Nunn & Clark,
Everett,	Scharfenberg & Luis,
Union Place,	Christern,
Metropolitan,	Breusing,
Prescott,	Firth & Pond,
Lafarge,	Hall & Sons,
Astor,	Sibell.
St. Nicholas.	Prox's music store and Rose's book store, Brooklyn.

THE PICCOLOMINI OPERA LIBRETTO.

An elegant edition of the Opera Libretto, containing the original Italian, with a correct English translation, as performed by

MLLE. PICCOLOMINI

At Her Majesty's Theatre, London, and at the Academy of Music, New York, has been expressly published for the performances of Mlle. Piccolomini. The Piccolomini Opera Libretto contains also a biographical sketch of Mlle. Piccolomini and Six Pages of Music, containing the Gems of the Opera, expressly arranged for this edition.

PRICE, 25 CENTS.
For sale at the regular Ticket Offices.

MINIATURE PHOTOGRAPHS OF MLLE. PICCOLOMINI,
Taken from life, by Silsbee, Case & Co., Boston, for sale at the Academy.
PRICE, 25 CENTS.

HERALD PRINT.

Piccolomini on stage.

covered with Brussels carpets and filled with sofas, armchairs, and divans for promenade during the *entr'acts*." Additionally, the floor of the auditorium proper was laid
with matting, "so as to deaden the sound of locomotion and impart to the house during the winter months an air of luxurious comfort." And on opening night, wrote
Burkhardt (*Dispatch,* October 23, 1858): "A large number of additional burners and the
lighting of that border of gas jets which lines the upper ceiling (which are but rarely
lighted) shed an unwonted lustre upon the gay scene below."

His contract with Lumley, announced Ullman, permitted only twelve Piccolomini appearances in New York—to be followed by a tour of the more important
cities, then back to London in March 1859. At her first appearance, as Violetta in *La
traviata,* Piccolomini was assisted by a new baritone, Emanuele Florenza, making his
debut as Germont; Luigi Stefani as Alfredo; the fine Spanish dancer Teresa Soto, just
returned after a long and lucrative absence in California and South America;[198] a
chorus of 100 singers, of whom sixty were students at the Academy's "gratuitous sing-

[198] Allegedly having accrued on her travels a large fortune in cash and jewels.

ing school," established three months earlier under Anschütz's direction; and an orchestra of "upwards of sixty Professors," conducted by Verdi's pupil Emanuele Muzio,
making the first appearance of his eventful stay in the United States.[199]

It was an unprecedentedly brilliant event: "Long before the opera commenced,"
reported the *Herald* (October 21, 1858), "the streets in the vicinity of the Academy
were choked up with carriages, and Irving Place fairly floated in crinoline.[200] Within,
every place was occupied,[201] the lobbies, aisles, and corridors being almost impassable. . . . Everybody was there."

October 20. . . . Murray Hoffman had got a seat for me at the Academy of Music
and would take no excuses, so I went with him to the Piccolomini's debut in *Traviata*.
Seats in parquet. House jammed. Opera put on the stage far better than it deserves.
There was the superfluous imbecility of a ballet *(pas seul)* by some strapping, black-
eyed Spanish woman—a bullfighter's bride. Orchestra and chorus well drilled and
strong. Opening chorus of W——s and W——mongers[202] quite effective. The Piccolomini's reception was uproarious; she was called out over and over again, and bombarded with bouquets. Nice looking little body[203]—acts with archness and spirit in a
fresh, unconventional way, sings well enough for Verdi's music, and grins at the audience rather too much. She will make no profound impression unless she confines herself to lighter roles—Zerlina, or Rosina in the *Barber,* or the heroine of *Don Pasquale,*
or of the *Elisir d'amore.* She would do such work delightfully, I think. She is said to
be a very respectable little lady.[204] The baritone (name forgotten) [Florenza][205] was

[199] As part of the package deal for Piccolomini, Muzio had been engaged to share conducting
duties with Anschütz, who had just returned from a profitable three-week tour of the West with
Formes.

[200] "Fashion in her most brilliant vestments had possession of Fourteenth Street," reported the
Times (October 21, 1858). "From 7 o'clock to 11, when the performances came to an end, the thor-
oughfares vibrated with the equipages of the fortunate, and the *trottoirs* were as gay and animated as
a ballroom."

[201] To accommodate those who had been unable to procure tickets, Ullman had put 1500
"standee tickets" on sale. "The standing visitors," complained the *Albion,* "are permitted to take possession of every inch of that space which is specially reserved for passing to and fro, and from their
numbers on great occasions necessarily block off the view of the stage, as well as impede locomotion" (November 13, 1858, p. 547).

[202] The obscene word *whore* and its variants were evidently inadmissible, even in the privacy of
one's own diary.

[203] Not to be construed as a comment on Piccolomini's diminutive physique but merely as a
contemporary locution: Strong might just as well have said, "nice looking little person," or "little
lady."

[204] Much was made of Piccolomini's respectability; she had come to the United States in the
bosom of her family—father, mother, and younger sister and brother. On October 30 the *Evening
Post* informed its readers that she had taken a pew near the altar at St. Stephen's (Dr. Cummings's)
Church, adding gratuitously that she had narrowly missed becoming an Abbess in an Italian convent,
but that despite having chosen a less saintly career, she still maintained "her devotion for the religion
of her ancestors."

[205] As Germont, the newcomer Florenza was judged by Fry to be "a remarkable acquisition."
Except for a tendency to "overweep his music," he was in every other respect admirable. "His solo
called forth a thundering encore, and from that moment his success was assured" (*Tribune,* October
21, 1858). But not for long.

very effective. Tenor (Stefani) was vociferous beyond what was written, though Verdi wrote it.

~~~

Strong's description of Piccolomini's debut barely conveys the extraordinary excitement of the occasion, an excitement probably unequaled since the frenzied early days of Jenny Lind's visit in 1850.♪ Piccolomini utterly vanquished her audience; she "won all hearts by her exquisite grace, beauty, and innocent, arch simplicity," gushed a smitten Watson. "She is a lovable little darling, and wins the kindly sympathy and the affectionate interest of all who see her, and creates an irresistible desire in all to come again and again within the circle of her fascination" (*Leslie's,* October 30, 1858, p. 345).

"With a petite figure and a lovely brunette complexion . . . a charming, rosy, tempting mouth;[206] an exquisitely molded hand and arm, and that indescribable fascination of manner which we call captivating," infatuatedly reported Wilkins (*Herald,* October 21, 1858), "it was no great wonder that la Piccolomini vaulted at once into the affection of the audience. Everybody said, 'How charming she is,' and then waited to hear her sing. When she took up the air of the *Brindisi* from *Traviata,* she looked like a duodecimo Hebe.[207] She dashed through it with true bacchanalian fervor. . . . It was received with a storm of applause as sharp as a volley of musketry."[208]

But if anyone expected to hear polished vocalization from Piccolomini they were doomed to disappointment. As the critics agreed, she possessed a fresh, pure, warm, and sympathetic voice, capable of expressing an unlimited range of emotions, but, like others of the new breed of singers "who have grown up with the Verdi operas," her object was to give "an intense dramatic expression to the music without troubling . . . with the niceties of execution."

With her extraordinarily mobile face, her acting was magnificent, "a study for the connoisseur. It is as perfect as a *chef d'oeuvre* by an old master," continued Wilkins. "Her adieu to her lover was an outbreak of her whole sorrowing heart. The suffused

---

[206] "*Her mouth,* while she sings," wrote N. P. Willis, "*plays the most delicious pantomime* possible to conceive! The eye of the spectator is so pelted with kisses . . . that it is absolutely bewildering," leaving the onlooker with the sensation of having been personally and privately kissed by those "pouting . . . pulpy little red lips." Willis's review, appearing in the *Home Journal* (October 23, 1959), was promptly reprinted (November 6, 1858) in the new *Saturday Press, A Weekly Journal of Literary, Dramatic, and Musical Intelligence.* Edited by Henry Clapp, Jr. (1814–1875), known as the "King of the bohemians," the *Saturday Press*—generally memorialized as a fount of sophisticated, witty, and devil-may-care criticism by a choice group of free spirits—now seems more an exercise in sophomoric contrariety, not untinged with ethnic bias (largely directed against Ullman). The "frolicsome lads" who contributed during its brief existence were Clapp's fellow-bohemians: Fitz-James O'Brien, soon replaced as music and drama critic by Edward G. P. Wilkins of the *Herald,* Thomas Bailey Aldrich, William Winter, Walt Whitman, Mark Twain, and the somewhat less frolicsome William Dean Howells. Ada Clare,♪ the notorious "Queen of bohemia" (but not Clapp's consort) contributed some breathless prose from time to time. The *Saturday Press,* founded in October 1858, survived only two years; it was revived for a few months during 1864–65, then silence.

[207] A felicitous locution that Burkhardt later appropriated, referring to her as a "little *duodecimo* Leonora" in the abominable *Trovatore.*

[208] According to Burkhardt: "The enthusiasm of the audience shook the very walls of the temple" (*Dispatch,* October 23, 1858).

eyes, trembling hands, quivering frame, and words broken with sobs were irresistibly touching."

Watson, a Johnny-come-lately modernist, passionately defended the new approach to opera that Piccolomini (and Gazzaniga) so brilliantly personified. For some years now, he wrote, the more advanced opera composers—Bellini, Donizetti, and Verdi—had aimed to "progress from the artificial to the real . . . replacing the wooden idols—with their glitter and their glare of meretricious ornament and meaningless *fioriture*—with living, breathing, human realities." The more rigid critics had deplored the modern shift to melody, "to the exclusion of the profound harmony, the noble counterpoint, and the abstruse, complicated elaboration of thought which are the glories and the attributes of high art" of the past.

Not that Watson lacked "heartfelt reverence" for "the prophet-like inspirations of Mozart, Beethoven, and Weber"—but he responded more spontaneously to "those expounders of the human heart, Bellini, Donizetti, and Verdi," composers perhaps not so scientific as the great masters of the past, but of more immediate appeal to the contemporary ear. "Thousands who eagerly devour the passionate outpourings of Byron," he wrote, "would yawn over the majestic flow of Milton—the last appealing to the intellect, the first to the passions."

While Bellini and Donizetti had continued to employ the elaborate ornamentation of their musical forebears, it was Verdi who had effected the great operatic breakthrough, replacing intricate vocal gymnastics with dramatic declamation and artistic finish with earnest realism, thereby giving to opera a greater vitality than it had ever before attained. Verdi's works demanded none of the "nimble-go-lucky fandangos and fal-de-lals," which in any case could be more perfectly performed by a music box than by a human. It was therefore unfair to criticize Piccolomini, or any other exponent of the Verdi school, for lacking that which was not required in the operas they performed (*Leslie's,* October 30, 1858, p. 345).

The other critics, no less captivated by Piccolomini's powerful charisma, sought equally to extenuate her vocal limitations. She was not to be judged by conventional standards. "If we try to analyze what it is that gives her pre-eminence, we must at the outset discard . . . ordinary considerations," wrote Seymour (*Times,* October 21, 1858). Granted, her vocal powers were in no way comparable to her "immense histrionic capacity, which embraces so wide a range of emotion that it overshadows everything else. . . . It is this rare gift," he declared, "which distinguishes true from conventional art, and we have seldom seen it more wonderfully manifested than in the case of Mlle. Piccolomini. . . . Her entire performance is, in fact, a protest against conventionality.[209] . . . to say that this independence of model is mere talent would be absurd. It is genius of the best kind, because creative and absolutely free from the taint of imitation."

Modern opera no longer required "that immense executive finish which was once essential to success," deplored the *Albion* critic, who admittedly had had more than

---

[209] "No doubt, in Mdlle. Piccolomini we have a marked individuality, something apart from the conventional appearances on the stage," wrote Hagen. "We have seen the *rôle* of Violetta by Mesdames LaGrange, Gassier, Gazzaniga, and Colson, and yet there was not one air, one single phrase, which Mdlle. Piccolomini did not give quite differently from her predecessors in the same character" (*Review and Gazette,* October 30, 1858, p. 339).

enough of *La traviata* by now. "Singing, in point of fact, is falling into abeyance, and histrionism has taken its place. The crop of brilliant singers that burst into roulades during the reign of Rossini has long been harvested and consumed."

It was "the intense and passionate music of Verdi, although sometimes exaggerated and vulgar," that was "more in accordance with the energy and velocity of our time, and, simply for this reason, it [had] superseded all other music." Requiring a minimum of musical skill, it could be respectably performed by only moderately gifted artists. This explained the numerous successful impersonators of Violetta; particularly it explained Piccolomini's "unprecedented career" (*Albion,* October 23, 1858, p. 511).

Of the other members of the cast, virtually lost in the Piccolomini uproar, the baritone Florenza received unanimous praise; he was admired, despite his continued tendency to overgild the lily. Señorita Soto was warmly welcomed back, and Muzio was saluted as a valuable acquisition to the opera scene. Unlike other conductors, wrote the *Albion* critic, "he possesses an intuitive feeling for the relative importance of harmonic passages, and an inherent love and respect for the human voice. His accompaniments are beautifully clear and wait on the voice like a tidy handmaiden, not as a lazy, lagging loafer. . . . We are heartily glad that a good Italian conductor has at last been found, and . . . that a fine orchestra has been provided for him."[210] The critic noted as well a marked improvement in the chorus, and he gave great credit to Ullman for the opulence of his staging.

After two sold-out repetitions of *La traviata* (October 22 and 25) Piccolomini appeared in—or rather, joyously romped through—her second opera, *La figlia del reggimento,* on October 27 and 29. The recently returned Carl Formes was the "massively grotesque" Sergeant Sulpizio,[211] and a newly imported tenor, Giuseppe Tamaro [1824–1902], "condescended" to sing the comparatively unimportant role of Tonio.[212]

Although Piccolomini's *Figlia* was even more ecstatically received than her Violetta, to the *Albion* critic the overall critical assessments of her vocal capabilities revealed a certain "marvelous caution." It was obvious, he wrote, that his colleagues were "hugely disappointed," but unwilling to "pitch in" because it would have harmed the cause of opera—a fragile flower, at best.

Fry, who only a week earlier had saluted Piccolomini as "a beautiful, finished, and fascinating artist," now bluntly asserted that although *La figlia* provided an excellent vehicle for displaying her cleverness as an actress, it also revealed her lack of the "vocal supremacies" requisite to a true *prima donna.* "We have had so many artists of high desert that it is useless to attempt to set up those as great who are not," he wrote. It would, he added, in antithesis to the *Albion,* be harmful to the Academy if her quality were to be "overstated" (*Tribune,* October 28, 1858).

The *Musical World* (November 6, 1858, p. 706) patronizingly referred to her vocal limitations: "Piccolomini is a dear little girl, and gives, we confess, 'a full and fair

---

[210] An orchestra apparently chosen by young Theodore Thomas, who functioned as the Academy's orchestra contractor as well as its concertmaster.

[211] "It is something to see such an astonishing little flirt as Piccolomini, especially in contrast with the massive loyalty of the ponderous Formes" (*Albion,* October 30, 1858, p. 523).

[212] Due to delayed arrivals of various new singers from Europe, explained Ullman, Tamaro had obligingly consented, on short notice, to study and appear in the comparatively minor role of Tonio, a role scarcely suitable for his debut.

equivalent' for every note that she fails to touch."[213] Her acting, however, "was roguish to a degree and minute even to a fault"; it was wonderful how she seized on the "juvenilities of a part and [raised] them to the most enjoyable womanhood."[214] (Whatever that meant.)

"The actual fact about Piccolomini," wrote Seymour, "is that she is a most fascinating young actress. Beyond this judicious acknowledgement, criticism cannot well go. The cultivated ear rejects the tradition that she is a great singer. . . . There is a graceful vivacity in her performance which is irresistible. Her youth, her diminutive stature, her pleasing features, her coquettish airs, her pleasing impudences—these are the batteries she directs against the audience, and they are so potent that criticism feels uncomfortable when thinking of anything else. We can understand perfectly how the sternest pens have been mollified by such witchery." But vocally considered, "the effect was an average one, and no more" (*Times,* October 28, 1858).

It was thus a great astonishment to everyone when, after a further repeat of *La traviata* on October 30, Piccolomini was announced to appear on November 1 and 3 as Leonora in *Il trovatore*. An example of Ullman's brilliant managerial adroitness, wrote Burkhardt (*Dispatch,* November 6, 1858), this extraordinary piece of casting newly aroused the public curiosity to see what she would do in a radically different kind of role. Both performances were played to capacity audiences.[215]

As Strong, musing on the Greek classics, observed in his journal (October 28, 1858): "Only think of the struggle for seats to hear Sophocles' new tragedy, and our eagerness for a place on a first night of Verdi's *Rigoletto* or *Traviata* or *Masnadieri!!!* Alas for the nineteenth century of progress and enlightenment." Oddly enough, Piccolomini surprised everyone with her Leonora. Although "the little charmer [was] not the Leonora of Verdi's conception, nor of ours, nor of anybody else's," wrote the *Trovatore*-hater, Burkhardt, yet she possessed, "in this, as in all other roles, originality and individuality, from first to last, from head to foot—a distance of at least five feet nothing" (*Dispatch,* November 6, 1858).

"Who would suppose that Piccolomini would be good in the 'Trovatore'?" incredulously demanded the *Musical World* (November 6, 1858, p. 706). It was barely possible; yet it was true. She appeared "to very decided advantage in that much overdone work," singing the role with less effort than seemed possible and illuminating it in ways hitherto unprobed. A miracle![216]

---

[213] Usually substituting a charming toss of the head for an inaccessible high note, it was observed. N. P. Willis was particularly struck with the "full and captivating equivalent which she gave, with a toss of her pretty fingers, for every note she despaired of reaching; but she is perfectly aware of it, and simply so delights *the eye,* at that particular moment, with the bewitching grace and coquetry of a gesture, that the expectant *ear* forgets to be disappointed! The most strenuous '*bravo*,' in fact, is likeliest to be heard from the audience at the point artistically the faultiest" (*Home Journal,* October 23; *Saturday Press,* November 6, 1858).

[214] A fanatical Watson furiously attacked his colleagues for their refusal to acknowledge Piccolomini's perfections in *La figlia,* as in everything else she attempted (see *Leslie's,* November 6, 1858, p. 361).

[215] "It was difficult to find even standing room at any point from whence a view of the stage could be had," reported Wilkins (*Herald,* November 2, 1858). The great crowds drawn to her performances attested not only to "her hold of the public heart" but to the public recognition of her extraordinary gifts, "however they may puzzle and mystify the critics."

[216] For this production the Azucena was Elena D'Angri, who had rejoined Ullman's opera company "for a few nights" before purportedly departing on a trip to Europe; the Manrico was Stefani,

But Darcie, who until now had limited himself to an ostinato of run-of-the-mill abuse of Ullman and comparatively mild denigration of Piccolomini, now went to work in earnest. Piccolomini's attempt to sing Leonora, he wrote, was a "lamentable failure, which even her most ardent admirers were compelled to admit." It could not be dismissed "as a miscalculation on her part": it was undoubtedly a cynical trifling with the public by her manager. Darcie "sympathized" with Piccolomini, who was reputed to be an exemplary daughter and a devout Catholic. But more was needed to make a *prima donna.* "We want voice—voice—voice!" he ranted. Voice and a knowledge of how to use it. Perhaps several years of study would enable Piccolomini to try some of the lighter roles. "But never in this city," he stormed, "let her repeat the experiment of interpreting Grand Opera!" (*Porter's Spirit,* November 6, 1858, p. 160).

On November 4, Ullman presented his stars—Piccolomini, Formes, Tamaro, Louis Gassier (temporarily on loan to Ullman while awaiting his summons to Havana), and Florenza—in a concert of opera arias at the Brooklyn Athenaeum; on November 5, he gave a "Gazzaniga Night" at the New York Academy of Music in farewell tribute to Gazzaniga[217] (also waiting to rejoin Maretzek's company in Havana), who created a furor with her "last performance in New York" of *Lucrezia Borgia* and the last act of *La favorita.* Appearing with her were Tamaro, the long absent tenor Domenico Lorini,♪ Louis Gassier, and Gasparoni.

The following day Piccolomini repeated *La figlia del reggimento* at a full-priced "Gala Matinée"—her only one, it was announced, due to the exigencies of this "first epoch" of the opera season. A miscellaneous program was additionally presented, with Gazzaniga giving a post-valedictory performance, in costume, of her famous Spanish song *La naranjera* and, with Lorini, again the fourth act of *La favorita.* Selections from *Semiramide* with D'Angri and Gassier had been announced, but were canceled because of D'Angri's indisposition. No reserved seats were put on sale for this daytime event, but the new private boxes might be purchased in advance at any of the twenty authorized ticket offices, variously priced at $8, $10, and $12. An audience of some 4000— mostly women—reportedly attended, braving the rain, the doubled price of admission, and the remorseless struggle for seats.

"Two years ago, when the experiment of day performances was first made, no one could be induced to patronize them," editorialized the *Times* (November 5, 1858). But now, "by cultivation and sensible management, they have become the best patronized and most fashionable of entertainments." In view of the extraordinary response to this matinée, Ullman decided to present another on the following Saturday. And, despite "epochal exigencies," again with Piccolomini.

But the "Little Napoleon" had even greater things up his sleeve. With resounding fanfare he announced an all-star, superspectacular, "Grand *Don Giovanni* Night" to follow on November 8, a production that would eclipse any past production of the work "in America, or in any European city, not even London and Paris excepted."[218]

---

crippled by a hoarseness that elicited hisses from an unsympathetic audience; and the Count di Luna was Florenza, who, according to the *Musical World,* was merely passable, but according to Darcie, the best Count di Luna he had ever heard.

[217] Now lauded as one of the great artists of the day, Gazzaniga, on her return to the Academy of Music was welcomed by a house "as crowded as any Piccolomini night."

[218] Usually mounted as the last resort of a faltering opera season, this opulent mid-season *Don Giovanni* proclaimed the extraordinary degree of assurance to which Ullman had attained.

Added to his magnificent singing cast and a solo by Señorita Soto, the new production offered a chorus of 400 singers, of whom 300 represented the student body of the Academy's free singing school, and, under Anschütz's direction, "three distinct orchestras, numbering upwards of 100 musicians"—two bands appearing onstage in the ballroom scene with the 400 chorus singers—to play, synchronously, on the right, "La Gavotte," on the left, "The Ländler," and in the pit "The Minuet."[219]

For this extraordinary production Ullman trusted, in heartwrenching appeal, that an understanding public would "cheerfully" accept his increased prices of admission: parquet $1.50, reserved seats in the parquet and balcony $2.50 and $2, family circle, converted to reserved seats, $1, and amphitheatre fifty cents. To foil the speculators, the boxes would be sold at auction, with only the box-office price accruing to Ullman;[220] the aggregate premiums to be turned over to Mayor Tiemann for charitable distribution.

On November 10, Strong attended the second "Grand *Don Giovanni* Night,"[221] deriving from it both musical sustenance and food for anti-opera sentiments.

November 11. . . . Last night Ellie and I, with Miss Rosalie [Ruggles] and [the American painter] Louis Remy Mignot [1831–1870], heard *Don Giovanni* at the Academy of Music. Zerlina, Piccolomini; Donna Anna, Gazzaniga;[222] Elvira (forgotten) [Angiolina Ghioni],[223] very respectable. Don Ottavio's music decently rendered by one Tamaro[224] and Don Giovanni's by Gassier; the Commendatore [Wilhelm Müller]♪ uncommonly good—his voice audible above the trombones of the finale; Formes was Leporello.[225] Piccolomini's acting was very nice and coquettish—especially in *La ci darem* and *Batti, batti*—but there are amateurs in New York who could render Zerlina's music as effectively. She is a graceful actress and sings decently well, and that is all that can be said about her.[226] This furore, mostly got up by Mr. Ullman's skillful engineering, is absurd and will be short-lived.

[219] The two onstage orchestras, commented the *Saturday Press* (November 13, 1858), were "so tremendously out of perspective" that they gave the reviewer "the strabismus to look at them. They are as much out of drawing," commented the critic, "as Mr. Ullman's advertisements are out of taste."

[220] An "exploded humbug," sneered Darcie. Only thirteen bidders had attended the auction (held in the Rotunda of the Merchants' Exchange). The premiums averaged 25 cents, he claimed, the highest being $3 (*Porter's Spirit,* November 13, 1858, p. 176). But the *Musical World* (November 20, 1858, p. 738) reported average box-office receipts of $3000 for each of the four *Don Giovanni* performances, "about twice as much as the gross receipts of all the New York theatres put together." The total first-night receipts, reported the *Musical World,* amounted to "upwards of five thousand dollars."

[221] *Don Giovanni* was performed on November 8, 10, 12, and 15 (the last performance returned to original prices); it might have run indefinitely, it was felt, had Gassier, the Don Giovanni, not been summoned to Havana to join Maretzek's company.

[222] Still here, explained Ullman, because Maretzek had so far been unable to secure her steamship passage to Havana.

[223] Just arrived, Angiolina Ghioni, a highly praised mezzo-soprano, was another of the singers included in last summer's deal with Lumley.

[224] Misidentified as "Tamais" in the published *Diary* (II, 421).

[225] Gasparoni, the Masetto, was replaced at the next performance by Coletti.

[226] Never had the role of Zerlina been so admirably rendered, wrote the *Evening Post* (November 9, 1858): "LaGrange, Bertucca, Sontag, and all the other representatives of this character must consider themselves eclipsed by Piccolomini." Burkhardt went even further: she eclipsed not only the

Though *Don Giovanni* in concert room or parlor is always more and more noble and transcendent, it is a little disappointing on the stage, I think, because its music is too exalted for the barbaric foolery wherein we think we delight, and which we honor and applaud as "Opera," or "Lyric Drama." Its glorious melodies are degraded and the effect impaired by their accompaniment of idiotic puppet-show behind the footlights. I don't refer to this production in particular but to opera *per se*. What we call "good" acting only makes the misalliance more conspicuous. If the swine be a fine, large, fat specimen of his dirty kind, you are only the more offended by the jewel or gold in his snout, and the less disposed to admire it. Donizetti's and Verdi's music being mostly poor and shallow, its degradation is less disgusting. But Mozart's celestial melodies, condemned to the office of illustrating the conventional absurdities and imbecilities that make up a representation of this or any other opera, are somewhat lamentable to hear—like a chorus of angels diligently harping and hymning the accompaniment to a Chinese comedy, or to a troupe of trained monkeys and dancing bears.

For his second Gala Matinée, on November 13, Ullman presented a double bill of a caliber usually reserved for major evening events at the Academy. Although it was again a rainy day, another capacity audience assembled to hear the return, after an absence of nine years, of Rosine Laborde,♪ a reigning *prima donna* at the Astor Place Opera House in the late 1840s and more recently a star at the Paris Opéra and a guest star in Rio de Janeiro. Madame Laborde appeared as Norma,[227] the role with which she had dethroned Teresa Truffi, the incumbent queen of the Astor Place Opera House in 1848.♪ As the second feature of the program, Piccolomini and Maggiorotti, a debutant *basso buffo* from Lumley's company, gave the first performance in America of *La serva padrona* (St. Petersburg 1781) by the "old-fogy" composer Giovanni Paisiello (1740–1816),[228] a short, merry work made to order for Piccolomini's special assortment of piquant attributes.

Although Laborde's voice showed the wear and tear of the intervening years, wrote the critics, her always formidable vocal virtuosity had, if anything, increased. "Her trill is magnificent," wrote Hagen. "In fact, such a chain of trills as she exhibited in the first act of *Norma* could hardly be reproduced with the same evenness and smoothness on the piano-forte" (*Review and Gazette,* November 27, 1858, p. 371).

Piccolomini as Serpina, in *The Domineering Housemaid* (as it was translated), was almost unbearably bewitching. As an enthralled out-of-town correspondent for *Dwight's* wrote (November 27, 1858, p. 276): "The little princess tripped upon the stage, looking like a child of fourteen, in a short petticoat looped up with cherry colored ribbands, which showed to great advantage her pretty, childlike feet and

above named Zerlinas, but Persiani, Bosio, and Alboni (*Dispatch,* November 13, 1858). But Darcie, who had also heard Persiani, Bosio, and Louisa Pyne (in English) in the role, rated Piccolomini's performance about on a par with "a second-class chambermaid at Wallack's" Theatre (*Porter's Spirit,* November 13, 1858, p. 176).

[227] With Ghioni as Adalgisa, Lorini as Pollione, and Domenico Coletti as Oroveso.

[228] In this work Elise Siedenburg joined Piccolomini in an incongruously interpolated "Quarreling Duet" from Auber's *The Mason and the Locksmith,* and, in lieu of Paisiello's original finale, Piccolomini even more incongruously sang "The Piccolomini Waltz," composed for her by Emanuele Muzio.

ankles.[229] In five minutes the eyes and hearts of 'four thousand spectators' were irrevocably captivated. 'Did she pelt them with her kisses?' . . . Not oppressively. Was she beautiful?' No. 'Was she a great artist?' I cannot tell. She was charming in a way so exclusively her own that it would be quite unavailing to talk about it. She was so young, so innocent, so blooming, so confidingly frank and coquettish and piquant, so winning, so arch, so graceful, that her presence was like a beam of morning light or a breath of morning air."

Building momentum, on November 17 Ullman followed his *Don Giovanni* triumph with a spectacular triple bill: *La figlia del reggimento* with Piccolomini, *et al.;* the second act of *The Barber of Seville* with Laborde,[230] Lorini, Florenza, Coletti, and Maggiorotti; and to conclude, Piccolomini and Maggiorotti in *La serva padrona.* On November 18, Thanksgiving Day, another Gala Matinée with a dual bill: *La traviata* with Piccolomini and a repeat of the second act of *The Barber of Seville* with Laborde and her show pieces; and on November 19 a single performance of *Robert le diable,* billed as a second Gazzaniga Night.

November 20. . . . Last evening . . . after dinner we heard *Robert le diable.* Alice, Gazzaniga; Isabella, Laborde; Bertram, Formes; Robert, a stick whose name I've forgotten [Lorini].[231] Pleasant evening enough, but I can't work myself into cordial admiration of Meyerbeer's music. *Grâce* is certainly a fine, original musical thought, but the rest of the opera mankind would "willingly let die," I think. The little phrase of the "gambling scene" is fresh and vigorous, but how is it *economized* and repeated and made the most of! Mozart would have presented it once and then laid it aside.

~~~

On November 20, seeking new worlds to conquer, Ullman brought opera for the first time to the emerging town of Brooklyn. To accomplish this historic breakthrough, wrote the Brooklyn theatre historian, Gabriel Harrison (1818–1902), a special stage was constructed in the Brooklyn Athenaeum; it was "furnished with scenery, footlights, and drop curtain . . . [it measured] about thirty feet wide inside of the proscenium by twenty-two feet deep; and, although small and cramped . . . [its shortcomings] could well be overlooked in the exciting thought that Brooklyn had really reached an opera performance" (cited in Odell, VII, 197). Performed on this momentous occasion were *La figlia del reggimento,* a part of *Lucia di Lammermoor,* and *La serva padrona,* sung by Piccolomini and her colleagues. Ullman, who had already announced his intention of giving weekly performances of opera in Brooklyn the following season, was so encouraged by this first response that only a few days later, on November 25, he was back at the Athenaeum with a complete performance of *The Barber of Seville,* conducted by Muzio and featuring Madame Laborde.

[229] ". . . very—very—Italian feet," disparaged Darcie (*Porter's Spirit,* November 13, 1858, p. 176).
[230] In the lesson scene, in addition to *Una voce poco fa,* Laborde sang "The Carnival of Venice" with Paganini's variations *di bravura* for violin. "There are few such perfectly trained voices at the present day, very few that could attempt the variations on the eternal 'Carnival of Venice' and get through the simplest with the skill that Madame Laborde displays in the most difficult," wrote Seymour (*Times,* November 18, 1858). As a finale, she sang the spectacular Rondo composed by Maretzek in 1849 for her virtuoso portrayal of *Linda di Chamounix.*
[231] The German tenor Hugo Pickaneser was the Raimbaut and Teresa Soto the phantom abbess.

By now, yet another controversy was raging around Ullman. For a variety of alleged reasons, he had again become the target of systematic and progressive journalistic
abuse, this time by the French language newspaper *Le Courrier des États Unis*. On November 17, a frazzled Ullman published a card in the various papers, lashing out at the
Courrier's three editors, LaSalle, Masseras, and the patrician de Trobriand, in vehement
denial of their latest charge—that he had oversold the Academy for the past two Gala
Matinées, cruelly subjecting the ladies to unspeakable inconvenience in causing them
to fight for nonexistent seats. Although the Academy "comfortably" held 4000
people—at a pinch 5000—defensively claimed Ullman, he had stopped the sale of
tickets when 3800 had been purchased, because at the previous matinée he had seen
"so many ladies who did not like to go up to the amphitheatre standing in the passages
and lobbies."[232]

For more than a year now, wrote Ullman, taking up the cudgels, he had disregarded the abuse the *Courrier* had heaped upon him because the paper was too insignificant to be noticed. But recently they had taken to insulting Mlle. Piccolomini "in
the grossest manner," like *Porter's Spirit,* disputing her claim to the name of Piccolomini, and daily sending their paper to her apartment at the Union Place Hotel to
make sure she did not miss the insults. This could not go disregarded, he stormed.
Surely the public would never countenance this villainous persecution of a young and
innocent girl.

The *Courrier,* once a reputable newspaper, had miserably deteriorated under the
management of the "three hungry Frenchmen,"[233] as Ullman felicitously dubbed the
present editorial trio. "I have had the misfortune to displease all of them," he wrote:
"Trobriand, because I will not permit my artists to sing at his sugar and water soirées,[234] and to be blackmailed to the tune of a couple of airs and a duet per week;
LaSalle because I do not advertise as largely in his paper as in the *Herald, Times, Tribune, Express, Post,* etc.; Masseras because I used to address the free admissions to the
Editors, and not to him alone—he being greatly in want of opera tickets for purposes
to me unknown, and asking only the moderate number of eighteen reserved and best
seats per week, at $2 each. With all these requests I refused to comply, and continued
to send four tickets to the editors, over which, I am told, the three hungry Frenchmen
have been fighting as only excited Frenchmen can do, until they got tired, when they
combined their united forces and fell upon me and my artists, which assaults I an-
swered by stopping both advertisements and free tickets."[235]

A "distasteful personal squabble that had no right to be inflicted upon the public,"
maintained the *Times* (November 20, 1858). The combatants were equally culpable,
and the *Times* would have nothing further to do with the sordid mess. The other papers reveled in it, particularly the ultra-precious *Saturday Press,* which on November

[232]"Imagine the delights of a visit to the opera," sardonically wrote the *Musical World* (November
13, 1858, p. 722), "with every aisle blocked up and all the seats submerged in a sea of crinoline."
[233]The epithet was quickly picked up by the gossipy New York press and done to death, as they
had earlier overdone "youth, beauty, and genius."
[234]Occasionally attended, as we know, by George Templeton Strong.
[235]"Mr. Ullman regards Prima Donnas in the light of merchandise," commented the "Lounger"
(George William Curtis) in *Harper's Weekly* (December 4, 1858, p. 771). "If you don't like my Prima
Donna, you insult me. If you insult me, I cut off your admission and insult you back again."

20 attacked Ullman with a virulent, red-hot anti-Semitism that put George Wilkes's most poisonous outpourings to shame. On November 20, too, Ullman published another indictment of the three hungry Frenchmen, quoting in lengthy detail their libels of Mlle. Piccolomini, who, they asserted, was in fact not a Piccolomini but only a Clementini.

But suddenly, by November 22, as the *Evening Post* reported, hostilities were suspended: "Both Ullman and Masseras published conciliatory cards signifying that 'Mars has given place to Apollo'; that Mr. Ullman may call Piccolomini a Princess or a Grand Sultana, if he chooses, and that hereafter the 'three hungry Frenchmen' can appease their appetites and drink their sugar and water undisturbed."

This rapprochement coincided with the presentation, on November 23 and 24, of Mozart's *Le nozze di Figaro* (Vienna 1786), erroneously claimed by Ullman to be its first performance in the United States.[236] Strong was enthusiastically present.

> ***November 26.*** . . . Heard *Nozze di Figaro* for the first time Wednesday night [November 24]. With us, Mrs. S. B. Ruggles and Mignot. Formes as Figaro and Florenza as the erratic Count, were excellent. Piccolomini sang Susanna's music nicely enough and was saucy, pert, petite, piquant, and "aggravating."[237] Ghioni made a respectable, mechanical Countess, and the other parts were decently filled.[238] Music beyond my expectations, which were high. That it is of the same exalted order with the music of *Don Giovanni* is manifest, even on a first hearing. But it's useless to platitudinize about it. Grammar must be enriched with a new double-extra super-superlative degree of comparison before I can do justice to Mozart, on the whole, the greatest of composers.
>
> Admitting that Handel's sublimities of choral effect—the inspirations of *Israel in Egypt* and the *Messiah*—cannot be matched in [Mozart's] works, that he had no faculty for the uncanny depths and intensities of Beethoven's greater orchestral compositions, he outdoes both in every other kind of creative power and in the exuberance and the loveliness of his creations. Amen.

⌐⌐

The critics were less ecstatic. While, of course, dutifully recognizing Mozart's genius, it was generally felt—contrary to Strong—that the *Marriage of Figaro* was less sublime than *Don Giovanni*. Rather, asserted the *Evening Post* (November 24, 1858), it was "one of those quaint, old-fashioned operas that suggest the days of powdered heads, ruffled sleeves, and broadswords. The music is melodious and agreeable, the vocal portion being replete with quiet melody, while the orchestra is carefully elaborated." But,

---

[236] More precisely, its first more or less authentic performance in Italian. An 1819 English adaptation—Sir Henry Bishop's—of *The Marriage of Figaro* had, in fact, been successfully given at the Park Theatre as early as 1824, with a cast that included the Covent Garden actor/singer William Pearman (Figaro), Mrs. Holman (Susanna), Mrs. Bancker (Cherubino), Miss Johnson (the Countess), and Henry Placide (the "boozy" Gardener) (*New-York American,* May 12, 1824).

[237] In the opinion of the *Albion* critic (November 27, 1858, p. 571), Piccolomini, who was vocally unequal to the role, wore thin as the opera progressed. Although her dramatic concept of Susanna was "perfect," the charm of her coquetry dwindled from act to act: her first act was "delightful, the second amusing; the third a little tedious; the fourth a bore."

[238] By Minna von Berkel (Cherubino), Joseph Weinlich (Dr. Bartolo), William Müller (the Gardener), and Ernest Perring (Don Basilio); Anschütz conducted.

unlike *La traviata* (which in current performances was anachronistically set in the eighteenth century), Mozart's score seemed to carry one back several centuries, while Verdi's jolted one out of that world, making one aware of listening to the "fresh, noisy music of today instead of the quietly-flowing harmonies of the olden time. The opera contains some exquisite melodies and a vast amount of recitative," wrote the *Post* critic, "which, however interesting to an audience familiar with the language, is considered as the signal for conversation in our auditorium." The critic hoped that at the second performance "the audience will wait to the conclusion, and not mar the effect of the beautiful finale by leaving in the midst of it, as was the case last night."[239]

Although *The Marriage of Figaro* had been composed only some seventy years earlier, wrote Hagen, it was difficult for contemporary audiences brought up on Bellini, Donizetti, and Verdi to adapt to Mozart's obsolete musical style. *The Marriage of Figaro* belonged to "a different epoch of art, where the musical ideas, as well as their treatment, must be different from our own, according to the laws of time and natural progress." What Hagen missed most in the work were "real dramatic effect, contrasts in the coloring, and sharp musical characterization of the different persons who figure in it. . . . In *Nozze di Figaro,* where everybody and everything ought to be light and pleasant, [Mozart] neglected to use the more delicate shades of color in order to produce variety. All goes on in the same strain of fluency, most remarkable in itself, but rather too much of one and the same good thing for three [*sic*] long acts" (*Review and Gazette,* December 11, 1858, p. 386).[240]

"Regarded as a dramatic production, the work is . . . absurd," declared the *Albion* (November 27, 1858, p. 571). "Instead of laughing with the author [Beaumarchais or Da Ponte?], we are tempted to laugh at him." And although Mozart's slow pieces— "melodious, tender, and crowded with gentleness"—are enjoyable and "scarcely show age," he continued, "the rapid ones are unmistakably antiquated; anything quicker than an *andante* is dull. . . . Anything duller than [the ensemble pieces] we do not desire to hear. The effort to pronounce the greatest number of notes in the shortest space of time, and to maintain a constant chattering with some respect to the laws of harmony—but none to the soul of melody —these are the comic features of Mozart's music. . . . According to modern ideas of propriety, such a score would more than suffice for a serious opera."

Only Seymour—although he agreed with his colleagues that the score of *Le nozze di Figaro* was more suited to a serious plot than to a comic one—perceived it to be "a masterpiece." "In fullness, freshness, and intention it is not inferior to *Don Giovanni,*" he maintained (*Times,* November 29, 1858). "There is the same felicity of learned orchestration, the same descriptive tenderness in humble phrases of characterization." Affecting the critic's (and biographer's) assumed prerogative of omniscience, he continued: "Mozart never saw a joke in his life; he could gambol like a child, and in this way achieved a certain playfulness. But it was a very sensitive vivacity, and as often ended in tears as in smiles. . . . Hence, the music is frequently lovely, but never light. You cannot take it in a foaming draught as in the case of Rossini."

---

[239] "The opera improves with acquaintance," wrote the same critic after the second performance. And, happily, "judicious cuttings allowed the audience to leave at a reasonable hour."

[240] The opera's original four acts had been telescoped into three.

Leslie's, Dartmouth College Library

Marietta Gazzaniga.

Piccolomini, wrote Seymour, was dramatically a splendid choice for Susanna but vocally insufficient, as, evidently, the prompter was not.[241]

Yet another Gazzaniga Night followed on November 26, again with *Robert le diable*—this time a farewell benefit that spilled over to a Gala Matinée the following day,[242] consisting of an act of *Ernani* (Piccolomini), an act of *La sonnambula* (Laborde), and *La naranjera* (Gazzaniga in costume).

As the season neared its end, commented the *Times* (November 29, 1858) Ullman, "like a skillful postilion . . . reserved a gallop for the last stage of his journey." Before sending Piccolomini on a flying trip to Philadelphia for an appearance with

[241] The prompter "appears to be oblivious of the fact that his services are needed solely for the actor, not the audience," continued Seymour. "A gentleman of less stentorian propensities would materially contribute to the enjoyment of the front part of the house."

[242] Those holding tickets for the evening performance were admitted to the following day's matinée as well. For those attending only the matinée the admission was $1. This time the doors were opened at 12:30 P.M. to allow the ladies an extra half-hour to find seats.

Strakosch's company,[243] on November 29 he presented her in *Lucrezia Borgia*,[244] a venturesome bit of casting, even for Ullman. In her treatment of this preposterously inappropriate role,[245] Piccolomini's supporters found much to praise, her detractors more to criticize. All in all, it was not a memorable occasion.

On December 1 came a repetition of *Le nozze di Figaro*, allowing Strong—in a long ramble—to indulge to his heart's content in his propensity for making musical comparisons.

December 1. . . . Miss Leavenworth and Mr. S. B. R. dined here. . . . Then we went to hear *Nozze di Figaro*, from which we've just returned, and I'm still tingling and nervous from undergoing that most intense and exquisite music. It's not so *potent* merely, but the dose is of such heroic magnitude! Donizetti could dilute any ten bars of it into two grand operas. Don't think I've ever enjoyed *Don Giovanni* so keenly, though parts of that opera far exceed anything in this or any other. This perhaps seems, as a whole, fresher and more genial and glowing from being lighter and less grave. Where can one match *Non più andrai* (especially as Formes gives it),[246] and what has Mozart written that embodies so much of the vigorous, kindly bonhomie, in which Haydn is supreme, than the concerted music of the second act—especially one quartette that suggests the celestial *Non ti fidar, o misera*, of *Don Giovanni* (though very far from it in sentiment), and nearly lifts a man out of his boots with the electric pungency of some of its phrases. *Voi che sapete*—it surely runs even *Vedrai, carino* very hard. The opening duo of the third act—the first chorus—the most lovely little duo in the fourth (Figaro and Susanna)—*Pace, pace, o mio tesoro*. Life becomes more valuable after one has heard and grasped as a firm possession these priceless gems of musical thought.

Query: If that lovely popular melody "Araby's Daughter" (popular when the undersigned was a twelve-year-old, and in which he used to revel then and long thereafter) be not a development of a phrase that occurs early in the fourth act of *Nozze di Figaro?*

Piccolomini sang *Deh vieni* very prettily, but not as Mozart wrote it. She could not sing certain low notes of the air and had to substitute certain other notes of her own invention.[247] But she works so hard and is so clever and self-possessed and "cunning" and spicy a little Susanna that one has to pardon her for taking liberties even with Mozart. Ghioni (the Countess) sang *Dove sono* accurately and well, but without life and earnestness, and it seemed quite tame and flat. Formes was admirable throughout, and the Count (Florenza) very satisfactory.

---

[243] Ullman/Strakosch relations had apparently been mended (if indeed they were ever truly severed).

[244] With Ghioni as an unsatisfactory Orsini, Tamaro an unsatisfactory Gennaro, and, most unsatisfactory of all, Formes as the Duke Alfonso.

[245] The childlike Piccolomini as the mother of an adult son put a great strain on the auditors' credulity, it was noted.

[246] "For the sake of a little additional applause," disapprovingly observed Seymour, Formes repeated it in German. Was this proper or respectful to the other singers? "If it is optional to sing in any language the singer may select, we do not see why Mr. Perring should not sing in English, Mme. Laborde in French, and Mme. D'Angri in Greek" (*Times*, November 29, 1858).

[247] Strong's familiarity with the score was doubtless acquired in sessions at home with Ellie at the piano.

. . . Mr. S. B. R. seemed refreshed by the music and by its souvenirs of the Park Theatre ages ago, when the English version of this opera reigned and "drew" at that long perished institution.

Artists in music (especially "opera-tives") are at a disadvantage, compared with poets and painters, in their chance of being known to posterity. Printing makes every book that is not absolutely worthless (and many that are) accessible to everyone for indefinite generations. Photographs, engravings, and copies disseminate all over the world the conceptions of the painter. But to make a great musical work known—to submit it to inspection—to make it *accessible* to those who desire to know it, at any given period, requires combination and organization and preparatory labor, and is possible only at a few points of the earth's surface. where the material is to be found.[248] Before even a symphony or overture can be fairly rendered, some two score, at least, of skilled mechanics must be found, each qualified by a lifetime of preparatory drill and by a month of special training and rehearsal. To evoke and make manifest the creations that lie hidden in the score of an opera by Mozart or Gluck, there must be troops of singing men and singing women, cunning fiddlers and flutists, scene painters and lamplighters, a theatre, a *prima donna* or two, basso, baritone, etc., etc., at so many hundred dollars a night, and a great deal besides. Without all these complex and costly conditions the beautiful composition over which its author toiled so long, and on which he rested his hope of fame, is practically null and non-extant, except so far as amateurs and pianofortes keep alive a dim sense of its existence. A pity the finest operas are not given as concert music, like oratorios, complete, or omitting only recitative.

This lovely *Nozze di Figaro,* though so famous and so brilliant, melodic, and popular, has been unheard and unknown in New York till 1858, except in a mutilated and mangled English version twenty-five years ago. It may sleep now for another generation, or until another performer turns up with special qualifications for one of the parts—like little Piccolomini's for that of Susanna.

What chance is there of my ever knowing the *Zauberflöte?* with its preposterous plot to deter all managers from the experiment of producing it[249]—Gluck's *Orfeo*— Weber's *Oberon*—the *Matrimonio segreto,* etc., etc.—especially while the stage is occupied by Verdi, Donizetti, and Co., making occasional room for respectable, diligent artificers like Meyerbeer.

Every author of symphony or opera should produce his work with a rope around his neck. If the work be merely creditable and clever—not truly great and genial—he should be hanged. For by bringing it into the world he has helped to lessen the few opportunities accorded to mankind of hearing the great masterpieces of music that are to most of us as if they had never been. Why should Gade and Wagner write symphonies and overtures? If they devoted themselves to sawing wood instead, my chance of knowing Beethoven and Mozart would be better.

～～～

After a performance of *La traviata* on December 3, Ullman climaxed his remarkable season with a magnificent revival of *The Huguenots* on December 4 and 6, provid-

---

[248] For better or worse, an obsolete limitation.

[249] Strong could have heard it in 1855, when it was performed in German at the *Stadt-Theater.* Earlier, in addition to its English adaptation by Charles E. Horn, presented at the Park Theatre in 1824, it had been given in French at the Chatham Theatre in 1831.

ing a vehicle for the last-minute debut of Mlle. Euphrosine Poinsot, heralded as a principal dramatic *prima donna* from the Paris Opéra.

December 6. . . . Miss Mary Ulshoeffer and Mignot dined with us, and we heard
the much lauded *Huguenots,* Carl Formes was Marcel, Laborde Marguerite, Mlle.
Poinsot Valentine. She is new —gawky and lank—sings with feeling and power—acts
well.[250] Opera effective (dramatically), with horses, costumes, and gunpowder. Don't
care much for it. Meyerbeer's musical thoughts are commonplace and unlovely. Being
a most skillful and painstaking mechanic in music, he elaborates them and sets them
off to the utmost possible advantage by the most erudite artistic management of voices
and orchestra, but they are not worth it. All his ingenuity of construction—novelty
and brilliancy of instrumental effect—fail to compensate for the poverty of his conceptions. There is no *song* in his melody, no *revelation* in his harmony. There is this material
dissimilarity (among others) between Meyerbeer and Mozart: that whereas the former
is evidently writing *at* an *audience,* and toiling to excite admiration, the latter is evidently working on a plane far above any given human assemblage and pouring out
thoughts that he knows to be true and beautiful without much concern about the *recognition* of their truth and beauty. Mozart knew that *Don Giovanni* and the *Nozze di
Figaro* were great and lovely creations. All he wanted was to *bring them forth.* Meyer
beer had no such conviction about *Robert* or the *Huguenots.* What he sought was to
produce an effect—to make an impression—to be recognized as a great composer.
One feels that his every semiquaver is deliberately and skillfully aimed at an audience.

December 8. . . . With Mr. and Mrs. Lewis Rutherford and Ellie to Piccolomini's
[farewell] benefit last night. *Lucia.* Brignoli[251] and Florenza doing the *he*-parts in that
idiotic caricature of Walter Scott's novel. Full house in spite of rain, "Grand Ovation,"
the newspapers call it—presentation of a $1000 bracelet—pretty little broken English
speech by the Princess *Pic*[252] and a procession of firemen to escort the little lady to
her hotel with torches and Roman candles—Mose paying spontaneous homage to the
"Queen of Lyric Drama." Ullman understands the art of humbug; he's the P. T. Barnum of opera. Little *Pic* is very charming, but not quite charming enough to justify
Pierre Marié[253] in carrying on about her like an enamored donkey and parading his
long ears before the public with a simplicity too ostentatious to be touching.

---

[250] At her debut Mlle. Poinsot, the Valentine, upon being shot in the final scene, "forgot in the
excitement of the moment to fall in the right place." To avoid being struck by the falling curtain,
"the dead Valentine partially raised herself and instead of drawing back, came forward," and was thus
embarrassingly left lying in front of the curtain. Anschütz gallantly came to her rescue, leaping over
the footlights and helping her to escape. A sensation!

[251] Desperately in need of a tenor, Ullman had procured Brignoli from Strakosch.

[252] As she concluded her little speech, a shower of leaflets descended from the upper tier inscribed with the following *poésie:* "Gifted one—from a gifted Land! / Fair rosebud of a lineage
grand! / Spoiled child of Music, Grace and Art! / So loved by all! Say, must we part? / Must Violetta
now no more / Our smiles and tears at will explore? / Must thy fresh voice, so sweet, so bright /
Our ravished souls no more delight? / Pretty Serpina, pert of manner— / Superb Lucretia—sweet
Susanna— / Must these delicious friends of ours / Leave us to tears—ere many hours?" (*Evening
Post,* December 8, 1858).

[253] Referred to by Strong as "poet and banker," the ardent Peter Marié is listed in the New York
City Directory as a broker.

Piccolomini's farewell, like Gazzaniga's, overlapped to the following day, when the whole vast production of *The Huguenots* was repeated at a monster matinée. Following the custom of giving a novelty at a closing performance, the first performance in America of an act of Donizetti's *Les Martyrs,* a reworking in French of *Poliuto* (Paris 1840) was announced but had to be canceled, "in consequence," as the *Evening Post* put it, of the "alleged indisposition" of Lorini.

Immediately after the matinée Ullman's company took off for Boston.[254] In the following profusion of summings–up, it was the critical consensus that this had been the most successful opera season ever conducted in New York.[255] In the seven weeks of its duration, according to the *Evening Post* (December 9, 1858), its twenty-five performances had netted some $70,000. It was generally agreed that Piccolomini was not so much the idol as the pet of the city, that Poinsot was the best new artist to join the company, that Laborde was an unrivaled virtuoso, Ghioni a careful singer but lacking in dramatic power, Formes as great in German music as he was poor in Italian opera, but supreme in his Meyerbeer characterizations, Florenza a good and tasteful baritone, Tamaro awkward and generally unsatisfactory, and that Lorini had a sweet voice and was improving but was out of his class in this company.

It was noted that the company was topheavy in sopranos and sadly lacking in contraltos and tenors, but that Ullman had artfully chosen his repertory to minimize this deficiency. He was praised for the lavishness of his productions,[256] although only one "new" opera had been produced, *Le nozze di Figaro,* a work too antiquated to be adopted into the repertory. (*La serva padrona,* although entertaining, was "too trifling to be dignified with the name of opera.")

It was generally appreciated that Ullman, with his superb showmanship, had wrought unheard-of wonders. As *Trovator* wrote: "Mr. Ullman has certainly the most remarkable talent for keeping up an excitement . . . much of his success is owing to the excellent tact he evinces in his managerial system. It is not humbug . . . nor does *tact* rightly express it; so let me call it managerial genius. In the first place there are the advertisements! . . . They are not merely bold announcements of operatic facts, but they are delicate missives that appear to be concocted solely for the private ear of each individual reader. The manager therein appeals to your pride, to your liberality, almost to your conscience. He argues and reasons, with respectful pathos, to prove why you

---

[254] A lively trip, according to a fellow traveler on the steamer *Connecticut:* "The Opera Company, numbering something over a hundred, kept up a prodigious jabbering on the boat—French, English (or *Ingleesh,* rather), Italian, German, and whatnot. Formes took two of the ballet or chorus women under his special charge, and amused them and others all night with stories and imitations of cats and dogs and a kind of trumpet solo upon his nose. Others sang, and very finely, too—in the hold, having first obtained inspiration from various bottles of wine, brandy, etc. Tamaro's stateroom seemed to be the headquarters for liquor, but although many of the Italians and Germans were exhilarated, none were disorderly. The *prime donne* kept apart mostly, and Ghioni derived comfort from a lap dog. On the [train] from Stonington to Boston, the chorus people took possession of the best car, and filled it with tobacco smoke. It was altogether a funny company" (*Tribune,* December 14, 1858).

[255] Darcie reported it to have been a dire failure and predicted that the tour would be an even greater fiasco.

[256] Despite which, as the *Albion* critic complained, the *Huguenots* orchestra had lacked a necessary harp: "Considering the prosperity of the season," he wrote, the management might surely have afforded this essential, even if a horse had to be left out (*Albion,* December 11, 1858, p. 596).

should pay double the usual price. He hints at future novelties; he talks mysteriously of future wonders. Gazzaniga will appear tonight—Piccolomini the next, and then, oh! unexampled condescension, the two will appear together. Then Mme. Laborde will appear, and Mlle. Poinsot will appear, and so, between debuts and revivals and novelties, the poor opera-goer is kept in a constant whirl of excitement. Then, when the house is crowded at double prices, what does the incomprehensible Ullman do but reduce the rates of admission to the old standard—and this too, when there was no apparent necessity for so doing. . . . The little man fully deserves his title of the Napoleon of managers" (*Dwight's,* November 25, 1858, p. 269).[257]

Accordingly, before leaving for Boston, Ullman tantalizingly made it known that, beginning January 6, immediately after the Boston engagement, his company—Piccolomini and all—would be back at the Academy for a brief season of six consecutive nights before going to Philadelphia and then on to Havana and New Orleans, not to return until May. This would be the last chance until then to hear them in their new operas—Balfe's *The Bohemian Girl* and Flotow's *Martha,* both in Italian—and in his great productions of *Don Giovanni, Robert le diable, The Huguenots,* and, particularly meaningful to Strong, *Le nozze di Figaro.*

In anticipation:

December 10. . . . Jem Ruggles dined here and spent the evening reading music—*Martha* and *Nozze di Figaro*—with Ellie.

---

[257] But Darcie, in an all but obscene attack, attributed to Ullman the official odor of an "operatic skunk," a stench with which he had polluted Piccolomini, and she—"dear, conceited, fascinating little impostor, is made a scapegoat of her unscrupulous Hebrew hirer" (*Porter's Spirit,* November 27, 1858, p. 208).

OBBLIGATO: 1858

The cosmopolitan character of this city is in no way better shown than in its public amusements. At Wallack's on Tuesday and Friday one might imagine himself at the Paris Vaudeville or Varieté, while if a trip to Germany is needed one has only to cross to the Bowery, where there are numberless theatres and concert halls of the Teutonic order.

New York Herald
June 28, 1858

At the height of the Atlantic Cable festivities—in ill-considered competition with both Maretzek at the Academy and Strakosch at Burton's Theatre—yet another season of opera befell the opera-drenched city, this time opera in English. Opening at Wallack's Theatre on September 6, a new company, directed by the eminent English violinist Henry C. Cooper and consisting of Cooper's wife, Annie Milner, a newcomer to the opera stage, the old-timers Mr. and Mrs. George Holman, David Miranda, a new English tenor, F. Rudolphsen, a basso from Boston,[1] and Charles Guilmette, opened with Balfe's *The Bohemian Girl.*♪♫ Presenting a repertory of five operas, a nightly change of bill was advertised for the duration of their two-week engagement.[2]

But, as the *Albion* critic observed (September 11, 1858, p. 439), rather than a repertory of English operas, their offerings turned out—with the sole exception of *The Bohemian Girl*[3]—to consist entirely of such tried and true Italian chestnuts as *La sonnambula, Lucia di Lammermoor, L'elisir d'amore,* and *Il trovatore,* all decked out in ill-fitting English garb.[4] It was, in the critic's opinion, "a mistake to limit the stock to this

---

[1] In Boston, Rudolphsen had first been known as a fine horn player in the Germania Society and the various theatre orchestras, and later as a concert singer variously under the names of Signor Rodolfo and Herr Rudolph (*Dwight's,* September 25, 1858, p. 207).

[2] Fry—albeit jubilant at the prospect of opera in English—disapproved the plan: "Under such a desperate regimen the pieces cannot be adequately well done; and a success achieved in a well-composed opera may not be attached to a second- or third-rate one of the repertory," he wrote (*Tribune,* September 11, 1858).

[3] The scarcity of English musical stage offerings was blamed on the lack of English operas available in print.

[4] With recitatives converted to ungainly spoken English dialogue sans accompaniment (*Dwight's,* September 25, 1858, p. 207).

Wallack's Theatre, which devoted several weeks to operas
in English, did advertise other offerings.

much-hackneyed [English] work, and still more of a mistake to patch up a deficient *répertoire* with Italian operas, too well known in a southern accent to bear transplanting to a northern tongue."

More bluntly, Hagen asserted that the English opera literature contained little worth doing beyond Balfe's *The Bohemian Girl* and William Vincent Wallace's *Maritana;* the remaining choices were necessarily limited to translations of French or Italian operas. "But how is it to be expected," he demanded, "that in large cities like New-York, people will pay for a counterfeit when they can hear the original for nearly the same money?"[5] How could one prefer Miss Milner as Amina when for the same price one could hear Madame Gassier in the same role; or Miranda as Edgardo in preference to Stefani; or the "poor apology for an orchestra at Wallacks" to the fine orchestra at the Academy?[6]

Not that Hagen wished to disparage the merits of Cooper's singers: "Miss Milner is quite acceptable in oratorios and some concert pieces," he conceded. "Mr. Miranda has a good voice, Mr. Rudolphsen the same, and Mr. Guilmette is an intelligent singer, although rather too declamatory. But in Italian opera all these artists are out of place, and as, for want of the so-called English operas, they have to give the former, we repeat, all their struggles will in the end neither benefit their reputation nor their purses" (*Review and Gazette,* September 18, 1858, p. 291).

It was, nonetheless, the consensus that Miss Milner compared favorably with Louisa Pyne, at least vocally: her minor histrionic shortcomings would surely be ironed out with further stage experience. Miranda, with a sweet and powerful tenor voice and a fine appearance, was welcomed to the local music scene; Rudolphsen, a good basso, was similarly welcomed; and Guilmette again demonstrated his eminently intelligent artistry, although he tended to be pompously declamatory "to the point of tedium."[7] As for Cooper, Fry regretted that he conducted his meager orchestra with a "stick." "If occasionally he would drop [it] and take up his violin for a solo bit, it would enhance much the interest" (*Tribune,* September 11, 1858).

Eclipsed during the second week of their run by the ruthless Maretzek/Strakosch

---

[5] Tickets for the Cooper English operas were fifty and twenty-five cents.
[6] An opinion shared by most of Hagen's colleagues and apparently by the public as well.
[7] Watson deplored Guilmette's "absurd introduction of *outré* and ridiculous ornaments in simple ballads" (*Leslie's,* September 18, 1858, p. 249).

warfare, on September 18 Cooper's English Opera Company completed their sparsely attended New York season, and departed for a short engagement in Boston (see *Dwight's,* September 25, 1858, p. 207).

Only two weeks later—immediately upon the termination of Strakosch's season at Burton's—another English opera troupe materialized. On October 4, under Burton's management, the Lucy Escott English Opera Company—still suffering the aftereffects of a trying voyage from England—made their overhasty debut at his theatre.

Mrs. Escott (formerly Eastcott),♪ a native of Springfield, Massachusetts, had—since her undistinguished concert appearances in 1851—been studying in Europe and acquiring credentials at opera houses in Italy and England, notably at the San Carlo and the Drury Lane Theatres. Her present company, reportedly popular in England, included a Miss Emma Heywood, a contralto from Drury Lane; a Miss Harriet Payne, from Covent Garden, probably the second soprano; the long absent American tenor (a former pupil of James G. Maeder) Henry Squires,♪ "from the German, Italian, and English Operas"; Brookhouse Bowler, second tenor, from Drury Lane; Aynsley Cook, basso, from the London Opera House; Charles Durand, billed simply as "the celebrated English baritone"; and to conduct, a Mr. Edward Reyloff,[8] of undisclosed origin. William Burton, who had imported the company (doubtless on the strength of these credentials), informed local "lovers of music" that "printed notices of the professional career of Escott and the other members of the company" might be viewed at the theatre box office.[9]

The Escott company ill-advisedly—indeed, disastrously—opened their season of English opera with *The Troubadour (Il trovatore).*[10] A most unfortunate choice, wrote Seymour, who questioned the wisdom of opening a season with that work in any version but the original Italian. Besides: "We have had good singers in the leading *rôles,* and every regard has been paid to the proper illustration of the choral and instrumental parts. It is somewhat hopeless, therefore, for an English company—never too strong—to measure itself against the Academy and its legions."

Mrs. Escott, the Leonora, was doubtless a "charming singer" but her voice was too light for the role; Squires, the Manrico, was "laboring under an attack of illness"; Durand, the Count di Luna, sang his role well enough but suffered by comparison with his "Italian predecessors." Seymour trusted that their ensuing efforts would redeem the company from the "laborious and tiresome blunder" of their debut (*Times,* October 6, 1858).

But Darcie was implacable: "Now, if anything more fatuous and insensate than such a selection for the debut of an English Opera company can be imagined," he fumed, "we should like to know what it is. Here, at this very theatre, we last week

---

[8] Instead of George Loder,♪♪ now back in London after a long sojourn in Australia, who—it had been rumored—would conduct the Escott company.

[9] Despite the heavy expenses of presenting this company, involving a full orchestra and chorus, new scenery and costumes, and all the requisite accessories, the prices of admission would remain the same, advertised Burton: dress circle and parquet fifty cents, third tier twenty-five cents, orchestra or stall chairs $1, and balcony seventy-five cents.

[10] Referred to by Burkhardt as "that most abominable of Italian abominations, the sledgehammer and nightmare *Trovatore* of Signor Verdi . . . now, alas, dished up to us with English melodramatic dialogue for the *recitatives*" (*Dispatch,* October 9, 1858).

had such a performance of the same opera [by Gazzaniga, Brignoli, and Amodio] as even the first Italian companies of Europe could scarcely hope to surpass . . . when here comes, to just follow them and provoke the most painful kind of contrasts, a moderately good-looking woman, with a thin, strained quality of soprano, deficient in tone, limited in register, and meretricious in style, with a manner of acting that has neither piquancy nor passion, and an unpleasant confidence in bearing that would have been insufferable, had it not been thrown in the shade by the still more abominable egotism of the baritone." If, as reported, Escott and Squires were excellent in *The Bohemian Girl* and *Maritana,* then "let them adhere to that style and leave Verdi to those who understand and can interpret him. It is no use arguing the matter," argued Darcie, "the fact is patent that Italians who come on with messages have more voice and knowledge of music than the very best of English or American aspirants to operatic fame." Darcie excepted Adelaide Phillips, Louisa Pyne, and Sims Reeves (*Porter's Spirit,* October 9, 1858, p. 96).

The Bohemian Girl was indeed played on October 6 and 8, but upon its repetition (with *Maritana* announced to follow on October 11), Burton, without warning or apology to cast or public, peremptorily closed his theatre, and the Escott season came to an abrupt close. Protesting this cruel and unprofessional treatment in a card appearing in the various newspapers on October 14, Lucy Escott accused Burton of wanton breach of contract, "on the faith of which she was induced to leave England, declining most favorable engagements there." Mrs. Escott stated her company's willingness yet to fulfil their agreement with Burton. In vain.

The incident was widely discussed in the papers. Mostly sympathetic to the performers, the critics felt that not enough time had been allowed—after their rigorous voyage and its various resultant ills—to prepare for a first appearance worthy of themselves and a New York audience. The various members of the troupe were evidently capable professionals, but it was strongly felt by all that Italian opera was distinctly out of bounds for English performers.

Wilkins (*Herald,* October 12, 1858) went even further, declaring so-called English opera, once beloved of the American public, to be irretrievably passé: "In the early days of the American theatre nothing was more popular than the old-fashioned English operetta of the 'No Song, No Supper'♪ or 'Love in a Village'♪ order. An actress who could sing tolerably and act well was always sure to make a sensation, and generally caught a rich husband." Upon the success of these operettas, English composers began to "steal right and left from the repertories of the Italian and French comic Opera," creating a new bonanza for such actor/singers as the Woods,♪ the Seguins,♪♪ and even the French-oriented Anna Thillon.♪ More recently, however, the Pyne/Harrison company, "though highly esteemed, failed to reap any pecuniary reward, and within the [present] month two English opera companies have sought for the favor of a metropolitan audience, which would not take the trouble to go and hear them. Many ingenious persons have puzzled their brains," to find excuses for this "frigidity on the part of the public, but none of them have hit the nail on the head."

"It is not that the artists are mediocre," explained Wilkins, "or that they injudiciously pit themselves against the Italians in English versions of hackneyed operas. It is simply that the taste of the public has changed, and that nobody cares now for the English Opera when the Italian article can be had for the same price." While, ten or twelve years before, it had been "hard work to muster an audience for Italian Opera sufficient to fill Palmo's old place in Chambers Street" or the Astor Place establishment," ♪♫ nowadays we enthusiastically supported two opera companies performing at the same time, at Burton's and at the Academy, either house accommodating more people than the two old houses combined.

"The Italian opera is the fashionable amusement of the day," stated Wilkins, "not only in New York, but in Boston, Philadelphia, Baltimore, and the other provincial cities, when they are lucky enough to get it. . . . Fashionable people think it is the thing to say they have been to the opera, but are not so fond of saying that they have assisted at the acting of an English play" (much less an English opera!).[11]

Fashionable people felt privileged, however, to attend private performances by their social peers of an opera in English, *Flora, or, The Gipsy's Frolic,* by the Upper-Ten poet/librettist/composer Dr. Thomas Ward (1807–1873). Given for charity, the opera was performed four times at Ward's house at University Place,[12] where, reported the *Musical World* (July 10, 1858, p. 435), the drawing room was transformed into a "small opera house *pro tem.* The stage was at one end, with the footlights and other necessary appurtenances of scenery, etc. The orchestra was composed of a pianoforte and an Alexandre organ; the former being played by Mr. [William] Dressler, the conductor, and the latter by Mr. Timm," the only professionals involved in the production. "The composer, on being called before the curtain, [recalled] the trials and troubles of an amateur opera manager, greatly modified, however, in his own case, by the kindness and cheerful cooperation of the friends who had assisted him. He declared his conviction that a great amount of amateur music existed in the city of New York,[13] which, if brought together and cultivated, would do credit to the metropolis."

The writer (Richard Storrs Willis?) would have liked to dwell on the qualities of certain of the amateur performers but delicately desisted, for "this could hardly be done without trespassing on that privacy, which should be well guarded in the case of private performances in a private house."

Over the entire year, only a single performance of a single German opera was heard—at least, a French opera sung in German—Boieldieu's *La Dame blanche.*[14] Excellently performed on August 25 by Minna von Berkel, Joseph Weinlich, Hugo Pickaneser, and a number of their compatriots, it was announced as the first of a series of German operas to alternate with the programs of French dramatic offerings, vaudevilles, and ballets presented since May at Metropolitan Music Hall (as the hall at 585 Broadway was renamed). For some unexplained reason (doubtless monetary), after this single performance the opera project was for a time dropped (*Musical World,* quoted in *Dwight's,* September 18, 1858, p. 197).

The absence of German opera was, however, more than offset by the extraordinary proliferation throughout the summer of out-of-doors German festivals in which music played a major role. The annual celebration of *Pfingst-Montag* (Pentecost Mon-

---

    [11] It should be borne in mind that the *Herald,* at this time, was Ullman's (and the Academy's) fondest propagandist.
    [12] Composed some years earlier, the work had first been performed at Huntington, Long Island, by a group of Ward's amateur friends (*Dwight's,* June 18, 1859, p. 95).
    [13] As, for example, George Templeton Strong's past and future "Mass-meetings." ♪
    [14] Unlike Verdi in English, Boieldieu in German seems to have ruffled no critical feathers.

day) on May 24, due to "disagreements between some of the *bundes* with others," was held this year in two different places: Conrad's Yorkville Park (Eighty-sixth Street at the East River) and Jones's Wood (a rural area extending from Sixty-sixth to Seventy-first Streets, bounded by First Avenue and the East River). Early in the morning, according to prescribed ritual, "the different Societies of the *Sängerbund* [the faction bound for Yorkville] assembled at the Metropolitan Rooms [160 Hester Street], and, forming a procession, marched with their bands of music to the [City Hall] Park, and passed in procession before the Mayor and Common Council. Thence the line of march was taken up the Bowery to the foot of Tenth Street, East River, where a boat waited to convey the procession to the foot of Eighty-sixth Street.

"But already the Second, Third, and Fourth Avenue cars were literally packed with Germans, young and old . . . on their way to the scene of festivity, and by one o'clock several thousand persons were assembled on the ground. The number gradually increased until later in the day, when there could not have been less than 10,000 persons present and participating in the amusements of the day.

"And these were diverse. The various singing societies, numbering nearly a score, took their stations in various parts of the ground,[15] and from time to time sang their glees and choruses with fine effect. . . . Dodworth's two bands were present, and each in turn performed some of their finest pieces, and comprising several of the unique compositions introduced by Musard. Wherever was music was found the dance, whether on the grass or within the walls of [Conrad's] house. . . . Sailing and rowing on the East River also constituted a pleasant amusement." Athletic exhibitions and competitions abounded. And beer. "Tens of thousands of cataracts of real lager [were] poured into . . . unfathomable caverns [and] keg upon keg was exhausted" (*Tribune,* May 27, 1858).

Also according to ritual was the visit, late in the afternoon, of the Mayor (Daniel F. Tiemann) and his retinue; he "reviewed the *Turner* Rifles, ackowledged cheers," and made a speech glorifying Germans and things German. (Mayor Tiemann was half German.)

And the breakaway group: "Regarding themselves as slighted in the general arrangements, several associations established themselves at Jones's Wood, a little below, and celebrated on their own account," reported the *Evening Post* (May 25, 1858). "Music, rowing on the East River, and athletic exercises were the order of the day. Copious potations were made from a huge wassail bowl, filled, we believe, with *Lager Bier.*" At about four in the afternoon the Mayor appeared, was cordially received, exchanged mutually laudatory speeches with the celebrants, and made his departure (presumably headed for Yorkville). "The fun was kept up till seven o'clock, when the merrymakers, some three thousand in number, retired to the boats and were soon wending their way homeward."

Probably inspired by the public predilection for such out-of-doors events, it was resolved a week later, at a meeting of local musicians presided over by Carl Anschütz,[16] to hold a many-faceted, grand music festival "for charitable purposes" toward the end

---

[15] Each with its own tent.

[16] Currently enjoying a brief respite from both Ullman, who was in Europe, and Musard, whose short-lived promenade concerts were scheduled to begin at the Academy on July 12.

of June. Beginning with a huge concert at the Academy of Music, it would be followed the next day by an even more huge "pic-nic at some convenient rural spot." All the instrumental musicians in New York and environs were invited to participate, as were all the singing societies (*Tribune,* May 31. 1858).

The response was staggering. Crowding the Academy stage at the concert on June 27, an orchestra of more than three hundred volunteer musicians,[17] under the dual concertmastership of Joseph Noll and Theodore Thomas, purportedly represented "all, or very nearly all, of the instrumental performers of New York and vicinity, comprising members of the Philharmonic, the Italian Opera, the Musical Fund Society, all the different orchestras of the city theatres, and also of all the various [military] bands." In addition, three hundred members of the city's foremost German singing societies appeared with their respective conductors; a quartet of the best solo singers currently present in the city or neighborhood participated; and "the most celebrated conductors now in the country"—Anschütz, Bergmann and Maretzek[18]—conducted at both the concert and the "Grand Rural Festival, or Pic-nic," held the following day at Jones's Wood.[19]

During the hectic preparations for this colossal undertaking, the complicated details of sectional rehearsals at various locations, involving hundreds of musicians, were administered by F. B. Helmsmüller,♪ secretary of the project, and transmitted to the players through notices in the newspapers. The prevailing mood was reportedly one of high exhilaration. Beginning with Anschütz, who tirelessly contributed his talent, labor, devotion, and even the Academy (allotted him for his overdue benefit), the dominant concept of the undertaking (at least, according to Burkhardt and Hagen) seems to have been one of idealism, mutual good will, and philanthropy[20] (albeit the prospective beneficiaries were never precisely identified).[21]

The musical concept was no less grandiose. The great feature of the Academy

---

[17] Allegedly restricted to that number by space limitations: many who had volunteered and rehearsed were "reluctantly compelled to 'hang up their fiddle and the bow' and become listeners instead of performers" (*Dispatch,* July 3, 1858).

[18] Who had completed his Commonwealth opera season only the day before.

[19] "What a pity," observed *Harper's Weekly* (June 19, 1858, p. 387) (probably George William Curtis), "that the Central Park is not yet completed, with all its casinos, its music-halls, and fountains!" These alluring future features of Central Park, to be designed, under the superintendence of Frederick Law Olmsted (1822–1903) and Calvert Vaux (1824–1895), by the music-loving architect Jacob Wrey Mould (1825–1886), had only recently been approved (in April).

[20] It was "entirely an affair of love," wrote an overbrimming Hagen, "love to do good to suffering brethren, and to the great cause of that art which comparatively has made more progress in this country than in any other. Not one of the hundreds and thousands who participated in this grand enterprise, who lent their talent, labor, and knowledge to it, was paid, and the whole proceeds are destined for [unidentified] benevolent purposes." At the going rates, estimated Hagen, payment for the donated services would have amounted to nearly $100,000 (*Review and Gazette,* July 10, 1858, p. 211).

[21] Watson, piqued at what he considered a snub by the festival managers, referred to the charity as one about which he had vaguely heard but actually knew nothing (*Leslie's,* July 10, 1858, p. 87). But Burkhardt, a passionate supporter of the undertaking, wrote in the *Dispatch* (on June 19): "The object of the festival is one of universal charity, and although the final disposal of the profits accruing has not yet been made public, we believe that . . . the proceeds will most probably find their way into the treasuries of the 'Musical Fund' and the 'Musical Mutual Protective' Societies, two excellent associations for the support of sick, aged, and infirm members of the musical profession."

concert—occupying the entire second part of the program[22]—was Beethoven's Ninth Symphony, no less, not heard in New York since its single performance (in English) conducted by George Loder♪♩ at Castle Garden in 1846.♪[23] With Anschütz at the helm, it was now performed by the huge orchestra, the huge chorus (embracing members of the *Allgemeiner Sängerbund,* the *Liederkranz,* the *Arion* Society, and the *Harmonia* Society of Hoboken), and the quartet of soloists, Mesdames Caradori and Zimmermann, and—replacing Formes and George Simpson, who were originally announced—Pickaneser and Weinlich.[24]

Unfortunately, as all the critics noted, the multitudes onstage considerably outnumbered the scanty audience. The poor attendance was generally attributed to the public's reluctance to attend a performance on a Sunday (unless it was labeled "sacred");[25] it was also blamed on the intense heat—close to 100 degrees. Watson blamed the prices of admission—outrageous, he claimed, for a Sunday concert.[26]

Nor—except for the tribal ecstasies of Hagen and Burkhardt—did Beethoven's reputedly incomprehensible Ninth receive the unmixed commendation of the New York press. Seymour, who, like his compatriots, regretted "the unfortunate necessity of giving the concert on the Sabbath,"[27] was lukewarm: the first and second movements, although of interest to musicians, he wrote, were "not attractive to the multitude," but the "glories of the third movement [were] perceptible to everyone," and the fourth, "in which Beethoven introduces the voice in elucidation of his musical ideas"—when superbly performed, as it had been by Anschütz and his forces—was grand and imposing and afforded a pleasure that was "almost overwhelming"[28] (*Times,* June 28, 1858).

But in the opinion of the *Albion* critic: "Compared with some symphonies of Mendelssohn, and even Gade, the three first movements are plain and readable to the well instructed instrumentalist of the present day. Only in the fourth movement do we find the composer grasping at effects more or less beyond the range of the conductor's *bâton.*"

Proceeding to debunk Beethoven, he wrote: "There are works by celebrated

[22] The first part comprised Weber's Overture to *Oberon* conducted by Anschütz and repeated by vociferous demand of the audience; the chorus "O Isis and Osiris" from *The Magic Flute* (*Sängerbund* conducted by E. Weber, a Philharmonic violist); Schumann's Overture, Scherzo, and Finale, op. 52 (Bergmann); "The Heavens are Telling" from *The Creation* (*Liederkranz* conducted by Agricol Paur); and the Coronation March from *Le Prophète,* the hit of the evening, dynamically conducted and encored by Maretzek, who was "greeted with shouts of welcome."

[23] Hagen erroneously referred to a prior performance by Bergmann of the Ninth Symphony, probably a confused reference to a performance that had been announced during Bergmann's fleeting conductorship of the Harmonic Society in 1856,♪ but to my knowledge never given.

[24] Formes was reported to be ill; no excuse was made for Simpson.

[25] The event was pooh-poohed by the chauvinistic Briton at the *Albion* (July 3, 1858, pp. 319–20). Not only did he condemn the immorality of a Sunday performance—a practice piously shunned by Anglo-Saxons but embraced by Teutons—but he belittled the whole effort as inferior to the great triennial festivals at Birmingham in numbers, quality, and beneficence.

[26] They were opera prices: seats in the parquet $1; reserved seats fifty cents extra; family circle fifty cents; gallery twenty-five cents.

[27] Largely attributable to the number of volunteers from the theatre orchestras who were employed on all the other nights of the week.

[28] Following the symphony, Anschütz was showered with bouquets and presented with a laurel wreath, which he modestly (and rightfully, according to the *Albion* critic) declined.

composers which appear to be surrounded by a sacred halo and to be protected by an art-divinity perfectly incomprehensible. The world has long since sunk into a state of big-eyed wonder at the genius of Beethoven and has made up its mind to wink at any shortcomings. In the particular instance of this work, it [the world] persists in regarding it as his greatest, whilst those who hear it as persistently refuse to believe anything of the kind."

Under Anschütz's direction, the first three movements had been played "with moderate skill," considering the musicians had to miss rehearsals in order to fill their job demands at this "steamboat-excursion time of the year." In fact, the third movement, in which "the Master regains his old strength and throws a chain of melody around the audience which it is impossible to break," admittedly had been quite excellently played.

But in the last movement (in which the double basses went rhythmically astray at the start): "So long as the singers are confined to a simple melody and its harmonies, the result is massive and grand. But Beethoven aims for a profound agitation, a wild delirium of joy, and soon exercises his voices in such a way that it is barely possible to keep them together. The wisest men are ignorant of certain things, and Beethoven, cloud-compeller as he was, knew nothing whatever about writing for the voice" (*Albion,* July 3, 1858, pp. 319–20). Blasphemy!

At nine o'clock the following morning—with the thermometer soaring yet higher—the members of the four singing societies flourishing gorgeous banners, together with the various festival committees and a number of invited guests, great numbers of brass players, and several military bands, assembled at the Metropolitan Rooms. Forming companies under the various Marshals of the Day and accompanied by two "mammoth bands" they set forth on the ceremonial march to City Hall Park, then up the Bowery to Grand Street, where they boarded waiting steamboats for the voyage to Jones's Wood. Additionally the steamboats *Ohio* and *O. M. Petit,* scheduled to make three round trips to Jones's Wood during the day, picked up passengers at Delancey, Tenth, and Twenty-third Streets, at five cents a trip. The Second and Third Avenue railroad lines' fare was the same.

"The rush to the scene of action was something tremendous," wrote Darcie. "Every conveyance, either by land or water,[29] was thronged, from early morn to dewy eve; and it is stated that, in addition to the regular tickets issued for the Sunday performance, over thirty thousand persons paid admission [twenty-five cents] at the gates during the day"[30] (*Porter's Spirit,* July 3, 1858, p. 288).

Although the vast attendance was predominantly German—demonstrating, as the *Tribune* observed (June 29, 1858), "all the affectionate and naif demonstrations of German life in the open air—mother, father, children, babies—without false shame and with an *abandon* truly national"—other nationalities were also represented, particularly American. Indeed, American participation had been earnestly solicited, as indicated by the presence of such native luminaries as William Henry Fry and Stephen A. Douglas (1813–1861), the Senator from Illinois, both of whom made brief but stirring speeches.

---

[29] And on horseback, by "private conveyances" (which were allowed to enter the Jones's Wood grounds at the Seventy-second Street gate), and on foot (*Dispatch,* July 3, 1858).

[30] In his enthusiasm, Burkhardt estimated a crowd of from sixty to seventy thousand; Hagen reported forty thousand (*Dispatch,* July 3; *Review and Gazette,* July 10, 1858, p. 211).

Mayor Tiemann and his "corporate authorities," who had been invited, this time, however, defaulted.

Performed on a huge platform under the trees, and variously conducted by Anschütz, Bristow, Rietzel, Bergmann, Noll, and Weber, the musical program—during which was interpolated Fry's address and a speech in "learned German" by a Professor Füster of Vienna—consisted of Carl Maria von Weber's Overture to *Euryanthe,* a *Fackeltanz* by Meyerbeer, the Hunter's Chorus from *Euryanthe* sung by the *Sängerbund,* the Overture to Verdi's *Nabucco,* the March from *Tannhäuser,* and, principally, a hair-raising rendition of "The Star-Spangled Banner" by more than 2000 performers: 1400 members of the singing societies, 300 in the band, and 300 "members of the procession," supplemented by great numbers of joiners-in from the audience.

After the concert the gigantic platform was "arranged" for the Grand Ball to follow, and the pic-nickers danced to the strains of a quadrille orchestra of eighty musicians until closing time, seven P.M., when the multitude peaceably departed for home. Astounding quantities of beer were consumed. The *Albion* critic reported that Jones's Wood had been rimmed with "*Lager-Bier* stands," and that the dispensers of beer had further appropriated every inch of shade within the grounds: "only in the burning sun [was] the visitor . . . out of reach of the bar keeper, for it was only there that *Lager-Bier* would not keep." Rather than a festival for charitable purposes, this "beer orgie"[31] resembled a "gigantic speculation for the diffusion of various maltings," he wrote, thus it was no wonder that people who had come for the music hurriedly departed, upon encountering an overwhelming crush of guzzling humanity, solidly "matted on the turf."

Yet, despite the prodigious consumption of beer (purportedly "the drink which cheers but not intoxicates"), it was remarked that the behavior of this vast throng of pleasure-seekers—as at all such out-of-doors German festivities—was exemplary, leaving the police, scattered about the grounds and in boats, with nothing to do but witness the festivities. Indeed, even the fault-finding *Albion* critic admitted that "the hearty joviality of the scene was its principal attraction."

Heeding the public demand for a repeat of the enjoyable event (and quick to recognize a good thing when they saw one), Anschütz and Maretzek[32]—temporarily at loose ends—lost no time in announcing a three-day "Mammoth Music Festival," with elaborate extramusical embellishments, to take place at Jones's Wood,[33] August 2 through 4. Billed additionally as a "*Fête Champêtre* and Fancy Fair," the event, described by Burkhardt (*Dispatch,* August 14, 1868) as "a new and more intellectual style of enjoyment," would include such carnival attractions as balloon ascensions and fire-

---

[31] "1300 kegs were ordered for the occasion, which, as each keg contains 120 glasses, was equal to 156,000 pints of the beverage," but the demand at last exceeded the supply (*Times,* June 29; *Dwight's,* July 3, 1858, p. 111). Light wines, soda water, and lemonade were also "in great request."

[32] With the apparent backing, among others, of the much maligned John C. Jacobsohn (*Times,* August 10; *Porter's Spirit,* August 14, 1858, p. 384).

[33] The locality was perfect, wrote the *Herald* (July 7, 1858), easily accessible by "cars and steamboats on all sides," and, if successful, the festival might lead to the construction of a grand concert hall and gardens, similar to the delightful Surrey Gardens in London. "Something of the kind [was] needed here, combining artistic and physical enjoyment, and Jones's Wood, barring its [unromantic] name, [was] just the place for it."

works, jumping in sacks and climbing the greased pole. Prize competitions would be held for the best *Sangverein* and *Turnverein.*

Indicating dissension in the German music community, Helmsmüller, who apparently had not been included in the present arrangements, published a card disclaiming any connection with the Mammoth Festival. "Everybody will be delighted to hear it," waspishly retorted the *Times* (July 31, 1858). "The 'United Musicians,' on [the previous] occasion, did not distinguish themselves, and it is honest and straightforward of their Secretary to let the public know that they are not to mar the Mammoth Festival. The orchestra engaged by Maretzek and Anschütz is *paid* to do its duty."[34] (Evidently, indiscriminate philanthropy had its drawbacks.)

In an answering disclaimer (July 27), the "Management" of the coming festival not only denied any connection with the past effort and any of its officials, but acidly stated that the prospective "Mammoth Orchestra" of two hundred musicians included no unpaid or voluntary members; it represented instead a handpicked body of professional musicians, whose aggregate pay alone—exclusive of astronomical expenditures for fireworks, prizes for contests, balloon ascensions, and a thousand and one other disbursements—was greater than the total expenses of the previous festival.

Frustratingly, after a heavily persistent buildup in the papers, the Mammoth Musical Festival, for all its tantalizing wonders, had to be postponed to August 9 because of a stubborn spell of rain. By then the transatlantic cable had been joined (on August 5), and the city was plunged into its frenetic celebration of that, alas, ephemeral achievement, thus immeasurably contributing to the success of the Mammoth Musical Festival.

Darcie vividly sets the scene. On the morning of August 9, he writes: "Soon after ten o'clock, the visitors began to arrive [at Jones's Wood] in goodly numbers, by road, rail, and river conveyance; and as the day advanced, the throng increased until something like 8000 persons, bent on enjoyment, had assembled. The arrangements for the *fête* were excellent and on the most extended scale. The beautiful grounds, embracing a space of nearly sixty acres, were dotted with tents, marquees, booths, and refreshment stands, whilst the gigantic terrace for the concert and open-air ball loomed large in the center of the grounds, the pendant flags of all nations fluttering in the summer air and giving life and gaiety to the scene. In addition to these attractions there were giants, dwarfs, acrobats, tall men, and obese women, rendering the [resem blance] to a European fancy-fair complete" (*Porter's Spirit,* August 14, 1858, p. 384).

And *Trovator:* "In the evening it was worth something more than the twenty-five cents admission to visit Jones's Wood. The sylvan grove was illuminated with calcium lights [provided by the lighting expert Professor Grant], while innumerable stands for the sale of lager, fruit, candies, and soda ornamented, or encumbered, the grounds. Then there were establishments where for three cents you could get a ride upon one

---

[34] Furthermore, wrote the *Times,* "It is not the intention of the managers to convert the grounds into an extensive *Lager-Bier* garden [apparently a major bone of contention], but to supply them merely with unusual attractions appropriate to a musical festival." The *Albion,* still rankling over the discomforts of the earlier event, agreed. Labeling the previous festival "nothing but a *Lager-Bier* orgie," he wrote: "Barrels will not, we are glad to say, be accommodated with the only seats in the garden, nor will every shade tree be converted into an impromptu bar-room" (August 7, 1858, p. 380).

of a company of stump-tailed revolving horses; there were places where you could win a pint of peanuts by engaging in shooting a pop-gun at a target for a cent a shot." But the greatest attraction was the "huge platform for dancing, with overhanging trees, and calcium lights, and a little moonlight feebly struggling through the foliage. The orchestra was excellent, and everybody danced with everybody, and there was much fun." Although there was a lot of "jabbering in Dutch," wrote *Trovator,* it was difficult to tell whether the Germans or the Anglo-Saxons predominated (*Dwight's,* August 21, 1858, p. 165).

Not so Darcie: "It was at first imagined that this *fête* would . . . exhibit strong Teutonic proclivities," he continued, in *Porter's Spirit,* "but this was a *fête* intended for all New York, and not for the gratification of any peculiar set of citizens."

Not only was it a nonpartisan event, but, in the *Times's* opinion, it was an unprecedentedly American occasion: "Remove ten thousand Germans from an extraordinary musical festival; replace them with an equal number of Americans, crowd an ample orchard with human beings intent on wholesome amusement and determined to enjoy themselves at any sacrifice, and you have an idea of the gay picture presented yesterday at Jones's Wood" wrote the *Times* (August 10, 1858). "At first the attendance seemed slim. When the concert began there were not more than two thousand persons present, but they came, and came, and came, until the garden was filled, so that the merriment which preceded the fireworks, and the fireworks themselves, were witnessed by many thousand persons. We doubt very much if there has ever been such an assemblage of Americans before."

The phenomenon was attributed to Maretzek, who had made it his mission to "nationalize the musical festival in America." In wooing an American following, continued the *Times,* he had "incurred a vast disgrace" with the German musical community:[35] "Hundreds of his musical countrymen maintained that [the occasion] should be German and nothing but German.[36] But Mr. Maretzek was vain enough to believe that if he knocked down a score of *Lager Bier* stands[37] and gave the space to the public, they would, if American, discover the difference between a mere orgie and an entertainment of a pure and unexceptionable character. The result has proved that he was right. Seven-eighths of those present were Americans, and the entertainment passed off with triumphant *éclat.*" (And apparently with a considerably reduced consumption of beer.)

Yet, the program of the opening concert consisted, with only one exception, exclusively of German music: Festival Overtures by Lachner and Joseph von Arx (a local musician), Mendelssohn's Wedding March, Wagner's *Tannhäuser* Overture, the inevitable Coronation March from *Le Prophète,* two potpourris by the German composer Carl Zulehner (1770–1841),[38] and, as the *pièce de resistance,* the Anvil Chorus from *Il trova-*

---

[35] Maretzek, a quintessential citizen of the world, was accused by his irate compariots of having "lost his nationality" (*Dispatch,* August 14, 1858).

[36] According to Burkhardt, the Germans boycotted the festival (*Dispatch,* August 14, 1858). For example, the *Turnverein* competition did not materialize because the *Turner* elected not to compete.

[37] The discord seems in no small way to have hinged on the restricted number of beer stands permitted within the bounds of Jones's Wood for this event.

[38] Zulehner is thought by the editors of the Köchel Catalog, sixth edition (1964), to have been the composer of the spurious "Mozart Twelfth Mass."

tore, conducted by Anschütz, Maretzek, Angelo Torriani, and Theodore Thomas, with Carl Prox and G. Washbourn Morgan boisterously wielding the mallets.

The performances, wrote the partisan *Times,* were as close to perfection as one could desire. "Compared with it, the music of the previous festival was mere hand-organ work." But *Trovator* maintained that, rather than the principal feature of this musical festival, music was just another of its many pleasant attractions, about on a par with the dancing and fireworks.

Contrary to *Trovator,* the *Times* reported that, upon the conclusion of the concert, not one, but five dance bands "in the various parts of the garden struck up, and those who were disposed to dancing enjoyed themselves to the full. In every corner of the garden was a full band, and the moment one ceased another began." This continued until a little before eight o'clock, when a magnificent display of fireworks created by the celebrated brothers Joseph and Isaac Edge, "the fire kings," "commenced to make their way to the heavens." Most exciting was the finale, a set piece portraying the consummation of the Atlantic Cable-laying—the meeting of the two ships at sea—and culminating in a thrilling finale abounding in flags and ornaments and finally crowned with the motto: "Blessed be Providence; the Cable is laid." A spectacle that eclipsed anything the *Times* had ever seen done with light!

Lending their benedictions to the festival—and ceremonially received, of course—were the mayor and other representatives of officialdom. And on the final day an audience of ten to fifteen thousand persons assembled to hear four singing societies with unfamiliar names compete for a handsome Mammoth Silver Goblet, about 20 inches high. Apparently hastily improvised to replace the German singing societies, who, like the athletic societies, had defected from the Mammoth Festival,[39] the competing groups—all small—were the Amphion, led by Carl Prox; the Confluentia, under Theodore Thomas, the *Vierblätteriges Kleeblatt* (Four-leaved Shamrock) conducted by Emanuel Grill, and the Quadricinium, again under Prox. Each group sang two pieces, one comic and one serious, and at the end of the program they united in a hymn "This is the Lord's Day," conducted by Theodore Thomas. Upon the goblet being awarded (with requisite speechmaking by Henry C. Watson) to the aptly named *Vierblätteriges Kleeblatt,* a male quartet, it was promptly filled with *Steinwein* and passed around among the victors, the German opera singers: Quint,♪ Beutler,♪ Pickaneser, and Müller, all of whom, much to the amusement of the audience, mightily quaffed thereof, as did their conductor Grill. Various instrumental pieces were interspersed among the choral offerings,[40] and the concert ended with the clamorous Anvil Chorus, clamorously encored, as usual.

With out-of-doors Musical Festivals now proclaimed "all the rage," it was not surprising that a three-day continuation of the Mammoth Festival at Jones's Wood was promptly announced. This time billed as a "Grand Telegraphic Musical Festival" in honor of Cyrus W. Field, the supreme hero of the moment, it commenced, after an intervening day of recess, on August 13. Stressing the American theme, the musical highlight of this reprise—in addition to "The Electric Telegraph"—was a descriptive

---

[39] At Conrad's Yorkville Park, on August 25, the *Liederkranz* Society autonomously presented, at four P.M. "A Summernight's Dream," consisting of "promenade music" by Noll's Band, at six o'clock a vocal and instrumental concert conducted by Agricol Paur, and at midnight a *bal champêtre.*

[40] One of them being a timely item, "The Electric Telegraph," by one Kuhner.

work for band by V. Streck, "The Battle of Bunker Hill," subtitled "A Military Picture Musical," tracing the progress of that historical episode from "The Appeal to Arms" to the final victorious "Hymn of Freedom." It was announced that the work would be performed "in the center of the grounds with (recalling Jullien) Shelton's and Grafulla's Brass Bands advancing from the corners toward the conductors": Maretzek, Anschütz, Torriani, Thomas, Grill, Prox, and von Arx. (Did they conduct in succession, episode by episode, or ensemble?)

For the grand finale, falling on a Sunday, "two of the Most Superb Sacred Concerts which have ever been given in the United States" were announced (the extra concert probably to compensate for the sabbatical absence of the usual weekday attractions). For a single twenty-five cent ticket one could hear both concerts, scheduled for two and six P.M. Unfortunately, it rained, and the double-pronged event had to be postponed until the following Sunday, August 22,[41] by which time it had been expanded into a triple-pronged event, still for the single admission price of twenty-five cents. The segments were presented at 2:30, 4:30, and 6:30 P.M. Where else could one enjoy so much superb music for only eight and a half cents a concert? exulted Burkhardt (*Dispatch,* August 28, 1858).

The triple event (advertised as "Three Mammoth Sacred Concerts") came off on August 29 with "the Grandest Band of Wind Instruments ever assembled in the United States," comprising, in the first segment, the Washington Band led by Thomas G. Adkins;♩ in the second, Shelton's Band led by Claudio Grafulla; and in the third, presumably a combination of the two. The programs, loosely denominated sacred, included—among the instrumental offerings—band arrangements of an unspecified overture by Beethoven, excerpts from *The Magic Flute* and Mendelssohn's *Athalie,* the *Miserere* from *Il Trovatore,* and two pieces by Zulehner: a "Grand Polymelos" (a slick, sacred-sounding disguise for "potpourri") and a Grand Finale. Weinlich sang airs from Rossini's *Stabat Mater* and Mendelssohn's *St. Paul,* and a nameless chorus, billed only as "the Singing Societies,"[42] delivered the standard choral blockbusters: "The Heavens are Telling" from *The Creation,* the Hallelujah from *Messiah,* the Prayer from Rossini's *Mosè,* and Martin Luther's Hymn, *Ein' feste Burg.* The conductors, as usual, were Anschütz, Maretzek, Theodore Thomas, Mosenthal,♩ Torriani, Prox, and von Arx.

On the very next evening Maretzek opened his problematical fall season of opera at the Academy (with Pepita Gassier and Ernest Perring in *La sonnambula*), and soon after, Anschütz departed on a three-week concert tour (or as Ullman announced it, a series of "Mammoth Musical Festivals"), with Formes and a large and impressive assisting company.[43] Talk of a continuation of the Mammoth Festivals at Jones's Wood thus came to naught.

---

[41] In the meantime, on August 16, the giant first festival of the Bloomingdale *Turner* Society was scheduled at Jones's Wood, to be attended by numberless athletic, singing, and social societies from New York, Williamsburg, Brooklyn, Morrisania, Hoboken, Hudson City, Jersey City, and Union Hill. Athletic contests, speeches, and band music provided by Scheld's Band were the features of the program.

[42] Probably an amalgam of the competitors in the recent prize contest and/or members of the currently unemployed opera chorus.

[43] Consisting of the American soprano Hattie Andem, a Madame Schumann from the Vienna Imperial Opera, Ernest Perring, and an orchestra chosen from the front ranks of the Academy of Music orchestra and the Philharmonic Society, including, among others, Theodore Thomas, Joseph

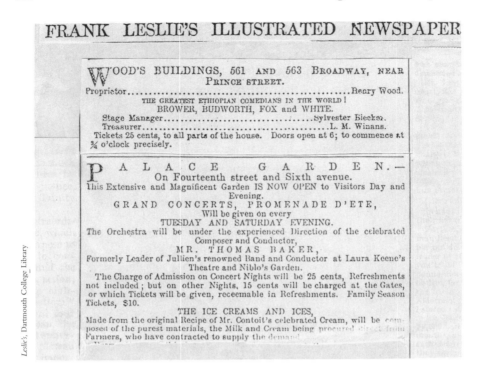

It is evident from such advertisements that there was plenty of entertaining activity available.

New Yorkers were not, however, deprived of more open-air music, fireworks, balloon ascensions, and other favorite summertime diversions, albeit in an urban location. Situated at Sixth Avenue and Fourteenth Street, the Palace Garden—a distant echo of Castle Garden—covering a "tastefully laid-out" expanse of 60,000 square feet,[44] had, since July 1, been dispensing these delights, together with superior ice creams and other confections fabricated on the premises under the guidance of the veteran foreman of Contoit's New York Garden.[45] Open every afternoon and evening except Sundays, the Palace Garden featured concerts directed by Thomas Baker on Tuesdays and Saturdays, at the admission price of twenty-five cents, refreshments not included; on non-concert days the tickets were fifteen cents, redeemable in refreshments.

As the former concertmaster of promenade concerts in London under such masters as Jullien and the elder Musard, Baker, a resourceful musician and tireless arranger,

Mosenthal, Carl Bergmann, and Xavier Kiefer. Concerts were booked for Pittsburgh, Wheeling, Columbus, Cincinnati, Dayton, Lexington, Louisville, St. Louis, Chicago, Milwaukee, Detroit, etc.

[44] Replete with "splendid decorations, gas jets, variegated lamps, fountains, statuary, shrubbery, illuminations. . . . The grounds . . . seem to have been transformed into a fairy scene," wrote the *Dispatch* (July 3, 1858).

[45] A favorite—indeed legendary—resort of an earlier day, located on Broadway, between Leonard and Franklin streets.

apparently possessed the particular (and elusive) knack for putting together programs that appealed to the popular taste. With his "choice orchestra" he presented great miscellanies of opera music, dance music, arrangements of popular songs, trick solo bits, ballet music, comic music, and more.

Notably, on July 22, as part of a widely diversified musical program, Baker presented his own "American Quadrille," composed, *à la* Jullien, on "Ethiopian melodies" by Stephen Foster: "Maggie by my side," "Gentle Annie," "Oh! Boys, carry me along," "Willie, we have missed thee," "Ellen Bayne," "Massa's in the cold, cold ground," "Hard Times," and, as a finale (deserting Foster), "The Arkansas Traveler." In another medley, "Music for the Million," Baker included—among popular English tunes and Italian opera arias—"Massa's in the cold, cold ground," "Nancy Till," and "Jordan is a hard road to travel"; and—continuing to rummage in Jullien's bag of tricks—"'The Sleigh Ride,' accompanied by bells, whips, etc." Evidently Messrs. De Forest and Tisdale, the proprietors and managers of Palace Garden, were as well attuned to the popular taste as was Baker: "The Palace Garden is by far the best attended place of recreation in the city," reported the *Times* (on July 10, 1858). "An excellent balloon ascension[46] took place here on Friday; on Saturday there was a concert and a fine display of fireworks. From three to five thousand people enjoy nightly the well-arranged attractions of this excellently conducted garden. It is precisely the place we have wanted in New-York, and its success is really a matter of congratulation."

At the height of the Cable celebration, in August, the whirl of "well-arranged attractions" at the Palace Garden included balloon ascensions, female choruses, male choruses, a "Veiled Songstress," a company of Iroquois Indians, and a thousand colored lights multiplied in glittering pendant lusters and mirror reflectors. Dodworth's Military Band and Cornet Corps, combined with the Palace Garden orchestra and conducted by Harvey Dodworth, performed on Mondays, Wednesdays, and Fridays; Baker's concerts continued to be given on Tuesdays and Saturdays.[47]

Earlier in the year, in March, Dodworth's peripatetic band had given Sunday evening "sacred" concerts for fun-loving New Yorkers at the Santa Claus, a new drinking and entertainment establishment at 596 Broadway. The day following its opening on March 6, the Santa Claus's proprietor, R. W. Williams, in vivacious prose, advertised: "Hurrah for the Santa Claus. Magnificent opening of Williams's Mammoth Billiard and Concert Saloon . . . Last evening, glees splendid, songs of the first class, dancing unexceptionable, extempore singing, every verse setting the audience in a roar—and all went merry as a marriage bell."[48]

And a week later (March 12): "Have you been to the Santa Claus to hear Miss Julia Barton, the most powerful singer in the Union? Also the celebrated extemporaneous singer, Mr. Harrison? If not, go tonight, as there is an entire change of programme."

---

[46] For those wishing to witness the inflation of the balloon, an operation requiring about an hour, the admission was advanced to fifty cents.

[47] To meet the change of seasons, on October 22, Messrs. De Forest and Tisdale opened their newly constructed Palace Garden Pavilion, seating 2500 persons, with a musical program that presented, among other attractions, the mysterious Veiled Songstress and the "celebrated pianist" and recent child prodigy, Mr. Sebastian Kook.♪

[48] Aided and augmented by the contents of an "uncommonly well-stocked" bar.

On May 1, Williams, who changed his seductive advertising copy as frequently as he did his attractions, promoted his Santa Claus as a concert saloon featuring "Opera, ballet, concerts, minstrels, and gymnasts." His current headliner was a "Bohemian Olio," presenting the musical high points of *The Bohemian Girl,* featuring, among its other allurements, a Miss Frothingham as Arline, a Mr. Eldridge as Thaddeus, and singing and dancing gypsies;[49] also on the program were the German acrobat Siegrist and his dog Lager in "wonderful feats, Brindley on the flying cord, W. N. Smith, the champion bones player, and Mr. West, the inimitable Irish comedian from Barnum's." Tickets were twelve cents, the standard price of admission to concert saloons. For a period Santa Claus apparently thrived.

Doubtless encouraged by the vast crowds of transients attending the cable celebration, such alcoholic concert saloons—too multitudinous to enumerate—proliferated at a giddy pace, as did the countless German beer-and-entertainment resorts.

Later in the year, on November 13 a phonetically spelled Madame "Vittersheim," in high-flown terms announced the opening of her new concert and drinking saloon, upstairs at 409 Broadway. Superior musical entertainment would be offered by the former Madame Elisa Valentini, now Madame Antonio Paravalli, "who stands without rival in beauty of voice, transcendency of musical talent, and dramatic sentiment, united to a wonderful execution."[50] The twenty-five-cent admission covered "one glass of refreshment."

Only a week after it opened, the establishment was newly advertised as "Valentini's Concert Saloon," and Madame Wittersheim, now identified as Valentini's partner, announced the added attraction of "Italian pasta dishes, such as macaroni, risotti, etc.," concocted by the celebrated Italian chef, Signor Arata. Italian delicacies daily from nine to five; concert every evening at nine o'clock.

The temples of minstrelsy enjoyed a banner year, with Buckley's Serenaders (assisted by Bishop Buckley's sensational trained horse Mazeppa) holding forth at their Opera House and later at 444 Broadway, Bryant's Minstrels at Mechanics' Hall, and Wood's Minstrels (ceasing to be Christy and Wood's with the breakup of the partnership in May),[51] with its passing parade of George Holland, T. D. Rice, and Eph Horn, at Wood's Buildings.[52] Budworth's Minstrels appeared at the Olympic Opera House, and Matt Peel's Campbell's Minstrels at the old standby at 444 Broadway, currently renamed Minstrel Hall.

At the Franklin Museum, where appeared twenty-seven young lady "Model Artistes" in a twice-daily, "beautiful exhibition of statuary, unequaled in the world," a "female opera troupe, composed of ladies," sang a selection of "negro melodies."

Other varieties of ethnic balladry were dispensed at Mozart Hall—on January 14

[49] In August, Williams advertised: "Have you seen the musical olio from the *Daughter of the Regiment?*" featuring the actress/singer Julia Barton.

[50] "LaGrange, Alboni, Grisi, and the rest of them may as well retire from the stage," caustically commented the *Evening Post* (November 11, 1858).

[51] In June, apparently to spur business after George Christy's departure, Henry Wood advertised a list of places where "silver tickets" worth twenty-five cents, good for admission to his theatre, could be procured in advance, to obviate the boredom of standing in line at his box office.

[52] Where in June a splendid ice-water fountain was installed.

*The all-but-defunct Crystal Palace had closed its doors
to all but an occasional private party, such as this one,
so well covered by* Leslie's Illustrated Newspaper.

by Lucy Williams, the Welsh Nightingale,[53] and on February 24 by Agnes Sutherland, the Scottish Nightingale. Miss Williams's assisting artists were the Welsh baritone and song composer John Rogers Thomas (1829–1896), who was honored with a triple encore, and a Mr. J. M. Abbott who accompanied at the piano. In September, reports Odell (VII, 190), Miss Williams announced four appearances at the Apollo Rooms.

[53] Lured to the United States with false promises of a Jenny Lind promotion by agents of Barnum's Museum (no longer in Barnum's possession), Lucy Williams had found herself in the ignominious position of singing at the Museum—not a disreputable place, but not a genteel one either. She had recently freed herself and was attempting, by giving concerts, to amass enough money to return home (*Dwight's,* January 23, 1858, p. 341).

Miss Sutherland appeared under the patronage of the Highland Guard and Caledonian Club and was assisted by Mr. Walter Relyea, "the eminent and only male soprano," formerly with Madame Anna Bishop and Miss Catherine Hayes,♪ and a Mr. Cumming, who atmospherically sang "some of the gems of Scotch and Jacobite airs in full Highland costume." H. C. Becht♪ presided at the piano, and Robertson's Quadrille Band accompanied and also played "several favorite pieces."

On September 23, Stephen C. Massett,♪ "the First California Troubadour," gave his long-and-loudly heralded one-man show at Niblo's Saloon. Active on the New York stage in the 1840s, in 1849 Massett had emigrated to gold-rush, entertainment-hungry San Francisco, where, under the alias of "Jeems Pipes of Pipesville," he attained great celebrity as a song writer,[54] author, and entertainer. Making a virtue of necessity (assisting artists being locally nonexistent at the time), Massett had evolved a multifaceted solo entertainment that embraced song, recitation, mimicry (of his theatrical and musical colleagues), and personal reminiscence. Returning now from an around-the-world tour that had included Australia, India, and England, Massett, in his present show, "Song and Chit-Chat of Travels in Many Lands," enchanted a capacity audience with his singing "in the popular style"[55] and with his fascinating monologue, consisting of travel anecdotes—comic and tragic—reminiscences, witty imitations,[56] and a stirring rendition of Tennyson's poem "The Charge of the Light Brigade." Massett repeated his entertainment at Niblo's on September 28. There was talk of continuing performances at Dodworth's, but Massett went on tour instead.

In April the Hutchinson Family, John W. and Asa B., absent for the past year, now with the addition of Lizzie C., returned from their tour of the West and gave three concerts in rapid succession—on April 6, 9, and 13 at Mozart Hall. Reviewing the first, the *Times* (April 7, 1858) urged those who had not yet heard the Hutchinsons to seize the present opportunity. Their program, much the same as usual, elicited "rounds of applause and peals of laughter, as in the olden time": "The unquestionable earnestness which characterizes some of the pieces, and which is highly pathetic in spite of ultraism [radicalism]; the utterly reckless absurdity and buffoonery of some of the pieces; the wild, unkempt, prophetic look of the singers; the extraordinary harmony, unisons, and accompaniments they adopt; and the marvelously dry and chip-like speeches they address to the audience are circumstances in the Hutchinsons' entertainment which give it a peculiar and thoroughly enjoyable character."

In September, Dodworth's Cornet Band performed nightly at the American Institute's Great Annual Industrial Fair, held for the third consecutive year at the Crystal Palace.♪ The Institute's official takeover (in July) of that derelict structure had been hotly denounced in the *Tribune*[57] (July 3, 1858) as an illegal, money-grabbing manipulation involving not only the Institute's administrators but various city officials. The investigation that the *Tribune* demanded never came to pass (if one were indeed in-

---

[54] Massett was credited with the composition of some fifty-six songs and ballads.

[55] Particularly appealing to "the general public, who dearly love simple and intelligible music," wrote Watson (*Leslie's,* October 2, 1858, p. 281).

[56] Among them burlesques of Henry Russell,♪ William Dempster, and of Anna Bishop's performance in San Francisco (in 1850) of "Home, Sweet Home."

[57] It should be remembered that Horace Greeley, the *Tribune*'s publisher, had been a principal motivator and original supporter of the Crystal Palace in 1852.

Once called an architectural marvel and claimed to be fireproof,
the Crystal Palace—one of the glories of New York—was destroyed by fire.

tended), for on October 5—despite its vaunted iron-and-glass incombustibility—the Crystal Palace burned down to the ground, according to the *Herald* (October 7, 1858), in a mere forty minutes.

By a lucky chance, on the afternoon of October 5, as George Templeton Strong, an ardent pyrophile, was returning to the city from Great Barrington, bringing "Ellen and her babies, and her Abigails, and Miss Josephine [Strong] safe back to town by five. . . . There was an alarm of fire as we emerged from the tunnel at 31st Street, and a majestic column of smoke was marching southeastwardly across the blue sky, and men said the Crystal Palace was on fire. So when we reached the 27th Street depot I put the party in charge of James (the waiter known as *PAM* from the likeness he bears to portraits of a British statesman),[58] who met us there, and 'fled fast thro' sun and shade,' up Murray Hill in pursuit of the picturesque *magna comitante caterva* [great gathering throng]. Up every avenue a miscellaneous aggregate of humanity was racing on this same errand. So scampers a wide area of yellow fallen leaves down the street of Barrington when smitten suddenly by a strong wind from the northwest. Over our heads was rising and wreathing and flowing onward this grand and ominous torrent of vapor, glowing with golden and coppery tints imparted by the setting sun. . . . It was the Crystal Palace. But before I got there the dome, roof, and walls had gone down. Only a few iron turrets were standing and some fragments of wall that looked like the wreck of a Brobdignagian [*sic*] Aviary. The debris was still flaming and blazing furiously. I contemplated the bonfire awhile and then came off, being tired and wanting my dinner.

[58] Meaning Lord Palmerston (1784–1865).

"So bursts a bubble rather noteworthy to the annals of New York," mused Strong. "To be more accurate, the bubble burst some three years ago, and this catastrophe merely annihilates the apparatus that generated it. Don't know how the fire broke out.[59] The building must have burned up like a pile of shavings" (Private Journal, October 5, 1858; *Diary,* II, 416).

It was sobering to contemplate, wrote the *Herald,* that the greater number of public and private buildings constructed within the past five years, thought to be impervious to fire, had been built of iron. And ships, as well. The *Herald* cited the recent shocking destruction by fire of the transatlantic ship *Austria,* whose sides—like the walls of the Crystal Palace—had collapsed as if they had been made of wood.

Feared lost in the maritime disaster was Theodore Eisfeld, returning from his annual vacation in Europe. "The *Austria* of the New York and Hamburg line burned on her voyage hither," wrote Strong in his private journal on September 27. "Crew and passengers between 500 and 600, of whom it seems but 67 are saved. Names of survivors not yet known and the story imperfectly reported. She seems to have burned up like tinder, and I think it will be found that officers and crew behaved ill, Poor Theo. Eisfeld was a passenger. He was nervous and not at all the man for a struggle with fire and water and a panic-stricken crowd, so I fear we shall have no 'Quartette soirées' this winter."[60]

The music community, stricken at the news, was relieved to learn, on September 28, that Eisfeld—albeit severely injured—had been among the few survivors[61] picked up at sea by the French bark *Maurice.* Because he was too badly hurt to proceed to the United States, Eisfeld was brought to the island of Fayal in the Azores, where he was warmly received and solicitously cared for, as he relates in a letter from there, dated October 4, vividly describing the disaster (see *Dwight's,* November 13, 1858, p. 259).

With the Philharmonic season scheduled to open on November 20, Carl Bergmann was appointed to replace Eisfeld as conductor.[62] And because, following their contretemps with Ullman on April 24, there was no possibility of their renewing their lease for the Academy,[63] the Society—after a search of likely performance places[64]—leased Niblo's Theatre, with a far smaller capacity than the Academy's, for their 1858–59 season.

---

[59] Arson was suspected; the American Institute offered a reward of $3000 for the capture of the perpetrator.

[60] If the "quartette soirées" were the extent of Strong's regret, he might have found consolation in the Mason/Thomas matinées, about to begin a new series on November 23 (discussed below).

[61] Only seventy-eight of the more than five hundred on board were saved.

[62] Bristow replaced Eisfeld on the Philharmonic executive committee (Philharmonic Archives).

[63] "The lessee of the Academy having declared that on no account will he allow the Philharmonic Society again to occupy the said building—for reasons which the reader may deduce for himself, as they are not known to us—our choice remains between Cooper's Institute, Burton's, or Niblo's Theatre, and the City Assembly Rooms, one of which places will probably be selected, until a regular Music hall, so much needed in our city, shall have been built" (New York Philharmonic Society Annual Report for 1858).

[64] At the Philharmonic directors' meeting on September 4, a committee consisting of Timm, U. C. Hill, and Daniel Walker was appointed to find a place for next season's concerts, the rent not to exceed $2000 (Philharmonic Archives).

Further grievances against Ullman were reviewed in the Philharmonic's Annual Report for 1858: his misleading (not to say deceitful) use of the term "philharmonic" in advertising his Academy concerts and his repeated false promises to permit his great stars—Thalberg, Vieuxtemps, and Formes—to appear with the Philharmonic Society, always ending in some last-minute, transparently trumped-up denial.

Yet, continued the report, despite these frustrations—and despite the "economic crisis" that had darkened the beginning of the 1857–58 season—the Society's concerts (henceforth to be increased to five a year) and their public rehearsals had been fully and enthusiastically attended; the membership had increased, as had the board of directors; the orchestra had grown from eighty to ninety actual [performing] members;[65] the classic and modern repertory performed had fulfilled the Philharmonic's loftiest intentions; and—cause for congratulations—Brooklyn had acquired (with due recognition to its "mother institution in New York") a Philharmonic Society of its own.[66]

In their search for a concert hall, on July 24 the New York Philharmonic had tested the acoustics of the innovative underground auditorium at the recently completed Cooper Institute (Cooper Union for the Advancement of Science and Art). "A towering edifice [designed by Frederick A. Peterson] of Romanesque architecture, built of brownstone, with four fronts, on Third-avenue, Seventh-street, Fourth-avenue, and Astor Place . . . the large hall in the basement of the building is 100 by 90 feet in dimensions," described the *Times*, "and will seat comfortably—when the iron chairs, with cushioned backs and seats, similar to those at the Academy of Music, which are now being manufactured for it, are in their places—3000 people. This huge chamber extends under the sidewalk, which forms a portion of its roof, and through which, by means of glass lights,[67] it will receive its supply of light from heaven during the day. In the night time, gas blazing forth from numerous chandeliers will supply the place of sunshine."

Conceived as a free school for working-class students, the Institute was designed to be self-supporting through income derived from the rental of stores and offices on the ground and second floors. "The third floor forms one large lecture room, furnished with semicircular iron seats with velvet cushions, and mahogany desks. The fourth floor is occupied by study rooms, recitation rooms, chemical laboratory, etc. On the fifth floor, accommodations are provided for the Female Academy of Design and artists' studios. The cornerstone of the Institute was laid in April, 1853, and the building has been completed at an outlay of $350,000" (*Courier and Enquirer*, April 6, 1858). The farsighted creators of this grand concept were Peter Cooper (1791–1883) and his gifted son-in-law Abram Hewitt (1822–1903).

The Philharmonic's trial run, free to the public,[68] was performed by an orchestra

---

[65] Each of whom received a dividend of $80 for the season from gross receipts of $9,651.50. "$80 was but poor pay for sixteen public and eight private rehearsals and four concerts," wrote Watson (*Leslie's*, October 9, 1858). "Still, the [hard] times considered, the success was very flattering to the Society."

[66] With Eisfeld appointed as conductor. During his absence, Joseph Noll took over the baton of the Brooklyn Philharmonic.

[67] Small squares of glass set into the pavement.

[68] For which passes to the performance were distributed at Scharfenberg and Luis's music store on Broadway.

of "thirty to forty musicians" conducted by Joseph Noll (the Philharmonic's concert-master for the ensuing season), assisted by an unfamiliar pianist whose name the critic for the *Musical World* (July 31, 1858, p. 481) could not catch (there were no printed programs).[69] In his opinion the hall was well suited to musical performance, except that the ceiling was too low for the size of the room, which, although it did not harm the acoustics, gave "a feeling of oppression to the beholder."

But Burkhardt found the sound unsatisfactory: "Nothing except the brass instruments was audible at the other end of the room. . . . We could scarcely hear the strings at all. The walls, moreover, were uncomfortably damp, and the access to the hall is not as pleasant or inviting as the Philharmonic audiences would seem to require. Perhaps the new hall being built in the rear of the Palace Garden may answer the Philharmonic purposes better," he suggested (*Dispatch,* July 31, 1858).

Thus, for lack of a more fitting place, on November 20 the Philharmonic Society and their subscribership squeezed back into the insufficient space of Niblo's Theatre, to an *obbligato* of complaints from the press: "When will that celebrated hall be built of which we never hear the end or see the beginning?" carped the *Albion* critic (November 27, 1858, p. 572). Nor did he (or his colleagues) approve of the Philharmonic's "injudiciously selected" opening program,[70] consisting of three first performances: Niels Gade's Fifth Symphony, op. 26 (1852), with its obtrusive piano *obbligato,* finely played, however, on a fine Steinway Grand by Henry C. Timm;[71] Spohr's Quartet Concertante, op. 131, played by Edward Mollenhauer, Joseph Noll, George Matzka,[72] and Frederick Bergner (a work in which the solo instruments were similarly all but drowned in the surrounding orchestral accompaniments);[73] and Rossini's scintillating Overture to *The Siege of Corinth* (Paris 1826), a redeeming finale to a "dismal" evening.[74] The soloists were Hattie Andem, who sang (or attempted to sing) an aria from Mozart's *La clemenza di Tito*[75] and, inappropriately, but more successfully, "The Harp in the Air," from William Vincent Wallace's *Maritana;*[76] Philip Mayer, who sang an aria

---

[69] The pianist—just arrived from Europe—played a concerto by Beethoven with "remarkable vim"; despite his rather harsh tone, he was on the whole a "first class artist." Noll conducted the Overture to *Euryanthe* in excellent style, but was far less satisfactory in an uncertain performance of Beethoven's Second Symphony.

[70] "People have grumbled that we have had too much Beethoven. It was, we are sure, to punish these unquiet spirits that the management resolved on giving a programme with nothing absolutely great in it" (*Musical World,* November 2, 1858, p. 754).

[71] To the *Albion* critic, the effect of Gade's symphony was "simply that of a long solo by Mr. H. C. Timm."

[72] Matzka replaced Joseph Burke, who had been invited to participate, but had declined (Philharmonic Archives).

[73] "Nobody appreciated it, few listened, and the majority chattered," wrote *Trovator* (*Dwight's,* November 27, 1858, p. 278).

[74] "Rossini's overture seemed to wake up the sleepers and quiet the chatterers," wrote *Trovator,* who throughout the concert had himself found it "hard work to triumph over my somniferous propensities."

[75] "Miss Andem should not have selected the Aria from *Titus,*" wrote Hagen, "as she has not as yet the technical means to give it due justice. And if this music is not performed in a superior manner," he added, "its antiquity makes itself felt rather too forcibly" (*Review and Gazette,* November 27, 1858, p. 371).

[76] "It is a standing reproach to the Philharmonic that it invariably has the worst singers in the City instead of the best," caviled the *Albion* critic. "The Directors would shudder at the idea of having

from the opera *Guttenberg* by Ferdinand Fuchs, and a song *Überall Du* by Ignaz Lachner (1807–1895), the latter with horn *obbligato* played by the cellist/hornist C. Brannes, "deservedly encored"; and Louis Schreiber, who splendidly played a movement of his *Fantasiestück* for *cornet à pistons*.[77] Whatever the cavils, Bergmann, however, received high praise for his masterly handling of the orchestra.[78]

Apart from his duties at the Philharmonic, Bergmann conducted a new series of biweekly Sunday evening "sacred and classical" concerts[79] at the City Assembly Rooms—a kind of continuation of his memorable series in 1856. With the Philharmonic musicians Edward Mollenhauer (violin), Louis Schreiber (cornet), H. Schmitz (French horn), and F. Rietzel (flute) as soloists, the *Arion* and *Teutonia* singing societies conducted by E. Weber, and an orchestra of forty, Bergmann's first program, on December 12, ranged from Beethoven's Fourth Symphony to Litolff's showy *Robespierre* Overture.♪ The lone item suggestive of "sacred" music was a choral work, "The Chapel," by one Becker, probably Albert Becker (1834–1899), sung by the *Arion* Society.

At the second concert of this series, on December 26, Bergmann presented, in addition to the *Tannhäuser* Overture and a Concert Overture by Rietz, such novelties as Schumann's Fourth Symphony in D minor, op. 120; and, with the *Arion* and *Teutonia* Societies, choral passages from Wagner's *Rienzi,* heard for the first time in America,[80] and from Beethoven's *Fidelio;* Anetta Caradori sang an aria from *Der Freischütz* and an unspecified German song.

Bergmann continued his cello-playing activities as well. Like many of his Philharmonic colleagues, he played in the opera orchestra at the Academy and doubtless toured with them as well, for it was not until the third concert in the new series of six "Classical Matinées" given by the former Mason and Bergmann—now Mason and Thomas—chamber group (reactivated after nearly two years of silence) that he resumed his place as their cellist.♪ As before, the group consisted of William Mason, piano, and a string quartet consisting of Theodore Thomas, Joseph Mosenthal, George Matzka, and, substituting for Bergmann during his absence on tour, Charles Brannes, from the Philharmonic.

Running neck and neck with Eisfeld's (pre-shipwreck) series of chamber-music

---

a Polka played after the Symphony, yet the effect could scarcely be more ludicrous than that produced by the combined efforts of bad singing and trashy music" (*Albion,* November 27, 1858, p. 572).

[77] Despite all the "vulgarity and parade" associated with the cornet, wrote the *Albion* critic, Schreiber's superlative performance on that instrument justified its presence at a Philharmonic concert.

[78] But: "The orchestra was somewhat weaker than usual, owing to an operatic performance in Brooklyn [the first, with Piccolomini in *La figlia del reggimento* and *La serva padrona*] which deprived the Society of some of its best instruments" (*Musical World,* November 27, 1858, p. 754).

[79] A series depending for its success on "our German residents," wrote *Trovator,* "as few of our American citizens will go to a concert on Sunday evening" (*Dwight's,* January 29, 1859, p. 347).

[80] The New York music community owed thanks to Bergmann for his tireless explorations into the newest repertory, wrote Hagen (*Review and Gazette,* January 8, 1859, p. 3): "It is all very well to say that the master symphonies of Beethoven cannot be heard too often, but if we are again and again treated with them, of what earthly use are then the efforts of our modern composers? Besides," added Hagen, "the musician, as well as the amateur, in our days, can—just as little as the man of letters— claim to be called educated if he is not acquainted with the works of distinguished living authors."

soirées, the Mason/Thomas matinées, starting at one P.M., were given in the lecture room of the Spingler Institute.[81] Tickets were $4 for a single admission to the series, or $10 for three admissions; $1 for a single concert, or $2 for three single tickets.

At their first concert, on January 30, a reportedly good-sized audience heard a varied program consisting of Beethoven's String Quartet in D major, op. 18, no. 3; a trio in F major for piano, viola, and cello, op. 3, by the contemporary German composer Robert Volkmann;♩ Schumann's String Quartet in A minor, op. 41, no. 1; and piano solos played by Mason—Chopin's Étude, op. 10, no. 7; Liszt's transcription of Weber's *Schlummerlied,* and Adolf Henselt's Étude, op. 2, no. 6, *Si oiseau j'étais* (or, according to Hagen, *Flieg, Vöglein, flieg*).[82]

"From the first to the last number, [the program] presented almost all the lights and shades of that school of music which modern esthetics have called the romantic," wrote Hagen (no master of stylistic lucidity). Volkmann's trio, apparently a first local performance, disappointed Hagen—being frothily Viennese instead of weightily Northern Germanic. To Seymour, too, Volkmann's work "pretended to nothing and accomplished nothing," but ——t—— thought it "full of pleasing melodies and quite taking, though not at all deep." Hagen thought the Liszt transcription especially delicious; Seymour thought it a mass of "technical trash." More significantly, ——t—— was struck by the group's great improvement since last heard; it was obvious that they had been earnestly practicing during the interim. Their playing, he reported, created "universal enthusiasm" (*Review and Gazette,* February 6, p. 35; *Times,* February 1; *Dwight's,* February 6, 1858, p. 358).

On February 27 at their second matinée[83] they presented Haydn's String Quartet in B-flat; Beethoven's Trio in D, op. 70, no. 1, for piano, violin, and cello; and the seldom played Octet for four violins, two violas, and two cellos, op. 20, by Mendelssohn. The extra violinists were Henry Appy♩ and Julius Eichberg, the other extras, both members of the Philharmonic, were Augustus Besig, violist, and Henry Luhde, cellist.

Mendelssohn's Octet deserved to be heard more often, wrote Hagen; it was "a highly interesting work, full of fine traits, especially in the quick movements," if not in the Andante. He noted the resemblance of its Scherzo to *A Midsummer Night's Dream,* a resemblance traceable throughout Mendelssohn's subsequent output, he wrote. A zealous promoter of the Steinways' increasingly popular instruments, and doubtless in reaction to ——t——'s continuing condemnation of them, he bestowed an extra accolade upon the piano used in this concert, although it was heard only in the Beethoven trio (*Review and Gazette,* March 6, 1858, p. 67).

[81] A school for young ladies, it was a bad choice of concert hall, demanding the ascending of numerous steps and the ringing of a bell to be admitted, which, complained Seymour, "in these unheroic days [was] asking too much of the mere critic" (*Times,* February 1, 1858). But ——t—— described the space as "a small hall, amphitheatrically arranged, which is tolerably good for music" (*Dwight's,* February 6, 1858, p. 358).

[82] Mason's splendid playing had been marred by his piano, a harsh and disagreeably loud Steinway that ——t—— claimed to have recognized as the same objectionable instrument that had spoiled Goldbeck's recent performance (*Dwight's, ibid.*).

[83] Postponed from February 13 because some of the performers were absent "with the Italian Opera Company in Baltimore."

The third program, on March 13, with Bergmann now restored to the group, included Schumann's Sonata in D minor for violin and piano, op. 121, played by Mason and Thomas, Beethoven's String Quartet in E minor, op. 59, no. 2, and the ("Italian") Trio for piano, violin, and cello by the contemporary German composer J. C. Louis (or Ludwig) Wolf (1804–1859). A trivial work, wrote Hagen, the Wolf trio was a superficial compound of Reissiger, Hünten, and Italian opera. It gratified Hagen that the public showed far less enthusiasm for it—although it was written in the popular style—than for the profound works of Beethoven and Schumann (*Review and Gazette,* March 20, 1858, pp. 83–84). The *Musical World* (March 20, 1858, p. 179), which found Schumann's sonata to suffer from "an excess of shade and too little sunlight," thought the Wolf trio—after its rather uninteresting first two movements—to improve "into something quite attractive," giving the impression of "a very wide-awake man as the composer."

At the fourth matinée, on March 27, the quartet played Mozart's String Quartet in D major, "no. 10," the Andante and Variations from Schubert's String Quartet in D minor ("Death and the Maiden"), and the Scherzo of Cherubini's String Quartet, no. 1, in E-flat; Mason, Thomas, and Bergmann played Beethoven's "Archduke" Trio, op. 97, and Mason and Timm played Schumann's rarely performed Andante and Variations for two pianos, op. 46.

Hagen observed that Schubert, in the "Death and the Maiden" variations, showed "great richness of imagination [and] more melody than Schumann, but less depth of conception" (*Review and Gazette,* April 3, 1858, p. 99). The critic for the *Musical World* (April 3, 1858, p. 211) confessed his aversion to variations: "No kind of writing requires more genius—and yet, in no field does stupidity oftener essay its commonplaceness." In his opinion the greatest composer of variations was Reicha, next came Beethoven. Schumann, although not in their class by any means, had been quite successful in this work for two pianos. At any rate, Schubert's variations, which followed, were "not so deep-thought and far more commonplace."

On April 10, at the fifth matinée—the best-attended of the season, so far—Schumann's String Quartet in F, op. 41, no. 2, was played, then Beethoven's "Kreutzer" Sonata, op. 47, splendidly performed by Thomas and Mason, then Bach's D-minor Concerto for three claviers played by Mason, Scharfenberg, and Timm on three Steinway grands; Thomas, Mosenthal, Matzka, Bergmann, and the Philharmonic double bassist C. Preusser made up the "orchestra."

The Bach concerto, locally performed for the first time by virtually the same group in 1856,[84] continued to present problems to nineteenth-century hearers, curiously ill-attuned as they were to the music that had gone before them. "It is one of those compositions which *must* be heard several times to be appreciated," wrote Hagen. "It is full of melody, only less catching than those who borrowed largely from the old masters, especially Mendelssohn," he cloudily added. "No doubt, without Bach, all our great modern composers, Schumann included, would appear much poorer" (*Review and Gazette,* April 17, 1858, p. 114).

To ——t—— it was "a strange, quaint composition, bringing up before the

---

[84] And recently less well performed by Gustave Satter, with pianists Jan Pychowski and Robert Goldbeck, and with E. Mollenhauer, Eisfeld, Reyer, and Bergner supplying the orchestra (see below).

mind gorgeous pageants of stately lords and ladies in powder, starch, and stiff brocade, with the straight-laced [*sic*] deportment, measured tread, and yet, withal, transcendent manly or delicate beauty which no ungraceful forms of fashion can conceal." Particularly, ——t—— was delighted with the three pianists, who played "as if they had one body and soul, and the notes were so marvelously intertwined that it was almost impossible to distinguish one piano from the others" (*Dwight's,* April 17, 1858, pp. 22–23).

On April 17, for the last matinée of the series, a predominantly retrospective program included Beethoven's String Quartet in F minor, op. 95, Handel's Fugue in E minor, and Mendelssohn's *Rondo capriccioso,* op. 14, for piano, played by Mason and encored with his popular "Silver Spring"; also the less familiar Chaconne from Bach's Fourth Sonata for unaccompanied violin, with a virtually unknown piano accompaniment by Mendelssohn (published in 1845), was played by Theodore Thomas; and as a grand finale to the series, Schumann's Quintet for piano and strings, op. 44, was repeated.

Particularly in the Beethoven Quartet, wrote ——t——, did the string players display the great strides they had made since 1856, when they had "'scratched' off this very piece in a most heart- and ear-rending manner"; indeed it was hard to believe they were the same performers. As they now played it, the work—generally thought to be incomprehensible—"belied its reputation." Too, they gave a beautiful rendition of Schumann's Quintet, particularly Mason, who also shone in his solos. But the high moment of the occasion was Theodore Thomas's performance of the Chaconne by Bach. Though young, Thomas unmistakably bore the "stamp of genius," wrote ——t——; he was destined to rise high in the world of music. "His tone is pure and full, his command of his instrument is very great, and his interpretation of the music he plays most faithful and artistic." Bach's Chaconne was a strange and baffling work, needing to be heard many times to be understood; yet even on first hearing, it invited the listener to know it better. Difficult to play, and without "regular forms or themes to assist the memory," young Thomas performed it magnificently, without faltering, from memory. Thomas was to be praised, too, for his uncompromising "real Art-love and reverence; he never plays any but *good* music." It was efforts like these concerts, with their high standards of performance and choice of repertory, that would eventually redeem true Art and defeat the Humbug rife in our land. It pleased ——t—— to report that the little hall, scantily filled at the beginning of the series, had come to be so crowded that a larger hall would be demanded for, hopefully, the group's succeeding winter season (*Dwight's,* May 1, 1858, p. 40).

And indeed, on November 24—with Eisfeld out of the running—the Mason/Thomas group began an uncontested winter series of six Classical Matinées at Dodworth's Hall. "The calamity which detains Mr. Theodore Eisfeld in the Western Isles does not, fortunately, deprive us of the rare luxury of Chamber Music," wrote the *Albion* critic (November 27, 1858, p. 571). But he regarded the catholicity of the Mason/Thomas programs as "eccentricity": "They run into all sorts of extremes for the sake of the unconventional," he wrote, "espousing the extreme future and the remote past with equal devotion. In Tuesday's programme we had a [string] Quartette by Schumann [in A major, op. 41, no. 3], as an indication of the sort of music our descendants are to suffer, and a Chaconne by Bach as a warning of what our ancestors have gone through. . . . The truth about Schumann is that certain aesthetical ideas about composition became engrafted in his mind before he commenced writing music, so that every piece is more or less an experiment. He changes ground constantly, because composition is a meditative process with him, not an inspiration. Hence, all those abominable dissonances which prevail in his harmonies, if we may use the word in such a connection." As for Bach's Chaconne, played by Thomas, this time "with milk and water accompaniments by Schumann"[85] (excellently played by Mosenthal), it was "an absurdity . . . an antiquated Étude, fit only for the closet of a violin student."

The *Albion* critic took more kindly to the remainder of the program, which consisted of Beethoven's Sonata in A major for cello and piano, op. 69, played by Bergmann and Mason ("as lovely and perfect a work as can be") and Schubert's Trio in B-flat, for piano, violin, and cello, op. 99 ("very good but somewhat long").

About the Schubert trio, Hagen agreed: "If Schubert's chamber music could be condensed into half of its length, it would offer the greatest interest to the musician as well as to the amateur," he wrote (*Review and Gazette,* November 27, 1858, p. 371). "Unfortunately, all his noble inspirations, his great riches of melody and harmony, are spoiled by the want of knowledge to finish at the right places. The unfortunate composer lacked appreciation for aesthetical forms, and only thus can we account for the fact that one of the most gifted creative musicians that ever lived ranks only second to the really great masters of the art." Hagen vastly approved, however, of Bach's Chaconne, terming it "colossal in its conception and treatment, grand in its details, full of depth and sublime aspirations, in fact, one of the greatest solos for the violin which have [*sic*] ever been written."[86]

Both Hagen and the *Albion* critic highly praised the performers (with Hagen bestowing extra praise on the "exquisite" Steinway piano used in the proceedings), but the critic for the *Evening Post* (November 25, 1858), although appreciative of the general effort, suggested that the addition of a vocalist, as in the bygone Eisfeld *soirées,* would greatly enhance the interest of these concerts.[87]

Early in 1858—a time abounding in both Eisfeld *soirées* and Mason/Thomas matinées—the critical brotherhood collectively frowned upon the *Tribune* for its inflated announcement, on February 20, of Dr. Guilmette's forthcoming "classical, instrumental, and vocal" concert on February 24 at Dodworth's Rooms. Chief among Guilmette's attractions was the then recently arrived English violinist Henry C. Cooper,[88] who

[85] In 1853, Schumann—outdoing Mendelssohn—composed piano accompaniments, first published in 1854, for all six of Bach's sonatas for unaccompanied violin. His accompaniments for Bach's six sonatas for unaccompanied cello have apparently remained unpublished.

[86] Willis, on the other hand, suggested that if violin solos were to be presented at these concerts, "a proper selection be made for this purpose. An antiquated morceau like this Chaconne is simply wearying" (*Musical World,* December 4, 1858, p. 771).

[87] In his review of the second Mason/Thomas matinée at the Spingler Institute, ——t—— had advised Eisfeld to follow their example and eliminate the vocalists from his *soirées:* although vocal performances varied the programs, he wrote, "the variety is not a pleasant one, and had better be dispensed with" (*Dwight's,* March 13, 1858, p. 396).

[88] The other participants in this concert, besides Guilmette and Cooper, were Annie Milner, Charlotte Bird, an American singer, Robert Goldbeck, who played some of his own compositions, and William A. King, who presided at the piano.

would, "for the first time in America," be heard with three members of Eisfeld's quartet party—Noll, Reyer, and Bergner—in performances of string quartets, one by Mozart and the other an unspecified modern work. "We mention this," stated the *Tribune,*
"because such a complete quartet has never been heard heretofore in this country."

The puff could hardly have been more pointed: the unidentified modern work to
be so unprecedentedly performed was a composition by the *Tribune*'s staff editor and
music critic William Henry Fry, his puzzlingly numbered "Eleventh Quartet."[89] Following its performance, the *Tribune* (February 27, 1858) again avoided specific mention
of Fry's quartet, choosing to state that "there was but one opinion among critics . . .
that never before was such artistic quartette playing heard on this side of the Atlantic."

Fry's colleagues, in fact, elaborately reviewed his quartet in varying terms of soph-
istry and euphemism. "Mr. Fry," wrote Seymour (*Times,* February 26, 1858), "is a native composer who, from the discouraging circumstances which encompass the pursuit
of art in America, has sought and obtained fame in other paths." The critic reviewed
Fry's past musical achievements, then turned his attention to the quartet: "The peculi-
arities of everything that emanates from Mr. Fry's pen are originality and quaintness.
The former he displays in a superabundant vein of melody . . . the latter in a strange
mingling of unexpected force and out-of-the-way erudition. In the Quartet played last
night, the first movement[90] illustrates the latter phase of Mr. Fry's idiosyncrasy. Every
instrument is individualized and expresses its meaning with volubility, but in a language not easily understood. . . . A little more familiarity with the musical harmonies
used by Mr. Fry," stated the critic, "would doubtless enable us to understand as well
as enjoy this very weird and remarkable fragment."

The slow second movement, which began and ended "logically," was followed by
an Allegretto, "a lovely little fairy in the old style, and intended, we should suppose,
to recall an Arcadian past." The quartet's last movement was "brilliantly conceived and
worked out with every regard to the vast capabilities of modern performers." The mechanical difficulties of the work were very great, reported Seymour, and it was "but
justice to Messrs. Cooper, Noll, Reyer, and Bergner to say that such quartet playing
. . . had never before been heard in this City."[91]

In the *Courier and Enquirer* (February 27, 1858), Richard Grant White, not only
a fellow-critic but a fellow-composer, deftly wielded his well-practiced, double-edged
dagger in subtle demolition of Fry's quartet. Crediting Fry's *Stabat Mater* with a "tenderness and poignancy which have not been surpassed by the strains of any composer
of this generation, except, perhaps, Schubert," White wickedly expressed the wish—
now that he had heard Fry's Eleventh Quartet—that he might hear the ten that had
preceded it.

[89] Upton (*Fry,* pp. 320–21) lists a completed "Tenth Quartet" and five unfinished, unnumbered
quartets or fragments of quartets by Fry, also sketches for a sextet for strings and a trio for piano,
violin, and cello.

[90] Apparently Fry's repudiation of the four-movement form in symphonic works♪ did not extend
to chamber music.

[91] A statement to which an infuriated Burkhardt retorted: "We know not what '*such* Quartet
playing' may mean, but we were once [in 1846] at a classical Quartet Soirée♪ . . . in this city, when
the quartet consisted of Messrs. Camillo Sivori,♪ [Michele] Rapetti,♪♪ [Alfred] Boucher,♪ and Pop-
penberg,♪ four names at least equal in fame to the four mentioned above. We have not since heard
'*such* Quartet playing in this City'" (*Dispatch,* February 28, 1858).

The Eleventh, he continued, would not have been an expression of Fry's "moral and mental idiosyncrasy" if it were not eccentric and vigorous, with a current of deep human tenderness," and, proclaimed White, "eccentricity, when it has the power to justify itself, becomes originality." Of the four movements, White preferred the Adagio, not only because of its "square, nobly pathetic" leading melody, but because it seemed the most clearly thought out and highly finished, while at the same time it was "less ambitious of novelty."

Although Fry was "too good a contrapuntist to require lessons at our hands," White nonetheless proceeded to give him a lengthy, schoolmasterish going-over, suggesting that "what is grammatical and well-looking on paper may not be pleasing when put into sound; that it is possible to make the inner parts of a quartet too elaborate as well as too difficult." For example, he instructed, "it is best, in writing melodic passages for the bass (except when the theme itself is given by the violoncello) to let them [the inner voices], nevertheless, decidedly mark the fundamental harmony of the passage. . . . Mr. Fry's composition abounds in thought and in learning, which are perhaps most apparent in the opening movement, [yet] the instruments seemed to us a little overburdened; but that may have been our want of acquaintance with the work, or even sufficient quickness of apprehension."

Then the *coup de grâce:* "Instead of a *Minuetto* or a *Scherzo,* Mr. Fry wrote a fantastic movement in 2/4 time [the *Times*'s "lovely little fairy"]. This we think an error of judgment. In a composition consisting of four parts, two of which are sure to be in quadruple time, the ear craves a movement in quick triple time; and this is best obtained in the old *Minuetto,* or in the *Scherzo* with which Beethoven replaced it." (Words calculated to gall Fry, the uncompromising modernist and fervent Mozart and Beethoven-basher.)

In the *Musical World,* R. Storrs Willis, Fry's erstwhile adversary[7] (who had "most reluctantly" been called away from the concert before Fry's quartet was performed), nonetheless wrote (from hearsay) that the first movement was "a veritable nest of snakes—the instruments coiling and squirming and intertwining in a most labyrinthine fashion; and yet [in] a succeeding slow movement, which is a square, consecutive, beautiful piece of writing, [it was] as though a man had come to his senses from previous champagne, and now were talking coherent and charming sense to you. Long live Fry," patronized Willis: "He is full of 'youth and juice'—enthusiasm for Art and glorious charity and kindness for all artists—with a fire in his brain (though smoke sometimes envelops it), which makes him luminous when it does clearly break forth, and stamps him a man of genius" (*Musical World,* reprinted in *Dwight's,* March 13, 1858, p. 393).

Earlier, on February 11, Henry Cooper appeared at the Grand Miscellaneous Concert of the New-York American-Music Association, the second event of their third season, given at Hope Chapel. Inappropriately billed—considering the Association's primary rationale—as "late violinist to H. B. M. Victoria, Queen of England," he played his own Fantasia on *La Fille du régiment* and his "Recollections of Scotland." A recent emigrant, Cooper exemplified—both by his presence and his choice of repertory—the altered philosophy of the Association since their beginning. As a gratified Hagen observed (*Review and Gazette,* February 20, 1858, p. 51): they were at length willing to admit "compositions hitherto not deemed eligible to their programmes (on the ground that they were not native works)." Also appearing on the program was the American soprano Fanny Stockton, who sang an *Ave Maria* by her teacher Carlo Bassini,♪ and, with Mrs. Westervelt, Mr. Peck, Dr. Guilmette, and chorus, an anthem, "Hide not thy face," by the Boston organist Samuel P. Tuckerman;♪ Mrs. Brinkerhoff sang William Vincent Wallace's "The Winds that waft my sighs to thee"; Richard Hoffman played two of his piano pieces, "Twilight," a reverie, and a *Marche funèbre;* Charles Guilmette sang a Grand Sacred Aria, "Jérusalem," by an unspecified Labarre; and the Association's chorus, with *obbligati* by Miss Stockton and Mrs. Brinkerhoff, concluded the program with an enthusiastically received Drinking Chorus by Dr. Thomas Ward; William A. King presided at the Steinway. A trio for piano, violin, and cello, by George Felix Benkert (1831–?), a prolific Philadelphia composer,[92] was scheduled to be played by Messrs. Berti, Simon, and Bergner, but was not performed.[93]

"The Directors have at last taken a step in the right direction," rejoiced Hagen, who was willing to foresee a prosperous future for the Association if—instead of giving only a single work by a foreign composer—"they would let us have at least four or five standard pieces of good, sound music," and fewer of the inferior American works they had hitherto espoused. Hagen would have preferred, at this concert, for instance, to have heard Hoffman play anything by one of the old masters rather than "his own tone fancies," or Cooper to have offered, instead of his compositions, something by Molique, de Bériot, or Mendelssohn.

Appended to the foregoing review was a surprising postscript: "Since writing the above, we regret to learn that the Directors have concluded to disband the Society, and that this was their final concert." Hagen permitted himself a final I-told-you-so: "Had they adopted the policy which we always advocated, and which they themselves at last acknowledged to be the most beneficial to their interests, they would not have been compelled to close for want of patronage."[94]

The rumor of their demise was immediately pounced upon and spread far and wide by the gossip-mongering press, but it soon proved to be false: on April 30 the *Times* sheepishly admitted to having made an "obituary blunder." The New-York American-Music Association was not only "alive and kicking," but about to give the final concert of their third season at Dodworth's Hall that very evening.

Hagen professed to be pleased that the Association still existed: "We can not afford to lose them just yet," he wrote (*Review and Gazette,* May 15, 1858), "as they offer to American composers the only chance to make such of their works known as have not yet attained a high degree of excellence and finish." The American pieces on the program were Benkert's previously announced trio, the Scherzo and Finale of Hommann's violin and piano sonata, and vocal works by Samuel O. Dyer, William

[92]Benkert had returned to Philadelphia in 1856 after five years of study in Germany with Lindpaintner.

[93]But all in all, an "eminently successful" concert, reported the *Courier and Enquirer* (February 12, 1858): "The audience were in the best humor, and the artists were so frequently encored that the entertainment was prolonged to a late hour."

[94]"The New-York American Musical Association, though embodying many excellent views on our musical wants," wrote the *Musical World* (April 10, 1858, p. 228), "was started in too narrow a manner to include the intelligent foreigner as well as [the] native, and was moreover indiscreetly engineered in many of its details."

Mason, and a Recitative and Aria from James G. Maeder's opera *The Peri*.♫ Alien music by Donizetti, Loder, and Mendelssohn completed the program. The performers were the soprano Hattie Andem, the young tenor George Simpson, and James A. Johnson's vocal Quartet Party. Gustav Satter, announced to appear, defaulted at the last minute and was apparently replaced by Aptommas. Too many singers, complained Hagen, but at least the four American works heard "afforded good hope for the development of talent and skill on the part of some of the composers."

The concert was more stringently reviewed in the *Musical World* (May 8, 1858, p. 291) by an obliging friend of the editor, who was unable to attend. "The program," wrote the deputy, "chiefly consisted of a very poor Trio for Piano, Violin, and Violoncello, by G. F. Benkert, which, but for the masterly handling of Messrs. Berti, Simon, and Bergner, would hardly have been tolerable. . . . While we wish to see the native music of America advanced in this community, we think that the Direction might find better compositions to bring before the public than the Trio above mentioned."[95] In general, the reviewer took a position opposite to Hagen's: "While we have such good composers as G. F. Bristow, William H. Fry, and others, surely we need not be troubled with the indifferent compositions of *naturalized* citizens."

During the ensuing hiatus in the American-Music Association's activities (for a lengthy hiatus in fact did follow) American and near-American musicians—both composers and performers, singly and collectively—continued their upward struggle. On June 3 at Dodworth's Hall, Guilmette, evidently a man of uncommonly versatile musical interests, presented a new cantata, *The Forest Melody,* by George Henry Curtis,♪♫[96] set to "twelve of the most beautiful lyrics by the first of American poets, William Cullen Bryant." Guilmette and Maria Brainerd sang the principal parts, assisted by a cast that included the fine contralto Mary Hawley, the Misses Westervelt, Charlotte Bird, and Ada and Fanny Robjohn; Curtis presided at the piano (*Review and Gazette,* June 12, 1858, p. 178).

On October 27, Charles Jerome Hopkins, now referred to in the *Musical World* as the "ex-president" of the New-York American-Music Association,[97] gave a "complimentary" program at Dr. Parker's Fourth Avenue Presbyterian church, consisting of selections from Hopkins's forthcoming collection of sacred tunes. Not only did he perform his own arrangements[98] but also music by his father, John Henry Hopkins, the illustrious Protestant Episcopal Bishop of Vermont, and by his brother, the Reverend John Henry, Jr., editor of the *Church Journal.* Jerome Hopkins's *Gloria in excelsis,* a long and elaborate work for chorus, with soprano and tenor solos and a fugued Amen, was "effectively" performed, with William Dressler (organist of the church) conducting and with Hopkins at the organ (*Times,* October 30, 1858).

Irrepressible Jerome Hopkins appeared again on November 12 at Chickering's

[95] "Mr. Benkert's trio is an ambitious composition but is exceedingly unequal in its excellence," wrote Watson. "It lacked consecutiveness, continuity of thought, and above all, originality" (*Leslie's,* May 15, 1858, p. 379).

[96] Curtis was currently the organist and choir director at the 14th Street Presbyterian Church.

[97] Hopkins had been warmly reviewed in the Philadelphia press for his recent organ performances in that city (*Times,* October 30, 1858).

[98] "It has become a recognized procedure to steal the material for religious music," wrote the *Musical World* (November 6, 1858, p. 707), "and overlooking the obliquity of this strange fact, we have only to add that Mr. Hopkins has done his work well."

new Rooms (Broadway and Fourth Street), this time playing the piano in a program of his secular compositions for piano, violin, and voice; he was assisted by one of the violin-playing Mollenhauers, probably Edward, and the soprano Hattie Andem. In the *Tribune* (November 15, 1858), William Henry Fry was stricken with his usual inability to write a straightforward or commendatory review of a fellow American composer. He began by criticizing Hopkin's piano playing as being too weak to "render effectively what he designs. The age of promising pianists is over," wrote ultra-modern Fry. "Nothing but excellence will answer."

Nor did Hopkins's compositions meet with Fry's favor. Dissatisfied with his melodic writing, Fry examined the essential components of melody; "There is absolutely no half way in a melody," he wrote. "It has either the divine spark or it is a failure." Fry summoned forth a procession of successful and unsuccessful melodists as examples: "Handel was not a good melodist. Mozart—less his want of determined accent and dramatic passion—was. Haydn was a melodist. So were Bellini and Donizetti. So was Weber. Beethoven could not construct a popular vocal or condensed passionate declamatory melody. Rossini can. Auber can write certain qualities of melody. Verdi is a melodist." Whether or not Hopkins could write as good a melody as the best of them, Fry was not prepared to say; only the public could be the judge; the critics knew only "just enough to be blind to a new melody."

Hopkins's violin and piano duet fared better with Fry than his piano pieces. Although its first movement was "vague and dreary," the second had more shape and purpose, albeit "the variegation of the motive at the end was excessive." Fry dispensed up-to-date advice for composing an accompaniment ("The art of writing accompaniments is [knowing] not so much what to put in but what to leave out"); a string quartet ("What Mr. Hopkins needs is to write many quartets for stringed instruments; that is the best gymnastic exercise for carrying musical weights"); a song (in one of Hopkins's songs, the "running passages were not fast enough for brilliancy [nor] slow enough for insipidity. They wrote so scores of years back. Composers have learned better since. Music has advanced.")

Fry advised Hopkins to avoid opera: "nothing but the stage itself will teach that most difficult of musical arts, in comparison with which all else is trifling." Fry ended on a generous note: "Oratorio, however, which is comparatively easy work, is before him. His energy and enthusiasm are admirable, so let him 'go ahead.'"

The few other concerts given by American performers—predominantly women and almost invariably singers—presented a recurrent cast of assisting artists, most often colleagues from the American-Music Association, the Harmonic Society, and the Mendelssohn Union. That rivalry existed where all should have been sweet concord is demonstrated by the pair of competing concerts on February 16: Hattie Andem's at Mozart Hall, assisted by Henry Cooper, Aptommas, George Simpson, Guilmette, with W. A. King replacing George Frederick Bristow as "conductor"; and Miss Dingley's at Dodworth's Hall, with Mary Hawley, Ernest Perring, Mr. McConkey, and a chorus (presumably members of the Mendelssohn Union) directed by G. Washbourn Morgan. Tickets to each of these concerts were fifty cents.

Fanny Stockton, making her concert debut at Dodworth's Hall on April 6, was assisted by Edward Mollenhauer, Jerome Hopkins, and the singers William Schubert

Leslie's, Dartmouth College Library

Interest in an instrument that could not go out of tune stimulated others besides the Key Harp inventors. A String-Clamp Piano made by Driggs & Tooker was claimed to have the same advantage and is shown here being demonstrated.

and George Wooster; William A. King presided at the piano. Although the *Times* (April 7, 1858) bore down rather heavily on the young debutante's failings, with many an ultra-technical cavil, the *Tribune* of the same date described her as a "stout, pretty young lady with Circassian eyes, hair, and complexion, making one forget her voice under so much artillery of belleship." The critic, probably Fry in one of his breezier moods, nonetheless found her voice to be a "good, pure, sympathetic soprano—not grand or dazzling, but winning and mellifluous." Wooster, with a baritone voice of "great purity and expression," although "inexperienced in the Tuscan dialect," showed promise of becoming a valuable artist.

On April 23 at Dodworth's, Ureli Corelli Hill,♪♫ assisted by C. F. Hill, demonstrated his invention, advertised as his "beautiful and wonderful Key Harp,♪ played like a piano, but without strings,[99] and which cannot get out of tune." Vocally assisting on this occasion were Fanny Stockton and the baritone George Wooster, with William A. King presiding at the keyboard.

On April 27 occurred another conflict: Maria Brainerd's concert at Dodworth's Hall versus James G. Maeder's Grand Concert and Entertainment at Mozart Hall. Miss Brainerd's program spanned the gamut from Handel to Verdi to Thomas Moore to the

[99] "This instrument has a manual like the piano forte, and in its compass is about the same, but instead of striking strings the hammers descend on a series of tuning-forks. [They] do away with wires and tuning is unnecessary. . . . We heard the Key-Harp . . . and were charmed with the ethereal quality of the sound produced, but disappointed in its volume" (*Times,* April 22, 1848).

latest pianistic acrobatics contrived and performed by the showy Gustav Satter; her other assisting artists were Aptommas and the highly praised tenor William Henry Cooke; Dr. Beames, who apparently had a lifetime stranglehold on Miss Brainerd, his former pupil, inevitably provided the accompaniments at a Steinway grand.

Maeder's concert was fraught with novelty. Not only did his pupils perform, but also Joseph Burke and Richard Hoffman, and in the second half of the program three eminent actors—William Burton, John Brougham, and Charles M. Walcot. Maeder's wife, the beloved actress/singer of an earlier era, Clara Fisher Maeder♪♫ sang the Scottish ballad "Kelvin Grove," and Alfred Sedgwick and his little son Charles, exquisitely played their bass and treble concertinas.

In May, the Sedgwicks presented a private "concertina *soirée*" at N. P. B. Curtis's music emporium (Broadway and Broome Street), playing Sedgwick *père*'s arrangements for treble and bass concertinas of Weber's Overture to *Oberon,* the Andante and Variations from Beethoven's Septet, op. 20, a Fantasia on *Il trovatore,* and, with piano, the Second Trio by the German composer Franz Hünten (1793–1878).[100] Mrs. Anna Warren, George Simpson, and William H. Dennett, an American basso, sang arias and ballads by Donizetti, Maeder, and Braham.

On June 17, one of the Misses Gellie appeared at Dodworth's Hall, assisted by "several distinguished artists," and on October 26, at Niblo's Saloon, Miss Kate Dean, a pupil of Antonio Bagioli, made her debut, assisted by the tenor W. H. Cooke, the violinist Edward Mollenhauer, the cornetist Louis Schreiber, and the pianist W. T. Evans. A fair amount of advance publicity accompanied this debut—both for Bagioli, whose local importance as a teacher of singing was equated with that of the Paris *Conservatoire* in Europe, and for Miss Dean, daughter of an upstate New York farmer, whose gifts were loudly heralded. Although she received considerable critical approval and predictions for a brilliant future—not only for her voice and the way she used it, but for her splendid "physical attractions"—Miss Dean was not heard from again.

In April and May the Harmonic Society, in alliance with Ullman, as we know, gave performances of *Messiah* and *Elijah* at the Academy of Music. On September 1 they contributed to the official Atlantic Cable ceremonies at the Crystal Palace with a giant concert for which they enlisted the participation of the various music associations of New York and adjoining cities.

To accommodate those who had failed to gain admittance to the concert in the overwhelming crush, the program was repeated on September 10, with the added attractions of Carl Formes and the celebrated Drum Corps of the Seventy-first Regiment. Formes sang the "Porter's Song," from *Martha,* the so-called "Trumpet Song" from *Messiah,* and, with Francis H. Nash, "The Lord is a Man of War, from Handel's *Israel in Egypt.*" During the intermission the Drum Corps played "The Drum Polka," evidently a sensational piece for percussion. The program featured two celebratory odes by a Mrs. Ann S. Stephens: "The Cable," sung to the tune of the "Star-Spangled Banner," and "All Hail," to an undisclosed tune. Additionally, Formes sang a "Hymn

---

[100] "The concertina is a wonderful instrument for one of such small compass, and the playing of Mr. and Master Sedgwick is calculated to exhibit its power to the fullest extent," applauded the *Musical World* (May 22, 1858, p. 322).

of Peace," with words by the actor John Brougham, set to music by one Clement White, an Englishman recently arrived in New York. The remainder of the program consisted of the overtures to *William Tell* and *Fra diavolo* and of choruses from Haydn's *The Creation* (the evocatively titled "Achieved is the Glorious Work"), *The Seasons,* and the Hallelujah Chorus from *Messiah.* The concert was conducted by G. F. Bristow; admission was twenty-five cents.

On December 25, again at the Academy of Music, the Harmonic Society gave their annual performance of *Messiah,*[101] with Misses Maria Brainerd, Harriet Westervelt, and Lizzie Coleman, and Messrs. George Simpson and Philip Mayer. Tickets were fifty cents; reserved seats fifty cents extra; annual subscriptions, admitting the purchaser to the Society's rehearsals (at Dodworth's Hall) as well as their concerts, were available at five dollars each.

Far better in ——t——'s estimation was the *Liederkranz's* performance of the *Creation* on December 28 at the Cooper Institute, with Madame Caradori valiantly assuming the ailing Madame Zimmermann's role in addition to her own. Herr Urchs, the Adam, was also good, but the less said about the other two gentlemen, the better.[102]

The venturesome Mendelssohn Union, on April 22, 1858, at the second concert of their fourth season—this time at Metropolitan Music Hall—presented the first performance in America of the oratorio *Jephtha and his Daughter* (London 1856), by the German composer Karl Reinthaler (1822–1896). With a chorus lopsidedly consisting of forty male singers and twenty females, wrote the *Musical World* (May 1, 1858, pp. 277–78), the "preponderance of bass and tenor effect . . . nearly crushed out the soprano and alto parts." *Why* this occurred was a mystery, wrote the nettled reviewer. The cast—Mrs. Crump, Miss Hawley, Dr. Guilmette, and Mr. Perring—and the chorus did nobly with a score "as full of discords as a midnight concert of feline serenaders is of ecstatic screams and moon-defying madness. . . . Mr. Reinthaler waylays his main themes with discordant countersubjects and suspensions in a manner truly assassin-like. He is also minor-mad. A full, plump major common chord is as rare with him as a sight of heaven's sunny sky is in an equinoctial storm." Only "occasional gleams of flowing melody would peep out from Mr. Reinthaler's drear array of recitatives and discordant harmonies, piled like Ossa upon Pelion; but they were like angel's visits, few and far between," declaimed the reviewer.

For their next concert, on May 27, the Mendelssohn Union again shifted their location—this time to the new underground hall of the Cooper Institute, anticipating Noll's Philharmonic tryout there by two months. "We have a repugnance to apartments under ground," admitted the *Albion* critic, "and it was not without misgivings that we descended the ample stone staircase of the Cooper Institute, but when at length we reached the lowest depth of that generally protracted building and found ourselves in an apartment of truly regal proportions, we lost all thought of Basement, and Vault, and Dungeon, with which our mind was previously filled. It is a magnifi-

[101] They gave "their annual performance of *Messiah,* complete with their annual faults," sourly wrote ——t—— (*Dwight's,* January 15, 1859, p. 332).

[102] Although the solos "were entrusted to feeble hands" and the recitatives "mutilated in a surprisingly commonplace way," perversely wrote the *Albion* critic (January 1, 1859, p. 7): "It was really a delicious entertainment of choral music, the best in some respects that we have had in this city."

cent apartment," wrote the critic, "cold and chaste, but comfortable. Twenty-five hundred armchairs are provided for visitors, and in an emergency a thousand more might be crowded in. The acoustical properties of the building are decidedly good, as they should be, seeing that the only materials used are stone and iron—substances in themselves musical." For "monster" choral events, he wrote, the Hall of the Cooper Institute was the "only place in New York worth considering."

On this occasion the Mendelssohn Union performed the setting of the Ninety-fifth Psalm, "Come, let us sing," by Mendelssohn, a composer, wrote the *Albion* critic, toward whose music a strange antipathy existed in America. He attributed this dislike to the same "German resistance that in earlier days had despised Beethoven as a madman. It may happen that in a quarter of a century or so, the Teutonic mind will be sufficiently manured to receive the seeds of good judgment concerning this composer [Mendelssohn], who, more than any other, gives expression to the sentiment of the nineteenth century." The second part of the program, excellently conducted by G. Washbourn Morgan, consisted of Rossini's *Stabat Mater.*

For the fourth concert of their season, on June 28, again at the Cooper Institute, the Mendelssohn Union performed choruses from Mendelssohn's incidental music to Racine's play *Athalie* and Beethoven's score to Kotzebue's *The Ruins of Athens.* Beethoven came off less well than Mendelssohn, wrote the *Tribune* (June 30, 1858) because the piano could not approximate the quality of the orchestra accompaniments as written by Beethoven. The performances by the Misses Dingley, Hanley, Hawley, and Demount, Messrs. Parker and Wernecke, with Berge at the piano and Morgan conducting, "with a few exceptions," were excellent. The writer commented on the splendid acoustics of the hall and its agreeable coolness in the warm weather. With the anticipated acquisition of an organ, it was an ideal place for the performance of choral music.

On Thanksgiving evening, November 18, again at Cooper Union (aptly advertised on this occasion as "the Hall of the Union"), the Mendelssohn Union, this time with a "large and select" orchestra of Philharmonic players conducted by G. Washbourn Morgan, gave Mendelssohn's *St. Paul.* The solo singers were Madame Zimmermann, Mary Hawley, Charles Guilmette, and a Mr. C. R. Adams, an "excellent" tenor from the Boston Handel and Haydn Society. The performance was so "flatteringly" received that it was repeated on December 2, "on the same grand and liberal scale," with the same cast except that George Simpson replaced Mr. Adams, who apparently had returned to Boston.

What with the number of concerts by the various choral and chamber-music groups and their offshoots—and particularly with Ullman's sensational concert extravaganzas offering dazzling combinations of chorus, orchestra, and the latest opera stars for a fifty-cent admission—it is understandable that comparatively few musicians were tempted to give autonomous concerts in 1858. Among the venturesome few (predominantly pianists) was the Countess de Bienville, as she was now billed, who made her second appearance at Dodworth's Rooms on January 9, assisted by unspecified "Eminent Artists from the Opera." Again presenting an eclectic program—the first performance in America of Mozart's Piano Sonata, "no. 15," Herz's "Carnival of Venice," Thalberg's "Home, Sweet Home," and "the beautiful septuor from *Lucia di Lammer-*

moor, by Listz" (*sic*)—Madame de Bienville's concert for some reason received minimal notice, and she seems quietly to have faded from the scene.

Madame Graever-Johnson, on the other hand, received unstinting acclaim, not only for her performance of Litolff's "Concerto Symphony" with the Philharmonic, but for her concert that followed at Dodworth's on January 19. Announced as the first matinée in a series of three,[103] on this occasion Madame Graever, an unquenchable missionary for Litolff, repeated his Trio, op. 47—this time with Henry Appy and Bergner; she played two of her own piano compositions, *La Prière d'un ange* and *La Chasse;* with Appy, a Fantasia on *Oberon* for piano and violin by Éduard Wolff (1816–1880) and Vieuxtemps; and again solo, *La campanella* by Wilhelm Taubert (1811–1891) and the *Grand Galop chromatique* by Listz (*sic*); Madame Graever was further assisted by Annie Milner and Ernest Perring. Again, ——t——, who couldn't imagine a greater female pianist than Madame Graever, unless it were Clara Schumann or Wilhelmina Clauss, was overwhelmed by her blending of masculine fire and force with feminine delicacy, tenderness, and soul. Yet, for all that, Madame Graever again proved the axiom that "woman's creative genius seldom equals her imitative and reproductive powers": she would have done better to omit her two compositions, which, in —— t——'s opinion, were "beneath all criticism. . . . The fair *pianiste,*" he wrote, "should not endanger her laurels by mixing weeds among them" (*Dwight's,* January 23, 1858, p. 341).

Madame Graever was again saluted as "undoubtedly the best lady-pianist" to have reached these shores, when—late in the year, amid a flurry of (mostly piano) concerts following the opera's departure for Boston)[104]—she launched her 1858–59 season at Dodworth's on December 10. With Joseph Noll and Frederick Bergner she gave the first American performance of Litolff's Second Grand Trio; alone she played a Beethoven piano sonata from op. 31, a Gavotte and Musette by Bach, Handel's "The Harmonious Blacksmith," Mendelssohn's "Spring Song," Thalberg's *Mosè* Fantasia, and Liszt's *La regata veneziana* (from *Soirées musicales, c.* 1837). Madame Graever's performances were "faultless," wrote the *Albion* critic (December 18, 1858, p. 607): she paid due regard to the "*quantity,* as well as the quality of tone." Her vigor, wrote Fry, was positively "unfeminine" (*Tribune,* December 14, 1858). She was assisted on this occasion by the splendid contralto Annie Kemp, by a Mr. Hudson, the possessor of "a still, small voice," and by Henry C. Timm, who accompanied.

In March, Gustav Satter, who had taken up residence in Boston after his New York triumphs in 1855, was back for a purported performance with the Philharmonic of his new Symphony in E for piano and orchestra[105] (*Dwight's,* February 13, 1858, p. 366). Instead—in addition to appearing at two of Eisfeld's *soirées* (March 23 and April 13, see above) and at a scattering of other people's concerts—Satter gave a series of three concerts at Mozart Hall with armies of assisting artists: on March 11 with the soprano Henriette Eben (the former Henriette Behrend), her new husband, the Philharmonic flutist Felice Eben, Jennie Twitchell, a well-known Boston contralto, Ed-

---

[103] She announced a following evening concert on February 8.

[104] "When the *impresario* is away, the pianos will play," warbled the *Albion* critic (December 18, 1858, p. 607).

[105] In 1857, Satter was elected an honorary member of the New York Philharmonic Society.

ward Mollenhauer, and Robert Goldbeck; on March 28 with Hattie Andem, Mollen-
hauer, Eisfeld, Noll, Bergner, Pychowski, and Goldbeck;[106] and on April 3 with
Bertha Johannsen, Louis Schreiber, Mollenhauer, Frederick Bergner, and Candido
Berti.

A blockbuster pianist of the acrobatic school, Satter astounded the audience at his
first concert with his pianistic feats, particularly in his showy transcription of the Overture to *Tannhäuser,* with which he opened the program.[107] Yet, wrote Hagen (*Review
and Gazette,* March 20, 1858, p. 840), although he possessed "great execution, a crispy
touch, extraordinary endurance, and excellent musicianship," Satter was an erratic performer: he played "by fits and starts," especially when not held within bounds by a
partner or a conductor. "He has all the requisites for a very great player," wrote Hagen,
"but as yet he is only a curious and not a great pianist."

Less tolerantly, Watson—who sardonically congratulated Satter on his "noble
candor" in acknowledging himself the world's greatest pianist—denounced his "slovenly and inarticulate execution" (despite his extraordinary technique) and his "passages
of power, [which] were a perfect jumble of discords, prolonged by the loud pedal. . . .
No circumstance," spitefully commented Watson, "could ever place him where he
could possibly reach Thalberg's coat-tail" (*Leslie's,* March 27, 1858, p. 267).

Except for a charity concert on January 16, Robert Goldbeck, who during the
past year had been devoting himself mainly to composition and teaching, did not appear until December,[108] when he gave a series of three concerts at which he exhibited
the compositions he had created during the interim—in addition to his Second Trio
for piano and strings, op. 39 (first performed on January 16)—a *Scherzo eroico* for piano
and violin, and a variety of shorter pieces for the piano.

Goldbeck's series commenced on December 2, when, with Edward Mollenhauer
and Bergner, he repeated his second trio, a work that some of the critics found inscrutable, others merely run-of-the-mill; from Fry it elicited an obscure lesson in composition (*Tribune,* December 14, 1858). At his following two concerts—at Dodworth's on
December 9 and Cooper Institute on December 23—the trio was again repeated, as
was Goldbeck's "charming" suite for piano, "Three Romantic Souvenirs": "Maho-
pac," "A Day at Middlehope," and "Lake Saranac."[109] He played two of his Études for
piano, his less praiseworthy fantasias on *Il trovatore* and the Coronation March from *Le
Prophète,*[110] an improvisation on *La Marseillaise,* some Nocturnes and the *Berceuse,* op.
57 (1843), by Chopin, and—apparently beyond his scope—Beethoven's "Appassio-

---

[106] On this program Satter, with Goldbeck and Pychowski, at three Steinways, accompanied by
Mollenhauer, Eisfeld, Noll, and Bergner, anticipated by a month the Mason/Thomas performance
of Bach's Concerto for Three Claviers.
[107] Additionally, Satter played his Grand Fantasia on *Ernani,* and, with Goldbeck, Liszt's transcription for two pianos of *Les Préludes;* Madame Eben and Miss Twitchell sang various opera arias
and ballads; Mollenhauser played a "Grand Concerto" by Paganini and his own Indian suite, entic-
ingly titled "Dreary Sounds of Wigwam Life" (Dreamy Sounds?).
[108] Goldbeck had been announced to appear at Paul Julien's farewell concert on March 30 but,
taking offense at being "patronizingly" billed as a "talented young pianist," had refused to perform.
[109] "Mr. Goldbeck's imagination is delicately rose-tinted," wrote the *Albion* critic (December 11,
1858). "His compositions are fragrant trifles, very complete and enjoyable."
[110] He is fond, however, of trying his hand at *bravoura* pieces, and in these he does not shine to
advantage" *(ibid.).*

nata" Sonata, op. 57.[111] Goldbeck's assisting artists, besides those already named, were Hattie Andem, Kate Comstock, and Dr. Guilmette; G. W. Morgan accompanied the singers; tickets, at one dollar, admitted two (a new variation on an old theme).

Yet other pianists materialized toward the end of 1858. On November 12 the former piano prodigy, William Saar,[♪] now eighteen years old and just returned from four years of advanced piano study in Germany, made his local debut as an adult at Dodworth's Hall—audaciously without benefit of assisting artists. "A pianist with a very wide range of style may attempt, and successfully, the awful experiment of giving a concert with nothing else than the piano," carped the critic for the *Musical World* (November 20, 1858, p. 789). "Gottschalk, although deficient in breadth," he wrote, "was capable, by his immense *finesse* and elegance, of making an evening delightful. Mr. William Saar is not."

Young Saar, the critic went on, lacked the requisite "style, variety of expression, or exquisiteness, or grandeur" for carrying off a solo evening. Admittedly he possessed a more than adequate technique, played very few wrong notes, and seemed to have an inkling of the "middle parts." Furthermore, supposed the critic, it was something that one so young felt—or thought he felt—himself capable of playing such widely differing and challenging works as Bach's *Fantaisie chromatique,* Chopin's *Polonaise concertante,* and Liszt's *Rhapsodie hongroise,* and actually getting through them "in good time." "But here our admiration must cease." It was good, but not good enough. "We have passed the days of mere dexterity in piano playing. Execution as such is rococo. We demand perfection, not only in the fingers but in the souls of our pianists. They must be bards, not mechanics." And not extroverts. Surely Saar must have known that ending his mazurka with a *glissando* that swept the keyboard from top to bottom did nothing to enhance it.

But the ideal pianistic attributes, and more, were possessed by the fifteen-year-old Portuguese piano prodigy Arthur Napoleao (1843–1925), who made his North American debut at Dodworth's Rooms on November 23. Despite his extreme youth, Napoleon (as his name was transcribed) was by now a veteran concert-giver, having—since his first sensational public appearances in Lisbon at the age of six—crisscrossed the European continent, England, Ireland, and, more recently, Brazil and other South American countries, creating great excitement wherever he went. He had played for—and been petted by—most of the royalty in Europe and had been highly lauded and testimonialized by Rossini, Meyerbeer, Herz,[♪] Moscheles, Liszt, and by Charles Hallé, with whom he had studied in Manchester (see *Dwight's,* January 1, 1859, pp. 319–20).

Arriving in New York at the highest pitch of the Piccolomini fever, without benefit of competitive ballyhoo, Arthur Napoleon's debut was sparsely attended. *Trovator,* who immediately became his most fervent champion, attributed the absence of a Napoleon furor to the nefarious plottings of "a clique against him, and that certain newspapers, greedy for opera tickets, are not very exuberant in their praise, their lukewarmness being more agreeable to a certain operatic autocrat" *(ibid.).*

But, as *Trovator* foretold, once Napoleon had been heard, his success was instantaneous. Not since the breathtaking first appearances of little Adelina Patti in 1851[♪] and

---

[111] A misnomer, wrote Fry, who found it to be a work totally lacking in passion—but then, passion was an attribute foreign to Beethoven.

of Paul Julien in 1852♪ had a musical prodigy created so great an excitement. "A more decided success we have seldom been called upon to record," wrote the critic for the *Evening Post*[112] (November 24, 1858). Although only fifteen, Arthur Napoleon exhibited the "result of careful study and laborious practice, besides being marked by all the fire and feeling of true genius." This was particularly evident not only in his own "magnificent" Fantasy on *The Bohemian Girl,* but also in Chopin's *Polonaise* in A-flat, op. 53, and pieces by the London/Viennese pianist/composer Ernst Pauer (1826–1905).[113]

Napoleon had "conquered the mechanism" of the piano "in the fullest sense," wrote the *Albion* critic (November 27, 1858, p. 571), including "the judicious use of the pedals, an accomplishment which excellent pianists sometimes neglect but good musicians never. It was more than wonderful to hear this stripling play Thalberg's *Sonnambula* Fantasia[114] and Chopin's *Polonaise.* . . . With much of the force of manhood, he has all the delicacy of an almost feminine youth.[115] His phrasing—to use a cant word—is what it should be—the clear and chaste expression of a musical idea. . . . In clearness of execution he leaves little to be desired. He possesses an enormous hand[116] . . . and a wrist that will bear octave passages *ad libitum.* In a word, he is a genuine prodigy, and one that we are sure the public will appreciate and enjoy."

And a skeptical R. Storrs Willis, who went to the concert more "out of curiosity to see the sort of child that tickles Europe than of desire to hear Arthur Napoleon," remained to be overwhelmed: "Arthur Napoleon is an extraordinary performer," wrote Willis (*Musical World,* December 4, 1858, p. 771); "His touch is exquisitely full of tenderness; his precision almost unerring; his power more than respectable, and his rounding of musical thought perfectly delightful."

But Hagen—giving no credence to Napoleon's brilliant European reputation—curtly dismissed him as a talented young man who would doubtless some day become a superior player, but who "for the present lacks style and abandon, two qualities which cannot be obtained but in the riper years of an artist" (*Review and Gazette,* November 27, 1858, p. 371).

At his following three concerts—given at Dodworth's on November 30, December 7, and December 14, Napoleon's repertory consisted predominantly of opera fanta-

---

[112]Later disclosed to have been none other than *Dwight's Trovator.*

[113]At Napoleon's first and second concerts the "accessories," as the *Post* critic contemptuously dubbed his assisting artists, were Claudina Cairoli, W. H. Dennett, replacing the originally announced Perring, and a Theodore Schallehn, who accompanied. Tickets were $1; tickets "admitting schools" fifty cents. Appearing at the third and fourth concerts were Cairoli, George Simpson, and the long absent Signor Oswald Bernardi; the "conductors" were Schallehn and James G. Maeder. Tickets continued to be $1, with $2 tickets admitting a gentleman and two ladies.

[114]But the *Evening Post* critic (November 24, 1858) advised Napoleon to avoid comparison with Thalberg by omitting Thalberg's compositions or works that Thalberg had played.

[115]Arthur Napoleon was described as a slight youth of modest demeanor, with "a one-sided nervous gait; pale, delicate countenance, and slender form; long, dark hair carelessly pushed behind his ears, and black Spanish eyes, well contrasted by the very paleness of his face." He was fluent in French, German, and English as well as Spanish and his native Portuguese; was as virtuosic a chess player as a pianist, and was said to write novels for his private amusement (*Dwight's,* February 19, 1859, pp. 375–76).

[116]Despite his deceptively delicate appearance, he possessed "a hand to take the steam out of Dreyschock himself," wrote Richard Storrs Willis (*Musical World,* December 4, 1858, p. 771).

sias: on *La traviata* by the Czech composer/pianist Wilhelm Kuhe (1823–1912); on *Il trovatore* by the Dutch composer Joseph Ascher (1829–1869); on *I puritani* by Herz; on *L'elisir d'amore* and *Mosè* by Thalberg; on *I Lombardi* ("Jérusalem") by Gottschalk: and on *Lucia di Lammermoor* and *Lucrezia Borgia* by Napoleon himself. And, to the critics' wonderment, everything from memory! He also played the Andante from Herz's Third Piano Concerto, Prudent's *Le Reveil des Fées,* Pauer's *La Chasse* and *La Cascade,* Thalberg's "Home, Sweet Home,"[117] and Gottschalk's *Marche de nuit* and "The Banjo" (works that he had encountered since coming to the United States).

"His style is more like Gottschalk's than that of any other pianist that has been here," declared *Trovator* (*Dwight's,* December 4, 1858, p. 284). Yet, in his review of Napoleon's third concert in the *Evening Post* (December 1, 1858)—after lauding his magnificent performance of Thalberg's Fantasia on *L'elisir d'amore*—*Trovator* had added Gottschalk to his former admonition (that Napoleon avoid Thalberg's compositions). The prodigy would do well to avoid all Gottschalk music in his future programs: although he played the *Marche de nuit* well, "as far as execution goes," it lacked that "certain dreamy fascination that probably no other player [but Gottschalk] could impart to it."[118]

On November 27 another "Lady-Pianist" joined the pianistically overcrowded scene: Madame Louise Abel, "a very finished, neat, and lady-like pianist from the Paris *Conservatoire,* who claims to be a pupil of Chopin, made her debut at a private *soirée* at Chickering's new Warerooms" (694 Broadway, at Fourth Street), reported the *Albion* critic (December 11, 1828, p. 583). Not a sensational pianist, but nonetheless equal to the technical demands of everything she performed, in her unobtrusive way Madame Abel was "a thoroughbred player of the very best school," wrote Willis (*Musical World,* December 4, 1858, p. 771). Madame Abel intended to become a teacher, a profession for which she was eminently fitted. Willis recommended her to "such of our friends as wish their children well instructed on the piano." Madame Abel would make her mark as a performer as well.

Another Parisienne, Emma Wellis, a pupil of Adolphe Adam and a virtuoso exponent of what was apparently an advanced version of the Alexandre organ, had earlier been heard (unfortunately during the first Piccolomini excitement) on October 14 at Dodworth's and on October 21 at Niblo's Saloon. The new model of the Alexandre was described in the *Tribune* (October 15, 1858) as a "chamber organ about the size of a cabinet piano" with two keyboards, one producing the sound of an organ and the other of the piano. Its diminutive size and price made it an especially desirable instrument for small churches, but also for the drawing room, where its "soft persuasiveness" would bring welcome relief from the "hammering decision" of the perpetual piano.

Mademoiselle Wellis, a young artist, possessed unlimited skill in producing "every possible effect, and an amount of light and shade truly surprising on an instrument

---

[117] A choice of repertory that Willis found too palpably aimed toward the public's predilection for light and showy pieces. "Art requires an effort more self-sacrificing, and good taste suggests that the two be combined," he pontificated. To Willis, the presence on Napoleon's third program of such lightweight composers as Ascher and Pauer placed Napoleon "on a lower level than is his by right" (*Musical World,* December 4, 1858, p. 771).

[118] Napoleon and Gottschalk were destined in later years, to become friends in Brazil, where Napoleon published great quantities of Gottschalk's music.

216   *Strong on Music: Repercussions*

managed by mechanical means," continued the *Tribune*. "Her combinations and manipulations are as delicately perfect as it is possible for them to be," wrote the *Albion* critic (October 15, 1858, p. 500). She makes the instrument sing." Mlle. Wellis was assisted at both her concerts by Maria Brainerd, Signor Bernardi, and E. Mollenhauer; Henry C. Timm accompanied. (Where was Dr. Beames?)

With Ullman in control of the available operatic forces, few concerts remained to be given by Italian opera singers. Among them was the farewell concert of the tenor Pietro Bignardi, who was returning to Europe upon the conclusion of his engagement at the Academy of Music. Appearing on March 23 at Niblo's Saloon, Bignardi attracted a thin audience despite the impressive array of Academy stars lending their assistance: de LaGrange, D'Angri, Formes, Tiberini, Labocetta, Ardavani, and Rocco, with Albites and Abella accompanying. "Signor Bignardi should not leave the United States," contended the *Herald* (March 24, 1858). "He has a fine fresh voice, and only needs to study to cultivate and develop his powers and enlarge his *répertoire* to achieve the success predicted for him on his first appearance here." Bignardi, however, departed.

On May 2, the young Italian tenor Antonio Alaimo presented himself in a concert at Dodworth's, assisted by Hattie Andem and Madame Bouchelle. Upon hearing Alaimo at a pre-concert musicale, ——t—— could not understand why he should sing in public, "or, indeed, in private, either" (*Dwight's*, May 8, 1858, p. 45). Among other birds of passage, on May 13 a nest of Italian prodigies, the Misses Antoinetta and Maria Erba, evidently singers, and their little eleven-year-old brother, Giovanni, a violinist, made their debut in an "Italian Concert" at Dodworth's, with the announced assistance of Tiberini, Gassier, Donizetti, and Nicolao. On November 18, at Dodworth's, a Mlle. Landi, billed as "Ex-Prima Donna of the Theatre San Carlo, Naples, and the Theatre Italien, Paris," made her American debut, assisted by Cairoli, Perring, Bernardi, a Mr. Edgard, billed as a *chanteur comique* of the [local?] French Company, and the pianist Harry Sanderson.

With Ullman's permission, Tiberini and Rocco were announced to appear at Paul Julien's farewell concert, on March 30 at Mozart Hall; his other assisting artists were Madame Chome, newly billed as the *prima donna* of the Brussels opera, and Goldbeck, who defaulted; as did Tiberini, pleading indisposition.

Young Julien, as the *Times* observed, had grown up in our midst since he was eleven, graduating from "the insignificance of a [little velvet] jacket to the full honors of a dress coat." Having for a period of years exhausted the farewell circuit in the United States, Julien, now eighteen years old, had more recently been touring in Venezuela and other South American countries. He had returned to the United States for a brief tour before again departing for Brazil. Julien was an extraordinary violinist, wrote the *Times:* "In tenderness and poetic impressibility [he] has rarely been surpassed." The attendance at his farewell concert was, however, meager: Formes was appearing at the Academy that evening in a performance of *Messiah*.

Charitable and complimentary concerts for the usual wide assortment of causes and honorees were performed by a repetitive cast of resident and opera musicians. On January 5 at Niblo's Saloon a representation of singers from the Academy of Music gave a Grand Concert for the benefit of the Italian Benevolent Society. Italian opera arias and ensembles galore were performed by D'Angri, Cairoli, Gassier, Labocetta (who not only sang, but played a cello *obbligato* to a song of Gassier's), Rocco, and Ardavani; Madame Graever contributed two Italian opera fantasias; Signor Abella presided at the piano.

On January 16 at Niblo's Saloon, Robert Goldbeck, together with the Welsh Nightingale Lucy Williams, Charles Guilmette, E. Mollenhauer, Feri Kletzer, Frederick Bergner, and the German *Liederkranz* under Agricol Paur, appeared in a Grand Vocal and Instrumental Concert to assist the Children's Aid Society in their new philanthropic function: according to —t— (as he was now abbreviated), the Society had recently opened "a branch office, from whence unemployed females [were] sent to the West to be provided with homes and work" (*Dwight's,* January 23, 1858, p. 340).

On January 21 a Grand Amateur Concert was given at the Baptist Church on Fifth Avenue at Thirty-fifth Street, for the benefit of the widow of Alexander F. Vache, a physician; the performers were Mrs. Beecher, the Misses Andem and Secor, and the Messrs. Alaimo and de Trobriand; Signor Manzocchi accompanied; tickets were one dollar.

On February 3 at Mozart Hall, a complimentary concert was tendered to the Welsh Nightingale by her compatriots of the St. David's Society; assisting, appropriately, were her countrymen Aptommas and J. R. Thomas; Vanderweide accompanied; tickets were fifty cents.

On March 7 a vocal and choral "Musical Fete" was given at St. Stephen's Church to raise money to pay off the remaining debt on its organ (built by Henry Erben). The event, a triumphant success, netted $1006. "This, with an additional hundred or so from the church treasury," asserted the *Musical World* (March 20, 1858), would suffice to liquidate the balance of the debt.

On March 22 the parishioners of Grace Church again manifested their devotion to their beloved soprano Mrs. Bodstein (the former Julia Northall)♪♫ with a complimentary concert at Niblo's Saloon. A choice event under the social tutelage of Sexton Brown, the distinguished participants, in addition to the honoree, were Madame D'Angri and Messrs. Gassier, Millet, and Appy; Morgan, the Grace Church organist, accompanied;[119] tickets were two dollars.

On May 5, to liquidate the "entire debt" of the Free Church of the Holy Martyrs, a choice matinée was presented at Niblo's Saloon by Madame Zimmermann (making her American debut on this occasion), the Misses Madeline and Mary Gellie, Miss Brainerd, and Messrs. Tiberini, Rivarde, and Aptommas; Signor Albites and Dr. Beames accompanied; tickets were one dollar.

On May 13, at the expiring Broadway Theatre, Thomas Dartmouth Rice was honored with a Grand Complimentary Testimonial by a great number of his burnt-cork colleagues.

On May 15 at Wallack's Theatre, an impressive roster of musicians joined with their thespian counterparts in doing honor to the actress Mrs. John Hoey upon her departure for Europe. As part of an elaborate farewell testimonial, a musical inter-

[119] The *recherché* event was "an homage of admiring amateurs," snobbishly reported *Raimond,* and it "was tendered like apples of gold on pictures of silver by not less admiring artists" (*Albion,* March 27, 1858, p. 151).

mezzo, bisecting two plays—Charles Mathews's *The Dowager* and Dion Boucicault's *London Assurance*—was performed by Annie Milner and Henry Cooper, Madame D'Angri, Carl Formes, and Ernest Perring; G. Washbourn Morgan accompanied.

On the afternoon of May 22, the Nursery and Child's Hospital inaugurated its new building (at Fifty-first Street near Third Avenue) with a concert for its own benefit. Appearing were Carl Formes, a Madame Schlarbaum, who played a piano duo with Henry C. Timm and a harp and piano duo with Aptommas, the Misses Gellie, a violin-playing Mr. Hagan (more probably Hagen),[120] Charles Brannes, the cellist, and Mr. Weismüller, a clarinetist.

On May 28, the new Church of St. Vincent de Paul, on Twenty-third Street, celebrated its opening with a Grand Concert organized by its organist and music director Mr. Gaspard [Dachauer].[121] The performers were Miss Brainerd, Mlle. Cairoli, and Messrs. George F. Bristow, Gassier, Mollenhauer, the veteran flutist John A. Kyle, and Dr. Beames.

On June 21 a complimentary concert and benefit was accorded the once popular singer Kazia Lovarny,♪♫ to take place upstairs at the Chinese Assembly Rooms (539 Broadway), where she was currently performing.

With the enthusiastic public response to the musical festivals at Jones's Wood, as the year progressed, the benefit events more and more took on festival-like characteristics. On June 29, at a vast afternoon and evening benefit at the Academy of Music for Theodore Moss, the treasurer of Wallack's Theatre, swarms of theatre folk participated, as did members of the current Italian and English opera companies—Amodio, Brignoli, and Gasparoni; Annie Milner, a Madame Krollman, and Henry C. Cooper; W. A. King accompanied.

But nothing approached in size and grandeur the three-day Grand Gala Festival at the Academy of Music devised by Ullman for the fund-raising campaign by the local branch of the Ladies' National Committee of the Mount Vernon Association to purchase Mount Vernon from its present occupant, John Augustine Washington.[122] Not that it was an altruistic gesture on Ullman's part. As explained in the *Tribune* (December 17, 1858), the Ladies' Committee would receive one-half of the net receipts after deducting the rental of the Academy, the advertising expenses, and all attendant services and expenditures; the remainder would accrue to Ullman.

As the earlier advertisements for the great event stated: "It is now some four years since public attention was first directed to the imminent dangers to which Mount Vernon was exposed. As regards its possession, all attempts made for the purpose of influencing Congress to secure the Home and Tomb of Washington as the property of the Nation had lamentably failed, and it was only when that eloquent and high-minded orator Edward Everett [1794–1865] forced the country to recognize the disgrace

[120] Theodore Hagen was a violinist and the founder, in 1858, of a string quartet—the Haydn Quartet—in Brooklyn.

[121] Dodworth's Band supplied the music at the annual festival for the benefit of the poor held by the Society of St. Vincent de Paul, at the City Assembly Rooms from October 26 through 30.

[122] John Washington had inherited the legal right to sell Mount Vernon to an unresponsive United States Government. His price for the Virginia property, comprising 200 acres of land, the mansion, gardens, landing place, and Washington's tomb, was $200,000.

Vera Lawrence

Efforts to raise money to buy Mt. Vernon, home of George Washington, were made by the Ladies' National Committee of the Mt. Vernon Association, which held dinners such as the one outlined on this menu.

which threatened it that they evinced any interest in its possession;[123] the result of that awakened interest was the foundation of a Ladies' National Committee, whose object was to raise means for the purchase of Mount Vernon. Though the labors of Edward Everett and others equally praiseworthy have realized a large fund, yet the object for which this Association was created has not yet been fulfilled—a larger amount is yet necessary. They believe that a series of festivals of the character now proposed, given throughout the entire country, will materially increase the fund." The public's support was earnestly solicited.[124]

Scheduled for December 14, 16, and 18, the dates were shifted to December 18, 21, and 22, possibly because of complications arising from Ullman's enforced absence with his opera company in Boston. Unable to be present, he had put the administration of the enterprise in charge of the problematical Henry Wikoff,♪♫ once again in the United States.[125] Despite his absence, the advertisements for the event bore the unmistakable stamp of Ullman at his most mellifluous, as did the festival itself, described in the publicity as an "intellectual carnival."[126]

On its first day—from half-past five in the afternoon until long past midnight— the combined stars and supporting companies of Wallack's and Burton's theatres and of Bryant's and Campbell's Minstrels appeared in a monster program comprising five full plays punctuated by various minstrel specialties, a recitation by John Brougham, and a "musical melange" by Mesdames Colson, Caradori, and Escott, Messrs. Bernardi and Durand, and Master Arthur Napoleon.

On the second day—or rather, evening—of the festival, a grand "full dress" (not fancy dress) ball was presented "upon a scale of unprecedented brilliancy." Musard, at last functioning in his true sphere of dance conductor, gracefully officiated, purportedly making what was unabashedly advertised as his first appearance in America (large type) as conductor of a ball (small type).[127] With a Mammoth Orchestra of 120 men and purportedly with his famed solo players (of whom only the cornetist Legendre had remained), Musard—again ballyhooed as *Le roi du quadrille*—was performing for the first time (in a ballroom, that is) his celebrated quadrilles, *Les Zouaves, Les Lancers,* The Gotham Quadrille, and the numberless other galops, polkas and such, works that in fact had comprised the bulk of his earlier concert repertory. Music for a preliminary

---

[123] Not exactly. True, Everett indefatigably toured the country with his spellbinding George Washington/Mount Vernon lecture, reportedly delivering it some 129 times and raising with it $69,064. But he had originally been recruited in 1856 by Ann Pamela Cunningham (1816–1875), who in 1853 founded the Mount Vernon Ladies' Association of the Union and made the redemption of Mount Vernon her lifelong mission.

[124] The transaction was at last consummated, appropriately, on February 22, 1859.

[125] "The Mount Vernon festival . . . is going on promisingly, as we hear, under the able management of Mr. Henri [*sic*] Wikoff, the 'Roving Diplomatist,' who has been engaged by Mr. Ullman to attend to the affair during his absence in Boston" (*Tribune*, December 17, 1858).

[126] "While we feel confident that the public will need no incentive to partake largely of the intellectual feast beyond the merits of its entertainment, few will visit the festival without bearing constantly in their breasts the pleasant sense that each is contributing a son's mite towards maintaining inviolate the home and tomb of the American who died childless that the nation might call him Father," spouted the advertisements.

[127] Musard, who had evidently been touring since his earlier debacle, had reportedly made a great hit in New Orleans, where there was no prohibition against the giving of masquerade balls.

promenade and auxiliary dance music was supplied by Joseph Noll and a second orchestra placed in the first circle.

For this quintessentially Ullmanesque production, the Academy was again specially decorated with statuary, natural flowers, and "eight magnificent chandeliers," supplemented by "appropriate devices in gas" to magnify the brilliance of the scene. At the rear of the stage hung a kind of scroll-work contrivance of gas jets forming the somber motto: "Woman Preserves His Home and Grave," and over the proscenium was placed a "representation of the homestead with the inscription beneath, 'Woman Gives Mount Vernon to the Nation.'" The walls were hung with flags of all nations, loaned by the commander of the Brooklyn Navy Yard and by colonels of the various New York regiments (all military men attending were requested to wear their uniforms, and, doubtless, their medals). And outside, two spectacular calcium lights swept the neighborhood from the Academy's exterior balconies fronting on both Fourteenth Street and Irving Place.

Dancing, for which the parquet had been boarded over to a level with the stage, began at half-past nine and continued until about midnight, when the participants, not numerous, rapidly dispersed. Although drawn from various social strata, it was reported that the dancers preserved perfect decorum throughout the evening (possibly because alcoholic beverages were prohibited).

The third night was more plentifully attended, for while tickets to the full three nights were three dollars, or separately at one dollar for the first night (no reserved seats) and two dollars and fifty cents for the second, one might attend the third night[128]—a monster concert conducted by Musard and Carl Bergmann (replacing Anschütz, who was in Boston with the opera company)—for a mere twenty-five cents: "in order that all may have an opportunity of contributing their mite to this truly national work."

Not that the program was unduly weighty. It was, in fact, a replica of the earlier Musard/Anschütz programs, with lightweight classics (Weber's Overture to *Oberon,* Mendelssohn's Wedding March, and Hérold's Overture to *Zampa*) conducted by "our very spirited Philharmonic conductor" Bergmann, and with Musard performing his old standbys—the "Zouves," the "Beef and Mutton Quadrille" (the "Cattle Show"), the "Express Train Galop," and, in honor of the occasion, an apparently new "Mount Vernon Polka."

Two nights later—on Christmas Eve—Ullman, taking advantage of the accumulated Mount Vernon momentum (and still retaining the decorations from the great ball), presented another Grand Monster Concert conducted by Bergmann and Musard, virtually duplicating the above program, but with the timely addition of Haydn's "Christmas" ("Toy") Symphony, with "solos for toy instruments."

As we know, the Harmonic Society's *Messiah* followed on Christmas night. Then, to cap this teeming musical year, on December 30, Bergmann, who had given the second of his new series of Sunday evening concerts on December 26, conducted a program of music by Beethoven (the Fifth Symphony), Mozart (chorus from *The Magic Flute*), Rossini (the *Stabat Mater*), and Wagner (the Grand March from *Lohengrin*) at a massive concert given for the benefit of the German Hospital by the German Society.

---

[128] With decorations held over from the second night.

Taking place at the Academy of Music, "very kindly tendered by Mr. Ullman free of charge,"[129] the participants were Madame Caradori, Messrs. Formes, Schreiber, and Mollenhauer, 300 members of the combined *Sängerbund, Arion,* and *Harmonia* Societies (the last from Hoboken), and an orchestra of eighty. Tickets, much to *Trovator's* disgust, were an inflated two dollars for the parquet, boxes, and balcony, one dollar for the second tier, and fifty cents for the amphitheatre.

Evidently no Germanophile, *Trovator* described the event in somewhat ethnically biased terms (in *Dwight's,* January 15, 1859, p. 333): "To be sure," he wrote, "there were some German demonstrations. Haydn's 'Creation' was given in German text by a German musical society, with German soloists, for the benefit of a German benevolent society, and before an exclusively German audience. Then another set of Germans hired the Academy of Music one evening and gave a $2-a-ticket-concert for another German benevolent affair."

---

[129] A courtesy not extended to the Mount Vernon ladies.

3

GTS: 1859

. . . although Verdi and Original Sin are fearful realities, Man *appreciates* true *music, at least, when he hears it in a well-lighted drawing room, on a comfortable chair, and among people of his own "set."*

George Templeton Strong
Private Journal
May 18, 1859

Private social concerts are becoming quite the rage.

Dwight's Journal of Music
June 11, 1859

January 7, 1859. . . . Murray Hoffman dined here, and we went together [to the Academy of Music] to hear *Nozze di Figaro.* . . . Very beggarly house. Mozart is repulsive, of course, to lovers of Verdi.

~~~

It was Mozart, however, who dominated the return of Ullman's opera company to the Academy of Music, replacing not Verdi but Balfe at the opening on January 6 of their "parenthetical," post-Boston season-in-transit. Because an ailing Brignoli had remained behind in Boston[1] (and lacking a suitable alternate tenor), it had been necessary to substitute *Don Giovanni*[2] for the loudly heralded local premiere of *La zingara,* as the recently Italianized version of Balfe's *The Bohemian Girl* was titled. The performance of *Le nozze di Figaro* that Strong heard on January 7 similarly replaced the announced first New York performance in Italian of *Marta* (Flotow's *Martha*).[3] On Janu-

---

[1] Ullman's lease of Brignoli extended through the Boston season and until January 27 at a rumored $2000 a month, with a "half clear" benefit at the close of the ensuing New York and Philadelphia seasons (*Herald,* January 3, 1859).

[2] Offering Fry another opportunity to lambaste Mozart as a composer of tiresome, inferior operas, in this instance "a mean and dirty one" (*Tribune,* January 8, 1859). It was performed by Piccolomini (Zerlina), Poinsot (Donna Anna), Ghioni (Donna Elvira), Florenza (Don Giovanni), Formes (Leporello), and likely Lorini as Ottavio.

[3] Announced to be sung by Laborde (Marta), Brignoli (Lionello), Formes (Plunkett), and Minna von Berkel (Nancy). Although scheduled and rescheduled, *Marta* was not performed during the present season.

223

ary 8, *Don Giovanni* was repeated at the Saturday matinée, and, finally, on the evening of January 10, with a reportedly recovered Brignoli back from Boston, *La zingara* was at last performed.[4]

A disappointment, wrote the *Albion* critic (January 15, 1859, p. 31): with its English dialogue transformed into uncomfortable Italian recitative and its indiscriminate, Italianate tamperings and interpolations (including an unsatisfactory replacement for Balfe's overture) by Emanuele Muzio, who conducted, *La zingara* amounted to nothing more than a good English opera disguised as a bad Italian one.[5] Nor did the predominantly mediocre performances improve matters (although dear little Piccolomini made a hit with her encore of "Marble Halls" in her piquantly broken English).

The *Evening Post* critic (January 11, 1859) charmingly evokes her rendition of this classic—her entrance, with "a sort of hop and skip step (sensation and applause); her arch look over left shoulder" to a stage box, wherein a "young man in small garrote shirt-collar, large, straw-colored whiskers, and white kids, in a high state of excitement, cries '*Bray-vo!*'

"Pic smiles to balconies; conductor flourishes baton, and orchestra plays symphony [introduction]," tersely continues the critic. "Upon which she sings, in her adorably mangled English, 'I dreamt zat I dwelt in marble halls.'" Upon reaching the final lines, after "three nods, shrug of pretty shoulders, and smiles all round balconies," she enunciates:

> But I also dreampt, vich please me mose,
> Zat you loaf me still ze same.

Then, "exuberantly to galleries, balconies, and everybody:

> Zat you *loaf*—zat you *loaf* me sti-l-l *ze same.*

(Applause—laughter—mirth.) Kids split to pieces in stage box, and a dress circle window smashed in by an individual in the lobby, anxious to see 'what it was all about.'"

On January 11 the St. George's Society took possession of the Academy with an elaborate Grand Festival: in the afternoon an operatic double bill—*La zingara* (a last-minute replacement for the hapless *Marta*) and *La serva padrona* (Piccolomini/Maggiorotti)—and in the evening a monster concert in two parts, the first an all-star miscellaneous program[6] and the second to comprise "the greater part" of *The Creation*, with Piccolomini—making her oratorio debut as Eve[7]—Formes as Adam, Laborde, Poin-

[4] With Piccolomini as Arlina, Brignoli as Thaddeus, Florenza as the Count, and Ghioni, Coletti, and Quinto in the lesser roles. Apparently part of his blanket deal with Lumley, Ullman's production of *La zingara* was given in the version with Balfe's additions and alterations specially devised for the recent production at her Majesty's Theatre "in honor of the Marriage of the Princess Royal of England."

[5] Fry, the fervent champion of opera in English, was, however, "glad to see Mr. Balfe in an Italian dress. Such a transmogrification," he wrote, "will contribute its quota toward the redemption of English music as being not good enough for grand opera" (*Tribune*, January 12, 1859). Darcie, too, thought this version an improvement over the original (*Porter's Spirit,* January 15, 1859, p. 320).

[6] Performed by Piccolomini, Caradori, Emma Heywood, Ghioni, Graever-Johnson, Poinsot, and Brainerd, and conducted by Theodore Thomas and Clare W. Beames.

[7] Sung with a "rare tenderness and with a precision of musical time and accent that [put] her detractors to shame," wrote the faithful *Albion* critic (January 15, 1859, p. 31). A great contrast, he added, to Formes, who sang correctly only "by accident."

sot, and Perring in the other roles, and with the German *Liederkranz* and the opera orchestra conducted by Anschütz. In deference to the Society's British constituency, the first part was programed to conclude with a gala performance of "God Save the Queen," sung in English by Piccolomini and Formes, with the chorus and orchestra.

Due, however, to a mighty backstage wrangle between the two superluminaries[8] over which of them would get to sing the second stanza of the anthem (apparently the only stanza either of them knew in English), Formes forcibly settled the matter. Suddenly materializing onstage with Madame Caradori, not Piccolomini, on his arm, he proceeded to render the second stanza, to the indignant boos and hisses of the audience. Directly upon the perpetration of this outrage, little Piccolomini, in a frenzy of frustration and rage, stormed onstage (but properly on the arm of the Society's president), loudly protesting her blamelessness. Determined to prevail, although the orchestra and chorus had by now dispersed, she triumphantly delivered the second stanza to the hastily summoned piano accompaniment of Ernest Perring. A sensation![9]

A pallid revival of *The Huguenots* followed on January 12[10] (Laborde/Poinsot/Ghioni/Formes/Tamaro/Coletti). And on January 13, the final night, Piccolomini bade a surprisingly underplayed farewell to New York with *La traviata*—positively her last performance, as the advertisements dispiritedly explained—"Mr. Ullman not having been able to obtain an extension of her contract [purportedly running only until March 20], her services being imperatively required by Mr. Lumley early in April at Her Majesty's Theatre."

Although Piccolomini's "farewell" called out the largest audience of the season, valedictory excitement for some reason was only lukewarm, the departing diva not being called out until the end of the opera. Indeed, summarized Watson (*Leslie's*, January 22, 1859, p. 120), the opera season had created little excitement. Not only had the weather been too bitterly cold to "permit the mercury of enthusiasm to rise in the musical thermometer, [but] the whole affair wore such a makeshift, fill-up-the-spare-time air that the public did not think it worthwhile to provide new dresses or don its opera cloaks for the occasion." The brief season had been "remarkable only for its disappointments. The promised operas were not given, in consequence of the indisposition—bodily or mental—of Brignoli; but nobody seemed to care much about the matter." Indeed, wrote Watson, the most vivid incident of the whole season had been

[8] Between whom a massive hostility apparently raged. It was "a new illustration of that bitter and unreasonable animosity which springs up between artists," commented the *Musical World* (January 22, 1859, p. 51). "One might suppose that two voices so utterly dissimilar as a basso and a soprano might travel on the broad road to harmony without any unpleasantness, but it seems impossible."

[9] "The funniest part of the business was to watch Formes and Piccolomini in the subsequent part of the evening, when they were singing the music of Adam and Eve in the oratorio of 'The Creation,'" wickedly observed Darcie (*Porter's Spirit,* January 22, 1859, p. 336). "In words, they had to dote upon each other; unhappily their action was not suited to the language that they uttered." (Darcie, like his colleagues, condemned Formes for his uncouth behavior.)

[10] Ullman might have been chastened by his experience in Boston, where he had undergone another of his unfortunate clashes with a newspaper critic. Under cover of a pseudonym, the formidable Mr. Edward House of the *Boston Courier* had devastatingly disparaged both the overblown ballyhoo for *Les Huguenots* and its disappointing production. Consequently being refused admittance to the theatre, the critic "knocked Ullman down and then passed in and took his seat" (*Evening Post,* December 31, 1858; also see *Dwight's,* January 1, pp. 314–17; *Porter's Spirit,* January 8, 1859, p. 304).

the "God-Save-the-Queen" flare-up at the St. George's Society benefit. A sorry epilogue to Ullman's brilliant successes of the preceding season.

The company proceeded to Philadelphia, where Piccolomini appeared only three times—in *La figlia, The Marriage of Figaro,* and *La traviata*—before, taking a few members of the company, and with Muzio as conductor and Lumley's watchdog to see to business matters,[11] she departed on a separate tour of Baltimore, Washington, and Richmond (*Dwight's,* February 5, 1859, p. 359). Although it had been announced that the troupe would then reunite and continue together along the eastern seaboard to New Orleans and Havana, the Piccolomini contingent suddenly switched their itinerary to the North and West.[12] Eventually, it was announced, they would descend along the Mississippi to New Orleans, where in early March they would rejoin Ullman and his company.[13]

Thus it came about that Piccolomini, now headed toward "Albany, Troy, Rochester, Toronto, Buffalo, and the West," was enabled to tuck in another farewell forever to New York, this time a double parting—on the evening of February 11 and the following afternoon—as Norina in Donizetti's *Don Pasquale.*[14]

February 13. . . . *Don Pasquale* Friday night with Ellie and Charley Strong and wife. Crowded house, but little Piccolomini was coldly received.[15] The opera contains nothing worth remembering, but some of its poor little melodies are quite pretty and pleasant to hear.

∼

Not an exemplary production, wrote the *Albion* critic (February 19, 1859, p. 91): "There was a feebleness about the performance at the Academy which entitles it to our silent commiseration. Piccolomini as Norina was as gay and coquettish as anyone in the presence of Maggiorotti [the Don Pasquale] and Lorini [the Ernesto] could be expected to be." Furthermore, wrote *Personne* in the *Saturday Press* (February 19, 1859): "The chorus was wretched, while the orchestra was picked up, like Falstaff's forces, here, there, and everywhere." *Don Pasquale* was "not so good with Piccolomini, Maggiorotti, Florenza, and Lorini, at two dollars, as with Bosio, Marini, Badiali, and Salvi, at fifty cents;♪ but while the latter sung to empty houses, the former, according to all

[11] Described by *Personne* in the *Saturday Press* (February 19, 1959), as "an extensive pair of mutton-chop whiskers sent here by Lumley to see that the dimes were forthcoming."

[12] Because, elucidated the *Herald* (February 9, 1859), "during February and March it pays better to give concerts in the provinces."

[13] Headed by Formes and including Poinsot, Laborde, von Berkel, and Florenza, with Anschütz conducting and Gustav Satter providing intermission music, Ullman's company opened in New Orleans on February 23 (*Dwight's,* March 12, 1859, p. 399).

[14] Given in contemporary dress and with minimal production requirements, it was an ideal vehicle for a small touring opera company.

[15] Not so, according to the *Times* (February 12, 1859). The production was not only a box-office smash—the two performances reportedly bringing in a fabulous $6500—but it was a role made for Piccolomini: "All the little ways that have made the lady popular are aggregated in the *rôle* of Norina. She fires off a perfect battery of witcheries, and with a skill which is appalling when contemplated from an exposed bachelor's point of view. . . . Without invoking the shade of Sontag,♪ we have no hesitation in saying that Mlle. Piccolomini is as good a Norina as the age can afford." The same could not be said of her colleagues, nor of the production, added the critic.

accounts, brought seven thousand dollars to the manager's till with a mediocre performance of an unpopular opera."

New Yorkers would thereafter be deprived of opera until April, when, reported the *Herald* (February 9, 1859), "the imperial Ullman" would return from New Orleans, "the indomitable Maretzek" from Havana, and "the mercurial Strakosch from the consecration of the magnificent Pike's Opera House" in Cincinnati.[16]

During this interval of operatic surcease, Strong, no devotee of opera (nor, for that matter, of publicly attended performances in general), reveled in the kinds of music-listening he preferred—with Ellie playing his favorite composers on the piano at home or attending a series of private musicales newly initiated by the musically indefatigable Mrs. Wolcott Gibbs (the former Josephine Mauran).♪ Patterned after Strong's cherished "Mass-meetings" of 1854–55,♪ Mrs. Gibbs's musicales consisted chiefly of readings of Strong's treasured Haydn and Mozart masses by members of the former group of musically and socially compatible amateurs. This time, however, the meetings were spread among the various members' houses.[17]

February 17. . . . Last night with Ellie at Mrs. Wolcott Gibbs's—Twenty-ninth Street—the first of certain little informal musical gatherings that promise to be very agreeable. The performers were Mrs. Gibbs, Mrs. Mary Wright, Ellie, and Mrs. Eleanor [Strong], with a tenor (one [William H.] Cooke) and a basso (the infallible Philip Mayer) professionally retained. Mrs. d'Oremieulx accompanied.[18] They sang the *Gratias agimus* and *Qui tollis* of Haydn's Sixteenth Mass [Hoboken XXII:12], the *Gloria* of Mozart's No. 1 [K. 317] (most refreshing it was to hear scraps of that music again), a couple of quartettes from Rossini's *Stabat Mater*, Dietsch's *Veni sancte spiritus*[19] (new to me and very lovely), besides sundry solos. About a dozen listeners were let in. . . .

February 24. . . . Poor Babbins's [GTS Jr.'s] illness cut off Ellie from Mrs. Wright's tonight, where Mrs. Gibbs and the rest of her little extemporized musical club were to have met and sung Mendelssohn's *Lobgesang* and the *Benedictus* of Haydn's Sixteenth Mass, etc.

March 1. . . . Met Ellie at Appleton's [book store] and walked with her uptown. She read music for me tonight—Haydn mostly.

March 5. . . . Mrs. Eleanor, Mrs. d'Oremieulx, and Mrs. Gibbs have been spend-

---

[16] With his excellent opera company—Mesdames Parodi, Colson, Strakosch, and de Wilhorst, and Messrs. Brignoli (no longer on lease to Ullman), Amodio, the American tenor Henry Squires, Ettore Barili, and Junca—the enterprising Maurice Strakosch had just concluded a successful opera season in Chicago and was about to inaugurate the newly completed Pike's Opera House in Cincinnati on February 22 with a season of twelve operas.

[17] Mrs. Gibbs's musicales were by no means unique. A "gratifying multiplication" of private music clubs had taken place at many of the most recherché homes of the city. The *Musical World* (May 28, 1859, p. 2) describes one such socially elevated event under the direction of Philip Mayer at the Fifth Avenue house of two unidentified ladies, where—assisted by Oehrlein, Beutler, and an unnamed French hornist, and by a chorus of amateur ladies (probably Mayer's pupils)—a program of German music had been performed. A delightful occasion.

[18] Replacing Henry C. Timm, who had accompanied at the organ for Strong's previous Mass-meetings.

[19] Pierre Dietsch (1808–1865) was the French organist, composer, and conductor who in 1861 would conduct the notorious first performances of Wagner's *Tannhäuser* at the Paris Opéra.

ing the evening here practicing Haydn, etc. with Ellie. . . . After the ladies had finished their vocalization, [they] settled the program of the next performance (on these premises next Friday), and spent a little time in denouncing their unfortunate tenor, Mr. Cooke, who labors under the melancholy delusion that any man blessed with a "fine organ" need not trouble himself to study his music, and who is therefore liable to blunders and breakngs down, as, for example, last night, in the lovely *Et incarnatus* of Mozart's Twelfth Mass, wherein his introductory solo was excellently well done, but he was "put out" the moment the other voices came in with the *Crucifixus, etc.,* and proceeded to sing something totally unlike the tenor part written by Mozart and produced the most dismal dissonance and Katzenjammer; *thereafter,* I say, Mrs. Gibbs and Mrs. d'Oremieulx sat down at the organ and gave us the Andante of the [Beethoven] C-minor Symphony and of Mozart's C-major (the "Jupiter"), four-handed, and then most of Mozart's E-flat on the piano. Glorious music, played with feeling and spirit and hearty appreciation seldom recognizable in professional performances, and without effort—offhand and accurately. It was an hour of special delight to me. At least, three Philharmonics were concentrated in it.

. . . Last evening spent very pleasantly in Twenty-second Street—Mrs. Eleanor's—at the third performance of the little musical society. About thirty outsiders [listeners]: among them Mrs. Seton, Miss Lizzy Clark, Bob Messenger, Mr. and Mrs. S. B. R., and snobeaginous George Bancroft. They sang some nice music: first movement of Rossini's *Stabat Mater,* the *Kyrie, Qui tollis,* and *Et incarnatus* of Mozart's Twelfth Mass, the *Agnus Dei* and *Benedictus* of a Mass in D by Cherubini—new to me—effective, but, I think, of lower grade than Haydn's and Mozart's ecclesiastical works—also the *Gloria* of Mozart's First Mass.

That *Kyrie* of Mozart's (No. 12) gains on one year by year.

> It begins in rocky caverns—as a voice that sings alone
> To the pedals of the organ, in monotonous undertone
> Anon from shelving beaches, And shallow sands beyond.
> In snow-white robes uprising, The ghostly quires respond, etc.

Perhaps that—the loveliest thing Longfellow ever wrote [from *The Golden Legend*]—was more or less suggested by this composition, which he must have heard done scores of times by musical Bostonians. Like many others of Mozart's best things, it seems to have been produced so easily—its purity, simplicity, and repose are so perfect that one underrates it at first. So one is tempted to despise the noble movement of the *Credo* (of the same Mass) ending with *descendit de coelis.* Each is so plain—anybody could have written it. But one comes by degrees to perceive that such work is of higher grade than even the intense and burning inspirations that Beethoven has embodied for the orchestra. If the office of Art be the revelation of Beauty and not the manifestation of strength, power, and passion, Mozart must out-rank Beethoven himself, though I should have scorned to concede it ten or fifteen years ago. But I don't rank Beethoven a single degree lower than I did then; I merely appreciate Mozart rather more justly. And certain of Beethoven's works: the second movement and the finale of the C-minor Symphony and the finale of the *Christus am Ölberge,* are embodiments of the purest and highest Art—blazing with a fever of conception and freedom of copious, vigorous, original expression that Mozart could hardly equal. (In the name of the Prophet, Bosh!)

March 12. . . . [Mrs. Gibbs's] musical club "performed" here last night to an audience of about sixty. The evening was on the whole pleasant, though I feared at one time that everything was going wrong, and "roared for the very disquietness of my soul," as the Psalmist hath it.

The best music they produced (not the best executed music) was Haydn's Second Mass [*Missa in tempore belli* (Hoboken XXII:9)], from the *Sanctus* to the end (the finest finale, I think, that Haydn ever produced. His choral works generally cool off and grow tame toward their conclusion—or rather, their strongest and most genial thoughts occur early, and the first half is apt to be the better. Witness the *Creation*, the *Seasons*, the *Seven Last Words*, and nearly all the Masses), the *Agnus Dei* (solo delightfully rendered by Ellie, who overcame her faintness of heart and trepidation most valiantly) and the *Dona pacem* of Mozart's No. 1. That surprised and delighted people by revealing the origin of the Grace Church Easter Hymn "Christ the Lord is risen today," an adaptation of W. A. King's, and a most tasteless one (it is from the *Andante maestoso* quartette of the *Dona*—not from its choral *Allegro*), and it suits the sentiment of Easter jubilation and triumph about as closely as the phrases of the "Dead March" in *Saul* would fit a *Gloria in excelsis*. The tenor solo, *Bell'adorata incognita,* from Mercadante's *Il giuramento,* was fairly done by Cooke; the lovely, luscious quartette and chorus from the same opera, *Vicino a che s'adora,* a cherished memory of 1847;[20] the first movement of Rossini's *Stabat Mater;* from Mendelssohn's *Lobgesang* a very respectable choral movement; and a four-handed organ performance (the Introduction) [to the *Lobgesang*] by Mrs. Gibbs and Mrs. d'Oremieulx; and Mendelssohn's little duet, *Ich wollte meine Liebe,* by Ellie and Mrs. Gibbs [completed the program].

The element of discord and distress was Mrs. ————, who sang flatter than ever. Poor little woman, how bright and pretty she looked, and how unconscious she was of the pangs and shudderings her false notes were producing. Joseph Haydn must have turned in his grave—or rather (since his honorable remains have doubtless become pulverulent long ere now) his ashes must have stirred and trembled under the dreadful murder of his *Agnus* and *Dona,* for which this lady was responsible. Her shortcomings were painfully appreciable—even by my blunt, obtuse ear.

April 2. . . . Last night at Mrs. Gibbs's—Twenty-ninth Street—another of our musical gatherings. Talked to Scharfenberg, Miss Mary Hamilton (Mount Vernon "Regent"),[21] and Mrs. [George Lee] Schuyler, George Bancroft, etc., and had a rather good time. Pity Bancroft is so intense and unmistakable a snob; it's so utterly gratuitous and superfluous. He *can* be very agreeable and instructive—is full of nice appreciation of books and of music. Why should he make such a beast of himself every day, with the lowest tuft-hunting and the silliest affectations?

The *Kyrie* of Haydn's No. 2, the *Qui tollis* and *Et incarnatus* of Beethoven's Mass in C. . . . All the music went respectably; some things were very well rendered; the *Gloria* in Mozart's No. 2 [K. 257] was excellently well done.

April 7. . . . Mrs. Gibbs here tonight, singing with Ellie, *inter alia,* a Mass by [the Swiss-born composer Louis] Niedermeyer [1802–1861] (who wrote that deadly sentimental *Le lac*) that seems vigorous and valuable.

———

[20] A sentimental souvenir of the days of Strong's courtship of Miss Ellen Ruggles.
[21] More precisely, Vice-Regent for the New York chapter of the Mount Vernon Association.

Temporarily descending from these beatitudes, Strong braved the rigors of the German *Stadt-Theater,* where, for the first time in the United States, on April 4, 6, and 8, an opera by the controversial Richard Wagner was being presented.

April 8. . . . Murray Hoffman dined here and I went with him to the little, dingy, sour-smelling Bowery *Stadt-Theater* to hear Wagner's *Tannhäuser.* Great crowd—Teutoni[22] and generally frowsy. Lieber[23] was there, and Wrey Mould[24] and Dan Messenger—being earnest enquirers after good music. . . . *Lagerbier* and cakes handed round between the acts.[25] Audience grimly attentive to the music, which is grim likewise.

First impression: the well-known overture is to the opera as portable soup[26] to beef—nearly all the nutriment and strength of the opera is condensed and concentrated therein—repetition of the overture phrases incessantly recurring throughout the three long acts; lack of fluent melody;[27] the attempt to give each several word its proper musical expression makes free-flowing song impossible; very bold instrumental effects, original rather than beautiful, and too continuously kept up. But the opera on the whole is decidedly impressive. Something of this is due to the libretto and plot—most unusually good, consistent, clear, and significant. Dramatically considered, it's the best opera I know—the only one, rather, that's not beneath contempt.

The performance [conducted by Carl Bergmann] was not to be found fault with, though the principal "artistes" [Siedenburg (Elizabeth), Pickaneser (Tannhäuser), Mrs. Pickaneser (Venus), and Isidor Lehmann (Wolfram von Eschenbach)] would have been sniffed at by the Academy of Music habitués. Orchestra unimpeachable; chorus [the

---

[22] According to the Teutonophobic *Trovator:* "It was exclusively a German affair. The performers and audience were German, and no notice was given in other than German papers" (*Dwight's,* April 9, 1859, p. 13). This last misstatement was energetically repudiated in the following issue of *Dwight's* (April 16, 1859, p. 22) by an indignant correspondent who reported not only that the event had been sufficiently advertised in the English language press but that, although the theatre was "not eligibly situated and [was] withal anything but an attractive spot," the performances had been attended by large and appreciative mixed audiences of Americans and Germans.

[23] Francis Lieber (1800–1872), the renowned German-born political scientist, teacher, and lecturer, was currently a professor of history at Columbia College.

[24] Before coming to the United States in 1853 to design and supervise the building of All Souls' Church (Fourth Avenue at 24th Street), Jacob Wrey Mould, the passionately musical English architect—misidentified in the published *Diary* (II, 445) as "Willy Marsh"—had translated into English the librettos and contributed informative introductions for *The Standard Series of Drama,* a published series of operas by Gluck, Mozart, Beethoven, Rossini, Spohr, and Verdi for which his friend William S. Rockstro had made piano reductions. His translations were performed in London and in distant Melbourne. In New York, as assistant to Calvert Vaux, Mould designed the terrace, bridges, music pavilion, and other decorative features of Central Park; he later assisted Vaux in creating designs for the American Museum of Natural History and the Metropolitan Museum of Art. It was Mould whose efforts brought about the first concerts in Central Park, begun in 1859. He is credited with having written music criticism for one of the New York newspapers.

[25] "Boys went through the aisles . . . selling lager in glass mugs and negotiating . . . for the sale of chunks of Swiss cheese," deprecated *Trovator* (*Dwight's,* April 23, 1859, p. 30).

[26] Portable soup, incorrectly transcribed as "potable soup" in the published *Diary* (II, 446), was a highly concentrated, water-soluble extract of beef used by travelers for nourishment en route.

[27] A lack remarked by all the critics.

Arion] the best I ever heard in Opera; *mise-en-scéne* most careful and elaborate. It was a very satisfactory evening and did *Deutschland* credit.

———

A labor of love, the production represented long and dedicated preparation. "A few Germans," wrote hotly Wagnerian Theodore Hagen in the *Review and Gazette* (April 16, 1859, p. 116), "led by our fine and well-bred musician Mr. Carl Bergmann, were anxious to produce in America what they justly considered the most abused work of the old world. They had only one singing society at their disposal (the *Arion*)—amateurs belonging to all classes of society. With these moderate means they commenced the rehearsals, which lasted for nearly two months. Meantime, a few of the singers of the late German opera troupe were willing to join the little party; the manager of the German theatre in the Bowery [Otto Hoym] also offered his aid, and thus, with very modest means, but with intelligence, energy, and real admiration for the beauties of the work, *Tannhäuser* was for the first time produced in America. . . . And in spite of the scanty means, the result was altogether satisfactory."

Devoting the greater part of his three-page paean to the plot of *Tannhäuser,* Hagen lauded Wagner's genius as a librettist[28] as well as an inspired creator of transcendent music—although, admittedly, the *Tannhäuser* score possessed a certain monotony, being written mostly in common time. But—defensively—"not only the German, but the American press have almost unanimously appreciated the excellence of the work, and even those who were opposed to Wagner and his music can not help acknowledging that the so-called 'Music of the Future' will do very well for the present, at least of America."

Indeed, a surprisingly large and supportive representation of the English-language press had attended the premiere.[29] Everyone praised the performances by the orchestra and chorus; Bergmann was highly lauded for his role in bringing about this splendid production; and the singers were generally thought to be more or less adequate. As for the opera itself, despite its melodic shortcomings it was recognized to be an important new work. Fry found its instrumentation to be "bold, rich, and dazzling," but he, too, pronounced Wagner to be deficient in musical ideas: "His melodies are mostly hobbling, and generally they are no melodies at all" (*Tribune,* April 15, 1859). "He does not apprehend musical suavity, cesural pauses, nice balances and compensations, and other things which go to make the magic of melody. . . . In a long waste of recitative we have occasionally a breath of melody, as in the 'Pilgrim's Chorus,'" a work Fry characterized as composed in the "Rossinian style,[30] very finely worked up and having a good melody, if mended where certain rests ought to mark the phrasing, but which do not." Fry apologized for being unable to give a more comprehensive musical analysis of the work, having been unable to "get a sight of the full score."

Darcie dismissed *Tannhäuser* in a single pungent paragraph headed "The Music of the Future." "Richard Wagner," he wrote, "who doesn't care a pinch of snuff out of

[28] The *Musical World* (April 16, 1859, p. 242) pronounced the plot to be excellent and to carry a good moral.
[29] Contrary to *Trovator*'s contention that no complimentary tickets were provided to non-German critics.
[30] An erratic judgment that was duly derided in the *Review and Gazette* (April 30, 1859, p. 131).

Formes's [snuff-] box about contemporary society and what that multitudinous noun may think of him, but who composes complicated combinations of harmony for the benefit of posterity, has just managed to get a hearing in this city. This opera of *Tannhäuser* was produced last week at the German Theatre, with [sounding like *Trovator*] a good German success. It is very scientific, but utterly destitute of melody" (*Porter's Spirit,* April 28, 1859, p. 128).

Six performances of *Tannhäuser* had been announced, but, due to insufficient funds, the opera was withdrawn after its third presentation. Revived on April 28 as a farewell benefit for Pickaneser, who was returning to Europe, the performance was delayed for some forty-five minutes while money was being scraped together from all over town to pay the orchestra, who demanded to be paid in advance. "Let this fact be borne in mind by those correspondents of *Dwight's Journal* who are so excessively Teutonic in their predilections," maliciously gloated *Trovator.* "These Art-loving Germans, who are supposed to be so devoted to music, refused to interpret one of the greatest works of one of their greatest music-apostles, simply because they were not sure of being paid for it" (*Dwight's,* May 7, 1859, p. 46).

April 10. . . . Theodore Eisfeld has returned from Fayal in good bodily preservation, considering the perils he has passed, but with a battered and weather-beaten exchequer. So a "Welcome Concert" was got up for him last night at the Academy of Music by the Philharmonic people. George Anthon dined here and we went together. *Sinfonia Eroica* and *Jubel* Overture. Blessed be the memories of Beethoven and Weber![31]

Ignoring Ullman's dispirited April opera season at the Academy of Music (see below), Strong continued to devote himself almost exclusively to the delights of home music.

April 14. . . . Last evening, *chez* Mrs. Charley Strong, rehearsal: *Kyrie, Gloria,* and *Qui tollis* of Haydn's No. 3 [*Nelson Mass,* Hoboken XXII:11] and *Agnus* and *Dona* of the Mass in D by Niedermeyer—a very noble movement. The whole Mass is far above what I took to be Niedermeyer's capabilities. The *Agnus* is rather dark, their prayer is a wail *de profundis,* a passionate cry of sorrow and of supplication almost without hope. Full of strange, keen, Beethovenesque phrases and slowly shifting, weird modulations, awfully suggestive of the legend of the ghostly Midnight Mass on All Souls' Eve, when priests and people come up from their home in the churchyard and fill the church. This *Agnus* might do for that occasion. But there is a very touching sweetness blended with all this; it fascinates me more and more at each hearing. Niedermeyer is to be spoken of with respect.

April 19. . . . Pleasant "concert" Friday evening at Mrs. Eleanor's.

April 23. . . . Tonight at Wrey Mould's funny little house in Twenty-sixth Street,

---

[31] Participating in the welcome to Eisfeld were Juliana May, Maria Brainerd, Philip Mayer, Sebastian Bach Mills (1838–1898), the splendid, newly arrived English pianist, Richard Hoffman, Joseph Burke, and the Philharmonic hornist Louis Schreiber; Bergmann conducted, except for a composition by Eisfeld, conducted by the composer.

hearing his little musical club. I think they outdo us. Organ and piano accompaniments, *eight-handed,* and difficult music clearly rendered at sight. Cherubini's Fourth Mass, a couple of movements from Mozart's Seventh [K. Anhang C. 106, spurious] (far the finest of his shorter masses, I think—certainly most lovely from *Credo* to Finale), parts of the [Mendelssohn] *Lobgesang,* and so on. Performers not generally "in society," I think—some of them semiprofessional—my old grammar-school teacher Dr. Quin among them.

May 7. . . . Scharfenberg promises to get up certain music on these premises next Friday: Beethoven's Septette and another by Hummel. I know but one movement of the latter—the Scherzo—not easily forgotten. I have not heard it since '43 or '44, but the simple beauty and pungency of its prominent phrases are not easily forgotten. That little bit of melody must belong in some *Volkslied;* Hummel could not have made it out of his own head. I hope the projected concert may prosper, for *its* sake.

May 16. . . . Thursday night [May 12] there was rehearsing here—Scharfenberg and his allies (Bergmann violoncello, Mosenthal first violin, Jacobi double bass, etc.). It was a little unpromising; the violins were sharp—had an acid reaction, to speak scientifically. The failures and Borborygmi[32] of the horn were cruel to hear. . . . [the event] came off Friday night . . . and went more smoothly. Hummel's Scherzo was received with acclamations. It does not pretend to be a great deal, but a more searching and drastic little dose of melody would be hard to find. There was a general movement and thrill as Scharfenberg and Co. modulated into that simple, hearty phrase in D major. The first movement (of the Hummel) is very spirited and stately; the Andante and Finale are brilliant and pleasant to hear, but impress me comparatively little. Scharfenberg did his laborious piano part ample justice. Beethoven's beautiful *Septuor* was fairly rendered and appreciated; each movement seemed specially delightful, except the last, for which I do not care twopence. There were about 120 auditors.[33] . . . People generally well-bred and not inclined to unseasonable loquacity, a majority of them being such as would rather listen to Haydn and Beethoven than exchange audible platitudes. If I believed twenty percent of the polite speeches that were made to me, I should say it was the most refined, brilliant, and delightful entertainment ever given in this town. But it was in fact very pleasant, the music being *great* and fairly rendered, and everybody being comfortably seated and the champagne successfully *frappé.*

Niedermeyer's *Agnus* came out grandly. It is undoubtedly very beautiful and deep. So seems the whole Mass, except where it has been spoiled by fugue-ifying. Writing a fugue (except as an exercise) should be punished by fine and imprisonment; the law can be repealed upon the advent of another Handel. When a church composer can produce nothing adequate to his text, he says: "Go to, let us make a fugue," and proceeds to enforce attention—not to his subject, but to his own private erudition in counterpoint—by constructing something that is commonly not music at all, but a mathematical problem embodied in sound—algebra made audible. And if he can introduce toward the end a vigorous phrase of clear melody and one or two effective contrasts of light and shadow, his fugue passes for something great and creditable.

---

[32] *Borborygm* is defined in the *Oxford English Dictionary* as "a rumbling in the bowels."

[33] A select group, among them George Bancroft, William and Edmund Schermerhorn, Ogden Hoffman, Miss Hamilton, "Howadji" Curtis and his mother, Eisfeld, and other noted New Yorkers.

By now Ullman had unmemorably come and gone. Having returned in early April from his ill-starred season in New Orleans[34] with a portion of his company,[35] he had engaged the great local favorite Madame Gazzaniga (just back from a triumphant season in Havana with Maretzek) and embarked on April 11 on a fragmented season[36] of perfunctorily performed chestnuts: *La traviata, Il trovatore, Lucrezia Borgia, La favorita.* "Dullness prevailed," wrote the *Albion* critic; except for Gazzaniga,[37] "a weaker company probably never played in this city"; nor was Anschütz a satisfactory conductor of Italian opera. The season's crowning fiasco was the first and last appearance on April 25 of Caroline Alaimo[38] as Norma. Touted as "one of the greatest of Italian *prima donnas*," she turned out to be an unexceptional singer, long past her prime and vainly pursuing what was described as an "eleventh hour" desire to reap "transatlantic laurels"[39] (*Albion,* April 30, 1859, p. 211).

On April 30, with the return of the Formes contingent from their tour, Ullman closed his "*ad interim, one-horse* season of opera" with a "Grand Combination Matinée,"[40] featuring at long last a "first and only" performance of *Marta* in Italian, with Theodore Thomas conducting. But only Laborde (Marta) and Sbriglia (Lionello)[41] sang in that language. To the critics' intense annoyance, both Formes (Plunkett) and Minna von Berkel (Nancy) had the bad taste to sing their roles in German.

Upon Ullman's departure, resourceful Maurice Strakosch, with his superior company,[42] took over the Academy of Music, just as he had taken over the management of Piccolomini following her break with Ullman in New Orleans. Obtaining from Lumley an extension of her American tour,[43] Strakosch brought her back to the Acad-

---

[34] Where Piccolomini had decisively broken with him upon her arrival in March.

[35] Consisting of Adelaide Phillips and the second-raters Tamaro and Florenza; they were later joined by Luigi Stefani and the long absent Filippo Morelli, and still later by Formes, who with another contingent (Laborde/Berkel/Sbriglia/Theodore Thomas) had been touring in the Midwest. Shortly after arriving in New York, Formes, too, broke with Ullman and returned to Europe, promising to be back soon with an opera company of his own.

[36] With all performances suspended for the duration of Holy Week.

[37] Although the widowed Gazzaniga had recently married the local opera maestro Luciano Albites, each of her performances was announced to be her last in the United States before returning to Europe to offer delayed solace to her fatherless child.

[38] Sister of the unremarkable tenor Antonio Alaimo, briefly heard in 1856.

[39] Mlle. Alaimo, one of Maretzek's less fortunate choices for Havana, was stopping over in New York to gather a few extra dollars before returning to Europe. Despite her failure in New York, Alaimo tarried in the United States, appearing subsequently in far-flung places with Parodi's touring opera company.

[40] A lifesaver to eternally pressed opera managers, the Gala Matinée had by now become a social phenomenon as well. On May 9, William Henry Fry wrote in the *Tribune:* "Thousands of ladies who cannot conveniently attend [the opera] at night avail themselves of the day performances, and the proportion of men to women is, say, one to twelve. It is a fine opportunity," crudely added Fry, no champion of women's independence, "to make a survey and perhaps a choice."

[41] Evidently temporarily on loan from Maretzek to tenor-poor Ullman.

[42] Strakosch, who now controlled the best singers, had also acquired Muzio, who, unlike Anschütz, was deemed to understand and do full justice to Italian opera.

[43] "It is impossible to understand the financial engagements of public singers," wrote the *Evening Post* (June 3, 1859). "Here is Piccolomini at one time under the management of Ullman, the next week enrolled in the forces of Strakosch, while all the time there is . . . a far-off Lumley who [has] a prior claim on the results of her efforts."

emy on May 4 for a season of farewell performances.[44] In nearly uninterrupted succession she appeared in all of her previous roles, suitable and unsuitable—*La traviata, Don
Pasquale, Lucia, La serva padrona, Il trovatore,* and *Don Giovanni*—and additionally in
three new ones, all by Donizetti: Adina in *L'elisir d'amore,* Leonora in *La favorita,* and
Paolina in *Poliuto* (or *Les Martyrs*)[45]★ announced as its first performance in America.[46]

Piccolomini—with her inexhaustible arsenal of coquetries and with "the ravishing smile with which she replaced every note she missed"—was, if possible, even more
bewitching than before as Adina.[47] Less suitably appearing two days later on May 13
in *La favorita,* she was pronounced to be "infinitely superior to what the public had
a right to expect from a singer of her class" (*Times,* May 14, 1859).[48] Indeed, it was
fondly stated that "wherever Piccolomini was most weak, she was most fascinating"
(*Albion,* May 7, 1859, p. 223).

On May 16, Strong, together with Ellen and the Charley Strongs, went to the
Academy of Music, not to hear Piccolomini, but Cora de Wilhorst, who was making
her purported last appearance on the opera stage as Elvira in *I puritani.* "That smallest
of *prima donnas* sings and acts very respectably,"[49] wrote Strong, but "the opera is poor
stuff; its so-called 'great' melodies seem to me specimens of a faint, sickish, nasty
sweetness like that of a rotten pear or a damaged banana or a pint of Diabetic [elixir]."

It was green-room gossip, tattled *Trovator,* that on this emotional occasion, de
Wilhorst at the last minute had absolutely refused to go on unless she was paid in advance. Because Strakosch "did not have the cash in his pocket," and because she was
adamant, Brignoli good-naturedly rushed off to his hotel, and "going to his trunk,
hauled out some gold eagles, rushed back to the Academy and poured [them] at Wilhorst's feet. Mercenary lady," concludes *Trovator,* "pacified, went on the stage and sang
like a nightingale" (*Dwight's,* June 4, 1859, p. 80). Following this episode, true or false,
Wilhorst departed on tour with one of Strakosch's concert companies; she would soon
reappear with his opera company.

Two days later Strong returned to the Academy to hear his beloved *Don Giovanni,*

---

[44] In a variant of the eternal farewell-forever dodge, a girlishly modest little card of impending
adieu, signed by Piccolomini, appeared in the amusement columns, avowing her love for her American public and her abject gratitude. "I would rather stay in this country than go to Europe," she
confided, "but one—even a spoiled girl—and a prima donna as well—cannot always have her own
way; so I must go on the first of June."

[45] Composed for the tenor Adolphe Nourrit to an Italian libretto adapted by Salvatore Cammarano from Pierre Corneille's play *Polyeucte* (1643), Donizetti's *Poliuto,* scheduled for its premiere in
Naples in 1838, was banned by the censor, who objected to its early Christian content. Adapted into
French by Scribe and retitled *Les Martyrs,* Donizetti's reworking of the opera was first produced at
the Paris Opéra in 1840.

[46] Its Italian version, perhaps. In the French it had been given in New Orleans in 1846, and in
English in 1849, disguised as an oratorio, by the Boston Handel and Haydn Society.

[47] Even the stolid Brignoli, as Nemorino, "actually exhibited alarming symptoms of vivacity,"
caustically observed the *Evening Post* (May 12, 1859).

[48] But not by Burkhardt, who maintained that casting Piccolomini as either of the Leonoras—
in *Il trovatore* or *La favorita*—was a tasteless joke on the part of the impresario, a joke too absurd to
merit serious criticism (*Dispatch,* May 14, 1859).

[49] According to *Trovator* (*Dwight's,* May 21, 1859, p. 63): "Mrs. Wilhorst . . . exhibited the most
delicious execution and a voice of increased power, but she acted so carelessly—without the slightest
effort to really act—that her performance was quite unsatisfactory."

presented with the casting ostentation that had become customary in productions of this opera. "It seems to be a mania with managers to crowd all the artists obtainable into this work," complained the *Times* (May 18, 1859). "Messrs. Maretzek and Ullman have done their best to make a reasonable cast unattractive, and now Mr. Strakosch perfects what they began."[50] Burkhardt was particularly offended by Muzio's "improvements on Mozart."[51] Strong did not share the critics' objections but had some of his own.

May 18. . . . With Ellie to hear *Don Giovanni;* sat in the parquette. Zerlina, Piccolomini, quite respectable, [her] acting very clever; Don Giovanni Gassier, Donna Anna Parodi,[52] Elvira Madame Strakosch, severally decent, or nearly so; Leporello Junca, remarkably bad,[53] Masetto, the adipose Amodio, who looked absurdly but sang well,[54] and Don Ottavio Brignoli, very uncommonly good. *Il mio tesoro* was sung with accuracy and grace, and encored deservedly. That air doesn't appeal to me very strongly, but it is a wonderfully artistic, original, elegant piece of melody, peculiarly appropriate to the gentlemanly Don Ottavio. *Vedrai carino* was also encored. It is too lovely and too pure and deep for Zerlina, with her coquettish *Batti, batti* and her very facile part in *La ci darem.* Perhaps a profoundly critical analyst of the Opera would say that Mozart meant the little flirt to be cured of her heartless love of aristocratic admiration at last, and waked up to an honest affection for her rustic bridegroom.[55] So mote it be, for poor Masetto's sake.[56]

. . . Friday's little musical performance [*chez* Strong on May 13] seems to have given much satisfaction. People stop me in the street to say how delightful and unusual it was. This is consoling and encouraging; it shows that although Verdi and Original Sin are fearful realities, *Man* appreciates *true* music, at least, when he hears it in a well-lighted drawing room, on a comfortable chair, and among people of his own "set."

[50] Darcie disgustedly referred to this production as "that dreadful *Don Giovanni,* with all the artists, male and female, crammed into its representation. . . . Why will operatic managers periodically inflict upon us this colossal nightmare of the lyric stage?" (*Porter's Spirit,* May 28, 1859, p. 208).

[51] "We had *Don Giovanni* on Wednesday, with an Italian conductor who has been most loudly and unnecessarily puffed of late, who is a pupil and friend of Verdi's, but who evidently," wrote Burkhardt with heavy irony, "has only a bowing acquaintance with a German composer of some reputation, by the name of Johann Chrystostomus Wolfgang Amadeus Mozart" (*Dispatch,* May 21, 1859).

[52] To present the best exponents of these roles, explained Strakosch, he had engaged Gassier and Parodi, not members of his company, to sing them at the huge fee of $200 a night each (*Dwight's,* May 21, 1859, p. 63).

[53] The Commendatore was sung by Nicolò Barili, Strakosch's half-brother-in-law.

[54] As Masetto, the outrageously obese Amodio "acted with much spirit and displayed a pretty fancy for pirouettes," wrote the *Times* (May 10, 1859). "A stupendous *pas* in the first act brought down the house and secured an encore."

[55] Strong never tired of seeking justifications for the lovely music that Mozart had heedlessly squandered on so morally reprehensible a character as Zerlina.

[56] "It is a little noteworthy that this opera—which has the most immoral and disgusting plot of any on the stage—should attract such crowded houses as it almost invariably does," wrote the *Evening Post* critic, presumably *Trovator* (May 17, 1859). "It is a work better calculated for the taste of the last century than the present. Yet it is repeatedly produced and draws so well this season that Mr. Strakosch has been obliged to suspend the free press, to the vast chagrin and indignation of dead-heads, who weep in sackcloth and ashes outside of the Academy doors."

May 26. . . . Dr. Hodges has just gone on a year's furlough to be spent at a sister's house near Bristol. I don't think he will return. His left hand has forgot its cunning—it has never recovered from the slight paralytic attack of last year. He can no longer rely on it for work upon his keyboards, and evidently considers his career ended. He called to bid me goodbye yesterday or the day before.[57] A very intelligent, pure-minded, amiable, crotchety, perverse old gentleman, with considerable talent and great accomplishments in his profession, but given over, unhappily, to absolutely unquestioning idolatry of the ungenial formalism and propriety and chilly, repectable decorum that constitute the sole and peculiar charm of Anglican Church Music.[58]

. . . Yesterday Mrs. Perkins of Boston (*née* Miss Lily Chadwick) dined here with Jem, and we attended the Opera—very full house; they said it was also a "brilliant" house, [the premiere of] Donizetti's *Poliuto,* or *I martiri.* Piccolomini, Brignoli, and Amodio. Music Verdi-esque, rather than Donizetti-oid, and a somewhat favorable and mitigated form of its bad type. There are grand [onstage] brass-band movements (suggestive of the Seventh Regiment executing a strategic movement up Broadway) and several lively, high-peppered duets and scraps of concerted music. The newspaper critics seem to have been profoundly impressed with the grandeur and genius of the work and write of it as sensible people might of a newly discovered symphony by Beethoven. I should say it was not Burgundy but a tolerable article of small-beer: music perhaps just about good enough to accompany and stimulate the usual Opera-box current of tattle and gossip.

～

As Strong remarked, the critics—probably from sheer relief at this blessed respite from the perpetual surfeit of *Traviatas* and *Trovatores*—were vehement in their praises of *Poliuto.* "The great operatic event of the year," the *Herald* called it (May 30). "Few operas have been produced of late years so well calculated to take a prominent place in the *répertoire,*" wrote the *Times* (May 26); "its success was tremendous. A more delicious work we have not listened to for some years. . . . In these days, when we have nothing but Verdi and Meyerbeer, a work like this is indeed a treat." And Fry, more guardedly: "If not destined as a whole to equal *Lucia* in popularity, it will hold a place on the stage for the excellence of various portions" (*Tribune,* May 26, 1859).

Little Piccolomini, incongruously draped in the statuesque robes of a patrician Roman matron, may not have achieved the sublimity of the divine Rachel (who had unforgettably performed Corneille's play in New York in 1855),♩ but she brought a certain womanliness to the role of Paolina, a rare quality not to be disdained, wrote the *Albion* critic (May 28, 1859, p. 259). Her most outstanding contribution, however, was her rendition, not so much of Donizetti's music, but of the showy, Verdi-like cabaletta composed for her by Muzio, cleverly exploiting her happiest characteristics.[59]

---

[57] The Trinity Vestry (of which Strong was a member) granted the ailing Dr. Hodges the sum of $500 to tide him over his year's leave of absence (*Dwight's,* June 4, 1859, p. 79).

[58] Strong's abiding musical *bête noir.*

[59] Burkhardt, the Verdi-hater, "could not approve of" Muzio's aria: "It is in Verdi's style," he wrote, "in fact a watery coagulation of that *maestro,* and out of place in Donizetti's work" (*Dispatch,* May 28, 1859).

The usually inanimate Brignoli (the Poliuto) not only sang magnificently, recalling Mario, but for once he evinced faint glimmers of life, a welcome improvement. Amodio, ludicrous in Roman drapery as the Proconsul Severus, provoked uncontrolled mirth with his entrance in a triumphal car laboriously dragged onstage by a quartet of struggling supernumeraries; all the same he sang superbly;[60] Nicolò Barili sang the secondary role of Felix.

The score of *Poliuto,* although abounding in brassy effects (indeed, the *Times* found the first act music to be "decidedly circussy"), was nonetheless almost unanimously judged to be "grand and delicious."[61] With its splendid staging, spectacular scenery (catacombs, an arch of triumph)[62] painted by the talented Hannibal Calyo for Maretzek's thwarted production of *Poliuto* intended for the year before, and its harp *obbligato*s played by Aptommas, the production was a triumph for all concerned.[63]

Poliuto was repeated on May 27,[64] and—after an intervening matinée of *Don Giovanni,*[65] followed by an act of *Lucia di Lammermoor,*[66] on May 28 (both with Piccolomini, of course)—it was again given for Piccolomini's farewell benefit on May 30, her "most positively last evening performance in America." On this momentous occasion the free list was again suspended;[67] in compensation, each purchaser of a reserved seat received a medallion photograph of Piccolomini as a souvenir, and better yet, at the end of the opera the little enchantress delivered an affecting little valedictory speech in her deliciously fractured English, ornamented by "shrugs, smiles, lifting of eyebrows, and kissing of hands to the audience," that sent them into raptures (see *Dwight's,* June 4, 1859, p. 80).

The following day the indestructible little diva gave her "most positively last *afternoon* performance," as Norina in *Don Pasquale,*[68] with Brignoli, Maggiorotti, and Ba-

---

[60] "Good stage management should avoid the risk of laughter," preached the *Albion* critic (May 28, 1859, p. 259), "especially with an artist so admirable (and portly) as Signor Amodio."

[61] It was among Donizetti's best scores, wrote Watson. Hagen, however, maintained that anyone who did not "laugh outright" at Donizetti's third-act music for the Christian martyrs should be handed over "to the authorities of the nearest lunatic asylum" (*Leslie's,* June 4, p. 11; *Review and Gazette,* June 11, 1859, pp. 178–79).

[62] Burkhardt, who highly praised Calyo's sets, would nonetheless have preferred the addition, in the last scene in the hippodrome, of a "few guards in flesh-colored tights and leopard skins and a show of dens or cages with even stuffed or painted wild beasts" (*Dispatch,* May 28, 1959).

[63] "The Strakosch Company at the Academy has been doing very well, and it ought to," wrote Darcie with forked pen, "for so good an opera has not been heard in New York since Maretzek's fall season in 1853. Piccolomini, though, should not try to sing in *La favorita* and *I martiri.* She fails dismally, and one feels all the more vexed with her for doing so, knowing as one does, how pretty and piquant she can be in *Don Pasquale* and operas of similar calibre" (*Porter's Spirit,* May 28, 1859, p. 208).

[64] By which time, hoped the nettled *Evening Post* critic (May 26, 1859), "the vociferous and officious prompter [would] learn enough to subside and not shout his instructions like a madman, thus drowning the voices of the artists on the stage."

[65] This time with Ettore Barili as Don Giovanni.

[66] With the excellent American tenor Henry Squires as Edgardo.

[67] Supposedly at the behest of Piccolomini's (Lumley's) agent. The house, although nicely filled, was therefore not crowded, reported the *Musical World* (June 11, 1859, p. 3).

[68] Of which the last act was entirely omitted, "without a word of apology or excuse," reported an irate and vengeful correspondent to the *Tribune* (June 2, 1859).

rili, and less appropriately as Leonora in the last act of *La favorita,* with Brignoli and Junca.

Piccolomini was leaving America just as she was beginning to be truly appreciated, regretfully wrote Wilkins:[69] "We might enter into a review of her career in this country, of the manner in which music critics have vacillated in their opinions . . . and then we might point to the circumstance . . . that the heart of the public has always been with her. There are some artists, 'grand, glowing, glittering,' who sing finely, answering all art conditions, but who never please the public—never give it a thrill under its waistcoat. . . . Piccolomini, going away, will leave sincere admirers who will often think of her piquant stage ways and pleasant manner which captivated the public at sight"[70] (*Herald,* May 30, 1859).

What Piccolomini in fact left behind was a sizable unpaid bill at the Everett House for lodgings for herself, her family, and two servants, amounting to seven people in all. As gleefully reported in the newspapers, her agent (Lumley's representative), Mr. Fish, was promptly arrested and jailed.

May 30. . . . Miss Josephine [Strong] and the eccentric [American architect] Richard Hunt [1827–1895] dined, and we went to the French Theatre[71]—dreary evening—five-act comedy full of the grandest sentiments—and in rhyme. French rhyme has, for me, a nauseating potency beyond ipecac. When this bore terminated, we were weak enough to stay for the last act of *Favorita,* a little bit of Opera to be executed by certain people no one had ever heard of and who, I hope, for their own sakes and that of the public, will not be heard of, or heard, again. Leonora (Madame Chome) looked like a large, elderly Irish chambermaid, and her clerical inamorato, the tenor [unidentified], who was all in white, like a sedate goblin hairdresser—the ghost of a hypochondriacal *friseur.* They acted worse than they looked and sang worse than they acted. . . . It was the vilest singing I ever listened to.[72] Half the audience fled soon after Leonora's lover set up his pipes. The first duo drove out another detachment, and Leonora went

[69] Watson, too, regretted her departure, just as she was beginning to show her true mettle: "In *Poliuto,*" he wrote (*Leslie's,* June 11, 1859, p. 27), "Piccolomini displayed greater powers, both as a vocalist and an actress, than on any previous occasion." And although Hagen maintained that public interest in Piccolomini had been dying out as the season progressed ("after a few weeks' longer stay she would scarcely be able to fill the theatre even with that liberal assistance of the free ticket system"), the box-office receipts for her farewell benefit reportedly amounted to a prodigious $6000.

[70] But Piccolomini was not memorable for her generosity of spirit: "We hear complaints of the lack of heart in little Pic," wrote the *Musical World* (June 11, 1859, p. 8), "she refusing to sing for any charitable group while here, or for the benefit of anything but her pretty self; and many protest that they are not a bit sorry she is gone."

[71] Currently the fad, the French repertory company at "cozy" Metropolitan Hall (formerly Buckley's Minstrel Hall), now under the joint management of Charles Sage and Fred Widdows, frequently concluded their programs of French plays and vaudevilles with musical entertainments of varying irrelevance.

[72] "Madame Chome, a talented artist whom we hear too seldom in public, sang finely," more charitably wrote the *Musical World* (June 4, 1859, p. 3), "but her assistants [still unidentified] were entirely inadequate to the task they had undertaken, and consequently did much to mar the performance of Madame Chome and the pleasure of the auditors."

through her last agonies, singing very false to nearly empty benches. We stood it out—
sat it out, rather—in resolute, charitable self-sacrifice. The two unhappy vocalists were
undergoing mortification enough—and our seats were conspicuous.

June 3. . . . Last night with Ellie, Mr. and Mrs. S. B. R., Mrs. Peters, Jem, Miss
Lily Clark, Graham, Walter Cutting, and Mignot to the Metropolitan Theatre, Broadway (late Burton's) to hear *The Gypsy's Frolic* (Dr. Ward's Opera), [a revival] in aid of
that pestilent, all-pervading Mount Vernon Fund,[73] which has become a social nuisance and made the Father of His Country a post-mortem Jesse Spunge.[74] One is constantly coming upon the Tomb of Washington, gaping fearfully for a slight donation.
The house was not very full,[75] but immense in quality, awfully genteel. It applauded
everything[76] with a vehement good nature that was not only imbecile but unsafe, for
the performers were very ready to be gracious and to construe our rash demonstrations
of approval into an encore, or demand for repetition, which was neither desired nor
desirable. The plot and libretto of the Opera are drivel. The overture is lively, but
scrappy, or shreddy, and insignificant. It was followed by two really pretty choruses,
and my hopes rose, but only to sink again below zero, and to stay there.

Dr. Ward seems to have studied good music, and gets himself up in something
distantly resembling the coat and breeches of a composer. He has a feeling for melody;
the phrases he adopts are good and pungent; some of his melodies are so distinct and
clear that they ought not to be stupid and tame, which they are, beyond dispute or
gainsaying—certainly not because of any classical severity in form or instrumentation.
Commonplace decoration is freely used: the orchestra is lavish in twiddling, jingling,
and crash.[77] But each movement seems the reflection of some higher and brighter luminary—frequently Mozart, and once or twice Bellini.

I think, however, that I've heard Operas quite as dull—perhaps duller—and this,
being the work of a wealthy, respectable middle-aged or elderly New York amateur
in music is creditable and meritorious. Neither Joe Kernochan nor Dan Fearing, nor
Charles H. Russell[78] could do as well if he tried. The example is good. Studying
any form of Art and producing a tolerable specimen of diligent work, after good mod-

---

[73] Whose spectacular efforts continued unabated. On March 4, when the noted orator Edward
Everett delivered his oration on "The Character of Washington," he was escorted to the Academy
and back to his lodgings by the 71st Regiment, marching to the stirring music of Dodworth's Band.

[74] Defying identification, "Jesse Spunge" presumably refers to a slang expression or a fictional
character who "sponged" off the bounty of his fellow-man—or, as in this case, largely of his fellow-
woman.

[75] So discouragingly sparse, in fact, as to cause the the cancellation of the second performance,
announced for the following evening.

[76] Following its most recent amateur performance, Dr. Ward's opera had been rated so great a
success by his "Mutual Admiration Society," that it was thought to be an ideal vehicle both to assist
the Mount Vernon Society and to establish Ward's reputation as an important composer. Indeed, it
was even thought a likely candidate for performance at the Academy of Music (*Dwight's*, June 18,
1859, p. 95). But to the irreverent *Saturday Press* (May 21, 1859) it was "as bad as a watering-place
belle of three seasons, who is continually flirting and never marrying, until nobody cares what becomes of her."

[77] "As to orchestration," wrote the *Evening Post* (June 3, 1859), "there is nothing beyond the
baldest accompaniments and an occasional blare of brass."

[78] Members of the Upper Ten equal in importance to Dr. Ward.

els, is not to employ one's time in the most ennobling or useful way, but it's better than concentrating one's faculties on dinners, carriage horses, and investments. The performers—professional, semiprofessional, and amateur—were mostly an inferior article.[79] Our little Cooke was the tenor. After the Opera, and after a rambling speech by the composer (which might have been spared), we repaired to Maillard's and ate ices.

⁓

Less tolerantly, the *Albion* critic cited a thousand and one reasons why such self-indulgent, misguided, fund-raising efforts were counterproductive: "The sooner that fund for the Mount Vernon Association is raised," he wrote, "the better for artists, critics, public, and its reputation."

The meager attendance at Ward's opera was unquestionably attributable to the opening on the same evening of Strakosch's new season with a sensational new *prima donna,* an event whose realization in itself epitomizes the flowering of contemporary impresarial skullduggery.

In early May, no sooner had the successful Strakosch/Piccolomini season taken hold at the Academy than Menace reared its ugly head in the form of a series of tantalizing little squibs appearing in the daily amusement columns. "Adelaide Cortesi,"★ read the first: "The Public are respectfully informed that the above named celebrated Prima Donna[80] will shortly appear in some of her great characters. Particulars hereafter." And another: "Pepita Gassier, returned to New York from her triumphs in Havana, will shortly appear in some of her most celebrated characters. Particulars hereafter." A parade of similarly intriguing little items systematically followed.

With this Machiavellian ploy did Max Maretzek—back from his latest Havana season with his opera company and at loose ends—gain his re-entry into the enemy-held Academy of Music. By the time he crowned his artful buildup with the announcement of a season of nightly opera performances[81] featuring the by-now legendary Cortesi, to open immediately at the Metropolitan Theatre, Strakosch (doubtless as unwilling as Maretzek to renew their cutthroat rivalry of the year before) was ripe for negotiation. Accordingly, a deal was struck: without further ado, Maretzek's impending season at the Metropolitan Theatre was tacitly dropped, Piccolomini's farewell season was completed without competition, and on June 3, immediately following her final exit from the Academy of Music, Strakosch—with all due fanfare—presented *his* new *prima donna* Cortesi, "one of the greatest living Lyric Tragediennes," in Pacini's

[79] Originally intended to be performed by a cast of amateurs, wrote *Trovator,* "as the eventful evening approached, most of these became frightened and backed out," and some professional talent was engaged: Adelaide Phillips, Lucy Escott, Catherine Lucette (a new arrival from England), Charles Guilmette, and W. H. Cooke (almost a professional); members of the Mendelssohn Union made up the chorus, and G. W. Morgan conducted (*Dwight's,* June 18, p. 95; *Albion,* May 28, 1859, p. 254).

[80] Celebrated in her native Italy, perhaps, but not here, nor in London or Paris; Adelaide Cortesi (1828–1899) had appeared in such far-flung places as St. Petersburg and Mexico. On the strength of her reported triumphs in Mexico, Maretzek had engaged her for his forthcoming 1859 winter season in Havana.

[81] Duplicating Strakosch's ruthless tactic during last year's hostilities.

Saffo.[82] Triumphantly ensconced in the conductor's chair, as of old, was "indomitable Max Maretzek."[83]

A masterstroke, applauded Darcie (*Porter's Spirit,* May 21, 1859, p. 192): "Max Maretzek must get up very early in the morning, very early indeed," he wrote. "His stratagem of pretending to take the Metropolitan as a rival to the Academy in the Italian Opera line of business, was a capital idea. Of course, Strakosch had to buy him off,[84] and so he [Strakosch] gets the responsibility of keeping a lot of capricious, quarrelsome Italians in good humour and big salaries for a month or so, at least. The fusion, too, makes Strakosch's company unusually strong. In addition to Piccolomini, Madame Strakosch, Madame de Wilhorst, Parodi, Amodio, Junca, Brignoli, and Barili, he now gets the Gassiers, Sbriglia, and Madame Cortesi."

Cortesi was almost unanimously acclaimed the greatest *prima donna* heard in New York within recent memory. Taking her first audience "by storm," she "walked on flowers, with which the stage was bestrewn most of the evening,[85] and the applause was vociferous," reported the enchanted *Musical World* (June 11, 1859, p. 3). Indeed, never before had the writer heard "such yells of enthusiasm."

"A more successful debut has seldom been achieved in this city," corroborated the *Albion* (June 11, 1859, p. 283). Madame Cortesi possessed a mezzo-soprano voice of "fine power and extensive compass. Now that dramatic intensity is the fashion," wrote the critic, "it is probable that this sort of voice will become the rage, for it possesses to a pre-eminent degree the tearfulness so essential to lyric expression, and so overpoweringly effective when used judiciously by a Gazzaniga or a Cortesi. . . . As an actress, Madame Cortesi is admirable. She never loses sight of the role, or thinks more of the singer than the heroine." The critic's only quibble—delicately expressed—was her occasional tendency in moments of searing passion to surrender herself too absolutely to her part, "and thus from excess zeal [to] overstep the bounds of art."

Less delicately, —t—, one of the very few who were "disappointed in Cortesi," stated that she was a "screamer" given to overacting: "Opening her mouth to a very inartistic extent," he wrote, "she screams out her notes with a degree of effort which is really painful to witness." Indeed, —t— feared she might burst a blood vessel.

---

[82] Strakosch trumpeted Cortesi's debut in a full, Ullmanesque column of fine print that was, in effect, a series of informative little essays: on his philosophy of artist-management (formerly a subject of controversy); on Cortesi's splendid physical attributes (slicing four years off her age); on her magnificent vocal and dramatic gifts; her purported Spanish ancestry; her purported studies with Rossini and Donizetti; then an "historical sketch" of the poetess Sappho and a synopsis of Cammarano's libretto. As William Henry Fry wrote in the *Tribune* (May 18, 1859): "Criticism is now an obsolete idea. Whoso would know the truth lyrically and vocally need not read the newspaper critiques but the handbill rhetoric."

[83] "The presence of Max Maretzek in the orchestra seems to be equally relished by the artists and the audience," wrote Watson (*Leslie's,* June 25, 1859, p. 59). "It is well enough to tolerate Italian adventurers [apparently meaning Muzio], with nothing to recommend them but their assurance or the favor of some *blasé* lady patroness when there is no one better to have; but when their betters come, let them be shipped at once to Coney Island, Washington Heights, or any other spot that will receive them."

[84] *Dwight's* (May 21, 1859, p. 63) published another version of the story: that Maretzek's proposed season at the Metropolitan Theatre had "fallen through," and that Cortesi, consequently at loose ends, had been picked up by Strakosch.

[85] Albeit all issuing from the same private box, observed the *Evening Post* (June 4, 1859).

And when she did not force her voice, he wrote, it assumed an unpleasant wobble (*Dwight's,* July 2, 1859, p. 109).

Hagen—German to his marrow—assuredly was not one to tolerate such Italianate excesses. "The new singer, Madame Cortesi, took the public, on the first night of her appearance, by storm," he wrote (*Review and Gazette,* June 25, 1859, p. 195). "The second night she increased this storm to a positive hurricane, which, however, on the third night became a dead calm, and on the fourth night the lady did not sing at all."[86] Hagen, with evident satisfaction, was referring to the unfortunate vocal disability that had overtaken Cortesi before her first week at the Academy had elapsed. "In this short career," he wrote, "lies the history of the whole school to which Madame Cortesi belongs," a category of vocalist that Hagen contemptuously lumped together as "these Verdi singers." Hagen likened them to the fireworks exhibited at Jones's Wood—a quick flash of brilliance and then extinction. They might possess "fine voices, passion, and intensity of feeling," but these qualities sputtered out when they were not supported by "such aesthetic laws as insure a good method of singing. A dramatic singer is not the one who screams most, who embraces with the greatest vehemence, who sobs as if she had the hiccoughs, and runs about the stage as if she wanted to play catch-me-not with the public," he wrote, obviously referring to Cortesi's histrionics. In Hagen's opinion "these Verdi singers" and the ignoble art they represented deserved each other.

But Seymour, more matter-of-factly attributing Madame Cortesi's incapacity to a bad cold,[87] wrote in the *Times* (June 13, 1859): "Her success, despite illness, is something to be wondered at. No singer has ever before created the *furore* at the Academy that this lady created on Wednesday last [as Paolina]. The public was completely carried away, bestowing double encores on the principal pieces. Even the players in the orchestra, who are usually very philosophical about prima donnas, became excited and followed the lady home to pay her the compliment of a serenade."[88]

"In the *Poliuto* she was magnificent," wrote *Personne* (Edward Wilkins) in the *Saturday Press* (June 11, 1859), so magnificent as to "seriously affect Brignoli's composure." Later, an overwrought Ada Clare (*Saturday Press,* October 1) would incoherently hail Cortesi as nothing less than a goddess: "Genius, thou only glorious image on this dusky globe!" she chanted. "We, the true hero-worshippers and the world's recognized fools, clasping thy feet, make offering to thee of all that we have—our living hearts! Perchance, in the ears of the Gods, these tributary heart-cries sound like voices of

[86] Hagen's reckoning is misleading: he apparently disregarded Cortesi's second appearance, again as Saffo, at the Gala Matinée on June 4, the day after her debut. Scheduled to sing *La traviata* on June 6, she was stricken with a throat ailment and was forbidden by her doctor to appear. The performance was canceled at the last minute; thus her sensationally successful following appearance, as Paolina in *Poliuto* on June 8, although her second night, was her third performance at the Academy. Sudden cancellations attributed to sudden illnesses later became Madame Cortesi's distinguishing characteristic.

[87] Her indisposition was variously ascribed to exhaustion, what with her killing schedule, to the treacherous New York climate, notoriously inhospitable to the Italian vocal apparatus, or perhaps to a glass of ice water that she was rumored to have heedlessly gulped down between the acts.

[88] Cortesi's style was vastly different from Piccolomini's, stated the fickle *Evening Post* (June 4, 1859): "One is an Amazon, the other a fairy; and after the long rule of the fairy it is a relief indeed to be under the more vigorous sway of the Amazon."

thunders, compared with which the clamorous acclamations of ten thousand heartless lips, nay, even the very artillery of heaven, may seem like the silence of planets extinct!"

To fill the gap caused by Cortesi's unfortunately lingering indisposition, Strakosch presented Pauline Colson, who appeared as Alice in *Roberto il diavolo* on June 9 and at the matinée on June 11, supported by Claudina Cairoli (Isabelle), Brignoli (Robert),[89] Junca (Bertram), and Henry Squires★ (Raimbaud); Maretzek conducted. Accompanied by the orchestra, Monsieur Werner, a debutant pianist, played Mendelssohn's *Capriccio brillant* during the intermission. The hastily-slapped-together production was adversely criticized, except by Fry (*Tribune,* June 10, 1859), who found much to praise in the various vocal performances, although the opera itself lacked sufficient musical "go," and by Watson, who was delighted with Colson's refreshingly simple and direct style, uncluttered as it was by exaggerated histrionics and devoid of trickery and claptrap— an obvious thrust at Madame Cortesi's intensity (*Leslie's,* June 18, 1859, p. 43).

With Cortesi still unable to sing the *Lucia* scheduled for June 13, a well-liked, and this time truly all-Italian *Marta* was substituted, with Pauline Colson, as Marta, delightfully singing in that language for the first time.[90] Madame Strakosch was charming as Nancy; the habitually "negligent" Brignoli was unusually animated as Lionello; and Junca was a funny Plunkett. Strakosch conducted.

It was gratifying perhaps to those who preferred the Italian to the so-called "gutteral German in which the opera was written," huffily wrote Burkhardt (*Dispatch,* June 18, 1859), but to him the production was a failure, as any translated opera was bound to be, for, he proclaimed: "The language of the libretto and the melodies must, from the first and forever, assimilate—must be, so to say, created for each other. Witness the botch made of Balfe's *Bohemian Girl* in an Italian dress; the absurdity of *Robert le diable* in English or German, and its harshness, even in Italian, to ears accustomed to the original French version; or Rossini's *Barbiere* in German, or the *Freischütz* in French, or even Verdi's *Trovatore* in English!" (An ever ongoing argument.)

Further disaster awaited the beleaguered impresario.

June 15. . . . Dined with Ellie yesterday at Mrs. Georgey Peters and went with her and Dr. Carroll to the Academy of Music. *Puritani: prima donna* the very distinguished [American] amateur Madame *[la Comtesse]* de Ferussac [the socially prominent] (Colonel Thorne's daughter) [making her debut in New York]. We expected a crowd and a grand excitement, but on entering our box—very late—twenty minutes be-

[89] Brignoli had behaved outrageously, complained the *Evening Post* (June 10, 1859). In the graveyard scene, as the spectral Abbess (Signorina Annetta Galletti, the new prima ballerina at Niblo's) endeavored to entice Robert to take the magic branch, "this Brignoli faced the audience and unrestrainedly laughed at the dancer." Arousing at first an answering nervous titter from the audience, Brignoli was roundly hissed. The illusion had been irretrievably destroyed.

[90] In the opinion of the *Albion* critic (June 18, 1859, p. 295), it was debatable whether Madame Colson and Junca truly sang in Italian, but if they were incomprehensible they were also vocally delightful in Flotow's elegant music. Who would have supposed, gratuitously added the critic, "that its author is one of the snuffiest, greasiest, dirtiest creatures in existence?"

hind time—we found two-thirds of the front boxes empty and the parquette sparsely sprinkled with people, *rari sedentes (et sudantes) in gurgite vasto*.[91] Curtain rose at last to the thinnest and most apathetic of houses, and the Countess de Ferussac must have been disgusted and mortified. But she went resolutely through her work, showed little embarrassment, made no mistakes in her stage business, sang very brilliantly for an amateur, and very poorly for a *prima donna*. Either she was afraid to let out her voice, or she has not power enough for the Opera House. The performance in aid of the Woman's Hospital could hardly have paid expenses.

~

The event was indeed a disaster, representing a grievous loss to Strakosch of $878. As he furiously informed the public in a lengthy and detailed card, it was a greater sum than the box-office receipts, amounting in all to merely $622. The scandalous ineptitude and indifference of the Upper-Ten patronesses of the event were entirely to blame, he charged.[92] As for Madame de Ferussac's performance, the critical press, albeit in atypically gentle terms, generally agreed with Strong.

Immediately following this fiasco, a financially depleted Strakosch closed his unfortunate season[93] with a spectacular, two-part benefit to himself, featuring in each section the now recovered Cortesi: on Friday evening, June 17, in her delayed Norma—a sensation—and the following afternoon in her magnificent Paolina; both performances were conducted by Maretzek.[94]

Despite these allurements, Strakosch's benefit attracted only a sparse attendance. The *Albion* critic (June 25, 1859, p. 307)—admittedly averse to the concept of self-awarded benefits by impresarios empowered to command the free services of their casts at will—confessed that he was not "plunged into inconsolable regret by the spectacle of a slim house" at both performances. His only regret was that "a remarkably fine performance of *Norma* escaped, in this way, the just recognition of the public." Cortesi's Norma, he wrote, was rendered "with a degree of impassioned emphasis for which we can find no adequate expression.[95] Musically and dramatically considered, the effect was superb."

Two post-season benefits still remained: on the afternoon and evening of June 22 the members of the opera community united in a huge effort to aid the widows and

[91] A sardonic Strongian variant on Virgil's "*rari nantes in gurgite vasto*" (*Aeneid,* bk. 1.1.118), transforming the original meaning—"A man or two can be seen swimming in the huge maelstrom"—to "can be seen sitting and sweating," etc. By reinstating the original text in the published *Diary* (II, 455), the editors are not only misquoting Strong but mistaking his intention.

[92] "The ladies of the *crème de la crème* had the pleasure of 'seeing their names in print' as 'patronesses,' were satisfied, and did not 'patronise,'" wryly observed Burkhardt, who had seen "many poor, bad, shy houses" during his career, but never one "so thin and desolate as on this 'extraordinary' occasion" (*Dispatch,* June 18, 1859).

[93] Financially unfortunate, that is. During the just elapsed short season Strakosch had presented sixteen opera productions, among them one new work *(Poliuto)* that promised "to take a fair rank in the modern repertoire" (*Evening Post,* June 17, 1859).

[94] The *Norma* cast included Amalia Strakosch (Adalgisa), Lorini (Pollione), and Junca (Oroveso); the *Poliuto* cast, as before, consisted of Brignoli, Amodio, and Nicolò Barili.

[95] "The words *beautiful, enchanting, bewitching, exquisite,* are . . . too feeble for Cortesi," wrote the tongue-tied *Musical World* (June 29, 1859, pp. 2–3). "There is a breadth, a vastness, that leaves her without comparison."

orphans of the fallen in the Italian War of Independence against Austrian domination. "Have the Operatic managers anything to do with it?" perversely queried Burkhardt. "If so, Austria has to be considered first, for all of them—Maretzek, Ullman, and Strakosch—are Austrians" (*Dispatch,* June 18, 1859). The *Musical World* (July 2, 1859, p. 2), too, commented on the anomaly of the chorus and orchestra, consisting mostly of Germans and Austrians, cooperating with the foe in this pro-Italian effort. "However, as they sang [and played] for pay, it is not likely they will get a black mark for it," dimly reasoned the *Musical World*.[96]

It was indeed a fervently Italian occasion. Wearing the red, white, and green Italian colors, Gazzaniga (still present and still a great favorite), Aldini, Stefani, Gasparoni, and one Francesco Gnone (a new baritone making his first appearance in the United States) gave a fine performance of *Il trovatore.* The afternoon concluded with the soul-stirring delivery by Amodio and Junca of the "Liberty Duet" from *I puritani,* accompanied by brandishings of swords and flags; the conductor was Nicolai (the former Nicolao).

In the evening *Poliuto* was performed, with Cortesi a thrilling Paolina, and Amodio no less thrilling, when, "with a noble scorn of the ridiculous," he made his triumphal entry into the ancient city of Mitylene with great attendant flourishings of American, Sardinian, and French flags; Muzio conducted (*Albion,* June 25, 1859, p. 307). The benefit netted the cause some three thousand dollars.

A few days later, on June 25, many of the same artists—Gazzaniga, Brignoli, Sbriglia, Amodio, Gasparoni, and the newcomer Gnone—united again to honor the perennial stage manager/comprimario Amati Dubreuil with a gala performance of *Ernani,* conducted by Anschütz. As a feature of the "Musical *intermède,*" which included solos and duets performed by the above artists, Formes had been announced to sing "The Wanderer," by Schubert, but, coyly explained the *Musical World* (July 2, 1859, p. 2): "He suited the action too closely to the word and proved *himself* a wanderer by sailing for Europe on that day instead of singing at the matinée."

During the ensuing period of comparative quiet, as Watson informed the readers of his gossip column in *Leslie's* (July 16, 1859, p. 107), yet another readjustment took place within the Academy hierarchy: "Strakosch and Ullman have become as loving as turtle doves, and have drowned all their past animosities in a draught of lager. Strakosch is going to Europe, while Ullman will remain in a comatose condition during the summer. . . . Strakosch and Ullman will open the operatic campaign in the fall in joint partnership."

After his lean period following Piccolomini's defection, Ullman had received a fresh infusion of cash—reportedly $20,000 —from the Academy stockholders, unwilling that the opera should cease. Uniting with Strakosch, currently his brother in adversity,[97] Ullman announced large plans for the following season. Not only was Strakosch

---

[96] Apparently, Parodi, who appeared at the evening performance, did not receive the same cooperation: she was forced to sing the *Marseillaise* and "The Star-Spangled Banner" with merely piano accompaniment and without chorus.

[97] "Both of them have lost lots of money lately, and probably a fellow-feeling makes them wondrous kind," unkindly wrote *Personne* (*Saturday Press,* June 25, 1859).

immediately off to Europe to engage new talent, but new scenery and costumes had been ordered from Paris, including "sixty splendid suits of plate armor for man and horse, from the atelier of L. Granger of Paris, destined expressly for the production of Verdi's new opera, *Les Vêpres siciliennes*" *(The Sicilian Vespers)* (*Times,* September 6, 1859). Duties alone paid on the importation of these and other properties amounted to nearly $3000, facts that were interpreted as guarantees that the management of the Academy would "really endeavor, during the coming winter, to give us opera on a scale worthy of the metropolis."

In the meantime, wrote Watson: "Max Maretzek is cultivating corn and potatoes on his Staten Island farm; Madame Gazzaniga is sojourning at Saratoga; Madame Cora de Wilhorst has taken a cottage at Newport for the summer;[98] Signor Brignoli is playing a fine engagement at Saratoga—his dashing horses and outriders are the admiration of the F.F.F.A.'s (First Families Fifth Avenue)." And Amodio was being "cruel to animals" by dashing around New York in a wheeled contraption drawn by a single "small quadruped." Amodio, in fact, was "snuffing" the country air at Staten Island, as were Junca and Cortesi; Colson was diligently studying new roles at her cottage at Utrecht, Long Island, and Adelina Patti, soon to make her world-resounding debut in opera, was summering with her family at their Westchester County house at Mount Vernon.

During this idyllic interlude, Ullman, in anticipation of the new season, announced the availability of the refreshment concession at the Academy, providing the gossipy *Evening Post* critic with material for a revealing little essay (July 26, 1859) on this seldom discussed amenity at the Academy.

Although only "a little sponge cake and pastry" were ostensibly available to lady occupants of the boxes during intermissions, he wrote, it was not generally known that a populous "lager beer cavern" existed underground beneath the Academy lobbies, "a long room . . . where, in a cloud of cigar smoke and amid the fumes of lager and liquor, the artists and their friends refresh themselves with copious libations. The conductor has a subterranean communication from the stage to the place, and—with Brignoli, Amodio, the members of the orchestra, and a number of the initiated *habitués* of the opera house—meets there his friends. . . . Between the acts of the opera the cavern is crowded, but as soon as the music commences, the rotund German drops his lager; the Frenchman shrugs his shoulders and says '*Mon Dieu*'; the Italian quotes Count Luna in *Trovatore* and sings '*Andiamo*'; the yellow Cubans and Spaniards give a twirl to their moustaches; the English or New York swell struts toward the stairs, and in a few moments the motley crowd are in the seats or lobbies, ready at the next fall of the curtain to return to their bibulous and garrulous recreations in the lager beer cavern."

In late June, Ellen and her sons went to Great Barrington for a protracted vacation, leaving a lonely Strong—between occasional weekend visits to Massachusetts—to abandon himself to self-pitying lamentations, sometimes in verse:

---

[98] Where Madame Frezzolini, who had returned to the United States in June, doubtless in the hope of being re-engaged for the opera, gave a concert. She was assisted by Harrison Millard, a substitute for Brignoli, who had declined to appear with Madame Frezzolini, ungallantly declaring that he had come to Newport "to enjoy himself" (*Evening Post,* August 9, 1859).

Pity the sorrows of a poor old Cove,
   Whoo-oo-oo!!
Condemned in solitude alone at home to pine,
   O Yow-yow-yow!!
Listless thro' slimy streets to loaf,
   Haa-a-a-ay!!!
And at some swinish restaurant to dine,
   Mie-aou-wow-wow!!!!

July 6. . . . Took Niedermeyer's Mass to Mrs. Gibbs's tonight. Spent an hour with her and her husband. She read it over for me. It is certainly a very grand work; strange it's so little known. The *Judicare vivos et mortuos, cujus regni non erit finis* is a great point. That particular passage is rendered as beautifully in no other mass that I know of. Its *Dona pacem* is the finest I ever heard, and among the finest pieces of ecclesiastical music I am acquainted with.

Mozart and Haydn commonly sacrifice the sentiment of the *Dona* for the sake of a brilliant, emphatic finale, and express the aspiration for peace by contraries, or by a violent contrast, using trumpet phrases and quick time and highly colored martial instrumentation: *vide* the splendid and spirited, but utterly inappropriate movements with which Haydn's No. 2 and Mozart's No. 1 conclude. Niedermeyer has done far better.[99] His *Agnus* and *Dona* are blended, as they should be, into one movement, and every note is in keeping with the sentiment; yet they make a most intense and impressive finale.

Probably an aesthetic Roman Catholic would reply that it is fitting that the prayer of the one and infallible Church should be a song of triumph, that in this traditional way of rendering the prayer in music, Art bears unconscious witness for The Church, as entitled to intercede for Man in perfect faith and full assurance. But if music have any language, and mean anything, a *Kyrie* and a *Gloria* should be unlike in musical expression.

July 9. . . . Dined at Delmonico's with Charley Strong; walked sweatily uptown; saw Miss Rosalie [Ruggles] a few moments, took a cup of coffee, read, and then strolled forth and visited the Palace Gardens [or Garden] (Fourteenth Street west of Sixth Avenue). A nice place enough—ice cream, orchestra, colored lamps, an occasional skyrocket, and a well-behaved set of people. Alas for old Castle Garden, with its salt sea breeze and its outlook over the Bay.

July 10. . . . Downtown to Trinity Church this Sunday. The sexton pressed me into service as penny-grabber; proceeds of my tour about three and sixpence. [Rev. Benjamin Isaacs] Haight preached drearily. The music was vile, though Hodges's *locum tenens*[100] boasts of it. Boys and men in the chancel, with a little melodeon. It seemed to me like a choir of newsboys accompanied by a hurdy-gurdy.

---

[99] Niedermeyer superior to Haydn and Mozart?

[100] Henry Stephen Cutler (1825–1902), a Boston church organist, had been appointed for six months to substitute for the ailing Hodges. Cutler's innovations were evidently frowned upon by members of the Trinity Vestry, among them Strong. As it turned out, Hodges—although he lingered until 1867—was, as Strong had foretold, unable to resume his duties at Trinity, and Cutler was appointed his permanent successor (Messiter, pp. 68, 72, *passim*).

The excavation for the reservoir in Central Park, as shown here, matches Strong's opinion exactly: "a ragged ulcer." But it eventually became a welcome addition to the Park—and to the New York City water supply.

July 25. . . . [moodily musing, following a visit to Great Barrington, over the futility of trying to grasp the ineffable beauty of a summer landscape] How sad for you that you cannot receive what God's Earth was meant to give you. It's a feeling that always comes with the perception of eminent Beauty; oftenest, I think, by very pure and noble music, and especially by Mozart's.

It is not necessarily accomplished by actual conscious enjoyment of what produces it. For example, *Il mio tesoro* in *Don Giovanni* is *to me* merely a most elegant, finished, frigid piece of artistic composition, emotionless, soulless, cold, and dead—like an exquisitely elaborated sonnet, or a marvel of conventional landscape painting. Yet, I never hear it without the most uneasy sense, or suspicion, of a subtle beauty that transcends my perception.

September 3. . . . With George Anthon at Central Park this afternoon. Dodworth's Band plays in "The Ramble"[101] Saturday afternoons, so there was a great assemblage there, and the Third and Sixth Avenue Railroad cars were crowded and comfortless. We dispensed with the music and surveyed the upper Park and the vast excavation that is to be the new reservoir. At present it's a deep, ragged ulcer with innumerable vermin—Celts and carts—crawling over its edge and about its bottom, and purulent secretions of pond and boggy spring water and morbid growth of embankment and derrick, hideous to behold.

～

From its earliest, most primitive stages, Central Park—now in active construction—was a source of interest, pride, and enjoyment to New Yorkers, and Strong was evidently no exception. Saturday afternoon concerts of popular music had been initiated in July through the efforts of the music-loving architect Jacob Wrey Mould. It

---

[101] In June the Central Park commissioners announced that "the part of the enclosure which has been named the Ramble is now prepared for the visits of the people. This is the part of the Park which is now the Old Reservoir, toward the northern end. It was lately a rough hillside broken by ledges of rock and bestrewn with boulders, but it is now a picturesque and attractive bit of landscape, with shrubbery and winding walks, and some fine outlooks toward the city and the Hudson River."

was an idealistic attempt, wrote the *Albion* (July 16, 1859, p. 343), "to combine the pleasure of breathing awhile in a beautiful locality, with the enjoyment of high-class music . . . not an 'artistic speculation,' the mildest term for the many money-making attacks on the ears and pockets of the million, with which we are all familiar." On the contrary, Mould, then assistant architect for the Park works, and a "worshipper of St. Cecilia," had raised funds sufficient to launch the series from a few of his public-spirited friends. But more money was needed "in order to make permanent during the summer season this admirable attraction to our citizens." The public's support was earnestly solicited to "do for our New York Park what governments generally do in the European continental capitals, and what individual subscriptions have done in London!"

September 19. . . . [spending a weekend with Ellie and the boys at Great Barrington] I took a vigorous nap on the sofa Saturday afternoon [September 17], and Ellie read Beethoven's sonatas for me in the evening. . . . [Sunday] Evening at the microscope,[102] Ellie accompanying with sketchy readings from Haydn's Masses.

⌁

Strong's loneliness during Ellie's absence, however, was not so desperate as to drive him to the Academy of Music, where, from September 12 to September 30, Maretzek catered to the tremendous annual influx of tourists[103] with a season of the tried-and-true Italian opera favorites.[104] Presented in league with Ullman and Strakosch, his company included—in addition to Cortesi, Stefani, and the Gassiers—the currently idle Strakosch luminaries, Pauline Colson, Amalia Strakosch, Brignoli, Amodio, and Junca. At the end of this engagement,[105] after a Gala Matinée,[106] at which appeared, as an extra attraction, the highly acclaimed pianist Sebastian Bach Mills[107]—they transferred to Boston.[108] There, resuming under the Ullman/Strakosch

---

[102] Along with music, Strong cherished a lifelong predilection for microscopy.

[103] To whom a visit to the opera was a sightseeing imperative. On the crowded opening night, vivaciously wrote the *Times* (September 18, 1859): "They were there in force from all lands and all habitations of men, lively Canadians, astonished-looking New Englanders, sternly imperturbable, heavily-bearded, slouch-hatted, and variously waistcoated Western men, and of Cubans, small, wide-eyed, distressingly civil, an infinite multitude. . . . There were the usual bohemians scintillating through the doorways and playing at Bengal tigers up and down the corridors." Not more than five boxes housed their usual occupants.

[104] The closest approach to novelty, wrote the *Albion* critic (September 24, 1859, p. 463), was the casting of Madame Cortesi, as Leonora in *Il trovatore*. The well-trodden repertory otherwise consisted of *Poliuto, La traviata, Lucia, I puritani, The Barber of Seville, Ernani,* and, of course, *Don Giovanni.*

[105] Tremendously successful, according to Watson (*Leslie's,* October 8, 1859, p. 297). On two successive Saturdays, September 24 and October 1, the box office had taken in (for "democratic," unreserved dollar tickets) respectively $1900 and "over $2500." It proved, wrote Watson, that "the people at large like to have an equal chance; they do not like to be overridden by wealth."

[106] A disaster, wrote the *Evening Post* (October 3, 1859): instead of the complete *Ernani,* only two acts were given; the promised act of *Poliuto* "subsided" into a duet for tenor and soprano; and Stefani, who was announced, did not appear at all.

[107] At the previous week's Gala Matinée the piano soloist had been young Arthur Napoleon.

[108] All except Luigi Stefani, who—as he announced in an aggrieved card—had been dropped because of a dispute with Ullman over money. According to the Boston *Post* (as reprinted in the *Saturday Press,* October 8, 1859), Stefani had been paid $1200 a month. The other singers' monthly sala-

banner and with Muzio taking over the baton (Maretzek being off to Havana), they opened a short season on October 3, preceding the grand opening of the autumn season on October 17 at the New York Academy of Music, with new artists whom Strakosch had—with great fanfare—brought back from Europe.

By that time Ellie had returned to town and Strong had resumed his customary musical routine.

October 15. . . . With [Ellie] at Mrs. Gibbs's Thursday night [October 13], and heard the two ladies read much good music, including that transcendent Mass of Niedermeyer's.

October 18. . . . Ellie read me some Beethoven. . . . Last night with Ellie and Mrs. Georgey Peters and [her brother] Edward Snelling to the Opera. *Trovatore.* It's mere drivel, utterly worthless and doubly exasperating because its nasty little apologies for melody have been so rubbed and ground into one by all manner of hand organs and hurdy-gurdies for the last three years. I half expected to see a monkey in a red jacket (or that illustrious artist Signor Brignoli, which is the same thing) come spidering along from the stage and clambering up into our box, with a tin saucer for pennies.

◄►

Strong neglected to mention that the occasion had been the tragicomic opening of the Ullman/Strakosch autumn season, blazoned far and wide as a radical departure from the philosophy that until now had governed impresarial activities in the United States. Rather than continuing to bow to European tastes and judgments by importing prohibitively expensive European artists of alleged worldwide repute (often, in fact, past their prime), Strakosch—in a brave gesture of American independence—had engaged as *prime donne* two unknown young Italian singers (at bargain prices), who, he informed the public, would earn their fame on American opera stages through the discriminating acclaim of American audiences. To a large extent, the press went along with his premise.

A few days before the opening, the revolutionary concept was laid out for public consumption in an Ullmanesque essay/advertisement of unprecedented length and—even for Ullman—of unprecedented confidentiality.[109] Besides indoctrinating the public in the new approach and disclosing the current precarious state of the Academy treasury, it glowingly introduced each of the new artists, announced the season's proposed repertory[110] (the Italian operas to be conducted by Muzio, the German by Berg-

---

ries were Cortesi $2500, Madame Gassier $2400, Madame Strakosch $600, Amodio $800, Brignoli $1500, Junca $800, Gassier $1200, Squires $400, and Rocco $400; Maretzek was paid $1000, Muzio $800, and the first violinist and first flutist, respectively, $50 weekly.

[109] "It may be unwise in us, certainly impolitic, to write thus against long and frequently duplicated advertisements by which we, among other newspapers profit," wrote Burkhardt, as publisher of the *Dispatch* (December 10, 1859), "but we must be candid. It is impertinent in a manager—it is, in fact, a reflection upon the sense and judgment of his patrons—to advertise his views and criticisms of his own artists and of the works he is about to produce. . . . Mr. Ullman's love of writing must have cost a small fortune during the campaign, while it kept sensible people who could think for themselves away in disgust."

[110] "We can see nothing but Verdi, Verdi's nightmare and bloodshed operas," ranted Burkhardt (*Dispatch,* October 22, 1859). "We have Verdi with murder and stake in *Trovatore;* Verdi with murder

Girvice Archer, Jr.

*Adelina Speranza, an eighteen-year-old
prima donna, who—because of a
cold—missed the opportunity to
perform at the opening of the season.*

mann, not Anschütz), boasted of the newly imported costumes and stage sets and what they cost, and even (earning Burkhardt's rebuke) taking a vindictive swipe at Formes, now out of favor.

The *Albion* critic (October 15, 1859, p. 499), clearly perceiving "the glowing pen of Mr. Ullman . . . in this tremendous document," wrote: "It explains in the longest possible way how the past seasons have failed and how the coming one must certainly succeed. The old story of high priced artists is once more harped upon." The public was blamed for the high salaries with its insistence on having "none other artists than those who have won the applause of London and Paris audiences. . . . Translated into plain English," wrote the canny critic, this gigantic "howl of management" merely signified that the Academy currently had no great celebrity to boast of.

The season was scheduled to open on Monday, October 17, with eighteen-year-

---

and the bag trick in *Rigoletto;* Verdi with revenge and murder in *Ernani;* Verdi with immorality and consumption in *Traviata;* we are threatened immediately with Verdi and great noise in the *Sicilian Vespers.* . . . Cannot we persuade our friends to put dear Verdi up in sugar, or salt, or the smokehouse for awhile and give us . . . a taste of Rossini, Bellini, Donizetti, *et al.?*"

old Adelina Speranza, the more favored of Strakosch's two baby *prima donna*s, making her debut in *La traviata*. But at the last moment the debutante unfortunately came down with a cold, compelling her hapless co-*prima donna,* one Philipina Crescimano—apparently unfamiliar with the role of Violetta—to make a hurried, unrehearsed, and entirely disastrous debut as Leonora in the *Il trovatore* performance so harshly criticized by Strong.[111] To add to the general catastrophe, at the very start of the performance, Amodio, the Count di Luna, who for some time past had been struggling with a progressive hoarseness, completely lost his voice and attempted—with a cornet supplying his part—to continue in dumb show, prompting hisses from an unsympathetic audience and further serving to unnerve the frightened young debutante. The baritone Ardavani, who happened to be on the premises, quickly took over Amodio's role, and quite creditably, it was noted.

On Wednesday, October 19, with Speranza still indisposed, Crescimano again appeared, this time as Elvira in *Ernani,* the role originally intended for her debut; but, alas, although slightly better,[112] her performance was scarcely more tolerantly received.

The occasion, however, was retrieved by the introduction of two new male artists of high quality: Gaetano Ferri,★ a devastatingly handsome baritone of superb vocal and histrionic capabilities, and Giorgio Stigelli★ (Italianized from Georg Stiegel) (1815–1868), a *robusto* tenor, less handsome than Ferri but of equally high, if not higher, artistic stature.[113] Both men should be regarded as interlopers, sardonically wrote the *Albion* critic, for both were well known on the opera stages of London and Paris (an exaggeration).

With Speranza's debut continuing to be delayed, and with Crescimano a calamitous failure, Madame Colson, who in most opinions should have been the leading *prima donna* in the first place, appeared on the following opera night, October 21, as an excellent Gilda in a generally praised performance of *Rigoletto,*[114] with Ferri and Stigelli respectively (and splendidly) filling the parts of Rigoletto and the Duke, and the returned *basso buffo* Luigi Rocco as Sparafucile. At the Gala Matinée the following day, *Marta* was performed by Colson, Madame Strakosch, Brignoli, and Junca, and, to round out the program, the last act of *Ernani* was given with the unfortunate Crescimano bidding her precipitate farewell to the local opera stage.

---

[111] Quite a number of persons, on arriving at the opera house and learning of the substitution, went away, reported *Trovator* (*Dwight's,* October 22, 1859, p. 240). And of those who remained, many left long before the final curtain.

[112] Not according to Burkhardt, who pronounced her "utterly unfit to play the prima donna upon the New York Academy boards, whatever she may have been in fifth-rate Italian towns" (*Dispatch,* October 22, 1859).

[113] Willis, in the *Musical World* (October 29, 1859, p. 3) recalled Stiegel's youthful debut at Wiesbaden years before, under the baton of Eisfeld.

[114] Particularly by avant-garde Fry (*Tribune,* October 24, 1859), who was "at a loss to know" why *Rigoletto* was so adversely criticized. "It is a great pity," he gibed, "that composers could not take a few lessons from adorers of the periwig school and learn how to put the audience to sleep and empty the benches." Never before, in Fry's opinion, had dramatic composition been so well understood as in the preceding few years, when "directness [had taken] the place of pseudo-ingenuity and formalism, and the business of the scene and the passion of the singer [were] things looked after exclusively, as they ought to be."

Girvice Archer, Jr.

*Gaetano Ferri, who had already achieved
a European reputation in opera.*

As Speranza—still an unknown quantity[115] —continued to be too ill to make her
debut, Strakosch and Ullman's failed operatic experiment become the target of spiteful
editorials; and audiences at the Academy fell off alarmingly. The resulting increase of
"D. H.s" ("deadheads") was undemocratically scrutinized by Burkhardt (*Dispatch,* October 29, 1859): "True," he conceded, "a large free list and a small army of extra D.
H.s are admitted necessities of Opera. Thumping fellows with big sticks and others
with large (often very dirty) hands and resounding palms are always worth their admission, including 'one Lager,' so we don't object. But, most amiable Ullman and *carissimo*
Strakosch, do please order the gentle Miller at the door not to pass ragamuffins and

---

[115] And evidently, if the *Herald* (October 27, 1859) is to be believed, a subject of hot dispute between Ullman, who wanted to send her back to Europe before she ever appeared, and Strakosch,
who resolutely insisted that, once heard, she would create a sensation.

lazzaroni, greasy, unclean organ-grinders, guiltless of fresh linen and with an overpowering smell of garlic, to the balcony and boxes.

"Fellows, aye, and women also, such as we saw in the prominent seats and boxes on Monday (even in absent stockholders' seats)," he continued, "would not be allowed to pass into the boxes of the Bowery [Theatre] or some of the Negro minstrels. Deadhead them, if you please, for the gallery, where their huge paws may be equally useful, and where the strong odor of garlic ascends to the roof, not spreads itself over the balcony and boxes."

The deadhead phenomenon was satirized in the *Philadelphia Evening Bulletin* (reprinted in the *Tribune,* February 24, 1859) at the time of Ullman's earlier Philadelphia season in a takeoff of Tennyson's popular poem, "The Charge of the Light Brigade."

> Down the street, up the street.
>   Cross the street, onward,
> Into the Opera House
>   Rushed the Five Hundred.
> "Charge?" was the leader's cry,
> "None!" was the proud reply;
>   On, on, to hear and see
>   Fair Piccolomini,
>   Into the Opera House
>   Marched the Five Hundred.

In desperation, the partners engaged Gazzaniga (reportedly on the verge of an extended tour of the United States) for six farewell performances, and on October 26, although herself stricken with a cold, she ill-advisedly appeared as Paolina in *Poliuto,*[116] a role indelibly associated in the public mind with her rival, Madame Cortesi. Although Gazzaniga, an abiding favorite, attracted a large and fashionable audience,[117] it was not one of her triumphs: unflattering comparisons with Cortesi were inevitable.

The following evening, October 27, an off night, Adelina Speranza, at last judged healthy enough to make her debut,[118] appeared in *La traviata.* In contrast to the management's offhand treatment of Crescimano, wrote the *Albion* critic (October 29, 1859, p. 523): "Everything in the way of puff and free tickets was reserved for Mlle. Speranza, and, thanks to these auxiliaries of theatrical success,[119] there was a brilliant audience to decide on the lady's abilities and applaud her achievements." It soon became apparent, however, that Mlle. Speranza "was destined to share the unhappy lot of her predecessor, Mlle. Crescimano." To the management's face-saving announcement,

---

[116] Evidently a pickup production: not only was it marred by "one of the worst bands that ever was heard on any stage," wrote the *Times* (October 28, 1859), but the piano accompaniment to the chorus of early Christians might just as appropriately have been given on a banjo.

[117] Not including Strong, however, who spent that evening blissfully listening to "Mrs. Strong and Mrs. Gibbs, doing Beethoven *(Christus am Ölberge)* and Niedermeyer's Mass and Spohr's *Faust* and Pergolesi's *Stabat Mater.*"

[118] Not according to *Trovator,* who claimed that she was still ill, but that, against her will, her tyrannical father, a remorseless singing teacher, forced her to appear *(Dwight's,* November 12, 1859, p. 260).

[119] Including, at the performance, bouquets galore and even a pair of doves released from the amphitheatre.

after the first act, that Speranza had not fully recovered from her illness, the critic was unsympathetic: "If this were true," he wrote, "the management was greatly to blame and is responsible for a failure which will, we suspect, be disastrous in its consequences." Although Speranza was young, pretty, and obviously knew her way around a stage, her infinitesimal voice, albeit fresh and sweet, totally lacked any semblance of cultivation.[120] "It is not easy to see how Mr. Strakosch could have supposed it possible that such a prima donna would suffice for a New York audience," indignantly wrote the critic.

After a repetition of the first act of *La traviata* at the following, not-so-gala matinée on October 29,[121] Speranza was dropped.

November 2. . . . Opera Monday night [October 31] with Charley Strong and Mrs. Eleanor, who dined here. Donizetti's *Maria de Rohan.*♪ Thinnest small-beer, but less objectionable than Verdi's rotgut—not much worse than Meyerbeer's staple article of stale champagne.[122] Yet it is marvelous that people who think they appreciate Mozart and Beethoven can sit out three hours and a half of the paltry commonplaces that make up this opera. Music is a wonderful thing in every point of view. Gazzaniga sang, and a very nice tenor, Stigelli, and a good baritone, Ferri (facetiously called *Fulltone* Ferry).[123] Ullman's force seems strong, but the season is a failure thus far. Speranza, who was imported for the purpose of raising a furore, is an utter failure, and "*Lasciate ogni speranza*" ["abandon all hope"], etc., is written on the portals of the Academy, according to Murray Hoffman.[124] They talk of producing the *Zauberflöte,* and I hope they may, but it will only mire the management deeper. Its music will be thrown away on audiences that tolerate Verdi.

~~~

Upon the culmination of the Speranza catastrophe, Strakosch was rumored to have retired in disgrace,[125] leaving "Napoleon" Ullman to redeem the Academy's fallen fortunes single-handedly. Desperately in need of novelty—a requisite commodity of which the New York opera public felt cheated—Ullman, for lack of more

[120] Mincing no words, Fry pronounced Speranza's debut a total failure. Piccolomini, at least, despite her abysmally crude vocalising, could occasionally turn out a fair bit of acting. "But where there is nothing—neither acting nor singing to rescue a reputation made in managerial cards, the case [was] hopeless. It would be much better," he wrote, "for the directors to omit the ordinary flummery of advertisement. . . . The public will not be dragooned into admiration" (*Tribune,* October 29, 1859).

[121] Also heard was Gazzaniga, who, indisposed or not, repeated her Paolina and—a redeeming feature—the quartet from *Rigoletto,* rousingly sung by Colson, Amalia Strakosch, Stigelli (a great improvement over the static Brignoli), and "the great baritone" Ferri.

[122] The production, in fact, was a hodgepodge of interpolations by Mercadante and others, noted the *Evening Post* (November 1, 1859).

[123] The misreading in the published *Diary* (II, 466) of *Terri* for *Ferri,* and consequently of *Fulltone Terry* for *Fulltone Ferry,* misses the point of the pun on the Fulton Ferry, a preferred means of access to Brooklyn.

[124] An overworked pun on poor Speranza's name that was being done to death by just about everybody.

[125] A rumor that Ullman vehemently denied in a long letter appearing in the *New York Tribune* on November 2, 1859: "Ever since last May, when our association was formed," he wrote, "the best understanding and harmony have marked our relations, and I trust that this union will stand beyond the time stipulated in our agreement and will ultimately become permanent." (As it turned out, Strakosch would soon play the trump card that saved the opera.)

promising material, fastened upon Carlo Beaucardé,★ a passé Italian tenor whom Strakosch had engaged in Europe and who had just arrived. Beaucardé had brought his Italian wife, Augusta Albertini,★ an opera soprano of the vehement school, who, although not engaged by Strakosch, hoped to pick up an engagement or two in the United States on her own. With the present unforeseen shortage of *prima donna*s, Ullman hungrily seized upon Madame Albertini, explaining to the public that she had all along been meant for the opera but that until now her engagement had been kept a secret for purely "managerial reasons." As a team, he claimed, Albertini and Beaucardé enjoyed a status in Italy equaled only by Grisi and Mario.

Beaucardé was nonetheless presented sans Albertini—eliciting only lukewarm approval as Fernando in *La favorita* and Gennaro in *Lucrezia Borgia* (November 2 and 4).[126] Puffing him in oddly equivocal terms, Ullman informed (or warned) the public that "Signor Beaucardé goes in Italy by the sobriquet of the 'inspired tenor.'[127] He is, therefore, not the same on every appearance. Should this be one of his 'inspired evenings,' he will produce an excitement immediately. If not, he will do so on another occasion; but succeed he must, sooner or later, as he has done everywhere" (*Tribune*, November 2, 1859).

November 4. . . . Just from the Opera with Ellie and Mrs. Georgey Peters. *Lucrezia Borgia*: Gazzaniga, [Amalia Strakosch], Beaucardé, a new tenor whom I like, though his voice has lost its freshness,[128] and that fattest bull of Bashan,[129] Amodio. I left the ladies in their box, in the second act, and went down to the footlights, where it was rather pleasant to watch Gazzaniga's fine, expressive face in the *Madre mia terzetto*. Rarely heard that very clever bit of trumpery better done. Wonder what the children of Israel did for an Opera in the wilderness.[130] They fill the parquette now, and all the lower tier, or dress circle.

November 7. . . . Dined with Charley Strong and went to Verdi's *Sicilian Vespers* [Paris 1855], first night—Brignoli, Colson, Ferri, [Junca], etc. Could detect no gleam of life or sense in the music; it seems mere rumbustious nullity.

. . . Gentleman in the lobby: "Sam, what *are* Sicilian Vespers?"[131]

---

[126] He was heard as well at the Gala Matinée, on November 5, repeating the last act of *La favorita* in a program that included a full performance of *Rigoletto* and one of "Never Judge by Appearances," one of the charming, currently popular "Parlor Operas," performed by Mr. and Mrs. Henri Drayton (see following OBBLIGATO).

[127] Meaning, in factual terms, a has-been singer subject to occasional, erratic flashes of bygone brilliance. He should have been introduced as an "expired" tenor, unkindly wrote a journalistic wag, after hearing Beaucardé.

[128] Beaucardé's voice, ambivalently wrote the *Albion* critic (November 5, 1859, p. 535) was "weak and unpleasant in quantity and quality; a battered wreck of something that was once shapely and grand. Judged by the usual art standards, it would not be too severe to say that he has no voice at all." Yet: "The clearness with which he phrases, the polished grace of his periods, the positive grandeur with which he delivers even the most paltry notes indicate the superb artist—and superb as an artist Signor Beaucardé is."

[129] A biblical region noted for splendid cattle and sheep.

[130] An anti-Semitic comment excised from the published *Diary*.

[131] If only the Gentleman in the lobby had perused the day's amusement columns, he would, thanks to Ullman, have known everything—historical, esthetical, and theoretical—pertaining to Verdi and Scribe's opera, set in the thirteenth-century War of the Sicilian Vespers.

In the parlance of the day, *The Sicilian Vespers* received a truly "sensation" production. Its spectacular sets, painted by Hannibal Calyo after the original Paris designs,[132] and its wonderful costumes and armor imported from Paris received unanimous acclaim. At the same time, however, reservations were voiced by some critics over the drastic changes Muzio had made in the score, doing away with some of its best music in order to squeeze it into three acts from its original four,[133] juggling the remaining arias from act to act, interpolating foreign material—such as an inferior *cabaletta* from Verdi's *Simon Boccanegra* (Venice 1857), sung by Colson in the first act—and omitting the ballet, of which only a tarantella was retained, and that fragment transplanted from the second act to the first.[134]

Of the singers, Ferri (as Guido di Montforte) was judged to be the best, Colson (Elena) was brilliant within her capabilities, but she was no dramatic singer, Brignoli (Arrigo) was phlegmatic, uncertain in his part, and looked ill at ease,[135] and Junca (Giovanni da Procida) according to the acidulous *Albion* critic, was able to "rise only to the position of a talented bore." The secondary roles were adequately filled by Madame Morra and the Signori Müller, Rubio, Ximenes, Crouza, and other members of New York's opera underground. Aptommas received featured billing for his playing of the harp *obbligato*s.

Muzio was generally lauded for his expert handling of the augmented chorus of eighty singers and orchestra of sixty-four players and, surprisingly—considering the extent of his customary musical depredations—for his fidelity to Verdi. Whether or not the work, considered by some to be Verdi's best opera, would remain in the repertory was moot; most critics thought it would. In the vain hope that it would pull the opera season out of its financial woes, *The Sicilian Vespers* received an uncommonly long run of seven virtually consecutive performances.[136] Surprisingly, Strong, for all his disdain, returned to hear the third of these.

But first:

November 9. . . . Ellie and I have just returned from a concert (at the City Assembly Rooms, Broadway above Grand Street), one of the performances commemorating Schiller's birth.[137] It was a great success. It gave me a new sensation, or rather, recalled the sensations of 1843, etc., when each successive Philharmonic [concert] marked an

---

[132] Particularly singled out was a mobile pleasure barge "of large dimensions, adorned with lamps and filled with men and women"; it was judged by Fry to equal anything Paris was able to offer in stagecraft (*Tribune,* November 8, 1859).

[133] The excisions amounted to about two-fifths of the score, reported the *Times* (November 8, 1859), but a long opera still remained.

[134] "The persistent *ictus* of the light-footed, delirious, Mediterranean terpsichoreanism is a study, as rendered by the brilliant composer," wrote Fry of Verdi's tarentella (*Tribune,* November 8, 1859).

[135] It was greatly to be regretted, wrote the *Albion* critic (November 12, 1859, p. 546), that Brignoli seemed to regard the stage of the Academy of Music "simply and solely in the light of a spittoon, erected by a liberal and enlightened public for his special accomodation and use."

[136] Its run was momentarily interrupted on November 17 for the debut of Madame Albertini, who appeared in an apparently unrehearsed performance of *Il trovatore* as Leonora to the Manrico of her husband, who had created the role at the opera's premiere in 1853. Although judged to be a "sensation singer," Madame Albertini's tenure at the Academy was short, as was her husband's.

[137] The centenary of Friedrich von Schiller's birth was being celebrated by German/Americans throughout the United States.

Leslie's, Dartmouth College Library

*In the 1850s Castle Garden had been the scene of operas: Jenny Lind
gave her first American concert here. But in 1859 it became the place
where visiting celebrities were received because it was spacious, cool, and on the water.
Here, with crowds on the balconies, an honored general is being welcomed.*

era by its new revelations.♪ There was a great, silent, appreciative crowd of Teutons, in a good room, listening to an admirable orchestra and a passable chorus doing a program of the first order. Began with the Overture to *Tannhäuser* [conducted by Eisfeld]. Never heard it so well rendered; its magnificent lights and shadows were fully brought out. It is something more than a mere prodigy of elaborate construction. I admit it at last to rank among works of the highest order. Ellie said its first movement (the grand Pilgrim-chant) seems hewn out of granite—a felicitous criticism. Then Philip Mayer sang a rather doleful solo from that opera,[138] and Satter, with the orchestra, did a concerto of Beethoven's (no. 4 in G, op. 58) that was brilliant and pleasant but a little below the Beethoven standard; and a vociferous chorus by some *Sängerbund* or other closed Part I.[139]

Part Second was Beethoven's Symphony, no. 9, the "Choral" Symphony [conducted by Anschütz],[140] all but absolutely new to me. I heard it some twelve or more years ago, vilely done at Castle Garden,♪ and afterwards by Satter and Timm on two

[138] "Our admiration for Wagner has not yet reached that point where we can admire his vocal compositions," wrote Willis of this unidentified aria (*Musical World,* November 19, 1859, p. 2).

[139] It was in fact the *Sängerbund.* Under Bergmann's direction they sang Julius Rietz's setting of Schiller's *Dithyramb,* a conscientious work, wrote Hagen, "but in works of art, a little genius is better than a good deal of conscience" (*Review and Gazette,* November 26, 1859, p. 372).

[140] The solos sung by Mesdames Caradori and Zimmermann and Messrs. Mayer and Steinway (William or Charles?), assisted by the *Liederkranz;* the score and parts were loaned for the occasion by the Philharmonic Society, as were the Philharmonic's "old tympanies" (Philharmonic Archives).

pianos,♪ but retained not a single phrase. My impressions of it were that it was long, outré, and dull, and I was surprised tonight to find that I was able to follow it throughout, and in some moderate degree to appreciate it. Beethoven meant it to be his greatest work. The first three parts are certainly on the grandest scale: they seem to contain as much thought as any two of his earlier symphonies. But they are not *inspired* in the same sense with the "Eroica" and C-minor. The Scherzo, however, is full of fire, and the slow movement that follows is of lovely melodic feeling. The fourth part, with its chorus, seems like an afterthought. It's built on a fine, sharp-cut melody and worked up into striking effects, but Beethoven is not at home with a chorus. He's an inverted Thomas the Rhymer[141] ("Harping can I none / For Tonge is chief of Minstrelsie"), an autocrat of the orchestra, but when he undertakes to deal with voices, no longer omnipotent and infallible.

Many things in this fourth movement are spasmodic and extravagant, and it's hardly worthy of Schiller's text.[142] But it has grand points: the first introduction of the subject by the basses and its growth and development as the whole orchestra is gradually brought to bear on it, and a little later, the beautiful, brilliant orchestra coloring given to the little *Tempo di marcia* modification of the same subject. This is a refreshing passage, for the whole work is a little deficient in fine instrumental coloring. There are masterly touches in the first and third movements, but generally the neutral tints of the strings are relieved only by tremendous dashes of scarlet from the brass—great, red-hot chords from the trumpets and trombones.

So much for a first impression. Scharfenberg tells me that the Philharmonic may probably get up this symphony for its last concert this [coming] season. If they do, rehearsals may help me to understand it better.

But it's refreshing to have heard a little Beethoven after all this Verdi and rubbish. What magic there is in [Beethoven's] collocation of two single notes!

⌒⌒⌒

Strong did not attend the remainder of the Schiller Festival, which culminated in a gigantic, five-hour-long tribute at the Academy of Music the following evening. The program consisted chiefly of declamations of Schiller's poems and *tableaux vivants* (twelve in number) representing his plays, enacted by players from the Stadt-Theater and accompanied and interspersed with music supplied by an orchestra of 100 conducted by Carl Bergmann. Among the musical works heard—complete and in fragments—were the Overture to *Egmont,* the Prelude to *Lohengrin,* the Overture to *Coriolanus,* the first movement of Schumann's Fourth Symphony, the Introduction to act two of *Tannhäuser,* a Funeral March by Bergmann, the *Gaudeamus igitur* Overture by Friedrich Schneider,♪ Liszt's *Les Préludes,* the *Egmont* Funeral March, Weber's "Jubilee" Overture, the Finale to *Don Giovanni,* and, in conclusion, the German chorale "Now Thank Ye All the Lord."[143]

---

[141] Thomas the Rhymer (or Thomas of Erceldoune) was a legendary Scottish poet and seer of the thirteenth century.

[142] Hagen disagreed: "If Schiller had done nothing else for our art but inspire Beethoven to write his *Ninth Symphony,* he would be endeared to every musician" (*Review and Gazette,* November 12, 1859, p. 356).

[143] After the opening *Egmont* Overture, Fräulein Grahn of the Stadt-Theater recited a "prize poem," then crowned, apparently with a laurel wreath, "a fine bust of Schiller, which was placed on a pedestal on the stage, surrounded by ladies and children in picturesque groups, while showers of

November 13. . . . Dick Hunt dined here Friday [November 11] and [we] went to the opera *(Sicilian Vapors)* [*sic*] with Ellie and Mrs. Georgey Peters.

November 18. . . . Ellie has gone to the Opera with Jem: "Sicilian Vapors." I'm saving myself up for *Zauberflöte* next week,[144] and I'd rather hear Six Cats in a Gutter and Two Pigs in a Gate than the "Sicilian Vapors."[145] Ellie spent an evening reading me the *Zauberflöte.* . . . The loveliest, purest, simplest music it seems. But how our Operatic people will condemn and deride it! And the ineffable silliness of the plot[146] and libretto will give them unfortunately abundant occasion to blaspheme.

. . . Last night there was a sound of revelry on these premises. A little dancing party of fifty odd. . . . Helmsmüller♪ pianized.[147]

November 20. . . . Yesterday I was wretchedly dyspeptic. Had to give up the evening's Philharmonic, which Ellie and I meant to attend for the sake of Mendelssohn's *Melusine* Overture and Wagner's *Lohengrin* [Prelude]. Schubert's Symphony [in C] was reported uninteresting by Ellie, who had attended the rehearsals.[148] But I felt too utterly bilious to go, and the weather was uncertain, so we spent a Darby and Joan[149] evening at home.

November 21. . . . Murray Hoffman dined here, and we marched to the Opera House through unexpected, pelting rain to hear the *Zauberflöte,*[150] from which I've just returned.

---

copies of the poem floated down from the upper galleries" (*Musical World,* November 19, p. 2; *Evening Post,* November 11, 1859).

[144] Although the coming production was announced as its first in the United States, at least the Overture to the *"Zauberflute"* (as it was billed) had been heard as early as 1817, when James Hewitt conducted it at a "Grand Oratorio" (sacred concert) at St. Paul's Church (*Evening Post,* December 11, 1817). In Charles E. Horn's English version *The Magic Flute* had been performed in 1833 at the Park Theatre; in 1853 it had been given in German in Baltimore by the local *Liederkranz,* and as recently as 1855♪ again in German in New York at the Deutsches Theater on the Bowery. William Henry Fry recalled a production in Philadelphia in 1843, sponsored by a Mr. William Norris and performed in English by Arthur and Anne Seguin (*Dwight's,* December 3, 1859, p. 287). In German it was currently part of the revolving repertory at the Stadt-Theater. The present production at the Academy was performed in Italian, except for the choruses, which were given in German by more than 100 volunteer members of the *Arion* Society, brought in by Carl Bergmann.

[145] This was the penultimate performance of its present run. *The Sicilian Vespers* was given for the seventh and final time at the following day's Gala Matinée, which offered also the *Miserere* from *Il trovatore* sung by Albertini and Beaucardé, an unidentified "grand, dramatic duet" sung by Albertini and Amodio, and the complete last act of *La favorita* with Gazzaniga, Ferri, and Beaucardé.

[146] Described in the *Evening Post* (November 22, 1859) as "such an incomprehensible jumble of fairy scenery, Egyptian rivers, monkeys, streams of lava, apes, ladies in black, spangled dresses, negroes, priests, flutes, serpents, and musical glasses as was never before met up with." The writer doubted if anyone off the stage (or on it) had any definite idea of what it was about.

[147] In September, Helmsmüller had advertised his return from Newport with his "Germania Orchestra," a misleadingly named ensemble of flexible size, available for "private parties, sociables, receptions, dances, etc."

[148] Inasmuch as Strong does not record his attendance at any other of the Philharmonic reheasals or concerts, the Philharmonic 1859–60 season is discussed in the following OBBLIGATO, where the complete program of this concert is found.

[149] The model old-fashioned couple of flawless morals, celebrated in an English ballad by Henry Woodfall (1739–1808).

[150] An event that doubtless would cause "a great German mass-meeting" to be convened at the Academy, foretold the *Evening Post* critic (*Trovator*).

House very full, considering the foul weather,[151] and inclined to be amiable and patronize Mozart.[152] It was funny to hear people talking during the *entr'acte*—comparing this with the *Sicilian Vespers* and pointing out their various merits and demerits—one was more *this* and the other more *that,* etc., etc.[153] As if one should undertake an analysis of the relative position in Art of *The Tempest* and Sylvanus Cobb, Jr.'s last sensation story in the *New-York Ledger!*[154]

It was very fairly done. Colson, the Queen of the Night; Stigelli Tamino, Ferri Papageno,[155] Junca Sarastro,[156] Gazzaniga Pamina, Monostatos the nigger Amodio. The unaccountable "lady Attendants" and "Three Beneficent Genii" rather poor.[157] Scenic effects and properties as contemptible as their silliness deserved.[158] As to the plot—the dramatic element of the Opera—human language is unable to express its idiocy. Let us hope that to the fashionable public of seventy years ago, for which it was written, it conveyed some gleam of a notion about Truth and Virtue (always with a big "T" and a big "V"), Illumination, Initiation, *Frei Mauererei* [Freemasonry] or something else. But a question arises: whether real music be not heard at less disadvantage when allied with a mere absurd, incoherent series of stage effects like those of the *Zauberflöte*—with the representation of something that can hardly pretend to be real or historical or in any way connected with the movements and doings of human beings at any era of this planet's existence—than when it illustrates and accompanies something equally unreal that claims to be a sort of caricature of real human passion and action?

Is not *Zauberflöte,* in fact, better for musical purposes (because more unreal and unnatural) than *Don Giovanni?* I incline to think so, and that the nearest practicable approach to dramatic music is in something like the Masques of Ben Jonson's time, or the formal, conventional, statuesque librettos of Gluck (if I am right as to the character

---

[151] And, more tellingly, despite the suspension of the free list.

[152] "The people got warmed up in some parts of the performance to a fair pitch of excitement, notwithstanding the pretty general disappointment in the character of the music," wrote Watson (*Leslie's,* December 3, 1859, p. 3).

[153] "Like the 'Sicilian Vespers,' [*The Magic Flute*] was mutilated to suit the dimension of the Procrustean programme furnished by the highly imaginative manager," wrote the *Albion* critic (December 3, 1859, p. 583).

[154] Sylvanus Cobb (1823–1887) was a phenomenally prolific and successful author of pulp fiction that for more than thirty years occupied the pages of Robert Bonner's "sensation" weekly *New-York Ledger.*

[155] Who persistently failed to synchronize his action with the device simulating the sound of the musical glasses, invented by Joseph Mosenthal and played by him in the orchestra pit (*Evening Post,* November 26, 1859).

[156] Junca was replaced for the remaining performances by Joseph Weinlich, who unfortunately was unfamiliar with the Italian text and who therefore struggled visibly and vainly to hear the prompter, for once stricken with inaudibility.

[157] Minna von Berkel sang the first lady attendant and the first boy (or "Beneficent Genius"); Mesdames Morra, Reichhard, and Bergner were variously responsible for the second and third ladies and the second and third genii.

[158] In contrast to *The Sicilian Vespers,* which had been magnificently produced and puffed, fumed Burkhardt, *The Magic Flute* had been "badly cast, not half rehearsed, shockingly mutilated, meanly costumed, and most shabbily put upon the stage." It would have "disgraced a village show shop" (*Dispatch,* December 10, 1859).

of Gluck's Operas). If the composer try to be realistic he must fail, and the more extravagantly *unreal* is his work, the less offensive will be his failure and the less will it mar his music. Everyone must see that a certain degree of "reality"—or "realizability"—excludes a subject from the possibility of being "lyrically dramatized." General Washington, Napoleon, Queen Anne, Lord Byron, and Mrs. Hannah More[159] are inconceivable as *bassi, tenori,* or whatnot, for a hundred years to come.[160] But Henry VIII, Catherine de Medici, Giovanni da Procida, Lucrezia Borgia—anybody sufficiently remote from us in time and accessories to have become unreal and romantic to us—can be endured when doing his or her work and telling his or her woes in B-flat, or some other key. A libretto cannot take you too far from common sense and real life —cannot hold the mirror too persistently far away from Nature. And probably no extant libretto fulfills that condition more perfectly than the libretto of *The Magic Flute.*

. . . Who could have written it?[161] Who was the gifted man that created Papageno and Papagena? Was he drunk or sober when he evolved the conception of the Three Ladies Attendant? How did he look when the Negro Monostatos first dawned upon him? Did he think Sarastro rather grand and imposing, and did he die undeceived? Did he mean to symbolize anything by the Queen of the Night, and if so, what? As to the music: having heard it but once, I will not try to be critical.[162] It's less elaborate than that of *Don Giovanni* or *Nozze di Figaro.*[163] Nothing in it is as carefully worked out as *Deh vieni, Dove sono, Non più andrai,* etc. It seems a mere succession of lovely, sunshiny, offhand memoranda of melody, with one or two serious, thoughtful choruses.

November 24. . . . *Magic Flute* again last night[164] with Mr. and Mrs. d'Oremieulx, who dined here. Ellie was delighted. It finds far more favor with opera-goers than I thought possible.[165] Our oracles of the lobby say that it is "very pretty," and then proceed to distinguish Mozart's music from Verdi's as undramatic and unimpassioned.

[159] It was *Miss* Hannah More (1745–1833), and she was a famed English Bluestocking, writer, and social reformer.

[160] No longer applicable in the twentieth century, with its operas inhabited by such contemporary historical figures as Mao Tse-tung, Malcolm X, Marilyn Monroe, Harvey Milk, and Rudolph Valentino.

[161] Only Hagen and the *Evening Post* critic seemed aware of the presence and influence of the actor/librettist Emanuel Schikaneder (1751–1812) in the creation and early performances of *The Magic Flute* (*Review and Gazette,* November 26, pp. 370–71; *Evening Post,* November 21, 1859).

[162] As Willis wrote in the *Musical World* (November 26, 1859, p. 2): "The music rather puzzled the admirers of modern music. Mozart cannot be appreciated in one hearing." Strong, as a connoisseur of Mozart—for all his determination instantly to appreciate the music—apparently took refuge in intricate dialectic to mask his uncertainty. Not until his third hearing of *The Magic Flute* did he finally decide that the music was positively celestial.

[163] Ullman's advertising copy equated *The Magic Flute* with *Don Giovanni* and *The Marriage of Figaro,* or "any other of Mozart's grand operas," and several of the reviewers remarked on their identical musical characteristics. Indeed, the critics' blanket complaint against Mozart's obsolete music was of its interminable sameness—its lack of passion.

[164] Upon inaugurating a crash schedule of nightly performances for the remaining two weeks of the opera season before leaving for Philadelphia, a disastrous, off-night performance of *Poliuto*—with Albertini and Beaucardé—was given on November 22, between the first and second performances of *The Magic Flute.*

[165] Wishful thinking on Strong's part. The production of *The Magic Flute* was another on the long list of that season's failures.

November 25. . . . Threatening snow all day . . . and as we left the Opera House just now, it was beginning to come down . . . we heard the *Zauberflöte* [its third performance]. . . . *Zauberflöte* is delicious, and Mozart the King of Melody, *jure divino.* His work is so simple and *true* that it seems easy, and one must know something of other composers to appreciate it. But how far below him are even Handel, Beethoven, and Haydn in fertility of deep and various melody; how much more has he given us of pure, bright musical thought than any other composer! More than Beethoven himself, though I fully admit Beethoven's C-minor, "Eroica," and A-major symphonies to be intense beyond—and far beyond—all other music.

There is a certain nobleness in the sentiment of [Mozart's] melodies very often that seems to me a special characteristic. I do not know that I have the right word for it. For instance, the little duo of Pamina and Tamino in the second act—when they are passing through certain torrents of lava floods or in some like peril (one hates to think of music so transcendent on the same day with such shallow trumpery and clap-trap)—*Wir wandelten durch Feuergluthen,* I think it is, in the German libretto. Words cannot express what that little unnoticed hint of melody seems to reveal; its dignity and sweetness are wasted in the desert air of the Opera House, but it might be the voice of those who shall "come with songs and everlasting Joy upon their heads"; it is worthy to be heard beside that "river, the streams whereof shall make glad the City of God." And think of its being allied to the paltry fooleries of this Operatic nonsense!

Note also the peculiar courtesy and dignity embodied in the music of salutation or adieu in [Mozart's] operas: in the first act of *this* and in the entry of the three masks into the ballroom (finale of the first act of *Don Giovanni*)—the grand stately manner of the old regime idealized in music. People call his work undramatic: "He's a great composer, no doubt, but he could not write *dramatic* music like Verdi's or Donizetti's." I suppose dramatic music to be music that expresses passion or emotion capable of dramatic representation. And no one has ever done that like Mozart, to my knowledge, unless it may be Weber in the *Leise, leise, fromme Weise,* Agatha's scene in the *Freischütz,* Look at *Batti, batti,* for example. Never mind its melodic beauty. Attend only to its narrative power, to the story it tells. Could words express more clearly the seriocomic, solemn sham penitence and apology of [Zerlina's] power over her clown of a lover, than its first movement, or the triumph of the little coquette, dancing round him and reiterating her *Batti, batti* when she has teased and wheedled him into reconciliation and submission, than its final *allegro?* Is not this unequaled as dramatic music? But our barbaric taste prefers that some roaring, spasmodic *allegro* that expresses rage by help of minor trombone chords, or some other crude, raw, harsh, gross embodiment of the some single passion in its most coarse exaggeration.

——

The Magic Flute was not a critical success. To a man, the critics rejected it, despite its concededly lovely melodies, as outmoded entertainment. "The day when such a work would make a sensation, if it ever was, is not now, and we have no hesitation in adding, never will be again," categorically proclaimed Seymour (*Times,* November 23, 1859). Mozart's purported genius was an exploded theory; to listen to his works was to court boredom. Nor did Mozart display judgment in his choice of collaborators: just as the libretto of *Don Giovanni* was indecent, so was the text of *The Magic Flute* positively idiotic. And the legend that Mozart was a great orchestrator was "twaddle."

With the great improvements in musical instruments since his time, the "melodious chirruping" of the Mozartean orchestra was hopelessly out of date.

Yet, confessed Seymour, in one sense, at least, *The Magic Flute* was "beautiful—rarely and wonderfully beautiful." Precisely because the human voice was an instrument not susceptible to technological improvement with the passage of time, Mozart's admittedly beautiful melodies, at least, would not go out of style. "Indeed, it would be hard to point to a single phrase of the entire vocal score which is not characterized by some especial happiness," wrote Seymour. With the exception, however, of the Queen of the Night aria, which the confused critic characterized as "probably the poorest specimen of that kind of writing that can be found."

Even Hagen allowed himself to waver, questioning whether Mozart, for all his genius, could appeal to present-day music-lovers who "swore by Verdi."[166] Although *The Magic Flute* possessed moments of compelling truth, there unquestionably arose, among its wealth of "melodious jewels," the need for climax, and climax was what it admittedly lacked (*Review and Gazette,* November 26, 1859, p. 371).

In the opinion of the *Albion* critic (December 3, 1859, p. 583), although the music expressed none of the "imbecile stupidity" of the libretto, and although it was "thoroughly beautiful," it lacked variety: "The character is forever the same, and, as we have said, not dramatic. We have become so accustomed to the demonstrative school that three or four hours of Mozart's introspective musings are decidedly wearisome. . . . Tradition raves about Mozart's instrumentation, and Dilettantism listens with mute but yawning jaws," he wrote. "It was very fine in its day, no doubt; so were the Fugues written by S. Bach [*sic*], but the world jogs on and vocal music only can live. Purcell's Ecclesiastical [sung] pieces are as fresh now as on the day they were written; his instrumental pieces are forgotten. So it is with Mozart; his melodies will live forever, but his dramatic and instrumental music is already dead."

An unidentified critic, quoted in *Dwight's* (December 31, 1859, p. 319), found *The Magic Flute* to be "soporiferous in its tendencies. It may be classical, and all that, but it is dull. It could not well be otherwise with such a plot. Such a rigmarole of absurdity is without a parallel. The music, to interpret such puerile, silly thought, ought not to be grand or beautiful. The opera does, indeed, abound in melodies and admits of occasional vocal displays which cannot but astonish an audience, but it can never be popular, and does not deserve to be."

And *Trovator,* who in *Dwight's* (December 3, 1859, p. 285), preposterously referred to *The Magic Flute* as a work that "a few *Lager-Bier* Dutchmen got delighted with," gleefully translated a "piquant criticism" by Régis de Trobriand in the *Courrier des États Unis.* Likening Mozart's score to "the peruke or wig or head-dress of my grandmother," de Trobriand elaborated: "The 'Magic Flute' is in music merely my grandmother's peruke. It has made ever so many conquests in days gone by . . . but its day is over; now it is only a quaint bit of antiquity, cold and sleepy, that we can only regard as a curiosity."[167]

---

[166] "To the modern opera-goers . . . the music sounds tame, and lacks the excitement found in the works of Verdi and his predecessors," wrote Watson (*Leslie's,* December 3, 1859, p. 3).

[167] Echoing de Trobriand, up-to-the-minute *Trovator* wrote in the *Evening Post* (November 22, 1859) that only in a "powdered wig, knee breeches, and a queue" could one enjoy Mozart's "old-fashioned and passionless" music: "In this costume only can one fully appreciate the disconnected

To which an infuriated Hagen thundered in reply: How dared "a dwarf, a nothing of the Trovator stamp, attempt to throw his spite upon Mozart, or . . . an ignorant Frenchman like Monsieur de Trobriand, who knows just as much about music as the very wig which he introduces in his criticism . . . sneer at any of the works of the great master" (*Review and Gazette,* December 10, 1859, pp. 385–86).

After a continuing exchange of insults and a disclaimer from the Germanophilic Dwight, who denied sharing the opinions of his Germanophobic correspondent *Trovator,* the feud eventually dissipated.

In his preoccupation with *The Magic Flute,* Strong seems to have been oblivious of the delirium that seized New York upon the opera debut on Thanksgiving Evening, November 24 (an off night), of little Adelina Patti,[168] now a grown-up young lady of sixteen. Not that her ultimate arrival on the opera stage had ever been in doubt. As the youngest and most phenomenally gifted member of an inordinately gifted family of eight opera singers—a veritable "nest of songbirds . . . she was born in music and [had] been steeped in music all her life," wrote *Trovator* (*Dwight's,* December 3, 1859, p. 284). "When a child, when most children's vocal abilities are limited to 'Patty cake, patty cake, baker's man,' and similar tuneful effusions, this Patti was warbling the melodies of Bellini and Donizetti, and putting her doll to sleep with opera cavatinas."[169] It had been merely a matter of time before she would claim her inevitable place in opera.[170] Nor was her debut at this time a complete surprise: it had been announced months before, upon the formation of the current Strakosch/Ullman partnership. It was only the prodigious magnitude of her initial triumph that created surprise, indeed, astonishment.

Since returning the year before from her concert tour of the Caribbean Islands with Gottschalk,[171] little Patti, according to *Trovator* (*Dwight's,* June 11, 1859, p. 87),

---

portions of the drama, the long recitatives with the piano-forte accompaniment, the elaborate fugue movements and quiet airs that formed, eighty years ago, the delight of the Vienna public." As for the solo and ensemble music, the public taste had "so materially changed since Mozart wrote that no one will ever expect *The Magic Flute* to become a popular opera again."

[168] The Patti excitement overshadowed the performance of the recently returned Madame Anna Bishop,♪♫ after seven eventful, globe-spanning years, at a special Thanksgiving Gala Matinée that very afternoon. Following a performance of *Lucrezia Borgia* with Albertini and Beaucardé—she gave, as of old, two of her "celebrated" *scena*s in costume—from *Norma (Casta diva)* and *Tancredi (Di tanti palpiti).* (The resumption of Madame Bishop's local career is discussed in the following OBBLIGATO.)

[169] Maretzek amusingly remembers a spanking administered to the tiny Patti when, at a rehearsal of *Norma* in Boston in the '40s, as one of Norma's children, she had insisted on singing along with her mother, Caterina Barili-Patti, the Norma, and her sister Amalia, the Adalgisa, both of whose roles she knew (*Sharps and Flats,* p. 42).

[170] On inquiring of Patti what she thought of her impending opera debut, wrote *Trovator* (*Dwight's,* December 3, 1859, p. 285): "She shrugged her shoulders and remarked that it made little difference. She knew it must come some time. . . . She did not dread it, but on the contrary anticipated the event with joy."

[171] Where she had enjoyed triumphs everywhere she went: "In Havana," wrote Watson, in one of the biographies of Patti that now flooded the press, "she sang, in costume, the duet in the 'Barber of Seville' with her brother [Ettore?] Barili. The enthusiastic Havanese made such a row in recalling her that she ran away frightened and could not be persuaded to go on the stage again. Throughout the [West] Indies she divided the honors with Gottschalk, and at Porto Rico had an offer of marriage (she was then fourteen) from the richest proprietor of the place" (*Leslie's,* January 7, 1859, p. 94).

Adelina Patti was hailed at the age of eight in the newspaper advertisement of her concert. By 1859 she was sixteen—and still going strong. Her sisters were also successful in their concerts: a talented family indeed.

Girvice Archer, Jr.

The First Appearance of the Greatest Musical Wonder of the present age, La Petite Signorina

ADELINE PATTI,

This gifted child, only 8 years of age, whose extraordinary Vocal powers and brilliant execution, have been themes of wonder and delight to all who have heard her, will appear to-morrow Wednesday Evening, May 12th, on which occasion she will sing the

Celebrated Echo Song, exactly as sung by **Mlle. Jenny Lind**, with other brilliant **Morceaux.**

PRICES OF ADMISSION

Dress Circle ....50 Cents
Parquet.. 25 Cents
Family Circle..One Shilling
Orchestra Seats...75 Cents
Private Boxes ....$3 and $5

had been "pursuing her studies in private, and now with a voice of great power for one so young, and with an excellent execution, [she was] anxiously awaiting her first appearance on the operatic stage. Her friends confidently expect," wrote *Trovator,* "that she will become a really great operatic artist; and she comes of such a musical family, has had so many advantages, and possesses so much innate musical talent that there is no reason to suppose that these anticipations will be disappointed."

Because of the series of disasters that had befallen the Academy, Patti's anticipated opera debut had been put off. As the *Herald* observed (November 26, 1859), referring to the Speranza/Crescimano debacle: "Strakosch had been considerably snubbed for his memorable Italian campaign, so there was very little said about Patti." The decision to present her in *Lucia di Lammermoor* was obviously a last-gasp effort on the part of the two impresarios to save the sinking Academy, although the *Herald* mischievously suggested that perhaps the importation of the inferior Italian singers had been "a managerial dodge of Christopher Columbus Strakosch and Napoleon Bonaparte Ullman to bring out some poor and cheap singers from Europe in order to give little Patti a better chance, and show our people—what they ought to know by this time —that we have no real occasion to go abroad for our singing birds." But whether it had been cleverness or desperation, the fact remained, exulted the *Herald,* that "this little girl, with the magic of her voice, dispels the clouds which obscured the operatic horizon, and the Opera is saved."[172]

Just prior to her debut, Patti appeared at two co-called "try-out rehearsals" of *Lucia*[173] at the Academy for invited audiences of musicians and critics. After the first, the *Musical World* (November 12, 1859, p. 5) predicted that she would cause "a perfect *furore*"—and besides, "she is so young and pretty, and [with Piccolomini gone] New York is really in need of a pet at present."

Watson, who heard the second "invitation rehearsal," more responsibly wrote in *Leslie's* (December 3, 1859, p. 3): "She has a delicious voice, good throughout, of a high register, and flexible to a marvelous degree; her education has been purely Italian,[174] though we have heard her sing English ballads with much sentiment and charming accent, and her pronunciation is soft and liquid. She throws much pathos and expression into the role of Lucia—more than we could have expected from one so young; but to one of her genius, nature makes many early revelations, and the mysteries of art are familiar by intuition."

A "genius of the first order declared itself," corroborated the *Albion* critic (December 3, 1859, p. 583) after her sensational opera debut, and "everyone felt the joy that genius alone can bestow." Not since Malibran in 1825–1827♪♫ had the city experienced such elation. Nor was there a dissenting voice: the critics outdid themselves in their raptures over Patti's gloriously fresh and pure voice, her faultless intonation, her breathtaking vocal virtuosity, her youth, her beauty, her grace, her unaffected capacity for lighting up a stage.

Her triumph was regarded as a triumph for America: Adeline (*sic*) Patti—brought up in New York (albeit amid polyglot opera folk) was proudly proclaimed to be an

---

[172] "And all this has been done by a girl just out of primers and pantalettes!" beamed the *Herald.*

[173] Doubtless with Brignoli and Ferri, the Edgardo and Ashton of her subsequent debut.

[174] Her music education, that is. Patti was fluent in English, French, and Italian, and had a more than nodding acquaintance with Spanish and German.

American girl. "Managers here make a great mistake when they fail to afford every opportunity to American aspirants in whatever form, because they suppose the public will swear by foreign names," preached William Henry Fry (*Tribune,* November 25, 1859).[175] "The name of Beethoven did not save *Fidelio* from being a bore to the public here," he pointed out, happily mounting his hobbyhorse. "*The Magic Flute* will not have a great run, even with the name of Mozart, chiefly because the acting drama is repulsive nonsense and dreary twaddle. So, too, the last batch of raw singers brought across the Mediterranean and the Atlantic, with puffs premonitory, puffs contiguous, and puffs postcedent. But Miss Adeline Patti, though an American without a transatlantic puff,[176] though a child brought up in the midst of us, has a positive, unqualified, rich success—because she merited it. The applause from a good audience was immense," wrote Fry. "Calls before the curtain and bouquets were the order of the night."[177]

Patti of course appeared at the Gala Matinée on Saturday, November 26, sweetening the final performance (the fourth in a week) of *The Magic Flute* with the third act of *Lucia*.[178] On the following Tuesday, November 29 (again an extra night), she repeated *Lucia*,[179] and on Thursday, December 1, another extra night, she surpassed her earlier triumphs—if that were posssible—with her breathtaking Amina in *La sonnambula.*

"It is clear that we have now one of those rare singers who appears at long intervals on the musical horizon, to revive not only the hopes of the managers but the enthusiasm of the public," rejoiced Seymour (*Times,* November 30, 1859). "Miss Adelina Patti, although she has appeared but three times before the operatic public, has taken her place among the first of the *prime donne.* Her execution is unbroken and faultless; her intonation absolute. . . . Indeed, the performance in every aspect was one of the very best we have ever seen in this City. Miss Patti's triumph may be regarded as complete in every respect."

Exceeding even her marvelous Lucia: "The audacity with which she attacked the most involved and rapid congeries of notes which the composer has so happily wrought to express the gush of the maiden's happiness . . . astonished and delighted her audience. The applause was overwhelming," wrote Fry (*Tribune,* December 3, 1859). If she did not express the utmost in hopeless, "passionate, heaven-forsaken . . . human love," as had the incomparable Mrs. Mary Ann Paton Wood[3] in the role in 1835, she nonetheless gave a supremely graceful, tender, and, at the end, dazzling, performance of the closing Andante and Cabaletta, the *Ah! non giunge.*[180] Little Patti was a "veritable prima donna," wrote Fry.

[175] Not that "Patti" was a noticeably native-sounding name.

[176] Indeed, for a wonder, Patti appeared unheralded by Ullmanian puff in any form.

[177] "The horticultural business was more extensive than usual," reported the *Herald* (November 25, 1859). And Watson, in *Leslie's* (December 3, 1859, p. 3): "The stage was literally covered with beautiful and costly flowers; so heavy was the floral shower that the sweet Adelina could not carry off a third, but with the assistance of two or three persons the stage was at length cleared and the tributes of admiration conveyed to the dressing room of the young prima donna."

[178] As before, she was supported by Brignoli (Edgardo) and Ferri (Ashton).

[179] *The Sicilian Vespers* had been performed on November 28.

[180] "In the celebrated *Ah! non giunge* she created the greatest sensation by her astonishing execution of high passages and the neatness of her vocal runs," wrote the *Evening Post* (December 2, 1859).

To R. Storrs Willis she recalled the great Bosio, whose recent untimely death in St. Petersburg was mourned throughout the international opera community.[181] Patti's upper tones possessed "a velvet quality which rendered them more pleasing than any soprano" Willis could remember. "She does not make the slighest exertion in singing them," he added, "but scatters her staccato notes about, with a toss of her little head, like a child at play." He hoped that she would be retired from active singing when her present engagement was completed and for a period devote herself to study, as she was still "too young, and her physique too delicate, for her to remain on the stage actively engaged in singing at present" (*Musical World,* December 10, 1859, p. 2). (Little did Willis reck of what indestructible stuff little Patti was made.)

Strong continued to be impervious to the great Patti excitement.

November 30. . . . Last night with Ellie at Mrs. Gibbs's, where Mrs. d'Oremieulx and Mrs. Wolcott Gibbs did *two* Philharmonic concerts with four hands on the piano. But during the slow movement of the "Jupiter" Symphony I was assaulted by unconquerable sneezings, and I sternutated an accompaniment—in no particular time—to that composition and to the "Eroica." Admirable pianists are these two ladies. I was catching a cold then and there, and caught it as one catches a Tartar.

. . . [William Stanley] Hazeltine and Jem Ruggles dined here and squired Ellie to the opera. I had no appetite for *Les Huguenots*.[182]

December 1. . . . This evening Ellie read music for me.

December 2. . . . [stricken with influenza] Noticed this morning as I passed a hand-organ man, who was serenely and implacably grinding out *Casta diva,* that the scrannel-pipes of his Engine of Torture were inaudible above A (I think)—absolutely nonexistent. Which was not only a philosophical observation but a proof that influenza, like any other misfortune, brings its compensating good.

. . . Rather wanted to hear the *Huguenots* tonight,[183] but I could not properly make myself a nuisance to the whole house by snorting and coughing an extemporized fantasia during the Opera, so I stayed at home. Jem dined here and went with Ellie.

On December 3, Patti was heard for the "positively last" time this season at a Patti Matinée, consisting exclusively of *La sonnambula.* As unnecessary added bait, tickets to this event were awarded gratis to holders of reserved seats for the previous evening's performance of *The Huguenots.* The company then took off for Philadelphia, where the ensuing Patti frenzy rivaled—if it did not exceed—the one in New York.

Upon their departure, Albertini and Beaucardé, who had been dropped from the company, announced a brief independent season of cheap opera at fifty cents a ticket,[184] to open at Niblo's Theatre on December 12. With Beaucardé as co-star and director, the cast included—besides Albertini—the contralto Martini d'Ormy, recently

[181] Indeed, it was the critical consensus that Patti was destined to fill the gap left by Bosio's death.

[182] Revived for two performances, on November 30 and December 2, with Gazzaniga, Colson, Amalia Strakosch, Stigelli, Junca (no rival to Formes as Marcel), Amodio, and Weinlich; the *Liederkranz* Society volunteered their services.

[183] With Mesdames Gazzaniga, Colson, and Strakosch and Messrs. Stigelli, Junca, Amodio, and Weinlich.

[184] "Cheap both in price and quality," wrote the *Albion* critic (December 10, 1859, p. 59). But he soon changed his mind.

returned from Europe, the tenor Alessandro Maccaferri, and the baritone Achille Ardavani; Anschütz was the conductor and Noll the leader. During their stay at Niblo's they gave performances of *Lucrezia Borgia, Il trovatore, La traviata,* and, at a concluding matinée on December 17, acts from all these works, and additionally an act of *La favorita* and a trio from *I Lombardi.*

Although not the greatest singers, wrote the *Albion* critic (December 10, 1859, p. 59), Albertini and Beaucardé were good artists, as were the others; they appeared to greater advantage in Niblo's smaller surroundings than at the Academy;[185] and their *Lucrezia Borgia* was as good a performance of that work as the writer could remember. Indeed, some suggested that a second-string opera company of this ilk would be a desirable addition to the New York entertainment scene, while others argued that the sophisticated metropolitan public was unlikely to be satisfied with mediocre performances. "In this city, the opera public is divided into two distinct classes," wrote the *Musical World* (December 21, 1859, pp. 2–3). "The one goes to hear everthing and then judges for itself; the other waits to hear if the first one was pleased and acts accordingly. The first public went to the opera at Niblo's; the second has not yet made its appearance there."

Instead, like Strong, people were flocking to the French Theatre to hear the newest rage, Sam Cowell (1820–1864), the "Musical Comedian."[186]

December 9. . . . Have been attending, with Ellie amd Jem and Murray Hoffman (who dined here) one of Sam Cowell's "Drawing Room Concerts" (so-called) that are given on the off nights of the French Theatre. "Lord Lovell," "The Cork Leg," and other specimens of genuine British song[187]—the muse of the cider-cellar and pothouse "Free and Easies." It was intolerably funny.[188] In costume. Not elegant, but decidedly low, comedy. Buffoonery, in fact. I'm weak enough to enjoy buffoonery when there is any true comic *vis* in it, and when it's free from essential coarseness and hints of dirt. This was excellent of its kind and thoroughly enjoyed by a full house. As an actor of broad comedy, this man rivals Burton.

December 14. . . . Last evening Mrs. Gibbs and Mrs. d'Oremieulx here (with their respective spouses) reading four-handed music for piano and organ: choruses from *Messiah* and *Israel in Egypt* and the memorable Finale of the *Christus am Ölberge (Mount of Olives)* and most of Beethoven's D-Symphony [the Ninth?].

December 19. . . . Ellie read music for me awhile tonight.

---

[185] "Notwithstanding the scenic paucity and the inefficiency of the chorus, the efforts of the principal singers were sufficient to awaken a hearty enthusiasm," wrote the *Evening Post* (December 14, 1859).

[186] The worthy son of the beloved English comedian Joe Cowell (1792–1874), Sam Cowell, who had been a child actor in the United States, had recently returned from England and since November 30 had been attracting crowds with his hilarious "musico-comico-dramatico-elegantissimo" character impersonations, given three nights a week at the French Theatre, currently under the management of H. L. Bateman, Cowell's theatrically illustrious uncle.

[187] Among them, "The Ratcatcher's Daughter," "The Bad Macbeth," "Bacon and Greens," and "Richard the Third," advertised as being "a long way from Shakespeare."

[188] "To see this man put his mouth away up toward his forehead, and then lower it to his chest, by some mysterious means, while he melodizes 'There was a Tall Young Oysterman,' or 'Lord Lovell, he stood at the Garden Gate,' is something to be remembered for a lifetime," wrote the *Dispatch* (January 12, 1861).

December 21. . . . . Attended one of Mr. Sam Cowell's "concerts" at the French theatre.[189] His "Lord Lovell" is almost *too* poignantly funny for endurance.

December 23. . . . went to Cowell's again. He is wonderfully clever and funny, but this is my third attendance and will suffice for the present. The house was full and there were people there we knew. People have begun to find him out, and he will become popular.[190] Though he deals in the very lowest comedy, there is not even a whisper or look of aught uncleanly in his performance, wherein he has the advantage of our theatrical people generally. For although the stage has greatly improved in that particular, one seldom hears a farce or comedy in which there is not some double entrendre or questionable joke that would not be tolerated in the presence of ladies elsewhere.

<center>~~~</center>

Although it had been announced that, upon the completion of their three-week season in Philadelphia, Ullman's company would proceed directly to Boston, it was found possible, purportedly to accomodate those who had been unable to obtain seats for Patti's performances in New York, to present two—positively only two—Patti evenings at the Academy on December 21 and 22. Assisted by Brignoli, Amodio, and Weinlich, she would be heard in *Lucia* and *La sonnambula.*

As the disenchanted *Albion* critic observed (December 31, 1859, p. 630): "When Mr. Ullman found it necessary to publish a 'card' for the purpose of assuring an incredulous public that only two performances could possibly take place at the Academy during the past week—when the veracious Mr. Ullman did this—everyone knew that some additional performances were in contemplation. This is called 'managing the public,' and for which the 'little Napoleon' of Fourteenth Street enjoys so enviable a reputation. Ordinary people who pay their dollars at the doors call it 'deceiving the public,' but 'managing' is undoubtedly the right word. One of these days we shall learn our duties, and need less of the fatherly, and very ungrammatical, management of that excessive and superfluous manager, Mr. Ullman."

And indeed, Ullman's "positively only two nights" were soon stretched to include four more nights of opera, somewhat clouded by the non-appearance of the basso and now war hero Augustino Susini,♪[191] who had been announced for three performances. "The cause of this is not illness, but vanity or obstinacy," angrily wrote Burkhardt (*Dispatch,* December 31, 1859). Not heard in the United States since 1855, "Susini was to appear as Silva in *Ernani* on Monday [December 26]. On that evening the house was

---

[189] To satisfy public demand, Cowell had also begun appearing on the alternate nights, at first at the old minstrel haven at 444 Broadway, then at the Palace Gardens. "He excels in character songs," wrote the *Albion* critic (December 17, 1859, p. 607) and in "that species of comicality which prevails in Covent Garden after the theatres are out. His facial displays are enormously funny; for a comic singer he sings well; and he makes up like a thorough artist. People who desire to laugh until they are afflicted with sharp pains in the side should go to Sam Cowell's, and they will not be disappointed."

[190] By now Cowell had taken over the French Theatre, appearing there six nights weekly. His assisting artists were the singer Mrs. Harriet Westervelt, James Hicks, an English concertist and conductor, and the highly acclaimed English pianist Sebastian Bach Mills.

[191] Susini had served as a major in the recent Italian War of Independence, receiving a decoration for valor from the King of Piedmont (*Evening Post,* August, 13, 1859).

Girvice Archer, Jr.

Augustino Susini carefully chose the vehicle in which he would make his debut, thereby disappointing those to whom he had made other commitments.

unavoidably closed.[192] On Tuesday he should have been the Leporello [with Patti portraying Zerlina for the first time in New York],[193] but the role suited him not to make his *debut* in (as he has been well known and has been heard here during the entire Grisi and Mario season, it would at best be only a secondary *debut*).[194] On the occasion of Patti's benefit [December 29],[195] Susini was announced as the Duke Alfonso in the

[192] Those who went to the Academy that night were greeted by a transparency at the Irving Place entrance "bearing the unsatisfactory inscription: 'No opera tonight'" (*Evening Post,* December 27, 1859).

[193] Hagen did not share in the general euphoria over Patti's Zerlina, nor, for that matter, over Patti. He did grant, however, that her Zerlina was an improvement over her previous efforts, or would have been if only she hadn't emulated her colleagues in wantonly altering Mozart's score, the worst offender being Gazzaniga, who was the "poorest Donna Anna" Hagen had seen for some time (*Musical Review and Gazette,* January 7, 1860, p. 1).

[194] A fine performance of *I vespri siciliani,* with Gazzaniga and the former cast, was given on December 28.

[195] A grandiose affair employing the entire company performing *La sonnambula,* with the young beneficiary as Amina, the first act of *La traviata,* with Colson and Stigelli, and the second act of *Lucrezia Borgia,* with Amodio replacing the unwilling Susini.

second act of *Lucrezia Borgia,* but again he would not make his *debut* in only one act. . . . Perhaps New York may hereafter be able to do without him."[196]

Aside from Patti's radiance, the post-season season had not been a glowing success:[197] "The week between the two great New York holidays is rather better for the Broadway bazaars than for the Opera and the theatres," explained the *Herald* (December 29, 1859). "Everybody is so busy buying bon-bons, and dry goods, and *bijouterie,* and preparing for the grand New Year's carnival that they have no time to think of anything else." Then too, it was the beginning of the ball season, "and while Terpsichore reigns, the rest of the glorious Nine may as well retire into obscurity. As far as the Opera is concerned," continued the *Herald,* "were it not for the attraction of Miss Patti, a fresh prima donna who has taken hold of the popular heart in the most surprising and wonderful way, and the aid of a grand artist like Madame Gazzaniga, the Academy during the week would be quite deserted."

Accordingly, the managers decided to concentrate upon one grand night, a benefit to the artist "who had saved their season as Marshal Macdonald saved the decisive Battle of Wagram." Following this massive event, and dispensing with the usual Gala Matinée, on December 30, the company left for opera-loving Boston, where—needless to say—little Patti conquered all hearts.

In New York, Strong devoted himself to the simpler joys of the Christmas season.

December 25. . . . Yesterday afternoon at three, attended the Children's Festival at Trinity Church, which was crowded. Choral service: carol by the children with accompaniment of the organ and of the chimes in the steeple was very pretty.

. . . It is curious that the musical conceptions of that hot-tempered, old bewigged Dutchman—the crotchets and quavers of the German organist Mynheer Handel, written down a century ago—should so illustrate and intensify the meaning of those glorious words of Holy Writ, and make them stand out from all their context as if printed by Divine Ordinance in capitals or red letters. No commentator so developed their significance. His "notes" elucidate them far better than Mant and D'Oyly.[198]

December 28. . . . Went with Ellie to Mrs. [David Colden] Murray's in the evening. Small musical party—rather dismal. The chief musician, [S. B.] Mills, the pianist, disappointed our hostess and stayed away,[199] which was very nice for him, but bad for the other people.

---

[196] In fact, once Susini began to appear, he was again recognized as an artist of the highest worth.

[197] According to Burkhardt, it was literally a dim interlude, "the house being kept in a state of semi-darkness, whilst the curtain was up and down. Was there anything the matter with the gas? Or was it merely a question of economy?" Surely the reduction of the orchestra and chorus was dictated by economy, and, added Burkhardt, an economy destructive to the presentations, especially the *Don Giovanni (Dispatch,* December 31, 1859).

[198] Richard Mant (1776–1848) and George D'Oyly (1778–1846), whose popular annotated Bible was first published in 1814.

[199] Mills was apparently detained at the French Theatre, where he was now appearing nightly with Cowell.

OBBLIGATO: 1859

The narrow pathway of art is so choked with impediments that it is not easy, as we know, for the best men to make their way on it. . . . It is a little too bad that a composer who can write successful operas and symphonies should have to place himself in the hands of a committee or a society in order to reap some of the rewards of his information and genius.

New-York Times
March 9, 1859

"To speak of the stated soirées of the Philharmonic Society without a mild complaining would be alike unjust to the Board of Directors, the Ladies patronesses, the gentlemen amateurs, and the private and immutable feelings of the critic," mischievously wrote the *Albion* critic (April 9, 1859, p. 175), following the fourth and penultimate concert of the Philharmonic's uncomfortably housed seventeenth season. He thereupon set about redressing this injustice by complaining (albeit not mildly) of the Philharmonic Board's internal politics and their ill-considered choice of Niblo's Theatre for their 1858–59 concerts. "There never was before, and probably never will be again, such a cozy little concern with so many unquestionable grievances wrapt up in it as this same Philharmonic Society," he wrote. "No one pretends that the [cramped] accommodations [and inaccessible downtown location] of Mr. Niblo's are adequate to the wants of the Society."

Their previous move to the Academy of Music had been a step in the right direction, but (referring the mighty contretemps of April 24, 1858) "small commercial higglings ensued between the lessee of the Fourteenth Street establishment and the Treasurer of the Society; the latter spoke threateningly of a new Music Hall . . . and Mr. Ullman said 'drat' the new Music Hall; whereupon the Society came indignantly downtown again."

Not only was Niblo's Theatre inconveniently located and an uncomfortably tight fit,[1] but it had recently housed such inappropriate attractions as James M. Nixon's circus troupe, and Van Amburgh's Menagerie. Consequently, on Philharmonic nights

---

[1] "A disagreeable, fat old gentleman persevered in poking us in the back with his knees all the evening, and rapped us on the head with his hat, and . . . *flapped* his coat appendages against our ears when he stood up," complained the *Musical World* (April 2, 1859, pp. 210–11).

Leslie's, Dartmouth College Library

*Niblo's was considered too cramped and inaccessible to be used for concerts,
but it seemed adequate for private parties such as this Yacht Club Ball.*

"whiffs of powerful perfume—which, if not actually from Araby the blest, emanate at
least from the quadrupeds of that favoured clime—[regaling] the nostrils of amateurs
and artistes with odious impartiality." Even worse was the intolerable "chatting mania"
that more mercilessly than ever possessed the Philharmonic subscribership, from the
"densely feminated parquette to the dome."

Coping with these hazards, on January 8, the Philharmonic, at their second concert of the season, presented as soloists Madame Graever-Johnson, who played Mendelssohn's Second Piano Concerto, op. 40 (according to Hagen, efficiently in the first
two movements, but, being a lady, greatly fatigued in the third),[2] and Bruno Wollenhaupt,♪ the gifted younger brother of the pianist/composer Hugo Wollenhaupt,♪♫ who
performed Mendelssohn's Violin Concerto with great feeling and bravura. Bergmann,
this season's conductor, gave Beethoven's Seventh Symphony, Weber's Overture to *The
Ruler of the Spirits,* op. 27 (1811), and a first local performance of Schubert's Overture
to his opera *Fierabras,* op. 76 (1823)—the last, in Hagen's judgment, "comparatively a
small work," not distinguished by "the depth and originality of its ideas." Additionally,
with the *Arion* and *Teutonia* Societies, Bergmann presented two works that he had pre-

[2] R. Storrs Willis agreed: "There is much of Mendelssohn that needs the delicate *finesse* of a
woman's mind and hand"; but the last movement of the concerto contains "some passages too obviously masculine and awkward for a lady player" (*Musical World,* January 15, 1859, p. 87).

viously given on December 26, 1858, at the second concert of his current Sunday night series at the City Assembly Rooms: the Prisoners' Chorus from *Fidelio* and a recitative and chorus from Wagner's *Rienzi,* the latter an early composition, defensively explained Hagen (*Review and Gazette,* January 22, 1859, p. 19), written long before Wagner had conceived of "the Music of the Future."

At the following Philharmonic concert, on February 12, a Miss Marie Elina Couran, a novice mezzo-soprano, sang an aria from *La favorita* and a sacred song "Consider the Lilies," by one Topliffe. She "ought not to have sung there," snapped Hagen, who blamed the Philharmonic directors for misplaced indulgence in admitting such inappropriate performers to their programs (*Review and Gazette,* February 19, 1859, p. 50).[3]

But Fry, in the *Tribune* (February 14, 1859), was disposed to be tolerant. Although he conceded that "more skill at times in connecting the registers" might have been desirable, it was nonetheless wonderful that a debutante "under the exorbitant trial of appearing before such a crowd for the first time in New York could do so well." (Miss Couran, of course, was an American.)

According to the Society's usage of presenting dual soloists, young William Saar was also heard on this occasion, playing the second and third movements of Chopin's Piano Concerto in E minor. Fry, a concerto-hater—although he credited Saar with rapidity and brilliance—as usual deprecated the piano as an instrument unfit for public performance, particularly when combined with an orchestra: "A piano player loses his electricity in the attempt to fill Niblo's Theatre," he wrote, "and the contrast of the short, unsustained notes of that instrument, heard in connection, or even in mere sequence, with the orchestra is adverse to the success of such virtuosism [*sic*] as Mr. Saar possesses."

Hagen flatly stated that Saar—lacking delicacy of touch and conception—should have been "the very last to perform anything by Chopin." This applied as well to Saar's performance of the Chopin-like Nocturne in E-flat by John Field, which, with Anton Rubinstein's brilliant Étude, op. 23, in C, comprised his solo group.

At this concert Bergmann conducted two highly contrasting symphonies: Haydn's No. 2 (*sic*) in D major and Schumann's No. 4 in D minor, op. 120, the latter a controversial work that Bergmann had introduced at his Sunday concerts in 1856 and had recently repeated on December 26, 1858, at the second concert of his current Sunday series;[4] the program concluded with Ferdinand Ries's Festival Overture and *Marche triomphale,* op. 172.

This increasingly rare opportunity to hear Haydn, surprisingly wrote Seymour (*Times,* February 15, 1859), was doubly welcome, because "latterly, there has been a little too much of the modern school noticeable in the programmes; this return to a purer and more quickly appreciable one was timely." In Haydn's day, explained Seymour, a baffled traditionalist: "pure melody and profound harmony were the essentials

---

[3] Indeed, at the following Board of Directors' meeting (March 12) it was resolved in the future to engage only the best singers, paying as high a fee as $100, if necessary (Philharmonic Archives).

[4] A series that to a great extent served Bergmann as a kind of trial laboratory for works he would later present at the Philharmonic. Then, too, his repetitions of these works at the Philharmonic allowed music lovers whose religious convictions forbade them to listen to concerts on the Sabbath to hear the important new music that was being unveiled on those proscribed occasions.

of good composition; in their place we now have dislocated rhythms and hideous dissonances. Like a dark background to Haydn's bright picture was Schumann's Symphony in D minor—a work of startling boldness, frantic color, and hazardous effect, doubtless good as an exhibition of orchestral manipulation, but wearisome from its excessive effect."

Scarcely more receptive to the new, R. Storrs Willis (*Musical World,* February 19, 1859, p. illegible) asserted that although Schumann was undoubtedly a complete master of contrapuntal and orchestral effects—of all the devices of modulations, transitions, harmonic imitations, knowledge of instrumentation; of consummate ability in the employment of dynamic means and endless other learned attributes—he "either despised melody, or was ignorant of it."

But Hagen, an impassioned apologist for contemporary German music—particularly for Schumann and for this symphony—wrote: "While Haydn's music shows the Symphony in its infancy, Schumann's represents it in its very last development." Haydn never got beyond his dictum that "'The whole art [of writing a symphony] consists in treating and pursuing a theme,' while the contents of Schumann's symphonies vary, just as the poetical subject varies. . . . Hear Haydn's symphony twice and the charm of its simplicity will weaken," wrote Hagen. "Hear Schumann's work ten times, and your interest will increase with each performance. If Schumann had written nothing but this symphony, he would rank among the very first among his brethren of art" (*Review and Gazette,* February 19, 1860, p. 50).

Not only was Schumann again heard at the following Philharmonic concert—on March 26, when his Piano Concerto in A minor, op. 54, was played by the important new pianist Sebastian Bach Mills[5]—but, rarity of rarities, the American composer, George Frederick Bristow, recipient of a recent testimonial concert by the Philharmonic and Harmonic Societies (see below), received the first performance of his Symphony in F-sharp minor, op. 26.

The Schumann Concerto, although new to the Philharmonic audience, had been performed for the first time in the United States by Mills at his American debut a month earlier, on February 20, at the sixth of Bergmann's Sunday night concerts. Hagen, present on that occasion, was amazed that the work had until then been "neglected by our pianists." Even for Schumann, he wrote in the *Review and Gazette* (March 5, 1859, p, 67), it possessed rare "freshness, spontaneity of feeling and invention, fluency, and originality of ideas," in the writing not only for the solo instrument but also for the orchestra, with which it continuously intermingled.

Mills, a young Englishman bearing optimal credentials—study with the English composer/pianist Cipriani Potter (1792–1871) in England and with Moscheles, Plaidy, Rietz, and Hauptmann at the Leipzig Conservatory—had instantly been recognized, even by Hagen, as a pianist of superlative gifts. "Surer, neater, and more correct playing we have not heard in a long time," he wrote. But, being Hagen, he recalled pianists with better tone and more delicacy and elasticity. And although Mills's execution with both hands was "solid and immense," he lacked the spontaneity of feeling that resulted from the "inspiration of the moment." And although he had "yet to learn the picturing

---

[5] The Philharmonic Board of Directors voted to pay Mills $50 for this performance, that is, "if his circumstances should require it" (Philharmonic Archives).

of that which he performs" (whatever that meant), and although he lacked gradation and colors—and although, and although, and although—it nonetheless had to be admitted that Mills played like a musician and deserved a hearty welcome from his American colleagues.[6]

Treating Mills's Philharmonic appearance as his local debut, Seymour (*Times,* March 28, 1859) unreservedly hailed the young pianist as, "in almost every respect, the most remarkable player we have had in this country." Mills splendidly represented the Liszt school, wrote Seymour, a school that regarded "an orchestral effect as the legitimate effect of all piano emulation. Massive combinations, demanding manual strength and digital dexterity; huge, fantastic designs, great certainty, and flexibility of touch—these are some of the characteristics of the Liszt school," he wrote. Mills possessed all these attributes and more: "We have never heard a more certain player," wrote Seymour; in addition to his execution, which was "immense and his technique so good that even in the most brilliant passages the grandeur of his tone [was] unimpaired," he was capable of delivering the "melody of a composition with such round, yet delicate, force," and (waxing as abstruse as Hagen) of imparting to his phrasing "such lustrous complexions and flushings" as had rarely, if ever, been equaled.

It was Mills's extraordinary performance of Schumann's "excessively difficult concerto," rather than the work itself, that had captured his audience, wrote Seymour, who found it to be a composition "full of recondite suggestions that have to be acted on by the player and explained in impromptu musical elocutions. Clever as it is," concluded Seymour, "it does not please." It was only in his solo, Liszt's paraphrase on Mendelssohn's *Midsummer Night's Dream* music—the "Wedding March" and "Dance of the Elves" (1849–50) (Searle 410)—that "all the strong points of Mr. Mills's mechanism became thoroughly apparent. There are few piano pieces that demand so much orchestral color as this, or demand greater presence of mind in the performer.[7] Mr. Mills played it faultlessly, and in response to a unanimous demand for an encore played Chopin's Polonaise in E-flat minor [op. 26 (1834–35)]. A success more deserved we have never witnessed."

Less heatedly, R. Storrs Willis (also unaware or disregardful of the earlier performance) referred to Schumann's Concerto as a "lengthy and well elaborated piece" with a "pianoforte part more difficult than effective." It was a work "only to be appreciated by the cultivated amateur or musician, to others rather dry." Indeed, Mills's performance of it had been warmly applauded "by the gentlemen of the orchestra as well as the audience. . . . His success was very decided," wrote Willis, "and places him at once, in the estimation of the New York musical public (which was fairly represented on that occasion) among the best of the first-class pianists who have visited this country" (*Musical World,* April 2, 1859, pp. 210–11).

[6] The *Saturday Press*—after ungallantly noting the participation at Mills's debut of Madame Caradori "and several other Pompeian relics," and after disparaging the City Assembly Rooms as "the very worst rooms in which to give a concert on the face of the earth"—hailed Mills as nothing less than a genius (March 5, 1859).

[7] Mills had played this work at his previous appearance, causing Hagen spitefully to remark that "a little variety in the repertory of this young pianist would be welcome" (*Review and Gazette,* April 2, 1859, pp. 98–99). Little did Hagen know how true he spoke: Mills unfailingly played this same work at each and every one of his numerous performances for the remainder of that year.

As a matter of historical record, Sebastian Bach Mills, over a long and lustrous career, was one of the highest ranking, if least remembered, pianists of the American musical nineteenth century.

Of Bristow's symphony, Hagen playfully observed that the rather "desperate" motto introducing its first movement:

> And now 'tis doomed to know the worst
> And break at once—or yield to song,

led him to expect that in the following movement "something or somebody would either break or sing." It turned out, instead, to be merely a run-of-the-mill "stormy Allegro moderato." The second movement was a Mendelssohnian *Scherzo* introduced by a fluttery, four-line stanza, titled "The Butterfly."[8] The third movement, a nocturne, exposed Bristow at his weakest, revealing his poverty of invention when it came to "real ideas," wrote Hagen. Moreover, a harp glissando, occurring in the last movement, an *Allegro con fuoco,* was played—according to the Philharmonic's niggardly custom—on the piano, in this case by Henry C. Timm on a Steinway grand. "Why, in New York, the piano forte must always replace the harp, we do not know," complained Hagen. The symphony was, however, well received, he conceded, and Bristow was given a pat on the head for his "hard studies, which we feel confident will be crowned with ultimate and legitimate success."

Seymour, although he pronounced Bristow's symphony to be "a work of meritorious execution in a technical point of view, found it frequently to be weak and ill sustained. The writer of a symphony should have a musical intelligence superior to the temptation of popular dance themes," he sternly wrote. "Mr. Bristow frequently surrenders himself to these pleasant inspirations and mars, we think, the happiness and value of his work as a classical composition."[9] Patronizingly, Seymour added: "It cannot be denied, however, that the symphony is most agreeable in its effect on a mixed audience, and hence the reason of its selection by the Society. With more opportunities to have his work performed, there can hardly be a doubt that Mr. Bristow would do much better than he has done in this work."[10]

For the final Philharmonic concert of the season, on April 30, Bergmann conducted Beethoven's Symphony No. 4, in B-flat, Weber's Overture to *Euryanthe,* and Liszt's *Les Préludes* (after Lamartine) a work he (Bergmann) had introduced at his Sunday concert on February 6. An excuse was made for the non-appearance, due to indisposition, of a new singer Madame Amelia F. Inman;[11] she was replaced at the last minute by a German male vocal quartet, of whose personnel Hagen recognized Philip

---

[8] According to Willis, a charming movement, of which a repeat was demanded.

[9] A criticism similar to those received by Bristow's *Rip Van Winkle* in 1855.♪

[10] Also heard on this program were two overtures: Beethoven's in C to *Leonora* and Marschner's to *Der Vampyr.*

[11] Madame Inman, "of the London concerts," had been heard on April 6 at Niblo's Saloon, assisted by Madame Caradori, Madame Eugénie de Lussan,♪ Harrison Millard, Philip Mayer, one M. J. Loretz, Jr., a pianist, and Señor Jaime Nunó,♪ who accompanied. Following Madame Inman's failure to appear at the Philharmonic, the *Evening Post* (May 2, 1859) suggested that fewer artists would suffer from last-minute indispositions if the Philharmonic were willing to remunerate them for their services. But apparently her illness had been no subterfuge: on May 18 the *Post* reported the death of Madame Inman, at the age of twenty-two.

Mayer, Beutler, and Oehrlein, who sang unidentified music of the Fatherland;[12] and by four Philharmonic musicians—the brothers Schmitz, French hornists, and Lotze and Schullinger, versatile members of the viola section, who played Weber's Quartet for French horns, heard at an earlier Bergmann Sunday concert. With the orchestra, Richard Hoffman played Mendelssohn's *Serenade and Allegro giojoso,* op. 43 (1838); also a pair of solos: Litolff's *Spinnlied,* op. 51 ("very trashy," wrote Hagen) and Chopin's A-flat Polonaise, op. 53, encored (much to —t—'s disapproval) with Hoffman's own fantasy on themes from *Rigoletto.* "In finish and elegance we know of no superior to Mr. Hoffman," wrote the *Albion* critic (May 7, 1859, p. 223). "He is only excelled in power by Mr. Mills."

Hagen, in a descriptive essay on Liszt's Symphonic Poem *Les Préludes,* appearing in the *Review and Gazette* (February 19, 1859, p. 51) following its first performance at Bergmann's concert, reminded his readers that the work had long since become familiar through numerous local performances in its version for two pianos. Furthermore, he wrote, the term "Symphonic Poem," although new and originated by Liszt, in fact designated no new art form: it applied equally to any number of contemporary works by Berlioz, Schumann, and Wagner. Indeed, reproachfully added Hagen, Liszt's piece was "more Frenchy" than one would have expected after his sojourn of more than ten years in Weimar conducting the works of Beethoven, Schubert, Schumann, and Wagner. Yet, despite its "Frenchiness," Hagen approved of *Les Préludes,* finding it "a very pleasing, highly interesting, and effective composition"; it had received an enthusiastic public reception (high praise for a first performance of contemporary music).

Not so, maliciously claimed the *Albion* critic. Although Liszt was a prolific composer for orchestra, there was in fact so little demand for his music that no publisher would take him on without a sizable guarantee. Indeed, helpfully suggested the critic, since Liszt had already expended such great sums on the "mere printing of heavy Symphonies that no one will even look into, to recuperate his exchequer, he might find it convenient to listen to the persuasive tones of an Ullman or a Strakosch" and come to the lucrative United States as a pianist.

As for *Les Préludes:* "As an exposition of the resources of modern orchestration, it is full of interest," the critic admitted, "but regarded in any other light it is a bewildering and clashy jumble of fragmentary ideas. It is too pretentious to please the ear and too empty to satisfy the mind.[13] . . . Liszt," he continued, "in all he does is essentially vulgar; his piano compositions are only remarkable for pretending to be what they are not—orchestra pieces."

The Philharmonic, at least, deserved credit for their faultless performance of the work, but they deserved no credit for their stinginess in persistently substituting the piano for the harp: "Our abject Society did not feel itself warranted," sneered the critic, "in going to the expense of a harp . . . the piano being free and the player more so" (*Albion,* May 7, 1859, p. 223).

In August, during the summer recess, the Philharmonic Board of Directors met to make plans for their 1859–60 season. Because they could not (or would not) deal

---

[12] The members of the quartet were paid $25 for this performance (Philharmonic Archives).

[13] Willis, on the other hand, found the work "more intellectually significant than musically beautiful" (*Musical World,* May 7, 1859, p. 2).

with Ullman for their (inescapable) return to the Academy of Music, Scharfenberg and Timm were appointed to negotiate with a Mr. Kingsland, representing the Academy stockholders. Thus bypassing Ullman, the Philharmonic reached an agreement to return to the Academy, this time with their public rehearsals shifted to Wednesday afternoons (doubtless to circumvent conflicts with the Saturday Gala Opera Matinées).

Reinstated at the Academy, on November 19 the Philharmonic presented the first concert of their eighteenth season (the concert Strong had been too indisposed to attend) to a large but not crowded house. Bergmann conducted Schubert's Symphony in C,[14] Mendelssohn's *Zum Märchen von der schönen Melusine,* Wagner's Prelude (or "Introduction," as it was programed) to *Lohengrin,* and Beethoven's *Fidelio* Overture; Stigelli, an extraordinarily musical singer, beautifully performed *Il mio tesoro* from *Don Giovanni* and his own song *Die Thräne,* encored by his great hit "The Brightest Eyes"; and Arthur Napoleon played his Grand Caprice for piano on airs from *Martha,* an ill-considered choice for the Philharmonic, as everyone agreed.

Oddly, Hagen, in his report of this concert (*Review and Gazette,* November 26, 1859, pp. 371–72), shrugged off the *Lohengrin* Prelude with a few remarks on its extreme difficulty, "exhibiting some of the boldest traits of modern instrumentation we have met with." But —t—, in *Dwight's* (December 3, 1859, p. 284)—although he agreed with Hagen that the Prelude was too short to be performed as an independent excerpt—more eloquently described it as "a bit of rich instrumental coloring, rising gradually from the merest thread of tone to a full gorgeous phrase of chords, from whence it dwindles down again to whence it came."

Schubert's symphony, on the contrary, suffered from excessive length: "Schubert," wrote Seymour (*Times,* November 21, 1859), "was a man of suggestive ideas: a symphony could be made out of his songs; and another out of the accompaniments to them." But although the themes of this symphony were exquisite, the work—even without repeats—consumed more than an hour to play, and was, suspected Seymour, "something of a bore to the majority of the subscribers. . . . Schubert, in his instrumental works," asserted Seymour, "never knew where or when to end, and their beauty is in spite of this characteristic, not by reason of it." Wagner's fragment, by contrast, although it was a "remarkable instance of successful orchestral coloring, [albeit] coarse and vulgar, did not possess a single popular characteristic [or] a precise intention of any kind."

To enumerate the remainder of Bergmann's formidable orchestral achievements for the year: at the third of his Sunday evening "sacred" concerts, on January 9, he conducted the first American performance of Anton Rubinstein's "Ocean" Symphony, op. 42 (a work disappointing to Hagen); also Berlioz's *Carnaval romain* Overture and Weber's Overture to *Euryanthe;* Theodore Thomas again played Schubert's Tarantelle, again to great acclaim; the *Arion* and *Teutonia* societies sang Mendelssohn's "Hymn to Art" *(An die Künstler),* op. 68 (1840), and the four Philharmonic musicians played Weber's Quartet for French horns, like Thomas, earning an encore.

At his fourth Sunday concert (January 23) Bergmann conducted Mozart's "Jupi-

---

[14]Listed in the program as "Schubert's Symphony in C, No. 1," but apparently the C-major Symphony, No. 9, known as "the Great."

ter" Symphony, Cherubini's *Medea* Overture, and Gluck's Overture to *Iphigenia in Aulis;* William Saar played Mendelssohn's *Serenade* and *Allegro giojoso* for piano and orchestra (later played by Richard Hoffman with the Philharmonic) and as a solo an unspecified Hungarian Rhapsody by Liszt; Frederick Bergner played a Fantasia for cello by Auguste Franchomme (1808–1884) and an arrangement of the Nocturne from Mendelssohn's *Midsummer Night's Dream;* and the Philharmonic musicians—Noll, Matzka, Boehm, Schmitz, Eltz, Brannes, and Bartels—played the variation movement of Beethoven's Septet.

For his fifth program (February 6), Bergmann conducted Beethoven's infrequently heard First Symphony, the first local orchestral performance of Liszt's *Les Préludes* (discussed above), and Mendelssohn's Overture to *Athalie;* Anetta Caradori sang "On Mighty Pens," from Haydn's *The Creation,* and Schumann's song *Widmung* ("Dedication"), op. 25 (1840), and the young pianist Miss R. V. Lebrecht♩ admirably played Mendelssohn's Piano Concerto in G minor and a *Galop di bravura* for solo piano by Julius Schulhoff.

At his sixth and final Sunday night concert (February 20), as we know, Bergmann gave the premiere of Schumann's Piano Concerto with Mills, who, on that occasion also played his warhorse-to-be, Liszt's paraphrase of Mendelssohn's *Midsummer Night's Dream* music; Bergmann repeated *Les Préludes* and conducted Nicolai's Overture to *The Merry Wives of Windsor;* the Philharmonic cornetist/composer Louis Schreiber played his *Adagio and Rondo* and his transcription of the Romance from *Tannhäuser;* and the *Arion* and *Teutonia* societies sang choruses from Lortzing's *Zar und Zimmermann.*♩

Following this well-attended event came Bergmann's even better attended post-finale benefit on March 13,[15] when he repeated Schumann's inscrutable Fourth Symphony and performed Gade's *Ossian* Overture and a new Concert Overture by Edward Mollenhauer;[16] Mollenhauer played his Fantasie for Violin; S. B. Mills played the first movement of Beethoven's E-flat Piano Concerto[17] and an unidentified piece by Chopin; and the *Arion* and *Teutonia* societies sang the Pilgrims' Chorus from *Tannhäuser.*

In mid-April, before the close of the Philharmonic season, an ambitious new series of ten monthly concerts was announced by a new organization, the Metropolitan Music Society.[18] Scheduled to commence in May at the Academy of Music under the associate conductorship of George Bristow, Harvey Dodworth, and Maurice Strakosch (the current Academy subtenant), the concerts were planned "on a scale of liberality never before attempted in this country," offering something for every taste, serious and

---

[15] Hagen hoped the income from the two final concerts would reimburse Bergmann for his losses on the earlier ones.

[16] Aside from his other multifarious musical activities, Mollenhauer served as music director at Burton's Theatre, and later remained in charge of the orchestra when the theatre was taken over in April by the actor/manager F. B. Conway and renamed the Metropolitan.

[17] Although Mills performed "very clearly and neatly, his conception of the Concerto was by no means in the Beethoven spirit," carped Hagen (*Review and Gazette,* March 10, 1859, p. 83). Satter had played the same concerto four years earlier with "more spirit and intellectuality."

[18] Reported in the *Saturday Press* (May 21, 1859) to have been founded by the Young Men's Democratic Club.

popular: an orchestra of eighty players (doubtless largely from the Philharmonic), a full military band of reed and brass instruments (of Dodworth's cohorts), the Harmonic Society, and a diversity of well-known soloists. And, "in addition to the fact that these Soirées [would] afford much-needed instructive and fashionable musical entertainment at a moderate price," the Society promised to "encourage and patronize, by their performance, the meritorious native and resident composers who have heretofore had but rare opportunities of placing their compositions before the public." The subscription price, admitting a gentleman and lady to the ten concerts, was five dollars; single tickets for single concerts were fifty cents.

At their favorably received first concert, on May 17, the new society presented an unspecified, doubtless representative, program, featuring the Strakosch artists de Wilhorst and Maggiorotti; also S. B. Mills and Edward Mollenhauer. Despite this promising beginning, between their first and second concerts the Metropolitan Society for some reason underwent a drastic change, as did their locale.[19] The ten ambitious original concerts at the Academy of Music were transformed to six promenade concerts "in the style of Jullien and Musard," to be presented June 21 through June 30 at the Palace Gardens and Hall.[20] The orchestra and military band were retained, but not the Harmonic Society; the altered and expanded roster of soloists now included—besides S. B. Mills and Edward Mollenhauer—Heinrich Mollenhauer and a group of first-desk brass and wind players from the Philharmonic and Dodworth's Band; the conductors were Bristow, Dodworth, and, instead of Strakosch, Carl Bergmann.[21] "In view of the fact that the Palace Gardens and Hall will accommodate a very large audience, and notwithstanding the very heavy expense attending the above liberal arrangements," tickets were reduced to twenty-five cents. As the *Times* commented (June 24, 1859): "An enterprise like this deserves success, for it is good and economical."

Yet, following their first appearance at Palace Gardens (driven indoors by rain),[22] the *Times* critic, for all his good will, felt impelled to offer fatherly advice: "We would suggest the propriety of giving more dance music and fewer solos," he wrote. "The managers must aim at liveliness. It will be their own fault, if, with judicious manage-

[19] A change most probably brought about by Strakosch's latest partnership with Ullman and his approaching departure for Europe to engage singers for their forthcoming disastrous autumn season at the Academy.

[20] The site in early May of the Grand Horticultural Festival, a six-day event to benefit the "poor orphan girls" of the Horticultural School. Among the attractions were floral exibitions, exhibitions of paintings, rare birds, and fireworks, a Grand Promenade Concert, a Grand *Soirée dansante* with dance music by the celebrated Seventy-first Regiment Band, a stream of addresses by the most prominent clergymen and orators of the city (among them Henry Ward Beecher and William Henry Fry), and on May 14, a concert (at twenty-five cents admission) by the singers Juliana May and Alessandro Amodio, the pianists S. B. Mills, William Mason, and Richard Hoffman, the violinist Joseph Burke, and the cornetist Louis Schreiber; Henry C. Timm presided at the piano.

[21] "The music chosen is of a quality to please all tastes—classic, operatic, martial, and Terpsichorean" reported the *Musical World* (July 2, 1859, p. 2). "About ten pieces are given at every concert for the sum of twenty-five cents. A half hour is devoted to intermission, refreshment, promenading, etc. The Garden is well supplied with tables, gas-lights, and the usual garden embellishments."

[22] "For an agreeable summer entertainment," wrote the *Times*, "no place would be more appropriate [than the hall]; it is half garden [being accessible to the garden by a row of thirteen adjoining arched doorways], yet wholly secure from those sudden pluvial onslaughts which are apt to harass the managers of places of open air amusement," to say nothing of drenching their clients.

ment, these entertainments do not prove immensely popular. They are the cheapest and most accessible things of the kind ever attempted, and by far the best. They deserve success."

But the Metropolitan Music Society quickly deteriorated. By July 9, 1859, the *Musical World* (p. 2) regretfully observed: "The performances were somewhat inferior—it must be remarked—to the earlier ones; the musicians became too familiar with the music, the place, and the audience, and grew careless, both in their music and their manners." The critic complained, too, of Dodworth's idiosyncratic tendency to conclude almost every piece—be it a march, quickstep, polka, or whatnot—with its trio; he was also offended by Dodworth's inappropriate use of the big and little drums in his band arrangements of sacred music.

On Sunday, June 26, the Metropolitan Society gave a redeeming "Grand Sacred Concert" at which Bergmann conducted Liszt's *Les Préludes* and accompanied Mills in Chopin's Piano Concerto in E minor; Dodworth conducted the band in arrangements of remotely "religious" orchestra pieces by Weber and Meyerbeer, also the *Cujus animam* from Rossini's *Stabat Mater* transcribed for euphonium, an ophicleide-like instrument new to the United States. Dodworth also conducted Louis Schreiber's cornet concerto, played by the composer, pieces for the Cornet Band, and Paganini's Violin Fantasy for one string on *Moses in Egypt,* played by Edward Mollenhauer.[23]

Others appearing with the short-lived Metropolitan Musical Society were Mrs. S. B. Mills, who, with her husband, played a piano duet by Moscheles;[24] the Four Leaf Clover Singing Society, now with an altered personnel; and Harry Sanderson, who, as before, was admired for his razzle-dazzle pianistic acrobatics but censured for neglecting the more solid aspects of his art in favor of "the polka and quickstep school to which he [was] too much given."

On the first of July, upon the departure of the Metropolitan Musical Society, Thomas Baker, still music director of the Palace Gardens, returned with an attractive nightly schedule, rain or shine: on Mondays, Wednesdays, and Fridays, promenade concerts and *soirées dansantes;*[25] on Tuesdays, Grand Concerts and fireworks; on Thursdays and Saturdays, Grand Promenades and Vocal Concerts; and on Sundays Vocal and Instrumental Sacred Concerts. Prominent artists were featured on Tuesdays, Thursdays, and Saturdays, and Palace Gardens soon became a valid presence in New York's world of music (and an off-season boon to unemployed artists). Appearing in July and August during Baker's sojourn were, among others, Arthur Napoleon, Maria Brainerd,

[23] "There is, in this city, a party of Sabbatarians whose pious scruples are greatly shocked because the German Gardens in the Bowery are open on Sunday nights," wrote Darcie (*Porter's Spirit,* September 17, 1859, p. 481). "Yet, by a singular inconsistency, they have not a word [against] the Palace Garden Sunday evening performances. What is a crime in the Bowery becomes a virtue in Fourteenth-street!"

[24] Following their earlier performance of the work at Mills's formal debut, at Niblo's Saloon on May 19 (see below), the *Times* critic (May 23, 1859) described it as "a dreadful duet by Moscheles, called 'Homage to Handel' [op. 91], but which might more properly be styled 'Homage to Ennui.'"

[25] Strict requirements governed gentlemen wishing to participate in the *soirées dansantes*. Only subscribers were eligible to dance; to become a subscriber the gentleman must submit his name, address, and a satisfactory reference; a force of police was present to expel anyone guilty of unseemly conduct; smoking on the dance floor was forbidden. Ladies and gentlemen were permitted, however, if they so desired, to wear their hats and outer garments—shawls, mantillas, etc.—while dancing.

Cora de Wilhorst, Minna von Berkel, Giuseppe Guidi, Louisa Francis (a singer of popular ballads), Agnes Sutherland, Guglielmo Lotti (a new German tenor), David Miranda, and Isidor Lehmann.

In September, upon Baker's departure to resume his duties as music director of Laura Keene's Theatre, Harvey Dodworth took over with his assortment of bands. Heard during his regime—in addition to return appearances by many of the above artists—was Gustav Satter, described as a performer of the "grimace and contortion school," who with one M. Davis, played an overture (probably Satter's), "To Washington's Memory,"[26] transcribed for two pianos, and with Arthur Napoleon another duo, Satter's *Tarentelle de concert*.[27]

By far the most noteworthy event of the Palace Gardens season was the highly publicized return to the American concert stage—after an interval of some seven adventuresome years of global wanderings—of the intrepid (and apparently indestructible) Madame Anna Bishop. Following the disastrous New York season of English opera that she had shared in 1852♪ with her Svengali, the harpist R. N. C. Bochsa,♪♪ the pair had made their way to California, where, for a period, they conquered gold-rush San Francisco. Then on to Australia, where in 1856 Bochsa died.[28] Undaunted by this catastrophe, Madame Bishop proceeded to South America, where, among other heroic exploits, she was reported to have crossed the Andes on muleback in fulfillment of professional engagements; then on to her native London, where she at last dared to show her face (and her voice) after an absence of some two decades (her deserted husband Sir Henry Bishop having died in the meantime). Before returning to New York she acquired a new husband, a Mr. Martin Schultz, "a well-to-do German merchant" of that metropolis, who, it was gossiped, had "followed the lady in her world wanderings, and whose assiduous and ambulatory devotion [had] at last been rewarded." (Little would subsequently be heard of Mr. Schultz.)

Watson, who effortlessly (and doubtless gainfully) resumed his former role of ardent Madame-Bishop-booster, attempted, as of old, to kindle the public's interest with thrilling tales of her fabulous worldwide triumphs and of the resultant great wealth that had "poured in upon her." And to propagandize for her instatement at the Academy:

---

[26] Patriotic and topical military pieces figured largely on the Palace Gardens programs, as they did at the Jones's Wood concerts. On August 13, at his benefit, Baker conducted a Grand War Symphony: *Italy and Austria,* composed by Julius Unger for the Jones's Wood Festival.

[27] Hagen eulogized not only Satter's virtuoso arrangement of the *Tannhäuser* Overture, "an astonishing piece of pianism which only very few pianists will be able to accomplish," but also his ineffably delicate performance, on a superb Steinway Grand, of his charming waltz *Les Belles de New-York* and of Weber's "Invitation to the Dance" (*Review and Gazette,* September 17, 1859, p. 290). (Hagen's insistent praise of the Steinways' pianos strongly suggests that he was one of the growing number of journalists who received tangible rewards from that forward-looking firm in return for favorable mention of their product.)

[28] In the various newspaper stories recounting Madame Bishop's spectacular adventures during the years of her absence, the writers (with the sole exception of the gossipy *Trovator*) tactfully managed to omit any mention of her "protector" Bochsa, with whom, over many years and in many lands, Madame Bishop—abandoning her husband and their three children—had unabashedly maintained a scandalous relationship.♪♪

Girvice Archer, Jr.

Anna Bishop, prima donna *in
both Italian and English opera, was also
an adventurous world traveler.*

"No engagement that Messrs. Strakosch and Ullman could make," he prodded, "would give greater satisfaction to the citizens of New York and the thousands of strangers now in the city than one which would enable Madame Bishop to appear in Italian opera at the Academy of Music" (*Leslie's,* September 16, 1859, p. 283).

Not the Academy, however, but the Palace Gardens Music Hall was the scene of Madame Bishop's comeback,[29] an elaborate event extending over three evenings of concerts, offering a kind of showcase for her great versatility.[30] Assisted by Arthur Napoleon and the peripheral Italian opera baritone, Francesco Taffanelli, and with Anschütz conducting a small but good orchestra, at the opening event, on September 10, Madame Bishop sang two English ballads (a genre in which she excelled), an unidentified grand opera aria by an unspecified Guglielmi, and, with Taffanelli, a comic duet from *L'elisir d'amore;* on the following night, a sacred concert, with the assistance of Madame Zimmermann and a chorus, she sang excerpts from Haydn's *The Creation* and Rossini's *Stabat Mater,* also Schubert's *Ave Maria* and Handel's "Angels ever Bright and

[29] As Burkhardt face-savingly explained (according to time-honored Bishop/Bochsa usage): "From all quarters brilliant offers of engagements poured in upon her; the enterprising manager of the Palace Gardens, however, outbid all others by his golden offers" (*Dispatch,* September 10, 1859).

[30] "The musical element of the metropolis was out in full force, and the audience was popular as well as critical," puffed the *Herald* after Bishop's first concert (September 11, 1859).

Fair"; and on September 14 she appeared in a "miscellaneous" program with the same assisting artists.

"Madame Anna Bishop looks younger than when last here," gushed Watson (*Leslie's,* September 24, 1859, p. 265). If her figure seemed a bit "fuller," its symmetry was "as elegant and perfect as ever," and her voice, if anything, had improved. It had "gained power without losing that marvelous sympathetic quality which was so great a fascination in days gone by, though [quickly recovering himself] not *far* off." Madame Bishop, wrote Watson, was "a first-class artist, one who could, as such, take rank in any city in the world."

By some coincidence, Watson's most extravagant claims of Madame Bishop's perfections—her untarnished youth and beauty and her undiminished—indeed enhanced—vocal powers were to a great extent corroborated by his fellow critics.[31] Even Hagen exhibited an atypically tolerant, indeed effusive, attitude toward Madame Bishop: he commented on her astoundingly youthful appearance—she looked not a day over thirty-two—although it was no secret that she had appeared twenty years ago with such bygone idols as Grisi, Viardot Garcia, Persiani, Rubini, and Lablache.[32] "And, we must say, she is, even at the present time, a noble representative of the art. We have not of late heard more correct singing.[33] Her method is excellent, her execution the same. She is at home in all styles and gives to each its due." Hagen was, however, impelled to add: "Her voice is of course neither fresh nor powerful, but it is still agreeable and pleasing." Whether or not she would do for opera was moot, but Hagen was quite sure that "as a concert singer, she [ranked] foremost" (*Review and Gazette,* September 17, 1859, p. 290). And although, perversely wrote the *Albion* critic (September 17, 1859, p. 451), Madame Bishop's voice was as thin as anything could be, because "twenty years of constant effort do not add to the richness of the human voice, however much they may increase the facility of management," it was nonetheless "beautiful, even in the delicacy of this thinness. That the lady is a grand artist is beyond question; we doubt if a more perfect vocalist has ever visited the United States."[34]

After these triumphs Madame Bishop departed with S. B. Mills and the opera baritone Vincenzo Morino on a tour of New England and Canada, and, for the month of October, Palace Gardens was monopolized by the American Institute Fair. As in past years at the Crystal Palace, concerts and walking music were supplied by Dodworth and his bands in various combinations.

[31] "The fair prima donna looked exceedingly well and sang as charmingly as ever," agreed Wilkins (*Herald,* September 11, 1859). "Her voice has lost none of its purity, sweetness, and flexibility, while, as a matter of course, her execution, always brilliant, has been improved."

[32] Madame Bishop had now reached the advanced age of forty-nine.

[33] "Mrs. Bishop preserves all the beauty of her voice," wrote *Trovator,* "and sings a ballad as perfectly as anyone I have yet heard" (*Dwight's,* September 24, 1859, p. 207).

[34] As the principal champion and embodiment of the Liberated Woman, Ada Clare expended paragraphs of overwrought prose on Madame Bishop, who exemplified for her an "Eastern fairy [from the Arabian Nights], who had charmed all the myriad singing birds in the forest into pouring forth their whole choral melody through her bright lips, leaving wood and grove desolate, sorrowful, silent." Young Arthur Napoleon, however (perhaps regarded as a potential Gottschalk), elicited even more extravagant paeans from the irrepressible Queen of Bohemia (*Saturday Press,* September 17, 1859).

Following the Fair, the entertainment at Palace Gardens offered, on November 8 and 10, a pair of concerts of popular and folk songs and recitations by the American soprano and future opera singer and actress, Fanny Stockton, accompanied at the piano by William Dressler and assisted by the *diseuse* Emily P. Lesdernier; and on November 18 and 19, by Elizabeth Taylor Greenfield, the "Black Swan,"♫ now in mid-tour, with a cast of unidentified "eminent artists."

On November 24, Thanksgiving Evening, a Monster Music Festival was announced for the Palace Gardens Music Hall, to feature Madame Bishop (who that very afternoon had appeared at the Gala Matinée at the Academy of Music). Her large assisting cast of predominantly native artists included, among others, the singers Mrs. J. M. Mozart, a fine oratorio soprano from Boston, now in the Grace Church choir, the Misses Gellie, Mary Hawley, Kate Comstock, and W. H. Cooke, Ernest Perring, and a Mr. Hubner, solo basso in the St. Francis Xavier choir; also promised were the pianists Robert Goldbeck and John Nelson Pattison (1845–1905), a native of Niagara Falls, just returned from study in Europe with Thalberg, Henselt, von Bülow, and Liszt; the harpist Aptommas; the Mendelssohn Union with their conductor G. W. Morgan; the new Guilmette Choral Society—a group of sixty singers under the leadership of Guilmette's star pupil, Harriet Westervelt—and, to accompany, William Berge and William H. Currie, organist of the Fifth Avenue Dutch Reformed Church. The Master Mind and "Director-in-Chief" of this extravaganza was Dr. Guilmette. To accommodate so great a throng of performers, and in expectation of a large audience, important structural "modifications" had been made in the hall, it was announced.

Wishful thinking, for, as the *Musical World* (December 3, 1859, p. 5) reported, the event turned out to be a doleful comedy of errors: among the missing were the Misses Gellie and Messrs. Perring and Hubner, and most of the Mendelssohn Union; William Dressler's new "Thanksgiving Anthem," heard that day at several churches, was replaced without explanation or apology by a short, "easy" *Sanctus;* a grand duo for two pianos programed for Morgan and Berge was tacitly omitted; the Bach Fugue scheduled for Pattison emerged instead as somebody's unidentified Mazurka; and Cooke forgot the words to the second stanza of his song. The remainder of the vocal solos fared somewhat better, except for Madame Bishop's first offering, "The Harp that once thro' Tara's Halls," announced to be accompanied on the harp by Aptommas, but heard with piano, because "this gentleman, who had just played a solo, rushed through the audience, out of the hall, and was seen no more."[35]

Following this fiasco, on December 13, 15, and 17, Sam Cowell, a sellout attraction at the French Theatre on alternate nights, appeared at Palace Gardens Music Hall with his "wonderfully mirthful portraits of eccentric London life," and with, as assisting artists, the pianist Arthur Napoleon, the London concertist James Hicks, and the *diseuse* Emily P. Lesdernier.

On Christmas evening Madame Bishop participated in the Harmonic Society's annual *Messiah* at the Academy of Music. In general, an unsatisfactory performance, wrote the persnickety *Musical World* (December 31, 1859, p. 2; reprinted in *Dwight's,* January 7, 1860, p. 328). Although Madame Bishop's voice sounded "natural," and de-

---

[35] The *Herald* (November 25, 1859), however, reported the event as "one of the very best concerts that has ever been given here."

spite her undiminished ability to render oratorio music with spirit, the critic took exception to her "peculiar enunciation," setting a bad example to the younger singers. For example: in "He shall bring peace unto the heathen," she persisted in singing "He shall bring peace unto the he-heathen"; the critic objected, too, to her introduction of roulades into Handel's music. With the exception of Miss E. Coleman, a soprano of growing prominence in the Society, who had done very nicely, the other solo singers, Mrs. Westervelt and Messrs. Simpson and T. J. Thomas, although correct, were cold, as was Bristow, who conducted "in his usual manner. . . . How we wished we were Santa Claus, or some other good *genie,*" the writer impulsively exclaimed, "to be able to endow this talented musician with a certain amount of fire and energy, which is all he needs to make a great reputation for himself, and without which he can never inspire either the orchestral or choral department under his control with the ideas of the composer."

Evidently this judgment did not represent the generally high regard in which Bristow was held in New York, for on March 7 the Harmonic and Philharmonic Societies, in both of which he had long served with distinction, joined together, and—with an impressive list of socially and politically important sponsors and a large cast of performers[36]—had accorded Bristow the overdue tribute of a Grand Testimonial Concert at the Academy of Music. As the advertisements summarized his achievements, Bristow enjoyed a recognition both in the United States and in Europe rarely accorded an American composer; his works had been performed on several of Jenny Lind's and Jullien's programs; his opera *Rip Van Winkle,* performed by the Pyne/Harrison Company, had enjoyed an unprecedented run of three consecutive weeks at Niblo's and was now purportedly about to be produced by them in London. Bristow's unceasing, selfless labors with the Harmonic Society had established for the Society its present high position and for himself "the respect and esteem of all with whom he has been associated, both as A Man and An Artist."[37]

The heterogeneous program, predictably abounding in double choruses from Handel and Mendelssohn oratorios coupled with a gallimaufry of instrumental and vocal solos and ensembles,[38] included surprisingly few works by Bristow: only a movement from his Jullien Symphony; the song "The Twilight Hour," from his *Rip Van Winkle,* sung by Mrs. Westervelt; and his little-known Overture to *The Winter's Tale,* composed in 1856 for William Burton's notable production of Shakespeare's play. This work, wrote *Trovator* (*Dwight's,* March 12, 1859, p. 397), with its "curious and interest-

---

[36] Including the singers Maria Brainerd, Madame Caradori, Mrs. Westervelt, Misses Coleman and Rhemmio, David Miranda, and Philip Mayer; the pianists William Mason, Richard Hoffman, and Henry C. Timm; the violinist Joseph Burke; the harpist Aptommas, and the Philharmonic cellist/hornist Charles Brannes. Joseph Noll shared conducting duties with Bristow.

[37] They might have referred as well to his distinguished contributions to the New York public schools, and, as the *Albion* critic disclosed (March 5, 1859, p. 115), to his "liberality and valuable services to the St. George's Society on occasions of its musical entertainments." Additionally, Bristow served as organist at St. George's Church.

[38] Including Schumann's "dislocating" Andante and Variations for two pianos, played by Hoffman and Timm. To the anti-Schumann *Musical World* (March 12, 1859, p. 168) it was "music which we think the composer must have invented while subjected to the pangs of the jumping toothache. Really, now," protested the writer (probably R. Storrs Willis), "where is the good of a writer being so shockingly dissonant?"

ing instrumentations and considerable melody," was the outstanding feature of the evening. Responding to its enthusiastic reception, Bristow delivered what *Trovator* referred to as a "rather confused speech, in which he had great difficulty in repeating the word 'reiterate.'"[39]

It was not a peak year for the Harmonic Society. They seem to have been heard in only two other major concerts, both benefits and both at the Academy: one for the Young Men's Christian Association on May 26, with *The Creation,* sung by Cora de Wilhorst (her oratorio debut), Miss Rhemmio, and Messrs. Perring and J. R. Thomas; the other for St. Ann's Church for Deaf Mutes,[40] on November 8, when they gave Mendelssohn's *Elijah,* with Maria Brainerd, Mrs. Westervelt, J. R. Thomas, and—a last-minute substitute for an indisposed Ernest Perring—the tenor George Simpson.

In contrast to this meager showing, the enterprising Mendelssohn Union appeared to greater advantage than ever. Following their success with *St. Paul,* they presented, at the Cooper Union,[41] on January 27, 1859, Rossini's opera *Moses in Egypt* as an oratorio. Translated into English by G. S. Parker, president of the Union, the work was performed by Maria Hadley, Mrs. Crump, the English tenor David Miranda, now a member of the group, Charles Wernecke, and Charles Guilmette;[42] G. W. Morgan conducted and William Berge lustily accompanied, all but exhausting the resources of a Steinway grand. But with merely piano accompaniment, however lusty, wrote the *Albion* critic (January 29, 1859, p. 55), the work lost "much or all of the unique colouring which belongs to Rossini's scores," particularly this one. He wished the Mendelssohn Union in the future "could afford to give no work without an orchestra."

The critic's wish was soon granted, for on February 21, at the Academy of Music, the Mendelssohn Union participated in—in fact sponsored—the first local performance of a widely discussed, indeed highly controversial, new work, a "Romantic Symphony," more accurately classified as a symphony/cantata, by Robert Stoepel (1821–1887), the gifted music director of Wallack's Theatre. An unconventional musical setting of Longfellow's popular poem *The Song of Hiawatha,*[43] the work's purpose, as the Academy program book described it, was to illustrate the "principal events narrated in the poem . . . selected for musical portrayal by means of descriptive orchestral

[39] A "neat speech," reported the *Musical World* (March 12, 1859, p. 168).

[40] After seven years of holding services at the University Chapel and in the Lecture Room of the New-York Historical Society, the St. Ann's congregation had purchased the buildings in Eighteenth Street near Fifth Avenue, formerly occupied by Christ Church. Primarily ministering to the needs of their deaf-mute parishioners, they conducted a service in sign language on the Sabbath, but also gave spoken daily morning and evening services.

[41] Described anew by *Trovator* (*Dwight's,* February 5, 1859, p. 359) as "one of the most remarkable concert halls in the world, because it is nothing more nor less than a large cellar, the floor thirty-five feet below the level of the street."

[42] As the *Evening Post* critic remarked (January 28, 1859), the principal singers were all members of local church choirs: Miss Hadley sang at Berge's church, St. Francis Xavier's (Sixteenth Street), as did Mr. Wernecke; Mrs. Crump sang at the Church of the Incarnation (Madison Avenue); and Miranda and Guilmette had just been engaged for the choir at Christ Church (Fifth Avenue).

[43] Although Stoepel was lauded for the originality of his concept, setting Longfellow's poem to music was apparently not a unique idea: in 1858 the *Evening Post* reported a performance in St. Louis of a setting of *Hiawatha* for mixed vocal quartet, piano, and orchestra, composed by one Emile Karst of that city.

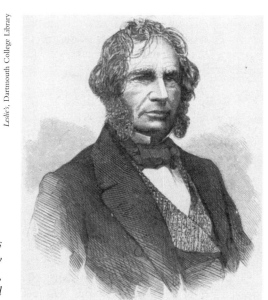

*Despite some criticism from journalists
of Stoepel's musical setting for Henry
Wadsworth Longfellow's* Hiawatha,
*the poet was pleased by it and
attended every rehearsal.*

pieces, choruses, and vocal solos. In order to sustain the continued interest of the work
in performance, as well as to elucidate the composer's meaning, the musical numbers
[were] connected by sections of the poem," declaimed, not sung, by the favorite actress
Matilda Heron, in private life Mrs. Stoepel.

Receiving an out-of-town tryout performance on January 8 in Boston (a Longfellow stronghold)[44] with the Boston singers Mrs. Harwood as Minnehaha, Harrison
Millard (1830–1895) as Hiawatha, and a Mr. Weatherbee as the Great Spirit, a chorus
drawn from the Handel and Haydn Society, a pickup orchestra conducted by Stoepel,
and, of course, with Miss Heron as the narrator, *Hiawatha* precipitated a long-drawn-
out journalistic bicker. Originating in the pages of *Dwight's Journal of Music* (January
15, 1859, p. 332, *passim*), the ultra-conservative Dwight and his correspondents found
the work monotonous, overlong,[45] and inconsequential, while the critics of the Boston daily press, enthusiastically hailed Stoepel's *Hiawatha* as a vital and important breakthrough in American music and one that would long endure. Even William Henry
Fry, after perusing the score, joined in the free-for-all, seizing, as usual, the opportunity (both in *Dwight's*, February 5, pp. 354–55, and the New York *Tribune*, February
23, 1859), to attack the old masters and their obsolete creations[46] and again to affirm
his fanatical adherence to the newest of the new, preferably the output of a native or

[44] Longfellow, who reportedly had attended all the rehearsals and readings of the work, professed
to be highly pleased with Stoepel's creation (*Evening Post*, January 11, 1859).

[45] Its first performance lasted three-and-a-half hours. The work's detractors recommended that
the narration be omitted, not only to shorten the work but to relieve its monotony.

[46] "The awful infliction" of Handel's oratorio, *Israel in Egypt,* wrote Fry, consisted of textually
"dismal rubbish set to twenty odd fugues . . . as lyrical as the multiplication table" (*Tribune*, February
23, 1859).

(like Stoepel) a naturalized American. *Hiawatha's* announced second performance in Boston did not take place.

Despite a reported personal loss of $1000 on the Boston experiment (according to Fry, $1200), an undaunted Stoepel—with the influential cooperation and sponsorship of the Mendelssohn Union[47] and heralded by widespread and spectacular advertisements—presented *Hiawatha* at the Academy of Music on February 21. Except for Charles Guilmette, who replaced Mr. Weatherbee as the Great Spirit, the cast of soloists remained the same: Matilda Heron was an eminently "womanly" narrator, evincing all through the work, as the critic for the *Musical World* could easily see (February 26, 1859, p. 131), pride in her husband's work and concern for his reputation;[48] Mrs. Harwood and Messrs. Millard and Guilmette acquitted themselves splendidly, as did the Mendelssohn Union and a fine orchestra of fifty players conducted by Stoepel.

Unlike their Boston brethren, the critics of the New York press, without exception, acclaimed Stoepel's work. Henry C. Watson, who, "at much personal sacrifice," had traveled to Boston to hear its first performance, was again enchanted with the "abundant and beautiful flow of charming, fresh, and quaint melody which pervades the entire work,[49] the poetic spirit in which it is treated, the marked individuality, the keen appreciation of national characteristics[50] . . . and the charm of the elaborate and exquisite instrumentation which enhances the beauty of the musical conception, as the artistic setting brings out the beauty of the gem" (*Leslie's,* January 22, p. 120; March 5, 1859, p. 217).

A second performance of *Hiawatha* was announced but withdrawn, purportedly because of Mrs. Stoepel's conflicting professional engagements.

At their following concert, on April 14, the Mendelssohn Union presented a full-fledged performance, with a "carefully selected orchestra," of Michael Costa's *Eli,* a work they had successfully introduced with piano accompaniment in 1856.♪ The solos were sung by Mrs. J. M. Mozart, Mary Hawley, David Miranda (in the *Albion* critic's

---

[47] They had in fact been rehearsing *Hiawatha* twice weekly since the beginning of the year, if not before. It was at first gossiped that Stoepel had engaged the Mendelssohn Union's services for $100, but it was soon made known that—with the possible exception of payment to the soloists—the Union had taken over the full production of *Hiawatha* as a project of their own. And, as Darcie commented (*Spirit,* February 26, 1859, p. 413), they "certainly made their arrangements in a very creditable manner."

[48] To the *Saturday Press* (albeit no admirer of Longfellow), her declamation "came in like silver bars in the golden tracery of the music . . . [she] gave the lines with exquisite clearness, delicious vocal modulation, and profound simplicity. When she laughed with Min-ne-ha-ha, it was really the music of the falling waters; flirting with Hiawatha was a combination of the tender tremulousness and Eve-like archness which the poet gives the rustic maiden. . . . The Heron was splendid in every way, proud, happy, handsome, and much applauded" (February 26, 1859).

[49] Tunes with "catchability," Seymour called them (*Times,* February 22, 1859).

[50] But of which nation? The *Musical World* (February 26, 1859, p. 131), although failing to detect any particular ethnic flavor in the work (it being an amalgam of "all styles"), at the same time lauded its "purely American newness." As to authentic Indian music, wrote the *Albion* critic (February 26, 1859, p. 103), the world knew little of it and cared even less. Thus, the composer had the field to himself. Anything was acceptable. "He might call a Negro melody Indian" and no one would be the wiser. But Seymour, in the *Times* (February 22, 1859), clearly detected war paint on the first bar of "Hiawatha's Fight with Mudgekeewis," a movement for orchestra.

opinion, "a long way" the best tenor in the city), James W. Alden, and the omnipresent Charles Guilmette; William Berge again presided at the piano and G. W. Morgan conducted.

"Mr. Costa, the distinguished Italian conductor of the opera in London, having failed as an operatic composer," wrote William Henry Fry (*Tribune,* April 15, 1859), "tried his hand at an oratorio." And because an oratorio was "infinitely easier to compose than an opera," Costa had succeeded. Indeed, surprisingly admitted Fry, he could hardly remember an oratorio "which excited, other things being equal, so much applause as this given last night, with a fine orchestra and chorus at the Cooper Institute." Its success, he extenuated, was doubtless due to the "capital interjections of a pleasing character to relieve the monologues, psalms, and prophetic gravities" typical of most oratorios, and particularly because it avoided "the old tie-wig, Italian flourishes which deform and stultify Handel's works." (Fry evidently detested oratorios as cordially as he did piano concertos.)

But it was precisely because of these characteristics that Hagen found fault with *Eli.* The work could lay no claim to being a real oratorio, he wrote. In form compounded of glancing resemblances to Handel, Mendelssohn, and to contemporary opera music, its essentially modern score lacked both unity of style and individuality. Hagen particularly resented the excessive fragmentation and duplication of syllables employed by Costa: "We really do not see the necessity, or appreciate the entertainment of hearing people sing, for ten or fifteen minutes, a quantity of sounds upon one syllable. Glorification of the Lord can be done musically in a far more efficient way" (*Review and Gazette,* April 30, 1859, pp. 130–31). *Eli,* despite its syllabic excessiveness, was repeated on April 21.

And in midsummer, on July 20, at 4:30 in the afternoon, the vivacious Mendelssohn Union—harking back to the popular musical steamboat excursions of the 1840s♪—boarded the steamer *Rip Van Winkle,* to which was hitched a "new excursion barge capable of accommodating twelve hundred persons," and set sail up the Hudson. Stopping off at Yonkers to pick up some suburban friends of the Union, they sailed on, mingling music with the scenic glories of the Palisades, as far north as West Point and the Highlands. Overtures were performed by Dodworth's Cornet Band, pianoforte solos by Sebastian Bach Mills, vocal solos by Harrison Millard, and choral music by the Mendelssohn Union, conducted by G. W. Morgan and accompanied by William Berge. The excursionists partook of choice nonalcoholic refreshments dispensed by a "first class caterer" and danced all the way back to Manhattan to the music of the Cornet Band. Admission to this delectable outing was two dollars for gentlemen, one dollar for ladies.

On October 29 the convivial Mendelssohn Union gave a "social *soirée* musicale and *dansante*" at Jones's New Assembly Rooms at 656 Broadway, two doors below Bond Street. The early part of the evening was devoted to "a few choice selections for piano-forte, solos, and choruses"; then on with the dance.

On December 8 the Mendelssohn Union opened their sixth season at the Palace Gardens Music Hall with a concert for the benefit of the St. Ann's Sunday School, the "proceeds to be applied to the purchase of Library and Recitation Books and for Clothing for the Destitute Children of the School." Their predominantly light program began with a performance of the Overture to *Masaniello* arranged for four pianos and Alexandre organ, resoundingly rendered on two Steinways and two Chickerings by five lady members—Mrs. Bordman, Mrs. William Berge, and the Misses Pearson, Condon, and Teresa Wernecke—and three gentlemen—G. W. Morgan, and William and Charles Berge—and on the Alexandre organ by William H. Currie. Morgan, Currie, and the Berge brothers performed Czerny's Piano Quartet (his op. 816!), and Morgan and W. Berge played a Fantasia on *Lucrezia Borgia* by an unspecified Dolmetsch. The remainder of their programmatic crazy-quilt included vocal solos performed by Mrs. Mozart, Mary Hawley, Louisa Francis, Dr. Guilmette, and C. Hubner; violin solos by Henri Appy (somewhat belatedly billed as the "solo violinist of the Jenny Lind Concerts"), a piano solo by G. W. Morgan, and oratorio choruses by the Mendelssohn Union accompanied by two pianos and Alexandre Organ. Pleasant, perhaps, wrote a stodgy critic for the *Musical World* (December 17, 1859, p. 7) but too "miscellaneous" for a choral society.

A similarly broad "sacred" concert had been given by the German *Liederkranz* at the City Assembly Rooms on April 24, conducted by Paur and featuring Joseph Weinlich (purportedly about to depart for Rio de Janeiro) and Sebastian Bach Mills. The program consisted of Beethoven's *Leonora* Overture no. 1, op. 138; a recitative and aria from Haydn's *The Creation* sung by Weinlich; Prudent's Fantasia on *Lucia* played by Mills; Schubert's eight-part *Gesang der Geister über den Wassern,* op. 167 (1820, revised 1821), by request; Mendelssohn's *Die erste Walpurgis Nacht,* sung by the *Liederkranz* at the Academy the previous February; and the by-now inevitable March from Wagner's *Tannhäuser.*

As always, members of the singing societies engaged in a wide range of auxiliary concert activities: often for philanthropic causes, sometimes to compliment an honoree, sometimes just for the sake of performing. Members of the Mendelssohn Union—the Misses Hadley and Demarest, Messrs. Wernecke, Hubner, Charles Berge, and Dr. Guilmette—on January 12 gave a concert of sacred and classical music at the Stanton Street Baptist Church under William Berge's direction. On April 5, at St. Paul's Methodist Episcopal Church (Fourth Avenue and 22nd Street), other members of the Union—Mrs. Mozart, Annie Kemp, Mary Hawley, C. and W. Berge, and G. Washbourn Morgan—presented a Mrs. S. H. Anderson (evidently a parishioner) with a complimentary concert of sacred music. By contrast, at Dodworth's Hall on March 29, Mrs. Harriet Westervelt and Charles Guilmette incongruously appeared for the joint benefit of two popular entertainers, Baptiste Panormo, a pianist, and the guitarist/minstrel Napoleon N. Gould, an alumnus of the original Christy's Minstrels.

On a far larger scale, the German *Liederkranz* and the *Allgemeine Sängerbund* combined en masse at the Academy of Music on February 18 in a Grand Benefit for the German Hospital Fund. Madame Anetta Caradori and the violinist William Doehler were the soloists, Agricol Paur conducted the choruses[51] and Franz (or Frederick) Kruger (a poor substitute for Bergmann, it was noted) conducted an orchestra led by Joseph Noll.

---

[51] Hagen reveled in the soldierlike precision of the singers' attacks, an object lesson that could not be too highly commended to the attention of the other vocal societies, he wrote (*Review and Gazette,* March 5, 1859, pp. 67–68).

Madame Caradori appeared, too, at the Church of the Immaculate Conception (Fourteenth Street near Avenue A), where, on February 27, under the direction of its organist Gustavus Schmitz, a predominantly sacred program was presented to help defray the cost of the church's new organ, built by Henry Erben. Members of the choir participated, as did the cornetist Louis Schreiber and an additional "grand choral society consisting of thirty male voices," accompanied by the ubiquitous William Berge.[52] So successful was this event that it was repeated a week later at the request both of "those who had heard it and those who had not."

Among the many well-known musicians who assisted in the various beneficent concerts was Harry Sanderson, who on May 2 contributed a piano solo to a program of sacred music for the benefit of the Sabbath School of the First Presbyterian Church, performed by the church's adult and juvenile choirs. The singers Maria Brainerd, Fanny Stockton, Adolphina Dressler, and William H. Dennett, the cornet virtuoso Louis Schreiber, and the concertinists Alfred Sedgwick and his son Charles appeared on January 25 at the Eighteenth Street Church (the future St. Ann's) in a Grand Concert, directed and accompanied by Clare W. Beames. As an added attraction "Little Ella" Burns, the sensational four-year-old *diseuse,* declaimed.

Little Ella, despite the *Tribune*'s bitter disapproval of such flagrant child exploitation, appeared on February 10 at the Academy of Music (donated for the occasion by Ullman) at a grand concert for her own benefit. Given under the sponsorship of the problematical mayor of New York, Fernando Wood, and a committee of influential citizens, the event was so enthusiastically attended that many ladies had to sit on the steps and gentlemen to stand in the lobbies and aisles. Assisted by William Mason and Robert Goldbeck, who together opened the miscellaneous program with the two-piano version of Liszt's *Les Préludes,* and Maria Brainerd, accompanied by Clare W. Beames, Little Ella "recited two or three poems embodying various sentiments, and in each evinced the most remarkable appreciation of their nicest shades of meaning . . . with the most remarkable emphasis, tone, and gesticulation." This was particularly true of a scene from *The School for Scandal,* wherein the infant Ella portrayed Lady Teazle "with wonderful skill and effect" to the Sir Peter of her mother[53] (*Times,* February 11, 1859).

The *Times* hoped that with the funds accrued from this event the child would be withdrawn from public performance and her "budding faculties [given] that due cultivation which they need." A vain hope. On December 27, Little Ella, declaimed more potently than ever at Dodworth's Hall, assisted by Harriet Westervelt, one Henrietta Noble, S. B. Mills, and Charles Guilmette.

Among the more fashionable benefits was the concert on February 18 for the House (or Institute) of Mercy given by the Misses Madeline and Mary Gellie (of the Calvary Church quartet choir) and Messrs. Cooke and Rivarde, Joseph Burke, Richard Hoffman, and Aptommas, with William A. King (the Calvary organist) and Ra-

[52] In April, Berge, together with the leading members of his choir, resigned from the St. Francis Xavier's choir, reportedly because the church elders objected to the unorthodox music he chose to perform there. In May they were reinstated.

[53] Little Ella's masterful readings, too, of Collins's "Ode to the Passions," General Morris's "My Mother's Bible," and William Cullen Bryant's "To a Water-Fowl" brought tears to many an eye, including Watson's (*Leslie's,* February 19, 1859, p. 185).

nieri Villanova accompanying on the piano and the Alexandre organ. To raise funds for the Calvary Free Mission Chapel, the Misses Gellie appeared again on October 20 at Niblo's Saloon, with William H. Cooke, Filippo Morelli, Gustav Satter, Louis Schreiber, John A. Kyle, Henry C. Timm, and William A. King. King was himself honored with a complimentary concert by the Calvary parishioners at Dodworth's Hall on November 3, assisted by the Gellies, William H. Cooke, Philip Mayer, and Louis Schreiber. On this occasion King brilliantly performed his improvisations and paraphrases on both a Steinway piano and an Alexandre organ, particularly excelling on the latter; Señor Nuno accompanied.

On May 31 at the Metropolitan Theatre, the elite Ladies Charitable Society of St. Vincent de Paul presented a concert under the direction of the organist Louis Dachauer and performed by Madame Eugénie de Lussan, Filippo Morelli, William Henry Cooke, and Edward Mollenhauer.

On June 9, members of the advanced class of the National Musical Institute, an establishment headed by Thomas D. Sullivan (*c.* 1826–1863) and soon to acquire Carl Anschütz as co-director, advertised a concert of sacred and classical music at the Cannon Street Baptist Church, "in aid of the funds of the Church." Selections from *Messiah* and works by Weber were performed by a male quartet; a Madame St. Laurent presided at the piano and Sullivan conducted.

The irrepressible champion of American music C. Jerome Hopkins "volunteered" an elaborate concert at the Palace Gardens Concert Hall, on November 29, ostensibly to assist the Building Fund for the Mission Chapel of the Church of the Incarnation (Madison Avenue and 28th Street), where Hopkins was currently the organist. Inevitably, the program included Hopkins's music,[54] in this instance "The Sailor's Return," a "descriptive ballad" sung by Charles Guilmette.[55] Also participating were Hattie Andem, Harriet Westervelt, George Simpson, Louis Schreiber, a vocal quartet party, and, of course, Hopkins; the accompanists were William Henry Currie and John S. Jameson, son of the well-known singer Mrs. Jameson and a pupil of William Mason.

Additionally, on November 30, Francis H. Nash conducted members of the Harmonic Society—among them Mary Hawley and the veteran Marcus Colburn—in a concert for the benefit of the Spring Street Church (Spring Street near Varick). John Nelson Pattison played piano solos and George Henry Curtis accompanied.

At the Ladies Fair, an elaborate two-week-long event at the Academy of Music, sponsored by the ladies of the Catholic Churches in New York to aid the Institution of Mercy, Harvey Dodworth and his band gave a Grand Concert on December 6. Securely in possession of the Academy for the first half of December, just as the first great Patti fervor had gripped the city, the Ladies Fair was the source of great chagrin to Ullman, who was thus forced at this untoward moment to remove his opera company to Philadelphia.

And on December 21, to aid the idled workmen of Lighte and Bradbury's burned-down Piano Factory (in Broome Street), a notable group of artists performed at Palace Gardens Music Hall: Madame Bishop, Beaucardé, and Albertini with mem-

---

[54] A dynamic self-promoter, on April 2 at the Church of the Messiah (Broadway), Hopkins, with the assistance of a group of vocalists, had presented several of his own compositions.

[55] Increasingly an exponent of Henry Russell's lurid ballads, popular in the '30s and '40s,' Guilmette also sang Russell's "The Ship on Fire."

bers of their recent opera company at Niblo's—Madame Martini d'Ormy and the Signori Maccaferri and Ardavani—also Arthur Napoleon and the National Musical Institute orchestra, conducted by Carl Anschütz and Thomas D. Sullivan.

As before, though in far fewer numbers, singers belonging to the two major singing societies were heard in independent concerts: on February 2, Miss Caroline Dingley at Mozart Hall with the assistance of Philip Mayer, the basso George McConkey, and Aptommas, and with George Frederick Bristow as accompanist; on April 26 at Niblo's saloon (under the patronage of "thirty or forty gentlemen of Calvary Church"), Miss Madeline Gellie, assisted by Miss Mary, Messrs. Cooke, Rivarde, Sebastian Bach Mills, William A. King, and Louis Schreiber, accompanied by H. C. Timm and Emile Millet; and on December 20 two events: at Dodworth's, Mary Hawley, with W. H. Cooke, John A. Kyle, Henry Appy, and Louis Schreiber, G. W. Morgan at the piano; and at the Hall of the Union, Hattie Andem, with S. B. Mills, Edward Mollenhauer, Ernest Perring, and Charles Guilmette, accompanied by William H. Currie. Blaming the inclement weather, Miss Andem solved the conflict by postponing her concert until December 24.

Mrs. Mozart, the admired Boston soprano who—after having completed the required period of study in Europe—had recently settled in New York, gave her first formal concert at Dodworth's Rooms on September 27. She was assisted by Mendelssohn Union familiars—the baritone J. R. Thomas, the omnipresent cornetist Louis Schreiber, the harpist Aptommas, and W. H. Currie, who accompanied. A fine singer of concert and oratorio music, Mrs. Mozart was commended for her especially felicitous performances of ballads, an insufficiently heard genre of music, wrote the *Musical World* critic (October 8, 1859, pp. 2–3), and particularly appealing to the masses.

The English singer and teacher, Madame Leati,♪♫ returning home after an uneventful residence in the United States since 1848, gave her farewell concert at Niblo's Saloon on May 7, assisted by S. B. Mills, Joseph Burke, William H. Cooke, Henry C. Timm, Charles Brannes, and, apparently, Mr. Leati.

With the Academy of Music management largely controlling the public appearances of imported singers, independent concerts by visiting foreigners were few. On January 7 at Niblo's Saloon. Cecilia Flores, a beautiful young Spanish mezzo-soprano, puffed as a pupil of Persiani, made her debut. On June 9 an event advertised as "Signor Clementi's Opera Concert" took place at Dodworth's Hall. Perhaps one of innumerable touring concert and opera companies that increasingly traversed the country, the polyglot group included the soprano Annie Kemp, the long absent bass/baritone Giovanni Leonardi,♪ Manuel Ruiz, a baritone, little twelve-year-old Giovanni Erba, violinist, and Antonio Morra, conductor. A second opera concert, this time managed by Ruiz, was given on June 23 at Dodworth's with such impressive assistance as Caradori, Brignoli, and Amodio; again little Erba played the violin and Morra conducted.

Among the instrumentalists, who seem mostly to have confined their efforts to assisting at their vocal colleagues' concerts, Aptommas, a man of seemingly boundless resourcefulness, on January 27 gave a solo matinée at Dodworth's Rooms, accompanied at the piano by A. Wöltge.♪ Following Gottschalk's example, Aptommas presented his audience with a huge list of dozens of compositions, mostly by Alvars but some by Aptommas's brother John Thomas, from which to choose the works they wanted him to perform.

Aptommas appeared again at Dodworth's Hall on February 24, with Caradori assisting and Wöltge again accompanying, and on May 19 with the assistance of Madame Abel at Chickering's Rooms. On October 15 Aptommas gave a concert at Niblo's Saloon, at which, recalling Thalberg, the stage occupied the center of the room, allowing the entranced listeners to be seated around it in a circle. Particularly entranced was the critic for the *Musical World* (October 22, 1859, n.p.) who ecstasized over the "magic tones [Aptommas] drew from his stringed treasure, filling with joy the listening ear as with sweeping hand he brought forth rich chords of harmony." In lightning descent from these lofty altitudes, the critic informed his readers that the chief impediment to the popularity of harp playing—the great expense of tuition—had now been removed with the establishment of Aptommas's new harp classes, costing about half the price of private lessons.

It was the pianists, however—primarily Sebastian Bach Mills—who largely dominated the concert scene in 1859. Immediately after his arrival early in the year, fresh from the Conservatory of Leipzig, and "without any preliminary flourish of trumpets," Mills, after his first appearance at Bergmann's Sunday night concert on February 20, virtually possessed the local concert scene.[56] He appeared at almost everyone's concerts, from the Philharmonic to the Palace Gardens to the Mendelssohn Union to the Little Ella and Sam Cowell entertainments. By May 19, when he at last made his formal concert debut at Niblo's Saloon, Mills was firmly ensconced as a virtually indispensable figure in the New York music community.

Appearing with Mills at his debut was his young bride (and recent schoolmate),[57] with whom, as we know, he played the Moscheles *Hommage à Handel;* also Maria Brainerd, accompanied by Clare W. Beames; George Simpson and T. J. Thomas, who, accompanied by James Gaspard Maeder, sang an assortment of ballads and arias; and Joseph Noll and Carl Bergmann, with whom Mills played an unidentified trio by Mendelssohn. Alone, he brilliantly played Thalberg's Étude in A (albeit not to Hagen's liking), but it was with Liszt's spectacular *Tannhäuser* transcription, evidently the 1848 Overture to *Tannhäuser* (Searle 442), that Mills brought the house down, only to surpass this *tour de force* with his even more electrifying encore, the Liszt/Mendelssohn *Midsummer Night's Dream* paraphrase.

Flinging all restraint to the winds, Watson, in his review of this performance, flamingly proclaimed Mills the world's greatest pianist, eclipsing even Thalberg in his mastery of the keyboard. Although barely twenty-one years old, Mills possessed not only the highest level of mechanical perfection—flawless scale passages, magnificent octaves, and tremendous power—but also, as his performance of Chopin's E-flat-

---

[56] "Few artists have had the rare good fortune to vault so speedily into a high place of public regard, even with the rare ability which Mr. Mills possesses," wrote Seymour (*Times,* May 23, 1859). "In a few months he has placed himself in the foremost rank of living pianists."

[57] In *Dwight's* (May 28, 1859, p. 71), —t— relates a romantic tale of young student love at Leipzig, the whisking away of the heroine by the disapproving mama, the pursuit to the United States by the ardent suitor, and a happy resolution.

minor Polonaise revealed, a marvelous capacity for "interpreting every style of piano composition" (*Leslie's,* May 28, 1859, p. 409). Mills was a man of "rare genius." In more restrained terms the other critics agreed that Mills was an extraordinary pianist, rarely equaled.

Outstanding among the other pianists of 1859, if on a more modest scale, was Madame Louise Abel, who quietly pursued her distinguished teaching and playing careers—at intervals performing music on the highest level at the less spectacular concert rooms of the city. At the Spingler Institute, on January 15, she gave a matinée, with the assistance of Philip Mayer and Edward Mollenhauer. Among other works, she played Beethoven's Piano Sonata in D (the "Pastoral," op. 28) and a "fragment" of Chopin's Concerto in E minor. "Sound and thoroughbred in all that constitutes a classic style," wrote the *Musical World* (January 29, 1859, p. 67), "it would be difficult—were we inclined—to find any fault with Madame Abel as an executant."

Appearing again on February 15 at a *soirée* at Chickering's Rooms, Madame Abel was assisted by a Miss Minna Lunau, who sang a "delicious" aria from *The Marriage of Figaro,* and by Edward Mollenhauer and Frederick Bergner, with whom she (Madame Abel) played a trio in A-flat major by Joseph Mayseder. With Mollenhauer she played the Andante and Variations from Beethoven's violin and piano sonata, op. 24 (1801); and alone Chopin's Étude in A-flat, op. 25, one of his two Mazurkas in B minor, and Gottschalk's immensely popular "The Last Hope." If her scintillating runs and passages in this last did not measure up to Gottschalk's breathtaking virtuosity, wrote the *Musical World* (February 26, 1859, pp. 180–81), Madame Abel nonetheless performed the work so splendidly as to merit an encore, another piece by Chopin, his Étude in F, op. 25. In the *Musical World*'s opinion, it was "the gem of the evening."

Madame Abel gave another of her choice *soirées musicales* at Dodworth's Hall on November 17, with the assistance of the violinist Bruno Wollenhaupt (with whom she played Beethoven's "Kreutzer" Sonata), a young mezzo-soprano Marie Krausch, and Aptommas; William Dressler presided at the Chickering.

In September, Robert Goldbeck, who since January had been conducting piano classes[58] in rooms over C. Breusing's music store (at 701 Broadway) announced the opening of his Piano Conservatory-cum-Music Hall (formerly Lyrique Hall, at 765 Broadway, between Eighth and Ninth Streets). Assisted by Perring and Aptommas, on October 27 and 29 Goldbeck inaugurated his new premises with a pair of concerts consisting of music by Schumann, Chopin, Parish-Alvars, Liszt's "*Miserere* after Palestrina," no. 8 of the *Harmonies poétiques et religieuses* (1853) (Searle 173), and Goldbeck. During November, with Mrs. Goldbeck reading recitations, Goldbeck gave nightly performances. In December they launched a new subscription series of joint "lyric recitals" with Mrs. Goldbeck reading poems by Longfellow, Browning, and Poe, and her husband playing music by Beethoven, Chopin, Liszt, and his own latest compositions.[59]

[58] His method was based on the principles practiced by the great *Conservatoires* in Europe, wrote Goldbeck in a self-promoting letter to the press in January, but it probably more directly followed Gottschalk's successful *Conservatoire de Piano* in 1856.

[59] The blending of oratory and music was apparently in the air. In January an apparently short-lived, new series impressively titled "The Oratorion" (or "Oratoreon") was announced by "Profes-

At the beginning of the year Arthur Napoleon, before going on an extended tour of the South,[60] gave a pair of farewell concerts at Niblo's Saloon, a *soirée* on January 21 and, with a different program, a matinée the following day. His assisting artists for these events were the little-known American soprano Anna Vail, the Spanish mezzo-soprano Cecilia Flores, the English tenor David Miranda, the German cellist Frederick Bergner, and a Richard von Schmidt, who "conducted." Due to "terribly bad weather," the attendance was limited, reported the *Herald* (January 24, 1859), but Napoleon's performance was truly wonderful, especially his rendering of his delightful new fantasia on *The Bohemian Girl*.

The *Musical World* (January 29, 1859, p. 67), on the other hand, angrily rejected bad weather as a perpetual excuse for a badly attended performance. The reviewer blamed Napoleon's miserable, niggardly management (unnamed) for having wrecked his brilliantly promising career in the United States. At a time when the public was conditioned to the spectacular offerings of an Ullman—the LaGranges, D'Angris, Thalbergs, and Vieuxtemps—Napoleon's "caricature" of such entertainment had no chance: "Fifth rate singers and an unknown pianist [von Schmidt] could scarcely be expected to excite the curiosity of the public." Although Napoleon had been critically adjudged a wonder, more than a good reputation was needed to attract audiences.

In June, Napoleon, under a new management—that of Bookstaver and Rosenberg—together with the Gassiers and Harrison Millard formed a new concert company and went off on a tour of New England and Canada. Less than a month later, after giving a few concerts in "Albany, Hartford, etc.," the troupe disbanded.

As we know, during the following summer months Napoleon appeared three times weekly at the Palace Gardens; he additionally assisted at concerts of all descriptions, and in December he assisted at the Sam Cowell entertainments at the French Theatre and at the Palace Gardens.

To round out the pianistic picture, on October 18 a transient Señor J. Gongora gave a "Spanish Concert" at Chickering's Rooms, with the assistance of Mary Hadley, George W. Wooster, George Matzka, Joseph Mosenthal, and Señor Lacosta, a "celebrated tragedian from Cuba." More memorably, on March 21, sixteen-year-old Adolf Neuendorff (1843–1897), the future pioneer conductor of Wagner operas and preeminent man for all musics, made his unheralded debut as a pianist at Dodworth's Hall. Billed as a piano pupil of Dr. Gustav Schilling (1801–1883), the noted German musical lexicographer then residing in New York, Neuendorff, who with his parents had emigrated to the United States in 1854, additionally studied violin with George Matzka (and, according to doubtful biographical information, also with Joseph Weinlich, with whom he more probably studied singing). At his debut Neuendorff was assisted by Weinlich and Edward Mollenhauer, by the Misses Drumm and Burns, sopranos (probably fellow vocal students of Weinlich's), and three fellow piano pupils of Schilling's.

---

sors" Bronson, elocutionist, and Colburn, Nash, and Curtis. The sessions, to take place at the Cooper Institute on Wednesday evenings (and at the Brooklyn Athenaeum on Fridays), would each consist of ten or twelve songs or recitations. Tickets were twenty-five cents each, or fifty cents for two ladies and a gentleman.

[60] Assisted by the singers Emma Heywood and Claudina Cairoli, and the violinist William Doehler.

Girvice Archer, Jr.

*Adolf Neuendorff, who started as a sixteen-
year-old concert pianist, later became a
pioneer conductor of Wagner operas.*

The Mason/Thomas matinées continued faithfully to carry forward the banner of chamber music. Their predominantly female subscribership, however, inspired an ostinato of contemptuous comment, principally from the *Musical World* (January 8, 1859, p. 19). Reviewing the second matinée of the current series, on January 3, falling on a Monday, the official "calling day" for Upper-Ten New York ladies, the critic caustically wrote, despite a tolerable turnout, that "this momentous fact, no doubt, interfered in some degree with the attendance. What a mysterious affair the ladies calling day is! Whom, on earth, do the dear creatures call upon? Clearly, if every lady makes a call, there can be none left at home to do the honors of the gay and festive occasion. The fun, we apprehend," wrote the critic from the Olympian altitudes of his masculinity, "must be found in the shuffling of cards, which unquestionably results from so much hollow courtesy." (Did he mean calling cards or playing cards?)

The Mason/Thomas program on January 3 comprised Beethoven's String Quartet in B-flat, op. 18, no. 6, splendidly played by Thomas, Mosenthal, Matzka, and Bergmann; two pieces for piano by Mason, his Ballade in B major and Étude in B-flat minor;[61] Schubert's ephemeral Tarantelle for violin,[62] spectacularly played by Thomas,

[61] "A ballad like this will contribute more to Mr. Mason's reputation than a bushel of *Études,* useful as the latter may be to one out of every ten millions of students," scornfully wrote the *Musical World* reviewer (January 8, 1859, p. 19), and added: "A composer so elegant and acceptable should write more often and more directly to the public."

[62] Although listed in the Pazdirek directory, no reference to such a Tarantelle has been found in Deutsch or in other catalogs of Schubert's works. The Tarantelle might possibly have been incorpo-

and a well-liked Trio in F major, op. 6, by the contemporary minor German composer Woldemar Bargiel (1828–1897),[63] played by Mason, Thomas, and Bergmann.

Listening to chamber music in this hall brought poignant thoughts of Eisfeld (at that time still in Fayal), wrote —t—, who deplored the public's indifference to the scheme proposed by Eisfeld's faithful colleagues—Noll, Reyer, and Bergner—that during his absence they would carry on his quartet *soirées* and send him the proceeds.[64] "Will you believe it," bitterly wrote —t—, "the requisite number of subscribers, small at best, could not be mustered" (*Dwight's,* January 15, 1859).

For their third matinée, on February 5 (a Tuesday), the Mason/Thomas program consisted of Schumann's Sonata in A minor for violin and piano, op. 105, a work, wrote Seymour (*Times,* February 10, 1859), through whose "comparative darkness" the artists at last managed to toil into the genial sunlight of Haydn's following String Quartet in D minor, no. 43 (*sic*).[65] Rubinstein's "impossible" Étude in sixths for piano, op. 23, no. 2, was "creditably" played by Mason, but, wrote the exasperated critic: "*Why* artists play *études* in a concert-room, we have yet to discover. They are dreary to a degree and [emulating Fry on Handel] mean no more than the multiplication table or a page out of a grammar." To make matters worse, the offensive étude was encored with a galop (Mason's *Galop fantastique*), "a little more impossible than the étude."

The concluding number, the "gem of the program," was Mendelssohn's posthumous String Quintet in B-flat, op. 87, splendidly given, with Augustus Besig of the Philharmonic playing the extra violin. A work of towering beauty, wrote Seymour, its Andante deserved to rank with the "grandest productions of any school."[66] It deserved, he wrote, an evening performance.

At the fourth matinée, on March 15, Mrs. Mozart, on this occasion making her first concert appearance in New York, sang the *Ah, mon fils* from Meyerbeer's *Le Prophète* and Schubert's *Lob der Tränen*. With a sympathetic and musical voice, she made a very agreeable first impression, wrote the *Musical World* (March 19, 1859, p. 179). In only one regard did she displease the critic (probably R. Storrs Willis)—her excessive use of the *portamento,* a common failing among singers and one that he hoped would soon go out of fashion, as had the "tremulousness in vogue some time since."[67]

---

rated into, or extracted from, Schubert's posthumous Sonata for violin and piano, op. 137, no. 1, whose last movement, is an Allegro vivace in 6/8 time.

[63] Bargiel was Clara Schumann's stepbrother and an ardent disciple of Robert Schumann.

[64] Upon first receiving news of Eisfeld's plight, the Philharmonic Society had immediately dispatched $500 to Fayal to "relieve him of any pecuniary embarrassment which might assail a stranger in a foreign land." This gesture testified both to the Philharmonic's generosity and to Eisfeld's worth, wrote Watson (*Leslie's,* November 6, 1858, p. 361).

[65] Hagen thought it would have been better had they begun with the Haydn Quartet and thus progressed from his simplicity to Schumann's "strange, deeply felt, and nobly conceived and executed music . . . for it is by contrast that we enjoy most" (*Review and Gazette,* February 19, 1859, p. 50).

[66] The *Albion* critic agreed. In a veritable rhapsody to Mendelssohn he wrote: "The Andante [of the Quintet] is one of the most exquisite things in music—far superior as an exhibition of stringed instrument writing than anything we can call to mind" (*Albion,* February 19, 1859, p. 91).

[67] Hagen made the same comment, but in characteristic Hagenese: although she had a fine quality of voice, he wrote, the delivery of her higher tones was faulty, showing an inclination to "illustrate in singing, as other people do, in morals, that the straight way is not the best" (*Review and Gazette,* March 19, 1859, p. 83).

With regard to Mendelssohn's *Variations concertantes,* op. 17, played by Mason and Bergmann, the critic reiterated his former censure of variations and their composers: "Mendelssohn is not a great variation writer," he wrote. "Nothing is easier to write than variations—and nothing is harder. Good variations require special and eminent genius. Reicha had it—Beethoven had it. But few others have ever possessed it."

Theodore Thomas being away on tour, Mason carried the weight of this program, performing with his brilliant pupil Jameson an Andante for two pianos, op. 6, by the German composer Carl Reineke (1824–1910), and with Mosenthal, Matzka, and Bergmann, Schumann's Piano Quartet in E-flat, op. 47. Ready with a separate quibble for each of these works, Willis's only unreserved praise was bestowed upon Steinway's superb pianos.[68]

For their fifth program, on April 26, Mason, Thomas, and Bergmann played Schumann's Trio in D minor, op. 63; Thomas played Berlioz's *Rêverie et caprice,* op. 8 (1839)—a work pronounced by Watson to be unsuitable for public performance, "being destitute of tangible melody and abstruse to a fault" (*Leslie's,* May 7, 1859, p. 361). Mason again played his Ballade in B major and Rubinstein's "impossible" Étude, op. 23, no. 2—"a work of difficulty to the performer and distress to the listener," wrote the *Albion* critic (April 30, 1859, p. 211). The program closed with Schubert's Octet, op. 166, for string quartet, contrabass, horn, clarinet, and bassoon, the bass and wind instruments played by Messrs. Preusser, H. Schmitz, Kuhlmann, and Goepel.

If the Octet was the *pièce de resistance* of the occasion, wrote the *Albion* critic, it was also unendurably long. "Schubert," he wrote, "was a man profuse in ideas and diffusive in treatment; he could create like a poet and spin out like a penny-a-liner." The critic suggested that the work constitute an entire concert, with a fifteen-minute intermission between the second and third movements "to enable the mind to free itself from the lugubrious, unrhythmetic [*sic*] effect of the former and prepare itself for the light and airy grace of the latter."

Reviewing this concert, the *Musical World* (May 7, 1859, p. illegible), still harping on the ladies, revealingly wrote: "The disadvantage of making daytime music for the ladies is the fact that they cannot applaud."[69] He forthwith set about, "between the pieces of the programme" (more probably during the interminable Schubert Octet), mentally to devise some permissibly ladylike "contrivances for purpose of applause— something of a miniature castanet style which might form part of the handle of a fan, or bouquet holder, and by which an audible demonstration could be made—distinctively ladylike and unobjectionable. The difference between the applause of the ladies and the ruder sex might thus be definitely marked," he happily continued, "and all artists be made immediately aware when they touched the sensibilities, and drew forth the enthusiasm, of the ladies. Charming idea," he applauded himself.

At their final matinée of the series, on May 17, the Mason/Thomas group opened with Mozart's Quartet for piano and strings in G minor (K. 478); Mason and Thomas played Schubert's *Rondeau brillant,* op. 70 (1826), an unfamiliar, Hungarian-sounding piece; Miss Adelaide Wollenhaupt (Hermann Wollenhaupt's sister), making her debut,

---

[68] "Really," he wrote, "the resonant, voluminous tone of these instruments is something luxurious to listen to."

[69] Ladies were apparently restricted to handkerchief-waving to express approval.

sang two songs, Mendelssohn's "Zuleika" and Rossini's *La separazione;* and the program closed with the first performance in the United States of Beethoven's String Quartet, no. 14, in C-sharp minor, op. 131 (1826).

"The program opened with Mozart's first quartette and closed with Beethoven's fourteenth, and nearly his last, a range sufficiently large for any taste," wrote Seymour (*Times,* May 18, 1859). "There is a respectable quaintness in Mozart's work which Beethoven's does not possess. In the one case, it is the staid but intelligible manner of the day in which he wrote; in the other the desperate eccentricities of an exhausted brain. A work so puerile as this of Beethoven's is more than wearisome; nothing is so provocative of locked-jaw [*sic*] as the dullness of clever men. In his third period the great master was frequently under a cloud. It is not without reason that this and others of the same sort have been rejected by the most eclectic of his admirers. Certain it is that anyone venturing to write so feebly in the present day would meet with a fate at once merited and salutary." (What might that fate have been?)

With the onset of summer, Yorkville and Jones's Wood (the latter now considerably enlarged) came to life. Jones's Wood opened on June 6 and 7 with a two-day Grand Rural Festival, Concert, and Pic-nic, given under the joint auspices of the New York Musical Mutual Protective Association and the American Musical Fund Society. The central event, a Grand Concert of popular favorites by Rossini, Mendelssohn, Meyerbeer, Méhul, Flotow, and Wagner, was performed by an orchestra of two hundred players, conducted by Theodore Eisfeld and Harvey Dodworth, together with the *Teutonia Männerchor* and *Uhland Sängerbund* under their directors, Messrs. Weber and Krüger. Dancing to the music of five different dance orchestras spotted throughout the grounds at five different dancing platforms, spectacular fireworks by J. W. Hadfield that fantastically lit up the woods, and, of course, the pic-nic, contributed to the "general good-time-having" (as Hagen expressed it) of the occasion. The festivities began with the ritual military and civic procession originating in Hester Street and leading eventually to the foot of Grand Street at the East River, where the steamboat *Erie* waited to transport the celebrants to the pic-nic grounds.

On June 17 the *Liederkranz* announced their annual Summer Night's Festival and *Bal Champêtre* at Conrad's Yorkville Park, with Paur conducting the choir and Noll in charge of the dance orchestra.[70]

To celebrate July 4, the theatrical entrepreneurs George L. Fox and James W. Lingard mounted a Mammoth Festival at Jones's Wood, attracting a day-long, "steady tide of population"[71] that exhausted all available means of transportation. Although the

---

[70] On August 8, the combined New York *Sängerbunden,* comprising some thirty-six singing societies, traditionally paraded through the streets of lower Manhattan, then boarded two steamers bound for Elm Park at Ninetieth Street and Broadway, and there held their annual festivities, musical and gymnastic.

[71] A motley crowd, reported the *Tribune* (July 6, 1859), it included, in addition to respectable holiday-makers, a sizeable contingent of "roughs and ruffians, rowdies, loafers, shoulder-hitters, and aspirants for pugilistic notoriety, pick-pockets, thimble-riggers that were continually offering to bet you couldn't tell which thimble the little joker was under, and all sorts of tricksters [roaming] at large through the grounds. . . . At intervals, fights were extemporized, but the knock-downs didn't amount to much."

The Steinway pianos were so praised for the quality of their tones that the makers built a larger factory, allowed visitors to inspect their work, and invited guests to a concert given by music professors who said that the sound was "something luxurious to listen to."

crowds were in a holiday mood and "lager beer flowed like water," the occasion was somewhat marred by the failure of its chief attraction, the inflation and ascension of the balloon *Louisa* by the renowned aeronaut Professor Pusey. And worse, during the course of the professor's futile efforts to inflate the obstinate *Louisa,* he was accosted—in full view of thousands of curious spectators—by a sheriff's deputy demanding payment of a thirty-dollar debt, an obligation the harassed aeronaut vehemently denied.

Despite this contretemps, there was still much to enjoy at this Fourth of July celebration. Although music was not the principal attraction (it being a non-German event), a splendid band was provided for all-day dancing; there were, besides, magic shows and feats of sword-swallowing, hobby horses and swings, throwing of balls and shooting of pistols, and "little or no drunkenness [was] anywhere observed." All in all, commented the *Herald* (July 6, 1859), contrary to the *Tribune,* "the Jones's Wood folks passed their Fourth in a most friendly and generous way," pleasant to reflect upon.[72]

Events at Jones's Wood did not, however, hit their true stride until the arrival on July 18 of the week-long, Grand Super-Mammoth Festival and Fête Champêtre. Although grandiosely credited to unidentified "Associate Members of the Great Congress Musicale," the event, advertised as "The Most Gorgeous Entertainment the World Has Ever Witnessed," seems once again to have been instigated by Maretzek and Anschütz.[73] Far exceeding last year's Mammoth Festival, it offered—in addition to a plethora of concerts by a two-hundred-member orchestra and multiple singing societies conducted by Maretzek, Anschütz, Bergmann, Bristow, Grill, Prox, and Unger (whose Grand War Symphony *Italy and Austria* was given twice), and by several military bands and a drum corps (Stoepel was announced to conduct sections of his *Hiawatha,* but defaulted)—a vast array of circus acts, equestrian, magic, acrobatic—Punch and Judy shows—all varieties of carnival entertainments—four dance bands doubling at eight dance floors—balloon ascensions—Hadfield's fireworks—and calcium lighting turning night into day. Even free transportation on board the steamboats *Satellite* and *John L. Lockwood* was included in the twenty-five cent admission.[74]

On Sunday, July 24, the entertainment was restricted, as before, to a Mammoth Sacred Triple concert, performed by the Mammoth Orchestra with a Mammoth Chorus, at three, six, and seven P.M. The Mammoth Festival was a resounding success, and an Autumn Mammoth Festival was devoutly hoped for. Notwithstanding the diversity of its attractions, wrote Burkhardt (*Dispatch,* July 23, 1859), the festival as an "art affair" deserved to be "affectionately" remembered forever. (It is perhaps a tribute

[72] Apparently not by the chagrined Messrs. Fox and Lingard. "Regretting the non-ascending of the Balloon" on the Fourth, and explaining that holes discovered in its surface had been to blame for its failure to become inflated, they handsomely invited the disappointed holiday-makers (and the general public) to be their guests at Jones's Wood on July 11, at a replay of the festival, complete with fireworks, dance orchestra, and a mended balloon.

[73] Assisted by Albert Maretzek, and by Messrs. Rullman, Charles G. Rosenberg, and—surprisingly—John Darcie.

[74] *Trovator,* however, pooh-poohed the festival as a "catchpenny" affair, doing little to advance the cause of good music with the lower classes of Germans and Irish and the New York rowdies who patronized it. Not that the music wasn't good; it was indeed too good for the audience, attuned as they were to the other attractions: the circus, pyrotechnical exhibitions, swings, revolving horses, etc. (*Dwight's,* July 30, 1859, p. 133).

to the festival's astute management that nowhere among its vast newspaper coverage was found a reference to beer.)

In July and August, as we know, crowds flocked, too, to Central Park, where free Saturday afternoon concerts by Harvey Dodworth and his band were "provided by a voluntary subscription of citizens." On July 9, Richard Storrs Willis, with a few friends, made the pilgrimage to the park. Contrary to Strong, Willis was enchanted by the wonderful progress made in the past year: "Trees of several years growth have been transplanted to beautify and adorn the extensive walks and drives, which are known as the 'Ramble,'" he wrote (*Musical World,* July 16, 1859, p. 3), "and it requires no great stretch of imagination to perceive what will be the future of the Park, judging from its present appearance. Near the Observatory, in the center of the Park, on an elevated rocky platform, Dodworth's Band delighted the assembled thousands with their charming music,[75] which sounded unusually sweet to us as we listened to it from a snug retreat under the shade of a beautiful tree. . . . There is no place," wrote Willis, "where an hour or two may be spent more pleasantly." Or more safely: "The Central Park Police, with their neat uniform, are present in large numbers to preserve order, and none need hesitate to visit it for fear of rowdyism, to which we are often subjected in some other places of popular resort."

The growing popularity of out-of-doors music—what with the activities at Jones's Wood and now at Central Park—suggested endless possibilities for further development along the same lines, wrote the *Herald* (July 29, 1859): "In all the public squares of the city, from the Battery to Knightsbridge, there might be similar means of recreation provided." Many of the city's military regiments and fire companies possessed their own bands who could give weekly concerts at the various squares, bringing the double benefit of providing the citizens with free entertainment and shaming the City Fathers into properly maintaining the currently neglected public spaces.

Homespun musical entertainment was dispensed at Niblo's Saloon on March 30 and succeeding evenings by an inflated reincarnation of the Old Folks troupe "from Massachusetts." Rechristened Father Kemp's Old Folks, the company, numbering "thirty-seven ladies and gentlemen, with their unique and superior orchestra,[76] all clad in costumes of 100 years ago," presented a program abounding in such gems of "Ancient, Sacred, Classic, and National Melodies" as "David's Lamentation over Absalom," "The Dying Christian," "Auld Lang Syne," "Old Hundred" (among numberless other hymns), also "The Star-Spangled Banner," "Hail Columbia," the "Marseillaise," and "God Save the Queen." Despite the enormous expense of supporting "the largest troupe in the world," announced modest Father Kemp, in his zeal to disseminate "Ye Music of Olden Time" he was "determined" to price the tickets within everyone's reach, twenty-five cents, fifteen cents for children.

In November, after touring far and wide, Father Kemp's Old Folks returned to New York and environs, appearing on November 11, 12, and 17 at Cooper Union;

---

[75] A classic band-concert mélange of popular music, dance music, marches, and opera medleys, including the *Tannhäuser* March, was offered.

[76] Featuring Grandsire Foss, "now going on 98 years old," and his great-grandson David, performing on "Ye Ancient Fiddles."

Father Kemp's Old Folks concert music. Favorite tunes were performed
by the "Old Folks," who claimed they gave more than nine hundred
concerts, receiving great admiration throughout the country.

on November 18, following a lecture on "American Social Life," by Timothy Tit-comb;[77] and again on November 19. On Christmas day they returned for a special holiday matinée at the Palace Gardens Music Hall.

Among other offerings of lighter musical entertainment, on April 7 at Dodworth's Hall the perennial William Dempster paid yet another of his annual visits to New York. As a feature of his "Lyric Entertainment," Dempster unveiled his latest creation, a musical treatment of another Tennyson poem,[78] this time of "The Princess" (1847). Partly set to music and partly declaimed, the work was, according to the *Evening Post* (April 8, 1859), not received with favor:[79] "Mr. Dempster's true vocation is not that of a public reader," wrote the *Post*.

Stephen Massett, in mid-tour—passing through New York on his way to the New England States and Canada—paused on June 16 to give an evening of his Jeems Pipes of Pipesville songs and monologues at Dodworth's Hall. Agnes Sutherland, "the Scottish Nightingale," sang her native ballads at Dodworth's Hall on September 29,

---

[77] Pseudonym of the famed New England writer and editor, Dr. Josiah Gilbert Holland (1819–1881).

[78] The *Evening Post* (February 23, 1859) records Dempster's recent visit to Tennyson at his home on the Isle of Wight, when Dempster reduced the poet to tears with his "pathetic" musical rendition of Tennyson's poem "The May Queen."

[79] An understatement: "To speak of Mr. Dempster's voice is mentioning a thing he does not possess," mercilessly wrote Hagen (*Review and Gazette,* April 16, 1859, p. 115). "Suffice it to say, the people were bored by long readings, the introductory lasting about twenty-five minutes. The people laughed, stamped, etc, but to no purpose. . . . When the tumult grew loud, Mr. Dempster, in a unique speech, begged the audience to be quiet, as he could not be thus interrupted, and stated that those who did not like it might leave the room, and the money would be refunded at the box office."

with Arthur Napoleon and Louisa Francis as assisting artists and S. Behrens as accompanist.

Throughout the year, musical entertainment of sorts was enjoyed, glass in hand, at a great variety of drinking establishments: at the Santa Claus, where Eva Brent had replaced Miss Frothingham in the olio of *The Bohemian Girl;* at Hitchcock's National Concert Hall (172 New Canal Street), where Maria Duckworth concurrently appeared in a rival version of the same attraction; at the Art Union Concert Hall (497 Broadway), where Julia Barton and W. B. Harrison warbled their ballads and duets in a company that included Raffaelle Abecco, a harp-playing tenor, and Tom Watson, comic and mimic. And again at the Art Union Concert Hall, where the sword-swallowing Great Greek Rhigos shared top billing with a Miss Annie Boardwell, who gave soprano selections from W. V. Wallace's *Maritana,* Verdi's *Il trovatore,* Bellini's *La sonnambula,* Balfe's *The Bohemian Girl,* and the latest ballads of the day; and where, in October, Thomas Dartmouth Rice, "the Old Original Jim Crow, the Father of All Negro Delineators," was seen in one of his final performances of *The Mummy.* At National Hall (150 Prospect Street) the best Extra Lager Beer was a special feature of the Sunday sacred concerts; at the Melodeon (the former Chinese Rooms, at 539 Broadway), vast concert programs presented armies of entertainers of all varieties;[80] at the Vauxhall Garden (199 and 201 Bowery, formerly Hoym's German Theatre), a "model company" included again Maria Duckworth and W. B. Harrison; and at the Hess Varieties (Seventh Street, opposite Cooper Union), the Broadway Varieties (127 Grand Street), and innumerable other "Varieties," torrents of entertainment flowed as profusely as did the liquid refreshments.

Most prominent of the myriad German music-and-lager establishments was the German Volksgarten (45 Bowery), where the musical programs ranged from popular waltzes and polkas and opera medleys to such esoterica as the "War March of the Priests" from Mendelssohn's *Athalie.* In September, Joseph Noll appeared at the Volksgarten with his National Guard Band; on Thanksgiving Day the chief vocal attraction was the eternally thwarted, but unquenchable, opera diva Madame Elisa Valentini. Admission to these establishments, exclusive of drinks, cost from ten to thirteen cents—in rare cases fifteen cents.

And the minstrel shows. "Ethiopian Minstrelsy never was better conducted than it is at present in New York," ballyhooed *Porter's Spirit of the Times* (January 1, 1859, p. 288). "Nearly all the talent in the profession concentrates here as to a natural metropolitan focus,[81] and the result is a variety and perfection of performance, impossible to be found in other places."[82]

The most constant of these attractions were Bryant's Minstrels, who occupied

[80] On the afternoon of July 4 the Melodeon presented a special holiday program at which the Female Minstrels, a compnay of "eight beautiful ladies" (apparently brought in from the Franklin Museum) performed "all their songs, choruses, witty sayings, comic doings, etc., etc." for an admission of fifteen cents.

[81] Concentrating in New York, perhaps, but, once there, shifting from company to company in a complicated game of musical chairs.

[82] Not so: the minstrel troupes seen in New York were usually seen as well over the length and breadth of the United States.

Mechanics' Hall (except for a three-week absence in July) for the remainder of the year and beyond, and Wood's troupe, who, although suffering a slump in 1858 following Henry Wood's breakup with his partner and star attraction George Christy, nonetheless ran on uninterruptedly, first in the splendid surroundings of "Wood's Minstrel Building" at 561–563 Broadway, then, in September—upon the sale of their "marble hall" to a bank—at the French Theatre (585 Broadway) for a few performances, then back at the old minstrel sanctuary at 444 Broadway.

The circumstances of the rift between George Christy and Wood were at last disclosed in Christy's confiding "Card to the Public," appearing in the papers on May 27. Ironically reminiscent of the mutual recriminations publicly exchanged in 1853, when Edwin Pierce Christy bemoaned George Christy's callous defection to Wood,♪ it was now G. Christy's turn to publish a public protest of his ill treatment at Wood's hands. It was his duty, asserted Christy, to explain the details of their recent litigation and his consequent temporary banishment from the local stage. The court had ordered Christy to abide by the agreement he had made with Wood upon their parting the year before (doubtless upon receipt of a sum of money), not to perform in New York for the period of eighteen months. Returning ahead of schedule from a tour of California and finding himself in need of funds, Christy had ignored the agreement and, with a company of sixteen minstrels, had begun a season on May 23 at 444 Broadway, a venue he advertised as "late George Christy's Opera House." Immediately, Wood procured a legal injunction barring Christy from performing locally until the expiration of the agreement. During this term of compulsory inactivity, Christy's partner R. M. Hooley ostensibly took over the management of the show, renaming it Hooley's Minstrels and presenting J. H. Budworth in Christy's stead. It was, however, advertised that Christy would be on hand at the theatre at each performance personally to greet his friends and well-wishers.[83] The show limped along for a short spell, then ceased.[84]

Promptly on the stroke of 8 P.M. on November 1, however, Christy, legally free since noon and again in command of a large company bearing his name, opened a successful engagement at Niblo's Saloon,[85] which ran nightly through the end of the year and far beyond.

In July the Buckleys—R. Bishop, George Swaine, and Frederick—returned from their wanderings and with a new *prima donna,* Julia Gould, opened for a summer engagement at the French Theatre (their former Opera House at 585 Broadway). Their programs—the usual miscellany of "new songs, solos, duets, choruses, dances, and mirth-provoking plantation scenes," invariably concluded with one of their highly vaunted burlesque operas: *La sonnambula* ("The Black Sleep Walker"), *Il trovatore, Lucrezia Borgia,* or *The Bohemian Girl.*

Attending a Buckley performance, Seymour (presumably) was prompted to write a lengthy essay in the *Times* (August 18, 1859), tracing the extraordinary evolution of blackface minstrelsy, from its humble beginnings—when a solitary performer sporting

---

[83] During this period of enforced inactivity, Christy was a contributor, as its publishers elatedly advertised, to *The Phunny Phellow,* a comic periodical selling for four cents.

[84] Advertised among its special attractions was a "Grand Concert à la Musard."

[85] Christy had engaged John M. Trimble, the eminent theatre architect, to alter the hall to suit the purposes of his show.

"a blackened face, a ragged coat thrown off the shoulder, and a pair of elaborately patched trowsers, with a shocking bad hat," delivered himself of an inferior song in bad doggerel referring to "passing events of the time"—through the intervening period of barbarous endurance contests billed as "negro dancing," executed to meaningless strumming of the banjo, to the present, civilized, evening-long productions that were currently going "full blast" at several theatres, performed by companies of "colored white men, in very decent apparel and of genteel demeanor," who leavened their skits and Ethiopian banter with ambitious glees and choruses and sometimes even with operas.

At the Buckleys' show, the jokes were amusing enough, as was the impersonation of an elephant, and the violin playing was quite fair; but the transposition into black-face of *The Bohemian Girl* was "poor and poorly done." Although the dialogue was "very well travestied, and the actors endeavored to sing the parts as correctly as it would be done in a veritable opera," their voices were just not equal to the task and the attempt was consequently ridiculous. "A lady singer with blackened face and arms executed the soprano part and mangled it as fearfully as a poor voice, falsely used, could do it." Yet, despite its shortcomings, wrote the critic, the Buckleys' show might serve as "a cheerful means of spending a spare hour—semi-occasionally."

English opera enjoyed a comeback in 1859, surprisingly enough with Lucy Escott, whose efforts in that medium had failed so disastrously the year before. But Lucy Escott had refused to be defeated, and apparently she had her supporters and well-wishers, for on April 4[86] she was tendered a complimentary concert at the Chickering Rooms,[87] with the distinguished volunteer assistance of Maria Brainerd, Harrison Millard, David Miranda, William Mason, G. W. Morgan, and Clare W. Beames. Mrs. Escott, who now enjoyed the sympathy of the press, many of whose members asserted that she had been unfairly treated by Burton, was praised for her performances of an aria from *Il trovatore,* the "Venzano Waltz Song," "Comin' thro' the Rye," and in duets with Millard and Miranda.

Shortly after this event, on May 9, upon the appointment of the actor/manager Edward Eddy to the management of Niblo's Garden, Mrs. Escott began a month-long engagement there, appearing, together with Miranda and Miss Heywood (of her ill-starred original troupe), in various English "operas" and operas in English: *Rob Roy, Guy Mannering, La Bayadere* (with Signorina Galletta and a *corps de ballet*), *The Bohemian Girl, The Beggar's Opera,* and—at Eddy's benefit on June 1—Dibdin, Sr.'s *The Waterman,♪* in addition to selections from *Der Freischütz, La sonnambula, Il trovatore, The Tempest,* and *The Bohemian Girl.*

In October, New Yorkers—public and critics alike—were captivated by an intriguing new species of miniature English opera with a French flavor, the so-called "Parlor Operas and Lyric Proverbs" originated by the fine American actor/singer Henri (né Henry) Drayton (1822–1872) and performed by Drayton and his equally accomplished

---

[86] The *Evening Post* (March 28, 1859) reports that Mrs. Escott had been singing in the choir at Dr. Chapin's Church of the Divine Unity while awaiting her benefit on April 4.

[87] Poorly promoted, complained —t— (*Dwight's,* April 16, 1859, p. 22), and thus poorly attended.

English wife.[88] A longtime expatriate, Drayton, a Philadelphian[89] with a beautiful and beautifully cultivated bass/baritone voice and with leanings toward French culture, had abandoned a promising career in his native land as a topographical engineer to pursue his musical education and subsequent career in Paris. Purportedly the first American to be accepted at the *Conservatoire,* Drayton had studied with Lablache and Ponchard, and, according to an enthusiastic review/puff in the *Home Journal* (October 22, 1859), the Parisians "found in Mr. Drayton a gifted and noble specimen of American": he became "one of the principal favorites of the best families in Paris." Following splendid successes in France, Drayton enjoyed even greater acclaim in England, where, married to the charming actress/singer Susanna Lowe, he initiated his urbane and amusing Parlor Operas.[90]

As always in New York, novelty was the crucial element: "A new idea, skillfully elaborated and pleasantly presented, is sure to be a success in a City fearfully nightmared, as this is, by all that is old and wearisome," wrote Seymour (*Times,* October 13, 1859). Thus, the Draytons were greeted with outstretched arms. Their first bill consisted of two one-act operas: *Never Judge by Appearances,* with a libretto by Drayton and music by Edward J. Loder, and *Diamond Cut Diamond,* an operetta by the popular Belgian composer Albert Grisar (1808–1869), the libretto translated from the French and adapted by Drayton.[91]

Opening on October 12 at the French Theatre, where they appeared on Mondays, Wednesdays, and Fridays, the Draytons were so successful that early in November they leased Hope Chapel, renamed it "Drayton's New Parlor Opera House," and—at twenty-five cents a ticket—proceeded to present nightly and Saturday matinée performances[92] of their little opera gems with proverbial titles ("a moral potion, done up in a casket of brilliants," the *Home Journal* called them): *Never Despair, Love is Blind, Never too Late to Mend, Better Late than Never, There's a Silver Lining to Every Cloud,* and *The Somnambulist,* a "duodecimo edition of *La sonnambula,* done up in 'Proverb' form"; also a pastiche, *Love's Labor Lost* (Drayton's libretto, not Shakespeare's) containing popular songs selected from the works of "Balfe, Dibdin, Lee, Hatton, Lover, Donizetti, Verdi, etc." In this piece, each of the Draytons portrayed four widely divergent characters.

In late December, during their last week at their Opera House before going on tour (commencing with seasons in Brooklyn and Williamsburgh), the Draytons acquired an assisting artist, a razzle-dazzle Dutch violinist of Spanish parentage, Señor Oliveira, who entertained during the intervals between operas. A product of the Bel-

---

[88] Rightly or wrongly, the *Albion* critic (October 15, 1859, p. 499) reported that the Draytons' American tour was "in the hands" of P. T. Barnum. According to their advertisements, the Draytons were managed by one George A. Wells.

[89] In Philadelphia, Drayton had studied with Edward Seguin.

[90] "Imagine sprightly conversation, superior voices, pleasant music, good costumes, and artistic fluency," wrote Fry, "and you have the entire of the evening's work" (*Tribune,* October 13, 1859).

[91] "In a literary point of view, they are mere trifles," wrote Seymour (*Times,* October 13, 1859): "The music is of the French school Frenchy." But if there were no memorable phrases, there was plenty of rhythmic vivacity, and mercifully little pretence. A small orchestra supplied the accompaniments.

[92] On the afternoon of November 5, as we know, the Draytons successfully performed *Never Judge by Appearances* at the Saturday Gala Opera Matinée at the Academy of Music.

gian *Conservatoire,* Oliveira at first played a movement of de Bériot's First Concerto but soon switched to musical fare more compatible with the popular taste: arrangements of opera airs and especially the grotesque variations on "The Carnival of Venice."[93]

The high point of the company's offerings, however, was Drayton's powerful rendering—at that grave period in the nation's destiny—of "The Star-Spangled Banner," providing an experience, feelingly wrote the *Musical World* (December 21, 1859, p. 2), that "would cure all disunionists to hear him sing those words."

[93] Señor Oliveira's future career unfortunately lay in the minstrel halls and drinking establishments of the city.

4

GTS: 1860

The history of opera is but a financial obituary.

New-York Times
October 21, 1860

*As for Brignoly, Ferry, and Junky, thay air dowtless grate, but I think
sich able boddied men wood look better tillin the sile then dressing their-
selves up in black close & white kid gloves & showtin in a furrin tung.
Mister Junky is a noble lookin man & orter lead armies on to Battle
instid of showtin in a furrin tung.*

"Artemus Ward"
New-York Evening Post
June 6, 1860

IN 1860, GEORGE TEMPLETON STRONG—haunted, like most Americans, by the en-
croaching menace of national dissolution—continued nonetheless to fulfill the customary occupations and preoccupations of his daily life: lawyerly duties in Wall Street,
Trinity Church business, Columbia College business, social communion with the best
people, opera-going, an occasional visit to the theatre, an occasional musicale at someone's house, delectable evenings at home listening to Ellen reading Beethoven's piano
sonatas, and—most delectable of all—the Philharmonic rehearsals and concerts that
permitted him to indulge his musical predilections, chiefly for works by Beethoven, to
luxuriate in prolix, post-mortem dissections of their content, and to conjecture, with
apposite German quotations, upon the composer's intent in creating them.[1]

Occasionally Strong broadened his accustomed orbit of socio-musical activity to
include a slumming expedition.

January 5, 1860. . . . Tuesday evening [January 3] we went to one of Wrey
Mould's little musical gatherings.[2] His *wee* parlors are uncarpeted and unfurnished:

---

[1] Pleasurable exercises, in which Strong was probably again prompted by his reading of Ruskin,
the fifth and final volume of whose *Modern Painters* was locally published during this year.

[2] Probably attracted to the "ugly and uncouth," but gifted (and apparently impecunious), architect Jacob Wrey Mould primarily because of Mould's passionate dedication to music, in May Strong

they contain nothing but a big organ and a grand piano. The chairs were evidently imported from the bedroom and the kitchen. But there were Burke with his violin, Mills at the piano, and Groeneveldt⌐ with violoncello, and they did full justice to a very elaborate and lovely work of Mendelssohn's, [Trio] (op. 66, I think). Item: there was good singing; item: Weber's *Euryanthe* Overture, eight-handed. It was all unconventional and outside the common social routine, and Mould's ardor in superintending was so genuine and intense, and the people he had assembled were so keenly appreciative of the music, that we found it refreshing. We had to leave early for a grand "conversational" blowout at [the astrophysicist] Lewis [Morris] Rutherford's.

January 7. . . . Tonight I went to the Philharmonic concert at the Academy of Music [the occasion of Eisfeld's return to the Philharmonic after his misadventure at sea] and seated myself in the gallery, or third story, which seems a good place. It was occupied mostly by men, a majority of whom behaved like lovers of music and had a talent for *silence.*

The Larghetto [and Finale] from Spohr's *Die Weihe der Töne* (the worse half of that symphony) went well enough.[3] Mendelssohn's [scena and aria] *Infelice* [op. 94], sung by Mrs. Anna Bishop, did not at all impress me.[4] Then came Schumann's ["Spring"] Symphony, No. 1, in B-flat [op. 38 (1841)]. Certainly very good: the Andante and Finale quite agreeable. *But* it seemed to me a specimen of the perfection to which "classical" music-manufacture may be carried by a composer of talent and taste. Artistic waxwork simulating Life so closely that I'm not quite sure whether it was in fact living or dead. I think it was in fact *dead* and a mere misty reflection of Beethoven; but I have heard it but once, and there may be something more in it.

Wagner's Overture to *Faust* opened part two.[5] I could make nothing of it.[6] Why should Wagner trouble himself to translate the sentiment of *Faust* into music? Beethoven has done that thing in the first movement of the C-minor Symphony.

> Da steh' ich nun, ich armer Thor!
> Weh! Steck ich in dem Kerker noch?
> O, dass dem Menschen nichts Vollkom'nes wird
>   Empfind' ich nun.[7]

---

successfully supported Mould's application to design the new Trinity Church Schoolhouse, over the powerful opposition (and resulting ire) of Richard Upjohn,⌐ the architect of Trinity Church.

[3] Played in memory of Spohr, an honorary member of the Philharmonic Society, who had died the previous October.

[4] Watson pronounced the work to be of "rare and peculiar beauty"; it was, needless to add, superbly sung by Madame Bishop, to whom he expressed gratitude for making it known (*Leslie's,* January 21, 1860, p. 115).

[5] Two helpings of the Music of the Future at a single concert signified "unnecessary cruelty" on the part of the Philharmonic program makers, wrote the *Albion* critic (January 14, 1860, p. 19). "After a symphony Schumann, to have an Overture Wagner is, to use the affecting expression of an American sufferer, like knocking a man down and then dragging him out to a worse punishment."

[6] An "eccentric and hard-to-be-come-at-understandably work, [but] with some strong and beautiful points," wrote Watson (*Leslie's,* January 21, 1860, p. 115).

[7] Strong has combined three separate lines from Goethe's *Faust:* the first: "And here, poor fool, I stand" (scene one, line 358); the second: "Woe! this dungeon still imprisons me" (scene one, line 398); the third: "O! that nothing can be perfect unto man, I realize now" (scene 14, lines 3240–42).

Beethoven's orchestra tells all that more clearly than Goethe's verse. That immortal first movement sings the Wail of Unrest and Heartlessness of Man, when all that mere Humanity can do is done; when *Philosophie, Juristerei und Medicin und auch Theologie* are studied out, conquered and exhausted, and the Conqueror feels that he is no wiser than before.

Then came Beethoven's "Emperor" Concerto, No. 5, in E-flat, op. 73♪ (second and third movements) [played by Gustav Satter]. Most lovely and refreshing, every note full of life, each phrase of melody genial and inspired.[8] Mrs. Bishop sang Schubert's *Ave Maria* rather badly,[9] and the concert ended with Weber's *Oberon* Overture, which I cannot hear too often.

What volumes of German legend are concentrated in the weird cadences of its opening movement! Then the fiery rush of the Allegro—like a column of Zouaves[10] storming a breach, "with the light of battle on their faces" and the pungency and beauty of the melodic phrases that are so exquisitely introduced by a repetition of the three notes with which the horn begins the overture. Weber's *Freischütz* transcends it, I suppose, in freshness and inspiration, but with that exception, this seems to me the finest overture extant.

January 10. . . . Ellie read me some music tonight. Beethoven's sonatas mostly. She seems pretty well.[11]

January 18. . . . Wall-Streeted with some diligence; wanted to come uptown early to hear Mendelssohn's A-Symphony (the "Italian"), but could not do it. Ellie heard the [Philharmonic] rehearsal and is enthusiastic in commendation.

January 30. . . . Ellie read Beethoven's sonatas for me tonight. They are very great, and she interprets them well—has improved very much in reading music.

While I was taking my very late breakfast this morning, Ellie and Mrs. Paulding were in the music room, and the glorious Andante of Beethoven's C-minor Symphony was in full blast, four-handed. Little Babbins sat near me in a big chair, his golden curls "making a sunshine" around him and his big eyes full of attention to the music. A picture-book lay on his lap neglected, His tiny finger was beating time, and each of the more salient phrases of melody was noticed with an ejaculation of "Poppa! That's *pitty!*" His feeling for music is singularly strong.

January 31. . . . Ellie read Beethoven's sonatas for me tonight.

February 1. . . . Uptown by great exertion by three-thirty for the Philharmonic

---

[8] Despite Satter's "too excessive appreciation of his own powers," wrote Watson (*Leslie's,* January 21, 1860, p. 115), he was an accomplished artist, and his performance of Beethoven's concerto—barring some ostentatious hurrying in the last movement—was excellent. For an encore Satter exquisitely played a transcription (probably his own) of the Menuetto from Mozart's E-flat Symphony, and for his solo his own Festival Polonaise in F-sharp, encored by his Variations on the Mermaid's Song from Weber's *Oberon.*

[9] If Madame Bishop sang Schubert's *Ave Maria* with "less than her usual conscientiousness," she nonetheless brought down the house with her encore, "The Last Rose of Summer." Eisfeld was warmly welcomed back, and Watson hailed the event, all told, as "one of the finest concerts, if not the finest, ever given by the New York Philharmonic Society" (*ibid.*).

[10] With their exotic, quasi-oriental uniforms and virtuosic drills, Zouave companies were currently a dashing, if fleeting, constituent of the American Army.

[11] Ellen Strong was again pregnant, and Strong was correspondingly anxious about her health. In May she would give birth to their third son, Lewis Barton Strong.

rehearsal with Ellie, Mrs. Gibbs, and Mrs. Paulding. Heard Mendelssohn's "Italian" Symphony. . . . I can't rate the Mendelssohn Symphony very high, but it is a beautiful piece of construction.

~~~

After five weeks of sensational Patti triumphs at the Boston Academy of Music[12] (as the Boston Theatre had been renamed upon its takeover by Ullman/Strakosch), a dazzling spring season was announced for the company's return to the New York Academy at the beginning of February. Its chief new attraction was a superproduction of Halévy's *La Juive* (Paris 1835), to eclipse even *The Huguenots* in spectacular scenery, suits of armor, and equine supernumeraries. Also promised were elaborate new productions of Auber's *Masaniello;* the American premiere of Verdi's *Aroldo* (Rimini 1857);[13] and perhaps Meyerbeer's new opera *Le Pardon de Plöermel* (Paris 1859), known in its Italian version as *Dinorah.*

But no sooner had the ambitious schedule been announced than Ullman issued a "counter-manifesto" informing the public that the season would be curtailed to two weeks, sans *La Juive;*[14] it would include, however, *I puritani* (with Patti), *Alessandro Stradella,* and *Der Freischütz,* all in Italian.[15] The company would then appear briefly in Philadelphia, Baltimore, and Washington, where little Patti was loudly demanded,[16] and in mid-April she would depart for London, where she would make her debut in *Martha* at Lumley's opera house.

Strong, who for all his disdain of Italian opera had evidently subscribed to the full season, attended the opening-night *Puritani* on February 6 and heard Adelina Patti for the first time. "Little Patti, the new *prima donna,* made a brilliant success," he wrote. "Her voice is fresh but wants volume and expression as yet—vocalization perfect."[17]

[12] So sensational that Gazzaniga, who had been engaged until May 1, 1860, at an exorbitant $2200 a month, in the desperate days of Crescimano and Speranza, was now considered superfluous. During the company's stay in Boston, Gazzaniga sued the impresarios for willfully preventing her from appearing, and for withholding her payment. "The management maintains," tattled the *New-York Evening Post* (January 30, 1860), "that, as the lady does not draw houses to cover the expenses, she is not worth—and is not entitled to—her salary." "If she fails to draw," commented the *Musical World* (February 11, 1860, p. 3), "it is not because her singing has deteriorated, but because the public is inconstant; the last pleases best. Novelty is the prime mover in crowding the Academy at all times." It was reported that Adelina Patti was paid a paltry $400 a month; Colson $1100, Brignoli $1200, and Stigelli $700.

[13] A revision of *Stiffelio* (Trieste 1850), it would in fact not be heard in New York until 1863.

[14] According to Burkhardt, who reacted furiously to this latest example of Ullman's perfidy, a score and parts of *La Juive* had already been shipped to Maretzek in Havana because "it cannot be produced here. And why?" demanded Burkhardt. "Because we could not discover any good in Verdi's *Sicilian Vespers,* are we to lose Halévy's *Jewess?*" (*Dispatch,* January 28, 1860).

[15] With the *Freischütz* to include the purportedly "new" recitatives by Berlioz that Maretzek might, or might not, have included in his less than successful production of *Il franco arciero (Der Freischütz)* in 1850.♩

[16] "We are to be cut down and reduced," wailed Watson, "we are to be curtailed of our musical season, and all because that little witch Adelina Patti has become so famous that every one wishes to hear her. This is too bad—it is unjust and ungenerous" (*Leslie's,* February 4, 1860, p. 147).

[17] In the cast with Patti, as Elvira (a new role), were Brignoli as Arturo, Ferri as Riccardo, and Susini, who at last made his reappearance in New York, and splendidly, as Giorgio. Under Muzio, however, "the chorus and orchestra were both decidedly and distinctly bad," reported the *Times* (February 7, 1860).

Little Adelina Patti, now sixteen years old, was honored by pictures on sheet music.

Both: Girvice Archer, Jr.

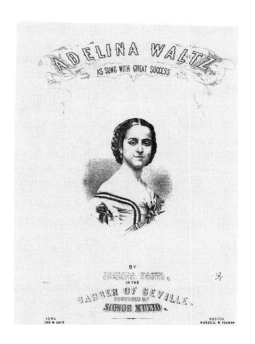

Vera Lawrence

THE LEONARD JEROME HOUSE

The house of Leonard Jerome (later the grandfather of Winston Churchill), containing a theatre that seated six hundred and a grand ballroom where Adelina Patti sang.

Among the critics, Patti's advent was largely regarded as a kind of divine benefaction. It had been a blessing in disguise, wrote the anonymous new reviewer for *Wilkes' Spirit of the Times* (February 11, 1860, p. 368), that the previous season, with its Speranzas and Crescimanos, had been so great a disaster, for it had brought us "our little Patti," whose genius might otherwise have remained hidden "within the narrow range of the home circle." Watson breathlessly agreed, but the prickly *Albion* critic had reservations: Patti was not without her shortcomings, he wrote (February 11, 1860, p. 67), partly due to her youth and partly to the combined pressures of too many performances and the enforced study of new roles under which she labored. To say nothing of "the still more burdensome pressure of metropolitan and provincial puffery."

February 10. . . . Opera tonight with Ellie and Mrs. Georgey Peters and her papa [Andrew S. Snelling]. *Der Freischütz* in an Italian version. The Germanism of that opera is so intense that any translation of its text is an injustice to Weber's memory, but its noble music can afford to be heard under disadvantages.[18] Max was Stigelli, and

[18] Charles Bailey Seymour differed. Despite here and there a spot of commendable orchestration and an occasional bit of "singable condescension," he wrote (*Times,* February 13, 1860), "the bulk

very good. Agatha (Colson) respectable. She knew how her music ought to be sung and tried hard, but had not the vigor it demands. Caspar (Junca) was pretty bad.[19] [Bergmann conducted.]

Query: if there ever existed a Caspar who could sing *Hier in ird'schen Jammerthal* as it ought to be sung; or an Agatha who would do justice to the glorious Allegro that follows her *Leise, leise, fromme Weise?* I enjoyed the evening; also Wednesday evening [February 8], when we had Charley Strong and wife in "our box" and heard *The Barber,* delightfully rendered. Little Patti made a most brilliant Rosina and sang a couple of English songs in the Music Lesson Scene, one of them ("Comin' thro' the Rye") simply and with much archness of expression.[20] This little debutante is like to have a great career and to create furors in Paris and St. Petersburg within five years. Brignoli was the Count; Amodio Don Basilio; Ferri Figaro; and Susini made a very satisfactory Dr. Bartolo. Have not heard that worthless, but fascinating, music so well rendered since the remote era of Bosio and Badiali at Castle Garden.♪

~

The only dissenter was, of course, Hagen, whose worst apprehensions were realized with Patti's Rosina. Obviously from overfatigue coupled with lack of technique, he claimed, her voice had deterioriated. Both her new roles, Rosina and Elvira (in *I puritani*), had been hastily slapped together; both were "uneven and little artistic." Although her natural endowments were great, she had so far accomplished little with them. Hagen compared Patti unfavorably with Madame de Wilhorst, who in his opinion was not only a superior artist but possessed a much finer voice. He counseled Patti to "study scales—chromatic as well as diatonic"—and to eschew "the aid of any of those movements of head which may do for Miss Piccolomini, who was no singer, but which will not do for Miss Patti, who ought to become a great singer" (*Review and Gazette,* February 18, 1860, p. 50).[21]

---

of the music is vocally impossible, a collection of passages that degenerate naturally into screams." Besides, it was difficult to decide which was the duller, Weber's "original German dialogues which connect the pieces or the intermediate recitatives of Hector Berlioz, which leave them centuries apart." To the *Albion* critic (February 18, 1860, p. 79), *Der Freischütz* was a hopeless bore in any language other than the original German, and even then it was a tiresome infliction, except for Weber's "really beautiful instrumental ideas."

[19] Both Madame Colson and Junca were, in fact, highly praised by the critics. But despite their admittedly commendable efforts, Hagen stoutly maintained that "the character, the poetry, the *couleur locale* of the music can only be felt and appreciated by Germans" (*Review and Gazette,* February 18, 1860, p. 51).

[20] The "winged *staccato* passages" decorating Patti's "Comin' thro' the Rye" were regarded among the high points of her completely wonderful Rosina, a role she had reportedly learned in six days. But the critic of *Wilkes' Spirit of the Times* (February 18, 1860, p. 384) found the introduction of an English ballad in a Rossini opera to be "in bad taste, and the effect not at all pleasing." More flexibly, Wilkins, in the *Herald* (February 9, 1860), wrote: "Such interpolations may offend the purists, but they always delight the popular ear. As half the fun of the 'Barber' is lost to those who do not understand Italian, it may be only fair that a little English be introduced as an offset." Patti also sang Sontag's "Echo Song" and, at the close of the opera, the "Adelina Waltz," a trifling substitution for Rossini's finale, composed for her by Muzio.

[21] In the meantime, Patti had appeared and triumphed at a crowded "Grand Patti Matinée" on February 11, when she repeated her Elvira in *I puritani*. The following day, a Sunday, Rossini's *Stabat Mater* was the feature of a fifty-cent sacred concert at the Academy, with Colson, Amalia Strakosch, Brignoli, Stigelli, Ferri, Amodio, Susini, Junca, Müller, and Quinto.

February 13. . . . Had to give up *The Barber* for a Trinity Church Vestry meeting, though I would rather have seen Dr. Bartolo than Dr. Berrian.

February 17. Jem Ruggles and William Christie dined here, and we went to the opera. *Freischütz* substituted for *Saffo* owing to Brignoli's indisposition, for which I hereby thank him.[22] Hardly a note of that opera *[Der Freischütz]* could be spared, except for Aennchen's music. Her role might be advantageously pruned and abridged.[23] The great points of the opera are, I think, these: the unsurpassed overture, a short chorus (of consolation to Max) in the first scene, the sextette of the finale, and the orchestral work all through, from beginning to end. All this seems to me music of the most exalted order, not merely great and beautiful, but so clear, plain, simple, sensuous (so far as music may be), and passionate, that every man who can distinguish "Pop Goes the Weasel" from "God Save the Queen" ought reverently to recognize its power and beauty the very first time he hears it. But it is all dull, old-fashioned, and flat to our opera-goers, except only Agatha's Scena, in which Colson's flexible voice calls out plaudits. . . . Wednesday [February 15] Peter Strong [a cousin] and his handsome Mrs. Mary dined here, and we took them to the opera. *Sonnambula.* Amina, Patti; her lover, Brignoli; the Count, Amodio. The performance was satisfactory, and the two ladies found the evening particularly pleasant.

February 21. . . . Opera last night. Ellie, Mrs. Georgey Peters . . . *Lucia:* Patti,[24] Stigelli [replacing Brignoli], Ferri.

━━━

At Patti's second performance of *La sonnambula,* on Washington's Birthday, a rousing musical tribute was paid to the Italian hero Garibaldi with intermission performances of two timely "patriotic *morceaux*" by Muzio: the first, his Overture in E for orchestra (a work, in fact, some time since composed for the Brooklyn Philharmonic) and the second, his rip-roaring "Garibaldi Rataplan," a "Grand Italian March,"[25] performed by everyone in the cast with Susini, an authentic veteran of the Italian War, martially flourishing the Italian tricolor.[26]

On February 24, Gazzaniga at last accomplished her delayed farewell with a per-

[22] *Saffo* had been announced as the ultimate farewell performance by Gazzaniga (who seems to have made up her differences with the management) before she departed on another ultimate farewell concert tour before yet another ultimate return to Europe.

[23] The *Evening Post* agreed (February 11, 1860). The critic was, however, greatly taken with Hannibal Calyo's scary stage set for the Wolf's Glen scene: "In the distance, snow-covered peaks lay gleaming in the moonlight, while in the foreground are rugged rocks, over which pours a foamy cataract." Within, "a mysterious owl of the most colossal dimension flaps his wings and emits red, lurid light from his eyes at regular intervals. During the forging of the magic bullets, unheard-of birds flit through the air; a gigantic skeleton . . . moves across the stage on a wagon, whose wheels move in pyrotechnic flashes, while divers skeleton horses and nondescripts course madly through the air and disappear." Moreover, a "decidedly villainous" smell of gunpowder pervaded the house.

[24] On February 18, at the second and "most positively" last Grand Patti Matinée, she repeated *The Barber of Seville.*

[25] In Boston the "Garibaldi Rataplan" had been "shouted between the acts [of *La favorita*] by the principals, secondaries, and choruses with much patriotic vigor, especially by Gazzaniga," reported *Dwight's* (January 28, 1860, p. 351).

[26] Rather he "staggered" under it "in a very pleasing and patriotic way," joshed the *Albion* critic (February 25, 1869, p. 91), who found the *Rataplan*—bellowed at the tops of everyone's lungs in an unequal struggle with the piccolo flutes and trombones—to be in musical essence "not remarkable for its freshness: it fell upon the ear 'like an old friend.'"

formance of *Saffo,* embellished at intermission time by the "Garibaldi Rataplan"; on February 25, at a Grand Farewell Matinée, Patti (yes, Patti), rematerialized in a post-farewell *Lucia di Lammermoor,* and Colson and Gazzaniga (yes, Gazzaniga) were heard respectively in single acts of *Der Freischütz* and *La favorita.* On Sunday evening, February 26, *Poliuto* was presented as an oratorio under its more religious-sounding alternate title of *I martiri,*[27]★ with Colson, Stigelli, Amodio, and the perpetual fillers-in, Müller and Quinto.

On February 27, Strong heard the season's final production, *Marta,* with Adelina Patti as Lady Harriet, Amalia Strakosch as Nancy, Brignoli as Lionel, and Junca as Plunkett. Of it Strong commented merely that it was "a very pretty opera."

The critics had more to say. As for little Patti, they wrote, she again surpassed herself (if such a thing were possible), although it was perceived by some that her voice was not sufficiently audible in the ensembles—a shortcoming to be expected, however, in one so young; with the passage of time it would right itself. The production, however—if one could so describe it—unleashed a barrage of pent-up journalistic ire against the blatant deceptions increasingly being foisted upon the public by Ullman and Strakosch. In the *Times* (February 28, 1860), Seymour deplored the deteriorating musical standards at the Academy: "By a slow but steady process of depletion the orchestra and chorus of that respectable establishment . . . are now almost totally inadequate to the just interpretation of any work containing many harmonic parts," he wrote. The subordinate parts were "always so negligently considered . . . that it is useless and unjust to dwell on the inefficiencies of Signor Müller [the Sir Tristram], who simply illustrates the rule of mismanagement by being intolerably bad."

Except for Patti, wrote Burkhardt (*Dispatch,* March 3, 1860), the Academy presentations "ranged from mediocrity downward to very bad." Instead of advancing toward greater perfection, Ullman's productions had sadly deteriorated since the splendid early days of *Robert le diable* and *The Huguenots.* Except for that "horrid *Vespers*" (Burkhardt's *bête noir*), every opera presented during the last few seasons had been "hurried upon the boards, scarcely rehearsed, if at all, carelessly costumed, badly put in scene, hurly-burly-hugger-mugger-rushed-out, grandiloquently announced, and carelessly performed." Nor was it the fault of the members of the company. "Overworked artists cannot do justice to themselves and [they] lose ambition," wrote Burkhardt, "and an overfed public becomes nauseated by the abundance of indifferent and bad food." Far better to present only three opera nights and one matinée a week, properly prepared, than this helter-skelter, insulting assault upon the public's judgment, patience, and credulity.

The truncated season concluded with a grandiose, two-day benefit to Patti, announced as positively the last opportunity for New Yorkers to hear her as Rosina (on March 2) and as Martha (March 3) before her April departure for England. For the overall monster event Patti would be joined by the entire company, who would vari-

[27] "Whether these [Sunday] entertainments will become popular is, however, doubtful," wrote the *Evening Post* critic (February 28, 1860). "The prejudice against Sunday evening entertainments is too strong here to be easily eradicated, and is participated in even by those who make no professions to religious fastidiousness. But there are a number of our foreign citizens who will patronize the Sunday night 'oratorio,' and we presume it is chiefly for them that this species of entertainment is provided."

ously combine, besides, in rousing performances of the "Liberty Duet" from *I puritani* and of Muzio's "Garibaldi Rataplan," the great hit of the moment.

Despite their complaints of the poor quality of the Academy's presentations, the critics continued to resent the company's early departure to Philadelphia and points south. "The opera now closes," sardonically observed the *Evening Post* critic on March 3, in his musical gossip column and rumor mill, "probably because the managers dread a success. The normal condition of opera managers is one of utter pecuniary depletion. Give them a chance of putting money in their purses and at once they will betake themselves to the less generous climes of Philadelphia and Boston [the classical targets of ridicule for the chauvinistic New York journalists], there to lose in lawsuits and empty houses the earnings of the New York season.[28] . . . The sudden flight of Ullman and his forces at this juncture" was downright perverse. With a star like Patti, adored by all, their departure was madness. During the just elapsed season of seventeen performances, wrote this reporter, Patti had appeared thirteen times,[29] Colson about six times, Gazzaniga once.

But never mind, consoled the writer; opera would not be absent for long: Maretzek would soon be returning with his great Havana company; Cortesi would not be far behind; and concerts would be restored to the concert-hungry scene. And it was persistently rumored that Maretzek was bringing Gottschalk back from Havana.

Strong, who most uncharacteristically had been neglecting the Philharmonic in favor of opera, now returned to the true faith.[30]

February 29. . . . Went alone to the Philharmonic rehearsal at the Academy of Music. Watched Hazeltine and pretty Helen Lane billing and cooing just in front of me, to the very appropriate accompaniment of Beethoven's lovely D-Symphony [no. 2, op. 36]. A sentimental gent would say that the handsome young couple and the glowing, joyous music were each a sort of commentary on the other.

March 3. . . . [Ellie] read me some music. My first introduction to [J. S.] Bach. My first criticism is that Bach, though old-fashioned and queer, evidently understood counterpoint and was able to produce clear and vigorous musical thought.

March 4. . . . Mrs. Gibbs and Mrs. d'Oremieulx spent the evening here reading quadro-manual piano and organ music.

[28] The formerly problematic New York opera season was now said to be financially successful, chiefly attributable to Patti.

[29] Not yet seventeen years old, she had by now mastered "seven leading operas," boasted Ullman's comparatively subdued advertisement for *Marta*.

[30] He had evidently not attended the Philharmonic concert on February 11, when Eisfeld had conducted Mendelssohn's "Italian" Symphony, Schumann's "abstruse" *Manfred* Overture, and the first local performance of Lachner's inconsequential Festival Overture, op. 30. The soloists had been S. B. Mills and Stigelli, a last-minute replacement for an ailing Madame Colson. Accompanied by Timm at the piano, Stigelli magnificently sang Beethoven's "Adelaide," his own song "The Tear," and, as encores, an unidentified *Lied* by Schubert and another of Stigelli's own compositions, "Lovely Night." With the orchestra, Mills, on one of Steinway's embattled overstrung grands, "flawlessly" played the Adagio and Finale of the Concerto in G minor, op. 60, by Ignaz Moscheles, his former teacher at Leipzig; his solo was Chopin's F-minor Fantasy, op. 49 (1840–41)—both works being heard for the first time in New York. Mills's encore, according to the *Musical World* (February 18, 1860, p. 3), was his own set of variations on "Poor Mary Ann," an old English tune.

March 14. . . . Philharmonic rehearsal at three-thirty. Beethoven's D-Symphony. . . . Ellie joined me there (Academy of Music), and we sat with Mrs. Wolcott Gibbs and little Gracie Paulding. . . . The D-Symphony is gorgeous. Pages of bosh might be written about it. It does not impress one with a sense of uncanny supernatural power, such as one finds in the "Eroica," the A-Symphony and the C-minor, but it is clear, healthy, genial, and sunshiny throughout, and in that respect is above all the three—except, of course, the C-minor, in which doubt and darkness are so magnificently developed into Light and Victory. *Der furchtbare Geist* [the fearful spirit], *Erbangen und Beklommenheit* [anxiety and oppressiveness], the *feindliche Princip* [the hostile principle],[31] etc. etc. are absent from this most *beautiful* of Beethoven's symphonies.

March 24. . . . With Ellie this A.M. at Academy of Music and heard the lovely D-Symphony rehearsed. How much thought and work are embodied in its transcendent *Larghetto!* That movement seems as if it might have been written as the musical exposition of some poem, or story—an impression Beethoven's music seldom produced on me. There is a *special* character about the sentiment of its phrases and their grouping that suggests correspondence with, or illustration of, some series of varied incident or imagery. Something of Goethe's or Schiller's, perhaps, but I cannot guess at the key. It might be *The Winter's Tale,* perhaps, or *The Merchant of Venice,* etc., etc. These plays are of about the degree of intensity embodied in this movement.

～

It is perhaps understandable that Strong—greatly as he cherished Beethoven—after four consecutive hearings of the Second Symphony, might want to forego a fifth at the concert,[32] conducted by Bergmann on March 24. More probably, he wished to avoid listening to the first American performance of Liszt's symphonic poem *Tasso: lamento e trionfo* (1849–54) (Searle 96), a work of which Seymour disgustedly wrote that although—like everything Liszt composed—it abounded in startling effects expertly wrought, such a composition might just as well have been improvised by any "well-informed orchestra," for all the musical quality it possessed. Indeed, that a well-informed orchestra could "endure such deliberate non-sequences as a matter of choice" baffled Seymour's comprehension. "We can account for it only on the ground that any new combination of instrumental effects becomes pleasing after a certain amount of familiarity. . . . Excessively tedious,"[33] reported Seymour, the work fell flat (*Times,* March 26, 1860).

The instrumental soloist of the evening was Madame Graever-Johnson, who brilliantly played Hummel's Piano Concerto in A minor, op. 85, and (inevitably) a piece by Litolff, his inconsequential *Souvenirs d'Hartzburg,* op 43. The vocalist was Pietro Centemeri, a greatly admired baritone "of the new Verdi school" and a soloist with the St. Stephen's Church choir, who sang an aria from Verdi's *Attila* and a *romanza* from Donizetti's *Maria Padilla.* The concert concluded with the overture to *Der Freischütz.*

---

[31] Favorite neuroses of the nineteenth century.

[32] An event presented by the "Association for the Promotion of Agreeable Gallantry," sarcastically wrote Seymour (*Times,* March 26, 1860), who added that the Philharmonic concert had been "talked through in a thoroughly satisfactory manner."

[33] "Nothing could be more incoherent and *outré,*" wrote —t— (*Dwight's,* April 7, 1860, p. 13).

At the close of his review Seymour announced that Beethoven's Ninth Symphony would be conducted by Eisfeld at the final Philharmonic concert of the season, on April 28. Music lovers were urged not to neglect the rehearsals. George Templeton Strong needed no urging.

April 4. . . . Met Ellie at the Academy of Music at three-thirty P.M. and heard the Philharmonic rehearsal of the Ninth Symphony. Begin to appreciate the Ninth Symphony. Strange I should have missed its real character and overlooked so many great points when I heard it last. An immense, wonderful work; it ranks among Beethoven's greater symphonies: embodies as much thought and labor as almost any two of them together.

The opening of the first movement is most grand and suggestive. The magic of those few random, simple notes is the genuine article, of which Beethoven possessed a monopoly. The amazing Scherzo, and the most lovely Adagio that follows it, are each unique in its way. How could I have got the notion that there was neither clear melody nor refined instrumentation in these three movements? They are wonderfully strong in both. Many of the melodic phrases are not only distinct and pungent, but beautiful in sentiment, and perhaps of higher order than many of Beethoven's bitter intensities. The melodic expression of the Adagio seems pure, calm, peaceful, celestial. Ditto as to certain phrases in the first movement. The instrumental effects are very novel and striking.

It is too profound and elaborate to be easily followed or understood at a glance, but it's not obscure. And though these three movements contain much that is strange, new, abrupt, and startling, I don't think they can be called extravagant.

But the fourth movement transcends my present capacities. It begins with a spasm (the Scherzo, by-the-by, begins with a sneezing fit), and then come certain recitatives for the basses and quotation from the previous movement, interspersed with titanic *tutti,* and then the basses begin that noble melody (and it *is* noble, though I think an *adagio* rendition of "Yankee Doodle" gave Beethoven the hint), which is repeated again and again, rising higher and higher in the instrumentation till it is delivered by the full orchestra with splendid effect. Dodworth's Band could give it with nearly equal effect, I suppose, but no matter. It is very good to hear—appeals to everybody— sets every head and hand to beating time involuntarily—is a good and appropriate expression of Schiller's glorious (though perhaps a little one-sided) "Song of Joy."

> Seyd umschlungen, Millionen!
> Diesen Kuss der ganzen Welt—
>
> . . . .
>
> Dieses Glas dem guten Geist!
>
> . . . .
>
> Wollust ward dem Wurm gegeben
> Und der Seraph [*sic*] steht vor Gott.

(These . . . lines, by the way, are a rather grand generalization!)[34]

[34] Strong slightly misquotes from Schiller's hymn *An die Freude* (1785), not noticing that the middle line ("Dieses Glas dem guten Geist") is not among those set by Beethoven. The five lines run in translation: "Be united, O ye millions / Brethren, share the kiss of love"; "Raise this glass to the Good Spirit"; "Pleasure to the Worm is granted / but the Cherub looks on God!"

Then follows the lovely little *Marcia* movement, reproducing the same subject, and then comes orchestral lunacy and chaos. The subject—*prestissimo* and *fortissimo*—trombones and trumpets plunging about amid the tumult and fury of the strings, etc., like mad elephants through a free fight, and making me feel as if Eisfeld, who led, was sticking knives into me. And I must say I know of nothing to justify the extraordinary and anomalous succession of orchestral *Snorts* with which the pretty *Tempo di marcia* passage is ushered in.

I think I see very clearly the difference between Beethoven's later works (meaning thereby this symphony, most of the Eighth and the Mass in D) [the *Missa solemnis,* op. 123 (1818–23)], and the products of the middle period. But I know too little of the technicalities of the art to attempt to define that difference. There may be less creative power and freshness in No. 9 than in the C-minor, for instance, but there seems to be a larger control (if possible) of musical language.

April 6. This being Good Friday, we went to Trinity Church. Even standing room could hardly be found—the aisles were crowded. As we could neither see nor hear, we came away before the sermon. The Choral Service, faintly heard, was impressive.

April 15. . . . Drove to Trinity Church this morning with Ellie and Johny and assumed possession of the old pew in the North Aisle. Very full congregation and of every degree, from the Astoroid type down to the English, or North-Irish, emigrant family party. Choral service was impressive; Ellie becomes reconciled to it. There was an Easter anthem; "But Thou did not leave his Soul in Death [*sic*]," solo; and "Lift up your Heads," chorus, from the *Messiah.* The former was most forcibly done by one of the choir boys, [William James] Robjohn [1843–1920] by name. I never before knew the vocal capabilities of boyhood—the male child's power of song. This little chap of eleven or fourteen sang his high soprano part without effort, with power and flexibility, and with a peculiar tone or quality of voice quite new to me.[35] The splendid chorus was accurately rendered, but Handel's great, massive effects demand a heavier chorus. A choir of twenty Archangels could not do them justice. They demand a great voice of much people, "as it were the voice of a great multitude and as the voice of many waters, and as the voice of mighty thunderings, saying: 'Alleluia! For the Lord God Omnipotent Returneth! [*sic*]'" One always feels the want of more power even when they are rendered on the largest scale. "The Glory of the Lord shall be Revealed," "For Unto Us a Child is Born," "Lift up your Heads," the "Hallelujah," etc., though executed with the utmost accuracy and spirit. are always unsatisfactory. No *finite* assemblage of *bassi, tenori,* etc. is sufficient for the inexpressible strength these sublime choruses embody. Ten thousand vocalists, with an orchestra to balance them, would fail. The immense inspiration latent in them can be adequately expressed only by the combined voice of all mankind in harmony.

By now, much to the delectation of the press, musical New York was agog over the latest outbreak of opera hostilities, with Max Maretzek at the Winter Garden (the renamed Metropolitan Theatre) and Ullman at the Academy of Music once again

[35] In later life, under the pseudonym of Caryl Florio, Robjohn, son of the organ builder William Robjohn, would become a well-known composer.

locked in mortal combat.[36] To retaliate for Ullman's duplicitious attempt to obtain a lease on the Tacón Theatre from Martí by offering Adelina Patti as bait, gleefully writes Maretzek (*Sharps and Flats,* p. 47): "I hired the Winter Garden Theatre, engaged [Ullman's] underpaid tenor Stigelli and his dissatisfied conductor Anschütz, added to my company Madame [Inez] Fabbri, in addition to Frezzolini and Gassier, opened the Winter Garden . . . producing *La Juive* before Ullman had time to finish his rehearsals, and followed in rapid succession with . . . [Verdi's] *Masnadieri* [London 1847] . . . and forced Ullman to shut the Academy of Music." Perhaps an oversimplification. Henry Watson (in *Leslie's,* March 24, 1860, p. 257) more immediately attributed the contest to Ullman's refusal, during his company's absence on tour, to sublease the Academy of Music to Maretzek.

Indeed, immediately upon Maretzek's announcement of his forthcoming season at the Winter Garden, Ullman/Strakosch, in what Watson called a "counterblast," suddenly returned to New York for an early spring season. Serene in their possession of Patti, a veritable "gold placer laying up ingots of the precious metal," as Watson inelegantly commented, the partners had become as "saucy [upon sniffing] opposition away off, as an Alderman [who] smells a fat contract."

Thus shut off from the Academy, regarded as the only suitable place for opera in New York, Maretzek, with murder in his heart, had again been forced into a substitute locale, wrote Watson. A peaceful coalition would have been better, but, he philosophized, "to effect a cordial union between opera managers would require the genius of a Palmerston."

It was no coincidence, then, that the rival opera seasons were announced to open on the same night—Easter Monday, April 9—Ullman's with Patti (whose purported departure for England was now put off until mid-May) appearing in *The Barber of Seville*[37] and Maretzek's with the Gassiers and a loudly proclaimed new tenor Achille Errani (1824–1897), fresh from their triumphs in Havana, in *Lucia di Lammermoor.*

In a pronunciamento of Ullmanesque grandeur Maretzek landed the first blows. Disingenuously denying Ullman's accusation that he was attempting "a factious opposition" to the opera at the Academy, Maretzek protested that if opera had indeed by now achieved the status of an established institution in the United States, he (or anyone else) was free to engage in it; if it had not, then there was no basis for argument. Maretzek boasted of his seniority in putting opera on a firm footing in the United States; he quoted "that acknowledged musical scholar and impresario Mr. Maurice Strakosch," who had claimed the Winter Garden's acoustics and sight lines to be superior to those at the Academy; he derided Ullman's idiosyncratic advertising tactics, but also emulated them—touting his brilliant new *prima donna,* the Austrian soprano Inez Fabbri (*née* Agnes Schmidt)[38] in what Burkhardt called "covered puffs." And above all,

---

[36] "It's the funniest thing in the world to note the bearing of the two managers toward each other," gossiped *Trovator* as the feud progressed (*Dwight's,* April 21, 1860, p. 29). "Ullman is a perfect St. Simon Stylites of dignity. He mounts upon a towering pillar of power and pride and, claiming to superintend *the* legitimate opera of New York, does not bestow a word of notice—even an expression of contempt—upon the newcomers at the Winter Garden."

[37] Again with Brignoli, Susini, Amodio, and Ferri.

[38] Since the beginning of March, when she had arrived from South America bearing the encomiums of Madame de LaGrange, who was then reaping triumphs in Rio de Janeiro, Madame Fabbri's name had been posted "in red and black all over the city" (*Evening Post,* March 3, 1860).

in contrast to Ullman's endless reiterations of the same tired old repertory, Maretzek promised productions of several "new" operas, among them Mercadante's *Il bravo* (Milan 1839) and principally Halévy's long awaited *La Juive*.

Ullman won the second round when Maretzek postponed his opening night to April 11. An enforced delay, smoothly extenuated Maretzek, because rehearsal time at the Winter Garden had been insufficient to satisfy his exacting standards. And indeed, when, on April 11, with dauntless Max dynamically leading a large and splendid orchestra comprising the best musicians in New York (carefully picked from the Philharmonic)[39] and a fine (and uncommonly pulchritudinous) chorus; with the Gassiers better than ever and with the new tenor Errani displaying a grace and elegance allegedly unknown since Salvi:[40] "All were so familiar in their parts," wrote Fry (*Tribune,* April 13, 1860), "that they proceeded as an individual utterance." Their performance of *Lucia di Lammermoor* represented the highest possible degree of operatic excellence.[41]

On that same evening, at the Academy of Music, little Patti enchanted her adorers with—for the first time in New York—her delicious Norina in Donizetti's *Don Pasquale.*[42] It was repeated on April 13, possibly to offset the thrilling debut at the Winter Garden on April 12 of Inez Fabbri as Violetta in *La traviata.*[43] Although Patti, as Norina, was deluged with breathless superlatives, it was Madame Fabbri, as the greater novelty, who received the lion's share of critical attention. She was in fact unanimously acclaimed—although neither young nor beautiful—as the greatest Violetta, vocally and histrionically, ever to have appeared in New York; her debut was "in every way important," wrote the exacting *Albion* critic (April 21, 1860, p. 187).

Seymour, like his colleagues, was completely overwhelmed by Fabbri's consummate command of the emotional, as well as musical, nuances of her role, ranging from youthful exuberance in the first act to the "spectral and vocal wreck of her former self" in the last. Her voice, a pure soprano of great volume, was capable of anything required in the score, wrote Seymour; her scales were even and true to pitch, her cadenzas sung with "neatness and dispatch," her trill faultless, her "delivery of sound open and grand," and her use of the *mezza-voce* in the last act was absolutely awe-inspiring (*Times,* April 13, 1860). She was truly a "sensation singer."[44]

At their respective Grand Matinées on the following Saturday, April 14, the warring opera companies repeated their respective hits of the preceding week: Maretzek's

[39] On opening night, Maretzek, upon entering the orchestra, was greeted with "the most hearty and tumultuous applause," reported Watson (*Leslie's,* April 21, 1860, p. 321). It was a demonstration, not of partisanship, he wrote, but of "respect and esteem for one of the most faithful and energetic musical managers that ever wielded a baton in New York."

[40] "In the general characteristics of voice and style he bears many resemblances to his illustrious predecessor," wrote Seymour (*Times,* April 12, 1860). With the malediction scene in the second act, which he delivered with "vehement musical emphasis," Errani brought down the house.

[41] Albeit, in the opinion of the *Post* critic (April 12, 1860): "The scenic effects appeared rather shabby, after the Academy of Music."

[42] With Brignoli (Ernesto), Ferri (Dr. Malatesta), and Susini (a superb Don Pasquale), and with "Venzano's Celebrated Bravura Waltz" as a sensational replacement for Donizetti's finale; Muzio conducted.

[43] With Errani as Alfredo and Ardavani as Germont; Maretzek conducted.

[44] Fabbri was, wrote Watson, echoing his colleagues, "one of the greatest of the many fine artists who have visited our shores" (*Leslie's,* April 28, 1860, p. 357).

Inez Fabbri, sensational Austrian soprano of great volume, singing at the Winter Garden and vying with "Little Patti," who sang the same opera at the Academy of Music. Sheet music reinforced Fabbri's fame.

stars giving the complete *Traviata* and one act of *Lucia;* Ullman's child-diva the *Don Pasquale* spectacularly embellished by the "Venzano Bravura Waltz."

On April 15, in a tongue-in-cheek editorial, the *Herald* assessed the heated opera situation. Referring to Maretzek as "a sort of operatic Garibaldi," the writer (presumably Wilkins) likened the Winter Garden operation to a revolutionary provisional government set up in opposition to the ultra-conservative regime of the magnates at the Academy. The general mood of the times was essentially one of belligerence, he wrote, and thus the opera duel was eagerly embraced by a public that thrived on contests, whether pugilistic,[45] political, or the increasingly imminent life-and-death struggle between North and South.

Comparing the opposing opera seasons, the writer observed that, after all, as "the managers on both sides are clever enough, and are perfectly well acquainted with each other's game, the contest is an exceedingly amusing one." Besides, with everybody rushing off in all directions to hear one opera or another, the managers were doubtless reaping a golden harvest. This was only fair: Ullman, who had suffered his ups and downs—mostly downs—would at last make a fortune; Maretzek would be able to purchase the greater part of Staten Island; and Strakosch be empowered to buy out August Belmont and "cut a dash among the heavy men on Wall Street." Emphatically not so.

On April 16, Strong noted in his diary that Ellen and friends had that evening attended and enjoyed a performance of *Ernani,* with Fabbri and Stigelli, at the "'opposition opera' at the Winter Garden."[46] On that same evening at the Academy, Patti was heard in *Lucia,* wonderfully performed, but, as the *Evening Post* noted, hardly a novelty. On April 18, Maretzek brought back the long absent Erminia Frezzolini[47] as Lucrezia Borgia; the Maffio Orsini was sung by one Anna Wissler, a new contralto from Philadelphia, the Gennaro by Errani, the Alfonso by Gassier. The following day, a Thursday, Maretzek—scooping Ullman's Grand Patti Matinée announced for Saturday—presented a Grand Gala Matinée comprising the whole of *Ernani* and an act of *La sonnambula,* the latter with Pepita Gassier and Achille Errani, probably programed in nose-thumbing defiance of the sensational *Sonnambula* sung at the Academy on April 18 by Adelina Patti.

April 18. After energizing in Wall Street with reasonable diligence, met Ellie at the Academy of Music and heard the second rehearsal of the Ninth Symphony. It

[45] The country was currently transfixed by the inordinately ballyhooed championship match between the American prizefighter John C. Heenan (1835–1873), "the Benicia Boy," and the English boxing champion Tom Sayers. Assuming international proportions, the match, which took place at Farnsborough, England, on April 17, was declared a draw, although Heenan had knocked Sayers down several times. This obviously biased decision was hotly denounced in the United States, where Heenan, upon his return, was feted as a national hero (see following OBBLIGATO).

[46] During this performance Fabbri's gauzy draperies brushed across the unprotected footlights and caught fire. With great presence of mind Stigelli extinguished the flames and saved her life. Throughout the frightening experience, both artists coolly continued in character as though nothing untoward were happening.

[47] In the summer of 1859, Frezzolini, accompanied by a retinue of servants, had, as we know, returned to the United States, in the vain hope of securing a reengagement at the Academy of Music. Contrary to reports of her vocal rejuvenation, her voice had supposedly deteriorated; she nonetheless continued to be regarded as one of the most fascinating artists on the opera stage.

clears and brightens wonderfully on nearer acquaintance. After dinner we called for Mrs. Georgey Peters, and with Willy [William Algernon] Alston [went] to the Academy of Music again. . . . The opera was *Sonnambula*.[48] Small-beer after Burgundy. Bellini's pretty melodies are "easy things to understand," but how flat and feeble and faded and Rosa-Matilda-esque they sound when one is fresh from trying to dig into that compact conglomerate of intensities, the Ninth Symphony!

Samuel Taylor Coleridge [1772–1834], in his *Table Talk*,[49] mentions some concert he had attended and how he didn't like some piece by Rossini: "It sounded to him like nonsense verses." But he could hardly contain himself when something of Beethoven's was played. Coleridge was no special amateur of music—does not seem to have cultivated his feeling for it—has said little about musical schools or styles—or of individual composers and their works. I do not remember any other criticism on musical art by him (he does allude to performers. [John] Braham, and perhaps others). But his genius and his intuition of Truth in art were profound and searching—hardly equaled in this age by any of our Anglo-Saxon race. Therefore, this *Table Talk* fragment of criticism is, to me, very significant. It shows that the recognition of something real, deep, significant in the highest music is *not* a mere vague form of transcendental, dilettanti talk, for the criticism is exquisitely felicitous. *Vide,* Rossini's overtures: *La gazza ladra, Semiramide, William Tell, The Barber,* etc., etc. They are delightful to hear—full of beautiful, fluent, original melody; elaborately finished; full of fine lights and shadows—but they mean nothing and suggest nothing. Harmonious nonsense versification is their precise analogy. Only in one *(William Tell)* do I remember any indication of a higher power, and that belongs, I think, not to Rossini, but to the Swiss yodel he has adopted and worked up most skillfully. Mere lifeless Art, beginning and ending in itself and existing for itself alone, seems to reach its highest point in Rossini. In one sense, he is the Goethe of music.

Compare anything he has written (or anything produced by the Verdis, Bellinis, and Donizettis) with any average work of Beethoven, Mozart, Haydn, Weber, or Mendelssohn. An immense essential difference is at once apparent. It is a generic difference, though I cannot define it in words; nor, I suppose, can anyone else. Musical criticism is beyond human language, just as vital forces transcend the capacity of chemical language. The reactions that convert proteins into muscular fiber—that transform pork and beans into human flesh and blood—that degrade the healthy human tissues into groups of cancer cells and fatty degenerations, tubercular deposits, are inexpressible by the vocabulary of $HO+NO^2+$, etc., etc., that deals so clearly with the phenomena of inorganic chemistry and expresses the facts of that science so fully and conveniently[50]—just so does articulate speech fail in the discussion of all high Art, and most

---

[48] In *La sonnambula*, Patti enjoyed her usual triumph, and was showered with an astronomical number of bouquets, reported *Wilkes' Spirit* (April 28, 1860, p. 128), "but Brignoli most ungallantly refused to pick them up for her"; he chose one or two and left the rest for attendants to clear away. Possibly, sardonically conjectured the reporter, Brignoli was able to detect the genuine bouquets from the "bogus managerial floral offerings, and in that case there [was] some method in his apparent churlishness."

[49] *Specimens of the Table Talk of the late Samuel Taylor Coleridge,* a collection of Coleridge's conversations, was compiled by his nephew H. N. Coleridge and published in 1835.

[50] Strong was indulging in a favorite game: attempting to transpose musical attributes into terms of his pet hobbies.

signally in musical criticism. The true significance and strength of a great musical work can be expressed in words only by a great poet, capable of reproducing in language—prose or verse—what the composer has told him through his orchestra. The critic cannot describe what the composer has done, for he has not the necessary apparatus. He must translate the composer's work—not from one language into another, but into language from a something above language. Hence the inexpressible imbecility of all our musical criticism. How can we expect the newspaper or the magazine hack critic to write anything but mere idiocy about *Don Giovanni* or a symphony of Beethoven's?

And I think I will not attempt any criticism of the Ninth Symphony tonight.

Our [critics'] criticism of symphony or overture is something like this, generally: "This magnificent composition opens with a fine *tutti* in 2/4 time, after which, by an abrupt modulation into B-flat, a remarkably bold subject is introduced by the *tromboni* in unison, with a brilliant accompaniment of clarionets and cymbals which gradually dies away and terminates in the subdominant chord of the original minor key. The resumption of this beautiful phrase by the first violins in triple time with kettledrums *obbligato* is made very effective by the emphasis the octave flute lends to the *crescendo.* But we think, with great deference to the genius of the composer, that the introduction of diminished fifths into the exquisitely touching *morceau d'ensemble* for the oboe, triangle, and double bass is an attempt to produce a startling effect at the expense of true artistic refinement," and so forth—about as valuable an illustration, or exposition, of what the symphony means and says, as Bull Anthon's' notes on the parsing and construction of the *Iliad* are of the genius of Homer and the significance of his epic.

April 19. . . . I am haunted by imperfectly remembered phrases from that Ninth Symphony.

— ⁓ —

With an opera company boasting such superb German artists (despite their Italianized names) as Fabbri and Stigelli, and including such excellent German conductors as Maretzek, Anschütz, and Richard Mülder (Fabbri's husband), it was inevitable that German operas would be performed in German at the Winter Garden.

April 20. Ellie . . . went with Hoffman and me tonight to the little Winter Garden (Broadway opposite Bond Street) and heard Flotow's *Stradella,* performed in German].♪[51] Nice performance;[52] everything notably good except the *music,* which is pretty but commonplace. House crowded—all Deutschland and all Judea, or all the inhabitants of all the *Judenschaften* [Jewish communities] of every capital in Europe, or as many of them as the little place would hold.[53] So we have two operas now—both fairly supported.

[51] In Fry's opinion, with *Stradella's* "entirely Italian" subject and French musical implications, despite its German provenance, the "interjection of the German language appeared out of place" (*Tribune,* April 23, 1860).

[52] Fabbri, essentially a tragic actress, showed a remarkable flair for "the fripperies and frivolities" of the light, "French" school (to which the German *Stradella* was generally relegated); Stigelli was, as always, excellent; Quinto, Müller, and Weinlich tolerably filled the smaller roles, and Anschütz conducted admirably.

[53] A sellout: "It is very rarely that we hear of money being turned away from the doors of an opera house, wrote Watson (*Leslie's,* May 5, 1860, p. 353). "A genuine overflow is a novelty, but in the present instance there was an undeniable rush, crush, and a vast number of disappointed pleasure seekers."

April 22. . . . To Trinity Church with Ellie (plucky little woman, awaiting her confinement within a fortnight). . . Church well filled. . . . Choral service was effective.

April 28. . . . Have heard the Ninth Symphony *twice* today—at rehearsal and concert—and as I have stood three hours in the crowded parquette this evening (the Academy was filled full), I am tired. But I would stand on one leg three hours more to hear the Ninth Symphony again!

Went to the rehearsal at ten A.M. . . . thence downtown . . . did some work—not enough to hurt me—and came uptown. . . . After dinner to the Philharmonic concert, as aforesaid, *solus.* Discoursed with Dr. Carroll, Mould, etc., etc., at intervals. Overture to the *Zauberflöte* was exquisitely played. Madame Johannsen sang *Ocean, du ungeheuer,* "that liest curled like a green serpent all around the World," Rezia's Grand Scena in *Oberon.* It corresponds to Agatha's *Wie nahte mir der Schlummer* in *Der Freischütz*—embodies a like transition of feeling—is cast on nearly the same mold—and demands nearly as much power. So Madame Johannsen did it less than full justice. Stigelli and Philip Mayer also favored us with solos. The former was down in the program for O *cara immagine* from the *Zauberflöte,* but he substituted a rather pretty German song,[54] which the audience applauded, asking no questions. The second part was the Symphony, which was well rendered throughout, except by the vocal quartette in the last movement. They got into terrible bewilderment, and no wonder.

This symphony begins to fascinate me. It resembles no one of its eight sisters, and in certain respects excels them all. I see no organic relation between its several movements, binding them together into one whole. The second and third are connected by a harmonious difference of sentiment (riotous joy and revel contrasted with serenity and perfect peace). But the first Allegro seems a strange introduction to the Hymn, *An die Freude,* of the Finale. I know nothing in music (not even the Seventh Symphony) more suggestive of some intangible horror of great darkness—not to be uttered in words—than the opening of that first movement. I have dreamed it scores of times, have felt the very essence of what Beethoven makes the orchestra do in that opening, when slumbering under the shadow of dyspepsia, have felt it scores of times.

And the ugly dream, of which this music is a sort of similitude, is in this wise: You are walking in darkness, solitude, and silence, nowhere and no whither, You are conscious of nothing but the presence of a vague terror:

> Like one that on a lonesome road
> Doth walk in fear and dread,[55]

eerie and shuddering with the intuition that something fearful is at hand. You feel that all creation is shuddering with you, that the ground you tread on and the air you breathe are instinct with the same all-pervading presentiment of some awful crisis close at hand. Then you hear faintly and far away the first whisper of its coming (two notes—E—A—breaking though the monotonous murmur of the violins) and then again a second—and then a third—this last time far down in the bowels of the earth. Then the shuddering grows keener, and the sense of horror masters you more and more, and the movement and approach of the unknown Enemy are quicker and

---

[54] Doubtless of his own composition.
[55] Samuel Taylor Coleridge: "The Rime of the Ancient Mariner," part 6, lines 446–47.

nearer, and gleams of uncertain lurid light come stealing in (as the flutes and violins open) that reveal nothing but their own uncanny presence. And the terror of the dream becomes more abject, and the palpitation more cruel, and the *Thing* you dread is stirring more energetically and drawing closer and closer, and the crisis is at hand (with the *crescendo* of the orchestra) and the agonizing panic of the dream is upon you, and you strive in vain to run or to cry for help, and then (with that sharp-cut phrase of the whole orchestra in unison) IT rises from the Earth, visible and tangible, and has you in its grasp, and the nightmare is consummated.

That is somewhat like what the orchestra says to me in the first section of that movement. I don't detect the logical connection of this impressive opening with the rest of the movement. It is the most elaborate of the four, full of vigorous thought and splendid effect, but I don't *understand* it. Perhaps the first movement of the C-minor Symphony is analogous in expression. There is certainly a general tone of unrest, oppression, fruitless aspiration, *Sehnsucht* [longing], blended with still darker elements; one grand dark *crescendo* is very memorable. But it is relieved by the loveliest phrases of melody that tell of soothing and consolation, glimpses of Hope and Peace and infinite Mercy penetrating the gloom. The movement attracts me and keeps my attention fixed, but I feel that I must hear it again and again before I understand it—that it is among the deepest of extant compositions.

The second movement is clear enough. Never was such a Scherzo. It is Comus and his rout—or the infinite revel and the Supermundane Beer of Walhalla—or the Triumph of Bacchus—or anything else that is utterly mad and wild and reckless and joyous. Its rush and tumult and intensity are most wonderful. Nobody but Beethoven could have sustained himself so long in such a flight. It stands absolutely alone, so far as I know. Not, too, the simplicity and triviality of the phrases on which the whole is built, the marvelous variety of form into which it is worked, and the perfect unity of the result. Very beautiful and happily contrasted in the trio, two melodic phrases, exquisitely worked up together and set off with the grandest orchestral effects. In this one finds (what is certainly missing in the rest of the symphony) the freshness, fluency, and geniality—the absence of all conscious effort—that characterize Beethoven's earlier works: symphonies, numbers Three, Five, and Seven.

Then the celestial Adagio! Standing alone, it would be perfect. But it is killed by the Scherzo, like Burgundy after Kirsch and Curacao. After the energetic brass and frenzied action with which one's nerves are still tingling, its quiet, lovely melodies seem tame and it sounds thin, like a chamber sextette. It would surely be more effective had it been painted in warmer orchestral coloring and with stronger lights and shadows. But it is the work of Beethoven, long deaf, retaining his faculty of musical thought unimpaired, but losing his power of appreciating contrasts of mere sound—the relative value of *forte* and *piano*. Intensely beautiful, nevertheless, and quite unlike anything else in the symphonies. Full of purity and nobleness. It might be a *Benedictus* or *Et incarnatus* of Mozart's, amplified and elaborated by a hand even more fine than Mozart's, and a faculty more exalted—if that be possible.

The fourth movement is of lower grade, though the clear, intelligible tune out of which it is mainly constructed will always make it attractive and agreeable. Given a nice, solid, tangible melody that one can whistle and an orchestra, there is no need of a Beethoven to produce what will set the heads of a miscellaneous Academy audience bobbling and make a lull in its chatter. It was well rendered by voices and orchestra, all but the solos and vocal quartettes [Mesdames Johanssen and Zimmermann], (Stigelli, Philip Mayer, etc.), which were sadly bungled.[56]

~~~

Far from sharing Strong's monumental intoxication with the Ninth Symphony, William Henry Fry in the *Tribune* (April 30, 1860) again expressed his objections to the antiquated, overlong four-movement symphonic form—with or without voices. In any case, wrote Fry: "Writing for the voice was not Beethoven's forte; this work, vocally, is below his usual standard, and is neither more nor less than a bore. It has, vocally, no climax, no intensity, no brilliancy, no declamatory function." Moreover, it was "screeching, cold, and unimpassioned and as great a nuisance as the 'new' Handel solos,[57] and we cannot say more." Indeed: "The common sense of the Americans makes them yawn over such inflictions as much as they do over stupid, musty oratorios."

If a few of the instrumental passages in the Ninth seemed "redolent of Beethoven's genius," obscurely commented Fry, "there [had been] a great deal of praise bestowed on works [equally] colossal, merely because the generic ideas are repeated many ways—high, medium, and low, loud and soft—on this instrument and that—or on many and few. These kaleidoscopic effects are awfully puffed in criticism, but really they are child's play to the composer who has any brains." It was the original *motivo*, or theme, something in which Beethoven was evidently deficient, that was nine-tenths of the battle, wrote Fry.[58]

While Strong was basking in the refulgence of Beethoven's Ninth Symphony, the opera rivalry steadily continued to escalate. On April 21, Maretzek announced a Super-Grand Gala Matinée featuring his three *prima donnas*: Frezzolini and Wissler in *Lucrezia Borgia,* with Errani and Gassier, and Fabbri in an act of Verdi's *Nabucco,* an opera not locally heard since 1848, when it had failed (under Maretzek's direction) at the Astor Place Opera House.♪ *Stradella* was repeated on April 23.

At the Academy "darling little Patti" continued to carry the full weight of the season on her delicate (but apparently sufficiently sturdy) young shoulders, appearing in *I puritani* on April 23, then in *Marta* on April 25, and at the matinée on April 28.[59] On April 27, at the Academy, one Laura Banti made a hail-and-farewell debut as Leo-

---

[56] The chief culprit was Stigelli, who as a last-minute replacement for one of the Mr. Steinways, originally engaged for the solo tenor part, was evidently not overfamiliar with his part (Philharmonic Archives).

[57] Apparently a reference to the newly issued, magisterial Handel edition by Friedrich Chrysander (1826–1901) (see *Dwight's,* March 24, 1860, p. 413).

[58] "The novelty of the Ninth Symphony, it is evident, no longer protects it from the yawns of a miscellaneous audience," agreed the *Albion* critic (May 5, 1860, p. 211): "An impression prevails that it is not only the longest, but the dreariest, of the master's works." Performed to the accompaniment of relentless feminine chatter, this was the worst rendition of the work the reviewer had ever heard: "The [solo] performers in the last part had a sort of steeplechase with the conductor," he wrote, "but the latter distanced them. It was very amusing to note how they dropped off, one by one, even Stigelli succumbing to the pressure."

[59] Again given in its ruthlessly truncated Italian version, this time with Adelaide Phillips a superior replacement for Amalia Strakosch as Nancy.

nora in *Il trovatore*,[60] a sorry rejoinder to Frezzolini's exquisite performance of the same role at the Winter Garden on April 25, with Stigelli a magnificent Manrico, and Anna Wissler displaying an opulent voice as Azucena.[61] (By now Ullman was reported to be in failing health—and small wonder.)

Despite his fabulous young star—and contrary to protestations in the press that the opera rivalry signified, if anything, a force for good in the city's musical life—Ullman suffered mortal injury from the cearseless barrage of successful productions fired from the Winter Garden. On April 30, a week before the unveiling of the Academy season's *pièce de resistance,* an elaborate revival of Rossini's biblical opera *Mosè in Egitto,* Maretzek brought forth his blockbuster production of *La Juive.*[62]

A coup! Not only was the production acclaimed musically and theatrically the "greatest success ever achieved in this city or country," but it was repeatedly observed in the press that Maretzek, unlike Ullman, had kept his promise and actually brought off a valid and sufficiently spectacular staging[63] of an important and monumental work.

Not possessing the easily assimilated melodies of a Bellini, Donizetti, or Verdi, *La Juive* would require several hearings for its magnificence to be appreciated by the ordinary listener, wrote the *Evening Post* critic. A modern opera, and especially one so elaborate, "should never be judged from a single hearing." A little pruning, too, would not be amiss: people did not enjoy being detained in the opera house until after midnight to hear the fifth and final act of an opera "so grand that it borders on the ponderous and heavy" (*Evening Post,* May 1; May 5, 1860).

The leading roles, wrote the *Albion* (May 5, 1860, p. 211), were magnificently realized by Fabbri and Stigelli. Both as singer and actress, Fabbri was a superb Rachel: "We have no one who can at all approach her; her conception of the *role* is always forcible and original, and she possesses the rare faculty of unfolding it, leaf by leaf, and preserving all the warmer hues for the right moment." Stigelli, as Lazaro (Eléazar), was no less extraordinary. Among the others, Minna von Berkel (Princess Eudoxia) was satisfactory, except when a cadenza was required; Weinlich (the Cardinal) did his "vocally chaotic" best; even Quinto (Léopold), "who has few friends and no admirers . . .

---

[60] Newly arrived from South America, Banti, a former pupil of Lorenzo Salvi in Bologna, had been scheduled, with the usual advance puffery, to make her debut on April 20 in *Norma* with Brignoli. Canceled due to his purported indisposition, by the time Banti made her debut a week later in *Il trovatore* (at Brignoli's benefit), she had become so hopelessly entangled in the toils of intramural opera mischief that, although her performance was commended (albeit mildly) by the critics, she was summarily dropped. Banti was "not quite up to the New York standard . . . but would probably make a hit at Philadelphia or Chicago, or at the second-story Opera House at Cincinnati," wrote Burkhardt, with the superciliousness that New York journalists reserved for the benighted provinces (*Dispatch,* May 5, 1860).

[61] Reported among the celebrities attending this performance were Albertini and Beaucardé (about to return to Europe), the Gassiers, and—surprisingly—Madame Maurice Strakosch.

[62] Erroneously announced as its first performance in New York, *La Juive* had been given in French at the Park Theatre in 1845 by a brilliant but unfortunate opera company from New Orleans,♪ where it had first been performed in 1844. In various English pastiche adaptations, *La Juive* had been heard in New York as early as 1838.♪

[63] As Fry commented (*Tribune,* May 2, 1860), the exciting visual elements of *La Juive*—the "cardinal, the bishops, priests, censer-boys, soldiers, peasant girls, dancers, a caparisoned horse, a caparisoned ass, pavilions mobile and fixed, banners, a Catholic festival, a Jewish Passover, a funeral procession"—were all integral to the plot, not dragged in as "mere decoration or surplussage."

succeeded in obtaining a few flutters of well-merited applause."[64] Anschütz, with an orchestra unequaled in the United States, conducted the work with "the ability of a true master of his art." Indeed, it would be "difficult to avoid apparent exaggeration of praise, so remarkable [was] the combination of sterling excellencies" offered in this production.

Burkhardt, in an outburst of misplaced chauvinism (*Dispatch,* May 5, 1860), gloated over the persistent failure of the Italian-dominated company at the Academy—with their Italian conductor and their "Verdi rubbish"—to effect a production of *La Juive,* while the all-German cast at the Winter Garden—with a German impresario, a German conductor, and a chorus and orchestra consisting mostly of Germans—had brilliantly succeeded in superlatively rendering a French opera in Italian, for the delectation of an audience of American Anglo-Saxons.[65] Except Strong, that is.

April 30. . . . Jem Ruggles dined here, and we went with him to the Winter Garden, where Charley Strong and wife and Mrs. Georgey Peters had seats next ours. Halévy's *La Juive.* We sat through three long acts of trumpet and trombone and then came off. Stage effects showy, house enthusiastic; but the music is absolutely without life—without, even, the galvanico-spasmodic simulation of life that makes Verdi's operas endurable sometimes.

<center>~~~</center>

Notwithstanding Strong, *La Juive* attracted four large audiences within a single week (April 30 through May 5). During this period, performances at the Academy were temporarily suspended to permit, it was claimed, full-time rehearsals by Muzio and the full company of *Mosè in Egitto*♪♫[66] (that is, of *Il nuovo Mosè,* Rossini's 1832 revision for Paris of his original *Mosè* of 1818). Heralded by flights of Ullmanian cajolery, the spectacular production was intended to dim the luster of *La Juive.* Opening on May 7 and consecutively repeated on May 9, 11, 12 (a Gala Matinée) and 14, except for the opening night *Mosè* was disappointingly attended.[67] Its "watery love story," wrote Fry (*Tribune,* May 15, 1860), was "as out of place as a declaration in a pew." Little Patti, as a "sugar plum of a Jewess, dressed in heartrending style,[68] could only

[64] "Certain roles could have been better filled by a portion of Mr. Maretzek's company, who were looking on and criticizing from the stage boxes," wrote the *Home Journal* (May 12, 1860), but in all other respects the production was splendid.

[65] The quip, apparently originating with W. H. Fry in the *Tribune* (March 2, 1860), seems to have caught on, being yet again repeated in a lengthy unsigned review of *La Juive* appearing in *Dwight's* on May 12 (1860, p. 54).

[66] With Patti (Anaïde), Madame Strakosch (Sinaïde), Brignoli (Aménofis), Susini (Moses), Ferri (Pharaoh), and Madame Anna Picker and Messrs. Dubreuil and Scola (back from his Latin American travels) in the lesser roles.

[67] The work was, after all, far from a novelty, noted Burkhardt; it had been frequently (and better) performed as an oratorio by one or the other of the singing societies. Furthermore, in the present production under Muzio, the score had undergone severe and not always judicious excisions (*Dispatch,* May 12, 1860).

[68] Contemporary usage for "attractively dressed." According to the *Evening Post* (May 8, 1860), Patti at first "looked lost in her large head dress, but after the first effect of this quaint costume passed away, it seemed to become her wonderfully. Coquettish curls fell gracefully over the white folds of the drapery, and certainly the costume did not effect her singing."

hang down her head and raise it to emit a lot of fast notes, but [could] not effect characterization, there being nothing to represent."

In Fry's opinion, the miracle of the Red Sea was well staged, but Watson (*Leslie's,* May 20, 1860, p. 401) described the canvas billows as "the funniest waste [expanse] of water that ever adorned even an Italian opera."[69] In his estimation, however, the role of Anaïde was Patti's greatest achievement so far; it suited her voice to perfection and revealed in her so great a musical aptitude and "artistic sentiment" as to convince him, beyond a doubt, that she was destined for a tremendous future.

Succumbing to progressively dwindling audiences, the Academy was the first to capitulate, suddenly announcing the close of its season on May 19. The final week's offerings included Gazzaniga's indispensable "farewell," this time with *La traviata* (May 15);[70] a performance of *Don Giovanni* for Patti's benefit (May 16);[71] an unstaged performance of *Mosè* at Dr. Henry Ward Beecher's musically fashionable Plymouth Church in Brooklyn[72] (May 17); and finally a "Grand Combined Farewell," offering, for the price of a single ticket, *Lucrezia Borgia* on May 18, and a closing Grand Gala Matinée of *Don Giovanni* the following day.

Surprisingly, Maretzek, the victor, immediately announced the close of his season at the Winter Garden, also on May 19.[73] As a parting shot (probably in tit-for-tat retaliation for *Mosè*), he announced for May 15—but, Ardavani being ill, postponed until the 16th—a sumptuous biblical spectacle of his own, Verdi's complete *Nabucco*[74] with Fabbri, who particularly excelled in the role of Abigail. Indeed, it was noted, with

[69] And not without untoward consequences. At the fourth performance of *Mosè,* reported the *Evening Post* (May 15, 1860), a succession of "startling phenomena" ensued when the waves of the Red Sea parted to disclose an individual in contemporary dress "unconcernedly strolling about the bottom of the sea." At the sound of laughter from the audience he "ran away in a state of great apparent perturbation." Worse was to follow: after the Israelites had duly passed through the parted waters, the unruly waves closed too soon, refusing to bury the pursuing Egyptians: "In vain did the poor wretches attempt with persistent pertinacity to burrow under the billows; the waves declined to cover them."

[70] Gazzaniga had sung "two or three times to empty houses, and with less than ordinary success," wrote Hagen (*Review and Gazette,* May 26, 1860, p. 162). She would doubtless continue to give farewell performances, just as she had for the past two years, he wrote, for although it was reported that Gazzaniga had really booked passage for Europe on a Cunard steamer, Hagen feared the rumor would once again prove to be "less Cunard than *Canard.*"

[71] Surprisingly poorly attended. The performances, too, with the exception of Patti's Zerlina, were poor. Indeed, wrote Burkhardt "more in sorrow than in anger," a worse cast (Gazzaniga, Brignoli, Ferri, Amodio, and Junca, the last a replacement for Susini, who probably "wanted to see *Nabucco* at the Winter Garden"), or a worse performance of *Don Giovanni,* had never been seen in New York (*Dispatch,* May 19, 1860). The *Herald,* on the other hand, reported a triumphant performance and the largest attendance, with accompanying largest box-office receipts, of the season (May 21, 1860).

[72] Dr. Beecher's church was now coming into its extraordinary musical importance: Maretzek and his operatic cohorts had given a Grand Sacred Concert there on May 8, and Patti had followed with a concert on May 10, assisted by Academy luminaries and by Sebastian Bach Mills.

[73] "How is it that . . . the usually shrewd Ullman and enterprising Maretzek strike their flags thus early and abandon the field when the most profitable period of the campaign [the tourist season] is at hand?" incredulously asked the *Herald* (May 18, 1860).

[74] The "scenery, costumes, and appointments—from the Babylonian brass band to the caparisoned steed of Nabucco—being all in complete order," wrote the *Herald* (May 21, 1860).

each new role Fabbri gained a new triumph. Rounding out the cast, Madame von Berkel was adequate as Fenena, Ardavani was a tolerable Nabucco, and Quinto, as Ismaele, was passable, as was Giorgio Mirandola, a new basso from an itinerant Italian opera company just arrived from Latin America, as Zaccaria; Richard Mülder conducted.

Nabucco was repeated on May 18, then again at the farewell Grand Gala Matinée on the 19th, and yet again on May 21, for Maretzek had now decided to extend his season at the Winter Garden for an unspecified period, probably through the summer. Having outlasted Ullman/Strakosch, indomitable Max was doubtless loath to forgo the opportunity—with the tourist season at hand, particularly potential with the impending visit to New York of the first Japanese legation to the United States[75]—to retrieve the losses (yes, losses) he had sustained on his "victorious" season.

Thus, in what the *Times* designated "a fresh spring-burst of opera," Maretzek continued with *Stradella, La traviata,* and *La Juive*—in the meantime making it known that two new operas were in "active rehearsal"—Mercadante's *Il bravo* and Verdi's *I masnadieri*.[76]

I masnadieri, the first novelty to be presented, was announced for May 29, to be conducted by Maretzek and, surprisingly, performed, not by his admirable company, but by Mirandola's unknown opera troupe.[77] This entrepreneurial aberration seems to have miscarried from the start. Pleading illness, Max, the usually indomitable, twice postponed the premiere, first to May 31, then to the evidently not-so-Gala Matinée on June 2, when *I masnadieri* was conducted by Anschütz. With this performance, about which the press seems almost by agreement to have maintained silence, Maretzek's victorious opera season came to an abrupt termination.

Only in *Wilkes' Spirit of the Times* (June 9, 1860, p. 224) did anything resembling a review of the inauspicious premiere appear (at least, to my knowledge). Noncommittally describing the performance as "not atrociously bad or exceedingly good," the critic pronounced the opera to be lacking in the "essential elements of popularity—telling melodies, grand cavatinas, and thrilling concerted pieces." It was by far "not Verdi's best."

The usually loquacious *Evening Post* reviewer, who had not attended the performance, merely repeated from hearsay that the new singers had "failed to make a favorable impression." But it was *Robin,* the *Albion*'s vivacious replacement for its suddenly departed music critic, who delivered the *coup de grâce:* "The last hours of the Maretzek

---

[75] To deliver their official ratification of Townsend Harris's 1858 treaty with Japan, some seventy Japanese dignitaries were sent to Washington in the summer of 1860, later to visit Philadelphia and New York. "There never will be again such a chance for managers to make money," salivated the *Herald* (May 18, 1860), before their arrival. "The curiosity to see these wonderful strangers will be so great that the bare announcement of their appearance at the Opera would be sufficient to engage all the places a week beforehand."

[76] An English version of *Il bravo* had been performed in Philadelphia in 1849 by the Seguins; *I masnadieri* had never before been performed in the United States.

[77] Newly arrived after an extensive tour, since 1852, of South America and the Caribbean, the leading singers of the troupe, besides Mirandola, were Signora Rosina Olivieri-Luisia, mezzo-soprano, and the Signori Enrico Rossi-Guerra, tenor, and Eugenio Luisia (Rosina's husband), baritone.

season," he wrote (*Albion,* June 9, 1860, p. 271), "were rendered unspeakably painful by a futile attempt to present Verdi's *I masnadieri.* But of the dead, why speak?"

The *Masnadieri* debacle accounts only partly, however, for Maretzek's seemingly sudden decision after all to declare a moratorium on his opera activities. His immediate acceptance of a paying job to conduct at the circus-master James M. Nixon's new midsummer extravaganza[78] at Niblo's Garden confesses to the insolvency with which he doubtless paid for his soul-satisfying demolition of Ullman.[79]

Perhaps Maretzek had little appetite for yet another tooth-and-nail struggle for operatic dominance when his former *prima donna* Adelaide Cortesi took the now idle Academy of Music for a short season, to commence on June 4. Under the management of her impresario husband, a Signor Servadio, Cortesi had been touring in the United States with Giuseppe Musiani,[80]★ a sensational *robusto* tenor with whom she had created a furor at Maretzek's most recent opera season in Havana. Having just completed a successful week of opera in Boston, Cortesi was bringing to the Academy her "Grand Combination" company, consisting of star members of the recently disbanded Strakosch/Ullman troupe[81]—Adelaide Phillips, Susini, and Amodio; also the stage manager/singer Dubreuil, and additionally our old acquaintances, the basso Cesare Nanni, the baritone (tenor) Giuseppe Tamaro, and the tenor Giovanni Sbriglia; Muzio conducted.

Maretzek had probably come to realize, too, that—largely through his own doing—New York had been force-fed beyond endurance with an indigestible glut of opera. As Burkhardt editorialized in the *Dispatch* (June 6, 1860), not only had Maretzek recently exceeded the limit with too many new operas at the Winter Garden, but in general, during the past two years, there had been too much opera in New York and too many opera managers. "One or two of these industrious and indefatigable gentlemen at a time are amply enough to satisfy a large city—even one that is larger than New York," wrote Burkhardt. "But Max Maretzek, Ullman and Strakosch, with the husband of Cortesi and half a dozen others, who have neither the chance nor the money to 'rush in like fools where wise men fear to tread,' are enough to squeeze dry the udders of that confiding milch cow, the public.

"Four months of Italian opera in the year are about all that Paris and London ask for," wrote Burkhardt, while for the past year New York had been exposed to a suc-

---

[78] Amid its multitudinous attractions—floral exhibitions, comedies, dramas, burlesques, ballets, and marching exhibitions by Amazonian Zouaves—a forty-minute intermission was devoted to the consumption of nonalcoholic refreshments, while promenading to the music of something ignominiously called Maretzek's "Cornet Band" and listening to favorite songs and ballads performed in English by Madame von Berkel and a Madame H. Eckhardt to the band's accompaniment.

[79] "The fact is," gleefully wrote *Trovator,* "that last season both companies were losing money and did not attempt to conceal it. But [each of] the rival managers took a fiendish delight in supposing that his opponent was losing the most. . . . Certain it is that the Academy folks 'caved in' and beat a retreat the first. Maretzek was however too exhausted by the contest to survive his victory very long" (*Dwight's,* June 9, 1860, p. 86).

[80] Musiani's most exploited accomplishment was his ability to sing a high C from the chest—the legendary *ut de poitrine.*

[81] Upon the breakup of the opera season, Adelina Patti, Amalia Strakosch, Brignoli, and Junca had gone on an extended tour of the United States under the management, and with the musical collaboration, of Maurice Strakosch.

cession of seasons, altogether "more than doubling that period of enjoyment." And besides—to attempt to surpass a period that had produced the Piccolomini furor, the
Patti furor, and the Fabbri furor! What new marvels could Cortesi offer, coming in,
as she did, at the "*finale* of the feast?"

Indeed, Cortesi's season survived barely a week. Attracting a pitifully small attendance on opening night *(Poliuto)*, an even smaller one on the second *(Il trovatore)*, and
with diminishing audiences at the following *Lucrezia Borgia* and the Saturday matinée
repeat of *Il trovatore,* her season collapsed after its fourth performance, on June 9. Its
untimely demise called forth the usual crop of editorials attempting to decipher the
great opera enigma.

The premature halt of the Cortesi season, however, was almost immediately rein-
terpreted to the public as merely a temporary suspension to permit preparations for a
Grand Gala Matinée on June 14 for the visiting Japanese dignitaries.

Generally regarded as oddities fit to be displayed at Barnum's museum,[82] the exotic ambassadors were subjected to a merciless onslaught of misdirected attention, en-
gendering colossal misunderstandings on both sides. Strong, an articulate spectator at
their welcoming parade in New York, wrote in his private journal on June 16: "From
early morning (or at least from the earliest hour of which I am personally cognizant)
the town was all agog about the Japanese ambassadors. Streets were already swarming
as I went downtown. Hardly an omnibus but was filled full. Every other person, at
least, was a rustic or a stranger. Flags everywhere. Small detachments of our valiant
militia marching, grim and sweaty, to their respective positions. Dragoons, hussars, and
lancers, by twos and threes, trotting about with looks of intense uneasiness. The whole
aspect of things indicated some great event at hand."

By mid-afternoon, Strong had grown "so sick of talk about the Japanese" that he
vowed not to see them, but he ran into a friend who persuaded him to "take advantage
of certain eligible windows in his office" which offered an unimpeded view of the parade route along Broadway. There, in company with an agreeable party of acquaintances, and fortified by an unlimited supply of strawberries and ice cream, Strong witnessed an "amazing turnout of horse, foot, and artillery. Ditto of aldermen in
barouches and yellow kids,[83] trying to look like gentlemen. The first-chop Japanese
[in their gorgeous robes] sat in their carriage like bronze statues, aristocratically calm
and indifferent. The subordinates grinned and wagged their ugly heads and waved
their fans to the ladies in the windows. Every window on Broadway was full of them."
As the procession passed, the great crowd closed in and followed it. "Broadway was
densely filled, sidewalks and trottoir both, for many blocks, and mostly with roughs,"
but the police maintained good order.

The local purveyors of entertainment on all levels—from Laura Keene to the
blackface minstrels to low-down concert saloon keepers—featured "Japanese" specialties on their bills. The Gala Japanese Matinée at the Academy of Music was no exception. Despite an uneasy postponement from June 14 to June 20 (when the performance was falsely reported in the *Herald* to have been canceled), every stale device of

[82] Visitors to Niblo's, where the official guests were invited to attend free of charge, were requested by the management not to "annoy the Japanese by crowding or staring at them" (*Evening
Post,* June 18, 1860).

[83] Not to be misconstrued as a reference to oriental children.

The Japanese ambassadors were met at Castle Garden and escorted by procession; the treaty that opened Japan to trade with the West was carried in a box on their floral car.

The ambassadors were then received by the Mayor of New York.

*The ambassadors were met by a band playing
in front of the home of J. G. Bennett,
publisher of the* Herald, *who entertained them.*

*The ambassadors reviewed the New York Volunteer Troops
in Union Square, near the statue of George Washington.*

public seduction in the Ullmanian bag of tricks was invoked. The opera chosen to edify the "uncultured heathen" was, most unsuitably, *Poliuto (The Martyrs),* drastically
pared down to accommodate the limited heathen tolerance.[84] As a special tribute,[85]
Muzio had composed a "Grand Japanese March" purportedly based—much to the
general journalistic amusement—on "original Japanese melodies,"[86] to be played during an intermission by the orchestra, augmented by thirty members of the Eighth Regiment Band, the Washington Grays.

"On hearing the march," gibed *Robin (Albion,* June 26, 1860, p. 295), "it became
clear that Mendelssohn had it in mind when he composed the 'Italian' Symphony."
Indeed, "If anyone hoped to see the Orientals leap up and weep when they heard the
melodies of their native land, that person must have been grievously disappointed. The
march was concluded," wrote *Robin,* "amid a decent silence from the audience [which
only emphasized] the frantic endeavors from someone behind the scenes to excite popular applause." In vain.

"On the whole, the Grand Japanese Gala Matinée was a failure," continued *Robin,*
becoming serious. "It could be nothing else." The event symbolized the cynicism to
which the opera game had sunk in America, a phenomenon that the writer bitterly
indicted as "a shallow pretense, a mockery, and a delusion. The arrangements [for this
occasion] began with untruthfulness, were carried on with insincerity, and were concluded with impolitic and stingy haste." Through such tactics, "art is not advanced, the
public confidence in managers is not increased. The strangers were not entertained; no
one was satisfied. Heigho! Are not we all nearly weary of this foolish imposture? When
shall we have an operatic enterprise conducted with simple fairness and a desire to advance the true in art?"

Throughout the preceding period of operatic turmoil, Strong—with the exception of a single visit to the Academy on June 8 to hear the Cortesi *Lucrezia Borgia*[87]—
addressed his musical attention solely to the music at Trinity Church.

May 20. . . . I like the choral service [at Trinity] better and better. It certainly fills
the church.

---

[84] And heathen reluctance. According to the *Herald* (June 21, 1860): "The chief ambassadors declined to go. . . . Many of the officers could not be made to understand where they were to go, others were deterred by the rain, and another party, having received permission to go out shopping, insisted that they must shop first and go to the theatre afterwards." The few who did attend arrived an
hour late, when, at last ensconced in one of the proscenium boxes of the grand tier, they attracted
"the earnest attention of the ladies, who seemed to lose all further interest in the performance."

[85] Surely the most massive musical commemoration of the visit was a Grand Symphony by the
unquenchable octogenarian Anthony Philip Heinrich. Titled *America's Welcome to Asia,* it had been
presented "through the Most Honorable Japanese Embassy to Kint-Siusama or Celestial Lord of Japan." Its movements were reported in *Dwight's* (May 19, 1860, p. 63): I. A "Grand Historic Overture:
Opening of the Sealed Gates to American Commerce; Exultation of the Two Worlds, Expressed by
a Grand Heroic March; II. The Children of Sensio Dai Sin Embark on the Ocean of Peace for a
Voyage to the Land of Washington; III. Rejoicing of Columbia." Apparently lost, the manuscript is
not listed in William Treat Upton's catalogue of Heinrich's works.

[86] Muzio had doubtless researched his themes from among the scholarly studies of that "eminent
Japanese authority," Monsieur Fétis,♪ joshed the *Herald* (June 21, 1860).

[87] Susini as the Duke and Cortesi as Lucrezia were good, wrote Strong (June 8, 1860); but Musiani as Gennaro was bad. Strong had no comment for Adelaide Phillips, the Orsini.

May 27. Whitsunday. To Trinity Church. Large congregation, though the day was chilly and uninviting. One Geary (a vicar choral, whatever that is, of Dublin Cathedral),[88] who has joined the choir as a volunteer, sang the anthem. "Comfort Ye" and "Every Valley" better than I have heard them sung since the era of Braham, twenty years ago. I care little for the florid aria, but "Comfort ye, my People" cannot be beat. It is the noblest production of its class in all the literature of music.

May 31. . . . Stopped at Trinity Church and discoursed Cutler, the organist. He has made up his mind—after some urgency on my part—to bring a little Haydn and Mozart into the service, and not to confine himself to the Smiths and Browns of the Anglican School—to substitute vigorous music for dull decorum and counterpoint. If this can be effected with the comparatively strong choir of Trinity Church, a daily dream of mine for the last twenty years will be realized.

June 13. . . . Last evening Cutler, the organist of Trinity Church, was here with little Robjohn, the first star of his choir. Also one Chase, belonging thereto, Mrs. Gibbs, Mrs. Paulding, Wrey Mould. I brought Cutler here to try over some things from Haydn's and Mozart's Masses (of which he is strangely ignorant, for a professional musician) and consider about adapting them to the services at Trinity Church. It has been my daily dream for almost twenty years—that noble music adequately rendered in the church service. They sang parts of Haydn's No. 1 and No. 6 [Hoboken XXII:10 and XXII:14], Mozart's No. 12, and Beethoven in C. Cutler was impressed by it—puzzled and astonished. It gave him a new sensation, and shook up the dull and decorous convictions of his Anglicanism. He accompanied badly, and no wonder, being unused to music of that force.

Little Robjohn is a nice, modest, self-possessed, intelligent English boy, quite worth cultivating. He is beginning to lose his beautiful boyish soprano and may make a fine tenor. He reads admirably, at least as well as Cutler, and did the tenor solo in the *Credo* of Mozart's little Mass with great effect.

June 16. . . . a small musical party at Dick Willis's. I suppose it was pleasant. I am sure getting out of the house into the open air was delightful. The atmosphere of the parlors was oppressive beyond carbonic acid.

June 24. Sunday. Trinity Church this A.M. with Ellie and Johny. Music went smoothly. The chanted psalms, versicles, and responses in the Litany are always effective. They impress me more and more. But the lifeless, unmeaning counterpoint of the Anglican *Te Deum* and *Jubilate* is intolerable.

On June 28, Strong brought his family to Great Barrington, Massachusetts, where—in the pleasant company of friends and acquaintances (among them the fashionable would-be diva, the Comtesse de Ferussac)—they would spend their accustomed extended vacation. After a bucolic weekend Strong returned to the hot city to celebrate a woefully solitary Fourth of July.

July 4. The day was ushered in, as the newspapers say, with the usual racket, which has not yet abated. I lounged downtown after breakfast and made an expedition

[88] Gustavus Geary from Dublin, with his daughter Mina, was currently giving "parlor entertainments" of the ballads of Thomas Moore at Mozart Hall. (See following OBBLIGATO.)

to Jersey City, partly for want of something to do, and partly to give Miss Rosalie Ruggles the latest news from Barrington. Sweltering hot day it has been, as I found out on my walk home after lunching at Delmonico's. After dinner I strolled out again and found my way to the North River, in the region of Bank Street, where the *Great Eastern* lies.[89] She loomed up, colorful in the twilight. It was too late to ask for admission (price one dollar). So I walked home again. Looked in at Palace Gardens (in Fourteenth Street) and looked out again very speedily. It was hotter than the hot street and presented no attractions but colored lamps, a dismal orchestra, and an occasional skyrocket.[90]

I am thankful to have got home tonight with both my eyes and without a rocket stuck through my body. The streets are really perilous, especially outside the fashionable district, where families have not left town. Blue and red balls from the Roman candles shoot about at every angle, producing lovely effects of light and shadow, but suggesting very possible mischief. Heavy rockets let off by inexperienced hands are whistling and rushing upward in front of every other house. . . . Packs of crackers explode under one's feet every minute, but that is nothing. I do seriously object, however, to rusty old pistols fired close to one's ears. . . . Though I walked in fear and dread, I "allow" it was a pretty sight. Every street, as far as one could see, was phosphorescent and coruscating.

Last night I dashed out of this lonesome house in desperation, and went to Laura Keene's to see the new "Japanese" burlesque or "extravaganza." Utter tomfoolery. but Mrs. [John] Wood and [Joseph] Jefferson helped it through with their irresistible *vis comica*. The music is very pleasant, lots of old popular tunes ("Buy a Broom" and the like) prettily rendered.

In a like fit of loneliness, on August 16 Strong sought distraction in a plebeian program of "Pantomime and Horse-opera" at Niblo's, but found, to his disgust and horror, that little children took part in the entertainment. As he somewhat immoderately put it, they were "butchered to make a Roman holiday."

September 12. . . . [at Great Barrington] Ellie assisted at a concert got up at the Town Hall by the indefatigable Madame de Ferussac for the benefit of the Roman Catholic Church. Madame la Comtesse sang, [also] Ellie. . . . The performance concluded with that jolliest of nigger melodies, "Dixieland,"[91] by the whole strength of

[89] The latest and most gigantic of giant ocean liners, the British *Great Eastern,* on exhibition since its arrival on June 28, proved to be a tourist attraction even greater than the Japanese ambassadors, and certainly more lucrative; in the first five days it was reportedly viewed by nearly 150,000 visitors at a dollar a visitor. The price of admission was later reduced.

[90] The level of entertainment at the Palace Gardens had somewhat deterioriated, wrote *Robin* (*Albion,* July 17, 1860, p. 331). Although "the coloured lamps, artificial rose miniature grottoes, and cheap scenery of the gardens [still] attracted the shilling throng, a brass band [now] blew and beat the popular airs of the day and of a great many days back. . . . When the band had blown itself out, and the 'Promenade concert'—so called because all remained seated—was ended, the 'Opera soirée' began." *Robin* wondered where all the "dreadful operatic vocalists" who infested the city's pleasure gardens came from; he commiserated with Donizetti for the brutal violence committed upon his music.

[91] The words and music of "I Wish I was in Dixie's Land" were composed as a walk-around for Bryant's Minstrels in 1859 by Daniel Decatur Emmett (1815–1904), then a member of the company.

the company, and I don't doubt the audience preferred it before Verdi, *Le Lac,* and the rest of the program. The concert was a brilliant success and netted a couple of hundred dollars.

September 14. . . . [back in town] Went with George Anthon and Walter [Cutting] to the opera. Heard three acts of *Martha* in the Cutting box. Patti and Brignoli did fairly. House full, but strangers mostly.[92] Music is pretty, but not very strong.

———

Throughout the months of July and August, except for a giant benefit for the Garibaldi Fund on July 11, New York remained mercifully free of opera. In a sense, however, the Garibaldi benefit presaged the shape of things to come at the Academy, demonstrating, as it did, the feasibility of collaboration by members of the opposing opera troupes: Frezzolini appearing peacefully with Musiani in *Lucia di Lammermoor;* Cortesi with Errani and Susini in the second act of *Lucrezia Borgia;* and to complete the catholicity of the occasion, Pauline Colson singing the Bolero from *The Sicilian Vespers* with the amalgamated chorus. With Muzio conducting, the proceedings closed, of course, with "The Garibaldi Rataplan," performed in grand ensemble.

A first intimation of radical change in the prevailing philosophy of mutually hostile opera management occurred when, early in August, Burkhardt hesitantly repeated a rumor that Maretzek had been engaged by Ullman/Strakosch to conduct at the Academy. "This," cautiously observed Burkhardt (*Dispatch,* August 4, 1860), "would argue a singular change in the personal politics of the opera." Upon confirmation of the rumor, Burkhardt, in less genteel terms, mused upon the bizarre turn of events. "It must be owned," he wrote, "that Operatic squabbles are the most laughable things in life. A great *tenor,* or a greater *basso,* or a magnificent *soprano,* or the most scientific of conductors, has a 'row' with the manager. . . . They abuse each other in the journals— or employ two of the hardest-tongued of the legal profession to take away each other's characters; or sometimes, in their bitterness, one writes a book about the other.[93] For three or four years they are at daggers drawn, when, one fine morning, the one offers the other an engagement. The potent medium of dollars and cents reconciles them, and the day after, they may be seen walking down Broadway, arm in arm, in the most amicable of manners. Max Maretzek, consequently, is again in contact as an *employé* with Mr. Ullman, under the joint Operatic firm of Ullman and Strakosch" (*Dispatch,* August 18, 1860).

And indeed, speaking for that firm in a card of Ullmanesque grandiloquence and confidentiality (despite Ullman's current absence in Europe on a talent-gathering expedition), a daring new concept was expounded. With the disastrous events of the spring season, the financially depleted combatants had doubtless come to realize that only by abandoning their cutthroat rivalry would operatic survival be possible. Thus, for the

---

So phenomenal was the song's success, both in the North and South, that a pirated edition of it was issued in New Orleans in 1860, before its legitimate publication in New York. In the ensuing controversy over the piracy, the New Orleans publisher offered to buy the copyright from Emmett for $5. "Dixie" was jealously claimed by both sides during the Civil War; it was reportedly played at the inauguration ceremonies of both Abraham Lincoln and Jefferson Davis.

[92] The papers reported the presence of a large contingent of visitors from the South during this final pre–Civil War opera season.

[93] Maretzek's *Crotchets and Quavers,* for instance.

coming season, the performing forces at the Academy would encompass "One Grand Constellation," an amalgam of the best existing operatic resources: the Academy company—Patti, Colson, Amalia Strakosch, Brignoli, Ferri, and Susini; the Cortesi company—Cortesi, Musiani, Barili, and Amodio (who had shifted his allegiance); and the Maretzek company—Fabbri, Errani, Stigelli, and Maretzek (but not Anschütz).

The participation of the former archfiend Maretzek was proclaimed in flowery encomiums: "Identified with the history of Italian Opera in the United States," went the announcement, "Mr. Maretzek is one of those rare public servants whose fidelity is as unimpeachable as their ability is undeniable, always at his post, ever ready for any emergency, deservedly a great favorite with the operatic public. The directors consider themselves fortunate in having been able to obtain Mr. Maretzek's exclusive cooperation during the whole of the ensuing season."

It was further announced that Ullman, soon to return from Europe, had engaged a galaxy of famous stars to appear at the Academy later in the season, chief among them the world-famed tenor Enrico Tamberlik (who defaulted) and—despite his earlier defection from Ullman's ranks—the basso Carl Formes, "whose former triumphal career in the United States renders eulogium altogether superfluous."

But even as the season began, discord loomed between Strakosch, in sole command of the Academy, and Servadio, very much in command of his wife's career—Academy or no Academy. On opening day Servadio announced in the papers that his arrangement with Strakosch/Ullman was merely temporary, calling for only two weeks of performances at the Academy by Cortesi, Musiani, *et al.*, after which, with the addition to their company of several new artists momentarily expected from Europe,[94] they would fulfill a number of engagements in several American cities before returning to Cuba for the winter season.

On September 3 the Academy season got off to a propitious start with Patti, "that pocket-Venus and diamond edition of all charms," enchanting a capacity audience with her delectable Amina in *La sonnambula;* Cortesi/Musiani followed on September 5 with a thrilling performance of *Poliuto,* Maretzek conducting; then Patti in *Lucia* on September 6; Cortesi in *Il trovatore* on the 7th; and a Grand Patti matinée with *La sonnambula* on the 8th.[95]

An embarrassment of riches, rejoiced the critics. Patti was more phenomenal than ever, Cortesi more excitingly dramatic; and Musiani regularly sent his audiences into fits of delirium with his unstinting applications of his trumpet-like *ut de poitrine.*

The second week, despite a drop in attendance, began promisingly. Patti exerted her familiar enchantment over a less than capacity audience as Rosina in *The Barber of Seville* (September 10); but something went seriously askew the following evening, when Cortesi, who had been announced for *La traviata,* appeared instead in *Il trovatore.* The substitution was officially attributed—with a cynical disregard of the public's intelligence—not only to an overwhelming demand for a repeat of that opera, but also

---

[94] Among them Amodio's younger and slimmer, but equally gifted, brother Federico, also a baritone.

[95] With daily performances at the Academy, wrote Watson, it was noteworthy that audiences nonetheless preferred to attend on the regular opera nights—Mondays, Wednesdays, and Fridays—while on the off nights, the attendance usually consisted of "groups of half a dozen each, scattered about, and nearly lost in the vast auditorium" (*Leslie's,* September 22, 1860, p. 273).

Adelaide Cortesi, so popular
that she was said to walk on
flowers showered on the stage
by her admirers.

Girvice Archer, Jr.

to Madame Cortesi's inability to sing Violetta because of indisposition. An incongruity, it was pointed out: how could Madame Cortesi have been too ill for Violetta, but not too ill for Leonora?

"The conscientious adherence of our managers to their programmes in times past had not prepared us for this remarkable *volte-face,*" complained Seymour (*Times,* September 12, 1860). It was "infinitely to be regretted that the system of extravagant promises and deceptive performances should not at once be abandoned by the *impresarii* at the Academy. The day of these things is past,[96] and the public is weary of them."

One of the "stalest humbugs" of opera management, wrote *Robin,* in a perspicacious indictment of the outrageous and insulting deceptions foisted upon the public by Ullman/Strakosch, with their false advertising tactics, their false promises of new

[96] Seymour was mistaken. The *Poliuto* that was announced for that very evening was metamorphosed, without warning, into a performance of *I puritani* with the more salable Patti as the attraction.

productions, the miserable quality of their staging (but what could one expect when supernumeraries were paid twenty-five cents a night?), the false excitement engendered by their box-office crew, who rushed to the doors of the parquet at the slightest suggestion of applause from within to "smite together their hands and cry bravo," and chiefly, their persistent pretence of being a beneficent force for the improvement of musical taste in the United States (*Albion,* September 16, p. 439; reprinted in *Dwight's,* September 22, 1860, pp. 202–3).

La traviata was rescheduled for September 13, and again the performance did not materialize. "The opera of *La traviata* cannot get itself sung this season," wrote Seymour (*Times,* September 14, 1860), calling attention to the "very curious but indubitable fact" that for a second time "Violetta was cut off before she was born." And without so much as an explanation, or even, this time, a substitution.

Following Patti's performance of *Martha* (mentioned by Strong on September 14), whereupon she immediately departed for a season in Philadelphia, it was announced, with a noticeable absence of the accustomed farewell fanfare, that Madame Cortesi would complete her interrupted engagement with a performance of *Norma,* unconventionally scheduled for the evening, not the afternoon, of Saturday the 15th. On the 14th Cortesi sent a doctor's certificate informing the management that she was (or would be) too ill to sing the following night. It was not until curtain time, however, that Parodi was announced as her substitute, much to the dissatisfaction of both public and press.

On the following Monday, September 17, the amusement columns displayed an advertisement for Fabbri's grand opening at the Academy that evening in *Lucrezia Borgia,* immediately followed by Strakosch's enraged denunciation of the perfidious contract-breakers Cortesi/Servadio, in turn followed by an advertisement for the grand opening at Niblo's Garden the following evening of Cortesi's brief season of opera,[97] with Musiani, F. Amodio, and with Anschütz conducting. Her opening vehicle was, of course, *La traviata.*

Servadio, who had pledged himself not to engage his troupe at any other New York theatre but the Academy, had no intention of fulfilling his part of the contract, accused Strakosch: "He did everything in his power to thwart and embarrass the management, subterfuges of all kinds being employed to keep Madame Cortesi from appearing in other than such operas as were least attractive, and when at length the directors insisted upon producing, and announced, more important works, the plea of indisposition was sent in, after requiring payment for such performances and too late to recast the opera or even substitute another performance, to avoid total public disappointment."

The opera war proceeded in a crescendo of venomous accusations and denials, supplemented by editorial side-taking, peppered with satirical commentary. The Cortesi offerings at Niblo's—splendidly performed and tolerably well attended—consisted, besides *La traviata,* of *Poliuto, Ernani,* and, as a parting production on September 27,

---

[97] Brief indeed: the engagement neatly filled the gap between their exit from the Academy and their opening in Boston on October 1. The Cortesi nights at Niblo's were Tuesdays, Thursdays, and Saturdays, alternating with the celebrated actor Edwin Forrest, who after a long absence had recently returned to the New York stage with a three-night-a-week season chiefly devoted to plays by Shakespeare.

*Edwin Forrest, the Shakespearean
actor, had just returned to New York
and alternated with Cortesi in her
brief season at Niblo's.*

to be repeated at the season's closing matinée on Saturday the 29th, the first performances in the United States of Pacini's *Medea* (Palermo 1843). Conducted by Servadio,
the work was judged (in *Wilkes' Spirit,* October 6, 1860, p. 80) to be good but not
great. But Cortesi, as Medea, was great both in her vocal delivery and her superb display of "a genuine and large-hearted [histrionic] power which we have rarely seen
evinced upon the lyric stage."

Robin, on the other hand, reported a "ragged and shabby performance." Although
Madame Cortesi unquestionably deserved credit for presenting a novelty, he wrote,
the work required more than good will and energy to be properly produced. *Robin*
accused Cortesi of having chosen *Medea* chiefly because it gave her the opportunity of
"rolling her eyes in a fine frenzy and of striking the attitudes in which she so much
delights. . . . Cortesi is great, even to sublimity, at times," he conceded, "but she often
takes that easy step from thence to the ridiculous, and after weaving her passion, is apt
to tear it to tatters." He had to admit, however, that the lack of a "symmetrical ensemble made her efforts to sustain the piece [seem] more extravagant than usual, [for] the
orchestra and chorus went hopelessly astray in brazen and clamorous disorder, and the
military bands on the stage were pathetically imbecile" (*Albion,* September 29, 1860,
p. 453).

On the final Saturday afternoon, continued *Robin* in the following issue of the
Albion (October 6, 1860, p. 475), "the Cortesi operatic enterprise came to an abrupt
and mysterious halt at the second act of *Medea,* having been strangled by 'a sudden

cold,' which seized the principal soprano." The crisis was apparently not entirely un-premeditated: "A knowledge of two facts complicates the mystery," wrote observant *Robin.* "First the music of the song with which Musiani kindly consented to fill the gap was laid out on the stands of the orchestra from the very commencement of the performance; in the second place, the boat for Boston, whither the troupe has gone, left at an hour which would have given Cortesi very little time to prepare for her voyage, had she concluded the programme she advertised."[98]

At the Academy in the meantime—albeit to distressingly small audiences—Fabbri, with Stigelli and with Maretzek conducting, held the fort with *Lucrezia Borgia* (September 17) and, again—with Stigelli and Maretzek—the embattled *Traviata* (September 20). To great fanfare, Pauline Colson appeared (September 19 and 21), with Stigelli, Ferri, Genebrel, a basso from New Orleans substituting for Susini, and with Muzio conducting, in a revival of *The Sicilian Vespers.*

Not a happy choice, wrote Seymour (*Times,* September 24, 1860): "The opera is by no means popular. It is characterized by a total absence of melody and poverty of thought, and [by] the usual resource to conceal these and other deficiencies—noise—the ever ready and welcome [makeshift] of imbecility. Having hardly recovered from the stunning din of big drum and cymbal, the braying of trombones and the lowing of ophicleides, being allowed to listen, on Saturday night [September 22], to the dulcet harmonies and flowing melodies of Mozart was like entering a grove of nightingales after leaving the roar and clang of a smithy." The instrumentality of this blessed surcease was *Don Giovanni,* and the dispensers of its healing strains were Fabbri (a magnificent Donna Anna), Colson (in Patti's absence a splendid Zerlina), Amalia Strakosch (a good-looking, but vocally inadequate, Donna Elvira), Stigelli (an excellent Don Ottavio), Ferri (a "stupidly depraved" Don Giovanni), Susini (a miscast Leporello), a chorus member Signor Maffei (a commendable Masetto),[99] and Müller (a run-of-the-mill Commendatore); Maretzek conducted. *Don Giovanni* was repeated on September 24.

On the 26th the long-heralded season of French Opera—or as *Robin* put it, "German opera sung in the Gallic language"—was launched, to a fashionable, predominantly French audience, with Meyerbeer's *Robert le diable.* Conducted by Maretzek, it was sung by Pauline Colson, charmingly in her element as an essentially Gallic Alice, Madame Bertucca-Maretzek, emerging from her retirement on Staten Island as an Isabelle who had vocally seen better days, and two French singers from the New Orleans opera, Messieurs Philippe and Genebrel—respectively the Robert and Bertram—collectively inadequate to the size of the Academy and the exacting demands of a New York audience. A "dreary" ballet corps, headed by a Mlle. Hélene (Mlle. Elena translated into French for this occasion) were, in *Robin*'s opinion, hardly worth the expense of their hire. Much as he hated taking "the bread of honest toil out of people's mouths," he wrote, "really the right women were not put in the right places when this saltatory troupe was made up" (*Albion,* September 29, 1860, p. 463).

A second performance of *Robert le diable* was announced for September 28, but instead, with no warning, as the *Times* angrily reported (October 1, 1860), "the curtain

---

[98] As the *Times* reported the incident (October 1, 1860): "The house being not of the most brilliant, Signora Cortesi caught, after the first act, one of those sudden illnesses for which this great *artiste* has so melancholy a facility, and she was seen no more."

[99] At the Monday night performance, Domenico Coletti took over the role of Masetto.

rose on the *Traviata*." What with the present chaotic state of affairs at the Academy and with Cortesi's outrageous exit performance at Niblo's, warned Seymour: "If opera managers and singers continue to play such extraordinary pranks with the public . . . the altars of song will soon become deserted."

It was a week of total failure for the Academy, wrote the *Spirit of the Times* (October 16, 1860, p. 80). "The struggle with their opponents [at Niblo's] was nothing but a succession of disasters. . . . Little Patti, who might have redeemed fortune, was singing in Philadelphia," whither "the gallant Strakosch" reportedly had fled. Ullman was in Europe. "Maretzek and Muzio, Muzio and Maretzek, were left here to do the fighting; and we must say they did a bungling job."

The mounting discontent with Strakosch's flagrant mismanagement of the Academy was exacerbated by Muzio's presentation on September 29 of a brutally butchered version of Verdi's *Nabucco*. Unlike Maretzek, who had faithfully presented the complete score the previous spring, wrote Burkhardt (*Dispatch,* October 6, 1860), Muzio had chosen to omit the whole of the last act, brazenly giving as his excuse that the work was traditionally performed that way in Italy. An act of vandalism, charged Burkhardt, it was not only a desecration of a fine work, but it deprived Fabbri of some of her most sublime effects.

Nor did matters improve when, on October 1, a large audience that had "perversely" braved the rain to hear the final performance of *The Sicilian Vespers* was treated, when the curtain went up, to another unannounced performance of *La traviata*. "Once and for all," thundered the *Times* (October 2, 1860), "we are utterly weary of the fracas, conflicts, mystifications, and resolutions of Irving Place, and we hope that the whole world of New York which cares anything seriously for music will take thought to itself as to the possibility of ending all this."

Indeed, so low had the Academy sunk by the time Ullman returned from Europe in late September, that—for all his faults—the formerly maligned, snubbed, and ridiculed little impresario was universally welcomed back and looked to as the sole hope of saving the ravaged opera. "Let us confess that we are pleased to hear of the return of Mr. Bernard Ullman," wrote his former tormentor Burkhardt (*Dispatch,* September 29, 1860). "We are obliged to own—granting him full possession of the vice of general impecuniosity [he hadn't paid his advertising bills] and the operatic advantage of a singularly querulous temper—he is undoubtedly the best musical manager, whether in concert or opera, now in the United States."

Returning to a nation deep in the throes of a crucial presidential election and—to complicate matters—finding himself without funds for staging a series of mandatory (and potentially lucrative) gala events to welcome the nineteen-year-old Prince of Wales (the future Edward the Seventh), currently on an ill-timed visit to the United States, Ullman decided (or was forced) to declare a moratorium on the disastrous New York opera season until after the election, and to address himself to the more immediately remunerative Prince of Wales festivities. He promised to reopen the Academy early in November with some of the artists he had engaged in Europe: Formes, D'Angri, and the young American mezzo-soprano Isabella "Incli" (Hinkley),[100] who had reportedly created a stir in overseas opera circles.

---

[100] The pretentious typographical transformation from *Hinkley* to *Incli* nettled the American press, far and wide.

But first, doubtless to raise a little necessary operating cash, Adelina Patti was brought back for three—inevitably stretched to four—performances of the two new roles she had been trying out in Philadelphia: *La traviata*[101] and *Linda di Chamounix.*[102] Her Violetta—generally regarded (despite Piccolomini's precocious fame in the role) as woefully inappropriate casting of a seventeen-year-old, however phenomenally gifted—was only a qualified success. Earlier hints that little Patti might not, perhaps, possess the tragic powers required of a full-fledged *prima donna* were now openly expressed. Although she threw herself into the music of *Traviata,* wrote Seymour (*Times,* October 4, 1860), "her reckless ecstasy of the first act and her despair of the *finale* savored more of the boarding school than of life, and it would be but idle to say that she either comprehended or pretended to create the role in its dramatic aspects."

The ratio of harsh criticism to praise of Patti's Violetta varied with the individual critic, but her emotional shortcomings were noticed by all. The burden of blame, it was agreed, rested with Strakosch, who, as Patti's professional mentor, was responsible for casting her in so unseemly a role.

Patti fared only marginally better as Linda, a role more suitable because less emotionally demanding.[103] Of course, wrote *Robin,* one made allowances for her youth, but he spoke for most of his colleagues when he expressed the fear that Patti was totally "wanting in that depth of feeling which is necessary to make her a great prima donna,[104] though it will not prevent her from gaining great popularity, much of a certain fame, and a very useful amount of money" (*Albion,* October 13, 1860, p. 487).

Hagen went further: Patti's appearances during the past season, he wrote (*Review and World,* October 13, 1860, p. 302),[105] only corroborated his original opinion of her. "The young singer, upon whom the management chiefly relied for the success of the season, has led to nothing but disappointment. Her talent is today the same as it ever was, but her training has been such that no lasting good can be expected from it. A few more attempts at Traviata singing, and voice and talent, together with a good many hopes for the future, will be gone forever."

Following her "farewell warble" in *Linda* on October 8, Adelina Patti was not heard in New York for more than two decades. When she would return in 1882—after an incalculable amount of "Traviata singing"—she would return as the world's undisputed queen of song.

Leaving the Academy to a corps of carpenters and designers who, under the finicky tutelage of Sexton Isaac Brown, made alterations and preparations for the coming

---

[101] Heard in New York on October 3 and 6, with Brignoli (Alfredo) and Ferri (Germont); Muzio conducted.

[102] On October 4 and 8. Also in the cast were Brignoli (who sensationally interpolated an aria from *Luisa Miller* in the second act), Ferri, Susini, and Dubreuil; Maretzek conducted.

[103] In fact, both roles, but especially the Violetta, had been "liberally cut by Mr. Strakosch to suit her as yet undramatic capabilities," wrote *Wilkes' Spirit* (October 10, 1860, p. 90).

[104] Throughout her life, Patti "allowed herself few emotions," much later wrote the pragmatic American *prima donna* Clara Louise Kellogg (1842–1916), for, she added, "every singer knows that emotions are what exhaust and injure the voice" (Kellogg, p. 30).

[105] In August the *Musical World* and the *New-York Musical Review and Gazette* merged, henceforth to appear—published by the Mason brothers amd edited by Hagen—as the *Musical Review and Musical World* (hereinafter cited as *Review and World*).

grand reception and ball in honor of the English Prince, the opera company hastened to Philadelphia, whither the princely party had by now progressed. There, instead of New York, for reasons best known to the managers,[106] the Prince was feted on October 10 with a super-grand gala performance of *Martha,* sung by Patti, Fanny Natali (*née* Heron, a favorite Philadelphia contralto), Brignoli, Formes, Nicolò Barili, and Maretzek, followed by the first act of *La traviata,* with Colson, Errani, and Muzio.[107]

"The house was sold out at increased prices many days before the appointed night,"[108] recalls Maretzek (*Sharps and Flats,* p. 48), the box-office receipts amounting to some $7000, and in addition about $3000 taken in by the managers' scouts acting as ticket speculators. "Ullman and Strakosch went there with gleams of hope in their breasts and the prospect of many more such nights. But behold!" exclaims Maretzek in unholy glee: "Next morning the treasurer declared that every penny had been paid out, upon orders from New York signed by Mr. Kingsland [representing the New York Academy landlords, to whom Ullman/Strakosch were heavily in debt]. Nothing was left for the artists, chorus, orchestra, and even for the supernumeraries, and I am witness myself that poor Ullman and Strakosch had that day not money enough to pay their hotel bill and return to New York!"

Upon this ultimate catastrophe, the teetering Ullman/Strakosch partnership collapsed;[109] the opera season at the Philadelphia Academy abruptly ceased, leaving the company stranded. Strakosch, retaining possession of little Patti, immediately departed with her on a tour of the South and West, leaving a penniless Ullman with the lease of the New York Academy of Music on his hands[110] and the hopeless responsibility of filling it with viable opera.

On October 11, upon the Prince's arrival in New York, the cumulative public excitement—far surpassing the earlier excitement over the Japanese ambassadors—fairly exploded. By ten A.M., wrote Strong, "people were stationing themselves along the curbstones of Broadway and securing a good place to see the Prince. . . . Shops were closed and business paralyzed. Wall Street deserted. . . . I lounged uptown at two o'clock, feeling my way through the crowd that filled Broadway. Omnibuses and carriages were turned into the side streets and all Broadway was one long dense mass of impatient humanity. All the windows on either side were filled.[111] Temporary platforms crowded, at five dollars a seat."

[106] Probably in the hope of removing their box-office receipts from the grasp of their New York creditors.

[107] The choice of program, it was grandly announced, accorded with the wishes of Lord Renfrew (the Prince's incognito), "to whom the repertoire was submitted for selection" (*Sharps and Flats,* p. 47).

[108] The box-office price of tickets was increased to an exorbitant $3, and ticket purchasers were admonished to attend the performance in full dress (*Evening Post,* October 5, 1860).

[109] "Rumor points to the secession of Mr. Strakosch from the management, and intimates that Messrs. Ullman and Maretzek intend to put up their steeds in the same stable," gossiped the *Times* (October 13, 1860).

[110] Ullman's lease of the Boston Academy of Music had by now expired.

[111] Fortunate possessors of windows on the parade route drove a brisk business in window rentals at up to five dollars a seat, and purveyors of jewelry, fans, and bouquet holders reaped a lively trade in supplying these fashionable essentials to the fortunates invited to the great ball. In a long newpaper column of Prince-of-Wales advertisements, two tickets to the ball were offered by a speculator for "not less than $200."

Despite his disdain for such plebeian goings-on, at three o'clock Strong joined friends at the New York Club (at Astor Place and Broadway), where they "watched and waited" for three hours to see the parade of welcome to the Prince.[112] "It was six o'clock and quite dark before the head of the procession reached us,"[113] he wrote. "We saw a six-horse barouche pass. We hurrahed. Ladies in the opposite windows waved their handkerchiefs. Little boys in the street hay-hayed. Elder loafers yelled, and the Prince was gone. Keen-sighted and self-confident men insisted that they had actually seen someone in scarlet uniform bowing his acknowledgments, but their assertions inspired no confidence. It was too dark to distinguish colors"[114] (Private Journal, October 11, 1860; *Diary*, III, 45–46).

The great reception and ball at the Academy of Music the following evening was not without incident. "The Academy," wrote Strong, who as a member of the select reception committee had arrived early, was "a brilliant sight, blazing with light and decorated with great masses of flowers." After the invited guests, reportedly more than three thousand paradigms of the "genius, talent, wealth, and beauty" of the city, were at last assembled—the ladies glittering with diamonds and resplendent in magnificient sartorial confections, the civilian gentlemen in sober dress clothes, the military gentlemen in dress regimentals festooned with decorations—the royal party arrived. The musicians, Noll's dance orchestra and Grafulla's Seventh Regiment Band, struck up "God Save the Queen" and "Hail Columbia," and a stately promenade began,[115] the promenaders—two by two—circling the room and making, according to Strong, their "murgeons [facial contortions] and 'jennyflexions'" as they passed the royal guest.

Suddenly, shattering the genteel murmur of small talk blended with the tinkle of discreet background music, a crash! A huge vase of flowers had toppled from the first tier to the floor below, spattering, but not injuring, the nearest celebrants. Before the astounded crowd had time to react, another vase followed. Then, to a thunderous detonation, two sections of the temporary flooring erected atop the parquet and stage areas of the Academy sank beneath the merrymakers' feet.

"Ellie went down into one of the pits and was frightened, but" wrote Strong, "did not lose her footing nor her self-possession. Of course, people crowded away from the dangerous region in all directions" but nobody panicked. "The promenade became impracticable and the Prince and his suite and most of the committee retreated

[112] Not that there was a dearth of elaborate parades during this period of heated electioneering. The city—indeed, the country—incessantly rang with the military music that paced marchers in the various political demonstrations. Particularly distinctive were the great torchlight processions of the pro-Lincoln "Wide-Awakes." As an enthralled Strong described one: "Each man [wearing an oilskin helmet and cape, carried] a torch or lamp of kerosine oil on a pole, with a flag below the light; and the line was further illuminated by the most lavish pyrotechnics. Every file had its rockets and its Roman candles, and the procession moved along under a galaxy of fire balls—white, red, and green." Strong had never seen so beautiful a spectacle devoted to a political cause (Private Journal, September 15, 1860; *Diary*, III, 41).

[113] As the procession neared Trinity Church, reported the *Tribune* (October 12, 1860), "the chimes rang out sweet and clear under the management of Mr.[James] Ayliffe, the experienced bell-ringer."

[114] On October 13, Strong witnessed the more luminous torchlight parade in the Prince's honor by an estimated force of five thousand New York and Brooklyn firemen, complete with fire engines.

[115] The promenade was a providential last-minute inspiration on the part of a committee member, to restrain the elegant assemblage from mobbing the Prince in their frenzy to get close and stare.

Leslie's, Dartmouth College Library

The Prince of Wales opening the ball in his honor at the
Academy of Music, where disaster almost ended the festivities.

to the reception and supper rooms." There they remained while "a score of carpenters and policemen and the illustrious Brown were energetically repairing the damage. Peering down into the oblong hole," Brown appeared to Strong as if "engaged in his ordinary sextonical duties at an interment" (Private Journal, October 15, 1860; *Diary*, III, 48, 49).

At last, reported the *Tribune* (October 13, 1860), after "two disturbed and dreary hours of repairing . . . two anxious hours of jarring sounds of propping timbers and hissing saws and clattering hammers [that] came unwelcome to the ears of the expectant merrymakers . . . the breach was covered, and the flimsy planks were pronounced secure. Treading warily at first, but soon more boldly, the company reassembled in its density."

With renewed courage, the determined souls who had weathered the catastrophe resumed the festivities, continuing the revel until five o'clock in the morning. "Got home at daylight, after nearly nine hours spent in a new pair of patent leathers," wrote Strong. "Very tired."

Attempting to capitalize on the crumbs of this glamorous occasion, Ullman, misleadingly advertising "the Prince of Wales Ball," recycled the event the following day, "at the urgent request of those who were unable to attend." Rather, contemptuously commented Burkhardt (*Dispatch,* October 20, 1860), Ullman provided "the adorers of 'powers and principalities,' who could not afford, or who were not fashionable enough to secure the opportunity of looking upon the face of the live Prince of Wales, the chance of looking at the boards he had danced upon, the room to which he had re-tired, the mended flooring over which he had trodden, and the fast fading flowers to which his princely nose had haply been inclined." From noon until seven P.M. some six to seven thousand curious people—at fifty cents a head—shuffled through the scene of last night's festivities to the accompaniment of last night's music, again played by Noll's and Grafulla's bands.[116]

Strong at last completed his welcoming duties at a crowded Sunday morning ser-vice attended by the royal party at Trinity Church on October 14, following which, to his relief, they departed. At least, wrote Strong, the occasion had been "marked by no gross indecency," even if "the music was dull. Cutler's 'Service in B' is among the most inane and insipid of extant musical compositions. The anthem, a psalm of [Benedetto] Marcello [1686–1739], was well rendered and respectable, though archaic and dry."

Perhaps to escape from his friends' interminable fond reminiscences of the Prince's visit,[117] Strong made one of his infrequent visits to the theatre, particularly resplendent that year with seasons by such legendary figures of the American stage as Edwin Forrest, Charlotte Cushman, Edwin Booth, Mrs. John Wood, and Joseph Jefferson.

October 19. Play-going with Ellie tonight at the Winter Garden. *Guy Mannering,* a dramatic distortion of Sir Walter Scott's [1815] novel. Miss Charlotte Cushman♪♫ was the Meg Merrilies,[118] supported by the worst sticks I ever saw on any stage. She is called very great in this role—the discriminating Dr. Carroll thinks it equal to any of Rachel's. She certainly makes up as the grisliest of hags. Her performance is intense and carefully studied—a few points in which Scott's words were preserved were effective and beautiful. Her attitudes were remarkably picturesque and striking. But it was almost all overdone and untrue, She was a Hecate or *Waldfrau,* perhaps, but not Walter Scott's Meg—nor any other possible woman.

The overture, a cento of Scotch airs,[119] was one of [Strong's sister] Eloise's piano pieces when I was a small boy. I remembered nearly every note. And I recognized an incident in the play, which I remember her telling me of, after she had seen it at the

---

[116] Losing no time, Hooley and Campbell's Minstrels, performing at Niblo's Saloon, presented a burlesque in blackface of the Prince of Wales's ball.

[117] Strong scornfully commented on the demeaning "toadyism" with which his upper-class friends responded to this thrilling brush with royalty.

[118] It was the great actress's benefit night, the ninth performance of her hugely successful present run in her famed role of Meg Merrilies. "How the management is prepared to accommodate the public we are at a loss to imagine," genially puffed the *Times* (October 19, 1860), "since on each occasion of its representation, sitting room—for those who came after the doors were opened—was a dream and delusion, while, before the curtain was raised, standing room became an imagination and a snare."

[119] Doubtless compiled and conducted by Edward Mollenhauer, music director of the Winter Garden.

The young Prince of Wales took time off from the celebrations (and the almost continuous entertainments of the city) to exercise at a Young Ladies' Institute.

The President honored the Prince of Wales with a reception in the White House.

old Park Theatre at least twenty-eight years ago. . . . Last night Ellie spent reading music for me.

October 20. . . . [returning home after a family visit to Barnum's Museum to celebrate little Johny's ninth birthday] Ellie read me some music: Haydn's "Last Words," and Beethoven's Symphony, and some scraps of *Zauberflöte.*

October 22. . . . Speaking to the Reverend William Berrian of the services at Trinity Church on the 14th; I asked him who composed the *Gloria in Excelsis* played that day. It is the same I've known since I was a boy—that one hears always in country churches—in fact the only Anglican *Gloria in excelsis* I ever heard, except one or two of Hodges's in Trinity Church and Trinity Chapel. He told me it was composed by Coates, the old sexton of Trinity some thirty years ago. This is curious and worth remembering, for I know of no piece of English church music that's half as effective and expressive as this familiar old composition. I remember that I used to *hope* for it at St. Paul's before I was fourteen years old. There is a flavor of "God Save the King" in its leading phrases.

～～

Scarcely had the Ullman/Strakosch partnership expired than the members of their derelict opera company split into two opposing—indeed, hostile—factions: the one, "Franco-Italian," under Muzio's direction, consisting of Colson, Susini, Ferri, and Brignoli; the other, German, headed by Formes and Fabbri, including Stigelli, with Anschütz as conductor and Richard Mülder as business manager. Each group was determined at all odds to gain control of the New York Academy of Music, but—to Burkhardt's and Hagen's intense satisfaction[120]—Formes and "Mülder Fabbri" prevailed.[121]

The rival Franco-Italian group vainly tried to secure the Winter Garden or Niblo's for a competitive run. Thus, cynically commented the *Times,* they were forced to "wait for the failure of the Formes division, to which they look with an anxious expectation, when Mr. Ullman promises them too an opportunity of disposing gracefully of any idle capital they may possess."[122]

On October 24—with a splendid performance under Anschütz's direction of Meyerbeer's *Robert le diable* in Italian—the German contingent reopened what they referred to (to the general amusement of the press) as the Academy's "momentaneously closed doors."

---

[120]Burkhardt and Hagen faithfully stoked the anti-Italian flames to an answering *obbligato* of anti-German heckling from the long absent *Evening Post* critic, now returned after extensive travels to the South and West. (The almost identical first-person descriptions of his visit to the Mammoth Cave in Kentucky, appearing both in the *Post* and, signed *Trovator,* in *Dwight's* (November 17, 1860, p. 269), confirm their common authorship although, regrettably, the critic's personal identity remains unknown.

[121]Ullman, wrote the *Times* (October 21, 1860), lent the dignity of his name to the undertaking, but only as their landlord, taking "no pecuniary interest . . . beyond the agreeable one of receiving his rent and reposing in a condition of lucrative taciturnity for a time."

[122]In the meantime, with the addition to their troupe of young Clara Louise Kellogg (see GTS: 1861), and presumably with Jacob Grau (1817–1877), a longtime hanger-on to the fringes of the opera world, as their behind-the-scenes man of business, they went on a concert and opera tour.

October 24. . . . . George C. Anthon dined here. With him and with Ellie and
Mrs. Peters to the opera. *Robert le diable,* tolerably rendered by Formes,[123] Stigelli, and
Fabbri, etc. Formes, they say, has lost his voice, but I cannot detect the change.[124] *Robert* is certainly not a great opera—that is, if we assume that Haydn's, Beethoven's, and
Mozart's music is great. It belongs to a different class, or order: *invertebrate music*—melodies and harmonies without backbone, of which class there are many genera—the
Donizetti, an analogue of the soft and shapeless mollusca—the Verdi, corresponding
to the hard-shelled, wooden-jointed crustaces, etc., etc. The particular type of baser
organization specially represented by the Meyerbeer genus is harder to indicate. Its feature should be indefinite multiplication of parts (as in some Annulata), complex organization and detail in each part, and the resulting whole feeble and of low grade in the
Animal Kingdom.

October 31. . . . . Am just from *Der Freischütz,*[125] with Ellie and Mrs. Georgey Peters. The lovely phrases of the finale are not quite out of my ears yet. Formes was
Caspar, Stigelli Max, [von Berkel Aennchen], and Fabbri the heroine. The best performance of the opera I have seen, though Fabbri misconceived her part[126]—took everything too slow and spoiled the glorious Allegro of her *Wie nahte mir der Schlummer*
scena by breaking it up into little bits of light and shadow instead of giving us the sustained rush of joyous melody which Weber meant it to be, and which she could have
made it if she tried. But in that scena perhaps—and in Caspar's drinking song certainly—Weber overrated the capacities of mundane voice, energy, and expression. No
mortal ever existed who could render them as they should be rendered and do full
justice to their intensity.

November 3. . . . . Ellie spent the evening reading music for me: *Freischütz,* "Eroica," etc.

~~~

"Aggravated by dyspepsia and grumblings of toothache," Strong evidently did not
attend the Philharmonic Society's celebratory seventy-fifth concert, the first of their
nineteenth season. Given at the Academy of Music on November 10 with Eisfeld conducting, the program included Schumann's problematical Symphony No. 2, op. 61

---

[123] Seymour, in the *Times* (October 26, 1860), regarded Formes's tremendous performance of
Bertram as "one of the destined traditions of the present age in lyric drama." And Fry, in the *Tribune*
(October 31, 1860): "He is never upon the stage for five minutes without making every one of his
hearers feel the wonderful magnetism of his presence, at once changing the entire atmosphere and
movement of the scene."

[124] It was widely noted that Formes had lost none of his power but also none of his propensity
for singing out of tune.

[125] Strong had bypassed the splendid performances on October 26, of *Martha,* sung in German
with Fabbri, Martini d'Ormy, Stigelli, and Formes, and on October 29, of *Les Huguenots,* in Italian,
given with the addition to the cast of Fanny Natali, a Vestvali-like contralto, making her New York
debut as Urbain, and Bertucca-Maretzek as a vocally played-out Marguerite de Valois. Fabbri,
Formes, and Stigelli surpassed themselves in the roles of Valentine, Marcel, and Raoul. The greater
and lesser secondary roles were filled by a representative assortment of local German singers.

[126] In this, as in every role she undertook, wrote the critics with a single voice, Fabbri surpassed
any *prima donna* previously heard in New York: "It is not extravagant to say," wrote Fry in the *Tribune*
(October 31, 1860), "that Fabbri has had no superior, when we consider her singing and action."

(1845–46), Mendelssohn's *Meeresstille und glückliche Fahrt,* op.27, and Beethoven's "Leonore" Overture, no. 1. The soloists were a Madame Schroeder Dümmler, a new German opera soprano said to have been imported by Ullman, who splendidly sang the
Va! dit elle from *Robert le diable* and Elizabeth's Prayer from *Tannhaüser,* and Joseph Noll,
who played Vieuxtemps's Second Violin Concerto, op. 19.

Although the occasion brought together "the faithful company of the musical
elect in large numbers," wrote Seymour (*Times,* November 12, 1860), "the serious political and financial complications of the day produced their effect and relieved the
throng from that outside pressure which, in past times, has so often swelled the coffers
of the Society at the expense of the comfort of their audiences.

"Schumann, Beethoven, and Mendelssohn were represented in the orchestral
program. The first of these composers, put on his trial for murdering harmony (of
which crime he is constantly accused by half the cosmopolite critics of the art), was
patiently heard through his Third [*sic*] Symphony and acquitted by a competent jury.
No unseemly applause, however, followed the verdict, and the approval won by this
composition was so modest in its sincerity that it seemed to have been rendered to the
masterly evolutions of Mr. Eisfeld and his musical Seventh Regiment[127] of performers,
rather than to the ideas of the divine Robert. This Third Symphony throws up here
and there a sweet or sparkling musical thought but lacks general spirit and fire."

"People say 'times are hard and dull,'" wrote Hagen (*Review and World,* November 24, 1860, p. 338), "and without question, even the first Philharmonic Concert
showed the signs of such a state. The audience was comparatively small. . . . There was
even less chattering, less tittering, less flirtation than usual, and alas! this is decidedly
the worst sign a Philharmonic concert in our city can offer; take it away and this responsibility of its permanency will fall upon the shoulders of the very few who attend
for the sake of the music and not for that of fashion and flirtation. It is for this reason
that we hope the political cloud, which has even thrown its shadow upon our Philharmonic Concerts, will soon pass away."

November 17. Mr. S. B. Ruggles dined here. Thereafter I played a game of chess
with Johny, and Ellie read me Mozart's Symphony in C, the "Jupiter." Why "Jupiter?"
It doesn't remind one in the remotest degree of anything in the history of that dissipated old deity. Perhaps so called because it was princeps and sovereign among symphonies (and among all orchestral compositions) at the date of its production. Only
four can compete with it now: Beethoven's C-minor, "Eroica," A, and D [Nos. 7 and
2]—and the second and third of these differ from it so generically and essentially that
they can hardly be compared together.

<center>~~~</center>

By now the opera scene had undergone a further series of transformations. On
November 2, with election day four days off, the Fabbri/Formes company, after four
successful performances at the Academy, abruptly announced the close of their season
with a performance of *Martha* for Formes's benefit. Rumors flew: that the company
were going on tour; that they would resume their performances at the Academy after

---

[127] New York's super-elite regiment.

the election excitement had died down; that the Muzio element was about to take over the Academy; that Ullman, ignited by the Fabbri/Formes success, had decided to try again at the Academy; that their season had all along been planned in collusion with Ullman as a trial run, if successful, to lead him back to the Academy.

And indeed, once again unleashing his most dazzling rhetoric, Ullman announced his comeback with an unprecedentedly magnificent production of Halévy's *La Juive,* to feature Fabbri, Stigelli, Formes, and Anna Bishop,[128] with Anschütz conducting— a production conceived on so lavish a scale (with what financial backing?) as to dwarf into insignificance Maretzek's spectacular achievement of the previous spring.

At this point, an apparently disgusted Maretzek suddenly sailed for Mexico (Cuba having been preempted by Cortesi/Servadio), to arrange for the extraordinary Mexican tour he so vividly describes in his *Sharps and Flats* (pp. 52–70).

Ullman, apparently undaunted by the *Herald*'s subversive propaganda disseminated on election day (November 6),[129] presented his *La Juive* on November 26, when Seymour wrote in the *Times:* "Mr. Ullman has lifted his little head once more above the troubled waters in which he has tumbled the past two months. The hope so long deferred, which has made sick the operatic heart, has come at last. *La Juive* is to be brought out tonight with even greater circumstance and crowds than distinguished its production at the Winter Garden last spring, where [giving a clue to Maretzek's payroll economies] the perfume of two hundred supernumeraries at ten cents each a night absolutely fumed everyone out of the house." Ullman's production promised, "in addition to a variety of acolytes and people of that class, no less than two cardinals, three archbishops, and four bishops."

Moreover, according to the advertisements, a chorus of sixty would be augmented by forty members of the *Arion* society expressly engaged for the Drinking Song; a Grand Mimic Sword Combat and other astounding acrobatic feats would be performed by distinguished athletes from several local *Turnvereine;* the stage was enlarged to accommodate magnificent new scenery by Calyo (the third-act set alone having cost $10,000); the more than 400 extras—dressed in "the richest *moyen age* costumes ever exhibited in this country, among them 64 suits of solid armor *(cap-à-pie)*"—included an emperor on horseback, with his crown and imperial insignia, eight imperial mounted princes all dressed in richest solid armor, twelve young girls dressed in white, twelve heralds dressed in gold and silver cloth, twelve trumpeters with pennants, and on and on, ad infinitum.

Preparations for his production of *La Juive,* claimed Ullman, had been in progress for more than a year and a half, and more than forty rehearsals, with chorus, orchestra, and principals, had been held since the beginning of October.

Sometimes spectators were permitted to attend.

---

[128]Determined to re-enter the opera field, Madame Bishop, together with Charles Guilmette, had been wooing Richard Mülder to form and manage an English opera company.

[129]Addressed to "Opera and Theatre Goers," the *Herald* (November 6, 1860) cautioned: "The prosperity of the metropolis will be seriously damaged if Lincoln is elected today, because its principal source of wealth, the Southern trade, will be cut off. Without a rich population, theatres cannot thrive, and the Opera becomes an impossibility. Look to it, then, that all you who relish the Opera and the drama vote against the sectional party of Abe Lincoln today."

November 24. . . . After dinner with Ellie to the Academy of Music . . . to the rehearsal of *La Juive.* Stigelli, Fabbri, Anna Bishop, Formes, etc.; a pleasant and funny evening. Opera in dishabille and a splendid revelation of bohemia. Formes, with his long locks and his rough coat, sitting on a table swinging his legs, taking snuff, talking German with the stage manager and occasionally jumping down and rushing across the stage to do a little bit of basso in B-flat—*Gran Dio*—or *Pietà*—or whatever it might have been, with one hand on his abdomen and the other extended in the regular opera pose—and thus resuming his seat and his conversation—Formes, I say, was fearful and wonderful to behold.

The opening night of *La Juive* (November 26) was an unmitigated triumph—its production, performance, attendance, reviews, everything! "Never did the New-York Opera House seem so truly a house of Opera" exulted the *Times* (November 28, 1860). And never did a more elegant and discriminating audience, filling the house to the rafters, evince such excitement. It was Ullman's moment of glory—his apotheosis—his justification—especially when, in response to calls from the audience, he was led out on the stage by Formes and Stigelli, a dwarf between two giants.

At last, opera, under Ullman's gifted management, gave promise of a secure future, rejoiced the critics, forgetting that they had ever ridiculed or reviled the "little Napoleon." Assuredly *La Juive* would enjoy an unlimited run. But it was Ullman's last hurrah. Only two days after its auspicious opening, when Strong went to hear its second performance (again finding it "a dull, heavy, dismal opera"), he heard it in a depressingly "thin house."

With each of its following performances, five in all, the houses grew thinner and thinner, and by the middle of the following week, Ullman was unable to pay his company. "It is my painful duty," he wrote to all the New York newspapers, "to announce to the public that I see myself compelled to close the opera. Notwithstanding the unanimity of approbation with which the 'Jewess' has been received by the press and the public, the receipts after the first night have fallen greatly below the expenses. This I ascribe to the precarious state of affairs in general, and to the disorganization into which the opera has fallen during my absence in Europe. Under these circumstances I cannot do otherwise but retire from the management and tender my best thanks for the generous aid I have received from the press, the artists, and all the employees of the opera."

Ullman's abrupt capitulation was received with a flood of editorials—retrospective, contemplative, speculative, and mostly regretful of the little impresario's defeat. "Alas! for our opera manager," wrote Hagen (*Review and World,* misdated November 24, 1860, p. 350). "With all his resources, he has been obliged to succumb. . . . He may console himself with the reflection that his last *coup de théâtre* was as brilliant as any man of talent can wish for. He has undoubtedly been the smartest manager we ever had."

Less sympathetically, the *Herald* reported (December 5, 1860): "The operatic union has dissolved, the singers and the fiddlers have seceded, the season has come to an inglorious and abrupt conclusion, and the little Napoleon, having already made several trips to Elba, is now packing up his things and marking his trunks 'St. Helena.'"

Fry bemoaned the city's lack of "so-called education" and artistic taste in failing to support Ullman's masterpiece of stage production (*Tribune,* December 4, 1860). The *Spirit of the Times,* formerly Ullman's most ferocious enemy, credited "the little Jewish Napoleon" with having been a manager of great astuteness, with the capacity for always coming right side up, no matter how drastic the upset: "Smashed one week with this company, he opened the next week with that."

And the anonymous current critic for the *Albion* (December 15, 1860, p. 595) asserted that although "Ullman was a man destitute of taste and thoroughly incapable in all that pertains to music . . . he knew the public and how to please great crowds of people. His advertisements were stupendous; a most wonderful combination of equine sawdust and aesthetic snuff."

But, continued the writer, the future of opera in New York was doomed as long as the stockholders insisted on retaining their stranglehold on the Academy: "Sooner or later, they *must* surrender their privilege of free admission. Two or three years more of ruin such as has attended the establishment from its opening to the present time and there will be few holders of stock who will care to be known as such."

And although Burkhardt had in the past professed "no manner of liking for the little *entrepreneur,*" he had nonetheless wished Ullman success for the "resolution and recuperative energy" he displayed in mounting his magnificent *La Juive* production against all odds (*Dispatch,* November 24, 1860). Now that the gallant little Napoleon had lost all, Burkhardt commiserated with him but allowed himself to be consoled by the fact that (without missing a beat) Fabbri, Stigelli, and Formes, at their own risk, were carrying on with the opera, to begin on December 7 with *Masaniello.* Their conductor would be young Theodore Thomas, who had covered himself with glory as a last-minute replacement for a purportedly ailing Anschütz at the last performance (on December 5) of *La Juive.*

As Mrs. Rose Fay Thomas tells it in her *Memoirs of Theodore Thomas* (p. 23), young Thomas, then 22 years old, had just settled in at home after a hard day's work, when he was abruptly summoned at curtain time to conduct *La Juive* because Anschütz had suddenly become ill. Being a man of action, Thomas seized the moment, although he had purportedly never before conducted an opera and was allegedly unfamiliar with this one (hard to believe, since he was concertmaster of the Academy orchestra and, in fact, why was he not playing there this very evening?). According to William Mason, however, from whose *Memories of a Musical Life* (pp. 200–201) Mrs. Thomas selectively extracted the anecdote, Anschütz, far from ill, had refused to conduct unless he was "paid what was due him." At any rate, the incident precipitated Thomas into his mighty conducting career, the first by an American, for despite his foreign origin—like Adelina Patti—Thomas was proudly claimed as an American.

December 7. . . . With Ellie and Charley Strong to the Academy of Music. Heard *Masaniello* for the first time (Formes, Stigelli, and Fabbri). Very creditably rendered. Auber's music is refreshing after Halévy's and Meyerbeer's leaden operas. It is fluent, melodic, and living. And the everlasting old tune of the second act ("Behold, how brightly the Morning"), wherein I took delight thirty years ago, is in fact a melody that would not have disgraced Mozart in the least. Why is it that all the music of the

Girvice Archer, Jr.

THEODORE THOMAS

last twenty years—everything I know that dates this side of Rossini's *Stabat Mater*—is deficient in melody?

Strong paid no further heed to the expiring throes of the opera at the Academy of Music. On December 10 the Fabbri/Stigelli/Formes/Thomas company valiantly presented *Stradella,* on the 12th *La Fille du régiment,* on the 14th *Robert le diable,* and at the sparsely attended Saturday matinée on the 15th ("resembling in its character a private reunion") again *La Fille,* then collapsed. "The latest operatic experiment has been nipped in the bud," announced the *Herald* (December 17, 1860). "The receipts fell far below the expenses, and the artists have been compelled to retire from the field."[130] The usual assortment of journalistic postmortems followed.

[130] Their losses amounted to some $2000, according to the *Albion* (December 22, 1860, p. 607).

Meanwhile, on November 25, Strong had found the music at the Sunday service at Trinity Church "as bad as usual. Cutler in D, or something—the dreariest platitudes." And on November 28, at the Academy of Music, he had heard Bergmann rehearse the "Pastoral" Symphony "very carefully and [also] an overture by Litztszstszt (I always forget how the consonants are grouped that spell his respectable name). It's a very long overture and very elaborately worked up," he wrote in his private journal. "There are brilliant passages, and the instrumentation throughout is admirable. I don't know its title [*Festklänge* (1853) (Searle 101)], and the composition itself furnishes no hint as to what the composer meant to say. It may have been an overture to *King Lear,* or the *Jungfrau,* or *Macbeth,* or *The Robbers,* or anything else.[131]

"The 'Pastorale' was delightful," continues Strong, "certain parts of the second movement excepted, which seem to me unworthy of Beethoven, and mere prettiness. But that symphony must rely on its first movement alone, if it claims to stand beside Beethoven's first-rate productions. That first Allegro is music of the very highest order and differs in genre from all the rest of the symphony."

Music at home, too, had lost none of its appeal.

December 9. . . . This evening we had a very pretty Miss Greenough of Boston and a brother of hers, also George C. Anthon, Dr. Lieber, Murray Hoffman . . . and others. . . . Miss Greenough is Bostonian and belongs, of course, to "one of the first families," etc., etc. She may perhaps cultivate music as her profession, being afflicted by severe impecuniousity. Has already studied somewhat in Europe and returns thither next spring. She sang for us after supper (*Voi che sapete,* among other things), displaying a fresh, sympathetic, cultivated voice and an unusual appreciation of music, as distinguished from vocalization. Though under twenty, she dares avow a preference for Mozart over Verdi and Meyerbeer.

December 13. . . . [Ellen being away on a brief visit to Washington with her father] George Anthon dined here. Then with him to Canterbury Hall, Broadway. Queer place. No women in the audience, which was made up mostly of raffish men drinking lager at little tables and smoking. The performances (ballet, gymnastics, singing, etc.) were respectable enough. Perhaps the ballet dancers' skirts were half an inch shorter than in the *Robert le diable* at the Academy of Music. There was some fair comic singing . . . and good music by a small orchestra [conducted by one Dave Braham].[132]

~~~

Evidently Strong, anxiously awaiting Ellen's return from Washington that evening, did not attend the Philharmonic concert on December 22. Besides the "Pastoral" Symphony and the Liszt *Festklänge,* Bergmann conducted Weber's "Jubilee" Overture. The soloists were Frederick Bergner, who played a *Grande Fantaisie russe* for cello by the prolific German cellist/composer Friedrich August Kummer (1797–1879), and S. B. Mills, who with the orchestra repeated Schumann's Piano Concerto, and as his

---

[131] Not so. Liszt was rumored to have composed his *Festklänge* to celebrate his forthcoming marriage to Princess Carolyne Sayn-Wittgenstein, an event that did not come to pass.

[132] Of the innumerable variety establishments flourishing in New York at the time, the entertainment at Canterbury Hall was considered the best.

solo played Liszt's showy new paraphrase on the Quartet from *Rigoletto* (1859) (Searle 434); like the *Festklänge,* it was a first performance in New York, rarely hospitable to works by Liszt.

The *Rigoletto* paraphrase, wrote an excessively harsh Seymour (*Times,* December 25, 1860), represented "an excess of vulgar and impotent treatment. Liszt is undoubtedly a great man, but when he approaches an Italian he is to be dreaded. Melody with a German [in those days anyone born in Central Europe was considered a German] is a flavor like garlic, or Worcestershire sauce, or red pepper, or any other condiment . . . with an Italian it is an essence which things, beautiful in themselves, yield spontaneously. Liszt is such an eminent musical swell, and has dined off the reputation of so many first-rate composers, that it can never be pleasant to see him gobble up a mere naturalist like Verdi.[133] This particular quartette has always been considered good, and we see no reason why it should be brought into disrepute by the oppressive patronage of a magnate who never yet touched a simple melody without strangling it."

And of the *Festklänge:* "All the acknowledged vices of harmony and harmonic progression are paraded as special boldnesses and eccentricities on the part of the composer. Rossini made fifths respectable; Liszt makes them intolerable. Beyond the affectation which one looks for naturally in everything from this great pianist's pen," Seymour surprisingly about-faced, there was, nonetheless, "great merit in this production; a peculiar and trenchant merit which will not bear analysis. The combinations are extremely varied; the transitions in *motivi* bold and happily effected; the various scraps of melody nicely introduced. In short, it is a work which proves that M. Liszt is as familiar with the gamut of a grand orchestra as he is with the keyboard of a piano."

On Christmas morning Strong attended services at Trinity Church with Johny, Ellie being housebound with a bad cold. There was a vast crowd to hear one of Reverend Francis Vinton's "sensation services," wrote Strong in his journal on December 27. Affectingly, morning prayer had begun, that Christmas Day, "not as the rubric directs, but with a Carol by the children, accompanied by the organ and the chimes."

But everybody was "depressed by the vague conviction that there [was] an uncommonly bad time coming," wrote Strong. It was not a festive Christmas.

[133] A protective attitude toward Verdi?

OBBLIGATO: 1860

The music for the day, just now, is all in the streets, guiding the march of torchlight processions of all parties, in turn, and the midnight air resounds with the cheerful sounds of innumerable full bands and the incessant roll of drums, while the blazing torches and ringing cheers for the different favorites of the day give to our quiet streets an unwonted life.

Dwight's Journal of Music
October 20, 1860

The story of 1860 is the story of a great nation marching to the music of bands, with flaring torches and with banners and with enthusiastic shouts, moving down a steep place into the sea.

Bruce Catton
The Coming Fury, 1961

COMPARED WITH THE operatic convulsions of 1860, concert-giving was at a low ebb. Except for the tried and true standbys—the Philharmonic, Mason/Thomas, the singing societies, and the increasingly audible C. Jerome Hopkins—comparatively few musicians were willing to undertake concerts at this time of economic and political uncertainty and the accelerating menace of war.

Reflecting a climate pervaded by parades, the most popular musical entity had become the military band. In New York, Noll's old Seventh Regiment (National Guard) Band had been reconstituted into an aggregation of forty handpicked musicians[1] under the command of the superlative band leader Claudio S. Grafulla♪♫ (1810–1880),[2] and on February 18, supplemented by the twenty-drum Seventh Regiment Drummer Corps led by Drum Major David Grafulla, the newly organized band made their bril-

---

[1] According to *Trovator*, an amalgam of Noll's and Shelton's bands (*Dwight's*, March 31, 1860, p. 6).

[2] "Although long noted for its band music, the 'excelsior' demands of the Seventh Regiment demand still better," explained the *Evening Post* (February 17, 1860). "The company is very large, and when marching, the music of Noll's band, though otherwise unexceptionable, is not powerful enough to be heard at the end of the line."

liant concert debut at the Academy of Music (currently under the Ullman/Strakosch regime). Their program, a wedding of two musical worlds, consisted of military and dance music, mostly composed or arranged by Grafulla,[3] and popular and operatic airs performed by the current Academy stars, Colson, Amalia Strakosch, Stigelli, Amodio, and Junca, and by the cornet virtuoso Louis Schreiber. Muzio and Bergmann conducted for the singers, and Maurice Strakosch presided at the piano.

At the close of the concert, reports the *Evening Post* (February 20, 1860), "the vast crowd, which filled seats, aisles, amphitheatre, and balconies,[4] was literally 'played out' to the appropriate air of 'Home, Sweet Home,' an interpolation on the printed programme, which was greeted with a general movement of feet—towards the points of egress."

Under the auspices of the Mercantile Library Association, the successfully revamped Seventh Regiment Band (doubtless wearing their new uniforms) made a second appearance at the Academy of Music on March 14, this time (no female solo singers being available) with the assistance of Ernest Perring and J. R. Thomas, the latter arousing the audience to a high pitch of emotion with his rendition of William Vincent Wallace and George P. Morris's timely patriotic song "The Flag of Our Union." Also assisting were the ubiquitous cornetist Schreiber and one Francis X. Diller, who played a baritone *obbligato* to Perring's aria from Donizetti's *Torquato Tasso*.♪ The concert opened with a Grand Overture by Rossini and closed with the *Attila* Quickstep, after Verdi, both arranged by Grafulla.

Doubtless with noses out of joint, Dodworth's hitherto unchallenged Seventy-first Regiment Band quickly followed with a concert at Cooper Union on March 31, assisted by S. B. Mills, Henri Appy, Harrison Millard, Samuel Meigs, a local baritone, and the indispensable Louis Schreiber.

On April 1, at the City Assembly Rooms, Bergmann presented his only Sunday evening concert of the season. His program consisted almost entirely of repeats: Schumann's Symphony No. 4, Liszt's *Les Préludes,* Beethoven's *Leonore* Overture No. 3, the Romance and Rondo movements of Chopin's E-minor Piano Concerto, played by Mills, and Servais's cello Fantasy, *Souvenir de Spa,* played by Frederick Bergner. The only novelty on the program was an early, pre-Music-of-the-Future choral piece by Wagner, *Das Liebesmahl des Apostel (The Lord's Supper)* (1843), a work written "in a hurry. . . . upon command for some festival or other when [Wagner] was in Dresden," defensively explained Hagen (*Review and Gazette,* April 14, 1860, p. 115). But any work by Wagner, however unrepresentative, had its salutary aspects: "If we restrict our knowledge only to works of a decided and indisputable merit, we fear we shall not know very much," mitigated Hagen. And if one tried, one could recognize in it "isolated melodic intimations of the author of *Tannhäuser.*" *The Lord's Supper* was sung by the *Arion* Society.

---

[3] Including Grafulla's arrangements of two "sprightly" quicksteps and his "Military Polka," all regarded as "model marching tunes."

[4] The attendance, estimated at about 4000, more than fulfilled the concert's purpose, to pay for the band's new blue and buff military uniforms.

On March 3, Mason/Thomas tardily inaugurated their fifth season, this time a short series of four *soirées* at Chickering's piano warerooms.[5] Their first program consisted of Schubert's posthumous String Quartet in G major, op. 161 (1826)—one of his "least satisfactory productions," complained the *Albion* critic (March 10, 1860, p. 115), who looked askance at posthumous publications in general. With its interminable repetitions and with "no apparent object except length," Schubert's quartet was a dry work, "barely saved by good playing." Far more agreeable was Beethoven's Trio in D major, op. 70, no. 1 (1808), beautifully played by Mason, Thomas, and Bergmann. Alone Mason played Chopin's Ballade in A-flat, op. 47, and as an encore, his own Barcarolle, a charming composition that the *Albion* critic preferred to Chopin's Ballade. The guest soloist was Stigelli, who was wildly encored after his magnificent renditions of his song "The Tear" and of Schubert's *Trockne Blumen* ("Faded Flowers"), from the song cycle *Die schöne Müllerin,* op. 25 (1823).

At their second *soirée,* on April 14, the Mason/Thomas group played Mozart's String Quartet in D minor, K. 421 (no. 2 of the Haydn set) (1783), and Schumann's Piano Trio in D minor, op. 63 (1847); Mason performed his Barcarolle, Ballade, and Nocturne for piano, and, as an encore, his *Danse Rustique;* Madame Eugénie de Lussan sang Mozart's *Voi che sapete* and Schubert's *Ave Maria;* and Theodore Thomas played Bach's Chaconne even more magnificently than before—and again, most unbelievably, from memory.

On April 21, for their third program the group performed Schumann's String Quartet in A major, op. 41, no. 3 (1842); Beethoven's String Quintet in C major, op. 29 (1801), with the second viola part taken by the Philharmonic violinist M. Schwarz; Mason, Thomas, and Bergmann played Mendelssohn's Piano Trio in C minor, op. 66, no. 2 (1845); and Mrs. Mozart sang the aria *O mio Fernando* from *La favorita* and a song by Franz Abt, "When the Swallows Homeward Fly" (inappropriate choices for the occasion, complained Hagen).[6]

Hagen was ecstatic, however, over the final program, on May 12, which included not only Haydn's String Quartet in D major ("The Lark"), op. 64, no. 5 (*c.* 1790), but two transcendent masterpieces, Beethoven's rarely heard Quartet in A minor, op. 132 (1825),[7] and his *Sonata appassionata* for piano, in F minor, op. 57 (1804), splendidly played by Mason. Hagen disapproved, however, of Thomas's reiteration of the *Rêverie et caprice,* op. 8, by Berlioz, who had displayed the effrontery to label Wagner's modulations "harsh and abrupt." At least in these characteristics, snapped Hagen, Berlioz was not inferior to Wagner. "People who live in glass houses," he proclaimed, "should not throw stones."

---

[5] A poor choice of venue, commented the *Albion* (March 10, 1860, p. 115): an elegant piano wareroom was not necessarily a good concert hall. And besides, any place fronting on Broadway was inevitably noisy. Some of the best pieces on the program had been obscured by a strident organ grinder just outside.

[6] In *Dwight's* (April 28, 1860, p. 38), —t— agreed.

[7] Erroneously "correcting" the opus number to 130, Hagen included a devoted analysis of Beethoven's Quartet, op. 132, in his review of the concert (*Review and Gazette,* May 26, 1860, p. 162), even supplying a sizable musical example, probably derived from the massive, recently published work (1859) on the Master by the German music scholar A. B. Marx (1795–1866).

Probably inspired by the current Maretzek/Ullman opera rivalry, and probably seeking to outdo Mason/Thomas, a group of well-known musicians banded together and—calling themselves the Chamber Concerts Union—announced a series of six *soi-rées* at Goldbeck's "snug little hall," to be performed on consecutive Tuesday evenings from March 20 through May 1.[8] Headed by not one but three pianists—Mills, Saar, and Goldbeck—and by Edward Mollenhauer, the group drew upon a fund of musicians from the Philharmonic: besides Mollenhauer, the violinists Doehler, Reyer, and Hahn, the cellist Brannes, the flutist Eben, and the hornist Schmitz; the assisting vocalists included, among others, Stigelli, Guilmette, Millard, Cooke, and the Misses Gellie. Emulating Mason/ Thomas, the Chamber Concerts Union's stated purpose was to perform important classical and contemporary ensemble and solo works by Beethoven, Schubert, Mendelssohn, Schumann, Chopin, and Liszt, as well as new works by Goldbeck and Saar. Insufficiently prepared and unenthusiastically received, the series—despite the high repute of its performers—was not renewed.

Mason/Thomas, on the other hand, announced an expanded sixth season, consisting of six *soirées* at Dodworth's Hall on Tuesday evenings, spaced approximately three to four weeks apart. At their first concert, on October 30, they played Beethoven's Piano Trio in C minor, op. 1, no. 3 (1793–95), Schubert's String Quartet in D minor ("Death and the Maiden"),[9] and Schumann's Piano Quintet, the last preceded by Chopin's Étude, op. 25, no. 11, played by Mason, who gave his own *Rêverie* as an encore.

Their second program, on November 27, consisted of one of Haydn's String Quartets in B-flat major, one of Mozart's sonatas for violin and piano in A major, Beethoven's "Razoumovsky" Quartet in C major, op. 59, no. 3 (1806), Theodore Thomas's bolero-like *Divertissement* for viola, played by George Matzka, and, as Mason's solo (probably sentimentally inspired), Liszt's Paraphrase (1853) (Searle 421) on the Andante Finale of the opera *König Alfred* (Weimar 1851) by Joachim Raff (1822–1882), a fellow student of Mason's at Weimar. Burkhardt found the transcription unworthy to be included in this splendid program; he also noted a certain "coldness" in Matzka and Thomas's playing in the Beethoven Quartet (not that they played it badly). Burkhardt attributed their unaccustomed detachment to fatigue, for they had borne the major weight of an exacting program (*Dispatch,* December 1, 1860).

Their demeanor more probably signified a backstage climax to the long-festering disagreement between Thomas and Bergmann, for with this performance Bergmann permanently broke with the group.[10] Fatuously referring to Bergmann's resignation as "a very annoying interruption," —t— accused him of emulating "our little sister Car-

---

[8] A subscription to the six concerts was $3, subscriptions for a family of three, $7; single tickets were 75 cents.

[9] A work so sublime as to elicit from Hagen (himself an avid quartet player) an elaborate analysis with three musical examples in the *Review and World* (November 10, 1860, p. 327).

[10] William Mason telescopes time in his reference to their break: "Before we had been long together," he writes, "it became apparent that there was more or less friction between Thomas and Bergmann. . . . The result was that Bergmann withdrew after the first year, and Bergner, a fine violoncellist and active member of the Philharmonic Society, took his place" (*Memories,* p. 186). Bergner, in fact, did not join the group until February 1861, when the delayed third concert of the series was at last given.

oline," a mindless reference to South Carolina's earth-shaking secession from the
Union only a week earlier, on December 20 (*Dwight's,* December 29, 1860, p. 318).

Concert-giving by the singing societies was noticeably curtailed in 1860. Among
the little that can be gleaned from the newspapers was the *Liederkranz's* concert on
May 19 at a crowded Academy of Music, when they presented the first performance
in America of Ferdinand Hiller's latest oratorio, *Saul,* op. 80 (1858). Joseph Weinlich,
a last-minute replacement for the suddenly ailing Philip Mayer, covered himself with
glory with his able performance—under the circumstances—of the difficult and unfamiliar role of Saul. Of the others, Stigelli was perfect as David, Madame Zimmermann
surpassed herself as Michal, Mr. Urchs was the Samuel (replacing another suddenly in-
capacitated, but unnamed, singer); the Messrs. William (or Charles) Steinway and Leopold Gilsa filled lesser roles. According to Hagen, Agricol Paur, who conducted,
coped successfully despite all difficulties (*Review and Gazette,* May 26, 1860, p. 162).[11]
    The Harmonic Society bravely offered a series of three concerts at Dodworth's
Hall. On April 14, with Bristow conducting and accompanying at the piano, they presented a concert version of his opera *Rip Van Winkle,♪* the principal roles sung by Maria Brainerd, Miss E. Coleman, George T. Atherton (a tenor), and J. R. Thomas; on
May 28, they gave the first American performance of William Sterndale Bennett's new
cantata, op. 39 (1858), on Tennyson's "The May Queen," the solos again sung by
Misses Brainard and Coleman and Messrs. Atherton and Thomas; and on July 30, they
revived Félicien David's once popular "Ode Symphony," *Le Désert,♪*[12] the recitations
declaimed by one Archibald Johnson replacing the actor John Dyott, who was ill, and
the vocal solos sung by Messrs. Tagliabeu and Mills, evidently members of the Society.
Following *Le Désert,* Bristow seated himself at the piano and treated the audience to
an "Arabic Fantasy" and "Dance of the Almées," said to have been taken down, almost
note for note, by David during his sojourn among the Arabs (1833–35). "It is needless
to say he [Bristow] played the curious music well," wrote Watson.
    In mid-October the Harmonic Society began rehearsals of Bristow's new oratorio
Praise to God, a work that would not be performed until the following February (see
OBBLIGATO: 1861), and on Christmas, at the Academy of Music, the Society, with Bristow conducting, presented their annual *Messiah,* this time with the distinguished assistance of Fabbri, Eckhardt, Stigelli, and Formes.

Unlike the year before, little official activity was reported of the Mendelssohn
Union (at least, insofar as I have been able to discover). They nonetheless held their
annual river excursion and concert on August 6, an event so exquisitely evoked by
Robin (in the *Albion,* August 11, 1860, p. 319) that it demands once again to be savored, at least in part: "At five of the clock," writes *Robin,* "a capacious barge and an
energetic tug left the city, bearing a company numbering about 250 of the sons and

---

[11] Although long and overdense, *Saul* was nonetheless a beautiful work, wrote —t— (*Dwight's,*
May 26, 1860, p. 70). Hagen, however, reported "a general leaving" by the audience before the last
of its three dense parts.
    [12] Not heard in New York for many years, Watson recalled its first performances in 1846,♪ when
George Loder had given it every evening for a week at the old Broadway Tabernacle (*Leslie's,* August
11, 1860, p. 177).

daughters of song. . . . Everybody knows what the Hudson is; all have sailed up the noble river when the shadows fall long amid the trees, heavy from the Palisades, when the slanting sunbeams tremble on the spires and high roofs of the villages along the eastern bank, when the delicious softness of the twilight throws over all things its dreamy atmosphere of beauty."

Having thus poetically set the scene, *Robin* proceeds to describe the concert: "Mr. Berge, the organist of the Church of St. Francis Xavier, played the accompaniments on a grand piano, and Mr. Morgan conducted. Selections from Mendelssohn's *Athalie,* Beethoven's *Ruins of Athens,* Wallace's *Lurline,*[13] Rossini's *Stabat Mater,* and other composers, were sung by Mesdames Berge, Coletti, and Chome, Misses Francis and Merrill, Messrs. Coletti, Werneke, Brookhouse Bowler, Seymour . . . and many others, together with a full chorus. . . . All sang *con amore* and with an expression never heard within four walls. While the music was going on, the twilight deepened into night, and the moon appeared. The barge and the tug were freighted with unspoken sentiment."

All the same, "love and the night air produce hunger, and there was a collation for all, which I may say all took advantage of. Then [Dodworth's] quadrille band attuned its instruments, and there was dancing, promenading, subdued conversation, and a general tranquil joy. Upon the bank of the river those who sat beneath their 'pines and fig trees,' or who waked from their early slumbers, must have shared the pleasure of the voyagers as the music floated up to them on the breeze. It was nearly two hours after midnight when the party once more set foot on Manhattan, and with enlivening talk and frequently renewed 'goodnights' scattered themselves over the city. For six months we will look back to this excursion with fresh delight, and then for six months we will anticipate another like it."

On November 24, at the City Assembly Rooms, the Mendelssohn Union repeated Mendelssohn's *St. Paul,* their great success of 1858, this time with Mrs. Mozart, Miss Hawley, Dr. Guilmette, and Mr. Millard as the soloists.

Among the more ephemeral music societies that fluttered by was the Burns Musical Society, an amateur orchestra reminiscent of the old Euterpean Society.[77] Conducted by one Jabez Burns, they gave their "second annual concert" on February 28 at the Bleecker Buildings (corner of Bleecker and Morton Streets). Their object, they advertised, was simply "the study and practice of music." The proceeds of their concert, at twenty-five cents a ticket (half price for children), would be set aside to fund other such events. Their weekly rehearsal meetings were held at Hitzelberger's Hall at 200 Eighth Avenue, where only well-recommended amateurs with "the necessary qualifications" were eligible to join.

Yet more fleeting was the Alpine Musical Association, which, despite its grandiose name, consisted solely of the veteran oratorio singer "Professor" Marcus Colburn and his accompanist, one H. G. Ovington. They gave a single Grand Concert at Mozart Hall on June 14, then silence.

---

[13] In mid-July the Mendelssohn Union had performed excerpts from William Vincent Wallace's latest opera *Lurline* (London 1860) for the first time in the United States at the concert and public reception tendered to Wallace by William Hall only the week before (see below).

On June 28 the even more pretentiously named National Musical Institute, formed in 1859, presented a Grand Vocal and Instrumental Concert at the Hall of the National Musical Institute, 765 Broadway (formerly Goldbeck's Hall), where students of the Institute shared a program with Madame Zimmermann, Ernest Perring, the violinist William Doehler, and the pianist John Nelson Pattison; Anschütz and Perring accompanied. Again, on November 29 at the same place, another students' concert was "aided and abetted" by Weinlich and Schreiber and a chorus of sixty singers guided and accompanied by Anschütz and F. Kruger.

On January 4, Arthur Napoleon, about to leave the United States, bade his farewell to New York with a concert at Palace Gardens Music Hall. The event did not "receive the patronage it merited," reported the *Evening Post* (January 5, 1860), despite its excellent program of Verdi arias sung by the tenor William H. Cooke (replacing an ailing Madame Martini d'Ormy) and a formidable list of piano pieces beautifully performed by Napoleon—Thalberg's fantasies on *L'elisir d'amore* and "Home, Sweet Home," Napoleon's Fantasia on *Lucia,* and a *Marche chromatique,* attributed to Liszt— and works for two pianos played by Napoleon and S. B. Mills. "He [Napoleon] sails on the 12th for Cuba, where he will probably do better than here,"[14] ruefully wrote *Trovator* (*Dwight's,* January 14, 1860, p. 333).

Far more gratifyingly received, Gustav Satter returned to Dodworth's Hall on March 28 with a supercolossal program that included, among other Satter arrangements and compositions, his unconventionally instrumented quartet for piano, two cornets, and *baryton* (euphonium). An interesting and effective work, wrote Hagen (*Review and Gazette,* April 14, 1860, p. 114), it was, however, fatiguing to the ears, with its unrelieved attack by all of the instruments all of the time.

Hagen might also have criticized the great length of the program: in addition to his quartet, Satter played his piano transcription of a prelude and fugue for organ by Handel, his blockbuster transcription of the Overture to *Tannhäuser,* and Beethoven's Sonata *Quasi una fantasia,* in E-flat, op. 27, no. 1 (1801); with John N. Pattison at a second Steinway, he played Schumann's Andante and Variations, op. 46, and Liszt's *Les Préludes.* Additionally, Bertha Johanssen sang songs by Cherubini, Spohr, Schubert, and, of course, by Satter—his ballad, "A Summer Night's Legend," and "The Bird in the Forest."

Also in January, C. Jerome Hopkins announced a "series" of two chamber concerts at Chickering's Rooms on January 17 and 23. At the first of these, Hopkins astounded his audience by performing from memory three Bach fugues ("one of them with its prelude"). It was "one of the most remarkable exhibitions of musical memory ever witnessed in this city," reported the awed *Evening Post* critic (January 18, 1860). Hopkins also played all, or part, of a Mendelssohn concerto (not identified), evidently with G. Washbourn Morgan at a second piano. His assisting artists, besides Morgan, were Hattie Andem, Charles Guilmette, and Edward Mollenhauer. The Andem and

---

[14] In Brazil, Napoleon would later enjoy an illustrious career as a composer, teacher, performer, and music publisher, notably as a publisher of Louis Moreau Gottschalk, with whom he would share a professional relationship and personal friendship during the final days of Gottschalk's regrettably short life.

Guilmette contributions consisted mainly of Hopkins's songs, not specifically named in the papers.

At his second concert, predominantly devoted to his own compositions, Hopkins was assisted by Mrs. Harriet Westervelt, again Guilmette and Mollenhauer, the Philharmonic cellist Charles Brannes, and Henry C. Timm, with whom Hopkins played his "Sepoy March," a duet for piano. The great feature of the program was Hopkins's Trio in D minor for piano, violin, and cello, a work the *Evening Post* critic (January 24, 1860) almost apologetically pronounced to be "not entirely satisfactory [in the] working up of the themes. . . . A trio," he wrote, should be "more than a series of melodic phrases alternating between the piano, violin, and violoncello, with each instrument in turn giving the accompaniment." Also, unlike Hopkins, who skillfully played its rather brilliant piano part, the others performed poorly.

Yet, extenuated the critic, it was not often that a young composer had "the energy and industry to compose a long and, to some extent, an elaborate trio and then produce it at his own expense." Hopkins deserved great credit for "the earnestness and honorable ambition that so far marked his musical career." One of his songs, performed by Guilmette, was certainly a composition that no composer need be ashamed of. Then too, Hopkins's awesome ability to perform Bach fugues from memory entitled him to special recognition.

Not one to languish in the background,[15] Hopkins announced three extraordinary "sacred and miscellaneous" concerts to be given in collaboration with the Harmonic Society at the Palace Gardens on August 14, 16, and 18. The participating artists were Hattie Andem, about to leave for Europe (presumably for vocal study), the former Annie Kemp (now Mrs. Brookhouse Bowler), George Crozier, an English tenor, and a Signor Montanari, a newly arrived *buffo* baritone[16] from the opera houses of Valencia and Madrid; Bristow was billed as the "conductor-in-chief" of the series; J. F. Stratton (or Stretton), the Palace Gardens music director, was the orchestra conductor; Henry Reyer of the Philharmonic the concertmaster; and W. H. Currie the "conductor at the piano."

The programs doubtless consisted largely of Hopkins's compositions. The first (the only one I was able to find) included—besides a smattering of opera arias and orchestra overtures—two Hopkins works for solo piano, his "caprice" for two pianos mystifyingly titled "Ruling Passion Strong in Death," two songs with orchestra accompaniment, and an ambitious "Concert Anthem" for solo soprano, contralto, and tenor, with chorus and orchestra.

Adversely reviewing the series in the *Musical Review and World* (September 9, 1860, p. 267), Hagen—progressively honing his curmudgeonly traits—allowed Hopkins the right, if he so wished, to congratulate himself on his energetic labors, but certainly not to delude himself that they had accomplished "a good deal for the advance-

---

[15] In the meantime, on February 22, reported the *Evening Post,* the enterprising Hopkins had given the first matinée ever to take place in Newark.

[16] Apparently more *buffo* than baritone. Of Montanari, who, with his wife, was currently a regular Palace Gardens attraction, Burkhardt left-handedly puffed (*Dispatch,* September 1, 1860): "Signor Montanari is a buffo artist of more than common merit and by himself would more than justify a stranger for his visit to Palace Garden. As a vocalist he is not much, but as a comic vocalist he is singularly and absurdly humorous."

ment of the cause of good music in this country."[17] Although Hopkins's compositions displayed certain "inventive powers," wrote Hagen, he had not learned, despite his years of study,[18] to make the most of his ideas. Nor had he even learned how to orchestrate. Americans were interested only in results, generalized Hagen, and were unwilling to undergo the painstaking, laborious study needed for acquiring valid musicianship. He proceeded to map out a system of properly humble, step-by-step musical education suitable for Americans.

Hopkins, undaunted, countered with yet another *soirée* at Chickering's Rooms in November, the program again consisting chiefly of his own compositions, this time with a sprinkling of Bach and Clementi. He was assisted by Dr. Guilmette and William Saar.

On December 20, with the assistance of the tenor Harrison Millard and a vocal quartet, Hopkins introduced a new (and short-lived) concert room, Ebitt Hall, at 55 West 33rd Street. On this occasion he grouped a "left-hand solo" by Maurice Strakosch with his own distinctively named compositions, "Pearl Drops" and "Wind Demon." "Strakosch's composition, such as it is," observed Hopkins's staunch supporter Burkhardt (*Dispatch,* December 29, 1860), "is only adapted to show off the mechanical dexterity of the pianist, but the other pieces gave Mr. Hopkins an opportunity for developing the amount of poetical feeling which he possesses in his fingers as well as in his brain."

The few other concerts of 1860 were mostly performed by redundant representatives of the local music community. Early in the year, on January 6, the tenor William H. Cooke, assisted by the Misses Gellie, Charles Guilmette, Harry Sanderson, and Frederick Bergner, essayed his first "Grand Concert" at Dodworth's Rooms. On February 2, Cecilia Flores appeared at the French Theatre with the singers Ernest Perring and Joseph Weinlich, the pianist John N. Pattison, and the flutist John Kyle; Bristow accompanied. At Cooper Union on February 23, a "beautiful contralto," Mrs. James H. Barclay, a pupil of Mrs. Seguin, made her debut with the assistance of Satter, Cooke, Guilmette, Schreiber, and Henry C. Timm, who presided at the piano.

On March 27 a ramshackle affair, ballyhooed as a "Grand Brilliant Concert," took place at Hope Chapel with a cast of unknown performers: a Señor Alcina, billed as "the greatest living Spanish tenor"; Messrs. Harvey and Herbert, duo-pianists, purportedly without parallel "for brilliancy and execution"; William B. Harvey (of the piano duo), "the great violinist and composer," and a Señor Morales, their musical director. "Humbug," angrily protested the critic for the *Musical World* (April 7, 1860, p. 4), referring to the false superlatives freely flung about by every two-penny adventurer to hit town. "Well, we went to hear the greatest living Spanish tenor. He proved to be barren of ordinary talent. . . . Mr. Herbert was a very indifferent solo performer, and his accompaniments were miserably played. Mr. Harvey seemed to have some talent

---

[17] Franz Liszt, on the contrary, who had heard of Hopkins's intrepid leadership of the American Music Association ("whose three years existence was so untimely cut off by the panic of 1857," wrote *Trovator*), had reportedly sent Hopkins a letter of commendation for his pioneering efforts (*Dwight's,* January 14, 1860, p. 333).

[18] According to Burkhardt, Hopkins was "almost exclusively self-taught" (*Dispatch,* August 25, 1860).

Girvice Archer, Jr.

*Another talented Patti, Carlotta, received great
acclaim for her accomplishments and was
honored with sheet-music portraits.*

both for piano and violin, but as he played nothing without the assistance of Mr. Herbert, he could not possibly produce any effect." As for Señor Morales, the Musical Director, "we puzzled ourselves to know what this Señor directed since he did not appear."

On May 31, Mary Gellie, assisted by Ardavani, Satter, Schreiber, and Mosenthal, gave a concert at the City Assembly Rooms. On October 9, James G. Maeder presented his annual concert, at which appeared Maria Brainerd, Mrs. Mozart, George Simpson, Charles Guilmette, Stephen C. Massett, George Wooster, Dr. Clare Beames, and Mrs. Maeder, the beloved Clara Fisher of the earlier New York stage.

Far more memorable was the official concert debut, on October 25 (concurrent with the short-lived Fabbri/Formes opera venture at the Academy of Music) of Carlotta Patti (1835–1889), another of "our" Adelina's gifted older sisters. "A concert for which many have long eagerly looked is at last definitely announced," heralded the *Tribune* (October 22, 1860). "Miss Carlotta Patti will make her first public appearance in New York at Dodworth's Saloon on Thursday evening. Aside from the interest attaching to the debut of a member of a remarkable family, expectation has been raised by the reports which those who have heard her in private give of the uncommon musicality of Miss Patti."

And indeed, wrote Seymour, following the event: "Miss Patti's debut was hardly a debut, for she has long since earned her place in the estimation of the genuine amateurs of New-York,[19] and the public ratification of her rank as a born mistress of that

[19] And of San Francisco, where she had appeared both as a pianist and a singer in 1855 (Martin, pp. 63, 283, n. 63).

musical art which seems to come with their breathing in her family was the merest matter of course"[20] (*Times,* October 26, 1860).

In a follow-up article on October 29, Seymour explained that Carlotta Patti would long since have assumed her rightful place in opera had not "a slight physical defect [a congenital lameness] prevented this, in every sense, charming girl from appearing on the [opera] stage." Rather than an impediment, however, her handicap, in Seymour's opinion, had "thrown around her a tender interest which has lent to her success an additional delight." Carlotta Patti's success was immediate and unequivocal. Indeed, wrote Seymour, "she is pronounced by the most accomplished critics even superior to her sister [Adelina]. Her style is as charming for simplicity of expression as for its grateful truth of intonation. She sings without pretence or affectation, leaving the melody to make its own impression. In this age of vocal degeneracy it is indeed a pleasant thing to meet such brilliant and unerring execution and such flowing, natural, and graceful ornament as are combined in Carlotta Patti."[21]

Carlotta Patti was assisted at her debut by the currently disposessed Franco/Italian contingent of Ullman's tottering opera company: her sister Amalia, who sang "Kathleen Mavourneen"; Pauline Colson, who sang the Bolero from *The Sicilian Vespers* and her great hit, the "celebrated French Laughing Song" *(L'Eclat de rire)* from Auber's opera *Manon Lescaut* (Paris 1856);[22] Brignoli, who sang the Serenade from *Don Pasquale,* and, with Ferri, a duet from *Belisario;* and Susini, who sang an aria from *I Lombardi.* The debutante was heard in the finale of *La sonnambula,* with her sister Amalia in a duet from *Saffo,* and with Ferri in a duet from *Il barbiere.* She did not, however, join in the concert's grand finale, the quartet from *Lucia di Lammermoor,* sung by Colson, Brignoli, Ferri, and Susini. Muzio "directed" the event, meaning he accompanied at the piano, and William Saar, obviously a fish out of water in this company, played two of his own compositions and Liszt's *Rigoletto* Paraphrase.

Less eventfully, on November 2 the Boston tenor, Harrison Millard, gave his annual concert at Dodworth's Rooms, with the cooperation of his townswoman Mrs. Mozart, S. B. Mills, Henry Appy, and a Mlle. Montmorency;[23]★ and on the 14th, Samuel Meigs appeared at Hope Chapel, assisted by J. R. Thomas and a group of little-known vocalists, presumably amateurs, assisted by members of the Harmonic Society and the *Schillerbund.*

At the Westminster Church (22nd Street between Sixth and Seventh Avenues), George Frederick Bristow presided at the piano, on April 12, at a lecture concert by the "Blind Preacher," the Reverend W. R. Milbern, who spoke on "What a Blind Man Saw in England." A vocal quartet, apparently derived from the Harmonic Society, supplied appropriate auxiliary music. On May 8, at a so-called "reception" at the

[20] In *Dwight's* (November 3, 1860, p. 255), —t— wondered "where will be the end of this talented family. Its name seems to be Legion, and if it continues to turn out an artist every year or two, we shall fairly be flooded with Barilis and Pattis."

[21] "Her voice," wrote *Robin (Albion,* October 27, 1860, p. 511), "is one of those thrillingly pathetic organs which move the soul from its most silent depths."

[22] The first of three highly acclaimed operas composed on the famous novel *L'Histoire de Chevalier des Grieux et de Manon Lescaut* (1731) by the Abbé Antoine-Francois Prévost (1697–1763); the second (Paris 1884) was by Jules Massenet (1842–1912); the third (Turin 1893) by Giacomo Puccini (1858–1924).

[23] An alternate pseudonym for the American actress/singer Kate Duckworth, who as Catarina Morensi would soon earn great acclaim as an opera singer.

Union Theological Seminary Chapel (University Place), Dr. Guilmette's students performed exercises in recitation, address, and music,[24] assisted by Mrs. Harriet Westervelt and the Guilmette Choral Society. And on June 11, at Hope Chapel, the actress Mary Agnes Cameron gave an "elegant entertainment" consisting of music and recitations. Miss Cameron was musically assisted by Charles Guilmette and histrionically by J. E. Nagle and Miss Alice Granger; "Professor" G. W. Morgan accompanied at the piano.

A program of Scottish ballads was presented at Dodworth's Hall on February 16 by the tenor George Simpson, with the collaboration of Mrs. Mozart, J. R. Thomas, the Sedgwicks, father and son, and James G. Maeder. A series of English concerts immediately followed at the Theatre Français on February 20, 24, and 27, the programs consisting of seldom heard glees, ballads, quartets, and male choruses sung "in our own language" by Mrs. Mozart, Mary Hawley, Messrs. Cooke, Henry Draper (a baritone), a double male quartet (probably from the Mendelssohn Union), John N. Pattison, who brilliantly played a group of piano solos, and G. Washbourn Morgan, who conducted a small orchestra. Complaining because no composers had been listed[25] in the printed program, Seymour nonetheless found it "a positive luxury to hear a well-sung ballad after the severe surfeit of Italian music which we have lately experienced in the concert-room and elsewhere" (*Times,* February 21, 1860).

At Mozart Hall on May 9, Gustavus Geary and his daughter Mina, recently arrived vocalists from Ireland, began a season of concerts devoted mainly to Thomas Moore's "Irish Melodies" (composed 1807–34), with spoken program notes contributed by Geary. Goaded by his patronizing explanatory remarks, the nettled *Evening Post* critic remarked (May 15, 1860) that the singer needed no posters to announce "from what bright isle of the sea he [hailed]. . . . None but a son of the Emerald Isle could ever have the cool assurance to act toward an American audience as though they were plunged in the profoundest abysses of ignorance in regard to everything relating to Thomas Moore.[26] . . . But when at the piano," admitted the critic, "Mr. Geary dissipates the smiles caused by his somewhat superfluous speechmaking. He has a noble tenor voice of considerable compass and cultivation, and sings with great taste and expression. In Moore's 'Melodies' he pronounces the words distinctly, though with an indescribably Irish r-r-roll on the *r*s. . . . Geary is what he claims to be—an admirable and first-class ballad singer, while at the same time we have heard many artists of pretension sing Italian opera music with less effect."

Billed as the "Irish Nightingale," Miss Mina, although inappropriately dressed in "affectation of very tender years," nonetheless possessed a beautiful voice, and used it with "charming taste and with true sympathetic fervor." The Gearys were so great a success that on June 30, before they departed on a tour of the Northern and Western states, they were honored with a Grand Complimentary Concert at the Winter Gar-

---

[24] On June 27, Guilmette's music class at the Cooper Institute (apparently a different class) held their commencement exercises in the Lower Hall of that institution. Guilmette delivered an address on the "Abuse of Music," reported the *Musical World* (July 7, 1860, p. 3). The principal soloists were warmly applauded, but the reviewer criticized the choice of program, the music being generally too difficult for the student performers.

[25] One of them being Dr. Ward, whose Serenade from *The Gypsey's Frolic* was delightfully sung by Mr. Cooke.

[26] In 1803, Moore had traveled in the United States and Canada on his return home from a failed diplomatic assignment in Bermuda.

den, at which Edward Mollenhauer conducted an orchestra, Anschütz and Morgan alternately conducted a chorus, and Berge played accompaniments on "Chickering's best grand."

To round out the ethnic picture, on November 22 the Hutchinson Family, with John and the reclaimed Abby—and with the new members Fannie, Henry, and Viola—appeared in a concert of their good old American ditties at the Cooper Institute.

On July 11 a musical welcome, or "ovation," was tendered to William Vincent Wallace, a favorite naturalized American, by his friends and publishers William Hall and Son upon his arrival on a flying visit to the United States. A representative number of Wallace's large circle of friends, admirers, and well-wishers taxed the capacity of the Halls' music establishment at 543 Broadway, where they were regaled, first with a program of Wallace's compositions—principally excerpts from his new opera *Lurline* (published in the United States by the Halls)—performed by Mesdames Cooper (Annie Milner), Brinkerhoff, Mozart, and Bouchelle, Miss Hawley, Messrs. Geary, Millard, Werneke, Simpson, and J. R. Thomas, and members of the Mendelssohn Union, with William Berge accompanying.[27] An elaborate collation followed, copiously spiked with a "vinous artillery" that unleashed a torrent of witty toasts and speeches by James Hall and the guest of honor (who reportedly was forced to stand on a slippery chair in order to be seen by all) (*Leslie's,* July 28, 1860, p. 147).

In direct contrast to the falling off of independent concert-giving, benefits—great and small—were given for an ever growing number of causes. Ullman-like persuasion was wielded in the advertisements for a New Year's Day concert to benefit the Church of the Immaculate Conception (14th Street near Avenue A), directed by the go-getting William Berge: "The pleasure and delight that will no doubt be enjoyed at this Sacred Concert," went the come-on, "may have the effect of effacing from the hearts and memories of many the sorrows and disappointments of the past year and replacing them by more cheering and brilliant hopes for the New Year." Performing at this spiritually redeeming event were members of the Mendelssohn Union and Henry Appy, still continuing to bill himself, a decade after the fact, as "the solo violinist to Jenny Lind in her tour through America."

On January 19, at the Dutch Church (5th Avenue and 21st Street), members of the Mendelssohn Union, together with members of the church choir—among them Mrs. Westervelt and Dr. Guilmette—and also one of the Misses Gellie, Mr. Cooke, the cornetist Louis Schreiber with a "private cornet quartet," G. W. Morgan and W. H. Currie, all performed for the benefit of the church's organ fund.

To aid in "paying the heavy debts" of the German Reformed Protestant Dutch Church (in Forsyth Street), a concert of sacred and secular music was given at the Cooper Institute on April 12 by Mesdames Zimmermann and Grosz, a Miss Albrecht (a soprano), a Mr. Hartmann (a minor tenor from Maretzek's Havana company), and the Philharmonic hornist Henry Schmitz; the conductor was Gustavus Schmitz (Henry's brother), organist of the Church of the Immaculate Conception.

On April 15, Louis Dachauer directed and accompanied a sacred concert for the

---

[27] On this occasion Berge "abdicated the organ for the evening in favor of one of [Spencer B.] Driggs's♪ new patent pianos" (*Times,* October 19, 1860), presumably one of the overstrung grand pianos, concerning whose origin a bitter feud raged between Driggs and the Steinways.

joint benefit of the Society of Saint Cecilia and the Sanctuary Society of the Church of St. Vincent de Paul. The performers were Madame Eugénie de Lussan, the sisters Gellie, Mary Hawley, Ferdinand Dachauer, and the combined choirs of the St. Cecilia Society and St. Vincent's.

At the City Assembly Rooms, the Gellies again assisted—together with Ardavani, the cornetist Louis Schreiber, the pianists Gustav Satter and J. N. Pattison, and with W. A. King and Joseph Mosenthal to accompany—at a concert for the benefit of the House of Mercy. The following day George Washbourn Morgan gave a Grand Organ Exhibition and Concert at the new Broadway Tabernacle (Broadway and 34th Street) to raise funds for building the Tabernacle Mission House. And on May 10 a benefit for the Music Fund of the Chelsea Presbyterian Church (22nd Street near 9th Avenue) enlisted the talents of Fanny Stockton, Madame Franz Stoepel (Kazia Lovarny), George Wooster, Louis Schreiber, Charles van Oeckelen♩ (pianist and automatonist), and one Louis Schmidt, who accompanied them in a mixed program.

Complimentary concerts to individuals included an event on January 17 for the singer/composer J. R. Thomas, tendered by his colleagues Mrs. Mozart, George Simpson, George W. Morgan, and James G. Maeder. "We have not many composers in America, and it is the duty of the public to support the few that can honestly claim the name," earnestly puffed the *Times* (January 14, 1850). "Mr. Thomas's compositions are hummed and whistled by the masses, from Maine to Florida, and we hope, for the sake of a gift that gives so much and produces so little, that Mr. Thomas's first concert will be adequately recognized by the public."

On a different plane, the German *Volksgarten* advertised a Gala Night on April 13 for the benefit of their "favorite prima donna, Signora Eliza Valentini-Paravalli." As the second part of the program, the unquenchable Valentini performed the fourth act of *Il trovatore* assisted by her husband and pupil Antonio Paravalli and a chorus and orchestra. For this glamorous event, the *Volksgarten*'s usual admission of six cents was raised to ten cents, reserved seats twenty-five cents.[28]

There were, as we know, junior benefits as well: for example, a concert at the Cooper Institute on May 21, ostensibly a benefit for Little Martha Davies, the well-known "Sunday School vocalist." Little Martha would be supported by the "celebrated Tremaine Family," consisting of her eight little Sunday School contemporaries, by Little Alonzo, the comedian of the troupe, and by "about 400 children from the Sunday Schools in New-York and Brooklyn."

On an even larger scale, on November 10, for the benefit of the City Missions, a chorus of one thousand juveniles "blended their voices in song" at the Academy of Music, where once "Gazzaniga had warbled, Piccolomini sung, Patti trilled, and Cortesi caroled" (*Times,* November 23, 1860). That a fair-sized (though not enormous) audience attended was scarcely to be wondered at if a thousand children sang, since it was safe to say, benignly computed the *Times,* that "each child had an average of one parent, one aunt, and one uncle. . . . The little performers were so tastefully attired, that the sight would have been a most pleasing one to the eyes, even had not the sound been eminently pleasing to the ears, and the applause which the little company received would have been sufficient to make Maretzek, on a similar occasion, stand on

---

[28] Later in the year the *Volksgarten* advertised a burlesque of *La Juive* at a six-cent admission.

his head in grateful acknowledgment." The *Tribune* (November 24, 1860), too, commented on the delighted parents "whose affection prompted their applause. The mode of instructing children to sing," continued the reviewer, "has so much improved that they read little melodies at sight from the blackboard, and keep time like watches."

Musicians and show folk, as always, willingly came to the rescue of their less fortunate fellows. To aid the widow and four bereaved children of a recently deceased Academy official, a large contingent of actors and musicians staged a huge Double Festival Benefit on March 10 at the Academy of Music, generously donated for the occasion by Ullman and Strakosch. In the afternoon the stars of the city's four principal theatres—Wallack's, Niblo's, the Winter Garden, and Laura Keene's—presented scenes from their current hits; in the evening Beaucardé and Albertini (then still members of the Academy company), with other musical stars, and with the Academy chorus and orchestra conducted by Muzio, gave a complete opera (unnamed) followed by a concert. Tickets for the afternoon or evening segments were fifty cents each.

On May 22 members of the currently opposing opera companies—Gazzaniga, Wissler, Tamaro, Amodio, Dubreuil, and Muzio—came to the aid of the still ailing, and now destitute, Adelina Speranza, with a performance of *Il trovatore*. Again Ullman donated the use of the Academy for the occasion.

To add musical spice to an all-star, all-dramatic afternoon-and-evening benefit for the Dramatic Fund Society at the Academy of Music on April 17, a "Grand Operatic Bouquet" was interpolated, consisting of arias from *The Sicilian Vespers* sung by Madame Gassier, an aria by Stigelli, the "Liberty Duet" (with flags) by Amodio and Junca, an English ballad by Amalia Strakosch, and, as a grand climax, the "Garibaldi Rataplan" sung by "the choral power of the Academy of Music." The conductor, needless to say, was Muzio.

For the benefit of the Widow and Orphan Fund of the New York Fire Department, on October 30 the current Niblo's manager James M. Nixon staged a supercolossal, predominantly Anglo-American, extravaganza at Niblo's Garden. Performances of two popular English plays by the Niblo's stock company were followed by a vocal and instrumental concert performed by Mesdames Bishop, Mozart, and Westervelt, Messrs. Miranda, Simpson, and Rudolphsen, Dr. Guilmette (who received special billing), the pianists C. Jerome Hopkins, George W. Morgan, and T. Augustus Hogan,♪ and the Niblo's conductor John Cook.

And again the Italian opera community rallied to the assistance of the mortally stricken *basso buffo* Mauro Assoni with a "Grand Italian Opera Concert" at Dodworth's, on December 21, wherein appeared Erminia Frezzolini, Amalia Patti Strakosch, her sister Carlotta (her second local public appearance), their half-brother Nicolò Barili, and the Signori Stefani, Centemeri, and Müller; also von Breuning, a new German pianist, and the cellist Alessandro Biscaccianti.♪♫[29]

The most spectacular, and probably the noisiest, benefit of all was the Grand Testimonial to Harvey Major, the one-armed cornetist of Dodworth's Band, who—as the

---

[29] Biscaccianti had most likely accompanied his wayward wife Eliza♪♫ when she returned to the United States in 1858, doubtless in search of an engagement at the Academy of Music. That this did not come to pass was a source of bitter disappointment to her many admirers in her native New England, where she toured extensively before making her way back to California—and that, too, only temporarily.

result of sunstroke—had suffered a further disablement, a paralysis of the lips that prevented him forever after from playing the cornet. In a sweeping gesture of sympathy,
a vast supporting aggregation of military bands—Grafulla's Seventh Regiment Band,
Dodworth's First and Second Bands, the Eighth Regiment Band, Robertson's Band,
and the Drum Corps of the Seventh, Ninth, Twelfth, and Seventy-first Regiments—
together with Maria Brainerd, Mrs. Mozart, George Simpson, Harrison Millard, J. R.
Thomas, Stephen C. Massett, S. B. Mills, Louis Schreiber, and Edward Mollenhauer—
in all, some two hundred performers—appeared on Major's behalf on December 13 at
the Academy of Music.

Upon the arrival of summer, announced by a monster *Pfingst-Montagsfest* at Jones's
Wood,[30] and by various kindred festivities at Conrad's and Elm Park, two new
German pic-nic resorts were opened: Columbia Park, 79th Street at the East River,
where "sacred" concerts were given on Sundays, and Broadway Park, on the rural
West Side, 94th to 96th Streets opposite Elm Park, where—for the benefit of the German Free School (Fourth Street near First Avenue)—a two-day "pupil-fest" was held.
After a pleasurable sail up the Hudson in a double-decker barge, its participants made
merry with the music, dancing, games, beer-drinking, and other out-of-doors delights
endemic to the German summertime psyche (*Evening Post,* June 15, 1860).[31]

At least one decidedly American event took place at Jones's Wood—the great
"Reception Festival" on August 15, to celebrate the return of the public idol John C.
Heenan from his recent pugilistic exploit in England (see preceding chapter). Directed
and organized by the showmen James M. Nixon and Henry Wood on behalf of a
group of sporting speculators, a gladiatorial amphitheatre had been erected in Jones's
Wood, with seating accommodations for 3000 viewers, to permit, it was hoped, "ladies
and family parties to witness the exciting and chivalric emulations between the knights
and champions of the 24-foot space." There was besides, it was stated, standing space
for 50,000 additional viewers.

Because the object of the event—aside from conferring a well-merited compliment upon the hero (and capitalizing on his inordinate publicity)—was to educate the
uninitiated in the finer points of pugilism, a program of edifying preliminary matches
filled the morning. It was punctuated at noon by a "national salute" of thirty-one
guns, and again at one P.M. by a "royal salute" of seventeen guns. To fill the intervals
between salutes and boxing matches, Harvey Dodworth and his full band of sixty musicians played medleys of patriotic tunes and arrangements of works by William Vincent Wallace, Gungl, and Meyerbeer.

At three in the afternoon the Champion, accompanied by a retinue of friends and
admiring hangers-on and followed by his "daring opponent," made his spectacular entrance to the grounds, driving through a triumphal arch decorated with the national

---

[30] Lustily celebrated by the twenty singing societies belonging to the *Allgemeine Sängerbund,* supplemented by countless *Turnvereine,* military bands, rifle societies, glee clubs, drum corps, and countless other German social amalgamations, to say nothing of a holiday-making, indigenous population.
(For a vivid eyewitness account of the event, see the *Times,* May 29, 1860.)

[31] An unfortunate gap in available files of the *Staats-Zeitung,* not supplied by other contemporary
German language newspapers, demands a curtailment of description of many succeeding German-
oriented summer events.

colors and bearing Heenan's motto: "May the best man win." First circling the arena to allow himself to be seen by all, mighty Heenan proceeded to thrill his audience, first with a "simulation" of the "Great Contest" in England, then taking on, one by one—in "friendly encounter"—each of the "professors" who had sparred in the preliminary bouts. To conclude the celebration, the "Mammoth Band" resumed their concert with something called the "Divertimento from *Lohengrin*" and ended with a *Jubel* Overture, anachronistically reported to have been composed by Lindpaintner (deceased in 1856) for the launching of the *Great Eastern* (in 1858). To crown the day's thrills, the *Jubel*'s finale was accented by the firing of cannon.[32]

Palace Gardens opened its summer season on June 12 with a huge extravaganza. On the following day they presented a concert featuring a Madame Johanna Ficher, soprano, "from the German and Italian operas," a Miss Della St. Marc, possessing so extraordinary a contralto "that she may be called a lady tenor," an authentically male tenor Herr Hartmann, and a Mr. Brauny, characterized as a "sonorous and pleasing bass"; Mr. F. Ficher, presumably Johanna's husband, accompanied. On June 15 they followed with a promenade concert and *soirée dansante,* advertised as "the first hop of the season"; on June 19, Miss Myra Rosella, a "talented young lady aeronaut," ascended skyward in a balloon; and from June 26 to June 30 the Ronzani Company, comprising a ballet corps of twenty young ladies, presented Domenico Ronzani's grand ballet, "The Fountain of Love."

On July 2, Palace Gardens celebrated its anniversary, a gala event that purportedly had "never failed to attract less than 5000 ladies." Special offerings for this occasion included a timely Japanese Lantern Fete, a magnificent display of fireworks, the usual delicacies, and J. F. Stretton's "orchestra band" playing—among lighter items—arrangements of music by Reissiger, Wagner, Meyerbeer, and Verdi. On July 4 the Independence Day program so severely disparaged by Strong was given three times. Later in July, Madame Ficher returned, this time sharing the bill with the tenor George Crozier, a Miss Ella Wren, with little Martha Wren and little Fred Wren, a Lilliputian "Comic Wonder"; W. H. Currie accompanied. As the season progressed, they were followed by the Lubin Brothers, "necromancers, ventriloquists, and table-rappers."

In August and September, as we know, the Montanaris performed at Palace Gardens, as did Anetta Caradori, and also Mrs. George Holman with her "Juvenile Parlor Opera Troupe" of miniature thespians and musicians. And on August 19, a "sacred" concert was performed by a motley crew: Madame Ficher, Julia Melville (of the concert saloons), George Crozier, and one G. C. Rexford, a baritone; W. H. Currie accompanied.

And, at the nadir of the August doldrums, *Robin,* who only recently had cruelly deprecated Palace Gardens, now asserted (probably under editorial duress) that it was "a really delightful place and much frequented." It had, he backtracked, provided the locale for C. Jerome Hopkins's fine series of concerts, which "gave enjoyment to many

---

[32] Heenan's great achievement had by now received the ultimate accolade: in May the superb comedian Joseph Jefferson, at Laura Keene's Theatre, hilariously impersonated Heenan in an English farce *The Benicia Boy* and, beginning June 18 and for the following week, the minstrels Jerry and Dan Bryant appeared, presumably in blackface, as Heenan and Sayers in something billed as a burlesque "Irish-American Opera."

and added to [Hopkins's] own reputation." Furthermore: "A variety of music, called light, has been performed at the same establishment through this week. Fortunately," added the incorrigible critic, "the audiences have not been exacting, and the convenient situation of the concert-room allows one to retire into the shade of the coloured lamps and trees when he has heard enough of the vocalism" (*Albion,* August 25, 1860, p. 403).

As before, the 1860 Fair of the American Institute was held at Palace Gardens, where, as in the past, nightly concerts by Dodworth's Band were a feature of the exposition.

And again, through the musically uplifting efforts, and under the guidance, of the music-loving architect Jacob Wrey Mould, Dodworth's Band resumed their Saturday afternoon concerts in wonderful Central Park, albeit not until August 25. For this, the concerts' second season, the "music stand" was moved from the Ramble to the north end of the Mall, a change approved by all. Under Mould's salutary musical leadership, wrote the *Times* (September 1, 1860), "new and choice arrangements of themes from the finest works of the best composers—Beethoven, Mendelssohn, Spohr—will in this way become the familiar friends of our population."

"All classes of New York society were represented at yesterday's [Park] concert," reported Wilkins (*Herald,* September 23, 1860), "from the aristocracy down to the little democrat, *sans* coat, *sans* shoes, *sans* almost everything, but with an expression that clearly demonstrated his republican and independent spirit. For some time previous to the beginning of the music, the people were scattered through the Park, rambling through the Ramble, or watching the graceful movements of the swans;[33] but scarcely had the overture commenced than there was a grand rush, and in a few moments there were at least five thousand persons gathered around the performers, while outside of these again, were stationed a large number of carriages, the largest number that has ever been there on a Saturday afternoon. As the owners of vehicles seldom leave them, it forms quite a pleasant feature of the concerts to see so large a number of carriages grouped about, filled with the beauty and fashion of New York."[34] The program consisted of overtures, marches, and dance music arranged from works by Strauss, Meyerbeer, Donizetti, Mendelssohn, Wallace, Verdi, and Rossini.

Surpassing even the pleasure gardens as places of popular entertainment—musical, comedic, alcoholic—the variety establishments, or "concert saloons," continued to multiply so rapidly and to employ such vast hordes of entertainers as to discourage individual identification (nor are they of primary consequence to the purpose of this chronicle).[35]

Continuing to be regarded as the best of these resorts was Canterbury Concert Hall, which in June took over the dingy premises of Mozart Hall and transformed them—at a purported expenditure of $6000—into a "palace of glass, in a blaze of

---

[33] An exotic installation, whose vicissitudes were closely monitored in the newspapers.

[34] Further stretching the audience was the lone rowboat plying the lake, wherein as many as six occupants—frequently ladies—might drift placidly upon the waters and enjoy the music, at the expenditure of ten cents an hour.

[35] For a representative listing of the concert saloons and their offerings, see Odell, VII, *passim;* or better yet, see the amusement columns in the various contemporaneous New York papers.

beauty, splendor [and] magnificence." Throughout the year Sam Cowell was a frequent attraction at Canterbury, as was—in December—the sensational actress/poet/adventuress Adah Isaacs Menken (1835?–1868), who, despite rumors to the contrary was briefly married to John C. Heenan.

Most prominent among the vast numbers of variety-cum-drinking-houses were again the Melodeon, the Art Union Hall, Hitchcock's, Vauxhall, Monahan's, and the Gaieties, where the most beckoning and loudly touted attraction was a corps of "Pretty Waiter Girls."[36] The German beer gardens of the Bowery and Yorkville continued to proliferate and to flourish seven days a week, drawing the sharp condemnation of the more straitlaced Anglo-Saxon citizenry over the stupendous quantities of sabbatarian beer-drinking committed within their atheistic precincts.

The three blackface troupes that dominated the field in 1860 were George Christy's Minstrels, who continued to play to packed houses at Niblo's Saloon until late July, when they departed on a long tour, not to return for nearly a year; Hooley and Campbell's Minstrels, whose ranks included several breakaway members of George Christy's troupe (with whom Christy had fallen into yet another acrimonious newspaper dispute, and who briefly appeared in June at the former French Theatre before triumphantly taking possession of Niblo's Saloon upon Christy's departure), and Bryants' Minstrels, who appeared virtually uninterruptedly throughout the year at Mechanics' Hall, and who possessed, along with the blackface superstars Eph Horn and Dan Emmett, the greatest and most politically significant song hit of the era, Emmett's walkaround "Dixie's Land."[37]

Among the lesser minstrel troupes performing in 1860 were the Hayti Minstrels, appearing in February at Onderdonck's Hall (405 Grand Street); Budworth's Minstrels, seen in April at the Bleecker Buildings; and Charlie White's company, who in May briefly inhabited a new Charlie White's Opera House (at 598 Broadway).

On September 19, 1860, with the death of Thomas Dartmouth Rice♪♫ (b. 1808), blackface minstrelsy lost its most celebrated early exponent, if not its true progenitor.[38] In the nearly three decades (since 1832) when he first sprang into international fame

[36] The least of whose functions included—according to *Bayard,* the pseudonym for Genio C. Scott of *Wilkes' Spirit of the Times* (October 12, 1861, p. 96)—plying the customers to insensibility with liquor. For the rest, he thundered: "The open shamelessness of some of these saloons would astound the keeper of a Water Street dance-cellar, while the imposing array of 'waiter-girls' would seem to have been brought from that sailor-frequented locality."

[37] Reviewing the Bryants' holiday show, the *Dispatch* (December 1, 1860) reported Mechanics' Hall "crammed with Thanksgiving hundreds, and the song ["Dixie's Land"] repeating its numerous triumphs." Transcending the minstrel shows, at a pre-election Republican meeting, reported the *Tribune* on October 26, "'Dixie's Land' was sung, with some new [political] words."

[38] Rice's obituaries credited the origin of blackface entertainment not to him, but—bypassing George Washington Dixon—to the comedian Thomas H. Blakely,♪ who, before Dixon, sang "Coal Black Rose" at the Park Theatre as early as 1828. Singing in blackface was in fact known as far back as the eighteenth century. The genre probably enjoyed its first popular vogue in the United States with the War of 1812 song "Backside Albany" (1814), by the American grocer/composer Micah Hawkins (1777–1825), and again with Hawkins's "Massa Georgee Washington and General La Fayette" (1824), both sung in blackface by the popular actor "Mr. Robertson" (Hopkins Robinson); see my "Micah Hawkins, the Pied Piper of Catherine Slip" (*New-York Historical Society Quarterly,,* April 1978, pp. 138–65).

with his phenomenally popular "Jump Jim Crow," "Daddy" Rice had swung from the heights to the depths and back again, or rather, as the *New-York Mercury*'s obituary (reprinted in *Dwight's,* September 29, 1860, p. 215) stated: "Rice was not satisfied with having mounted the ladder of fame in his profession, and scarcely had he reached the topmost round when he fell; not at one plunge but bumping and catching upon the rounds as he descended."[39] Although he had devised a genre of entertainment that swept the country (and beyond), would survive the Civil War, and—in one form or another—endure over the best part of a century, Rice lived to see his particular style of minstrelsy looked upon as archaic. Yet, despite the paralysis that disabled him for the last ten years of his life—and despite the "frequent indulgence in liquor" to which the obituarist attributed his downfall and his death "in the lap of poverty" at the age of fifty-two—Rice attempted to continue performing wherever and whenever he could wangle an engagement: he had appeared at the Canterbury Concert Hall until the onset of his final illness, only two months before his death. Learning that he was seriously ill and in parlous need, reported the *Herald* (September 21, 1860), his colleagues had been planning a benefit to assist him. Too late.

Although music of one kind or another was employed in most stage productions of 1860, no out-and-out musical production of note seems to have been offered at any of the legitimate theatres. In March, the former child star Kate Bateman appeared at the Winter Garden in her mother's dramatization of Longfellow's poem *Evangeline* (1847), a production for which William Henry Fry composed an overture and Edward Mollenhauer, the Winter Garden's music director, provided incidental music. Because Fry's overture sought musically to depict Longfellow's poem rather than Mrs. Bateman's altered version, to which a happy ending had been appended, the overture did not build to the requisite brilliant finale, and was thus coolly received, wrote *Trovator* (*Dwight's,* April 14, 1860, pp. 21–22). "It bears about the same relation to the conventional overture that a poetic recitation bears to a drama," wrote the critic. Anyway, he added: "At present, Mr. Fry is so engrossed in politics that he pays no attention to music."[40]

As we know, Thomas Baker compiled lively potpourris of relevant folk tunes for the ethnic productions at Laura Keene's Theatre—Irish for Dion Boucicault's great hit *The Coleen Bawn,* pseudo-Japanese for topical "Japanese" items concocted during the Japanese ambassadors' visit.[41] On November 1, to share a bill with Moliere's *La Malade imaginaire,* translated as *Physic and Fancy, or, The Hypochondriac* (for which the orchestra performed "a choice variety of operatic selections"), Miss Keene, probably at Baker's suggestion, staged another period piece, a new version of *The Beggar's Opera* (London 1728) mercilessly squeezed into one act, with a Miss Melvin as a transvestite Captain Macheath. The original *Beggar's Opera* by John Gay (1685–1732), wrote Fry (*Tribune,* November 5, 1860), had created an astonishing upheaval in the London of its day, with its daring underworld locale, its disreputable cast of characters, and its sixty-nine song

[39] "He danced with the negro grace, and the finishing touches of his 'breakdowns' even exceeded those of the laziest Virginia negro," eulogized the *Mercury.*

[40] Throughout the following year Fry was in negotiation with the State Department for the post of Secretary to the American Legation at Turin, capital of the newly united Italy. The appointment was approved but came to naught, probably because of Fry's ill health.

[41] Baker also composed topical dance tunes, for example, "The Prince of Wales Polka."

A Brady portrait of the unbearded candidate Abraham Lincoln.

texts—most of them politically subversive—fitted to familiar tunes. All London had hummed them and ladies had caused them to be inscribed on their fans; the Archbishop of Canterbury had inveighed against them. *The Beggar's Opera* had created what Fry called "a flutter and a buzz."

In the present production, however, out of its original three acts, "all the pithy dialogue, a majority of the characters, most of the songs, and all of the plot have been carefully cut and left on the shelf," wrote Fry. "Two young women [Misses Melvin and Willoughby], neither of whom has much voice or style, come upon the stage, sing a few snatches of old-fashioned melody, besides one of Stephen Glover's songs, and something by Balfe. . . . These songs are connected by scraps of entirely independent and meaningless dialogue. And this dramatic stupidity is called the 'Beggar's Opera!' Miss Keene cannot be congratulated upon the 'revival.'" (*The Beggar's Opera* would need to skip a century before resuming its place on the worldwide stage, albeit in alien guise.)

It was, however, the tremendous political spectacles that possessed the great

Leslie's, Dartmouth College Library

Pro-Lincoln Wide-Awake torchlight parade with band music.
Strong viewed it from one of the windows at Tiffany's.

American public as the fateful election campaign of 1860 escalated to its explosive conclusion. In New York, on October 3, the pro-Lincoln Wide-Awakes staged their
greatest national super-torchlight-parade of the campaign, an event reported to have
been witnessed by more than half a million spectators. One of them was George
Templeton Strong, who had rented a second story window at Tiffany's shop on Broadway, where, with Ellie and some friends, he witnessed the grand spectacle. "It was brilliant and successful . . . elaborate and splendid, but cold and mechanical," wrote
Strong, not yet a Lincoln advocate (Private Journal, October 5, 1860; *Diary,* III, 43).

Leslie's, Dartmouth College Library

*The second division of the Wide-Awake parade marched
around the park up to Town Hall, with a
sign about what Uncle Sam could do.*

Hardly cold and far from mechanical, according to the multiple-column report of the event in the pro-Lincoln *Tribune* (October 4, 1860), with its spread of breathless headlines: "Monster Torchlight Parade. 20,000 Lincolnites in Line. Seventy Acres of Republicans. Over Half a Million Spectators. Immense Enthusiasm. Grand Pyrotechnic Display. The City all Ablaze. Banners, Devices, and Emblems of the Procession. Scenes in Fifth Avenue, Broadway, the [City Hall] Park, and the Bowery. Grand Finale. The Great Wide-Awake Demonstration."

Bands of music were heard from every direction, summoning from every quarter of the city "soldiers of the torch . . . to the rallying point." Overlooking Madison Square, the chief mobilization point, the Fifth Avenue Hotel was ablaze with light from roof to basement, with every window framing "a bevy of delighted gazers," many in evening dress. As the incoming trains and boats and wagons from all over discharged their cargoes of young men, "all duly armed and equipped with torch and cape . . . the glee clubs struck up their telling campaign songs, and when the rolling chorus was taken up by hundreds of voices, the effect was wonderfully fine"[42]—martial music, torchlight, fireworks, cheers, drumbeats, heartbeats, overflowing crowds, violent political passions, all woven into a gigantic symphony of mass emotion.

Only a week later, on October 11, every window on Broadway was crowded with cheering spectators of the parade to welcome the Prince of Wales. And on October 13, Strong watched "part of the Firemen's procession in honor of the Prince pass up the Fourth Avenue. It was very brilliant, with torches, colored lights, and so forth." he wrote. "On Madison Square,[43] where they no doubt displayed all their resources of Roman candles and portable fireworks, it must have been a really attractive spectacle" (Private Journal, October 13, 1860; *Diary* III, 49).

And on October 23: "Tonight's anti-Lincoln, or Fusion, torchlight procession was 'a big thing.' It was more numerous than any political demonstration I have ever witnessed," wrote Strong in his journal (*Diary* III, 53). "It began to pass no. 24 Union Square [Mr. S. B. R.'s residence] (where I joined Ellie) a little before ten. We got tired of lanterns, Roman candles, red shirts, and the like by a little after eleven, and came home. The rear guard had not then reached Union Square. We could see the distant line of lights still flowing down Fourteenth Street. It's now a quarter past twelve, and band after band is still audible as the procession goes down Fourth avenue. Its route was up Broadway, through Fourteenth Street, and then down Fourth Avenue and the Bowery. The Fusionists have certainly turned out in great force. There goes 'Dixie's Land'—another band is passing the corner. . . . Here come more drums. . . ."

---

[42] Ever prone to broadcast their political sentiments in song, Americans outdid themselves during this presidential campaign, with its four candidates. (For an overview of the prodigious outpouring of topical and patriotic music issued on both sides during this period, see my *Music for Patriots, Politicians, and Presidents*, pp. 340–435).

[43] Site of the Fifth Avenue Hotel, where the Prince and his party were staying.

5

GTS: 1861

O say, did you see, by the dawn's early light,
What so proudly we hailed at the twilight's last gleaming;
Those broad stripes and bright stars which on Moultrie at night
O'er the ramparts of Sumter so gallantly streaming
And rockets may glare and bombs burst in mid air,
They'll but prove thro' the night that our flag is still there!
Oh say that the Star-Spangled Banner shall wave
O'er the land of the free and the home of the brave!

As sung by Isabella Hinkley at the New York
Academy of Music, February 4, 1861

ON JANUARY 1, 1861—hard times notwithstanding—the now dormant Academy
of Music was momentarily awakened for the "grand farewell" of Formes, allegedly again about to leave for London to fill an engagement at Covent Garden after his
unrewarding second adventure in the United States. On this valedictory occasion he
was heard in *Martha* and the second act of *Stradella,* both presumably sung in German,
with the assistance of his compatriots, Bertha Johannsen, Madame Eckhardt, and the
Teutonic Italians, Stigelli and Quinto. As an added attraction Formes sang his old war-
horse, Schubert's "The Wanderer"; Theodore Thomas conducted.

"Whatever may have been the reasons for the series of failures in management
during the present season at the Academy of Music," wrote Burkhardt (*Dispatch,* January 5, 1861), "it is evident that they have not arisen from the state of the money market, as was evidenced by the large audience that assembled to bid Carl Formes farewell. . . . Scarcely a place was vacant. Mademoiselle Johannsen, himself, and Stigelli
managed to cram the house in every part, and the result must have been a handsome
addition to the banking account of the German basso, which, by all we hear of non-
payment and ill encores since his second advent to this country, must have counted at
a somewhat low figure."

Perhaps the success of this event gave the German singers fresh courage, for on
January 11 they ventured another farewell benefit, this time for Stigelli, who was departing for an engagement in Havana. Their program consisted of *Stradella* in full and
the fourth act of *La Juive.* Formes—apparently still with us—unabashedly made another "last appearance," performing in both operas and joining with Stigelli and Ma-

395

dame Johannsen in what was becoming, in these politically explosive times, the mandatory performance at all public entertainments of a patriotic song, almost invariably, as on this occasion, the "Star-Spangled Banner."[1] The event was thinly attended and the outlook for opera bleak. But behind the scenes, amid widespread lamentations over the prospect of an opera famine,[2] extraordinary plans were hatching.

Early in January the Franco/Italian troupe, now organized as a cooperative known as the "Italian Artists' Association," or "Associated Artists"—still consisting of Colson, Brignoli, Ferri, and Susini, with Muzio as director and Jacob Grau apparently in charge of their business affairs—at last gained a lease of the New York Academy of Music, a "limited lease" for a season of eight opera performances. For the alternate nights they announced a concurrent season of six operas at—wonder of wonders—the newly completed Brooklyn Academy of Music.

A source of monumental pride to the residents of that devout community,[3] Brooklyn's Academy of Music celebrated its opening with a double festivity: on January 15 a Grand Gala Concert performed by the Associated Artists[4] and the Brooklyn Philharmonic under Eisfeld, with Muzio conducting the "vocal portion," and on January 17 a Grand Promenade and Ball.[5]

Although the supercilious New York press treated provincial little Brooklyn's cultural pretensions with amused condescension, Burkhardt, at least, regarded the inaugural concert as "one of those entertainments which can never be forgotten, because interwoven with the musical portion of the entertainment was the exhibition of a just pride on the part of the inhabitants of our nearest sister city for having erected a place

---

[1] "The triumph of the evening was the singing of the National song by Carl Formes and the company. With the flag of the Union in one hand and with a voice and air that thrilled with lofty patriotism and found an echo in every heart present, Formes sang this well-beloved song—the starry ensign of our country's glory fluttering in folds around him—and his cheering notes awakened the wildest and most unbounded enthusiasm. Shout upon shout rent the air. Patriotism gleamed from the eyes of the young men, while the mothers and daughters of America felt all the influence of that glorious moment, the whole being thrilled with emotion" (*Wilkes' Spirit,* January 12, 1861, p. 329).

[2] The Irving Place Opera House (Academy of Music), seemed doomed to become "the permanent and undisturbed residence for rats," wrote a prematurely despairing Burkhardt (*Dispatch,* January 12, 1861).

[3] "Built by Brooklyn hands, by Brooklyn bricks, and by money from Brooklyn pockets," proclaimed S. B. Chittenden, President of the Brooklyn Academy board of directors, in a notoriously chauvinistic speech at the inaugural concert. Only the architect had been imported from New York, he boasted (*Evening Post,* January 16, 1861). Because, retorted the New York press, none could be found in Brooklyn. (Brooklyn did not become a borough of Greater New York until 1898.)

[4] All but an ailing Susini, whose replacement, Coletti, "murdered" Leporello's aria *Madamina* (*Review and World,* January 19, 1861, p. 14).

[5] To which more than 1400 tickets were sold. "The interior of the building," reported the *Tribune* (January 18, 1861), "had been beautifully decorated with flowers and evergreens, and was brilliantly illuminated. . . . A dancing floor had been laid down, extending from the back of the stage over the entire parquet, forming a large and elegant ballroom. The stage was transformed into a red, white, and blue tent. . . . Ladies and gentlemen roamed about the building, or participated in the 'mazy'[dancing]. . . . Attached to the Academy is a large supper-room, wherein various tables were laid with all sorts of refreshments, which were served out at all hours on the restaurant principle of 'pay for what you eat.'"

of amusement which will bear favorable comparison with any similar establishment in the world" (*Dispatch,* January 19, 1861).[6]

Burkhardt described the sister city's Academy as "semi-Gothic" in style[7] and "though somewhat heavy, very effective." Smaller than the New York Academy,[8] the house was able to hold up to 2200 persons in its parquet, balcony, and two galleries; it possessed bronzed iron seats upholstered in crimson rep, uniformly good sight lines,[9] and a tastefully simple interior decorated in harmonious tones of red, yellow, and blue, and displaying minimal gilt-work and even less carving. Indeed, approvingly noted Fry (*Tribune,* January 14, 1861), "there are no symbolical figures . . . no plaster images, no little cupidons with dumpy bodies, no muses nor sprawling figures of women blowing long trumpets, which have hitherto been deemed indispensable in opera houses and concert rooms, nor even the semblance of a harp or any other musical instrument."[10]

The building comprised—besides the main auditorium with requisite dressing rooms, chorus room, and green room—a smaller concert hall and a "baronial" kitchen. The generous stage dimensions and backstage equipment represented the latest in theatrical design, and ample storerooms housed a stockpile of stage sets painted by the gifted Hannibal Calyo—reportedly superior to those at the New York Academy—able to accommodate a large prospective repertoire: *Lucrezia Borgia, Lucia di Lammermoor, Il barbiere di Siviglia, Linda di Chamounix, La sonnambula, Maria di Rohan, Don Pasquale, La figlia del reggimento, Norma, Ernani, Stradella, Martha, L'elisir d'amore,* and *Il giuramento.*[11]

The ground on which the Academy stood, strategically located on Montague Street near the convergence of "all the railroads that run through Brooklyn, Williamsburgh, and the adjoining districts," had cost $40,000. The first estimated cost of

[6] Architecturally favorable, perhaps, but philosophically doubtful. In his bigoted oratory at the gala opening concert, President Chittenden had pronounced a rigid ban on all such vicious entertainment as spoken drama and opera, particularly the evil opera *La traviata.*

[7] The eminent Bohemian/American architect, Leopold Eidlitz (1823–1908), an ardent exponent of the Gothic revival style, had been chosen to design the Brooklyn Academy over several competitors—among them Jacob Wrey Mould, according to the diary of Mould's friend and colleague, Alfred Jansen Bloor (entry for April 19, 1859) (New-York Historical Society).

[8] Indeed, smaller than many New York theatres, it was defensively pointed out in the New York press.

[9] Instead of a large central chandelier, obstructing the view from the topmost gallery, the Academy was brilliantly lit throughout by clusters of gas jets—so brilliantly, in fact, that when the lights were turned up for the first time, as the *Tribune* reported (January 18, 1861), the delighted first-night audience spontaneously burst into "three hearty rounds of applause followed by a 'tiger'" (contemporary term for a decisive extra cheer).

[10] "Our neighbors across the water have at last received of their wealthy citizens a building, which they call Academy of Music, and which in size appears to be a little larger than our Winter Garden," wrote Hagen (*Review and World,* January 19, 1861, p. 14). "In fact," he disparaged, "it looks very much like any theatre on Broadway, with this difference, that we have seldom seen in any building of this kind such a profusion of red and brown colors," a statement that earned him the condemnation of the sassy new musical columnist *Timothy Trill,* a pseudonym for C. Jerome Hopkins (*Dispatch,* January 26,1861).

[11] And supplemented by general utility props of versatile application: a wood, a garden, Gothic room, palace, ruins by moonlight, street, village, rustic chamber, temple, landscape, and vestibule (*Herald,* January 14, 1861).

construction—$180,000—had been exceeded by $20,000, but every cent had been paid by subscriptions and by additional assessments on the stockholders; the Academy was opening miraculously "without a shilling of debt upon it."

"Our friends across the water have now their own opera house," patronized the *Home Journal* (January 26, 1861). "It seems all very nice at present, but I fear that ere long they will be asking, 'What shall we do with it?' If they make it pay, they will do more than has either New-York, Cincinnati, or Boston, but even London or Paris. I would with pleasure wish them success, but I understood that the proprietors neither desired nor expected aid from the press."

To satisfy the musical demands of an unprecedented profusion of opera houses,[12] five weekly performances were scheduled—three at the more sophisticated New York establishment and two at the fledgling Brooklyn Academy.[13] And to accomplish this ambitious schedule the company was expanded to include a Signorina Elena,[14]★ a soprano newly arrived from performances in Brazil; two Americans, Miss Isabella Hinkley (or Hinckley) of Albany, New York, a mezzo-soprano fresh from European successes; and the greatly admired Boston contralto Adelaide Phillips (a third American, young Clara Louise Kellogg, was impatiently waiting in the wings); also, after a period of absence, the "robustious" tenor Luigi Stefani; a new baritone Francesco Ippolito (or Ypolito), a member of Maretzek's Mexican company, and the veteran bass/baritone Domenico Coletti. The former orchestra and chorus of the New York Academy were conducted by Muzio; William Döhler was the concertmaster; Frederic Hensler♪♫ the chorus master; and Carlo Scola, the sometime opera tenor, was the stage manager.

On Monday, January 21, the Associated Artists launched their ambitious "transriverine" enterprise at the New York Academy[15] with—much to Strong's delight—a revival of Mercadante's *Il giuramento,*♪♫ a work that awoke in him fragrant memories of his courtship of Miss Ellen Ruggles at the lamented Astor Place Opera House. Unfortunately, Ellen was prevented by illness from sharing the sentimental reunion.

January 21, 1861. . . . With Miss Rosalie [Ruggles] and Mrs. Georgie Peters to the Opera tonight to hear that lovely, well-remembered *Giuramento,* a precious souvenir of '48. We [Strong and Ellen] had not heard it for eleven years, and Ellie counted on going, but her cold was too bad. She did not complain, though it was a sore disappointment. Colson [as Elaisa] did very fairly in what used to be Truffi's role; Brignoli [as Viscardo] was a poor substitute for the rough voiced, nervous, sympathetic Benedetti♪♫ of old Astor Place evenings; Ferri [the Manfredo] an improvement on Beneventano.♪♫ [Adelaide Phillips was the Bianca.] The music has great merit. It did not disappoint me, as it was likely to do under the circumstances. I should call this the first

---

[12] And to satisfy feminine sartorial demands, L. Birns, a milliner at 581 Broadway, advertised (in the amusement columns): "Opera, Great amusement for the Ladies—Opera Bonnets at half price."

[13] Where tickets for the parquet, dress circle, and balcony, like those in New York, were $1; $1.50 for reserved seats; a full subscription for the six performances was $7.50; boxes ranged from $20 (ten seats) to $6 (four seats); subscriptions to boxes (four seats) were $40; family circle seats were fifty cents; seats in the amphitheatre, twenty-five cents.

[14] Identified in the *Herald* (January 1, 1861) as Miss Ellen Conran, a "veritable daughter of Erin."

[15] A dismal opening: the *Albion* (January 26, 1861, p. 49) reported a "miserably unattended house" with "row after row of empty benches."

of second-class operas (within my knowledge, that is). I put in the first class *Don Gio-vanni, Nozze di Figaro, Zauberflöte,* the *Barber,* and perhaps *Fidelio.* Also *Der Freischütz.*

The music [of *Il giuramento*] is not homogeneous. There are shallow melodies in it, almost as bad as Donizetti's best, and creaking, mechanical melodies that foreshadow Verdi. But there are also passages of great beauty and power, unlike anything else that I know. The lovely concerted piece with chorus in the first act *(Vicino a che s'adora),* and the first tenor solo *(Bell'adorata* something), and the quartette in D-flat, led off by the baritone, are very great in their own way. It's not the best way. If Mercadante wrote this opera in Naples, his semi-tropical music is characteristic of the place and its atmosphere of voluptuous languor. But though it's far beneath Mozart and Beethoven, it expresses and embodies something good or bad,[16] and is, so far, of higher order than Meyerbeer and Halévy.

Il giuramento was unexpectedly repeated for the opening of the Brooklyn Acade-my's opera season the following evening (January 22)[17] when the originally scheduled *La traviata* was unconditionally banned by what the *Times* (January 21, 1851) tactfully called the stockholders' "conscientious scruples." As Clara Louise Kellogg recalls in her *Memoirs* (pp. 69–70), several agitated meetings had been held following the Brooklyn Academy's inaugural concert, when President Chittenden had exploded his "sensa-tional speech arraigning the plot of *Traviata* and protesting against its production in Brooklyn on the grounds of propriety, or rather, impropriety; it was finally resolved that the opera was objectionable. The feeling against it grew into a series of almost religious ceremonies of protest and . . . it took Grau a year of hard effort to overcome the opposition."[18]

Il giuramento was performed a third and final time at the New York Academy on January 25, when Strong and a now recovered Ellie were present. Again a "lamentably thin house," he wrote, "but a satisfactory performance."

In the meantime, a Philharmonic concert was in the offing, with fresh opportuni-ties for the game of musical comparisons so dear to Strong's heart.

January 23. . . . [went] to the Philharmonic rehearsal (Academy of Music) on my way uptown this afternoon. Began with a well-known symphony of Haydn's (in F or B-flat) [in B-flat], the best among the few of his symphonies I have had the opportu-nity to hear. Every movement is most genial and delicious. How honest, healthy, and true is all his music! Upon my word, I seriously think that the general neglect of his

[16] Not so, wrote the *Albion* critic. Mercadante's music belonged to a school, he wrote, wherein "it was not essential that sorrow should be dismal or joy gay" (*Albion,* February 26, 1861, p. 491).

[17] Attended by the First Lady elect, Mrs. Abraham Lincoln, who sat in one of the stage boxes accompanied by her son and surrounded by friends. When her presence became known, she was visited in her box by more than 300 persons (*Tribune,* January 25; *Dispatch,* January 26, 1861).

[18] The Puritan morality that banned the performance from the Brooklyn Academy's chaste boards of what Hagen derisively called the "soul-elevating musical drama of *La traviata*" found noth-ing amiss in permitting, on the opera off nights, the overwhelmingly popular, learned "lectures" on the breaking of wild horses by the virtuoso English horse-trainer John S. Rarey. Rarey's sessions con-cluded with practical demonstrations of his art upon a ready stock of savage equine subjects (*Review and World,* January 19, 1861, p. 14). (A vivid description of a Rarey horse séance at the Brooklyn Academy is found in the *Herald,* January 25, 1861).

works by musical people and the general preference of Beethoven's intensities to the pure, kindly, and vigorous heartiness of Haydn, is a symptom of the moral diseases that oppress this generation, and strictly analogous to the Byronisms and Wertherisms that have now nearly disappeared. Of course, Beethoven is the greater or the stronger composer. So Byron is stronger than Cowper.[19] But if we knew of two men only this—that one delighted in Cowper and the other in Byron—I think we should infer that the former was the healthier minded of the two.

To be sure, the Cowperism does Beethoven obvious injustice. The C-minor Symphony is a most magnificent testimony against (what I call) Byronism, which is grandly enunciated in its opening, only that it may be triumphantly put down and suppressed by the glorious and perfect development of reaction in the second movement and the finale. The D-Symphony [Beethoven's Second] and the Septuor and scores of his compositions beside are as genial and healthy (perhaps) as Haydn's style of work, and certainly of larger power and grasp. And it's for the "Byronism"—the unrest and unhealthiness of his music—that we generally glorify Beethoven. That's his special characteristic in estimate. We value him not for the repose of his strength, nor for the unequaled energy of his healthy action, but for his weird, uncanny intensities and his paroxysms of despairing gloom—for the immortal Seventh Symphony, and the Overture to *Egmont,* and the first movement of the C-minor Symphony.

I think I could write an essay to show that Haydn's art is the highest and best—on the whole—for a world of men with homes and duties, business, and affections. He is thoroughly *human* always. Mozart in his highest range is *super* human. His noblest melodies carry one out of the commonplace region of work and care to which the great majority of mankind is doomed to belong—into the cloister and the cathedral. Their special characteristic sentiment is most appropriately expressed by white-robed choristers. And this is true even of his *buffo* music—of Leporello's part in *Don Giovanni,* and of minuet or scherzo in his quartettes and symphonies.

[and back to the Philharmonic rehearsal] After Haydn came a symphony of Schumann's [the "Rhenish," No. 3, in E-flat, op. 97 (Düsseldorf 1850)]. Left it unfinished; I was frozen out: the house was inhospitably cold. First movement emphatic and respectable; second (Scherzo) pleasant and effective. The credit of the nice, fresh, melodic phrase to which its effectiveness is due may belong to the composer,[20] but I think he owes it to some Scotch jig-tune or other. If so, he has worked it up very cleverly. I wonder that none of our symphony writers has taken up the Nigger-melody. "Oh Susanna, don't you cry for me"—"Carry me back to old Virginny"—"Rosa Lee"— "Dixie's Land," etc., etc., have a very special character, an *aroma* as yet unknown in "classical" music. A composer of respectable ability could make himself a reputation

---

[19] William Cowper (1731–1800), the English poet, whose didactic celebrations of the simple, everyday joys are the direct antitheses to Byron's fevered romanticism.

[20] Certainly not in the opinion of the *Albion* critic, who had "yet to meet with six sane people who are ready to admit that Schumann is great either as a melodist or as an instrumental colourist. According to our judgment, he is the least meritorious in these respects of any German writer. Liszt, who is unimportant as a composer, is his superior, and Wagner, with a simple instrument of each kind, would make a better effect than Schumann with an entire orchestra of eighty" (*Albion,* February 9, 1861, p. 67).

by embodying it in symphony or overture. What a scherzo could be made of "Jordan is a hard road to travel!!!"[21]

January 29. . . . Ellie read music for me tonight, and especially passages from that very noble Mass of Niedermeyer's.

February 2. . . . Philharmonic rehearsal this morning with Ellie. Concert tonight by myself. Betook myself to the sky-gallery, which I observe is favored by Scharfenberg and others as the best place in the house for those who go to hear. Lots of Germans there—"professionals" apparently—following the orchestra through copies of the score. Schumann's symphony [its first performance in America] was effective, the second movement especially.[22] There may be gleams in it of real life—of something beyond mechanism. If not, life is most cleverly and dexterously simulated. The Haydn Symphony (No. 2 in B-flat) most genial, beautiful, and pellucid. What is there in music much lovelier than the Adagio and the delicious, kindly, joyous Minuetto—so full of exuberant, rollicking, healthy fun? Wagner's *Tannhäuser* Overture—particularly unlike anything Haydn ever thought of, but a very substantial composition, beyond all gainsaying—closed the concert.[23]

I cannot imagine why the composers of our day are so utterly unable to produce anything like a sound, hearty, jolly scherzo—why their best work is always something grand and gloomy, and generally more or less morbid in its gloom, as, for example, this *Tannhäuser* Overture. A good, frank, careless *laugh* has not been embodied in music for years past, to my knowledge. What was there in Haydn's era of decomposing shams and progressive Revolution and general Unbelief to make him (and his fellows, in their degree) more healthy-minded and happy than the composers of this age? I ask for information and pause for a reply.

~

More interested in the relative moral and/or emotional merits of Byron versus Cowper, and/or Beethoven versus Haydn, or of their comparative merits in various other juxtapositions than in opera—at least, Italian opera—Strong had not attended the highly acclaimed debut at the New York Academy, on January 23, of the young American *prima donna* Isabella Hinkley in *Lucia di Lammermoor* (repeated in Brooklyn the following evening). Miss Hinkley (?–1862), daughter of a prominent Albany doctor, had received her primary music education at home from the local church organist,

---

[21] A revolutionary, indeed, prophetic idea, coming from Strong.

[22] The second movement was singled out by —t—, also, who called it "a gem, so quaint and thoroughly original." He complained, however, of the Philharmonic's too frequent performances of the selfsame Haydn symphony, depriving the public of ever becoming acquainted with some of Haydn's other—indeed more beautiful—symphonies (*Dwight's,* February 16, 1861, p. 375). Hagen, who devoted an elaborate historico-musicological analysis to Schumann's symphony, rebelled against the inappropriate insertion of Haydn's simplistic music—albeit "equally artistic in its way and certainly enjoyable at a proper time"—between the symphony by Schumann and Wagner's Overture to *Tannhäuser* (*Review and World,* February 16, 1861, p. 41).

[23] The remainder of the program, conducted by Eisfeld, consisted of works for men's chorus sung by the German *Liederkranz* and conducted by Agricol Paur: Conradin Kreutzer's *Frülingsnahen* ("Approach of Spring"), encored with Mendelssohn's *Der frohe Wandersmann,* op. 75, no. 1 (1844), and Schubert's *Nachthelle* ("Nocturnal Radiance"), op. 134 (1826). Louis Schreiber played his *Fantasia capricciosa* and Eisfeld's *Élégie cantabile,* both for cornet.

George William Warren (1828–1902).[24] In 1857 she had gone to Italy to study opera with the eminent Pietro Romani (1791–1877) and fifteen months later commenced her professional career in the opera houses of Germany, Belgium, and Holland, earning favorable reviews, as occasionally reported in *Dwight's.* Ullman had heard her in Paris in 1860 and engaged her for his (thwarted) coming opera season. As a member of Muzio's successor company, she was an instant success.

"Miss Isabella Hinckley may congratulate herself on having achieved one of the most successful *débuts* ever won in this City," wrote Seymour in the *Times* (January 24, 1861). Her first effort left no doubt that she was intended for a great career. "Her voice is a soprano of the best class, unusually full, large, and dramatic . . . and especially brilliant in the upper register," this despite her "defective" manner of producing it, "leading to a peculiar style of mouthing, which is known as churchey,[25] which in a small room is effective, but in a large theatre intolerable."[26] It was, however, only a minor defect, and easily overcome. More significantly, wrote Seymour, Miss Hinkley possessed "the true artistic temperament"; her delivery of a simple scale emerged not as a mere mechanical exercise but as "a chain of pearls, each link giving to its fellow a borrowed light." And, "whilst cheerfully awarding her a very emphatic success [for her Lucia], and hailing her as the best gifted of the many American *débutantes* we have had of late, we are sure we shall yet see her to greater advantage. Her *physique* and her voice alike point to a higher range of feeling than that elicited by Donizetti's work."[27]

C. Jerome Hopkins, thinly disguised as *Timothy Trill,* in a column devoted to native opera singers (*Dispatch,* February 9, 1861), wrote that Isabella Hinkley was a better actress (and had a better figure) than Cora de Wilhorst, more "stage-ease of manner" than [Adelina] Patti, and that her voice was "smooth, limpid, and equal in all registers." *Trill* reported that at her debut she had contended with "more jealousy and antagonism of feeling in the audience" than he had ever witnessed,[28] but she had shown magnificent courage and emerged triumphant.[29] Miss Hinkley immediately followed her dual debut with two tightly spaced performances of *Il trovatore,* at the New York Academy on January 29,[30] and in Brooklyn on the 30th.

Isabella Hinkley's second appearance, wrote Watson (*Leslie's,* February 9, 1861, p.

[24] Since 1860, when he assumed the post of organist at the Church of the Holy Trinity in Brooklyn, Warren had ostensibly become the new Brooklyn correspondent for *Dwight's,* writing under the pseudonym of "Jem Baggs."

[25] Otherwise known as defective diction.

[26] The *Albion* (February 2, 1861, p. 55) commented on the same failing, the result of defective training, but not insurmountable. Indeed, it was the only detectable flaw in the otherwise delightful combination of excellences that Miss Hinkley embodied.

[27] Apart from her beautiful voice, wrote *Trovator,* "She is young, pretty. In person she is of good height, excellent figure, brown hair, superb teeth, and possesses an expressive and pleasing face. When on the stage is quite free from affectation, but tries to act well, and for a novice is quite successful" (*Dwight's,* February 2, 1861, p. 350).

[28] Probably a subjective opinion: the other critics commented, rather, on her painful stage fright, not overcome until the Mad Scene.

[29] "I would like, had I time, to give a more extended analysis of Miss Hinkley's performance," added susceptible *Trill*/Hopkins, "in which I might be betrayed unawares into a few expressions of admiration for her sweet face, fine eyes, abundant hair, and charming smile (the personation of sunshine), but the physical 'points' of a Prima Donna are beneath the notice of an Art-critic."

[30] Where, for reasons of economy, no bell tolled in the *Miserere* scene.

179), was even more triumphant than her first. Demanding as the role of Leonora was, "she surmounted all the difficulties with ease, and sustained her power throughout. Young as she is," he added, "she gives evidence of a high and distinguished musical capacity." Not only was her vocal execution surpassingly fine (only her *"trillo"* displeased Watson, being "stiff and uncertain"), but among her great endowment of gifts and attributes, Isabella Hinkley possessed "intention," investing her art with a keen and cultivated perception of dramatic values.

Too, Adelaide Phillips, the Azucena, was magnificent. "We feel no little pride," wrote Watson (unregenerate Briton though he was), "in being able to point to two such artists . . . who can take their stand upon perfect equality with the most self-satisfied Italian artist in our operatic firmament. Some of our uneducated, servile critics may insolently pat them on the back or arrogantly patronize them," wrote Watson (faintly echoing the malevolent Watson of old³), "but their intrinsic merits place them far above the power of ignorance or arrogance to crush or belittle."

On January 28 the season's only performance of *The Sicilian Vespers*,[31] excellently sung by Madame Colson, *et al,* was presented, not in New York but in Brooklyn, where, much to the New York critics' chagrin, the crowds at the Academy so greatly exceeded the feeble attendance at Fourteenth Street that the performance schedule was reversed, with the three weekly performances being shifted to Brooklyn.

"Opera thrives in Brooklyn, whilst it starves in New-York," wrote a mortified Wilkins in the *Herald* (January 29, 1861). "Last night the *Sicilian Vespers* drew another crowded house, notwithstanding the doubts expressed that another representation [Miss Hinkley's performance of *Il trovatore* on January 30] so close upon that of Saturday would attract. M. Muzio has struck a rich musical mine and is determined to work it. . . . Undeterred by the apprehensions uttered by many that he will exhaust the enthusiasm of the Brooklynites, he announces two more representations at the new house next week—the *Trovatore* on Wednesday [January 30] and *Martha* on Friday [February 1]. . . . On Thursday [January 31] the Signorina Elena makes her debut in the *Lucrezia* at the New York Academy.[32] This will be the only performance given there again this week, so that the metropolis finds itself in the humiliating position of playing second fiddle to the sister city, which [twisting the knife] supports opera three nights in the week, while New York can only support two."

"For some reason there is a lull in the attention given to the musical drama in this city," wrote Fry. "Meanwhile, in the high-vaulting Brooklyn, unexpected resources and profits come forth, for in the Academy, just created there, we find as much attention given the Muses as there is neglect experienced now by the heavenly choir in this

---

[31] Now omitting the first-act Tarantella to spare expense.

[32] Not an auspicious debut. "In *Lucrezia Borgia* we have heard here Mesdames Grisi, Sontag, Steffanone, and others of world renown," boasted Fry (*Tribune,* February 2, 1861), "and any new claimant for honors in that character must not fail to make the 'points' which are fresh in the memories of the audience. In these we do not find Madame Elena [who in fact was ill, having recently undergone surgery] up to the mark. She has a pleasant exterior, with some stateliness of bearing, but does not exhibit the qualities of a tragedian in acting. Her voice is a mezzo-soprano of fair quality, and she has some facility, but she cannot give the music with effect." To make matters worse, "Signor Susini was out of voice, and Signor Stefani exceeded himself in certain outbursts which were not altogether musical. The celebrated trio was probably sung worse on this occasion than on any other representation of the present century" (*Times,* February 1, 1861).

tight little island. Every performance [in Brooklyn] thus far has been a success," he al-most accused. "On Saturday night, mauger the snow, the Brooklyn musical fanatics turned out in crushing numbers and dazzling gaiety to enjoy the woes of *Lucia di Lam-mermoor* and her unfortunate tenor of a sweetheart"[33] (*Tribune,* January 28, 1861).

The unexpected phenomenon amused the *Albion* reviewer (February 2, 1961, p. 55) because, he wrote, "there has been a journalistic disposition to 'make fun' of the musical excitement which undoubtedly prevails in the City of Churches.[34] The nov-elty of a new house has perhaps had something to do with it; but acknowledging this, the Brooklynites, who were always called staid and strait-laced and prim, have ex-ceeded the New Yorkers in mere abstract enthusiasm. . . . Without Brooklyn, at this crisis, there would be no opera in New York." Unthinkable!

February 4. . . . Just from an unpremeditated evening at the Opera with Ellie and Miss Rosalie. Sat in the parquette. *Barber of Seville* nicely done by Brignoli and Co.[35] The Rosina, a Miss Hinkley, a debutante of a week's standing. She looks, sings, and acts well enough. In the Music Lesson Scene she introduced "The Star-Spangled Ban-ner." The audience all stood up and made a great uproar.

. . . Last night a shoal of people came here and among them Scharfenberg, who wants to get up a series of musical evenings—string quartettes, trios, and so forth—a goodly device, in which I shall cheerfully cooperate.[36]

⇒

As to Miss Hinkley's patriotic interpolation in the Lesson Scene, according to the *Herald* (February 5, 1861): leaving Brignoli and Susini at the piano, she advanced to the footlights, sang a waltz by Pacini and followed it with the "Star-Spangled Banner" in a timely new version, reflecting the national consternation over the present impasse at Fort Sumter. As she was about to begin the refrain, an occupant of one of the pro-scenium boxes handed her a flag, whereupon the audience rose "and the national air was received with every demonstration of regard. In response to an unanimous encore, Miss Hinkley sang the first stanza of the original version [probably to make amends

---

[33] And to heap bouquets—"sincere Brooklyn bouquets"—and plaudits on their new favorite, Isabella Hinkley.

[34] For example, the sardonic comments of the novelist/editor Charles F. Briggs,' quoted in the *Home Journal* (February 16, 1861): "The aristocracy, the wealth, the talent, the beauty, the fashion of Brooklyn, it seems, rush three nights out of the week to the Academy of Music in Montague Place, dressed almost to death. The sale of white kids has been tremendous; several tailors who were on the point of bankruptcy have been put upon their feet by the demand for dress-coats; the dealers in bouquets have realized fortunes; hack drivers are full of orders, and the milliners and mantua-makers are half wild." Briggs estimated that if all the opera cloaks sold since the opening of the Brooklyn Academy were laid end-to-end, they would cover the whole of Long Island.

[35] Positively "slaughtered" by Brignoli (Almaviva), Ferri (Figaro), Susini (Bartolo), and Coletti (Basilio), wrote Seymour (*Times,* February 5, 1961). Only Isabella Hinkley, the Rosina, was at all bearable, although she, too, did not totally escape Seymour's displeasure.

[36] "A very pleasant custom is getting in vogue in regard to private musical *soirées*," wrote the *Eve-ning Post* critic (April 13, 1861). Instead of subjecting guests to the agonizing efforts of remorseless amateur musicians, "musical hosts incline to the sensible idea of hiring first-class musicians for the evening and treating the guests to a really good concert." Not only Scharfenberg but the Mason/Thomas group had recently participated in several such private *soirées*.

for her faltering delivery of the new version], after which the performance proceeded as usual."

If it was necessary in these precarious times to accept such an "absurd interpolation" in an opera, raged Hagen, he was reluctantly willing to accept it, but only "on condition that it be well sung." And even though the "Banner's" range was beyond Miss Hinkley's vocal capabilities, she might at least have "deigned to make herself familiar with some portion of the words. . . . For an American *prima donna* to sing one of the national airs without the slightest spirit, haltingly, and at a loss for each succeeding word until it was supplied by the prompter, was something for which the waving of a miniature Stars and Stripes did not compensate. That the words were new for the occasion is no excuse at all" (*Review and World,* February 16, 1861, p. 40).

February 6. . . . Opera tonight with Ellie [and] Mrs. Georgey Peters. . . . The Opera was *Martha*—somewhat curtailed and done with great spirit and heartiness.[37] Though the music is thin, it is good and pleasant to hear now and then.

February 13. . . . After dinner Ellie read Haydn for me.

February 18. . . . Just from Scharfenberg's (36th Street), where was the first of our series of musical evenings. Sixty or seventy present. One is half-ashamed to note the fact as anything remarkable, but the power of snobbery over New York is so far weakened that the so-called "best people" are glad to be invited to the house of a seller of music at retail[38] (who happens to be a refined and cultivated gentleman and lover of art). Our program was (1) Quartette in B-flat by Haydn. Satisfactory, the last movement especially so. (Then was intercalated a solo by Philip Mayer—the "Evening Star" song from *Tannhäuser.*) (2) Trio, no. 1 in D minor, Mendelssohn, Scharfenberg at the piano.[39] Andante and Scherzo very lovely. (3) Quartette in D minor, Mozart [probably K. 421, Haydn set, no. 2]; delicious from beginning to end, each movement fragrant with that special *bouquet* of melodic feeling that belongs to Mozart alone. The trio in the third movement is a gem, and brought an encore.

～～～

On February 9 a performance of *Ernani* (Colson/Stefani/Ferri/Susini), followed by an act of *Lucia* (Hinkley, etc.), was given in Brooklyn; *Lucrezia Borgia* was performed there on February 12, with a considerably recovered Signorina Elena. But difficulties with the intractable Brooklyn directors loomed. "There was danger a week ago," wrote Seymour, his pen dipped in venom (*Times,* February 5, 1861), "that New-York might become a sort of suburb to Brooklyn, so fervently did the newly ignited operatic fires burn in that city, and so dimly were they kept alive here. To avert this

---

[37] By Colson (Lady Harriet), Phillips (Nancy), Brignoli (Lionel), Susini (Plunkett), and Coletti (Sir Tristram).

[38] This was indeed a major concession: the private music-making enjoyed by Strong and his friends in years past had taken place solely at their respective homes, untainted by vulgar commercialism. *Timothy Trill* raged against the upper classes, who exhibited "a great willingness to form diminutive musical mutual admiration societies in their own *clique* . . . especially when an oyster and champagne supper is sure to follow" (*Dispatch,* March 30, 1861).

[39] Strong does not identify Scharfenberg's instrumental colleagues.

calamity the directors of the Montague-street Academy have been kind enough to raise the rent of their house." It was unfair of them, argued Seymour, to exact from managers the same rent ($250 a night) as for the Fourteenth Street establishment, where the seating capacity was greater, the scenery and costumes superior and more abundant, and a music library of more than a hundred operas available. Muzio nonetheless renewed his lease of the Brooklyn Academy for six more performances.

And with good reason: the Associated Artists were in fact staking their all on a spectacular production of Verdi's latest opera *Un ballo in maschera (The Masked Ball)* (Rome 1859), a work they had been intensively rehearsing for some time past. With its extraordinary history, *Ballo* provided the penny-a-liners with rich material for their voluminous advance synopses and comments, and later for wordy reviews and more synopses. Basing his text on Scribe's libretto for Auber's 1833 opera *Gustave III, ou, Le Bal masqué*—a work depicting in its last act the assassination in 1792 of that unfortunate Swedish monarch at a masked ball—Verdi's librettist Antonio Somma had transposed the opera's locale to Naples, where *Un ballo in maschera* was scheduled to be premiered at the San Carlo Opera House in 1859. Upon the refusal of the Neapolitan censors, and later the Roman censors—in that period of volatile political upheavals—to permit the enactment of a ruler's assassination,[40] it became necessary once more to change the scene. The politically uncontroversial *terra incognita* of seventeenth-century Boston was chosen, and the ill-starred hero recast as an imaginary English governor of that Puritan colony, one Riccardo, Count of Warwick. Appearing in the opera were Pauline Colson as Amelia, the object of the Governor's misdirected passion; Adelaide Phillips in blackface[41] as Ulrica, the sinister fortune teller; and Isabella Hinkley, radiant as the page Oscar. Brignoli played the hapless Count of Warwick; Ferri was Reinhart (*né* Renato), his confidant and assassin; and Coletti and Dubreuil contributed to the Yankee atmosphere as two conspirators named Samuele and Tomaso.[42]

Among the production's extra attractions were three bands of music (two playing from behind the scenes), a grand ballet divertissement devised and directed by Signor Ronzani, and, most titillating of all, the announcement that a few members of the audience, wearing dominoes and masks, would be permitted onstage to mingle with the cast in the last-act ballroom scene.[43]

At the American premiere of *Un ballo in maschera,* on February 11, the New York

[40] Too close for comfort, with the recent attempt, in 1858, to assassinate the French Emperor Napoleon III by the Italian revolutionary Felice Orsini.

[41] "A specimen of feminine Sambo," crudely commented *Wilkes' Spirit of the Times* (February 16, 1861, p. 384).

[42] Promptly dubbed Sam and Tom, they were probably intended to evoke Samuel Adams and Thomas Jefferson, joked Fry (*Tribune,* February 12, 1861); he regretted the absence of a Ben (Beniamino?) to symbolize Franklin in this jumble of incongruities. In a heavy-handed travesty of the plot, Fry ridiculed the silly and ignorant concept, as did his colleagues, of setting a masquerade ball in Puritan seventeenth-century Boston. He nonetheless found important musical felicities in the score, which he subjected to one of his painfully minute dissections.

[43] The advertisements for *Ballo* requested "such of its patrons as may wish to be upon the stage during the scene of the Masquerade" to apply to the management for cards of admission, a limited number of which were available at no additional charge. The management would supply dominoes and masks, if needed.

A Brady photograph of Isabella Hinkley, most gifted of American debutantes, noted for her introduction of the "Star Spangled Banner" in an 1861 production of The Barber of Seville.

Isabella Hinkley as Oscar in Un ballo in maschera; *she proved that Ullman had been wise to choose her when he was in Europe engaging artists for the Academy of Music.*

Academy, once again radiant with the Prince-of-Wales-ball illumination, presented a brilliant scene reminiscent of an Ullman opening night.[44] All New York was present, reported Wilkins: "The high and the low [and] the middle strata of metropolitan society appeared in grand array—pretty women, budding maidens, and buxom matrons, antique dowagers, venerable spinsters, grave judges, heavy merchants, and ponderous bankers. Young America pervading the lobbies and . . . private boxes, snuffy professors, wild looking pianists, inchoate *prime donne,* magnificent artists without engagements, sapient critics, and *blasé* dilettanti were all mixed up in one grand *olla podrida,* talking in as many tongues as the celebrated artificers of Babel, and representing as many cliques and shades of opinion—political, artistic, and societal—as there are several sovereignties on the continent of Europe" (*Herald,* February 12, 1861).

Muzio's judgment was triumphantly justified: *Un ballo in maschera* was a huge hit. Bringing it out, wrote the *Albion* (February 23, 1861, p. 91), had been a "masterstroke of policy. It seems to have awakened the public interest in music, and it has given new life to an enterprise which was in a very exhausted condition. There can be no doubt that the new opera has made a genuine success—a success altogether independent of puffing and claqueing—based on the double foundation of its own intrinsic merits and its very admirable performance.[45] . . . The impression made upon us by the music," declared the critic, "is one of unmixed pleasure. It is full of melody, tender, passionate, sparkling, and joyous, and the melodies are full of ideas, not mere pretty platitudes but themes with brains in them. They all bear unmistakably the genuine Verdi stamp. . . . The flow of thought is tinctured throughout with the Verdi idiosyncrasies,[46] but the general treatment of the subjects is of a vastly higher order than usual. . . . In dramatic effect, in powerful contrasts, Verdi stands far above all competition. He is the great melodramatist of opera, but the really great thoughts which startle the imagination and still satisfy the judgment redeem his compositions from the charge of mere claptrap."

The critic was delighted as well with the production: "Signor Muzio has given

[44] "It was about time that the public should give over the secession from the Academy in Irving Place," sardonically observed Fry in what had become contemporary lingo, "unless they wish to set up a fresh musical Confederacy in the Independency of Brooklyn."

[45] And chiefly on the basis of its novelty, New York was "essentially a go-ahead city," wrote up-to-date *Wilkes' Spirit* (February 23, 1861, p. 400). In contrast to benighted Brooklyn, the "suburban capital of Long Island," where any opera—however ancient—was an exciting novelty, "antiquity in music [was] at the present at a discount in New York . . . where we do not endure [such old chestnuts as] the 'Barber' or submit gladly to 'Lucrezia Borgia'. . . . But when 'Un Ballo in maschera' is produced, we rush to see it—we crowd the house in every part—night after night and matinée after matinée, it will be the shine for some two weeks to come."

[46] "It is less Verdesque than any of Verdi's operas, *La traviata* excepted," maintained *Wilkes' Spirit* (*ibid.*), "while the orchestration is, perhaps, the most perfect—that is to say, the least objectionable—of any which has proceeded from his pen." The critic admitted to being haunted from time to time by snatches of its melodies, suggesting that with sufficient rehearing *Ballo* might take "a high rank among enjoyable operas." Too, with repetition the performances had vastly improved over what he—contrary to his colleagues—had pronounced to be a poor first performance: Muzio was now conducting it "with more certainty, probably inspired by the satisfaction of the audience, who, had they been Gallic or Teutonic, would have hissed it off the stage on the first night, on the score of its orchestral deficiency—to say nothing of the style in which some of the vocalists executed their music."

the first proof of that ability which has been claimed for him," he wrote. "He has exhibited patience and perseverance and an intelligence to direct the energy of others, which has resulted in a performance of a degree of excellence rarely achieved in our theatres." Everything was superb: the cast, the chorus, the orchestra, and the wonderful sets; the ballroom scene was "the richest and most brilliant interior we have seen on the stage for a long time."

Seymour, too, devoted a full column of fine print to detailed description and praise of the opera, its production, and (with qualifications) its performance.[47] In it, he wrote, "Verdi attempts more vehemently than before, and as we think, more successfully, the portrayal of dramatic passion. His concerted pieces are never merely exercises for the display of so many voices; they are always well-devised contrivances for the exhibition and illustration of the varied emotions of the scene. . . . We are disposed to regard the work as one of the best dramatic productions of the modern Italian stage and as a certain monument to the genius of the composer" (*Times,* February 12, 1861).

Even Hagen was compelled to admit that some parts of the score indicated an effort on Verdi's part "to raise himself above that cheap and vulgar style of patch-working with which most of his former effects were produced. The short, melodic bits, thrown mostly into the sharp dance rhythms, are not altogether predominant; there is occasionally an attempt at more breadth of melody. . . . The treatment is better, the orchestration is richer, the instrumentation less coarse and vulgar, and the second act, especially, offers some fine points of fluent and characteristic music." Recovering himself, Hagen hastened to add that although Colson and Phillips had done well, the "performance offered little scope for laudatory remarks"; the ballroom scene had been "a very shabby affair"—although the cast was "painstaking . . . unfortunately this alone makes no artists"—and the scenery "offered nothing remarkable" (*Review and World,* February 16, 1861, pp. 40–41).

Un ballo in maschera was in fact a phenomenon, receiving an almost unheard-of total of nine performances by February 25,[48] with "not even a partially bad house," observed Burkhardt (*Dispatch,* February 23, 1861). "Indeed the oftener it is acted the more appreciative and brilliant are the audiences. Pretty soon," he predicted, "the gems of the opera will be set into barrel organs and will be retailed all over the city at marvelously low charges."

Although, as the *Albion* critic remarked in his follow-up article (February 23, 1861, p. 91), *Un ballo in maschera* had "more than saved the fortunes of the season at the New York Academy of Music," much of the credit was due to the unprecedentedly civilized management of the opera enterprise. In telling contrast to Ullman's "fantastic tricks and low devices, his impudent puffs of his own artists and his abiding faith in the stupidity of everyone save himself," wrote the critic, "the Associated Artists conduct their business in a very quiet and gentlemanly way; advertise sufficiently but not

---

[47] Seymour observed, as did his colleagues, that the cast, although praiseworthy and well rehearsed, showed signs of first-night nerves and would improve with future performances.

[48] Seven of them consecutively given at the New York Academy before it was played in Brooklyn (on February 10 and 23), where it was hoped it would revive the operatic fervor, by now beginning to sag (*Herald,* February 18, 1861).

extravagantly; work assiduously; and by attending to their own business have made it profitable."[49]

Of greatest moment during the run of *Ballo* was the attendance at the New York Academy on February 20 of President-elect Abraham Lincoln, briefly stopping over in New York on his way to Washington for his inauguration.

February 20. . . . Lincoln arrived here yesterday afternoon by the Hudson River R.R. from Albany. I walked uptown at 3:30. Broadway crowded, though not quite so densely as on the Prince of Wales's *avatar* last October. The *trottoir* well filled by pedestrians (vehicles turned off into the side streets) and sidewalks by patient and stationary sight-seers. Above Canal Street they were nearly impassable. At St. Thomas's Church I met the illustrious cortege moving slowly down to the Astor House [Lincoln's hotel] with its escort of mounted policemen and a torrent of rag-tag and bobtail rushing and hooraying behind. The great rail-splitter's face was visible to me for an instant, and seemed a keen, clear, honest face, not so ugly as his portraits.

〰

That Lincoln was expected at the opera was by no means a secret: his attendance had been announced in that day's advertisements.[50] Not arriving at the Academy until after the curtain had risen, he had so quietly made his entrance that it was not until well into the first intermission that the audience at last, according to the *Herald* (February 21, 1861), spotted the "plain black cravat, the neat shirt collar turned over the neckcloth, the incipient whiskers, and good humored face that sat so demurely" in a stage box in the second tier. A mighty ovation ensued, with shouting and cheering and universal waving of feminine handkerchiefs and tossing aloft of masculine hats.

"At first the object of this genuine outburst of patriotic feeling sat as still as when he first entered, only occasionally bowing from his seat," continues the *Herald,* "but as this did not seem to satisfy the clamorous audience, he presently arose to his feet, and his tall sinewy form was then seen in its full proportion, towering above his friends in the box a full head and shoulders, like Saul among his brethren." Pandemonium!

When at last, after successive waves of high emotion, the audience became comparatively quiet, the curtain rose to disclose "the whole force of the opera troupe on the stage with their unrolled musical scrolls, preparing to enchant their audience with the deservedly beloved National hymn, 'The Star-Spangled Banner.' With one of the artistic flourishes of Muzio's magic baton, the harmonious tones of the accompaniment trembled through the orchestral instruments and resounded through the house." Restraining the audience's reflexive demonstration, Isabella Hinkley advanced to the foot-

---

[49] "The Associated Artists of the Italian Opera have to congratulate themselves upon a very fine week's business with the new opera," wrote Wilkins (*Herald,* February 18, 1861). "The matinée on Saturday [February 16, the third performance of *Un ballo in maschera*] was the best since Piccolomini's time, and brought the aggregate receipts of the week up to near eight thousand dollars, and the share of the associates will be double their salaries under the old regime. They have taken the Academy for two months more, and a very active spring campaign may be expected." (An overoptimistic supposition, as it turned out.)

[50] As had the other added attractions of the evening: the Prince-of-Wales-ball lighting and Muzio's Galop substituting in the ballroom scene for Verdi's less catchy dance music.

A reception for President Lincoln upon his arrival in New York by special train on his way to his inauguration in Washington.

The Mayor of New York receives President Lincoln.

lights and, partially turning toward Mr. Lincoln, sang the first stanza. Then, as the great ensemble spiritedly took up the chorus, "a splendid Union American banner, blazing with the full glory of the thirty-three stars, was dropped from the proscenium with an effect that words can scarcely convey.

"The second verse was sung by Miss Phillips, and so on alternately with Miss Hinkley," all to deafening applause. Then, "before the applause subsided, Muzio started the other national song 'Hail Columbia,'" following which "cheers were given for Lincoln from the upper boxes, followed by cheers for Muzio and the opera singers, after which the excitement gradually subsided, and the opera was allowed to proceed."[51]

Departing as quietly as he had entered, Lincoln slipped out of the Academy before the last-act assassination scene. He would make good the omission four years later in another theatre.

Although still at the height of its popularity, *Un ballo in maschera* was withdrawn after its ninth performance to permit the long-awaited New York debut of Muzio's nineteen-year-old American pupil and protégée Clara Louise Kellogg. It was not, however, Miss Kellogg's first public appearance, nor even her first appearance at the Academy. In single-minded pursuit of a career since childhood, Miss Kellogg, with influential patronage, had studied singing with a galaxy of the best imported opera masters: Millet, Manzocchi, Albites, Rivarde, Errani, and Muzio;[52] she had been instructed in stagecraft by Muzio and Laura Keene.[53] In 1860 (April 19), billed as Louisa Kellogg, she had unsuitably appeared in an unofficial, unstaged "public rehearsal"[54] of *Poliuto* (obviously in hopeful imitation of Adelina Patti's triumphant "tryouts" in 1859). A handful of kindly critics scattered among the thousand or so invited guests agreed, despite Miss Kellogg's undeniable talent, to reserve judgment of her abilities until she appeared as a fullfledged professional.

Because this disappointing non-verdict did not warrant an immediate formal bow to the public[55]—especially not with the current delirium over little Patti (to say nothing of the raging Ullman/Maretzek hostilities)—Kellogg's debut was put in abeyance for a time. In October 1860, following the dissolution of the Strakosch/Ullman forces, she was taken along on the Associated Artists' concert and opera tour of the South and Midwest as a musical maid-of-all-work: "A sort of preliminary education," as she recalls in her *Memoirs* (pp. 22–29).[56]

[51] Two days later on Washington's birthday, at the following performance of *Un ballo in maschera*, Muzio again stoked the patriotic flames with his stirring special arrangement of "Hail Columbia."

[52] Yet, in a wildly diffuse column intended to celebrate America's advantages over Europe's as an "art school," Timothy Trill boasted that Clara Louise Kellogg was in no way indebted to Europe for her musical training (*Dispatch,* March 16, 1861).

[53] And with the solicitous interest of Charlotte Cushman.

[54] It was not even a dress rehearsal, reported the *Evening Post* (April 20, 1860): "The other artists were dressed in prosaic suits and shawls and took no definite interest in the action of the piece."

[55] In her *Memoirs* (p. 72), Kellogg candidly admits that with this ill-advised performance she came "tragically near to failure, as I had not then the physical nor vocal strength for the part."

[56] "I was a general utility member of the company and sang to fill in the chinks," writes Kellogg. "We sang four times a week, and I received twenty-five dollars each time." Throughout the tour, Kellogg's inexorably straitlaced mother, who tagged along, "never let me out of her sight."

Clara Louise Kellogg.

Clara Louise Kellogg in the title role of Martha—a long delayed recognition of her talent.

Miss Kellogg's choice of Gilda *(Rigoletto)* for her New York debut,[57] at the New York Academy on February 27, signified a rare boldness and deviation from the beaten track, wrote Seymour (*Times,* February 28, 1861), for most debutantes usually began with *Lucia* and ended "somewhere in the immediate vicinity."[58] Possessing a voice of "good quality, not very full in the lower part but round and satisfactory in the upper," Kellogg particularly impressed Seymour with her ability (after overcoming her stage fright)[59] to "strike a tone with energy," more important nowadays, he contended, than the capacity to "sing a scale trippingly." But chiefly, he wrote, she possessed the indefinable "secret of the lyric stage and with practice [would] certainly obtain a high position on it."

Burkhardt, who reported a "substantially respectable, if not flatteringly fashionable," audience, leniently accepted Kellogg's faulty lower-voice production as being "susceptible of great improvement by practice and culture" (*Dispatch,* March 2, 1961). Whatever their separate quibbles, the critics agreed on one point—that an important career awaited Miss Kellogg. And indeed, great improvement was noted in her second performance of Gilda at the Grand Gala Matinée at the New York Academy the following Saturday afternoon, March 2, when a complete performance of *Rigoletto* shared the program with the last act of *Un ballo in maschera.*[60]

On March 1, as the twin opera seasons approached their close, *Don Giovanni* was presented at the New York Academy (repeated the following evening in Brooklyn), with Colson (Donna Anna), Signorina Elena (Donna Elvira), Hinkley (Zerlina), Stigelli (Octavio), Ferri (Don Giovanni) Susini (Leporello), and Coletti (Masetto). Evidently poorly prepared, despite its fine cast it was judged among the worst performances of the work within local memory.

March 1. . . . This evening to the Opera—alone—*Don Giovanni*—a slovenly performance. But it's among the greatest of Musical works and far the best of operas. Each several movement seems the finest thing of its kind ever written. It's a long string of gems and nothing else. Not one solo or concerted piece but of the very highest order. This can be said of no musical production of equal bulk that I'm acquainted with— not even *The Messiah.* Much impressed tonight by the concerted music, e.g., the heartbreaking duet *Non ti fidar, O misera* and the sextette *Sola in bujo loco.* Each contains material that any living composer could dilute into six popular operas or creditable symphonies. And what perfect purity of celestial expression is in the melodies—*Vedrai, carino,* for instance!

[57] With Adelaide Phillips as an admirable Maddalena, Stigelli, back from Havana, as the Duke of Mantua, Ferri as Rigoletto, and Coletti as Sparafucile.

[58] The *Evening Post* critic thought it a questionable choice. Infrequently heard, *Rigoletto*—obviously selected in this instance to satisfy the insatiable New York appetite for novelty (and also because Miss Kellogg had been assiduously preparing it for the past nine months)—was a poor choice for a debutante because it prompted unflattering comparisons with the great singers who had been heard as Gilda. Yet, admitted the critic, "there would be some fault like this found with any opera that might have been selected" (*Evening Post,* February 28, 1961).

[59] She was remarkably self-possessed, giving no sign of stage fright, disagreed the *Evening Post.*

[60] In the meantime, on February 26, *I puritani* had been performed in Brooklyn, with Hinkley, Stigelli, Susini, and Ettore Barili.

March 4. . . . With Ellie at Richard Willis's. Number two of Scharfenberg's Musical parties. It went off well. Haydn Quartette, no. 43 in D minor; Beethoven Trio, op. 97, in B-flat (Scherzo and Andante very great); Mozart Quartette, no. 10, in D (first movement the best). Two songs by [Philip] Mayer. One of them (by Sebastian Bach) vigorous and melodic, its archaism hardly noticeable. The other, a "pleasing," shallow sentimentalism of Lachner's, enthusiastically received and honored with an encore. . . . Am very weary. Have been standing up all the evening.

March 6. . . . With Murray Hoffman to the Philharmonic rehearsal at the Academy of Music at half-past-three. Beethoven's most splendid and impressive Seventh Symphony. I do not appreciate its fourth movement, but all the rest (and especially the Allegretto and Scherzo) cannot readily be matched, to my knowledge or belief.

—

Strong evidently did not attend the concert, given on March 16, with Bergmann conducting. In addition to the Beethoven Symphony, the program included "the usual dose of Schumann," the first local performance of his Overture to *Genoveva,* op. 81 (Leipzig 1850). It was a "dictatorial overture, urging the claims of Slumber," wrote Seymour (*Times, March 18,* 1861), "claims which no one listening to Schumann's music would willingly dispute." Also heard was Berlioz's Overture to *Les Francs-Juges;*♪♫ Edward Mollenhauer brilliantly played his flashy Violin Concerto in A for the first time; and Richard Hoffman superbly "resuscitated" Mozart's "antiquated" Concerto in D (K. 466? 537?) with Hummel's cadenzas, also a first time; his two unfamiliar solos were *La Passé,* op. 47, by the Bohemian composer Ignaz Tedesco (1817–1882) and a *Grande Polonaise* in F by the Dutch composer Ernst Lübeck (1829–1876).

By now the Associated Artists had entered the final week of their season: on March 4 they presented *Un ballo in maschera* in New York; on March 5 *Rigoletto* in Brooklyn; on March 6 *Poliuto* had been announced for New York but had to be canceled because Madame Colson and several other members of the cast were ill (the house was consequently dark); on March 7, at the New York Academy, Clara Louise Kellogg scored her first triumph in *Linda di Chamounix;*[61] on March 8 a final *Ballo in maschera* was performed in New York; on Saturday, March 9, at the closing Grand Gala Matinée (New York), *Linda di Chamounix* was repeated;[62] and at the grand Gala finale that evening in Brooklyn—a performance of *Norma* for Miss Hinkley's benefit—Anna Bishop[63] came to the rescue at the last minute, replacing the still ailing Colson as Norma; Hinkley was the Adalgisa,[64] Stigelli the Pollione, and Susini the Oroveso; the

---

[61] With Adelaide Phillips as Pierotto, Brignoli as Carlo, Ferri as Antonio, and Susini as the *Prefetto.*

[62] Unfortunately, with Martini d'Ormy—without benefit of a rehearsal—as Pierotto in substitution of an ailing Phillips.

[63] Madame Bishop had just concluded a disastrous season of English operas at Niblo's (see following OBBLIGATO).

[64] At the end of the opera, reported the *Tribune* (March 11, 1861), Miss Hinkley was showered with applause and bouquets: "As she left the stage, a splendid basket filled with the choicest flowers (to which was attached a magnificent diamond cross) was presented to her from one of the stage boxes."

last act of *Rigoletto* followed, with Kellogg, *et al.* The Associated Artists immediately departed for Boston on a specially chartered boat. They were expected back for Easter Week before going on to Philadelphia and points west.

Their season, Wilkins summed up in the *Herald* (March 11), had been singularly successful: "It is the first instance on record in this country," he wrote, "where a combination of operatic artists have been able to sustain themselves without bickering." The *Home Journal* (March 16, 1861) found the season memorable for "having introduced three *prime donne* not of Italian birth." Besides: "The management deserve mention for honesty in not marking as 'reserved' seats those that were not sold," and added, "the gems from Verdi's *Un ballo in maschera* have found their way to our musical families, and the street organs are playing them to the ears of the public."

March 12. . . . Murray Hoffman dined here, and we went down to the plebeian *Stadt-Theater* in the Bowery,[65] where we saw *Orpheus in der Unterwelt* [*Orphée aux enfers* (Paris 1858)], a funny extravaganza that has had a great run in Paris. Music by the celebrated "Offenbach" (whoever he is), rather piquant and Frenchy. It contains one or two appropriations from Haydn, scraps of *Volkslied* (e.g., *Guten Mond, Du gehst so stille*) and lovely larcenies from the *Zauberflöte*.[66]

March 22. . . . Murray Hoffman dined here and Scharfenberg came in afterwards to arrange the programme of the proposed quartette concert on these premises Easter Monday. He kindly read me some music (movements from Beethoven's sonatas, etc.), which it was good to hear.

March 24. . . . [Palm] Sunday. To Trinity Church with Ellie and Prince John. . . . There was an anthem "by Cutler" (op. x + y) that was above his average, but mere manifest Handel-and-water.

March 29. . . . Good Friday. . . . Trinity Church was crowded. People stood in the aisles. After the sermon a *Miserere* (said to be Allegri's), unrubrical but effective.

April 2. . . . [a busy day and a walk through the snow] then came off our little quartette concert—the fourth of Scharfenberg's series. The illustrious [Sexton] Brown reports 110 percent [on the social score]. . . . The best music they played was Beethoven's Quartet [op. 18], no. 5, in A, especially its second and third movements. The second movement of the Mendelssohn Trio was melodic and genial.

The illustrious Brown is very funny. Toward the close of the evening he came in out of the weather and took a seat in the hall, Mosenthal and his colleagues were working away at the rather dry final Allegro of the Mozart quartette, when some

---

[65] Where, among prodigious numbers of German plays, an occasional opera was produced with the best local German opera singers—among them, earlier in the year, *Die Zauberflöte* with Mesdames Caradori and von Berkel and the German tenor Lotti, and *Der Freischütz* with Caradori, Quint, and Weinlich.

[66] *Orpheus,* by Jacques Offenbach (1819–1880), was performed by members of the *Stadt-Theater's* stock company—the Meauberts, husband and wife, Madame Methua-Scheller, and the Herren Krilling and Klein; it seems to have been the first presentation in the United States of that delectable work. With its nine consecutive performances (Odell, VII, 343) it was as great a success, in its way, as *Un ballo in maschera.* Later, in June—following the great *Tannhäuser* fiasco in Paris in March—Bergmann revived that problematical work, much to Hagen's satisfaction, at the *Stadt-Theater* with Madame von Berkel, and Messrs. Quint, Lehmann, Graf, Friedeborn, and Lotti (see *Review and World,* July 6, 1861, p. 159).

coachman outside, impatient for his "company," rang the front door bell (and no wonder, for there was a great deal of weather about, and it must have been dull work waiting on the sidewalk). Brown tramped to the door—opened it—and addressed the indiscreet disturber of his peace in a whisper of concentrated wrath: "G——D—— your soul, what do you mean by interrupting me in the middle of the finest *Shirt-so* they've played tonight!"

April 5. . . . Ellie and I are in daily council with Scharfenberg over the project of getting up a Mass with some small orchestral accompaniment for the next little musical meeting—the last of the series. We have settled nothing and are uncertain as yet even whether the voices can be got. First we contemplated Mozart's lovely little [Mass] No. 7, which is written for a very small orchestra (stringed quartette, horn, bassoon, and clarionette), but the orchestral parts are not to be had. (I observe that Arndt doubts the genuineness of that Mass.[67] But the internal evidence seems to me conclusive: the *Sanctus, Benedictus, Et Incarnatus,* and *Agnus Dei* are intensely Mozartoid.) Then we considered the shorter [Mozart] *Requiem,*[68] written for nearly the same instruments, but Ellie is not satisfied with the composition. It certainly is weak in spots. Next, Niedermeyer's most noble Mass in D, but that's for full orchestra and very fuguey and difficult. And Haydn's infallible No. 6 seems now our only chance. Probably we shall accomplish nothing, after all.

On April 8 the Associated Artists returned from their successful season in Boston, where they had remained an extra week,[69] stealing it from their New York/Brooklyn schedule. Opening at the New York Academy with *Un ballo in maschera,* sung by the original cast (except for Coletti, who was replaced by Ettore Barili as one of the conspirators), they next presented *La sonnambula* on the 9th in Brooklyn, with Kellogg as Amina[70] (a disappointing, last-minute substitution for her greatly admired *Linda di Chamounix*); then *La Juive* in New York on the 10th, using Ullman's magnificent sets, with Colson triumphant in Fabbri's role of Rachel[71] (repeated in Brooklyn on the 11th); in New York on the 12th, *Linda di Chamounix* was again enchantingly performed by Kellogg;[72] on the 13th, a Saturday, the company repeated *Ballo* at their farewell Grand Gala matinée in New York and that evening they ingloriously performed *Mosè in Egitto* in Brooklyn.[73] Not to waste the intervening Sunday before their scheduled opening in Philadelphia on April 15, they gave a low-priced, unstaged "ora-

[67] A justified doubt: the Mass, K. Anhang C 1.06, is spurious.

[68] K. C 1.90, another spurious work.

[69] Their four-week season in Boston was rumored to have netted them an unlikely profit of $25,000 (*Times,* April 8, 1861).

[70] A hastily concocted, ill-advised effort, injurious to Miss Kellogg, who did not triumph, reluctantly reported the *Albion* (April 13, 1861, p. 175).

[71] And with Hinkley as the Princess Eudoxia, Scola as Leopold, Susini as the Cardinal, and Stigelli in his great role of Eleazar.

[72] "A memorable treat," wrote the *Albion* (April 20, 1861, p. 187). Especially piquant was Muzio's "Clara Louise Polka," replacing Donizetti's duet at the end of the opera. "I never thought much of it," wrote its insufficiently grateful dedicatee in later years (Kellogg, *Memoirs,* pp. 88–89).

[73] With Hinkley (Anaide), Phillips (Sinaide), Stigelli (Amenofi), Ferri (Pharaoh), and Susini (Moses).

torio" performance of *Mosè* in New York the following evening, to the distant *obbligato* of secessionist cannon firing the opening salvos of the Civil War at Fort Sumter.

During the latter part of the foregoing week, reported Wilkins (*Herald,* April 15, 1861), "the Opera, as well as the theatres, had suffered materially from the war excitement, and the performances in Brooklyn had failed to remunerate the artists. Our friends across the water," he caustically added, had "evidently recovered from their severe attack of musical enthusiasm."

But, as the Associated Artists learned upon their arrival in Philadelphia, not only in Brooklyn had opera instantaneously become an anachronism. On that day, April 15, President Lincoln issued his proclamation of war, and on that same day Muzio, a realist, announced the termination of the Associated Artists' activities. As the *Albion* rather flippantly reported (April 20, 1861, p. 187): "The manager's proclamation and the President's made their appearance simultaneously. . . . Messrs. Muzio and Co. have retired into private life." More responsibly he added: "In the midst of scenes of such excitement as now prevail, it is, of course, impossible for art to flourish." Muzio, in the meantime, he wrote, would probably be off to Europe to engage singers for the following season.

As indeed he might, for a goodly number of the opera singers immediately fled the country, among them Madame Colson, Adelaide Phillips, Stigelli, Marcel Junca—also the Draytons (who had successfully been touring far and wide) and Mrs. William Vincent Wallace.[74] Brignoli and Susini were reported to be momentarily departing, but for a variety of reasons[75] they remained in the no-longer United States.[76] Adelina Patti, who had been touring under the management of Maurice Strakosch[77] since his breakup with Ullman, and who had been announced for Maretzek's impending Mexican tour,[78] defaulted at the last minute (professing her fear of Mexican bandits). She went instead, with Strakosch and her father, after three sensational appearances in Havana—on April 1, 2, and 5—to London, where greener fields beckoned, as Maretzek bitterly relates in *Sharps and Flats* (pp. 50–52).

Strong, like every responsible American, Northern or Southern, was consumed

---

[74] *Dwight's* New York correspondents, *Trovator* and —t— immediately joined the exodus; Dwight himself had gone to Europe the year before, in July 1860, not to return until November 1861. Also departing were Eisfeld and Mosenthal, but only briefly, to participate in a great "Singing Festival" in Nuremberg during the summer (*Review and World,* June 6, 1861, p. 149).

[75] In Susini's case, his courtship of Isabella Hinkley, which resulted in their marriage on October 31, 1861.

[76] "Of the *prime donne* of last season," wrote *T.W.M.,* a spasmodic substitute in *Dwight's* (August 31, 1861, p. 175) for the absent *Trovator* and —t—: "Hinkley and Kellogg are the only ones who have not been frightened away by the war, if we except Madame Fabbri-Mulder, who is, we believe, rusticating in the Canadas. Muzio, Susini, and the Barilis are at present sojourning in New York, calmly awaiting the course of events." As for Brignoli, who was "rusticating" at Long Branch: "He drives the fastest team on the road, and is evidently well pleased with himself and the rest of mankind."

[77] Since February, Strakosch had been advertising in the New York papers that Patti would be returning to New York for a few farewell appearances before departing for Europe. She didn't.

[78] With a fine company consisting—besides, as Maretzek believed, little Patti—of Madame d'Angri; the Natali sisters Fanny and Agnes; Stefani, Errani, Sbriglia, and Testa, tenors; Ottaviani and Ippolito, baritones; Biacchi and Rocco, basses; Abella and Nicolai, conductors; Maretzek's brother Albert, general manager; and his friend Alfred Joel, advance agent.

by the devastating events that had overtaken the nation. His private journal eloquently records and discusses the war's progress—his agonies and exultations over defeats and victories. Understandably, he engaged in a variety of official and quasi-official and patriotic activities, making occasional trips, most often in the company of his influence-wielding father-in-law Mr. Ruggles, to Washington—chaotic with office-seekers and influence-pedlars.[79]

In January, Strong purchased a Maynard Carbine (at the expenditure of $47.50), although his nearsightedness, as he admits, prevented his accuracy in handling a gun. In April he helped organize, and was elected president *pro tem* of, the New York Rifle Corps, a volunteer patriotic group; although a novice, he nonetheless participated in their drilling sessions. "I've found out what 'Eyes Right!' means. I've long wanted to know the purport of that familiar but mystic phrase," he wrote in his private journal (April 24, 1861).

At the very beginning of the war, Strong, with Ellen and a select party of friends, paid an agreeable visit (ostensibly a visit of inspection) to the military installation at Governor's Island, where raw army recruits were sent for rudimentary training before being drafted into regiments and shipped off to the various scenes of military action (see *Harper's Weekly,* May 4, 1861, pp. 271, 285).

April 15. . . . Expedition to Governor's Island this morning. Ellie and I, Charley Strong and wife, Dan Messenger, Christie, Miss Kate Fearing, Tom Meyer, and one or two more. Officer of the day was Lieutenant Webb (of Maine), whose guests we were. He treated us most hospitably and had out the Band, playing an hour or two for our own delectation. The programme included that jolliest of tunes, "Dixie Land," and "Hail Columbia." We took off our hats while the latter was played. Everybody's patriotism is rampant and demonstrative now.[80]

. . . [back from Governor's island at five P.M.] to Scharfenberg's tonight. The last of our series of concerts. Ellie was tired out and stayed at home most reluctantly. The programme was excellent. (1) Haydn Quartette in G, the Adagio and opening Allegro very lovely and the whole composition full, broad, and vigorous, a specimen of Haydn's very best style of work. (2) Hummel's Quintette in D minor, his memorable op. 74 arranged (by him) for piano and stringed quartette from his original septuor. The beautiful, genial melody of the trio in the second movement asserts itself emphatically

---

[79] Among the office-seekers was William Henry Fry, whom Strong met on one of these trips. Strong found him "very clever, and, I think, consumptive [true]; he's after some diplomatic post [Secretary of the Legation in Turin] and relies much on that terrible cough, the result of speech-making over much of New York and Ohio in the last [presidential] campaign" (Private Journal, March 17, 1861; *Diary,* III, 111).

[80] Strong not excepted. On April 18 he wrote in his diary: "The national flag is flying everywhere; every cart horse decorated. It occurred to me that it would be a good thing to hoist it on the tower of Trinity—an unprecedented demonstration, but these are unprecedented times." With the approval of the church hierarchy, Strong procured a large flag ("20 by 40") from the obliging shipping magnate Robert B. Minturn, who supplied as well a rigger to help hoist it. At half-past two on the afternoon of April 19, "it went up, the chimes saluting it with 'Hail Columbia,' 'Yankee Doodle,' and 'Old Hundred,' and a crowd in Wall Street and Broadway cheering" (*Diary,* III, 124–25). Various other churches, and at least one synagogue, henceforth hoisted flags, if not to such appropriate background music.

even when rendered on this reduced scale. (3) Beethoven Quartette [op. 18], no. 4 in C minor was delightful and Mozartesque. Phrases occurred in its charming second movement that seemed souvenirs of *Tace ingiusto core* in the second act of *Don Giovanni.* During the entre'acts we talked politics, of course.

April 19. . . . George Anthon dined here. Evening spent in listening to Scharfenberg and a dozen "professional" people rehearsing Haydn's lovely Mass, No. 2 [fittingly, the *Missa in tempore belli*], for our next "concert."

April 25. . . . We have given up our musical party, the second rehearsal for which was to have been held tomorrow night. This is no time for parties. We shall want all our spare cash and perhaps a little more before we have established the proposition that the People of the United States constitute a great *Nation,* and not merely a great *Mob.*

<div align="center">~~~</div>

Nor apparently was it a time for concert-going. Strong missed the fifth and final Philharmonic concert of the 1860–61 season, rehearsals and all. Given at the Academy of Music on April 20, the diverse program, conducted by Eisfeld, comprised a Mozart Symphony in G minor (K. 550?) and Beethoven's Overture to *Egmont;* Maria Brainerd sang Mendelssohn's *Infelice,* op. 94; William Saar played an *Illustration dramatique* of *Tannhäuser* for solo piano; and the German *Liederkranz,* conducted by Paur, performed Mendelssohn's cantata *The First Walpurgis Night,* op. 60.[81]

"The music of the drum and fife is fast superseding all others," wrote —t—, and the Philharmonic was no exception. At this concert, he reported (*Dwight's,* May 4, 1861, pp. 37–38), "almost everyone, lady or gentleman, wore the red, white, and blue in some shape. The members of the *Liederkranz* were all decorated in a similar way," as was Miss Brainerd, who wore "a sash of the Union colors across her breast. When she had finished her aria there was a call from various quarters for the 'Star-Spangled Banner,' upon which Mr. Eisfeld came forward and announced that the piece would be sung by Miss Brainerd and the *Liederkranz,* with accompaniment of the orchestra, at the end of the programme, and that the audience were requested to join in the chorus."

When Miss Brainerd reappeared, "sheets of paper with the words of the song were distributed among the audience, the American flag was suspended from the proscenium, and the orchestra played the introduction to the 'Star-Spangled Banner.' Unfortunately, it had been set in too high a key for Miss Brainerd, and her rendition consequently suffered." But the choruses were "grand," and "four or five verses were sung; and during the last the enthusiasm rose to the highest pitch. Flags and handkerchiefs were waved, cheer followed cheer, and there was a tumult such as the decorous, sober, Philharmonic has never yet witnessed. It was soul-stirring and exciting to the last degree, yet," feelingly wrote —t—, "underneath lay the mournful thought of how many of these brave, large hearts would be stilled, how many others would bleed with anguish before another winter would reassemble some of us within these walls!"

Strong's patriotism entrapped him—against his better judgment—in a burdensome and embarrassing project.

---

[81] In which a "Mr. Steinway" was singled out by —t— as the best of the *Liederkranz* soloists (*Dwight's,* May 4, 1861, pp. 37–38).

Girvice Archer, Jr.

Maria Brainerd.

May 14. . . . [following a meeting on legal business] Maunsell Field⌐ seized on me to say I had been appointed (query, by whom?) on a committee to issue proposals by advertisement and award a prize for a National Hymn, or popular and patriotic song appealing to the National Heart.[82] Was such a thing ever heard of before????!!!!!

I went to the meeting at the Chamber of Commerce building. Field was there, Arthur Leary [an influential merchant], [John Romeyn] Brodhead [a noted historian], George William Curtis, the Howaji, and Richard Grant White. Talked it over and adjourned to Thursday night. General [John Adams] Dix [the recent Secretary of the Treasury and now an army officer], [John J.] Cisco [a fellow lawyer and fellow Trinity Church vestryman], Charles King [President of Columbia College], Hamilton Fish [former Governor of New York] and others are on the Committee [as honorary members], so I shall be ridiculous in decent company.

"Wanted by the American Nation, a *Marseillaise.* Any poet having one to dispose of will please apply to etc., etc.; at etc., etc.; on or before etc., etc." Or: "$250 Re-

---

[82] "Music is frequently martial," commented the *Times* (May 19, 1861). "It is one of its most inspiritng moods. Just now, however, it seems to fall beneath the exigencies of the time. We are deficient it seems, even in a National hymn [as if the "Star-Spangled Banner" didn't suffice!], and a reward is offered for a good one."

ward. A Tyrtaeus[83] is urgently required by the People. If he be about, anywhere, he will please call on etc., etc., by whom a reasonable compensation for his services, not exceeding the amount above named, will be promptly paid." Or, in the *Herald* advertising column of Wants: "$250 worth of Genius and Inspiration embodied in patriotic Music and Words. Apply to, etc." This is among the funniest things ever undertaken by mortal man. Never mind. There is possibly one chance in ten million that it may bring out something good.

   May 16. . . . National Anthem Committee here tonight from eight till twelve, Arthur Leary, Maunsell Field, George Curtis, Richard Grant White, and Brodhead. We settled a form of advertisement, after much verbal criticism. Field is a fearful proser. We stand a good chance of being consumedly laughed at.

<center>~~~</center>

   Of far greater significance, in early June President Lincoln created the United States Sanitary Commission, progenitor of the American Red Cross, and Strong was appointed its treasurer.[84] In this important and exacting capacity, Strong would faithfully and selflessly continue to labor for the duration of the war.

   June 22. . . . Dined at the Union Club, on Dr. Van Buren's invitation, with the New York [Sanitary] Commissioners and old Dr. [Valentine] Mott. Much pleasant talk with Bellows and Olmsted. Came away at eight to attend meeting here of our absurd "National Hymn Committee." (Four or five large bales of patriotic hymnology were deposited here this afternoon by our express wagon.) There were present Governor Fish, Luther Bradish, John R. Brodhead, Maunsell Field, Dick [Richard Grant] White, and others. Charley Strong happened in and acted as amateur assessor.

   We got through possibly a third of our job between eight and twelve-thirty. There are 1,156 "hymns," many of them with music. The great majority were consigned to the great rubbish bin (or clothes-basket) after reading the first three lines. A few were put aside as meritorious and worth looking at, and a few others as brilliantly absurd and therefore worth saving. We came across no production to which we could think of awarding a prize.

   June 26. . . . Last evening [Ellie] spent with us (Dick White and George Curtis and others of the National Hymn Committee) and had a good time: we disposed of bushels of rubbish. This committee is responsible for the production of an enormous bulk of commonplace, watery versification. Fortunately, two-thirds of the trash is already consumed with fire. But there remains an immense pile of poetry with music to match still to be inspected.[85] It's clear, I think, that we get no National Hymn. Perhaps

---

   [83] A Greek poet of the seventh century B.C., Tyrtaeus was sent to inspire the Spartans, with his stirring martial poetry, to win the Second Messenian War.
   [84] The Reverend Dr. Henry W. Bellows (1814–1882), the Commission's president, and Wolcott Gibbs, a member of its executive committee, were Strong's close friends. Frederick Law Olmsted, the gifted designer and administrator of Central Park, was its potent General Secretary.
   [85] The response was overwhelming, at least to the overburdened members of the Committee. In a letter dated June 21 addressed to the *Review and World* (July 6, 1861, p. 163), Maunsell Field announced that some 1150 submissions had been received, that no more would be accepted, that the ulimate decision would be publicly announced, and that personal inquiries would be disregarded.

we may secure a dozen bits of second-rate lyric that charitable people may justify for publishing.

June 28. . . . Tonight Committee on National Anthem met here. Was there ever before a committee appointed to carry out a design so irrational and improbable?[86] There were George William Curtis, Richard Grant White, J. R. Brodhead, and myself. Also as outside assessors, Mrs. Ellie, Miss Rosalie, Mrs. D.C. Murray, George Anthon, Willie Graham, Charley Strong, and Scharfenberg. Scharfenberg came by invitation to help us pass on the vast amount of musical work (380 and upwards) sent in by competitors. We got through with about one half. Generally rubbish—a score or two reserved for further examination. The evening was pleasant, however, and the supper table jolly.

June 29. . . . Morning spent in Sanitary Commission business and evening here, with the National Anthem Committee. Scharfenberg assisted again. We got through, at last, with our preliminary inspection of the great rubbish heap of contributions, seriatim. Of course, there is nothing—neither verse nor music—that comes up to the standard required. We had no right to expect a suspension of the laws of nature. About three pecks of music and poetry are reserved for further inspection, as not manifestly commonplace or ridiculous or stolen. But we shall find nothing of value.

July 2. . . . After dinner to Richard Grant White's (186 South Street), where were old [Gulian] Verplanck [(1786–1870) literary and political luminary], George William Curtis, and Maunsell Field of the National Anthem Committee. We examined a score or two of efforts that had been laid aside as not manifestly rubbish, on our former inspection. Of these we condemned only about one half, a very tender and merciful judgment. It is conceded that no one of our 1,275 contributions answers the conditions of our advertisement and deserves the prize, but it is thought we may publish the best of them. *Not one* seems to me worth preserving, but there may be a dozen or so that the public would buy.

～

The sorry progress of the National Hymn contest continued to be a favorite object of ridicule in the press, with editorials, letters to the editors, and derisive barbs galore. "The Committee, whose hard fate it is to examine the various contributions by upwards of 2,000 competitors for the grand National Ode, have rejected all but fifteen of the manuscripts as worthless," erroneously reported the *Times* (July 21, 1861), continuing, "Even this remarkably small residue is not spoken of with enthusiasm," and caustically adding, "What a frightful destiny to examine bad musical compositions and worry through ungrammatical chords in [hot] weather like this!"

Obviously a fiasco, the project's ultimate resolution—or rumor of one, if a

---

[86] The *Albion* (June 1, 1861, p. 259) furiously attacked "that insane Committee which purposes to procure a new National Anthem by paying a ridiculously small price for it, and exacting conditions which place the poet at a disadvantage with the musician, and the musician at a disadvantage with the poet." And for a niggardly prize of $250 for either text or music, or $500 for both! Among the rights retained by the committee was the privilege of arbitrarily wedding any text to any tune "according to their Royal pleasure, and owning their copyright to the exclusion of the author or authors." Furthermore, they proposed publication of a collection of the entries, without payment to the authors, thus "appropriating a large number of manuscripts for no other reason in the world than that they have bought and indifferently paid for one."

lengthy report in the *Times* (July 28, 1861) is to be believed—was a performance of the surviving songs at a concert in New York and one in Brooklyn and let the public be the judge, although how that judgment would apply, the *Times* was at a loss to say. Whether or not this expedient was resorted to, in September a publication, *National Hymns: How They are Written and How They are Not Written, A Lyric and National Study for the Times,* was issued by the publishers Rudd and Carleton. Edited by Richard Grant White, it contained—in addition to a selection of entries from the competition (including submissions by R. Storrs Willis, C. Jerome Hopkins, and J. R. Thomas) an apparently objective account of the competition and the committee and a brief essay on national hymns, using "God Save the King" and the *Marseillaise* as paradigms.[87]

In mid-July Ellen and the boys went to Savin Rock, Connecticut, for their first wartime vacation. Strong made flying visits there whenever he could free himself from his demanding Sanitary Commission duties, which required frequent trips to over-crowded Washington and sobering inspections of various military hospital installa-tions—and in the meantime coping with his multitudinous professional and extra-professional responsibilities in New York. As the summer progressed he became more and more despondent over the succession of military catastrophes that had befallen the Union.

August 28. . . . Morning papers announced another disaster.[88] . . . We have been and are dispirited, dependent, and intensely disgusted with the Administration. I was so blue that I thought it charity to Ellie not to go to Savin Rock this afternoon. Dined with Charley Strong and George C. Anthon, and loafed awhile at that rather disrepu-table Canterbury Hall."[89]

September 16. . . . [stopping over in Baltimore, en route to Washington on Sani-tary Commission business] Sunday morning I went to the Roman Catholic Cathedral, a great, shabby, ugly building, and heard Mozart's Mass, No. 1 (of Novello's edition) [K. 317], fairly rendered. The elegant *Agnus dei* (soprano solo) and the *Dona pacem* quartette, with its intense choral finale, were worth the journey to Baltimore. Why should Papishers enjoy an undisturbed monopoly of this glorious music?

~~~

Except for military quicksteps and patriotic songs, music—glorious or other-wise—was in diminishing supply in New York. There had been a vague rumor, quickly dispelled, that Ullman—intrepidly attempting a comeback—was planning a summer season of opera at the New York Academy of Music. He had, in fact, suc-

---

[87] In October a seemingly identical publication, titled *The Book of the National Hymn Committee,* was advertised by a different publisher, George W. Elliott, to be issued by subscription at the price of one dollar. Again edited by Richard Grant White, the volume would comprise a selection from the best and worst (the latter allegedly for amusement value) of some 1200 contest entries, and again an essay by White on national hymns with a selection of the best European national anthems. The project apparently did not materialize.

[88] A report, later discredited, that General Daniel Tyler had suffered an important defeat in West Virginia.

[89] Where a "Magnificent Military Pantomime, 'The Southern Refugee, or False and True,'" shared the bill with the blackface antics of J. H. Budworth.

ceeded in gaining leases of both Academies for the ensuing fall and winter seasons and
had gone to Europe to engage new singers. In September, in a radical switch, he
opened the New York Academy (and soon after, the Brooklyn Academy), not with
opera but with the supervirtuoso magician or, as Ullman seductively billed him, "the
greatest living *préstidigitateur,*"[90] Herrmann, fresh from a sensational season in Havana.[91]
(Ullman was reported at this point to have entered into a long-range partnership with
Don Francisco Martí♪♫ and also—wonder of wonders—with Max Maretzek.)

Herrmann was sold to the public in vintage Ullmanese. Overflowing with heartfelt sincerity, the confiding impresario begged the public to remember that during the
past fifteen years of his managership he had brought to America the greatest musical
artists, from Sontag to Piccolomini, Sivori to Vieuxtemps, Herz to Thalberg. His object in presenting Herrmann by no means suggested a mercenary desire for profit, but
rather Ullman's idealistic conviction that Herrmann was a great and unique artist
whose "appearance has been a new revelation in the art of prestidigitation, as that of
Jenny Lind has been in singing."

And indeed, Herrmann,[92] an affable and urbane devil's deputy with a gift for
witty verbal improvisation, took New York (and Brooklyn) by storm—not least the
critics, whom he utterly bewitched at a series of preliminary private *soirées.* So rapturously did the critics herald Herrmann's miraculous feats that Ullman was happily compelled—following Herrmann's debut at the New York Academy on September 16—
to publish an "apology" to the public for the "overcrowded state of the Academy last
evening." Neither he nor any other manager, he wrote, could have foreseen, "in the
present disturbed state of business," such an overflow audience. Evidently more tickets
had been sold than the Academy had seats.[93]

Filling the intervals between Herrmann's wondrous feats, the opera orchestra,
conducted by Theodore Thomas, performed popular musical favorites:[94] the overtures
to *Masaniello* and *Zampa,* the March from *Tannhäuser,* Mendelssohn's Wedding March,
and also the "Herrmann Polka," composed in tribute to the magician by "the celebrated Strauss [presumably Strauss the younger] of Vienna."

Like all New Yorkers, the Strongs went to the Academy to see the "grand Préstidigitateur." "Very brilliant performance, mostly quite inexplicable," wrote Strong on
September 27. "One or two of his tricks without machinery or appliances are awful
and alarming."

On that very evening Herrmann introduced his talented wife, Rosalie, who not
only displayed astounding powers of "double vision" (clairvoyance) but—a product of

[90] A term that captivated the public fancy: "People have become familiar with the name of
'Prestidigiteur,' and a few reckless and roistering blades toy with it in their cups," joked the *Times*
(October 4, 1861).
[91] Where he had occasionally shared a program with Gottschalk.
[92] Thought to have been of Spanish or French origin, Carl Herrmann (1817–1887) in fact was
born in Hanover, Germany.
[93] At the outset tickets were a blanket fifty cents. With Herrmann's huge success, the scale was
adjusted to a fifty-cent admission, with twenty-five cents extra for reserved seats (highly recommended because of the crowds), and twenty-five cents for the amphitheatre, a special bargain.
[94] An incident in Thomas's early career that is bypassed by Thomas's biographers, himself included.

the Paris *Conservatoire* —was an accomplished singer and pianist. At her benefits, at the New York Academy on October 23 and in Brooklyn the following evening, her performances with Theodore Thomas of de Bériot and Osborne's brilliant violin and piano fantasy on *William Tell* established her as a "perfect mistress of her instrument" (*Herald,* October 24, 1861). Assisting at both benefits was Carlotta Patti, who sang arias from the "Sicilian Vespers" and the "Magic Flute," and, of course, Herrmann himself, who brought the house down with four breathtaking new tricks.[95]

Herrmann's magical presence afforded Ullman a providential reprieve, permitting him to maintain the two Academies while he attempted to scrape together the wherewithal to support the somewhat shadowy opera season he had promised for the following January.[96] With credit depleted and small likelihood of finding new backers at this time of war, Ullman conceived an audacious scheme for raising the necessary funds: he would give a few nights of opera in New York and Brooklyn as benefits to himself (something he had virtuously shunned in the past) and apply the proceeds to his future opera season.

In floods of heartwrenching verbiage, Ullman drenched the amusement columns with pleas to the Academy stockholders and the public to patronize his benefits,[97] if only in recognition, he pointed out (and not without reason), of their debt to him for "the satisfaction of having heard Sontag, Piccolomini, D'Angri, de Lagrange, Gazzaniga, Adelina Patti, Laborde, Formes, Thalberg, Sivori, Henri Herz, Vieuxtemps, and various other musical celebrities, and to whom I have given the splendid spectacles of a *Juive,* the *Vespers,* the *Huguenots,* etc." Ullman put his trust in the "generosity and liberality" of the American national character; he had no doubt that the public would respond, "if not in acknowledgment of long and faithful services, [then] to avoid the bad moral effect the closing of the opera for an entire season would produce in the South and Europe."

And respond they did. The Directors of the Academy nobly supported Ullman, reported Burkhardt in the *Dispatch* (October 12, 1861): "They say he shall be sustained; that rebellion shall not interfere with opera; that there is a necessity for keeping open the Academy, not only for the amusement it affords stockholders and music-loving citizens, but to show—despite a Civil War that calls half a million men to the field, despite the treasure promptly found to supply their necessaries and war's expensive requisites—we are not compelled to close our institutions of art and intellectual amusement, or debar citizen's their usual pleasure of a season's opera."

As to the public response: "Who would have thought," wrote Hagen (*Review and World,* October 26, 1861, p. 254), "when seeing the display of beauty, luxury, and brilliancy—the costly dresses, the diamonds of the ladies, the latest fashions in their most gorgeous styles, the smiling faces, the merry, although subdued, laugh of the girls when something 'very funny' was whispered to them by their young and 'elegant' attendants, the perfect unconcern with which the fathers listened to the 'inspiring' music

[95] He began his performance with the favorite "Flying Photographs," in which, instead of playing cards, he "threw 200 of Madame Herrmann's photographic likenesses."

[96] Purportedly to include the celebrated European singers Mesdames Giuseppina Medori and Anne Charton-Demeure (1824–1892), also Madame D'Angri, the basso Biacchi, and the other stars of Maretzek's current Mexican company, including Maretzek himself.

[97] At $1 a ticket, fifty cents extra for reserved seats.

of Verdi—who would have thought that a fierce war is raging in the land, upon the result of which hangs the fate of this great and glorious nation?"

Ullman's plan called for two performances in New York and two in Brooklyn,[98] featuring the remaining stars of the Associated Artists—Hinkley, Kellogg, Brignoli, and Susini, with Muzio conducting. They appeared in *Ballo in maschera,* in New York on October 17 and in Brooklyn on the 19th,[99] with Clara Louise Kellogg assuming Colson's former role of Amelia, Amalia Patti as Ulrica, Isabella Hinkley enchanting as ever as the Page, and a Signor Giuseppe Mancusi (recently arrived from Havana) "no improvement on Ferri" as Reinhart/Renato.[100]

The second pair of benefits, a double bill consisting of purported first American performances of Donizetti's *Betly* (Naples 1836) and Victor Massé's comic opera *Les Noces de Jeannette* (Paris 1853),[101] was announced for October 21 and 22, but had to be postponed to October 28 and 29 because the company failed to return from their intervening performance in Philadelphia in time to rehearse the two unfamiliar works. Turning the postponement to advantage, they repeated *Ballo* on October 21 (a great improvement over the earlier performance) and again, following their presentation of *Betly* on October 25, at a grand gala farewell "combination matinée" on October 26, featuring a "prestidigitorial entr'acte" by Herrmann, clarvoyance and piano playing (again the *William Tell* duet with Thomas) by Madame Herrmann, and a "concert" by Carlotta Patti, assisted by her sister Amalia, at which Thomas played a violin solo and Muzio accompanied at the piano "with false notes ad libitum" (*Dwight's,* November 9, 1861, p. 254).

October 28. . . . We went to the Opera. Full house and two little operas given: *Les Noces de Jeannette* [in French, with Clara Louise Kellogg, Signorina Elena, and Dubreuil], which was utter drivel, and Donizetti's *Betly* [in Italian, with Isabella Hinkley], which seemed high art by contrast.[102] On the whole, a very feeble performance. Lasted from eight until near twelve. If there were 2000 people in the house, some 8000 hours of human life—equivalent to nearly a year—(more than a year if sleeping time be allowed for) were absolutely wasted on this imbecility.

———

Although the press frequently reported continuing disagreements between Ullman and the stockholders of both Academies, he nonetheless announced a big winter opera season definitely to commence in January, as planned, upon arrival of various

---

[98] With two concurrent performances in Philadelphia and four to follow in Boston.

[99] With Herrmann occupying the adjoining evenings.

[100] "Accustomed as we are to the powerful voices of Ferri and Amodio," wrote the *Evening Post* (October 18, 1861), "Mancusi falls a little below the standard." Less politely, Hagen likened his singing to that of a man "who could not clear his throat of the last meal he took, and as satisfactory as this, on some occasions, may be to himself, it is by no means pleasant to those who have to witness this somewhat novel process of digestion" (*Review and World,* October 26, 1861, p. 255).

[101] Fragments of *Betly* had been heard at various concerts in the '40s; *Les Noces de Jeannette* had been performed in English as *The Marriage of Georgette* by the Pyne/Harrison company in 1855.

[102] Hagen agreed: "Strange to say," he wrote (*Review and World* (November 9, 1861, p. 267), "Donizetti's music to *Betly* was, for once, a relief." At least, it made no pretences and sounded, by comparison, like music.

These three talented Patti sisters—
Adelina (top left), Amalia (top right), and
Carlotta (at right)—were on hand to give
concerts and provide music for the public
during the war.

artists from Europe, Mexico, and Havana. And although the most recent local opera company had purportedly disbanded, with Brignoli and Susini supposedly about to leave for glamorous engagements in Europe and Muzio to depart with the others for a season in Havana, matters took a surprising turn. Suddenly, on November 1, Jacob Grau[103] stepped out of the shadows and issued a card informing the public that he had succeeded in "retaining in this country, for the present (so that Italian Opera may be given)," Hinkley (now Signora Susini), Kellogg, Brignoli, and Susini. With Anschütz to accompany them on the piano (Muzio being off to Havana), they were about to embark on a tour of one-night stands to include Newark, New Haven, Hartford, Springfield, and Worcester; on December 8 they were engaged to open the new opera house at Buffalo, then to proceed to Toronto, Montreal, and Quebec. Country managers wishing to engage them for operas, concerts, or oratorios were invited to communicate with Grau at 11 West 18th Street.

Inheriting Ullman's difficulties with the intransigent boards of directors over their rent demands, Grau solved these problems simply by keeping his troupe on the road, performing each night in a different place. Their programs, in two parts, consisted of a concert (assisted by the cellist Henry Mollenhauer) followed by an act from a favorite opera, unstaged but in costume. "As the company give six performances a week without a chorus or orchestra," observed the *Herald* (November 11, 1861), "it will be seen that their expenses are small and easily met." Failing to reach an agreement with the stockholders, Grau continued to tour his company for the remainder of the year.

Ullman, in the meantime, had rented Niblo's disused Theatre,[104] where he purposed to present dramatic entertainments. Instead, on December 24, he installed Herrmann, plucked from mid-tour, for a two-week engagement. Although Ullman would make a further attempt at opera production in 1862, his great days of operatic glory were over, and Grau's were in the ascendant.

While these events were taking place, and despite the exigencies of war, Strong and the Philharmonic, at least, remained constant.

October 26. . . . Philharmonic rehearsal [for the first concert of the 1861–62 season] this afternoon. Beethoven's C-minor Symphony. Not at the Academy of Music this season but at [the new] Irving Hall (corner of 15th Street and Irving Place), a much better place for music.[105] Attendance very small, comparatively, which is also an

---

[103] A Central European like his fellow impresarios, Grau (1817–1877) had emigrated from Austria to the United States in 1847. After an apprenticeship of knocking about in the corridors and alcoves of the concert halls and opera houses, he had at last found employment, first with Ole Bull and Thalberg, then with Strakosch at the inauguration of Pike's Opera House in Cincinnati in 1859. Then, according to his obituary, for three years Grau was the joint lessee, with Ullman and Maretzek, of the Academy of Music, an item not publicized at the time. Grau's obituary names him, too, as having managed both the legendary Prince of Wales's Ball in New York and also the preceding grand gala at the Philadelphia Academy in the Prince's honor.

[104] Niblo's had been standing vacant since June.

[105] Apprehensive over the general falling-off of music events and audiences, the Philharmonic, as a safety measure, had moved to the much smaller and cheaper Irving Hall, opened in January by the creative and enterprising entrepreneur, Lafayette F. Harrison. The Philharmonic's scaling-down applied as well to the orchestra personnel. To suit the smaller space, it was decided at a Board of

improvement. There is no chattering. Irving Hall is not a rendezvous for flirtatious boys and girls, as the Academy has been. The Symphony was gloriously rendered [by Bergmann]. One of its great points—the transition of the third movement into the magnificent opening of the Finale—came out most clearly and forcibly.

October 27. . . . To Trinity Church with Ellie, Miss Rosalie, and Johny. . . . For anthem we had one of Marcello's psalms ("O Lord our Governor"). A brilliant exception to the usual trash of Cutler's programs, but to the average musical ear utterly without meaning or impressiveness. As for the *Te Deum* and *Jubilate*—Snooks in X flat— they were as usual, utterly worthless, devoid of melody, of harmonic effect, and of contrasts of light and shadow. I could sit down at the organ and make music as effective and significant by the hour. An average or a first rate Anglican *Te Deum* reminds one of a penitential psalm, but it does not even express penitence and contrition otherwise than by monotony, dullness, and dreariness. The music of Trinity Church is a disgraceful waste of money. I shall return to Trinity Chapel next Easter.

November 3. . . . Trinity Church with Johny. . . . Music as usual. Most abundant in quantity and most exasperating in its dull, imbecile, lifeless quality. Every dollar spent on music in Trinity parish is wasted. Our dismal, commonplace *Te Deum*s, *Gloria*s, and *Jubilate*s warm no devotion. They are weaker and worse than any music I know. Their degradation is below that of even Verdi in secular music. But there is no remedy.

November 5. . . . Tonight with Ellie and Mrs. D.C. Murray to one of Mason and Thomas's Classical Soirées; a quartette of Mozart's (in G major, no. 1) [of the Haydn set, K. 387] was very lovely. The rest of the programme not impressive.[106]

November 9. Feel comparatively jolly today, notwithstanding dismal wet weather, grievous dyspepsia, and grave anxiety about the fate of our naval expedition, which is still unknown.[107] The jollifying agency is potent: Beethoven's C-minor Symphony, which I have heard twice today, namely at morning rehearsal and at the Philharmonic concert (with Ellie) tonight. What a glorious—perfect—inspired—and inspiring— work it is! Clearly, I think, the first of orchestral compositions. New points show themselves at every performance. I never appreciated the third movement until today.

Each movement is the greatest of its kind ever written. Each has an organic relation to the others. Each seems the most intense embodiment conceivable of its own sentiment, and there is a steady climax of intensity that culminates at last in that transcendent, triumphal final march—about which there is no use talking: it is a Revelation of Beauty and Majesty that cannot be conveyed in words. It is too exalted to cele-

---

Directors meeting on November 15 to invite certain older members of the orchestra to resign— among them the veterans Helfenritter and Windmüller (violinists), Boucher and Walker (cellists), and Goodwin (violist) (Philharmonic Archives).

[106] The rest of the program consisted of Schumann's String Quartet in F major, op. 41, no. 2; Beethoven's Piano Sonata in E-flat, op. 31, no. 3, played by Mason; and Schubert's *Rondo brillant,* op. 70, for violin and piano, played by Thomas and Mason. This was the first concert of their seventh season (their first mentioned by Strong). The remaining Mason/Thomas concerts of 1861 are discussed in the following OBBLIGATO.

[107] Strong was referring to the Battle of Fort Royal Sound, South Carolina, on November 7, at which a great Federal armada was victorious.

brate any finite conquest or victory—it is appropriate only for the final consummated triumph of Good over Evil—or Life over Death.

What a wonderful passage is the little *crescendo* that links the third movement with this tremendous Finale! At the last repetition of the characteristic, sharp rhythmical phrase of the former, the orchestra introduces a new element (somewhere in the bass) into its last chord—a most weird note that is held and held for two or three bars, and on which certain queer little modifications of the first phrase of that movement begin to build themselves, quicker and quicker—more and more intensely *minor,* and eager and nervous and hurried—as if a swarm of little imps of darkness were scuttling out of the way, as they saw what was coming. The upward swell and pressure of the orchestra seems to keep them in countenance, and *then* come the resplendent, glowing major chords of that unspeakable March. Compared with this, Haydn's "Let there be light" is but the burning of a gas-burner.

We had also a concerto of Chopin's—piano (Mills) and orchestra, in F minor, op. 21 [(1829) "first performance"], which did not interest me.[108] Timm rates it very high. Berlioz's Overture *Carnaval romain,* pretty and odd, and Wagner's *Rienzi* Overture.♫ This is worth hearing again. It is elaborate, vigorous, and melodious. But I think it includes a little clap-trap, and it is spotty, broken up into little bits of light and shadow.

December 22. . . . [after a strenuous spell of Sanitary Commission work in both New York and Washington] Last night with Ellie at the Philharmonic concert. Mozart's Symphony, No. 5 ["in D," K. 45?]. Not very strong except its little gem of a third movement. Mendelssohn's "Fingal's Cave" Overture and a rather dreary violin concerto of Beethoven's, op. 61 [(1806) played by Edward Mollenhauer].[109] The [Mendelssohn] overture is very great, quite on a level, I think, with the best things in Beethoven's "Pastoral" Symphony. The first movement of that symphony and this overture are, I think, the greatest of what we commonly call "descriptive" composition. The adjective is erroneous unless it is meant to indicate mere base imitative music. This overture is not descriptive. It merely suggests the same emotions that are pro-

---

[108] Nor, apparently, did Mills's solo, Henselt's outmoded Variations, op. 1, on Donizetti's *Le philtre (L'elisir d'amore);* or the other soloist, Miss Abby Fay, a favorite Boston soprano, who—to Hagen's intense disapproval—sang a recitative and cavatina from *La sonnambula* and a cavatina from Pacini's opera *La niobe* (Naples 1826). If Pacini's obsolete cavatina had to be heard, railed Hagen, let it, at least, be performed with whatever life and spirit it contained, not the "dry and pupil-like singing of the notes, as Miss Abby Fay gave us. . . . Where there is no manifestation of soul, of life or intelligence, there may be utterances of tones . . . and yet there is no singing." And the Boston favorite, Miss Fay, had "not yet learned how to sing" (*Review and World,* November 23, 1861, p. 279).

[109] Its first complete performance in New York; Vieuxtemps, as we know, had played the first movement in 1858. The Directors, at their meeting on November 16, 1861, resolved to persuade an unwilling Mollenhauer to play the entire concerto because the Mozart Symphony was "very short" (Philharmonic Archives). The concerto created little notice. Hagen commented that it required "a very intellectual, spirited, not to say bold, rendering in order to captivate the interest of the listener to the end." Joachim had commanded the "granitic" quality required; Mollenhauer's "technical ability was, of course, tested on the occasion to his entire credit" (*Review and World,* January 4, 1862, p. 3). The other soloist was Pietro Centemeri, the splendid baritone of St. Stephen's, who sang an *Aria da chiesa* by the Italian composer Alessandro Stradella (1639–1682), accompanied by the Alexandre Organ, and a *romanza* by Donizetti, with horn *obbligato* played by Henry Schmitz. Additionally, Eisfeld conducted Liszt's *Les Préludes.*

duced by certain material phenomena; and that is all music can do or ought to attempt in the descriptive way. It seems to me to do this with wonderful intimacy and power. I know how vague and subtle all musical criticism must be,[110] from the impossibility of subjecting its aesthetics to any tangible test on which any two people can be sure they agree—how much room there is for mere fancy in any attempt to define the significance of any musical work. But it seems to me that this overture speaks unmistakably of the seashore and the surf and the seabreeze. It is pervaded by the smell of salt water. It somehow suggests the keen wind of Nahant—the monotonous roar of the breakers—their reflux in sparkling bits of broken water among the ridges of rock—the bracing salt air—the loneliness and nakedness of an iron-bound shore. It reminds one of the way he felt when he was last at the seaside, and it does this without the smallest attempt at any imitation of rolling surf or whistling wind. It was admirably rendered tonight, all the lights and shadows perfectly brought out, and without exaggeration.

～～～

There was no further opportunity for musical solace during that bleak Christmas season—at least, not for Strong, who for once did not record a family celebration. On New Year's Eve he dejectedly wrote in his private journal: "Poor old 1861 just going. It has been a gloomy year of trouble and disaster. I should be glad of its departure were it not that 1862 is likely to be no better."

---

[110]Vague, perhaps, but not necessarily subtle. The "Hebrides" Overture, wrote the *Albion* critic (December 29, 1861, p. 619) was correctly performed but without any feeling for the composer. The work represents "a restless striving after a poetic impression (Mendelssohn went to the Hebrides, remember?) and needs the deliberation of a genial elocutionist, not the mechanical grind of a mere timist." The critic had never heard the work given with greater precision, nor with less effect. Beethoven's Violin Concerto, he wrote, was superbly played by Mollenhauer and the orchestra. The cadenza—"one of the most difficult to play and unpleasant to hear"—was a marvel of what the Germans call *technik*. And in Liszt's tone poem, "the weight Mr. Eisfeld gave to certain interior and subsidiary rhythms of the work was most excruciating."

OBBLIGATO: 1861

Everything in musical circles has received a sudden shock. . . . The war feeling is dominant, and no one has heart for music as amusement.

New-York Evening Post
May 15, 1861

People must be amused, and no possible number of Bull Run defeats can repress the natural craving of the Yankee mind for a little fun.

Wilkes' Spirit of the Times
October 31, 1861

DISREGARDING THE INEVITABLE curtailment of music activity as war loomed closer, on January 5, 1861, C. Jerome Hopkins made his debut as *Timothy Trill* in the *New York Dispatch* with a blistering indictment of New York's musical institutions and the "inconsistencies with which this great, famous city abounds, especially in the details of its much-boasted artistic advantages."

Assuming William Henry Fry's all-but-discarded mantle as the *enfant terrible* of the New York musical press—but sporting a vividness all his own—*Trill* painted a sorry picture of the local music scene. To begin with, he deplored the absence of concerts aiming to encourage "a healthy musical taste among the masses." In Germany, and particularly in Austria, he wrote, excellent open air concerts were given free to the public two to six times a week, and operas and orchestra concerts of good quality could be heard for an admission price of twelve cents. Their closest approximations in New York were "the nuisance known as street-organs" and the shoddy offerings at the infamous "concert saloons"—Canterbury Hall, the Gaieties, the Melodeon, etc.—hardly suitable places to take one's sister, wife, or sweetheart.

As to the more "expensive musical luxuries of our city," *Trill* vehemently rejected Ullman's dictum that opera developed a "'pure taste' in our fashionable youth." Rather, claimed *Trill,* it made "coxcombs" of our young men. Opera, he wrote, "conduces to musical flatulency and encourages superficiality of musical achievements. It dulls the perceptive faculties when anything deeper than a false *roulade* or a steam-whistle sort of a vocal screech is to be appreciated."

Opera had its deleterious effects, too, on our "female youth." At the opera house, contended *Trill,* the "fashionably disgusting old dowagers of society transform many of Nature's sensible and noble-minded female youth into sad specimens of crinolined, animated syllabub, who, being accustomed to make LaGrange or Grisi their ideals of all that is lovely in woman, forthwith set out to imitate them, and boast that if they *can't* make bread or cook a beefsteak, they *can* scream '*grand scenas,*' or sigh soft 'arias' as an offset to their deficiency in the other department." *Trill* (evidently no advocate of women's rights) wondered if these young ladies had an inkling of their "excessive repulsiveness to those individuals they most [sought] to fascinate and please—namely young men! If they *had,* how they would evacuate the parlor and drawing room and rush to the kitchen range and dairy tubs!"

The Philharmonic fared better in *Trill*'s estimation; unlike Fry, he was tolerant of their Germanic orientation, He also praised Eisfeld and his "charming Quartette of conscientious Art-interpreters," whose pioneering and self-sacrificing efforts had introduced New York music lovers to the best in chamber music. *Trill* similarly lauded the Mason/Thomas *soirées* and Bergmann's "miniature Philharmonic" concerts at the Assembly Rooms, but he regretted that a large number of non-German music lovers were deprived of good music because Bergmann persisted in giving his concerts on the forbidden Sabbath.

Of the Harmonic Society, New York's foremost and largest singing group, their efforts, wrote *Trill,* were handicapped by the lack of a regular orchestra and by their fuddy-duddy programing of obsolete choral works, particularly those by Handel. Like Fry and other up-to-the-minute music critics, *Trill* had little tolerance for antique oratorios. "Why do not the Harmonic take a lesson from their former failures and boldly attack modern works?" he demanded. The contemporary English composers Sterndale Bennett, George Alexander Macfarren, Henry Leslie (1822–1896), Michael Costa, and John Farmer (1836–1901), the Europeans Ferdinand Hiller and Ad. Rubenstein [*sic*], and the Americans J. M. Deems (of Baltimore), W. H. Curtiss [*sic*] (of Brooklyn), and the Harmonic Society's own popular and able conductor, the versatile Bristow, could surely "afford enough material to stretch their 'laryngial extensors' for a good while to come. I do not believe in this blind Pagan adoration of old things because they are old," proclaimed *Trill.* "Our fathers were doubtless good in their time, and perhaps better for their *Anno Domini* than we are for ours; but some of these one-ideaed, narrow minded Art-bigots would believe that the chord of the Diminished Seventh resolved on the Tritone, if they thought Handel had said so, and would walk off the end of a yard-arm, plop into the water, if they were only told to do it by their musical Divinity."

As far as programing went, the Mendelssohn Union was more advanced than the Harmonic Society, but "its influence has been sadly contracted," wrote *Trill,* "and it is not to be mentioned with the [Harmonic], as yet, as an instructor of the public." For himself, *Trill* had "little faith in the ultimate healthy influence of a Choral Union whose birth," he asserted, "was in the hotbed of strife and bitterness, and whose very mainspring is the spirit of opposition. If they should add their young life to the old bones of the Harmonic and repent their *secession,* the coalescence must be productive of the most beneficial results."[1]

---

[1] According to the choral conductor and music historian Frédéric Ritter (1834–1891), the Mendelssohn Union had been formed by defectors from the Harmonic Society. "There was no difference

As to individual concerts: "Now and then, the spasmodic artistic throes of some resident teacher results in a concert," wrote *Trill*. Although Carlotta Patti's recent debut (on October 22, 1860) had been hailed as a great success, to *Trill* it was merely "a long-winded succession of inevitable Verdi, sung by Italians with voice enough to raise the roof off an ordinary-sized barn, and *this* condensed into the limited space of Dodworth's Hall! I would as leave be put to bed with a live gong, a dozen well-blown fish horns, and a shouting fire captain exercising his lungs on a speaking trumpet, as to hear Ferri and Susini in such a small room. At this concert the only refreshing change in the programme was William Saar's piano playing and the female singing. There was little variation in the composers' names, from Verdi to Bellini and to other Italians, but 'twas very like the change of diet with that man who had bread and cheese for breakfast, cheese and bread for dinner, and *both together* for supper!"[2]

Nor did audiences escape *Trill's* censure, although, as he admitted, they could hardly be blamed for growing restive at the recent benefit for Harvey Major (at the Academy, December 13, 1860), a "mongrel occasion" at which seventeen pieces had been offered, some more than twenty minutes long. Drowning Mrs. Mozart and Harrison Millard's "charming" duet from *Rigoletto* in an "improvised whispering accompaniment"—and similarly Theodore Thomas's violin solo and S. B. Mills's piano playing—the audience responded more warmly to the military bands. Not, however, from appreciation of Harvey Dodworth's "*delicate scoring,* but because there were 'so many drums,' and there was *such* a noise! Nor," cynically added *Trill*, "do I believe the [band's] red jackets were without their effect."

With the onset of hostilities, theatrical and musical amusements ceased to attract audiences, and theatre after theatre closed its doors. Attendance became barely "tolerable," reported *Wilkes' Spirit of the Times* (May 4, 1861, p. 144), "and the audiences exhibited the utmost restlessness—the drums and fifes which constantly pass the doors calling out on each occasion the major part of the male portion to the sidewalk."[3]

As art for art's sake waned, members of the city's music community more and more frequently joined forces with the regimental bands in performing the patriotic songs that materialized in a deluge of sheet music, dime songsters, and penny broadsides. On January 12, when the Seventh Regiment National Guard Band and Drum Corps, under Bandmaster Grafulla, gave their second concert of "new and classic band music," the assisting artists, accompanied by a "powerful and efficient orchestra" under Theodore Thomas, were Mesdames Colson and Mozart and Messrs. Formes and Stigelli.

---

of aims, only that of activities and conductors," he wrote. Indeed, several members of both societies frequently attended each others' rehearsals, and sometimes even appeared at each other's concerts (Ritter, p. 298).

[2]By no means did Carlotta Patti adhere to the chauvinistic musical diet described by *Trill*. Appearing with the German singers von Berkel, Formes, and Stigelli, and the English pianist Mills in a "Great National Concert" of international scope at the new Irving Hall on January 22 (opened on January 8), Patti and her colleagues offered the first American performance of an aria from Meyerbeer's new opera *Le Pardon de Ploermel* (Paris 1859), plus songs and ensembles by Beethoven, Mozart, Schubert, Flotow, and Verdi, and concluded with "The Star-Spangled Banner," soul-stirringly delivered, as usual, by Formes.

[3]"Drums are the only instruments in vogue just now," asserted the *Albion* (May 11, 1861, p. 223), "and, as the result of their performances may not be judged by the pleasure that they give to the cultivated ear, we shall not presume to criticize them."

On February 21, at Irving Hall, the Germanic *Arion* Society's annual fancy-dress ball presented patriotic tableaux representing "Columbia receiving the homage of all peoples and nations on earth," and, doubtless sardonically, "Miss South Carolina meeting with King Cotton." Two days later at the same hall Harrison Millard presented a "Concert of National Songs and Anthems of All Nations," with the assistance of Mlle. Montmorency (the former Miss Kate Duckworth and future Mlle. Morensi) and Messrs. Simpson, Centemeri, Mills, Aptommas, and Massett, with Bristow conducting a chorus of fifty men's voices accompanied by a full orchestra, Dodworth with his Military and Cornet Bands, and with J. Gaspard Maeder and William McKorkell accompanying at the piano.[4]

Grand as it was, this event was dwarfed by Bristow's giant patriotic Musical Festival at the Academy of Music on May 25, in aid of the Volunteer Defense Fund. The printed program of twenty-two numbers (too many to analyze, complained Fry) was decorated with a Union flag "emblazoned in colors" and the "Dix word of command."[5] The "lovely women" participating in the event—Madame Kazia Lovarny Stoepel (who was making a comeback) and the Misses Hinkley, Brainerd, and Lizzie Parker (erstwhile *prima donna* of the Boston Handel and Haydn Society)—were "dressed with heart-rending taste," wrote Fry; they "swelled their throats like Mocking Birds on the Fourth of July, trying to imitate the distant notes of the bugle playing the 'Star-Spangled Banner,' as was the custom with Southern birds. Stalwart men like Brignoli and Susini, looking like two Italian heroes, declaimed so proudly in their native tongue respecting liberty and country that the audience accepted it as so much English. Indeed, a little gunpowder would hardly have added more to the flamboyant intensities of the occasion." Fry listed the individual contributions of the aforementiond ladies and of Messrs. William Doehler, J. R. Thomas, Aynsley Cook (or Ainsley Cooke), one Busch (a composer from Copenhagen), and G. W. Wooster; also Eben, Mills, Muzio, Beames, Timm, and Bristow. In his review, Fry additionally traced the genealogy of "Yankee Doodle" and his "Maccaroni" (*Tribune,* May 27, 1861).

Yet more impressive was the Grand Military Festival given for the benefit of the Regiment's families by Colonel Louis Blenker's First German Rifle Regiment. Opening on May 17 at the Academy, the featured attractions were Isabella Hinkley, Anna Bishop, Brignoli, the *Arion* and *Teutonia* societies, the former opera orchestra conducted by Muzio, the chorus and band of the Regiment, who performed Charles Fradel's "First German Rifle Regiment March," and a Presentation of the Colors by a Committee of Ladies. The festival was continued at Jones's Wood from May 21 to 23, where the attractions were the New-York *Turner* Association, the *Sängerbund,* the *Turner* Rifles, and again Colonel Blenker and his German Rifle Regiment.

"The pavement in Broadway is battered with the steady tramp of pedestrians keeping step to the martial strains of military bands leading new-fledged warriors to the field of glory; and the possible widows of these same warriors begin to excite attention," wrote the *Albion* on June 1, 1861 (p. 259). "Music—a very handy and willing

---

[4] In May, Harvey Dodworth announced publication of Harrison Millard's patiotic song "Flag of the Free." Concurrently, among the great outpouring of military and patriotic publications, the printing house of Baker and Godwin issued "The Star-Spangled Banner" on 7-by-10½-inch postcards in "illuminated Printing," an item they touted as "the Best Thing Out."

[5] General John A. Dix, an honorary member of the National Hymn Committee, was chairman of the committee for this concert.

servant—has been called upon to do something for them. We have had patriotic Concerts (an excellent one on Saturday of last week under the direction of Mr. George F. Bristow) and Concerts for the benefit of the families of different regiments (like the one given by the German Rifles). In entertainments of this kind the public still continues to take a certain amount of interest; but when the word 'patriotic' is omitted from the bills there is a fearful exhibition of empty benches. And so it happens that no programme is complete now without at least one National song among the pieces, as a substitute for this precious word. The way in which the 'Star Spangled Banner' waves in the musical firmament is certainly a caution to its foes."[6] The *Albion* then proceeded with its scathing condemnation of the National Anthem Committee, quoted in the preceding chapter.

On June 22 the members of the recently disbanded Associated Artists—Isabella Hinkley, Amalia Strakosch, Ettore Barili, Augustino Susini—with the pianist S. B. Mills and the "opera orchestra" under Theodore Thomas, appeared in a "Grand Opera Concert" at the Academy, to assist the Regimental Fund of the elite United States Guard Regiment (the former British Volunteers).

The overarching patriotic effort embraced the sister arts as well. For the benefit of the Patriotic Fund, from June 22 to July 1 the Institute of Fine Arts (625 Broadway) combined an exhibition of "The Reading of the Declaration of Independence" by the American painter, Peter Frederick Rothermel (1817–1895), advertised as "A Picture for the Times," with a series of nightly *soirées musicales* performed by a group of transient musicians from the Paris *Conservatoire.* Both attractions could be enjoyed for the price of a single ticket—twenty-five cents.[7]

Patriotic concerts were also privately given. On June 4, Mrs. C. Mears Burkhardt (Mrs. Charles Burkhardt) gave a recherché concert at her new school (222 Madison Avenue) for the benefit of the New-York Volunteers. If those who crowded the premises, even the stairs, were unable to hear, wrote Hagen (*Review and World,* June 6, 1861, p. 149), at least they "had the satisfaction of seeing some very elegant and excited people, which in some cases was decidedly preferable." At any rate, wrote Hagen, some excellent playing by William Mason and Theodore Thomas compensated for all the singing.

The first wartime Fourth of July was celebrated at the Academy of Music, "by the special invitation of our citizens," with an oration on "The Great Issues Now Before the Country" by the Honorable Edward Everett. The Seventh Regiment Band, recently returned from the front, joined by a choir from the Institution for the Blind, contributed stirring performances of the "Star-Spangled Banner," "My Country, 'tis of Thee," and "The Army Hymn," the last with words by the beloved American poet Oliver Wendell Holmes (1809–1894), set to the tune of "Old Hundred." The entire proceeds of the concert were pledged to the relief of the families of the New-York Volunteers.

At the Palace Gardens the Fourth was celebrated with a magnificent display of

[6] Not least as waved by Madame Bishop, who developed what amounted to a supplementary career singing Wallace and Morris's song "The Flag of Our Union."

[7] "The North," an Arctic canvas by the celebrated American painter Frederick E. Church (1826–1900), was also currently exhibited for the benefit of the Patriotic Fund at the Goupil Galleries (772 Broadway).

fireworks by the Messrs. Edge, a Grand Drill by the Palace Garden Zouaves, songs by "Colonel Fred and the Daughter of the Regiment," and patriotic selections by J. P. Stratton's Military and Serenade Band. Immediately thereafter, the Palace Gardens was pressed into service as the headquarters for Colonel John Cochran's Volunteer Regiment.

Farther afield—among the concerts, benefits, serenades, memorials, lectures, charity bazaars, fairs, publications, panoramas, dioramas, and souvenirs purportedly inspired, or at least motivated, by patriotic sentiments—was a celebration at Clinton Hall of Shakespeare's birthday (performed on April 23, in fact the anniversary of the Bard's death), when the English elocutionist and lecturer J. H. Siddons recited a dubiously relevant selection from Shakespeare's "Warlike Scenes," as well as his own poem "Fight for the Union"; his colleague Charles Maturin additionally delivered Tennyson's "The Charge of the Six Hundred" (*sic*), and Madame Bishop sang "Hail Columbia," "Home, Sweet Home," and, of course, "The Flag of Our Union." At their repeat performance the following night Madame Bishop added Stephen Massett's patriotic song "Our Good Ship Sails Tonight."

On May 4 at Dodworth's Hall a *Soirée musicale et literaire,* featuring "the patriotic verse of American poets," was given by the French actor Edmond Pillet, with the assistance of Robert Goldbeck, who played his "Union March" for piano.

At the Lyceum (720 Broadway), opening on July 25, the popular entertainer R. J. de Cordova recited his poem "The Rebellion and the War" to an evocative background of "dissolving" battle views, portraits of heroes, past and present, and a patriotic musical score, arranged and played on the Alexandre Organ by Charles van Oeckelen.

Throughout the remainder of the year, patriotic concerts, particularly by military bands, continued to dominate the dwindling musical scene: on August 7 the Seventh Regiment Band serenaded Major-General John Ellis Wool as he passed through New York to assume his new command at Fort Monroe. On August 15, postponed from a rainy August 14, the Seventy-ninth New-York Highland Regiment presented a Monster Festival and Pic-nic at Jones's Wood for the benefit of the families of fallen and disabled members of their company; at the same place, on September 5, they held their "Shooting Games" for the same cause.

On October 31 a contingent of German musicians, represented by Mesdames Johannsen and von Berkel and Messrs. Quint, Müller, Reichard, and Weinlich, with one Mathias Keller conducting an orchestra of sixty, gave a "Grand Union Concert" at the Academy of Music, devoted predominantly to Keller's greatly ballyhooed patriotic songs. The following evening an Italian group consisting of Carlotta Patti, her sister Amalia Strakosch, her half brother Ettore Barili, the tenor Alessandro Maccaferri,♪ and a new English pianist, Adam Touhay, with Theodore Thomas conducting, appeared at the Academy for the benefit of the families of the d'Epineuil Zouaves. On November 7, at Irving Hall, an oration was delivered at the presentation of the colors to the Fifty-eighth Regiment of New-York State Volunteers, followed by a Grand Instrumental and Vocal Concert under the direction of Carl Anschütz. On December 7, at the Academy of Music, the Twenty-second Regiment Band, under Frederick B. Helmsmüller, gave a "Grand Military Concert" (offering, in fact, a strictly civilian program for their own benefit), with Johanna Vollandt, a debutante from the Leipzig Conservatory, S. C. Campbell (*né* Cohen), a baritone (the Campbell of Hooley and Campbell's Minstrels), the pianist Robert Goldbeck, four brass and wind soloists, and Carl Bergmann, who conducted the orchestral works on the program.

Not that the regimental band musicians—for all their activity—were thriving. It was reported in the *Tribune* (December 11, 1861) that "at the urgent request of many members of the [Seventh] Regiment, and for the purpose of encouraging the members of the band through the winter months, the Bandmaster [Grafulla] has obtained permission to use the large room in their armory (near Tompkins Market) for a certain number of concerts," the first to be given on December 14.[8] On December 16 they performed for the Union Bazaar (a charity event at the City Assembly Rooms), and again at the Bazaar's closing concert, when R. Storrs Willis's "celebrated National Anthem" (his entry in the great National Hymn contest) was sung by a "powerful chorus."

"Besides the regular musicians attached to the regimental bands," reported the *Evening Post* (July 22, 1861), "a large number of our resident musicians have left, or will leave, for the war. About a dozen churches yesterday were deprived of the services of their organists who had gone on with the 7th, the 71st, the 12th, or the 6th. Mr. G. W. Morgan, the organist of Grace Church, goes with the 8th on Tuesday [July 23].[9] Mr. Millard, the well-known singer, went with the 71st, the band playing, as they marched down Broadway, his air 'Viva l'America.' Mr. Mayer [Samuel D., not Philip], the solo tenor of Trinity Church also departs with the 7th,[10] and various choirs are represented by their singers among the bands of patriots who have hastened to the defense of our country's honor."[11]

On August 14 a solemn requiem was celebrated at St. Bridget's Catholic Church (on Tompkin's Square) for the fallen of the Sixty-ninth Regiment at the battle of Stone Bridge (first Bull Run campaign, July 20–21). With the new St. Bridget's organist, Agricol Paur—phonetically identified in the *Tribune* (August 15, 1861) as Mr. Powers, the leader of the *Liederkranz* Society—presiding at the organ, Mesdames Stephani and Klein and Messrs. Hartmann and Graff, assisted by a splendid choir of twenty-five

---

[8] Early in the year—probably for the same pragmatic purpose—the Seventh Regiment operated a gymnasium on East 8th Street, where the "best of our citizens [might] go to improve their muscles." There was space, besides, for seven hundred seats, permitting public exhibitions of "Concert and Gymnastic" exercises. A concert by the Seventh Regiment Band under Grafulla would be followed by "gymnastic feats [performed to a background of string music] (embodying the most difficult, and at the same time interesting, trials of skill in the development of grace and dignity)" (*Dispatch,* February 9, February 16, 1861).

[9] Morgan soon returned from service—not with the Eighth but the Seventy-first Regiment—slightly wounded in the leg but able to resume his duties at Grace Church, where his absence had been "much felt," wrote *T.W.M.* (*Dwight's,* August 31, 1861, p. 175).

[10] "The Civil War was just beginning," recalled the longtime Trinity organist and choirmaster Arthur H. Messiter in his 1906 history of Trinity Church (p. 87); "Excitement and enthusiasm were running high, and the choir of Trinity Church had to give—or, as it fortunately happened, to lend only—some of its members for service. On the 19th of April [1861] the Seventh Regiment started for Washington, having in its ranks Messrs. Mayer and Congdon [a bass in the Trinity choir]; in two months they had returned in sound condition. Two other men followed a few days later in another organization."

[11] "We hear various rumors about some of our prominent musicians having gone to the wars," wrote Hagen (*Review and World,* May 11, 1861, p. 114). "We know not how much truth there is in the stories, but we wish all who go a lively campaign and a safe return."

singers (including members of the *Liederkranz*), sang Mozart's Grand Requiem Mass "in the best manner possible."

A solemn Mass was held, too, on July 13, at a crowded St. Stephen's Church, for Alessandro Amodio, who, shockingly, had died at sea of yellow fever as he was returning from a singing engagement in Mexico. For this memorial the music was mainly composed by the newly installed St. Stephen's organist Antonio Morra,[12] and impressively sung by Isadora Clark, Pietro Centemeri, Federico Amodio—Alessandro Amodio's brother—and his bereaved colleagues at the opera, among them Susini, Quinto, and Ardavani.

Late in April the music community was further impoverished by the loss of the city's two grand old men of music: the eccentric eighty-year-old composer Anthony Philip Heinrich,♪♫[13] and the pioneering organ builder and peppery composer and organist Peter Erben,♪ who was ninety-two. And in May, Edward G. P. Wilkins, the promising playwright, gifted essayist, and well-liked music and drama critic of the *Herald,* suddenly died of pneumonia.[14]

Amid these somber events, the members of the music and theatre communities strove (with diminishing success) to function with some semblance of normalcy. Early in the year the English showman James M. Nixon, then still in possession of Niblo's, persuaded Professor Anderson, "the Wizard of the North," to put aside his magic wand for a bit and appear on three of Edwin Forrest's off nights—January 22, 24, and 26—in a dramatization of Sir Walter Scott's novel *Rob Roy.* Appearing in this production, given with Sir Henry Bishop's 1818 musical score, were the survivors of the former Lucy Escott and Milner/Cooper English opera companies: the bass/baritone Aynsley Cook, the tenor Brookhouse Bowler, and the contralto Annie Kemp (now Mrs. Bowler). The singers would then form the supporting cast for the following season of English opera—on Forrest's off nights—that indefatigable Madame Anna Bishop had finally succeeded in putting together.[15]

[12] Formerly the organist of St. Patrick's, Morra was now replacing Charles Wels at St. Stephen's. In a general shuffle, Centemeri would henceforth be replaced in the St. Stephen's choir by Ettore Barili ("an especial favorite of Dr. Cummings") reported *T.W.M.* (*Dwight's,* August 31, 1861, p. 175). The choir—in fact a vocal quintet—would henceforth consist, besides Madame Isadora Clark and Barili, of Madame Beyer (contralto), Signor Quinto "(or Herr Quint)" (baritone), and Signor Morra, Sr., the organist's father (basso).

[13] Poverty-stricken in his old age, Heinrich was looked after by friends during the months of his last illness, reported *Dwight's* (May 11, 1861, p. 47).

[14] Besides a number of produced plays and his several years of music and drama criticism for the *Herald,* Wilkins had contributed to *Harper's Weekly Magazine* under the pseudonym of "The Bohemian," and more recently, as *Personne,* he had written "airy and sparkling *feuilletons* for the *Saturday Press*" (*Harper's Weekly,* May 18, 1861, p. 61).

[15] Madame Bishop had been honored on January 18 with a Monster Benefit "Farewell" Concert at Irving Hall, offered by her singing colleagues Frezzolini, von Berkel, Kate Comstock, Quinto, Rudolphsen, Müller, J. R. Thomas, Bowler, and Aynsley Cook; the pianists S. B. Mills, John Nelson Pattison, William Saar, and Augustus T. Hogan; the violinist William Doehler, the cellist Alessandro Biscaccianti, the elocutionist Stephen C. Massett (who recited Tennyson's "The Charge of the Light Brigade"), and W. McKorkell, who played the Alexandre organ. The event concluded with a "grand finale, called 'The Star Spangled Banner.'"

The season, wordily announced Nixon, was planned to satisfy the public's desire for "the time-honored songs, ballads, and melodies incidental to English musical pieces of the olden times," as well as for more recent works, presented in "a style of elegance and with an array of talent such as has not been witnessed in this city for many years." It was Nixon's optimistic plan to "bring out a fresh opera every week." Tickets were fifty cents.

Opening on February 12, Madame Bishop's season had the misfortune to coincide not only with the first *Ballo in maschera* excitement, but also with the onset of Lent. Nor was her opening vehicle, *Linda of Chamouni* [*sic*], a novelty. Madame Bishop's supporting cast, besides the Bowlers and Cook, included the Germans Anetta Caradori, Johanna Ficher, and Joseph Weinlich; also a Miss Kate Fisher, a Mrs. Le Brun, and two unfamiliar male singers, Martin and Gonzalez; Anschütz conducted an orchestra of thirty musicians and—a bone of contention—a shabby chorus of thirty singers who had seen better days.[16]

Madame Bishop's season did not fare well. Although the critics dutifully paid their customary lip service to her miraculously preserved powers, a chorus of complaints arose on the subject of her meager audiences. *Wilkes' Spirit* (February 23, 1861, p. 400) blamed her choice of tired repertory for her poor houses. Her management had made radical mistakes, wrote the critic: "In the first place they should not have rushed into work at the time the Italians were open. Then they should have procured at least one of the new hit Operas in London before they opened—[Wallace's] *Lurline* or [Macfarren's] *Robin Hood* [London 1860]—and have forced it upon the stage as speedily as possible. . . . As it was, the curtain was raised on the first night of the *Linda* merely to a fairly filled house; we will not presume to say with how many 'dead-heads' the paying audience was interlarded. On Thursday the audience was very thinly scattered over the Garden, and on Saturday it was sparse in the extreme."

"There is a prejudice against Anglicized versions of foreign operas," wrote Seymour (*Times,* February 13, 1861), "but why, we are at a loss to explain. In Germany and France all the newest works are given in the natural tongue; only in England and America do we cling to the skirts of the Italians for our singers and our operatic music. The power of emancipation from this musical thralldom has commenced in the first-named country, and England may fairly boast of a good *repertoire* of native music and of singers to interpret it."

Exonerating only Madame Bishop—who of course had never sung more deliciously, or acted more superbly, or dressed more magnificently—Watson blamed the season's failure on the "want of sufficient rehearsals [that] was very evident in the slovenly execution of the antediluvian and mastodonic chorus and the somewhat impromptu band" (*Leslie's,* February 23, 1861, p. 211). The second performance of *Linda*

---

[16] Although the *Times* (February 13, 1861) pronounced the chorus "sufficiently powerful" and the *Spirit* (February 23, 1861, p. 400) thought them "fair" in sound if not in appearance, the *Dispatch* (February 16, 1861), after according Madame Bishop the required Madame-Bishop compliments on her eternal youthfulness, physical and vocal, launched into a tirade against the company, the production, and particularly the chorus—acceptable in voice, perhaps, but "terribly witch-like in look and manner. Has the stage manager of opera no power to make singing women dress themselves in cleanly and otherwise befitting garments, and wash their hands and faces?" he demanded.

was, however, greatly improved, and Watson hoped for a continuing improvement that would "meet with so liberal an encouragement from the public that an experiment [a euphemism for failure] may be turned into a success."[17]

"Perceiving the necessity of getting up something in which she had never appeared before," wrote the *Dispatch* (February 23, 1861), "after wisely dropping the hackneyed opera of *Linda*," Madame Bishop (perhaps rashly) chose for her second attraction a role she had never before performed—Arline in Balfe's even more hackneyed *The Bohemian Girl*. "With two weeks' hurried study of the music and one or two hasty rehearsals she contrived to accord it that grace, force, finish, and fervor for which she has made herself eminent, dramatically as well as musically," wrote Burkhardt. For this production David Miranda was added to the company as Thaddeus; Aynsley Cook was the Devilshoof, Brookhouse Bowler the Florestan, and the mysterious Mr. Gonzalez, a "very intolerable, not to be endured, in fact, Count Arnheim."

The *Albion* critic, evidently no partisan of the star system, took exception to the exaggerated publicity accorded Madame Bishop.[18] "If we pinned our faith to the advertisements," he wrote (February 23, 1861, p. 91), "she is not only the prima donna, but everything else connected with the company, for, with the exception of her name, none other is mentioned [a slight overstatement]. Is not this a little old-fashioned? Do people go for the purpose of hearing Madame Bishop only, or with the intention of listening to a work that is to be justly interpreted in all its parts? It seems to us that New York is rather too large a place for entertaining the vain delusion that one artist can draw."

For her third attraction Madame Bishop chose another overripe chestnut, an English version of *La sonnambula,* to whose first performance she attracted, according to the pro-Bishop *Dispatch* (March 2, 1861), "a critical and well-filled house and [to] the second . . . a crowd." Notwithstanding these claims, and despite her thrilling delivery of "The Flag of Our Union" (incorporated into the opera's finale), and despite her brave plans, which included productions of *The Merry Wives of Windsor, Lurline,* and *Robin Hood,* Madame Bishop's season came to a close after just two more performances—on March 2 of *Fra diavolo* with Henry C. Watson's faded sister Eleanor making her belated debut as Zerlina,[19] following which Madame Bishop, impersonating the Goddess of Liberty, performed "The Flag of Our Union," and on March 4 of *The Bohemian Girl* for Aynsley Cook's—not Madame Bishop's—benefit.

Among the postmortems, the *Albion* deplored the "pitiful condition of vagabondage" to which English opera had been reduced in this country. As an experienced artist, argued the writer, Madame Bishop—given the chance—might very well have es-

---

[17] Following the second performance of *Linda,* the *Evening Post* (February 15, 1861) reported various alterations: "The duet in the second act between the Marquis and Linda is omitted, and in its place Madame Bishop sings her admired song 'Banks of Guadalquivir'♪♫ and the tenor introduces a pleasing ballad. Again, in the last act the baritone introduces Balfe's air 'Light of Other Days,' and for the *finale* to the opera the *prima donna* sings a waltz by Ricci." As an even further attraction, she would soon add "The Flag of Our Union" to every performance.

[18] Not least, *Timothy Trill'*s embarrassingly adulatory column in the *Dispatch* (March 6, 1861), giving a worshipful account of Madame Bishop's astounding global career, but adeptly managing to omit any mention of Bochsa.♪♫

[19] As the *Albion* ungallantly suggested, the debutante had "perhaps, waited too long" to make her debut (March 9, 1861, p. 115).

tablished an opera company capable of performing a few of the many new works now "easily obtainable in England." True, it was rumored that a further season was in the offing, but: "Such things are always stated at the end of an unsuccessful season"; it was what the Americans called "coming down easy." But whether Madame Bishop's company would "ever be resuscitated or not, it [was] clear that the cause of English music [had] received another blow" (*Albion,* March 9, 1861, p. 115).

Burkhardt, baffled at the sudden termination of Madame Bishop's season at Niblo's, solicitously feared for "the future professional movements of that best of *sfogato sopranos*" (*Dispatch,* March 9, 1861). But he reckoned without Madame Bishop's boundless gumption, for, on April 19, at the Academy of Music, no less, the intrepid lady awarded herself the Grand Complimentary Benefit that had been denied her at Niblo's—an extravaganza consisting of a full performance, with her Niblo's company, of *The Bohemian Girl,* conducted by Anschütz; her Grand Scena in costume from *Tancredi;* and, as an extra attraction, the final performance in the United States of the great tightrope dancer Blondin, "the Hero of Niagara," who was returning to Europe. Parquet tickets were one dollar, amphitheatre twenty-five cents.

Less than a month later, on May 13, Madame Bishop launched a well-publicized series of nightly "chamber" (or "drawing-room") concerts at the newly renovated Stuyvesant Institute, with a company that included the singers Kate Comstock, George Crozier, and J. R. Thomas, the youthful concertinist Master Charles Sedgwick, and his father Alfred, who played both the concertina and the piano and who acted as musical director and conductor for the series. On May 25, Madame Bishop added to her cast the latest juvenile pianistic sensation, little Willie Barnesmore Pape (1850–?), "pronounced by Thalberg 'the Greatest Musical Wonder in the World.'" Her programs, comprising "national, patriotic, and home ballads, will draw good audiences if any entertainment can do so at this time," gloomily predicted the *Herald* (May 13, 1861). Admissions ranged from twenty-five to fifty cents.

Although concert-giving suffered a drastic decline in 1861, not all musical activity ceased. The established institutions—the Philharmonic, the Mason/Thomas concerts, and, albeit with less than their former frequency, the Harmonic Society and the Mendelssohn Union—persisted. At Irving Hall, on January 10, 1861, Bristow conducted the Harmonic Society in a Grand Concert for the benefit of the St. John's Chapel Industrial School. Performed by Maria Brainerd and Messrs. G. W. Haselwood (or Hazelwood), Eben, Wooster, and Beames, the program consisted of gems from the operas and Félicien David's *The Desert.*

Of greater immediate interest, on January 29, and again on February 28, the Harmonic Society, under Bristow's direction, at last performed his long-awaited new oratorio, *Praise to God.* Accompanied by an orchestra doubtless recruited from the Philharmonic, the solos were sung by Mrs. Jameson, Maria Brainerd, Haselwood, and J. R. Thomas.

"The production of a work of American art at a time when politics and the clash of contending parties magnetize the public is not fortunate for the artist," wrote William Henry Fry (*Tribune,* February 26, 1861). Nor, in Fry's opinion, was Bristow's composition a particularly fortunate example of native art. Lacking "scenery, dress, decoration, and histrionic beauty," wrote Fry, a work "restricted to its poetry" suffered a disadvantage in creating "effects." Bristow had set his lengthy work entirely to the text of the Protestant Episcopal *Te Deum,* whose words "are distinguished for want of coloring or variety, being in a single strain, with hardly a word admitting music beyond the exultant. Expressing nothing dark, passionate, or erotic," wrote Fry, the result was bound to be monotonous, although he admitted that "despite these radical defects of the subject, Bristow [had] composed a work copious as to detail and large as to scope." Several of its nineteen sections had elicited "hearty encores" from a discriminating audience. Nonetheless, adopting his usual schoolmarmish attitude toward Bristow, Fry could not resist pointing out, among the work's many faults, that in the soprano solo, "where [the word] 'heaven' is essayed, it should have been emphasized by a change to the major from the minor mode."

At least, the "style of the music is modern," granted Fry; "the accompaniments partake of the Spirit of Mendelssohn and Spohr without being copies of any school." And in general: "The whole work will compare favorably with the classics, beside being free from old-fashioned crudities."

But to that other fervent modernist, Hagen—although he agreed that the work was boundlessly monotonous, and in any case not an oratorio—the score was by no means modern. It belonged, he wrote, to "a past period of our art: Bristow's motives, his modulations, his whole treatment indicate this." It was lacking, too, in "a large style, great ideas, power." Bristow had been "willingly guided by the hand of Mendelssohn, for instance, without even making an attempt to move independently." Although Bristow's music was smoothly and expertly wrought, it contained nothing original, nothing exciting, no "stirring discords" (*Review and World,* March 2, 1861, p. 51).

And although the *Albion* agreed that Bristow's work was no oratorio (a form the critic defined as "a sacred drama, having action, or, at least, a dramatic contrast of emotions"), in his opinion, Bristow merited a higher position in American Art than he enjoyed: He was, claimed the critic, the best composer the country had produced, and indeed the only one (except Fry) whose works had been performed and praised by Jullien.

The writer deplored the level to which sacred music had sunk in America. "There is probably no country in the civilized world where sacred music occupies so low a station as it does here. If we go into the Churches we hear frivolous music sung by a quartette of voices [the current fad in church choirs],[20] accompanied by an organist who would be rapturously appreciated in a lager beer cellar. . . . If we go into the Concert room we hear, once a year, the 'Messiah,' and semi-occasionally a Cantata performed in a rudimental manner by a small number of ladies who are no doubt highly respectable and delightful companions, but hardly first-class artists, even in a choral point of view."

It was obvious that Bristow had regarded the creation of this work as "a matter

---

[20] In the *Dispatch* (April 6, 1861), *Timothy Trill* mercilessly dissected the church choir situation, especially the Quartet Choir, which, unless flawless, was downright unendurable. "Away," he cried, "with those pretentious, semi-barbarian imitations of Church Quartets, away with conceited young minxes who consider themselves Madame Bodsteins and Miss Gellies, merely because they have given a concert or two, and who valiantly pit their lilliputian artistic claims against the moral sense of duty of Music Committees and Rectors." Abandoning his alias, Hopkins gave at least three public readings at Clinton Hall of his "humorous dissertation" on church choirs and church music in general (*Tribune,* May 15, 1861).

of love rather than prospective profit"; his "oratorio" testified to his devotion to the school it represented. But despite Bristow's "fresh and original, singularly unborrowed ideas, his manner of conveying them [was] identical with that adopted a century ago." And while the critic found nothing wrong with this method, it was nonetheless true that "in the present day, when Art is moving forward with giant stride, it is at least curious to come across a work that ignores progress and boldly swears by the models of the past."

Notwithstanding his reservations, the writer concluded that Bristow's oratorio was "the best work of its kind that we have heard or seen, after the great masters. It does not try to get away from Handel, but, on the contrary, draws closer to him in every great emergency. Judged, then, by the Handelian standard, Mr. Bristow's 'Praise to God' deserves to rank as a great production" (*Albion,* March 2, 1861, p. 103).

The Harmonic Society crowned their year of predominantly patriotic efforts with their annual *Messiah* at Christmas, this time scaled down to Irving Hall, with Maria Brainerd, Madame Kazia Lovarny Stoepel, and Messrs. G. F. Ilsley and J. R. Thomas[21] singing the solos, Harvey Dodworth playing the trumpet obbligato, C. W. Beames presiding at the piano, and George Frederick Bristow conducting a "powerful Orchestra."[22]

Reviewing the performance, Fry suggested—because so little of the antiquated *Messiah* was of contemporary interest—that it should be blended into a potpourri with works by Haydn, Mendelssohn, Spohr, Costa, and others. "Why the public should be dragged into the tooty-tooty violinism of Handel and the meanest and stupidest form for vocal music, the fugue, by the hour, is not clear. In England, where the worship of old bones is part of the rubric, it does answer—but for a young country with genius, the antique opiate is an overdose" (indignantly cited in *Dwight's,* January 4, 1862, p. 319).

Without wishing to "enter into any controversy with the editor of *Dwight's Musical Journal,*" Fry continued the argument in the *Tribune* (January 13, 1862): With the exception of the *Hallelujah Chorus* and "He was despised," needled Fry, "pretty much every other piece, we take it, must be a moldy bore to ears educated to the refinements of logical musical form, of pure and grand statement of vocal method, of vocal declamatory style, of musical rhythm integrated with, and born of, regular and flexible poetical measures and not dreary prose, taken higgledy-piggledy, without connection, progress, climax, and culmination—the whole drowned in dreariest fugues, the fossils of an early age, when Apollo's rays had not produced the highest forms of grace and beauty."

The Mendelssohn Union made even less of a showing in 1861. On January 8, a "select chorus" from the Union, conducted by George W. Morgan and accompanied by William Berge, had assisted at the delayed opening of Irving Hall,[23] a concert by

---

[21] J. R. Thomas and Gustavus Geary also jointly advertised their availability on Christmas morning to "engage with a choir, either separately or together."

[22] For the mandatory patriotic offering, they sang Bristow's new National Hymn, "Keep Step to the Music of the Union," published by Harvey Dodworth.

[23] The Grand Opening of Irving Hall, originally planned for December 18, 1860, had to be postponed when the touring Associated Artists, announced to appear, were unable to return to New York in time. Once opened, as we know, on January 8, Irving Hall supplanted both Dodworth's and Niblo's Saloon as New York's favorite concert-giving place.

Mary Hawley. Also assisting were George Simpson, Charles Werneke, Henri Appy, and a piano- and organ-playing Mr. Beale from London. The Mendelssohn Union subsequently appeared at the City Assembly Rooms on April 6 in their unstaged performance of William Vincent Wallace's opera *Lurline*. The *Evening Post* (April 8, 1861) praised Mrs. Reese and Dr. Guilmette, who sang the leading roles; also Morgan, who directed, Berge, who accompanied, and principally the enterprising Union for bringing out a fresh work instead of "adhering so closely to the oratorio music, which is excellent in itself but is never popular with a New York public." But Watson—Wallace's faithful friend—although aware of the careful preparation by the "choral department," found the principal performers to be "by no means equal to the tasks allotted to them" (*Leslie's,* April 20, 1861, p. 339).

That the Mendelssohn Union was not flourishing is further indicated by the brochure distributed at this performance, announcing a reduction in ticket prices for their forthcoming season. But by October, with no further performances, their eighth season consisted solely of private weekly readings of "Oratorios, Operas, and Masses."

Conversely, on January 22, a group of professional and amateur singers who had been meeting privately to practice madrigals and glees, gave a public concert of high quality at Dodworth's Hall, in compliment to a member of the group, William H. Walter, organist of Trinity Chapel. A "great treat," wrote a "trusted correspondent" of the *Dispatch* (obviously Hopkins): "Never before, we venture to say, has [better] part-singing been heard in this city." Indeed, particularly with their scrupulously true *a cappella* singing, they "put to the blush" most of the local singing societies, except, perhaps the *Arion*. The highly praised performers were Mrs. Jameson, Miss Hawley, Dr. Guilmette, and the Messrs. Hall and J. A. Johnson; "piano quartets" were rendered by Messrs. Connolly, During, Jameson, and Walter himself.

The event had been highly successful too "in a pecuniary point of view," continued the reporter, "*malgré* the discouraging apathy of the Reverends, the clergy of Trinity Parish, not one of whom so much as purchased a ticket, though nearly all were present at the concert (thanks to the 'complimentaries'), and this, notwithstanding the fact that Mr. Walter has been in Trinity Parish and a *communicant of the Church* for twelve years. Something," he added, "which can be said of so few church organists, alas" (*Dispatch,* February 2, 1861).

So successful was this concert that it was repeated on February 1 at Dodworth's, this time to honor Mrs. Jameson, at that time a solo singer at Dr. Cheever's Church of the Puritans. But such efforts were few and far between. Except for the Philharmonic, lamented —t— (*Dwight's,* February 16, 1861, p. 375), "there has rarely been such a dearth of musical matter to record in our good city as there is this winter." And, even worse, the few events that did take place were "hardly advertised, and the givers thereof [being] very chary with their favors to the press, few persons knew of them" (meaning that without paid-for advertisements and free tickets, few critics reviewed them).

In January the brotherly colleagues Anschütz and Bergmann announced their joint conductorship of three distinctive symphonic/choral concerts of old and new music at the increasingly popular Irving Hall—on January 24, March 28, and April 18—to be performed by the *Arion* Society and an orchestra of "fifty chosen artists" from the Philharmonic. "For a concert of Philharmonic proportions," approvingly commented the *Times* (January 21), their subscription price of $1.50 for the complete series (reserved seat included) "is surely cheap enough."

At their first concert Bergmann conducted Beethoven's Fourth Symphony, Liszt's *Les Préludes,* and the first American performance of Meyerbeer's "Schiller March," a work composed in 1859 for the Schiller Centenary Celebrations in Europe. Under Anschütz's direction the *Arion* sang two songs by Franz Abt; also Julius Rietz's *Altdeutscher Schlachtgesang* (translated as "Warrior's Song"); "Rolland's Rock," a ballad by Reissiger; and—another first performance—Schumann's Festival Overture on the *Rheinweinlied* for tenor, chorus, and orchestra, op. 123 (Düsseldorf 1853). Additionally, Louis Schreiber brilliantly played his new *Capriccio fantastique* for *cornet-à-pistons* and orchestra.

A splendid concert, reported Seymour (*Times,* January 26, 1861), but, unfortunately, heard by only the few brave souls who had defied sleet and blizzard to be present. The orchestra, he wrote, was "superb," and the *Arion,* perhaps the best vocal association in New York, had performed with great spirit, seemingly undismayed by the dreadful weather or the meager attendance.[24] Except for the Meyerbeer March, which he considered unworthy of a place on this fine program, Seymour urged that the concert be repeated for the benefit of those who had been unlucky enough to miss it. This transpired at Irving Hall on February 3.

For their second program, about twenty members of the Ladies' Chorus of the New-York *Singakademie* joined forces with the gentlemen of the *Arion*[25] in the Pilgrims' March and Chorus from *Tannhäuser.* Bergmann conducted the orchestra in Schumann's Fourth Symphony,[26] Liszt's "Goethe March" *(Festmarsch zur Goethejubiläumsfeier)* (1849, 1857) (Searle 115), a first local performance and according to —t— "the least enjoyable number of the programme," and the Overture to *Die Zauberflöte.* Noll, the concertmaster for the series, gave an inadmissably rough performance of the Mendelssohn Violin Concerto; Henry Mollenhauer more agreeably played two movements of an unfamiliar cello concerto by Georg Goltermann (1824–1898); and the *Arion*—in addition to the *Tannhäuser* music—beautifully sang Schubert's "Song of the Spirits on the Face of the Waters" *(Gesang der Geister über den Wassern).*

By their final concert —t— unabashedly reversed his earlier statement and declared that "there has been no winter in my recollection when we have had so many really good concerts" (*Dwight's,* May 4, 1861, p. 37). With the Ladies' Chorus again

---

[24] It was rumored, reported Hagen (*Review and World,* February 2, 1861, p. 29) that the first *Arion* concert "did not pecuniarily meet with favor on the part of the public . . . most probably on account of the wretched state of the weather. Whether the concert was successful or not, we can not say," spitefully added Hagen, "not having received an invitation to attend."

[25] Only on rare occasions were women permitted to intrude on the inviolate maleness of the *Arion* Society.

[26] Because Bergmann was the conductor, fumed the *Albion* (April 6, 1861, p. 163), "Schumann—the most stupendous bore that music has ever produced—occupied the place of honor" on the program. "A little of Schumann goes a long way," wrote the critic. "To have him thrust down our throat at every Philharmonic Concert and at every second-rate *soirée* . . . was intolerable." As were Bergmann's repetitive performances, not only of the hated Schumann but of Liszt, Berlioz, and Wagner, all calculated to "provoke, first lockjaw, and second the enquiry, 'is there nothing good in music but what these gentlemen write?'"

assisting and the piano part only adequately played by one W. Barth, a member of the *Arion,* Beethoven's Fantasie for piano, orchestra, and chorus, op. 80 (1808), was heard for the first time in New York.[27] Directed by Anschütz, the *Arion* additionally sang the Drinking Chorus from Halévy's *La Juive,* the first performances of a *Thürmerlied* by the German composer Gustav Rebling (1821–1902), and "The Church," a work for *a cappella* chorus by one Becker, probably Albert Becker (1834–1899), a noted composer of sacred music; Bergmann conducted Mozart's "Jupiter" Symphony, the first American performance of Otto Nicolai's Festival Overture on *Ein' feste Burg* (1844), and Berlioz's thrilling "Rákóczy March."

On a different plane, the *Arion*'s fun-loving progenitor, the *Liederkranz,* held their great pre-Lenten revel at the City Assembly Rooms on February 11. The *Tribune* (February 13, 1861) vividly recreates a scene of unmitigated merrymaking: "It was estimated that [in the course of the evening] there were between 4000 and 5000 people on the floor. In each gallery was stationed a band of fifty musicians, performing alternately marches and music for dancing. The members of the society, as well as their guests, entered into the spirit of the affair with zest, and all went merry as a marriage bell.

"The festival was opened at 9 o'clock in the evening with a grand carnival scene and procession, which passed around the room several times between the crowded lines. An elegant chariot, in which was seated a Teutonic damsel, gorgeously dressed and *en masque,* was drawn at the head of the column by six boys, attired in the most hideous costume that art could devise."

Next came a group of Zouaves, followed by "clowns, harlequins, acrobats, kings, queens, courtiers, pages, señoritas, men on stilts fourteen feet high, boys on skates, giants, dwarfs. . . . Mephistopheles, the Prince of Darkness, followed close upon the heels of two monks who were distributing lithograph copies of a Madonna.

"Nearly one half of the company was in fancy dress and mask, which added greatly to the brilliancy of the scene, and about a quarter more wore masks and dominoes. During the carnival scene gymnastic performances were given, and several grotesque dances took place, the most amusing of which was the one performed by four bonnie boys. Among the musical selections were a pot-pourri from *Der Freischütz, Trinklied* from *Undine,* potpourris from 'The Prophet,' 'Il trovatore,' and the 'Hopp, Hopp, Hopp Galop' from 'Silberman.'

"About 12 o'clock, at the close of the carnival scene, all masks were removed, when dancing was commenced in good earnest, and the quadrille, waltz, schottische, galop, polka, lancers, Varsoviènne, etc., followed in rapid succession. Toward 2 o'clock many sought their carriages, but a large proportion of the company remained and made a night of it."

On August 21 the *Liederkranz* belatedly held their annual "Summernight's" concert and festival at Jones's Wood. "The moonlight was now and then dimmed by a passing cloud," rhapsodized Watson (*Leslie's,* August 31, 1861, p. 243), "but otherwise it was all that a poet could desire. The sound of the German tongue, and the full swell

---

[27] It had been performed in Boston in 1848 by the Handel and Haydn Society, with the orchestra of the Musical Fund Society and with the English singer/pianist/composer John Liptrot Hatton² at the piano.

of German melodies, gave the East River a Rhenish appearance, and it only wanted some old ruined towers on lofty rocks to convert New York into *Das Vaterland*." The vivacious *Liederkranz* Society announced another concert and ball for November 28, again at the Assembly Rooms.

On February 5, at Dodworth's Hall, Mason/Thomas gave the delayed third concert of their sixth season, with Frederick Bergner appearing in Carl Bergmann's place for the first time. He "filled his post," wrote —t—, "in a manner which made it impossible for anyone to regret the change" (*Dwight's,* February 16, 1861, p. 375). The program consisted of three chamber works: the first performance in the United States of the String Quartet in E-flat (1814) by Luigi Cherubini♪♫[28] (more interesting than pleasing, wrote —t—), Schubert's Trio in E-flat, for piano, violin, and cello, op. 100, and Schumann's String Quartet in A minor, op. 41, no. 1 (1842). To —t— the Schumann quartet was like "an old beloved friend, ever fresh in beauty and originality, and always welcome"; Hagen agreed, even if "that fluency of melody which Schubert could command was not given to [Schumann], his enthusiastic admirer and . . . faithful restorer."

At their following concert (the fourth of the series), performed on February 26 at a crowded Dodworth's Hall,[29] Mason, Thomas, and Bergner played Schumann's Piano Trio in G minor, op 110 (1851); Bergner performed a *Morceau de Salon,* a bit of virtuosic fluff by the Austrian cellist and composer Josef Stransky (1810–1890); Mason played his *Deux Rêveries—Au Matin* and *Au Soir*—and introduced his Chopinesque *Valse-caprice;*[30] and the program ended with Beethoven's First Razoumovsky Quartet, op. 59.

The Schumann trio, wrote Seymour (*Times,* February 28, 1861), was even "more barren than the ordinary run of Schumann's ambitious nothings," although its treatment was ingenious: "Every phrase is nursed, and coaxed, and wheedled, and bullied into every possible position that mechanical skill can give it on the staff." The work might probably make sense to a musician scrutinizing the score, he wrote, but "to the mere listener it is a dreary business."

"After Schumann's trio," he wrote, "anything would be cheerful, and thus the graceful gambols of the violoncello in the hands of Mr. Bergner created a positive *furore.* . . . [Stransky's] piece was a most pleasing fantasie and was charmingly rendered."[31]

But in Hagen's opinion, Schumann's trio was one of his "very best compositions," possessing "all that humor . . . and that originality, those fine traits of genius, that beautiful blending of the music given to the three instruments, and especially that nat-

[28] One of his six quartets, not three, as various New York musical journalists misinformed their readers.

[29] So crowded that many had to stand throughout the performance.

[30] Encored with his *Danse rustique.* "Mr. Mason is very happy in his piano-compositions," wrote —t—; "they are always attractive and of infinitely more sterling value than most works of our young composers, which," he added, "unfortunately, is not saying much, after all" (*Dwight's,* March 9, 1861, p. 399).

[31] Not so, wrote —t— *(ibid.).* Permissible at a miscellaneous concert, perhaps, but not at an event where none but the most elevated music was to be expected.

uralness of conception and freshness of idea" typifying the works belonging to Schumann's first period as an instrumental composer[32] (*Review and World,* March 2, 1861, p. 51).

At their fifth *soirée,* assisted by the Philharmonic violinist Augustus Besig, they presented, for the first time in America, Mendelssohn's posthumous String Quintet in B-flat, op. 87 (1849); Mason repeated Beethoven's "Moonlight" Sonata, op. 27, no. 2;[33] with Theodore Thomas he played Raff's "chaotic" Sonata for violin and piano, op. 73, following which the program "refreshingly" closed with Mozart's String Quartet in C, (K. 465, no. 6 of the Haydn set).

Although the *Albion* critic lauded Mason/Thomas for having, "during their brief career . . . given us more new and curious works, in addition to those of standard excellence, than have ever been produced in this city by all the other classicists put together," he rebelled mightily, as usual, against the unfamiliar works on the program. Mendelssohn's quintet, he wrote, was more curious than pleasing. Having been put aside by Mendelssohn as "unsatisfactory to himself," after his death it had been "fished out by his literary executors and published." Like most posthumous works, wrote the critic, the quintet was "more remarkable for skill of treatment than originality of idea" (*Albion,* March 30, 1861, p. 151).

Turning his attention to Raff, the critic wrote: "Mr. Raff slashes with his pen, right and left. Fragments of melody, groups of disconsolate chords, whole battalions of passages not one whit better than finger exercises, a broken and defeated army of rhythms—these are the materials he has tumbled together, and in a way which, it must be confessed, is not without its wild picturesque effectiveness." Raff's "Grand Sonata," he wrote, would more appropriately have been named "War Dance."

At the sixth and final Mason/Thomas concert of their sixth season, judged to be the best they had ever given, they performed Beethoven's String Quartet, the "Harp," op. 74; Thomas masterfully played the legendary "Devil's Trill" Sonata by Giuseppe Tartini (1692–1770) for the first time in America,[34] and with Mason, the program closed with Schumann's Piano Quartet, op. 47.

By November, when George Templeton Strong attended the first concert of the seventh Mason/Thomas season (see GTS: 1861), the war had taken its toll of the critical population. With —t— and *Trovator* safe in Europe since midsummer, for the remainder of the year *Dwight's* New York correspondence dwindled to the barest of minimums; and because the New York daily papers had little space to spare for anything except war news, the first two concerts of Mason/Thomas's seventh series were advertised, but sparsely reviewed.

Their well-attended opening program, at Dodworth's Hall on Novemmber 5, as we know, consisted of Mozart's G-major String Quartet (K. 387); Schumann's String

---

[32] Only a moderate Schumann fancier, —t— found the work "very difficult to understand." It was "acknowledged to be one of [Schumann's] weakest compositions of the kind," he wrote *(ibid.).*

[33] A "charming" work, wrote Seymour (*Times,* March 28, 1861), played by Mason with "much delicacy." Seymour was "glad to perceive among our best artists a growing disposition to restore these delightful compositions to their proper place in the concert-room."

[34] Performed in a manner to satisfy even those who had heard it played by Joseph Joachim, magisterially wrote —t— (*Dwight's,* May 11, 1861, p. 47).

Quartet, op. 41, no. 2; Beethoven's Piano Sonata in E-flat, op. 31, no. 3; and Schubert's *Rondo brillant,* op. 70, for violin and piano.

At their even better attended second "classical *soirée,*"[35] at Dodworth's on December 3, they played a Haydn String Quartet in G; Beethoven's "Razoumovsky" Quartet, op. 59, no. 2; an unfamiliar Trio for strings and piano in B-flat minor, op. 5, by Robert Volkmann;♪[36] and, for Mason's "conscientiously played" solo, Schumann's three *Romanzen* for piano, op. 28 (1839).

From January to mid-April the self-celebrating composer/pianist Gustav Satter indulged his egocentricity with an extraordinary series of concerts at Dodworth's Hall, principally devoted to his own compositions and transcriptions.[37] At the first event—reviewed but not dated[38] in the *Musical Review and World* of February 2, 1861 (p. 28)—Satter, with S. B. Mills at a second Steinway, played two original works, an "Overture" and a *Tarantelle de concert,* then, following a fine performance with Theodore Thomas of Beethoven's "Kreutzer" Sonata, Satter played his pyrotechnic *Illustration* of *La Juive* and his Grand Paraphrase on Beethoven's incidental music, op. 113 (1811), for Kotzebue's play *The Ruins of Athens.* The other assisting artist, Mrs. Mozart, wrote Hagen, added "to a fine soprano a good deal of execution" in songs by one of the Fescas and Charles E. Horn and an aria by Donizetti.

At his second *soirée,* on February 19, Satter repeated, "by request," his paraphrase on *La Juive;* he played Beethoven's "Moonlight" Sonata "with most wondrous execution, and, for the most part, exquisite taste," wrote —t— (*Dwight's,* March 2, 1861, p. 391), also two groups of solo pieces including a "Song Without Words" by Mendelssohn, Satter's transcription of the Minuet movement from a Mozart Symphony in E-flat (designated as no. 6), a Nocturne by Chopin, Liszt's Paraphrase on the *Lucia Sextet,*[39] William Mason's "Cradle Song," Gottschalk's recently published mazurka, *Printemps d'Amour,* op. 40 (1855),[40] and, to complete the program, an improvisation on themes suggested by the audience—from *Ernani, Il trovatore,* and *Lucrezia Borgia.* This time the assisting artists were Aptommas and, substituting for Stigelli, one G. C. Rexford, purportedly a debutant bass singer (formerly heard at Palace Gardens), who detracted from his good voice with his amateurish "airs and gestures."

[35] Signifying, wrote Hagen, that "the taste for good music has spread in this city, in spite of the very unfavorable times. . . . Nay, people seemed to relish the music more than usual, being anxious to forget, in the harmonious strains of our best masters, the discords and troubles of the present times" (*Review and World,* December 7, 1861, p. 291).

[36] Although an essentially modern work, wrote Hagen (*ibid.*), Volkmann's Trio contained "plenty of recitativos, tremolos, *sforzandos,* etc.," but artisically applied and thus acceptable.

[37] Numbering well into the hundreds, as listed by *Timothy Trill* in the *Dispatch* (February 16, 1861).

[38] The casual announcements in the newspapers of Satter's concerts frequently omitted their dates. For example: "Among the forthcoming concerts may be mentioned Mr. Satter's *soirée* at Dodworth's some evening (probably Wednesday) in Easter Week" (*Evening Post,* March 26, 1861).

[39] Hagen had heard it "performed better. . . . Mr. Satter spoiled the effects of the runs for the left hand by a too liberal use of the pedal" (*Review and World,* March 2, 1861, p. 52).

[40] *Printemps d'Amour,* Doyle, D-125; *Piano Works,* IV, 253. In the course of this series Satter performed other new piano works by contemporaries: *Drusenthal,* a "too fantastic" fantasy by Robert Goldbeck, *Sentiment poétique* by John Nelson Pattison, and "Midnight Barcarole" by C. Jerome Hopkins.

Thereafter, apparently beginning on February 28, Satter switched to solo matinées. A wise move, wrote —t— (*Dwight's,* March 9, 1861, p. 399), who reported a greatly increased attendance, mostly of enthusiastic ladies.[41] Not only were assisting artists dispensed with, but, in imitation of Thalberg, the piano was placed in the center of the hall, by which arrangement," caustically observed the *Albion,* "every lady is enabled to fall instantly in love with some portion of the dear artist's person. . . . It is obvious that the most he can do between the pieces is to hold brief conversations with the fairest of the fair, and so rivet the fetters by exciting the jealousy of the others.[42] Mr. Satter, whose retiring disposition is equal to any emergency," sardonically remarked the critic, "behaved with a dignity which would not have been unbecoming" to the greatest Turk on the banks of the Bosphorus.

"Who would not be an artist, especially an unmarried piano player," sighed the writer, as he turned "in sorrow, to a contemplation of the programme." Satter's transcription for piano of the *William Tell* Overture, he wrote, was in all respects inferior to Liszt's, but, admittedly, Beethoven's Piano Sonata in A-flat, op. 26 (1801), had been "played superbly and with a tenderness and delicacy perfectly irreproachable." Satter possessed the fortunate faculty for making old works seem new, a quality the critic applauded, for he was not among the "grumblers" who resented any liberties a true artist might choose to take in "renewing" a traditional piece of music.

This program included "Chopin's Impromptu," loosely identified as "the regular one" (op. 66?), which Satter played "with the velocity of the Presidential Express train"; also *Jeunesse,* a *Mazurka brillante,* op. 78 (1859), by Gottschalk, "a quaint and original thing,"[43] and *La Voix du coeur,* a so-called "*Poesie*" by Satter, endlessly long and a merciless bore. Although the piece offered many beckoning opportunities for coming to a close, the composer had skillfully eluded them, wrote the *Albion.* An interminable mass of incoherence, Satter's *Poesie* consisted, in equal parts, of Introduction and Coda.

To add insult to injury, Satter followed this trial of endurance with his *Tannhäuser* Overture transcription, and yet worse: "At the request of several ladies, the *grand Seigneur* (who charges a dollar for listening to four of his pieces) gave an improvisation on melodies from Italian operas. Nothing can justify this outrage except the provocation," wrote the *Albion* critic, and Satter, a gallant man, displayed his boundless gallantry by complying with the request. Gallantry notwithstanding, the injured critic

[41] "There were hardly twenty gentlemen in the room," wrote —t—.

[42] "Perhaps between the pieces Mr. Satter did as much execution as when he had his hands on the keyboard," ambiguously commented the *Times* (March 4, 1861).

[43] Composed in 1859 during Gottschalk's sojourn in the mountains of Matouba, Guadaloupe, *Jeunesse* (D-78; *Piano Works,* III, 215) was published in New York by Hall in 1860. Its designation as "Tennessee" in —t—'s review of this concert in *Dwight's* (March 16, 1861, p. 407) should settle a twentieth-century difference of opinion over the work's possible dual identity. Robert Stevenson (as cited in Doyle, p. 294) claims that "*Tennessee* handwritten resembles *Jeunesse*" (but fails to say where he had seen the manuscript); Robert Offergeld elaborately conjectures that Gottschalk might have composed "Tennessee" in 1857 and named it for the side-wheeler then plying the West Indian Islands. Offergeld also states that the manuscript was lost, and the piece never published (*Centennial Catalogue,* 263). Later in the series Satter played another Gottschalk piece, "Columbia, *Caprice américain,*" op. 34 (1859) (D-38; *Piano Works,* II, 105), a work freely based on Stephen Foster's "My Old Kentucky Home" (1853).

thought "a law should be passed to make improvisation on the piano a penal offense" (*Albion,* March 9, 1861, p. 115).

Satter's close proximity to his feminine audience had its reverse side as well. At the second, less well attended, matinée, on March 8, reported —t— (*Dwight's,* March 16, 1861, p. 407): "there were sundry very restless spirits, who, by constantly changing their seats, or standing up in the middle of the room, close by the piano, and consulting about the best place, not only annoyed other people but obliged Mr. Satter to make a very inappropriate pause between the movements of [Beethoven's] 'Pastoral' Symphony in Liszt's two-hand arrangement" (1837) (Searle 464/6). In annoyance, he refused a request for an improvisation at the end of the concert, and justifiably, for the program had included, besides the "Pastoral" Symphony, his fantasies on *The Hugue-nots* and *Don Pasquale,* his ballade "Lorely," a Chopin waltz, and Hopkins's "Midnight Barcarole."

Undaunted, Satter, on March 19, again performed "a most remarkable and delicious improvisation," when—together with the violinist Henri Appy and the guitarist Sebastiany (*sic*)—he assisted at an unusual concert at Dodworth's Hall given by the latter-day Maelzel,[²] Charles van Oeckelen—or rather by van Oeckelen's musically gifted Automaton and two others of his uncanny creations, the "Clavier Oboe" and the "Clavier Contrabasso," wind instruments played by means of piano-like keyboards.

The Automaton, a mechanical clarinetist "somewhat larger than life," reported the *Evening Post* (March 20, 1861), "is dressed in the old court costume of three centuries ago. In response to the applause which greets its appearance it bows to the audience, turning its head slowly in doing so. At the proper moment it places the instrument, to all appearances a normal clarionet, to its lips and plays a few musical phrases, lowers the instrument to allow an interlude on the pianoforte, surveys the audience, nods, and soon resumes its playing [of a fantasy on Weber's *Preciosa,* another on *Der Freischütz,* and an *Air Varié* by de Bériot]. The inventor asserts that the music is really made by the clarinet, and in view of this, the manipulation of the fingers of the Automaton is truly astonishing, for scales and rapid chromatic passages are played with unerring facility and correctness." Following the concert, the Automaton's interior arrangements were exhibited to the astounded audience.[44]

If Satter's public performances were extraordinary, hearing him in private was even more special, wrote *Trovator,* who in March visited the pianist at his home. Dominating Satter's large parlor at 154 Waverly Place was the cherished Steinway grand piano that had accompanied him on his tours of North and South America over the past two years. "It was a treat indeed to hear his admirable fantasia on *La Juive,* and his brilliant arrangement of *Ernani* airs, some pieces of his own composition and . . . a wonderfully long and difficult Fugue of Handel's, composed for some festival at Westminster Palace. All these he played from memory," wrote the awestricken critic. "He never uses notes when playing before anyone." And, unlike his colleagues, in order to devote himself totally to "concert-giving and practice," he did not teach (*Dwight's,* March 23, 1861, p. 416).

On April 4, Satter gave his fifth matinée as a benefit for the German Hospital

---

[44] The other two instruments would have "taken" better, wrote the reviewer, had their repertory not consisted of "dry extracts from Spohr."

Fund, an event mostly patronized by German ladies. Assisted on this occasion by John N. Pattison, he played his *Marche triomphale* for two pianos, alone he played his transcription of Weber's Overture to *Oberon* and Liszt's "stupendous arrangement" of Beethoven's Fifth Symphony (1837) (Searle 464/5). As an encore, he sensationally improvised on themes from seven German operas, among them *Martha, Der Freischütz, Don Giovanni,* and *Tannhäuser,* all "interwoven with each other in a very skillful manner," wrote —t— (*Dwight's,* April 20, 1861, p. 21). His other assisting artists were Emma Rowcroft, a new English soprano, and Henri Appy.

The following day, apparently having exceeded saturation point, he gave an anticlimactic, poorly attended final matinée. "The programme was not as interesting as usual," wrote —t— (*ibid.,* p. 22), "as, for the first time in any of these matinées [despite Satter's seemingly limitless repertory], three out of the six pieces played were not new." The repeated works were his *Tannhäuser* transcription, his Fantasy on *Don Pasquale,* and Liszt's Fantasy on the Sextet from *Lucia.* The unfamiliar works were Anton Rubinstein's Prelude and Fugue, op. 53, no. 5, and Brahms's Variations on a Theme of Schumann, op. 9 (1854),[45] both superbly played, as was Chopin's Waltz in A-flat, op. 34.

This event by no means signified Satter's departure. On April 18 at Dodworth's Hall, together with Emma Rowcroft and Charles Morra, a pianist, he assisted at Aptommas's matinée.[46] On May 23 at Dodworth's Hall he assisted at a concert by Mary Gellie, as did Ettore Barili, Louis Schreiber, and Miss Gellie's vocal teacher Émile Millet.

Even to his friends and admirers, Satter was an anomaly, a musical Jekyll and Hyde. Acknowledged an exquisite interpreter of the classics—Mozart, Beethoven, Bach, Schubert—Satter willfully demeaned his art, wrote *Timothy Trill* (*Dispatch,* February 16, 1861) with his cheap, keyboard-thumping paraphrases of orchestral works and opera tunes intended purely to seduce an unworthy, musically uninformed public. True, Satter was following the custom of his time, but he did so "without obtaining any such great popularity among the heathen who usually attend concerts, as did de Meyer, Herz, or Thalberg." Indeed, wrote *Trill,* Satter's "technicality and profundity as a thorough musical scholar have *actually stood in his way.*"

Reviewing Satter's final matinée on March 15, when he had performed—in addition to his solo piano transcription of Mendelssohn's "Scotch" Symphony—a group of minuets by Haydn, Mozart, and Beethoven, his Fantasy on Schubert's "Serenade" and "The Eulogy of Tears," and his paraphrase on *La traviata,* his long-suffering admirer, —t—, at last turned on him for his blatant transgressions against good taste. The *Traviata* paraphrase was "the merest show piece," wrote —t—, "and unworthy of one who is capable of so delighting the critical as Mr. Satter. Anyone claiming the name of artist ought never to lower himself to please even a portion of the public. Even modern Italian Opera airs can be worked up with genius and need not be spoilt by ornaments and variations entirely inappropriate to their character." To "dress up" Schubert's beautiful melodies, or "the sublime chorale *Ein' feste Burg ist unser Gott* [in the *Huguenots* para-

[45] This might have been the first public performance of Brahms's Schumann Variations. According to Margit McCorkle's Brahms catalogue (Munich 1984), the first concert performance of the work was given by Hans von Bülow in Berlin in 1879.

[46] Aptommas and his wife were about to take a class of students on a tour of Europe.

phrase] in a fancy costume of roulades, trills, etc., thus being robbed of all its grandeur and solemnity [was] still less excusable. Such clap-trap performances should be beneath the dignity of one who can interpret the 'Pastoral' and 'Scotch' symphonies, Beethoven's Sonata, op. 28, Chopin's Impromptu, and the like compositions, as Mr. Satter can" (*Dwight's,* March 23, 1861, p. 415).

Perhaps it was not only poor judgment but overweening hubris that accounted for Satter's failure to attain the success he so avidly sought in the United States. With the outbreak of hostilities, he returned to Europe. He would be even less successful when he returned to the United States in 1875.

The timing of Satter's series and its persistence might have signified, too, his desire to scoop Louis Moreau Gottschalk, whose imminent return from the Caribbean was being widely advertised by his new manager, Max Strakosch.[47] Assisted by Carlotta Patti, Gottschalk was announced to give concerts in New York immediately upon his return, which was momentarily expected.[48] Only after long-drawn-out suspense was it announced in late May that Gottschalk, a Southerner by birth (but not by politics), had decided (not unreasonably) against risking the dangerous voyage from Cuba in the present climate of belligerence.[49]

Few other pianists attempted concert-giving in 1861. Madame Louise Abel, after an absence from public playing, returned to perform more admirably than ever at her interesting *soirée musicale* at Chickering Hall on February 21. With Frederick Bergner, she played Chopin's little-known Polonaise for Cello and Piano, op. 3 (1829) and Gounod's too well known *Méditation* on J. S. Bach's C-major Prelude from the *Well-Tempered Clavier*—a work less successful with cello than with violin, commented —t— (*Dwight's,* March 9, 1861, p. 399). Alone, Madame Abel masterfully played the first movement of Beethoven's "Waldstein" Sonata, op. 53 (1804), Chopin's Polonaise in C-sharp minor, op. 26, no. 1 (1834–35), and a charming Étude on a Barcarole by Weber, one of a set of six studies on themes from *Oberon* by Camille Stamaty♩ (misspelled "Stamatz" in *Dwight's*). Bergner scored a great hit with his salon piece by Stransky (repeated at the Mason/Thomas concert a week later) and Centemeri gave his usual distinguished performance in arias from Donizetti's *Maria Padilla* and Meyerbeer's new opera *Le Pardon de Ploermel*.

On April 23 at Dodworth's Hall, Centemeri jointly appeared with Madame Abel's pianistic opposite number, Madame Madeleine Graever-Johnson. Hagen commented most favorably upon her performance with Edward Mollenhauer and Carl Bergmann

---

[47] Upon Maurice Strakosch's departure—following his break with Ullman—for points South and on to Europe with Adelina Patti, his younger brother Max (1834–1892) assumed his managerial interests in the United States.

[48] Gottschalk's advance publicity leaned heavily on his fabled prowess as a Lady-Killer. "We have seen women kiss a piano because his fingers had touched the keys," panted the *Dispatch* (April 13, 1861). And the *Albion* (April 6, 1861, p. 163): "Be it known to men and the vulgar masses in general, that this Gottschalk is a great favourite with the ladies, and when he crieth 'Behold me!' they go and gaze upon him with awe and wonder." All the same, wrote the critic: "Gottschalk is the only pianist now living who has a style of his own. Let us greet with high approval and extreme kindness any man who possesses originality."

[49] And despite the sacrifice of the $800 a month purportedly to be paid him by Strakosch (*Dispatch,* May 4, 1861).

of Beethoven's Trio, op. 1, no. 3; less so upon an étude and a prelude by Chopin, chiefly because of her too copious use of the pedal. Stephen Heller's Caprice for piano, op. 33, on Schubert's song, "The Trout," was, however, excellently played, and, in her inescapable piece by Litolff, this time a "very weak *Caprice de concert* on *Lucrezia Borgia,* she displayed considerable technique." Centemeri, as always, sang well, if on this occasion a little too vigorously for the size of the hall. Madame Clara Brinkerhoff, just back from a trip to Europe, also assisted, singing English, German, and French songs "in their respective tongues with taste and discrimination." Particularly gratifying to Hagen was her "fragment from *Lohengrin,*" which he embraced as "a very acceptable novelty in our concert-room" (*Review and World,* April 27, 1861, p. 99).

On April 29, closely following the onset of hostilities, Sebastian Bach Mills gave his long-postponed concert at Dodworth's Hall. As the *Dispatch* explained (April 27, 1861): "The state of the political world has been such as to materially derange Mr. Mills's first intention." But the concert was worth waiting for. Among the participating artists were Edward Mollenhauer and Bergmann, who with Mrs. Mills played Beethoven's Trio in D (op. 70?); with Schreiber, Matzka, Mosenthal, and others, they supplied the orchestral accompaniment for S. B. Mills's performance of Chopin's E-minor Concerto. Additionally, presumably with Mollenhauer and Bergmann, Mills played an unspecified trio by Schumann; his solos included Henselt's fantasy on *Le Philtre,* and C. Jerome Hopkins's "Wind Demon." The *Dispatch* commended Mills on his bravery in attempting a concert in such times.

Foolhardiness rather than bravery seems to have impelled young Adam Touhay, described in the *Dispatch* as "a young sprig of a John Bull," to seek his fortune as a pianist in wartime America. In reviewing his first (and apparently last) Grand Concert, on September 24, the writer (exuding the unmistakable aura of C. Jerome Hopkins) cruelly dredged up the most egregious musical failures of the past few years—the sorry attempts at singing by Carlo Jacopi♩ and Juliana May♩—with which to compare Touhay's positively criminal violations of the fundamental musical decencies. He had exhibited the audacity to "show us benighted New Yorkers how Weber's *Concertstück* ought to be played (after Mason), [Chopin's] *Fantasie impromtpu* (after Mills), and the *La Juive* Fantasia by Satter (after *Satter*)! Oh! ye Gods!"

Advising Touhay (a graduate of the Leipzig Conservatory) to confront "a *knowledge of his own ignorance,* and then take to five-finger exercises," the writer indignantly concluded: "Such exhibitions are disgraceful in a refined community like ours, but are hardly to be wondered at when the public press draws so little distinction between charlatanism and high art, and systematically permits their great artists to be insulted by lavishing equal encomiums upon the most undoubted and presumptuous upstarts. . . . Bah!"[50]

Solo violinists were even more rare than pianists. Henri Appy, together with John N. Pattison and assisted by George Simpson and Charles Fradel, gave a highly praised

---

[50] The critic (doubtless Hopkins) was probably fuming over the dulcet review Touhay had received in the *Tribune* (September 26, 1861), crediting him with "a fine touch, intrinsic healthful vigor, free from spasm or overaction," and excellent training. In the *Tribune's* opinion, Touhay was "a very valuable addition to our stock of good pianists, who, despite the multiplication of instruments, are yet not numerous."

concert at Chickering's Rooms on April 2. Pattison, described as "a clever exponent of the Leopold de Meyer school," played a Bach fugue and a Mozart *fantasia* and *menuetto,* both without notes, displaying, wrote the *Dispatch* (April 6, 1861), "a musical memory as rare as it was remarkable." The star of the evening, however, was Appy, whom the reviewer named "the best solo violinist now in this country."

On April 6 at Irving Hall, the brilliant young violinist Bruno Wollenhaupt, assisted by his older brother Hermann, Centemeri, and an orchestra conducted by Bergmann, followed his successful Philharmonic debut with a Grand Concert, his first. The program opened with Weber's Overture to *Oberon,* so magnificently conducted by Bergmann as to eclipse any previous performance of it in New York, gushed Watson (an *Oberon* expert since childhood, when he appeared as an elf in its first performance in London in 1826♩). With the orchestra, Bruno Wollenhaupt played Vieuxtemps's Concerto in E, op. 10, in some respects—wrote an overbrimming Watson—even better than had Vieuxtemps himself, thus causing the audience to break out in applause at each pause in the music.[51] With his brother at the piano, Wollenhaupt brilliantly played a dashing Hungarian air by Heinrich Ernst♩ and his own variations on Félicien David's charming *Les Hirondelles;* Centemeri sang arias from Verdi's *Attila* and the—by then—apparently inescapable *Le Pardon de Ploermel;* the concert concluded with a fine performance of Beethoven's Second Symphony (*Leslie's,* April 20, 1861, p. 339).

Undaunted by Gottschalk's non-appearance, Carlotta Patti, apparently under Max Strakosch's guidance, presented a Grand Concert of her own at Dodworth's Hall on May 30. Again largely a family affair, she was assisted by her sister Amalia Strakosch, by Brignoli, and by her Barili half brothers—Ettore, who sang, and Antonio, who "conducted" at the piano.[52]

Despite "a good deal of singing by Madame Strakosch and Messrs. Brignoli and Barili, done in the usual style, which is not always to our taste," wrote Hagen (*Review and World,* June 6, 1861, p. 135), Carlotta Patti's concert was "very successful. Miss Patti sang well, better than we have heard a great many renowned singers do it—better than often her sister [Adelina] did, the present pet of the London public.[53] But what she cannot do, as yet, is—trilling. The trills in the *Bolero* of the *Sicilian Vespers* presented some very curious and vacillating outlines which might be called shaky."[54]

Elizabeth Taylor Greenfield, still billed as "the Black Swan," gave two virtually unadvertised, frustratingly unreviewed, concerts at the Bleecker Buildings (264 Bleecker Street) on March 21 and 27.

In May, two years after her crushing failure at the Academy of Music, Adelina

---

[51] Young Wollenhaupt played this difficult and complicated work—as he did everything else—from memory. "This is as it should be," approved Hagen, "but it is not often done," especially with a very long concerto such as the Vieuxtemps (*Review and World,* April 13, 1861, p. 87). It was a practice that was beginning to catch on.

[52] Carlotta Patti's appearances with the Herrmanns, later in the year, suggest that a kind of rapprochement might have been reached between Ullman and the brothers Strakosch.

[53] Reports were rife of Adelina Patti's senasational triumphs in England.

[54] In September, Carlotta Patti advertised her availability as a teacher of singing, either at the pupil's residence or her own, at 345 West 22nd Street. By November she referred all concert managers' inquiries regarding her availability as a singer—with or without a supporting concert company—to Max Strakosch, at 116 West 11th Street.

Speranza, at last emerged from her protracted illness, and, ostensibly devoured by self-blame, attempted to redeem herself. Giving a concert on May 2 at Irving Hall (postponed from April 16), she was tepidly praised in the *Dispatch* (May 11, 1861). She was assisted by her mother Assunta Speranza, an opera contralto of purported reputation in Europe, Gaetano Ferri (who suffered an incapacitating attack of hoarseness and recovered from it, all within the space of a half-hour), and also Susini, Guglielmo Lotti, Richard Hoffman, and Ranieri Villanova. Having never before been "fairly heard by our New York public," wrote the *Herald* (May 3), Speranza "made a favorable impression," and had "every reason to be gratified with the result of the evening's performance."[55] But there was more to it than that. As the *Herald* had earlier intimated (April 11, 1861), Adelina Speranza's reappearance was intended to win her an engagement with the Associated Artists. By the time she sang, as we know, the troupe had disbanded.

During the earlier part of the year, despite the precarious times, a small procession of musical newcomers had come and gone. On January 24, Miss Louisa Frances O'Keefe (a version of the ballad singer Louisa Francis?), announced as a singing and piano-playing pupil and protégée of Madame D'Angri, appeared at Dodworth's Hall, assisted by George Crozier, Dr. Guilmette, William H. Currie, and "a private Glee and Madrigal Society." On January 18, Emma Rowcroft, English and therefore heavily puffed in the *Albion,* sang at Dodworth's Hall, assisted by Rivarde, Joseph Burke, and Richard Hoffman. Subsequently appearing at a matinée at Dodworth's on March 12, assisted by Annie Kemp, George Crozier, J. R. Thomas, S. B. Mills, William Saar, and Aptommas, Miss Rowcroft was praised for her "internal singing." On March 5, one Adeline Leserman, a pupil of Manzocchi, appeared at Irving Hall, assisted by Madame Zimmermann, Vincenzo Morino, William Saar, Noll, Bergner, and Anschütz.

On March 11, the veteran violinist/conductor Michele Rapetti proudly assisted at his daughter Cecilia's debut. With her excellent and well-cultivated mezzo-soprano voice, Cecilia Rapetti possessed the Italianate capacity to thrill, wrote the *Evening Post* (March 12, 1861), a capacity denied to American singers, excellent though they might be in matters of technique and execution. Thus, her numerous Italian airs were as admirable as her single English song was not. Besides her father, who played several violin solos, the debutante was assisted by Harrison Millard, Richard Hoffman, and by Villanova, who brilliantly exhibited the capabilities of the Alexandre Organ with a fantasy on themes from *The Sicilian Vespers.*

One J. M. V. Busch, a native of Copenhagen—having secured not only the eminent patronage of Archbishop John Hughes of New York, but of the Bishops of Brooklyn and Newark and the Reverend Pastors of the Roman Catholic Churches of New York, Brooklyn, Newark, Jersey City, and Hoboken—presented a Grand Sacred Concert at Irving Hall on March 26, "in artistic conformity with the season of Lent." Performed by a quartet of less than optimal solo singers—Johanna Ficher, Octavie Gomien, George Frederick Clarendon, and Anton Graff—and with a chorus of combined Catholic church choirs and apparently a pickup orchestra under Busch's direc-

[55] To Hagen her concert only "confirmed the impression this lady made in her debut at the Academy of Music" (*Review and World,* May 11, 1861, p. 114).

tion, the program consisted of his religious compositions and of Schubert's Twenty-third Psalm and *Ave Maria,* both with accompaniments orchestrated by Busch. The pièce de résistance was Busch's *Stabat Mater Dolorosa,* for solo vocal quartet, chorus, and orchestra, dedicated to Bishop Hughes. In April a repeat of this *Stabat Mater,* with Madame Bishop, Mlle. Gomien, and Messrs. Millard and Weinlich as soloists, was casually announced for a second performance "some evening this month, place and time hereafter to be appointed."

Sacred and classical music was performed on February 13 at the Madison Avenue Baptist Church by Mrs. Mozart, Mrs. J. H. Barclay, David Miranda (of the Church's choir), and Dr. Guilmette, with G. Washburn Morgan conducting and Messrs. Beale and Currie accompanying at the organ. Morgan conducted a choir and played the organ at a sacred and classical concert on April 13 at Calvary Baptist Church (23rd Street between Fifth and Sixth Avenues), when his assisting vocalists were the Gellie sisters and George Crozier. The Gellies assisted at Louis Dachauer's concert at Dodworth's Hall on April 18, together with Miss Montmorency, a Mlle. C. Gélin, the Messrs. Rapetti, Millard, and Ferdinand Dachauer, the cellist Brannes, and a grand choir.

A testimonial concert was tendered to Guilmette by his class at the Cooper Union on February 20, when the honoree was announced to sing a Grand National Anthem expressly composed for the occasion, the words by "an eminent Episcopal clergyman" and the music by C. Jerome Hopkins. The Harmonic Society, conducted by Bristow, with Maria Brainerd (accompanied by C. W. Beames), the Misses Hawley and Montmorency, the Messrs. Millard, William Saar, and George W. Morgan, and others, appeared at Irving Hall on March 12 for the benefit of Frederick Widdows, the former manager of the now defunct French Theatre.

Benefit concerts abounded. On March 21, at Dodworth's Hall, a concert to assist the Italian and German Industrial School, connected with the Chldren's Aid Society, was performed by Emma Rowcroft, Madame Graever-Johnson, an anonymous "lady amateur," and Messrs. Mayer, Schreiber, Hagen (presumably in his capacity of violinist), and Brannes. That same evening at the Academy of Music, the American Dramatic Fund Association gave their great annual benefit, the principal attraction being *Macbeth,* performed by Charlotte Cushman, Edwin Booth, and Joseph Jefferson, no less, with a dazzling cast that included Madame Bishop in a role unflatteringly designated as "Principal Singing Witch"; after the play she sang "The Flag of Our Union." The box-office receipts came to $2040, reported the *Herald* (March 25, 1861), of which the Fund netted about $1700.

Again at the Academy, on March 29, a "Grand Caledonian Festival" for the Benevolent Society of the Thistle was given by Professor Anderson, the "Wizard of the North," and sponsored by the New York Caledonian Club in collaboration with the officers of the Seventy-ninth Regiment. The huge cast participating in a vast program, consisting mostly of Professor Anderson's magic spells and a myriad of Scottish songs and dances, included Agnes Sutherland, George Simpson, Sam Cowell, Ainsley Cooke (*sic*), and the concertina-playing Sedgwicks, father and son.

To aid the Ladies' Hebrew Benevolent Association, Madame Zimmermann and Messrs. Bernhard, Weinlich, Henry Mollenhauer, and Carl Anschütz appeared at Irving Hall on May 13. And on June 13, on the eve of her departure to Canada, Mina Geary gave a twenty-five-cent concert for her own benefit at Hope Chapel, where she and her father had just completed a season with General Tom Thumb. Miss Geary was assisted by Madame Johanna Ficher, little Master Willie Barnesmore Pape, and a ten-year-old violin virtuosa, Mademoiselle Mathilde Toedt, a pupil of Edward Mollen-hauer.

As always, juvenile entertainers were in good supply, particularly the little Sunday School Vocalists, sponsored and directed by the piano manufacturer and music publisher Horace Waters. On March 3 they were heard at Irving Hall, together with 150 of A. P. Peck's little charges from the Protestant Half Orphan Asylum. On March 25, again at Irving Hall, a complimentary concert featured "Nine Celebrated Sunday School Vocalists" and other little prodigies under Horace Waters's aegis, appearing for little Miss Mary F. Thoms, "a promising young vocalist in her own right."

On April 15, to raise funds for the St. Ann's Church library and to stock it with recitation books, a group of adults—Mr. and Mrs. William Berge, Berge's brother Charles, G. W. Morgan, William Currie, and others—joined forces with the "Wonderful Myers Children" and the pupils of the St. Ann's Sunday School at Irving Hall. High among the attractions at their concert were recitations in their "beautiful sign language" by the children of the Home for Deaf Mutes. On April 18 a children's concert took place at Palace Gardens for the benefit of the Bethany Mission School.

On July 2, in advance celebration of the Fourth of July, L. A. and G. P. Benjamin presented their class of 1000 children at the Cooper Institute in a program of songs that "portrayed the present state of the country, as well as its past glories." Thirty-four "appropriately dressed" young misses represented the Union, other little students impersonated President Lincoln, Secretary of State Seward, the "seceder Jeff Davis," John Bull, and Napoleon; other groups represented Germany, Russia, Italy, Hungary, Switzerland, and other countries, "with occasional responses from a real Yankee, terminating in a Grand Tableau, 'Triumph of Union Over Rebellion.'"

At the Church of the Puritans on May 30, Horace Waters presented twelve of his little protégés in a concert for the benefit of the "Imperial Zouave Regiment," with a Professor Abbott (Asahel Abbott⌐?) presiding at the organ. And on September 29, Waters, with his Sunday School Vocalists, donated one of their "very interesting" sacred concerts to the Shepard Rifles, headquartered at Palace Gardens.

On August 3, amid increasingly depressing war news, the *Tribune* announced the welcome resumption of the Dodworth Band concerts in Central Park, "so great a source of enjoyment to the multitudes who [last year] could not escape from the city during the sultry months." Because, justified the *Tribune,* "the work of suppressing a rebellion brings with it the seriousness of war, it furnishes no excuse for lugubriously ignoring rational recreation."

Among the improvements to the Park made in the past year, the *Tribune* (August 7) listed the Terrace, which no longer suggested only the bare outlines of its future "finish and harmony"; the "swans and waterfowl [that] sported gracefully on the lake"; and "the pleasure boats [that floated] throughout the devious course of the lake, landing at the cave." Other improvements were a marquee to shield concert-goers from the sun, increased seating accommodations, a lengthened carriage drive, and a hydrant of special construction that would supply "thirsty souls" with "filtered ice water."

Because a great number of the customary male escorts were off in the fighting

Currier & Ives view of the Drive in Central Park.

Music Stand on the Mall in Central Park,
where free Saturday afternoon concerts were given.

lines, continued the *Tribune* (August 12), the vast audience attending the first concert (August 10) consisted mostly of ladies, whose colorful attire gave a brilliant appearance to the event. The large awning, or tent, provided for their protection from the sun was inadequate, however, to the size of the attendance, and worse, the canvas shelter under which the musicians played had the unfortunate effect of deadening the sound. "The laws of acoustics will not be trifled with," wrote the *Tribune,* "and a cotton ceiling is the death of music and oratory." Until "the golden period when the trees grow in the Park" (a matter of some thirty years), the writer (Fry?) urged the construction of a well-designed wooden shell that would diffuse sound, not destroy it. He also recommended the enlargement of the lake, in his opinion "an apology for a sheet of water in the Summer and a wretched place for skating in the Winter."

At the third Park concert the *Tribune* (August 25) reported an audience of not less than 25,000 and a "magnificent turnout of equipages." Not less than 20,000, more modestly reckoned the *Evening Post* reporter (August 26), who suggested that future concerts begin an hour later, at 5:30 P.M., to obviate the need for the awning over the band, which indeed deadened the music and prevented those only a little distance away from hearing it at all. Moreover, the writer foresightedly suggested that the "avenue railroad companies 'do the handsome thing' to the public and their own pockets by employing the band at the Park three times a week for the remainder of the season."

For the fourth concert, on August 31, an experiment was tried: the band occupied a "music stand" erected on the edge of the lake. It was hoped that "the water and the surrounding hills" would successfully diffuse the sound.

The Park concerts continued regularly through September, if not longer. As late as November 2 the *Tribune* announced a concert in Central Park, weather permitting, to commence at 2:30 P.M. Dodworth's repertory for the series, it should be added, spanned the traditional park concert fare, from arrangements of the classics and opera potpourris to popular tunes; it notably included Dodworth's composition (played on September 14), whimsically titled, "Bunch of Melodies, Strung on Chords."

Following a summer otherwise devoid of music, the new season tentatively began with a sacred concert on August 29 by W. A. King for the benefit of the Reformed Dutch Church at Mott Haven, an exhibition by G. Washbourn Morgan and Edward G. Jardine of a magnificent new Jardine organ on September 19 at the 23rd Street Presbyterian Church, and a Grand Musical and Dramatic Soirée by Cecilia Flores, assisted by J. H. Brown, dramatic reader, on September 27 at Dodworth's Hall.

Things picked up ever so slightly in October and November. On the afternoon and evening of October 3 the massive Annual Festival for the benefit of the Roman Catholic Orphan Asylum held forth at the Academy of Music with a cast that spanned the entertainment spectrum from Bryant's Minstrels to Chanfrau's sophisticated histrionics to Herr Cline's acrobatic feats on the *Corde Elastique* to opera and concert music performed by Mesdames von Berkel and Johanna Ficher, Herr Lehmann, and Harry Sanderson. On October 22 the Boston singer, Lizzie Parker, giving a farewell concert at Irving Hall, assisted by Brignoli, Ardavani, Susini, and S. B. Mills, before departing for music study in Italy, received such persuasive professional offers that she decided to change her plans and pursue a local career instead.

On November 27 at Irving Hall, in aid of the Christ's Church Industrial School, Mrs. Mozart gave her third annual concert, assisted by George Simpson, J. R. Thomas, and Edward Mollenhauer, with Carl Wels, Frank Gilder, and William Dressler, pianists, and Mollenhauer's wonderful little ten-year-old violin pupil, Master Bernardo. On November 29, Frederick, the least noticeable of the Mollenhauer brothers, and Jules Roussel, a French actor, presented a Grand Musical and Literary *soirée,* assisted by Edward Mollenhauer, Louis Schreiber, and Heinrich Gelhaar, a pianist.

A sacred vocal and organ concert for the benefit of the Free Protestant Church of the Redemption on East 14th Street was given by Mary Hawley, George Simpson, and G. W. Morgan on December 12. On December 19, Gustavus Geary presented his "Grand Annual Concert" at Irving Hall, with a cast that included Mrs. Mozart, Mina Geary, George Simpson, S. C. Campbell, little Willie Barnesmore Pape, Napoleon Gould, the guitarist/minstrel, and G. W. Morgan, who conducted and played the piano. On December 23, again at Irving Hall, Maria Brainerd (and the inevitable Beames) appeared with S. B. Mills and Dodworth's Cornet Band, for the benefit of the little Meyers sisters, Louisa and Josephine, who also performed.

The Upper Ten, too, engaged in goodly causes. As *Linda,* an apparently ladylike substitute for the *Albion*'s music critic, put it (*Albion,* December 24, 1861, p. 607): "The long repressed social tendencies of the [upper class] New York public, deprived of the customary outlet of balls and Opera, have of late vented themselves in full force on Charity Balls and Charity Concerts." Several "zealous and indefatigable women," resolving to raise badly needed funds for The Nursery and Child's Hospital, had mounted an amateur musical entertainment at a grandiose Murray Hill home generously loaned by a Mr. Clark. So successful was the event that they were obliged to repeat it.

Heading a mixed cast of professionals and amateurs were Madame Graever-Johnson, who, with three lady amateurs, very creditably played two "piano quartets," and Madame de Ferussac, who, though not a professional, was musically entitled to "pass the indefinable barrier which separates the amateur from the artist" (or so she evidently continued to hope). Madame Ferrusac's performances of arias from *Norma* and *La traviata* revealed her excellent method but also, alas, her loss of "freshness and accuracy of tone."

Of the gentlemen participants, the social tenor William Henry Cooke, as always, exceeded "comment or eulogy" with his beautiful voice and admirable method; and for the alien touch, Philip Mayer, "an artist and professor of distinction, assisted by three German gentlemen, sang some characteristic glees in their native dialect, combining the patriotic, sentimental, and descriptive." But the great sensation of the concert was "Mr. [R. Storrs] Willis's National Anthem, which—being fortunately rescued from the oblivion of that fatal basket, whereto it had been consigned by the late inexorable Committee on Patriotism—burst forth . . . in lofty strains, kindling in every heart a gleam of the noble enthusiasm which had inspired it."

A far from disinterested Willis, reviewing the event in the first issue of his ultra-genteel little gossip sheet, *Once a Month,* ambitiously subtitled *A Paper of Society, Belles-Lettres and Art* (January 1862, p. 4), paid tribute to "that huge-hearted liberality which proffered a private mansion for a purpose most laudable, it is true, in itself, but one that must have put a private family to exceeding discomfort for at least a fortnight, and turned their elegant mansion upside down." Not many private families, he permitted himself to say, "would let the general public (even though composed of our New York well-behaved 'best') inside their doors to such a thronging extent as did Mr. Clark—to whom, therefore, be all praise from the lovers of charity." Willis had equally elegant words of praise for Scharfenberg, who accompanied and "firmly" held things together, for Mr. Rakerman (*sic*), who rendered cheerful and friendly service, and for Philip Mayer, who —although his chorus was composed of a private club of uptown ladies and gentlemen sponsored by an "art-loving lady-amateur of Murray Hill"—modestly refused to be credited as their leader. "The amount realized by both these concerts," wrote Willis, "was $1500."

For more plebeian listeners, the original Hutchinsons, John W. and Abby—with their recently added kin, Fanny, Henry, and Viola—gave concerts on January 31 at Ebitt Hall and on February 6 and April 18 at Hope Chapel. The Continental Old Folks, "all attired in costumes of a hundred years ago," with a "Grand orchestra and Full Brass Band," made a tour of the local church circuit: appearing on April 3 at the South Baptist Church; on October 25 at the Methodist Episcopal Church (85th Street between Third and Fourth Avenues); on November 5 at the Bethany Baptist Church (55th Street and Lexington Avenue); November 7 at Morrisania Hall, in the suburb of Morrisania; November 8 at Washington Hall, Astoria, and on and on.[56]

The Alleghanians, now consisting of Caroline Hiffert, Maria Boulard, Franz Stoepel, G. Galloway, and J. M. Boulard, together with a company of Swiss Bell Ringers, returned from their four-year round-the-world tour and opened at Barnum's on August 4. There, and later at Hope Chapel—where on October 14 they began a run of forty-eight nights—they greatly pleased "large audiences by their homely melodies and the clear music of their bells. These performers," wrote the *Tribune,* October 21, 1861), "take hold of the public heart in something of the way of the Hutchinsons, who were the delight of a generation, and give the family party that abstains from the ruder shows what it desires of entertainment."

Of like respectability, the Peak Family of vocalists and harpists, together with a company of Lancashire Bell Ringers (who exquisitely performed on two hundred silver bells), were a Christmas Week attraction at Niblo's remodeled saloon. Tickets to both entertainments were twenty-five cents for adults, children (admitted only to matinées), ten cents.

Attempting to put a good face on the decline of show business in wartime New York, *Bayard* editorialized in *Wilkes' Spirit of the Times* (October 31, 1861, p. 413): "While the number of places of amusement in active operation is sadly diminished . . . still, those that are open are, for the most part, doing a good business. The audiences are made up principally of strangers, soldiers and their friends, contractors, jobbers, and the others whom the exigencies of the war have brought to the city being largely in the preponderance. Where the strangers in the city can be enumerated by tens of thousands, it would go hard, indeed," wrote *Bayard,* "if there were not every night a few hundreds with the disposition to go to the theatre, and with a sufficiency of the indispensable cash to ripen the will into the deed. . . . People must be amused, and no possible number of Bull Run defeats can repress the natural craving of the Yankee mind for a little fun."

---

[56] The equally peripatetic Father Kemp's Old Folks similarly dotted the environs.

Leslie's, Dartmouth College Library

With musical productions in decline during the war, the Academy of Music put on shows of acrobats and minstrels—all well attended.

Thus—as theatre after theatre closed its doors and magicians and acrobats invaded the Academy of Music—the minstrel shows, concert saloons, and beer gardens catered to a large influx of out-of-towners, many in New York on war business and seeking big-city thrills. To attempt only the barest indication of the labyrinthine shiftings and interminglings of the minstrel folk: for the better part of the year the Bryant Minstrels continued to attract crowds to Mechanics' Hall, taking time off only briefly after the sudden and lamented death of Jerry Bryant (of "a congestion of the brain"), and later for renovation of their overworked theatre.[57] Hooley and Campbells' Minstrels continued their run at Niblo's Saloon until March.[58] They were succeeded in April by Lloyd's Minstrels, who stayed until June, when Niblo's shut down until December. Sans Campbell, Hooley's Minstrels then reappeared at the Stuyvesant Institute in October, remaining there until the following spring. Campbell in the meantime trans-

[57] Serving the apparently limitless contemporary capacity for irreverence—no matter what the subject—on their return, in August, the remaining Bryants elicited "roars of laughter" with their screamingly funny travesty of "Bull Run," a spectacular dramatization of that military debacle currently running at the New Bowery Theatre. In the Bryant version, "Cousin Jeff" was played by Eph Horn and "Uncle Abe" by Dan Bryant (*Dispatch*, August 31, 1861).

[58] Their programs contained at least one new musical burlesque, "Ten Minutes at the Academy of Music."

ferred his "ballads and Tyrolean warblings" to Bryant's, and, in between, as we know, appeared at vocal concerts. George Christy, back from his long tour, preempted Irving Hall from mid-May to early June with nightly performances, then followed Madame Bishop's "drawing-room concerts" at the Stuyvesant Institute, where he remained until August. In October, a lesser group, Sharpley's Minstrels, uneventfully took over the Stuyvesant Institute with a single feature, topically titled "The Great Ethiopian Confederacy."

But it was the alcohol-dispensing concert saloons, with their superabundance of entertainment, that attracted the greatest crowds. As the *Tribune* (August 19, 1861) explained, the general shutdown of theatres throughout the Union had forced hordes of entertainers of all descriptions to flock to New York, where—merely to survive— many accepted underpaid employment in places formerly beneath their notice. The English opera singers, David Miranda, Brookhouse Bowler, and Aynsley Cook, blackened their faces and appeared with the minstrel troupes; they appeared at the concert saloons as well, as did the singers Agnes Sutherland, George Crozier, Johanna Ficher, and others. The noted choreographer Paul Brillant devised ballets for the American Concert Hall (444 Broadway); the ballerina Annetta Galletti danced at the Broadway Music Hall (483–485 Broadway) and at the Melodeon, where also appeared the Ronzani Ballet. Sam Cowell, after a long sojourn at Canterbury Hall (which in April relocated to the premises of the former French Theatre at 585 Broadway),[59] attempted an experiment in self-management. Taking over the old Stuyvesant Institute and suggestively renaming it the "Boudoir Pantheon," he presented an ephemeral series of "parlor entertainments." Replaced in May by Madame Bishop's series, Cowell immediately transferred to the Melodeon, where he more successfully performed his repertory of comic songs. At the Gaieties the entertainment was becoming more and more focused on the illicit seductions of the no-longer merely "Pretty," but now the *Prettiest Waiter Girls.*

Throughout this first year of the war, the drama and music columns veered from black despair at the demise of theatre and music activity in New York to a kind of whistling-in-the-dark false euphoria over how things were really not so bad, and how they would soon be picking up. On August 19, when the war was still young, the *Tribune* editorialized: "But two of our regular city theatres . . . survive the combined effect of the war and the summer season. One by one, the others have closed their doors, only to reopen them, let us hope, with renewed spirit at the beginning of the fall." That two theatres were still open (soon to close) proved "that the depression produced by the critical condition of public affairs [was] not so widespread but that some portions of the community [displayed] the sense and spirit to enjoy themselves while they could.

"Evils are invariably worse in anticipation than they are in reality," babbled the *Tribune*. "A year ago the bare idea of a civil war that would last for six months in this land, without producing the most widespread desolation and paralyzing all the life springs of business, could hardly have been conceived of. . . . And yet two armies of from a quarter to half a million each are in the field, and hostilities are being carried

---

[59] In September, Canterbury Hall presented a blackface burlesque of *Un ballo in maschera.*

on without producing one tithe of the misery and suffering that might have been supposed inevitable. It is not wise, therefore, to be too easily frightened. There are panics among communities as well as among armies, and they are equally foolish and fatal in both.

"The moral of all this is that people should put the best face on things, be happy while they can, patronize the theatres and places of amusement as much as ever. . . . All communities, as well as individuals, have their rainy days, but they ought never to lose sight of the comforting reflection that

Behind the clouds is the sun still shining.

6

GTS: 1862

After the first excitement of the war-fever was over, people in large cities, as if to counteract the effects of the terrible suspense caused by the uncertainty of ever-occurring battles, began to flock in crowds to places of amusement, in order to seek temporary forgetfulness of the terrible drama that was being enacted on the battlefield. The opera, as well as the theatres, for a time reaped an abundant harvest.

Frédéric Louis Ritter
Music in America *(1890)*

OBSERVING AN INVIOLABLE social ritual, on New Year's Day Strong went calling on friends and acquaintances—"some forty, including calls by pasteboard." It had been a pleasant enough day, he wrote in his private journal on January 2, "but in these times one cannot get over the presence of national peril. Even when one gives up the whole day to mere amusement, he is haunted by a phantom of possible calamity and disgrace."

The war impinged on all aspects of domestic life. Spending a quiet social evening with the Wolcott Gibbses, "Mrs. Gibbs and Mrs. Strong played four-handed music, while Gibbs and I talked Sanitary," wrote Strong on January 15.

Strong's all-absorbing duties at the Sanitary Commission increasingly brought him face to face with the brutal realities of war. He made frequent visits of inspection to camps and field hospitals, was an indispensable member of the Commission's deputations to Washington in their unceasing struggle with bungling officialdom, and, for local consumption, he wrote editorials urging "a reformation in the Medical Bureau." On January 11, following a Sanitary Commission meeting at the Century Club, Strong turned over to Charles Anderson Dana,♪ the managing editor of the *Tribune,*[1] "another roll of manuscript thunder against that wretched Medical Bureau, which he says shall appear editorially." Preoccupied with his official and professional duties and his gnawing anxiety over the progress of the war, Strong had little time or inclination for the sparse smattering of music events that constituted the wartime music scene in early 1862. Thus he missed the Philharmonic concert at Irving Hall[2] on February 1, when

---

[1] Soon to resign from that paper after fifteen years of faithful and distinguished service.
[2] Because the modest capacity of Irving Hall had been overtaxed at the last Philharmonic concert, the *Home Journal* (February 1, 1862) advised the hall's proprietor/manager, Lafayette F. Harrison,

Bergmann again conducted Schumann's Fourth Symphony, op. 120, also the first local performance of Brahms's Serenade no. 2, in A, op. 16 (1859), and Weber's *Ruler of the Spirits* Overture. The soloists were the baritone Signor (or Herr) Federico Ridolfi, who sang "It is enough" from Mendelssohn's *Elijah* and an aria from *I puritani;* Ernst Hartmann, a new arrival from Berlin, who played the first movement of Beethoven's C-minor Piano Concerto and the first local performance of Liszt's Polonaise in E (1851) (Searle 223); and Henry Schmitz, who played *La Solitude,* a nocturne for French horn by Eisfeld, also a first performance.

By now somewhat inured to Schumann's vagaries, the critics did not, however, take kindly to Brahms's new Serenade. As far as the *Albion* was concerned, it "might have been omitted without driving the subscribers to desperation. It is written for sixteen of the drowsiest instruments in the orchestra and enjoys the advantage of having five movements—any one of which," remarked the critic, "is sufficient to demand the interference of the police" (February 8, 1862, p. 67). To the *Home Journal* (February 15, 1862), its "five dreary movements," striving to imitate Haydn's obsolete style, were enough to "drive the most stoical mad."

William Henry Fry, ignoring Brahms's reprehensible excursion into the eighteenth century, concentrated his critical/editorial pronouncements on his favorite musical *bêtes noires:* the oratorio, the symphony, and the piano. "When Schumann does not identify music with nightmare, he is well worth listening to," magnanimously conceded Fry. "Our idea of music is the beautiful, as a rule; the hideous may be used as mustard and cayenne." As always, belittling any form of non-operatic musical creation, Fry, the eternally frustrated opera composer, expounded on the inferiority of symphonic writing conpared to opera. The composer of symphonies, he wrote, "is not restrained by words, the breath of the singer, or the necessities of producing at every turn excellent popular effects (otherwise the opera treasury-box would be empty), but being pure, free sound, is comparatively so easy in its production by the yard, whereas opera composing is beset with troubles at every step. Symphony writing, which can deal in time, and eternity, if you choose, and reverie and independence, ought not to be so unattractive as it generally is. There ought to be more well-defined, accented dramatic melody, ten to one, than there is; and then the public would esteem symphonies at a higher rate, and moreover, the symphonies would deserve to be so held."

As to oratorio: the air from Mendelssohn's *Elijah,* well sung by Signor Ridolfi, was "about as near a logical melody as oratorio writers can or will come; the theory of oratorio composition being first to take prose for words, though lyrical music demands measured poetry as much as a fish does water; and next, if a well-defined melody occurs to the composer, to knock in the head immediately. It is remarkable," observed Fry, "that the piano-forte illustrators, such as Thalberg, Liszt, and others, avoid oratorios, generally, for themes, as they would snakes. But the fountain of the grand piano-forte school, Thalberg's arrangement of airs from *Moses,* finds its ecstasy in the 'Prayer,' because Rossini had the brains to put a distinct melody in this invocation in an opera also given oratorio-wise. Composers who can only sermonize, that is, write oratorios,

---

to provide camp stools, "which are so conveniently removed and so conveniently placed in every available corner, for, to enjoy music, even the very best, is a task when one is obliged to stand the whole evening."

might take a hint from the illustrious maestro and give us square melodies of eight-bar divisions. If the time of these can be altered and they be twisted into quadrilles, so much the better for the quadrilles."

Young Hartmann, a pupil of the renowned German pedagogue Theodor Kullak (1818–1882), was "a nice young performer," although "his use of the pedals might be mended and his trill improved." Fry appreciated Beethoven's concerto, particularly because it was "mercifully in one movement" (a shocking but revealing lapse on the part of this musical savant). He condescendingly commended it for possessing some melody and a first and second theme, albeit not passionate, "for passionate quasi declamation on the piano—its highest function—is a thing of later date, and came in with piano-forte opera monographs."

The perfect example of this latter phenomenon, wrote Fry, was Liszt's paraphrase on the *Lucia* Sextet, in which "the old school, fluent, logical, and not nightmarish as it is, appears surcharged with tame surplus matter—diatonic runs and generally filling-up 'utility business,' which makes it pale and tame in comparison. The *delice* of piano music—what takes off from the prose of the keys' dead wood—is drawn from heaven's great instrument, alongside of which all others are starved mockeries—the Human Voice Divine" (*Tribune,* February 3; partially reprinted in *Dwight's,* February 15, 1862, p. 365).

New Yorkers and Brooklynites had been granted a tantalizing sample of the Human Voice Divine with a so-called "opera season" of four performances that Jacob Grau—having effected a kind of truce with the directors of both Academies—had mounted from January 14 through 17. With his traveling concert and opera company, consisting of Kellogg, Hinkley, Brignoli, Mancusi, and Susini, augmented by Amalia Patti-Strakosch and Barili (presumably Nicolò), and with Anschütz conducting a hastily picked-up chorus and orchestra,[3] Grau presented, on the successive nights, *Il barbiere* (Brooklyn), *La traviata* (Irving Place), his notoriously hard-fought *Traviata* (Brooklyn), and, replacing *Barbiere, Un ballo in maschera* (Irving Place).[4]

It was Grau's spectacular triumph over the Brooklyn Academy's iron-willed Board of Governors that particularly intrigued the critics. Although the directors had proclaimed with might and main that the highly moral Brooklynites would never tolerate a local performance of the infamous *Traviata,*[5] not only did the largest audience ever seen at the Brooklyn Academy brave knee-deep slush and snow to hear Clara Louise Kellogg as the controversial Violetta,[6] but, as the *Times* noted (January 17, 1862): "Very many of the clergy of the City and all the *habituées* of the [Brooklyn] Philharmonic were there."[7]

---

[3] As late as January 11, three days before the opening, Grau advertised for "Ladies and gentlemen of the Choruses and gentlemen of the Orchestra desirous to be engaged" to apply at the Academy of Music from 10 A.M. to noon.

[4] Following this "season"—in effect, an extended stopover on their tour—the company immediately proceeded to Philadelphia and Washington.

[5] In their zeal, they went so far as to distribute anti-*Traviata* leaflets to passengers in the Brooklyn "cars."

[6] With Brignoli as Alfredo and Mancusi as Germont.

[7] And fashionable habituées: "Brooklyn affects more of the opera waistcoat and tie, as well as the more fatal feminine toilet, than New-York," wrote Fry (*Tribune,* February 3, 1862).

Dreadful weather had imperiled the Irving Place opening (January 15), when Kellogg had sung the embattled role for the first time. Although her Violetta was highly praised, the critics generally agreed that she had heedlessly squandered her beautiful, but still fragile, vocal resources in her headlong performance of the first act, to the ensuing impoverishment of the high moments in acts two and three. But Seymour (*Times,* January 27, 1862) was confident that, with experience, Violetta would surely become one of Kellogg's best roles.

Like *Timothy Trill,* Fry joyfully hailed Kellogg as a shining example of what could be accomplished with "all-American" musical training: "This young New-York lady," he wrote, "whose travels have hardly been beyond the Island [of Manhattan], and who has been indebted to home culture for all the Italian and vocal culture she has, appeared to much advantage. She has strengthened her voice considerably by her practice in the foreign opera-house over the ferry and the grand musical theater at Buffalo," he joked. "She is now distinctly heard above the orchestra in the remote parts of the house. . . . Miss Kellogg has improved. Her Italian is crisper and more to the manner born" (*Tribune,* January 16, 1862).

The New-York *World,* a fresh presence on the local journalistic scene,[8] found Kellogg's Violetta to possess "grace and spirit" but to be lacking in "that fervor and intensity with which other singers have made us familiar." Musing on the eternal enigma that was opera, the critic wrote: "The opera is a plant which is quite too sensitive for the rudely-changing temperature of these latitudes. A single slim audience and it shrivels; another and it closes tightly over its vibratory petals and remains shut till the sunshine of crowded parquette and circles calls it into life again. Its vitality has always been feeble in this country and its purse only best when the community is prosperous and has plenty of money wherewith to purchase tickets and gloves and bouquets and opera cloaks. So that this year it evanished like the aurora—it went out in a blaze of benefits, which are understood to have ruined the beneficiare [Ullman]. Mr. Grau gives us another gleam of the rhythmic halo,[9] whereafter it is probable that, musically speaking, all will be dark as before" (January 17, 1862).

But hardly had this brief operatic interlude concluded than Grau announced another, a two-week (six-performance) opera season to begin on January 29, again to be shared by both Academies. It was not until the day before it opened, however, that he announced "a combination with Mr. Max Maretzek," who would henceforth "take charge of the musical department of the enterprise."

It was not a harmonious combination. As Maretzek tells it: having at last managed to borrow money enough to bring his tattered company back from their disastrous Mexican tour (vividly recounted in *Sharps and Flats,* pp. 52–70), he had returned to New York with six dollars in his pocket, just enough to pay for his night's lodging in

---

[8] Founded in 1860 as a rigidly moralistic daily newspaper, it was not until a year later, upon its merging with the *Courier and Enquirer* (whose pugnacious editor James Watson Webb had been appointed United States minister to Brazil), that the *World,* under the able editorship of Manton Malone Marble (1835–1917), began to accept music and theatre advertisements, and in 1862 to publish reviews (see Mott, *American Journalism,* pp. 350–51).

[9] Although the *Albion* (January 18, 1862, p. 162) referred to Grau as "the Bedouin of managers . . . on whose head Ullman has set a price," it is more than likely that some sort of alliance might have existed between them.

Manhattan before embarking for home on Staten Island. "I had hardly time for the welcome of my own family," he writes, "when Mr. Jacob Grau arrived at my humble cottage, and in a very patronizing manner, condoling warmly with my misfortunes, offered me an engagement from three to six years as a conductor of his opera company. Mr. Jacob Grau, who ten years before this time had been selling opera librettos for me outside Castle Garden, had worked his way to becoming manager himself, which," contemptuously, "was no difficult task after the departure of Strakosch and Ullman for Europe and during my absence in Mexico.

"I respect any man, who by his merit, or even by a stroke of fortune, betters his social position," declares Maretzek, "and I do not think it any dishonor if a manager accepts a place as conductor or agent under adverse circumstances any more than if a President of the United States, having returned to private life, and in practicing law, accepts a fee from one of his former employees. But I felt hurt at the manner in which the offer was made, as if it were a charity, when I knew well that only some necessity could have made him apply to me. I would have refused, but the thought of paying my draft to Spofford and Tileston[10] made me pliable; but instead of an engagement of six years, I offered my services for six weeks.

"'Six weeks!' he said, with a contemptuous smile, 'What can you do after that? What do you intend to do?'

"'I intend for next season to have the greatest and most complete opera company under my management,' I replied." And that is precisely what Maretzek did do. But all that in good time.

Always a great favorite with New York audiences, Maretzek was enthusiastically welcomed back. "If we will but honestly recall the numberless *bad* performances that have taken place during Mr. Maretzek's absence," wrote Seymour in his review of the opening *Martha*[11] (*Times,* January 30, 1862), "and remember too, that art has steadily retrograded since he abandoned the field to less competent, but far noisier, competitors, it will be conceded that there was nothing more than a graceful recognition of positive merit in the hearty applause which greeted that gentleman on his appearance in the orchestra last night. And the opera went so smoothly, and with so much spirit, that a blind man might have known a new chief was at the head of the musical forces." Even the public's latest darling, Clara Louise Kellogg, appearing for the first time as Lady Henriette (Lady Harriet) profited by Maretzek's superlative musicianship: "The freshness of youth was for once uncrushed by an avalanche of instruments," wrote Seymour, "and the result was, of course, a distinct success."[12] Amalia Strakosch as Nancy, Brignoli as Lionel, Susini as Plunkett, and Barili as Tristan were also in top form. It promised to be a memorable season.

But it was not to be. According to the *Albion* (February 8, 1862, p. 67), an inopportune snowstorm had "rather subdued amusements, [for] when the sleigh-bells jingle, a number of vagabond musical parties usurp the public ear and set it awry for

---

[10] The Spofford and Tileston steamship line had accepted a note from Maretzek for the transportation of his company back from Cuba.

[11] "A light and agreeable opera to all save the critic who has to write about it," complained the *Albion* critic (February 2, 1862, p. 55).

[12] Kellogg's rendition of "The Last Rose of Summer" was the equal of Adelina Patti's, wrote the *Herald* (February 3, 1862).

anything higher than tin trumpets and laments on the subject of 'John Brown.' The latter effusion, indeed," the critic took occasion to note, "is the lyric novelty of the season, and if the Academy really did represent the taste of the community, this would find a place on the [opera] conductor's desk."

As to the opera season, the killing nightly schedule was taking its toll of the singers, physically and morally. Despite Maretzek's presence, the level of performance sank to an all-time low. Isabella Hinkley in a new role—Leonora in *Il trovatore* (January 31 at Irving Place)—was respectable only by comparison with the miserable efforts of her colleagues, and the quality of Grau's productions was generally so "feeble and degrading" as hardly to be "guessed at by people outside the building."

"In times like these," conceded the writer, "when Art is in danger of disappearing altogether from among us, it will not do to be too particular with the quality of the musical dish placed before us,[13] but," he protested, "we have at least a right to demand that proper care be bestowed on its preparation." Instead, one or two leading members of the company had refused utterly to attend rehearsals, regarding them as "the last fragment of an exploded despotism, and clearly superfluous in the case of eminent genius and talent like their own." Maretzek, for all his ability, had been unable to bring the *Trovatore* performance to an acceptable degree of respectability. "Signor Brignoli was lazier, more dawdling, more indifferent than usual. In the second act he did not even put himself to the trouble of changing his dress, and indeed, throughout the work, he stalked through his part as if it were a prodigious bore—as indeed it was. Signor Mancusi meant well, without doubt, but his intentions were not realized. . . . Mrs. Strakosch was the gypsy. Ahem!"

In Brooklyn, on Saturday, February 1, *Don Pasquale,* with Susini as the Don, was a last-minute replacement for *Martha,* because of Kellogg's indisposition. On Monday, the 3rd, *La traviata* was presented at Irving Place, with the new baritone Francesco Ippolito making his local bow as Germont. "It is a good sign in a young artist," perversely reasoned the *Albion (ibid.),* "that he sings too loud to please the greater part of the audience. It shows that he is not deficient in resources and can tone down without disappearing altogether." But although Ippolito possessed an "old-fashioned baritone voice, circumscribed by rude blasts and fearful gustiness in the upper part and an arctic coldness . . . in the lower," between these extremes he possessed a "temperate zone of very refreshing kind," and for this reason the writer was disposed to welcome him as "successor to poor Amodio."

Lucia di Lammermoor was performed in Brooklyn on February 6;[14] *Linda di Chamounix* at Irving Place on February 7;[15] *La traviata* in Brooklyn on the 8th,[16] and, to

[13] "Large and expensive companies have given way to small and inexpensive ones," wrote Fry (*Tribune,* February 3, 1862). "The chorus is cut down; the orchestra is reduced; the *prime donne* are of New-York manufacture—plain names like Kellogg and Hinkley, without any foreign sound. . . . This opera we believe is about as good as the public will pay for and enable the manager to grow rich in a short time. The public want some music, and they are disposed to take small favors."

[14] With Hinkley (Lucia), Brignoli (Edgardo), Ippolito (Ashton), and Barili (Raymond).

[15] With Kellogg (Linda), Amalia Strakosch (Pierotto), Mancusi (Antonio), Brignoli (Carlo), Susini (the Prefect), Rubio (Intendant), and Dubreuil (Marquis de Boisfleury).

[16] "Brooklyn's favorite opera," sardonically wrote Seymour (*Times,* February 10, 1862), was performed by an ever-improving Kellogg, with Brignoli, Mancusi, and Barili. "No other opera draws such crowded houses, and on no occasion do the good people so liberally patronize librettos and bouquets as when *La traviata* is on the bills. . . . Mr. Grau deserves from Brooklyn hearty recognition

close the season, *La sonnambula*[17] at Irving Place on February 10, with Clara Louise Kellogg charming in her new role of Amina (if a bit overwhelmed in the second act). On February 15, at Irving Place, Grau presented a Grand Gala Matinée with *Martha.*

"We must not look a gift horse in the mouth," admonished Fry in a rambling summation of the deterioriated opera situation and several loosely related topics (*Tribune,* February 10, 1862). "The operas at the Academy have been, owing to the war, simply a spasm. They were not designed or performed by the contractor for the season, Mr. Ullman, who prudently withdrew, owing to the belligerent storm and the colossal tax." Taking advantage of the situation, Grau had picked up the "operatic waifs" and, working his way through "the lands of the Puritans," had finally arrived at the Academy of Music of this "deserted city."

"A large opera house demands large means," continued Fry; the Academy was really too big for a small company with small voices. "Accordingly, this last week, with a small orchestra, blighted chorus, and singers generally wanting in power for such a wide *enceinture,*" the opera had been unutterably dull, to say the least.

Perhaps to compensate for the fractured social show at the opera house, the Strongs planned an ultra-recherché private musicale, to which they invited the Uppermost of their Upper-Ten friends and connections.

February 9. . . . Tonight Scharfenberg here, Murray Hoffman, [his brother] Wickham Hoffman, and others. A musical performance comes off tomorrow night on these premises, organized by Mrs. Ellie. I do not know the program, but fear it includes Verdi.

February 12. . . . Monday night's party was pleasant. About one hundred [guests]. William Astor, Dick [Richard Grant] White, George Bancroft, a Mrs. Chickering from Boston, Brigadier General [Julius] Stahel[18]—epaulettes and all—my nice little nephew Henry Derby (a Harvard sophomore), pretty Miss Caroline Strong, Mrs. Mott [another Bostonian] and Mrs. McVickar, Mr. and Mrs. George Miller, Madame de Trobriand with a little rosebud of a daughter, Miss Charlotte Wilson, Mrs. Christine Griffin, beautiful Mrs. John Kernochan, Brignoli (!!!), who came in late after the Opera, Mrs. Jones, etc., etc.

The vocalizers were Miss Reed of Boston, Barry, and Cooke, now a divinity student. We had some good four-handed piano playing by Scharfenberg and someone else, and a nice trio of Schubert's—caviar to nine-tenths of the audience. Most of the program sad rubbish.

~~~

Nestled among the pages of Strong's journal is the program of the musicale, elegantly printed in French, its margins bestrewn with Strong's less elegant private comments on its content. An opening group of "*morceaux de piano à quatre mains*" by Schu-

---

of his services. He has kept all his promises, broken no engagement, and given them *Traviata* twice. What more can they ask?"

[17] A comfortingly familiar work, obviating the need for consulting a "badly printed libretto, compared with which a catalogue of a Geological Museum is light and entertaining," quipped the *Albion* critic (February 15, 1862, p. 79).

[18] A Hungarian-born Civil War hero.

bert, played by Scharfenberg and "someone else," were "Bosh"; the assorted vocal solos and ensembles by Donizetti, Verdi, and Arditi were mostly "Rubbish"; a Chopin Nocturne and Liszt's *La campanella,* played by the anonymous pianist, were more "Rot." Only Miss Reed's "very good" performance of Gluck's *Che faro senza Euridice* and Schubert's Trio in E-flat, op. 100, for piano, violin, and cello, played by Scharfenberg and his cohorts, received Strong's approval. The latter, he noted, was "a fine composition thrown away on an audience, two-thirds of which it bored fearfully."

On February 8 a smaller, less starchy musical party was given at Louis Descombes's piano warerooms in East Ninth Street. The host was Louis Moreau Gottschalk, who at last had safely negotiated his passage from Cuba and was about to play his return concert amid torrents of Ullman-like publicity generated by Grau, now become Gottschalk's co-manager with Max Strakosch.[19] Purportedly to renew old ties, some twenty-five members of the music community had been invited, music journalists included. Among them was R. Storrs Willis, who in his *Once a Month* (February 1862, pp. 21–23) vividly describes the memorable evening, with Gottschalk, a courtly and elegant host, regaling his guests with epicurean delicacies, superb Havana cigars, and magical, spur-of-the-moment performances of his entrancing new compositions.[20]

Late in the evening the opera troupe—at least, its male component—arrived, having that evening closed their Brooklyn season with *La traviata,* whereupon "the pleasures were prolonged to the small hours, the Aetnas of tobacco cloudily ascending and the blue-seal corks talking to each other with a continuous sauciness." Indeed, so compelling was the mood, wrote Willis, that journalists who had been deadly enemies for years past were lulled into dulcet brotherhood: "The typographical hatchet was buried in one or two instances, and in several others the imaginary hatchet suddenly dissolved in the smoke of Gottschalk's superb Havanas and floated off with the tones of his dashing measures." If only the South could be similarly influenced, sighed Willis, "without our using the hatchet of conviction with such reluctant severity as we have of late!"

And if only the critical naysayers would cease their censure of Gottschalk for playing only his own compositions to the exclusion of the sacrosanct German classics! Willis reports (or fantasizes) a three-cornered exchange between *We,* representing the "American impartial [meaning pro-Gottschalk] party," *You,* symbolizing the condemnatory "German party" (could Hagen have been invited?), and *Gottschalk* himself, who—after listening to *We* and *You*'s apparently inexhaustible quibbling over what he did or did not represent, of what he was or was not capable, and of his importance or lack of

---

[19] Grau's epical announcement of Gottschalk's return concert on February 11 was on a par with Ullman's most virtuosic promotional prose. Virtually a biographical essay, it traced Gottschalk's career from his early triumphs in Europe (complete with lauds by Adolphe Adam, Berlioz, and Fiorentino) to his sensational recent exploits in the Antilles.

[20] He caused the piano to sound "as if every key were cut from the tusk of an inspired elephant," ecstatically reported the *Home Journal* (February 22, 1862). Gottschalk played his *Murmures éoliens,* op. 46 (*c.* 1858–59) (Doyle, D-102; *Piano Works,* IV, 81), and, with Richard Hoffman's admirable assistance ("as if he needed assistance!"), his *Ojos criollos,* op. 37 (*c.* 1859), for piano, four hands (D-105; *Piano Works,* IV, 109), and his four-hand transcription of Rossini's *William Tell* Overture (*c.* 1850–54) (D-160; *Piano Works,* III, 73).

importance in the greater musical scheme of things—passionately expounded his musical credo: in effect, his rejoinder to the carping Dwights and Hagens of the world.[21]

"Understand then that I am simply Gottschalk, and nobody else," he declared. "I could not be other, if I would—and I certainly would not be, if I could. I compose just to suit myself, and if my way please you, I am delighted—if not, I cannot help it.

"The Germans and their music I don't much like—with exceptions, of course. A sonata of Mozart sounds thinnish to me, of only Homeopathic potency, and *very* 'mildly drawn.' Those little bits of melodies in one hand and little bits of accompaniments in the other—don't ask me to like them—I cannot.

"Gentlemen, the end and aim of art is to please, not to instruct, or indoctrinate, or anything of the sort. If I succeed in pleasing, what matter how, or by what means? And I must do it in my own way. Every man has his way, and just to the extent that mine is successful, call me an artist.

"And why this endless comparison?" he demanded. "A flower, if it charm at all, charms because it is like itself, and not in proportion as it resembles some other flower. . . . Let us artists blossom out as we will and follow the leading of our instincts as to what is beautiful and what will please. Time will test us and our works sufficiently—be sure of that. Therefore, my Teutonic friend, swear by your German worthies and only by them, if you will. This is a free country, and nothing could be more free than individual taste and fancy. Only don't think it is necessary, liking *them*, to hate *me*. Indifference, it strikes me, is quite as strong a feeling as the case justifies; and indifference (let me confidentially tell you) is a much severer trial to men of sensibility than hate."

Gottschalk then disclosed that he was planning a book, "whether of life or art, or both, is not quite clear," wrote Willis. "He showed us the material, however, very promiscuously heaped in a trunk, and filling it to the brim."

Most likely this "material" consisted largely of Gottschalk's journal, written in French during his recent adventuresome years in the West Indies. Together with his account of his ensuing wartime concert tours and beyond, a chastened version of the journal, rendered into English under his sister Clara's stern editorship, was eventually published in 1881, twelve years after Gottschalk's death, as *Notes of a Pianist.*♪

Writing of his fervently acclaimed return concert after a five years' absence, Gottschalk confesses (February 15, 1862): "I played badly. I felt too much emotion for my fingers and my mind not to be affected by it. I recognized among the audience all the well-disposed physiognomies of unknown friends who, during my long series of concerts at Dodworth's Hall in 1855, constantly had encouraged and sustained me, and had been the first to contribute to the success of *Marche de nuit*♪ and *Last Hope*,♪ which I had [then] just composed. Richard Hoffman, one of the rare brotherhood of the piano, who has always given me proofs of good fellowship, had lent me his cooperation to play my *Guillaume Tell* [Overture] and *Ojos criollos*" (*Notes*, pp. 44–45).

Although no stranger to show business, Gottschalk was nonetheless irked by his

---

[21] Naming no names, in his journal, *Notes of a Pianist* (Behrend edition, hereinafter cited as *Notes*), pp. 45–46, Gottschalk's entry for February 15, 1862, mildly refers to Dwight as "an old [Unitarian] minister who does not understand music" and, less mildly, to "Mr. H." [Hagen], as one who "continues to distill from his sourish little pen the personal spite that he pours out every week [every fortnight] through his little musical drain."

Gottschalk, sure of himself in
spite of criticism and carping.

managers' excessive promotional tactics: "My impresarios, Strakosch and Grau, having discovered that my first concert in New York on my return from Europe in 1853 took place on February 11, decided to postpone my reappearance for some days so that it might take place on February 11, 1862—a memorable coincidence, of which the public (whom it did not interest the least in the world) was informed through all the newspapers."

Impresarios, wrote Gottschalk, treated their artists as so much negotiable merchandise, taking the credit (and profit) for their successes and making them the scapegoats for anything that went awry. Grau, in fact, had contrived a neat scheme for presenting Gottschalk with fitting grandeur while at the same time keeping his opera company intact and employed at minimal expense. Closing his opera season, as we know, at the Irving Place Academy on February 10, he presented the "Grand Gottschalk *rentrée*"[22] the next evening at Niblo's Saloon,[23] with his opera stars Hinkley,

[22] For which tickets, at the usual dollar for admission, and fifty cents extra for reserved seats, were on sale at Beer and Schirmer's, the successors to Breusing's music store at 701 Broadway.

[23] An outdated venue, but far less expensive than the Academy, and easier to fill. Grau justified his choice of Niblo's Saloon in his concert advertisements, sentimentally explaining that it was the hall in which the "greatest pianists who have visited America," especially Thalberg, had enjoyed their

Susini, Mancusi, and Brignoli (an old friend of Gottschalk's from Paris days)[24] to assist with an assortment of favorite arias and ensembles from popular operas by Donizetti and Verdi. Also present were Richard Hoffman, who played duets with Gottschalk on one and two pianos, Henry Mollenhauer, who filled the interstices with showpieces for cello, and Maretzek, whose grandiose title "Director of Music and Conductor" served as a euphemism for "piano accompanist."

Gottschalk's return was unanimously acclaimed (except by Hagen) "the great musical event of the season." On first appearing, reported the *Herald* (February 12, 1862): "The lion of the evening, with his breast decorated by a profusion of orders," received a tumultuous welcome from a brilliant audience that filled every inch of space at Niblo's.[25] In the first part of the program he played, with Richard Hoffman, his spectacular four-hand transcription of the Overture to *William Tell* (encored by "The Last Hope"); in the second he was heard in his bravura solo transcription of the Quartet from *Rigoletto* (now lost), his *Murmures éoliens,* and his so-called *Fabliau* ("medieval tale"), *Pastorella e cavalliere,* op. 32 (*c.* 1859),[26] which, in response to "immense applause," he encored with his *Marche solonelle (Apothéose),* op. 29 (*c.* 1856)[27] ("by far the most difficult piece that he executed during the evening," wrote the *Herald*); and finally, by request, he played "'The Banjo,'♪ with that peculiarity of touch which he alone possesses."

Everyone was struck by the "wonderful improvement that hard study and practice [had] made in his execution," continued the *Herald*. "Poetry and sentiment he never lacked. He has attained since we last heard him—some five years since—a marvelous power in giving expression to the creations of a fancy cultivated to a point of which there have been few examples in his profession."

---

greatest successes. To say nothing of its being the very hall in which Gottschalk, by a "curious coincidence," had made his New York debut exactly nine years earlier, to the day. The *Albion* critic (February 15, 1862, p. 79) thought Niblo's Saloon an unfortunate choice for Gottschalk's concerts, not only because it was inaccessible but because the "minstrel stage" constructed for George Christy in 1859 had rendered it inappropriate as a proper concert hall.

[24]Hearing Brignoli in *Martha,* Gottschalk wrote (*Notes,* pp 52–53): "This favorite tenor still has his beautiful voice, and has preserved, notwithstanding the progress of an *embonpoint* that annoys him, the aristocratic appearance that—with his fine hair and his handsome white neck—has given him so much success with the ladies. Notwithstanding the defects with which his detractors reproach him, he is an artist whom I admire above all singers—who are all, for the most part, uncouth. He understands music and knows how to judge a musical work. His enemies will be much astonished to learn that he knows by heart Hummel's Concerto in A minor, which he studied when, as a child, he thought of becoming a pianist, and which he still plays in a charming manner. He knows how to sing, and if it were not for his fear of the public, which paralyzes all his powers, he would be classed among the best singers of the age. Besides," added Gottschalk, "he is careful of his grooming, which, among artists, is one of the rarest qualities, and which I place among the most brilliant of those possessed by Brignoli. I knew him in 1849 in Paris, at the period when, still quite young, he made his debut under the amorous aegis of the beautiful Madame R."

[25]Hagen, an Iago among critics, professed to be "rather disappointed" at the "only moderate" size of the audience, and this despite "the extraordinary exertions of the Press to produce a sensation in favor of this pianist" (*Review and World,* February 15, 1862, p. 39).

[26]Supplied with a note-by-note scenario, *Pastorella e cavalliere* (D-114; *Piano Works,* IV, 193) was published by Hall in 1862.

[27]*Apothéose* (D-5; *Piano Works,* I, 9).

The *Times* (February 12, 1862) more precisely defined the ways in which Gottschalk had grown: "Mr. Gottschalk returns to us with his character more matured and his artistic mind stronger," wrote Seymour. "His gems are not strung at random, but polished and presented with the skill of a master. His style is more distinct and charming, and his way of rendering it seemed to us to be more perfect. The Overture to *William Tell* is the work of a thoughtful writer who knows his own capacity and does not hesitate to tax it to its greatest extent. It is filled with effects of the most startling character, effects enormous in their difficulty, that are hardly likely to descend to other pianists.[28] Mr. Gottschalk's endurance is as remarkable as his cleanness of touch and delicateness of articulation: in the most rapid passages he never becomes incoherent; never by accident makes a false use of the pedals or attempts to cover a blemish with a bang. All that he does is honest and perfect." Seymour also dangles a tiny clue to the content of the lost *Rigoletto* transcription: "The *Rigoletto* Fantasie deals with the Quartette in a broad and generous way and is singularly fresh in its adornments." Yet more tantalizingly, the *Albion* (February 15, 1862, p. 79) pronounced it "altogether better than Liszt's [*Rigoletto* Paraphrase] in point of effect, and yet it is totally different in the means by which it is produced."

Even Hagen—albeit grudgingly—pronounced the *Rigoletto* Fantasie, like the *William Tell* Overture, to have been very well written for the piano. But Hagen persisted in his earlier condemnation of Gottschalk: "Just as we then considered him a first-rate pianist, so do we now; but his style not having changed in the least, we cannot help confessing again that we do not admire it. We find a want of variety and an overdose of sweetness in it, which is not to our taste. We willingly hear him in his *Marche de nuit* and in his *Pastorella e cavalliere,* and even his 'Last Hope'; but then, having become quite familiar with his individuality, we should like to hear something else." Hagen condescended to offer advice: "Mr. Gottschalk's technical ability is such as to enable him to play many pieces by Chopin and other writers. Why does he not intersperse his Programmes with these pieces? This would increase the impression of his own compositions and offer a general relief from that monotony which now his performances must invariably produce" (*Review and World,* February 16, 1862, p. 39).

Later intensifying the attack, a wide-eyed Hagen noted that there had generally been "considerable surprise in musical circles that Mr. Gottschalk did not play a few compositions by the classical masters, such as Beethoven and others." This seemed to him unfair, he protested, since nothing in Gottschalk's background or capabilities—aesthetic or technical—would have equipped him to so much as approach the sonatas of Beethoven's second period, to say nothing of the third; or Mendelssohn's concertos; or even Schumann's minor compositions. Hagen disingenuously suggested that with Gottschalk's "natural capacity for technics" he might succeed, after a few years' diligent study of Clementi's *Gradus ad parnassum* and Bach's "Well-tempered Clavichord," in technically mastering the simpler of the aforementioned classics, "although he will never grasp and appreciate the ideas contained in them." Perhaps, helpfully suggested Hagen, he might occasionally be able to tackle a piece by "good writers for the parlor,

---

[28] Hagen conceded that the *William Tell* transcription was "very well written" and "superbly played." It would make, he suggested, a welcome addition to the scanty existing repertory of easy examination pieces for young lady boarding-school students.

such as [Julius] Schulhoff,♪ whose music is easily understood, and yet by no means trivial. There are also the minor compositions by Chopin and some music by Weber, which, we think, Mr. Gottschalk would be able to perform satisfactorily" (*Review and World,* March 15, 1862, p. 63).

At his second concert, at Niblo's Saloon on February 12, Gottschalk played his *Marche solonelle (Apothéose),*[29] his Grand Fantasy on Donizetti's *La favorita,* op. 68 (*c.* 1859),[30] and, with Richard Hoffman, his *Ojos criollos.*[31] On the very next night Gottschalk and his company repeated their first program at the Brooklyn Athenaeum, and the night after that (February 14) he was back at Niblo's Saloon, playing his Grand Paraphrase on the *Miserere* from *Il trovatore,*[32] often confused with the superspectacular two-piano *Trovatore* transcription that he had performed with Thalberg in 1856.♪ Also he repeated the *Ojos criollos* and, again by request, "The Last Hope" and "The Banjo."

Grau, to preserve his opera franchise, mounted a Grand Gala Matinée at the Academy of Music on Saturday, February 15, with Clara Louise Kellogg (not a member of the Gottschalk galaxy) as Lady Harriet in *Martha.* Then, on February 17 and 18, Gottschalk—heralded anew by a fresh collection of panegyrics culled from twelve of New York's leading newspapers—reappeared at Niblo's Saloon for a pair of farewell concerts before allegedly going on tour.

"The excitement of the past week in fashionable musical and journalistic circles was the return of the eminent pianist Mr. Gottschalk," wrote Seymour in a follow-up editorial in the *Times* (February 17, 1862). "Every one with an opinion to utter has been careful to deliver it," and the collective wisdom added up to "a loud chorus of praise." Gottschalk, as a young American artist, had reason to be proud of his triumph, a triumph rarely falling to the lot of even the most deserving.

It was particularly gratifying, wrote Seymour, that the excitement over Gottschalk was truly merited, and "not a cheap incense burnt to the gods of our own making." As a composer Gottschalk was unique: "He cannot be likened to anyone who has preceded him, nor does he resemble anyone who is here now. What light he possesses is his own, not the refraction of another luminary. In his style he differs as widely from the German school as the latter does from the Italian—a blessed divergence [a sly thrust at Hagen] too vast to be measured in a sentence. . . . His music does not even *look* like anyone else's. . . . And yet it is never eccentric, albeit frequently learned and abstruse; never lopsided or vulgar, or pedantic, or trivial."

Having listed the numberless felicities of the Gottschalkian composing magic, Seymour at last turned to Gottschalk's no less superb pianistic attributes: "Nature has been kindly toward him in the way of fingers and otherwise bestowing upon him the precise kind of strength that he requires. . . . He is able to introduce passages of great force after exhausting the usual difficulties, and at a point where other players would

[29] Probably the same work, conjectures John Doyle (p. 192), as the "Fragment" of the legendary Concerto in F minor—similarly designated a *Grande marche solonelle*—that Gottschalk had performed in Brooklyn in 1856.

[30] *La favorita* (D-54; *Piano Works,* II, 203), posthumously published by Hall in 1871.

[31] Rounding out the program, the vocalists sang excerpts from Mercadante's *Il bravo,* Flotow's *Martha,* and from five Donizetti operas: *Don Pasquale, Maria di Rudenz, Lucia di Lammermoor, Linda di Chamounix,* and *La favorita;* Mollenhauer played a Fantasie for cello by Servais.

[32] *Miserere du Trovatore, Paraphrase de Concert* (D-97; *Piano Works,* IV, 53).

desire to leave off. Nothing can exceed the pearly distinctness of his scales, the evenness and limpidity of his trills—single and double—the smoothness with which his
fingers travel over thirds and sixths, or the agile willingness of his wrists in octaves."
And although all good pianists were expected to understand the use of the pedals, it
was Gottschalk, who, "by a deft combination of force and mechanism," truly made
them the means of creating a "peculiar musical atmosphere in which to sink drowsily
to thought or mount vigorously to action. . . . We have said enough to show that we
regard Mr. Gottschalk as one of the greatest artists now living," declared Seymour.
"His genius in some respects is exceptional and places him apart from other men."

At his following concert (February 17) Gottschalk, departing from his custom of
playing only his own music, "embroidered" (improvised?) upon a *Polka de concert* for
two pianos, with its composer, his gifted pupil and prospective touring colleague Harry
Sanderson, at the other piano. Of his own compositions Gottschalk played his Reminiscences of *Lucrezia Borgia,* another lost work,[33] his nocturne, *Reflets du passé,* op. 28
(1853?), his mazurka *Jeunesse,*♩ op. 70 (1859),[34] and his Fantasia *di bravura* on *La favorita.*

It was not until Gottschalk's "final" concert, on February 18, that Strong, who
derived his musical sustenance from a different fountainhead, momentarily capitulated
to the pervading Gottschalk fever, but not before he had refreshed his eternal dialogue
with Beethoven.

February 15. . . . At half-past three to the Philharmonic rehearsal. Irving Hall. *Eroica.* Appreciated it all, except that preposterous fugue in the second movement. What
can it mean, and why was it put there, and isn't it dreary? But after the C-minor, this
is surely the greatest of symphonies.

February 17. . . . To Scharfenberg's (63 West 36th Street) with Ellie and Miss Rosalie tonight. Small musical party, including George Bancroft, Mrs. Camilla Hoyt, Miss
Mary Hamilton. . . . Mozart's Quartette, no. 1 in G [K. 387?]. Very lovely. Andante
and Minuetto specially clear and beautiful. Schubert's Trio, no. 2 in E-flat (played here
last Monday) was nice. Not specially clear, genial, or popular, except the third movement; that is a gem. Schumann's Quartette [op. 41?], no. 1, in A, an asphyxiating bore.
Miss Reed sang [Gluck's] *Che farò senza Eurydice* and *Il va venir* from [Halévy's] *La Juive.*
Have known the latter for some ten years or more, and pronounce it deliberately to
be among the most leaden and offensive specimens of modern Opera music.

February 18. . . . Tonight with Ellie, Miss Rosalie, and Mrs. D. C. Murray to
Gottschalk's concert at Niblo's Saloon. He has great command of the piano and could
render real music admirably if he chose to play it.[35] But he prefers pseudo-musical
manifestations of physical strength and dexterous manipulation. His feats are surpris-

---

[33] Probably the *Lucrezia Borgia: transcription du finale* that Gottschalk had played on January 15 and
March 8, 1856, at the third and eighth concerts of his memorable 1856 series of concerts.♩

[34] *Reflets du passé* (D-129; *Piano Works,* V, 11). *Jeunesse,* as the *Times* (February 19, 1862) reminded its readers, had frequently been played by Satter (see OBBLIGATO: 1861).

[35] Strong evidently read the *Musical Review and World.* The distasteful music that Gottschalk had
chosen for this occasion included his *William Tell* Overture, with Harry Sanderson replacing Richard
Hoffman as his partner, his *O ma charmante, épargnez moi* (O my Charmer, Spare Me), op. 44 (*c.* 1861)
(D-107; *Piano Works,* IV, 113); his *Suis-moi!* ("Follow Me!"), op. 45 (*c.* 1861) (D-150; *Piano Works,* V,
223); his *Pastorella e cavalliere;* and his *Rigoletto* transcription. Nor did Strong have ears for the singers'
contributions, an assortment of opera arias and ensembles by Verdi, Mercadante, Donizetti, and
Rossini.

ing. But I think those of the Hanlon Brothers[36] and other like athletes more exciting, and those of Herrmann the "Préstidigitateur" more amusing.

March 2. . . . [returning to his natural element] Yesterday afternoon I heard the *Eroica* at the Philharmonic rehearsal. Specially impressed by the second movement. Every note (except in its impertinent fugue) translucent and of intense significance. The Scherzo is not what the old programs of 1843 described it: "the return of the French soldiers" *(und Heimwerts schlägt der sanfte Friedensmarsch)* [and homeward drives the gentle march of peace] but a holiday or festival spree in camp. The fourth is the return of the victorious army to its capital—Paris or Vienna—celebration, bustle, and excitement—cannon-shot—signal that the column is near the gates (the single notes that follow the opening *tutti*)—gradual swell of martial music (into the simple melody characteristic of the movement) mingled with phrases that suggest joyful recognition and welcome of the restored son or brother—vigorous modification of the melody into something that suggests plebeian jubilation in its wildest form, through which comes piercing the original melody, high up in the orchestra, as if the fife were heard through and above the roar of the mob. A most pungent and powerful little bit of melody it is, with a most special "nutty" aroma, like that of old Madeira. It underlies the whole movement. It reappears (at the change of time) as a majestic and mournful expression of sorrow—in the midst of exultation—for those who have fallen with honor. This may be bosh, but to me it seems very manifest and real.

⌁

Apparently Strong did not attend the Philharmonic concert, on March 15, when, in addition to the "Eroica," Eisfeld conducted Marschner's Overture to *Der Vampyr*♪♫ and a first performance of *Deux Morceaux symphoniques pour orchestre et piano* by Robert Goldbeck, who played the piano solo. Hagen was tolerant of these performances—and in varying degrees of *Ländliche Szene,* a Fantasie for bassoon by the German composer Neukirchner, played by the Philharmonic bassoonist Paul Eltz—but was relentless in his condemnation of a hapless Miss Ludecus, who unwisely attempted Mendelssohn's *Infelice,* op. 94, and Schumann's *Widmung,* op. 25, no. 1. "Why must we always be annoyed in our Philharmonic concerts with poor singing?" he raged. "If the society cannot afford to pay for a singer (but we think it can), then let it at least avoid to make these concerts a field for all kinds of singing lessons" (*Review and World,* March 20, 1862, p. 74).

Nor was Strong present at the fifth and final Philharmonic concert of the 1861–62 season, on April 26, when Eisfeld conducted Schubert's great Symphony in C (lasting, without repeats—as Hagen's neighbor informed him—forty-three minutes), the first local performance of Liszt's symphonic poem *Orpheus* (1853–54) (Searle 98), and Beethoven's Overture to *Fidelio.* Bruno Wollenhaupt played the first movement of the *Concerto militaire,* op. 24, by the Polish violin virtuoso and composer Karol Lipiński (1790–1861); Richard Hoffman, "by particular request" (a phrase to which Hagen took particular exception), played Mozart's Concerto, "No. 8" in D (?), with Hummel's cadenzas; and F. Letch, a Philharmonic trombonist, played a concertino for trombone (another first performance) by the German composer/violinist Ferdinand David.♪

Gottschalk, in the meantime, had bade his "positively" final farewell to Brooklyn

---

[36] Popular acrobats whose spectacularly named "Zampillaerestation" exploits had been a sensation at the Academy of Music in December 1861.

on February 19 and was scheduled immediately to depart for concerts in Philadelphia, Baltimore, and Washington, stopping off, en route, for an appearance in Newark on the 21st. But Grau, who apparently could not bear to interrupt the lucrative Gottschalk steamroller, announced two Grand Gottschalk post-farewell farewells at Niblo's Saloon: on February 20, with Carlotta Patti replacing Isabella Hinkley as his star assistant, and—after snatching a flying trip to Newark on the 21st—a "Grand Gottschalk Matinée" on February 22, a Saturday.[37] At this Gala, recalling Thalberg's remorseless ubiquity, Gottschalk performed his "Gems" between the acts of an opera, a scaled-down production of *Don Pasquale* performed by Hinkley, Brignoli, Mancusi, and Susini, with Maretzek accompanying, presumably at the piano.[38]

So rapturously were these events received that Grau—abandoning his overworked farewell ploy—announced four additional Grand Gottschalk Galas: at Niblo's Saloon on February 26; then (after tucking in a rapid jump to Hartford on the 27th) at the Fourteenth-Street Academy of Music on February 28 and March 1, the latter a Grand Gottschalk Gala Matinée; followed by a Grand Gottschalk Gala Night at the Brooklyn Academy on March 3.

"Tonight Mr. Gottschalk will give his eighth concert at Niblo's Saloon, assisted by the opera artists [again in a performance of *Don Pasquale*],"[39] wrote a nettled William Henry Fry in the *Tribune* on February 26. "A 'Grand Gala Opera Night,' whatever, in the name of English and sense that may mean, will take place at the Academy on Friday [February 28],[40] and the same tremendous thing in Brooklyn on Monday [March 3].[41] We were requested to record a final concert for Mr. Gottschalk. What, in the name of art, is this deception practiced on the press and public for? Who speaks for him? Such humbug shall be stopped as far as our columns are concerned. If an artist believes in himself and his art, let him not be 'exploited' after this fashion." The exploitation nonetheless continued profitably, with no discernible complaint on the part of the exploitee.

At the Niblo's concert Gottschalk, with two of the Mollenhauers, played a group of works now lost: his Two Tarentelles for piano, violin, and cello,[42] and the tantalizing "Fragment" of his Concerto in F minor. He also played his Fantasy on *La favorita*

---

[37] Washington's Birthday was spiritedly celebrated in wartime New York, wrote Strong, with "parade, jubilation, universal efflorescence of flags. . . . Tonight there was a quasi-illumination in all the houses around Gramercy Park; the front window blinds and shutters were thrown open and the gas lit in every story" (Private Journal, February 22, 1862).

[38] In a hopelessly garbled mass of errata, Loggins (p. 188) transforms this February 22 matinée at Niblo's Saloon into a fictitious evening event at the Academy of Music with Clara Louise Kellogg, not Isabella Hinkley, singing the Norina in *Don Pasquale,* and with Gottschalk creating a frenzy with his performance, against a background of American flags, of his patriotic piece "The Union" (see below).

[39] Loggins again transposes the locale of this event to the Academy and the opera to *Lucia* with Kellogg, confusing it with a performance that did not take place until February 28.

[40] When Kellogg made her inauspicious debut as *Lucia* in a shoddy production, despite Maretzek, who this time presided over a small orchestra. "We have seldom seen *Lucia di Lammermoor* worse performed in this city," wrote the *Herald* (March 3, 1862).

[41] Not exactly the same tremendous thing. In Brooklyn on March 3 the opera was not *Don Pasquale* but *Betly,* with Isabella Hinkley. Gottschalk, too, added his *Danza,* op. 33 (1857) (D-41; *Piano Works,* II, 163), to the program he had performed at the Niblo's concert (see below).

[42] Numbered 201 in the Offergeld catalogue, the work is listed as "Piano Trio: Two Tarantelles." Never published, no manuscript of it is known to have survived.

and, for the first time, his fascinating *Souvenir de Porto Rico (Marche des gibaros),* op. 31 (*c.* 1857–58).[43] But by far the greatest sensation of the evening was his patriotic Civil War piece "The Union," op. 48 (1862),[44] a spectacular medley of "The Star-Spangled Banner," "Yankee Doodle," and "Hail Columbia," bearing a timely dedication to Major General George B. McClellan.

Scarcely had the Brooklyn Grand Gottschalk Gala been consummated than Grau announced two more Grand Gottschalk Galas for March 6 and 8 at the New York Academy.[45] This time, however, he was unable to juggle a further deferment of Gottschalk's overdue concert commitments in Washington,[46] Baltimore, and Philadelphia, and thus Gottschalk's New York adorers were consigned to a fortnight of enforced Gottschalk-deprivation.

Worse, upon his triumphant return to New York in mid-March, Gottschalk was announced for only a single "positively last concert" at Niblo's Saloon on March 17[47] before going on a tour of the Midwest. On this occasion, with Sanderson at a second piano, he played his transcription of Méhul's "The Chase of King Henry"♩ and, probably to thumb his nose at Hagen, what appears to have been his embellished version of the "March Finale" of Weber's *Concertstück.* Solo he played his *Jeunesse, Danza,* and *Marche des gibaros;* also he accompanied Brignoli in a *Sérénade* that he had purportedly composed for the singer and dedicated to him.[48]

A single last concert, except, that is, for a loudly trumpeted *matinée d'instruction,*[49] to take place at Irving Hall the very next day. For this event, using the Thalberg matinées as a model, two pianos facing in opposite directions were placed at the center of the room. Thus positioned (according to the advertisements) within easy "eyeview" of each listener: "The special [pedagogical] object of these entertainments [was] to present to the eye, as well as the ear, of the spectator the method by which modern effects are produced on the piano-forte." The circular seating arrangement in the hall, although space-consuming, was intended, it was explained, to "enable Mr. Gottschalk to converse with those present, and to explain what they may desire to have made clear to them."

At this event Gottschalk, unassisted, was announced to perform five pieces and then play whatever the audience chose to select from his repertory.[50] Three of the an-

---

[43] *Souvenir de Porto Rico. Marche des gibaros* (D-147; *Piano Works,* V, 199). Gottschalk is said to have composed this work for his versatile teen-aged touring partner Adelina Patti, who played its first performance in Ponce in 1858 (see Doyle, p. 324).

[44] "The Union" (D-156; *Piano Works,* V, 265).

[45] Since February 11, reported the *Dispatch* (March 9, 1862), Gottschalk had given twelve concerts in New York, three in Brooklyn, one each in Hartford and New Haven, two in Philadelphia, and three, to sold-out houses, in Washington.

[46] One of his first acts on reaching Washington, wrote Gottschalk, was to swear a solemn Oath of Allegiance to the Union (*Notes,* March 5, 1862, p. 55).

[47] With Carlotta Patti, Brignoli, Mancusi, and Sanderson, and with Carl Bergmann replacing Maretzek, who had departed, or was about to depart, for Havana.

[48] A switched dedication. The work was originally composed in Cuba in 1861 as a *Serenata a Paulina M.* With new texts in English and French, and with a dedication to Brignoli, it was published by Hall in 1863 as "Idol of Beauty" *(Viens, O ma belle)* (D-71).

[49] Ambiguously advertised both as a single event and the first of a series.

[50] "The plan of the entertainment is excellent," approved the *Times* (March 18, 1862), "and to the lady admirers of the great pianist will be peculiarly attractive, for Mr. Gottschalk not only supplies

nounced pieces—a strange gallimaufry—were of Gottschalkian origin: an otherwise unidentified *Polka de concert,* his arrangement of "God Save the Queen," op. 41 (1850/1860?), and his *Polonia, Grande caprice de concert,* op.35/43 (1859).[51] Also listed were Chopin's Funeral March and finally a Polonaise by "Fradle" (doubtless a reference to the New York musician Charles Fradel).

On his return to the United States, Gottschalk had been astonished to find New York in 1862 "at least as brilliant as when I left it in 1857." In Cuba, he wrote, he had been told that in wartime New York "the theatres are closed; that the public finances and private fortunes are exhausted; that the North is a prey to famine" (*Notes,* p. 51). By the time Gottschalk arrived, an astounding renaissance of concert and opera activities, largely attributable to Grau, was under way. And not only in New York. "Gottschalk has added himself to all Herr Grau's enterprises, whether of opera or concert," wrote the *Home Journal* (March 15, 1862); and Grau had now expanded his activities to embrace, as separate entities, a Gottschalk concert tour of the Midwest[52] and yet another miniature opera season to begin on March 19 at the New York Academy. His opera company included Kellogg, Hinkley, Amalia Strakosch, Brignoli, Mancusi, and Susini, with Anschütz to conduct; and with the beautiful and gifted Spanish dancer, Isabel Cubas, her partner Juan Ximenes[53] and a "powerful corps de ballet" were present to provide the ancillary choreographic embellishments until now largely shunned in America.

Thus, at the opening offering, *Un ballo in maschera,* instead of volunteers from the audience participating in the last-act masked ball, Cubas and her group performed a "spirited terpsichorean divertissement"[54] of a brilliance "never yet received in America." Also performed in the ballroom scene was a waltz, composed, of all people, by Brignoli, the evening's Count of Warwick.[55]

"Opera goers have a capacity for Verdi that is perfectly surprising," observed the *World* (March 20, 1862) in its review of the opening. "Notwithstanding the Lenten fast, notwithstanding the War, notwithstanding the impending shower of taxes, the Academy presented last night a magnificent spectacle. Everybody knows the *Ballo* as well as the multiplication table, yet its performance on the opening night of the vernal season brought out the largest audience that ever listened to its—by turns—positively good, comparatively indifferent, and superlatively bad, music.[56] . . . The fact that pro-

---

the entire musical entertainment, but mingles with his audience, and takes their suggestions as to the additional pieces that may be required at his hands."

[51] "God Save the Queen," or "America, *Morceau de concert*" (D-62; *Piano works,* II, 275); *Polonia. Grand Caprice de concert* (D-124; *Piano Works,* IV, 231).

[52] With a revised company consisting, not as Behrend states (in *Notes,* p. 54) of Hinkley, Brignoli, Susini, Mancusi, and Maretzek, but of Carlotta Patti, the tenor George Simpson, the baritone Luciano Morino, the pianist Harry Sanderson, and Carl Bergmann to accompany.

[53] Cubas and Ximenes had been performing at the Winter Garden and other New York theatres for a good part of the past year.

[54] Superimposing an incongruous Iberian flavor upon the already superimposed New England locale of the opera.

[55] With Kellogg (Amelia), Hinkley (the Page), Amalia Strakosch (Ulrica), Mancusi (Renato/Reinhardt), and Barili (Samuele or Tomaso).

[56] "A bad opera of a bad school," wrote the *Dispatch* (March 23, 1862).

fessional terpsichoreans, instead of fun-seeking amateurs, did the business of the masquerade scene doubtless added materially to the receipts of the house. And certainly the improvement was a marked one. The ballet company numbered nearly a hundred.[57] . . . Aside from the opera, the ballroom scene well repaid one for attending. A pleasing trifle in the shape of a waltz, composed by Brignoli, was introduced in the fourth act and met with success."

The following evening (March 20) the company appeared in *Masaniello,* with Señorita Cubas brilliantly assuming the pantomimic role of Fenella, the Dumb Girl of Portici.[58] On the 21st, *Martha* was performed with Clara Louise Kellogg as a delectable Lady Harriet, and with Cubas, Ximenes, and company bringing a whiff of old Spain to Richmond Fair. On the 22nd at the Grand Gala Saturday Matinée, *Masaniello,* the hit of the season, was repeated, and again on the 24th.

On March 26, Eugénie de Lussan,[59] billed as an American *prima donna,* made her long-awaited opera debut as Leonora in *La favorita.*[60] Too long awaited, judged the *Albion* (March 29, 1862, p. 15). Considering "how easily singers with no voice become popular in this country," mused the critic, "who could help—listening to her—trying to account for the tardy acquisition of so full a voice to the lyric stage? . . . Here was one that some years since would have electrified the town; and yet it has been permitted to overripen and spoil for lack of a gatherer."

Madame de Lussan had been ill-advised, too, in her choice of role for her debut, a role dramatically taxing for a performer of far greater dramatic endowments and wider stage experience than she possessed.[61] She was a singer—"a voice, and nothing more," wrote the critic. And that voice, a mezzo-soprano "of good compass and excellent sonority," sympathetic in quality and powerful, was marred by a lack of precision, uncontrollable wobble, infidelity to pitch, and other ills palpably the penalty for years of vocal abuse.

On March 27 the Grau company brought *Masaniello* to the Brooklyn Academy for a single performance, and the night after that, with great fanfare, Madame Elena D'Angri was welcomed back to the New York Academy after an absence of some three years. For her return she chose one of her most celebrated roles, Rosina in *The Barber of Seville,* enhancing it, in the lesson scene, with "The Elena Waltz," a vocal *tour*

[57] Doubtful.

[58] "To Señorita Cubas belongs the success of the evening," wrote Seymour (*Times,* March 21, 1862), "her Fenella being characterized by grace, force, and intelligence—qualities not often found united in representatives of that part." The audible members of the cast were Hinkley (Elvira), Brignoli (Masaniello), Susini (Pietro), Barili (Donello), and Rubio (Alfonso). Brignoli's waltz, now sporting a provocative title, "The Cage of Love," was performed by the orchestra during the interval between the second and third acts.

[59] Madame de Lussan, a Brooklynite, was a former pupil of Elisa Valentini.

[60] With Brignoli (Fernando), Susini (Baltazar), and Mancusi (Alfonso), and with Anschütz conducting. During the second act, Cubas, Ximenes, and their dancers performed a Grand Spanish Divertissement, and between the third and fourth acts Cubas danced her "celebrated Spanish national *pas seul, El olé.*"

[61] Even Steffanone, in the "plenitude of her great physical power," had faltered in the role by the time she reached the fourth act, recalled the *Dispatch* (March 30, 1862). The writer, probably Burkhardt, attributed de Lussan's tremolo largely to stage fright. With that voice, she was capable of much better efforts, he wrote.

de force composed for her by her husband Pedro Abella; as a finale, she sang the *Non più mesta* from *Cenerentola.*

Her voice had lost none of that "power, richness, and flexibility which won her deserved favor on her first appearance here in connection with Thalberg, and which soon placed her in a position nearer to the rank of Alboni than any other contralto who has ever sung in this city," wrote the *Dispatch* (March 30, 1862), presumably Burkhardt.

D'Angri appeared again the following day at Grau's Last and Grand Combination Matinée, but, disappointingly—because of a necessary shift of program due to Susini's worsening hoarseness—not as Pierotto in *Linda di Chamounix* but as Lucia di Lammermoor, and again with the interpolations of Abella's waltz and the *Cenerentola* finale. "Our readers will excuse us if we say nothing of *Lucia,*" meaningfully wrote the *Dispatch.* Between the acts and following the opera, Cubas and her "*corps de ballet, so called,*" performed various works of Spanish origin.

Immediately following this somewhat anticlimactic finale, the company, dancers included, went to Boston for "a few nights." On their return, presumed the *Times* (March 31, 1862), they would probably present small operas at Niblo's Saloon—"an experiment which can be conducted with safety until a larger plan of operations is hit upon." Maretzek was reportedly soon to be leaving for Europe to engage—with Martí's backing—artists for Havana, and, continued the *Times,* "on his success the future management of the Academy may depend."

Strong, whose duties at the Sanitary Commission kept him from hearing much music, was reduced to Cutler's unsatisfactory efforts at Trinity Church.

April 13. . . . At Trinity Church this morning. Thanksgiving sermon by [the Reverend Frederick] Ogilby [following recent Union victories at Shiloh and elsewhere]. Music a shade better, or less bad and unmeaning, than usual.

April 20. . . . At Trinity Church . . . music was vile. "Anthem by Cutler," the organist. His platitudes are always offensive, but they are sometimes, as today, absolutely maddening. He likes to select, as the text for his insane counterpoint, words doubly consecrated by Handel's music, e.g., "He shall feed his flock like a Shepherd," "O thou that bringest glad tidings to Zion," "And He shall reign for ever and ever," "King of Kings and Lord of Lords."

The contrast between Handel and Cutler would be sufficiently aggravating anyhow, but Cutler writes a servile, base imitation of Handel, but far less close an imitation than the counterfeiter tenders with his pewter half-dollar. It is as if I were to set about writing a poem on Waterloo and began:

> There was a crowded party late at night,
> And Brussels (that large town) had gathered then
> Her most distingué people. Candle light
> Shone on fine women, likewise on fine men,
> And they were having a "high old time" generally, when
> Somebody thought he heard a gun go off somewhere,
> And people stopped dancing, and then they began again,

But another gun went off nearer, clearer, deadlier
than before.
And everybody said, "What a bore. It *is,* it is,
the cannon's opening roar," etc., etc.[62]

If I could compel a large congregation to sit and listen to such bosh every Sunday, I
should be an affliction analogous to the organist of Trinity Church.

〜

On Easter Monday, April 21, Grau, back from Boston, reopened the Irving Place
Academy for "his briefest season yet"—three nights (albeit interspersed by two more
in Brooklyn). Now under the musical direction of Emanuele Muzio, back from Havana, Grau's company—lacking Isabella Hinkley, who was pregnant—consisted of
D'Angri, Kellogg, Brignoli, Mancusi, Susini, and especially featured the two male stars
of Muzio's recent season at the Tacón Theatre: Giuseppe Tombesi,★ a highly praised
new tenor, and the familiar and greatly admired baritone Gaetano Ferri. The Tacón
prima donna Adelaide Basseggio had been announced to open the season as Leonora in
Il trovatore but unfortunately had fallen ill and was obliged to cancel her engagement
and return to Europe. The opening-night honors thus fell to Tombesi, who covered
himself with glory as the Duke of Mantua in *Rigoletto,* as did Ferri in the title role;
Clara Louise Kellogg was the Gilda, and Elena D'Angri was a "remarkable" Maddalena.

Although not a thrillingly novel choice of opera for an opening, wrote Seymour
(*Times,* April 22, 1862), this *Rigoletto* performance nonetheless offered "such a dish of
novelty, actual and comparative, [as] is rarely placed before the musical epicure." The
newcomer Tombesi, "young, handsome, spirited,[63] and conversant with the business
of the stage," continued Seymour, "is gifted with an excellent and sympathetic voice
of considerable compass, which he manages as though trained in a good school. . . .
He took and held the ears of the house." Tombesi was a great acquisition, and it was
hoped that Grau would engage him for future seasons.[64] As for the others, Ferri's admirable Rigoletto was too well known to need further comment, D'Angri left one
wishing that Maddalena had more to do, and Kellogg, always delightful as Gilda, "ver-
ily caught inspiration by contact with [these] genuine and impulsive artists."

On April 22, at the Brooklyn Academy, *La favorita* was superbly performed by
D'Angri and Tombesi; on the 23rd at Irving Place, Kellogg made her bow as an en-
chanting *vivandière* in *The Daughter of the Regiment,*[65] with Brignoli unusually alert as
Tonio;[66] on the 24th, a dark night at both Academies, members of the company as-

---

[62] A Strongian takeoff of Byron's "Childe Harold's Pilgrimage" (1816), canto 3, stanzas 21 and 22.
[63] The contrast with the phlegmatic Brignoli could not have been more marked, it was asserted.
[64] Especially if Brignoli went to Europe, as was rumored.
[65] Rather than a regiment, she was the daughter of "a corporal's guard," and rather than the Gallic tricolor, she wore the "red, white, and blue of America," patriotically interpreted the *World* (April
24, 1862).
[66] "Stimulated, perhaps, by the presence of a rival, [Brignoli] sang with special care and success."
A lively war of words was being waged between Brignoli's loyal supporters and those who were disgusted with his stolid, lazy indifference, to say nothing of the ungainly "two hundred and odd
pounds of *avoirdupois*" that he had acquired (*Albion,* April 26, 1862, p. 199).

sisted at a nearby Gottschalk concert. On the 25th the brief season at the New York Academy came to a close with *La favorita* and on the 26th the Brooklyn season concluded with *The Daughter of the Regiment.*

"With such splendid artists, the performances should have attracted better houses," wrote the pro-Grau *Herald* (April 28, 1862). "Our public, however, is capricious in these matters, and Mr. Grau has done well to give it leisure to cultivate a more generous disposition in his regard."[67]

Scarcely could it be called leisure. No sooner had Grau launched his short opera season than he fervently began advertising "positively only two concerts," at Niblo's Saloon on April 30 and May 2, by Gottschalk,[68] briefly in New York between tours.[69] Assisted by his touring companions Carlotta Patti, Henry Mollenhauer, and Harry Sanderson, with Tombesi and Ferri as guests and with Muzio as music director, the first concert—apart from Gottschalk's always magnificent playing[70]—was, in the opinion of *Linda* (*Albion,* May 3, 1862, p. 211), "much better than the preceding ones." *Linda* credited the improvement to Muzio's accompaniments, "a most agreeable innovation on the slovenly [piano] playing of Bergmann and Maretzek, which," she wrote, "in destroying the equanimity of the singers [had] interfered naturally with their success and the consequent enjoyment of the audience." Too, Carlotta Patti had created an outstanding sensation with Muzio's spectacular showpiece *L'Amour Polka,* as had Tombesi with *La donna è mobile.*

But it was Gottschalk who dominated the excitement. His performance of his *William Tell* transcription, with Sanderson at the second piano, graphically evoked for *Linda* the "frowning majesty of Swiss scenery, its glaciers and snow-capped peaks" and other well-known features of the Swiss landscape, just as his *Pastorella e cavalliere* strongly suggested to her Whittier's poem "Maud Muller" (1854). *Linda* was particularly gratified by Gottschalk's rendition of the slow movement of Beethoven's *Sonata pathétique,*[71] a performance that led her, albeit timidly, to wonder if "an occasional interpolation of the works of other composers would not lend additional zest to his own compositions, which are of too delicate and exquisite fibre for everyday wear."

At this concert Gottschalk also played his *Polonia,* his *Valse poétique (Sospiro),* op. 24 (1855), his *Minuit à Séville,♪* op. 30 (1851–52), and, with Sanderson, a first New

---

[67] Excepting Tombesi and Ferri, who were soon to leave for Europe, and Muzio, who was about to join the Gottschalk forces, Grau lost no time in sending his company on a tour of one-night stands in Albany, Troy, Rochester, and Buffalo, then on to Washington.

[68] Attended by Ellen Strong, as her husband noted in his private journal.

[69] Gottschalk's Midwestern tour had been badly timed: "My concerts are not very profitable," he wrote on April 18, 1862, in mid-tour. "We are in Holy Week, and neither the Episcopalians nor the Catholics go to concerts in the second half of Lent" (*Notes,* p. 59). The war, too, was ever present: in the same entry Gottschalk told of encountering, on his travels, "a convoy of wounded from the last battle—Pittsburg Landing [Shiloh] . . . a heart-rending sight."

[70] "He appeared to be in the vein and rendered his several *morceaux* with great dash and spirit, and to much and richly deserved applause" (*Dispatch,* May 4, 1862).

[71] If the inclusion of Beethoven's sonata was intended to appease Hagen, it was a resounding failure. "Mr. Gottschalk has returned to us and given several farewell concerts," wrote Hagen (*Review and World,* May 10, 1862, p. 113). "At one of them he attempted to perform one of the easiest movements by Beethoven, the Adagio from the *Sonate pathétique,* but signally failed."

York performance of his Cuban dance, *Reponds-moi,* op. 50 (1859), in its four-hand version, another hit.[72]

At the May 2 concert Gottschalk unveiled his *Illusions perdues (Fantôme de bonheur),* op. 36 (*c.* 1859),[73] a work described in the *World* (May 5) as "a plaintive little morceau, very suggestive, though unpretending"; he again performed his *Pastorella e cavalliere;* a composition listed only as "Trovatore" (apparently his arrangement of the *Miserere*); and his lost *Fantasia di bravura* on *La Fille du régiment* (1855?).[74] With Mollenhauer he played two movements of a work programed as Mendelssohn's cello and piano Sonata in B-flat (op. 45) (1838) but suspected of being a work of his own (see *Dwight's,* May 10, 1862, p. 45).[75] And with Muzio replacing Sanderson, he repeated his *Reponds-moi,* enthusiastically encored, as was everything he played.

Yet, "without wishing to be classed as German-minded," the pro-Gottschalk *World* (May 8, 1862), like *Linda,* would have liked him to "give us some of his interpretations of works by [other] contemporaneous composers. Liszt's later productions, for instance, are not so well known in the concert room here as they perhaps deserve to be. Some artists have a fear of the public, or of themselves, in place of needful respect." Gottschalk was not of that inferior ilk, and thus we had a right to expect him to "venture upon broader fields of chamber music than is usually done by musicians of a less catholic taste."

Against such suggestions, Fry indignantly defended Gottschalk, who was "capable," he wrote (*Tribune,* May 5, 1862), "of playing every style of music which is worth performance. His execution is faultless. He understands the value of shading, from extreme softness to extreme loudness, no amount of massive force wearying his strong fingers. He has a poetic nature and quick perceptions. We are told that he does not play *Chopin,* however. Who then does? What is the mystery, the fire, the melody, the harmony in one author, beyond all others, that nobody can play him?"

It was, of course, inevitable that Gottschalk's "positively last" appearance, on May 2, should turn out to be an "ante-final" appearance. Thus, on May 5, he surpassed all his previous efforts with yet another program that climaxed with his performance—with Sebastian Bach Mills—of the supercolossal two-piano fantasy on themes from *Il trovatore* that he had performed with Thalberg in 1856.♪[76] Not only was it "the event of the evening," wrote the *World* (May 8, 1862), it was "the event of Mr. Gottschalk's whole series of concerts thus far. To undertake the *Trovatore* Duet, players must feel themselves admitted among the first-form people of the art world. Gottschalk laid down some rugged passages for his companion as well as himself, but the difficulties were passed over with astonishing ease, without unseemly physical exertion." Indeed, Mills had magnificently risen to the occasion, surprising even his friends with the grandeur of his performance. Gottschalk had never before been so ably assisted.

---

[72] *Sospiro. Valse poétique* (D-142; *Piano Works,* V, 141); *Minuit à Séville. Caprice* (D-96; *Piano Works,* IV, 39); *Reponds-moi. Dí que sí. Danse cubaine. Caprice brillant* (D-131; *Piano Works,* V, 29).

[73] *Fantôme de bonheur* (D-51; *Piano Works,* III, 175).

[74] *La Fille du regiment* (D-76/B).

[75] Might it have been it a hoax, similar to the hoax Gottschalk was rumored to have played on Dwight in 1853?♪

[76] Believed by some to have been jointly composed by Gottschalk and Thalberg, the work had aroused no particular critical enthusiasm when it was first played in 1856.

It was an event "to be remembered in the annals of art in this country, to hear these two glorious artists perform this duet, and the effect on the audience was stupendous," reported the *Dispatch,* ostensibly employing the vocabulary of C. Jerome Hopkins. "Thunderbolts, lightning, clouds, sunshine, poetry, storms, the perfume of violets, the music of rippling brooks, boisterous crashes of mountain torrents, the twittering of innocent birds, the blue-eyed babble of heaven-born and heaven-destined children were all pictured in this masterly composition, and never before have we been so impressed with the utterly perfect union of consummate virtuosity and tender poetic expressiveness as on this occasion." Mills, who deserved great praise for the care he had bestowed on his part, "left Thalberg quite in the shade . . . and it was difficult to believe that he [Mills] had only first seen [the score] on the Saturday evening previous."

A work of formidable length, lasting about twenty minutes, at least half of the *Trovatore* Duet had to be repeated to satisfy the audience, which, wrote the critic, "became decidedly boisterous in its expression of intense delight."

In addition to this memorable *tour de force,* Gottschalk played his *Ricordati* (Nocturne), op. 26 (*c.* 1856), and three lost works: his *Fantaisie* on the *Lucia* Finale, his *Fantaisie* on *Un ballo in maschera,* and his *Caprice burlesque* on the song *Marlborough ("Malbrook, s'en va-t'en guerre").*[77] The following day he departed for Washington. But still more was to come.

Upon the termination of Grau's "contract," or rather, his sublease of the Academies following Ullman's collapse, it became clear, wrote the *Herald* (May 19, 1862), that, with his unconventional method of producing frequent short seasons of popular operas with modest forces, he had financially succeeded where impresarios more given to the grand gesture had invariably failed.

Not that Grau had not exhibited great courage as well as remarkable astuteness. Entering what was at best a risky profession at a time when the country was plunging into a horrible war, "when a paralysis had rendered inert the great business efforts and interests of the country; in the midst of these drawbacks, and undismayed by forebodings, Mr. Grau inaugurated a season of musical entertainments—uncertain enterprises at the best of times—and grasping a first success, made it the basis of future and greater successes."

Now, after eight months of his dynamic management, having presented (according to the *Herald*) 215 performances, of which eighty-five were complete operas—twenty-seven in New York, twelve in Brooklyn, fifteen in Boston, nine in Buffalo, seven in Philadelphia, four in Washington, two each in Albany, Troy, and Hartford, and one each in Baltimore, Chicago, Milwaukee, Detroit, Cleveland, and New Haven—Grau was "the first operatic manager who had fulfilled all his engagements and closed a season without having been—or declaring himself to have been—'ruined.'" He could boast not only a balanced ledger, but handsome surpluses accruing to the Academy directors, his artists, and himself. He could also boast of everyone's good will, "something for an opera manager to say in these difficult times." (Or any times.)

---

[77] *Ricordati,* variously subtitled *Nocturne, Méditation,* and *Romance* (D-133; *Piano Works,* V, 43); *Lucia di Lammermoor Sextette* (Offergeld 136); *Marlborough. Caprice burlesque* (Offergeld 160); *Un ballo in maschera Fantaisie* (Offergeld 18).

Grau's extraordinary achievement was celebrated on May 20 with a great farewell concert by Gottschalk, whose contract with Grau had also expired; the assisting artists were Carlotta Patti and the members of Grau's erstwhile opera company—D'Angri, Brignoli, Mancusi, Susini, and Muzio, who accompanied them on the piano in a great number of Italian opera arias. "Gottschalk's last concert" was judged by the press to be his greatest concert of all. Not only did he repeat the tremendous *Trovatore* Duet with Mills, but, with William Mason at the other piano, he played Thalberg's equally grandiose two-piano transcription of themes from *Norma*, the other great showpiece he had performed with Thalberg in 1856. Aside from these two blockbusters, Gottschalk thrillingly performed his *Marche funèbre,* op. 61/64 (1853–54),[78] and a work alternately programed as "Caprice by Chopin and Schumann" or "Caprice by Chopin."[79] Immediately following this massive leave-taking came the announcement, on May 23, that upon the completion of their contract with Grau, Gottschalk and Brignoli had formed a partnership with Max Strakosch and that their first entertainment—including a performance of *La figlia del reggimento,* with Kellogg, Brignoli, and Susini, and with Muzio as music director—would be presented as a Gala Matinée the following day at Niblo's Saloon. Between the acts, Gottschalk would play his *Fantasia di bravura* on *Jérusalem,* his *Fantasia* on *Un ballo in maschera* (again advertised as its first performance), and Chopin's Étude in F minor and Valse in A-flat.

"The audience filled the Saloon to overflowing and seemed pleased with everything that was done," reported the *World* (May 26, 1862), "despite the meager chorus and such apologies for scenery as the stage afforded."

Directly following this modest gala,[80] the Gottschalk/Brignoli troupe took off for Philadelphia, Baltimore, and Washington, then to several New England cities,[81] a journey compellingly described in *Notes of a Pianist* (pp. 62–80, *passim*).

Upon Grau's temporary departure from the managerial scene, a sixteen-year-old soprano, Miss Emelie C. Boughton, with great advance fanfare, appeared at the Academy of Music in a family production of *La traviata.* Besides her parents, she was supported by Vincenzo Morino and a chorus and orchestra conducted by Carl Anschütz. As an extra attraction, between the first and second acts Miss Emelie was announced to sing, by special request, "her much admired song of 'Cherry Ripe' in appropriate costume." Originally announced for April 2, the debut was unfortunately postponed twice because of the young *prima donna*'s indisposition. She finally appeared on May 22, and the following day Seymour, in the *Times,* reported that "her Violetta was most certainly an unconventional rendering of the part." But her method unfortunately

---

[78] *Marche funèbre* (D-90; *Piano Works,* IV, 1).

[79] Attaching extraneous titles to existing compositions was commonly done. In his journal, for instance, Gottschalk refers to his performance of Chopin's Prelude in D-flat "under the name of *Méditation religieuse*" (June 3, 1862; *Notes,* p. 75). The "'Caprice' by Chopin" might have been one of Chopin's Scherzos.

[80] Gottschalk writes of an ensuing performance by this company at the Philadelphia Academy of Music of *La favorita,* with de Lussan, Brignoli, and Susini, followed by an act of *Lucia,* with Kellogg, with a chorus that had consisted entirely of "four Germans" (*Notes,* p. 73).

[81] With, according to Gottschalk's journal (June 3, 1862), a company—apparently a variable commodity—that included Madame de Lussan and Francesco Amodio (*Notes,* p. 75).

lacked "certainty, precision, and finish," and although she had a warm and potentially sympathetic voice, she most emphatically needed study before attempting a career.

If the critic dealt gently with Miss Emelie, he did not hesitate to "remonstrate seriously with the paternal Boughton, the Alfredo of the occasion. Upon what pretence he has ventured before the public it would be hard to say. A *tenore* with a 'remarkably' small voice and a 'remarkably' small amount of skill, dressed in a quaintly absurd manner, and moving in a singularly automatic fashion, we might perhaps have said nothing about him but that 'harsh justice' may in this case prove 'sweet mercy,' and possibly induce him to terminate his own operatic career forthwith."

Gottschalk, who apparently witnessed the performance, gives a more vivid account: "Mr. B., a furrier who has made more than two hundred thousand dollars by selling beaver skins from Canada and bearskins from the Rocky Mountains, has become almost a theatrical monomaniac. He is forty-five years old, with a small, sourish voice. He has a daughter sixteen years old, pretty but singing false, and a wife forty years of age, who sings badly. With these elements he has formed an Italian opera company in which he is tenor *assoluto,* his daughter *prima donna,* and his wife contralto. It must be admitted that his operas are got up regardless of expense; but imagine *La traviata* by a merchant of otter skins and his interesting family!

"Their debut took place at the Academy of Music," continues Gottschalk. "The eccentricity of the thing had drawn an immense crowd; all the rabbitskin merchants strutted there. They applauded Mr. B., whose acting was adorable, and all won success in bursts of laughter. They were recalled. Miss B. managed to appear the same evening in four marvelous costumes that cost, it is said, five thousand dollars. The father, B., dressed absurdly. In the first act he was muffled up in a troubadour's cloak and funnel-shaped boots that reached to his waist and gave him the appearance of a mock scavenger. Besides, he was not willing to sacrifice to the demands of the stage a magnificent pair of whiskers. We are going to have *Il trovatore* in a few days, Madame B. singing Azucena. I have known people less crazy who were sent to the madhouse" (*Notes,* pp. 76–77).

Miss Boughton was, however, fervently defended by *Timothy Trill,* whose somewhat deranged diatribe against her critics, originally appearing in "a Brooklyn paper," was reprinted and refuted in the *Dispatch* (June 1, 1862). Perhaps she was not yet a Laborde or a Piccolomini, *Trill* had ranted, but she was far better than many of the singers recently praised by the critics, particularly Madame de Lussan, who had received scandalously gentle treatment after making a downright fiasco. And the father's shortcomings should have been overlooked "in view of his love for his daughter," for whom he was willing to make untold sacrifices. Preposterously lashing out in all directions, *Trill*/Hopkins gave intimations of his extreme eccentricity to come.

Early in May the government assigned a hospital ship, the *Ocean Queen,* to the Sanitary Commission and issued an urgent call for surgeons and nurses and needed equipment. After a great deal of pro-and-con debate, Ellen Strong, "at her own earnest request," and overcoming her husband's misgivings, volunteered and—together with a group of women of her caste, accompanied by their serving women—departed for the war zone. For the remainder of the month Strong—blaming himself for having let her go—mingled his anxiety over the war with his gnawing fears for Ellen's safety,

Leslie's, Dartmouth College Library

*Volunteers being trained at the City Hospital in New York. The women had to be over
thirty and receive a month's training to become nurses recognized by the government.*

with only her infrequent cheerful letters and an occasional hearsay report to reassure
him. As he awaited her return, at the conclusion of her tour of duty, he wrote on May
26: "God grant that her hard work and exposure of the last three weeks may have done
her no harm. Olmsted gives great praise to her energy, intelligence, and willingness in
a P.S. in a letter received today. . . . I thought I rated her rather high, but I have never
done her half justice in all these years, and I have never known till now the resolute
pluck and capacity for usefulness that are in her pretty little delicate, fragile person."
On May 28, Ellen returned, jolly, invigorated, and mercifully free of the malaria or
typhoid that Strong had so greatly feared. Strong's relief at her safe return did not,
however, mitigate his response to the music at Trinity Church.

June 1. . . . Church with Ellie and Johny. The *Te Deum* was extraordinary—
screeching, cranky, monotonous, dismal—sounded on a singly repulsive melodic (or
dys-melodic) phrase. It was like my notion of a Feejee funeral chant. Learned on enquiry
that it was by the venerable [Thomas] Tallis [*c.* 1505–1585].[82] Never heard any of his
music (?) before, and pray to be delivered from the same in *saecula saeculorum*. What
an outrage to inflict this excruciating, semi-barbaric trash on people, some of whom,
at least, have heard and can appreciate real music. Antiquity is venerable, of course,
but what should we say to Cutler if he adopted a facsimile of the organ of the tenth
century? And a defective instrument is not near so irritating as a crude or feeble composition. I know little or nothing of sixteenth-century music, but this production was

---

[82] A choice of composer, despite Strong, that speaks well for Cutler's musical inquisitiveness.

strongly suggestive of *Verdi*. That raises a curious question, which I should like to investigate.

━━

Early in June, Bernard Ullman—interrupting his well-publicized impresarial negotiations in Europe[83]—materialized in New York and announced a Grau-length opera season of six performances[84] at the Academy of Music. On returning to the United States, as he confided in his advertisements, he had been dismayed to learn that during his absence only twenty-four opera nights had been given at the Academy instead of the thirty required by the terms of his lease. As a man of honor, he was therefore supplying the missing six performances, to be presented on the "Castle Garden plan," that is, with "the very highest talent in the country in one Grand Festival Entertainment Accessible to All Classes" for only fifty cents, one dollar for reserved seats, and twenty-five cents for the amphitheatre.

On each of six consecutive evenings beginning on June 11, he would offer, at these bargain prices, an "Immense Combination of a full grand and complete opera by the best artists [the currently unemployed members of the Gottschalk/Brignoli/Strakosch troupe—Kellogg, D'Angri, Brignoli, Susini, *et al.*]; a concert by the Great Pianist Gottschalk; and a performance by the Wonderful Herrmann,[85] all on one and the same evening."

The opening night, a Wednesday, was tremendously attended. As the *Albion* reported (June 14, 1862, p. 283): "Triple attractions—namely Opera, Gottschalk, and Herrmann—at prices reduced to one half, served to crowd the house in a degree but rarely seen." The opera was *Lucrezia Borgia,* introducing in the title role a new *prima donna,* Madame Comte Borchard, a French soprano popular in New Orleans. She had been mentioned some time since as a potential member of Grau's opera company, but had not yet appeared locally. Now that she had been heard, she received moderate praise and less moderate blame in varying degrees. Her voice, wrote the *Times* (June 12, 1862), "perhaps not in its first youth" was lacking in freshness, but still capable of excellent vocalization; the *World* (June 12) thought her method "a trifle antique and her rendering of certain bravura passages hardly pleasing"; *Dwight's* somewhat waspish new correspondent, *Alma,* referred to her voice as "a high soprano, clear, but not of telling quality; of considerable acquired flexibility, but cold and full of mannerism"[86] (June 21, 1862, p. 93). D'Angri, Brignoli, and Susini, who appeared with her, deserved unequivocal praise, also wrote the *Albion.* "Would that we could honestly say the same of the new prima donna." But with Gottschalk[87] and Herrmann each working his par-

[83] Chiefly efforts to import two world-renowned artists to the United States: the German soprano Therese Tietjens (or Tietiens) (1831–1877) and the Italian tragedienne Adelaide Ristori (1822–1905).

[84] Presented in collaboration with Ullman's partner and doubtless his backer, a Mr. Palmer? (was it Cortlandt Palmer, charter member of the Academy board of directors?).

[85] Gottschalk had previously shared public appearances with Herrmann in Havana, and sometimes had even played duets with Madame Herrmann.

[86] "Her costume, too (Lucrezia *en crinoline!*), was not only historically incorrect," complained *Alma,* "but so unbecoming as to give a ludicrous coloring to some situations, regarded in operatic tradition as tragical."

[87] Playing his *Trovatore* transcription (the *Miserere*) and his *Murmures éoliens*.

ticular magic, "whoever went away doubtful whether he had had his fifty cents' worth, must have been exceedingly hard to please."

On the second evening (advertised as "the most positively last night but four") Clara Louise Kellogg appeared as Lady Harriet in *Martha,* a role that fitted her "like a garment. The music she gets over as easily as she would her alphabet," wrote the *World* (June 13, 1862). D'Angri, Brignoli, and Susini were excellent, and although the orchestra might have been stronger, with Theodore Thomas as concertmaster and Signor Abella wielding the baton "with commendable nerve" (liveliness), the score was well interpreted. Between the second and third acts Gottschalk played his Fantasy on *La favorita* and created his usual furor with "The Union"; Herrmann "filled the void" between acts three and four.

"Everybody, however, does not sit through the entire combination entertainment, which," noted the *World,* "looks as though it were possible that too much of several good things is being offered to the satiated public. Mr. Ullman in reality is giving more for a half dollar than New York ever got before for two dollars."

A second new *prima donna*—none other than the versatile and captivating Madame Rosalie Herrmann—made her debut on June 13 as Maria in *La figlia del reggimento.* "The wand of the great Magician has not apparently endowed Madame Herrmann with any wondrous spell of enchantment," unkindly quipped the *Albion* (June 21, 1862, p. 295). But in the opinion of the *World,* no debutante since Clara Louise Kellogg had so enchanted a New York audience. "Madame Herrmann," wrote the smitten critic, "has all the essential qualifications for becoming a pet with opera-goers, belonging as she does to the Piccolomini school. Her figure is petite, her face beautiful and expressive, her action coy and natural." Her soprano voice, he added, was sympathetic and clear, with a powerful upper register, and her acting was wonderful. "In deference to her alliance with the accomplished prestidigitator," added the reviewer, "we presume Madame has been pet-named the 'Little Bewitcher'" (*World,* June 16, 1862).

Madame Herrmann reappeared in a condensed version of *La figlia* at the Gala Matinée the next day, sharing the bill with a full performance of *Lucrezia Borgia* with Madame Borchard. Brignoli, who was indisposed, was admirably replaced in both operas by Giovanni Sbriglia,[88] "a graceful and amiable" artist with a young, well-trained, and melodious voice of extended register. Gottschalk and Herrmann, of course, triumphantly performed during the intermissions.

So great was the "jam" at this matinée, so great the "crush of crinoline" and the "array of beauty under millinery coverings," gossiped the *World* (June 16, 1862), that "one [unnamed] distinguished artist nearly tarnished his fame, owing to the distractions placed before him."

Midway through this extraordinary season, Fry—silent until now—took serious issue with its demeaning treatment of Opera: "The performances of a Summer season are often of such a disheveled, touch-and-go kind—being appeals to travelers and the floating population—that they are not properly to be judged by the rules accorded to the standard of Winter exhibitions, for if they are, they are wide open to an eager and a nipping air of criticism. To go to the theater—an opera house—nay more, an Acad-

---

[88] Sbriglia was currently appearing daily with a distinguished concert company at Nixon's new Cremorne Gardens (see below).

emy of Music—and find that the music of the opera is considered of small attraction, and that a misplaced piano solo and the customary tricks of juggling are necessary to keep the muse out of the almshouse, is a sorry sight. Perhaps this is the lower deep of the opera, and it may take a rise; but we doubt it. A community vulgar enough to admit of such things requires a thorough course of civilizing treatment before a hope for better things can be attained"[89] (*Tribune,* June 16, 1862).

Seymour, too, regarded the Grand Festival Entertainments and their audiences with jaundiced gaze, or, at least, with pen dipped in acid. Reviewing the following opera, *Il trovatore,* sloppily presented on June 16 with Madame Borchard as Leonora, Sbriglia again replacing the still ailing Brignoli as Manrico,[90] and Federico Amodio assuming his lamented brother's most celebrated role as the Count di Luna, Seymour wrote (*Times,* June 18, 1862): "The audience, which was the largest of the present season, was very good-natured. It evidently came to enjoy itself. When the opera could not begin [on time], it accepted *Prestidigitation* in its place. As Brignoli did not sing, they took Sbriglia with the most polite indifference—they relished *la* Borchard, and they applauded Amodio, while they gossiped and chatted between the acts in a way that Gottschalk alone could still for a time."

Sbriglia, in fact, was not only a very acceptable Manrico, wrote Seymour, but he sang his recitatives "with something approaching to care and taste—qualities which we had begun to forget the existence of in Italian recitative—at least, among Italian *tenori.*"[91] And Madame Borchard's Leonora was a great improvement over her Lucrezia, showing greater assurance and a younger and fuller quality of voice. Indeed, Seymour ranked her among the best Leonoras we had heard in New York. Elena D'Angri was, as in everything she sang, superb as Azucena. Federico Amodio, regarded as a debutant,[92] faced the inescapable fate of being compared with his brother, a comparison most often based upon their comparative girth,[93] by which he was variously classed as less good, as good, or better than the lamented Alessandro.

The *World* (June 17, 1862) described him as "young and very handsome," with a full and clear voice of real baritone register, extending easily to G, or maybe A-flat. He would improve, possibly, "and if he does," qualified the *World,* "he will edge very near the class of artists who deserve to be called unrivaled." Appearing again the following night as Antonio in *Linda di Chamounix,* another of his brother's outstanding roles, Federico Amodio was judged to be "a very satisfactory baritone."

Advertised as "The Last Night of the Great Fifty Cents Combination" (that is, the last night before the great closing Gala for Ullman's benefit), *Linda di Chamounix* was sung by Kellogg, who outdid herself as Linda, and Brignoli, who reappeared in

---

[89] A comment brutally relevant in the last decade of the American twentieth century.

[90] Sbriglia was certainly as good a tenor as Brignoli, wrote Hagen (*Review and World,* June 21, 1862, p. 146), but not at a fee of $225, which was extracted from the management because no other tenor was available. They might just as well have given *Il trovatore* without a tenor, for all the difference it would make.

[91] A direct swipe at Brignoli.

[92] Despite his having appeared with Adelaide Cortesi in her brief but vivid season at Niblo's in 1860.

[93] "The new baritone Amodio, whose vocal dimensions, as compared with his departed brother's, correspond exactly to his diminished corporeal proportions," observed the *Albion* (June 21, 1862, p. 295).

great form as Carlo. As usual, when threatened by a rival, he endeavored "to do away with the favorable impression made by Signor Sbriglia," wrote the *World* (June 18, 1862). Madame D'Angri was the best Pierotto ever heard in New York, and Susini, as the Prefect, had recovered from the hoarseness that had plagued him for the past six months.

Gottschalk, as always, caused a furor with his *Pastorella e cavalliere* and "The Banjo." "Mr. Gottschalk's genius is not of a nature to suffer from contact, and is ever capable of asserting itself triumphantly, however trivial may be its surroundings, however inveterate personal prejudice," wrote *Linda* in the *Albion* (June 21, 1862, p. 295). "But," she quibbled, echoing Fry, "we must confess that the Academy of Music was not constructed with reference to the piano, or the glory of pianists, and that necromancy is not a fitting pendant to high art." Nonetheless: "With these obstacles to contend with, due homage must be rendered to the talent that possesses the key to popular enthusiasm, and at the same time can kindle the fastidious natures of the most aesthetical Dilettanti."

For the grand finale—Ullman's benefit—on June 18, *Il trovatore* was repeated, Madame Herrmann performed excerpts from *L'elisir d'amore,* Gottschalk sensationally played several of his works (unidentified), and Herrmann, purportedly about to leave for England, revealed (or promised to reveal) the secret of his baffling Ring Trick.

With their season, editorialized the *Dispatch* on June 22, the Messrs. Ullman and Palmer had "right royally" fulfilled their promises, providing a species of entertainment "of a character heretofore unknown to the lyric stage, [although] some of the critics have felt inclined to regard [it] with disfavor. They object to the introduction, *entreacte,* of the performances of Herrmann, the prestidigitator, on the ground that it is unseemly and out of taste, and tends to lower the estimate in which operatic performances have been held in this country." The *Dispatch* believed that if Ullman were asked for his opinion, he would silently (and smilingly) point to the "fiscal results as an explanation of his tactics."

Evaluating the many ways that music had profited by Ullman's unorthodox treatment, the *Dispatch* world-wearily concluded: "We suppose that cessation from labor by the members of the late combination is the next thing on the programme." And indeed, not until late September would any of the opera singers again find employment at the Academy of Music.

Gottschalk, purportedly without assisting artists, departed on an extended tour, and by July 24 the *World* reported that he had given "no less than forty highly successful concerts" in New York State, New England, and Canada, including Quebec, Montreal, Toronto, Kingston, and Ottawa. "The trip was undertaken entirely at Mr. Gottschalk's own risk, his engagement with Messrs. Grau and Strakosch having expired some time since."[94]

In mid-June, a time of serious military reverses for the Union, Ellen, again accompanied by her faithful maidservant Annie, sailed with a contingent of nurses on a newly commissioned hospital ship, the *St. Mark.* Where her earlier mission had been

---

[94]But who was the booking agent who set up the tour, preceding Gottschalk from place to place? Might it have been the budding impresario, Diego di Vivo (1822–1898)?

Volunteer nurses attending the sick and wounded
in a U.S. General Hospital in Washington, D.C.

to inspect and report to the Sanitary Commission on general medical conditions, shortcomings, and needs, this time she was headed for active duty at McClellan's headquarters in Virginia. To Strong, heavy laden as he was with anxieties and responsibilities, it was blessed surcease—in her absence—momentarily to lose himself in the music he loved most.

June 23. . . . Tonight to a concert [by the Philharmonic] at the Academy of Music. It was got up spontaneously by the young men of the Mercantile Society Library for the benefit of the Sanitary Commission. Tolerable house—guess we shall net $1000 and upwards. The wonderful Seventh Symphony was on the program and, of course, covered a multitude of sins—solos, vocal and instrumental—*fiorituri* and bosh.[95] The overtures to *Tannhäuser* and *Euryanthe* also are not to be heard every night.

The Symphony was well enough rendered. Its second movement certainly stands alone—unrivaled in its way—as an expression of hopeless supplication in sorrow of a despairing cry from the Depths and from a horror of great darkness. One might write about it for pages, but what he wrote would be nonsense to everyone but himself, so

[95] The vocal sinners were Clara Louise Kellogg, who sang *Les Rossignols* from Victor Massé's light opera *Les Noces de Jeannette* and as an encore "The Last Rose of Summer," and Elena D'Angri, who sang the inevitable "Elena Waltz" followed by a highly dramatic performance of the mandatory "Star-Spangled Banner." The instrumental transgressors were Sebastian Bach Mills, who played the second and third movements of Chopin's Concerto in F minor, and Louis Schreiber, who played his popular salon piece for cornet à piston, *Effusion du coeur*.

intangible and incommunicable is the message addressed by the highest musical art to each individual that feels it.

Then the grand, mournful march that comes "sweeping by," like Tragedy, "with sceptered pall," silencing the festal phrases of the Scherzo—the few massive chords that connect these two parts of the third movement and lead the orchestra back from D major to F—the roaring triumphant chaos and anarchy of the fourth movement— what do they all mean? There must be—or must have been once—in Beethoven's heart—a key to this wonderful symphony.

~~~

On July 11, Ellen returned from the battlefields—tired but cheerful—and on that same day, together with Dr. and Mrs. Peters, she was off to Newport to engage rooms for the inviolable summer holidays. On July 24—Strong being indispensably required at the Sanitary Commission—she and her sons, escorted by their waiter John, departed for their usual lengthy vacation, leaving Strong to face another forlorn summer, with only small occasional distractions to relieve his loneliness, his heavy labors, and anxieties.

July 19. . . . Charley Strong came in, and Otis Swan [a prominent New York attorney], to inspect our big parlor organ.♪ He [Swan] contemplates building something of the sort. Brought with him an artiste, one Connolly [organist of St. Mark's Church] to try the instrument. I plied Connolly with Haydn's and Mozart's masses, and he did them full justice.

August 22. . . . At "Cremorne Gardens," Fourteenth Street, tonight. Spent an hour watching an idiotic Pantomime of the Ravelesque school in its crowded little theatre. *Eheu, eheu, eheu* [Alas, alas, alas (Latin)].

~~~

Strong might have chosen any of several entertainments offered twice daily (except Sundays) at the Cremorne Gardens, a highly successful new pleasure spot opened in June by the creative supershowman James M. Nixon. Located on the site of the former Palace Gardens (more recently a military installation), the locale had been extensively altered to include a proper theatrical stage in the concert room, now grandly renamed the Palace of Music, also a "Gorgeous" Turkish Pavilion, a Hall of Flora, a Japanese Tower, a Chinese Pagoda, and—a special attraction—beckoning pathways winding through lush plantings of evergreen trees and flowers, illuminated by multicolored lights, and dotted with fountains.

Music, and music of an excellent quality, was virtually omnipresent. At the Palace of Music—where Strong had evidently witnessed the unsatisfactory pantomime— concerts were performed, with daily changes in programs, under the expert direction of Thomas Baker by Grau's former stars: Carlotta Patti, Amalia Strakosch, Amati Dubreuil, Achille Ardavani, and Giovanni Sbriglia. Each concert was followed by a ballet or pantomime performed by Isabel Cubas[96] and Señor Ximenes with their ballet corps.[97] Baker additionally conducted daily out-of-doors promenade concerts, their

---

[96] Soon to become Mrs. James M. Nixon.

[97] Other dancers and choreographers occasionally appeared: Costa (or Carolina) Theleur, Monsieur Wiethoff, Mademoiselle Hélène, and Signor Ronzani.

pauses filled with opera music and popular tunes played by Kopp's Grand Military Brass Band.

Consonant with Nixon's circus background, splendid equestrian and acrobatic feats were performed at the Turkish Pavilion by Louise Tournaire, the Conrad Brothers, and other virtuosos of the sawdust ring; the Hall of Flora housed a ravishing horticultural display; and, for the younger generation, the juvenile favorites Commodore Foote and Colonel Small "held a levee" every afternoon.[98]

All kinds of refreshments—ices, creams, jellies, fruits, cakes, cigars, etc.—were served by "attentive waiters," but, most emphatically, "no liquors of any kind, spiritous, vinous, or fermented" would be permitted on the premises, "in compliance with a newly-passed ordinance prohibiting the sale of liquor in places of amusement" (see following OBBLIGATO).

Furthermore: "In consequence of the thousand and one applications from parties desirous of having the various establishments connected with the Cremorne Gardens for the purpose of giving sacred concerts on Sundays . . . the manager deems it necessary to give this notice to the public: that the Garden and everything connected with it is closed to the world on Sundays." This dictum was soon rescinded.

On July Fourth, despite untoward news from the front, from ten in the morning to ten at night three complete shows were run consecutively at Cremorne Gardens. The program at the Palace of Music featured Carlotta Patti singing her new hit, "The Nightingale," composed for her by Muzio, and with the assistance of all her vocal colleagues, of course, "The Star-Spangled Banner"; additionally, Madame Strakosch sang "The Flag of Our Union"; Cubas repeated her celebrated *Madrilena,* and presented a new ballet *Medora;* two new topical compositions by Baker were heard, his "Grand National Union Fantasia" and (recalling Handel or anticipating Stravinsky) "The Fireworks Polka," dedicated to the Messrs. Edge, whose spectacular pyrotechnics concluded the day-long celebration.[99]

With its cornucopia of fine entertainments, Cremorne Gardens attracted a superior attendance. There, wrote the *Tribune* (August 25, 1862), "soft-colored lights ooze through the evergreen clusters, [and] people move, mingle, loiter, sit here and there, laugh aloud, and yet are not a bit shocked at themselves.[100] With all the gay illuminations, with the timid sparkle of the fountains, the ceaseless motion of the multitude, the moonlight above and the light of mirth and enjoyment below, the sight is about the most cheerful and refreshing that New York can now afford."

In recognition of his valuable contribution to the city's well-being, on September 8, Nixon was tendered a complimentary testimonial by a group of influential citizens.[101]

---

[98] A single twenty-five cent ticket admitted the pleasure seeker to all these wonders except the children's show in the afternoon, for which the admission was fifteen cents. Reserved armchairs in the Palace of Music were twenty-five cents extra, as were "orchestra armchairs."

[99] Later in the month Cremorne Gardens exhibited the Messrs. Edge's thrilling fireworks depiction of the great *Monitor/Merrimac* battle.

[100] Apparently a reference to the war.

[101] A feature of the event was a spectacular Chinese festival illuminated by "1000 Chinese lamps, 1000 Chinese lanterns, and 1000 Chinese reflectors of variegated colors." So successful was this extravaganza that it was repeated every night for a week.

Enjoying an unprecedented success, and with Carlotta Patti, a highly potential young *prima donna,* under his wing,[102] Nixon—probably not unmindful of Grau's recent success—had begun to cast covetous eyes toward opera production and the unoccupied Academy of Music. On September 1 he expanded his musical cast to include—in addition to the Patti sisters, Sbriglia, and Dubreuil—the recently bereaved Susini,[103] and Emanuele Muzio, who succeeded Thomas Baker as music director at the Palace of Music.[104] This move inspired great speculation in the press concerning Nixon's possible opera plans, and indeed he soon announced four performances of Italian Opera, three at the Fourteenth Street Academy of Music and one at the Brooklyn Academy,[105] to be given, he stated, "for the express purpose of introducing in Opera that truly great artist, Mlle. Carlotta Patti."

Public speculation now shifted to conjecture over the feasibility of an opera career for Carlotta Patti, whose unfortunate lameness had until now prevented her from attempting dramatic roles. Nixon sought to reassure the public on this score: "Whatever anxiety may have existed as to the personal hazards of this undertaking, has," he delicately announced, "been happily removed." With the aid of a mechanical device invented by a Dr. Ceccarini, "a surgeon in high esteem among the foreign population of New York," Carlotta Patti would henceforth be able to move about as if she had never been lame, reported *Dwight's* (August 23, 1862, p. 167).

But this, alas, was not to be. Reviewing her performances at the Academy—as Amina in *La sonnabula*[106] on September 22, as Lucia on the 26th, in mixed offerings at the gala matinée on the 27th, again as Lucia on the 29th (her single appearance in Brooklyn),[107] and at an extra performance for her benefit on October 4 as Elvira in *I puritani*[108]—the critics for the most part lauded her superb vocalism but delicately forbore to refer to her apparently unmitigated lameness. Concluding a long, musically commendatory review, Fry wrote: "We have not spoken of Miss Patti as a dramatic artist for well-known reasons, but confined ourselves to a view of her vocal ability,

---

[102] And with the outdoor pleasure-garden season approaching its end.

[103] On July 5, young, vivacious, gifted, admired Isabella Hinkley Susini, twenty-three days after having given birth to a daughter, died of a fever diagnosed as typhoid. Susini, who had tenderly cared for her during her terrible last illness, was in a "state [of grief] bordering on insanity," reported the *Dispatch* (July 6, 1862).

[104] On September 1 at Cremorne Gardens, Muzio, a man adaptable to his times, conducted his orchestra of "thirty first-class musicians from the Academy of Music" (as against Baker's two dozen musicians of undisclosed provenance) in the first performance of his latest stirring topical composition, "The Uprising Galop."

[105] During which time the Palace of Music would be taken over by Maria Brainerd (with, of course, Dr. Beames), and the singers George Simpson and J. R. Thomas.

[106] With Sbriglia (Elvino), Susini (Rodolfo), the American soprano Fanny Stockton (Lisa), the veteran Madame Avogadro (Teresa), Mancusi (Alessio), and Ximines (the Notary). Scola was the stage manager, Dubreuil his assistant, and Muzio conducted.

[107] With Brignoli (Edgardo) and Ardavani (Ashton).

[108] In the belief that Maretzek had leased the New York Academy for six months, from September 29 on, explained Nixon in a card, he had scheduled only four local performances for Carlotta Patti, with out-of-town engagements immediately to follow. But Maretzek's plans had been changed, and Nixon was taking advantage of the Academy's unexpected availability to present her in another role before departing for an opera season in Boston. The *Puritani* cast included Brignoli (Arturo), Susini (Giorgio), and Federico Amodio (Ricardo).

which is very remarkable, so far as agility, certainty, and pure method extend. We do not know anyone who can execute the rapidities or calmer suavities of the difficult part of Amina with greater ease" (*Tribune,* September 23, 1862).[109]

Most, but not all, of the critics were similarly evasive. But *Zincalo,* one of *Dwight's* parade of ephemeral New York correspondents, calling a spade a spade, wrote (September 27, 1862, p. 204): "It would be hardly fair, in view of Mlle. Patti's infirmity, to measure her rendition of Amina last night from a very critical point of view. The sleep-walking scenes, calling for little else than a fixed tranquillity of voice and action, were most successfully sustained; in the finale of the second act, where famous *prime donne* usually concentrate their best powers of tragic action, Carlotta Patti was, as ever, a finished concert singer and not much more." Although the Italian doctor's invention had slightly ameliorated her lameness, her limp was still "painfully perceptible," and she had been obliged to lengthen her costume to conceal the mechanism. "If she would discard the hoop, so out of place in characters like this," wrote *Zincalo,* "her halt would be even less apparent; the hoop, as she moves, accentuates every step."

Valiant Carlotta Patti was even less gently treated in Boston.

Yet a further opera effort had been emerging upon the fragmented opera scene. On January 24, wedged between the first and second of Grau's miniature opera seasons, an even shorter season of German opera in German had flashed by at the Brooklyn Academy. Consisting solely of a performance (or two) of *Der Freischütz,* it had been mounted and conducted by the German musician and music dealer Carl Prox. The cast had included the German actor/singers, Mesdames Schroeder-Dümmler and Schreiner-Kronfeld, Messrs. Rudolphi (Ridolfi?), Weinlich, Oehrlein, and Kronfeld, and a chorus of sixty singers selected from the choruses of the Italian opera, the Brooklyn Thalia, and the Independent Turner Rifles. This "experimental season" had been so well received that Prox was encouraged to venture into Manhattan, rent Wallack's disused old theatre on Broadway and Broome Street,[110] grandly rename it the New-York Athenaeum, and open it (alas, only momentarily) on February 22 with, again, *Der Freischütz,* sung by the same cast.

Following Prox's thwarted effort, German opera was dormant until May, when the same singers—together with Madame Johanna Rotter, a vivacious new *prima donna* from the court theatre *(Hoftheater)* of Darmstadt—surfaced at the old *Stadt-Theater* on the Bowery. Under the musical direction of the Philharmonic violinist F. Herwig, the troupe alternated with the theatre's dramatic cast, offering a wide opera repertory that included Flotow's *Stradella* and *Martha,* Donizetti's *The Daughter of the Regiment,* Hérold's *Zampa,* Lortzing's *Zar and Zimmermann,* Weber's *Der Freischütz,* Mozart's *Die Zauberflöte,* Bellini's *La sonnambula,* and Auber's *The Mason and the Locksmith (Le Maçon).* If the performances were not exactly first-rate, wrote *Alma* in *Dwight's* (June 21, 1862, p. 93), it was still "something" to have Mozart's *Magic Flute* "within auditorial

---

[109] Hagen chose to be more terse: "Miss Carlotta Patti made her debut as Amina in *La sonnambula.* The house was crowded, and everybody seemed more than satisfied with the singing of the young lady. To judge from this first appearance, it is more than likely that her career as a dramatic singer will not be long" (*Review and World,* September 27, 1862, p. 233).

[110] In September 1861, Wallack had moved uptown to a handsome and commodious new theatre at Thirteenth Street and Broadway.

possibilities, even on the Bowery, when the principal Opera House in New York, with something like resources, clings to a stale and worn-out répertoire."

Doubtless following these developments with more than casual interest was Carl Anschütz, recently inactive except for such meager crumbs as Grau chose to throw in his direction, and—in the absence of anything better—wasting his formidable gifts on such happenstance phenomena as the Boughtons. In mid-September, with the backing of his own singing society, the *Arion,* Anschütz initiated a season of German opera[111] at Wallack's old theatre, now renamed the German Opera House. Assembling a company of tried-and-true German singers, including not only Rotter, Lotti, Weinlich, Quint, *et al.,* but Bertha Johannsen, Madame Zimmermann, and the Herren Graf and Hartmann, Anschütz proceeded—bypassing the usual introductory fanfare—to establish a durable and surprisingly successful German opera presence in New York.

"Mr. Carl Anschütz, anxious to do something for the art of his country," exulted Hagen (*Review and World,* September 27, 1862, p. 231) "has undertaken the very difficult task to give us, at Wallack's small, but convenient, old theatre, a season of German Opera." Few truly German operas had been performed in America, wrote Hagen, the majority having been French or Italian works translated into German. It was Anschütz's purpose to make American audiences aware of German opera beyond *Martha* and *Der Freischütz.* He planned to produce, among others, such seldom-heard masterpieces as Beethoven's *Fidelio,* Nicolai's *The Merry Wives of Windsor,* and—still unperformed in the United States—Mozart's *Elopement (sic) from the Seraglio (Entführung aus dem Serail)*[112] (Vienna 1782).

Thus, after launching his undertaking, albeit with such chestnuts as *Martha* (September 15),[113] *Der Freischütz* (September 22), *The Child of the Regiment* (October 8), and Lortzing's *Zar und Zimmermann* (October 9), Anschütz—again refreshingly bypassing the "puff preliminary"—announced four consecutive performances of *Die Entführung* for October 10, 13, 15, and 17.

October 15. . . . Murray Hoffman dined here, and we went to Wallack's old theatre, now a German Opera House, and heard the *Entführung aus dem Serail* for the first time and under disadvantage, our seats being within whispering range of the Big Drum. But many lovely things were perceptible, as in a glass darkly. I hope to hear it again. There are an exquisite tenor solo, a delicious, cosy drinking song, and a lovely finale for the soli and chorus—[as] antiphonal as Reverend Vinton and his chorus boys

---

[111] A so-called "cheap opera," with tickets at twenty-five, fifty, and seventy-five cents, and boxes at five and six dollars.

[112] Unperformed as a staged production, that is. In 1860, Anschütz had given it in a concert version, as part of a series of "operatic recitals" at the Brooklyn Atheneum, with Mesdames Eckhardt and Ficher and Messrs. Cooke, Hartmann, and Weinlich (see Mattfeld, *Handbook,* p. 30; Odell, VII, 300). Performed in the same series were *Der Freischütz* and *Fidelio,* sung by Berta Johannsen and Giuseppe Tamaro.

[113] Despite the "rage in high Teutonic circles for Herr Wagner," the attendance at the opening *Martha* showed that "the popular German heart clings defiantly to Auber, Flotow and von Weber," wrote Fitz Hugh Ludlow in the *Home Journal* (September 27, 1962). "When you entered the packed house, you wondered where anybody would find room to clap his hands, but that difficulty was obviated by extending those members aloft over the head, the net result being enforced by *bravos,* compared with which the applause of the Academy was as Mrs. Winslow's Soothing Syrup."

at Trinity Church. These came out clearly and well defined; everything else somewhat blurred.

October 17. . . . Ellie and I and Murray Hoffman, who dined with us, went to
hear Mozart's *Entführung* again. Well worth hearing it is, and includes many beautiful
things worthy its composer, but much of it is written in a bravura style of extravagant
vocalization that Mozart must have disapproved at heart.[114]

For the most part the critics approved the *Seraglio,* as it was promptly nicknamed.
Despite their generally patronizing attitude toward Anschütz's singers it was agreed—
albeit with individual quibbles—that they were trying to do their best and that the
work had been acceptably enough performed.[115] In an appreciative and scholarly review, *Arsace,* evidently familiar with the *Seraglio,* marveled anew at its "richness and
variety of coloring"; he poked fun at the *Herald* for finding Mozart's score, belonging
as it did to another time, to be "neither rich in melody nor orchestral effects," and of
interest merely as a quaint curiosity. Even Hagen found the overture—composed some
eighty years earlier—"rather thin and old-fashioned" to present-day ears, "especially
in its Presto movement" (*Review and World,* October 25, 1862, p. 255).

The moment was ripe for Anschütz and his effort. "If Italian Opera is destined to
lead a precarious and exciting life at the Academy during the war," wrote Seymour
(*Times,* October 8, 1862), "German opera is making itself comfortable in its snug quarters" at Wallack's former theatre, where the Muse might "find her reward in the opportunity of hearing opera sung less for show than for love." And surely, reasoned Seymour, Beethoven and the other great composers had existed for "more elevated
purposes than to put lazy people agreeably to sleep or attract crowds to a bazaar."

For Anschütz, a musician of high ideals and uncompromising standards, the enterprise was a supreme labor of love and a fulfillment. Not only did he unsparingly
dedicate himself to the greater glory of German opera, but, concurrently, at his well-
attended Sunday sacred concerts—performed by members of his opera company, by
the *Arion* Society, by distinguished guests from the Philharmonic, and by guest artists
of the caliber of S. B. Mills and Madame Anna Bishop—he essayed to conduct all nine
of Beethoven's symphonies, a monumental undertaking.[116]

A small, nervous man, "with long black curling hair just tinged with grey, a quick
nervous eye, and a pair of arms which have discovered the secret of perpetual motion,"
described *Trovator* (briefly restored to *Dwight's,* December 6, 1862, p. 285), Anschütz
was "a musician of the first water, and art is to him bread, meat, *Lagerbier,* sweet pota-

---

[114]Agreeing with Strong, *Arsace,* another of *Dwight's* fleeting New York correspondents, mingled encomiums with reservations over the role of Constanze, in which, "with its heroic flights and
passages in alt, [Mozart had] sacrificed something of truth and beauty to the prevailing taste of his
time and . . . to the great vocal abilities of the singer [Katharina Cavalieri] for whom the part was
written" (*Dwight's,* October 25, 1862, p. 240).

[115]By Johannsen (Constanze), Rotter (Blondchen), Lotti (Belmont), Quint (Pedrillo), and
Weinlich (Osmin), replaced in the role by Graf after the first two performances.

[116]By mid-November he had come as far as Number Six, reported *Dwight's* (November 15,
1862, p. 261). Oddly, Strong, for all his worship of Beethoven, seems not to have attended any of
these performances.

toes, and caramels—lodging and washing. He lives for Art and by Art. He sleeps with Art, or rather, stays up all night with it, for . . . as soon as the opera is over, he goes to the manager's room and copies music all night, preparing from a piano score the orchestral parts of the next new opera. He has already, in less than forty opera nights, produced a dozen operas and intends to produce a dozen more this season, thus introducing to our musical public works which but for him would never have been heard of."

Perhaps heard of, but for the most part not recently—and rarely, if ever, performed so authentically. In addition to repeat performances of the operas already given, on October 22, Anschütz very successfully presented a German version of Boieldieu's *Jean de Paris.*[117] "It is not presumed that this company is the best that can be got together," qualified Seymour (*Times,* October 27, 1862), "but it is, at all events, better than any other that has ever been formed in this city. With due encouragement and a decent amount of kindliness from the German press, it can easily be made into something of permanent value to the world of art. Italian music has so monopolized the public ear," wrote Seymour, "that few are aware of the wealth of the German *répertoire.* There are plenty of delightful works worthy of a place in the public esteem. . . . It is impossible to find a better conductor for the purpose than Mr. Carl Anschütz, and hence, all that has been done so far has been marked by rare artistic feeling."

October 25. . . . Philharmonic rehearsal this afternoon. Beethoven's Symphony in B-flat (No. 4), one of the two that I know but little, but it turns out to be a very noble symphony. For about one hour I forgot all about the War and the Sanitation Commission and was conscious of nothing but the marvelous web of melody and harmony and pungent orchestral color that was slowly unfolding. Though deep and elaborate, the symphony is very clear and I followed it all without effort on this first hearing. It is *Beethoven,* every note, but, except perhaps in the first movement *Haydnoid* in sentiment. The second movement seems transcendently beautiful; Haydn's purity and heartiness expressed in Beethoven's more copious vocabulary. The Scherzo and Trio are full of lovely melodic phrases and the jolliest thing Beethoven ever wrote for an orchestra. One of these phrases is reproduced, by-the-by, with telling effect in the last movement of the Seventh Symphony. After this symphony there was an overture of [Ferdinand] Hiller's, "A Christmas Eve Dream" or some such title [*Ein Traum in der Christnacht* (1845)]. Very pretty and carefully constructed, but coming after Beethoven it was mere *dudelei.*

. . . Last night with Murray Hoffman to the German Theatre. Heard Boieldieu's *Jean de Paris* in a German version.[118] That opera has its good points, in the third act

---

[117] Although announced as a first performance in America, *John of Paris* had been heard at the Park Theatre in 1816 in Sir Henry Bishop's English version (London 1814), adapted from Boieldieu's opera (Paris 1812). Presumably based on Bishop's adaptation, it had been presented in 1855 by William Burton at his little Chambers Street Theatre.

[118] Appearing in *Johann von Paris,* which opened on October 22, were Madame Johannsen (Princess of Navarre), Madame Rotter (Olivier, the Page), Graf (the Seneschal), Quint (Johann von Paris), Kronfeld (Pedrigo, the Innkeeper), and a Miss Clemens (the Innkeeper's Daughter). Costa Theleur and Monsier Wiethoff performed a *Grand Pas de deux* in the third act.

especially,[119] but they are too few to compensate one for three hours of mephitic atmosphere and absorption of carbonic oxide into one's blood and bones in that ill-ventilated little theatre.

November 8. . . . At the Philharmonic rehearsal with Ellie this morning at ten. . . . Tonight . . . to the [first] Philharmonic concert [of the twenty-first season, conducted by Eisfeld], at Irving Hall. Beethoven's Fourth Symphony, heard twice today, is very great. How we should glorify it if he had never given us the C-minor, the "Eroica," and Number Seven! Its strongest movement is the third, which is first-rate. The most lovely Trio very Mozartesque in sentiment. The fourth movement is brilliant and delightful, but nothing more. The first is more characteristic of its author. There are examples in it of a special faculty Beethoven enjoyed, viz., that of closing a musical phrase or sentence, or paragraph (how hard it is to write intelligibly about music) with a conclusive sledgehammer-blow by a couple of sharp-cut and massive chords. Certainly Beethoven's orchestral work differs from all others (Mozart's and Haydn's included) in that it possesses a *virulence*—intensity—emphasis—pungency—or *something*—to be found nowhere else.

Schubert's Piano and Orchestra ["Wanderer"] Fantasie (op. 15)[120] was very good—the first of his instrumental productions that has seemed to me worthy to be ranked with his noble *Lieder;* Schumann's "Descriptive Overture" to *Manfred* was bosh—nonsensical sound and fury—as worthless as the talk of a young dry-goods-shop apprentice trying to be Byronical; Mendelssohn's Violin Concerto (op. 64) [played] by [Edward] Mollenhauer was tolerable; Hiller's concluding overture was rubbish; and now I'll go to bed.

— ~~~ —

In October, Gottschalk, absent on tour since July,[121] returned to New York and—apparently by an arrangement between Strakosch and the increasingly important concert impresario Lafayette F. Harrison—gave a series of four concerts at Harrison's newly redecorated Irving Hall. For this series, with Harrison's brilliant young assistant Theodore Thomas acting as music director, Gottschalk was surrounded by a new company: the fine Boston contralto Jenny Kempton, a pupil of Elena D'Angri, the popular composer/singer J. R. Thomas, and, from the Philharmonic, the trumpet virtuoso Louis Schreiber and a quartet of string players—Noll, Matzka, Bergner, and Anton Reyer—with Henry C. Timm to accompany. Theodore Thomas both directed the proceedings and played violin solos.[122]

Probably to silence the persistent criticisms of Gottschalk for playing his own

---

[119] Like everything that Anschütz produced at the German Opera House, *Jean de Paris* was a popular hit, and although it was a French opera, the admiring *Albion* critic (October 25, 1862, p. 511) predicted that in the future, people would say, as they respectfully lifted their hats: "Honour to you, Carl Anschütz; you are the Founder of the German Opera."

[120] Played by William Mason in Liszt's transcription for piano and orchestra (*c.* 1851) (Searle 366). Mason's solo was Chopin's Ballade in A-flat, op. 47; as an encore he played his "Silver Spring."

[121] With time out for a vacation at Saratoga Springs, where, under the auspices of the patriotic Ladies' Society of Congress Hall, he had given a concert in aid of sick and wounded soldiers, netting the considerable sum of $800 (see the *Dispatch,* September 30, 1862).

[122] With Timm present to accompany, what was left for Thomas to direct? disingenuously wondered *Zincalo* (*Dwight's,* October 11, 1862, p. 223).

compositions to the exclusion of the classics,[123] it was announced that his Irving Hall programs, as planned by Thomas, would offer a "novel" combination of classical and lighter music.[124] Thus, at the first concert, on October 2, Gottschalk momentarily deferred to the "classics" by playing Chopin's preludes in C and D-flat and Adolf Henselt's étude *Si oiseau j'etais,* then returned to his own compositions, giving his "burlesque" of *Marlborough s'en va-t'en guerre* (again announced as a first performance), his *Berceuse,* op. 47 (*c.* 1860–61),[125] his *Minuit à Séville,* his *Rigoletto* transcription, and, as an encore, his *Murmures éoliennes.* Mrs. Kempton sang a cavatina from Mercadante's *Il giuramento,* a ballad by J. R. Thomas, and with him a duet from *Lucia di Lammermoor;* Theodore Thomas gave a sensational performance of Vieuxtemps's violin fantasy on *Lucia;* and Schreiber impeccably performed a cornet piece attributed to Beethoven. An unidentified string quartet played by Noll and his associates, while good in itself, seemed to the *World* reviewer (October 4, 1862) "as much out of place as a mourner in a ballroom."

But Gottschalk! "It seems to us that Mr. Gottschalk plays better and better every time he appears before the public," wrote Fry in the *Tribune* (October 6, 1862). "His digital dexterity now seems to have arrived at its perfection." As had his extraordinary capacity for handling octaves with immense force and rapidity, and his lightness of touch—a veritable "spray of sound." "It may safely be said," added Fry (notoriously no lover of piano sounds), "that Mr. Gottschalk has extracted from the piano all that it is capable of in resonance, delicacy, chord-combinations, octaves, and individual sequences of notes."

On October 3, with the same company (and probably the same program),[126] Gottschalk was tumultuously received at the Brooklyn Athenaeum, then again at Irving Hall on October 4, 7, and 9. His program for the last of these events, according to the *World* (October 10, 1862), included his "Chase of King Henry" and his *Ojos criollos,* both played with Harry Sanderson at the second piano; solo, he played his Mazurka *Jeunesse,* his *Chant,*[127] his Fantasy on *Le Carnaval de Venise,* op. 89 (1850);[128] and to close, again with Sanderson, his Overture to *William Tell.* As an encore Sanderson played his charming polka, "Bridal Eve" (a gracious gesture on Gottschalk's part, it was noted).

Immediately following these latest triumphs Gottschalk departed, as the *World* put it, "to assault the classical fortress Boston," a city he had conspicuously avoided since

---

[123] A complaint most recently voiced in the *Albion* (October 4, 1862, p. 475): "The public may have rather too much of oft-repeated pieces; nor can brilliant variations upon very commonplace themes attract the genuine lovers of music."

[124] A programing concept brilliantly elaborated nearly a decade earlier by Jullien,♩ in whose orchestra an alert young Thomas had played.

[125] *Berceuse,* Cradle Song (D-20; *Piano Works,* I, 179).

[126] Contrary to custom, Harrison, as manager of the series, regrettably did not list the programs in his advertisements of these concerts.

[127] But not specifying if it was his *Chant de guerre,* op. 78 (*c.* 1857–59) (D-29; *Piano Works,* I, 249), or *Le Chant du Martyr, Grand caprice religieuse* (*c.* 1854) (D-30; *Piano Works,* I, 263), or the *Chant du soldat, Grand caprice de concert* (*c.* 1855) (D-31; *Piano Works,* II, 1). Or it might have been his popular *Souvenir de Porto Rico,* alternately subtitled *Chant gibaresque.*

[128] *Le Carnaval de Venise. Grand caprice et variations* (D-27; *Piano Works,* I, 221).

his celebrated contretemps with Dwight in 1853.♫ Now, after a systematic softening-up campaign of concerts embracing the Boston periphery and coming as close to the Athens of America as Roxbury, but always bypassing the tantalized cultural stronghold, Gottschalk was at last ready to administer the *coup de grâce* to Dwight. Played up for all it was worth in the gossip columns, the affair had by now attained the redundant (and profitable) notoriety attending a particularly juicy scandal in the remorseless grip of late-twentieth-century media.[129]

"Mr. Gottschalk has entered Boston once more and [on October 11] played in the elegant *salon* of the Chickerings," reported the *New-York World* (October 13). And he had conquered! "The editor of *Dwight's Journal* has in his last issue [October 11, 1862, pp. 222–23] undertaken to prove that his severe attacks upon Gottschalk nine years ago were merely kindly criticisms, and [has] reproduced the [1853] articles as proof thereof. The manner in which the hero-pianist [had been] handled in these *critiques* . . . can hardly be considered affectionate. . . . Gottschalk is forcibly reminded, and frequently, that his compositions are not to be compared with Chopin's, Liszt's, Henselt's, or Beethoven's. . . .

"Neither Mr. Tennyson or Mr. Longfellow, has ever been blamed, even impliedly, because their poems are surpassed by Shakespeare and Milton," acutely observed the writer, "yet these poets are esteemed highly. If Mr. Gottschalk were to write like the classicists he would be pronounced a plagiarist. Writing as he does, with wonderful originality, he is scoffed at because he does not follow the beaten track."

Not until art emancipated itself from the "slavery, the detestable terrorism exercised over music and its disciples by the intellectual hobby-riders of Germany, England, and America," asserted the writer, would there be any hope of "modern genius being widely acknowledged."

In the face of Gottshalk's tremendous present success in Boston, Dwight—embarrassed and openly on the defensive—sought to exonerate, or at least to justify himself. Reviewing Gottschalk's current concerts in his journal (October 18, 1862, pp. 230–31), Dwight testified to a pianistically reformed Gottschalk (albeit still an insignificant composer).[130] Despite Dwight's protestations of good will, Gottschalk never regarded him with anything but contempt, as expressed in the sharp little stabs that continue to be dotted throughout his *Notes of a Pianist*.

"Gottschalk seems to have pleased everybody in Boston," happily reported the partisan *World* (October 10, 1862), "except two squeamish critics, one of whom intimates that the piano-forte is Mr. G.'s hobby—a fact that will probably startle a good many who have heard him play. Chickering's room was found too small to accomodate the rush that occurred at every performance, and so Max Strakosch was compelled to present his ward in the Melodeon."

Following his conquest of Boston, and subsequently his renewed conquest of Philadelphia, a victorious Gottschalk returned to New York to give a "second series"

[129] Even up to the time of this writing (1995) Gottschalk aficionados are prone to attribute exaggerated importance to the Dwight episode, to be unaware of—or to ignore—the fact that Dwight, an incurably rigid apostle of the narrowest musical orthodoxy, was by far not the only critic to fault Gottschalk for neglecting the classics.

[130] Despite his ostensible efforts at conciliation, Dwight pronounced Gottschalk's *William Tell* transcription "abominable."

of four concerts at Harrison's Irving Hall—on October 21, 23, 28, and 30—followed by a single *matinée d'instruction,* assisted by Carlotta Patti, on November 1.[131] With Theodore Thomas again as music director, Gottschalk's concert company for this series consisted of Madame de Lussan, Fanny Stockton, Mary Hawley, a transitory Madame Goessel, and Abella's prize pupil, the promising tenor William Castle,[132] also the Philharmonic flute virtuoso Felice Eben; and, at the second piano—instead of Sanderson—Eugénie Barnetche, "a charming appearing young pianiste from Paris," who successfully negotiated the fabled difficulties of Gottschalk's *Il trovatore* duo.[133]

"It has been maintained by experienced managers and artists of long suffering that the days of popular concerts were at an end, that three-decker programs, with *fantasias* all over them, like buttons on a page's coat, were no longer attractive to the public," wrote Seymour (*Times,* October 22, 1862). "Mr. Harrison, in his admirable series of entertainments, goes far to upset this theory. In reviving the palmiest days of miscellaneous music, he has also restored to the concert-room its ancient reputation of being the most harmless place where worldly delights can be enjoyed."[134]

"Profuseness and excellence were combined with admirable discrimination in last evening's programme," wrote Seymour following the opening concert of the series. "Mr. Gottschalk has rarely been heard to greater advantage, being received, of course, with the usual fervor"; he was, as always, "inimitable."

After concluding this unusually brilliant and successful season, reported a New York correspondent of *Dwight's* (November 16, 1862, p. 261), "Mr. Gottschalk has withdrawn from our sight—hearing rather—and is concertizing around the country with Carlotta Patti. Won't his manipulations astonish the country people! As to his selections, it makes no difference; the 'Banjo' will be as acceptable as Chopin's loveliest."[135]

Anschütz, too, continued to pile success upon success, adopting into his repertory splendid new productions that attracted not only great numbers of German music lovers, but also—as the *Times* noted (November 2, 1862)—members of the "American part of the musical community." On October 31 he presented a German adaptation of Adolphe Adam's *Le Postillon de Longjumeau;*[136] on November 10 an authentic *Magic*

---

[131] Tickets for Gottschalk's Irving Hall concerts were fifty cents, reserved seats fifty cents extra. Purchasers of one or two tickets to the *matinée d'instruction* received as a gift "a splendid portrait of Mr. Gottschalk, engraved in the highest style of the art, by Messrs. Sarony, Major, and Knapp, from a photograph by J. Gurney and Son; printed on heavy paper; size, 34 × 24 inches."

[132] A recent graduate from the ranks of Christy's Minstrels, formerly known as Reeves.

[133] The number of accompanists appearing at this series struck *Dwight's* correspondent *Cenerentola* as "amusing." In a game of musical chairs, reported the critic (November 15, 1862, p. 261), Abella played for Castle, Timm for Thomas, Thomas for Eben, and Muzio for Carlotta Patti.

[134] Probably a reference to the current law prohibiting the sale of alcoholic beverages at the disreputable concert saloons (see following OBBLIGATO).

[135] On returning to New York in December, at the conclusion of this tour, Gottschalk wrote in his journal: "I have given eighty-five concerts in four months and a half. I have traveled fifteen thousand miles by train. At St. Louis I have given seven concerts in six days; at Chicago five in four days." Gottschalk had sometimes given concerts in two different towns on a single day; it was his ambition, he wrote, to increase the number of towns to three (*Notes,* undated).

[136] In an English version *Le Postillon* had been performed at the Park Theatre in 1840; in French it was played at Niblo's Theatre in 1843 by Julie Calvé and a splendid visiting French company from New Orleans.

Flute;[137] and on November 24, *Fidelio* (given with the "same perfection as 'The Magic Flute'").

By now the dormant purveyors of Italian opera had awakened, and conflicting rumors of coming Italian opera seasons began to fly thick and fast. In September, Ullman, who, despite the war, had been freely shuttling back and forth across the Atlantic, had unconditionally announced to an expectant public that—after long and arduous overseas negotiations—the reigning European diva, Madame Therese Tietjens, would positively appear at Niblo's in November. But at the last moment Madame Tietjens was unwilling to risk the voyage in wartime,[138] and a finally defeated Ullman, conclusively bereft of his backers, cut his local ties, and in December departed for Europe.

Maretzek, who, as we know, had announced a substantial pre-Havana season at the Academy with his new company, had suddenly whisked them off to Havana, at the behest of Martí, his backer.[139] Thus, conditions were ripe for Jacob Grau once again to gather up the pieces and announce a ten-performance season of Italian opera at the Academy of Music,[140] relieving Ullman (with whom he was most probably in collusion) of the three *prima donna*s that Ullman had brought over from Europe.

Although freshly imported, two of them were Americans—indeed, New Yorkers—who had been establishing opera careers abroad. Madame Ginevra Guerrabella, *née* Genevieve Ward (1838–1922), despite her ferocious stage name, was the granddaughter of a former mayor of New York,[141] and Virginia Lorini was the former Virginia Whiting,♪ absent from the local scene since her promising early appearances with Maretzek more than a decade earlier.[142] The third, Angiolina (*née* Angel) Cordier, billed as a French *chanteuse légere,* had "maintained her ground during the Picolomini furor" in New Orleans in 1859 (*Herald,* November 3, 1862).

As the *Home Journal* pointed out (November 8, 1862), the war presented a rare opportunity for native operatic talent. Not only were Mesdames Guerrabella and Lorini featured at the Academy of Music, but the gifted young American contralto (or

---

[137] "The attempts heretofore made to produce this Opera having been very incomplete," announced Anschütz's advertisements, "this will be the first time in America that this immortal work is presented to the public with the original libretto by Schickaneder, and without curtailment."

[138] Adelaide Ristori, too, had been promised by Ullman but did not appear until the following year, after Ullman had left the country.

[139] At about the same time, Maretzek's brother, Albert, had assembled an opera company for Santiago de Cuba, consisting of Mesdames Borchard and von Berkel, and the Signori Sbriglia, Ippolito, and Rocco, with Bergmann as conductor.

[140] With the help of reductions in both the high rentals demanded by the Academy directors and the singers' salaries. "We are not in the habit of eulogizing the 'powers that be' at the Academy," wrote Burkhardt (*Dispatch,* November 2, 1862), "but their generous conduct in seconding the efforts of Mr. Grau to give us this refined and almost indispensable amusement deserves the praise of all lovers of the Divine Art."

[141] Taken abroad by her mother to study music, Genevieve Ward at the age of eighteen had been the victorious pursuer in a chase ending in St. Petersburg with a shotgun marriage to an unwilling Russian nobleman, Count Constantine de Guerbel. Immediately forsaking her husband but adopting an elaboration of his name, in 1859 Guerrabella made her debut in Paris as Donna Elvira in *Don Giovanni.* In 1861 she sang with the London Phiharmonic, and now, steered by Ullman, she was back in New York, about to become one of Grau's *prima donna*s.

[142] In Europe, where she had achieved high professional repute as the possessor of a superbly beautiful voice, Madame Lorini at the same time had amassed so prodigious a mass of weight that her appearance bordered on the grotesque.

mezzo-soprano), Catarina Morensi, a pupil of Ettore Barili, earlier known to us as Kate Duckworth and/or Mlle. Montmorency; also the alto Fanny Stockton; and the ex-minstrel tenor William Castle. Rounding out Grau's company were Pasquale Brignoli, Alessandro Maccaferri, Federico Amodio, Augustino Susini, and Ettore Barili; Muzio was the conductor and musical director and Carlo Scola the stage manager.

Ushered in with appropriate fanfare, the season opened on Monday, November 10, with Guerrabella, reported to be an uncommonly beautiful woman, as Violetta in *La traviata.*[143] A superlative actress, she portrayed a singularly ladylike Violetta. "It is seldom," wrote the *Times* (November 11, 1862), "that one sees on the Italian stage a Violetta who so completely charms the audience and wins their sympathies." But— not that she didn't sing well and with excellent taste—the critics agreed that her voice was insufficient to the demands of the role and the dimensions of the Academy of Music. "Extremely fine, delicate, and penetrating," her voice nonetheless had no body, wrote the *Albion* (November 15, 1862, p. 547).

On November 12 (and again at the Grand Gala Saturday Matinée on the 15th) Guerrabella appeared to better vocal advantage as Leonora in *Il trovatore.*[144] Kate Morensi, making her debut as Azucena (in a makeup that "wickedly obscured and disfigured her countenance") was hailed as "another American artist of whom the Metropolis may well feel proud. She has a voice of superb quality and so abundant that it seems to issue forth without effort. Nature has lavished all her vocal riches on this charming person. . . . Study cannot fail to place her in the foremost rank of living contralti. As it is, we doubt if a finer voice has ever been heard at the Academy of Music" *(ibid.).*

On Friday, November 14, Virginia Whiting Lorini, the third of the native divas, made so brilliant a debut as Norma[145] that the much-touted premiere of *Dinorah,* the Italian version of Meyerbeer's *Le Pardon de Ploermel,* scheduled for November 18, was postponed to the following week to permit its repetition. "Madame Lorini is gifted with a magnificent soprano voice of pure, bell-like, and voluminous quality," wrote Hagen. Even if it occasionally revealed the ravages of time, it was still "an uncommonly fine voice." Being Hagen, however, he immediately atoned for this excessiveness by calling attention to Madame Lorini's lack of "real style and of that 'repose in motion' which is proof of a thorough musical control." Then, too, he added: "Perhaps the considerable *embonpoint* of the lady interferes with an easy and fluent delivery, as well as with her acting"[146] (*Review and World,* November 22, 1862, p. 279).

On Wednesday, November 19, Guerrabella inauspiciously appeared as Maria in a poor production of *La figlia del reggimento.*[147] "The adventure, in all respects, was so singularly unfortunate that we shall not lose time by speaking of it," wrote the *Albion*

---

[143] With Brignoli as Alfredo and Amodio as Germont.

[144] With Brignoli as Manrico and Amodio as the Count di Luna.

[145] With the vocally resplendent Morensi as Adalgisa, Maccaferri as Pollione, and Susini as Oroveso.

[146] Fry referred not only to her "fine, pure, smooth, elegant soprano which presents all the registers with equal success," but also to her "amplitudinous person" (*Tribune,* November 17, 1862). Fitz Hugh Ludlow (1836–1870), writing music and drama reviews for the *Home Journal,* suggested that she might very well be "the largest *prima donna* on any stage," but also, he atoned, "one of the best" (*Home Journal,* November 29, 1862).

[147] Wherein, as a special feature of the music lesson scene, she was announced to sing the Rondo from Balfe's latest opera, *The Puritan's Daughter* (London 1861).

Girvice Archer, Jr.

Ginevra Guerrabella as Violetta
in La traviata.

(November 22, 1862, p. 559). "Suffice it that Madame Guerrabella did not add to her reputation; that Signor Muzio seemed to have lost control of all of his forces; that a large portion of the opera was omitted; and that everyone, with the exception of Signor Susini as Sulpice, sang and acted and played badly." Particularly Brignoli as Tonio.

On November 21, with Virginia Lorini as Lucrezia and Kate Morensi as Maffio Orsini,[148] a powerful *Lucrezia Borgia* was presented to a crowded and appreciative house. And on the following evening an unprecedented crowd stormed the Academy, where a Grand Evening Gala offered Guerrabella in *La traviata,* Lorini and Morensi in the first act of *Norma,* and all three American divas in a spectacular performance of "The Star-Spangled Banner." The eager thousands who fought their way into the suffocatingly packed Academy were not there for the music, however, but to catch a glimpse of General McClellan, who was in the city, and, who, it was rumored, planned to attend the gala. With the spread of the rumor he remained away, and the audience was forced to make do with Mrs. McClellan and Mrs. Lincoln.

The opera season was doing so well, quipped the *Herald,* (November 24, 1862),

---

[148] And with Brignoli as Gennaro, and Barili, substituting for Susini, as the Duke Alfonso.

following this event, that Grau had every prospect of "becoming a millionaire[149] and transforming the Academy of Music into a private residence." The *Dispatch* (November 23, 1862), however, reported Grau to be a heavy loser and predicted his ruin unless he could repeat such audience-grabbers as the McClellan fiasco.

The very next night (November 24) the General and his lady, accompanied by members of his staff, did indeed attend the Academy for the mightily ballyooed pre-miere[150] of Meyerbeer's pastoral opera *Dinorah.* Of its many wonders—its plot, a bizarre concoction endlessly synopsized in the papers; its new *prima donna* Mlle. Cordier;[151] its "all-star" cast (Morensi/Stockton/Brignoli/Amodio/Susini); its "Grand Symphonic and Choral Overture" (with an "Invisible Chorus"); its "Reaper's Song"; its "Hunter's Song"; its "Shadow Song"; its magnificent sets and stage effects designed by Calyo—of all these the most titillating marvel, by far, was a goat, a real live goat, whose prospective presence in the opera inspired a vast dissemination of facetious goat-lore in all the papers. It was reported that Ullman, Brignoli, and Grau were vying for possession of the goat; that the goat might be previewed in front of the Academy, where it was customarily tethered; that the goat was being coached in its role by Ull-man; that the goat had vanished but was later discovered in nearby Gramercy Park, earnestly rehearsing its role; that Ullman had dispatched the goat to Grau from Eu-rope, together with Mlle. Cordier and the score of *Dinorah,* and that Grau—after in-stalling Mlle. Cordier in a French boarding house and placing the score with a copyist to extract the parts—had conceived a paternal affection for the goat, so great that he had adopted it, engaged a servant and a hairdresser to care for it, and paraded it up and down Broadway, decked out in a necklace and a satin dressing gown embroidered with the message: "DINORAH—THIS EVENING AT THE ACADEMY OF MUSIC."[152]

Aside from the goat, *Dinorah* promised longed-for musical novelty to a blasé pub-lic: "There is a well of pleasure," anticipated the *World* (November 22, 1862), "in the mere fact that we are to be invited to an opera whose melodies are as yet untattered and untorn, whose overture is not instrumentally seedy, and whose tableaux are not as familiar to us as the Broadway stages. Either Verdi, Donizetti, or Bellini has been the standard dish of the Academy, year after year, and there are numbers of thoroughly unmusical stockholders who can hum the 'Anvil Chorus,' 'Libiamo,' 'Di provenza,' 'Casta diva,' and half a dozen other *arias* with as much ease as if reciting the multiplica-tion table."

But *Dinorah* was not gladly received. *Orfeo,* another of *Dwight's* transitory New York correspondents, mercilessly pounced on the work (*Dwight's,* December 6, 1862, p. 285), calling the score "made, cold, sought-for, far-fetched. . . . Beside such music

---

[149] It was feared that Anschütz ran the same risk: not only did people buy tickets to his satisfying performances at the German Opera House, playfully wrote the *Times* (December 8, 1862), but they persisted in "sending checks to Mr. Anschütz, so that there is a strong possibility of his becoming a millionaire before the end of the week."

[150] Touted in prose strongly redolent of Ullman.

[151] It seems more than likely that Ullman, tarrying in New York, retained a behind-the-scenes financial interest in this production, for which he had personally brought Angiolina Cordier to the United States.

[152] More realistically, the services of a local, amateur goat were solicited in newspaper advertise-ments appearing on November 15, 1862: "ACADEMY OF MUSIC. Wanted, a Goat for the new opera, DINORAH. A good price will be given for a well trained animal. Apply at the stage door."

as this (the heaviest of light operas)," he wrote, "Bellini's melodies are golden and Rossini's operas classic."[153] The plot, too, was "very tiresome and undramatic." True, Angiolina Cordier was a pleasing singer and an interesting actress—indeed the only redeeming feature of the evening. And indeed, Morensi sang the first goatherd's music with a "sonorous contralto" (that nonetheless needed further training); but Brignoli was even more awkward than usual and "sang ill";[154] Susini had only one air; Amodio would be a good singer when he learned to dispense with that "senseless *tremolo*." The score had been much cut, the *mise-en-scène* was "fourth rate," the orchestra "insufficient," the chorus "miserable." As for the choral *Ave Maria* "interlarded" with the orchestra, ridiculously announced as "invisible," *Orfeo* wished it had been inaudible as well.[155] Strong, who heard the second performance of *Dinorah*, tended to agree.

November 27. . . . Academy of Music last night with d'Oremieulx and Mrs. d'Oremieulx, who dined here. The Opera was Meyerbeer's *Dinorah*. Its idiocy and imbecility as a *dramatic* work are amazing, but not much below the usual operatic standard. Nobody knew what the people on the stage were supposed to be doing, and nobody cared to inquire. The grand feature of this specimen of the Lyric Drama and of "High old Art" is a white goat—a real live goat—that trots across the stage now and then and is watched by the audience with keen interest. Some future Meyerbeer will electrify an Opera-House-full of cultivated amateurs by introducing a drove of real pigs, or beef-cattle. The music is rather pretty—for Meyerbeer—but his constant strain and struggle for effects and novelty by all manner of trivial claptrap on the stage and in the orchestra is too manifest.

~~~

Presented three times during its first week, by its fourth and purportedly final performance, on December 1, *Dinorah* had at last found a champion in the *Herald* (December 1, 1862). An authentic *opéra comique* in its original French, maintained the writer, the work had lost all its fun in the Italian translation. Yet, he wrote, it had already become a great favorite with New York operagoers; Grau would be making a great mistake to withdraw it.[156]

Scarcely coincidental was the inclusion in the same column of Ullman's fatherly open letter to Brignoli, dated November 30, publicly consoling the tenor for the universally bad reviews his Corentino had received. "Corentin, in the French opera of *Le Pardon de Ploermel* (an *opéra-comique*), is quite a different personage from Correntino in the grand opera of *Dinorah*," wrote Ullman. "The one is a raw and half-idiotic peasant, with long, straggling yellow hair and an ungainly walk; the other a peasant of the Nemorino or Elvino style." It would be just as unfair, reasoned Ullman, to blame Brig-

---

[153] In Hagen's opinion, any of Liszt's "so-called Symphonic Poems" was a masterwork compared with this miserable score (*Review and World,* December 6, 1862, p. 292).

[154] Brignoli was assaulted by the critics for his inept and "frigid" performance as the bagpiper Corentino, a role for which he was totally unsuited. Hagen pronounced his performance (also Amodio's as the goatherd Hoël) "abominable" *(ibid.)*.

[155] Fry's gigantic blow-by-blow "analysis" of *Dinorah,* occupying a large part of the *Tribune* on November 25, was reprinted in full in *Dwight's* (December 6, 1862, pp. 284–85).

[156] That several fellow journalists now shared this opinion suggests that a certain amount of "persuasion" might have been siphoned to the critics by Grau (and from behind the scenes by Ullman?).

noli for wearing "a neat jacket and clean shoes in *L'elisir d'amore,* instead of wearing wooden shoes fitted with straw, as in *Le Philtre,* which is the same opera in French."

Threaded among the performances of *Dinorah* were a *Trovatore,* with Guerrabella, on November 25, and, on Thanksgiving night, November 27, a fifty-cent, "cheap" performance[157] of *Lucrezia Borgia,* with Virginia Whiting. On December 1, as we know, *Dinorah* was repeated at the New York Academy; on December 2, *Lucrezia Borgia* was performed in Brooklyn, and on December 3, in New York, Guerrabella appeared as Leonora in a revival of *La favorita.*

December 3. . . . went to the opera. *Favorita.* Donizetti's music is low grade, but the old tunes of fourteen years ago are pleasant to hear, just as the newly arrived visitor at Willard's Hotel [in Washington] experiences an agreeable emotion when he sees on his wash-stand the identical old Cockroach whom he knew intimately and pursued in vain during his last preceding sojourn there. It is all very nice and pretty, but it differs in kind—*toto genere*—from the music of Beethoven, Haydn, and Mozart, in that it conveys no impression and expresses no emotions that cannot be defined, or at least approximately, in words. The prerogative of the highest music is the utterance of ἄρρητα ῥήματα, ἃ οὐκ εξον ἀνθρώπῳ λαλῆσαι [from the Greek New Testament, 2 Cor. 12:4, literally translated "unspeakable words, which it is not permissible for a man to speak" (Ed.)].

I use St. Paul's words without irreverence, I think. He speaks of a Revelation, which the wooden machinery of human language cannot describe. Our version seems wrong. Instead of "which it is not lawful for man to utter," I would substitute "which man is incapable of uttering," and "of expressing consistently with the laws and limitations of articulate speech." Everyone feels this imperfection of human language in times of strong emotion. A restless night of lively dreaming, when reviewed on awaking, produces a score of keen, distinct, but speedily perishing impressions that are incommunicable, which the law of human language forbids one to communicate—which it is *unlawful* to utter in words. ("Unlawful" is sometimes—unhappily, not always—synonymous with "impossible.") Musical language begins where articulate language stops. It undertakes to tell its audience something they cannot be told by words. For this undertaking Donizetti and Co. fail. Beethoven and Co. succeed.

Look, for instance, at that fearful Allegretto of his Seventh Symphony. No created thing in Nature or Art speaks more clearly and intensely. It says what nobody ever heard, save from an orchestra playing that movement. But who could translate its meaning, whatever that may be, into prose or verse?

December 6. . . . Went to the Opera . . . had the satisfaction of finding *Trovatore* substituted for *Favorita,* owing to somebody's indisposition. That Opera, like most of Verdi's, is worse than worthless. It is actively and positively aggravating, offensive, and disgusting, from beginning to end. It was followed by a grand struggle for carriages,

---

[157] The *Herald* critic took exception to the term "cheap," calling it a "stigmatizing" designation that was unpleasant to the "hyper-fashionables, the *élite,* whose taste for music is not sufficiently great to cause them to overlook that fatal word 'cheap.'" Rather than "cheap," this performance had in fact been truly "grand," with every member of the cast rising to exceptional heights, even Brignoli. The designation "cheap" for fifty-cent presentations was henceforth superseded by the more face-saving "popular."

which I endured for half an hour, wading through the slush, before ours could be found and brought up.

With Ellie and Miss Rosalie at the Philharmonic rehearsal, Irving Hall, half-past-three. Stayed as long as I could and heard three movements of Gade's beautiful symphony, [No. 1♪]—the same that was produced about six years ago. I wanted something to take away the taste of *Trovatore*. If it's not first-class music, it's an excellent imitation. I know of no orchestral work since Beethoven—nothing of the Schumanns, Hillers, Wagners, etc. (unless, perhaps, the *Tannhäuser* Overture)—that comes near it.[158]

⌒⌒⌒

In the meantime, with the performance of *Dinorah* in Brooklyn on December 4, Grau had come to a rude parting with his Brooklyn landlords. "A financial dissonance having been engendered between the trustees of the Montague Street Academy and Mr. Grau," reported the *World* (December 8, 1862), "it is understood that no further enterprises of an operatic nature will be undertaken this season." And derisively added: "This retaliatory measure will possibly necessitate a general return to the indigenous amusements of the sister city—base-ball, tea parties, and crossing the ferry."[159]

In Manhattan *Dinorah* was given a final performance on December 8, the following night *Norma* was presented in a "popular" (no longer "cheap") performance, and on December 10, *Un ballo in maschera* was revived, with Guerrabella as Amelia, Morensi as Ulrica, Cordier in the lamented Hinkley's role of Oscar, Maccaferri (replacing an ailing Brignoli) as the Count of Warwick, Amodio as Reinhardt, and Barili and Dubreuil as the conspiratorial Tom and Sam. In the ballroom scene Madame Marzetti and Monsieur Tophoff performed a mazurka to music especially composed for the production by Muzio, and with the *corps de ballet,* they danced to his "Grand Ballo in Maschera Gallop." Thus, wrote Strong on December 11: "Went with Ellie and Miss Rosalie to hear the *Ballo in maschera,* at which performance I was, happily, not required to assist."

For the penultimate performance of his remarkably successful wartime opera season, Grau offered an Ullman-like Grand Combination and Gala Night (December 12), featuring a complete *Ernani* with Virginia Lorini (Elvira), Maccaferri (Ernani), Amodio (Don Carlos), Susini (Sylva); also the "Shadow Song" from *Dinorah* sung by Cordier and the fourth act of *La favorita* with Guerrabella and Brignoli.[160] The following day the season officially closed with a Gala Matinée of *Ballo* with the three American *prima donnas*—Guerrabella, Lorini, and Morensi—appearing together for "the first and only

---

[158] "Gade, to be sure, had a few ideas of his own, and the Scherzo of this particular work is an instance of how well he could use them," wrote the *Albion* critic (December 27, 1862, p. 619). "The only trouble is that he coddles them too much and repeats them fearlessly, without any, or with but little variety of treatment; whereas Beethoven, with all his passion for repetition and indifference to length, never said the same thing twice, never touched a theme without adding to its beauties or reflecting some hidden charm that it possessed."

[159] The *Times,* too, took up the cudgels for Grau, writing (December 8, 1862) that the powers at the Brooklyn Academy had extorted from Grau an extra $300 for each of the four poorly attended performances he had brought to "that cheerful Mausoleum of Art, the Brooklyn Academy of Music."

[160] At least, the last act of *La favorita* was announced: *T.W.M.* in *Dwight's* (December 20, 1962, p. 301) reports, however, that Madame Guerrabella sang instead the *Brindisi* from Verdi's *Macbeth*.

time at a matinée." But this finale was only a prelude to the ultimate Grand Finale on
December 15, a huge event for Grau's benefit, tendered to him following an exchange
of exquisitely ceremonial open letters by his grateful and devoted company. Preceded
by an act of *Ernani, I puritani* was given complete, with Cordier as a highly praised
Elvira, and with Brignoli as Arturo, Amodio as Riccardo, and Susini as Giorgio. The
last act of *La traviata,* with Guerrabella, Maccaferri, and Amodio, had been announced
to follow, but, as the *Times* (December 16, 1862) rather unfeelingly reported: "An apology had to be made for Madame Guerrabella, who, having met with an accident, was
unable to sing. Hence, an act of 'Traviata,' announced for performance, was happily
annulled."[161] The evening closed with Morensi and Amodio singing a new patriotic
hymn composed by a local clergyman, Charles Hodge. An anticlimax, unkindly remarked *T.W.M.:* not only did it fail to meet with the success its composer anticipated,
but "to a large majority, it seemed very stupid."

In their uncommonly benign summings up the critics generally agreed that—despite the war—Grau had succeeded, where other impresarios had failed, in conducting
a profitable and mutually congenial season of Italian opera. Instead of his originally announced ten-performance season, he had satisfactorily presented a total of twenty-six
performances in the space of little more than a month: nineteen evening performances
and three matinées at the New York Academy, and four presentations in Brooklyn; he
had introduced four new *prima donna*s, three of them Americans, and one new opera.
He was now off to Philadelphia, where—together with his other repertory—he
would present his "cage of larks" (and his goat) in *Dinorah.* And—best news of all—
they would be back at the New York Academy on January 5 with Clara Louise Kellogg in farewell appearances before her purported departure for London, where, reported the *Herald* (December 17, 1862), under Ullman's management, she had been
engaged to sing at Her Majesty's Theatre at the extraordinary salary of 30,000 francs
($6000) for twenty-four performances. As it turned out, Kellogg would indeed enjoy
a great success in London, but not until 1867.[162]

Ullman did not go silently, nor should he have been expected to do so, contended
Fitz Hugh Ludlow in his "Masks and Music" column in the *Home Journal* (December
20, 1962): "New York art owes too much to Ullman to refuse him an opportunity of
explanation [of his recent failed projects]. We would gladly accord room to the man
who foreran his time by putting 'The Huguenots' on our Academy stage in a style of
splendor scarcely surpassable anywhere abroad—the man who has many large artistic
ideas and impregnable faith in the future of his operatic ideals. To such a man, when
Finance, Art's stern unyielding tyrant, withholds practicability as yet from his highest
conceptions, does art owe all manner of gentle sympathies, nursings, and encourage-

---

[161] "Such lengthy and mixed performances are very rarely enjoyed for the reason that the audience tires, and even the best artists grow weary and dispirited," wrote *T.W.M.* in *Dwight's (ibid.).*

[162] During her second professional season, explains Kellogg in her *Memoirs* (p. 120), "an *impresario,* a Jew named Ulman [*sic*], had made me an offer to go abroad and sing in Paris and elsewhere.
Being very eager to forge ahead, it seemed a satisfactory arrangement, and I signed myself to sing
under Ulman's management *if I went abroad* any time in three years. When I came to think it over, I
regretted this arrangement exceedingly. I felt that the *impresario* was not the best one for me. To say
the least, I began to doubt his ability. . . . By 1867, however, my Ulman contract had expired, and I
was free to do as I pleased."

ment. He has done for her more than he has for himself—he is in some sense a sacrifice to her—let her therefore be grateful."

Ludlow proceeded to convey the "marrow," if not the space-devouring verbiage, of Ullman's valedictory card, in which he acquitted himself from blame in the derelictions of Therese Tietjens and Adelaide Ristori, both under contract to him to visit America, neither of whom had appeared. It was perfectly reasonable on both their parts—for personal as well as professional reasons—he wrote, to refuse the risk of visiting a country at war. By mutual consent, he asserted, the engagements of both had been postponed, not canceled, until the following year, when everyone expected the war to be over.

In the fullness of time, both ladies eventually did arrive, but not managed by Ullman, who would not return to the United States until 1875, when he would bring Hans von Bülow for his historic American tour.

It was Anschütz—with the high integrity of his offerings—who immeasurably triumphed above the erratic operatic doings of 1862. "The German Opera has become a fixed fact in New York and may be ranked among our most popular places of amusement," wrote the *Herald* (December 1, 1862). "The manager, Mr. Carl Anschütz, shows great taste and discrimination in his choice of opera. . . . He gives us opportunities to hear the admirable works of Mozart, of Beethoven, of Auber," and most recently a most pleasing comic opera, *Der Wildschütz (The Poacher)* (Leipzig 1842), by Lortzing. Splendidly performed by the company's principal singers, the chorus, the orchestra, and by a chorus of fifty children, it was another great success.

In December a group of prominent German/American citizens honored Anschütz with a testimonial performance, a tribute both to his "efforts to diffuse a taste for classical music in New-York" and his "efforts in the production of German opera on a scale of splendor and artistic costliness never before attempted in this city." On this festive occasion, a performance of *Fidelio*[163] on December 11, Anschütz was feted with "a grand ovation. . . . Numerous presents and a variety of testimonials were showered upon him," reported the *Dispatch* (January 14, 1863). "Madame Methua Scheller of the *Stadt-Theater* (dressed in elegant taste for the occasion), delivered to him, in her usual graceful manner, a neat bouquet of classical verses . . . and handed the astonished and overcome beneficiary a costly *baton* of silver and gold, tastefully ornamented with names of leading Masters and the initials C. A. set in diamonds.[164] . . . The audience, composed of the *élite* of German society mostly, with a good sprinkling of Americans, gave vent to its approbation by a burst of thundering applause."[165]

December 21. . . . Went out in the cold last night to hear Gade's beautiful symphony rendered by the Philharmonic Society [second concert of the 1862–63 season] at Irving Hall. Sent off Ellie and Miss Rosalie in charge of [eleven-year-old] Johny as

---

[163] With the collaboration of the *Arion*.

[164] *Trovator,* in advance of the event, reported an additional gift of "a purse containing almost a thousand dollars" (*Dwight's,* December 6, 1862, p. 286).

[165] During the remainder of his extraordinary season, which continued until January 10, 1863, when he took his company to Philadelphia, Anschütz added still another new production, Konradin Kreutzer's *Das Nachtlager von Granada.*⁀⁀

escort and, finding, after they had gone, that I could spare an hour or so, I posted after them, but was unable to join their party in the crowded concert room. It was Johny's first experience of an orchestra, and of duty as escort to two ladies on a nocturnal expedition. He performed his duty creditably, and seems to have appreciated the music in some degree.[166]

December 24. . . . Christmas Eve. . . . Streets more crowded, shops fuller than I have ever known them. This looks unlike a State of War and still more unlike disposition for self-denial and earnest prosecution of War. . . . Christmas is a great institution, especially in time of trouble and disaster and impending ruin. *Gloria in excelsis Deo et in terra pax* are words of permanent meaning, independent of chance and change, and that meaning is most distinctly felt when war and revolution are shaking the foundations of Society and threatening respectable citizens like myself with speedy insolvency.

December 27. . . . Christmas went off comfortably. . . . Trinity Church was artistically decorated. . . . The Christmas service was long. Its music was dismal in quality, and its execution produced acute suffering.

---

[166] On this momentous occasion, besides Gade's symphony, Johny heard Beethoven's *Leonore* Overture, no. 3, and Liszt's symphonic poem *Tasso* conducted by Eisfeld, Mendelssohn's *Capriccio brillant* for piano and orchestra and a Prelude and Fugue in A minor by Bach played by John Nelson Pattison, and a *Scena italiana di concerto* composed by Eisfeld and the *Non piuα andrai* from *Le nozze di Figaro* sung by Pietro Centemeri.

OBBLIGATO: 1862

Fifty years hence John Brown will be remembered as the Hero, a Representative Man of this struggle—up to 1862. . . . A queer, rude song about him seems growing popular:
    John Brown's body lies a-molderin' in the grave,
    John Brown's body lies a-molderin' in the grave.
        Glory Hally Hallelujah,
        Glory Hally Hallelujah,
        But his soul's a-marchin' on.

                  George Templeton Strong
                  Private Journal, February 4, 1862

IF JACOB GRAU RULED the fragmented wartime opera scene in 1862, it was Lafayette F. Harrison, the presiding spirit of Irving Hall, who—with his dynamic approach—created a vibrant new dimension in concert-giving. Innovatively employing the gifts (and doubtless the suggestions) of his young assistant and protégé, Theodore Thomas, as violinist, conductor, program maker, and artists' liaison, Harrison attracted large audiences to Irving Hall with a steady stream of attractive concert offerings catering to many levels of taste at minimal ticket prices.[1]

As Fry remarked, in summing up the events of the musical year (*Tribune,* December 15, 1862), Harrison represented a new breed of impresario:[2] "It is a matter of considerable importance to the advances of concert and other music," wrote Fry, "that a gentleman of the singular enterprise and liberality of Mr. Harrison should be proprietor of the chief music hall of the city, one that nestles,too, in the very academic bosom of the muse, being close to the opera house and the cynosure of taste, fashion, and art. Mr. Harrison, of whom we wish to speak with the euphoria simply his due, does not wait for all artists to give concerts at the Hall. He coincides, cooperates, nay, under-

---

[1] Never exceeding fifty cents and sometimes offering three tickets for a dollar.
[2] Harrison's previous qualifications to be a concert manager are not known. He is listed in the New York City Directory for 1855 as an employee at the Custom House, and in 1860 as a contractor located at 27 Pine Street.

takes solely, we learn, those entertainments for the public. This is a new phase of concert-hall keeping. We know of operatic managers, but we do not know of another person who is a concert manager, a lessee of a music hall, independent of all other attractions, having the audacity to act like Mr. Harrison."[3]

Harrison had displayed the quality of his audacity early in the year, on March 27, with an elaborate single-day Music Festival at Irving Hall, consisting of a concert at one in the afternoon and another at half-past seven in the evening. His roster of performers, all of whom, in various combinations and capacities, were frequently heard at Irving Hall,[4] represented a veritable who's who of the local music community: from the opera, the singers Isabella Hinkley, Amalia Strakosch, Brignoli, Susini, and Mancusi (with a credit to Grau); the concert-givers Maria Brainerd, Mary Hawley, Mrs. J. E. Thomas, Mina and Gustavus Geary, J. R. Thomas, George Crozier (about to return to England), S. C. Campbell (still a part-time minstrel with the Bryants),[5] and Federico Ridolfi; the pianists S. B. Mills, William Mason, Hermann Wollenhaupt, and William Saar; the violinists Bruno Wollenhaupt and, of course, Harrison's music director, Theodore Thomas (appearing both as a soloist and with his colleagues of the Mason/Thomas quartet); also, from the Philharmonic appeared the bassoonist Paul Eltz, the clarinetist Edward Boehm, and Carl Bergmann in his cello-playing persona. George F. Bristow conducted a "powerful chorus" from the Harmonic Society; Harvey Dodworth conducted his Military Band; and Carl Anschütz presided over a full orchestra. The accompanists were Dr. Clare Beames and Henry C. Timm.

Harrison's festival was enthusiastically hailed in the press: "It does not often happen," wrote Fry in the *Tribune* (March 27, 1862), "that so sumptuous a bill is offered to the public, or that a festival of such proportions is placed within the pecuniary reach of the masses." And the *World* (March 25, 1862) agreed that "this community has long needed a man of Mr. Harrison's ability and perception to institute concerts and musical reunions after the manner of those with which Exeter and St. James's Halls, London, have been identified."

The festival proved to be "a distinguished success in every point." The afternoon program, consisting of eight pieces,[6] reportedly attracted an audience of about 800; the evening concert, with a huge program of twenty-five pieces—each performed by a different artist—was heard by about 2000 persons. And, wonder of wonders, it all went off without a hitch: "Everything announced was carefully given, and every promised artist appeared with the most surprising punctuality. When it is borne in mind," marveled the *World* (March 31, 1862), "that a large chorus, an orchestra, a military band, and twenty-five select instrumentalists and vocalists united in giving the fes-

---

[3] Suggesting that Harrison ran what was in effect an integrated, self-contained artists' management/booking agency/production enterprise that enabled him to draw on his own network of artists for his own productions at his own concert hall. He was also equipped to supply prospective concert-givers with a ready-made concert setup: hall, assisting artists, publicity, management, everything.

[4] Appearing sometimes as concert-givers, sometimes as reciprocal assisting artists.

[5] In addition, Campbell, a versatile performer, had earlier in the month successfully undertaken the role of Uncle Tom in a highly praised production of *Uncle Tom's Cabin* at the New York Athaneum (as Wallack's old theatre was briefly called), given with all the songs of the Howard production of 1853-7 and with a new overture by Koppitz.

[6] Regrettably—except for Schumann's Quintet for strings and piano played by the Mason/Thomas group at the afternoon concert—the further content of the programs has eluded me.

tival, it will be seen that the fact of no drawback whatever occurring argues favorably for Mr. Harrison's skillful management."

The success of this event—and doubtless Theodore Thomas's persuasion—encouraged Harrison, among his more popularly attuned productions,[7] to venture a further experiment, a concert on May 13 wherein Thomas irrefutably asserted his growing stature as a conductor and an innovative program maker. "Gotten up" by Thomas, wrote the *World* (April 23, 1862), the event promised, "in point of excellence, to completely distance anything attempted in New York for a long time."

The program was indeed venturesome, offering for the first time in the United States Wagner's Overture to *Der fliegende Holländer (The Flying Dutchman)* (Dresden 1841) and—more to the critics' liking[8]—Meyerbeer's overture and entr'acte music to his brother's play *Struensee*♩ (Berlin 1846).[9] Conducted by Thomas, both works were performed by an orchestra of sixty[10] first-rate musicians (doubtless chiefly from the Philharmonic), with Joseph Noll as concertmaster. For the *Struensee* music they were joined by the Teutonia Choral Society, directed by Joseph Mosenthal.

Also a departure from the beaten path was Liszt's transcription for piano and orchestra of Schubert's "Wanderer Fantasy," played by William Mason (in anticipation of his performance of it with the Philharmonic in November), and Moscheles's *Les Contrastes* for two pianos, eight hands, op. 115, a work "scientifically but monotonously" performed by Mason, S. B. Mills, Ernst Hartmann, and Robert Goldbeck (*Herald,* May 14, 1862). Additionally, Bruno Wollenhaupt gave a fine performance of the Violin Concerto in A minor by Bernhard Molique,♩ and Madame de Lussan sang two opera arias.[11]

As suggested by Thomas himself, this event has come to be regarded as the first great, definitive musical statement of his unparalleled career. Never one to underestimate himself—and neglecting to mention Harrison's important role in the proceedings—Thomas later wrote in his *Autobiography* (p. 50): "In 1862, I concluded to devote my energies to the cultivation of the public taste for instrumental music. . . what this country needed most of all to make it musical was a good orchestra and plenty of con-

[7]Such as a Grand Irish Concert on March 20, sponsored by the Society of the Friendly Sons of St. Patrick, wherein Gustavus Geary, assisted by Mrs. Mozart, Mina Geary, Messrs. Crozier, Seymour, and J. R. Thomas, and others, were heard in songs by Thomas Moore. On May 25, again at Irving Hall, Geary and a group of colleagues commemorated the eighty-third anniversary of Moore's birth with more selections from his *Irish Melodies.*

[8]Not according to the staunch Wagnerite, Hagen, who reported that Wagner's overture had been preferred by the audience, probably because of its descriptive program note, which Hagen quoted in his review.

[9]The *Struensee* Overture had been introduced by Carl Eckert in 1852, when Alfred Toulmin had played its harp *obbligato,* as he did again on this occasion. Fry vastly preferred Meyerbeer's score to Wagner's *Flying Dutchman* Overture, a work he described as "ingeniously destitute of melody," whose main feature was "*ghostly rumpus.*" In contrast, "harmony and melody were not abolished in Meyerbeer's *Struensee,* and there was reference to the beautiful." (Fry's review was scornfully quoted in *Dwight's,* May 24, 1862, p. 63.)

[10]According to the papers, an orchestra of sixty; according to Rose Fay Thomas, Thomas's widow, and Ezra Schabas, in their respective biographies of Thomas, forty players.

[11]Madame de Lussan appeared in place of the recently arrived Madame Comte Borchard, who had been offered the engagement but had declined to be heard for the first time in New York in anything but opera (*Herald,* April 28, 1862).

certs within the reach of the people." Quoting this passage in her *Memoirs of Theodore Thomas* (pp. 24–25), Rose Fay Thomas refers to the May 13 concert as nothing less than the beginning of a new musical era in America, "the first Thomas Concert."

Embroidering upon this interpretation, Thomas's more recent biographer, Ezra Schabas—apparently unaware of Harrison's existence, or disregardful of it—devises a scenario wherein a penniless Thomas, having resolved to make this country musical, bravely, "without any financial backing, rented the two-year-old Irving Hall, a nondescript, already rundown, building just off Union Square, to conduct an orchestral concert on May 13, 1862. Hiring an orchestra of forty, he engaged several soloists and an amateur choir, the Teutonic [*sic*] Choral Society, and, thanks to his experience with the Mason-Thomas concerts, directed the advertising and ticket selling." So enthusiastically was this concert received, writes Schabas (p. 16) that Thomas forthwith engaged Irving Hall for a second concert some four months hence.[12]

More accurately, this "second concert" celebrated Harrison's reopening of his hall, on September 18, after a massive and highly publicized renovation of its visually unsatisfactory, albeit acoustically acceptable, interior.[13] Previewing it at a private showing for distinguished guests, the *Times* (September 25, 1862)[14] perhaps excessively proclaimed the new Irving Hall the most beautiful music hall in the United States, "or, perhaps, the world."[15]

At the gala reopening, Thomas ventured even deeper into the programmatic unknown with the first known American performance of a symphony by Carl Philipp Emanuel Bach (1714–1788), an act of daring in that day of intolerance toward music composed in the preceding century.[16] He conducted also Weber's Overture to *Oberon*, again the *Struensee* music with Toulmin and this time with Mosenthal's Teutonia Choral Society, and appropriately, Auber's "Inauguration March in the Form of an Overture," composed for the opening of that year's Great London Exhibition. Elena D'Angri sang the *Ah! mon fils* from *Le Prophète* and, inevitably, Abella's "Elena Waltz"; and

---

[12] John Tasker Howard, among the more adulatory of Thomas's adulators, in both *Our American Music* (pp. 384–85) and the *Dictionary of American Biography* (IX, 424), erroneously states that in 1862 Thomas "had an orchestra of his own, with which he gave concerts."

[13] "Irving Hall, 'cross-the-way neighbor' of the Academy, one of the most useful, and at the same time uncomfortable, concert rooms in New York, has undergone very important changes," wrote *T.W.M* in *Dwight's* (September 20, 1862, p. 200). "After having been sealed up for several weeks, it is thrown open to the public entirely remodeled and in a most elegant and comfortable style."

[14] Particularly admired—indeed, "hailed with joy"—was the spectacular new ceiling painted by the eminent theatre designer Giuseppe Guidicini, described in the *Times* (September 10, 1862) as a veritable "picture gallery" of the immortals. The beautiful drop curtain painted by the versatile opera baritone/painter Giovanni Garibaldi also reportedly produced joyful reactions.

[15] "The courage of Mr. Harrison in going to such a large expense at the present time as the redecoration of the Hall demanded is worthy of remark," wrote the *Dispatch* (September 14, 1862). "He has emphatically made it the most elegant, as it was formerly the [acoustically] best, Music Hall in the city, and we sincerely trust that his success with it will justify him in the almost prodigal use of capital which he has made."

[16] Composed in "the blessed A.D. year 1776," contemptuously wrote Fry (*Tribune*, September 20, 1862), the symphony was "a venerable old composition of an *Allegro, Largo,* and *Presto* . . . which has come down to this day only somewhat extended by other composers." An examination of the Fétis edition of C. P. E. Bach's works, suggested Fry, would confirm the fact that "strong, brave men lived before Agememnon."

William Mason masterfully played Liszt's transcription of Meyerbeer's "Schiller March" (1860) (Searle 549).[17]

"Taken as a whole," wrote Seymour (*Times,* October 22, 1862), "the concerts now being given by Mr. Harrison at his beautiful hall [Gottschalk's sensational second series was currently in progress] are by far the best that we have had in the City for many years, being as remarkable for their cheapness as their excellence. It is not strange that they are attracting the undivided attention of the musical public and reversing the theories of management."

But Harrison was yet to produce the most extraordinary of all his attractions, Miss Teresa Carreño (1853–1917): "The latest novelty offered by Mr. Harrison is in the shape of a little girl," announced Fry (*Tribune,* December 15, 1862).[18] "This most remarkable child is only eight years of age, and yet plays on the piano in a style sufficiently advanced to be agreeable to good ears. She essays pieces of an ambitious structure." But the mechanical difficulties that little Carreño so easily vanquished were "the least part of her merit. It is the expression which she throws into the work before her," wrote Fry. "Phrasing, as it is technically termed, is an art possessed but by few adults in song or playing, yet this child has a remarkable taste that way. Of course, a child cannot be expected to play as well as a skilled adult," backtracked Fry, "but, given the extremely youthful years of the little pianist, it is a most remarkable and interesting performance."

This was a comparatively restrained description of the amazing child who, in fact, had totally ensnared the critics in a web of wondering disbelief. On October 27 the *Herald* had rhapsodized over the little "musical phenomenon," recently arrived in the city from Caracas, Venezuela.[19] Although in all other respects a child, little Teresa, musically tutored chiefly by her father, an exiled Venezuelan diplomat, "plays the works of Thalberg, Prudent, Goria, and other modern composers with a facility of execution that is truly wonderful.[20] Her reading of the difficult compositions which she plays is entirely her own, she being too young to have made studies of interpretation.[21] This is in all cases refined, and often original and striking. Her power of touch, execution, and style of phrasing are such that if one were to hear without seeing her, it would be difficult to make him believe that it was the performance of a child." Indeed, it was suspected that her age might have been falsified, and a certificate of birth

---

[17] A work that—together with Auber's "Inauguration March"—inspired Hagen's most scathing condemnation in the *Review and World* (September 27, 1862, p. 230).

[18] Teresa Carreño was not the first child prodigy to have crossed Harrison's managerial path. On January 11 little Willie Barnesmore Pape and the violin prodigy Master Bernardo had jointly appeared at Irving Hall, and on April 28, Harrison had presented another piano prodigy, eleven-year-old Master Isaac Rice from Philadelphia, a pupil of Carl Wolfsohn (1834–1907) of that city.

[19] Not from Brazil, as Odell erroneously states (VII, 528).

[20] According to *Dwight's* (January 24, 1863, p. 343), little Carreño had brilliantly mastered Thalberg's forbidding Fantasy on *Norma* when she was seven years old.

[21] Not too young, however, to have received a few lessons from her idol, Gottschalk, at whose concerts she had been seen childishly gamboling about, as poet and journalist Fitz Hugh Ludlow (1836–1870) charmingly discloses (see below). Amid the great body of Gottschalk apocrypha propagated by Loggins is the fuzzy fable that Gottschalk had performed in Caracas on his earlier travels, and that he had exerted his influence, transmitted through her father's reports of his playing, on impressionable four-year-old Teresa Carreño, then too young to be taken to concerts (Loggins, p. 175).

was solicited from the Spanish consul to verify that she was indeed only eight years old (*Dwight's* December 13, 1862, p. 294).

Harrison first presented little Carreño on November 7 at Irving Hall at what appears to have been a private (or quasi-private) *soirée* for an invited audience. Seymour, despite his avowed disapproval of infant prodigies, was overwhelmed, writing in the *Times* (November 10, 1862) that her charming warmth of temperament and "calm intellectual perception of what she [had] to do and how to do it" imbued her playing with a "spirit and clearness, amounting almost to style." These precocious qualities and her uncanny digital correctness and discipline permitted her to play Thalberg's difficult compositions "with facility and with extraordinary power for a child who cannot yet reach the pedals with her toes."[22] Seymour cited, too, her performance of an enchanting "little French theme, imbedded in fragrant garlands of many-colored notes, which . . . could hardly have been given better by any performer now before the public."[23]

And Fitz Hugh Ludlow in the *Home Journal* (November 22, 1862) confessed that he had not expected to see "that little eight-year-old hand strike any larger chord than fifths. Having never known her before, except as an almost baby playing about the benches at Gottschalk's concerts, we looked, at the farthest, for some remarkable trills—what our Boston friend Dwight would call *twiddling in piccolo*.[24] Our surprise may be imagined when she gave us some specimens of octave playing admirable for precision, rapidity, and power, and we discovered hardly a spot in the child's whole execution which could be called weak." From Ludlow we learn that on this occasion she played Thalberg's Variations on Themes from *Norma*, an unidentified somebody's *Souvenir of Trovatore* and also an *Ernani caprice*. Proving that she was not performing by rote, "she played a waltz and one of her own Spanish dances, which possessed decided idiosyncracy—almost as truly so, indeed, as Gottschalk's *Bananier*, which she gave as an encore."

At her official debut, which followed on November 25 at Irving Hall: "A sprightly girl of eight years wrought such miracles of music upon the pianoforte as to evoke [from a large and discriminating audience] the most rapturous enthusiasm at first. Then," continued the *World* (November 27, 1862), "when the truths of the case presented themselves more clearly and the realization of her extreme youth increased, a sense of profound astonishment seized every spectator. Could it be possible that fingers just freed from sporting with dolls and toys were capable of producing chords of sensitiveness, runs and trills of such delicacy and finish? The intellect struggled against what the senses averred, but eyes and ears triumphed."

[22] William Mason (*Memories*, p. 271) affectionately remembered his first impressions of little Carreño in the early sixties, "both from her artistic playing and her charming appearance in short dresses and 'pantalets,' the fashion for children of that day."

[23] "Even Gottschalk himself might well be proud of the laurels she has already won," wrote the *Dispatch* (December 7, 1862).

[24] A scornful reference to Dwight's recent review of Gottschalk's "abominable" paraphrase for two pianos on the *William Tell* Overture, performed by him in Boston with the eminent local organist and pianist Benjamin Johnson Lang (1837–1909). Gottschalk, "at his more brilliant instrument," vindictively wrote Dwight, "piled upon it such *tours de force* as served to illustrate his own virtuosity rather than the overture, now trilling and twiddling, with senseless, painful repetition, in those piccolo octaves" that he allegedly preferred (*Dwight's*, October 18, 1862, p. 231).

Carreño opened the program with Hummel's *Rondo brillant* (op. 98), with an accompaniment played by a quintet consisting of Mosenthal, Matzka, Bergner, and the Philharmonic double-bassist C. Preusser; her solos were Thalberg's formidable *Mosè* Fantasy, a Nocturne by Theodor Döhler, and Gottschalk's *Jérusalem;*[25] as one of her encores, she played Thalberg's "Home, Sweet Home" Variations.[26] She was deluged with flowers, wrote the *World,* "some of which were presented by gentlemen of the Wall-Street-and-gold-spectacle pattern, and others [doubtless stage-managed by Harrison] by children of her own brief age."[27]

Carreño's first-rate company of assisting artists were Madame D'Angri, William Castle, and Theodore Thomas, with Signor Abella as accompanist.

For the remainder of November little Carreño and Gottschalk alternated their concerts at Irving Hall: Gottschalk appeared on November 23; Carreño on November 25; Gottschalk on the 28th, Carreño on the 29th.[28] On November 30, Gottschalk gave the final concert of his series, then departed on tour. The Carreño concerts continued: on December 2,[29] December 4, and on December 9 a fifth, purportedly last, concert. This event was so mobbed that the sale of tickets had to be stopped, and Harrison was "forced" to announce a sixth concert on December 11, to be followed by a Saturday matinée at noon on December 13,[30] purportedly for the edification of the juvenile population, and "positively" Carreño's last performance. This was, of course, followed by another, a final grand complimentary concert to celebrate her ninth birthday at the Academy of Music on December 22, again with D'Angri, Castle, Thomas, and Abella, joined by S. C. Campbell. The "completely filled" Academy had "hardly presented so gay an appearance since the gala days of Piccolomini," wrote the *Times* (December 26, 1862).

Harrison's management of Carreño apparently ended with this final triumph: she departed on "a tour of the provinces," to begin in Boston, where, as *Dwight's* reported (January 24, 1863, p. 343), she "created a sensation."

Seymour had doubtless spoken for many well-wishers when—following Carreño's first *soirée*—he had expressed the "greatest apprehensions" for her future if she engaged in an arduous concert career at this early stage of her life: "So much genius should be devoted to study and spared to art, not dissipated in the idle adulations of friends and the well-intentioned, but seldom well-considered, applause of the public" (*Times,* November 10, 1862).

Hagen, predictably, looked on her public appearances with dire forebodings: "We

[25] An interpretation acquired at the master's knee: "Shortly after her arrival in New York, she had an interview with Gottschalk, and played a piece with him for four hands. In *six* days she learned by heart his *Jérusalem* and his *Bananier,* and upon Gottschalk's return from giving some concerts in Boston he gave her instructions for her more finished execution" (*Dwight's,* January 24, 1863, p. 343).

[26] Regrettably, following her first two appearances the contents of her programs ceased to be listed in the newspapers.

[27] Tickets to the Carreño concerts were one dollar; 50 cents for chldren.

[28] On November 29 she played Thalberg's *Barcarolle,* Prudent's Fantasia on *Lucia,* Mendelssohn's *Rondo capriccioso,* and a Fantasia on *I due Foscari* by the French composer Henri Rosellen (1811–1876).

[29] From her third concert on, an extra charge of ten cents was added for reserved seats.

[30] At which Jenny Kempton replaced Madame D'Angri, who was to appear with the Brooklyn Philharmonic that evening, as also was Carreño (see below).

consider this a very cruel proceeding. Why not leave the poor child to the quiet continuation of her studies, especially as there seems no pecuniary necessity for her appearance in concerts?" To launch her prematurely on a public career, he darkly prophesied, would "certainly stay the progress of her studies . . . poison her mind, and . . . *never enable her to grasp the artistic responsibilities of her profession*" (Hagen's italics). She might possess talent but certainly never genius. Only one child genius, Mozart, had appeared in history, and that's the way Hagen was determined it should remain (*Review and World,* November 22, 1862, p. 279).

True, after her third concert Hagen conceded that little Carreño, no doubt, had remarkable talent (December 6, 1862, p. 293). But, he qualified, "some of the pieces she played were much too difficult for her; on the other hand, others [Gottschalk's?] were so insipid and stupid that they are little apt to improve her taste, especially as they were received with the same applause as all the others. We still think," concluded Hagen, "it would have been better for the future of the child not to appear in public just now."

This opinion was unearthed many decades later by Marta Milinowski, Carreño's fanatically partisan biographer, who harshly accuses Harrison not only of ruthless child-exploitation for his own selfish gain, but of perpetrating a series of frauds on the father, Don Manuel Antonio Carreño, whom she portrays as a proud but gullible hidalgo. Although Milinowski extenuates the "ambition" that led Don Manuel to permit the exploitation of his wonderful child, she accuses the "insatiable Mr. Harrison" of tricking him into permitting (in addition to seven previous appearances) "a farewell concert on Teresita's ninth birthday" and of misrepresenting the event as a benefit for her. "Not realizing to what he was committing himself," she oversimplifies, "Manuel Antonio politely consented."

Not only was the Academy "filled to the last inch of standing room," continues Milinowski, "but hundreds were turned away, everybody being very naturally under the impression that he was contributing his share to a handsome birthday present for the child who so lavishly squandered her gift of music. . . . But of the tremendous receipts of that evening's concert neither father nor daughter ever saw a penny." And— an ultimate act of villainy: "Even the birthday present that Mr. Harrison in a sheepish moment had promised Teresita was not forthcoming" (Milinowski, pp. 10, 35–36). The author gives no source for this damaging testimony; nor does she attach similar blame to George Danskin, who took over Carreño's management in 1863, when she transferred her multitudinous concert-giving activities to Boston and environs.

Gottschalk, himself a former child prodigy, enthusiastically approved of little Carreño's career and sought to advance it. In a letter to Harrison from Cincinnati, where his tour had taken him, Gottschalk wrote (December 12, 1862): "I really am delighted to hear that you are doing so well. Little Teresa seems, according to what I see in the papers, to be quite the *furor* now. I am very much pleased with it. She is not only a wonderful child but a real genius. As soon as I am in New York, settled down and at leisure, I intend to devote myself to her musical instruction.[31] She *must* be something

---

[31] But only briefly. Although Gottschalk aficionados claim Carreño as a pupil of Gottschalk, Gottschalk himself—in a letter to his friend Espadero in Cuba, where she gave concerts in 1863— wrote: "She is a genius—I have only been able to give her five or six lessons [but] she already achieves a thousand miracles" (cited in Milinowski, p. 52).

great and she *shall* be" (holograph at Dickinson Music Library, Vassar College; quoted in Milinowski, p. 35).

Gottschalk's faith in Carreño's enduring greatness was more than justified. Despite the naysayers, she enjoyed, over the succeeding five decades, an unrivaled fame as a superlative pianist, popular composer, great teacher, and international beauty and *femme fatale.*

Meanwhile at Irving Hall, Madame de Lussan, who had been touring with Gottschalk, was presented in a "first" concert of her own on November 20, assisted by an ephemeral Madame Erminia Carrere, billed as a "pupil of Thalberg," a Monsieur de la Perrière, tenor, Theodore Thomas, violinist, Joseph Mosenthal in an unspecified capacity, and Emanuele Muzio as music director and piano accompanist. On December 18, Eugénie Barnetche, too, followed her auspicious first appearance with Gottschalk with a "First Grand Concert," assisted by Carreño's company—Madame D'Angri, William Castle, Theodore Thomas, and Signor Abella. On December 25, Annie Salembier, a French actress/singer who had assisted at a Carreño concert on December 2, gave her official first concert, assisted by George Simpson, Domenico Coletti, J. N. Pattison, and William Berge.

In January and February venturesome Harrison, in addition to balls and lectures at Irving Hall, booked a season of French plays, *Les Soirées françaises,* under the direction of the actor/director Paul Juignet, at which were featured musical interludes by the singers Ridolfi and Garibaldi and the violin child prodigy Mathilde Toedt. On February 27 the juvenile Myers Sisters, Josephine and Louisa, gave dramatic readings there at their Grand Vocal and Instrumental Concert and Literary Entertainment,[32] with the musical assistance of the Irving Hall alumni: Maria Brainerd, S. B. Mills, Gustavus Geary, and Dr. Clare Beames.

From November 10 through 15 "the antique bonnets, grey beards, and cracked voices of Father Reed's Old Folks"[33] took over the hall for a series of five concerts,[34] interrupted only by a Grand Dramatic and Musical *Soirée* presented on November 12 by Nina Foster, *diseuse* and exponent of "Saloon Theatricals." Fitz Hugh Ludlow

---

[32] Little Miss Josephine had successfully appeared as Little Eva in a recent Winter Garden production of *Uncle Tom's Cabin.* Desiring to become "better known," the sisters later announced a series of dramatico-musical events at Dodworth's Hall, to begin on November 13.

[33] The *Times* (November 10, 1862) identified Father Reed as the "venerable musician, in white hair and yellow stockings, who may have been noticed on the principal walks of the city." His Old Folks were described as "resurrectionists of popular art [who] dig up the festive morsels that used to regale the palates of our forefathers and, with an antique sauce of strange costumes, serve them up for the enjoyment of the present generation." They sang church music of the preceding century with "clever effect," wrote the *Tribune* (November 11, 1862). "The costumes and manners of the vocalists [added] much to the verisimilitude of the performance [and] some semi-burlesque imitations of the usual style of antique psalmody excited great merriment and applause."

[34] A competitive group of twenty-five ladies and gentlemen, identifying themselves as the *original* Father Kemp's Old Folks, appeared in a series of three performances at the Cooper Institute on December 22, 24, and 25. They were scooped by the Bryant Minstrels' takeoff of "Ye Old Folks Concert" with Dan Bryant as "Old Daddy Hemp." On Christmas Night a company of "Young Folks" materialized at the Methodist-Episcopal Church in Eighteenth Street (near Eighth Avenue) to give a concert of "solos, duetts, and choruses, interspersed with recitations and dialogues."

(*Home Journal,* November 22, 1862) reported that Miss Foster, in addition to reciting the *Parrhasius* of N. P. Willis and several of the "most exquisite scenes" from *Romeo and Juliet,* enacted the characters of both Sir Peter and Lady Teazle in the "Scolding Scenes" from Sheridan's *The School for Scandal.* Foster's musical assistants were a Mrs. Farnham, an amateur pupil of Antonio Barili,[35] who commendably delivered the "Shadow Song" from *Dinorah;* William Castle, the former minstrel, who once again won his listeners with his delicious voice and the exquisite pathos with which he used it; Harry Sanderson, who, emulating Gottschalk, played only his own compositions— fantasies on *Rigoletto* and *Semiramide* (according to the *Times,* on *Un ballo in maschera*), his "Bridal Eve Polka," and his newly composed "Irving Quickstep" dedicated to "Harrison of the Hall"—and Theodore Thomas, who rushed to the concert directly from his first rehearsal as the newly appointed associate conductor (with Eisfeld) of the Brooklyn Philharmonic.

"Mr. Harrison's concerts have all proved successes," wrote the *Dispatch* (November 11, 1862). "We congratulate him. He has proved that even when the opera is in its full blast, a good concert will command large and appreciative audiences." And not only good concerts originated by Harrison. At Irving Hall on February 9 the *Arion* Society, conducted by Anschütz and Bergmann, performed a choice program of unfamiliar German choral works: Schubert's "Song of the Spirits Over the Waters"; his *Nachtgesang im Walde* ("Night Song in the Woods") accompanied by four horns, op. 139b (1827); Schumann's *Der Rose Pilgerfahrt* ("Pilgrimage of the Rose"), op. 112 (1851), also with four horns; and—the hit of the evening—Liszt's spirited *Reiterlied* (Hussar's Song) for men's chorus (1841) (Searle 72). A formidable roster of assisting artists—Bruno and Hermann Wollenhaupt, S. B. Mills, Henry Mollenhauer, the German actor/singer Isidor Lehmann, Joseph Weinlich, and several members of the *Arion*—contributed a wide assortment of solos.

Hagen boasted of the *Arion's* venturesomeness and high purpose. Even in Germany, he pointed out, the singing societies "contented themselves" with chestnuts by such mediocre composers as Franz Abt and Friedrich Wilhelm Kücken, while the great works of such masters as Schubert remained unheard. But here, he wrote, "the *Arion,* the *Liederkranz,* and other clubs dig up the treasuries of the old masters and hunt after those of modern authors, perform them as well as they can, and, what is still better, feel a real gratification in this task" (*Review and World,* February 15, 1862, p. 40).

Returning to Irving Hall on March 16, the *Arion* participated in a Bergmann Sunday "sacred" concert that offered first performances in America of a Grand Scene from Wagner's *Rienzi* and Liszt's symphonic poem *Orpheus* (1854) (Searle 98).[36] Additionally

---

[35] Carlotta Patti's half brother, Antonio Barili, had recently returned to New York after ten years as director of the opera in Mexico City and once again had established himself as a highly respected vocal teacher.

[36] Another of Liszt's baffling "fugitive orchestral works," wrote the *Dispatch* (March 23, 1862), "all of which are characterized by an individuality certainly startling, but which abound in monstrosities of harmonic modulation, progressions, prolongations, and instrumental technics which one has to woo a long time before he can regard them as particularly tame or tractable, but which [switching course in midstream] we cannot help admiring and regarding with an affectionate interest and a longing to take him into his bosom to pet and fondle until better acquainted." And, concluded the ambivalent *Dispatch:* "The work had a great success."

the *Arion* repeated Liszt's *Reiterlied;* S. B. Mills repeated his hardy perennial, the Schumann Piano Concerto,[37] and essayed de Meyer's acrobatic Fantasie on *Lucrezia Borgia;* Louis Schreiber played his *Effusions du coeur* for *cornet à pistons;* Bergmann played his "Sounds from the Alps" for cello, and conducted Weber's Overture to *Euryanthe* and the *Leonore* Overture, no. 3, by the "tone-God" Beethoven. On April 6, together with the ladies of the *Singakademie,* under the direction of Frederick Kruger and an orchestra conducted by Joseph Noll, the *Arion* returned to Irving Hall for a performance of Schumann's *Paradise and the Peri,♪* revived in March by the *Liederkranz.*

In July the members of the *Arion* embarked on a twelve-day concert-giving junket, appearing as far afield as Rochester, Niagara Falls, and Buffalo, where S. B. Mills, Henry Mollenhauer, Louis Schreiber, and others of their company were joined by the estimable Buffalo *Liedertafel* (*Dwight's,* August 2, 1862, p. 141).

Later in the year, as we know, the *Arion* became a vital ingredient of Anschütz's German opera productions, appearing both in the operas and in weekly Sunday evening concerts. Additionally, at the German Opera House, under Anschütz's direction, they presented an orchestral/choral program on December 16, that included—in addition to Schumann's First Symphony and Weber's *Jubel* Overture—unfamiliar contemporary German works: "On the Open Sea," for baritone solo, men's chorus, and orchestra by the German choral composer Ferdinand Möhring (1816–1887), "Nightly Wanderings" by Franz Abt,♪ and "Spring Greeting to the Fatherland" by one of the Lachners. The vocal soloists were the stars of Anschütz's opera company: Madame Johannsen and Messrs. Hartmann and Lotti; S. B. Mills played a work by Chopin and a Tarantella of his own composition; Louis Schreiber played his *Élégie* for *cornet à pistons* and orchestra.

On November 18 at Irving Hall the *Liederkranz* launched a four-concert subscription series[38] devoted chiefly to rarely heard works. Accompanied by a "Grand Orchestra of forty artists," conducted by Agricol Paur, and with Madame Johanna Rotter as soloist, they gave a splendid performance of the first-act Finale *(Ave Maria)* of Mendelssohn's unfinished opera *Loreley,*[39] also Ferdinand Hiller's (not Schubert's) setting for full chorus of Goethe's *Gesang der Geister über den Wassern,* and, for men's chorus, a *Hymne an die Musik* by Vincenz Lachner (1811–1893) and a *Sturmes Mythe* by Franz Lachner;♪♪ Bruno Wollenhaupt played Mendelssohn's Violin Concerto and Vieuxtemps's *Fantaisie caprice;* the orchestra opened the concert with Niels Gade's *Michelangelo* Overture, op. 39 (1861), apparently a first local performance, and closed it with Johann Christian Lobe's *Reiselust* Overture.♪

Unlike the German singing organizations, the Harmonic Society's efforts dwindled exceedingly in 1862. After appearing on March 27 at Harrison's music festival, they returned to Irving Hall on Easter Monday, April 21, with Bristow's *Praise to God,* presented as a "Grand Te Deum" in celebration of "Recent Victories of the National

[37] "Hardly a novelty," snorted the *Dispatch (ibid.),* to whom Mills sounded "mechanical after our late Gottschalk experiences."

[38] Their untrammeled, fancy-dress-ball activities continued undiminished, with an event on February 15 and another on November 27, both at the City Assembly Rooms.

[39] Madame Rotter was also heard in Schubert's *Ave Maria* and, as an encore (much to Hagen's disgust), Carl Eckert's "trashy and empty" *Air Suisse.*♪

Army." The soloists were Mesdames Mozart and Stoepel and Messrs. G. F. Ilsley and J. R. Thomas; Henry C. Timm was the organist, Eben played the flute solos, Harvey Dodworth the trumpet solos, and Bristow conducted. The military heroes, Lieutenant General Winfield Scott ("if in the City and well"), General Anderson, and "other eminent men" were expected to attend.

This event might have been Bristow's swan song as music director of the Harmonic Society. Because their internecine discords were not confided to the public,[40] it came as a shock when, in September, it was abruptly disclosed, with no explanation, that Bristow, the Society's longtime, highly regarded director, had resigned. "Rumors are afloat," trendily gossiped the *Dispatch* (September 14, 1862), "that the time-honored Harmonic Society and the youthful [more precisely, inactive] Mendelssohn Union are about to join forces for the supression of discord and discouragement of musical secession from their ranks. If this is done, and if an able conductor can be found who will take a pride in the success of the undertaking, we may expect great things of them this season."

Bristow was accorded appropriate valedictory praise: "It is due to his ability and perseverance that [the Harmonic Society] has existed so long." And, true or false: "The Society is in a more prosperous state, financially, than it has been for years," wrote the *Dispatch*. "Success to them."

It was immediately announced—not surprisingly—that George W. Morgan had accepted the music directorship of "the city's only remaining American singing society."[41] Thus, the Harmonic Society's *Messiah,* by now an indispensable Christmas Night ritual in New York, materialized at Irving Hall without a further hitch. It was excellently performed by Mesdames Mozart, Coleman, and Kempton, Messrs. Simpson and J. R. Thomas, with a splendid orchestra chosen by Felice Eben and led by Theodore Thomas, and with E. J. Connolly, the new Harmonic Society organist, presiding at a "large-sized Harmonium, producing the tone of a 16-foot pedal pipe, manufactured by the celebrated firm of Carhart, Needham & Co, No. 97 E. 23rd Street," all under the directorship of George Washbourn Morgan.

An independent choral performance, the first hearing of the Danish composer J. M. V. Busch's *Stabat Mater,* announced for April 24 at Irving Hall, fared less well when the composer was forced to cancel at the last minute because he lacked the funds to pay the pickup chorus and Dodworth's orchestra. To add to his humiliation, Mrs. Brinkerhoff, who—with Octavie Gomien (alto) and Messrs. Durant and Gonzalez (respectively tenor and basso)—had been announced for the solos, publicly washed her hands of the event with an unfeeling card informing "her friends and the public that she had withdrawn her name from the programme of Mr. J. M. V. Busch's concert, as he finds he is utterly unable to fulfil his engagement to the public as regards an orchestra and chorus for the performance of the 'Stabat Mater,' as advertised."[42]

---

[40] "Extended notice of theatrical [and musical] subjects is, at this particular moment, not only unnecessary, but impossible," explained the *Times* (May 19, 1862), "because war news crowds out everything that has not a direct bearing on the great struggle on which the whole energies and attention of the country are engaged." Yet, added the *Times,* the theatres were "tremendously prosperous."

[41] Not counting the shadowy Glee and Madrigal Society that infrequently surfaced to regale their devotees with "venerable glees and madrigals."

[42] Not until June 1, 1862, at the Church of St. Vincent de Paul, was Busch's *Stabat Mater* at last heard. Mrs. Brinkerhoff—apparently willing to let bygones be bygones—after all sang the soprano

Not every performing group appeared at Irving Hall. Despite Theodore Thomas's professional ties with Harrison, the Mason/Thomas chamber-music concerts continued, as before, at Dodworth's Hall. On January 28 (the third concert of their seventh season) their program consisted of Mozart's Quintet in E-flat for winds and piano, K. 452 (1784), played by Mason and, from the Philharmonic, Ohlemann (oboe), Goepel (clarinet), Gewalt (horn), and Eltz (bassoon); Beethoven's Sonata in A for cello and piano, op. 69 (1808), was performed by Bergner and Mason; Schubert's Fantasie for violin and piano in C major, op. 159 (1827), by Thomas and Mason; and Beethoven's String Quartet in C minor, op. 18, no. 4, by the quartet—a program that transported Hagen to the loftiest regions of ecstasy (*Review and World,* February 1, 1862, pp. 26–27).

Nor was he less ecstatic over their following program, on February 25, consisting of Haydn's String Quartet in G, op. 77, no. 1,[43] Beethoven's Sonata in A, op. 101, played by Mason, Schumann's second Trio for strings and piano in F, op. 80 (1847), with Mason, Thomas, and Bergner, and Schubert's Quintet in C, op. 163 (1828), for two violins, viola, and two cellos, the second cello played by one of the versatile brothers Schmitz from the Philharmonic.

At their fifth concert, on March 25, Mason, Boehm, and Matzka performed Mozart's Trio for clarinet, viola, and piano in E-flat, K. 498 (1786); Mason and Thomas were heard in Schumann's second Sonata for violin and piano in D minor, op. 121 (1851); and the quartet played Spohr's *Quartette brillante* in E, op. 43, and Beethoven's String Quartet in F minor, op. 95 (1810). The Spohr quartet amounted to little more than a showy violin solo accompanied by three subsidiary instruments, caviled Hagen. Fluent and melodious, perhaps, but the "motivos are by no means such as we like to hear in chamber music" (*Review and World,* March 24, 1862, p. 75). How different was Schumann's sonata, with its large ideas and unsurpassable workmanship. As for the Beethoven quartet, words were inadequate.

For the last concert of their seventh season, on April 29, Mason, Thomas, Matzka, and Bergner played Mozart's Quartet in G minor for strings and piano, K. 478 (1785); with the Philharmonic cellist Ludhe, the quartet repeated Schubert's String Quintet, op. 163; and with Mason, they repeated Schumann's Quintet for strings and piano, op. 44.[44]

On December 23, still at Dodworth's Hall, Mason/Thomas launched their eighth season. In a heartfelt, year's-end letter to *Dwight's* (appearing on January 3, 1863, p. 318), —t—, recently returned from Europe, wrote: "In these sad, cloudy days, music, to those who love it, is a true comfort and solace, and never have I felt this more than at Mason and Thomas's first Soirée last Tuesday, A Quartet of Beethoven [op. 18,

---

part, summoning, emotionally wrote Hagen, "that deep feeling and artistic conscientiousness for which she is distinguished, and which is ample proof of the deep interest she must have taken in the composition" (*Review and World,* June 7, 1862, p. 134).

[43] Haydn's melodies "warmed the [audience's] hearts and made everybody satisfied," wrote Hagen, although, he pointedly added, "we suppose the proprietor of the hall calculated upon the effect of Father Haydn's music as a substitute for some other more substantial means to warm the room" (*Review and World,* March 1, 1862, p. 50).

[44] With great nostalgia Hagen remembered his first hearing of Schumann's Quintet (vastly superior to Schubert's), when Clara Schumann had performed at home shortly after her husband had composed it.

no. 1], Quintets of Hummel [for strings and piano, op. 87] and Mozart [K. 516, with extra viola played by Zeiss], and Schumann's lovely *Fantasiestücke* [for piano, op. 12, nos. 2, 3, and 4 (1837)], among them the mysterious *Warum?,* were so finely interpreted that the listener could enjoy their beauties without alloy, and be wonderfully cheered by what he heard."

Yet more chamber music was heard that year. Unwisely attempting to compete with Mason/Thomas, in February a group consisting of S. B. Mills and Edward Mollenhauer, with Henry Mollenhauer (cello), and—from the Philharmonic—M. Schwartz (second violin) and Zeiss (viola), ill-advisedly commenced a rival series of five "classical soirées" at Dodworth's Hall. At their first concert, on February 3, they played Beethoven's String Quartet in E minor, op. 59, no. 2, Schumann's growingly popular Piano Quintet and, as the requisite novelty, the Mendelssohn-like Sonata for violin and piano in D minor, op. 21, by Niels Gade. Mills additionally performed an unidentified something by Chopin, and Henry Mollenhauer a piece by Romberg.

"A brilliant affair," applauded the *Dispatch* (February 9, 1862). "An entertainment the like of which is seldom given in this city," acclaimed the *Sunday Atlas* (quoted in *Dwight's,* February 15, 1862, p. 366); "Schumann's wonderful Quintette in E-flat was performed beautifully," wrote Hagen (*Review and World,* February 15, 1862, p. 39), even though the first movement was perhaps taken a little faster than the composer had intended it.

But by their second, perhaps less well-prepared, *soirée,* Hagen was less enthusiastic. This time the group unveiled the second of Cherubini's six all-but-unknown string quartets, a work Hagen described (*Review and World* (March 1, 1862, p. 50) as "one of those *morceaux de fine bouche,* exceedingly interesting to the musician but altogether 'caviare' for the uninitiated. It seemed rather so for the performers themselves," he pointedly added. The remainder of the program—Beethoven's Sonata for cello and piano in A, op. 69, and Schubert's Trio for strings and piano in B-flat, op. 99—was correctly played, but "without that artistic finish and that unity in sentiment and conception which can only be attained by severe studies, mutual enthusiasm, and long practice." Hagen noted also (repeating the eternal cavil of string players) that "the piano part was, as a rule, too predominant." Mills played piano music by Liszt; with Henry Mollenhauer he performed an unidentified cello and piano sonata by Beethoven; Bach's Chaconne, scheduled for performance by Edward Mollenhauer, was not heard.

The Chaconne was played at their following *soirée* on March 14, but the most interesting offering on that program was Weber's rarely heard Quartet for strings and piano in B-flat, op. 8 (1809). An anonymous correspondent, reviewing the concert for the *Review and World* (March 29, 1862, p. 75), noted that both the Adagio and Scherzo of Weber's quartet were derived from melodic material that he had less deftly used in an earlier composition for piano, posthumously published as *Les Adieux* (op. 18).

The program included, too, Beethoven's String Trio in G, op. 9, no. 1 (*c.* 1797); two of Schumann's *Fünf Stücke im Volkston* (Five Pieces in the Folk Idiom) for cello and piano, op. 102 (1849), played by Henry Mollenhauer and Mills; and, for the finale—purportedly by request—Mills tackled the acrobatics of Leopold de Meyer's Fantasy on *Lucrezia Borgia.* Hagen-like, the correspondent grumbled: "Mr. Mills might have been 'requested' to play something better than this piece, for, though it was rendered very finely, we thought the inevitable *brindisi,* or, in plain English, drinking song, was entirely out of place in this 'classical soirée.'"

The Schumann-hater at the *Albion* (March 22, 1862, p. 139) pronounced the program "somewhat *bizarre*"; it "seemed to grope among the masters for impossible novelties," such as Weber's Quartet and Schumann's "wretched" cello and piano pieces, he wrote. "Weber's success in chamber music was never very marked, and after a few experiments, which are almost forgotten now, he abandoned the desire to write it. His mind was too bold and daring for the jading limits of any kind of composition that required a tenacious observance of form. It was like expecting a scene painter to become at once a good bank-note engraver." Weber's quartet possessed many good ideas, "but their effect was that of a rambling, discursive, and frequently charming *potpourri,* very popular in its character but not in the slightest degree severe or classical." The performances of this and the other works on the program, however, could not be sufficiently praised. In this writer's opinion the Mills/Mollenhauer group were worthy opponents of Mason/Thomas.

But *Alma,* reviewing Mills/Mollenhauer's final *soirée,* given on May 17, reported (*Dwight's,* May 24, 1862, p. 64) that "Beethoven's fine F-minor quartet (opus 95) was not played with the unity of expression and equality of tone, the light and shade, always demanded by the quartet, and by such a quartet in particular. Mr. E. Mollenhauer's *Concert Étude,* an excellent see-what-can-be-done-with-the-violin!, was a little out of place. Either Beethoven or Mollenhauer must suffer by such close comparison." More to *Alma*'s liking were Mendelssohn's Variations for cello (not violin, as incorrectly listed) and piano (the *Variations concertantes,* op 17).♪ Charmingly performed by Henry Mollenhauer and Mills, they were a pleasing "relief" to the "more serious music" on the program. Anton Rubinstein's Trio in B-flat, op. 52, no. 3, presented the usual problem encountered when hearing new music: "Experience has taught us the folly of criticising any work of importance after a first hearing only," wrote *Alma,* "so let it suffice to say that the Trio struck us as most interesting, but of unequal merit; the beautiful somewhat weakened by the infusion of the mediocre." Alma did not discuss S. B. Mills's performance of Beethoven's Piano Sonata in D, op. 10, no. 3 (1796–98), but according to Seymour it was a wonderfully precise and graceful rendition (*Times,* May 19, 1862).

On March 18 at Dodworth's Hall, Friedrich, the least visible of the Mollenhauers, gave a "Grand Soirée Musicale" of his own, with the collaboration of Mrs. Brinkerhoff, S. B. Mills, and the Herren Brannes, Matzka, and Heinrich Gelhaar.

Other concerts at Dodworth's Hall included a less than successful series, on April 4, May 19, and June 30, by Ernestine de Villiers, a French pianist settled in Brooklyn. "As the great Préstidigitateur would say," sneered Hagen, her debut was "'very useful' in order to show How Not to Play the Piano." Hagen delicately declined to name the artists who had been "inveigled to assist on an occasion so unworthy of their artistic merit"[45] (*Review and World,* April 12, 1862, p. 86).

---

[45] They were S. B. Mills, J. R. Thomas, E. Mollenhauer, his pupil little Master Bernardo, and Achille Ardavani. At her following concerts, the undaunted Madame de Villiers was assisted by Madame D'Angri, Amalia Strakosch, Giovanni Sbriglia, Federico Ridolfi, William Doehler, Robert Goldbeck, Charles Wels, Charles Brannes, and Ranieri Villanova (playing the Alexandre Organ).

In March, without so much as a farewell concert, Madeleine Graever-Johnson, the highly regarded pianist, abruptly departed this war-torn land. Her elegant opposite number, Madame Louise Abel, announced a "farewell concert" at Chickering's Rooms on April 22, but evidently decided to remain in the United States a while longer. At this concert she played an unidentified sonata by Beethoven, Chopin's Scherzo in B-flat minor, op. 31, and his Waltz in A minor, op. 34, no. 2. She was assisted by Mrs. J. M. Abbot, a soprano of future renown, and by Federico Ridolfi and Theodore Thomas.

Beginning on May 5 at Dodworth's Hall, recalling the gift concerts that had flourished in 1851,♩ a week of "presentation concerts" featured Mrs. Mozart, J. B. Thomas, Gustavus Geary, S. B. Mills, the eleven-year-old violinist Matilde Toedt, and, not least, 122 gifts to be distributed among the audience. Along with other valuable articles, the prizes included a splendid "renewed" Pianoforte (on display at Firth, Pond's), a Grover and Baker's sewing machine, and an elegant Gold Watch. Tickets, at one dollar, were on sale at the music stores, the hotels, and at the door.

Mary Gellie sang at Niblo's Saloon on May 22, assisted by her sister Madeline, Ardavani, one Julius Werner, and Louis Schreiber, and accompanied by Miss Gellie's teacher Émile Millet and William Dressler. On November 5, Elizabeth Taylor Greenfield, the "Black Swan,"♩ gave a concert at the Stuyvesant Institute, assisted by her pupil Mrs. Brown, the "American Nightingale," and "Professor" Kook, the erstwhile prodigy.

At Dodworth's Hall on August 8, the inextinguishable Signora Elisa Valentini Paravalli announced her tenth grand pupils' Concert, yet again featuring the recurrent debut of her pupil/husband, the "great tenor" Antonio Paravalli. Whether or not this debut took place, another followed on October 12, when the Signora again fondly identified the debutant as a "pupil of Signora Paravalli, who unites a chest voice, high to C, to the best size and looks for the lyric stage." Appearing with Paravalli were several of his classmates, including a phenomenal ten-year-old *prima donna* contralto and a seven-year-old ballerina.

As hospital ships brought increasing numbers of battle casualties to the already overcrowded New York hospitals, the horrible facts of war assumed a new immediacy. The New York music community responded with an outpouring of concerts in aid of needy, sick, and wounded soldiers: at the Academy of Music by the Seventh Regiment Band on May 19; at Dodworth's Hall on May 27 by Antonio Barili, his pupils, and the opera singers Sbriglia and "Spalito" (Ippolito?); at Cooper Institute on May 28 (and again on December 23) by George Frederick Bristow with Kazia Lovarny Stoepel, Miss Kissy Stoepel, Miss Lizzy Coleman, Messrs. J. R. Thomas, Felice Eben, and Edward Boehm, and a chorus of 250 of Bristow's Cooper Institute students; at the City Assembly Rooms, on June 30, by 150 pupils of the Colored Grammar School No. 2 (Laurens Street), who performed *Esther, the Beautiful Queen,*[46] and again at the Acad-

---

[46] The oratorio composed by William B. Bradbury♩♩ in 1856 to a libretto by Chauncey M. Cady. This was, in fact, a repeat performance of *Esther* for the gifted class of Colored Grammar School No. 2; on June 9 they had given it (at the City Assembly Rooms) for the benefit of the Colored Orphan Asylum.

emy, on November 20, by more than five hundred public-school children from the Thirteenth Ward, who shared the stage with Dodworth's musicians under the direction of the pedagogue Thomas D. Sullivan.[47]

Washington's Birthday was commemorated that year with a Grand Concert to aid the Widows and Orphans of the New-York Volunteers. Performed by the Seventh Regiment National Guard Band and Drum Corps at the Academy of Music, the assisting artists were Carlotta Patti, Edward Mollenhauer, Louis Schreiber, and one S. Drews (or Drewes); the conductor, of course, was Grafulla. On May 11 the trumpet virtuoso Louis Schreiber, assisted by Edward Mollenhauer, S. B. Mills, the *Arion* Society, and an orchestra of fifty conducted by Bergmann, presented a painfully personal benefit concert—for Schreiber's brother Charles, who had been gravely wounded at the Battle of Belmont (Missouri) on November 7, 1861.[48] On December 9 Father Reed's Old Folks appeared at Irving Hall in a Grand Patriotic Concert sponsored by the Ladies' Rose-Hill Soldiers' Relief Association, to aid sick and wounded soldiers in Bellevue Hospital.

Nor did needy civilian causes go unheeded. In January, Herrmann the *Préstidigitateur* handsomely donated the proceeds of his four final performances at Niblo's Garden to a variety of charities: on January 3 to the Society of St. Vincent de Paul; on January 4, a Saturday, his afternoon and evening performances to the German Ladies Association for Widows and Orphans; and on January 6 to aid the Nursery and Child's Hospital. Herrmann returned on May 30, again to donate a performance at the Academy of Music to the French Benevolent Society of the Ladies of St. Vincent de Paul.

On January 31, Maria Brainerd, Clare Beames, John Kyle, and George F. Bristow appeared at a free Grand Sacred Concert and Organ Exhibition at the Methodist Episcopal Church (East Seventeenth Street). To assist their stricken and needy colleague, the violinist George Schneider, his Philharmonic brethren, Noll and Schwartz (violins), Bergner (cello), Eben (flute), and Letsch (trombone), with the baritone Ridolfi, the Harmonia Society (of Hoboken?), and an orchestra conducted by Bergmann, united for a concert on February 15 (*Times*, February 17, 1862). On February 20, Elizabeth Taylor Greenfield, the Black Swan, gave a concert at the Abyssinian Baptist Church for the church's benefit. On February 23, a concert for St. Joseph's German Catholic Church, 125th Street and Ninth Avenue, was presented at the Convent of the Sacred Heart in suburban Manhattanville. Under the direction of Gustavus Schmitz, the gifted organist of the Church of the Immaculate Conception (whose compositions were heard on this occasion), the soloists were the sopranos Mesdames Chome and Grosz, the baritone Ridolfi, and the Philharmonic hornist Henry Schmitz, Gustavus Schmitz's brother.

---

[47] After Sullivan opened the program with the Overture to *Le nozze di Figaro*, "The curtain then raised, disclosing the 500 [*sic*] children of the Thirteenth Ward public schools seated in picturesque order and beautiful array," reported the *Dispatch* (November 23, 1862). "They opened the vocal part of the program [with songs of the war], and did themselves and their tutors justice throughout."

[48] On this occasion Mollenhauer's masterly performance of Beethoven's Violin Concerto—particularly his rendition of Vieuxtemps's magnificent cadenzas—aroused so great a furor that Mollenhauer was forced to take bows for a full five minutes before the concert was permitted to continue (*Dispatch*, May 18, 1862).

William Berge and Henri Appy contributed the musical portion of a dramatic and musical *soirée* at Dodworth's Hall on March 13, sponsored by the Ladies Benevolent Society for Providing Work and Clothing for the Poor. At a Grand Concert at the Academy of Music on March 18, to assist the Graham Old Ladies' Home and the Industrial School Association and Home for Destitute Children, Clara Louise Kellogg and Madame Schroeder-Dummler (sopranos), Ludwig Quint and William Steinway (tenors), Fred. Steins (basso), Louis Schreiber *(cornet-a-pistons),* Carl Bergmann and the Philharmonic, led by Joseph Noll, and the German *Liederkranz,* conducted by Agricol Paur, joined in a performance of Schumann's *Paradise and the Peri.*

On March 31 the chorus of 150 "Colored juvenile singers" of the Colored Grammar School No. 2 appeared at the Cooper Institute for the joint benefit of the weekly *Anglo-African* and a proposed "Mechanical School for colored youths of both sexes." In a gesture of ethnic friendship, they appeared again at the Cooper Institute on May 26 for the benefit of "Loyal Indians."

On April 22 at Irving Hall, Gustavus and Mina Geary appeared with the children of the Sunday School of St. Ann's Church in a program of duets, choruses, and recitations. Again at Irving Hall, on May 22 the Gearys, Mrs. Mozart, J. R. Thomas, S. C. Campbell, and Henri Appy, directed by William Berge and assisted by his brother Charles, performed for the benefit of the New York Catholic Library Association.

On June 17 at the Trinity Methodist Episcopal Church (Thirty-fourth Street), Maria Brainerd, Clare Beames, Felice Eben, and the St. Bartholomew's quartet choir appeared at a Concert-*cum*-Strawberry-and-Ice-Cream-Festival apparently for the benefit of the church. Tickets for the concert were twenty-five cents; strawberries and ice cream were extra.

At the Sixth Annual Festival of the Society of St. Vincent de Paul for the Benefit of the Poor—from October 21 through 24 at the City Assembly Rooms—Dodworth's Band played nightly promenade concerts. On October 22, Madame Stephani, assisted by vocal and instrumental colleagues, appeared at the Cooper Institute for the benefit of the Janes Methodist Episcopal Mission. A Grand Concert at the Church in Twenty-third Street was performed on November 6 by Mrs. R. S. Jameson, Mary Hawley, Marcus Colburn, Charles Wernecke, Alfred Toulmin, and, taking turns at the organ, W. A. King, William Berge, and John S. Jameson. For the benefit of the Mission School, No. 190, its students, assisted by Horace Waters's Celebrated Sunday-School Vocalists, gave a concert of Sacred, Patriotic, and Miscellaneous Music at the Cooper Institute on November 11.

Father Reed's Old Folks appeared on March 10 at the Presbyterian Church (First Street between First and Second Avenues) for the benefit of the church; apparently for their own benefit they gave concerts on April 3 at the Church of the Redemption (Fourteenth Street, opposite the Academy of Music) and on May 8 at the Bleecker Street Universalist Church (corner of Downing Street).

An extraordinary complimentary "Organ Matinée" was tendered by Grace Church on April 3 to its organist George Washbourn Morgan. The program, not exclusively sacred, included Morgan's transcription of the Overture to *William Tell,* "as remarkable a transcription for the organ," commented the *World* (April 7, 1862), "as is that of Gottschalk for the piano."

At a widely publicized event to honor the great acting star Kate Bateman, who was completing a triumphant dramatic season at the Winter Garden, a musical interlude was offered on May 31 by Amalia Strakosch, Carlotta Patti, Edward Mollenhauer, and the piano prodigy Willie Barnesmore Pape.

At Thomas Baker's benefit, at Laura Keene's Theatre on June 5, Baker unveiled his New Grand Union Overture. His program additionally included Haydn's *Toy Symphony,* complete with toys, and also Baker's Gift Polka, a copy of which was presented to every lady in the audience. As a special added attraction, Señorita Cubas and Señor Ximenes, with their dance company, presented a new Spanish ballet.

On June 7, Carlotta Patti, with the Signori Sbriglia and Garibaldi and little Willie Barnesmore Pape, appeared at Niblo's Saloon to honor the opera baritone Achille Ardavani. And—farther afield—on August 4 the Italianate foursome, Amalia Strakosch and Carlotta Patti, Sbriglia and Muzio, lent an exotic touch to the Grand Testimonial Festival to honor Professor Anderson, the Wizard of the North, sponsored by the Caledonian Society, the Benevolent Society of the Thistle, and the Burns Club.[49]

Less festively, a concert to honor the memory of the lamented Isabella Hinkley, was proposed by the *Herald* shortly after her death early in July but postponed until a more propitious season for concert-giving. The concert seems not to have taken place.

As might be expected, military band concerts were frequently given as benefits for wounded soldiers and their families, but sometimes purely for entertainment. At the Academy of Music on January 3, entertainment in military trappings was dispensed by Helmsmüller and his Twenty-second Regiment Band and augmented by his Germania Dance Orchestra (presumably sharing many of the same players), J. R. Thomas, William Castle, and Signor Abella. At his following concert, on March 22, again at the Academy, Helmsmüller was assisted by Clara Louise Kellogg, substituting for the then ailing Isabella Hinkley, by Signor Mancusi, S. C. Campbell, and by a Herr Otto Spindler, who played his own Valse and Rondo for oboe. Also heard were William Saul, trombonist, and Friedrich Dietz and Fritz Washausen, cornetists, in a *Trio concertant* with orchestra accompaniment credited to one Diethe (Dietz?).

Of special interest among the gallimaufry of opera arias, ballads, marches, and dance music that comprised Helmsmüller's program was his descriptive piece "Drums and Trumpets, or, A Parade on Broadway," a series of "Tableaux" evidently patterned after Carl Lenschow's once-famous "Panorama of Broadway in 1848." The work's topical, if somewhat redundant, sections musically depicted a "Drum Corps and Band Approaching"; "Cavalry Band, Third Regiment"; "Seventh Regiment Drum Corps and Band"; "Seventy-first Regiment Drum Corps and Band;" and finally, "Twenty-second Regiment Drum Corps and Band." In December, Helmsmüller, shifting his venue to Irving Hall, launched a new series with his band, his Germania Orchestra, and Jenny Kempton and William Castle, accompanied by Abella.

In November and December, Grafulla and his band were heard in a series of four Promenade Concerts at the Seventh Regiment Armory.

[49] At this event "Mademoiselle Carlotta Patti and Madame Strakosch both sung deliciously, and *The* Carlotta was, as she always is, the very best concert vocalist we have ever listened to," wrote the *Dispatch* (August 1, 1862).

As for Fourth of July festivities, although the *Tribune* (of June 28) had outdone itself in optimistic predictions of an old-time celebration with business-as-usual fireworks, patriotic tunes chimed from the Trinity steeple, and a heavy theatre attendance, on July 7 a chastened reporter wrote: "The murky nature of the army news during the greater portion of the past week operated unfavorably upon theatrical receipts. The public were too anxious about the effect of the congeries of battles before Richmond to be excited by the mimicry of the stage. The realities of the moment were too terrible to admit of any divided thought. All that was above and beyond the day's labor for bread, or duties of whatever nature, were expended in eager solicitude for the fate of the gallant army of McClellan.[50] With the [better] news [of the Battle at Malvern Hill], which came on the Fourth of July, public feeling becomes more cheerful, and with it a disposition to enjoy the *dolce far niente* of the playhouse."

But, continued the *Tribune,* "the Fourth—such a theatrico-patriotic symposium for country-cousins coming to town,[51] and for the various classes who do so enjoy a holiday—was a wilted affair as regards jollity, noise, fun, and ecstasy. But little powder was burnt; the fireworks failed to excite by their multitudinous chromatics and cunning lurid mottoes and devices. . . . It was the first Independence Anniversary which was hedged in with misgivings."

Despite the *Tribune*'s report of a theatrically barren Fourth, many theatres offered special holiday bills.[52] At Niblo's a performance with Caroline Richings of *The National Guard,* as James Robinson Planché's English adaptation (London 1830) of Auber and Scribe's opera *La Fiancée* (Paris 1829)⁾ was renamed, was followed by a spectacular Grand Patriotic Allegory, with Peter Richings portraying Washington, the Father of His Country, and his daughter, Caroline, as the Goddess of Liberty, singing "The Star-Spangled Banner."

In contrast to the spasmodic appearances and disappearances of Grau's operas, Miss Richings, from mid-April through mid-July, reaped triumph upon triumph at Niblo's with an attractive repertory of English operas: besides *The National Guard*— Balfe's *The Enchantress* (an especially great hit), Auber's *The Syren,*[53] Donizetti's *The Daughter of the Regiment,* and *The Night Dancers,* as John Maddison Morton's adaptation of Adolphe Adam's ballet *Giselle* (Paris 1841) was renamed. Caroline Richings's fine supporting cast included, besides Peter Richings, the old-timers James G. Maeder, Mrs. Maeder, James Dunn, and the dancers Galletti and Tophoff.

Of the popular singing groups, the Hutchinson Family, on receiving the permission of General McClellan and the approval of Secretary of War Simon Cameron, had

[50] Recently repulsed by Lee in their attempted advance on Richmond.

[51] Like the concerts, the theatres had enjoyed a remarkable rebirth in 1862, with a succession of brilliant seasons by Lester Wallack, Laura Keene, Kate Bateman, James W. Hackett, Edwin Forrest, and Edwin and John Wilkes Booth—to name only a few.

[52] Presiding over the orchestra pits were Robert Stoepel at Wallack's, Edward Mollenhauer at the Winter Garden, Harvey Dodworth at Niblo's, William T. Peterschen at Barnum's theatre, and, of course, Thomas Baker at Laura Keene's.

[53] Alternately spiced up, as its run progressed, with unlikely interpolations of the *Casta diva* from *Norma* and the final scene of *La traviata.*

Girvice Archer, Jr.

Caroline Richings in Daughter of the Regiment.

begun "what they hoped would be a series of concerts through the camps across the Potomac. . . . They were audacious enough," reported the *Tribune* (January 23, 1862), "to sing Whittier's noble song, commencing 'We wait beneath the furnace blast' [to the tune "Ein' feste Burg"]. A Dr. Oakley of the Fourth New Jersey made so noisy an expression of his scorn for the Anti-Slavery spirit," furiously continued the *Tribune,* "that General Franklin revoked the license of the choristers—a simple method of avoiding dangerous disorder. General [Philip] Kearney had the Family ranged before him and judiciously informed them that 'he thought just of much of Rebels as of Abolitionists.' General Franklin also ventilated his opinion that the song was 'incendiary and deserved to be suppressed.'"

This unexpected setback did not deter the Hutchinsons from performing the song at their subsequent New York concerts—on January 31 at Dodworth's Hall, on February 6 at the Church of the Puritans (for the Daughters of Deceased and Disabled Volunteers), on February 14 at the Spring Street Church, then later at the Rose-Hill Methodist Episcopal Church, at the Free Will Baptist Church, and at Professor Mattson's Church "Uptown" at 41st Street near Sixth Avenue.

On December 11 the *Times* announced a radical change in the Hutchinsons' personnel and style: "With the old name, a new group has presented itself to the public. Asa and Abby are yet of it, but the others have passed to other and more harmonious spheres. In their places a trio more harmonious stands.

"Miss Lizzie, a bright-eyed, sweet-faced, modest-mannered girl of perhaps fifteen summers, sings easily a strong, well-balanced, methodical alto, which needs only culture to carry her to a higher rank than that of a family balladist.

"Master Fred, a well-made, Hutchinson-haired, strong-voiced youngster, manages the tenor, and 'little Denny,' a mere child, who at seven o'clock ought to be kissed and sent to bed, puts in his little oar at all times and in all places, greatly to the edification of the elder portion of the audience and the glee of the little folks."

The Alleghanians, with personnel unchanged and still collaborating with the Swiss Bell Ringers in a repertory of English, Irish, Scottish, German, and Spanish ballads, and a variety of opera arias and cavatinas, gave a successful season at Stuyvesant Hall in May. In August and September they shared the bill at Barnum's American Museum with such attractions as the Connecticut Giant Girl, weighing 618 pounds, a Den of Living Monster Serpents, and Ned, the Learned Seal.[54] The Peak Family, with their band of Lancashire Bell Ringers, reportedly drew crowds to Niblo's Saloon over the New Year's holidays.

During the musically dormant summer months—particularly with the exceptionally hot weather that this year plagued the city—parched New Yorkers fled in droves to the out-of-doors amusement places. The torrid weather had "established the fact, if there existed any doubt of it," wrote the *World* (July 7, 1862), "that theatricals do not refrigerate. There is a fortune in store," the writer foretold, "for the man who shall furnish us with an Arctic Opera House, an Anarctic Theatre, the Icelandic Pavilion, or the Freezing Garden."

Lacking such futuristic remedies, New Yorkers flocked to Jones's Wood, Cremorne Gardens, and Central Park for relief from the heat and for amusement. Jones's Wood, in particular, was the scene of great numbers of concerts and pic-nics, many originated by and for citizens of German origin for charitable causes.[55] On July 14 some 15,000 persons reportedly attended the great Pic-Nic and Summer Night's Festival at Jones's Wood sponsored by the *Frauenhilfe Verein* for the benefit of the German Hospital.

About noon, when the celebrants began in arrive, they were greeted by the delightful music of Hirschmann's band of twenty musicians,[56] wafted from the balcony

---

[54] An accomplished mammal who, according to the Barnumesque come-on, "plays the organ, kisses his keeper, shoulders the musket, shakes hands with the ladies, throws them kisses, etc." Among the other curiosities at Barnum's was Franz Stoepel's "newly invented Piano-Forte of wood and straw."

[55] And often excessively promoted. "Your turn to be drafted may soon come!" threatened an advertisement. "Therefore aid the sick and wounded in whose behalf a FESTIVAL AND PICNIC will be given at Jones's Wood on August 20. Good Music! Good Speakers! Grand Concert! Bal Champêtre! Tickets 50 cents, admitting a gentleman and ladies. For sale everywhere."

[56] "Professor" A. Hirschmann, a former member of Dodworth's Band, regularly conducted free band concerts at Jones's Wood.

of Sommers's Hotel overlooking the East River. "The adjacent spacious dancing floors were soon filled with joyous groups of German ladies and their friends in gala attire," described the *Times* (July 15, 1862), "and the afternoon was devoted to polkas, quadrilles, waltzes, and innocent mirth, another fine brass band alternating with Hirschmann's in keeping up the spirit of the scene.

"The substantial viands and beverages of German usage, of course, performed their part, and the inevitable brigade of fat and rosy children, ever present at the revels of Teutonia, added a happy feature to the tableau. The day was exceedingly beautiful, and the aspect of the woodland retreat, with its gay banners and picturesque groups, reflected by the bright waters of the neighboring river, dotted with sails and studded with green islands, formed a picture worthy of the painters Claude [unidentified among many landscape-painting Claudes] for softness of outline, and of [David] Teniers [1610–1690] for hearty life."

Twenty-five German singing societies took part in the celebration: the *Rheinische Sängerbund, New-York Sing-Academie, Uhlandbund, Colonia, Schillerbund, Frohsinn, Social Reformer Liedertafel, Fidelia, Teutonia, Mozart Männerchor, Germania, Hoboken Quartette Club, Amphion, Sängerrunde, Apollonia, Mozart Verein, Social Reformer Gesang Verein, Concordia Männerchor, Melomaie, Orpheus, Yorkville Männerchor, Union Männerchor, Allemania, Lyra Männerchor,* and the *Bloomingdale Eintracht.*

"Toward eight o'clock," continues the *Times*, "the real throng of the festival began to arrive, and by nine o'clock the scene was one of fairyland—the woods sparkling with colored lanterns and crowded with joyous groups, the illuminated dancing floors, the river reflecting the whole scene upon its unruffled surface, and then the wholesome mirth pervading the entire *fête* made it all and more than had been predicted: a midsummer night's revel worthy of the participants and the occasion."

At about nine o'clock, at the inevitable concert, music of the *Vaterland* was performed by Hirschmann's apparently indefatigable band and by the various singing societies, singly and en masse. The revels then began in earnest, permitting, as the *Times* poetically put it:

> No sleep till morn, when youth and pleasure meet
> To chase the glowing hours with flying feet.[57]

Similar events at Jones's Wood continued throughout the summer and beyond. By August 14, as the *Herald* reported: "There have been held this year at Jones's Wood, up to this time about forty festivals, being a larger number than any summer for three years past, and although the season is about closing, the success of this place of amusement does not show much signs of a decrease."

Perhaps less flamboyant, but no less popular—and no less lyrically rhapsodized in the press—were the Dodworth Band concerts in Central Park. On June 6 the *Tribune* (strongly suggesting William Henry Fry in lightsome mode) merrily announced: "The musical festivals at the Central Park—always sure to attract immense throngs of auditors—are to be renewed on Saturday next at four o'clock in the afternoon, just at the hour when the great metropolis throws aside its laboring oar and betakes itself to re-

---

[57] It was exotically reported that the German Hospital netted "many golden obolus from the merrymaking of the day."

laxation and repose. The scores of thousands of juveniles relieved from their school-rooms, their books and their discipline; the banker from his discounts, the broker from his stocks, and the merchant from his salesroom; men, women, and children; gentle-men, ladies, and darlings; fops, fools, and philosophers—if there are any of the three latter classes in our fair city—are all released and can take a course, if they please, in the Park.

"At such a time the divertisement of a rich musical entertainment affords as much pleasure to the ear as the scenery does to the eye, and multiplied gratification is afforded. . . . If that mythical personage vulgarly styled 'the Clerk of the Weather,' will only sweep away the rain-clouds, and gently veil the sun in a gossamer of soft and fleecy vapors, it will be just in keeping with the caprice and convenience of the fifty thousand Gothamites who are engaged to be present."

Harvey Dodworth's opening program, appropriately beginning with an original "Central Park March," indeed offered an ample assortment of opera gems and waltzes, galops, and marches by a wide array of composers ranging from Donizetti to Verdi, Weber to Wagner, Gungl to Kuhner.[58]

At the other end of the entertainment spectrum were the indecent attractions offered at the disreputable underground concert saloons that threatened to overrun the city. Speaking for the responsible community, an outraged *Bayard,* in an outraged col-umn headed "Our Frightful Plague Spots" (in *Wilkes' Spirit,* January 18, 1862), hotly denounced "those terrible children of Hell, which are ruining hundreds of our young men and covering the fair fame of New York with a mantle of shame. . . . The wick-edness of such places [consisting, behind a facade of sleazy entertainment, of the en-ticements and accomodations—alcoholic and beyond—of their "Pretty Waiter Girls"] is indescribable without using language that would outrage decency," blasted *Bayard.* "They richly deserve burning to ashes, and every proprietor and manager should go to the penitentiary for life."

In early January, as public indignation mounted,[59] a bill was introduced at the State Senate in Albany for the purpose of preserving "public peace and order in Public Places of Amusement in the City of New York [and dealing] a vigorous and final blow against the dens of vice, which under the style of 'Concert Saloons,' infest the cellars and halls in nearly every block on Broadway" (*World,* January 11, 1862). The bill, fur-ther explained the *World,* was designed to "sweep out of existence at once the cor-rupting and disgusting public exhibitions which have disgraced the city and tempted our young men to ruin for many a day."

On January 21 the *World* was gratified to report the confiscation by the police of the indecent transparencies that adorned the entrances to the concert saloons—"dis-gusting placards, done in crimson and blue and yellow" obstructing the walkways and placed in such a manner as "to require no little skill to pass them without personal contact."

[58] In April, Dodworth's ubiquitous band supplied intermission music for the *Soirées magiques,* performed at the Academy of Music by the linguistically versatile Lubin brothers, Frederick and Je-rome, who billed themselves as *Ascomoteurs extraordinaires.*

[59] Incited, claimed the heavily pro-concert-saloon *New-York Clipper,* by theatre owners and legit-imate purveyors of variety entertainment (see Slout, *passim*).

In February, Canterbury Hall vainly attempted to appease public censure by advertising that it now employed only "Men Waiters, Men Waiters." The Gaieties, however, brazenly continued to feature not only the *Prettiest* Waiter Girls, but a supplementary ballet corps of fifty ladies, unequaled for their "Beauty, Talent, and Grace," fortified by an additional troupe of female minstrels, who dispensed a program of edifying "Moral Entertainment." "Without a visit to the Gaieties, a visit to New York is wasted," was their advertising slogan.

All to no avail. The final blow fell in April when—despite an inordinate amount of "lobbyng and filibustering" by the concert saloon owners—the State Legislature passed a law prohibiting the sale of alcoholic drinks in any place supplying entertainment, with the threefold penalty of loss of entertainment licence, imprisonment in the penitentiary from three months to a year, and payment of a fine not less than $100 and not more than $500.

The *Times,* following a tour of the defeated concert saloons on the first night of their proscription (April 25, 1862), reported, with fine tongue-in-cheek irony: "Broadway disclosed a most unusual spectacle. No more was the light that shed its radiance o'er the arts of the fair attendants visible. The gas meters were in a state of eclipse. The Cyprian attendants had likewise lost their effulgence, for darkness reigned where there was wont to be

> —dancing, masking,
> And various other things—for asking.

"Lager became stale, flat, and unprofitable. . . . The high-strung fiddle nearly snapped its strings, while the banjo and trombone seemed to echo the dull sound as a few stray pennies dropped into the empty money drawers."

At the Melodeon, because it possessed a theatrical licence, the show—or a form of the show—went on, but only temperance drinks were served by small boys, while the immobilized waiter girls, decked out in their seductive best, helplessly looked on from the sidelines. "Of course," taunted the *Times,* "any ladies who wish to come and see the performance, and pay as other people do, can obtain admission." And: "If they are afraid to go home alone and wish a male protector from the rudeness of the street, they are at liberty to secure him. It is not supposed that any law will prevent that."

On this first night, as the *Times* reported, the dispossessed waiter girls were present at all of the places visited. According to the proprietor of the Melodeon, the enforced dismissal of his employees sentenced at least 1100 people to destitution.

The vanquished resorts greeted the situation with a mingling of compliance and defiance, the Gaieties being the last eventually to capitulate. Before long, however, ingenious loopholes were devised and put into operation, and slightly disguised versions of the concert saloons were back in operation within a year. But for the present, to all intents and purposes, the concert saloons had ceased to function. Or so it seemed.

Blackface minstrelsy, however, remained impervious and inviolable through thick and thin. In March, Hooley's Minstrels, installed at the Stuyvesant Institute since the previous October, permanently shifted their operations to the upcoming town of Brooklyn. On May 21 the Profession lost one of its revered founding fathers with the shocking suicide of Edwin Pierce Christy (b. 1815), retired from the stage since 1854.

A victim of paranoia, Christy—obsessed by the fear that the rebels would soon arrive and seize all his worldly possessions—threw himself from a second-story window and died of his injuries two days later.

From January to July—and again from September through the remainder of the year and beyond—Bryant's Minstrels were an immovable fixture at Mechanics' Hall, the old E. P. Christy stronghold. Among their musical burlesques and travesties—in addition to "Ye Old Folks Concert"—were takeoffs of *Un ballo in maschera* and an item titled *Il captivo trovatore*.

On June 23, upon the eviction of Canterbury Hall from 585 Broadway,[60] George Christy took possession of the premises. Two weeks later, on July 2, his former partner and remorseless adversary Henry Wood announced the opening (on July 7) of his own new theatre, at 514 Broadway, opposite the St. Nicholas Hotel. Proudly describing it in architectural detail, Wood also made it clear in a card in the entertainment columns (probably as a reminder or warning to George Christy) that he, Wood, and no other, was the originator and owner of Wood's Minstrels and that he would tolerate no imitators: "There is scarcely a town of any importance in the country that does not boast its band of Wood's Minstrels," he boasted, "and while I take this as an indubitable proof of the popularity of my company, I cannot at the same time commend the dishonesty of those who, for the sake of a little temporary success, are willing to sail under false colors. I wish it to be distinctly understood that I am the originator, as I am the sole and only proprietor, of Wood's Minstrels, either in this city or elsewhere, and should I at any time decide to travel with my company, I will notify the press . . . over my own signature."

On July 24, George Christy, apparently still beset by professional difficulties, responded with a confidential declaration of his own, similarly in the entertainment columns: "On my return from the Western country, where I have been professionally engaged for the past two years," he asserted, "I determined to settle down and make New York, my native city, my abiding place for the remainder of my life. With this end in view, I acquired the premises at 585 Broadway, which I found completely dismantled and laboring under the ban of municipal conscription."

Christy's elaborate alterations and repairs to the hall, he stated, included provisions for its enlargement "should circumstances arise, such as the approach of the millenium upon the conclusion of our present unhappy political difficulties. . . . I owe the good people of this city much (pecuniarily and otherwise)," he wrote, "and shall strive to pay my debts, both professional and honorable ones, by every means within my power," but, defiantly, "should it be necessary for me to take advantage of the bankrupt or any other act, I shall do so with perfect complacency, and assurance that I am not alone in the boat."

In November, M. C. (not S. C.) Campbell, a veteran of both Christy's and Wood's troupes, announced his takeover of the now disused Palace of Music at the Cremorne Gardens, where he would appear with a new company of Campbell's Min-

[60] On May 5 the police descended on the Canterbury, where, defying the law, illicit waiter girls were still found dispensing drinks while entertainment was going on. "Fifteen girls and twelve men, including the man in charge of the saloon, the barkeeper, and some of the performers, were arrested and taken to the station house, where they were locked up for the night," happily reported the *Tribune* (May 7, 1862). Exit Canterbury.

strels. After requisite alterations to the hall his Minstrels opened on November 10, only to depart a month later for Chicago.

On December 22, back from triumphs in England, Buckley's Serenaders—with their *prima donna* Miss Julia Gould, their Burlesque Opera Troupe, and a Brass Band— took over the Palace of Music Hall. Their odd choice of a Christmas entertainment was a three-act burlesque in blackface of *Lucrezia Borgia.*

Henry Wood's holiday fare, too, was opera-inspired: a blackface travesty on *Dinorah, or Le Pardon de Ploermel,* renamed *Dinah—The Pardon Pell-Mell.* Adapted by Wood, not only were the plot and score of *Dinorah* "preserved in very modified form," reported the *Herald* (December 23, 1962), but the Academy cast, not omitting the goat, were "burlesqued very laughably, and yet delicately." It was a production, wrote the critic, that should make Jacob Grau look to his laurels.

And finally, to crown the endlessly diverse musics of 1862, on December 31 the chimes of Trinity Church loosed a flood of harmonious sound upon the midnight air, pealing out a medley of well-loved, homely tunes, strung together by George Frederick Bristow and discoursed by James Ayliffe. Thus—to the comforting strains of "Hail Columbia," "Yankee Doodle," "Old Dog Tray," "Evening Bells," "The Last Rose of Summer," "Columbia, the Gem of the Ocean," and finally, "Home, Sweet Home"— did New Yorkers face the sorrows and perils of another year of war.

APPENDIX

by Thomas G. Kaufman

1857

p. 11   Teresa Parodi, a pupil and disciple of Pasta, had a fairly important career, taking part in several tours of the United States. In 1859–60 she toured with her own company—singing Elvira (in *Ernani*), Norma, Lucrezia Borgia, and Rosina (in Rossini's *Barber*)—starting in Canada in July 1859 and continuing to many Midwestern and Southern cities until summer 1860.

p. 11   Mario Tiberini was an Italian tenor, noted for being the first Alvaro in the revised version of *La forza del destino* (Milan, February 27, 1869). He had a long and distinguished career: debuting in 1852, touring the Caribbean for some years, giving concerts in North America in late 1856, going back to Cuba, and returning to the U.S. in 1857 until early 1858. He took part, as did Claudina Cairoli (see below), in the tour headed by Luigi Corradi-Setti, from New Orleans up to St. Louis, Cincinnati, and Pittsburgh.

p. 11   The three Barili brothers were Ettore, a baritone; Nicolò, a bass; and Antonio, a conductor (John Cone, *Adelina Patti* [Portland, Amadeus Press, 1993], pp. 10, 67). Ettore was the most important of the brothers, having had an Italian career during the late 1840s and early 1850s. After two seasons in Mexico City (which were followed by tours of the provinces), he sang in New York in 1859 with Piccolomini, later with Cortesi, and in 1860 with Adelina Patti. Nicolò had sung in Mexico City with Sontag in 1854, with Antonio Barili conducting, and was a member of various companies singing in New York, also taking part in a number of U.S. tours, such as with the Parodi company (see above), in the 1850s and 1860s.

     The given names of singers were not always identified in the press, as in the case of the Barili who sang at the New York Academy in early 1857. There is compelling evidence, however, that Ettore sang with the Roncari company in Mexico City from October 1856 to mid-February 1857, while Antonio was the director of the Sociedad Filarmonica (Olavarria y Ferrari, "Resena historica del teatro en Mexico" [Mexico City, *Editorial Porrua*, 1961], pp. 647–48). Further, since Ettore was again in Mexico City for the 1857–58 season (*ibid.*, p. 650), and Antonio was a conductor, it can be assumed that the unidentified Barili performing in the Grand Oratorio at the Academy on October 4, 1857, (discussed later) was Nicolò.

     Cone (p. 67) also states that Gottschalk had described Antonio as a *basso cantante*.

He was active, however, as a conductor in Mexico City throughout the 1850s, and is listed as such in the index of the "Resena historica."

p. 11   Filippo Morelli (also known as Morelli-Ponti to distinguish him from several other singers named Morelli) created the role of Wolfram at the premiere of the Paris version of *Tannhäuser*. He toured the United States extensively (returning in 1863–64), and also performed with his own company in Caracas in 1858.

p. 34   Anna de LaGrange, an internationally famous French soprano, sang in most of the major opera houses of Europe. She also sang in South America from 1858 to 1860, and spent several seasons in the United States, first in 1855–58, and finally in 1867–68, even touring briefly in autumn 1867 with her own company. She had a wide and varied repertory, and thought nothing of singing both Norma and Lucia in the same season.

p. 43   Louis Gassier, French bass, sometimes mistakenly called Éduard, was married to the Basque soprano Josefa Cruz-Gassier (see below). Like her, much of his career was spent in Paris, London, and the British provinces, often with his wife as part of the same company. He continued for quite a few years after she died, and also sang a few more seasons at the Bolshoi theatre in Moscow than she did.

p. 43   Domenico Labocetta was at the Teatro Nuovo in Naples from 1843 to 1845, at which time he created the role of Guglielmo in Mercadante's *Leonora*. He then sang five performances of the same composer's *Il bravo* at La Scala in 1846, and was one of the leading tenors with the Italian companies in Berlin from 1846 to 1851, when he returned to Naples, this time at the San Carlo. Before reaching New York, he spent some seasons in Brazil and elsewhere in South America.

p. 47   Carlo Scola had sung briefly in Boston in August 1854. He arrived in San Francisco later that year, remaining there for the first half of 1855, and then sang in Lima in 1856.

p. 54   See under Barili brothers, see p. 11 above.

1858

p. 143   Giuseppina Gassier, Basque soprano, born Josefa Cruz-Fernandez, made her debut in Palermo in October 1847. Louis Gassier (see above) was also in Palermo that season; they apparently met then, and eventually married, singing together for quite a few more years until she died in Madrid in 1866. In Venice in 1850, she created a role in Luigi Ricci's *I due ritratti,* not the Ricci brothers' *Crispino e la Comare* as has been stated elsewhere. In addition to singing in the U.S. and Havana in the 1859–60 and 1860–61 seasons, she often sang in London, Paris, and the British provinces. In the 1861–62 season she was at the Bolshoi theatre in Moscow.

p. 143   Luigi Stefani, an Italian tenor with a relatively brief career, sang mostly in smaller Italian cities during the late 1840s and early 1850s, then appeared as Macduff at La Scala in winter 1854. He sang leading tenor roles (including Alfredo, Manrico, and Faone in *Saffo*) at the San Carlo during the 1855–56 season, and spent the next few seasons in Mexico City and Havana, finally coming to the U.S. in late 1858.

p. 151   Although best known as the teacher of singers such as the De Reszke brothers, Pol Plançon, and Lillian Nordica, Giovanni Sbriglia also had a distinguished career as a tenor. He sang in New York and other East Coast cities in 1858–59, then toured the U.S. with Teresa Parodi's company in 1859–60, being the first Poliuto in Chicago, Cincinnati, and several other towns.

p. 152   Cesare Nanni had been the leading bass at La Scala in the 1855–56 season, and also had sung in many other Italian cities (Bologna, Trieste, Turin, etc.) as well as the Teatre del Liceu in Barcelona in the 1857–58 season.

1859

p. 235   When *Poliuto* was announced during the nineteenth century, a considerable portion of *Les Martyrs (I martiri)* was frequently included in place of the original music, sometimes to the point that what was given actually came closer to the later work. *Poliuto* had been first composed for Naples in 1838–39, but banned by the censors. *Les Martyrs* (Paris 1840) was a drastic revision, with much new music, some important textual changes to existing music, and changes in the names and functions of some of the secondary characters. The differences were perhaps even greater than those between Verdi's *I Lombardi* and *Jérusalem*. Generally, there could be two ways of confirming that a "mixed" edition was used: Felix being sung by a bass, as is the case with *Les Martyrs* (he is a tenor in *Poliuto*), and/or a reference to how well the tenor sang the "Credo," which is an important textual change from *Poliuto* to *Les Martyrs*.

p. 241   Adelaide Cortesi made her debut in Florence in 1847 in *Gemma di Vergy*. She was a *prima donna assoluta* at La Scala in the late 1840s, then in St. Petersburg, Naples, and other Italian cities. When she was in Venice in 1850, she took part in the premiere of the revised version of Pacini's *Medea*, the leading role of which was destined to become one of her favorites, along with Norma, Saffo, Gemma, and Lucrezia Borgia. She first came to the Western hemisphere in the 1857–58 season, touring Mexico for two successive years before singing in New York City and Havana in 1859–60, then in New York (again) and Boston later in 1860. After spending much of 1861 in the Caribbean, she married a wealthy banker and retired.

p. 244   Henry Squires, an American tenor who reportedly sang in southern Italy in the 1850s, made a London debut at the Surrey theatre in 1857 as Manrico, later singing Masaniello and Edgardo. After extensive tours of the British Isles, and then a number of appearances in New York and elsewhere on the East Coast, he went to the Midwest with Strakosch in winter 1859. Following a long season in San Francisco in the spring and summer of 1860, early in 1861 the company left for Australia, where he was the leading tenor through the 1860s.

p. 253   Gaetano Ferri was one of the leading "Verdi baritones" of the mid-nineteenth century, and the creator of Egberto in *Aroldo*. After making his debut in Piacenza in 1839, he sang in the leading opera houses of Europe for the next twenty years. He toured the U.S. under Emanuele Muzio's baton from 1859–61, with appearances in all the major East Coast cities, as well as a few in the Midwest, such as Chicago, Cincinnati, Pittsburgh, and St. Louis. He was in Havana in 1861–62, returning to New York and then to Europe, after which he sang primarily in Spain.

p. 253   Although Giorgio Stigelli had been born in Germany and had made his debut in Vienna in 1841, his principal career was in Italy and Italian opera houses outside that country. He frequently sang in Naples, where he created the role of Icilio in Mercadante's *Virginia*. He sang in the U.S. during the 1859–60 and 1860–61 seasons, but then returned to Vienna, where he sang at the *Hofoper* in 1861–62.

p. 257   Carlo Baucardé was born in Florence in 1825, although his family was originally French. His first known appearance was in the title role of Mercadante's *Il bravo* in his native city in October 1847, later singing other roles there and in Naples. In 1848 he created Poliuto in Donizetti's opera when it was finally given at the Teatro San Carlo that year. Verdi heard him some years later, and was sufficiently impressed to select him as the first Manrico for Rome in early 1853. When Baucardé interpolated a high C in *Di quella pira* in Florence later that year, Verdi was evidently less impressed, and refused to engage him for the premiere of *Aroldo* in 1857, saying that he wanted to have nothing to do with lunatics. His only North American appearances came in 1859–60, by which time he was well past his prime. But he continued singing, mostly in Spain, Paris, and Italy, into the mid-1860s.

p. 257   Augusta Albertini generally sang with her husband, Carlo Baucardé (see above), although, unlike him, she did not create any major roles.

1860
p. 324   See under *Poliuto/I martiri*, p. 235 above.

p. 342   Like Carlo Baucardé, Giuseppe Musiani was noted for his brilliant chest high notes, and specialized in operas such as *Poliuto, Il trovatore, Lucrezia Borgia,* and *Norma*. During the 1850s he sang primarily in Italy, but also spent two seasons in Bucharest. He came to Havana for the 1859–60 season, singing in New York and Boston later in 1860. He returned to the Caribbean in 1860–61 (Havana, Port au Prince, and Caracas), then went back to Europe, singing at the San Carlo in the 1861–62 season.

p. 381   Keltie Morensi, who had previously sung under several stage names, toured the United States again during the 1864–65 season, becoming the first U.S. Preziosilla, in Verdi's *Forza del destino*. She later sang extensively in major European cities, including London (Covent Garden in 1866 and 1867), Barcelona, Paris, Berlin, and Brussels.

1861
p. 398   Ellen Conran returned to Ireland by late 1861, and toured the British Isles with Giulia Grisi.

1862
p. 488   Before coming to the United States in 1862, Giuseppe Tombesi had sung primarily in lesser Italian theatres such as the Teatro Paganini in Genoa. He was in Havana during the autumn and winter of 1861–62 before coming to New York. In the next (1862–63) season he sang Carlo in *I masnadieri* at the Teatro Regio in Turin. Later, he was the leading tenor for an extended season in Mexico City in 1865–66, and in Havana again in 1867.

BIBLIOGRAPHY

BOOKS, ARTICLES, AND PAMPHLETS

Aldrich, Richard. *Musical Discourse* (New York, Oxford Univ. Press, 1928).

Anon. *History of the Liederkranz of the City of New York, 1847–1947, and of the Arion, New York* (New York, Drechsel Print Co., 1948).

Arditi, Luigi. *My Reminiscences,* ed. Baroness von Zedlitz (New York, Dodd, Mead, 1896).

Asbury, Herbert. *The Gangs of New York: An Informal History of the Underworld* (New York, Knopf, 1927; rpt. Capricorn, 1970).

Austin, William W. *"Susanna," "Jeanie," and "The Old Folks at Home": The Songs of Stephen C. Foster from His Time to Ours* (New York, Macmillan, 1975).

Barnum, Phineas T. *Struggles and Triumphs; or, Forty Years' Recollections of P. T. Barnum* (Hartford, Burr, 1869; ed. George S. Bryant, 2 vols., New York, Knopf, 1927).

———. *Selected Letters of P. T. Barnum,* ed. A. H. Saxon (New York, Columbia Univ. Press, 1983).

Barzun, Jacques. *Berlioz and the Romantic Century,* 3rd ed., 2 vols. (New York, Columbia Univ. Press, 1969).

Beers, Henry A. *Nathaniel Parker Willis* (Boston, Houghton, Mifflin, 1885).

Bender, Thomas. *New York Intellect: A History of Intellectual Life in New York City, from 1750 to the Beginnings of Our Own Time* (New York, Knopf, 1987).

Berlioz, Hector. *Memoirs of Hector Berlioz from 1803 to 1865,* trans. Rachel S. C. Holmes and Eleanor Holmes, rev. and ed. Ernest Newman (New York, Knopf, 1932).

Brown, T. Allston. *A History of the New York Stage from the First Performances in 1732 to 1901,* 3 vols., (New York, Dodd, Mead, 1903).

Bull, Sara C. *Ole Bull: A Memoir* (Boston, Houghton Mifflin, 1883).

[Byrne, Julia Glass]. *Gossip of the Century: Personal and Traditional Memories—Social, Literary, Artistic, etc.,* 2 vols. (London, Ward & Downey, 1892).

Carse, Adam von Ahn. *The Life of Jullien* (Cambridge, Eng., Heffer, 1951).

Catton, Bruce. *The Coming Fury* (Garden City, Doubleday, 1961).

Chase, Gilbert. *America's Music: From the Pilgrims to the Present,* 3rd ed. (Urbana, Univ. of Illinois Press, 1987).

Chorley, Henry F. *Thirty Years' Musical Recollections* (London, Hurst & Blackett, 1862; ed. Ernest Newman, New York, Knopf, 1926; rpt. Vienna House, 1972).

Curtis, George William. *Early Letters of George William Curtis to John Sullivan Dwight:*

Brook Farm and Concord, ed. George Willis Cooke (New York, Harper, 1898; rpt. AMS Press, 1971).

————. *From the Easy Chair,* 3 vols. (New York, Harper, 1891–94).

Davison, J. W. *Music during the Victorian Era, from Mendelssohn to Wagner,* ed. Henry Davison (London, Reeves, 1912).

Dizikes, John. *Opera in America: A Cultural History* (New Haven, Yale Univ. Press, 1993).

Elson, Louis C. *The History of American Music* (New York, Macmillan, 1904; rev. Arthur Elson, Macmillan, 1925; rpt. Franklin, 1971).

Epstein, Dena J. *Music Publishing in Chicago before 1871: The Firm of Root and Cady 1858–1871* (Detroit, Information Coordinators, 1969).

————. *Sinful Tunes and Spirituals: Black Folk Music to the Civil War* (Urbana, Univ. of Illinois Press, 1977).

Erskine, John. *The Philharmonic-Symphony Society of New York: Its First Hundred Years* (New York, Macmillan, 1943; rpt. in *Early Histories of the New York Philharmonic,* Da Capo, 1979).

Fay, Amy. *Music-Study in Germany* (Chicago, McClurg, 1880; rpt. Dover, 1965; Da Capo, 1979).

Field, Maunsell B. *Memories of Many Men and of Some Women: Being Personal Recollections* (New York, Harper, 1874).

Forbes, Elizabeth. *Mario and Grisi: A Biography* (London, Gollancz, 1985).

Gottschalk, Louis Moreau. *The Piano Works of Louis Moreau Gottschalk,* ed. Vera Brodsky Lawrence, introd. Robert Offergeld, 5 vols. (New York, Arno/New York Times, 1969).

————. *Notes of a Pianist,* ed. Clara Gottschalk Peterson, trans. Robert E. Peterson (Philadelphia, Lippincott, 1881; ed. Jeanne Behrend, New York, Knopf, 1964).

Groce, Nancy. *Musical Instrument Makers of New York: A Directory of Eighteenth and Nineteenth Century Urban Craftsmen* (Stuyvesant, N. Y., Pendragon, 1991).

Harris, Neil. *Humbug: The Art of P. T. Barnum* (Boston, Little, Brown, 1973).

Haswell, Charles H. *Reminiscences of an Octogenarian of the City of New York* (New York, Harper, 1896).

Hegermann-Lindencrone, Lillie de. *In the Courts of Memory, 1858–1875* (New York, Harper, 1912; rpt. Da Capo, 1980).

Herz, Henri. *My Travels in America,* trans. Henry Bertram Hill (Madison, State Historical Society of Wisconsin, 1963).

Hewitt, John Hill. *Shadows on the Wall; or, Glimpses of the Past* (Baltimore, Turnbull Bros., 1877).

Hibben, Paxton. *Henry Ward Beecher: An American Portrait* (New York, Doran, 1927).

Hoffman, Richard. *Some Musical Recollections of Fifty Years* (New York, Scribner, 1910; rpt. Information Coordinators, 1976).

Hornblow, Arthur. *A History of the Theatre in America from Its Beginnings to the Present Time,* 2 vols. (Philadelphia, Lippincott, 1919).

Howard, John Tasker. *Our American Music: A Comprehensive History from 1620 to the Present,* 4th ed. (New York, Crowell, 1965).

Howe, Granville L., and W. S. B. Mathews, eds. *A Hundred Years of Music in America* (Chicago, G. L. Howe, 1889; rpt. AMS Press, 1970).

Huneker, James G. *The Philharmonic Society of New York and Its Seventy-Fifth Anniver-*

sary: A Retrospect (New York, Philharmonic Society, 1917; rpt. in *Early Histories of the New York Philharmonic,* Da Capo, 1979).

Ireland, Joseph N. *Records of the American Stage from 1750 to 1860,* 2 vols. (New York, Morrell, 1866; rpt. Blom, 1966).

Kellogg, Clara Louise. *Memoirs of an American Prima Donna* (New York, Putnam, 1913; rpt. Da Capo, 1978).

Klein, Hermann. *The Reign of Patti* (New York, Century, 1920).

Krehbiel, Henry E. *The Philharmonic Society of New York* (London and New York, Novello, Ewer, 1892; rpt. in *Early Histories of the New York Philharmonic,* Da Capo, 1979).

LaBrew, Arthur R. *The Black Swan: Elizabeth T. Greenfield, Songstress* (Detroit, La-Brew, 1969).

Lahee, Henry C. *Annals of Music in America: A Chronological Record of Significant Musical Events from 1640 to the Present Day* (Boston, Marshall Jones, 1922).

————. *Grand Opera in America* (Boston, Page, 1902; rpt. AMS Press, 1973).

Lawrence, Vera Brodsky. *Music for Patriots, Politicians, and Presidents: Harmonies and Discords of the First Hundred Years* (New York, Macmillan, 1975).

Loesser, Arthur. *Men, Women and Pianos: A Social History* (New York, Simon & Schuster, 1954).

Loggins, Vernon. *Where the Word Ends: The Life of Louis Moreau Gottschalk* (Baton Rouge, Louisiana State Univ. Press, 1958).

Lott, Allen R. *The American Concert Tours of Leopold de Meyer, Henri Herz, and Sigismund Thalberg,* 2 vols., Ph.D. dissertation, City Univ. of New York (Ann Arbor, University Microfilms International, 1986).

Lowens, Irving. *Music and Musicians in Early America* (New York, Norton, 1964).

Lumley, Benjamin. *Reminiscences of the Opera* (London, Hurst & Blackett, 1864).

Maretzek, Max. *Crotchets and Quavers; or, Revelations of an Opera Manager in America* (New York, French, 1855; rpt. Dover 1968).

————. *Sharps and Flats* (New York, American Musician Publishing Co., 1890; rpt. Dover, 1968).

Martin, George. *Verdi at the Golden Gate: Opera and San Francisco in the Gold Rush Years* (Berkeley, Univ. of California Press, 1993).

Mason, R. Osgood. *Sketches and Impressions, Musical, Theatrical and Social (1799–1885), Including a Sketch of the Philharmonic Society of New York, from the After-Dinner Talk of Thomas Goodwin, Music Librarian* (New York, Putnam, 1887).

Mason, William. *Memories of a Musical Life* (New York, Century, 1901).

Messiter, A. H. *A History of the Choir and Music of Trinity Church, New York* (New York, E. S. Gorham, 1906).

Metcalf, Frank J. *American Writers and Compilers of Sacred Music* (New York, Abingdon, 1925).

Milinowski, Marta. *Teresa Carreño: "By the Grace of God"* (New Haven, Yale Univ. Press, 1940).

Milne, Gordon. *George William Curtis and the Genteel Tradition* (Bloomington, Indiana Univ. Press, 1956).

Mott, Frank Luther. *A History of American Magazines,* 5 vols. (Cambridge, Belknap Press of Harvard Univ. Press, 1938–68).

————. *American Journalism: A History of Newspapers in the United States through 250 Years, 1690–1940* (New York, Macmillan, 1941).

Ogasapian, John. *Organ Building in New York City, 1700–1900* (Braintree, Mass., Organ Literature Foundation, 1977).

Palmer, William Henry [Robert Heller]. *Melody Magic,* ed. Harry L. Clapham, with biog. sketch by Henry Ridgely Evans (Washington, D.C., Clapham, 1932).

Pearse, Cecilia, and Frank Hird. *The Romance of a Great Singer* (London, Smith, Elder, 1910; rpt. Arno, 1977).

Pemberton, Carol A. *Lowell Mason: His Life and Work* (Ann Arbor, University Microfilms International Research Press, 1985).

Pleasants, Henry. *The Great Singers* (New York, Simon & Schuster, 1966; rev. ed., 1981).

Ridgeway, Thomas. "William Henry Fry, the First American Composer of Grand Opera" (*Publications of the Genealogical Society of Pennsylvania,* Oct. 1943, pp. 120–35).

Ritter, Frédéric Louis. *Music in America,* 2nd ed. (New York, Scribner, 1890; rpt. Franklin, 1972).

Rockstro, W. S. *A General History of Music* (New York, Scribner & Welford, 1886).

Root, Harvey W. *The Unknown Barnum* (New York, Harper, 1927).

Ross, Joel H. *What I Saw in New-York; or, A Bird's Eye View of City Life* (Auburn, N. Y., Derby & Miller, 1851).

Ryan, Thomas. *Recollections of an Old Musician* (New York, Dutton, 1899).

Saxon, A. H. *P. T. Barnum: The Legend and the Man* (New York, Columbia Univ. Press, 1989).

Schabas, Ezra. *Theodore Thomas: America's Conductor and Builder of Orchestras, 1835–1905* (Urbana, Univ. of Illinois Press, 1989).

Schmidgall, Gary. *Shakespeare and Opera* (New York, Oxford Univ. Press, 1990).

————. *Walt Whitman: A Gay Life* (New York, Dutton, 1997).

Schonberg, Harold C. *The Great Conductors* (New York, Simon & Schuster, 1967).

————. *The Great Pianists* (New York, Simon & Schuster, 1963; rev. ed., 1987).

Shanet, Howard. *Philharmonic: A History of New York's Orchestra* (New York, Doubleday, 1975).

Slout, William L. *Theatre in a Tent: The Development of a Provincial Entertainment* (Bowling Green, Ohio, Bowling Green Univ. Popular Press, 1972).

Smith, Mortimer. *The Life of Ole Bull* (Princeton, Princeton Univ. Press, 1943).

Southern, Eileen. *The Music of Black Americans: A History* (New York, Norton, 1971; rev. ed., 1983, 1997).

Stendhal (Marie-Henri Beyle). *Life of Rossini* [1824], trans. and ed. Richard N. Coe (New York, Criterion, 1957; rev. ed., Orion, 1970).

Still, Bayrd. *Mirror for Gotham: New York as Seen by Contemporaries from Dutch Days to the Present* (New York, New York Univ. Press, 1956).

Stoddard, R. H. *Recollections, Personal and Literary,* ed. Ripley Hitchcock (New York, Barnes, 1903).

Strong, George Templeton. *The Diary of George Templeton Strong,* ed. Allan Nevins and Milton Halsey Thomas, 4 vols. (New York, Macmillan, 1952).

Sutoni, Charles. *Piano and Opera: A Study of the Piano Fantasies Written on Opera Themes* in the Romantic Era, Ph.D. dissertation, New York Univ. (Ann Arbor, University Microfilms International, 1973).

Thomas, Rose Fay. *Memoirs of Theodore Thomas* (New York, Moffat, Yard, 1911).

Thomas, Theodore. *Theodore Thomas: A Musical Autobiography,* ed. George P. Upton, 2 vols. (Chicago, McClurg, 1905).

Thompson, Oscar. *The American Singer: A Hundred Years of Success in Opera* (New York, Dial, 1937).

Toye, Francis. *Rossini: A Study in Tragi-Comedy* (New York, Knopf, 1934; rpt. Dover, 1987).

Trotter, James M. *Music and Some Highly Musical People* (Boston, Lee & Shepard, 1878; rpt. Johnson, 1968).

Upton, George P. *Musical Memories: My Recollections of Celebrities of the Half Century, 1850–1900* (Chicago, McClurg, 1908).

Upton, William Treat. *Anthony Philip Heinrich: A Nineteenth-Century Composer in America* (New York, Columbia Univ. Press, 1939; rpt. AMS Press, 1967).

————. *William Henry Fry: American Journalist and Composer-Critic* (New York, Crowell, 1954; rpt. Da Capo, 1974).

Wagner, Richard, and Franz Liszt. *Correspondence of Wagner and Liszt,* trans. Francis Hueffer; rev. W. Ashton Ellis, 2 vols. (London, Grevel, 1897; rpt. Vienna House, 1973).

Wallace, Irving. *The Fabulous Showman: The Life and Times of P. T. Barnum* (New York, Knopf, 1959).

Wecter, Dixon. *The Saga of American Society: A Record of Social Aspiration, 1607–1937* (New York, Scribner, 1937, 1970).

Werner, M. R. *Barnum* (New York, Harcourt, Brace, 1923).

White, Richard Grant. "Opera in New York" (*Century Illustrated Monthly Magazine,* June 1882, pp. 193–210).

Whitman, Walt. *Specimen Days & Collect* (Philadelphia, R. Welsh, 1882–83).

Winter, William. *Old Friends, Being Literally Recollections of Other Days* (New York, Moffat, Yard, 1909).

BIBLIOGRAPHIES, BIOGRAPHICAL DICTIONARIES, ENCYCLOPEDIAS, ETC.

Baker's Biographical Dictionary of Musicians, 5th ed., rev. Nicholas Slonimsky (New York, Schirmer, 1958).

Cyclopedia of Music and Musicians, ed. John Denison Champlin and William Foster Apthorp, 3 vols. (New York, Scribner, 1888–90).

Dictionary of American Biography, ed. Allen Johnson and Dumas Malone (New York, Scribner, 1928–58).

Dictionary of American Negro Biography, ed. Rayford W. Logan and Michael R. Winston (New York, Norton, 1982).

Doyle, John G. *Louis Moreau Gottschalk 1829–1860: A Bibliographical Study and Catalog of Works* (Detroit, Information Coordinators, 1983).

Dox, Thurston J. *American Oratorios and Cantatas: A Catalog of Works Written in the*

United States from Colonial Times to 1985, 2 vols. (Metuchen, N.J., Scarecrow, 1986).

The Encyclopedia of New York City, ed. Kenneth T. Jackson (New Haven, Yale University Press, and New York, New-York Historical Society, 1995).

Grove's Dictionary of Music and Musicians, ed. George Grove (London, 1878–80); *American Supplement,* ed. Waldo Selden Pratt (New York, Macmillan, 1920); *Supplementary Volume to the Fifth Edition,* ed. Eric Blom (New York, St. Martin's Press, 1961); *The New Grove,* ed. Stanley Sadie (London, Macmillan, 1980).

Homberger, Eric. *The Historical Atlas of New York City* (New York, Holt, 1994).

Jones, F. O. *A Handbook of American Music and Musicians, Containing Biographies of American Musicians and Histories of the Principal Musical Institutions, Firms and Societies* (Canaseraga, N. Y., Jones, 1886; Buffalo, Moulton, 1887; rpt. Da Capo, 1971).

Kaufman, Thomas G. *Verdi and His Major Contemporaries: A Selected Chronology of Performances with Casts* (New York, Garland, 1990).

Kutsch, K. J., and Leo Riemens. *Grosses Sängerlexikon,* 2 vols. (Bern, Franke, 1987).

Loewenberg, Alfred. *Annals of Opera, 1597–1940,* 3rd ed. (Totowa, N.J., Rowman & Littlefield, 1978).

Macmillan Encyclopedia of Music and Musicians, ed. Albert E. Wier (New York, Macmillan, 1938).

Marcuse, Sibyl. *Musical Instruments: A Comprehensive Dictionary,* corr. ed. (New York, Norton, 1975).

Mattfeld, Julius. *A Handbook of American Operatic Premieres, 1731–1962* (Detroit, Information Service, 1963).

————. *A Hundred Years of Grand Opera in New York, 1825–1925: A Record of Performances* (New York, New York Public Library, 1927).

————. *Variety Music Cavalcade, 1620–1969: A Chronology of Vocal and Instrumental Music Popular in the United States,* 3rd ed. (Englewood Cliffs, N.J., Prentice-Hall, 1971).

Moore, John W. *Complete Encyclopedia of Music, Elementary, Technical, Historical, Biographical, Vocal, and Instrumental* (Boston, J. P. Jewett, 1854; Appendix, Ditson, 1875).

National Cyclopedia of American Biography (New York, James T. White, 1898–1984).

The New Encyclopaedia Britannica (Chicago, Encyclopaedia Britannica Co., 1974–).

The New Kobbé's Complete Opera Book, ed. George H. Lascelles, Earl of Harewood (New York, Putnam, 1976).

Nicoll, Allardyce. *A History of English Drama,* 6 vols. (Cambridge, Eng., Cambridge Univ. Press, 1952–59).

Odell, George C. D. *Annals of the New York Stage,* vols. 6–7 (New York, Columbia Univ. Press, 1931; rpt. AMS Press, 1970).

Offergeld, Robert. *The Centennial Catalogue of the Published and Unpublished Compositions of Louis Moreau Gottschalk* (New York, Stereo Review, 1970).

Partridge, Eric. *The Macmillan Dictionary of Historical Slang* (New York, Macmillan, 1974).

Redway, Virginia Larkin. *Music Directory of Early New York City: A File of Musicians, Music Publishers and Musical Instrument-Makers Listed in New York Directories from*

1786 through 1835, together with the Most Important New York Music Publishers from 1836 through 1875 (New York, New York Public Library, 1941).

Southern, Eileen. *Biograhical Dictionary of Afro-American and African Musicians* (Westport, Greenwood Press, 1982).

Weichlein, William. *A Checklist of American Music Periodicals 1850–1900* (Detroit, Information Coordinators, 1970).

NEW YORK DAILY NEWSPAPERS

(Unless otherwise noted, the following newspapers have
been read for the years covered in this volume.)

Evening Mirror, ed. Hiram Fuller. 1857–59.
Evening Post, ed. William Cullen Bryant.
Daily Times, ed. Henry Jarvis Raymond.
Daily Tribune, ed. Horace Greeley.
Herald, ed. James Gordon Bennett.
Morning Courier & New-York Enquirer, ed. James Watson Webb. 1857–61.
New Yorker Staats-Zeitung, ed. Oswald Ottendorfer.
World, ed. Manton Malone Marble. 1861–.

PERIODICALS

(published in New York, unless otherwise indicated)

The Albion; or, British, Colonial, and Foreign Weekly, ed. John R. Young. 1857–.
Dwight's Journal of Music: A Paper of Art and Literature [Boston] (weekly), ed. John Sullivan Dwight. 1857–.
Frank Leslie's Illustrated Newspaper (weekly), ed. Frank Leslie, with Henry C. Watson and E. G. Squier. 1857–.
Harper's New Monthly Magazine, ed. Henry J. Raymond. 1857–.
Harper's Weekly: A Journal of Civilization, ed. Theodore Sedgwick (1857–58) and John Bonner (1858–63). 1857–.
Home Journal (weekly), ed. George Pope Morris and Nathaniel Parker Willis. 1857–.
Musical Review & Musical World (fortnightly), ed. Theodore Hagen, 1860–. (A continuation of *New-York Musical Review & Gazette* and *New-York Musical World*.)
New York Clipper (weekly), ed. Frank Queen. 1857–.
New-York Dispatch (weekly), ed. Charles Burkhardt. 1857–.
New-York Musical Review & Gazette (fortnightly), ed. Theodore Hagen. 1857–60. Merged 1860 with *New-York Musical World* to form *Musical Review & Musical World* [see above].
New-York Musical World: A Literary and Fine-Art Paper (fortnightly), ed. Richard Storrs Willis, Edward Hodges, and Augustus Morand. 1857. Continued as *The Musical*

World, 1858–60. Merged 1860 with *New-York Musical Review & Gazette* to form *Musical Review & Musical World* [see above].

Once a Month: A Paper of Society, Belles-Lettres and Art, ed. Richard Storrs Willis. 1862.

Porter's Spirit of the Times (weekly), ed. William T. Porter and George Wilkes. 1857–61. Continued by (and overlapping with) *Wilkes's Spirit of the Times,* ed. George Wilkes, 1859–.

Putnam's Monthly Magazine of American Literature, Science, and Art, ed. Charles F. Briggs, with George William Curtis and Parke Godwin. 1857.

Saturday Press: A Weekly Journal of Literary, Dramatic and Musical Intelligence, ed. Henry Clapp, Jr. 1858–.

Spirit of the Times: A Chronicle of the Turf, Agriculture, Field Sports, Literature, and the Stage (weekly), ed. William T. Porter. 1857–61. Appeared concurrently with *Porter's Spirit of the Times* [see above].

ARCHIVAL MATERIALS

NEW-YORK HISTORICAL SOCIETY LIBRARY

Hone, Philip. Diary. 1838–51.
Strong, George Templeton. Private Journal. 1835–75.

NEW YORK PHILHARMONIC ARCHIVES

Minutes of board of directors' meetings, account books, annual reports, 1850–.

INDEX

By Marilyn Bliss

Asterisks designate persons who settled permanently in the United States; "premiere" and "debut" refer to first performances in New York. Page references in italics refer to illustrations. Alphabetization of titles ignores definite articles in all languages; leading function terms (as, and, of, *etc.*) are also ignored. No distinction has been made between attributed and signed criticism under the critic's name.

Herz, Henri (1802–1888), Austrian/French pianist/
    composer/piano manufacturer, 49, 121n
    "Carnival of Venice," 210
    Fantasia on *I puritani,* 215
    Piano Concerto No. 3, 215
    pupils of, 213
Herzog, C., Philharmonic double bassist, 88
Hewitt, Abram (1822–1903), American industrial-
    ist/politician, 195
Hewitt, James (1770–1827), English★ composer/
    conductor/publisher, 261n
Heywood, Emma, English contralto
    performances
        concerts, 224n, 301n
        with Escott English opera troupe, 176, 301
Hicks, James, English concertinist/conductor,
    272n, 289
Hiffert, Caroline, popular vocalist, 95, 464
Hill, Ureli Corelli (1802–1875), American conduc-
    tor/violinist
    invents Key Harp, 207
    on Philharmonic committee, 194n
Hiller, Ferdinand (1811–1885), German composer/
    conductor, 434
    Ein Traum in der Christnacht, 506, 507
    Gesang der Geister über den Wassern, 531
    Saul, op. 80, American premiere, 375
    Symphony, 119
Hinkley (or Hinckley), Isabella (?–1862), American
    mezzo-soprano, 355, *407*
    appearance, 402n
    benefit, 415
    biography, 401–2
    birth of daughter, 502n
    death, 502n, 539
    marriage to Susini, 418n, 429
    on Associated Artists' roster, 398
    performances
        with Associated Artists opera company, 402–5,
           406, 414, 415, 417n
        concerts, 436, 437
        debut, 401–2
        at Gottschalk concerts, 477
        with Grau opera company, 429, 470, 473,
           483n, 485
        at Irving Hall Music Festival, 522
        of "Star-Spangled Banner," 395, 404–5, 410, 412
        with Ullman opera company, 427
    pregnancy, 488
Hirschmann, A., bandleader, 542n
Hodge, Charles, clergyman/composer
    hymn, 518
Hodges, Dr. Edward (1796–1867), Trinity Church
    organist
    as co-editor of *Musical World,* 51
    on Mendelssohn Union, 79–80
    forced retirement, 248n
    as Trinity Church organist, 141n, 237, 248, 362
    works, "Consecration Anthem," 73
Hoey, Mrs. John, actress, farewell testimonial, 217
Hoffman, Murray, lawyer and Strong's friend, 31,

    55, 67, 68, 103, 223, 230, 256, 261, 271, 334,
    369, 415, 416, 474, 504, 506
Hoffman, Ogden, New York politician, 233n
Hoffman, Richard (1831–1909), English★ pianist/
    composer
    performances
        at Bristow testimonial concert, 290n
        chamber music, 9, 109
        concerts, 84–85, 87, 208, 232n, 284n, 296, 458
        with Gottschalk, 475n, 476, 478, 480
        with New-York American-Music Association,
           204
        as Philharmonic soloist, 281, 283, 415, 482
        in Strong's home, 130
    works
        Fantaisie, 73
        Fantasy on themes from *Rigoletto,* 281
        Marche funèbre, 204
        "Twilight," 204
Hoffman, Wickham, acquaintance of the Strongs,
    474
Hogan, T. Augustus, pianist, 385, 440n
Hogg, James (1770–1835), Scottish poet
    The Queen's Wake, 119n
Holland, Dr. Josiah Gilbert (1819–1881), American
    writer/editor, 310
Holland, George, comic actor
    blackface performances, 190
    as blackface performer, 98–99
Holloway, Mr., concert singer, 79
Holman, George, actor/singer, 174
Holman, Mrs. George, actress/singer, 166n, 174, 387
Holmes, Oliver Wendell (1809–1894), American
    poet/physician, 437
"Home, Sweet Home." *See under* Bishop, Henry
    Rowley
Hommann, Charles (c.1800–c.1862), American
    composer
    Sonata for violin and piano, 204
    String Quartet in D minor, 73
Hone, Philip (1780–1851), diarist, one-time New
    York mayor
    on Broadway Tabernacle, 101
    on Rossini, 105
Hooley, R. M., George Christy's partner, 312
Hooley and Campbell's Minstrels. *See* Blackface
    minstrelsy
Hope Chapel. *See under* Performance places
Hopkins, Charles Jerome (1836–1898), American
    clergyman/musician/critic. *See also Timothy
    Trill*
    performances
        concerts, 297, 371, 377–79, 385
        as organist, 205
        "sacred and miscellaneous" concerts, 378,
           387–88
    personality, 493
    as pianist, 206
    as president of American-Music Association, 74,
        75
    private *soirée,* 83

Zeiss, violist, 534
Zeller (or Zeiller), composer
　songs, 109n
Zerrahn, Carl (1826–1909), German★ flutist/con-
　　ductor
　as Boston Philharmonic conductor, 6n
　as Handel and Haydn Society conductor, 108n
Zimmermann, Madame (Anschütz's wife), singer
　defaults, 209
　performances
　　with Anschütz German opera company, 504
　　of Beethoven's Ninth, 181
　　with Bishop, 287
　　concerts, 375, 377, 383, 458, 459

　debut, 217
　with Mendelssohn Union, 210
　as Philharmonic soloist, 337
　promenade concerts, 139
　Schiller centenary concert, 259n
Zincalo, Dwight's New York correspondent
　on Carlotta Patti, 503
　on Thomas's direction of Gottschalk concerts,
　　507n
Zulehner, Carl (1779–1841), German composer/
　　teacher
　possible composer of "Mozart's Twelfth Mass,"
　　185n
　potpourris, 185, 187